THE SEARCH for Personal Freedom

NEAL M. CROSS
University of Northern Colorado
ROBERT C. LAMM
Arizona State University
RUDY H. TURK
Arizona State University

THE SEARCH FOR PERSONAL FREEDOM

A text for a unified course in the Humanities

VOLUME ONE

Prologue: The Integrated Humanities, Greece: The First Humanistic Culture, Rome: The International Culture, Judaism and Christianity: The Star and the Cross, The Age of Faith

FOURTH EDITION

WM. C. BROWN COMPANY PUBLISHERS
Dubuque, Iowa

Library of Congress Catalog Card Number: 70-190086

ISBN 0-697-03106-3

Third Printing, 1973

Printed in the United States of America

Contents

Foreword

■ This fourth edition of this book is the product of testing in the kiln of classroom teaching through three previous editions. In our time particularly, life changes so rapidly that teaching materials must be constantly reevaluated to keep them abreast of new moods, new demands. Even Greek literature—so firmly established—needs to be reinterpreted and scrutinized. For example, when we were making selections for the third edition of this text, Euripides' *Bacchae* did not seem of great importance. Since then, however, a release of the Dionysiac element in human nature has made the play particularly pertinent, and so it is included in this edition.

Viewed simply as art history, music history, world literature, and history of philosophy, this book is unashamedly superficial. It is not intended to be a history of the arts, nor is it intended to be an "introduction" to those disciplines in order to impart an academic vocabulary that can be used later in more specialized courses. The contention of the authors is that a course in the unified humanities—not as history or introduction—has a validity in its own right.

In such a course, *man is the center:* his problems, his wonderings, his confusion of experience, his experience with beauty. The postulate is that in the arts—where irrelevancies of experience are cut away and where new relationships are perceived and presented in visual, auditory, or verbal form—that true meaning for experience can be found. The artist is forever the interpreter and the creator of human life. As an individual sees a wide variety of meanings in the happenings of his life, he is more and more able to make sound value judgments—and in the late twentieth century we need sound value judgments far more than we need sophisticated computers or megamegaton nuclear devices.

The principles which have guided us in preparing this edition are these: First, we have tried to move man in his infinite complexities more to the center of attention than in previous editions. For example, we have tried to humanize the music sections, making the music simpler than before, and treating it as an expression of human hope, aspiration, triumph, and vision of beauty. Second, we have tried to create better balance between literature, the visual arts, and music than was achieved in previous editions. Thus, the art sections have been greatly expanded. Third, we have constantly kept in mind that this is a book for the last part of the twentieth century. Ideas of a "gentleman's" knowledge of past art have been discarded in favor of a rigorous and disciplined search for meaning in our own time and for our own students and teachers.

Naturally, a single course cannot cover the field. The materials presented in this book are simply intended to give the student a start toward viewing the arts in a humanistic light, and to begin to give him some of the myriad meanings in a few of life's experiences. It is hoped that this work will cause him to begin to ask questions about things which he never knew were there to be questioned. It is hoped, too, that he will be given the skills in thinking that will enable him to find some of the answers to his questions and eventually to formulate tentative and growing answers of his own through study and creation in the arts.

The text is organized chronologically, utilizing the traditional framework of the Greek, Roman, medieval, Renaissance, seventeenth, eighteenth and nineteenth centuries, and the twentieth century. We feel that a sense of change and development is of extreme importance, a sense that can most naturally be presented in a chronological approach. The section dealing with the Western world since 1914 has been greatly expanded and it is now treated as the soil in which a new cultural life is growing and on which the old patterns of the nineteenth century are being destroyed.

For reasons of space we have dealt only with the Western world. The teacher's attention, however, is called to new companion volumes on non-Western cultures. Each unit in *The Search* starts with one or more chapters in which the world-picture of an epoch is presented, since artists work within a definite *weltanschauung*, interpreting or changing it. Then the unit moves on to a consideration of the arts themselves as testimony to man's creativity. In such creativity men have found their freedom in the past, and are finding it now. Hence the theme of this book.

Acknowledgments

■ The authors are indebted to the following authors and publishers for permission to reprint selections from their works:

Charles Scribner's Sons. Reprinted by permission of Charles Scribner's Sons from *The Aeneid of Virgil*, pages 87-112, translated by Rolfe Humphries. Copyright 1951 Charles Scribner's Sons.

Maurice A. Crane for permission to reprint his translations of two of the *Odes of Horace.*

Dell Publishing Co., Inc., for permission to reprint George Thomson's translations of the "Agamemnon" and "Eumenides." Reprinted from *Aeschylus* edited by Robert W. Corrigan. Translated by George Thomson. Copyright © 1965 by Dell Publishing Co., Inc., and used by permission of the publisher.

Desclee & Cie Editeurs S.A., Tournai, Belgium, for permission to reprint selections from the *Liber Usualis*, Copyright © 1961 by Desclee & Cie, Tournai.

Frederick Ungar Publishing Co., Inc., for permission to reprint a selection from Book III, Prose 10 of Boethius, *Consolations of Philosophy*, James J. Buchanan, ed. Copyright Frederick Ungar Publishing Co.

George Braziller, Inc., for permission to reprint from *Judaism*, by Arthur Herzberg, ed., pp. 73-74. Copyright 1961, by Arthur Herzberg; reprinted with the permission of the publisher.

Grove Press for a brief selection from D.H. Lawrence, *Lady Chatterley's Lover.* Reprinted with the permission of the publisher.

Holt, Rinehart and Winston, Inc., for Robert Frost's "Stopping by Woods on a Snowy Evening," from *The Poetry of Robert Frost* edited by Edward Connery Lathem. Copyright 1923 by Holt, Rinehart and Winston, Inc. Copyright 1951 by Robert Frost. Reprinted by permission of Holt, Rinehart and Winston, Inc. For A.E. Housman's "With rue my heart is laden," from *A Shropshire Lad*—Authorized Edition—from *The Collected Poems of A.E. Housman.* Copyright 1939, 1940 © 1959 by Holt, Rinehart and Winston, Inc. Copyright © 1967, 1968 by Robert E. Symons. Reprinted by permission of Holt, Rinehart and Winston, Inc.

Houghton Mifflin Company for several selections from Henry Adams, *Mont St. Michel and Chartres;* and for twenty-two lines from Isabel Butler's translation of *The Song of Roland.*

The National Council of the Churches of Christ in the U.S.A. The Scripture quotations in this publication are from the Revised Standard Version of the Bible, Copyrighted 1946 and 1952 by the Division of Christian Education of the National Council of the Churches of Christ in the U.S.A. and used by permission.

New American Library, Inc., for Pluto's "Phaedo," from *Great Dialogues of Plato*, translated by W.H.D. Rouse and edited by Philip G. Rouse and Eric H. Warmington. Copyright © 1956, 1961 by John Clive Graves Rouse. Reprinted by arrangement with the New American Library, Inc., New York.

W.W. Norton and Co., for permission to reprint a selection from Oliver Strunk, *Source Readings in Music History.* Copyright © The W.W. Norton Co., New York, 1950 and Faber and Faber Ltd., London for British Empire Rights.

Oxford University Press for three selections from "Antigone" and "Oedipus the King" from *Three Theban Plays by Sophocles*, new translation by Theodore Howard Banks. Copyright, 1956, by Theodore Howard Banks. Reprinted by permission of Oxford University Press, Inc.

Penguin Books Ltd., for the complete play, *The Bacchae* from Euripides: *The Bacchae and Other Plays* translated by Philip Vellacott. Copyright 1972 and reprinted by permission of Philip Vellacott and Penguin Books Ltd.

Random House, Inc., Alfred A. Knopf, Inc., for Elinor Wylie's poem, "Sanctuary." Copyright 1921 by Alfred A. Knopf, Inc., and renewed 1949 by William Rose Benet. Reprinted from *Collected Poems of Elinor Wylie* by permission of the publisher.

Thomas Nelson and Sons, Ltd., for permission to reprint a selection from W.H.D. Rouse's translation of Homer's *Odyssey.* Thomas Nelson and the New American Library are publishers of the British and American editions respectively. Reprinted by permission of the publishers.

Time, the Weekly Newsmagazine, for permission to quote from the *Time* article: "On Running New York" from the issue of November 1, 1968. Reprinted by permission from *Time*, the Weekly Newsmagazine. Copyright Time, Inc., 1968.

A. Watkins, Inc., New York, for permission to reprint *Hell* from Dorothy Sayers' translation of Dante's Divine Comedy. Copyright 1949, Dorothy L. Sayers.

Wilbur Daniel Steele and Harold Matson for permission to reprint Mr. Steele's story, "The Man Who Saw Through Heaven."

World Publishing Company. A selection from *The Greek Experience* by C.M. Bowra. Copyright © 1957 by C.M. Bowra. Reprinted by permission of The World Publishing Company.

UNIT I

PROLOGUE: The Integrated Humanities

CHAPTER 1

The Humanities: Revolution and Relevance

■ "They were the best of times, the worst of times. . . ," wrote Dickens in *The Tale of Two Cities.* And so, it seems, is the last third of the twentieth century. We see all about us the destruction of an old way of life, a destruction which overwhelms many people by the terror of it all. On the other hand, it's an exciting time. The humanist, in particular, sees the sprouts of a new culture, a warmer way of life, springing up in the midst of boredom, confusion, and chaos. To see and to participate in the creation of a new civilization can make life exhilarating. Surveying our years, most people experience both despair and excitement. It is the best of times, the worst of times.

Very deliberately in this chapter we attempt to make a general and controversial survey of the years in which we are living. Then, to give perspective on our chaotic period, we have interpolated Wilbur Daniel Steele's short story, "The Man Who Saw Through Heaven." As a parallel, our present culture now finds itself at about the same spot where Mr. Diana, Steele's hero, was when he created his first mud sculptures. Around him and within him lay the wreckage of all his old beliefs. Yet he *was creating*, giving a shape and a meaning to his experience, developing a new and viable life out of the rubble and sterility of the old.

I

In this last third of the twentieth century, government frequently fails to govern well, economic systems no longer provide the desired flow of goods and services to all mankind,[1] moral codes

1. Providing goods and services to black, brown, red, and yellow people and to the chronically impoverished is a late twentieth-century demand upon our economic system not dreamed of in the colonial nineteenth, and the system has bogged down.

which were enunciated by our Victorian grandfathers are replaced by the "new morality" or "situational ethics." If one can believe a segment of a new generation of students, education does not educate relevantly. The institutions which our culture built and which, in turn, preserve the culture, crack, crumble, and, in spite of all sorts of patch-jobs, seem ready to tumble down.

In terms of much adult personal life, our culture has become so stylized and encrusted that we can no longer express the deeper needs within us; our loves, our hates, our anxieties remain bottled up. Loneliness and alienation, the themes of so much recent literature, result from the conventionalized masks which our culture forces us to wear—the kindly-but-stern-professor-mask at school, the dutiful-husband mask at home, the smiling-all-is-well mask in our ordinary business dealings, the let-us-sit-down-and-be-sweetly-reasonable-mask when we meet with committees. Our life of once quiet desperation now cries for an expression which our stifling culture denies.

Although one hopes that there are many exceptions, it seems that the average adult spends the days of his years in routine, seemingly pointless, and repetitious activities—selling groceries, clothing, cars or real estate; driving large machines or small ones; pumping gas—for no visible end except a mirage-like, status-dictated income, a split-level house, and two cars in the garage. When the gas is pumped for one day, when the typewriter is covered, the groceries sold and the store locked, the television set remains to stupify the mind until bedtime. In terms of institutions, personal expression, and the workaday world, our culture, the "Establishment," has brought us to these ends.

The Establishment may be defined as the dominant mode of life in any culture, preserved and expanded by the force and weight of the combined institutions of the time and place. In the eighteenth century, particularly in the United States with the Declaration of Independence and the Constitution, our present establishment emerged as a revolutionary hope for the freedom of each person. For many years, fed by virile confidence and enthusiasm, and with vast virgin territories into which life could expand, it fulfilled that hope. Now it would appear that the hope and the enthusiasm have grown old, tired, and hardened in the arteries. A new culture based on life-values seems to be emerging. In the meantime, the goals of life have become material rather than human, and most men believe that they will find their freedom with increased wealth or the material things that wealth can buy: automobiles, a private swimming pool, an electric toothbrush. Let us make no mistake, these products are good, and they add greatly to our creature comforts. Thousands of lives have been saved, millions prolonged, by the medicines of our civilization. Yet even in these comfort-giving, life-saving efforts, we have polluted our planet to such an extent that all life may be choked out within the next century. The establishment has become dominated by power structures which mass-produce their products for a mass market and thus force conformity of hopes and desires on the population as a whole. The entire structure has become weighted down by a vast bureaucracy in which paper-workers have forgotten the original purpose of their work and keep themselves busy, their numbers growing, by passing papers back and forth among themselves.

Within this system, personal freedom has imperceptibly shifted its meaning to competition between individuals for material goods and status. ("Your name on the door deserves a carpet on the floor.") The Establishment professes to love peace, yet in its demand for uniformity either at home or abroad, it frequently uses terrible violence to suppress variation and to force "noncivilized" peoples into its mold. Because it strives for efficiency, it reduces people to numbers, for numbers can be machine-handled more quickly than persons. The establishment consists of the forces of government, of economics, of a great deal of education, of highly institutionalized religion, and of the family, banded together to promote these conforming, material values.

It is the purpose of this chapter, not so much to tell how we got this way as to point out that we are in the midst of a tremendous cultural change. At the moment it seems that the revolution is directed against our formal institutions, immoral wars, irrelevant education, racism, smug religion, pollution of our planet, and politico-economic failure to eliminate poverty. It is the contention here that these aspects of revolution are symptomatic; even the most violent of the activists are striking out against symptoms. The real change, for good or bad, seeks to replace the whole structure and fabric of Western culture as we have built it since the Renaissance. We are facing no minor cultural adjustment which can be resolved by a change in the voting procedures or even a change in the economic system. (Communism aims at material values with more fervor than does present-day capitalism and subordinates the individual with much greater weight.) Confronting us is a ground swell of change as great as that which men faced at the time the Roman Empire collapsed or in the transition between the Middle Ages and the Renaissance.

This book and the course for which it is a text, recognize the need for revolutionary change. (It makes precious little difference, by the way, whether or not one "favors" the revolution or not; one might as well favor or oppose the rising and setting of the sun.) The authors have long contended that our dominant cultural pattern is sterile and fruitless. The way of life which was so good for the upper-middle-class European in the mid-nineteenth century has run its course, and now serves to bind life rather than to set it free. The whole purpose of this book is to aid individual students to find personal freedom as they cut away the deadwood of the old pattern of life, saving all those things which are good, and in an orderly and knowledgeable way to create a new pattern which is fertile and life-giving.

Throughout this chapter two common fears will be disregarded. First, the threat of any nuclear device will not be considered. If someone explodes the bomb, all other problems will dissolve in a mushroom cloud. Second, many conservatives fear a general Communist take-over, and they talk of campus and city violence as being inspired by Communist agents. This may or may not be true, but it is beside the point here. Finally, we shall discuss problems in the United States only, though similar confrontations exist in greater or lesser degree throughout the Western world.

In considering the idea of a "cultural pattern," we would do well to select an example sufficiently removed from us in history so that we can examine it objectively. In looking at such a pattern, three things seem to be important: the concept of reality which was held at the time; the institutions which were built on that concept; and the method which was used to gain new knowledge, since the method of gaining knowledge always determines the *kind* of knowledge which is gained and shapes it into conformity with the method itself. As our example we may take Western men in the Middle Ages, who built walled villages and eventually walled cities. In almost the same pattern, they built a walled culture. Their concept of God as Reality was their solid foundation. Feudalism and manorialism, providing narrow but substantial political and economic systems, formed the walls on either side. The ceiling on their culture was Scholasticism, their method of discovering new knowledge, which accepted the Scriptures and the writings of the Church Fathers as the mother lode of all knowledge, with Aristotelian logic as the means of refining new knowledge from the mother lode. Scholasticism, it is to be noted, kept all thought within the framework of the walled culture. As long as the raw material for intellectual investigation lay in religious sources, and the method of "progress" was a closed deductive one, all new knowledge was necessarily oriented toward the medieval conception of God.

All that is past. From the time of Descartes, certainly from Newton's time, we have built a new cultural pattern. Descartes divided all phenomena into measurable and nonmeasurable classes. The nonmeasurable he thrust out of the realm of most intellectual consideration. From his time on, the quantitative elements of life would be the proper subjects for investigation and discovery. Sir Francis Bacon and others gave us what has since always been called "*the* scientific method" of treating this material. With material things as the mother lode of all knowledge, and with the inductive method of discovery, we have built the cultural pattern of the twentieth century, a pattern which may now be as narrow and as binding as the walled culture of the Middle Ages.

If we may continue to speak in analogies, it would seem that our present cultural pattern is like a pipe-line. Like a pipe, it is open-ended, and the people of this culture move with ever greater acceleration down the pipe. The confining wall in the main stream of our present civilization is our concept of reality, which consists only of those things that can be weighed and measured; the motive force is the antiseptic intellectualism of the scientific method. Because this culture is in constant motion, though always within the ever-narrowing confines of its pipe-line, we have the illusion of inevitable progress. One of the hardest concepts to comprehend in the twentieth century is that change by itself is not necessarily progress, a lesson which history fails to impress upon us.

Parenthetically, one wonders how much our idea of progress is conditioned by our concept of time as a constantly flowing stream. Newton, one remembers, assigned to God the duty of maintaining an even flow of time and space, and this idea has been a postulate in our cultural picture ever since. Of course other concepts of time are equally tenable; certainly in the Middle Ages when time was marked only by church bells and the silent flow of sand in an hourglass, Western man was not obsessed with the onward flow of time. Our concept is peculiar to the West. The Hindus and Buddhists think of time as a vast, still ocean on whose surface individualized phenomena rise, appear, and sink. Neither men of the Middle Ages nor Oriental men made "progress" in the Western sense. We, with a watch on the wrist, with ubiquitous clocks, and with calendars staring from every desk, impose an order on time and shackle it within our pipe-line. We ride the evenly flowing river of time, feeling that we must be going somewhere. (We do not know where, but we define the destination in terms of greater and greater affluence for all men.) We call that motion toward our dreamed-of materialistic utopia "progress."

The nature of this "progress" is indicated by the predictions of future "breakthroughs" as made by Dr. Olaf Helmer and J.J. Gordon, respectively senior mathematician and consultant to the Rand Corporation. These developments, with median dates, are as follows:

1. Biological agents to destroy enemy's will to resist 1975
2. Manned Mars and Venus fly-by . . .1978
3. Directed-energy weapons (laser, particle beams) 1980
4. Drugs to produce personality changes 1983
5. Primitive forms of life created in the laboratory 1989
6. Regional weather control 1990
7. Automated voting (legislation by plebescite) 2000
8. Hereditary defects controlled by altering genes 2000
9. Facsimile newspapers printed in the home 2005
10. Drugs to raise the level of intelligence 2012
11. Brain-computer link to enlarge man's intellect 2020
12. Breeding intelligent animals for low-grade labor 2050

Five of these twelve "breakthroughs" have direct bearing on the human being, but none of these five has any concern with the quality of life itself. As a matter of fact, those concerned with drugs to produce personality changes and the control of intelligence are, in effect, expressions of our desire to tinker with the human personality so that, if it cannot be free, it will at least be happy with its bondage. The brain-computer link is even more frightful in that it automatically ties the human mind to the machine, and limits the process of thought to mechanized channels.

In our time it would seem that the highly sophisticated computer, particularly with the development of "artificial intelligence," is the ultimate symbol of our culture. Ideally we can solve any problem in the world by feeding relevant data into the computer and collecting an answer at the far end of the machine. One is apt to forget how the "relevant" data are chosen. Actually any large problem is broken down into a very great number of small questions which can be answered with either a "yes" or "no." These many questions constitute the data which the computer digests; its solution is the aggregate of the thousands of partial answers. No one stops to think whether the answer to some of these atomized questions could be "maybe" instead of an absolute positive or negative. Or, if the answer to several of these atom-questions is "maybe," by how much is error compounded when the final solution comes from the machine? Let us grant that the computer can place men on the moon and bring them back within a hundred yards of a target on earth. In this realm of knowledge we deal with absolute and truly measurable forces. But in predicting an election? The computer can do this fairly accurately, since, in elections, it deals with large averages, actuarial statistics, rather than with the precise predictions of individual behavior. In computerizing a marriage? In any of the affairs of men? In the Middle Ages one hears that a favorite topic of debate among scholars was the number of angels that could dance on the head of a pin. We can consider the computerizing of problems concerned with individual human responses to experience as fruitfully as we can debate that old question. The computerized solution to intricate human concerns and the problem of the angels represent the sterile dead ends of two methods of thought. Yet the dream of the dominant segment of our rationalistic, pipe-line culture is eventually to computerize all of the questions which beset us.

So here we are in the last third of the twentieth century, enclosed in our pipe-line culture. We can see forward and backward, but we have only a glimpse of what may lie outside the walls. Progress is defined in terms of material things. (Serious men with human intelligence design bumper guards or concealed headlights as evidence of progress in automotive design. No one stops to ask why headlights should be concealed, or why bumpers, originally designed to protect the body of a car, need "guards.") Curiously, the more we study our environment, the thicker we make our surrounding wall, for all of our knowledge is filtered through the process which we have developed for the discovery of new knowledge. It is always of the same *kind* as before, narrowing and limiting human vision. Herein lies the ultimate significance of McLuhan's medium as message. Our medium does not consist merely of the television tube, the radio, the newspaper or magazine, or all of our methods of communication put together. The systems of communication simply express the basic medium: our way of thought. This way accepts reality as the measurable only, and deals with it through nonhuman, depersonalized, intellectual methods. This medium shapes whatever message we receive from all of our pursuits of knowledge. Thus our vision becomes ever more limited, our living space more and more cramped.

In our century we have been offered the inkling of a glimpse outside the thick walls of our pipe. Einstein was among the first to see outside when he proclaimed time and space, mass and energy, not as absolutes, but as functions (manifestations or appearances, really) of each other. The principle of complementary truth which views light and electrons as either wave or quantum phenomena, with the corollary that we deal only with the contradictory manifestations of light and electrons—the "real" light or the "real" electron being beyond the grasp of the human mind—takes us outside the realm of measurable truth. Indeed, Einstein and Infeld's *Evolution of Physics* makes clear the possibility of a view from outside our cultural framework.

The Einstein-Infeld book clearly suggests that all of our natural law in scientific realms, formerly believed to be so solid and absolute, is hypothesis made within the present limits of human intelligence and cultural framework. Our most basic belief in a "reality" which is solid and measurable is pulled out from under us. True reality, in Einsteinian terms, lies somewhere "out there" in a dimension which cannot now be plumbed by the mind of man. Einstein and all of the higher scientists in recent times have had to scrap the old scientific method as well as the basic concept of reality simply because the data with which they deal—atomic structure and space stretching to infinity—cannot be gathered and subjected to the types of experiment which were the significant steps of the old method. As nearly everyone knows, the methods employed by these scientists consist of exercises in higher mathematics carried on in the study rather than in the field or laboratory. Only occasionally can the *results* (as in $E = mc^2$) be checked by scientific extensions of our senses.

Not only in the realm of physics, but in other areas of knowledge, too, have we been offered the inkling of a glimpse outside our cultural limits. The general semanticists have warned us that our thought is still based on Aristotelian logic which tends to classify phenomena into larger and larger units, polarizing thought into generalizations which ignore differences between things. A generalization, like a map of a territory, tends to distort the territory which it represents. Since our thought process is almost entirely verbal, we deal with maps placed upon maps placed upon maps. If at the base of a thought process the distortion of a territory is slight, by how much has it grown when slight distortion is piled upon ever greater distortion? The problem is identical to the computerizing process mentioned earlier, for the computers are built in the image of our present process of thought. For more than two thousand years one intellectual map has been used as a basis for another, and that for still another. By now, how far wrong are our answers? When we think about problems of war, of poverty, of race relations, what kinds of answers could we find other than those derived by our Aristotelian minds? We do not know; we cannot even define the questions clearly.

In psychology, Freud gave us a glimpse of dimensions of the mind beyond the simplified patterns which we had known before and which we still use in our purely intellectualized consideration of problems. Before Freud, the behaviorists conceived a model of mind not much different from a telephone switchboard—or a computer. An impulse came in and the message was carried to appropriate nerves and muscles. Although modern psychologists have fairly well discredited Freud, they can never return to the switchboard model of mind. Any new picture must at least contain provisions for depths and dimensions beyond the superficial rational processes, for racial memory, and for libidinous impulses far removed from the favorite image of our thought process as a kind of neat and tidy intellection.

Our contact with the Oriental world has given us a peek outside our cultural prison, for here we have come to know a culture built on completely different foundations from our Graeco-Judeo-Christian tradition. We in the West have known of the Orient from the time of Alexander the Great, but our sympathetic attempt to understand its sources and traditions dates only from the Paris Exposition of 1889 when the late impressionist artists were first delighted with the possibilities of Eastern painting. From that time, Buddhist and Hindu cultures, principally, have been presented to English and American audiences in translation, in the work of several philosophers, and even by such popular novelists as Maugham, Huxley, and members of the Beat generation of the 1950s in their preoccupation with Zen Buddhism. From these sources we in Western civilization have come to know something of a cultural pattern completely different from our own—a pattern in which time is not considered as a stream and in which the differentiation between objects, a basic concept of Western thought, is obliterated. Many other differences exist, but these two are suggested here as fundamental.

Thus, in the last third of the twentieth century we find ourselves in a narrow and binding cultural pattern. Within this pattern only those things which were solid and measurable have been accepted as real, only such things have been accepted as the raw material for human thought. The human mind has been considered as a dry, cold thinking-machine whose ultimate expression is the computer. In the middle of the nineteenth century, Thomas Henry Huxley expressed the common belief when he spoke of the intellect as a "clear, cold, logic engine, with all of its parts of equal strength, and in smooth working order; ready, like a steam engine, to be turned to any kind of work, and spin the gossamers as well as forge the anchors of the mind; whose mind is stored with a knowledge of the great and fundamental truths of Nature and of the laws of her operation. . . ." This view has shaped our pipe-line culture so that its walls encrust on the inside to allow the human being less and less room for life itself.

Einsteinian physics, general semantics, Freudian psychology, and a beginning grasp of Oriental philosophy have allowed our vision to escape from its pipe-line cultural prison, and have allowed us to begin to see ourselves from other platforms than the rational, materialistic viewpoints within our own structure. In the meantime, the institutions which are characteristic of our own pattern have failed badly.

This, then, is where we find ourselves in the last third of the twentieth century, except that we have not considered the symptoms of change and the all too frequent repressive reaction of the establishment. While it sometimes seems as if the revolution is being carried out entirely by young people, the generation gap is much more apparent than real. Many men and women well over the age of thirty have felt the aridity of our present way of life quite as keenly as have the young. Leaders in business and industry, ministers, teachers, and many others have involved themselves in the process of cultural change, seeking to avoid purely destructive violence on the one hand and fascist overreaction on the other. The promoters of cultural change are to be found in all age groups; the illusion of youth-revolution comes about largely because the violence of many of the youth activities is more television-prone than is the great ground swell of change in the whole population.

II

Symptoms of change can be roughly categorized in five groups. First one saw the overt attacks on the establishment—early "happenings," the "Free Speech" movement at Berkeley, the black riots in cities and on campuses, and the white riots like those of Students for a Democratic Society. Second were the beatniks or hippies as dropouts from the establishment. Third, some academic attempts at revolt revealed themselves in the form of sensitivity sessions and multimedia teaching. Fourth has been the realization that our present way of life violates the natural order of the planet so that the air, the water, and the earth may become incapable of sustaining life. Fifth has been the revolt in the arts in such plays as *Dionysius in '69* and *Che!*, conceptual art, and the new music of the electronic and computerized varieties. In most of the arts, particularly music, we see one impulse which attempts to ally itself with the machine-culture and to exploit and perhaps even to destroy traditional man-made works, and another which has attempted to strike out against the artery-hardened institutions of our pipe-line culture.

In all of the five groups of symptoms listed we see an attack against the reduction of persons to computer-numbers, and against the personal loneliness and alienation which comes about as highly stylized forms of expression and communication encase individual personalities in a mask so thick and warping that each individual looks and speaks like every other individual (like rows of packaged cereals on the supermarket shelf), while deeply personal emotions and warmth of individual expression fester beneath the hardened mask.

An analysis in depth of the five groups of revolts against our pipe-line culture is not possible here, and would only result in series of generalizations which would lack solid evidence for support. One can list a great number of recent books which have made an exhaustive analysis of the aspects of revolt in society and the arts. However, as one examines the different kinds of art and social events, a number of common characteristics emerge. The first of these is violence. Those who engage in such activities are striking against a culture which smothers them, and are trying to build a social structure in which they can find themselves. But their effort is incomplete because they cannot yet see what a new culture can be.

A second characteristic of all the phenomena noted is escape from society. Whether one is discussing the hippies, the use of hallucinatory drugs, or academically respectable multimedia teaching sessions, the entire effort lies in the direction of removal from the limits of our cultural pattern. The hippies deny materialistic values in life. The split-level, two-car rewards of conformity do not attract them. In the use of drugs—now a widespread phenomenon not confined to any particular group in society—and in the multimedia experiments, the goal is removal of the self from the boundaries of time and space which rational Western society accepts as postulates, and upon which most of our institutions are based.

The third characteristic of the various movements is the return to the irrational, Dionysiac element of our nature. Many of the revolutionaries turn their backs upon intellect and upon elaborate structures of language as the embodiment of intellection. They glorify sensation, and communication through feelings of the body. They choose the act which releases feeling rather than the planned and patterned activity which has produced so much Western "progress."

All of the five trends noted have one element in common. They all reject the narrow, cold rationalism (essentially a false interpretation of true rationalism, which considers the whole man and the total environment in its intellectual process) which has built our pipe-line culture. All of the trends seek to establish the freedom of the individual to create and to be himself.

A new culture is in the process of gestation, but its birth is still a long way off. The most obvious trends and characteristics of our time may be negative and destructive. Yet, as will be shown later in this chapter and illustrated throughout this book in its analysis of cultural change, nihilism, destruction and negativism are an essential part of the growth process. Francis Thompson, the poet, once asked the question of God, "Ah! must Thou char the wood ere Thou canst limn[2] with it?" In many cases the answer seems to be in the affirmative. For a person who is conventionally minded, much of our analysis may lead only to pessimism. Yet, as the barbarism of the Gauls was necessary to invigorate the wornout society of the Romans, so the forces of protest against the establishment represent new human energy—unleashed, undisciplined, but leading to a new and strong cultural pattern based on the quality of living itself and on human rather than materialistic values.

III

This book has at least two purposes: (1) to help the student begin to find his own personal freedom and (2) to help him in the construction of a new society with an emphasis on human and life-giving values rather than materialistic and repressive ones. Fortunately both can be approached through the arts and philosophy, for they are the means of discovery which explore human experience and yield new meanings for that experience and new significance to life itself.

First, what do we mean by personal freedom? A very simple analogy may help make this idea clear. One may consider the expert swimmer and the person first learning to swim. The learner does a tremendous lot of splashing and gets almost nowhere. The expert moves through the water with a minimum of disturbance, makes it look easy, and gets where he is going. So the person with a measure of freedom moves through life knowing himself and the medium through which he is traveling, knowing the goals he wishes to reach, and he reaches them with a minimum of disturbance. The freedom we are talking about is not conditioned absolutely by political, social, and economic surroundings, although such factors may help or hinder the person. One can imagine a political prisoner in Siberia whose knowledge of himself and whose personal values permit him to be a free and independent spirit in the most squalid of surroundings. His goals are not those of *going* somewhere, or of *getting* some material thing, but of *being* a particular person. The movement of the person toward *Being* measures his approach toward the personal freedom of which we are talking.

A person can come to know himself, can establish an ever-expanding personal philosophy which encompasses his value system, and can know the substance of the life through which he travels almost solely through the arts. Of course direct experience with all of life might seem to be a better way, but we all know that such experience often gives us dusty and confused answers, and, further, if anyone waits for enough immediate sensation he would be 99 years old before the search ever got started. Chapter 2 will discuss this personal humanistic value of literature, music, and the visual arts in more detail. Here let it be said only that the sincere artist confronts the great problems of human experience, explores them, cuts away the irrelevancies that confuse us in direct experience, and leads us to new meanings. The greatest artists often present us with a visible symbol of the highest human being, as in Michelangelo's statue of "David," as in the Parthenon, or as in Dante's *Divine Comedy*. The individual, having made these meanings and these exaltations of the spirit a part of himself, can make more and more discriminating value judgments, and is on his way in the search for personal freedom.

In approaching the second of the goals of this book, the building of a culture on human values, one needs to know how a culture is built. Philosophers of history have found many patterns which seem to account for the growth, flowering, and decay of civilizations. In this book we are using a very modified and simplified form of the "culture-epoch" theory as a framework upon which to arrange our materials. This theory is neither more nor less "true" than any of a half-dozen other theories which attempt to account for the changes which have occurred throughout the recorded story of mankind.

According to the culture-epoch theory, a culture is founded upon whatever conception of reality is held by the great majority of people over a considerable period of time. This is true even though the majority may not be aware of any concept of reality or, more probably, take it so much for granted that they are not aware that it is simply a human idea, held on faith. Thus, for most people at the time this is written, a typewriter is real, a physical tree is real, and all things which can be seen, heard, smelled, felt or tasted are real.

As a matter of fact, a number of scientists, philosophers, and religious thinkers have given us different concepts of reality which have been widely held. These thinkers have contemplated the millions of forms of life, many of them bearing resemblances to others, yet each one different; they have examined the forms of earth, air, fire and water; they have wondered about the processes of change by which a tree today may, at some time in the future, disintegrate into earth and reappear in some totally alien form. They have watched such nontangible things as sunlight and air becom-

2. Limn: to draw or paint, i,e., to create. (From "The Hound of Heaven.")

ing leaf and branch. Pondering these things, they come inevitably to the ultimate question: "What is the nature of reality?"

To reach an answer, their questions usually come down to a few profound inquiries, some of which may be given here. For example they might say, "We see change all around us. We see grass eaten and turn into cow. We see cow eaten and turn into man. We see man disintegrate and turn into earth. If all these changes can take place, what are the universal elements of which all things are composed?" Or they might say, "We see an individual human, John Doe, as baby, as youth, as adult, as senile old man, as corpse. From one moment to the next, he is never the same. Yet he is always the same, John Doe, a distinct being. Can it be that nothing is permanent, that reality is a process rather than a thing or group of things? If we have change, then, *how* does the process take place? And more important, we know that we live in a world of constant change, but what force *directs* the process?"

"Nonsense," retorts another group of thinkers. "That which is in a constant state of flow cannot be real. Only that which is permanent and unchanging can be real. What, then, in the universe is permanent, unchanging in itself, yet is able to transform itself, manifest itself, or produce from itself the countless forms which we see around us?"

These are some of the basic questions which the pure thinker contemplates, and his answers are various concepts of reality.

Based upon one idea of reality which seems to be irrefutably true, other specialized thinkers build the different thought-structures which underlie our visible institutions. These include a philosophy of justice from which particular forms of law and government spring; a philosophy of education which dictates the nature of our schools and the material taught in them; a religious philosophy which becomes apparent in churches and creeds; and an economic philosophy which yields its particular ways of producing and distributing goods and services, including the token-systems which are used as money. Other philosophies and institutions could be named, but those listed are some of the chief ones which affect our daily living. When these are formed, we have a complete culture, but always by the time such a pattern is established, we have forces at work which tend to destroy it.

The destroyers are new pure thinkers who note inconsistencies within the idea of reality itself, and who question postulates or find contradictions within them.

From these new thinkers (philosophers, scientists, religious men) comes a new idea of reality so convincing that it cannot be brushed aside. It must be accepted. Suddenly the whole structure of the culture finds itself without foundation. The justice and the law that were appropriate in the old culture no longer fit on the new foundation; the old education is no longer appropriate; old religious beliefs no longer describe man's position in relation to God; old ways of making things and distributing them no longer suffice.

At this time men are plunged into a *period of chaos*, the first step in the formation of a new epoch.

The symptoms of the period of chaos lie around us now in such profusion that they scarcely need description. In the latter part of the twentieth century this is where we live. New and shocking ideas, new moralities, and new beliefs are produced. The entrenched members of the establishment hang onto the old ways and preach them or enforce them by police methods with more ardor than ever before. The great number of people, caught between the old and the new, do not know what to believe or how to act. At such a time as this we witness a retreat from society of a significant segment of the population, a retreat to whatever sort of safe haven is most popular at the time and which seems to protect them most from the storms that rage within the world of men. In other words, we see in the 1970s a period of chaos.

Out of this confusion, the second period within a culture-epoch begins to emerge, *the period of adjustment.* At this point the great artists, whether they be painters, writers, sculptors, composers of music, or creators in some other medium, make their highest contribution to society. Phidias, Aeschylus, Dante, the designers of the great Gothic churches of the twelfth and thirteenth centuries, Michelangelo, Beethoven, Goethe—these men begin to suggest the new line, the new shape and pattern for a new culture.

Perhaps two ideas need to be stressed about the role of the artist in the development of a cultural pattern. First, the artist does not necessarily know all about new ideas of reality. For example, the artist in our time does not necessarily know all about Einstein's theory. The artist is simply a man of greater sensitivity than others, and with great skill in the medium in which he works. As a sensitive man he feels, probably more keenly than the rest of us, the tensions of his time—the pulls of this belief and the pulls of another contradictory one—within himself. His nature as artist will not let him rest until he has explored the confusing experience of man and discovered some meaning, some significance, therein. The great artist is always the *composer* (whether he be musician, writer, painter, choreographer, architect, or sculptor), the man who puts things together in new relationships and finds new meanings for man's experience.

A second idea that we need to recognize about the artist's contribution to the formation of a cultural pattern is that it is not his subject matter so much as his basic structure which yields the cultural meaning. For example, one may compare the structure of a Norwegian stave church with that of the Parthenon in Athens. The subject matter of both is roughly the same: they are both temples built for the worship of a god. But what a difference! The stave church is disproportionately tall, a mass of sharp, angular lines looking more than anything else like an arrow shot into the skies. The Parthenon is low, horizontal, calm, and coolly rational. Its curved lines are so carefully calculated in terms of optical science as to appear absolutely straight to the human eye.

It comes down to this: Styles in beauty change as the basic characteristics of people change. Or perhaps it works the other way; perhaps as new glimpses of beauty are caught by the artists, people themselves change to conform to the new beauty.

However it may happen, the artist, especially in the period of chaos and early in the period of adjustment within a culture-epoch, feels the stresses, the tensions, and the turmoil of the period within himself. He explores the conflicts within himself—which are the conflicts of the general population as well—and creates new structures, new designs, which synthesize the elements of conflict and give new meaning to man's experience. Some of these works of art, probably depending upon the individual artist's breadth of vision and ability to compose his insight into significance, are seized upon as symbols of new pattern and new truth in society. They express the new idea of beauty and truth.

At this point another element of the population—we may call them the "intellectuals"—enter the picture. They are people like ourselves, college students and faculty members, government officials, ministers, business executives, and many others who think seriously about things and who, like the artists, have been troubled by the conflict of their times. They still are working within the period of adjustment in an epoch. They become aware of the new meanings and new patterns which the artists have produced, and they start reshaping these designs into new philosophies of justice, of economics, of religion, and the like, and begin to build concrete institutions out of the philosophies that they have created. Slowly through their work order emerges out of the chaos.

When their work is finished, we come to the third period within a culture-epoch, the *period of balance*. At this point, the idea of reality, the philosophies which underlie our basic institutions, and the institutions themselves are all in harmony. Early in a period of balance, life must be very satisfying; everyone must know the reason for getting up in the morning to face the day. But if balance lasts too long, life begins to get dull. The big jobs all seem to be done, and decadence, boredom, and world-weariness may set in. As we look back upon the end of the Greek epoch, the Roman interlude, indeed, to the end of the Victorian period, boredom and decadence seem to be present.

But change comes inevitably. At the beginning of the twentieth century physicists were assuring young men that the great discoveries in physics had all been made and that only little tidying-up jobs remained. At the same time, Einstein was beginning his work, which was to supersede all of our knowledge in the area of physics. Just when men have been certain of everything in their periods of balance, new pure thinkers come along to upset the whole apple cart into a new epoch.

A word of caution should be appended here. This systematic description of an epoch makes it sound as if artists only function in a time of chaos or adjustment, or as if philosophers quit philosophizing until their proper time came around. This, of course, is not true. While the epoch does divide itself into three rough periods, all of the functions occur with greater or lesser impact throughout the entire time period.

In this book, the various periods of history will be treated in the following way: The rise of Athenian democracy in the fifth century B.C. and its rapid decline will be treated as one culture-epoch. The Roman period from the time of the rule of Julius Caesar will be regarded as an attempt to maintain rationalistic Greek times, under law, and backed by strong military authority. It does not constitute an epoch of the type we have been describing. Because of their far-reaching importance, Judaism and Christianity will be treated separately, though inadequately because of limited space. Actually the teachings of Jesus represent the work of the pure thinker, and the Christian concept of God was a new concept of reality which served as the foundation for the Middle Ages. The Middle Ages, dating from about A.D. 450 to 1450 will be considered as a complete epoch. The time period from 1450 to the early twentieth century really constitute another epoch, with the Renaissance as a large segment of the period of chaos within it. Because the Renaissance, using the approximate dates of 1450 to 1650, presents so much of interest for the student of humanities, however, it will be treated as a separate time period. Then, with the clash of rationalism and romanticism and the final emergence of the Faustian man we will consider the period from about 1650 to the early twentieth century as a complete epoch. The last unit of this book will look as carefully as possible at cultural change with which we in the twentieth century are so deeply involved.

The humanities *are* the arts of literature, painting, music, sculpture, architecture, and the dance, and the discipline of philosophy which permeates all of the arts and finally unites them all. As set forth in Chapter 2, the arts, taken together, are a separate field of human knowledge with their own area of exploration and discovery, and with a method of their own. So these volumes will concentrate on the great artistic production of each of the time periods outlined above. Each unit is planned to give a chapter or two to the social, scientific, religious and philosophic climate of the period in which the artists were working, for the artist usually accepts the scientific and social world-picture of his time. Following these introductory discussions, direct attention will be given to the arts themselves, with enough examples of each of the arts to reveal the new answers to the great questions of mankind, the new patterns, structures, and meanings which the artists found for life in their time. It is to be hoped that by this treatment the student will be able to trace the development and changes through history of the problems which plague us so sorely in our own time. Equipped with this knowledge of the great answers which have been found in the past and which shape the way we live today, having come to know the great expressions of humanity revealed at its fullest, the student should be well on his way to find his own freedom and to build a new culture based on human values.

The Man Who Saw Through Heaven

Wilbur Daniel Steele

People have wondered (there being obviously no question of romance involved) how I could ever have allowed myself to be let in for the East African adventure of Mrs. Diana in search of her husband. There were several reasons. To begin with, the time and effort and money weren't mine; they were the property of the wheel of which I was but a cog, the Society through which Diana's life had been insured, along with the rest of that job lot of missionaries. The "letting in" was the firm's. In the second place, the wonderers have not counted on Mrs. Diana's capacity for getting things done for her. Meek and helpless. Yes, but God was on her side. Too meek, too helpless to move mountains herself, if those who happened to be handy didn't move them for her then her God would know the reason why. Having dedicated her all to making straight the Way, why should her neighbor cavil at giving a little? The writer for one, a colonial governor-general for another, railway magnates, insurance managers, *safari* leaders, the ostrich farmer of Ndua, all these and a dozen others in their turns have felt the hundred-ton weight of her thin-lipped meekness—have seen her in metaphor sitting grimly on the doorsteps of their souls.

A third reason lay in my own troubled conscience. Though I did it in innocence, I can never forget that it was I who personally conducted Diana's party to the Observatory on that fatal night in Boston before it sailed. Had it not been for that kindly intentioned "hunch" of mine, the astounded eye of the Reverend Hubert Diana would never have gazed through the floor of Heaven, and he would never have undertaken to measure the Infinite with the foot rule of his mind.

It all started so simply. My boss at the shipping-and-insurance office gave me the word in the morning. "Bunch of missionaries for the *Platonic* tomorrow. They're on our hands in a way. Show'em the town." It wasn't so easy when you think of it: one male and seven females on their way to the heathen; though it was easier in Boston than it might have been in some other towns. The evening looked the simplest. My friend Krum was at the Observatory that semester; there at least I was sure their sensibilities would come to no harm.

On the way out in the street car, seated opposite to Diana and having to make conversation, I talked of Krum and of what I knew of his work with the spiral nebulae. Having to appear to listen, Diana did so (as all day long) with a vaguely indulgent smile. He really hadn't time for me. That night his life was exalted as it had never been, and would perhaps never be again. Tomorrow's sailing, the actual fact of leaving all to follow Him, held his imagination in thrall. Moreover, he was a bridegroom of three days with his bride beside him, his nerves at once assuaged and thrilled. No, but more. As if a bride were not enough, arrived in Boston, he had found himself surrounded by a very galaxy of womanhood gathered from the four corners; already within hours one could feel the chaste tentacles of their feminine dependence curling about the party's unique man: already their contacts with the world of their new lives began to be made through him; already they saw in part through his eyes. I wonder what he would have said if I had told him he was a little drunk.

In the course of the day I think I had got him fairly well. As concerned his Church he was at once an asset and a liability. He believed its dogma as few still did, with a simplicity, "the old-time religion." He was born that kind. Of the stuff of the fanatic, the reason he was not a fanatic was that, curiously impervious to little questionings, he had never been aware that his faith was anywhere attacked. A self-educated man, he had accepted the necessary smattering facts of science with a serene indulgence, as simply so much further proof of what the Creator could do when He put His Hand to it. Nor was he conscious of any conflict between these facts and the fact that there existed a substantial Heaven, geographically up, and a substantial Hot Place, geographically down.

So, for his Church, he was an asset in these days. And so, and for the same reason, he was a liability. The Church must after all keep abreast of the times. For home consumption, with modern congregations, especially urban ones, a certain streak of "healthy" skepticism is no longer amiss in the pulpit; it makes people who read at all more comfortable in their pews. A man like Hubert Diana is more for the cause than a hundred. But what to do with him? Well, such things arrange themselves. There's the Foreign Field. The blacker the heathen the whiter the light they'll want, and the solider the conception of a God the Father enthroned in a Heaven of which the sky above them is the visible floor.

And that, at bottom, was what Hubert Diana believed. Accept as he would with the top of his brain the fact of a spherical earth zooming through space, deep in his heart he knew that the world lay flat from modern Illinois to ancient Palestine, and that the sky above it, blue by day and by night festooned with guiding stars for wise men, was the nether side of a floor on which the resurrected trod.

I shall never forget the expression of his face when he realized he was looking straight through it that night. In the quiet dark of the dome I saw him remove his eye from the eyepiece of the telescope up there on the staging and turn it, in the ray of a hooded bulb, on the demon's keeper, Krum.

"What's that, Mr. Krum? I didn't get you!"

"I say, that particular cluster you're looking at—"

"This star, you mean?"

"You'd have to count awhile to count the stars describing their orbits in that 'star,' Mr. Diana. But what I was saying—have you ever had the wish I used to have as a boy—that you could actually look back into the past? With your own two eyes?"

Diana spoke slowly. He didn't know it, but it had already begun to happen; he was already caught. "I have often wished, Mr. Krum, that I might actually look back into the time of our Lord. Actually. Yes."

Krum grunted. He was young. "We'd have to pick a nearer neighbor than *Messier 79* then. The event you see when you put your eye to that lens is happening much too far in the past. The lightwaves thrown off by that particular cluster on the day, say, of the Crucifixion—*you* won't live to see them. They've hardly started yet—a mere twenty centuries on their way—leaving them something like eight hundred and thirty centuries yet to come before they reach the earth."

Diana laughed the queerest catch of a laugh. "And—and there—there won't be any earth here, then, to welcome them."

"*What?*" It was Krum's turn to look startled. So for a moment the two faces remained in confrontation, the one, as I say, startled, the other exuding visibly little sea-green globules of sweat. It was Diana that caved in first, his voice hardly louder than a whisper.

"W-w-will there?"

None of us suspected the enormousness of the thing that had happened in Diana's brain. Krum shrugged his shoulders and snapped his fingers. Deliberately. *Snap!* "What's a thousand centuries or so in the cosmic reckoning?" He chuckled. "We're just beginning to get out among'em with the *Messier*, you know. In the print room, Mr. Diana, I can show you photographs of clusters to which, if you cared to go, traveling at the speed of light—"

The voice ran on; but Diana's eye had gone back to the eyepiece, and his affrighted soul had re-entered the big black tube sticking its snout out of the slit in the iron hemisphere. . . . "At the speed of light!" . . . . That unsuspected, that wildly chance found chink in the armor of his philosophy! The body is resurrected and it ascends to Heaven instantaneously. At what speed must it be borne to reach instantaneously that city beyond the ceiling of the sky? At a speed inconceivable, mystical. At, say (as he had often said to himself), *the speed of light*. . . . And now, hunched there in the trap that had caught him, black rods, infernal levers and wheels, he was aware of his own eye passing vividly through unpartitioned emptiness, *eight hundred and fifty centuries at the speed of light!*

"And still beyond these," Krum was heard, "we begin to come into the regions of the spiral nebulae. We've some interesting photographs in the print room, if you've the time."

The ladies below were tired of waiting. One had "lots of packing to do." The bride said, "Yes, I do think we should be getting along, Hubert, dear; if you're ready—"

The fellow actually jumped. It's lucky he didn't break anything. His face looked greener and dewier than ever amid the contraptions above. "If you—you and the ladies, Cora—wouldn't mind—if Mr.—Mr.—(he'd mislaid my name) would see you back to the hotel—" Meeting silence, he began to expostulate. "I feel that this is a rich experience. I'll follow shortly; I know the way."

In the car going back into the city Mrs. Diana set at rest the flutterings of six hearts. Being unmarried, they couldn't understand men as she did. When I think of that face of hers, to which I was destined to grow only too accustomed in the weary, itchy days of the trek into Kavirondoland, with its slightly tilted nose, its irregular pigmentation, its easily inflamed lids, and long moist cheeks, like those of a hunting dog, glorying in weariness, it seems incredible that a light of coyness could have found lodgment there. But that night it did. She sat serene among her virgins.

"You don't know Bert. You wait; he'll get a perfectly wonderful sermon out of all that to-night, Bert will."

Krum was having a grand time with his neophyte. He would have stayed up all night. Immured in the little print room crowded with files and redolent of acids, he conducted his disciple "glassy-eyed" through the dim frontiers of space, holding before him one after another the likenesses of universes sister to our own, islanded in immeasurable vacancy, curled like glimmering crullers on their private Milky Ways, and hiding in their wombs their myraid "coal-pockets," star-dust foetuses of which—their quadrillion years accomplished—their litters of new suns would be born, to bear their planets, to bear their moons in turn.

"And beyond these?"

Always, after each new feat of distance, it was the same. "And beyond?" Given an ell, Diana surrendered to a pop-eyed lust for nothing less than light-years. "And still beyond?"

"Who knows?"

"The mind quits. For if there's no end to these nebulae—"

"But supposing there is?"

"An end? But, Mr. Krum, in the very idea of an ending—"

"An end to what we might call this particular category of magnitudes. Eh?"

"I don't get that."

"Well, take this—take the opal in your ring there. The numbers and distances inside that stone may conceivably be to themselves as staggering as ours to us in our own system. Come! that's not so far-fetched. What are we learning about the structure of the atom?—a nucleus (call it a sun) revolved about in eternal orbits by electrons (call them planets, worlds). Infinitesimal; but after all what are bigness and littleness but matters of comparison? To eyes on one of those electrons (don't be too sure there aren't any) its tutelary sun may flame its way across a heaven a comparative ninety million miles away. Impossible for them to conceive of a boundary to their billions of atomic systems, molecular universes. In that category of magnitudes its diameter is infinity; once it has made the leap into our category and become an opal it is merely a quarter of an inch. That's right, Mr. Diana, you may well stare at it: between *now* and *now* ten thousand histories may have come and gone down there. . . . And just so the diameter of our own cluster of universes, going over into another category, may be. . ."

"May be a . . a ring . . a little stone . . in a . . a—ring."

Krum was tickled by the way the man's imagination jumped and engulfed it.

"Why not? That's as good a guess as the next. A ring, let's say, worn carelessly on the—well, say the tentacle—of some vast organism—some inchoate creature hobnobbing with its cloudy kind in another system of universes—which in turn—"

It is curious that none of them realized next day that they were dealing with a stranger, a changed man. Why he carried on, why he capped that night of cosmic debauch by shaving, eating an unremarkable breakfast, packing his terrestrial toothbrush and collars, and going up the gangplank in tow of his excited convoy to sail away, is beyond explanation—unless it was simply that he was in a daze.

It wasn't until four years later that I was allowed to know what had happened on that ship, and even then the tale was so disjointed, warped, and opinionated, so darkly seen in the mirror of Mrs. Diana's orthodoxy, that I had almost to guess what it was really all about.

"When Hubert turned irreligious. . . " That phrase, recurrent on her tongue in the meanderings of the East African quest to which we were by then committed, will serve to measure her understanding. Irreligious! Good Lord! But from that sort of thing I had to reconstruct the drama. Evening after evening beside her camp fire (appended to the Mineral Survey Expedition Toward Uganda through the kindness—actually the worn-down surrender—of the Protectorate government) I lingered a while before joining the merrier engineers, watched with fascination the bumps growing under the mosquitoes on her forehead, and listened to the jargon of her mortified meekness and her scandalized faith.

There had been a fatal circumstance, it seems, at the very outset. If Diana could but have been seasick, as the rest of them were (horribly), all might still have been well. In the misery of desired death, along with the other contents of a heaving midriff, he might have brought up the assorted universes of which he had been led too rashly to partake. But he wasn't. As if his wife's theory was right, as if Satan was looking out for him, he was spared to prowl the swooping decks immune. Four days and nights alone. Time enough to digest and assimilate into his being beyond remedy that lump of whirling magnitudes and to feel himself surrendering with a strange new ecstasy to the drunkenness of liberty.

Such liberty! Given Diana's type, it is hard to imagine it adequately. The abrupt, complete removal of the toils of reward and punishment; the withdrawal of the surveillance of an all-seeing, all-knowing Eye; the windy assurance of being responsible for nothing, important to no one, no longer (as the police say) "wanted"! It must have been beautiful in those few days of its first purity, before it began to be discolored by his contemptuous pity for others, the mask of his inevitable loneliness and his growing fright.

The first any of them knew of it—even his wife—was in mid-voyage, the day the sea went down and the seven who had been sick came up. There seemed an especial Providence in the calming of the waters; it was Sunday morning and Diana had been asked to conduct the services.

He preached on the text: "For of such is the kingdom of Heaven."

"If our concept of God means anything it means a God *all*-mighty, Creator of *all* that exists, Director of the *infinite*, cherishing in His Heaven the saved souls of *all space and all time.*"

Of course; amen. And wasn't it nice to feel like humans again, and real sunshine pouring up through the lounge ports from an ocean suddenly grown kind? . . . . But—then—*what* was Diana *saying?*

Mrs. Diana couldn't tell about it coherently even after a lapse of fifty months. Even in a setting as remote from that steamer's lounge as the equatorial bush, the emberreddened canopy of thorn trees, the meandering camp fires, the chant and tramp somewhere away of Kikuyu porters dancing in honor of an especial largesse of fat zebra meat—even here her memory of that impious outburst was too vivid, too aghast.

"It was Hubert's look! The way he stared at us! As if you'd said he was licking his chops! . . . . That *'Heaven'* of his!"

It seems they hadn't waked up to what he was about until he had the dimensions of his sardonic Paradise irreparably drawn in. The final haven of all right souls. Not alone the souls released from this our own tiny earth. In the millions of solar systems we see as stars how many millions of satellites must there be upon which at some time in their histories conditions suited to organic life subsist? Uncounted hordes of wheeling populations! Of men? God's creatures at all events, a portion of them reasoning. Weirdly shaped perhaps, but what of that? And that's only to speak of our own inconsiderable cluster of universes. That's to say nothing of other systems of magnitudes, where God's creatures are to our world what we are to the worlds in the atoms in our finger rings. (He had shaken *his*, here, in their astounded faces.) And all these, all the generations of these enormous and microscopic beings harvested through a time beside which the life span of our earth is as a second in a million centuries: all these brought to rest for an eternity to which time itself is a watch tick—all crowded to rest pellmell, thronged, serried, packed, packed to suffocation in layers unnumbered light-years deep. This must needs be our concept of Heaven if God is the God of the Whole. If, on the other hand—

The other hand was the hand of the second officer, the captain's delegate at divine worship that Sabbath day. He at last had "come to."

I don't know whether it was the same day or the next; Mrs. Diana was too vague. But here's the picture. Seven women huddled in the large stateroom on B deck, conferring in whispers, aghast, searching one another's eye obliquely even as they bowed their heads in prayer for some light—and all of a sudden the putting back of the door and the in-marching of the Reverend Hubert . . .

As Mrs. Diana tried to tell me, "You understand, don't you, he had just taken a bath? And he hadn't—he had forgotten to—"

Adam-innocent there he stood. Not a stitch. But I don't believe for a minute it was a matter of forgetting. In the high intoxication of his soul release, already crossed (by the second officer) and beginning to show his zealot claws, he needed some gesture stunning enough to witness to his separation, his unique rightness, his contempt of matchflare civilizations and infinitesimal taboos.

But I can imagine that stateroom scene: the gasps, the heads colliding in aversion, and Diana's six weedy feet of birthday suit towering in the shadows, and ready to sink through the deck I'll warrant, now the act was irrevocable, but still grimly carrying it off.

"And if, on the other hand, you ask me to bow down before a God peculiar to this one earth, this one grain of dust lost among the giants of space, watching its sparrows fall, profoundly interested in a speck called Palestine no bigger than the quadrillionth part of one of the atoms in the ring here on my finger—"

Really scared by this time, one of the virgins shrieked. It was altogether too close quarters with a madman.

Mad? Of course there was the presumption: "Crazy as a loon." Even legally it was so adjudged at the *Platonic's* first port of call, Algiers, where, when Diana escaped ashore and wouldn't come back again, he had to be given over to the workings of the French Law. I talked with the magistrate myself some forty months later, when, "let in" for the business as I have told, I stopped there on my way out.

"But what would you?" were his words. "We must live in the world as the world lives, is it not? Sanity is what? Is it, for example, an intellectual clarity, a balanced perception of the realities? Naturally, speaking out of court, your friend was of a sanity—of a sanity, sir—" Here the magistrate made with thumb and fingers the gesture only the French can make for a thing that is matchless, a beauty, a transcendent instance of any kind. He himself was Gallic, rational. Then, with a lift of shoulder: "But what would you? We must live in the world that seems."

Diana, impounded in Algiers for deportation, escaped. What after all are the locks and keys of this pinchbeck category of magnitudes? More remarkable still, there in Arab Africa, he succeeded in vanishing from the knowledge and pursuit of men. And of women. His bride, now that their particular mission had fallen through, was left to decide whether to return to America or to go on with two of the company, the Misses Brookhart and Smutts, who were bound for a school in Smyrna. In the end she followed the latter course. It was there, nearly four years later, that I was sent to join her by an exasperated and wornout Firm.

By that time she knew again where her husband-errant was—or where at least, from time to time in his starry dartings over this our mote of dust, he had been heard of, spoken to, seen.

Could we but have a written history of those years of his apostolic vagabondage, a record of the towns in which he was jailed or from which he was kicked out, of the ports in which he starved, of the ships on which he stowed away, presently to reveal himself in proselyting ardor, denouncing the earthlings, the fatelings, the dupes of bugaboo, meeting scoff with scoff, preaching the new revelation red-eyed, like an angry prophet. Or was it, more simply, like a man afraid?

Was that the secret, after all, of his prodigious restlessness? Had it anything in common with the swarming of those pale worms that flee the Eye of the Infinite around the curves of the stone you pick up in a field? Talk of the man without a country! What of the man without a universe?

It is curious that I never suspected his soul's dilemma until I saw the first of his mud-sculptures in the native village of Ndua in the province of Kasuma in British East. Here it was, our objective attained, we parted company with the government *safari* and shifted the burden of Way-straightening to the shoulders of Major Wyeside, the ostrich farmer of the neighborhood.

While still on the *safari* I put to Mrs. Diana a question that had bothered me: "Why on earth should your husband ever have chosen this particular neck of the woods to land up in? Why Kavirondoland?"

"It was here we were coming at the time Hubert turned irreligious, to found a mission. It's a coincidence, isn't it?"

And yet I would have sworn Diana hadn't a sense of humor about him anywhere. But perhaps it *wasn't* an ironic act. Perhaps it was simply that, giving up the struggle with a society blinded by "a little learning" and casting about for a virgin field, he had remembered this.

"I supposed he was a missionary," Major Wyeside told us with a flavor of indignation. "I went on that. I let him live here—six or seven months of it—while he was learning the tongue. I was a bit nonplussed, to put it mildly, when I discovered what he was up to."

What things Diana had been up to the Major showed us in one of the huts in the native kraal—a round dozen of them, modeled in mud and baked. Blackened blobs of mud, that's all. Likenesses of nothing under the sun, fortuitous masses sprouting haphazard tentacles, only two among them showing pustules that might have been experimental heads. . . The ostrich farmer saw our faces.

"Rum, eh? Of course I realized the chap was anything but fit. A walking skeleton. Nevertheless, whatever it is about these beasties, there's not a nigger in the village has dared set foot inside this hut since Diana left. You can see for yourselves it's about to crash. There's another like it he left at Suki, above here. Taboo, no end!"

So Diana's "hunch" had been right. He had found his virgin field indeed, fit soil for his cosmic fright. A religion in the making, here before our eyes.

"This was at the very last before he left," Wyeside explained. "He took to making these mud pies quite of a sudden; the whole lot within a fortnight's time. Before that he had simply talked, harangued. He would sit here in the doorway of an evening with the niggers squatted around and harangue'em by the hour. I knew something of it through my houseboys. The most amazing rot. All about the stars to begin with, as if these black baboons could half grasp *astronomy!* But that seemed all proper. Then there was talk about a something a hundred times as big and powerful as the world, sun, moon, and stars put together—some perfectly enormous stupendous awful being—but knowing how mixed the boys can get, it still seemed all regular—simply the parson's way of getting at the notion of an Almighty God. But no, they insisted, there wasn't any God. That's the point, they said; there *is no* God. . . Well, that impressed me as a go. That's when I decided to come down and get the rights of this star-swallowing monstrosity the beggar was feeding my labor on. And here he sat in the doorway with one of these beasties—here it is, this one—waving it furiously in the niggers' benighted faces. And do you know what he'd done?—you can see the mark here still on this wabble-leg, this tentacle business—he had taken off a ring he had and screwed it on just there. His ring, my word of honor! And still, if you'll believe it, I didn't realize he was just daft. Not until he spoke to me. 'I find,' he was good enough to enlighten me, 'I find I have to make it somehow concrete.' . . . 'Make what?' . . . 'Our wearer.' 'Our *what, where?*' . . . 'In the following category.' . . . His actual words, honor bright. I was going to have him sent down-country where he could be looked after. He got ahead of me though. He cleared out. When I heard he'd turned up at Suki I ought, I suppose, to have attended to it.

But I was having trouble with leopards. And you know how things go."

From there we went to Suki, the Major accompanying. It was as like Ndua as one flea to its brother, a stockade inclosing round houses of mud, wattles, and thatch, and full of naked heathen. The Kavirondo are the nakedest of all African peoples and, it is said, the most moral. It put a great strain on Mrs. Diana; all that whole difficult anxious time, as it were detachedly, I could see her itching to get them into Mother Hubbards and cast-off Iowa pants.

Here too, as the Major had promised, we found a holy of holies, rather a dreadful of dreadfuls, "taboo no end," its shadows cluttered with hurlothrumbos of Diana's artistry. What puzzled me was their number. Why this appetite for experimentation? There was an uncertainty; one would think its effect on potential converts would be bad. Here, as in Ndua, Diana had contented himself at first with words and skyward gesticulations. Not for so long however. Feeling the need of giving his concept of the cosmic "wearer" a substance much earlier, he had shut himself in with the work, literally—a fever of creation. We counted seventeen of the nameless "blobs," all done, we were told, in seven days and nights before their maker had again cleared out. The villagers would hardly speak of him; only after spitting to protect themselves, their eyes averted, and in an undertone, would they mention him: "He of the Ring." Thereafter we were to hear of him only as "He of the Ring."

Leaving Suki, Major Wyeside turned us over (thankfully, I warrant) to a native who told us his name was Charlie Kamba. He had spent some years in Nairobi, running for an Indian outfitter, and spoke English remarkably well. It was from him we learned, quite casually, when our modest eight-load *safari* was some miles on its way, that the primary object of our coming was nonexistent. Hubert Diana was dead.

Dead nearly five weeks—a moon and a little—and buried in the mission church at Tara Hill.

Mission church! There was a poser for us. *Mission church?*

Well then, Charlie Kamba gave us to know that he was paraphrasing in a large way suitable to our habits of thought. We wouldn't have understood *his* informant's "wizard house" or "house of the effigy."

I will say for Mrs. Diana that in the course of our halt of lugubrious amazement she shed tears. That some of them were not tears of unrealized relief it would be hardly natural to believe. She had desired loyally to find her husband, but when she should have found him—what? This problem, sturdily ignored so long, was now removed.

Turn back? Never! Now it would seem the necessity for pressing forward was doubled. In the scrub-fringed ravine of our halt the porters resumed their loads, the dust stood up again, the same caravan moved on. But how far it was now from being the same.

From that moment it took on, for me at least, a new character. It wasn't the news especially; the fact that Diana was dead had little to do with it. Perhaps it was simply that the new sense of something aimfully and cumulatively dramatic in our progress had to have a beginning, and that moment would do as well as the next.

Six villages: M'nann, Leika Leikapo, Shamba, Tara and Little Tara, culminating in the apotheosis of Tara Hill. Six stops for the night on the road it had cost Diana as many months to cover in his singular pilgrimage to his inevitable goal. Or in his flight to it. Yes, his stampede. Now the pipers at that four-day orgy of liberty on the *Platonic's* decks were at his heels for their pay. Now that his strength was failing, the hosts of loneliness were after him, creeping out of their dreadful magnitudes, the hounds of space. Over all that ground it seemed to me we were following him not by the word of hearsay but, as one follows a wounded animal making for its earth, by the droppings of his blood.

Our progress had taken on a pattern; it built itself with a dramatic artistry; it gathered suspense. As though it were a story at its most breathless places "continued in our next," and I a reader forgetting the road's weariness, the dust, the torment of insects never escaped, the inadequate food, I found myself hardly able to keep from running on ahead to reach the evening's village, to search out the inevitable repository of images left by the white stranger who had come and tarried there awhile and gone again.

More concrete and ever more concrete. The immemorial compromise with the human hunger for a symbol to see with the eyes, touch with the hands. Hierarchy after hierarchy of little mud effigies—one could see the necessity pushing the man. Out of the protoplasmic blobs of Ndua, Suki, even M'nann, at Leikapo Diana's concept of infinity (so pure in that halcyon epoch at sea), of categories nested within categories like Japanese boxes, of an over-creature wearing our cosmos like a trinket, unawares, had become a mass with legs to stand on and a real head. The shards scattered about in the filth of the hut there (as if in violence of despair) were still monstrosities, but with a sudden stride of concession their monstrousness was the monstrousness of lizard and turtle and crocodile. At Shamba there were dozens of huge-footed birds.

It is hard to be sure in retrospect, but I do believe that by the time we reached Little Tara I began to see the thing as a whole—the foetus, working out slowly, blindly, but surely, its evolution in the womb of fright. At Little Tara there was a change in the character of the exhibits; their numbers had diminished, their size had grown. There was a boar with tusks and a bull the size of a dog with horns, and on a tusk and on a horn an indentation left by a ring.

I don't believe Mrs. Diana got the thing at all. Toward the last she wasn't interested in the huts of relics; at Little Tara she wouldn't go near the place; she was "too tired." It must have been pretty awful, when you think of it, even if all she saw in them was the mud-pie play of a man reverted to a child.

There was another thing at Little Tara quite as momentous as the jump to boar and bull. Here at last a mask had been thrown aside. Here there had been no pretense of proselyting, no astronomical lectures, no doorway harangues. Straightway he had arrived (a fabulous figure already, long heralded), he had commandeered a house and shut himself up in it and there, mysterious, assiduous, he had remained three days and nights, eating nothing, but drinking gallons of the foul water they left in gourds outside his curtain of reeds. No one in the village had ever seen what he had done and left there. Now, candidly, those labors were for himself alone.

Here at last in Tara the moment of that confession had overtaken the fugitive. It was he, ill with fever and dying of nostalgia—not these naked black baboon men seen now as little more than blurs—who had to give the Beast of the Infinite a name and a shape. And more and more, not only a shape, but a *shapeliness.* From the instant when, no longer able to live alone with nothingness, he had given it a likeness in Ndua mud, and perceived that it was intolerable and fled its face, the turtles and distorted crocodiles of Leikapo and the birds of Shamba had become inevitable, and no less inevitable the Little Tara boar and bull. Another thing grows plain in retrospect: the reason why, done to death (as all the way they reported him) he couldn't die. He didn't dare to. Didn't dare to close his eyes.

It was at Little Tara we first heard of him as "Father Witch," a name come back, we were told, from Tara, where he had gone. I had heard it pronounced several times before it suddenly obtruded from the native context as actually two English words. That was what made it queer. It was something they must have picked up by rote, uncomprehending; something then they could have had from no lips but his own. When I repeated it after them with a better accent they pointed up toward the north, saying "Tara! Tara!"—their eagerness mingled with awe.

I shall never forget Tara as we saw it, after our last blistering scramble up a gorge, situated in the clear air on a slope belted with cedars. A mid-African stockade left by some blunder in an honest Colorado landscape, or a newer and bigger Vermont. Here at the top of our journey, black savages, their untidy *shambas,* the very Equator, all these seemed as incongruous as a Gothic cathedral in a Congo marsh. I wonder if Hubert Diana knew whither his instinct was guiding him on the long road of his journey here to die. . .

He had died and he was buried, not in the village, but about half a mile distant, on the ridge; this we were given to know almost before we had arrived. There was no need to announce ourselves, the word of our coming had outrun us; the populace was at the gates.

"Our Father Witch! Our Father Witch!" They knew what we were after; the funny parrot-wise English stood out from the clack and clatter of their excited speech. "Our Father Witch! Ay! Ay!" With a common eagerness they gesticulated at the hilltop beyond the cedars.

Certainly here was a change. No longer the propitiatory spitting, the averted eyes, the uneasy whispering allusion to him who had passed that way: here in Tara they would shout him from the housetops, with a kind of civic pride.

We learned the reason for this on our way up the hill. It was because they were his chosen, the initiate.

We made the ascent immediately, against the village's advice. It was near evening; the return would be in the dark; it was a bad country for goblins; wouldn't tomorrow morning do? . . . . No, it wouldn't do the widow. Her face was set. . . And so, since we were resolved to go, the village went with us, armed with rattles and drums. Charlie Kamba walked beside us, sifting the information a hundred were eager to give.

These people were proud, he said, because their wizard was more powerful than all the wizards of all other villages "in the everywhere together." If he cared to he could easily knock down all the other villages in the "everywhere," destroying all the people and all the cattle. If he cared to he could open his mouth and swallow the sky and the stars. But Tara he had chosen. Tara he would protect. He made their mealies to grow and their cattle to multiply.

I protested, "But he is *dead* now!"

Charlie Kamba made signs of deprecation. I discerned that he was far from being clear about the thing himself.

Yes, he temporized, this Father Witch was dead, quite dead. On the other hand he was up there. On the other hand he would never die. He was longer than forever. Yes, quite true, he was dead and buried under the pot.

I gave it up. "How did he die?"

Well, he came to this village of Tara very suffering, very sick. The dead man who walked. His face was very sad. Very eaten. Very frightened. He came to this hill. So he lived here for two full moons, very hot, very eaten, very dead. These men made him a house as he commanded them, also a stockade. In the house he was very quiet, very dead, making magic two full moons. Then he came out and they that were waiting saw him. He had made the magic, and the magic had made him well. His face was kind. He was happy. He was full fed, these men said, without any eating. Yes, they carried up to him very fine food, because they were full of wonder and some fear, but he did not eat any of it. Some water he drank. So, for two days and the night between them, he continued sitting in the gate of the stockade, very happy, very full fed. He told these people very much about their wizard, who is bigger than everywhere and longer than forever and can, if he cares to, swallow the sky and stars. From time to time however, ceasing to talk to these people, he got to his knees and talked in his own strange tongue to Our Father Witch, his eyes held shut. When he had done this just at sunset of the second day he fell forward on his face. So he remained that night. The next day these men took him into the house and buried him under the pot. On the other hand Our Father Witch is longer than forever. He remains there still . . .

The first thing I saw in the hut's interior was the earthen pot at the northern end, wrong-side-up on the ground. I was glad I had preceded Mrs. Diana. I walked across and sat down on it carelessly, hoping so that her afflicted curiosity might be led astray. It gave me the oddest feeling, though, to think of what was there beneath my nonchalant sitting-portion—aware as I was of the Kavirondo burial of a great man—up to the neck in mother earth, and the rest of him left out in the dark of the pot for the undertakings of the ants. I hoped his widow wouldn't wonder about that inverted vessel of clay.

I needn't have worried. Her attention was arrested otherwheres. I shall not forget the look of her face, caught above me in the red shaft of sundown entering the western door, as she gazed at the last and the largest of the Reverend Hubert Diana's gods. That long, long cheek of hers, buffeted by sorrow, startled now and mortified—Not till that moment, I believe, had she comprehended the steps of mud-images she had been following for what they were, the steps of idolatry.

For my part, I wasn't startled. Even before we started up the hill, knowing that her husband had dared to die here, I could have told her pretty much what she would find.

This overlord of the cosmic categories that he had fashioned (at last) in his own image sat at the other end of the red-streaked house upon a bench—a throne?—of mud. Diana had been no artist. An ovoid two-eyed head, a cylindrical trunk, two arms, two legs, that's all. But indubitably man, man-size. Only one finger of one of the hands had been done with much care. It wore an opal, a two-dollar stone from Mexico, set in a silver ring. This was the hand that was lifted, and over it the head was bent.

I've said Diana was no artist. I'll take back the words. The figure was crudeness itself, but in the relation between that bent head and that lifted hand there was something which was something else. A sense of scrutiny one would have said no genius of mud could ever have conveyed. An attitude of interest centered in that bauble, intense and static, breathless and eternal all in one—penetrating to its bottom atom, to the last electron, to a hill upon it, and to a two-legged mite about to die. Marking (yes, I'll swear to the incredible) the sparrow's fall.

The magic was made. The road that had commenced with the blobs of Ndua—the same that commenced with our hairy ancestors listening to the nightwind in their caves—was run.

And from here Diana, of a sudden happy, of a sudden looked after, "full fed" had walked out—

But no; I couldn't stand that mortified sorrow on the widow's face any longer. She had to be made to see what she wanted to see. I said it aloud:

"From here, Mrs. Diana, your husband walked out—"

"He had sunk to idolatry. *Idolatry!*"

"To the bottom, yes. And come up its whole history again. And from here he walked out into the sunshine to kneel and talk with 'Our Father Which—' "

She got it. She caught it. I wish you could have seen the light going up those long, long cheeks as she got it:

"Our Father which art in Heaven, Hallowed be Thy Name!"

We went down hill in the darkness, protected against goblins by a vast rattling of gourds and beating of goat-hide drums.

CHAPTER 2

A Common Basis for Understanding the Arts

■ In the humanities we take art seriously. In the Victorian period and early in this century, the arts were regarded as "the finer things of life" and were respected as a sort of polish which the upper-class and upper-middle-class person received as a part of his education. Art was show-off stuff, valuable precisely because it was of no practical good. As a matter of fact, in the 1920s and 1930s the upper-middle-class child showed his status by wearing braces on his teeth and by taking piano lessons until he eventually learned to plunk out the "Moonlight Sonata" with little thought beyond the mechanical problem of getting his fingers on the right keys. Another status symbol in the home was having a beautifully bound volume of *Swinburne's Complete Works* lying on the coffee table, never opened, certainly never read, but advertising the good taste (and the opulence) of the owner. As a matter of fact, this whole attitude toward art might well be called the coffee-table school of appreciation. This attitude is still the standard one. But, as indicated in our description of a culture-epoch in Chapter 1, we now recognize that the great artists actually create the pattern for a way of life, and that lesser ones have much to communicate that is important to us as individuals. Artists refine the raw experience of life and give us its meaning in a highly personal, intellectual-emotional way.

One might well ask what area of the universe is the darkest and most completely unknown. Africa? The solar system? Not with our recent rocket explorations. Probably the most incomprehensible area in the universe is yourself. If you are a normal member of the human race, you are constantly asking yourself such questions as, "Who am I?" "What am I really like?" "What do I mean, and why do I exist?" It is the artist who can keep supplying fuller and fuller answers to these questions.

Several years ago the writer read a paragraph which puzzled him, and which he could not believe. The paragraph, written by an important Shakespearian scholar and literary critic, made the statement that in his tragedies Shakespeare had made discoveries as important as those made by any scientist. Such an assertion is hard to accept, even by a person whose chief interest is a study of literature and the arts in general. It is only after some years of thought that the truth of the statement becomes apparent; yet this idea can give us a basis for understanding the arts, and is presented here for that purpose.

At the risk of making too sweeping a generalization, we might think of the problem in this way: In the sum total of human knowledge the natural sciences explore the world outside of men; the social studies, with their methods of investigation, make discoveries about man's actions as he works together with other men in various groups, organizations and communities; and the arts and humanities probe the area of inner meaning—man's fears, hopes, loves, delights as he—the individual—and society act and react within their world. All sincere art is exploration, and its discoveries are as significant as are those in the natural sciences and the social studies. The discoveries which any artist makes are always expressed both as concept (the loves, hates, and delights spoken of before), and percepts, the sense-apparent objects and materials which he uses and arranges to create the meaning which he seeks to express.

Largely because of differences in media, the arts differ from each other in many ways. Certainly a nonmaterial time-art such as music, which exists only as long as it is heard, is different from a space-art (which also exists only in the time when we see it) which expresses itself in visual symbols. Both are separated from literature, which has its existence in word-symbols to which the reader brings meaning. Although these variations among the arts are important, their similarity is even greater. The common basis of them all is their exploration by means of sensory percepts into the emotion, the mind, and the personality of man and the discovery of meaning therein. D.H. Lawrence's statement about the novel is equally applicable to all the arts:

> And here lies the importance of the novel, properly handled. It can inform and lead into new places the flow of our sympathetic consciousness, and it can lead our sympathy away in recoil from things gone dead. Therefore, the novel, properly handled, can reveal the most secret places of life: for it is in the *passional* secret places of life, above all, that the tide of sensitive awareness needs to ebb and flow, cleansing and freshening.[1]

An examination of this common basis is the purpose of this chapter.

The artist deals with highly relative materials, for artistic truth is largely individual. It depends as much upon the background and personality of the artist as it does upon the raw material of experience, and both depend upon the background and the sensitivity of the members of the audience. One might take, for example, the treatment which two artists make of the same theme—let us say the futility of the life of a woman who, in herself, is a complete blank, but who moves from man to man, husband to husband, and lives only as she reflects these successive men. For concrete evidence, see Dorothy Parker's story, "Big Blonde," and Chekov's story, "The Darling." Although the experience is the "same" in both stories, the feeling of the two artists is quite different, and the experience of the reader, too, is very different as he relives the same thing in two different forms, created by two different artists. The reader might protest, "But one of them must be right about this kind of woman, and one of them must be wrong." Actually, both are right, and any other artist who treated the same material with a different insight might also be right. This discovery is almost entirely a personal matter, and the corollary is that the realm of truth in personality and experience, the area of truth in the arts, is inexhaustible. The person who appreciates any work of art grows with each new facet of experience which he lives through with the artist, and growth in this sense is limited only by the ability-for-experience of the beholder.

Not always recognized is the fact that the artists in literature, painting, sculpture, music and the other arts have a method of investigation in their field of knowledge which we may call the method of intuition or insight. In much the same way that the scientist starts out, the artist becomes aware of a problem in the realm of human experience, or he senses some aspect of the human personality which is dark and unknown. Put more simply, he feels the need to create, and this compulsion is the first step in the artistic method. As a second step he begins to gather his materials, both conceptual (idea-stuff) and perceptual (physical-stuff: visual images, sequences of sound, etc.). The third step is the appropriate arrangement of his materials, which comes as an insight or an intuitive perception of new and varied relationships among the materials with which he is working. Since he is dealing with a problem of relationships, the truth which he seeks takes the shape of arranging his materials in proper order with respect to each other. In other words, the form (arrangement and relationship) is a very necessary part of artistic truth; this form involves the arrangement of incident, character, or images in literature, of visual

1. D.H. Lawrence. *Lady Chatterley's Lover.* (Stockholm: Jan Forlag, 1950), p. 128.

elements in painting or sculpture, of sounds or themes in musical composition so that they arrive at the point which the artist has felt by insight. In other words, this is the step we call *composition*, a term which is common to all of the arts. From this step the art-object emerges—a song, a pot, a picture, a poem—which has both an aesthetic and a utilitarian function in the world (and frequently the best of the utilitarian productions have a very high degree of aesthetic value). But how can the artist check the results of his exploration? That is the job of the members of his audience. After the composition, the artist turns his creation loose in the world. Many people examine it, both in terms of its subject and explicit meaning, and in terms of the form in which it is presented. If the work is composed in such a way that the members of the audience *live through* the experience themselves and find that the artist has made a true statement of the experience in all of its relationships, then the discovery of the artist is accepted as a truth wrested from the dark ignorance of the human condition in the world. Two of the tests which might be applied are these: First, is it new? If the meaning (a combination of idea and formal structure) is old and trite, the art work may be comfortable, but not of much artistic value. Second, is the emotional content proper for the subject? If the treatment is sentimentalized, then it is probable that the artist lacked either sincerity or a steady view of life.

One caution: The test of artistic truth cannot be made by the general public, although their criticism may be valuable. A scientist, for example, would not allow the validity of his conclusion to be tested by a plumber, a newsboy, and a meat cutter. He asks that his truths be tested by the experiments of scientists who are his equals in scientific knowledge. There is a little difference between the scientist and the artist, but the difference is not too marked. We could argue that since the butcher, the baker, and the candlestick maker are human personalities, they might be accepted as valid critics of the artist's discovery. To a certain extent this claim is true. On the other hand, certain people can read with more discernment than others. Some are excellent at understanding the language and symbolism of painting, sculpture, or music. And, perhaps more important, some people are more sensitive than others to the problems of personality and experience. These people, those who can understand the medium of expression and who are sensitive to human problems, must constitute the group of judges for the validity of a work of art.

The next question for consideration is the nature of the raw materials for artistic investigation. These are sometimes hard to see. Most obvious are the many facets of such emotions as love, hatred, jealousy, contentment, sudden apprehension of the beauty in nature or people, and other emotional reactions. As a matter of fact, these materials from life are so common that it is probable that the great bulk of art is made from them, but there is much more material which has been explored in literature, art, and music. Artists present their explorations as experience which the members of the artistic audience may live through. Take, for example, the psychological experience which confronts a young prince who has been humanely educated, who faces a problem of evil involving the murder of his father, the king, and the unfaithfulness, even incest, of his mother. (In other words, the problem Shakespeare explored in Hamlet.) The artist feels this problem within himself and composes its elements and its solution. Psychology and literature often run parallel to each other; the former gives facts, the latter gives truth-to-life. This truth is achieved because we become personally involved in the work of literature, live through the complexities of the problem with all their attendant, opposing emotions, and sense the logic, the rightness, and the freedom of the solution when it is reached.

Perhaps one more consideration is neccessary before we turn to examples of the explorations and discoveries of the artists. This consideration is that of the place and importance of form. Let us put it this way: Human experience is seldom simple or direct. Rather, its importance is usually clouded with events of no importance, many of which are totally irrelevant. Perhaps the best illustration of this may be found in the artist who is painting a landscape. His purpose is not to make a direct copy from nature—a camera might provide a more exact representation than a human being. Rather, the painter is seeking to interpret an experience with beauty. The natural scene, however, is cluttered with objects detracting from the impression which the artist seeks. Consequently, he leaves many out, he rearranges in his mind and on his canvas the objects which *he* sees, so that the picture, when complete, is not a copy of nature, but a picture of beauty, with the natural objects selected and arranged to make the meaning clear. But no critic, nor commentator, perhaps not even the artist himself, could give us a definite, final statement as to what that "meaning" is. Perhaps it is a sense of the importance of peace, quiet, repose; perhaps it is the wonder of organization, order, design; perhaps it is the sheer joy of contrasting colors, the delight in appearances of objects, their texture and feel; perhaps the pleasure of a thing of beauty. If it could be expressed definitely in words, the picture would not be necessary, but since it cannot, it is the only means by which the artist can share his delight in the world. And the imperative need to share it, to get it "said," is the quality that makes the artist; he does not only what he can, but what he must. Somehow, that creative urge, which everyone shares to some extent, is communicated to an audience; theorists of "aesthetic experience" do not agree on the "how": it helps little to say that the picture "speaks for itself." However little understood the process, the fact remains that people throughout the years have enjoyed (the word is too weak: they have *needed*) the making of pictures and the looking at them. The great point is that the good artist has made the picture do something to the beholder, partly through the subject matter, partly through the form of the picture itself.

It is interesting that it is this element of form which all of the arts have in common, and it is this which gives them the "living-through" quality which we have noted as distinctive of artistic truth. It is the process, not the end result, which is important. It is the form, not the final statement, which yields artistic truth. This is not to say that the artists' final point is unimportant. It is to say that its importance lies in having gone through the experience with the artist and having arrived with him at the discovery which he finally wishes to communicate. With this in mind, let us examine some examples of art to see how the artist has discovered truth from the chaos and darkness of the human personality and its experiences.

Painting and literature are roughly equal insofar as definiteness of meaning is concerned. Literature uses words which have a fairly distinct meaning in their context: the meaning is approximately clear. The images which the painter uses have about the same "vocabulary," and one can learn to read a painting in much the same way that one learns to read a poem. In both arts a single work may have several levels of meaning, ranging deeper and deeper from the simple surface meaning, and careful readers can uncover greater and greater depth of significance as they work through the symbols put down by the artist. In both arts the interpretations are somewhat personal, depending upon the critical ability of the reader or the viewer and upon his background. The response, however, *must be* within the limits set by the artist. In the arts, as in most other things, we can arrive at some very wrong interpretations.

Music is almost pure form, and it is seldom that a definite "story" interpretation can be given to a musical selection. Most untutored listeners have one of two responses to music. When they think they are listening carefully and intelligently, they arrive at some sort of story, which usually sounds something like this: This person is in love, and then his girl leaves him, and right at the end she comes back and everything is dandy. The other listening attitude is simply to bathe in the sound without distinguishing anything. Usually, the latter listener finds his attention wandering off in a thousand directions before a musical selection of any length is finished. In other words, he finds himself paying attention to everything except the music.

But music, except for program music, which has a story to tell in sound and often employs sounds found in ordinary life (and the composer's "story" is not necessarily that of the listener), is pure form in sound. It is one of the "time arts," which makes it particularly elusive since, by the time it is heard, it is gone. For this reason we are devoting a special chapter to an introduction to music. Music makes greater demands on its audience, both in knowledge and attention, than do any of the other arts. The knowledgeable and attentive listener, however, finds that living through a musical selection yields as much meaning for life's experiences as do any of the other arts. In its structures one may find the grandeur of Bach, the intricate ornamentation of a Handel oratorio, the deceptively simple single-line melody of Gregorian chant, or the protest which is sometimes characteristic of good jazz. Whatever the significance of a musical selection, it is the composition that counts. As much as in any of the other arts, perhaps more, the musical composer must arrange his material so that the listener lives through an experience which lies deeper than words or the recognizable subject matter of painting. It is this process of composition which leads to "living through," our concern in this chapter since it is the common basis for all the arts.

EXAMPLES FROM LITERATURE

In order to see how this intricate interrelation of meaning and form is accomplished in literature, we can use some very simple illustrations for analysis. For example, a creative writing class once tried to make an "absolutely beautiful" line of poetry. This is what they came up with:

> Rainy evening. Idle. Only music. . .

Most people would agree that this is a very pretty line. But what makes it so? You might ask yourself where the heavy accents fall. And then, what about the vowel sounds? Suddenly what appears at first to be only a nice lazy line begins to look like the work of a craftsman, for we discover that we are running down the long vowel sounds, exactly as they come in the alphabet A, E, I, O, U, and that these sounds occur exactly on the heavy accents. Now what about consonant sounds? The consonants are *r*, *n*, *v*, *ng*, *dl*, *l*, *m*, hard *c* (a *k* sound). We could have had *p*, *b*, *k*, *g* and all the rest. Are the ones which appear in the line purely accidental choices? Not on your life. Except for the last *c*, all the consonants are "liquid" consonants. The term is self-explanatory; they flow along without creat-

Colorplate 1. **Where Do We Come From? What Are We? Where Are We Going?** —*Paul Gauguin*

Courtesy Museum of Fine Arts, Boston.

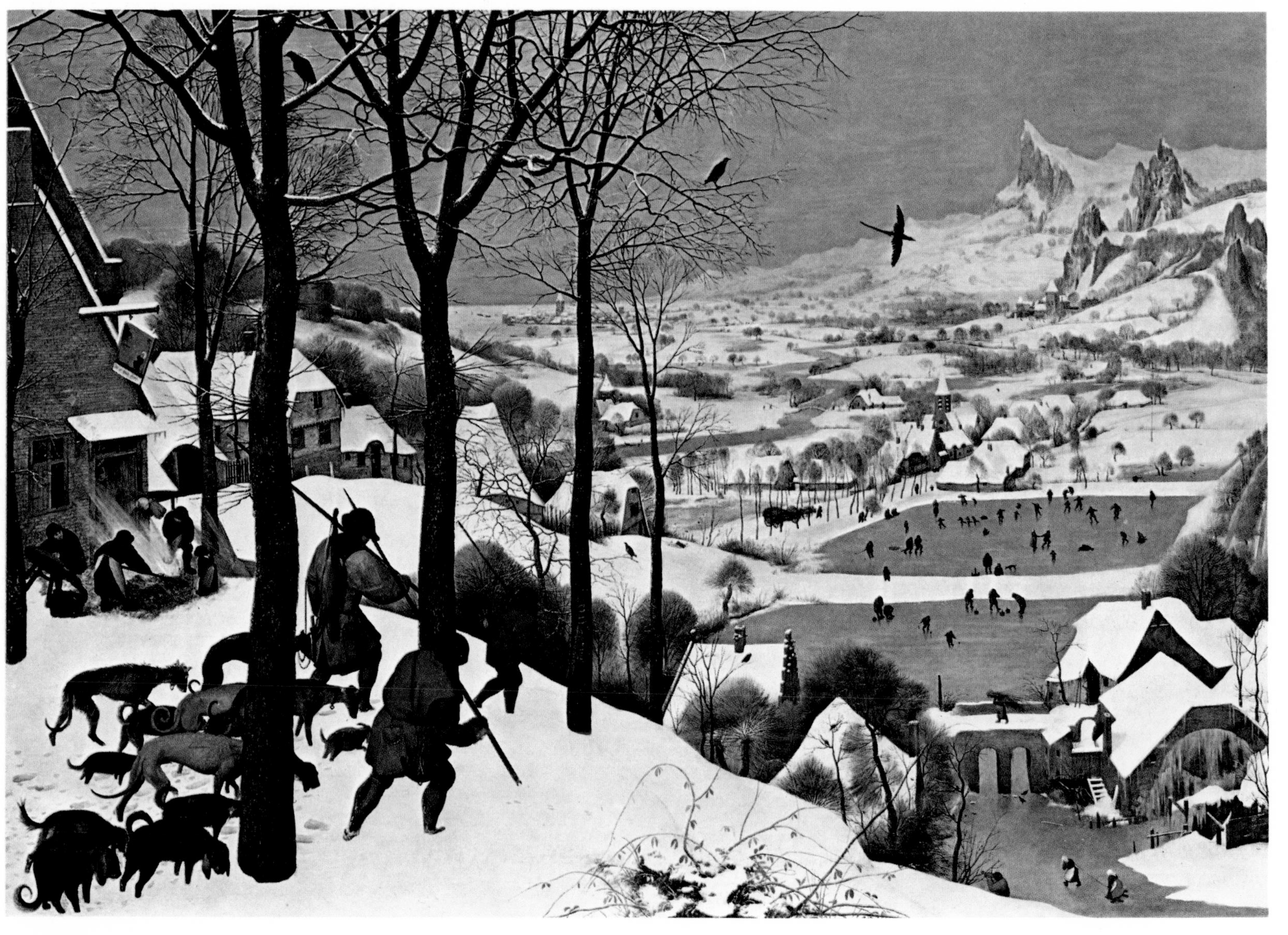

Colorplate 2. **Winter (Return of the Hunter)**—*Pieter Brueghel*
Kunsthistorisches Museum, Vienna
Courtesy Art Reference Bureau.

Colorplate 3. **The Watermill with the Great Red Roof**—*Meindert Hobbema*
Courtesy Art Institute of Chicago.

Colorplate 4. **The Starry Night**—*Vincent van Gogh*
Courtesy The Museum of Modern Art, New York. Lillie P. Bliss Bequest.

Colorplate 5. **Composition #3**—*Wassily Kandinsky*

Courtesy The Museum of Modern Art, New York. Mrs. Simon Guggenheim Fund.

Colorplate 6. **Portrait of Louis XIV**—*Hyacinthe Rigaud,* Louvre

Courtesy Art Reference Bureau.

Colorplate 7. **Girl Before a Mirror**—*Pablo Picasso*

Courtesy The Museum of Modern Art, New York. Gift of Mrs. Simon Guggenheim.

ing much stoppage. Only the last one (the *c* in *music*) is of a different sort, and it is put there exactly because it *does* stop the line. We have here a line which doesn't "say" much in terms of making a declaration or asking a question, but it certainly creates a mood. And the mood is created because of a lot of hard work in choosing sounds carefully and distributing them in terms of accentuation.

As another example, a student in the same class wrote a five-line poem about the Cain and Abel story. Here are the first two lines:

> Oh Cain, you slay in vain. You may not stay.
> East of Eden, East of Eden, flee for. . . .

Notice not only the vowel music, but the change in rhythm between the first and second line. Using the same pattern you might try to write the last three lines.

The examples given above are really only one-finger exercises in the craft of writing poetry. Now we can choose a complete poem for the same kind of analysis to see the intricate relationships of form that create a sum of meaning greater than the arithmetical addition of the meanings of the words themselves. We might choose A.E. Housman's deceptively simple, eight-line poem, "With Rue My Heart is Laden."

> With rue my heart is laden
> For golden friends I had,
> For many a rose-lipt maiden
> And many a light-foot lad.
>
> By brooks too broad for leaping
> The lightfoot boys are laid;
> The rose-lipt girls are sleeping
> In fields where roses fade.

Of course Housman is saying that he grieves for the friends of his youth, now dead. Where does one attack the *form* of a poem like this. You might ask yourself why he chose the word *boys* in the second stanza when he used *lads* in the first. Then examine the first line of the second stanza:

> By *b*rooks too *b*road for *l*eaping

Perhaps you begin to see that he chose *boys* in the second line to make an alliterative pattern with *brooks* and *broad*. What of the *l* in the first line of the second stanza? Suddenly one discovers that it forms a similar pattern with *lightfoot* and *laid* in the second line. In the first line of the second stanza we have two *b*s, one *l*; in the second line, two *l*s, one *b*. Is this purely accidental on the part of the composer? Try the last two lines of the first stanza, with its *m*s and *l*s. The same pattern reveals itself and, furthermore, the alliterative *l* of the first stanza carries over to repeat itself in the second stanza. In other words, the middle four lines of the poem form a unit by themselves, created by the alliterations.

But that's not all. Examine the rhymes: *laden, maiden, leaping, sleeping; had, lad; laid, fade.* The first four of the rhymes listed here (lines 1, 3, 5, 7 in the poem) are what is called "feminine" endings; that is, they end in a dropping-off syllable that gets almost no accent at all. The second group of rhymes (lines 2, 4, 6, 8 of the poem) are "masculine" endings; they end sharply on the accented syllable. This is strengthened even further by Housman's use of end punctuation after the lines with masculine endings. Reason? Look at the subject matter of the lines with feminine endings and that of the lines with masculine endings.

One more example, this time in prose, for it is easy to jump to the conclusion that poets take this much care with their sounds, but that prose writers do not have to. In the story by Wilbur Daniel Steele, we find the following sentence:

> Accept as he would with the top of his brain the fact of a spherical earth zooming through space, deep in his heart he know that the world lay flat from modern Illinois to ancient Palestine, and that the sky above it, blue by day and by night festooned with guiding stars for wise men, was the nether side of a floor on which the resurrected trod.

An unskilled writer tried to communicate the "same" meaning with the following sentence:

> Although he accepted in his mind the fact that the earth was a sphere travelling through space, yet in his deepest emotions he knew that it was flat and that the sky was the under-side of the floor of heaven.

Why, for example, does Mr. Steele say that the world "lay flat from modern Illinois to ancient Palestine" instead of simply saying that it was flat, as the other writer did? Perhaps he wanted to suggest an expanse of time, from the modern world back to the time of Christ, as well as an expanse of space. Why did he describe the sky as he did rather than plainly using the word *sky*, as the unskilled writer did? There is the possibility that while he was stating a fact about a man's belief concerning the physical structure of the earth he also wanted to suggest a religious significance to the belief. So he mentioned the stars and the wise men to flood our memories with the story of the birth of Christ. The two sentences differ in at least one more phase of meaning. The unskilled writer's sentence has no rhythm, while Steele's sentence reads in long undulations of sound. This kind of rhythm puts us in a philosophic frame of mind which creates the kind of atmosphere which he wanted. It is for such reasons that the author chose exactly the words he did, and arranged them as he did. For its purpose in the story it is a much better sentence than that of the unskilled writer.

These literary examples are given here to show how the form of a work conveys a meaning much larger than the words themselves, and how, in each case, this form is used to explore a meaning of human experience interpreted in deeply personal terms. Similar illustrations from the other arts follow, and more examples for your own analysis are given in the exercises at the end of the chapter.

AN EXAMPLE FROM MUSIC

Music is sound moving in time, and therein lies its magical mystery. While listening to an unfamiliar piece of music the listener does not know where the music is going until it gets there, that is, ceases to sound. From silence to sound to silence, and what takes place in between is a mixture of sound and silence which is comprehended only in retrospect, after one musical section has followed upon another until silence reigns again. Readers can reread difficult passages in a book and art lovers can study a painting for hours, but music listeners have one ride on a merry-go-round. There is no way to stop the music or freeze a beautiful sound, even though some critics are fond of referring to architecture as "frozen music." Nothing is ever that simple.

Music is a structural art built by the composer out of a multiplicity of materials; he picks and chooses tones, colors, textures, rhythms and patterns just as a writer selects words and phrases which best suit his purpose and the painter chooses lines and colors. Rarely are these infinite choices deliberately calculated or contrived, except in so-called "bad" art. The artist, each in his own way, is seeking to express himself, to communicate some feeling, truth or emotion about his experience as he perceives it.

Music is the envy of many artists because it is so abstract that it can never pretend to represent anything specific, or exactly portray one iota of the sensible world in which we live. Music is *free*, truly free, to soar to the heights or descend to the depths of intellectual-emotional experiences. This unfettered freedom is the constant delight of all good musicians and experienced nonmusicians (listeners). It is also the cause of utter despair of teachers and students who have yet to learn the basic skills and thus the joys of listening to music with some degree of understanding. Only after understanding can there by any real "appreciation," and this appreciation need not include approbation; many experienced listeners can understand and even appreciate music which they really do not enjoy. But then, how can a person know whether or not he dislikes a novel if he is illiterate?

Literacy in music is no more a common heritage of all mankind than is the ability to read and write. To become a reasonably knowledgeable listener is not very difficult because the listener has only to learn to "read"; the "writing" is left to professional musicians. And what is there to read in music: notes, scales, intervals, keys, chords? Not at all; these are merely the "grammar" of music and not its content. The listener begins with the larger units of music, with its structure. In the fullness of time a certain minimal knowledge of musical grammar will fall into place within the overall picture of musical design. For example, the following musical phrase has a beginning and an incomplete and unsatisfying ending:

Ein feste Burg

However, when the next phrase is added we have the completion of a musical idea, even though something less than a complete composition:

The two phrases add up to a musical period or relatively complete musical idea called, for convenience, letter *A*. Then, for purposes of balance the period (or paired phrases) is repeated before proceeding to the next section (section *B*). This section retains the strong, stern character of the first section but introduces several new ideas for contrast (phrases indicated by dotted lines):

Formal Structure: *Ein feste Burg*

SOME EXAMPLES FROM PAINTING

A common plaint among laymen is that they cannot understand "modern art" and that they prefer "realistic" works, that is, painting and sculpture that tell a story, look like something, and are easy to understand. The sad truth is that most people have never learned to understand much of anything about any kind of art, are very vague as to what "realism" might be, do not know the story related in most figurative painting and sculpture (painting and sculpture presenting natural objects) and, if they do, are unaware that subject matter cannot make the art object beautiful, life-enhancing, or valuable by itself. Most painting, sculpture, and architecture seem to be easily understandable, but the qualities that make one work superior to another need to be learned, just as they must be learned in music and literature.

Some people refuse to take art seriously, being convinced that it is all a matter of taste. They fall back on that old bromide "There is no disputing taste." We answer, "Nuts." Taste is a learned, not innate, ability and all statements to the contrary are delusive and established in self-defense to soothe the ego. The vocabulary, subject matter, materials, and techniques of the visual arts, however, cannot be reduced to the confines of this book, which serves a broader purpose, though imparting basic knowledge of the visual arts, stimulating aesthetic response, and encouraging further investigation into the arts are part of that purpose.

It is regrettable that in this century the words "beauty" and "beautiful" have taken on a narrow meaning for the general public, a meaning of "prettiness" and "niceness" which makes the words "beauty" and "beautiful" incomprehensible to many people when they are applied to a highly abstract painting by Picasso, a nonobjective orgy of bright, explosive and intermingling colors by Kandinsky, miles of earthwork constructions in the wilderness, or mounds of earthworks on the parquet floors of distinguished museums, and sculpture that moves, screeches, or destroys itself. For the moment, then, let us discard these words and investigate a fundamental term, aesthetics. A survey of dictionaries to discover the meaning of the word "aesthetics" generally will only add to the confusion, for the word is usually defined as a sense of beauty, love of beauty, or philosophy of beauty. It would seem that we are on a merry-go-round until we realize that the opposite of aesthetic is anaesthetic, which is the diminuation and/or loss of communication and excitement of ideas and emotions, irrespective of what these ideas and emotions might be. The quality of art is determined by how well the ideas and emotions have been communicated.

Man is by his very nature a sentient, communicative being—a creator, an artist. All men create, but seldom produce anything unique, life-enhancing, or enduring. In this book the authors are concerned with the fine arts of literature, music, painting, sculpture, and architecture. But we must be aware that there are many other arts, including the art of cooking, the art of dancing, the art of gardening, and the art of living.

The French painter Paul Gauguin (go-Gan; 1848-1903) never saw a scene such as he portrayed in "Where Do We Come From? What Are We? Where Are We Going?" (Pl. 1), nor has or will anyone else. Certainly he drew the images of the gentle islanders, their birds and dogs, the beautiful landscape, from the world about him. But these perceptions could have been captured by a camera, which would have given us a clearer, more detailed, visually accurate representation. Gauguin, however, produced a painting in which his perceptions were simplified, distorted, abstracted, to present his vision of mankind asking the eternal questions. Carefully observe in Plate 1 that the bodies vary in color from gold to brown to red; that the trees are undulating patterns of blues and purples; that there is a systematic interweaving of shapes and colors. Patterns, shapes, lines, and colors are so arranged as to establish a mood of enduring silence, gentleness, and reflection. Although the title aids us in understanding Gauguin's vision, it is not necessary for understanding the mood, the spirit of the painting. Obviously, this painting could not have been called "Joy and Celebration," for it does not convey that mood. Likewise, "Natives on the Beach," its elementary subject matter, fails to express the feeling this painting evokes. Of course philosophers, scientists, theologians, and historians have written books on the very questions Gauguin uses as his title and motif; this text will pursue these questions relentlessly. However, Gauguin painted instead of wrote, because line value, shape, form, color, and texture were his materials, which he used in repetition, opposition, dominance, and subordination, to produce a painting of unique rhythm and harmony.

How different, but equally challenging, is the "Return of the Hunters" (Pl. 2) by the Flemish painter, Pieter Brueghel (BROO-gull; 1525-69). Two moods are conveyed in this painting: the coldness and bleakness of nature, and the warmth and activity of man. This painting is a wonderful study in linear and aerial perspective, for Brueghel was a master of illusion, convincingly conveying on a two-dimensional surface the illusion of the third dimension. Linear perspective is based on our visual memory that tells us that two parallel lines eventually seem to meet in the distance; aerial perspective relies again on a visual memory that tells us that objects seem to become obscure, faint, as we increase our distance from them. Our eyes tell us lies and Brueghel repeated the lies of visual memory. In this painting, which also is called "Winter," our eyes are directed to the distant snow-covered mountains by strong diagonal lines which lead away from the picture plane; likewise, people, buildings, even the mountains decrease in size and clarity as we move away from the returning hunters at the lower left-hand side of the painting. We have been brought up to understand perspective and proportion and thus appreciate Breughel's mastery accordingly. An ancient Egyptian would not have understood this painting, since his art did not use these principles of perspective, and proportion was determined for him by the importance of the personages represented. Different cultures see and express themselves with different conventions.

Brueghel's work is considered a masterpiece not only because of his technical virtuosity, but because the artist presented an image of his time, of life as he saw it. The day may be cold, the hunters and their dogs bent with fatigue after a long and arduous hunt, but within this little hamlet there is a variety of activity that shows the warmth and delights of human life. Breughel presents a microcosm under the guise of a deceptively simple genre scene.

The Dutch painter Meindert Hobbema (MINE-dirt HOB-a-moh; 1639-1709) records a gentler nature in "The Watermill with the Great Red Roof" (Pl. 3). This scene of a countryside with soft, downy clouds in a baby-blue sky, gnarled trees with fuzzy foliage, sparkling water falling gently into the still pond, has a lyric quality which is enhanced by backlighting the scene. There is a gentle gradation from dark to light from foreground to background. Hobbema refined his work so that we can hardly see the brushstrokes. The artist disappears in the image he creates. The artist is concerned with the beauty of domesticated nature as revealed by light. The scene is calm, quiet, and peaceful—a scene such as Wordsworth recounted in many poems.

The Dutch artist Vincent Van Gogh (van-GO; 1853-90) was no pastoral lyricist. He wanted to paint the world, man, and nature, with all the love, passion, and excitement that he failed to convey in personal relationships. In "Starry Night" (Pl. 4), nature is shown to be violent: the moon and stars of brilliant oranges and yellows are glowing, burning whirligigs which leave trails of golden streaks as they speed through the sky, which also moves in dashes, spots, and streaks of a variety of assertive blues. In the foreground the top branches of a cypress shoot into the sky like flames seeking to reach the highest heavens, devouring the very air in their pursuit. No camera could ever reproduce this scene; all knowledge of perspective and of natural color is disregarded; optical illusions and visual truths are forsaken. Van Gogh painted the scene, not as he saw it, but as he felt it. And he painted it in heavy pigment (impasto) into which he gouged and scratched, so that in addition to the strength of color and violence of lines, the painting is rich in animated surface texture. Even cursory observation makes us keenly aware of the artist's physical activity in creating the work, and thus heightens our emotional response. Not for a moment, however, should we think of Van Gogh as a madman, the popular conception of this great artist. Van Gogh was a driven man, indeed, but he planned his paintings in great detail, as his writings prove, and in this case he purposely established the small hamlet with its buildings composed of quiet squares and rectangles in the lower foreground to contrast with the turbulence of the heavens and the cypress. This painting relies very little on perception, very much on conception, in this case through very personalized abstractions.

The word "abstract" in relation to art is greatly misunderstood and commonly misused. All art is abstract—even the most naturalistic. Take a photo of a friend from your wallet and ask yourself how realistic it is. Quite obviously your friend's body or head is not flat, not small enough to put in a wallet, and is not black, white, and grey. This photographic likeness is just that: a likeness or an abstraction of your friend. The painter or sculptor has always used abstractions in his art, and society, as a group or as individuals, determines the degree to which it will accept these abstractions. Therefore there are many degrees of abstractions, just as there are many languages, which are oral and written abstractions. Among some primitive tribes a high degree of abstraction from visual reality is so accepted that the primitives cannot recognize photographs of themselves or friends, but do "see" themselves and others in geometric signs and symbols. Some critics persist in claiming that the greatest art is that which is most illusionistic, that is, art which conveys the most convincing illusions of physical bulk and texture, visual recognition, and sense of three-dimensional space. Some of the greatest painters and sculptors in history have been superb illusionists, but illusionism by itself has little merit. There is no art form more illusionistic that the sculptured figures in a wax museum, but these figures lack vitality in that they resemble corpses rather than human beings.

When a painter chooses to forsake the perceptual word completely and paints his canvas with shapes, lines, and colors that draw upon no natural counterpart, the painting is called nonobjective. Wassily Kandinsky (va-SILL-ee can-DINski; 1866-1944), a Russian painter, is often heralded as the first nonobjective artist. Without disclaiming his brilliance and importance to the development of modern art, it is important to note that the pottery painters of the geometric period of ancient Greece, the monks responsible for the medieval "Book of Kells," the mosaicists who designed and executed the beautifully patterned floors of the public buildings of Byzantium, weavers from all periods of history, and your grandmothers who made patchwork crazy-quilts, were among the many thousands of artists who worked nonobjectively long before Kandinsky appeared upon the scene.

It was Kandinsky and the Dutch painter Piet Mondrian (Pete MOAN-dree-ahn; 1872-1944) who were the great pioneers of modern nonobjective art. Mondrian became the forerunner of the geometric nonobjective school and Kandinsky of expressionistic nonobjective art, both styles being carried to new and further directions by avant-garde artists today. Kandinsky's "Composition #3" (Pl. 5) has all the turbulence of Van Gogh's "Starry Night" without the subject matter drawn from nature. Colors and shapes move, impinge upon and obliterate each other in this dynamic composition. For those who say, "I can't understand this kind of painting," here are a few questions: (1) Is this painting quiet or lively? (2) Is this painting somber or gay in mood? (3) Is this painting dull or bright? If your answers are (1) lively (2) gay in mood (3) bright, you do understand the basic nature and elements of this painting. Keep asking questions of this type about any painting or work of art and you will learn a great deal. All that is needed is time and perseverance. One note of caution: the fact that you understand or do not understand a work of art does not necessarily make it a good or bad work.

We are brought to the problem then of how does one look at and judge a work of art? Just as with music and literature, there is no easy answer, but perhaps the following guide will be of some assistance:

First, look at the work and ask yourself what you *see*. Inventory the painting, not just the figurative parts but for all the shapes, colors, lines, textures, spaces, and notice the manner in which these elements are put together, that is, the composition.

Second, almost at the same time you are asking yourself what you see, ask yourself what you *know*. There is an immense difference between seeing and knowing. For example, you might *see* a figure of a haloed man with a white beard carrying a key, but you might *know*, also, that the halo represents sainthood and that the key is the attribute (or symbol) through which we recognize St. Peter. You might see a tree form, but only special knowledge will define that particular tree as an oak, aspen, or willow.

Third, ask yourself what the artist was attempting to do. It is at this point that most amateurs falter, quite naturally. But the artist sets a mood for a painting, describes items in certain ways through color, shapes, lines, arrangements of many elements to create certain effects. For example, Brueghel bent the back of his hunters to indicate their weariness, Van Gogh painted stars in bright colors to make them seem like glowing orbs, and Kandinsky used white extensively to set off the bright reds, blues, and yellows of his painting. Each art work, be it painting, sculpture, architecture, or craft item, has a composition which should function to make all parts work together in rhythm and harmony. The rules for judging any work are implicit in the work itself.

Fourth, judge how well the artist solved the problems he set for himself. Remember that even the "Divine Michelangelo" goofed sometimes and that some tenth-rate artists turned out single works of inestimable merit. Do not hesitate to be critical. Do Brueghel's hunters give a convincing impression of weariness? Does the little and quiet hamlet afford a balancing contrast for the "Starry Sky?" At this point you are evaluating or appreciating the painting, making a judgment on the basis of all that you *see* and *know*, and an analysis of how well the artist resolved the problems he set for himself.

You have just received an elementary lesson in criticism. Try it often; you'll improve with practice.

Do not be discouraged or embarrassed if some of the world's greatest masterpieces leave you cold. If you can recognize the obvious merit of a work of art but find that is has qualities distasteful to your temperament, you are developing discriminating personal taste. It is altogether possible to recognize the greatness of Raphael and Van Gogh and at the same time dislike them because Raphael's figures are too saccharine for you and Van Gogh's paintings much too wild for you to live with comfortably. If you find, also, that you like paintings which have little artistic merit but are predominately orange (your favorite color) or whose subject matter is cats (and you love cats), recognize that there often are factors in a work of art which you value over the purely artistic values. In any case, you should begin to know how and why a work moves you. This is part of the process of learning how to judge a painting and yourself. Aesthetic understanding and appreciation is a give-and-take process involving you and the work of art. In undertaking the problem of criticism you should become a more knowledgeable, humanized individual.

Only a historian would know that the portrait (Pl. 6) by Hyacinthe Rigaud (RIE-go;1659-1743) of the imposing old man with the flowing wig, sumptuous robes, and red-heeled and red-ribboned shoes was the famous Louis XIV of France. Still, practically anyone would know that this gentleman was an overdressed, important personage posing in an elaborate setting. The French artist wanted to impress the viewer with the magnificence of the "Sun King," the elegance of his costume and majesty of his pose. Observe the artist's mastery in describing the fabrics, which are masterpieces of illusion. This is a beautiful painting of a homely old man, although the artist used every trick in the trade to deemphasize the face. It is relatively easy to appreciate the quality of this painting, but it is difficult to like it because contemporary taste rejects the over-blown extravagance of garb and ceremonial authoritarian poses. Remember that this painting was produced for a palace and now resides in a palace museum. It was not meant to hang over a television set and, despite its beauty as a painting, would have little relevance in most homes.

The Spanish artist Pablo Picasso (PAB-lo pea-KAH-so; 1881-) painted the "Girl before a Mirror" in 1932 (Pl. 7). Like most of his works it is a very controversial painting which most people do not understand and even today is seldom called beautiful. A cursory examination would reveal only a series of circles and triangles in bright colors and patterns working on the picture plane. Perhaps you need to be told that the girl on the left is shown both in full-face and profile. Look carefully and you will see a profile view in pink and then its merging with a yellow side to describe a face frontally, a device now used by many comic strip artists. Picasso is telling us that he *knows* that each individual has profile views as well as a frontal view, that he is painting not only what he actually sees but what he knows to exist in a combination or "Picasso-view." That the colors of these sections do not coincide and are different again from the profile reflection in the mirror again makes no difference to Picasso because, in the last analysis, this painting is a highly abstracted study of a woman presented from many viewpoints and brightly colored and patterned to achieve a complex decorative composition. Pattern and color are the keys to this painting, but the psychological interpretations which may be made are numerous. This painting still seems new, unique, and very intriguing; Picasso has created new forms, a new way of seeing and presentation. Those of us who have been brought up with Picasso's works find them easy to understand, and we enjoy this painting for its decorative qualities, mystery of interpretation, and bold innovations. Art styles change as people's basic ideas and characteristics change. Picasso is one of the great men of our time who not only reflects but produces these changes. All innovations seem heretical, even crazy, but later they become part of the mainstream of life, and eventually are superseded by new and seemingly wilder innovations.

All the works illustrated and discussed were composed to communicate ideas and emotions; all differ from each other in style, degree of abstraction, perceptual and conceptual understanding of man and nature. It is hoped, even anticipated, that you will appreciate or learn to appreciate each of these works, but it is unlikely you will like each of them. Remember, nevertheless, that each artist is sharing with you his vision of the world, his way of seeing, and to do so he has had to learn how to use the materials and elements of art in composition.

SUMMARY

In such fashions as those illustrated, the artist, whatever his medium—music, painting, literature—has made form the vehicle of idea, has made the raw materials of his art acquire significance by arrangement and handling. It is a different kind of meaning from that of the scientist, which can be perceived and measured in an objective world, for this sort of meaning can be known only by the individual who can see the relationships the artist has formulated, and who can find them valid in terms of his own experience. It is not an easy process, sometimes; and just as the effectiveness of the scientist depends upon two things—the validity of his discovery, and the ability of the beholder to understand or comprehend it—so the effectiveness of the artist depends upon the validity of his discovery, and the sensitivity of the beholder to apprehend it. "I don't get it" is no refutation of either Einstein or Bach.

Not everyone will derive the same kind or degree of satisfaction from a particular art form, obviously; but the educated person owes himself the obligation of knowing that "there is something in it," even if that "something" does not move him deeply. And perhaps, with deeper acquaintance and wider knowledge, that "something" will become clearer and of greater value than before.

In this chapter we have made the assertion that the artist is an explorer and discoverer in the realm of the human personality. The artist uses the method of intuition and composition. The artist's raw material lies in the human personality and in human experience, with their vast and unknown reaches, their disrupting conflicts. The artist gives form to the component elements of personality and experience, and in so doing yields his artistic truth. No matter whether we speak of literature, of painting, of sculpture, of music, or any of the other arts, this concept of creating form out of chaos is the single common basis and foundation for all aesthetics.

Exercises

1. George Meredith's poem, "Dirge in Woods" is given here together with two other versions which attempt to say the same thing. What differences in the meaning do the differences in form create?

Dirge in Woods

George Meredith

A wind sways the pines
    And below
Not a breath of wild air:
Still as the mosses that glow
On the flooring and over the lines
Of the roots here and there.
The pine-tree drops its dead:
They are quiet as under the sea.
    Overhead, overhead
Rushes life in a race
As the clouds the clouds chase:
    And we go,
And we drop like the fruits of the tree,
    Even we,
    Even so.

A Second Version

Pines in the wind are swaying.
    It is quiet down below;
Not one wild breath is straying
    Above the mosses that glow
Among the roots in wandering lines
    Upon the forest floor.
The needles quietly fall from the pines,
    Fall, and are no more.
As darkly green, as stilly quiet
    As under the sea, this place.
Look! overhead, in restless riot,
    The rushing clouds' wild chase!
But like the needles we shall fall,
    Nor run in life's swift race;
We all shall die—all, all.

A Third Version

Above, wind in the pines;
below, stillness—
quiet as the mosses
creeping over roots.
    The pine needles drop, drop,
quiet, dead.
Overhead, the rushing clouds
chasing each other.
    We too die and become
quiet: drop like dead leaves,
like a dying wind
vanish into silence.

Here are three ways of saying the same thing: or nearly the same thing. Yet two of these ways are definitely inferior, although the words repeat, the ideas are like, and the "meaning" is similar. What makes the difference?

Perhaps a fourth way of straight prose without versification, could convey the "meaning" more clearly, if by "meaning" we understand only the words and what they refer to; but there is—or should be—more to a poem than the words and their immediate, surface significance. For part of the stuff of the poem is its pattern, arrangement, design; the form is significant as well as the meanings of the words. It is to see better the effective form of one that we look at the other poorer versions.

Which one sounds most like a sermon, a teaching with a moral rather than like a poem? Which one is sing-song, so monotonous that your ear is distracted from meaning by the regularity of expected sound? Which one most effectively presents the three successive ideas, "Trees . . . Clouds . . . Ourselves"?

In the first version, what is gained by the short second line?

What is the effect of the succession of vowel sounds in "st*I*ll *A*s th*E* m*O*sses that gl*O*w"? (*the* is thə, not thi)

What is the effect of repeated sounds in "glow . . . flooring . . . over"?

Why is "overhead" repeated, and "clouds" (in the eleventh line)? Also the *r* sounds, and the sibilant *s*'s?

What is gained by the short line, "and we go"?

What is the effect of the near-repetition in the last two lines?

Again one might well ask, what does the poem gain by being a *poem*? It is not merely by the dictionary meanings of the words employed, but by the patterns of sound and arrangement, that the poet has achieved a meaning.

2. Here, again, we might compare the writing of an expert and a rank amateur in terms of meanings which lie beyond pure sense meaning. Both the stanza from Matthew Arnold's "Dover Beach" and the paraphrase of it "mean" the same thing in that they deplore the loss of faith in the world. But what additional overtones and undertones of meaning does Arnold get? In what specific ways does he achieve them?

A. The Sea of Faith
Was once, too, at the full, and round earth's shore
Lay like the folds of a bright girdle furled.
But now I only hear
Its melancholy, long, withdrawing roar,
Retreating, to the breath
Of the night wind, down the vast edges drear
And naked shingles of the world.

B. Once men the world around believed
In other men and God.
But faith's now lost, men are deceived,
And earth's a dusty clod.

3. Here is Robert Frost's lovely poem, "Stopping by Woods on a Snowy Evening."

Whose woods these are, I think I know.
His house is in the village though;
He will not see me stopping here
To watch his woods fill up with snow.

My little horse must think it queer
To stop without a farmhouse near
Between the woods and frozen lake
The darkest evening of the year.

He gives the harness bells a shake
To ask if there is some mistake.
The only other sound's the sweep
Of easy wind and downy flake.

The woods are lovely, dark and deep.
But I have promises to keep,
And miles to go before I sleep,
And miles to go before I sleep.

Notice how the choice of words in a poem, once it is done, seems right, almost inevitable. In the twelfth line one accepts the word "easy" as an adjective describing the wind. What other adjectives could Frost have chosen? Why do you suppose he selected the rather unusual word, "easy"?

In answering these questions, you might notice some of the music of the poem. For example, look at lines three and four. In line three we find the words "will" and "stopping"; in line four, the words "watch" and "fill." Do you notice the cross-rhyme: "stop" and "watch," "will" and "fill"? In lines seven and eight we have something of the same thing with the words "between" and "evening." Now look at lines eleven and twelve to see why the choice of the word "easy." You might notice the pattern of end-rhymes, too. Where does the word that ends line three of each stanza find its rhyme? What is the effect, and author's purpose, of having all four lines of the last stanza rhyme? As one begins to discover these rather hidden elements, a simple-seeming poem becomes a complicated fabric of rhyme and music, most of which has its effect on the reader even though he is not conscious of it.

4. Raphael painted his "Madonna della Seggiola" within a circle: why he did so does not especially matter—probably because he wanted to! But the decision once made, the problem of the arrangement within that circle was his to solve. (How he did, the picture shows.) Suppose that he had chosen some other arrangement of the Mother and Child: suppose he had (like Cimabue) presented her and the Babe face-on. Suppose he had turned the infant the other way. Being Raphael, he probably would have made a better design of it than the following sketches would indicate!—but whatever the design he might have effected, the new picture would not have done what the present one does: it might have been better or worse; it would certainly have been different. The "Madonna of the Chair" is what it is because it was designed the way it is; the flowing curves fitted together with their interweave of movement give the painting its

quality of "coziness" (if the word may be forgiven), its intimately human appeal. The mother is not the "Virgin Enthroned," the baby is not God Incarnate, in this picture; the majesty and awe of the subsequent story are foregone to portray the most understandable, the most appealing of human relationships—simply Mother and Child.

Consider some other possible arrangements, not with a view of bettering or worsening Raphael's design, but in the hope of understanding more fully what this form, this arrangement, accomplishes. (There's even a circle for you to try your hand in.)

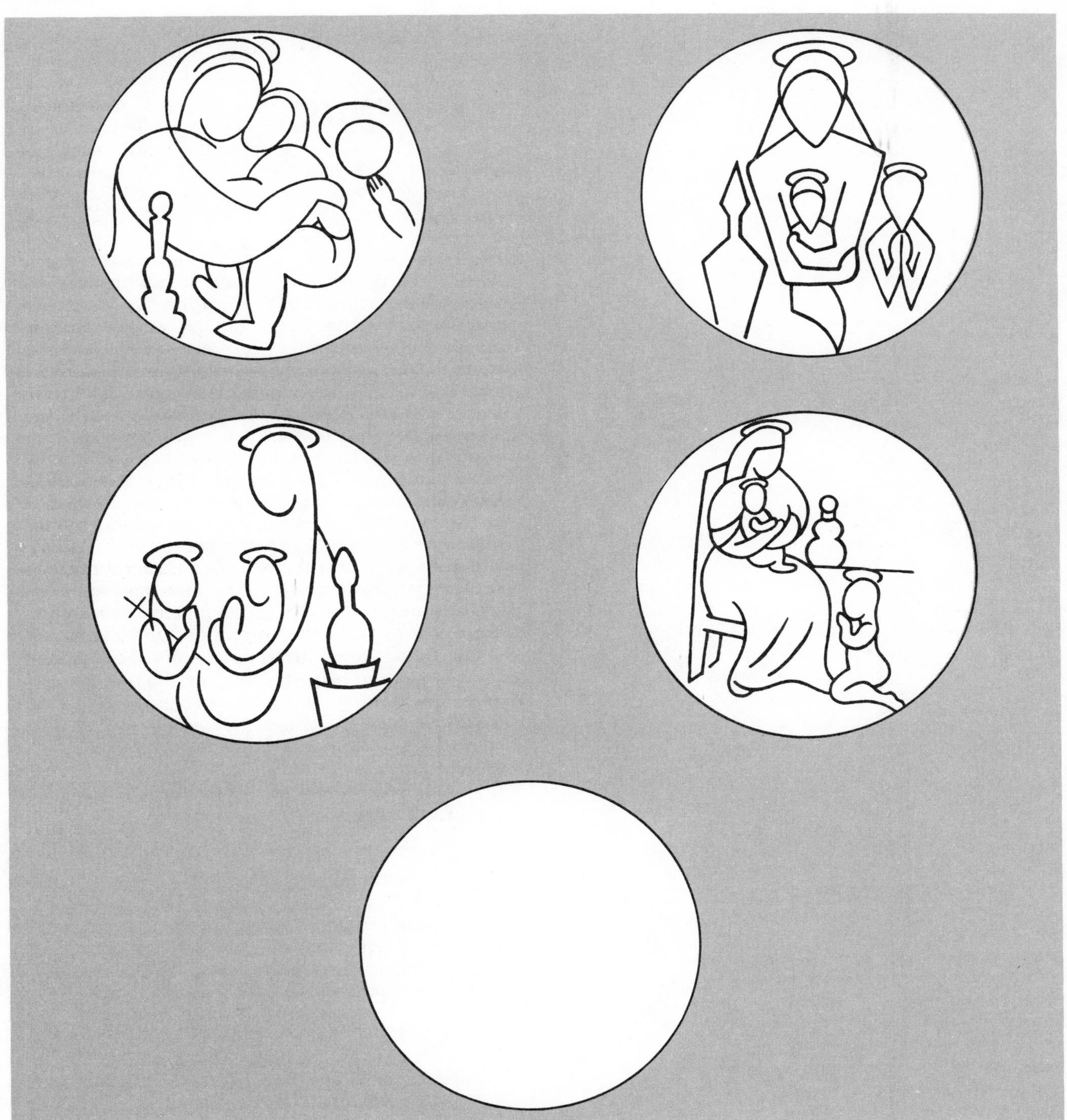

CHAPTER 3

An Introduction to Music Listening

■ Music is a form of communication which has existed in every culture known to man. The responses to music are sensory, emotional, and intellectual. The sensory responses seem to be common to all mankind. The emotional responses are dependent on the beliefs, customs, and conventions of society and on the unique experiences of the individual. The intellectual response can range from zero (a "tonal bath") up to and including the ability of a Mozart to not only perceive and understand everything happening in a piece of music he heard only once, but the technical ability to write down the entire piece from memory, as he heard it, and as it was. This is not to suggest that everyone, or even anyone, can be educated and trained to this fantastic level of achievement. There is no limit, however, to the amount of understanding to be derived from listening to music; the more knowledge you bring to listening the more you will hear, the more you will understand and, perhaps, the more pleasure you will experience. True appreciation is a result not of mindless exposure but of knowledge, a genuine aural, intellectual and emotional understanding of music as a unique, nonverbal, time-art.

Music is a nonverbal medium of structured sound moving in time, as well as a social art reflecting the customs and values of past and present. Simply by closing one's eyes and otherwise blocking out the contemporary world one can listen to, say, a Beethoven symphony and be instantaneously transported to the Vienna of 1805. No amount of reading *about* either Beethoven or Vienna can substitute for the *sound* of the music. The key word for this kind of involvement is *listening*.

Listening is developed by listening; music is learned from music; musical experience is gained only by listening to music. Reading or hearing a lecture *about* music is undoubtedly a prerequisite for developing a knowledgeable awareness of music in all its aspects, but by no means a substitute for the actual musical experience. In this respect, music differs little from other art forms. Just as verbal descriptions and even blueprints of a notable piece of architecture can do no more than prepare one for *experiencing* the building as one moves about in and through the actual structure, so does music require the *hearing* of the various combinations of musical sounds and silences, colors and textures, as they, in a manner of speaking, move about in and through the conscious and even subconscious aural perceptions of the listener.

Experiencing music involves a varying combination of *sensory*, *emotional*, and *intellectual* responses. The lively beat of a stirring march can literally increase the pulse rate of a parade watcher (sensory response). Listening to a somber funeral march can bring about feelings of depression and sadness (emotional response). The organized sounds of the tonal architecture of a complex symphonic composition can appeal directly to an intellectual awareness of unity, varied repetition and coherent and logical structure (intellectual response). These responses, however, rarely if ever exist independently. The same symphonic composition can also stimulate the physical response of the listener in passages with great excitement and volume (sensual response), can remind him of a familiar song of his own past, thus releasing memories associated with that particular song (emotional-associational response), and can produce feelings of joy or sorrow (emotional response) while also appealing intellectually to his sense of order and logic.

Because of wide variations in the physical makeup of different individuals and the uniqueness of individual experiences, the sensory and especially emotional responses can be as many and varied as there are people in the audience. On the other hand, the intellectual response will tend to vary according to the amount of knowledge and experience that each person brings to the music. It follows then that people can be educated to a greater intellectual awareness of the various elements of music without losing either their inherent physical responses or experiential emotional and associational responses. There is no such thing as knowing so much as to *spoil* the music, a frequently heard rationale for not studying music; nor is there any known limit to what people can learn about music, as attested to by veteran concert artists who study the music of Bach and Mozart all their lives.

THE LISTENING EXPERIENCE

Listening to music begins and ends with the question: What do you hear? This is an objective question which has nothing whatever to do with a story you may think the music is telling, random associations the music may invoke, or any meaning you may attribute to the music. The question, What do you hear? can be taken literally. If you heard, for example, a recording of a baritone singing a French song accompanied by a tuba and a piccolo it is likely that "what you hear" is tuba and piccolo accompanying a baritone song in the language of France, providing of course that you could hear and recognize French, songs, baritone voices, tubas, and piccolos.

Assuming you cannot read music and you have no knowledge of musical terminology (or think you have no such knowledge) it is nevertheless possible to hear, recognize and identify many basic, important elements in a piece of music. The following outline represents the initial stage in an objective approach to music listening. Part A specifies some basic categories of things to listen for; Part B, three conclusions which could be drawn from the information in Part A.

Listening Guide (First Stage)

1. Listening outline
   a. Medium
      (1) Vocal (Text: English, Latin, German, French, other)
      (2) Instrumental
      (3) Vocal and instrumental
   b. Tempo: very slow, slow, moderate, fast, very fast
   c. Loudness: soft, medium loud, loud, combination
   d. Number of performers
      (1) Solo
      (2) Ensemble
         (a) Small (2 to 5 performers)
         (b) Medium (6 to 20)
         (c) Medium large (21 to 59)
         (d) Large (60 to 100 or more)
   e. Rhythm
      (1) Regular beat (or pulsation)
      (2) Pulsation seems to be either irregular or indistinct
   f. Texture
      (1) One melody, unaccompanied
      (2) Melody with accompaniment
      (3) Simultaneous melodies (two or more)
   g. Form: sacred, secular

2. Conclusions
   a. Possible period: A.D. 600-1450; 1450-1600; seventeenth century; eighteenth century, nineteenth century; twentieth century
   b. Possible style: symphony; concerto; sonata; mass; cantata; oratorio; opera; jazz; art song; folk song; madrigal; other

c. Possible national origin: England; France; Germany; Italy; Hungary; United States; Austria; other

Exercises

Your first listening experiences based on the *Listening Guide* will preview some of the musical selections to be studied, music which includes a variety of styles and a time span of about ten centuries. For best results, your listening should be as objective as possible and follow this pattern:

1. Listening Outline
   a. Write a vertical column of letters from *a* through *g* corresponding with the categories in the *First Stage* of the *Listening Outline* (see below).
   b. Follow the *Listening Guide*, writing down your answers for each letter.
   c. Always determine the medium first. It is best to answer each question in the order given, but you may prefer following your own sequence. In this case, try to do it the same way every time.
   d. Do not leave any blank spaces. An incorrect guess is better than no answer at all. Follow the procedures; correct answers come later as your continued listening experiences are reinforced by an increasing fund of factual knowledge about music and its materials.

Record I

1. Listening Outline
   a.
   b.
   c.
   d.
   e.
   f.
   g.
2. Conclusions
   a.
   b.
   c.

Record II

(etc.)

2. Conclusions

After completing the seven listening categories, make a column of three letters (see above) and hazard a guess as to approximately *when* the music might have been written, the *type* or *style* it may be, and the possible *national origin* of the music or composer (check the *Listening Guide* for the possibilities).

The goal of the *Listening Guide* is to provide you with enough concrete information to make the three educated guesses which are referred to as *conclusions.* Up to this point it is presumed that you have comparatively little information on which to base these educated guesses; however you can make some logical deductions based on what you are able to hear plus the following clues which can help you reach your conclusions:

a. The language used in a song usually identifies the country. Names of places (New York, London, etc.) can help pinpoint a locale.
b. The use of Latin usually (but not always) indicates some kind of sacred music.
c. Symphony orchestras, string quartets, and pianos did not exist before the eighteenth century.
d. Opera did not exist before the seventeenth century.
e. Jazz did not exist before about 1890 and is still mostly of American origin.
f. A cappella (unaccompanied) choral music was common in the sixteenth century, but became quite rare until revived in the twentieth century.
g. Solo songs (with instrumental accompaniment) were numerous through the sixteenth century but declined for the next two centuries. They became important again in the nineteenth and twentieth centuries. The instrument used for the accompaniment provides a valuable clue.

FUNDAMENTALS OF MUSIC

The first experiences in objective listening help demonstrate that everyone possesses the ability to identify some of the characteristics of music as outlined in the *Listening Guide*. Increased knowledge and awareness of the materials of music can only serve to increase the listening capabilities. Fortunately, there is no regression in listening-learning experiences, only progression!

The basic materials of music (notes, melodies, chords, etc.) are no less susceptible to study and analysis than are the materials of language (alphabet, words, phrases etc.). Learning to read a language is a necessary preamble to reading a nursery rhyme, a newspaper, or the plays of Shakespeare. Learning to read music is just as obviously a prerequisite for studying a popular song, polka, symphony, or opera.

Since our purpose is to attempt to instruct reasonably literate listeners, an esoteric knowledge of the complexities of musical notation is neither necessary nor desirable. Our goal is to acquire an understanding of the elements of music (rhythm, melody, harmony, and tone color), and to hear how these elements are combined into meaningful units. The procedure, then, will be to commence with the characteristics of sound, and work our way through the elements of music, musical notation, and principles of organization until we begin to arrive at a practical and functional understanding of the language of music.

CHARACTERISTICS OF SOUND

Musical sounds, or tones result from a vibrating string (piano) or column of air (trumpet). Setting a string into vibration or motion by striking it will generate sound waves which radiate from the source in an expanding sphere. When these physical disturbances of the air (sound waves) reach the ear, they are perceived as a tone, or musical pitch (highness or lowness of sound). A specific pitch is heard because strings and air columns vibrate in a regular pattern at a fixed rate. Irregular patterns of vibrations such as the squeak of chalk on a blackboard or the rattle of pots and pans are heard as noise.

Using the single note of middle C on the piano (see piano keyboard illustration on p. 36), striking it firmly, and holding it for five seconds can demonstrate all four characteristics of musical tones (see bottom of page).

The frequency of middle C is the number of complete vibrations the string will make in one second, in this case 256 cps (cycles per second). These 256 vibrations are heard as a musical pitch, or tone. The amplitude refers to the size of the vibration; the farther the string is displaced from its position of rest, the greater the amplitude of vibration and the louder the tone that is heard. In terms of this illustration, a duration of five seconds has been prescribed, which means simply that the tone has a length, or duration of five seconds. The overtone structure of a set of piano strings (middle C has three strings) is that characteristic by which we know we are hearing a piano rather than a violin or harp; we hear the tone color which results from the overtone series.

The *overtone series* is a physical phenomenon common to all vibrating strings and air columns. Strings, for example, vibrate throughout their entire length and produce the musical pitch, or *fundamental tone* that we *seem* to hear, for example, the brilliant tone of a violin results, in part, from a strong 2nd partial (rather than the fundamental pitch) whereas a synthetic fundamental pitch (possible on the Hammond organ) tends to confuse the listener; a violin *seems* to be higher-pitched than a pure, synthetic tone produced on the Hammond organ. The relative disorientation of the listener is a result of the relative strength (or absence) of the overtone series.

The vibrating string (or air column) vibrates in segments: halves, thirds, fourths and so forth. Each segment produces its own pitch, each of which is higher and softer than the fundamental pitch. This can be illustrated as follows:

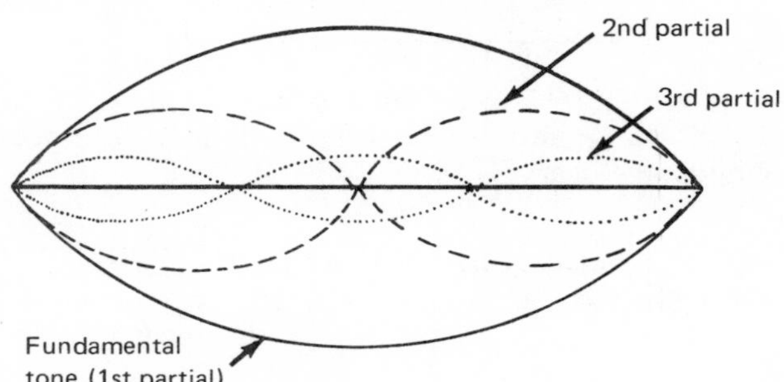

Using middle C as the fundamental tone (1st partial), the 2nd partial is 'c' above middle C and the 3rd partial is 'g' above that 'c'. These overtones proceed in a regular pattern upward from the fundamental pitch until they pass out of audible range. The pattern of overtones never changes but the relative strength (loudness) of the individual partials varies, depending on whether the vibrating body is string or air column and how this body is set in motion.[1]

MUSICAL NOTATION

Pitch

The essential elements of our notational system were devised some ten centuries ago and sub-

1. Overtones are discussed further in connection with Greek music and musical instruments.

FOUR CHARACTERISTICS OF MUSICAL TONES

Physical Characteristic		Psychological Characteristics
frequency (number of vibrations per second)	→	pitch
amplitude (width of string vibration	→	intensity or loudness
overtone structure	→	tone color or *timbre*
duration (5 seconds in this case)	→	length of time tone is audible

sequently altered and augmented to become a reasonably efficient means of communicating the composer's intentions to listener and performer. The system is based on the first seven letters of the alphabet and can best be illustrated by using a segment of the piano keyboard. The pitches range from low to high, from A through G in a repeating A—G pattern.[2]

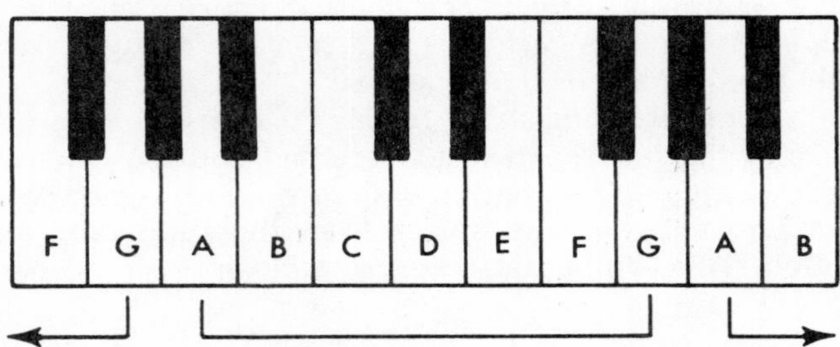

In order to know which of the eight As available on the piano is the intended note, the following is necessary:

1. use a musical *staff* of five lines and four spaces;
2. use a symbol for a musical pitch, i.e., *note;*
3. place the notes on the staff;

4. indicate by means of a *clef sign* the *names* of the notes.

Clef (French, *key*) implies that the key to precise placement of the notes is the establishment of the letter name of *one* of the lines or spaces of the staff. There are two clefs in common use. Both are ornamental symbols derived from the letters G and F. The solid lines are the present clef signs and the dotted lines their original form:

The clefs are placed on the staff to indicate the location of the letters they represent. Although the clef sign can specify G or F on any staff line or space, they are usually confined to one location on the staff. The lower portion of the G clef curls around the second line to indicate the location of G; the two dots of the F clef are placed above and below the fourth line to show that this is the F line.

Once the five-line staff has received its pitch designations of G or F, the *staff* is subsequently identified as *treble*, or *bass staff.*

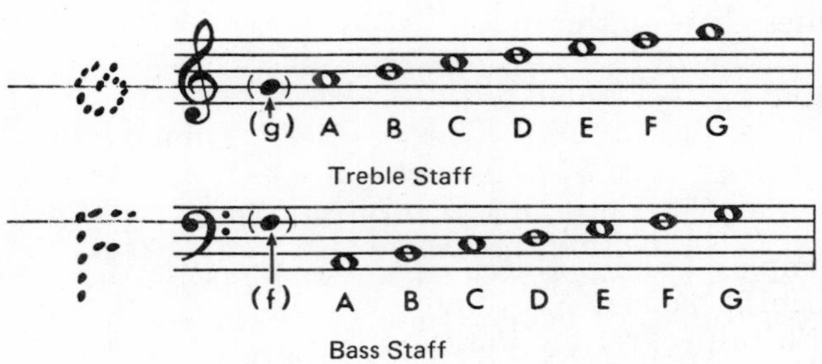

Both these staffs (or staves) are segments of a complete system of eleven lines and ten spaces called the *great staff:*

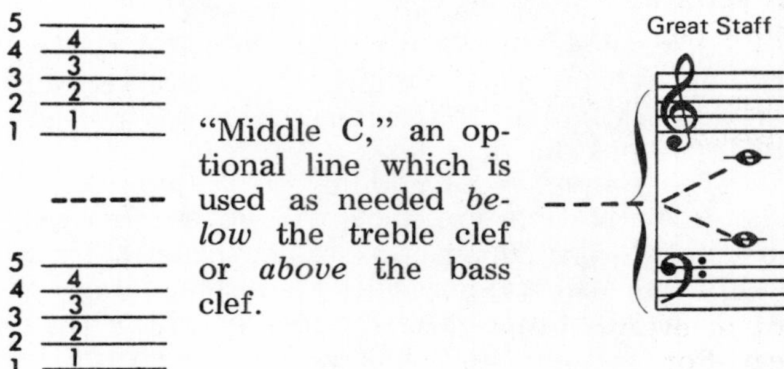

"Middle C," an optional line which is used as needed *below* the treble clef or *above* the bass clef.

Loudness (Intensity)

Composers did not indicate how loud or how soft the music was to be performed until about the year 1600. This particular element will therefore be taken up in conjunction with musical development in the seventeenth century.

Duration

The notation of the length of time of musical sounds (and silences) was developed in conjunction, more or less, with the notation of pitch. The modern *note-value* system consists of fractional parts of a whole unit, or *whole note* (𝅝), expressed in mathematical terms as 1/1. A *half note* (𝅗𝅥) is one-half the whole unit, or 1/2; a *quarter note* (♩) is one-quarter the unit, or 1/4 and so forth.

2. The pattern A—G (rather than C—B) is used because it begins with the first letter of the alphabet.

The *name* of the note value indicates the *number* of notes in the whole-note unit: There are four quarter notes (4 × 1/4 = 1/1), eight eighth notes (8 × 1/8 = 1/1), etc.

With note values smaller than the whole note, the relationships remain constant: There are two quarter notes in a half note (2 × 1/4 = 1/2), two eighth notes in a quarter note (2 × 1/8 = 1/4), etc.

Rhythmic notation is both relative and fixed. The duration of a whole note is dependent on the tempo (speed) and notation of music. It may have a duration of one second, eight seconds or something in between. The interior relationships, however, never vary. A whole note has the same duration as two half notes, four quarter notes and so forth. The mathematical relationship is fixed and precise.

The *Reference Chart: Note and Rest Values* at the end of this chapter outlines the basic system and should be consulted as necessary.

RHYTHM

Rhythm, one of the four elements of music is easier to hear than to define. It can be heard in the complex noise patterns of a city, the click of train wheels on rails, a ping-pong game or the castanets of a Spanish dancer. Essentially, rhythm is the organization of musical time, that is, everything that takes place with respect to the duration of sound and silence, musical tones and noise, accent and nonaccent, tension and relaxation. Rhythm is an indefinable *something* that is greater than the sum of its parts.

Rhythm is the name of the whole and is not to be confused with *beat,* which results from a certain regularity of the rhythmic patterns. Beat, or pulse, can be compared with heart beat, or pulse rate. The beat will usually be steady but it may temporarily speed up or slow down. It may be *explicit* (the uniform thump of a bass drum in a marching band) or *implicit* (resulting from combinations of rhythmic patterns). As soon as one duration follows another, there will be rhythm but not necessarily beat. Certain types of music (such as Gregorian chant) do not produce the regular pulsation called beat.

When beats are produced by the music in a repeating pattern of accents, the result is *meter. Metered* music is *measured* music, with groupings of two, three, or four beats (or combinations of these) in each *measure,* or *bar.*

TIME SIGNATURES

When there is a regular pattern of accented and unaccented beats, it is customary to use a *time signature* in which the upper figure indicates the number of beats in a measure and the lower figure (though not in every case),[3] the unit of beat, that is, the note value the composer has selected to symbolize one beat. For example:

2 = two beats per measure (duple meter)
4 = ♩ unit of beat (quarter note receives one beat)

3 = three beats per measure (triple meter)
8 = ♪ unit of beat (eighth note receives one beat)

4 = four beats per measure (quadruple meter)
2 = 𝅗𝅥 unit of beat (half note receives one beat)

All of the above time signatures indicate *simple* meters in which beat units are divided into even numbers of notes per beat (2, 4, 8, etc.). *Compound* meters such as $\frac{6}{8}$, $\frac{9}{4}$, and $\frac{12}{8}$, have an uneven number of notes (usually three) per beat.

MELODY

A melody is a horizontal organization of pitches or, simply, a succession of musical tones. Melodies may move with:

conjunct (stepwise) motion

3. See Chap. 16 on medieval music, and particularly the exercises connected with that chapter.

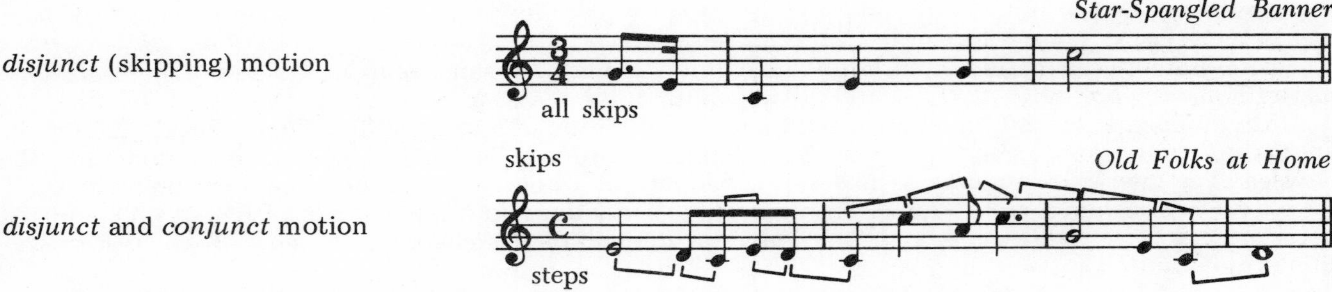

In addition to describing the types of melodic motion, melodies may also be described by the range they encompass: the distance between the lowest and highest notes of a particular melody. *Ranges* may be:

HARMONY

Harmony exists when two or more pitches are sounded simultaneously. It can also be described as a vertical organization of pitches. Because harmony was developed during the Middle Ages it will be discussed in greater detail in conjunction with the development of medieval music.

Reference Chart: Harmony

Six different vertical organizations (individual harmonies):[4]

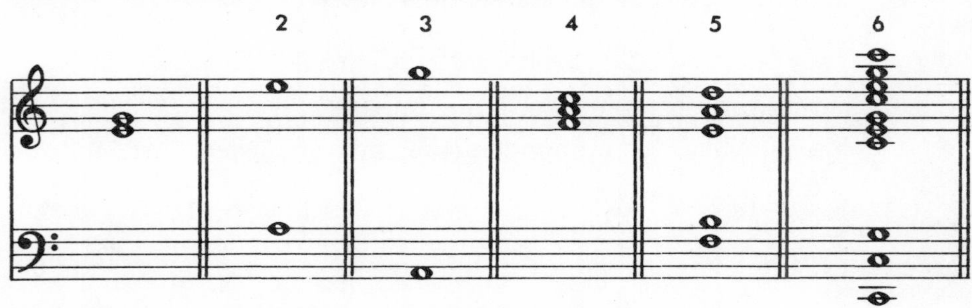

Horizontal organization (melody) combined with harmony:

4. Harmony is developed further in Chap. 16 on medieval music.

Reference Chart: Note and Rest Values[5]

Note Value	Symbol	Rest Value	Symbol
Double whole note	𝅜	Double whole-note rest	𝄺
Whole note (basic unit)	𝅝	Whole (note) rest	𝄻
Half note	𝅗𝅥	Half rest	𝄼
Quarter note	♩	Quarter rest	𝄽
Eighth note	♪	Eighth rest	𝄾
Sixteenth note	𝅘𝅥𝅯	Sixteenth rest	𝄿

Rhythmic notation uses certain conventional symbols and terms including *notehead*, *stem*, *flag*, *beam*, *tie*, and *dot*.

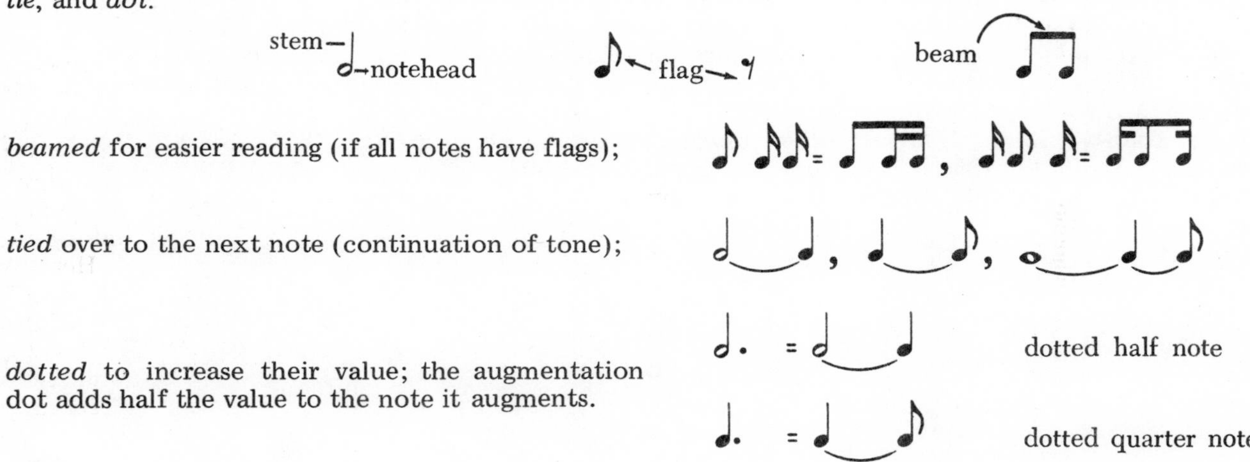

beamed for easier reading (if all notes have flags);

tied over to the next note (continuation of tone);

dotted to increase their value; the augmentation dot adds half the value to the note it augments.

Record List

Following are some suggested recordings for the music used in Exercises in Listening. Because records are constantly going out of print, alternate selections are given wherever possible. Records are listed by composer, composition, title of record album (if different from the title of the composition, performer or performing group, record company and catalog number). All records are 12 inches, 33 1/3 LPs unless specified otherwise. Catalog numbers for monophonic records are listed first, followed by the stereo number (if any).

1. Bach, J.S., Fugue in G minor, Schweitzer, Angel COLC-89.
   or: Recordings of Bach's organ works by Biggs, Weinrich, Richter, Walcha, Dupre, etc.
2. Bartok, B., *Concerto for Orchestra*, Ormandy, Philadelphia Orch., Columbia ML-6026; MS-6626.
   or: Szell, Cleveland Orch., Columbia ML-6215; MS-6815.
   Bernstein, N.Y. Phil., Columbia ML-5471; 6040.
   Leinsdorf, Boston Sym., Victor LM-2643; LSC-2643.
3. Beethoven, L.v., Symphony No. 5, Ormandy, Philadelphia Orch., Columbia ML-5098.
   or: Munch, Boston, Sym., Victor VIC-1035; VICS-1035.
   Bernstein, N.Y. Phil., ("How a Great Symphony Was Written"), Columbia ML-5868; MS-6468.
   (and many others).
4. Bennet, John, "Thyrsis, Sleepest Thou?", *Masterpieces of Music before 1750*, Vol. 2, Haydn Society 9039 (3 volume set, 9038/9040).

5. This chart is to be specifically applied in Chaps. 8 and 16 on Greek and medieval music.

5. Brahms, J., Symphony No. 3, Reiner, Chicago Sym., Victor LM-2209; LSC-2209.
   or: Szell, Cleveland Orch., Columbia ML-6085; MS-6685.
   Karajan, Vienna Phil., London 9318; 6249.
6. Debussy, C., "Voiles," *Preludes for Piano*, Books One and Two, Horowitz, Columbia ML-5941; MS-6541.
   or: Casadesus, 2-Columbia ML-4977/8.
   Gieseking, 2-Angel 35066, 35249.
   Bachauer, Mercury 50391; 90391.
7. Gabrieli, G., "Et Ecclesiis," *History of Music in Sound*, Vol. 4, Victor LM-6029.
   or: Stokowski, Victor LM-1721.
8. Haydn, F.J., Quartet in F Major, Allegri Quartet, Westminster 19111; 17111.
   or: Amadeus Quartet, Westminster 9033.
   Janacek Quartet, London 9385; 6385.
9. Scarlatti, D., Sonata in C Major, Longo 104, Valenti, Harpsichord, 3-Westminster 1010; S-1010.
   or: Kirkpatrick, 4-Columbia SL-221.
   Landowska, 2-Angel COLH-73, 304.
10. Schubert, F., "Gretchen am Spinnrade," *A Lieder Recital by Schwarzkopf and Fischer*, Angel 35022.
    or: *Marian Anderson Sings Beloved Schubert Songs*, Victor LM-98.
11. Jazz: "Kyrie Eleison" from *Jazz Suite on the Mass Texts*, Victor LPM-3414; LSP-3414.
12. Jazz "This Here," Cannonball Adderly, *Quintet in San Francisco*, Riverside 311; 1157.
    or: Cannonball Adderly, *Greatest Hits*, Riverside 416; 9416.
13. Sequence, "Victimae paschali laudes," *Masterpieces of Music before 1750* (henceforth referred to as *Masterpieces*), 3 volumes, Haydn Society 9038/9040.
14. Spiritual, "Didn't It Rain," *Newport 1958: Mahalia Jackson*, Columbia CL-1244; CS-8071.
    or: Mahalia Jackson, *Greatest Hits*, Columbia CL-2004; CS-8804.
15. Trouvere song, "Or la truix," *Masterpieces.*

UNIT II

GREECE: The First Humanistic Culture

CHAPTER 4

Early Greece: Preparation for the Good Life

■ As nearly everyone knows, it was in Greece, particularly in Athens for a short time in the fifth century (c. 500-400 B.C.), that human life developed a quality which has seldom if ever been equaled. Here, for the first time—and most gloriously—personal freedom was achieved for a large percentage of the population, with a sense of justice embodied in laws, and a political system which gave the individual the greatest possible freedom compatible with the coherence of the social group. Here, too, was a sufficient amount of wealth and leisure to allow the individual to develop his capacities to the fullest, and a sufficient challenge in the differences between the various city-states and between the individuals within them to keep many persons keenly alive in the development of their full selves.

It would be convenient for the reader, and certainly for the writer, if the development to the apex of culture had proceeded in some sort of regular progression from the beginning of our knowledge about the Greeks until the culmination during the reign of Pericles (PAIR-i-kleez) in Athens; if all of the statesmen who brought change to the Greek social structure had been high-minded men with a clear vision of the ultimate goal of human values. Unfortunately this is not the case. Greek history—even Greek geography—represents the ultimate in confusion, and even the statesmen who made the greatest contributions in the development of the social structure were often self-seeking politicians, not above taking bribes or committing treason to accomplish their purposes. Out of all of this confusing history the evolution of a society devoted, even for a brief time, to human values becomes a tribute to the toughness of the human spirit.

This chapter will attempt to trace the development of Greek society from its earliest beginnings to the fifth century in what is necessarily an

Figure 1. Greece and the Ionian coast.

oversimplified version. Eventually the focus will be on the city of Athens, where the highest development took place and where ideas which were generated throughout Greece came into greater conflict than they did in their places of origin. This will necessarily be a long chapter, since the whole Greek period covers 2,000 years, and this chapter will cope with 1,500 of them. This was a lively, even a brawling culture, whose history is hard to trace. Furthermore, during the two millenia of the epoch the seeds—and some of the finest flowers—of all Western art and philosophy reveal themselves.

In the first place, let it be clear that there never was a nation called Greece. Instead, we find a group of people who called themselves Hellenes (HEL-e-neez), united by a common language, with several dialects, by a common though diversified religion, and a common heritage. Politically these people lived in independent city-states, each with its own form of government. Frequently we find alliances between these small states, and in the fifth century Athens put together a very loose Athenian Empire, opposing a strong coalition of city-states whose allegiance was to Sparta. Greece was not even confined to a single geographical location. The map shows that the mainland of Greece is the tip of the Balkan peninsula, joined by a narrow isthmus to a fairly large land mass known as the Peloponessus (pel-uh-puh-NEES-us). This is the heartland. But Greece was invaded from the north in the twelfth and eleventh centuries (1199 to 1000 B.C.), and many of the mainlanders fled to the Asiatic coast of the Aegean (i-JEE-an) Sea and the islands off the Asian coast to form a flourishing Greek cultural center with many important cities. Later, in the seventh and sixth centuries (699 to 500 B.C.), land poverty on the mainland encouraged many of the city-states to send out colonies to occupy new land. As a result, a great number of Greek cities were formed all the way from Byzantium (bi-ZAN-tshum, or bi-ZANT-e-um), along both shores of the Mediterranean Sea, in Sicily, and in Italy. For example, Syracuse in Sicily and Paestum (PES-tum), near Naples, were both important Greek cities. Although these cities were so widely dispersed, and although they were frequently at war with each other, their common culture, heritage, religion, and language gave them a sense of brotherhood as Hellenes, while people of the rest of the world were regarded as barbarians or strangers. These Hellenes maintained a feeling that they were somehow different and better than the barbarians, a sense which created a sort of unity in the vast diversity, and a pride which led to the accomplishments mentioned earlier.

THE GEOGRAPHY OF MAINLAND GREECE

Mainland Greece was a hard country in which to live. Ranges of mountains divided the area so that communication across the countryside was difficult in the extreme. Furthermore, according to our earliest records, the mountains have been so eroded that little farmland was available. Only in the north do we find broad and fertile plains. For the remainder, sheep and goats grazed on the mountain slopes, and bee-culture was common. The valleys between the mountains offered small areas of arable land, and it was in these valleys that the first villages appeared which would later unite to become city-states. In these valleys the chief crops were olives and grapes.

Nor was the climate conducive to easy living. In the winter great storms blew down from the north bringing torrential rains and, on the mountain peaks, a good deal of snow. The summers were extremely hot and dry.

One other geographical factor influenced Greek life: this was the closeness of the sea. Nowhere is the sea more than a few miles distant, and communication by water was frequently much easier than overland travel.

All of these factors contributed to the Greek character. In a hard land, people must be ingenious and clever to survive. In a land where nature yields little, people must turn to man-made objects in order to make a living. As compared to other early civilizations, the Greek population contained many more artisans and artists than peasants. Finally the proximity of the sea always offered the possibility of trade and commerce (and piracy) as a source of livelihood. Such commerce always broadens horizons; in addition to the bartering of goods, the traders barter ideas and bring them home. It is never possible to attribute the character of a people to geography and climate alone, yet the factors mentioned here must have done much to shape the personality of the Hellenes.

SOME STEPS IN GREEK HISTORY

The first people about whom we have much information and who lived in Greek lands were the Minoans (mi-NO-uns), so named after the fabled King Minos (MI-nus) who lived on the island of Crete. These were probably not "Greek" people, in that their language, as far as one can tell, does not seem to be related to the Indo-European family. (Of this language we have only clay tablets in the "Linear A" writing, which has not yet been deciphered.) This Minoan Culture existed from about 2600 B.C. to about 1125 B.C., and reached its peak somewhere around the year 2000 with the building of the great palaces and the surrounding towns of Knossos (KNAWS-us), Phaistos (FEST-us), Mallia (MAL-ya), and others.

We know a great deal about this culture because of the excavations of Sir Arthur Evans and other archeologists. From Evans' excavations and reconstructions of the palace at Knossos we see that this was an extremely rich culture and a highly sophisticated one. The basis of the prosperity seems to have lain in trade and commerce, for we have abundant evidence of trade with Egypt and the Asian coast of the Aegean sea. On the island of Crete, at least, life was peaceful, for the palaces were not fortified, and the Cretans seem to have trusted to their maritime power to ward off enemies. This sense of peace is enforced by the art of the time, for the paintings depict athletic contests (the famous bull-dance), women gossiping, cupbearers, and the like, rather than scenes of war. The designs on jars and vases were ornate and colorful, utilizing fish and animal designs, one of the most common of which is from the octopus, since the flowing tentacles offered an infinite possibility for involved and convoluted spirals and circles, patterns which entirely cover the surface desired.

The religion of these people seems to have been a fertility cult and a worship of the earth goddess. This, in turn, led to a matriarchal form of government, with the essential power lying with the queen as the earthly representative, indeed, the incarnation of the earth mother. A part of this worship involved the tradition of the year-king, a tradition that the king married the queen for a specified time—a year, four years, perhaps some other length of time—after which he was killed and the queen took another husband. This custom relates to the concept that the earth (the queen) must be refertilized to maintain continuing prosperity. It is important to mention this here because of the belief of many scholars, particularly Robert Graves, that much of Greek myth arises out of the clash between this earth worship and the matriarchy which it produced and the worship of the sky gods, a religion which was brought into Greece by the people whom we will know as the Mycenaeans (mī-se-NE-uns), the first of the true Greeks, whose worship venerated the male, and male symbols, rather than the female.

So much has been discovered about the Minoan culture that it could be described at very great length, however the student is directed to such fictional works as Mary Renault's book, *The King Must Die*, for a real grasp of the nature of this civilization.

The fact is that for many years (from about 1900 B.C. onwards) a group of tribes from northern Europe had been slowly invading and infiltrating Greece. By the year 1600 they occupied all of the Greek mainland including the Peloponessus where, at Mycenae (mi-SEEN-ee), their Great King established his palace and fortress. These were warlike peoples, [one of the Great Kings was Agamemnon (ag-a-MEM-non)], who naturally came into contact and conflict with Cretan culture, and some time between the years 1400 B.C. and 1125 they conquered Crete. A persistent story and much archeological evidence suggests that the fall of Crete was speeded by a violent earthquake which wrecked the palace at Knossos and much of the Aegean world, including the sinking of at least half of the island of Thera (Santorini) into the sea. Whatever the cause may have been, the power of Crete was broken, and the Mycenaean Greeks became the overlords of the Aegean world.

The deciphering of clay tablets in the "Linear B" script (accomplished in 1953) showed that these Mycenaeans were true Greeks. They spoke a Greek language, worshipped the pantheon of sky gods whom we recognize as the Greek gods, and created the heritage which was to unite the Hellenes, for they were the ones who fought the Trojan War which, centuries later, was to become the subject of the Homeric poems and the core of the Hellenic tradition. This Mycenaean culture lasted from the sixteenth century through the twelfth century (1599 B.C. to 1100 B.C.).

As far as the facts of this culture are concerned, we know a considerable amount. The people established themselves in small, warlike independent kingdoms whose king lived in a strongly fortified but rich palace. Each king was independent, administering his rule through a group of officials who supervised the farmlands, collected taxes in produce, managed religious celebrations and sacrifices, and otherwise handled all the affairs of government. Although each king was independent, each owed a rough allegiance to the high king at Mycenae; although, as seen in Homer's Iliad (IL-ee-ad), a local ruler could disobey the high king—as Achilles (uh-KIL-eez) did with Agamemnon—and not be forced to follow the ruler. Each king had a group of well-armed troops, and the nobles rode chariots into battle, although most of the fighting was done on foot.

These people carried on extensive trade, mostly among the islands and Asia Minor, although their influence extended throughout the Mediterranean world. Gold, ivory, textiles, and spices were bartered for the local products, and the number of gold ornaments and cups found in the royal tombs at Mycenae and at other great palaces attests to the rather barbaric wealth of these kings. In general, the prosperity of these people seems to have depended upon trade, commerce, and barter, a fact which is to be remembered as we see this civilization decline in later years.

This was a society in which the masculine virtues were honored, evidence for which is given in the Homeric poems. Although Homer wrote his poems late in the ninth century or early in the eighth, his poetry seems to reflect with considerable accuracy all the rest of the knowledge which we can piece together about the Mycenaeans.

The chief virtues of the early Greeks were

physical courage and the preservation of individual honor. These qualities are shown time and time again in the Iliad, as when Diomedes (di-uh-MEED-eez) broke from the ranks of his troops and ranged through the Trojan forces risking everything in individual combat. Or by Achilles, who, by twentieth-century standards appears to be a pouting boy when Agamemnon takes his girl, Briseis (bri-SEE-us), from him, but was in reality the Greek hero whose personal honor had been affronted. He refused to fight, not from cowardice or pique, but simply because Agamemnon had insulted his pride and belittled him in front of the entire Argive (the Greeks, led by the king from Argos) army. The hero must retaliate, and he did so by refusing to fight until he was moved, not by loyalty to his cause or his king, but by the grief which he felt at the loss of his friend Patroklus (pa-TRO-klus). The greatest example of all is the death of Hector in Book XXII of the Iliad. Here was a man, the greatest and strongest of the Trojan warriors, who could easily have shirked this last individual battle. His aged father pled with him to stay within the city walls; earlier, in a touching scene with his wife and his little child he admitted that he knew that he and his city were doomed. Yet, when the time came, he had to assert himself in a glorious action which would test all of his powers to the utmost, fulfill all of his capacities, and finally bring him immortality, not in heaven, but in the minds of men. For these Greeks, human worth and dignity lay in total self-fulfillment, usually on the battlefield where their exploits would bring death, perhaps, but certainly fame among their fellows and among people to come after them as their deeds were recounted in song and story.

Another aspect of the Greek character, much admired throughout the history of the people, was the use of a wily and tricky intelligence. For this quality, Odysseus (o-DIS-yews) stands as the supreme example. Thus, when Odysseus finally won his way home to his kingdom of Ithaca he was put ashore disguised as a beggar. Here Athena (uh-THEE-nuh) met him and heard his lying tale. Her response was typical of the Greek attitude:

> "What a cunning knave it would take," she said, "to beat you at your tricks! Even a god would be hard put to it.
>
> "And so my stubborn friend, Odysseus the arch-deceiver, with his craving for intrigue, does not propose even in his own country to drop his sharp practice and the lying tales that he loves from the bottom of his heart. But no more of this: we are both adepts at chicane. For in the world of men you have no rival as a statesman and orator, while I am pre-eminent among the gods for invention and resource."

And a few lines later:

> "How like you to be so wary!" said Athena. "And that is why I cannot desert you in your misfortunes: you are so civilized, so intelligent, so self-possessed."

Perhaps in our time we cannot so admire the man who was so smoothly deceitful to gain his own ends; even in classic Greece Euripides (you-RIP-i-deez) despised these qualities as he pictured a rather despicable Odysseus in the drama Philoctetes (fil-OK-ti-teez). But for the Greek of the heroic age, this was simply another example of the idea of self-fulfillment. Odysseus had been given the quality and the capacity for sharp intelligence, and it was his purpose, man's purpose, to utilize all of his capacities to their utmost. He would be a fool, shirking his own fate, not to use this ability.

GREEK RELIGION IN THE HEROIC AGE

The worship of the Olympian gods forms one of the most curious religions that we know of. This religion had no "revealer," divine or mortal; no Christ, no Mohammed, no Buddha. Neither did it have any sacred book such as the Bible, the Koran, or the Talmud. As far as we know, it simply grew as a collection of myths which were honored in various ways throughout the Greek world. Even the myths varied greatly, so that no single version of the history and the nature of the gods exists. Hesiod (HEE-see-ud) in his book *Theogony* (thee-OG-uh-nee), and other writers as well, attempted to systematize the story of the gods, but with only minor success. Vastly simplified, the genealogy of the gods can be presented in the following way: In the beginning was Chaos, composed of void, mass, and darkness. From Chaos emerged a male god, Uranus (YUR-uh-nus), who represented the heavens, and a female god, Gaea (JEE-ah), who represented earth. These gods had three types of offspring, one of which was the Titans, who represented earthquakes and other catacylsms of the earth. Kronus (KRO-nus), one of the Titans, led a revolt against his father and overthrew him. (It is interesting that from the drops of blood of Uranus sprang the fearful hags known as the Furies, whose duty it was to pursue anyone who had shed the blood of his kindred; this type of superstition was important because it helped hold the clans together.) Kronus took his sister Rhea (REE-uh), another representation of the earth goddess, as his wife, and from this union, although not without some difficulty, came the Olympian gods. The difficulty alluded to was the fact that Kronus had a prophecy that one of his children would overthrow him; to prevent this he swallowed all his children at birth (Kronus, of course, may be thought of as Time, which swallows all things). By a trick, Rhea saved Zeus (rhymes with *juice*) from being swallowed, and spirited him away to Crete, where he grew to manhood. Then Zeus led the prophesied revolt and, aided by some of the Titans, managed to shut up his father in the dark cave of Tartarus, but not before Kronus had regurgitated the other children, Demeter (di-MEET-er), Hera (HEAR-uh), Pluto (PLEW-to), Poseidon (po-SID-on), and Vesta (VEST-uh). Zeus then took Hera as his wife, and from this union came such gods and goddesses as Apollo, Athena, Aphrodite, Artemis, and others.

In addition to these, many entirely local gods and nymphs presided over particular streams and groves, and were locally worshipped. The whole Greek pantheon represents a most confusing array.

No less confusing are the stories of the actions of the gods; we see Zeus almost constantly pursuing (and seducing) some mortal girl; all of the gods quarreled jealously among themselves; they all had favorites among the mortals, as we saw Athena protecting Odysseus; and they used all sorts of trickery to foil each other's designs for the success of their favorite mortals. How could such a group possibly be revered and worshipped?

If one can understand this worship, even faintly, then he may come to know something of the Greek character, and particularly some of its love for the very process of living. The gods were regarded as a race infinitely superior to men in that they were completely powerful, immortal, and always young and beautiful; they had the same characteristics as men, but in a higher category. If men sometimes showed wisdom and nobility, so did Athena, or Apollo (uh-POL-o), but to a vastly superior degree. If men were sometimes lustful, Zeus was much more so, and in his power, much more successful. If men were skilled craftsmen, so was Hephaestus (hi-FES-tus); if men were crafty and skillful, so was Prometheus (pro-MEE-thee-us)—but the skill, wisdom, lust, or whatever quality one may choose, of the gods was infinitely beyond that of mortals. For the Greek man, death was a sort of dark oblivion, but the gods had life forever, and life in full beauty, full youth, and complete power.

The worship of these gods during Mycenaean times and later may illustrate the point, for the formal ceremonies were always feasts. Animals were sacrificed, and a portion of the meat was burnt upon the fire. The rest was roasted and eaten by the men performing the sacrifice. Wine was drunk, with a certain amount poured out first as a libation to the gods. Then the feast proceeded, with the assumption that the god was present as a guest at the meal, and that he enjoyed such things as well as the mortals did.

In what must seem to be a very diverse religious practice, one aspect of the life with the gods is of great importance. The Hellenes were never a priest-ridden group of people, as were the Egyptians. To us their religious practice seems inchoate, but it allowed plenty of room for freedom of thought. We will see later that in political organization these same Greeks were not downtrodden by political despots, or, at least, never for very long. The Persians were, and culturally they produced only the monuments of a totalitarian state. In both religion and politics, the Greeks maintained the widest possible latitude for thought, questioning, and experimentation which, though turbulent and unstable, produced a great humanistic value system.

Such, greatly simplified, was the Olympian religion which existed from the fifteenth century throughout all of Greek history. During classical times and later, doubt may have existed about the nature and the presence of the gods, but the vast majority of people, probably excluding some of the intellectuals, believed in the gods, and for almost every important state decision one of the oracles was consulted, usually the oracle at Delphi. That the answers given by the oracles were frequently riddles which could be interpreted in any of several ways did not shake the faith of the people in the oracles themselves.

In this bewildering complexity of gods and men, what determined the events and the fate, or doom, of any individual? Here, as before, we must rely on Homer who wrote centuries after the heroic age, and none too certain himself of the answer to the question we have posed. In the first place, they had a vague belief that each man, or each hero, had his own *moira* (MOY-ruh), or pattern of life, which he would fulfill. This may be illustrated as a sort of jigsaw puzzle which the hero's life would fill in—with the added complexity that the individual never knew what the picture would be when it was finished, nor would he know when it was completed. Within the individual life we have the three forces of free will as determined by character, accident, and the intervention of the gods. These worked together, and sometimes in opposition, to determine the course of a man's life, and nothing could be counted on as certain until death finished the picture. (A much more mature consideration of this problem than Homer's is found in Sophocles' *Oedipus* [ED-i-pus or EED-i-pus] *the King*, p. 148.) Frequently the gods intervened and brought tragedy to a man when he overstepped the limits of human action, and out of pride, attempted to act in the realm of the gods. Such action almost certainly brought about a doom. But for the most part it seems that in the heroic age a man's character *was* his fate. The man did the things he did, receiving their attendant consequences, because he was the kind of man he was. Thus Achilles, in spite of all sorts of ruses to outwit his predicted fate, had his short and glorious life just because he was the kind of person to whom personal honor was all important, because he took great risks in the hope of winning great fame. Odysseus, on the other hand, lived a long life not only because of his heroic strength, but also because of his ability to talk, to deceive, and to plan ahead for survival.

Such, then, is a suggestion, at least, of the nature of the Mycenaean civilization, the culture in which the Trojan War occurred, in which Agamemnon, Menelaus (men-uh-LAY-us), Helen, and the other fabled Greeks actually lived.

This Mycenaean culture began its decline in the twelfth century (the 1100s) as a result of many factors: a forced closing of trade with the Middle East and a series of wars between the kingdoms within the Mycenaean groups and, most importantly, an invasion from the north by a group called the Dorians. These last were a people of the same racial stock as the Mycenaeans, but who were just now forced to migrate south because of the complicated folk-movements of the time. They slowly occupied the mainland of Greece during the twelfth to the tenth centuries, overcoming the already spent civilization which they found there. Two important consequences followed. First, a long "dark ages" descended upon Greece in which there was little cultural or artistic creation. Second, retreating from the Dorians, the inhabitants of the Greek mainland emigrated to the Asiatic coast of the Aegean Sea where, in the course of time they developed a number of Greek cities in an advanced state of civilization. Because these last people spoke the Ionian dialect of Greek, this region became known as the Ionian coast, and was later to become the home of the earliest Greek philosopher-scientists, as well as a land which was a sort of military football between the kingdom of Lydia and then of Persia (the great Asiatic powers) and the city-states of Greece. We know little of Greece until the ninth century (800s).

THE ARCHAIC PERIOD

These dark ages move almost imperceptibly into the Archaic (ar-KAY-ic) times of historic Greece. We know quite a bit about the life of the period through the poems of Hesiod (HEE-see-ud), *Works and Days.* Hesiod was a farmer in Boeotia who, except for once winning a poetry contest, seems to have known nothing but bad luck. He gives us a picture of a landed aristocracy whose chief occupation was to squeeze the small farmer. Life was a continual round of jobs to be done with little or no reward or future in the work. Justice lay in the hands of the aristocrats who rendered their decisions almost entirely in terms of who could offer the largest bribe. Hesiod was always reverent towards the gods, but he neither expected nor got any reward in this life except for continuous toil, and Hesiod's plight was the common lot of most of the Greeks of his time.

Of course the latter part of the ninth century or the early part of the eighth was also the time when Homer wrote. While Hesiod was describing the life of his own time, Homer's work describes the departed glories of the heroic or Mycenaean period which has already been discussed. We know little about Homer; he may have been one man, or perhaps two people were composing—one author composing the tragedy of the *Iliad*, another writing the adventure tale which is the *Odyssey.* These questions will probably never be settled for certain, nor is their answer important here. What is important is that the two books mentioned, the *Iliad* and the *Odyssey*, are the very center of the common Greek heritage. Greek ideals, the idea of Greek superiority over the barbarians, the overwhelming desire for personal honor were embodied in these works, and they became as close to a central religious book as the Greeks ever possessed. The works of Homer were memorized by every Greek schoolboy; they were recited at all of the great Greek festivals and games throughout the Hellenic world. Homer, of course, did not make up the stories which he wrote. The books were a collection of the legends which had their origins from time out of mind sung or recited by bards in the palaces. But they were brought together by the sure hand of a literary genius and transformed into the works which inspired the Greek mind from the time of their composition.

But to return to the times of Hesiod. We witness, first, the rise of a landed aristocracy who, by force and guile, seized most of the land from the poor farmers. Not the least of the ways of acquiring land by the aristocrat was to lend money to the farmer, who used his own person as security for the loan. When he was unable to pay his debt, his land became the property of the aristocrat and the farmer became a slave. Numerous forms of governments arose at this time; frequently the most powerful landowner became king, at other times the city-state was ruled by a committee of landowners, constituting an oligarchy. It was during this time that land-poverty, simply the fact that there was not enough land to support the population, became painfully evident.

As a result of this land-poverty the colonizing process which was mentioned earlier began to take place. Many city-states simply exported fairly large bands of adventurers to found colonies throughout the Aegean and Mediterranean world. Many colonies were established in northern Greece, including Byzantium, and a number of cities on the shores of the Black Sea. The present city of Marseilles in France was originally a Greek colony, as were a number of the cities of Sicily and Italy. The Greek world expanded greatly, and with the expansion came the development of trade and commerce among all of the Hellenic cities and an increasing flow of wealth into the original Greek cities. A large, important, and wealthy commercial class of people also began to form a part of the population of the cities, different from the landed aristocracy and opposed to them and different from the small-farmer group. This new group was to become a political faction to reckon with in the development of new governmental forms.

The first of the political changes came with the rise of *tyrants.* For us in the twentieth century, the term suggests the harsh military dictator, but at first, among the Hellenic cities, it was simply another word meaning "king." The tyrant was simply a man, sometimes chosen by the people, more usually a man who seized power and established himself as absolute ruler as long as he could hold office. Sometimes he came from the members of the old land-owning families, a man who discerned the "wave of the future" and grabbed power either by allying himself with the merchant class or the farming class and promising political reforms which would bring help to his political allies. Sometimes he rose from the merchant group; sometimes he was an outsider who came in to take over the rule of a city-state. No matter what his origin, he had to win over a good part of the population in order to try to hold his position, and he did this by effecting political, judicial or economic reforms which would make him popular with a fairly large segment of the population. From this movement toward tyranny came the earliest reforms which were to lead, in Athens and some other cities, toward eventual democracy. None of this development was uniform through the cities of the Hellenic world; in none of them was progress a steady evolutionary process. From this point on in our discussion, we shall focus our attention on governmental changes in the city of Athens, which, in most ways was to become the most glorious of the Greek cities. For our purposes in this chapter, we shall consider only the changes made under the rule of four leaders: Draco (DRAY-ko), Solon (SO-lon), Pisistratus (pie—SIS-truh-tus), and Themistocles (the-MIS-to-kleez). Furthermore, they will seem to appear as if they came in an orderly sequence, which is not the case. For example two of Pisistratus' sons attempted to follow their father in power, but one of them, Hipparchus (hip-AR-kus) was assassinated in 514, the other, Hippias (HIP-i-us), was exiled in 510. The course of leadership, like that of true love, never runs as smoothly as it appears in a book.

THE RISE OF ATHENS

In considering the political and economic development of Athens from the sixth century, it is well to bear in mind a rather curious power structure. Three political factions, largely determined by economic status, struggled for power; they were the old landed aristocracy, the poor farmers who eked out a living on marginal land, and the growing commercial class. In addition to these economic groups, Athenian life was dominated by four family-clans, originally of the aristocracy, who controlled the individual lives of their members, and, in a fairly large measure controlled, as well, the political developments within the city. As long as these four tribes remained powerful, political and economic advances would always be dominated by the traditions of the tribes.

The first of the reformers in the seventh century was an almost legendary figure, Draco, one of the early tyrants. His great contribution was to publish a code of laws. This simple act was a great step toward freedom. Hesiod, for example, had complained that the aristocrats who were the judges of his time were the only ones who knew the laws, and it appears that they made up the rules as they went along. An ordinary citizen involved in a legal suit about land or homicide really cast himself on the mercy of the judges who rendered decisions as they saw fit; decisions which depended upon the economic status of the litigants, their family connections, and the size of the bribe that could be offered. Justice cannot reside in such a system. Draco's Code, although it is reputed to have been very severe, did offer a single standard of justice for *all* people, and since the law was published, individuals within the state could know their legal rights. No matter how harsh the laws may have been, the publication of the laws became a step forward in developing a *rational* system of justice rather than one based upon tradition, privilege, and wealth.

The second of the great reformers, in the early sixth century, was Solon, a man whose name has come down to us as the synonym for a wise lawgiver. Like Draco, he was a member of the nobility, but evidently in his youth he had travelled extensively, and had developed interests in the possibilities of trade and commerce, and he also became aware of the injustice of land distribution in his native state of Attica. Perhaps his most important reform was to free all slaves who had reached that condition because of debt, and to abolish the custom that made debt-slavery possible. A man who sought moderation in all things, he was evidently pressured to break up the great estates and to distribute the land to the farmers, but he did not have sufficient faith in the poor and uneducated masses to take this step. He did, however, allow all people to become involved to some extent with the government. He limited the magistracies and important governmental offices to the upper classes, but he allowed members of the lowest class, even, to serve as jurors and thus he began a process of educating all people in the processes of social action and social change. In running the day-to-day affairs of Athens he established an administrative council of 400 members, and thus greatly broadened the civic responsibilities of the citizens.

In order to encourage trade and commerce, Solon adopted a much lighter coinage than Athens had used in the past, and also he imported many artisans, particularly potters, since pottery manufacture was one of the chief industries of Athens and one of its chief exports. These last reforms began a series of developments which were to break Athens away from an economic dependence upon agriculture and land, and to establish it as a city whose wealth depended upon man-made objects which are more or less independent of the uncontrollable forces of climate and nature.

The third great reformer to be considered here was Pisistratus, who came to power and controlled Athens for nineteen years in the latter part of the sixth century, from 546 onwards. In his economic reforms he was to follow the precedent which had already been set by Solon in that he broke up the large estates and distributed the land to the almost landless peasants. Since voting privileges and participation in the government were determined largely by economic status, this single reform did much to broaden the base for government and it allowed the people who had already been somewhat educated in social action by Solon's changes to take a more important role than before in the actual government of the state. He and his sons further increased employment by starting a number of great public works within the city. Perhaps the most important of Pisistratus' contributions to the city lay in the development of its art. Two of the greatest Hellenic poets of the time, Simonides and Anacreon, were brought to Athens, and Pisistratus and his sons also commissioned the preparation of the first careful edition of Homer's poems, which were later sung and recited at all of the important festivals and sacrifices within the city. This last step may not seem to be of great importance, but its significance is apparent when one realizes that the learning of these poems by most of the citizens and their recitation at public functions gave the people a sense of common heritage and a feeling of unity *as citizens of Athens* not as members of a particular family clan. These tyrants of Athens, consciously or unconsciously, were leading their city toward democracy, and, by educating them through increased responsibility, made them ready for active participation in a truly democratic government.

This government came into being with the reforms of Cleisthenes (KLICE-the-neez) who attempted to abolish the influence of the four old aristocratic tribes whose power had, for years, been the dominant political influence in Athens. To accomplish this he instituted ten new "tribes" whose membership was based simply on place of residence rather than upon heredity. In order to do this he first divided the city into "demes" or neighborhoods. These purely artificial units furnished the basis for the political structure. Then a number of demes were combined to form a tribe, of which there were ten within the city-state. Furthermore, the demes for any single tribe were selected at random, so that within any tribe one found neighborhoods composed of the shore (people connected with shipping and sea-faring trades), the city itself, and the rural areas. Thus no tribe was dominated by any single economic group. To make a not-too-exact analogy, we might think of the city of Detroit divided into ten political groups but within each group one would find neighborhoods from the inner-city, neighborhoods from the regularly employed working class, and neighborhoods from suburbs like Grosse Point.

Cleisthenes abolished the old Council of Four Hundred which had come into being with the reforms of Solon, and substituted a Council of Five Hundred, with fifty members representing each of the new political tribes. He did this since the old council had come to be simply the voice of the four traditional tribes, and Cleisthenes wished to break their hold upon political and judical matters. In the new government, each artificial political tribe nominated a large slate of candidates for the Council, from which 50 were selected by lot, on the theory that any citizen who was nominated (the nomination process eliminated the obviously unfit) was just as capable as any other citizen to administer the affairs of the state, so that actual membership could be left to chance.

The executive branch of the government was placed in the hands of a committee of ten generals who were elected yearly by the Council, and, in turn, this committee-of-ten was headed by a commander-in-chief whose term was also for a single year.

While Athens had been developing in these political ways, the rest of the Middle Eastern world was not standing still. The most important change throughout these years had been the growth of the great Kingdom of Persia, and all sorts of in-fighting between Persia and the Greek cities of the Ionian coast and the adjacent islands. The Persian king, Darius (da-RI-us), finally chose to make his world conquest complete by invading the mainland of

Greece, and in the year 490 completed his plans for the invasion. The great battle of this war was fought on the plain of Marathon where the Greeks (Athenians, in this case) met the overwhelming force of the Persian army. Under General Miltiades (mil-TI-uh-deez), Greek strategy prevailed, and in a swift dawn attack the Athenians drove the Persians back to the sea and into their ships with a loss, according to the historian, Herodotus, of more than 6,000 men. The Persians sailed their remaining forces to Phalerum, near Athens, to make another attack, but Miltiades rushed his army overland ahead of the Persians, who, seeing the shore protected, did not choose to land, but sailed away in defeat.

This was the first great Greek victory, which Herodotus and many others attributed to the new democratic spirit among the Athenians. The Persian army was pictured as a great mass of troops beaten into battle by the whips of their officers; the Athenians, as men spurred on by a love of their city and their personal honor into valiant combat. Greek pride in Hellenism as opposed to barbarianism was vindicated.

The Persians were not to give up easily, and a second invasion was planned, but held up for ten years while the Persians put down a revolt in Egypt. In 480, however, they effected their second invasion. In the meantime the Athenians had discovered rich silver deposits at Mount Laurium in Attica, and had achieved a fairly high degree of wealth. Themistocles (the-MIS-tuh-kleez), the commander-in-chief in Athens sent a delegation to Delphi to ask how best to meet the Persians in their second invasion, and was told that they should protect themselves with "wooden walls." Themistocles, with the usual Greek intellectual twist, believed that the Athenians could best protect themselves with a strong navy, and convinced his fellow citizens that the "wooden walls" were ships. Consequently, the money from the silver mines was used to build a strong Athenian navy which proved to be not only a military force, but also the determining factor in establishing Athens as a great commercial center. The Persian invasion of 480 was conducted on an even larger scale than the earlier war, for Herodotus estimates the Persian forces at 5,000,000 men—an obvious exaggeration, but indicative of the size of the invading army. This army crossed the Aegean Sea far in the north and marched down the Greek peninsula, closely attended by the great Persian navy. The first of the great battles was a Persian victory, but a glorious episode in the history of Greece. This was the battle at the pass of Thermopolae (ther-MOP-uh-lee).

Here, at a narrow pass between the mountains and the sea, 300 Spartans (now actually allied with Athens as a part of the fighting force) under their king, Leonidas (lee-ON-uh-dus), faced the entire Persian army and fought magnificently. As usual in Greek wars, they were betrayed by a traitor who showed the Persians an alternative route through the mountains so that the Spartans were surrounded, but even in the face of such odds, they kept on fighting until they were all killed. The inscription later carved on the tomb of the heroic Spartans, in tremendous understatement and compression of meaning, gives testimony to the spirit of the encounter:

> Go tell the Spartans, thou that passest by,
> That here, obedient to their laws, we lie.

In the meantime the Persian fleet sailing down the coast in support of the army had suffered defeats from the Greeks and from the storms, but it still overwhelmingly outnumbered the ships of Athens and its allies. Eventually this fleet reached the sea just off Athens near the bay of Salamis (SAL-a-mus), while the land army moved inexorably toward its goal. Themistocles abandoned the city and all of Attica, moving the population to the island of Salamis, and prepared to gamble everything on a single naval battle. By trickery he enticed the Persian fleet into the Bay of Salamis, where the fleet's very size was a disadvantage since in the narrow waters it was impossible to maneuver so many ships, and the Greek fleet attacked around the edges of the Persian ships and destroyed the Persians. The war continued for a year more on land, but the Persian army was finally defeated by the Spartans at the Battle of Plataea (pla-TEE-uh), and the Persian threat was broken.

It is almost impossible to overestimate the feeling of pride which the Greeks felt as a result of these victories. Persia controlled Egypt, the entire eastern end of the Mediterranean Sea, and all of the land as far east as India. The wealth of the Persian kings and their satraps is impossible to estimate. Yet a relatively few Greek men, poverty-stricken in comparison to the Persians, had beaten off the totalitarian enemy. The Greeks rightly felt that their tradition of personal freedom, their pride in personal honor, and the love which they felt for their cities had been the decisive factor. As, indeed, it was. Although the old aristocratic, oligarchical party continued in Athens, the years following the Persian wars marked the complete triumph of democracy in Athens. Suddenly the idea of freedom had worked.

For us in the Western world in the twentieth century, these far-off wars are of equal importance, for the Greek tradition—principally the concept of the worth of the individual person—survived and has given form to the ideas which we now hold as of greatest worth. If the Greeks had failed, that tradition might have been snuffed out.

ANOTHER QUEST FOR FREEDOM: THE PHILOSOPHERS

Developments in Greece during these preclassical times were not only political, economic, and military. One important phase of individual freedom is always the liberation of man's mind, allowing him to ask all the important questions of the gods and the universe, and to formulate new and original answers. This, too, had been going on during the time of more tangible and material progress of which we have been taking note. Curiously, the abstract speculation about the nature of the universe was a Greek phenomenon, one not found in other parts of the Western world. The Egyptians had made astronomical observations, but always for such practical purposes as the prediction of the flooding of the Nile upon which their agriculture depended. So, too, in Babylon a number of men had observed the stars, largely for use in making practical predictions about the affairs of the earth. But pure thought about the nature of things was uniquely Greek; Edith Hamilton attributes it to the very looseness of Greek religion, which did not dominate the thinking of the people by a priestly class. Such things can never be completely explained. Sometimes they happen, and the work of the Greek philosopher-scientists is the first example which we have in our civilization of the speculations of the "pure thinkers," who were discussed Chapter 2.

THE IONIAN PHILOSOPHERS

The first of the philosopher-scientists was a group which lived in the Ionian city of Miletus (mī-LEET-us) in the early sixth century, and their leader was a man named Thales (THA-leez).

The *questions* that these men asked are always more important than the answers which they found, for the questions are those which constantly return to challenge men's minds. The answers change as our knowledge of the universe becomes more varied.

One problem consistently bothered the philosophers of the Ionian (or Milesian) School. They were intrigued by the constant change of all the things which they could see around them. Earth changed to plant life; plant life changed to animal; wherever one turned, one observed movement from one form of existence to another. They postulated that there must be one single basic substance of which all the forms of being are made, so that the process of change is simply the transformation of the basic element. The first question which Thales asked, then, is, "*What is the single element, the basic stuff, of which the universe is composed?*"

His answer was that this basic element is water, for all things need water for their existence, and water itself changes when heated or cooled to a gaseous nature, steam, or to a solid state, ice. These things being true and observable by our relatively coarse sensory equipment, all sorts of other changes and transformations which are not sense-apparent, could take place in water. Other philosophers, following the line of thought first explored by Thales, argued for earth or air as the basic world-stuff. But, as we have said before, the questions are important, not necessarily the answers.

A second of the Ionians, Anaximander (a-NAKS-uh-man-der), a student of Thales, came up with the second question of importance, "*How do specific things emerge from the basic element?*" His answer, while it may seem unsatisfactory and vague, is probably more scientifically accurate than those of many of his contemporaries or successors. In the first place, he rejected the idea of a physical element such as water, earth, or air, and simply called his basic stuff "the Boundless." This, he suggested, was a form of being which we cannot perceive with our senses; that is, it permeates everything and surrounds everything. In specific answer to the question which he raised, he simply said that all forms which we can see—trees, living animal bodies, all specific things—are formed by "separating out" of this boundless element. Thus all forms which our senses can know, all physical things, simply coagulate out of the non-sense-apparent boundless, and eventually lose their form and disappear back into it.

A later philosopher-scientist, not strictly a Milesian since his native city was Ephesus on the Ionian coast, and since he was doing most of his work right at the end of the sixth century (500 B.C.) was the philosopher, Heracleitus (hair-uh-KLĪ-tus). Following the same line of thought as that of Thales and Anaximander, he raised a third important question, "*What guides the process of change?*" He would grant a basic element from which all particular forms emerged, but he felt there must be some sort of controlling force to keep the process of universal change in order so that, let us say, an elm tree always produces elm trees rather than hippopotamuses.

Heracleitus denied the possibility of existence, for he felt that the universe was in a process of flow, not fix. His basic belief is that nothing *is;* everything is *becoming*. Thus his famous statement that one can never step into the same river twice. The appearance of the river may be the "same," whatever that may mean, but by the time one has taken his foot out of the river and put it back, the water is changed, the bank has changed, nothing is exactly the same. The universe is in the same condition. Between *now* and *now* it has flowed, changed, varied; it is no longer the same even though its appearance may seem to remain.

Perhaps to illustrate this contention, he chose fire as his basic element. Thus one may watch a flame in a fireplace for a half an hour and say to one's companion, "I have been watching that same flame for thirty minutes." Actually, though the shape of the flame may remain fairly constant, the burning gas which is the flame is never the same, even for the smallest fraction of a second. Thus the universe envisioned by Heracleitus.

But such a universe needs a guiding force, for the human mind finds it hard to live with a picture of a changing world without some order and direction. So Heracleitus proposed a great "Logos" as the direct answer to his question of the guiding force. Now *logos* in Greek means *word.* (Thus, the Gospel according to John, originally written in Greek, starts with the sentence, "In the beginning was the Word"—*logos,* in Greek. But with John, as with Heracleitus, it obviously has a much more important significance than our word, *word.*) For Heracleitus it meant a great *Intelligence* which permeated the world and somehow guided the constant change of its flamelike element of which all things were composed. This sense of all things "knowing" what shapes they should take, what forms they should assume, is one of the great mysteries of the universe. (How does each maple leaf, different from every other maple leaf in the world, yet take a characteristic shape so that we can identify it at a glance? How does it "know" the form it must fulfill?) Heracleitus' assumption of a great Logos or Intelligence is not far from the assumption of a single God as an intellectual Principle in the universe.

The line of thought of these Ionian philosophers seems reasonable enough in their attempt to explain the element which is One, and yet so many; which seems to be always the same and yet so varied. However the basic assumption here is one of constant change, and furthermore, all of the conclusions which these thinkers reached are based on the testimony of the human senses. We see, hear, taste, feel, or smell the phenomena of the world and the changing nature of all things. The search for a basic element from which it is all made is essentially a quest for "That Which is Real."

But the human mind can take an entirely different tack in this same quest. For example, our mind can simply say that whatever is *real* cannot always be changing. The mind can equate *permanence* with reality and say that only those things, or that thing, which is absolutely permanent and unchanging is real. Furthermore, it can easily be proved that our senses cannot be trusted. We know that they give us varying reports about the "same" thing. For example, water at the same temperature as measured by a thermometer will be either "hot" or "cold," depending on the temperature of our hands as we feel the water. Perhaps only the "thought process," independent of the senses, can be trusted as a guide to truth. Here we have the difference between the scientist—a man who trusts his senses as they can be refined through such instruments as he can make—and the pure philosopher, one who trusts his mind alone to lead him to truth. This distinction appeared early in Greek thought.

PYTHAGORAS

Pythagoras (pi-THAG-o-rus) was perhaps the earliest philosopher, if one can accept the distinction made in the paragraph above, for Pythagoras accepted permanence as the basic criterion for reality, and eventually he tried to reach it through mental operation alone.

Pythagoras, like the other early philosophers, had his origin among the Ionian Greeks, since his birthplace was the island of Samos, off the coast, roughly between the cities of Ephesus and Miletus; yet his main work was done in Italy, for he moved from Samos to the city of Croton in Southern Italy in the year 530. Thus he was roughly contemporary, though slightly earlier, than Heracleitus.

In attacking the problem of a basic universal material, Pythagoras abandoned the idea of a *material* substance, and abandoned the idea that such a substance could be found through the use of the human senses, since our senses are so fallible. Instead, he moved toward the idea of a *pattern* or nonmaterial *idea* for all particular things. In so doing, he laid the framework for the work of the Eleatic (ee-lee-A-tik) philosophers and Plato, who will be discussed in the next chapter. It must be stressed here, as it will be in the discussion of Plato, that this nonmaterial *idea* which we are considering is not simply a mental picture in the mind of an individual but, instead, a permanent pattern for each type of thing which we can know, existing in some realm above the grasp of the human mind. It exists without any substance itself, but it shapes all matter into the things which we recognize.

In this search for that-which-is-most-real, Pythagoras was struck by the universality of mathematical relationships. For example, most of us know the formula in plane geometry which is called the "Pythagorean" theorem for the length of the hypotenuse of a right triangle. Here are three such triangles:

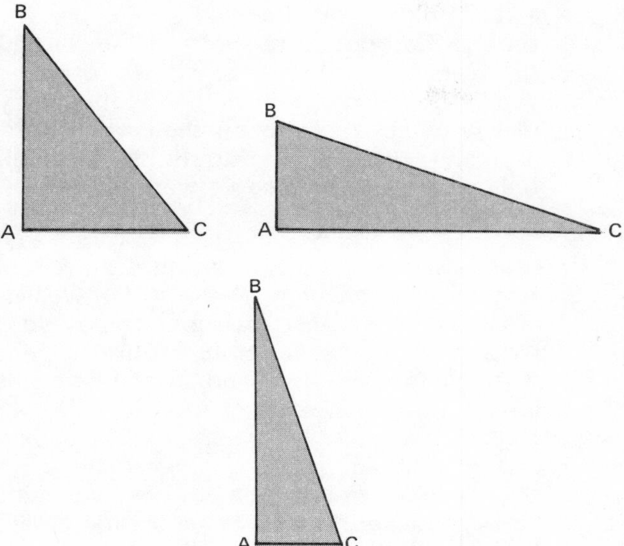

Although the triangles are dissimilar in appearance, one fact about them is true: $AB^2 + AC^2 = BC^2$. In Euclidean geometry this relationship was true before it was ever discovered, and it will remain true when there are no men on earth to be aware of it. Furthermore, it is true no matter what sensory conditions surround it. In the hottest furnace or the coldest refrigerator it is true. Here is an "idea" which has no substance, which exists entirely apart from men's minds; yet any shape which fulfills the equation is inevitably a right triangle. In this numerical relationship we have the pattern for a physical thing.

Or we might look at another field of learning, music, where Pythagoras laid the foundation for much of the study of musicology. Here he observed that the strings of a stringed instrument vibrated when they were plucked, and that this vibration caused the sound which we hear. Further, he observed that if one cut the length of the string exactly in half and plucked it, the vibrations were of the same width as before, but exactly twice as fast. Even further, when the shortened string was plucked, the sound produced was the "same" note as produced with the long string, but an octave higher than that note. Thus any musical note can be expressed as a mathematical equation, and any time we have the terms of the equation specified, the particular sound will come forth.

Even in the idea of number itself we can find some interesting speculations, for number is purely abstract, yet it can apply to everything which we can see and recognize. Take "twoness" for example. The number "2" is pure idea. It does not exist in any material form. Yet it can apply to all kinds of substance, and we can have two electrons or two elephants. This relationship can apply to all things, though it exists as idea only.

It was this kind of speculation which led Pythagoras to the conclusion that reality—that which is permanent, and that which transforms itself into all particular things—was mathematical relationship. If two such widely different things as a right triangle and a musical note can be expressed as mathematical equations, and if number can be applied to all phenomena which we can know, could it not be that *every* type of thing is the expression or embodiment of a mathematical relationship? Most of these are yet to be discovered, but they are there, like the Pythagorean theorem, awaiting recognition if the human mind can ever stretch so far.

With Pythagoras, then, we enter upon a wholly different type of philosophic speculation from that of the Ionians. These latter sought a physical element as the basis of all things; they trusted their senses to yield truth; they believed in the changeable nature of the universe. Pythagoras and all the philosophers who followed his line of thought believed that the one criterion for reality was permanence; they believed that form existed apart from substance; they trusted the intellect rather than the senses to lead them to truth.

SUMMARY

In all of these developments we find in Greece just at the beginning of the fifth century B.C. the emergence of a culture from chaos into a period of adjustment. A new political form, democracy, had emerged but was not yet tested, and in most of the Greek cities was opposed by a strong faction of the old aristocracy, the oligarchs. We have great pride, founded first upon the common heritage of the Hellenes which was expressed in the Homeric poems, then tremendously enhanced by the victories over the Persians. We have a varied and uncertain religious structure, and we see great philosophic speculation, dividing itself into two distinct avenues of inquiry into the nature of things. Here is the raw material for a great culture which needs to be formed and channeled by the artists, and made firm by institutions developed by the intellectual class. That development will be the subject for Chapter 5.

Bibliography

Note: The following books are chosen from thousands of books written on the subject of Greek culture, literally hundreds written within the last twenty years. We have chosen to list only a few general books, and a number of fairly recent translations. The teacher or the student will want to supplement this list with choices of his own.

I. General studies of Greek Culture: These works apply to the whole period through Hellenistic culture. They will not be listed at the end of subsequent chapters.

1. J.B. Bury, *History of Greece*, 2 vols., 1902. This is an older work, pretty much the standard history of Greece.
2. Francois Chamoux, *The Civilization of Greece.* A new and very handsome cultural history with excellent illustrations.
3. Finley Hooper, *Greek Realities.* An excellent general cultural history. The author attempts to strip away many of our romantic ideas about the Greeks, but where the Greeks were good, he gives them full credit. Very readable.

II. Translations of original material:

1. Homer, *The Iliad* and *The Odyssey*. Many translations, most of them good. Your authors prefer the prose translations of W.H.D. Rouse for their clarity and verve.
2. Herodotus, *The Persian Wars.* A new translation by Aubrey de Selincourt is excellent. This book is for the reader who has the time to find out more about the Medes and the Persians and the Egyptians than he wants to know, since Herodotus very slowly comes to focus on the Persian wars. A really charming, leisurely book which tells what all these people were *really* like.

III. Commentaries of one sort or another:

1. Aubrey de Selincourt, *The World of Herodotus.* The translator mentioned above has written a fine evaluation of the ancient world before 500 B.C. and an evaluation of Herodotus as historian.
2. Mary Renault, *The King Must Die.* The legend of Theseus is used as a vehicle for a fictionalized description of very ancient Greece. In addition to being a good story, the description of Cretan-Minoan culture is excellent (and exact from the archaeologist's point of view), as is the clash between the worshippers of the earth goddess and the worshippers of the male sky gods.

CHAPTER 5

Hellenic Athens: The Fulfillment of the Good Life

■ With the governmental reforms of Cleisthenes and with the defeat of the Persians, the emotions of pride, hope, and confidence motivated the Athenians. These were heightened by the role of leadership which Athens played in the formation of the Delian League, a confederation of some 150 city-states for the purpose of defense against further Persian aggression. Although the treasury of the league was maintained until 454 on the island of Delos (hence the name of the organization), Cimon (KI-mon), the archon of Athens, was the leading spirit in organizing the cities, and Athens, with its powerful navy, was the chief guarantor of protection to the member states. For a time each member of the league contributed ships and men; later most of them simply paid money into the treasury, leaving military affairs in the hands of Athens.

The city seethed with ideas. In the first place, the democracy of Cleisthenes was not unopposed. The old aristocratic segment of the population maintained itself in force and constantly challenged the democratic ideas, even though the leaders of Athens were usually members of the aristocracy who caught the new spirit and sided with the democrats. Beyond this political ferment of ideas, we have examined the philosophic ideas which were known to the intellectual element of the population: the philosophy of the Ionians, culminating in Heracleitus' belief in constant change, and the philosophy of Pythagoras, which held that true reality lay in mathematical relationships.

Two other philosophic schools came into prominence during the early and middle part of the fifth century. The first of these had its beginning in the city of Elea in Italy, and was known as the Eleatic School. Led by Parmenides (par-MEN-uh-deez), this group of philosophers simply could not tolerate the idea of Heracleitus that nothing *is;* that the universe was in a constant process of *becoming.* As the very basis of their thought they stated that whatever is *real* must be permanent and unchanging. If one turns the statement around, it may seem to be more logical: anything which constantly changes its state of Being cannot be real. Furthermore, they attacked the method of the Ionian philosophers by pointing out that the Ionians depended entirely upon their senses for the discovery of truth, trusting their sight, their sense of feeling, their hearing, the senses of smell and taste to lead them to valid conclusions. The Eleatics were quick to point out that the senses cannot be trusted. Of course this contention is easy to support; the sense impression that one receives depends quite as much on the state of the receiving sense organ as upon the thing itself. (The color-blind person sees a green traffic light as a sort of neutral gray; the person with "normal" sight sees it as green. Which is it really? For that matter, when one person sees "green" and another person agrees, are they really seeing the same color?) If the senses cannot be trusted as a guide to truth, what can? The Eleatic philosophers asserted that only the mind is a sure guide, and they could point to such truths as those found by the geometers like Pythagoras to support their theory that the mind, without the aid of the senses, can arrive at truth. As a matter of fact, these thinkers were much like the Pythagoreans, and form a sort of bridge between him and Plato, who will be discussed later. In the middle of the fifth century Parmenides visited Athens at a time when Socrates would have been about 20 years old. The two men could have met at that time.

A second type of philosophy which grew up fairly early in the fifth century was that of the completely material atomists. This line of speculation was first advanced by an Athenian, Leucippus (loo-KIP-pus), and was fully developed by his student, Democritus (di-MOK-ruh-tus), who lived from about 460 to 362. The atomists insisted that all things were composed of little chunks of solid matter so small that they could not be further divided. Furthermore, they stated that the entire universe existed in a constant blizzard of these atoms, oddly shaped, with hooks and eyes, knobs and holes, which fell through and around all things, permeating and surrounding everything. Thus the whole process of formation and transformation can be accounted for in terms of the falling atoms joining together and falling apart. Leucippus and Democritus called the force which directed this atomic drift "Necessity," which simply means that atoms fall in the way they do because they have to fall that way, and comes very close to our idea of chance or accident. Even the gods, said these atomic philosophers, were composed of these chunks of matter, and thus, were no more important (or immortal) than any other thing in the universe.

It is interesting, though parenthetical, to notice how these different philosophies have led to types of philosophy which are current in the twentieth century. Atomism leads to epicureanism, and then, by a long jump, to existentialism; the thought of Heracleitus is the forerunner of stoicism and then to deism; Pythagoras and Eleatic philosophy are the ancestors of the different forms of platonism and contemporary idealism.

Following the Persian wars, Athens was optimistic, hopeful, filled with democratic pride and a confusion of ideas. Furthermore, the entire city had been burned by the Persians and needed to be rebuilt. The possibilities for growth and progress lay everywhere, but direction for human growth was needed. In terms of the development of the spirit, Aeschylus (ESK-i-lus), the playwright-artist in a time of chaos and early adjustment, was to point the way.

THE DRAMA AND AESCHYLUS

Before speaking specifically of the plays of Aeschylus, it might be well to mention something about the history of the drama. It began in Greece, as it was to do later in the Middle Ages in Europe, as a part of the worship service. Originally the priest spoke individual parts, while a chorus chanted responses. An original and almost mythical dramatist, Thespis (THES-pis), began to transform this rite into secular drama during the Archaic period.

The theaters were always in the open air, with the seats for spectators ascending the side of a hill. At the bottom of the hill a round flat area (the orchestra) provided a space in which the chorus probably danced and chanted, and which had as its center the statue or altar of the god. Back of this, and facing the audience was a long low building (the skene) with a room at either end and a platform between the two rooms. The rooms were for dressing and storage, and it is probable that the chief actors performed on the platform above and behind the chorus.

The theater was a place of education and entertainment for most of the populace of a city-state, and the theaters were very large. It is estimated that the theater at Epidaurus (epi-DOW-rus), pictured in Figure 2, held 17,000 spectators. Many drama festivals were held throughout Greece, but the one at Athens in honor of the god Dionysus (di-uh-NI-shyus, and several other pronunciations) was the most important. Before the festival a number of playwrights would submit their plays to a board of judges and the plays of four dramatists would be chosen for presentation, each one on a different day. In Aeschylus' time, each dramatist

Figure 2. The Theater at Epidaurus.

submitted a trilogy (a series of three plays on one theme), and a satyr play which was a bawdy comedy presented at the end of the trilogy. A wealthy citizen paid the production costs for a playwright in the hope that his dramatist would win the first prize. A slight charge was made for seats at the drama, but in the fifth century, the city paid for the admission of any citizens who could not afford it. Thus, if a writer had a message which he wished to give to the entire population of his city, the drama was an almost perfect vehicle.

Aeschylus lived from 525 to 456 and was, therefore, a part of the great development of Greece as a whole, and Athens in particular. He was a soldier at the Battle of Marathon, a fact which he recorded on his tomb rather than that he was a dramatist. An aristocrat by birth, his drama presents a synthesis between the old ideas and those of the most enthusiastic democrats. Aeschylus has sometimes been accused of being much more of a preacher than a dramatist, for all of his plays carry a clearly stated message; yet Edith Hamilton points out that he was so much a dramatist that, when the dramatic form did not exist, he invented it. Certainly before his time the cast contained only one speaking-actor and the chorus. Aeschylus introduced a second speaking-actor so that we can have the possibility of dialogue, real conflict and resolution between two people and two ideas.

Aeschylus wrote about ninety plays, of which seven survive. Of these, only four will be discussed here: the trilogy called the *Oresteia* (aw-res-TEE-ya; the story of Orestes, son of Agamemnon), and the single play, *Prometheus Bound*, which remains from the Prometheus trilogy, *Prometheus the Fire-bearer*, *Prometheus Bound*, and *Prometheus Unbound*. All of these plays deal with the delicate problem of human freedom: the *Oresteia* with the relation of the individual to society as a whole and the development of a sense of justice within the city-state; the *Prometheus* with the scope and limit of man's freedom in relation to the gods. In all of Greek drama, the plot (the events of the play) was of small importance to the spectators, since all the plots were drawn from mythological stories which were known to all theatergoers. The audience was concerned with the author's treatment: how he shaped his materials to express the truth or the emotional experience which he wanted to communicate. The Greek myths, or the myths of any culture, for that matter, represent the effort of people to externalize and make visible some truths that go beyond verbalization, but are the basic truths by which the culture lives. Thus the manipulation of the mythical material by Greek drama reinterprets for the people their most basic beliefs.

The three parts of the *Oresteia*, *Agamemnon*, the *Libation Bearers*, and the *Eumenides* (you-MEN-i-deez), will be considered here as if they were three acts of a single play. (Too often critics, brainwashed by Aristotle's definition of tragedy, treat the *Agamemnon* as if it were a separate play in order to find a tragic hero among the characters.) The three plays together, however, are to be read here as a story of the evolution of a system of justice which was once dominated by tradition and fear and carried out by a system of personal revenge, but was transformed into a new justice which allowed the individual man maximum freedom within the framework and responsibility of a free society.

Agamemnon begins in what Aeschylus must have regarded as the rural district of Argos, in front of the palace of Agamemnon, on what should be the most joyous day in ten years, for word has just been received that Troy has fallen, the ten-year Trojan War is over, the Greeks have been victorious, and Agamemnon, the great king, is returning. It should be a day of rejoicing, but the watchman on the palace who first sees the signal fires announcing the victory mutters darkly about the evil deeds that have been going on within the palace; the chorus refuses to believe in the message of the signal fires and spends much of the first part of the play recounting the sacrifice which was a part of the beginning of the war.

Their particular concern is with the death of Iphigenia (if-i-je-NĪ-yuh), the daughter of Agamemnon and Clytemnestra at Aulis ten years before. The myth tells us that, at the beginning of the war, the brother kings, Agamemnon and Menelaus, had assembled the Greek army at the port of Aulis for embarkation to Troy, but after the troops were gathered the kings had offended the goddess Artemis (ART-uh-mis) who, in retaliation, refused to grant them favorable winds unless Agamemnon sacrificed his daughter. As commander-in-chief, Agamemnon could either call the whole war off and tell the troops to go home, or he could carry out the sacrifice. As a military leader, he chose the second course of action, one which would not endear him to his wife, Clytemnestra (klī-tem-NES-tra).

Also a part of the background of the drama is the long history of family killing within the House of Atreus (A-troos, or A-tree-us), Agamemnon's family. Although each generation had been marked by such an act of violence, the one which concerns us in this play is the act of Agamemnon's father, Atreus, who had quarreled with his brother, Thyestes (thigh-ES-teez), and then pretended to make a reconciliation. For the reconciliation banquet he caught all of Thyestes' children except one, killed them, and served them as the baked meats at the feast. The one who escaped was Aegistheus (i-JIS-thoos), Agamemnon's cousin, who, when Agamemnon had gone to war in Troy, had come to live with Clytemnestra in an adulterous relationship. This series of events, too, the chorus calls to our attention in the first part of the play. What should be a day of rejoicing at the return of the heroic and victorious king starts as a day when all the dark collective guilt of the past is dragged out into the awareness of the chorus and the audience.

Finally Agamemnon himself returns, accompanied by Cassandra (ka-SAN-druh), a princess from Troy who has received the unfortunate gift from Apollo that she can prophesy the future, but that no one will believe her prophesies. The last is not of immediate concern, though it will become important later in the play. What is of importance is that she has come on the same ship with the king, and now appears with him in his chariot. Of course Greek heroes were expected to take captive maidens as their mistresses, but the custom was that they would be brought home in a ship with the rest of the captured booty, and would serve as slaves in the household of their new master. Cassandra's appearance in Agamemnon's chariot is another act which will anger Clytemnestra.

Upon his arrival at the palace, Clytemnestra greets her husband so effusively that one recognizes this as a set speech, the sort of thing which is said when a returning hero is presented the keys to the city on the court house steps. Symbolically there follows one of the most important events of the drama, for the wife asks Agamemnon to enter the palace on a carpet dyed with a crimson (or purple) dye which is so costly that it is reserved for the gods. Agamemnon refuses at first, but is persuaded by his wife. The act shows a pride too great for men; this mortal is stepping out of his proper zone and into the area reserved for the gods. Quite aside from his human errors which angered his wife, this prideful act alone is sufficient to mark him for death.

After he has gone into the palace, we have one of the most interesting scenes of the play, for Cassandra tries to tell the chorus that Agamemnon is to be killed. Ranging back and forth in almost animal fury, probably in opposition to the strophe and antistrophe of the chorus, she tries to tell them of the murder which is being committed and to urge them to break down the palace doors and prevent the deed. Casting aside all of her prophetic regalia, she finally shouts, "I say you shall see Agamemnon dead!" The chorus remains dumb and stupid, refusing to act. Then Cassandra, knowing that she is to be murdered, meekly goes into the palace, hoping only that her death blow will be sure and swift.

Only when they hear Agamemnon cry out that he has been struck does the chorus nearly rouse itself to action. For the first time in Greek drama the members of the chorus speak as individuals, each with a short solo speech. The mood reaches a crescendo in the middle of this brief section when they are almost ready to break in and catch the murderers red-handed. Then apathy takes over, and at the end of the sequence they agree to wait until they really know what has happened. They do not have long to wait.

The palace doors are flung open, revealing the bodies of Agamemnon and Cassandra, with Clytemnestra proudly announcing that she has done this deed. The chorus mutters its protest, and Clytemenestra tries to calm them by suggesting that she is only the instrument of fate and the ancient curse on the house. Finally Aegisthus appears, rattles his sword a bit, and tells them to go home. The play closes as the chorus rather childishly tells the murderers just to wait until Orestes comes home to take his vengeance.

What does all this mean? It is interesting that the image most often presented in the play is that of a net or web. The purple carpet is referred to as a web, and Agamemnon has a net thrown over him in his bath so that he cannot resist while the murderous blows are being struck. Perhaps Aeschylus felt that this net was the old traditionalism, the belief in fate, and the idea of justice as revenge. Certainly the chorus is bound up in this web, since many of their speeches warn against pride, against wealth which breeds pride, and against any sort of innovation. Their wisdom follows the ancestral traditions which hinder action. If they had acted by breaking down the door of the palace, they might have done more than merely break through a door; they might have broken the barrier between themselves and freedom. Curiously, Cassandra tries to inspire them to act, but she cannot do it. She, too, is caught in the net. The key to this lies in her entrance into the palace to meet her known fate. Even the chorus admonishes her that to delay her death even by a short time is to gain a small victory, but she answers that the time of her doom has arrived. She, too, is enmeshed by a belief in a fate which rules her life. Of all the characters in the play, only Clytemnestra seems free to act as a human being. True, she falls back upon the curse on the House of Atreus at the end, but this is only to placate the chorus in terms which they can understand. But her action is murderous and destructive, a type of freedom which cannot be permitted to survive in a community of men. So, at the end of the first play we have two conditions of human existence: that of the chorus, which is always looking backward to tradition for guidance in their lives, and that of Clytemnestra, whose wild destructive freedom will destroy human society. Aeschylus' job in the remaining two plays of the trilogy is to free one segment of society and restrict the other.

The second play in the trilogy, the *Libation Bearers*, is principally a transition play designed to bring the problem to a head. Orestes as a young man returns from Phocis (rhymes with *focus*) where he has been reared. He bears with him the command of Apollo to kill his mother and Aegisthus to avenge the murder of his father. It is interesting that this is the command of Apollo, a member of the new generation of progressive gods. On the other hand, we have the old tradition coming from clan and tribal governments that anyone who spills kindred blood will be hounded to his death by the Furies. Orestes is caught between two seemingly equally forceful commands; in his killing of his mother, he is damned if he does, and damned if he doesn't. But he does return, and in what must be the most awkwardly handled recognition scene in the history of drama, he is reunited with his sister Electra (i-LEK-tra) and finally commits the murder. As the play ends he is set upon by the Furies and driven from the stage.

The word *Eumenides* may be translated as "The Gracious Ones" and the change of the Furies (the Erinyes [i-RIN-e-eez]) to the Eumenides is the point of the third play in the series. The scene opens in Delphi at the shrine of Apollo, the Furies temporarily sleeping, and with Orestes as a suppliant to the god having performed all the rites for the cleansing of guilt. He is told to go to the Temple of Athena on the acropolis in Athens where he will receive justice. The movement in the trilogy is interesting to note at this point. *Agamemnon* started in the darkness with the gloomy mutterings of the watchman and the chorus in rural Argos. Now, in *Eumenides* we come to full light in the city of Athens. Because of the clash of ideas, the city is the place where new thought is generated, and Athens is chosen not only because it was the leading city of Greece, but also because it was Aeschylus' own city. The patriotic gesture is the appropriate one.

In Athens the chorus of Furies lament that they, the older gods, are being shamed and dishonored, and predict that if Orestes is allowed to go free, children will murder their parents at will, and that they, the Furies, will bring a blight upon the land. It is at this point that Athena arrives, and after hearing the preliminaries of the case asserts that the cause is too grave for a god to decide, and too grave, also, for a mortal man. She then sends out for a jury of twelve citizens of Athens to hear the case and render a verdict. What appears to be a contradiction may be resolved in this way. A trial by a jury transcends the judgment of a mortal man since, in the course of time, a jury will build up a body of law which will provide a rational basis for judgment, and thus go beyond the limits of on-the-spot mortal judgment.

With the jury selected and sworn in, the evidence in the case is presented, with Apollo acting as attorney for the defense. A modern reader must admit that his case—that the mother is not related to the child, but is only a sort of animated baby-carriage—sounds pretty flimsy, but fortunately that is almost beside the point. After the presentation of evidence, Athena establishes the court, the Areopagus (air-ee-OP-uh-gus), and charges it with its duties for the rest of time. Her speech, though given in context on p. 144, may well be quoted here:

Here reverence
For law and inbred fear among my people
Shall hold their hands from evil night and day,
Only let them not tamper with the laws,
But keep the fountain pure and sweet to drink.
I warn you not to banish from your lives
All terror but to seek the mean between
Autocracy and anarchy; and in this way
You shall possess in ages yet unborn
An impregnable fortress of liberty
Such as no people has throughout the world.[1]

The tied vote of the jury follows, with Athena casting her vote for the acquittal of Orestes, who departs after a vow of perpetual alliance between Argos and Athens. We must agree that we have a curious dramatic structure here when the hero of the drama can walk out with only two-thirds of the play finished. The reader must realize that Orestes is not the hero; *the real hero is an idea of justice*—of people getting along with people in such a way as to promote freedom and happiness for all.

The last third of the play deals with the conversion of the Erinyes to Eumenides. These ancient and immortal hag-goddesses have real power which cannot simply be taken from them by force, and they start the dialogue with their usual threats of civil violence and sterility in the city of Athens. But Athena is the goddess of wisdom and also of persuasion, and she slowly reveals to the Furies the role that they can play and the worship they will receive as defenders of the city. Finally the Eumenides agree to accept their new role, and the drama closes with a procession, probably including the citizens of Athens, to the altar of the Eumenides on the side of the Areopagus.

As far as the significance of the play is concerned, Aeschylus probably had several specific messages for the Athens of his time. The court which Athena founds is the old Areopagus, which represented the conservative element of the city as opposed to the more democratic Council. Four years before the production of the play, the Areopagus had been stripped of much of its authority, and perpaps Aeschylus is protesting this action. On the other hand, he may be considering the development of the Areopagus as the real birth of the polis (PŌ-lis), the city-state, which through law, was to give people freedom under a democratic government. For us, this latter is the significant interpretation.

In terms of the problem which we noticed at the end of the discussion of *Agamemnon*, we have a much broader and more relevant meaning than the local Athenian one. The problem was that of bringing all of the people out of the net of bondage to tradition and fate and, at the same time, limiting the freedom of such a person as Clytemnestra. The universal significance which is our chief concern may be described in the following way:

The people, as represented by the old chorus in *Agamemnon*, are set free simply because their eyes are turned forward rather than backward. No longer do they act under the shadow of old tradition and old superstition, since each case is tried in terms of its own evidence, and decided in terms of a law which has been made by human beings. In *Eumenides*, Aeschylus is setting forth the idea that men are to establish the limits for their own zone of action, limits determined by the amount of freedom each person can have while still maintaining the freedom of others. The same thing applies to the Clytemnestras of this new world. Their acts will also be brought to this tribunal to be checked by the same standard. Mankind—at least mankind in Athens—is now free for individual action for the best interests of the person and the state.

One more point is of interest here. The Furies insisted on rule by fear, and one is tempted to discard the element of fear in this new order toward which Aeschylus is pointing. But Athena insists that a certain amount of fear is still necessary. While Aeschylus was optimistic about human nature and man's behavior in an atmosphere of freedom, he was not willing to go completely overboard with his hope. He knew that in spite of laws and courts there is in human nature a tendency to act completely selfishly, and without any consideration for the rest of men. To curb this tendency an inbred fear must remain, more deeply felt than the purely intellectual respect for law. A number of critics have seen in the conversion of the Furies to the Gracious Ones a sort of birth of conscience. If this is true, the conversion must be to a very sophisticated conscience rather than the old primordial cultural fear. This must be an ethical conscience, which, while incorporating some element of fear, is chiefly concerned with the safety, even the total welfare, of the group. Conscience, of course, is the internal regulating force within each individual by which the morality of the culture is

---

1. This prescription of a middle ground between anarchy and autocracy by Aeschylus and Athena is of particular interest in the twentieth century. In the November 1, 1968, issue of *Time*, New York's mayor, John Lindsay, is quoted, "I think New York *is* governable, but we've got to go through sound barriers. No one should be surprised at some of the things going on. In the Kerner Commission Report we pointed out that this polarization of extreme forces would occur. The centrists and the moderates have to keep fighting to keep the extremist elements from colliding head on and killing each other. That's what democracy is all about—trying to steer a middle peaceful course between chaos at one end and tyranny at the other."

Whether Mayor Lindsay knew that he was quoting Aeschylus makes no difference. The formula for just government in 458 B.C. (the date of the first production of the *Oresteia*) and A.D. 1968 remains the same: steering a middle course between the chaos of anarchy and the too strict regimentation of autocracy.

maintained. This may be the type of "fear" which Athena maintains; perhaps we do not stretch the meaning of the play to think of the conversion of the old superstitious fears into household gods as the beginning of ethical conscience. At least it is a point to think about.

With a consideration of the play *Prometheus Bound*, we come to one of the favorite games of many imaginative people. How did the play come out? Since our play is probably the second one of a trilogy, of which the third is lost, how did Aeschylus bring about a reconciliation of the opposed forces? The play is to be read as a conflict between the absolute and whimsical power of a god and mankind which hopes to grow and prosper, with Prometheus as its champion.

Here are some of the elements of the play which we know. Zeus thinks that he has absolute power (Power says, "None is truly free save only Zeus"). Yet we have also the prophecy that Zeus, in one of his many affairs, will breed a descendant who will overthrow him. Prometheus knows how this prophecy will work out; if he gives up his knowledge, Zeus may be forewarned and avert his downfall. Yet Prometheus in his own way is as stubborn, unbending, and generally ungracious as Zeus. To all this we may add one more factor: Prometheus created mankind and has given men certain gifts. Zeus, angered by this, wishes to stamp out the whole race of men. Thus the problem. What can we guess about a solution from the evidence we have in the existing play?

In the first place, Prometheus divulges in his talk with the daughters of Oceanus (oh-SEE-a-nus) that Zeus is not all-powerful, but is subject to "Necessity," which, in turn, is directed by the Fates and the Furies. He may not avoid what is destined. Furthermore, mankind has all the gifts which Prometheus had given. It is interesting that in the original myth, fire was the only gift. All the rest which Prometheus enumerates were devised by Aeschylus for this particular play, and for his own purpose in developing his particular idea for presentation to the citizens of Athens. Some of these gifts are blind hope (why *blind*?) which will cause man to cease the contemplation of his own death, a portion (why only a portion?) of reason, written language, mathematics, fire, and the working of metals.

These gifts suggest one aspect of the solution to the problem. One might well ask why, if Prometheus was so fond of man, didn't he give him Cadillacs, split-level homes with a swimming pool, automatic dishwashers, or the Athenian equivalents of all these gadgets which are supposed to make life easier and simpler? An answer might be that the actual gifts furnish the raw material by which mankind will develop his material things, his philosophies, and his science. The twentieth-century philosopher Lewis Mumford has written that man makes *things*, and by making them he, himself, grows. (Thus the man who invented the wheel must have felt at least a foot taller when he observed that it actually worked.) It may be that in providing these gifts Aeschylus was thinking not of man's comfort or his leisure, but his growth through the use of the new materials for invention and thought.

So, reading this play as one of the universal answers to the question of man's relation to his God, what can we surmise about the ending of the trilogy, remembering that Aeschylus did not hesitate to tamper with his original mythological material and change it, as he did in the *Oresteia*? In the first place, we know that Prometheus will not give up his secret just to secure his own freedom and relief from his torture. He submits almost boastfully to being chained to the rock, to being sent down to Tartarus, and to being raised later to be parched in the sun while the eagle tears at his vitals. These physical torments will not move him, yet he must have been moved to tell his secret, since Zeus did not fall. The solution to our problem must lie in a change in the nature of Zeus, the seemingly all-powerful god, yet subject to Necessity, and a chance for man's development under the transformed god. Most men have needed a God to give shape, orderliness, and sense to what otherwise might seem to be a meaningless universe; to give inspiration in life which might otherwise seem pointless. Thus Zeus will not be destroyed.

Aeschylus would not have transformed his Zeus into a loving God-the-Father (one of the aspects of the Christian God) for at least two reasons: First, starting with Zeus's original nature, such a transformation would have been too great; second, Aeschylus was a Greek, and the Greeks were much too rational to accept a really loving God. Instead he must have drawn upon one or more of the philosophies which were then current in Athens—the mathematical orderliness of Pythagoreanism, the permanence and intellectually sought reality of the Eleatics, the changing, logos-directed universe of Heracleitus, or the materialism of the very early atomists. It is the guess of your present authors (and only a guess, your opinion is as valid in this matter as ours) that Aeschylus somehow converted the "Necessity" to which Zeus was subject into the Logos of Heracleitus, and made Zeus realize that he must direct the world in terms of this great Intelligence. Aeschylus seems to have believed in change more than most men, so that the ever-flowing universe of Heracleitus would not repel him, and with intelligent change, man, too, would have the opportunity to grow in the directions which are indicated by the gifts of Prometheus. This is at least one possibility for the third play which concluded the trilogy.

THE ATHENS OF PERICLES

After the terms of office of a number of leaders such as Cimon and Ephialtes who made the laws of Cleisthenes ever more democratic, we come to the long and glorious rule of Pericles. Pericles was first elected as general-in-chief in 461 and, with the exception of two years when he was voted out of office, directed Athenian affairs until his death in 429.

One historian has estimated the population of Attica (the city of Athens and the surrounding territory which it governed) at about 230,000 people. Of these, 40,000 were free male citizens, the actual voting population which participated in the democracy; 40,000 were women who, at best, were second-class citizens; 50,000 were foreign-born, and 100,000 were slaves. One must remember that in all of our discussion of the glories of Athenian democracy, we are talking only about the 40,000 free men. The rest of the free people participated only on the periphery, and the slaves had no voice at all. Nevertheless it is a miracle of history that a small group of less than a quarter of a million people, in about a single century starting with the second defeat of the Persians, could have produced three of the great writers of tragic drama and one of the great comedy-writers in the history of literature, two or more of the philosophers whose ideas still give shape to our lives, great architecture, and magnificent sculpture. The music and the painting of the time are lost, but in the contemporary writings music is regarded as the highest and the best developed of the arts, and sculpture was thought of as a secondary art in comparison with painting.

Finally, and most significant of all, the people, at least in the first generation of this century, produced a life-style which in its freedom for the individual, coupled with a concern for the welfare for the state as a whole, has been envied and emulated by the Western world ever since. This was the life-style toward which the plays of Aeschylus pointed.

The ideal of this life-style during the middle fifth century is nowhere better stated than by C.M. Bowra (*The Greek Experience*, p. 44) who writes, "A man served his state best by being himself in the full range of his nobility, and not by sacrificing it to some abstract notion of political power or expediency." We see here the delicate balance upon which the best of Athenian life was built: the individual loved the city-state, the polis, as if it were his own family and served it completely. But his service was not to some "ism" or some party. Rather it was felt that the state grew and prospered if each man developed his own powers fully and expressed them completely, at the same time allowing other men to do the same. This, one may note, is a positive driving force which impels a man to the top of his ability and then raises that top for continued effort; it is not the negative denying force of a puritan, middle-class ethic.

Life at this time was largely out-of-doors. The courts and the council met on the Pnyx Hill, near the acropolis, and heard matters of state argued. More vigorous was life in the Agora (AG-uh-ruh), a level area at the foot of the acropolis, which was the marketplace for the city and also the place where the men went to meet each other and to argue politics and philosophy. Here, visiting teachers would lecture to any audience which they could attract, and one assumes that they did a thriving business. The Greeks were a dynamic and talkative people, and the issues of the day were thrashed out in the Agora with most of the free men listening and joining in the debate.

When not in the Agora, many men spent their time in the gymnasia. These were parks set aside for physical exercise not far from the city limits of Athens. These provided a running-track, a wrestling-ground, and other facilities for exercise, and provided, as well, for shady walks and places for discussion, since the ideal was the development of the whole man, with full development of both mind and body. Later, Plato's Academy and Aristotle's Lyceum were to be founded in surroundings like those of the gymnasia.

Home was the place where the Greek man went when there was no place else to go, and it is interesting that in all of the archeological remains, we have little indication of the nature of the private houses. Within the city they were probably not much more than shelters and sleeping rooms, together with work rooms for the women. The country houses were probably more spacious, but the lack of remains of house-architecture suggests the relative unimportance of women and the home in Greek life.

Pericles did not make many great changes in the government of the city. His role, instead, was to maintain the democratic values and the human values which had already come into being. In order to do this, he rebuilt the city as a proper home for these ideals. Probably the Agora was first rebuilt, since it formed a marketplace for ideas as well as things, and later he commissioned the building of the Parthenon (447-438) and other temples on the acropolis. The care with which the architects Ictinus (ik-TI-nus) and Callicrates (ka-LIK-ra-teez) shaped the building to conform to human standards rather than rigid mathematical and physical rules suggests the complete devotion of the Athenians to the standard of human values.

The balance which the Athenians found between individualism and the welfare of the state is a most delicate one, and one which can easily be upset. During Pericles' time a change began to take place, moving the balance more and more toward individuality, less and less to the general good. This is perhaps first noticeable in the international relations of the city, for it converted the Delian League into what really constituted an Athenian empire, and moved the treasury from the island of Delos to Athens. As a matter-of-fact, the Parthenon and other buildings were constructed with money which belonged to this treasury, and when member cities objected, they were simply told that if Athens was to assume the burden of protection for the league as a whole, Athens alone should be able to decide what to do with the money that was paid into the treasury.

As an international power, Athens became autocratic, and within the city, the older values of reverence to the gods and to the state, ideas which had been triumphant at Marathon and which Aeschylus had preached in his plays, moved toward self-centered individuality. This metamorphosis probably had its start with the teachings of the atomists like Democritus who argued for complete materialism, even with the gods, and ascribed all change to accident. In such a world, the only human goal can be material pleasure, since, with accident as the ruling force, nothing about the future can be predicted, and the gods who are material and subject to chance, offer no guidance or inspiration.

Probably taking their cue from the atomists, the leading teachers of Athens became the sophists (sof [o as in *hot*] -ists). This group had a leader in Protagoras (pro-TAG-uh-rus), a high-minded thinker and teacher whose chief pronouncement was that *man is the measure of all things.* Taken by itself, this is simply a sloganlike reassertion of the idea of human values which we have already praised so highly in this Greek state. But dangers also appear. If men, mankind, is the measure, then all may be well; if man the individual, I, am the measure of all, then whatever the individual person may choose to do or believe is proper. The later sophists moved toward this last position, teaching, for example, that the laws were merely a set of men's opinions, so that if any individual holds a different opinion, his conviction is as valid for him as are the laws. Much can be said in favor of the sophists' teachings, for they introduced a healthy questioning of the old traditions and the old veneration of the gods. On the other hand, their complete relativism, if taken seriously, undermined any coherence within the group and all thought or action became merely a matter of expediency.

Into this new and changing atmosphere came two of the great tragic writers to direct Athenian thought and feeling: Sophocles (SOF [as in hot]-uh-kleez) and his younger contemporary, Euripides (you-RIP-uh-deez).

SOPHOCLES

Of Sophocles' eleven remaining plays, *Antigone* (an-TIG-uh-nee) and *Oedipus the King* (ED-uh-pus, or EED-uh-pus) will be discussed here. Both deal with the Theban myth of the stranger, Oedipus, who came to the city, solved the riddle of the Sphinx, and became king of the city. Unwittingly he married his mother and fathered four children by her. The two sons were Polyneices (pol [as in *hot*] -uh-NICE-ees) and Eteocles (i-TEE-uh-kleez), the daughters, Ismene (is-MEEN-uh) and Antigone.

The plot of *Oedipus the King* concerns a plague in the city of Thebes, which the Delphic oracle says will be lifted only when the murderer of Laius (LYE-us), the former king, is discovered and punished. Oedipus, the new king who has, according to custom, married the widowed queen, Jocasta (joe-KAS-ta), swears to find this murderer in order to save the city. This is done in the face of two prophecies, one known to Jocasta and Laius, that their son would kill his father and marry his mother. Accordingly, when a son was born to them, they had the baby taken and exposed to die on the slopes of Mount Kithaeron (si-THEE-ron, or kee-the-RON). The second prophecy, known to Oedipus when he grew up in Corinth as the son of the king and queen there, was that he would kill his father and marry his mother. To avert this, he had fled the city of Corinth. On his flight he had had an altercation with an old man and his bodyguard at the place where three roads come together, and in a fit of rage Oedipus had killed the whole group. He had then proceeded to Thebes where he solved the riddle of the Sphinx, was chosen king by the populace, and married Jocasta. The play is riddled with irony, for the audience and the readers know that in the search for the murderer, Oedipus is searching for himself, and that the curse which he has pronounced on the killer of King Laius will fulfill itself on him. This expected event comes to pass; Jocasta commits suicide, and Oedipus blinds himself and exiles himself from the city. With these events the play of Oedipus ends.

In terms of the history of Thebes, *Antigone* takes place about 15 years after the events of *Oedipus the King.* Polyneices was driven from the city, and later returned with a military force from Argos to capture Thebes and set himself up as ruler. In the battle which ensued, the two brothers met and killed each other, whereupon the kingship was assumed by Creon (KREE-on), the uncle of the two young men. He ordered that Eteocles be given a proper burial since he died defending his city, but that the body of Polyneices be cast out to be eaten by the dogs and the birds. Antigone insists on giving her brother proper burial, and is condemned to death by Creon. In the tragic events which follow, Antigone is killed, Haemon, Creon's son, who is engaged to Antigone, commits suicide as does Creon's wife, Euridice (you-RID-uh-see). Creon is left at the end of the play humbled, but with insight into the tragic nature of human life.

The total impact of both plays, *Antigone* and *Oedipus the King*, has to do with the tragedy of existence and the greatness of the man who stands up squarely to face it so that his spirit rises above the physical events of existence and the traps which his own personality, accident, and the gods set for him. This impact, however, is an intellectual-emotional experience which can best be known by reading or seeing the plays themselves, not by academic discussion. The complete play *Oedipus the King* is given on p. 148.

Sophocles was also speaking about events and moods in the Athens of his time, and this level of meaning can be considered. The dramatist was a conservative, and his message to his fellow citizens is the need to return to the noble virtues of the men at Marathon and the time of Aeschylus.

Antigone is usually considered as a play in which two types of loyalty are opposed: Creon represents total loyalty to the man-made laws of the state; Antigone represents an allegiance to great and eternal laws of the gods. During the German occupation of Paris in World War II, the modern playwright, Jean Anouilh certainly presented that point of view with this version of the play, with Creon as a thinly disguised Hitler insisting that the laws which he made are the only ones which should be obeyed, regardless of any human decency or dignity. Sophocles, too, has Creon driven to this point when he argues:

> Therefore I cannot pardon
> One who does violence to the laws or thinks
> To dictate to his rulers; for whoever
> May be the man appointed by the city,
> That man must be obeyed in everything,
> Little or great, just or unjust.

The reader feels so strongly for Antigone when she faces this sort of fascist pronouncement that he tends to forget the one sidedness of her vision, her total obstinacy, and the fact that she rushes toward her own martyrdom in a way that makes that death inevitable. One sees her twisted sight, however, in such passages as the one in which the chorus of citizens has been trying to comfort her and is completely in sympathy with her. At that moment she turns on them to cry out:

> By our father's gods, I am mocked! I am mocked!
> Ah! why,
> You men of wealth, do you taunt me before I die?

As a matter of fact, she has been praised, not mocked. Her self-pity shows itself a few speeches later when she laments:

> Unwept, unfriended, without marriage song,
> Forth on my road I miserable am led;
> I may not linger. Not for long
> Shall I, most wretched, see the holy sun
> My fate no friend bewails, not one;
> For me no tear is shed.

She is wrong. Throughout the drama the chorus has been trying, somewhat timidly, to soften Creon's harsh ruling, and Haemon (HEE-mon) has pled with his father to spare her life until Haemon is suicidal, yet Antigone is literally hell-bent to support her own view and seek her own destruction. Her view of what is right is as twisted as that of Creon.

Perhaps we can get a glimpse of Sophocles' thought in two of the great choral odes of the drama. At one place they chant:

> Wise is the famous adage: that to one
> Whom the gods madden, evil, soon or late,
> Seems good; then can he but a moment shun
> The stroke of fate.

Earlier, in the great ode in which they consider the greatness of man, they conclude with the idea that the man alone is great "When he honors the laws of the land and the gods' sworn right."

The first of these quotations reminds one of Shakespeare's thought, that "He whom the gods would destroy, they first make mad." The question is to whom, in *Antigone*, does the statement apply: Creon, Antigone, or both? From one point of view, it would seem to include both; both are mad to some extent, to both evil (or at least half-truth) alone seems good. The whole truth is given in the second of the quotations above: that one must honor both the laws of the gods and the laws of the state. Then, indeed, does the city stand high. This, perhaps, is the message which Sophocles tried to communicate to a city which, in his opinion, was rapidly falling apart because the citizens accepted only half-truths as if they were complete.

Oedipus the King was produced almost a generation later than Antigone, and presents a vision of man much more profound and wise than that of the earlier drama. By the time of *Oedipus*, too, the teachings of the atomists and the sophists had gained a stronghold upon the intelligentsia of the city. The real meaning of the play lies in its exploration of man's fate; whether a man, because he is the kind of person he is, brings about his fate, whether he is a mere pawn of the gods, or whether the course of his life lies somewhere between these extremes. Of ultimate importance lies the question of the greatness of the human spirit as it faces and rises above the tragedy of existence. As mentioned before, Sophocles' exploration in these great problems can only be experienced within the drama itself. Here we shall only look at the level of meaning which deals with the temper of Athenian life at the time Sophocles wrote.

Professor Bernard Knox sees the play as an example of the power of the gods presented to the Athenians to stop them in their progress toward skepticism and atheism, and certainly this does constitute one level of meaning. Oedipus first quarrels with the ancient prophet, Tiresias (tie-REE-see-us), and ends up shouting angrily that all prophets are cheats. Several times Jocasta entreats Oedipus to put no faith in oracles, each time trying to show him how the oracles have lied. The final statement of her belief is given in the lines:

> Why should be afraid? Chance rules our lives,
> And no one can foresee the future, no one.
> We live best when we live without a purpose
> From one day to the next.

The thought here is almost exactly the day-to-day philosophy of the atomic materialists, but each time Jocasta attempts to prove that the oracles are useless, Oedipus receives a new jolt which points to the fact that he is the murderer whom he is seeking.

This scoffing at the prophecies from the gods has an interesting effect on the populace as represented by the chorus of Thebans. One of their odes is a plea for reverence to the gods, ending with these lines:

> If evil triumphs in such ways as these,
> Why should we seek, in choric dance and song,
> To give the gods the praise that is their due?
>
> I cannot go in full faith as of old,
> To sacred Delphi or Olympian vale,
> Unless men see that what has been foretold
> Has come to pass, that omens never fail.
>
> All-ruling Zeus, if thou art King indeed,
> Put forth thy majesty, make good thy word,
> Faith in these failing oracles restore!
> To priest and prophet men pay little heed;
> Hymns to Apollo are no longer heard;
> And all religion soon will be no more.[2]

But the oracles are upheld; faith is restored. From the moment of Oedipus' highest hope when the messenger brings news the king of Corinth has died and that the citizens there have chosen *him* king, he is dashed to the bottom of despair as he finally learns that he was the baby who was exposed to die, and that the old man whom he killed was his true father. Strained beyond endurance by her burden of knowledge, Jocasta commits suicide, and Oedipus, who has seen external things throughout his life, blinds himself as he comes to see himself and, with clear vision, sees truths which lie beyond the externals. He and the blind Tiresias, also one of the clear-sighted ones, reach equality at the end of the play. On this level of meaning this drama is a clear admonition that the gods are powerful and should receive worship and honor.[3]

EURIPIDES

The third great tragedian of Athens, Euripides, directed his tragic vision toward entirely different goals from those of his predecessors. Living under the shadow of Sophocles and choosing subjects for drama which did not suit the public taste, he was not popular in his time. It is a cliché to say that Sophocles showed man as he should be, and that Euripides showed man as he was, yet there is much truth in the statement, for the latter dramatist undertook an almost psychological-clinical examination of the motives of men and women. In *Electra,* which furnishes a good example since both Aeschylus and Sophocles wrote on the same theme, we see Orestes and Electra, not as the vehicles for developing an idea of justice, as in Aeschylus, nor is Electra a study of a woman possessed and driven almost mad by the indignities which have been heaped upon her, as in Sophocles, but as cold-blooded, scheming butchers bent solely upon revenge. Orestes, for example, insists on staying close to the borders of Argos so that if he is defeated, he can make his escape; Electra is a proud, disdainful aristocrat, looking down upon her peasant husband. In this play, too, we see another of Euripides' themes, the nobility of the poor, for the peasant is as good a man as one can find, stoicly putting up with the scorn which his wife piles on him.

In *The Trojan Women* Euripides shows us war as it really is. He does not treat the Trojan War as a glorious victory of the good Greeks; instead he chooses the time immediately after the victory and shows the misery of the once-proud women of Troy as they are parceled out to the conquerors, their heartbreak as they see their children murdered by the Greek "heroes." This theme would not have endeared him to the Athenians who accepted the Trojan War as the source of the great Hellenic tradition. In *Medea* two more of Euripides great themes appear: the strength and greatness of a woman, and the vileness of civilization itself. Medea is a savage woman consumed by love turned to hatred as she confronts the opportunism and the scheming falseness of her civilized Greek husband, Jason. As she arranges for the murder of her husband's intended bride, Creusa, and then murders her own children to wipe out any trace of the hated Jason, she becomes a magnificent rising

2. And to think that some believe that God died in the twentieth century!

3. Since this was written, a new book by Philip Vellacott, *Sophocles and Oedipus* (Ann Arbor: University of Michigan Press, 1971) gives a completely new interpretation of this play. Students should see this new work.

flame of hatred toward all of civilization and its phony, status-seeking schemes. For anyone who seeks to destroy the establishment, Euripides is the Man.

During the last two years of his life, Euripides exiled himself from civilized Athens and went to live in more primitive Macedonia, where he wrote the play, *The Bacchae* (BOCK-ee), in which he literally vomits all of the rationalistic civilization which he had known, which had rejected him, and which he had rejected. The play is given in full following p. 191.

The opponents in the play are the highly civilized, typically Greek Pentheus (PEN-thee-us, or PEN-thoos), King of Thebes, and the god Dionysus who, according to tradition, was born in Thebes, the son of Semele (SEM-uh-lee) and Zeus. Semele had been destroyed by the god's thunderbolt before the birth, but Dionysus had been taken from the mother's womb and reared by Zeus (sewed into his thigh, according to the myth) to become a god of power. The worship of Dionysus had spread throughout Asia, and at the beginning of the play Dionysus has assumed a homosexual role and come to Thebes to demand that his native city recognize him as a god and worship him. Dionysus is not only the god of wine, but he also represents all of the nonrational and emotional elements in a person or a civilization.

By the time the play has begun, all the women of Thebes including Pentheus' mother, Agave (a-GAV-ee), have been enticed into the hills surrounding the city to take part in the Dionysiac revels which, according to popular report, are of an orgiastic nature, but from the word of messengers are good and gracious as long as the women are not opposed; when opposition appears, however, the women with superhuman power raze villages, tear cattle apart with their bare hands, and destroy everything in sight.

Pentheus comes into the city to oppose the god and set everything back on its normal path. Dionysus is first imprisoned, but by an act of will frees himself and destroys his prison and Pentheus' palace. The king, not even noticing the smoldering ruins of his palace, attempts to argue with the god, who, by appealing to the morbid curiosity of Pentheus gains complete control over him, dresses him as a woman, and parades him through the streets of Thebes on their way to watch the revels of the women in the hills. Once there we get the report of the women becoming enraged at the spy and tearing his body completely apart. Blinded by the magic of Dionysus, Agave tears off the head of her son, believing that she is killing a lion barehanded. Only when she brings back the head to show it off in the city does her sanity return as she realizes the horror of the act she has committed.

Dionysus then ends the play, still as cool and effeminate as ever, by dispensing his justice. Cadmus, the grandfather of Pentheus, and Agave are exiled and transformed into snakes for having resisted the god, so that, with Pentheus' death and the destruction of his palace, we end in total ruin. The curious thing is that Cadmus and Agave have not opposed the god. Cadmus, it is true, adopted the worship largely because it would be mighty nice to have a god on one's family tree, but Agave had become a wholehearted worshipper. By any rational standards, her murder of her son and her banishment make no sense.

The usual interpretation of this play is that it represents the necessity for the recognition of the emotional element in life as well as the rational. According to this opinion, Euripides is pointing out the delicate balance that must be achieved between reason and intellect. On the other hand, this drama may represent the worship of the irrational. Its conclusion may be complete nihilism and confusion. The student is encouraged to read the play itself (p. 191) and form an opinion for himself.

ATHENIAN BACKGROUND AFTER PERICLES

Throughout the times of these dramatists, the cities of Athens and Sparta had each been growing in power until a confrontation between the two for dominance throughout the Hellenic world was probably inevitable. In 445 the two cities signed a pact for a 30-year truce, which was observed more or less for 14 years. In 431, however, the Peloponnesian War broke out, which, in its two phases was to last until 404 and Sparta's total conquest of Athens. Pericles believed that this would be a long war of attrition, and decided to abandon the land to Sparta, bringing all the people of Attica inside the walls of Athens, and trusting the Athenian navy to attack Sparta and her allies wherever a hit-and-run attack would do the most damage. Athens was almost immediately crippled when, in 430, plague broke out in the city and a third of the population died. Pericles himself died of the disease in 429. The conflict which followed furnishes almost a classic example of the stupidity of war. On two or three occasions Athens got the upper hand and could have made peace with Sparta without serious loss of honor, but the hawks within the government demanded total victory.

A number of Athenian acts during the war demonstrate the temper of the times. For example, in 416 the Athenians attacked the neutral island of Melos on the general principle that if you aren't for us, you are against us. The battle lasted a single day, with Athens winning, killing all the men on the island and selling the women into slavery.

In the following year Athens mounted a great attack on the city of Syracuse in Sicily; an attack which was foolhardy and almost doomed to failure. Of the three generals in command, Alcibiades (al-si-BI-uh-deez) represents an extreme, but a type, of the new egocentric individualism in Athens. His relativism and opportunism reflects the teaching of the sophists. In the first place, he left Athens under a cloud, for, after a series of farewell parties a number of the sacred shrines in the city were defaced, and it was generally supposed that Alcibiades and his followers committed this sacrilege. Before reaching Sicily, he defected to Sparta, and in Sparta became a leading citizen and military adviser. When he felt that his good fortune in Sparta was running out, he deserted to Persia, and, even later, he returned to Athens where he was greeted as a national hero and reelected to a generalship. This, as we have said, is an extreme case, but when such conduct could be tolerated, the moral fiber of the city must have been extremely weak. Almost parenthetically, in the Sicilian campaign, the Athenian navy was destroyed, and most of the men were enslaved and put to work in the mines belonging to Syracuse.

At any rate, throughout the Peloponnesian War, Athenian thought was dominated by the extreme individualism which was promoted by the sophists, and the war came to its conclusion in 404 with a Spartan victory. Then, during the fourth century, the government vacillated between the strong antidemocratic element in the population, the democrats, and a moderate element which sought to limit the voting power to a few thousand of the upper classes, but still maintain some sort of democratic voice.

THE CRITICS OF ATHENS: SOCRATES AND ARISTOPHANES

Probably the greatest questioner of the new value-system in Athens was the philosopher, Socrates, of whom we know little since he never wrote, and the only reports we have about him are from his pupils, principally Plato and Xenophon (ZEN-oh-fun). It is apparent, however, that he spent most of his life in raising embarrassing questions and demanding that the Athenians examine their motives for their way of life. He was an extremely popular teacher for a group of the intellectual young men who shared his views about the decay of the old value-systems, but he was certainly not popular with those whose motives were totally selfish. These last finally had him arrested on the charge of corrupting the youth of Athens; he was tried, convicted, and in 399 was put to death. This death truly marks the end of the great fifth century. The opinions of Socrates will be viewed in the next chapter, since it is quite impossible to separate his ideas from those of Plato who wrote down what purport to be many of the later dialogues of Socrates. At Socrates' trial, he described himself as the gadfly of Athens, and the description is probably very exact. He insisted that the only good life was the well-examined life, and he sought to help others by causing them to examine themselves by asking them what they meant by the words they used—what do you mean, "justice"?—and then by a series of other questions finally revealing to the person that he simply didn't know what he was talking about. His method was always the same: to ask a question and arrive at an answer which seemed to be true. Then, by further questions he would test each part of the original answer, paring away those parts which proved themselves to be false, until the original answer was refined to truth by the clear process of thought.

For Socrates, the end of the good life is happiness, which is not only the avoidance of ignorance and its fruits, but the virtue which comes from knowledge. To know rightly, to make right choices is virtue, for it alone can satisfy the reason. Knowledge and virtue are inseparable. And happiness is the result of worthiness that comes when enlightenment and knowledge result, as necessarily they must in this highest good, which we call virtue.

The other great critic of late fifth-century Athens was Aristophanes (air-i-STOF-uh-neez), the writer of comedies. An aristocrat and a conservative, he sought to make Athens aware of its faults through satire. He did great disservice to Socrates in one of the early comedies, *The Clouds*, by depicting Socrates as the leader of one of the sophist schools in which the student, for a fee, could learn either the right logic or the wrong logic. This was the picture of Socrates which the uneducated mass of Athenians held in their minds, and the image helped convict him.

Aristophanes wrote many comedies in which the leading figures of his time were lampooned, and balloonlike ideas were unmercifully pricked. Most of these comedies date pretty badly since the references to persons and events are unknown to most readers. The only play which still stands and is still played is the magnificent comedy *Lysistrata* (LIS-i-stra-ta, or lī-SIS-tra-ta) in which the war between Athens and Sparta, or any war, for that matter, is satirized. In this comedy, the Athenian woman Lysistrata enlists the aid of all Greek women to withhold their favors from the men until the war is stopped. In spite of minor revolts among the women, they manage to hold the acropolis, where they have sequestered themselves, until the men will promise anything, even giving up warfare, if the girls will only come out. The play reduces the whole problem of ideologies and national pride to one very basic human function, but perhaps if nations could give up arguing and get back to such basics, people might be able to find their way out of many seemingly insoluble problems.

Thus the great fifth century in Athens. It had started with the pride of victory over the Persians, with the triumph of democracy, and with the promise of the great life in the plays of Aeschylus. Within the early years of the leadership of Pericles that good life had been realized about as much as it ever can be. It ended in a time of military defeat; a time when selfish individualism was the dominant mood; a time when Athens could no longer listen to the voice of its best critic, and when even criticism-through-comedy turned from biting satire to simple comedy-for-amusement, which we see in the later plays of Aristophanes.

The highest assertion of the human spirit in these exhausted times came at the very end with the trial of Socrates and a glimpse of the philosopher as hero. In his *Apology* he spoke to his jury as a highly urbane and civilized man, disdaining high-flown rhetoric on the one hand, and sentiment on the other. Instead, he speaks almost in a conversational tone about his own life and his devotion to his own highest ideals for human conduct. Perhaps the highest statement comes after the vote has been taken which condemned him to death:

> . . . there are many other means in every danger, for escaping death, if a man can bring himself to do and say anything and everything. No, gentlemen, the difficult thing is not to escape death, I think, but to escape wickedness—and that is much more difficult, for that runs faster than death. And now I, being slow and old, have been caught by the slower one; but my accusers, being clever and quick, have been caught by the swifter, badness. And now I and they depart, I, condemned by you to death, but these, condemned by truth to depravity and injustice. I abide by my penalty, they by theirs.

Bibliography

Translations of original material:

1. Grene and Lattimore, *Greek Tragedy*, 3 vols., paperback. Very good modern translations of the more important plays of Aeschylus, Sophocles and Euripides.
2. Plato, *Great Dialogues of Plato*, trans. W.H.D. Rouse, Mentor Book. For this chapter, see particularly *The Apology*. The *Phaedo* given from pp. 167 to 190 is taken from this volume.
3. Thucydides, *History of the Peloponnesian War*. The Crawley translation given in the Modern Library edition is a good one.

General Works:

1. C.M. Bowra, *The Greek Experience*. Like the Edith Hamilton work listed next, this is an interpretation of Greek life at its best.
2. Edith Hamilton, *The Greek Way*. Probably the most popular of the recent interpretations of the Greeks.

Criticism:

1. H.D.F. Kitto, *Greek Tragedy: A Literary Study*. One of the older books, Kitto is practically the norm for all criticism of Greek tragedy.

CHAPTER 6

Greece: The Hellenistic Period

■ "The name Greek is no longer a mark of race, but of outlook, and is accorded to those who share our culture rather than our blood," said the Athenian orator Isocrates in 380. He pinpointed one of the most important of the changes in culture between the fifth and the fourth centuries. Greek culture, as it had changed, became the culture not only of the Mediterranean world, but of Egypt and the vast Persian empire as well.

It would not further our particular interests to consider all of the political and international development within the Greek states during the fourth century. Following the Peloponnesian War, Sparta became the dominant city for a time, then various cities including Thebes, Athens, and Corinth assumed leadership for as long as their political acumen and military strength could hold that leadership. Persia was constantly involved in Hellenic affairs and from time-to-time, largely through diplomatic skill and outright bribery, controlled the destinies of the various Greek cities. By the middle of the fourth century, however, King Phillip of Macedon had begun to move toward a Macedonian Empire which united all of Greece, accomplishing his purposes by military strategy and principally by a series of wily political and diplomatic moves. His brilliant son, Alexander, became king in 336, and in one campaign brought all of Persia (including the territory of modern Turkey) as far east as India, Egypt, and all of Greece into one vast empire. In doing so he carried Greek culture as it had been influenced by many foreign sources throughout the vast territory. Significantly he established at least a half-dozen new cities named Alexandria throughout the empire, and in these he built libraries and other centers of culture. The Alexandria which he built in Egypt was to supplant Athens as the cultural center of the world for centuries. The Hellenistic Empire lasted until

146 B.C. when Rome finally conquered the last Achaean League, but the influence of Hellenistic art and thought was to flourish throughout most of the Roman period.

Our concern during this time must limit itself to the developments in art which are discussed Chapter 7 and to the contributions of the two philosophers, Plato and Aristotle.

PLATO

Plato was born in 427, two years after the death of Pericles; he was a youth at the time of the Athenian defeat in the Peloponnesian War; and he was a student of Socrates. It is impossible to distinguish between Plato's and Socrates' thought in the early writings of Plato, for most of them are dialogues in which Socrates is the principal speaker. It is probable that Plato included much of his own thought in these dialogues, or, certainly, that he reported the thought of Socrates with which he was in agreement. Only in the later part of his life did he speak entirely for himself, as in *The Laws.*

Plato's thought about that-which-is-real is perhaps his most significant contribution to modern thought. In developing this he started with the work of Pythagoras and the Eleatic philosophers in that he accepted permanence and unchangeability as the basic criteria for reality, and he accepted the mind as the only way to approach a knowledge of the real. In so doing, he denied the reality of all the sense-apparent objects around us, whether they be trees, animals, human, or even such abstract concepts as the various manifestations of love or justice. All sense-apparent things he regarded as shadows of the Real, made imperfect by the alliance with material stuff. (See his illustration of this in the small excerpt from *The Republic* called "The Allegory of the Cave" on p. 165, and constantly referred to in *The Phaedo*, p. 167, since this idea of reality is the foundation upon which most of Socrates' ideas about death are based.)

For Plato, reality consisted of ideas or essences of all basic things which had their existence beyond the grasp of the human senses or even of the human mind. These ideas had no physical attributes, no material substance, but were the "pure form" for all things which we see and know in our earthly existence. One must bear in mind that these forms are not ideas-in-the-minds-of-people. Thus when one imagines the perfect tree or the perfect human being, we are not dealing with Plato's essences. The ideas had existence, they were unchanging, and were the source, in that they gave form, to all material things. But the material thing, because it is allied with matter or flesh is always a distorted or impure shadow of its essence.

Probably this is clear enough, but a homely illustration might not be out of order. We can imagine that an architect is commissioned to design a building. Probably it does not happen this way, but assume that one morning, after wrestling with the problems for some time, he suddenly sees the building in his mind perfectly, exactly as it should be. "Eureka," he cries. "This is *it.*" So he dashes off to the drawing board. In drawing the plans, he has to make some changes in his original idea. For example, he has to stack the plumbing on the various levels directly above what is below. By the time that the blueprints are finished, the building is no longer the same as it was when it was idea. Then comes the construction. Perhaps the builder faces a steel strike, and another material must be substituted for some of the steel members. The costs for the planned building may go beyond the money available, so sections must be cut out, and cheaper materials substituted for those in the original plan. But finally the building is complete and stands in its material form for people to see and use. When was the structure most real? A good argument can be made that it was most real when it was pure idea, and that it has become less real each time it became involved with substance or material. One suspects that the architect, at least, looking at the final product, will see it as only a shadow of what he had once seen in his mind. To avoid argument, let us accept these last statements as true. The physical building is but a clumsy manifestation of the "real" idea. Can we take another step now? Assume that the architect is God, and that the building is the universe. The ideas for all things existed in God's mind, and these forms, essences, or immaterial patterns exist forever, but, as they are mixed with material substance—wood, mineral, flesh—they become distorted and changed. Now, perhaps, we have Plato's belief about reality with but one more step needed. From our last picture subtract the picture of God, for, although Plato frequently spoke of the gods, and often of God, he did not believe that these ideas were created; they simply existed eternally.

For a further illustration of this concept of reality, the student is referred to Plato's dialogue, *The Symposium*, where the nature of love is discussed. The discussion turns on the thought that in the realm of ideas, there is one which is beauty—not a beautiful sunset, or a beautiful person, just pure beauty. Many physical things can reflect this idea, among them a person. So that when one says, "I am in love with Isabella (or Henry)" what he really means is, "I am attracted by beauty, and Henry (or Isabella) reflects that idea to me."

There are a great many important philosophic repercussions from this Platonic belief about reality. One of the most important is the separation of the soul from the body, and the belief that soul was related to the realm of the essences, and that body was evil because it imprisoned and distracted the soul. This has been a major bone of contention in all Christian religion, for St. Augustine, in formulating the first unified Christian theology borrowed a great deal from Platonism. Specifically, Plato believed that in the realm of ideas a hierarchy existed, starting at the bottom with the essences of plants and animals, and ending at the top with the idea of the good (the light or fire which one encounters in the allegory of the Cave). This good, translated into early Christian theology, became the concept of God as the highest and best pattern for all things, and the goal toward which all Christians should strive. The method of reaching it can easily become the method of despising the flesh as a hindrance to the soul in its aspiration.

The dialogue called *The Republic* gives us our best view of the Socratic-Platonic idea of the nature of man on earth, and the nature of his government. A much later treatise, *The Laws*, gives the purely Platonic view of the same matter, differing somewhat from the beliefs stated in *The Republic*. In the first place, it should be made clear that *The Republic* is not Plato's formation of an ideal state as such. Instead, it is a discussion between Socrates and his students concerning the nature of justice. Justice is not necessary when one has only an isolated individual, but it becomes more and more necessary within an ever-larger group. So, in *The Republic* the discussants formulate a picture of the luxurious state (one that goes beyond the provision of the barest physical needs of men) in order to seek out the illusive quality, justice, which exists to a greater or lesser degree in the interrelationship of people.

In regard to man himself, Plato felt that men were dominated by one of three qualities: appetite, spirit, or intellect. For this reason he divided men into three classes. Those who were essentially men of appetite were to be the workers, including all those who followed commercial pursuits. Men of spirit were to form the auxiliaries or soldier class, who had no property or money to distract them from their duty: the maintenance of order at home and protection from foreign enemies. The men of intellect were to be carefully educated to become the guardians of the state, the rulers, the philosopher-kings.

Education was to be the force which gave form to this state. The lowest class was to receive little or no education. The soldier or auxiliary group was to be taught gymnastics (to give them strong bodies, fit for their duties at all times), and music to make their personalities gentle toward their fellow citizens. Under the general heading of music, Plato included almost all of what we call the "liberal arts," including such reasoned and measured subjects as mathematics. In the discussion of this point, Socrates uses the example of the good watchdog as an illustration of his point, for such a dog is gentle toward his master and friends, but fierce toward enemies. The soldier class should have such a nature, with their quality of spirit tempered by the study of music. The guardian class should have all of the education of the soldiers, then study methods of reasoning, and finally philosophy. After their years of study they were to be subjected to all sorts of trials and temptations to test their strength of character and their ability to make decisions on an unselfish basis, in terms of the general good. At about the age of 50, after passing through this period of testing, the guardians would be called upon to rule the city. They would become the famous "philosopher-kings," and they would rule the state absolutely.

One notices immediately that this is a totalitarian state, with the exception that no madmen would ever be able to rule. But the society is divided into strict classes; and Socrates advocates a strict censorship of all stories and music which the students are to hear, so that only the best and finest will enter into their souls. The classes of citizens are not controlled by birth or wealth, however, for Socrates proposes the "great lie" which will be perpetrated on the citizens: all children will be told that the state is their mother, and they will be reared as wards of the city until they are about seven years of age. During these formative years they will be carefully observed in all their activities, and their chief characteristics noted. At the end of this time they will be divided into the three classes according to their natural ability.

Insofar as the ultimate question of the nature of justice is concerned, Plato and Socrates take the middle ground, the Golden Mean, which was ever a Greek ideal. In the qualities of men, wisdom should control the other qualities, so that appetite would be curbed to the point of temperance, spirit should be limited to the point of courage, and intellect should become wisdom. When these conditions are met, justice emerges. These: temperance, courage, wisdom, and justice were the great Platonic virtues. Later on, the Christians were to add faith, hope, and love to these to establish the seven cardinal virtues. The difference between the Platonic, intellectual virtues and the Christian emotional and spiritual virtues illustrates a fundamental difference between the hopes and aspirations of the two cultures.

ARISTOTLE

Aristotle came from a very different background from that of Plato, and, although he studied with Plato at the academy, his answers to man's important questions are quite different, perhaps because of the difference in youthful experience. Aristotle's father was a physician in northern

Greece, and, early in Aristotle's life was called to the city of Pella to serve as a physician in the court of King Phillip. Perhaps Aristotle's inquiring mind about sense-apparent things, his interest in experimentation, his concern in change rather than permanence, and his inability to accept the mind alone as a guide to truth came from his father's interest in similar things. As a matter of fact, exactly as Plato's thought had its source in the Eleatics and Pythagoras, Aristotle's mature conclusions have their roots in the Ionians.

Aristotle is one of the most extraordinary men of all time; the keenness of his intellect, the range of his interests and studies, the staggering amount of information and speculation in his enormous collection of writings, rouse the admiration and awe of any who read his work. Not the least of his distinctions was the fact that he served as tutor to the youthful Prince Alexander, and must have had a great influence on the brilliant career of that monarch. After this period of tutoring, Aristotle went to Athens and founded his own school, the Lyceum. With Plato, he was to shape the course of western thought: these two men are probably the most powerful influences from our Greek heritage.

As we have seen, Plato's quest for the permanent, the idea or form, rather than the actuality of experience, led him into a dualism that separates form from substance, soul from body. Aristotle, profoundly interested in the changing life about him, tried to reconcile the two. Perhaps the difference could be expressed in this way: when Plato wished to discuss his ideas of the state, he wrote *The Republic*, and later *The Laws*, theoretical speculations that construct the wholly imaginary idea of a state; when Aristotle wished to discuss his ideas of the state, he and his students collected and studied the constitutions of 158 Greek city-states as a prelude to the work known as *Politics*.

It is an impossible task, and not to the present purpose, to even mention the multitude of Aristotle's writings. His speculations ranged all the way from his logic, the proper process of thought, through biology, physics, metaphysics, ethics, law and politics, and literary criticism. In a very condensed and simplified form, some of his ideas about the nature of tragedy are given in the introduction to *Oedipus the King*, and a suggestion about the nature of his *Logic* is discussed in connection with the writing of St. Thomas in the Middle Ages. Only two of his ideas concern us here: one is his view of the nature of reality; the other is his idea of the conduct of life in the light of that view. These last are drawn from the *Nicomachean Ethics* and the *Eudemian Ethics*, summaries of his thought about the proper conduct of life as written by his son and one of his students.

For Aristotle, the abstract idea or form of Plato's teaching could not be separated from the matter or substance by which it was known; the two must somehow come together as different aspects of the same thing. Thus Plato's "ideal" chair did not exist for Aristotle apart from the actual wood and metal which composed it. A brick is a brick only when the "idea" brick and the clay composing it come together; then the brick is "real." The brick then may become the matter or substance of another "idea," and become house; and the house, in turn, may be substance to the idea of town or city. At every stage, the union of substance and form, of matter and idea, is necessary to constitute "reality"; but there is a progression, upwards or downwards. The substance that Plato is not concerned with becomes for Aristotle the basis for higher, more complex realities when it is informed by idea of form. Such, at least, is the direction of the difference between the two men; Plato's static view becomes more dynamic in Aristotle's teaching.

The process of change (which Plato never satisfactorily explains) is accounted for, by Aristotle, in his theory of enteleche (en-TEL-uh-kee; the Greek word is made of the particles en, "within"; telos, "purpose or end"; and echaia, "having, possessing"). That is to say, it is in the nature of things that they have within them a goal, a destiny, to fulfill: the seed becomes the plant, for that is its "enteleche"; the clay becomes the brick, for that is its "enteleche." The movement upward through increasing complexity is the "enteleche" of the universe; and the cause of the process, drawing all things toward their own perfection, is God, the First Cause, who moved all things without being moved: the "Unmoved Mover," in Aristotle's phrase.

The motive power of Aristotle's God is apparently not love, as Christianity might contend, nor will, as Judaism might argue; it is rather that there seems to be a cosmic yearning toward perfection, and that perfection is, by definition, God. Aristotle's customary view of the necessity for the union of both form and matter to constitute reality here breaks down (or more kindly, "transcends itself"?) for such a God must be pure form, with none of the inherent weakness or imperfection of the material,[1] God is the only instance where pure form is separated from matter.

1. "Such then is the principle upon which depend the heavens and the world of nature. And its life (i.e., the principle, or God) is like the best that we enjoy, and enjoy but for a short time; for it is ever in this state, which we cannot be. And if then God is always in that good state in which we sometimes are, this compels our wonder; and if in a better state, then this compels it yet more. And God is in a better state. We say therefore, that God is a living being, eternal, most good; so that life and a continual eternal existence belong to God; for this is God." (Aristotle, Metaphysics, XII, 7.)

How does one lead the good life? It is interesting to note that Aristotle makes no apology for thinking that it must begin with sufficient means; he holds no ascetic views on the matter, and quite matter-of-factly begins with an assumption of enough material possession to allow one the choice of doing as he would. Granted, however, the adequate wealth, what does one do? The enteleche of which he speaks implies that there is a goal, or end, reached when the person or thing is functioning properly—that is, in accord with its own inner purposes; when conditions permit such functioning, there is a highest good, a summum bonum, attained. The enteleche of man, then, would lead him to his own summum bonum, his own best functioning, the worthy and proper fulfillment of his humanity. And since man is for Aristotle the "rational animal," that fulfillment would be the life of reason. When he is living harmoniously, using his mind, functioning in family and state (for Aristotle also calls man a "political," i.e., social, animal), he has achieved his greatest good. Such a life has two implications, among many others, that concern us here.

One is that such a life will be a life of virtue, or excellence. But virtues may fail by being deficient, or by being carried to excess; the middle ground between is what is to be desired. Courage, for instance, is a virtue; but it may be perverted through deficiency into cowardice, or no less perverted by being carried to the excess of foolhardiness, mere rashness. Generosity is a virtue, but it can be carried to the excess of prodigality and wastefulness, or perverted through deficiency to stinginess. To mediate between extremes, to discover the "Golden Mean"—which it is to be noted is a relative and not an absolute matter—that is to achieve virtue.

The other implication, then, is that man's best use of reason is in the life of contemplation. He must have time to read, to talk, to think about the whole idea of excellence, that he may achieve the high-mindedness that is his summum bonum; the word that Aristotle uses is "magnanimity." Such a quality is not to be won in the heat and dust of the marketplace; though the good man will perform his duties as a member of society, still the life of action is not as good as the life of contemplation.

With this brief discussion of a few of the ideas of Aristotle, we come to the end of our background of Greek civilization in Greece itself. The Hellenistic culture was to flourish for many years in such centers as Egyptian Alexandria and Pergamum in Asia Minor. Indeed, much of Roman culture formed itself around Hellenistic principles.

Greek civilization had started within the shadow of superstition and tradition in archaic times. Slowly those bondages had been cut away until a very delicate balance was achieved between the freedom of each individual person and the welfare of the group in Athens early in the reign of Pericles. The philosophers, the authors, the artists of the time took an active part in politics, and conducted their affairs in the Agora, the marketplace.

But change is inevitable. In Athens it would seem that the knife-edge between individuality and the welfare of the group was too thin, the balance on it too precarious, for a group of people to maintain equilibrium for a long period of time. The skeptical sophists taught that complete individuality was the goal—violating Aeschylus' doctrine of the mean between autocracy and anarchy. The original strength of the city was sapped, but to give rise to a new and different kind of strength in the broadened horizons of Hellenistic culture. It is interesting that both Plato and Aristotle (except for their brief efforts to educate a king: Plato as tutor for the Syracusan Dionysius, Aristotle as Alexander's tutor) stood apart from politics and the vigorous life of the time; they deserted the active marketplace. They were contemplatives, aware that something had gone wrong, that the dream had somehow failed, and each in his own way, introspected into himself and his culture to discover what had failed. Probably nothing had really gone "wrong." Change had simply taken place in the cultural milieu, leading to new forms of life, new types of exploration into human existence, new forms of freedom.

The Romans brought about a different type of balance in civilization, and this will be discussed in the next unit of our work.

Bibliography

Translations of original material:

1. Aristophanes, *The Comedies of Aristophanes.* Fitts and Fitzgerald, eds. Excellent translations, done with a real sense of humor appropriate to the subject. For example, in Lysistrata, the girl from Sparta speaks with a fine Texas drawl.
2. Aristotle, *Nicomachean Ethics.* Any recent edition.
3. Plato, *Great Dialogues of Plato.* Trans. W.H.D. Rouse.
4. Xenophon, *The Persian Expedition.* Rex Warner's translation of the *Anabasis.* Light reading; what an excellent Sunday night TV movie for all the family this would make.

Fiction:

1. Mary Renault, *The Mask of Apollo.* Using a traveling actor as the central figure of the novel, Miss Renault gives a lively picture of the times of Plato.

CHAPTER 7

The Search for Freedom as Reflected in Greek Art

THE AEGEAN HERITAGE

■ According to Greek mythology, Daedalus (DE-da-lus) was the first and greatest of artists, a legendary Minoan artificer who created figures in wood, stone, and bronze that seemed to walk, animals of wood and leather that fooled dumb beasts, all manner of ingenious inventions for comfort and amusement, and that mysterious Minoan maze, the labyrinth that housed the fabled Minotaur. Although the story is fascinating, it is immaterial whether or not Daedalus existed, because the essential idea that the myth proclaims is the Greek urge and commitment to creative activity: to invent, design, sculpt, and build. The Daedalian Greek studied nature and used his discoveries not only to reproduce but to create new images and structures which he animated to give the illusion of vitality and life. The desire to create marks the Greek genius.

Unfortunately the story of Daedalus has an unhappy ending, but one which points to a primary aesthetic consideration of the Greek artists. Daedalus, according to one of the legends, had an undisciplined son named Icarus (IK-ah-rus), who prevailed upon his father to contrive wings made of wax and feathers which enabled the lad to soar, birdlike, in the sky. One day the proud aviator, heedless of his father's instructions not to fly too near to the sun, approached that glowing orb only to have his wings melted so that he plummeted to his death in the sea which now bears his name. This part of the myth stresses Greek insistence that the laws of nature must be recognized and respected judiciously, that is, according to reason. Thus, through the story of the sage artificer Daedalus and his hubristic son Icarus, we see reflected the Greek search for freedom in the arts through study of nature, invention, and obedience to reason. Myths are sometimes said to be charming lies; nevertheless, they are often lies that tell truth beyond appearance.

Obviously, the great art achievements of the Golden Age of Greece did not appear suddenly in full development, as Athena sprang full-grown from the head of Zeus. Archeologists and art historians have not been very successful in tracing the genesis and development of Greek art; despite involved studies and excavations, the experts have been proved wrong time and time again. For example, until the last century historians dismissed the *Iliad* as a fanciful, albeit brilliant, epic poem and smugly and resoundingly stated that Troy and Mycenae had never existed, that the hosts of Achaean and Trojan heroes were products of fertile, creative imagination. In 1871, Heinrich Schliemann, a wealthy German merchant who had a passionate love of the Homeric tales and Greek history, astounded the scholars in announcing that he had discovered Troy under a hill called Hissarlik in Troad, a city in the northwest corner of Asia Minor. During his excavations he uncovered more than 9,000 objects in silver and gold, the so-called "Treasury of Priam." Soon Schliemann's site was virtually inundated with archeologists who discovered a second, and then a third, and ultimately nine cities of Troy, one superimposed over another. Troy exists once again, although which of the cities is the Troy of which Homer sang is still a matter of controversy.

Schliemann went on to discover Mycenae (my-SEE-knee), that great citadel of Agamemnon, with its many royal tombs replete with skulls wearing golden masks and arm bones encircled with golden bracelets. But even before Schliemann died, other archeologists contended that this Mycenae predated that of the Homeric king, that the remains of Agamemnon were of a far earlier civilization, one contemporaneous with the great Minoan Age in Crete. The undaunted German, feeling the futility of argument and acknowledging the lack of positive identification jokingly renamed his Agamemnon "Schulze." Nevertheless, Schliemann started a movement which has drawn generations of scholars to the Aegean world, and they have discovered and are discovering masterworks of sculpture and architecture that continuously change our picture of prehistoric Greece and Greek art.

Only brief or undeciphered written records remain from civilizations which flourished in the Aegean world during the Bronze Age (c. 3000-1000 B.C.), but it is contended and seems highly probable that these early peoples of the Aegean world contributed to the development of Greek civilization and, thus, Greek art of the first millennium B.C. The three great Aegean civilizations of the pre-Greek period, although closely interrelated through trade, colonization, and conquest, had distinctive as well as similar artistic achievements. It has been customary to ascribe beginnings and endings for the Cycladic (SIGH-clodik), Cretan or Minoan, and Mycenaean or Helladic mainland civilization, but it is very unlikely that there were sharp cultural breaks in any of these civilizations. Rather, it is now believed that these were slow and general transformations of artistic forms and subject matter which, along with the development of completely new concepts and precepts, resulted in Greek art. Brief indications of some possible sources of the Greek artistic achievement should be studied with a generous attitude of receptivity tempered with as equally generous skepticism.

Before discussing the pre-Hellenic Aegean civilizations, it must be understood that the Greeks were keenly aware of the Egyptian civilization and were influenced by it, as were the Mycenaeans, Minoans, and Cycladians. Perhaps Plato was exaggerating when he said that Egyptian art had not changed in 10,000 years, but his statement indicates that he was very much aware of it; and many of its conventions were continued in Greece throughout the geometric, archaic (are-KAY-ick, severe, classical, and Hellenistic periods, albeit with refinements of animation which are uniquely of Greek character. (A "convention" is a way of seeing and depicting things in a manner which has been generally accepted or, in other words, commonly held values which have taken visual form. The sum of all conventions is "culture.")

The Egyptians utilized a post and lintel system of architecture, and a column with capital which was highly refined and widely used. Direct Egyptian linkage with Greek architecture is as probable as are Minoan and Mycenaean influences—and just as difficult to prove. It is in sculpture, however, that direct adaptation of Egyptian conventions can be shown. The statue of "Mycerinus (MY-sir-reen-us) and His Queen" from Giza (Fig. 3), which was completed about 2500 B.C., shares a common quality with practically every Egyptian statue depicting figure or figures life-sized, standing or sitting. The Egyptian sculptor took a cubic view of the human forms, preparing the statue by drawing its front and side views on the faces of a rectangular block, then working inward until the angular views met. The image that emerges is one of great clarity, but one that demands a 90° change of position on the part of the viewer every time he wishes to see another view. The Egyptian statue has a frozen quality and must be seen either from directly in front or from the sides to obtain the complementary profiles. Archaic Greek sculpture (Figs. 13-19) is noticeably similar, and one achievement of later Greek sculpture was the abolition of this limited manner of

Figure 3. "Mycerinus and His Queen" (slate, front view, black ground; fourth dynasty). Courtesy, Museum of Fine Arts, Boston.

Figure 4. "Offering Bearers from the Tomb of Sebek-hotep" (wall painting, tempera on mud plaster). The Metropolitan Museum of Art, Rogers Fund, 1930.

depiction and the development of the revolving view or what is commonly called "sculpture in the round." But even with this new development it is not until the late Hellenistic period that the sculptured figure is allowed to break out of the rectangular format used by the Egyptians.

In Egyptian painting, illustrated by "Offering Bearers from the Tomb of Sebek-hotep" (Fig. 4), and in Egyptian relief sculpture as illustrated in the "Portrait Panel of Hesire" (Fig. 5), an even more pervasive Egyptian convention may be noted. Egyptian painters and relief carvers invariably depicted the human body with face and legs in profile, eye and torso frontally; this depiction shows body parts in their most telling and easily understood view. This is the way the artist "knows" rather than the way he "sees" the body. Greek use of this convention is obvious in the "Helmeted Runner" (Fig. 19), and the "Mourning Athena" (Fig. 43), but only very close and careful observation will reveal that the "Discobolos" (dis-KOB-o-lus; Fig. 42), which is one of the best-known Greek sculptures, commonly considered realistic, maintains that convention into the Golden Age.

Between the Greek mainland and the island of Crete are approximately 220 small islands, of which the central and most famous is Delos, the legendary birthplace of Artemis and Apollo. The simple, but monumentally proportioned, marble head (Fig. 6), was created in the Cyclades about 2400 B.C., although its formal resemblance to the work of the twentieth-century sculptor Brancusi makes it seem very modern indeed. The anonymous Cycladic sculptor illustrated an artistic truth; that is, that all figurative art is abstract, a simplification of the body, of nature, of all that which is experienced objectively. In this work, the artist simplified to the degree that the sculpture is barely recognizable as a head. All artists determine the degree to which they carry their abstractions or, conversely, how diligently they pursue the illusion of visual reality. Neither extreme necessarily has merit in itself, for artistic value is not based on single elements. Nevertheless, until the Hellenistic period the Greek artist always emphasized formal qualities over sense-appearance. This will be explained and illustrated in detail later. What is important to remember about the Cycladic figure is that it is but one of a large number of similar significant works, all highly abstract, produced in the third millennium B.C.

The "Mask from Mycenae" (Fig. 7), whether it be of Agamemnon or "Schulze," is an outstanding example of highly-developed metal craftsmanship called toreutics (to-RUE-ticks), the hammering of metals into representational or plastic form. This death mask shows an Egyptian influence, for Mycenaean mercenaries assisted the Pharaohs in their struggles with the Hyksos during the seventeenth and sixteenth centuries B.C., came home

Figure 5. "Portrait Panel of Hesire" from Saqquara, c. 2650 B.C. Egyptian Museum, Cairo (Hirmer Fotoarchiv München).

Figure 6. "Cycladic Head," c. 2400-2000 B.C. National Archeological Museum, Athens.

Figure 7. "Mask from Mycenae," c. 1500 B.C. National Archeological Museum, Athens.

laden with Egyptian gold, and developed funerary practices similar to those of the Egyptians, including the burying of their illustrious dead with goods and ornamentation suitable to the status of the deceased. The concept of immortality, a life memorialized through a work of art, is basic to all Greek sculpture of the Golden Age.

The citadel of Mycenae, today in ruins, is still an impressive structure. Its massive walls of gigantic stones were said to have been constructed by the Cyclopes (SIGH-klo-pays), a mythical race of one-eyed giants. This is a romantic explanation for a colossal architectural achievement, but it would be difficult for contemporary architects to reproduce the citadel. Whoever built it, however, had a keen sense of military necessity, for the only revealed gate of the fortress is at the end of a rectangular area, three sides of which had high walls from which defenders could protect the entrance. The gate itself was a massive post and lintel construction with a wooden door banded and studded with metal; over the lintel stands a stone relief of two stately lions (now headless) flanking a symbolic Minoan column. It is from this striking carving that the entire gate unit takes the name "Lion Gate" (Fig. 8). Although the Mycenaeans' and Minoans' only major architectural achievement was in building palaces, open and airy in the case of the Minoans, closed and fortified in the case of the Mycenaeans, both peoples were master builders. The remains at Mycenae and Knossos give impressive proof that fashioning of stone and masonry construction was well practiced long before the construction of temples on the acropolis of Athens. Because the Greeks excelled in building temples and since there is strong evidence that the early Greek temples were made of wood, there would seem to be no direct Mycenaean and Minoan influence upon Hellenic architecture. On the other hand, the Greek transition from wooden to stone construction was so fast and so complete that the likelihood of a more than elementary background in the fashioning and handling of stone should not be dismissed lightly.

Figure 8. "Lion Gate" at Mycenae, c. 1250 B.C. (Hirmer Fotoarchiv München).

The remains of elaborate palaces and hundreds of mural paintings of great decorative elegance attest to the claim that the Minoan was one of the most highly-developed and artistic civilizations in history. Centered in the city of Knossos on the island of Crete, the Minoans held sway over most of the Aegean world, including part of the Greek mainland, nearly a thousand years before the siege of Troy. And throughout the third and second millennium B.C., even during the height of Mycenaean power, Minoan traders disseminated Minoan arts and ideas throughout the Aegean world. It well could have been of Crete that Homer and Plato were thinking when they spoke of a golden age in the dim past, for Minoan civilization was marked by body comforts, manifold refinements in clothing, manners, and art. Minoan pottery, whether painted with geometric patterns or representational forms, always shows a sophisticated unification of the form of the vase and the subject matter. Despite its known influence on Mycenae, it is impossible to show a direct Minoan influence upon Greek art. The "Snake Goddess" (Fig. 9), for example, is unlike any sculpture produced in Greece. Even if we accept the subject as a goddess rather than a priestess (both designations have legitimate bases), the Minoan anthropomorphism is more symbolic and decorative than humanistic. Greek sculptors would later stress positive and negative aspects of human qualities. The Minoans had a highly-developed sense of decorative line and color, and this quality may have been partially understood and utilized by the Greeks; but the Minoans showed little interest in the ethical values basic to Greek art.

Obviously, Minoan, Cycladic, Mycenaean, and Egyptian civilizations has some influence on the development of Greek art. The degree of influence, whether it was of artistic form or subject matter, probably will never be fully ascertained, nor is this knowledge necessary to enjoy Greek art. It is necessary only to recognize that the factors inherent in any work of art are diverse, that no art work is without a mixed pedigree, and that originality is a very rare commodity. Greek art, no matter what its sources, is marked by a unique combination of interest in structural form, mimetic accuracy, and visual animation, which makes it the first truly humanistic art.

Figure 9. Minoan statuette of "Snake Goddess" (right side; ivory and gold), sixteenth century B.C. Courtesy Museum of Fine Arts, Boston. Gift of Mrs. W. Scott Fitz.

THE GEOMETRIC PERIOD

The formative phase of Greek or Hellenic civilization, the period in which the homogenous elements of that great civilization were established, can be dated only vaguely. Generally the beginning has been established as around 1100 B.C., during the time of the Dorian invasion, and the ending occurs sometime in the period 700-660 B.C. In art this long period produced no significant buildings or substantive statues, for this was a period of great physical devastation and slow recovery. Military invasions always disturb the major arts: political and economic turmoil is not conducive to commissioning and producing large aesthetic monuments such as temples and life-sized statues. The Dorian invasion probably impoverished many of the artists and ended or limited for a time the transmission of technology. It is not surprising then that this period is chiefly one of applied or utilitarian arts: furniture, textiles, glassware and, above all, pottery. And because most of the pottery produced from c. 1000 to c. 700 B.C. emphasized geometric decoration, this time-span is known in Greek art as the geometric period.

Pottery had been practiced since the Stone Age and by 1800 B.C. the art of throwing on the wheel was practiced with great skill throughout the Aegean world. The Minoans produced superb ceramic pieces covered with lively representations of plant or marine life such as the famous "Octopus Vase" (Fig. 10). By the eleventh century B.C. the natural and curvilinear elements of Minoan pottery painting began to disappear and in the period of the ninth and much of the eighth century a highly-developed geometric convention of pottery decoration had evolved. Almost all Greek abstract decorative forms used in painting were developed and used then: meanders, horizontal bands, concentric circles, shaded triangles, wheellike patterns, swastikas, and zigzags. Moreover, animal and human figures were introduced, although these figures were schematized or patterned renderings, purely two-dimensional, and only depicted in full-front and profile views.

Figure 10. "Octopus Vase" from Crete, c. 1500 B.C. Museum of Candia, Crete (Hirmer Fotoarchiv München).

That this pottery was not simple but quite sophisticated, work of great aesthetic as well as utilitarian value, is evidenced by the "Geometric Vase with Prothesis" (Fig. 11), which was found in the Dipylon Cemetery in Athens. This vase is colossal in size, well over four feet high, and served as a grave monument: liquid offerings were poured into this and similar containers which had openings at their bottoms through which the libation filtered down to the honored dead. The main representational theme of the pot illustrated is a *prothesis*, or lying-in-state of the dead, a frequent theme of these funerary monuments. The head of the deceased is composed of a boxlike object with a dot in the center; his chest is a shaded triangle; his stomach and legs are assorted lozenge shapes; his arms and hands are lines such as those used for stick figures. He is surrounded by a patterned row of similarly composed men whose arms are raised in mourning or prayer. The secondary representational scene depicts warriors carrying shields or driving simple chariots pulled by graceful decorative horses. This scene depicts the funeral procession, or the funerary games, or both. In addition to these bands of figurative depiction, purely geometric decorative bands of diverse designs cover the rest of the vase from its lip to its foot. Although the artist who painted this vase (it was very unlikely to have been the same man who shaped the clay) used his limited repertory of pictorial shapes to produce an astonishingly varied effect, its aesthetic success owes much to the subtle relationship that the artist created in spacing the bands so that their weight and density relate effectively to the structure of the vessel.

Figure 11. "Geometric Vase with Prothesis," eighth century B.C. Metropolitan Museum of Art, Rogers Fund, 1914.

The history of Greek pottery and vase painting is highly involved, interesting to specialists and beginning students alike, and includes thousands of outstanding works by known and anonymous artists. However, the great artistic achievements of the Greeks in architecture and sculpture of future generations will be emphasized in the rest of this chapter, for their influence was germinal and has been all-pervasive thoughout the history of Western art. Nevertheless, the geometric period in pottery was an important interlude in Greek artistic development, for it was a period in which the Greeks began to find and develop the shapes, forms, abstractions, theories, and relationships which would largely determine the development of architecture and sculpture.

There is no architectural type which might be called geometric, but it is apparent that the temple as such was known to Homer (*Iliad*, I, 39) and foundations of temples dating from this period have been discovered in Samos, Eleusis, and other centers of Greek antiquity. Fragmentary terracotta models of temples from this period show that two important elements of the canonical temple were already present: the cella, or enclosed shrine, and a front porch supported by columns. By "canonical" is meant adherence to body of fundamental rules and forms that are essential to achieve the accepted concept of what an object, in this case the temple, should be. Moreover, the models and the excavated foundations indicate that the ground plan of most of these temples was rectangular. By 600 B.C., a time shortly beyond the geometric period, the temple had acquired all its essential forms and parts and the "canon" was completely realized.

Greek statuettes, although not very important or impressive when compared with substantive, life-sized stone sculpture, are among the most popular products of Greek art. Their very smallness enables one to hold and turn them around in his hands—a very intimate relationship. Although the geometric age in sculpture generally is defined as being the ninth and eighth centuries, one should remember that all the arts do not develop in the same manner and at the same speed. Thus, strict, general adherence to an artistic style and period cannot be followed. It is important to recognize, however, that small Greek sculpture in bronze,

Figure 12. Bronze statuette of youth, "Mantiklos dedicated me . . . ," 700-680 B.C. Courtesy, Museum of Fine Arts, Boston, Francis Bartlett Collection.

wood, ivory, and terra-cotta was produced throughout Greek history; and these works either predict or reflect stylistic changes and attitudes of developments in monumental sculpture and aesthetic theory. The bronze statuette shown in Figure 12 dates from c. 700-680 B.C. and is a votive offering representing a standing youth. On its thighs it bears the inscription "Mantiklos dedicated me to the Far-Darter of the silver bow, as part of his tithe. Do thou, Phoebus, grant him gracious recompense." This little figure is pompous in his stiff, erect, and exacting bisymmetrical pose; but the bulging of the thighs from the waist and protrusion of the shoulders show the beginnings of an interest in anatomical structure. This statuette is less formalized than the Dipylon Cemetery vase which was contemporaneous, and indicates a growing interest in naturalism which will become increasingly evident in the archaic period, into which all of Greek sculpture entered within half a century.

The geometric interlude produced little or no art which might be considered "great," but it was a period in which the Greek began to see and think and create as a Greek, not as a Minoan or Mycenaean or an Egyptian. Borrowings from those civilizations might be evident, but the vitality and new, unique forms used in art from the geometric period indicate that the Greeks were involved in an elementary process of producing an art which would not be bound strictly to established conventions, which would be the result of experimentation and invention, and, above all, which would be dynamic rather than static.

THE ARCHAIC PERIOD

It was in the archaic period (c. 660-480 B.C.) that the Greeks probably produced their first substantive marble sculpture and evolved the canonical Greek temple. Primarily it is because of these achievements that this period is called archaic, a word which derives from *archaios*, Greek for beginning or source. Today the word "archaic" usually is defined as "old-fashioned" or "out-of-date," but the primary meaning refers to the *archē*, the ultimate source. One should remember first that the Greeks built upon a tradition going back into Mycenae, Crete, Egypt, and Asia Minor; second, they had developed respect for the laws of nature; and third, they showed genius for coming to terms with tradition and the world in which they lived, even in the preceding geometric period. These accomplishments and attitudes, so apparent in the so-called minor arts of the geometric period, became manifest in the major arts in the archaic period.

Archaic Sculpture

From the archaic period, through the entire history of ancient Greek art, Greek sculptors evolved new modes or manners of representation that changed the conception of sculpture which had been held in Egypt and Asia Minor for thousands of years. They developed three-dimensional, large-scale sculpture which advanced continuously on the path of naturalism in the representation of the complex mechanism of the human body. The two main subjects represented were the standing male youth called the kouros (COO-rose) and the standing maiden called the kore (CORE-a). These subjects, probably adapted from Egypt and Mesopotamia, were repeated again and again, never with the intention of exact repetition, but with the achieved goal of constant innovation.

Compare the Egyptian statue of "Mycerinus and His Queen" (Fig. 3) with the "Kouros" from the Metropolitan (Fig. 13), c. 615-590 B.C., and the "Kore from Auxerre" (Fig. 14), c. 650-625 B.C., to see the dynamic nature of the evident change. Both kouros and the king are presented in strict, bisymmetrical frontality, with left feet a little advanced and arms held close to sides; the similarity of their broad shoulders, narrow waists, and small flanks is obvious also. The important differences are that whereas the Egyptian sculpture is supported by a pillar and wears clothing, the Greek kouros is completely freestanding and nude. Moreover, the Greek sculptor cut through the marble to

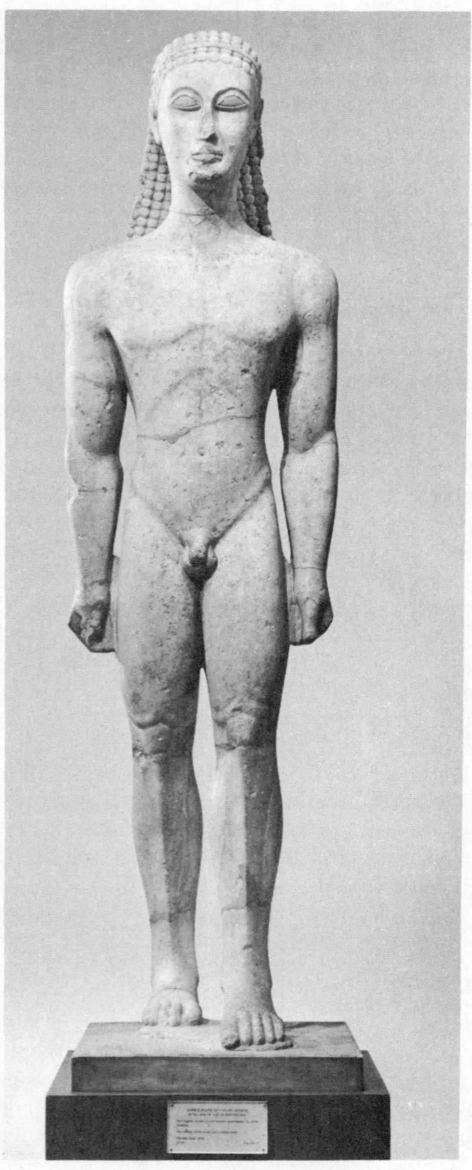

Figure 13. "Kouros," archaic marble statue of youth of the Apollo type, Athenian, 615-590 B.C. Metropolitan Museum of Art, Fletcher Fund, 1932.

Figure 14. "Kore of Auxerre," c. 650-625 B.C. Louvre Museum, Paris (Musées Nationaux).

allow real space to appear between the arms and torso, and between the legs. In fact, as there are no holes in the Egyptian sculpture and the figures project from a wall-like surface, it is really a high relief. The Greek sculptor allows an absolute minimum of meaningless stone to remain in his work, whereas the Egyptian sculptor allowed the stone to remain as neutral matter. This difference in representation testifies to Greek insistence on organic unity. The archaic kore seems somewhat crude or primitive in comparison to the Egyptian queen, even though she, too, is clothed. But, like the kouros, the maiden is freestanding, with arms separated from her torso by real space, and hair and anatomical details described in very geometrical patterns. The Greek subjects, the male youth and the maiden, and their concomitant different manners of expression (emphasis on the body and naturalism in the case of the kouros and emphasis on decorative formal qualities of materials and hair in the case of the kore) will force Greek sculptors to explore in different directions and eventually lead to the union and reconciliation of the divergent manners or modes of expression in the classical age.

It is pertinent to suggest that the ancient Greeks seemed to enjoy a unique visual sensibility that former peoples of the ancient worlds did not know or to which they did not give expression. Many factors may account for this and a few may be considered: the Greeks were the great geometers or reasoners who cast their ideas in visual shapes; Greek medical practice, as exemplified by Hippocrates, emphasized making and accumulating visual observation; the Greek gods were conceived in man's image, and, thus, were immediately accessible to artistic representation; and the Greek philosophers emphasized the development of the body as well as the mind. It is not surprising, then, that imitation of the visual, perceptual world would become important to the Greeks. Nevertheless, imitation was not the major interest, for the Greeks preserved and developed a remarkable sense of structural form which saved their art from complete submission to representational accuracy and, consequently, from triviality, banality and sentimentality.

The nude form comes into its own as a mode of expression in Greek art, but only for male representations, during the archaic period. The unclothed kouros, it must be stressed, was nude not naked. (In contemporary usage, "naked" implies shame, discomfort, a lack and need, whereas "nude" implies completeness, absolute acceptance of one's body without shame or pride.) The Greek was a seeker of truth about his mind and body; he sought truth through study and exercise of all his faculties; he found truth or beauty in that which was essential and basic. In modern phraseology, clothes do not make the man. It is significant that the Greek attitude to female representation was different, as were the general attitudes concerning the status of women.

The "Calf-Bearer" (Fig. 15) from the middle archaic period conforms to the ideal of physical perfection sought by the Greeks for themselves and the sculptural representation. This man wears a thin cloak, but since it fits him like a second skin, his strong vigorous body is emphasized rather than obscured. Note, also, that his anatomical and facial features are less strongly marked, much softer, and more naturalistic than those of the kouros from the Metropolitan. The "Hera of Samos" (HE-rah of SAM-us; Fig. 16), sometimes called "The Statue from Samos," has drapery rendering much more refined than that of the "Kore of Auxerre," which

Figure 15. "Calf Bearer," c. 575-550 B.C. Acropolis Museum, Athens.

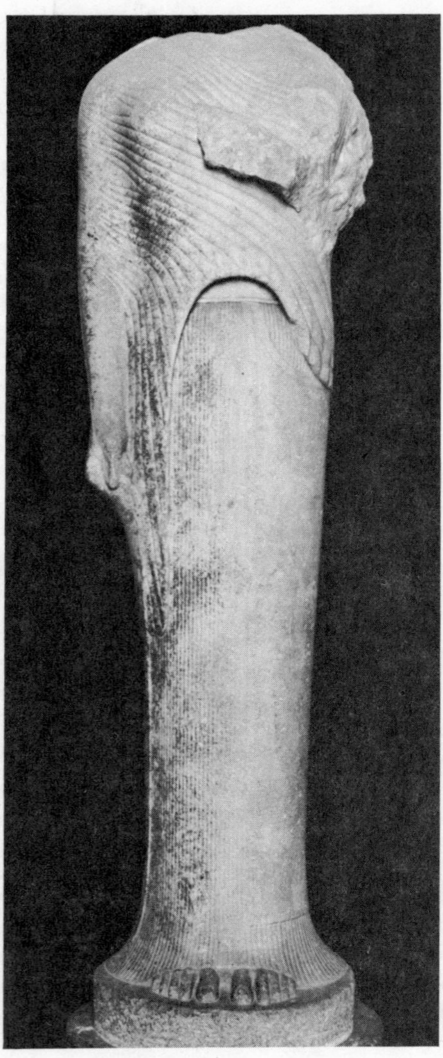

Figure 16. "Hera of Samos," c. 755-550 B.C. Louvre Museum, Paris (Musées Nationaux).

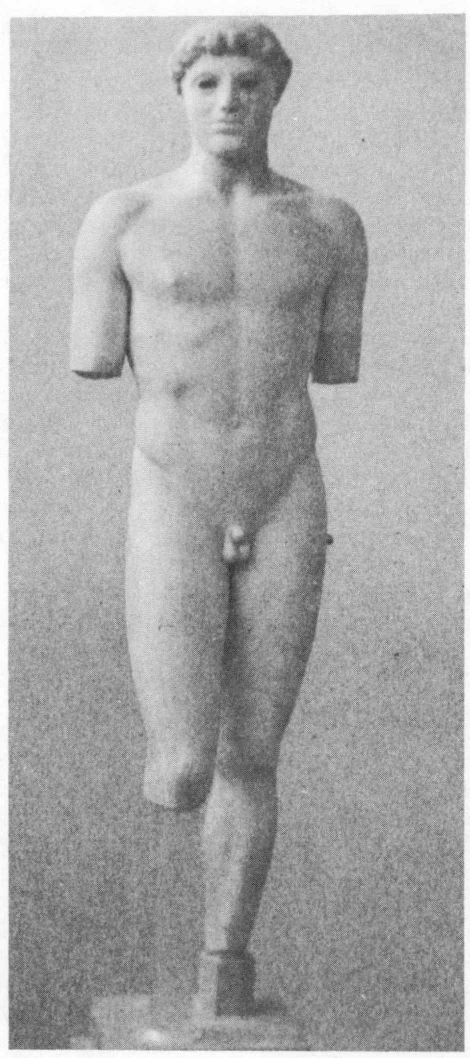

Figure 17. "Kritios Boy," c. 490-480 B.C. Acropolis Museum, Athens (Robert C. Lamm).

was produced no more than a hundred years before it. This kore, or Hera, is like a majestic column come to life and her clothing is draped in a smooth, continuous flow of delicately cut lines. Moreover, the clothing again reveals rather than conceals the body.

By the end of the archaic period there was a beginning of the dissolution of frontality and bisymmetrical construction which had characterized ancient sculpture for milleniums. The "Kritios Boy" (Fig. 17) shows not only a softening of muscular contours, but a stance which is less rigid and an anatomy which is well-understood. The vertebral column assumes the S-shaped curve and a slight turn is given to the head and the upper part of the body. Although the shoulders are presented frontally, the legs, especially the flanks, are no longer rendered symmetrically: the flank of the advanced leg is placed forward and lower than the receding one, which now takes on the weight of the body, as it would in physical reality. In effect, the Kritios statue and others of the same period indicate that Greek sculptors had attained almost complete knowledge of the complicated structure of the male human body. The late archaic "Kore" (Fig. 18) from the Acropolis Museum is a much more complicated figure than the previously illustrated maidens. This kore is noted for the superb rendering of heavy folds of the mantle and the crinkly folds of the chiton which move in diverse directions in effective contrasts. The gentle stylization of the hair is more elegant than the bold, direct stylization of the "Kore from Auxerre"; the drapery is more dynamic and varied in movement than in the "Hera of Samos." The figures from the late archaic period show mastery of two subject matters and two modes of expression. That this mastery was achieved in less than two centuries is astounding in itself; that this mastery would allow the sculptors of the next generation to combine representational and formal qualities in unique works is of greatest historical and aesthetic importance.

Figure 18. Archaic "Kore," c. 530-515 B.C. Acropolis Museum, Athens.

The six statues used to illustrate the development of three-dimensional sculpture of the archaic period could be replaced by many others of equally high quality and equal effectiveness for indicating the developments pursued. Moreover, hundreds of other pieces could have been used to illustrate the minute but relentless changes from one decade to the next. If all the kouros statues were placed in a row in the order of their manufacture and all the kore figures were placed parallel in a similarly organized row, the viewer would see a slow, ceaseless, and momentous change while walking between the marble monuments. The first figures would be very static, stiff, even crude; the last figures would be much more representational, dynamic, and animated. Moreover, the viewer would see color, for originally these sculptures were painted to increase the decorative and life-enhancing quality of the works. The beauty and wonder of much of art, especially Greek sculpture, depends not only upon our perceptual awareness but upon our ability to recreate them mentally.

In addition to the depiction of the kouros and the kore, the Greeks of the archaic period developed freestanding representations of the seated figure, the flying or running figure, the half-kneeling figure, and all of the above in relief representations. Relief sculpture is sculpture which is not freestanding but which is worked (cast or carved) so that it projects from a surface of which it is a part. It would be impractical to show the development of each of these modes, but it is imperative to know that no matter what the subject or the mode, the end of the period saw it developed to a high degree of naturalization and/or sophisticated stylization. One more example of archaic work is illustrated in the relief, a "Helmeted Runner" (Fig. 19) from about 500 B.C. Note that the figure still

Figure 19. Relief of "Helmeted Runner," c. 510-500 B.C. National Archeological Museum, Athens.

carries on the conventions first illustrated in the Egyptian panel of Hesire (Fig. 5) from about 2650 B.C. Although the figure is running and there is a scientific attempt at foreshortening by placing the abdominal muscle obliquely, the helmeted runner is depicted with face and legs in profile and torso and shoulders in frontality. Old conventions die hard in art and appear from time to time to indicate the awesome pressures and authority of tradition, even in an age noted for scientific advancement. It is confusing and provoking to recognize again that all art, by its very nature, implies convention and that all styles, all modes of expression, are conventions.

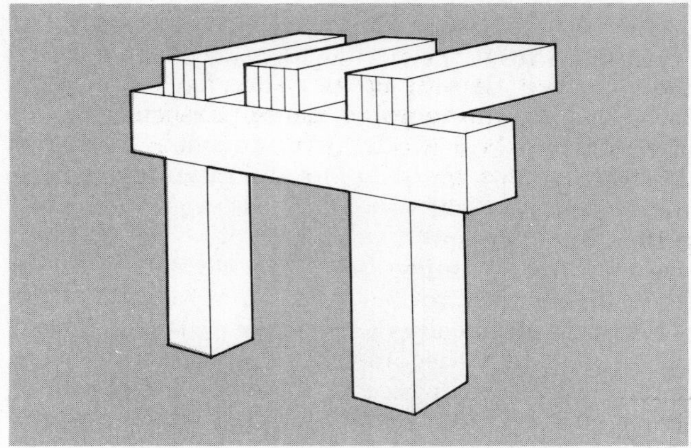

Figure 20. Post and lintel system.

Archaic Architecture

It is relatively easy to enjoy pottery without considering practical use; to admire a sculpture or painting without being overly concerned about the political, religious, or social message conveyed; to experience an object aesthetically without being concerned to any great degree with its utilitarian function. Architecture, of course, functions in an easily understood utilitarian way. Nevertheless, the "art" of architecture is not an art of utility—that is the role of engineering. Architecture is an art in that it provides a spatial presentation of solid and/or enclosed forms and has as its chief consideration aesthetic pleasure. In the strictest and most common sense of the word, architecture is not an imitative art, but it can be considered a representational art in that it represents a conventional object, and by extension a world of man's own creation. Visual representation of a concept which has no perceptual equivalent in nature, of course, anticipates Platonic philosophy.

To visualize a Greek temple is a simple task for most people; the basic image is of a low, one-story, rectangular building with alternating columns and spaces on all sides. Indeed, this is an adequate description of the basic structure, which is one of the simplest building forms ever devised and brought to high refinement. The amazing thing is that the canonical Greek temple had evolved by the seventh century, that is, within the archaic period, and that all temples from ancient Greece, including the Parthenon (PAR-the-non) of the fifth century B.C. and the Athenian Temple of Olympian Zeus of the first century B.C., are only refinements of the archaic architectural achievement.

To understand the Greek temple, it is imperative that the basic architectural system of post and lintel (Fig. 20) be explained. At each of four corners of the space to be enclosed, the builder puts posts into the ground and then places a beam called a lintel on top and across the posts. Roof beams called joists are then placed at regular intervals joining the opposite lintels, and these are covered to make a roof. The spaces between the posts are filled with walls, windows, and doors. This post and lintel system was first used in wood, then brick and eventually in stone construction. Almost all Greek building constructions, definitely all major buildings, were based on the post and lintel system.

A typical temple plan (Fig. 21) shows a *cella* (CELL-ah) or *naos* (NAY-as)—a central room where the statue of the deity was placed—provided with a columned porch; when, as usual, the porch was located at the front, it was called a *pronaos*; if there were a porch at the back also, it was called an *opisthodomos* (op-is-tho-DOME-os) and often served as a treasury. The larger and more important temples had rows of columns in front, in back, and even all around the cella and porch areas to form a *peristylon* (PAIR-is-stile-on) or colonnade. Since the Greeks did not worship as a congregation, the colonnade served as a shelter where worshippers could gather and walk about while somewhat protected from the elements.

Figure 21. Typical Greek temple floor plan.

This plan seems very simple, but a diagram of

a facade (fa-SOD; Fig. 22) indicates that a progression from the simple post and lintel system had occurred. A sloping or saddleback roof was developed for the temple because Greece is an area of much rain in winter and thus a flat roof is not satisfactory on a large building. This roof was covered with terra-cotta or marble tiles, equipped with gutters and rain spouts, and adorned with decorative sculpture. The triangular space at each end of the building thus roofed is called a *pediment*; the pediment wall is called a *tympanum* (TIM-pa-num) and was usually decorated with large-scale, high-relief, or freestanding sculpture. When the roof and the pediment areas were enlarged and thus made heavier, the exterior columns not only had to be increased in number but mathematically spaced to support the upper structure evenly.

Again refer to the façade plan to become familiar with the fundamental Greek temple structure and basic architectural terminology. Upon a stone foundation called a *stereobate*, a foundation surface area called a *stylobate* was formed. From this complex block foundation rose columns (shafts with capitals) which supported the lintel, now called an *architrave*. The ends of the roof joists appeared over the lintel and are called

Figure 22. Typical Greek temple façade.

triglyphs (TRI-gliffs), a term derived from the vertical groovings which were a decorative adaptation in stone of the natural pattern of wood joist ends. The spaces between these triglyphs were filled with plain or painted or relief rectangles called *metopes* (MET-o-pays). Over the metope-triglyph band was the triangular pediment which included a series of cornices and gutter tiles that prevented rainwater from falling upon pedestrians in the colonnade. They also served as decorative features strongly defining the upper portion of the building.

Even these simplified diagrams make it apparent that the various parts of the temple were interrelated to each other and to the whole in height, width, and depth. The interest of the Greeks in arithmetic and especially geometry is well known—the Greek temple is based on arithmetic and geometric systems of proportion. That these systems were a primary factor in the resulting beauty of the temple is obvious in viewing the existing temples, incomplete though they may be. Also, it is evident from the diagrams and the extant buildings, that the temple was a structure which defined space, not enclosed it. The interiors were relatively insignificant, but the exteriors presented a reposed, ordered, sculpturesque pattern sharply defined against the sky. The play of vertical columns and space, solids and voids, in opposition to the dominant horizontal shapes and lines, was balanced, rhythmic, harmonious. Like archaic statues, the Greek temples were essentially solid, patterned shapes meant to be viewed in four cardinal profiles. The temples were seemingly simple, direct, and though awe-inspiring, always implied human service and human understanding.

Although the relationship of the secondary forms to the totality of the building and the silhouette or space-defining quality of the Greek temple would be sufficient cause for great aesthetic appreciation, the refinements of the three orders of columns (Fig. 23) determined the general mode im-

Figure 23. Greek orders of columns: (a) Doric; (b) Ionic; (c) Corinthian.

posed upon the basic plan and gave these buildings their ultimate distinction. The Doric order is the simplest, heaviest, most restful of the classic Greek orders. The Doric column (shaft and capital) was placed directly upon the stylobate. Its shaft in length was approximately seven times its diameter, fluted, tapered toward the top; its capital consisted of an *echinus* (eh-KI-nus) or curved block under an *abacus* (AB-a-cuss) or square block which joined the architrave. Over the architrave was the Doric frieze, which consisted of the alternating triglyphs and metopes. The overall effect is massive, sometimes even ponderous, but each segment, be it shaft, capital, architrave, or metope and triglyph area, is sharply defined.

The Ionic order, in contrast, is graceful, lighter, and highly refined. The shaft of the Ionic column in length is approximately eleven times the diameter of the column, has a base in several tiers making a gentle transition from the stylobate to the shaft, softer flutes separated by a narrow band, and a capital with a pair of volutes or scrolls replacing the echinus and a small but highly-decorated abacus. The Ionic architrave is usually subdivided into three projecting bands, and the Doric metopes and triglyphs are usually replaced by a continuous sculptural frieze in the Ionic order.

The Corinthian order is a variant of the Ionic, but much more decorative, even opulent. Its column is slenderer and taller than the Ionic column and its capital is basically an inverted bell shape surrounded by rows of acanthus leaves, a rather marvelous and fantastic transition from the circular shaft to the rectangular architrave. The nature of the orders determined the entire expressive quality or mode of the temple, although its basic form was unique. One form and three modes of expression might seem a very limited architectural achievement, but the attainment of perfection or near-perfection is slow, tedious, and seldom achieved by *any* culture. For perfection of proportion and clarity of outline, subtlety of refinement, and visual appearance of solids and spaces in equilibrium, the Greek temple has never been excelled.

CLASSICISM: THE GREEK CONTRIBUTION TO ARCHITECTURE

Most of the ancient cities of Greece developed around an *acra* or fortified hilltop. As each city grew powerful and prosperous this people's hill or *acropolis* (ah-CROP-o-lis) became the center of religious and civic activity and was adorned with palaces for the rulers, governmental buildings, and temples dedicated to the proprietory god or gods of the city. The acropolis of Athens (Fig. 24), according to legend, had been the site where Poseidon and Athena contested for authority over the city; it was also the military citadel and burial place of the fabled hero-king Erechtheus, and the military citadel sacked and burned by the armies of Xerxes in 480 B.C. Shortly after the Athenian disaster, the Persian fleet was defeated at Salamis and Athens founded the Delian League and assumed hegemony over most of the Greek states. Although the Athenian Empire fell to Sparta in 404 B.C. and most of Greece was conquered by the Romans by 146 B.C., Athens remained the cultural center of Greece from the defeat of the Persians well into the early Middle Ages.

Figure 24. View of the acropolis at Athens (Robert C. Lamm).

The fifth century B.C. saw the Golden Age of Athens, that brief span of time in which, under the leadership of Pericles, the Athenians launched and fulfilled a building and art program surpassing anything the Western world had ever seen. In 450 B.C., the sculptor-architect Phidias was appointed overseer of all works on the Athenian acropolis and by 490 the Parthenon, Erechtheum, and Temple of Athena Nike had been built. For half a century the small rocky plateau (about 1,000′ long and 445′ wide) was a center of creative activity for the greatest painters, sculptors, and architects of the time. The ample funds of the Delian Treasury, entrusted to Athens for military preparedness, were lavished on the Athenian building program supposedly dedicated to the goddess Athena, but in reality dedicated to proclaiming the power, glory, and leadership of Athens in philosophy, politics, art and in the humanistic way of life.

The Parthenon (Fig. 25) was built under the direction of Ictinus (ick-TIE-nus) and Callicrates (cal-IK-cra-tease) between 447 and 432; its sculptural reliefs and the massive gold and ivory statue which it housed were created by Phidias and his assistants. Although the Parthenon was the largest temple ever built on the Greek mainland, and its refinements were so subtle that the building symbolized the Periclean ideal of "beauty in

Figure 25. Ictinus and Callicrates, Parthenon (view from the west), 447-432 B.C. (Robert C. Lamm).

simplicity," in basic plan it was still the archaic temple of the sixth century. Its architects invented nothing new; they merely saw more clearly how refined the temple form could be. Despite its great dimensions (228′ by 101′ with columns 34′ high), this building was still a simple rectangular box surmounted by a triangular prism and surrounded by columns. It was a building in which the Doric order reached perfection, and geometry was used in accordance with nature. That geometric and arithmetric proportions were used in the Parthenon is apparent when viewing the building or even its floor plan which is very simplified in Fig. 26. What might astonish the viewer is the fact that there are very few straight lines or true right angles in the building. The architects used slight deviations from mathematical regularity and symmetry for the purpose of optical corrections and to animate the rigid mathematical correctness of the standard norm. The secret of beauty which seems to govern natural forms was applied to this great temple—geometrical accuracy tempered by minute deviations.

Thus the cella walls lean slightly inwards, and the entablature leans outwards; the stylobate rises to 4 1/4″ at the center of the 228′ sides and to 2 3/4″ at the center of the 101′ short sides; all columns lean inward about 2 1/2″ except the corner columns, which lean diagonally, so much so that they would meet about a mile up in the sky if they were projected into the air; the cornice, frieze, and architrave are slightly higher at their center than their ends. The enlarged schematic drawing of some of these refinements (Fig. 27) seems strange indeed, but it accurately reflects these subtleties.

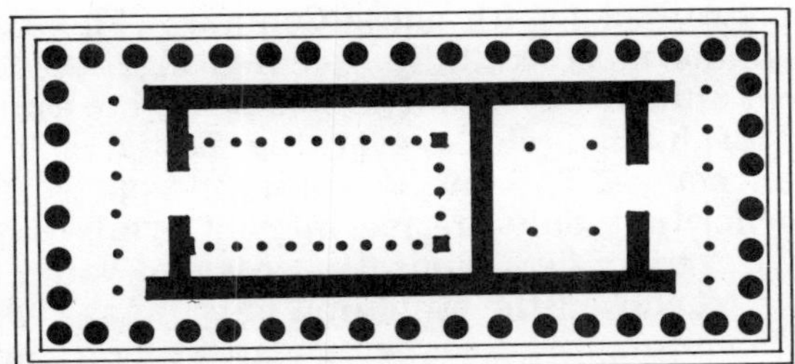

Figure 26. Simplified floor plan of Parthenon.

Figure 27. Schematic drawing of Parthenon refinements.

Let us proceed with this study of refinements. Each corner column is greater in diameter and over two feet closer to its neighbor than the rest. It is believed that these deviations or optical corrections were organized so that the corner columns, which are seen most directly against the sky, would seem thinner and farther apart. Practically all Doric buildings show some signs of "correction," for the Doric column of Greek antiquity always had a slight outward curvature called the *entasis* (EN-ta-sis). This entasis looks like a bulge a third of the way up the column in the early Doric temples, but in the Parthenon columns this curvature deviates from the straight line by only 11/16″ in the 34′ columns. Even the fluting of the Doric column had long before been established as a convention, not just of beauty, but for reasons of optical correction. Without fluting, from a distance, a column would appear to be flat and without sufficient solidity and rigidity to perform its support function.

In addition to these architectural refinements, whether they were for the purpose of optical correction or to animate the basic geometry and arithmetic of the building, the Parthenon was adorned with some of the most beautiful marble carvings of antiquity. A reconstruction of the east pediment (Fig. 28) illustrates the story of the miraculous birth of Athena who has just emerged from the head of Zeus to break the Olympian calm. All the

Figure 28. Reconstruction of east pediment of Parthenon (central section). Acropolis Museum, Athens.

gods at the center are astir, but Dionysus (Fig. 29) is just awakening at the left corner as the sun god drives his chariot into the scene and, at the opposite end, three goddesses (Fig. 30) are about to hear the good tidings as the moon goddess begins her nightly travels. Dionysus and the goddesses are freestanding, over life-size, carved in broad, clear planes and sharply delineated lines. Whether they were carved by Phidias or his assistants is of little concern, for these are masterpieces of monumentalized human form, graceful despite their amplitude, and animated—in the case of the goddesses by garments that reveal as well as decorate the bodies. A Parthenon metope depicting the "Combat between a Lapith and a Centaur" (Fig. 31) is one of the most skillfully executed high reliefs in ancient art and was meant to symbolize the ascendancy of human ideals over the bestial side of human nature. This and the other metopes of the Parthenon not only are magnificent symbols, but lively legendary depictions that provide a variety of figures to enliven the structural unity of the building. Their play of lines with emphasis on curves and diagonals contrasts effectively with the alternating verticles of the triglyphs and the horizontals

Figure 29. "Dionysus," from east pediment of Parthenon, c. 438-432 B.C. British Museum, London (courtesy, Trustees of the British Museum.

Figure 30. "Three Goddesses," from east pediment of Parthenon, c. 438-432 B.C. British Museum, London (Hirmer Fotoarchiv München).

Figure 31. "Lapith and Centaur," metope from the Parthenon, c. 447-443 B.C. British Museum, London (courtesy, Trustees of the British Museum).

of the architrave and cornice immediately above and below them. The inner frieze, about 3 3/4′ in height and over 500′ in length, ran along the outer walls of the cella. This marble bas-relief[1] depicted the Athenians and gods participating in the Greater Panathenaea celebration that took place in Athens every four years. This contemporary scene portrays a procession carrying a *peplos* (a large scarf worn draped about the body and woven for this ceremonial occasion) to the statue of Athena in the Parthenon. The horsemen (Fig. 32) ready their mounts to escort the young maidens and in the heavens the gods (Fig. 33) look on approvingly. Although the scene depicted has over 600 people in its 500′, it presents us with but one day's activity: this is "simultaneous narration" in which each character appears but once, doing one thing, and all activity occurs within a very short period of time. Thus the classic unities of Greek drama are also practiced in sculpture.

Figure 32. "Horsemen," from the west frieze of the Parthenon, c. 440 B.C. British Museum, London (courtesy, Trustees of the British Museum).

Figure 33. "Deities," from the frieze of the Parthenon, c. 440 B.C. Acropolis Museum, Athens.

It is unfortunate that the monumental gold and ivory statue of Athena by Phidias has disappeared. It must have made a fitting focus and climax to the architectural and sculptural edifice that proclaimed her power. The Parthenon symbolized the triumph of Greek culture over barbarians. It glorified Athena, the city of Athens, the Athenians, and the Athenian way of life.

The Erechtheum (er-eck-THEE-um; Fig. 34) built by Mnesecles (ne-SEE-clease) from about 421

1. The degree of projection of the sculpture from the surface is described as high or alto, medium or mezzo, low or bas. High relief is almost detached from the surface and low relief is only slightly raised.

Figure 34. Mnesecles, the Erechtheum (view from east), 421-409 B.C. (Robert C. Lamm).

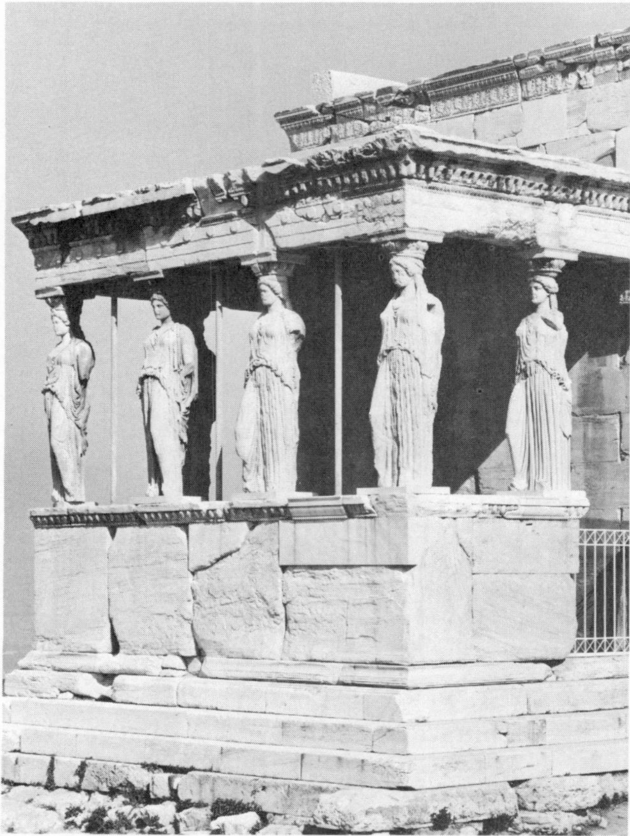

Figure 35. "Porch of the Maidens," Erechtheum (Hirmer Fotoarchiv München).

to 409, is a more complex building than the Parthenon and in many ways more elegant. Because it housed a number of deities, was the supposed site of the grave of Erechtheus, and was the shrine of a very old statue of Athena that supposedly fell from the heavens in ancient times, the architect had to design a temple with four rooms on two levels for the various cults. Three porticoes, each of different dimension and design, project from three sides of this graceful Ionic building. The view from the southeast had a row of six delicate Ionic columns that contrasted with the heavy, sturdy columns of the Parthenon a few yards away. It is the south porch (Fig. 35) however, with its six caryatids (karry-AT-ids) which is most acclaimed and well-known. This porch. only 10′ x 15′ has an architrave supported by young maidens whose drapery suggests the fluting of columns. They are grouped as if in procession, with three figures on one side slightly bending their right legs and those on the other side their left legs to give the appearance of life and animation. All columns suggest physical strain and, despite the individual beauty of these caryatid figures, substituting a representational, human form for a completely geometric form causes an undue strain on our imaginations and our kinetic empathy. Fortunately, architecture has been very sparing in the use of the caryatid or its male equivalent, the atlantes. As few sculptors have been able to achieve figures at once as powerful and graceful as those of the south porch of the Erechtheum, these caryatids remain supreme examples of this type of architectural sculpture.

Another Ionic temple on the Athenean acropolis, the Temple of Athena Nike (Figs. 36-37) was created by Callicrates in the period about 427-423 B.C. It is a small building, only 17′ 9″ x 26′ 10″, of Pentelic marble, but it is an exquisite example

Figure 36. Temple of Athena Nike (Hirmer Fotoarchiv München).

Figure 37. Temple of Athena Nike (Photo Courtesy Bohr).

Figure 38. Temple of Olympian Zeus, Athens, c. 174 B.C.-A.D. 174 (Hirmer Fotoarchiv München).

of architectural unity. Moreover, the contrast of the column and intercolumniation (spaces and solids) against the cella is more easily perceived in this little building than in the Parthenon or Erechtheum—and one of the greatest achievements of Greek architecture is made apparent. All Greek temple architecture, it has been noted previously, shows a lack of interest in space enclosure and indicates instead an emphasis on structural outline and form. What the Temple of Nike proves so well in addition is that the Greek temples were, in reality, sculptural concepts. Each temple complex was designed and built with a series of planear progressions from steps to columns to cella wall; and all the temple reliefs again are planear in organization. The Greek temple is both a large sculptural, geometric form with strong outline, and a four-sided, complex sculptural relief. The huge size of the Parthenon and the complexity of the Erechtheum make the subtlety of this sculptural conception fade or recede, but the Temple of Nike reveals the greatest refinement and one of the most unheralded aspects of Greek architectural genius.

In the fourth century B.C., the Corinthian order developed. The Corinthian is a variant of the Ionic, from which it is distinguished by its taller and slenderer columns and by its ornate capitals decorated with acanthus leaves. This order was little used by the Greeks until the late Hellenistic and Roman Periods, when it reached its full and opulent development. The ruins of the Temple of Olympian Zeus (Fig. 38), dating from about 174 B.C.-A.D., give a satisfactory idea of Greek use of this order while Greek concepts of moderation and harmony still prevailed. The Doric and Ionic orders, however, achieved their most perfect rendition in the temples of the Athenian acropolis, which have been a source of inspiration and life-enhancement for Western man since the fabled Golden Age.

CLASSICAL AND HELLENISTIC SCULPTURE

In the archaic period sculptors had concentrated their efforts on attaining complete knowledge of the male body in all its complicated structure and the ability to represent it as a coordinated totality; and in gaining similar knowledge and ability in representing the drapery, hair, and decorative accessories necessary in their representation of women. Through pursuing proficiency in male and female imagery and, thus, concomitantly in two different modes of expression, Greek sculptors gradually achieved mastery of both goals. This enabled them to combine these modes in the classical age. Classical sculpture, however, can not be considered naturalistic or realistic, if by those terms a photographic likeness is understood. Rather, Greek sculptors of the classical era combined visual perception of human and decorative forms with conceptual images highly abstract in their purity. Thus, the sculpture of this period is highly idealized and marked by a serenity that makes the figures represented seem to be the perfection of humanity, the essence of the form they portray.

Early Classical Sculpture, c. 480-450 B.C.

The sculpture of the early classical period often has been termed "severe," for it still has some of the rigidity of archaic works. Nevertheless, it is sculpture marked by an unequal distribution of weight which affects the whole figure, giving a sense of generalized movement and relaxed asymmetric balance not achieved previously. The "Charioteer of Delphi" (Fig. 39), c. 475 B.C., one of the most famous, large-scale, freestanding sculptures of antiquity, displays both the archaic tree trunk verticality, especially in the rendering of the chiton from the waist downwards, and the sense of bodily movement imparted by the turn of the head and upper torso, varying thicknesses and opposing rhythms of the folds of the upper part of the chiton, and the large curves which are composed by a blending of body turns and drapery folds. Moreover, the arm and hand holding the reins and the naturalistic feet with upturned large toes are graceful, naturalistic renderings. The "Charioteer" is shown in a severely calm attitude and gives no indication of an individual engaged in a grueling competition or of a victor being acclaimed. His face (Fig. 40) shows no emotion, but suggests perfect command of body and mind.

Figure 39. "Charioteer of Delphi," c. 475 B.C., bronze. Delphi Museum (Hirmer Fotoarchiv München).

Figure 40. Detail, "Charioteer of Delphi" (Robert C. Lamm).

The statue of "Poseidon" (Zeus?—Fig. 41), c. 470-450 B.C., is one of the finest Greek bronzes that has survived from antiquity. With daring originality, the sculptor depicted the god with legs and arms widely separated, as if in a majestic stance he prepares to hurl his trident or thunderbolt. The figure is stridently asymmetrical: legs, arms, even

Figure 41. "Poseidon (Zeus?)," c. 470-450 B.C., bronze. National Archeological Museum, Athens.

the head, turn in different manner and angles from the torso which, in turn, shows the various competing muscular strains and tensions. Unlike even the most naturalistic archaic statues, his body is not marked into geometric segments, but has indications of rippling muscles functioning under a taut skin. The gentle concavities and convexities of the surface receive and reflect light in a shimmering manner which further animates the figure. It matters little that if Poseidon's arms were lowered his hands would dangle at his knees, that his eyes are hollow sockets which once were filled with colored stones, that his hair, beard, and eyebrows are highly stylized, very linear. The figure expresses a totality of kinetic energy and an animation of surface which had never been attained previously.

It is important to remember that the "Charioteer" and "Poseidon" are original bronzes—and that they are substantial in size—for the Greeks of the archaic period had never, to our knowledge, attempted bronze works of such size and intricacy. These works are not solid castings such as were done in the archaic period, but hollow castings like those developed in Egypt and introduced to Greece in the seventh century, later to become a common method for large-scale works in the fifth century B.C. Basically, cast sculpture is produced by pouring molten metal into a mold. The most popular metal-casting process, one used extensively today by sculptors, jewelers, and dentists, is the lost wax or *cire-perdu* (SEAR-pair-due) process. In this process a wax model (sometimes with a plastic or clay core) is surrounded by a clay or plaster body, then molten metal is poured into the mold, melting and replacing the wax. Of course, this is a simplified description of a complicated process which has many variations. The system has many inherent difficulties, not the least of which are to develop a mold in which each area of the object to be cast is of similar thickness and to get the molten metal to all areas of the mold at approximately the same time. If the molten metal cools at different speeds because of thickness discrepancies in the mold or because of irregular pouring, the metal will crack or splinter, often beyond repair. That the Greeks were able to achieve outstanding bronze works in the fifth century B.C. shows an amazing technological advance in the arts, an advance to freedom of movement in sculpture that was not attained until much later in stonework. Most of the marble and bronze Greek sculptures that are displayed in museums, it must be emphasized, are Roman copies. In fact, only the "Hermes" of Praxiteles (prax-SIT-ill-ease) is generally conceded to be an original work by one of the great Greek sculptors. The authorship of the original Greek works such as the "Charioteer" and the "Poseidon" has not been determined and, as the Greeks left no written commentary on these pieces, it may be assumed with some justification that they were not considered to be among their most celebrated sculptural achievements. Recognizing that these and other anonymous works were not considered extraordinary, we can only dimly imagine what their "great" works were like—for example, the gigantic statue of Athena Parthenos (Athena the Virgin) which Phidias made of gold, ivory, wood, glass, and precious stones. This statue, which stood in the cella of the Parthenon, was forty-feet high and represented Athena standing, armed with spear, helmet, and shield, and holding a winged statue of Victory in her right hand. Travelers' accounts from the Roman Period tell of countless Greek statues of such size and magnificence.

According to ancient writers, the outstanding sculptors of the early classical period were Kalamis, Pythagoras, and Myron (MY-ron). We must dismiss the first two, because there are no known originals or even copies of their works extant. The "Discobolos" of Myron (Fig. 42), however, has come to us in many Roman copies and is featured in university art buildings and gymnasiums throughout the world in plaster copies. The "Discus Thrower" is shown in the act of throwing a discus, turning his head and body in a twisted yet harmonious pose, a

Figure 42. "Discobolus," Roman copy after Myron (Archives Wm. C. Brown Company Publishers).

Figure 43. "Mourning Athena," c. 470-450 B.C. Acropolis Museum, Athens.

pose which is impossible for the human body to reproduce with accuracy. Notice that the Egyptian convention of frontality is followed: the legs and head are presented in profile, the torso presented frontally. This is not immediately obvious for Myron has replaced the rigid angular forms of Egyptian sculpture with wide curves that animate, unite, and suggest naturalistic movement. One curve starts at the discus, moves through the shoulder, down the left arm and right leg; the other sweeps from the head, through the body and left leg, to rest at the base. Formal and representational qualities are combined to produce an idealized figure which reflects the harmony sought in physical activity.

The gravestone relief of "The Mourning Athena" (Fig. 43) again shows use of the Egyptian conventions, but this time not in a depiction of harmony in action but of a harmonious mental condition. Emotion is depicted here, but it is controlled emotion. The Greeks did not depict mankind photographically. Even in the early classical period mastery of relief and freestanding sculpture was bound by formal conventions, animated by ability to represent the factual, and controlled by desire to unite physical and mental truths in a life-enhancing product. As the classical period progressed, the sculptors would gain more technological know-how, opportunities to depict figures in a greater variety of poses and implied actions, and would replace severity by serenity, but the philosophic goal of harmonic proportion already had been achieved early in the fifth century.

High Classic Sculpture, 450-400 B.C.

The freestanding pedimental sculpture, high-relief metope, and the low-relief frieze of the Parthenon epitomize those sculptural types and modes. The serenity of the figures, naturalistic play of draperies, and masterful depiction of the human body, clothed or nude, make these works the culmination of centuries of artistic and philosophic search. With their completion, Greek sculptors could do no more than copy or find new areas of expression. Three additional works from this period will be presented, not because they are different but because they are of equal greatness and in the mode of the Parthenon sculptures. The "Nike" (as in the NIKE missile) relief (Fig. 44) from the parapet of the Temple of Athena Nike shows the same mastery of drapery, accenting the body rather than hiding it, that distinguishes the goddesses of the Parthenon pediment. It is included in this study of sculpture from the high classic era to indicate that mastery of body-revealing drapery extended from freestanding sculptures to relief sculpture, from large-scale representation to works of more intimate size.

Figure 44. "Nike," from the parapet of the Temple of Nike, c. 410-407 B.C. Acropolis Museum, Athens.

Figure 45. "Stele of Hegeso," c. 400 B.C. National Archeological Museum, Athens.

A sculptured gravestone called the "Stele (STEE-lee) of Hegeso" (Fig. 45) shows a standing serving maid offering her mistress, the deceased who is commemorated, a casket of jewels. The serenity of features is common to Greek sculpture of this era whether the subjects depicted are people in a glorious procession, a meeting of gods, or military activities of lapiths and centaurs. Moreover, note that the heads of the standing servant and her seated mistress are at approximately the same level. This is true, also, of the figures in the Panathenic frieze, whether they be sitting, standing, or riding horses. This isocephalic (I-so-se-FALL-ick) convention, that is, the tradition of keeping all heads on approximately the same level, brings to Greek relief art of the classic period a clarity that is exceptional, as it is so subtly done that the convention is accepted without disturbing one's sense of rightness.

Polycleitos (polly-KLIE-tus) of Argos was one of the most highly acclaimed artists of the Golden Age. Unfortunately none of his original works is extant, but the Roman copy of his "Doryphoros" (dory-FOR-os; Fig. 46), or "Young Man Carrying a Lance," is of sufficiently high quality for us to realize why the original became the model or "canon" for artists of his and the following generation. The young man is broad-shouldered and

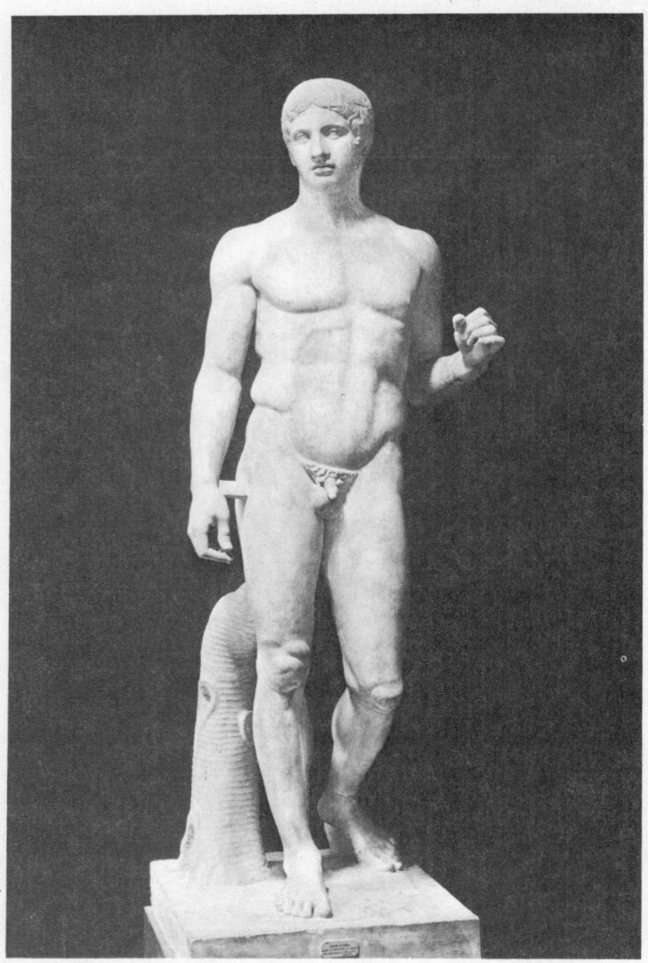

Figure 46. "Doryphorus," Roman copy after Polycleitos. National Museum, Naples (Alinari Art Reference Bureau).

broad-chested, a sturdy athlete. He rests his weight on the forward leg and places the other slightly sideways as well as backwards, thus gracing his body with a double S curve. In one hand he grasps a spear, the other is lowered but slightly separated from his torso. The youth is poised but relaxed. It is possible that Polycleitos wrote a book on proportion called, appropriately, *Canon*, and close observation of the Roman copy has confirmed that Polycleitos must have applied a strict ratio of proportion to all parts of the "Doryphoros." The beauty of proportion, the balance of artistic and natural form, the harmony projected of physical and mental equilibrium, which we find in this and all sculpture of the high classic period, are the elements that comprise its greatness. The sculpture and architecture of this period testify to a triumph of humanism in the history of man.

Late Classical Sculpture, 400-350 B.C.

It is sometimes difficult to distinguish sculpture of the early fourth century B.C. from that of the high classical period. Nevertheless, despite the sameness of serene facial expressions, easy balance of figures, and transparency of drapery, a more personal quality began to prevail. Expressions began to show a dreamy or high emotional quality; poses and skin renderings became more sinuous and sensuous; and drapery and other accoutrements were rendered more naturally. The idealization of the high classical period slowly was replaced by a naturalism which is superbly executed, often very pleasing but which, by its very nature, is seldom profound.

Praxiteles of Athens, Skopas (SKO-pas) of Paros, and Lysippus (lie-SIP-us) of Sikyon dominated the art of the fourth century, although it must be remembered that they were sculptors in an age which developed a plethora of skilled artists in all media who carried Greek artistic technology and ideals to the entire Western world. The Macedonian conquest of Greece under Philip, and then the conquests of Alexander the Great of the Near East, Asia Minor, Persia, and India were high points, not climaxes or beginnings of the spread of Greek ideals. The immediate source, however, of Hellenistic art, was the Hellenic work of the classical age.

The statue of "Hermes with the Infant Dionysus" (Fig. 47), c. 350-330 B.C., is the only large-scale, freestanding sculpture extant from the Greek classical period which has definitely been proved to be the work of a known master, although a few scholars contest even this attribution. Undoubtedly, Praxiteles created a masterpiece in this work, which has a textural surface representing skin that is so delicately modeled that the work is used as a standard by which Roman copies of this and other classical works are judged. "The Aphrodite of Cnidos" (Fig. 48) was the most famous work Praxiteles produced, but is available only in Roman copies. The Roman historian Pliny (XXXVI, 20) stated that it was the finest statue in the whole world. Moreover, he tells us that it was placed in an open shrine, and was visible and could be admired from all four sides. This reference by a Roman of the first century A.D. is valuable, not only for its evaluation of Praxiteles and his work, but also because it gives us an excellent idea of how an educated Roman looked at a work of art. Although the statue was freestanding, it seems likely that neither artist nor his public conceived or chose to see the statue in the round. Greek sculpture, like Greek architecture, was created to be seen from four cardinal points, a convention that bears marked similarity to that followed by Egyptian sculptors. Only very gradually did the sculptor

Figure 47. Praxiteles, "Hermes with the Infant Dionysus," c. 350-330 B.C. Olympia Museum (Hirmer Fotoarchiv München).

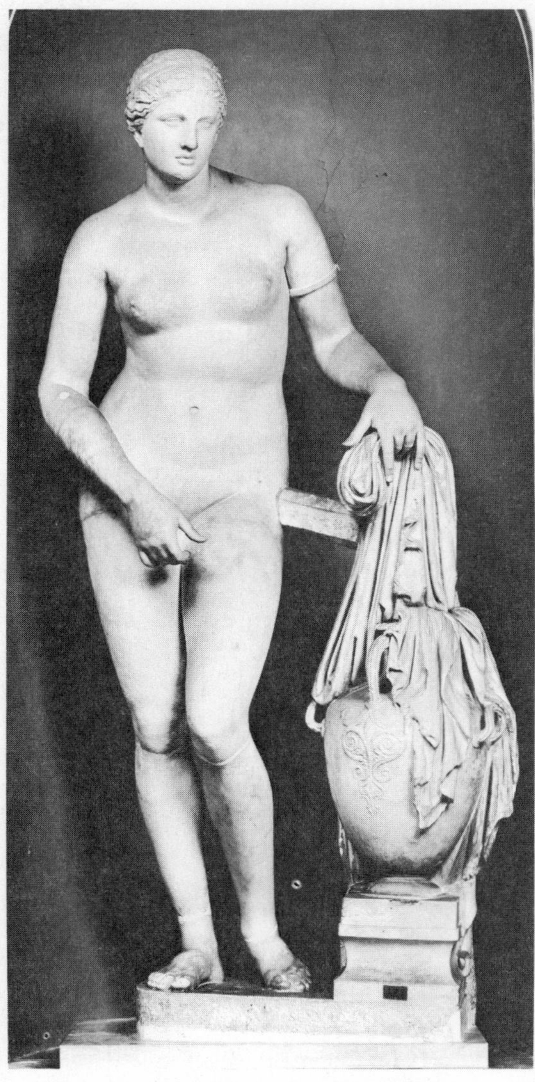

Figure 48. "Aphrodite of Cnidos," Roman copy after Praxitiles. Vatican Museum (Hirmer Fotoarchiv München).

and viewer learn to execute and view works in a 360° movement. Of course, we can view any freestanding sculpture in this way, but if the work was produced in a planear manner, we are demanding more of the work than the sculptor intended.

The bronze sculpture of a "Boy from the Bay of Marathon" (Fig. 49) is probably directly derived from Praxiteles' creations. Because of the inherent strength of bronze, the anonymous artist was able to dispense with the tree trunk and marble support bar which irritate the viewer and break the unity of the Hermes-Dionysus piece. Moreover, the bronze boy stands solidly on one foot, while the toes of the other foot barely touch the ground. Such freedom from base and support is extremely difficult to achieve and almost impossible to reproduce in marble sculpture. Still the poses of "Hermes" and the "Boy" are very similar, as are the modelings of surface and the melting gaze of the eyes.

Skopas, it is known, worked on the Temple of Artemis at Ephesus and the Mausoleum of Halikarnassos, but there are no existing works which can be definitely attributed to him. However, works from those sites have been uncovered which have the attributes of deep-set eyes, furrowed brows, and square head forms—generally very emotional attitudes—for which ancient writers acclaimed Skopas. The "Fight of the Greeks and Amazons" (Fig. 50), a section of high relief from the Mausoleum of Halicarnassus, could have been

Figure 49. "Boy from the Bay of Marathon," c. 340-330 B.C. National Archeological Museum, Athens.

produced by him or influenced by his work. The action is turgid and emotional; isocephalicism is replaced by a naturalistic view, effective as visual truth but lacking the artistic grace of the Parthenon frieze. A new convention has been developed and it must be judged by rules that are implicit in the work itself. One of the great problems and joys of art-viewing is comparing works of equally high quality in different conventions. The conclusion reached in doing so reflects taste or preference, whereas comparison of like works generally is a test of knowledge.

Figure 50. Scopas (?), "Fight of the Greeks and Amazons," from the east frieze of the Mausoleum, Halicarnassus, c. 359-351 B.C. British Museum, London (courtesy, Trustees of the British Museum).

Probably the most revolutionary sculptor of the late classical period was Lysippus, who was active from about 370 to about 300 B.C. His "Apoxyomenos" (apox-e-o-MAY-nos; Fig. 51) is as

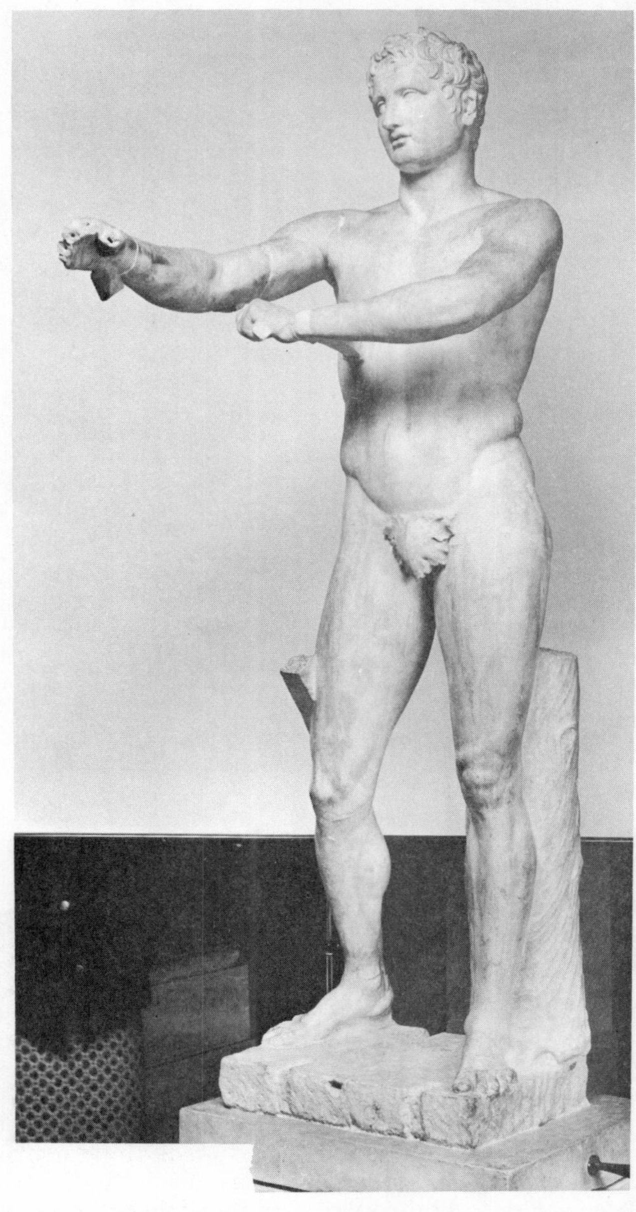

Figure 51. "Apoxyomenos," Roman copy after Lysippus. Vatican Museum (Hirmer Fotoarchiv München).

important for the fourth century as Polycleitos' statue of the "Doryphoros" (Fig. 46) was for the fifth, in that both established or epitomized sculptural canons. Lysippus introduced a new system of proportions in which the head was a smaller unit and the body much slenderer than in the system promulgated by Polycleitos. In addition, Lysippus developed a new sense of movement: trunk, head, and limbs face in different directions—this is sculpture conceived, executed, and meant to be viewed in the round. This revolutionary convention, as epitomized in the "Apoxyomenos," was not to be fully understood or excelled until the Italian Renaissance, 1,700 years later.

A number of original Greek marble and bronze sculptures from the fourth century have been preserved which, although not signed or attributed to any specific artist, are of extremely high quality and assist us in establishing the style of this period. The "Youth from Antikythera" (Fig. 52) is a radiant, commanding bronze that reflects the materialism and delicacy of skin rendition of Praxiteles and the elegance of proportion of Lysippos. In many respects he could be the "Boy from Bay of Marathon" grown to maturity. That the definitive history of Greek art has not and probably will never be written seems certain: both of these fine bronzes were discovered in this century and only in 1970 were parts of Praxiteles' "Aphrodite of Cnidos" discovered in the storerooms of the British Museum.

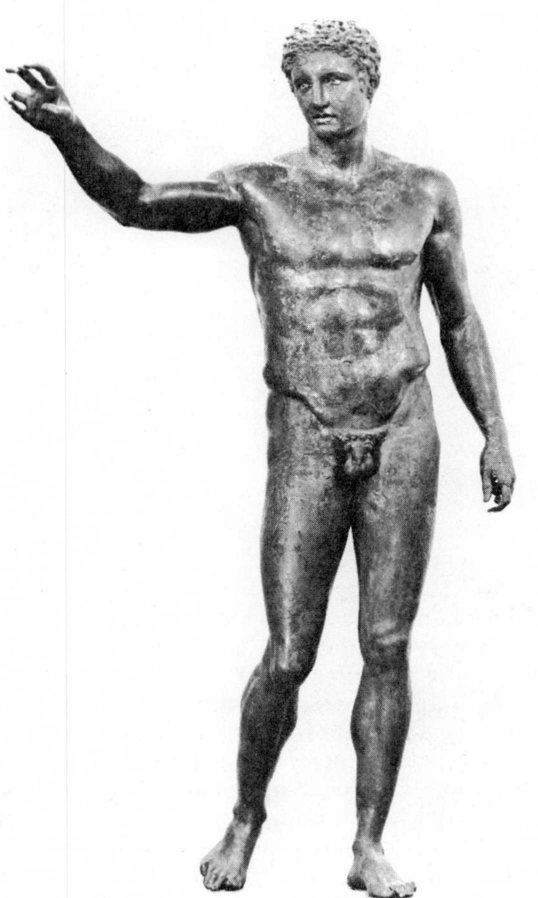

Figure 52. "Youth from Antikythera," c. 350-330 B.C. National Archeological Museum, Athens.

Figure 53. "Apollo Belvedere," Roman copy of a Greek work executed c. 350-320 B.C. (courtesy, Vatican Museums).

As has been stated previously, we know a great deal about Greek sculpture from Roman copies, some of which are excellent in craftsmanship. For centuries the "Apollo Belvedere" (BELL-ve-darey; Fig. 53) was thought to be an original Greek work and was heralded as the most beautiful statue of antiquity. We know now that it is a Roman copy of a work executed between 350-320 B.C. and have reason to suspect the original was a bronze unsupported by the tree trunk and foot wedge. Moreover, the skin treatment has little surface animation and his cloak and general pose is somewhat pretentious, even theatrical. This "Apollo" is one of the prettiest gods or men in the history of art, but while excelling in grace, he lacks depth of personality. By the time he appears in Greek art, the classical concept of harmony of mind and body is an outmoded convention. This is a sign of change. Is it a sign of decadence?

Hellenistic Sculpture, c. 350-30 B.C.

The military conquests of Alexander the Great were insignificant in comparison with the conquest of the Western world by Hellenic culture. Culture, in effect, became internationalized or Hellenized as Greek ideas spread to Alexandria, Rhodes, Pergamum, Rome, even to Gandhara in northwest India. As these ideas traveled, they changed (as they did in Athens, also), and there developed a conspicuous concern with the actual physical appearance and psychological character of the individual. No longer was the artist dominated by the concepts of harmony and idealization; rather, there was an ever-increasing interest in the varied nature of man. Thus, though the artists were very advanced technologically, often they turned to banalities and trivialities, to pathos, and to displays of virtuosity. The art of the Hellenistic Period has often been described as "decadent," and with some justification, for many of its products were crude plagiarism of works from the classical era, and much work produced was not life-enhancing. Nevertheless, Hellenistic artists succeeded in showing a broader view of man and his world than the classical Greeks had ever attempted. Above all, they called lie to the classical assertion of human perfectability.

The "Winged Victory of Samothrace" (SAM-o-thrace; Fig. 54), c. 200 B.C., is one of the most dramatic and compelling sculptures ever executed. The goddess stands erect against the buffeting wind and water which twist her draperies in violent movements. This is a virtuoso performance, no less great or impressive for being that, which marks a conscious aestheticism which was seldom seen in the classical era.

Genre sculpture, that is, works portraying activities from everyday life, were abundant, sometimes charming, more often cloying. Statues of little children at play, frisky cupids, pretty youths dressing or pulling thorns from their feet, and children with cute animals abounded. The "Child with a Goose" (Fig. 55), c. 200 B.C. is typical of these pretty, rococo-like knickknacks and of the taste of relatively large numbers of people, for this type of work was done in thousands of figurines as well as in life-scale sculpture.

Figure 54. "Winged Victory of Samothrace," c. 200 B.C. Louvre, Paris (courtesy Musées Nationaux).

Two statues from Melos dating from about 200-150 B.C. are statuesque, impressive, and world-acclaimed. The "Poseidon of Melos" (Fig. 56) is a very handsome, but rather prettified gentleman. The complexity of directions given to the work by the contrasting arm positions, the extremely heavy folds of drapery held rather insecurely over the lower part of the body, and the emphasis of flesh over muscle, makes the Poseidon seem theatrical in comparison with the strident bronze "Poseidon" (Fig. 41) from the early classical era. Likewise, the famed "Venus de Milo" (more appropriately the "Aphrodite from Melos"; Fig. 57) is a fleshy, albeit very sensuous, counterpart of the three goddesses from the Parthenon pediment (Fig. 30) or even the graceful "Aphrodite

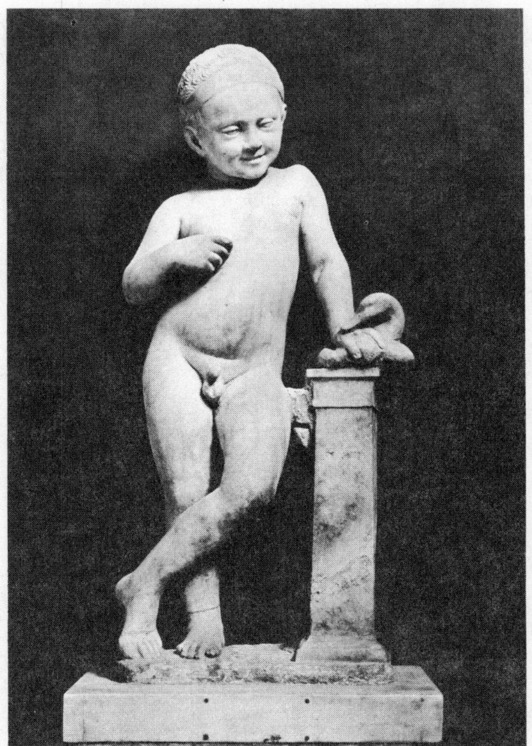

Figure 55. "Child with a Goose," c. 200 B.C. National Archeological Museum, Athens (Robert C. Lamm).

of Cnidos" (Fig. 48). The "Aphrodite of Melos" (Fig. 57) is widely heralded, but the abundant fabric of her gown and its heavy folds draw more attention than her body. Of course, the motif of clothes falling off a figure is awkward at best, but repeated observations of this work leave the impression that the goddess is rising from a laundry pile. If this criticism of the Melian sculptures seems harsh, it is meant to be. It is admitted, however, that for sheer sensuality these statues are conspicuous achievements.

For pathos, the over-life-sized statue of the "Dying Gaul" (Fig. 58), which is a marble copy of a bronze done in Pergamum, c. 240-200 B.C., has seldom been equaled, probably never excelled in sculpture. This depiction of a warrior is not concerned with heroics or with the beauty of the body; rather, the artist depicted a humble captive, defeated, slowly succumbing to an ignoble death. It is a matter-of-fact record without sentimentality; the Gaul in not a heroic symbol; he is a sentient human being. From Pergamum, also came "The Battle of the Gods and Giants" (Fig. 59), a relief segment from the Altar of Pergamum erected about 175 B.C. This is a highly emotional, intensely dramatic work, in which the combatants are contorted in anguish and action. Here we see a world of giants, an exaggeration of physical and emotional force, which will be seen again in Michelangelo's "Last Judgment." What a contrast when

Figure 56. "Poseidon of Melos," c. 200-150 B.C. National Archeological Museum, Athens (Robert C. Lamm).

Figure 57. "Venus de Milo," c. 200-150 B.C. Louvre, Paris (Robert C. Lamm).

compared with the serenity of the Parthenon frieze (Fig. 32-33). Both works, nevertheless, are supreme masterpieces in accomplishing their goals, and our comparison must not be invidious.

In 1506 there was discovered in Rome a huge marble sculptured group "The Laocoön" (lay-OK-o-on; Fig. 60), which we now know was created by Hagesandros (adg-e-SAN-dros), Polydoros (polly-DO-rus), and Athanodoros (a-than-o-DO-rus) of Rhodes about 160-130 B.C. Michelangelo was but one of the many artists and scholars to hail this great discovery, which for centuries was considered to be the epitome of Greek sculpture. Only in recent time have scholars realized that this work was

Figure 58. "Dying Gaul," Roman copy in marble of bronze executed in Pergamum c. 240-200 B.C. Capitoline Museum, Rome (Robert C. Lamm).

Figure 59. "The Battle of the Gods and Giants," relief segment from the Altar of Zeus at Pergamum, c. 180 B.C. State Museums, Berlin (Bruckmann—Art Reference Bureau).

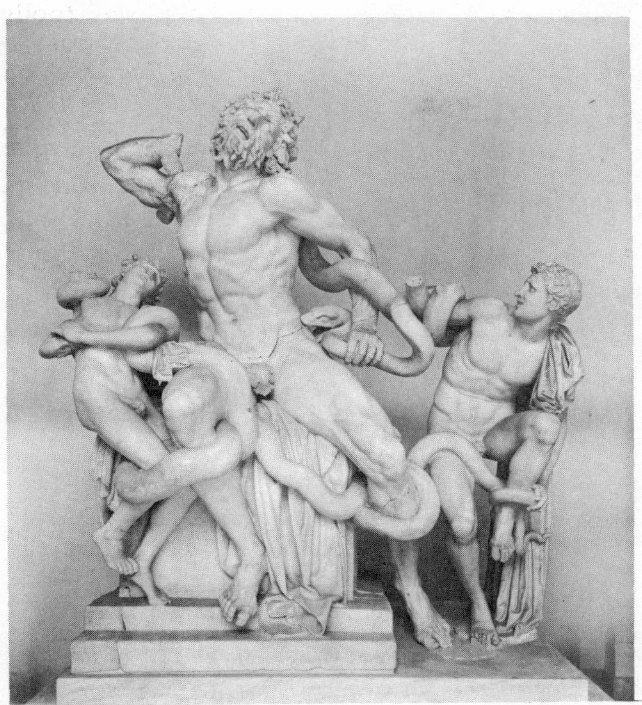

Figure 60. Hagesandros, Polydoros, and Athanadoros of Rodes, "The Laocoön," c. 160-130 B.C. (courtesy Vatican Museum).

a late manifestation of Greek genius, was, in fact, Hellenistic. A comparison of it with the works from the classical era makes it apparent that this was not a work from the serene Golden Age. Nevertheless, the general condemnation the "Laocoön" has received in this century is not warranted. The scene portrayed is the moment when Laocoön, the Trojan priest who had preached against allowing the wooden horse into Troy, has with his sons been beset with serpents sent by the gods to kill them. Laocoön and his sons writhe and struggle, their faces distorted with terror. Despite his highly-developed, muscular body, Laocoön is helpless before the power of the gods. There is a quality akin to baroque art in this work, although even baroque artists seldom were this melodramatic.

The artists of the Hellenistic Period produced works of great variety and displayed magnificent virtuosity. Often the works were slick, imitative, outright plagiarisms, banal, trivial, vulgar, and melodramatic. But, at the same time, these artists depicted the world they knew in telling terms: sensuous, pathetic, emotional, frankly pretty. With an historical and contemporary perspective, it is altogether possible and legitimate to make our own evaluations.

The Greeks of antiquity established the foundation for the development of Western art. Almost all contemporary artistic judgment and achievement requires that their work serve as thesis or antithesis.

Bibliography

Bieber, Margarite. *The Sculpture of the Hellenistic Age.* New York: Columbia University Press, 1961.

Well-written and well-illustrated book recommended for students with solid background in general field of Greek sculpture.

Boardman, John *et al. Greek Art and Architecture.* New York: Harry N. Abrams, Inc., 1967.

A good, general survey, well-illustrated.

Dinsmoor, William B. *The Architecture of Ancient Greece.* London: B.T. Batsford, Ltd., 1950.

Broad coverage and excellent bibliography.

Lullies, Reinhard and Hirmer, Max. *Greek Sculpture.* New York: Henry N. Abrams, Inc., 1960.

Excellent, short essay by Lullies; 282 magnificent photographs by Hirmer; splendid notes on all plates.

Richter, Gisela M.A. *Handbook of Greek Art.* London: Phaidon Press, 1960.

Every book or monograph by Richter is a major achievement and highly recommended. This particular book, well-illustrated and concise, is invaluable to any student of Greek Art.

Richter, Gisela M.A. *The Sculpture and Sculptors of the Greeks.* New Haven: Yale University Press, 1950.

Robertson, Donald S. *Handbook of Greek and Roman Architecture.* New York: Cambridge University Press, 1943.

Short, concise, easy to read, and illuminating. (Available in paperback edition.)

CHAPTER 8

Music in Greek Life and Thought

■ Music has often been called the language of the emotions, and the Greeks were emotional people. Their search for order in an apparently disorderly world parallels their intent to dominate their emotional energy through exercise of the power of reason. Greek rationality was not a cold, dispassionate approach to life and nature; it proceeded from recognition of the "appetites" as a basic part of the dynamic vitality of human existence which, if not controlled, rendered men no better than animals. Greek drama, poetry, music, and the plastic arts are charged with emotion, and experiencing, for example, a Sophoclean drama is a powerful emotional experience. But the Greek arts are much more than strong feelings and dark, turgid drives; they are rationally controlled compositions that are more than the sum of their parts, a recognition in many instances of things, not as they are, but as they should be.

The Greek arts are complex and multifaceted. They can be studied and understood on many different levels from the obvious to the profound. Music was far from the least of these Greek arts and considerable evidence leads us to believe that the Greeks considered music to be *the* most important of their multiple means of expression. Glaucon asked Socrates the question, "After music our youth are to be educated by gymnastics?" The laconic Socratic reply was a terse, "Certainly." The balanced combination of music and gymnastics provides for harmonious adjustment of body and soul: a sound mind in a sound body. Overemphasizing gymnastics makes men "more brutal than they should be." Overstressing music makes men "softer than is good for them."

Music, for the Greeks, implied all of the following:

1. The art of singing and playing music, an art which was enjoyed by all educated men. Public performance, however, was delegated to professionals who were less esteemed than the educated amateurs.

2. "Of the muses," thus encompassing all of the arts presided over by the muses. Misinterpretation of this particular reference has led to the false assumption that "music" as we know it was a minor art.

3. Music for the purpose of education, that is, performing and listening to music as a vital part of the ethical training necessary to inculcate virtue and "sobriety in the soul." This is the "ethos" of music which occupies such a prominent place in Greek philosophy.

4. Study of the scientific basis of music with the necessary emphasis upon acoustics, mathematics, and music theory.

5. Music (acoustics and mathematics) as a key to understanding the harmony of the universe (the Pythagorean "music of the spheres").

Apart from performance, educational and ethical considerations, and acoustical and mathematical principles (items 4 and 5 above) form the basis for most considerations of the fundamental importance of Greek music, not only during the Hellenic period but for many centuries to come. Pythagoras (sixth century B.C.) is traditionally credited with the discovery that the relationship of musical tones (or pitches) depends on the relative lengths of vibrating strings or air columns. Perhaps Pythagoras first noted the different pitches produced by variously sized blacksmith's hammers or the differences in pitch between small and large shields which the blacksmiths were beating into shape, but the acoustical principles involved can be demonstrated by using, as did the Greeks, a vibrating string.

Why all this concern with a vibrating string? Among several possible answers would have to be the Greek fascination with a demonstrable mathematical order in the universe, that is, the constant mathematical relationships between musical pitches (or notes) that are now referred to as the *overtone series*,[1] and all that this natural order implies. The Pythagorean discovery of the overtone series provided Greek thinkers with the indisputable fact that there was indeed, in nature, an immutable and eternal series of mathematical relationships which mankind could neither deny nor avoid. The existence of this mathematical relationship could and did provide some Greek philosophers (Plato in particular) with a reliance on mathematics that would lead eventually to the Platonic theory of immutable and eternal forms. However, Plato's forms were not the only derivative of the overtone series; Pythagoras himself interpreted the series as an indication of a mystical "music of the spheres," that is, the entire universe, as he knew it, functioning in accordance with the ratios of the component parts of the overtone series.

The important point to be made is that the Greeks placed their reliance on mathematics as a solid foundation for their metaphysical speculations as well as for their educational system (cf. Plato's Academy[2]). That their confidence in mathematics was grounded to a great extent on their understanding of the overtone series cannot be disputed, but one would suspect that Plato himself realized that his mathematics (beyond the overtone series) amounted to a tautology in the very fact that the mathematical symbols were man-made. Nevertheless, their knowledge of the overtone series was implicit in Greek speculative thought and a simple, basic understanding both of Greek philosophy and the place of the overtone series in the theory and performance practices of Greek music is, in ancient Greek terminology, a matter of plain "common sense" (necessary and useful).

The overtone series is composed of the tone (or musical pitch) actually heard (the *fundamental*) plus an unvarying series of pitches above the fundamental called *partials*, which pass beyond the range of human hearing.[3] The relative strength of the partials of the overtone series is quite important; for example, the Greek lyre produces very soft partials and thus a very light, clear tone, whereas the Greek aulos produces strong partials and a penetrating, pungent tone quality.[4]

The ramifications of the overtone series are quite complicated and need not concern us. It is important, however, to understand the elementary principles of this natural phenomenon in order to acquire some additional understanding of Greek philosophy, mathematics and music.

To illustrate the principle of the mathematical relationship of musical pitches (the overtone

1. Physicist Joseph Sauvenur (1653-1716) is credited with being the first to prove scientifically that *one* string or air column vibrated in simultaneous multiple segments to produce the fixed sequence of higher and softer tones known as the *overtone series*. The ancient Greeks enthusiastically exploited the mathematical relationships *between* strings (or air columns) but were unaware of the internal relationships of a single string.

2. A knowledge of mathematics was the only requirement for admission to Plato's Academy.

3. The number of partials is theoretically unlimited, but the higher partials are audible only to some animals, for example, a dog. Everyone is familiar with very high-pitched dog whistles which only Fido can hear.

4. A modern equivalent might be a comparison between the tone quality of a harp and that of an oboe. The relative strength of the partials (weak to strong) distinguishes the tone quality of lyre and aulos, harp and oboe. See the reference chart in this chapter, "Greek Musical Instruments."

series), let us assume that we have two strings of equal diameter under equal tension. String *a* (the fundamental tone or pitch) is 60 inches in length, while string *b* is 30 inches in length. String *b* is *half* as long as string *a* and will therefore have twice as many vibrations. If *a* has a *frequency* (vibrations or cycles per second, i.e., cps) of 64, then *b* will have a frequency (cps) of 128. In other words, *b* is to *a* as 128 is to 64 as 2 is to 1 (b/a = 128/64 = 2/1).

If the fundamental pitch is C, then the second partial will be the next highest C and the relationship will look like this:

String	Length	Frequency (cps)	Ratio	Notation
b	30 inches	128	2	c
a	60 inches	64	1	c

Although, as stated above, the overtone series is theoretically unlimited in terms of high-pitched partials, the following portion of the series will illustrate the basic concept:

String	Length	Frequency (cps)	Ratio	Notation
e	10 inches	384	6	g
d	12 inches	320	5	e
c	15 inches	256	4	c
c	20 inches	192	3	g
b	30 inches	128	2	c
a	(fundamental pitch) 60 inches	64	1	c

Pythagorean Tuning

Named after its reputed inventor, Pythagorean tuning has been in existence for nearly 3,000 years, and is still used today. Detailed analysis is not essential for our purposes, but some understanding of the principles of Pythagorean tuning is necessary because these help illuminate some mainstreams of Greek thought, particularly that of Pythagoras, Socrates, Plato and Aristotle. Greek philosophers felt the world could be understood in terms of a fundamental unity. The acoustical research credited to Pythagoras and his successors provided welcome *proof* of the existence of basic unity in the natural world.

A *monochord*, also ascribed to Pythagoras, was the device used to work out the tuning, in conjunction with the necessary mathematical computations. The monochord (Greek *monos*, "one"; *chorde*, "string") consists of a single string stretched lengthwise on a large wooden resonator and fastened securely at each end of the resonating box. Any note could be produced (after plucking the string) by sliding a movable bridge (fret) back and forth under the string, after first determining mathematically where the string was to be divided. The ratios between the various string lengths, as discussed earlier in this chapter, also apply to a single string which can be divided to produce shorter string lengths.

Pythagoras' personal religion developed from a kind of mystical ecstasy, but his theology was based on mathematics and the mathematical proportions of a vibrating string. For Pythagoras, the nature of ultimate reality was revealed in *number*, and the cardinal number was *one*, or *unity*.

The full length of a vibrating string stands for *unity*. The string is then divided by *superparticular ratios*, namely, those ratios in which the antecedent and consequent differ by *unity (one)*. The essential superparticular ratios were 2/1, 3/2 and 4/3, all differing by one and all related to the *oneness* (1/1) of the entire string.

The full length of the string is a unison (1/1) and represents unity, or *perfection*. The superparticular ratios of 2/1, 3/2 and 4/3 all differ by one (unity) and are therefore degrees of perfection. Because they stand nearest to unity, the P8, P5 and P4 are *perfect consonances*. The P8 (2/1) is more perfect than the P5 (3/2), and the P5 more perfect than the P4 (4/3). The unison, however, is the only true perfection and everything is related to it.

To summarize: The perfect consonances are unison, P8, P5 and P4. All other intervals are either imperfect consonances or dissonances.[5]

Reference Chart:
Divisions of a Vibrating String

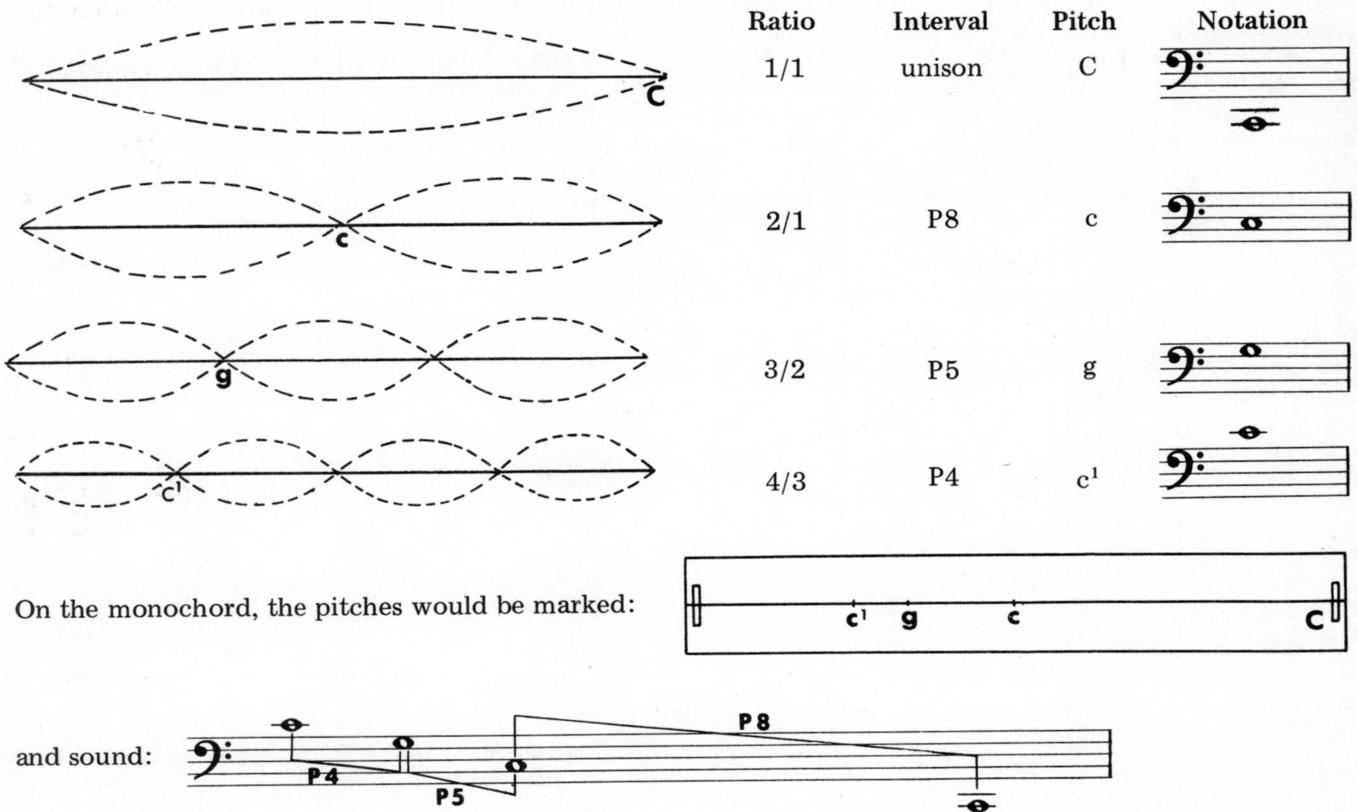

Ratio
Interval
Pitch
Notation
C
1/1
unison
C
c
2/1
P8
c
g
3/2
P5
g
c¹
4/3
P4
c¹
On the monochord, the pitches would be marked:
c¹ g c C
and sound:
P8
P4
P5

The string also divides into five and six parts to produce the 5th and 6th partials of the abbreviated overtone series outlined above.

Applied Tuning

The seven-stringed lyre could be tuned to a variety of pitches, but the diatonic scale on e^1 (e^1-d^1-c^1-b-a-g(f)-e) was standard. The missing note (f) was obtained by *stopping* the string: A finger was placed near the end of the e string to shorten the string and raise the pitch a semitone. All strings were the same length, but with larger diameters for the lower strings (as in modern violin and guitar).

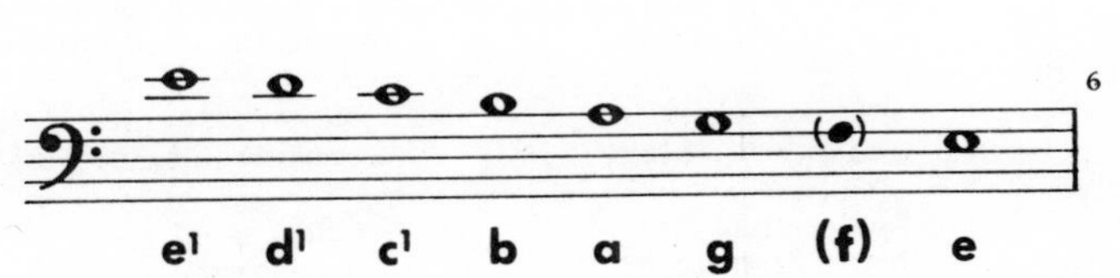

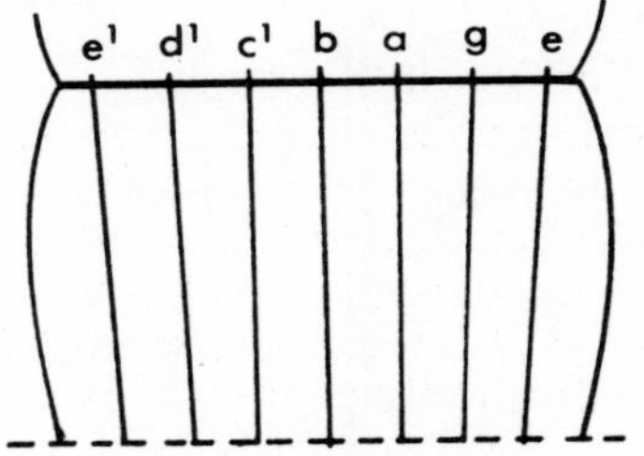

5. Additional superparticular ratios would be 5/4 and 6/5, which will eventually be added to the system as *imperfect consonances.* Larger superparticular ratios (9/8, 10/9, 16/15) and nonsuperparticular ratios (81/64, 256/243, etc.) are *dissonances.*

6. The scale is in descending order (high to low pitch). The Greeks, however, described this as an *ascending* scale because e^1 was the lowest string when the lyre was held in playing position. This literal description of high and low *strings* led to considerable confusion when scholars of the early Christian era attempted to unravel some of the complexities of Greek music.

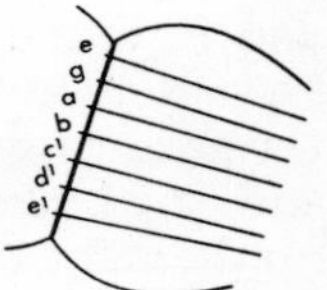

INSTRUMENTS

Lyre, *kithara* and *aulos*, each with its own special function, were the principal instruments of classical Greece. *Lyre* and *kithara* were different-sized plucked string instruments of similar construction which represented Apollo, the god of light, music, poetry, healing and so forth. The *aulos* consisted of two short tubes joined together in a mouthpiece with a double reed; it represented the emotional and expressive aspects of life presided over by Dionysus, god of wine and drama.

Lyre and kithara were dominant in Greek music to the same extent that the ideas they represented tended to dominate Greek thought: a balanced unity of opposing concepts[7] but with mind taking precedence over matter, soul over body, rational over nonrational, intellectual over emotional, classicism over romanticism, idealism over realism. Dorian (Apollonian) instruments and music were to provide ethical instruction and control over Phrygian (Dionysian) instruments and music.

Characteristics and functions of these instruments can be summarized as follows:

Greek Musical Instruments

Instrument	LYRE	KITHARA	AULOS
Basic form			
Tone production	string instrument	string instrument	wind instrument
Played	plucking	plucking	blowing through double reed into twin pipes
Size	small, hand-held	larger than lyre, hand-held	small, hand-held
Number of strings or air columns	usually seven strings	usually eleven strings	two pipes with up to eleven tone holes
Performance by:	amateurs (usually aristocrats)	professional musicians	professionals and amateurs
function	primarily to accompany solo songs	accompany solo and group singing	solo instrument and accompany group singing
location	home, school	social and public gatherings, plays	plays, orgiastic religious ceremonies, elegies
Tone quality	light, delicate, serene	louder than lyre but still delicate	loud, nasal, penetrating
Ethos (ethical quality)	intellectual, Dorian, Apollonian	intellectual, Dorian, Apollonian	emotional, Phrygian, Dionysian

7. Essentially Platonic Dualism: Reality=The Ideas and Phenomena.

GREATER PERFECT SYSTEM

The scale e[1] to e to which the lyre was tuned was the *Dorian octave*, the basic tonal arrangement around which the Greeks built an elaborate structure called the *Greater Perfect System* (GPS), one of the most complete theories of music ever devised. The GPS furnished a logical frame of reference for the music of the period. As such it is still another example of the Greek passion for reducing everything to an ultimate unity; in this case to a single comprehensive explanation for the varieties of musical practice.

The Greater Perfect System was built from a nucleus of the *Dorian tetrachord* (*tetrachordos*, "having four strings") consisting of two tones and a semitone.

Dorian tetrachord

The *Dorian octave* is composed of two Dorian tetrachords joined by a whole tone.

Dorian octave

The Greater Perfect System consists of the Dorian octave plus a tetrachord at each end:

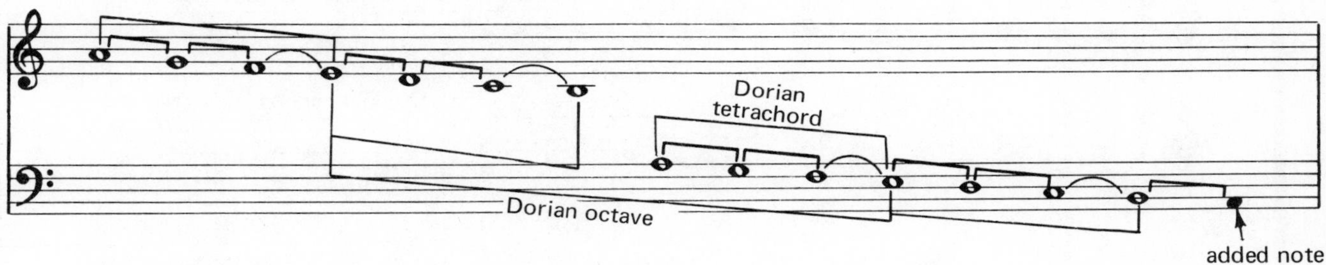

The system included all the diatonic pitches used by lyre, kithara and aulos. The low A (added note) was not part of any portion of the system. Its sole purpose was to round the system off to two complete octaves (a[1] to A), and thus further exemplify Greek preoccupation with balance, order and unity.

GREEK MODES

A composition played on a lyre tuned to the Dorian octave and using the notes of this octave is said to be in the Dorian *mode. Mode* may be defined as the *manner* in which musical tones are arranged in a scale (or ladder) or, to put it another way, mode refers to specific *arrangements* of tones and semitones in a ladder or scale. The four principal Greek modes are: Dorian, Phrygian (FRI-gee-un), Lydian and Mixolydian (mix-o-LID-e-un). (See the reference chart "Greek Modes" at the end of this chapter.)

In addition there are three related modes which are treated as lower versions of the four principal modes and which are named by using the prefix *hypo-* (lower): Hypodorian, Hypophrygian, Hypolydian (*lower* always means low strings of the lyre when held in playing position). These seven modes formed the Greater Perfect System, a system which was "greater" because it explained the manifold varieties of musical practices and "perfect" because it symbolized unity.

ETHOS

Of the four basic modes, the Dorian and Phrygian were probably the most popular and certainly they were the subject of much speculation by philosophers in regard to their moral and ethical implications and thus their subsequent effect upon the audience, and particularly the younger listeners. Dorian melodies supposedly communicated the Apollonian virtues of intellectual elevation and high moral and ethical standards. Phrygian melodies were very popular but were said by some philosophers to appeal to man's baser nature through their sensual allure and thus contribute to the corruption, in particular, of the youth. This is not to say that only Dorian melodies were permitted; as mentioned before, the Greeks were an emotional people whose life-style emphasized the inevitability of the appetites and the necessity for controlling these natural drives.

Of course, in the final analysis the ethical qualities ascribed to the Greek modes, have no basis in fact; nevertheless, the Greeks *believed* in the Apollonian virtues of the Dorian mode and the Dionysian irrationalism of the Phrygian mode. A contemporary analogy might be something like ascribing intellectual respectability and moral elevation to all of the so-called classical music of Bach, Beethoven, et al., while condemning all hard rock and acid rock as a menace to the moral values of our impressionable youth. Of course there is a difference in the *sound* of Beethoven when compared with acid rock, but this need not be a qualitative difference since all music must ultimately be judged upon the merit of a particular composition without special regard to other musical styles. That there *is* a difference in sound between the Greek modes, particularly when compared with the original mode of a familiar piece of music, can be illustrated by the following versions of the first phrase of *America:*

PERFORMANCE OF MUSIC

Greek music was always bound up with drama and dance and was indispensable for the proper presentation of poetry. Accompanying themselves on the lyre, singers presented recitations, rhapsodies, odes, lyric songs and epic poetry of Homer. Trained choruses sang the choral parts of Greek drama accompanied by kithara and aulos. Modern performances of Greek dramas do not include music, a practice almost comparable to operatic presentations without music. The music for *Oedipus the King*, *Agamemnon* and others has been lost, for reasons which will be explained later.

Melody, rhythm, and tone color (but not harmony) were the elements of Greek music. Rhythm was directly related to the rhythm and meter of poetry. The predominant tone color was the delicate string tone of lyre and kithara. The aulos, with its emotional and exciting tone, was used most effectively with songs of mourning and dramatic portions of religious ceremonies.

Melody was by far the most elaborately developed of the three elements. Because the Greeks practiced more than one tuning with seven different modes and used, in addition to the Dorian tetrachord previously illustrated, two other types of tetachords,[8] the same melody could appear in many different forms. For example, a melody could be performed in Dorian mode with Pythagorean tuning and diatonic tetrachords; then the mode could be changed, *or* the tuning, *or* the tetrachord, *or* any two of these, *or* even all three. Theoretically, it was possible to perform one melody in approximately 100,000 different variants. This staggering number of possibilities undoubtedly helps account for Greek fascination with the

8. The Dorian tetrachord could be divided into three different kinds, or *genera:* the diatonic version already discussed plus the *chromatic* and *enharmonic* varieties. All three *genera* were extended throughout the Greater Perfect System.

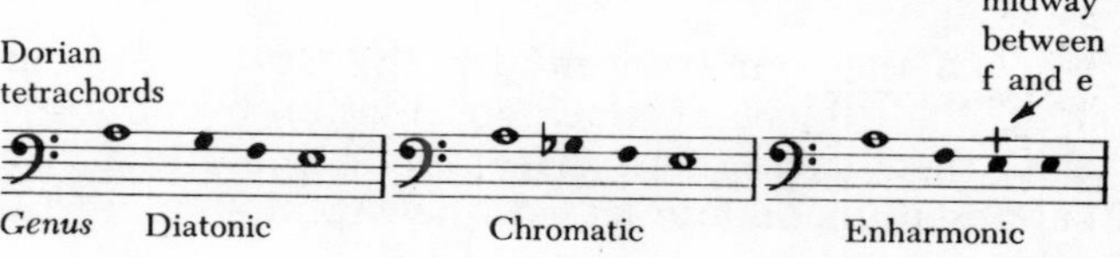

development and exploitation of melody.[9] These manifold melodic possibilities more than made up for the absence of harmony, that fourth element of music which did not begin its development until fourteen or fifteen centuries after the Golden Age.[10]

MUSICAL NOTATION

Almost all the written music of ancient Greece has been lost. Historians have tended to belittle the importance of music in Greek life, contending that a literate society which valued music would have certainly left a musical heritage. They argued, not illogically, that a civilization which leaves behind only five or six complete compositions and a like number of fragments can hardly be interested in that particular art form. To further compound these misconceptions there has been a tendency to minimize the purely musical importance of the essays on music in such literary sources as Euclid, Plato, Aristotle, Aristoxenus, Plutarch, Quintilianus, Nichomachus, Ptolemy, and others.

Music in all its aspects was so important that music theory and music notation reached a high stage of development; in fact, the notation was so well developed that later generations were unable to read it!

Because few Greek works survived in their original forms, posterity has had to rely on surviving copies of these works. When reproducing a Greek drama, for example, a scholar would copy the text but omit the accompanying intricate alphabet which symbolized the music. The Greek musical alphabet died out under Roman rule, and there was not an adequate notational system to take its place. There was no point, for the copyist, in copying a dead musical system and no possibility of transcribing Greek notation into another set of symbols. The net result of this dilemma was the copyists' omission of a musical system which had become incomprehensible, and the loss of Greek music forever.[11]

MUSICAL EXAMPLES

No music has survived from the Periclean Age. From a later period the "First Delphic Hymn" (c. 138 B.C.) is the most extended work known. Like much of Greek music it is in *quintuple* meter (a combination of triple and duple meters). The piece has three major sections, of which a portion of the first section is reproduced below. The example is *diatonic* (Greater Perfect System) and is in the *Phrygian mode*. Other sections of the piece are considerably more elaborate, with chromatic tetrachords and the like. The text setting is *syllabic* (a syllable for each note) except where the note beams (♫) indicate two notes to a syllable.[12]

Time: :30[13]

First Delphic Hymn c. 138 B.C.[14]

Translation of the first two sections of the text is as follows:

> Hark, ye fair-armed daughters of the loud thundering Zeus who dwell in the deep forests of Helicon! Hasten thither, to praise in song your brother Phoebus, of the golden locks, who high above the rocky dwellings of the two-peaked Parnassus, surrounded by the august daughters of Delphi, betakes himself to the waters of limpid Kastalis, visiting at Delphi the prophetic crag.

9. In terms of present-day possibilities a melody could be played on the piano in one tuning (equal temperament) and with possibly a dozen different scales or modes in general use.
10. The twelve tones of a chromatic scale on the piano give little indication of the pitches available for Greek melodies. Within one octave the Greeks could choose from about two dozen pitches, none of which (except the octave) coincided with the piano pitches.
11. Not even surviving manuscripts could tell the whole story because the Greeks are credited with improvising much of their music.
12. This music exists in recorded form but usually in the equal temperament of the piano keyboard, a practice which does no justice whatever to the song as originally performed. Many of the Greek tunings gave an oriental flavor to the music.
13. Performance time will be given for each musical example, in this case, 30 seconds. Since music is the movement of sound in time, the performance time of each illustration is an important factor.
14. T. Reinach. *La Musique Grecque.* 1926, p. 177.

> Lo, the famous Attica, with its great city, which, thanks to the prayer of the arms-bearing Triton, inhabits an unassailable region. On holy altars Hephaestus consumes the thighs of bullocks; together Arabian incense rises toward Olympus. The oboe [aulos] shrilly sounding brings forth music with varied melodies and the golden sweet-voiced kithara sounds with hymns.

The "Song of Seikolos" was found engraved on a tombstone in Asia Minor. It can be transcribed into a modern equivalent of eight measures of music. Probably because the song is an epitaph, the meter is duple, with none of the irregularity so typical of Greek meters. The beams and also the slurs in measures 4 and 6 indicate one syllable to these two-or three-note groups.

Time: :20

Phrygian mode

Seikolos Song (A.D. 1st century)[15]

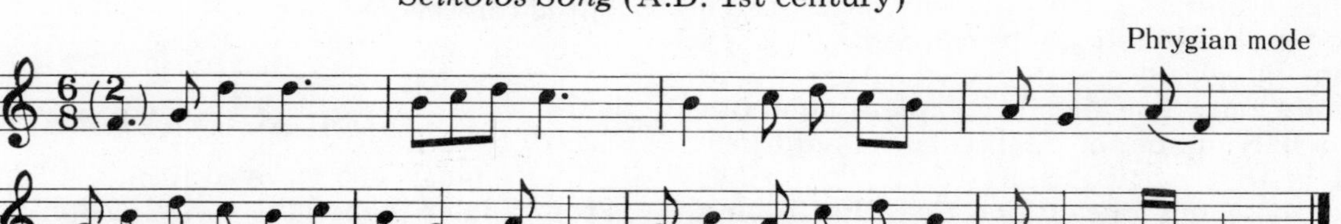

As long as you live, be cheerful; let nothing grieve you. For life is short, and time claims its tribute.

SUMMARY

The Greeks yearned for reassurance that they lived in a rational and orderly universe in which there were certain eternal truths and, most important, an appropriate place for mankind. They based their rather unique realistic idealism quite heavily upon the multifarious approaches to music in terms of education, emotional communication, the ethical life, applied science and metaphysics.

A proper balance of instruction in music and gymnastics provided the educational foundation for the citizens of ancient Greece. The study of music included the arts in general and music in particular, with special reference to its scientific basis (acoustics) and the comprehensive theory and tuning of music built on that basis. Music was also expected to further ethical instruction, which was designed to encourage rational behavior and intellectual control.

Through acoustics, the Greeks determined the mathematical relationships of sounding bodies and built a theory resting on the conception of the unity and perfection of the vibrating string. This eventually led to the metaphysical concept of a unified universe which could be perceived and understood by the rational logic of those philosophers who could go beyond the sensory data of the material world.

Derived from the unison of the vibrating string were the so-called perfect intervals of octave, fifth, and fourth (P8, P5, P4) from which the theory of Greek music was built. From the Dorian tetrachord came the Dorian octave, or actual playing range of the lyre. The Dorian octave was then provided with additional upper and lower tetrachords to establish the Greater Perfect System, a theoretical framework from which the seven modes could be derived. The Greater Perfect System (plus later theories of lyre tuning and a Lesser Perfect System) could then function as the single, unified reference for the vast body of existing music, to provide, in other words, a theoretical unity for the multiplicity of musical practices.

Music performance was allied with drama, dance, and especially poetry. Principal tone colors were the golden sounds of lyre or kithara (the instruments of Apollo) and the dark and pungent tone of the aulos (the instrument of Dionysus). Rhythm was almost entirely dependent on the rhythm and meter of poetry. Melody was developed to a fine art of subtle nuances selected from a vast range of compounded variations in tunings, modes and tetrachords. Harmony as such was unknown, but the melodic element has reigned supreme and unmatched by developments in Western music up to the present day.

The specialized art and craft of music notation achieved a notable degree of clarity and precision, almost all of which was lost during the centuries of copying and recopying Greek manuscripts. The precious little Greek music remaining can do no more than provide a tantalizing glimpse of the richness of Greek musical culture. Modern instruments and tuning (equal temperament) distort beyond all recognition even this hint of past

15. Ibid., p. 193.

achievements. Only performances on lyre, kithara and aulos in the original Greek tunings and in conjunction with poetry and drama can actually bring to life the glory that was Greece in the tonal art known as music.

Greek Modes

Tones and Semitones

Mode	Letter Names	Between Pitches	Notation
Dorian	e^1 to e	T T S T T T S	
Phrygian	d^1 to d	T S T T T S T	
Lydian	c^1 to c	S T T T S T T	
Mixolydian	b to B	T T T S T T S	

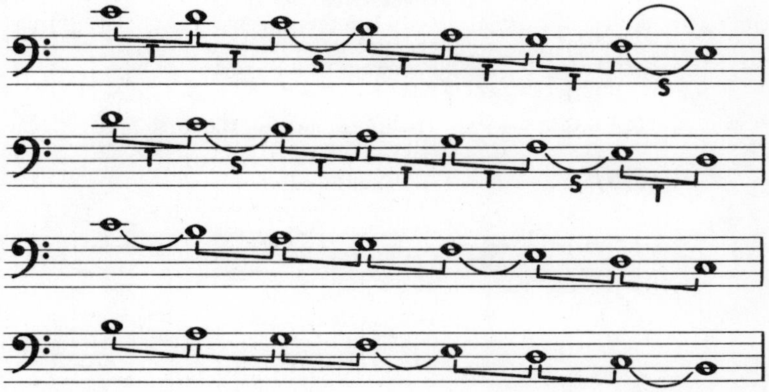

Record List

1. "First Delphic Hymn," *The Theory of Classical Greek Music*, vol. 1, Musurgia Records. *The Theory of Classical Music*, vol. 1 may be obtained through a large wholesale outlet such as those in New York.
2. "Seikolos Song," Ibid. Both (1) and (2) are also available in *History of Music in Sound*, vol. 1, RCA Victor LM-6057.
3. *Folk Music of Greece*, Folkways Album P-454. *Folk Music of Greece* is relatively contemporary but it does provide the listener with some of the character of ancient Greek music, though lyre, kithara, and aulos are not used. It *does* indicate the general flavor of Greek music as it might have been performed during the Hellenic and Hellenistic periods.

Bibliography

Strunk, Oliver. *Source Readings in Music History from Classical Antiquity through the Romantic Era.* New York: W.W. Norton & Company, Inc. 1950. Useful primary material about music excerpted from the writings of Plato, Aristotle, Aristoxenus, and others.

Time Chart for Greek Civilization

Time	Government and Politics	Philosophers-Scientists	Literature & Art
2000 B.C.	Cretan-Minoan culture. About 2600 to 1125 B.C.	Worshippers of earth mother.	Highly sophisticated frescoes. Octopus designs on pots.
1500 B.C.	About 1600 B.C. onward, infiltration of Mycenaean Greeks. Between 1400 and 1125 these people conquered Crete. The heroic age of the Trojan War.	Worshippers of the sky gods—the traditional Greek gods. Spoke a true Greek language.	Gold death masks and other gold ornaments date from this period.
1184 B.C.	Traditional date for the fall of Troy.		
1000 B.C.	Dorian infiltration. Colonization of cities on Ionian coast. "Dark Ages" from about 1050 to 850, merging into Archaic period. Towns ruled by traditions of blood-related clans.		1000 to 700 B.C. Geometric period in Greek art.
900 B.C.	Lycurgus molds Spartan law: two kings: young men in constant military training.		
800 B.C.	Land poverty causes colonization throughout Mediterranean world.		*Iliad* and *Odyssey* of Homer. Hesiod writes *Works and Days* and *Theogony*
700 B.C.	Revision of Spartan Constitution. Ephors rule.		
650-550 B.C.	Draco's Code: Written law. 621 B.C. Solon (638-558). Cancelled all debt; freed debt-slaves, established graduated income tax. Pisistratus (605-527 B.C.). Redistributed land. Homeric poems form Hellenic cultural tradition.	Ionian Philosophers a. Thales (water as world-stuff). b. Anaximander (the Boundless; separating out). c. Anaximenes Pythagoras (580-500 B.C.). Form found in numerical relationships.	660 to 480 B.C. Archaic period in Greek art. Sappho: woman lyric poet. Form of Greek temple fully established. Thespis: original dramatist.
550-500 B.C.	Cleisthenes (c. 507). Abolished blood clans substituting political demes. Assembly of all free Athenians. Senate of 500 members; ten generals administer law.	Heraclitus (535-475 B.C.) "No thing abides." Fire as world-element. Logos or Reason rules change.	
500-450 B.C.	Persian Wars 490-480 B.C. Themistocles (514-449 B.C.) Income from silver mines used for fleet which defeated Persia and made Athens supreme sea power. Delian League founded, later to be transformed into Athenian empire.	The Eleatic Philosophers. a. Parmenides (510-?). b. Zeno (488-?). Nothing changes. Our senses lie to us. Only reason can be trusted. The Mediators: Many elements. Change occurs by combination.	Classical Age (480 B.C.-c. 350) Charioteer of Delphi.

Time Chart for Greek Civilization (Cont.)

Time	Government and Politics	Philosophers-Scientists	Literature & Art
			Pindar (522-448). Odes to victors in Olympic games. Aeschylus (525-456). First tragic dramatist. Celebrated greatness of men and Athens.
450-400 B.C.	Pericles (490-429). Ruled in Athens 443-429. The height of Athenian glory. Rebuilt city after Persian Wars.	Democritus (460?-362?). All things made of atoms which drift through space following no law but necessity. Completely materialistic.	Sophocles (496-406). Second tragic dramatist.
			Euripides (480-406). Third tragic dramatist.
		Socrates (469-399). Teacher of Plato.	Herodotus (484-425). Historian of Persian Wars.
			Parthenon built, 447-438 B.C. Ictinus and Callicrates, architects. Phidias directed or executed sculpture.
			Thucydides (471-400). Historian of Peloponnesian Wars.
	Peloponnesian Wars (431-404).		Myron (480-407). Famed sculptor.
		The Sophists.	Polyclitus (460-412). Famed sculptor.
		Plato (427-347). Reality lies in the idea or essence of things. Virtues of temperance, courage, wisdom, from which comes highest good, justice.	Aristophanes (448-380). Writer of comic drama satirizing life of Athens.
400-350 B.C.		Aristotle (384-322). Collected and wrote down all wisdom of his time. Principle of enteleche or purposivity. All things exist as they are, but move into higher forms. There must be a *summum bonum* or highest good.	Praxiteles (390-330). "Hermes."
			Demosthenes 383-322). Orations to arouse Athenians against Phillip. Hellenistic art.
	Philip, King of Macedon, 359-336 B.C.	Epicureans—Pleasure the highest good.	
350-232 B.C.	Alexander the Great, King of Macedon 336-323 B.C.	Stoics—Virtue the highest good.	Apollo Belvedere.
			Venus of Milo.
	Rome conquers Greece 146 B.C.		Victory of Samothrace.

Literary Selections

Prometheus Bound

Aeschylus

This play is the second of three in which Aeschylus dealt with the problem of the clash between an absolute God who ruled by power, force, and fear, and mankind, which was growing in many skills and in reasoning ability. Obviously the two forces will be in conflict unless an understanding can be reached which will allow proper zones of action for each. Thus he is treating the problem of man's relation to God, one of the questions which we have spoken of as fundamental for human freedom. Aeschylus was trying to interpret for the people of Athens the importance and the meaning of a change from the old Olympian gods to a new idea of divine power.

Before the beginning of this play, Zeus had led a successful revolt against his father and had taken over the task of reigning over heaven and earth. (For the genealogy of the gods, see p. 47.) These are the group of gods referred to in the play as the "new gods in heaven." Kronos and his group were the "old gods." It is to be noticed and emphasized that Prometheus (pro-MEE-th[y]us), a Titan, together with Oceanus (o-SEE-a-nus), another Titan, aided Zeus. The rest of the group fought on the side of Kronos. Prometheus was given the task of creating man, which he did by rolling dust together. However, Prometheus favored man so much that he gave him many gifts. It was for this that Zeus had Prometheus chained to a massive cliff for all eternity. Prometheus, however, knows the secret which reveals the way in which Zeus will be overthrown. If Prometheus would reveal his secret, Zeus might free him from the rock. Thus we see the conflict of the play.

Read this play as a conflict between an absolute god (Zeus) and the champion of men (Prometheus). The play which follows this one and which offered a solution to the problem is lost. When you finish this play, noticing carefully the powers which men have acquired, you might try writing a sketch (or a full play) of the type which Aeschylus might have written.

The translation is a contemporary one by George Thomson.

(Scene. A rocky gorge in Scythia. Power and Force enter, carrying Prometheus as a captive. They are accompanied by Hephaestus.[1])

Power:
To this far region of the earth, this pathless wilderness of Scythia, at last we are come. O Hephaestus, thine is the charge, on thee are laid the Father's commands in never-yielding fetters linked of adamant to bind this miscreant to the high-ridged rocks. For this is he who stole the flame of all-working fire, thy own bright flower, and gave to mortal men. Now for the evil done he pays this forfeit to the gods; so haply he shall learn some patience with the reign of Zeus and put away his love for human kind.

Hephaestus:
O Power and Force, your share in the command of Zeus is done, and for you nothing remains; but I—some part of courage still is wanting to bind with force a kindred god to this winter-bitten gorge. Yet must I summon daring to my heart, such dread dwells in the Father's word.—(to Prometheus) O high magnanimous son of prudent Themis, against thy will and mine with brazen bonds no hand can loose I bind thee to this unvisited lonely rock. No human voice will reach thee here, nor any form of man be seen. Parched by the blazing fires of the sun thy skin shall change its pleasant hue; grateful to thee the starry-kirtled night shall come veiling the day, and grateful again the sun dispelling the morn's white frost. Forever the weariness of unremitting pain shall waste thy strength, for he is not born who can deliver thee. See now the profit of thy human charity: thou, a god not fearing the wrath of the gods, hast given to mortal men honors beyond their due; and therefore on this joyless rock thou must keep vigil, sleepless and weary-clinging, with unbended knees, pouring out thy ceaseless lamentations and unheeded cries; for the mind of Zeus knows no turning, and ever harsh the hand that newly grasps the sway.

Power:
It may be so, yet why seek delay in vainly spent pity? Feel you no hatred for this enemy of the gods, who hath betrayed to mortals your own chief honor?

Hephaestus:
Kinship and old fellowship will have their due.

Power:
'Tis true, but where is strength to disobey the Father's words? Fearest thou not rather this?

Hephaestus:
Ever merciless thou art, and steeped in cruelty.

Power:
It healeth nothing to weep for him. Take not up an idle burden wherein there is no profit.

Hephaestus:
Alas, my cherished craft, thrice hateful now!

Power:
Why hateful? In simple sooth thy art hath no blame for these present ills.

Hephaestus:
Yet would it were another's, not mine!

Power:
All toil alike in sorrow, unless one were lord of heaven; none is truly free, save only Zeus.

Hephaestus:
This task confirms it; I can nothing deny.

Power:
Make haste then to bind him in fetters, lest the Father detect thee loitering.

Hephaestus:
Behold the chain; it is ready to hand.

---

1. hi-FES-tus.

Power:
Strongly with thy hammer, strongly weld it about his hands; make him fast to the rock.

Hephaestus:
The work goes on, it is well done.

Power:
Harder strike them, tighter draw the links, leave nothing loose; strange skill he hath to find a way where none appeared.

Hephaestus:
One arm is fastened, and none may loose it.

Power:
Fetter the other, make it sure; he shall learn how all his cunning is folly before Zeus.

Hephaestus:
Save now my art hath never wrought harm to any.

Power:
Now strongly drive the biting tooth of the diamond-hard wedge straight through his breast.

Hephaestus:
Alas, Prometheus! I groan for thy pangs.

Power:
Dost thou shrink? Wilt thou groan for the foes of Zeus? Take heed, lest thou groan for thyself.

Hephaestus:
Thou lookest upon a spectacle grievous to the eye.

Power:
I look upon one suffering as he deserves.—Now about his sides strain tight the girth.

Hephaestus:
It must needs be done; yet urge me not overmuch.

Power:
Yet will I urge and harry thee on.—Now lower; with force constrain his legs.

Hephaestus:
'Tis even done; nor was the labor long.

Power:
Weld fast the galling fetters; remember that he who appraises is strict to exact.

Hephaestus:
Cruel thy tongue, and like thy cruel face.

Power:
Be thine the tender heart! Rebuke not my bolder mood, nor chide my austerity.

Hephaestus:
Let us go; now the clinging web binds all his limbs.
(Hephaestus departs.)

Power:
There, wanton, in thy insolence! Now for thy creatures of a day filch divine honors. Tell me, will mortal men drain for thee these tortures? Falsely the gods call thee Prometheus, the Contriver, for no cunning contrivance shall help thee to slip from this bondage.
(Power and Force depart.)

Prometheus: *(alone, chanting)*
O air divine, and O swift-winged winds!
Ye river fountains, and thou myriad-twinkling
Laughter of ocean waves! O mother earth!
And thou, O all-discerning orb o' the sun!—
To you, I cry to you; behold what I,
A god, endure of evil from the gods.

Behold, with what dread torments
I through the slow-revolving
Ages of time must wrestle;
Such hideous bonds the new lord
Of heaven hath found for my torture.
Woe! woe! for the present disasters
I groan, and for those that shall come;
Nor know I in what far sky
The dawn of deliverance shall rise.

Yet what is this I say? All future things
I see unerring, nor shall any chance
Of evil overtake me unaware.
The will of Destiny we should endure
Lightly as may be, knowing still how vain
To take up arms against Necessity.
Silent I cannot keep, I cannot tongue
These strange calamities. Lo, I am he
Who, darkly hiding in a fennel reed
Fountains of fire, so secretly purloined
And gave to be the teacher of all arts
And giver of all good to mortal men.
And now this forfeit for my sin I pay,
Thus lodged in fetters under the bare sky.
(The Chorus of the Daughters of Oceanus enter, drawn in a winged car.)

Prometheus:
Ah me! ah me!
O all ye children of Tethys,
Daughters of father Oceanus
Who ever with tide unwearied
Revolveth the whole world round,—
Behold now prisoned in chains
On the dizzy verge of this gorge
Forever I keep sad watch.

Chorus:
I see, O, Prometheus, thy body
In the toils and torture of bondage
Withering here on this rock;
And a mist as of terror, a cloud
Of tears o'erveils my eyes:
New helmsmen guide in the heavens,
And Zeus unlawfully rules
With new laws, and the might of old
He hath banished to uttermost darkness.

Prometheus:
Would that me too he had hurled,
Bound in these cruel, unyielding
Bonds, down, down under earth,
Beneath wide Hades, where go
The tribe of innumerable dead,
Down to the infinite depths
Of Tartarus! There no god,
No mortal would gloat o'er my ruin.
Now like a toy of the winds
I hang, my anguish a joy
To my foes.

Chorus:
Who of the gods is so hardened
To whom is thy sorrow a joy?
Who save only Zeus
But feels the pang of thy torments?

But he, ever savage of soul
Swayeth the children of heaven;
Nor ever will cease till his heart
Is satiate grown, or another
Snatches the empire by guile.

Prometheus:

Ay, and this Lord of the blessed
Shall call in the fulness of time
Upon me whom he tortures in bondage,
Shall implore me to utter the plot
That will rob him of honour and throne.
No sweet-lipped charm of persuasion
Then shall allure me, and never
In cringing fear of his threats
The knowledge will I impart,
Till first he has loosened these bonds,
And for all my anguish he too
Hath humbled his neck unto judgment.

Chorus:

Bold art thou, and calamity
Softens thee not, but ever
Thy thought is quick on thy tongue.
Terror pierceth my heart,
And fearing I ask what shore,
O wanderer tempest-tost,
Far-off of peace shall receive thee!
Stern is the son of Kronos,
And deaf his heart to beseeching.

Prometheus:

I know of his hardness, I know
That justice he holds in his palm;
Yet his pride shall be humbled, I think;
His hardness made soft, and his wrath
Shall bow to the blows of adversity;
He, too, in milder mood
Shall come, imploring of me
The friendship I willingly grant.

Leader of the Chorus:

Unfold to us the whole story. For what crime does Zeus so shamefully and bitterly torture you? Tell us, if there is no harm in telling.

Prometheus:

Painful are these things to relate, painful is silence, and all is wretchedness. When first the gods knew wrath, and faction raised its head amongst them, and some would tear old Kronos from his throne that Zeus might take his place, and others were determined that Zeus should never reign over the gods, then I with wise counsel sought to guide the Titans, children of Earth and Sky,—but all in vain. My crafty schemes they disdained, and in their pride of strength thought it were easy to make themselves lords by force. Often to me my mother Themis (or call her Earth, for many names she hath, that being one) had foretold in oracles what was to be, with warning that not by might or brutal force should victory come, but by guile alone. So I counselled them, but they turned their eyes from me in impatience. Of the courses which then lay open, far the best, it seemed, was to take my mother as my helper and to join my will with the will of Zeus. By my advice the cavernous gloom of Tartarus now hides in night old Kronos and his peers. Thus the new tyrant of heaven took profit of me, and thus rewards me with these torments. 'Tis the disease of tyranny, no more, to take no heed of friendship. You ask why he tortures me; hear now the reason. No sooner was he established on his father's throne than he began to award various offices to the different gods, ordering his government throughout. Yet no care was in his heart for miserable men, and he was fain to blot out the whole race and in their stead create another. None save me opposed his purpose; I only dared; I rescued mankind from the heavy blow that was to cast them in Hades. Therefore I am bowed down by this anguish, painful to endure, pitiable to behold. Mercy I had for mortals, but found no mercy for myself: So piteously I am disciplined, an ignoble spectacle for Zeus.

Leader:

Fashioned of rock is he, and iron is his heart, O Prometheus, who feels not indignation at thy disasters. Rather would I not have seen them at all, and seeing them I am sore of heart.

Prometheus:

To my very friends I am a spectacle of pity.

Leader:

Yet it may be—did thy transgressions end there?

Prometheus:

Through me mankind ceased to foresee death.

Leader:

What remedy could heal that sad disease?

Prometheus:

Blind hopes I made to dwell in them.

Leader:

O merciful boon for mortals.

Prometheus:

And more than all I gave them fire.

Leader:

And so in their brief life they are lords of flaming fire?

Prometheus:

Through it they will learn many arts.

Leader:

And was it for crimes like this Zeus—

Prometheus:

Tortures me, and ceases not nor relents.

Leader:

And is there no goal to the struggle before thee?

Prometheus:

There is none, save when it seems to him good.

Leader:

When shall it so seem? What hope? Seest thou not thy error? That thou hast erred, I say in sorrow and with sorrow to thee. But enough of that; seek thou some release from the conflict.

Prometheus:

How easy for one who fares in pleasant ways to admonish those in adversity. But all this I knew; with open eyes, with willing mind, I erred; I do not deny it. Mankind I helped, but could not help myself. Yet I dreamed not that here in this savage solitary gorge, on this high rock, I should waste away beneath such torments. Yet care not to bewail these present disasters; but descend to the earth, and hear of the woes to come and all that is to be. I pray you heed my word; have compassion on one who is now caught in the toils; for sorrow flitteth now to one and now to another, and visiteth each in his turn.

Chorus: *(singing)*
We list to your words, O Prometheus.—
Lo, with light foot I step
From the swift-rushing car; the pure air,
The highway I leave of the birds;
And now to the rugged earth
I descend. I listen, I wait
For thy story of pain and disaster.

(Oceanus enters, borne on a winged horse.)

Oceanus:
To thee I come, O Prometheus;
Borne on this swift-winged bird
That knoweth the will of his rider
And needeth no curb, from afar
I have flown a wearisome way,
Weary but ended at last.
I am grieved with thy grief; I am drawn
By our kinship, and even without it
Thee more than all others I honor.
I speak simple truth, and my tongue
Knows not to flatter in idleness.
Nay, tell me what aid I may render;
For never thy lips shall avow
Oceanus failed thee in friendship.

Prometheus:
Ho! What is this I look upon? What then, art thou too come to stare upon my ruin? What new daring has brought thee from thy ocean stream and thy rock-roofed unbuilded caverns hither to our earth, the mother of iron? Art thou come to view my fate with indignation for my calamities? Behold the spectacle! Behold me, the friend of Zeus, who helped him to a throne, now bowed down by his torments.

Oceanus:
I see, Prometheus; and, though thou art thyself cunning in device, I would admonish thee to prudence. Learn to know thyself, put on the habit of new ways, for there is a new tyrant among the gods. If still thou hurlest forth these harsh and biting words, perchance from afar off, Zeus sitting above, may hear thee, and thy present burden of sorrows will seem as the sport of children. But, O wretched sufferer, put away thy moody wrath, and seek some respite from thy ills. My advice may sound as the trite sayings of old, yet thou thyself canst see what are the wages of too bold a tongue. Thou hast not learned humility, nor to yield to evils, but rather wouldst add others new to thy present store. Take me for thy teacher and kick not against the pricks, for there rules in heaven an austere monarch who is responsible to none. Now I will go and make trial to win thy release from this grievous state. Do thou keep thy peace, and restrain thy blustering speech. Or knowest thou not in thy wisdom what penalties overtake an idle tongue?

Prometheus:
I give you joy that, having shared and dared with me, you have still kept yourself free of blame. I bid you trouble not your peace; his will is immutable and you cannot persuade him. Even beware, lest by your going you being sorrow upon yourself.

Oceanus:
It is clear your words dismiss me home.

Prometheus:
Your tears for me might win hatred for yourself.

Oceanus:
His hatred you mean, who newly wears the sovereignty?

Prometheus:
Ay, his; beware that you vex not his heart.

Oceanus:
Your calamity, Prometheus, is my teacher.

Prometheus:
Be gone, take yourself off, keep your present mind.

Oceanus:
I am gone even with your urgent words. See, the winged beast flutters the broad path of the air; gladly would he bend the weary knee in his stall at home.

(Oceanus departs as the Chorus begins its song.)

Chorus:
I mourn, O Prometheus, for thee,
I wail for thy hapless fate;
And tears in a melting flood
Flow down from the fount of my eyes,
Drenching my cheeks. O insolent
Laws, O sceptre of Zeus,
How over the gods of old
Ye wield despotic might!

Lo, all the land groans aloud;
And the people that dwell in the West
Lament for thy time-honored reign
And the sway of thy kindred, Prometheus.

Prometheus:
Think not I am silent through pride or insolence; dumb rage gnaws at my very heart for this outrage upon me. Yet who but I established these new gods in their honours? But I speak not of this, for already you are aware of the truth. Rather listen to the sad story of mankind, who like children lived until I gave them understanding and a portion of reason; yet not in disparagement of men I speak, but meaning to set forth the greatness of my charity. For seeing they saw not, and hearing they understood not, but like as shapes in a dream they wrought all the days of their life in confusion. No houses of brick raised in the warmth of the sun they had, nor fabrics of wood, but like the little ants they dwelt underground in the sunless depth of caverns. No certain sign of approaching winter they knew, no harbinger of flowering spring or fruitful summer; ever they labored at random, till I taught them to discern the seasons by the rising and the obscure setting of the stars. Numbers I invented for them, the chiefest of all discoveries; I taught them the grouping of letters, to be a memorial and record of the past, the mistress of the arts and mother of the Muses. I first brought under the yoke beasts of burden, who by draft and carrying relieved men of their hardest labors; I yoked the proud horse to the chariot, teaching him obedience to the reins, to be the adornment of wealth and luxury. I too contrived for sailors seafaring vessels with their flaxen wings. Alas for me! such inventions I devised for mankind, but for myself I have no cunning to escape disaster.

Leader of the Chorus:
Sorrow and humiliation are your portion: you have failed in understanding and gone astray; and like a poor physician falling into sickness you despond and know not the remedies for your own disease.

Prometheus:
Hear but the rest, and you will wonder more at my inventions and many arts. If sickness visited them, they had no healing drug, no salve or soothing potion, but wasted away

for want of remedies, and this was my greatest boon; for I revealed to them the mingling of bland medicaments for the banishing of all diseases. And the secret treasures of the earth, all benefits to men, copper, iron, silver, gold,—who but I could boast their discovery? No one, I ween, unless in idle vaunting. Nay, hear the whole matter in a word,—all human arts are from Prometheus.

Leader:
Care not for mortals overmuch, whilst you neglect your own profit. Indeed, I am of good hope that yet some day, freed from bondage, you shall equal the might of Zeus.

Prometheus:
Not yet hath all-ordaining Destiny decreed my release; but after many years, broken by a world of disaster and woe, I shall be delivered. The craft of the forger is weaker far than Necessity.

Leader:
Who then holds the helm of Necessity?

Prometheus:
The Fates triform and the unforgetting Furies.

Leader:
And Zeus, is he less in power than these?

Prometheus:
He may not avoid what is destined.

Leader:
What is destined for Zeus but endless rule?

Prometheus:
Ask not, neither set thy heart on knowing.

Leader:
Some solemn secret thou wouldst clothe in mystery.

Prometheus:
Speak no more of it; the time is not yet to divulge it, and the secret must still be deeply shrouded. Harbouring this I shall one day escape from this outrage and ignominy of bondage.

At this point, a long episode (here omitted) introduces Io, another victim of divine wrath. Beloved of Zeus, hated consequently by Hera, transformed into a heifer and tormented by a gadfly, she is being driven out of Europe and into Asia, crossing at the Bosphorus ("cow-crossing"). The point of the episode is twofold; it increases sympathy for Prometheus by showing the injustice of the gods to a fellow-sufferer, and it provides Prometheus a chance to foretell that from Io's progeny, after a dozen generations, his eventual deliverer will come.

Prometheus:
Yet shall Zeus himself, the stubborn of soul, be humbled, for the union he purposes in his heart shall hurl him to outer darkness from his throne of supremacy. Then at last the curse of his father Kronos shall be fulfilled to the uttermost, the curse that he swore when thrown from his ancient seat. All this I know and how the curse shall work, and I only of the gods may point out a refuge from these disasters. Therefore let him sit boldly now, trusting in his thunders that reverberate through the sky, and wielding fiery darts in his hands; they shall avail him naught nor save him from falling in ruin unendurable. A mighty wrestler he is preparing against himself, an irresistible champion, who shall search out a fire more terrible than his lightning and a roaring noise to drown his thunder, and who shall break in pieces that sea-scourge and shaker of the earth, the trident-spear of Poseidon. And Zeus, broken on this rock, shall learn how far apart it is to rule and be a slave.

Leader of the Chorus:
Thy bodings against Zeus are but thy own desire.

Prometheus:
I speak what is to be, and that is my desire.

Leader:
Must we look for one to reign above Zeus?

Prometheus:
Troubles more grievous to bear shall bow his neck.

Leader:
Thou tremblest not to utter such words?

Prometheus:
Why should I tremble whose fate is not to die?

Leader:
Yet he might still harder torments inflict.

Prometheus:
So let him! I am prepared for all.

Leader:
Yet the wise bow down to Nemesis.

Prometheus:
So worship, flatter, adore the ruler of the day; but I have no thought in my heart for Zeus. Let him act, let him reign his little while as he will; for he shall not long rule over the gods.—*(Hermes*[2] *enters.)* But I see here the lackey of Zeus, the servant of the new tyrant. No doubt he has come with tidings of some new device.

Hermes:
Thee, the wise, the bitter beyond bitterness, the thief of fire, who hast revolted against the gods and betrayed their honours to thy creatures of a day,—to thee I speak. The Father bids thee declare the chance of wedlock thou vauntest, that shall bereave him of his sceptre; and this thou art to state clearly and not involve thy speech in riddles. Put me not, O Prometheus, to double my journey; thou seest that Zeus is not appeased by dubious words.

Prometheus:
Haughty thy speech and swollen with pride, as becomes a servant of the gods. Ye are but young in tyranny, and think to inhabit a citadel unassaulted of grief; yet have I not seen two tyrants fall therefrom? And third I shall behold this present lord cast down in utter ruin. Do I seem to cower and quail before these new gods? Hardly, I think; there is no fear in me. But do you trudge back the road you came; for all your pains of asking are in vain.

Hermes:
Yet forget not such insolence has brought you to this pass of evil.

Prometheus:
Be assured I would not barter my hard lot for your menial service.

Hermes:
It is better no doubt to serve this rock than to be the trusted herald of Zeus.

Prometheus:
I but answered insult with insult.

Hermes:
You seem to glory in your present state.

2. HUR-meez

Prometheus:
What, I? So might I see my enemies glory,—and you among them!

Hermes:
You blame me too for your calamities?

Prometheus:
In simple sooth I count all the gods my foes, who requited my benefits with injuries.

Hermes:
Your madness I see is a deep-rooted disease.

Prometheus:
If hatred of foes is madness, I am mad.

Hermes:
Who could endure you in prosperity!

Prometheus:
Alas, prosperity!

Hermes:
Zeus has not learned that cry, alas.

Prometheus:
Time growing ever older, teaches all things.

Hermes:
It has not taught you wisdom yet.

Prometheus:
Else I should hardly talk with you, a slave.

Hermes:
It seems you will not answer the Father's demands.

Prometheus:
My debt of gratitude I fain would pay.

Hermes:
You have reviled and scorned me as a child.

Prometheus: *(in supreme anger)*
And are you not simpler than a child if you hope to learn aught from me? There is no torment or contrivance in the power of Zeus to wring this utterance from me, except these bonds are loosened. Therefore let him hurl upon me the red lightning, let him confound the reeling world with tempest of white-feathered snow and subterranean thunders; none of these things shall extort from me the knowledge that may ward off his overthrow.

Hermes:
Consider if you shall profit by this.

Prometheus:
I have considered long since and formed my plan.

Hermes:
Yet subdue thyself in time, rash fool, to regard thy present ills in wisdom.

Prometheus:
You vex me to no purpose, as one might waste his words on a wave of the sea. Dream not that ever in fear of Zeus's will I shall grow woman-hearted, and raise my supine hands in supplication to my hated foe for deliverance from these bonds;—it is not in my nature.

Hermes:
Though I speak much, my words will all be wasted; my appeals have no power to soften and appease your heart, but champing the bit like a new-yoked colt you are restive and struggle against the reins. There is no strength of wisdom in your savage mood, for mere self-will in a foolish man avails nothing. And consider, if thou disregard my words, what a tempest of evils, wave on wave inevitable, shall break upon thee; for first the Father will smite this rugged cliff with rending of thunder and hurtling fires, and in its harsh and rock-ribbed embrace enfold thy hidden body. Then after a weary age of years once more thou shalt come forth to the light; and the winged hound of Zeus, the ravening eagle, with savage greed shall tear the mighty ruin of thy limbs, feasting all day an uninvited guest, and glutting his maw on thy black-gnawed liver. Neither look for any respite from this agony, unless some god shall appear as a voluntary successor to thy toils, and of his own free will goeth down to sunless Hades and the dark depths of Tartarus. Therefore take heed; for my words are not vain boasting, but all too truly spoken. The lips of Zeus know not to utter falsehood, but all that he saith he will accomplish. Do thou consider and reflect, and regard not vaunting pride as better than wise counsel.

Leader:
To us Hermes seems to utter words not untimely; for he admonishes you to abandon vaunting pride and seek for wise counsel. Obey him; it is shameful for a wise man to go astray.

Prometheus: *(chanting)*
All this ere he uttered his message
I knew; yet feel no dishonor
In suffering wrong from a foe.
Ay, let the lightning be launched
With curled and forked flame
On my head; let the air confounded
Shudder with thunderous peals
And convulsion of raging winds;
Let tempests beat on the earth
Till her rooted foundations tremble;
The boisterous surge of the sea
Leap up to mingle its crest
With the stars eclipsed in their orbs;
Let the whirling blasts of Necessity
Seize on my body and hurl it
Down to the darkness of Tartarus,—
Yet all he shall not destroy me!

Hermes:
I hear the delirious cries
Of a mind unhinged; his prayer
Is frenzy, and all that he doth.—
But ye who condole with his anguish,
Be quick, I implore, and depart,
Ere the deafening roar of the thunder
Daze and bewilder your senses.

Chorus:
Waste not thy breath in vain warnings,
Nor utter a word unendurable;
For who art thou in the pathway
Of evil and falsehood to guide me?
Better I deem it to suffer
Whate'er he endures; for traitors
My soul abhorreth, their shame
I spew from my heart as a pest.

Hermes:
Yet remember my counsel in season,
And blame not your fortune when caught
In the snare of Disaster, nor cry
Unto Zeus that he throws you unwarned
Into sorrow. Yourselves take the blame;

Foretaught and with eyes unveiled
You walk to be snared in the vast
And implicate net of Disaster.
(Hermes goes out. A storm bursts, with thunder and lightning. The rocks are sundered; Prometheus slowly sinks from sight, while the Chorus scatters to right and left.)

Prometheus:
Lo, in grim earnest the world
Is shaken, the roar of thunders
Reverberates, gleams the red lightning,
And whirlwinds lick up the dust.
All the blast of the winds leap out
And meet in tumultuous conflict,
Confounding the sea and the heavens.
'Tis Zeus who driveth his furies
To smite me with terror and madness.
O mother Earth all-honored,
O Air revolving thy light
A common boon unto all,
Behold what wrongs I endure.

Exercises

1. In the early part of the play, Power says, "None is truly free, save only Zeus." Look through the rest of the play to find out how exact this statement is. Is Zeus himself completely free?

2. In the introduction to his *The Condition of Man*, Lewis Mumford writes of man as building his civilizations as a child builds sand castles on the beach. The civilizations are always destroyed with the rising of the tide, but man continues to build each day anew. Man, says Mumford, is the only one of the animals who consciously can impose work on himself.

   Does this statement of Mumford's have any relation to Aeschylus' statement about Death and blind hopes? What, exactly?

   So now can you explain why this gift of blind hope (why *blind*, by the way?) is important to mankind?

3. Notice the pattern of Prometheus's gifts. We might arrange them in this way: Blind hopes, a portion of reason (why only a portion?), language, numbers, fire, etc. If so, and remembering that according to the legend, fire was the only gift that Prometheus gave to man, what seems to be the idea that Aeschylus had about man's development? Why, for example, didn't he give them Cadillacs, yachts, and garbage disposals?

   In the same preface referred to above, Mumford makes the point that man creates things, which may or may not be of too great importance, but that in making things, man himself grows. Does this idea have anything to do with this series of Promethean gifts?

4. Having considered all of these factors, you might speculate on the solution which Aeschylus may have worked out for his problem in the third play. For example, what are the limits of the power of Zeus, of Prometheus, of Man? What ideas of the philosophers did Aeschylus have to work with? In developing some sort of a solution, you need not be afraid of altering the status of the gods. See, for example, what Aeschylus did to the Furies in *Eumenides*.

Agamemnon

Aeschylus

This is the first of a series of three plays by Aeschylus, called the Oresteia (aw-res-TEE-ya). Exactly as Aeschylus explored the question of the relation of men to God and the universe in *Prometheus Bound*, he investigates in these plays the question of man's relation to other men. He is asking the question, "What is justice?" In the first of the plays he presents the old idea of justice and men's freedom of choice as it probably existed in the period of chaos. In the second of the plays (omitted here) he carries the question further. In the last of the series he presents a new idea of justice and explains the meaning of it to his Athenian audience as they approached the period of balance in their epoch. To understand this series of plays, one needs to know a little about the history of the dynasty of kings who ruled in the land of Argos. Since Atreus (A-troos, or A-tree-us) was one of the early kings in this dynasty, the family line is called the House of Atreus.

Atreus, ruler of the kingdom of Argos, quarreled with his brother Thyestes (thī-ES-teez), and banished him. Later, Thyestes sought reconciliation. Atreus pretended forgiveness and invited his brother to a feast. Secretly, however, he killed the two elder sons of Thyestes, and served them as roast meats to their father, who unwittingly ate the flesh. When Thyestes discovered the treachery of Atreus, however, he again departed from Argos with his remaining son, Egistheus (i-JIS-thus), leaving behind him an abiding curse on all the House of Atreus.

The sons of Atreus, Agamemnon (ag-uh-MEM-non) and Menelaus (men-i-LAY-us), married the sisters, Clytemnestra (klī-tem-NES-tra) and Helen, daughters of the King of Lacedemon. Helen left her husband, fleeing to Troy with Paris, and Agamemnon rallied all the forces of Greece to help his brother win her back. The fleet could not leave from Aulis (AW-lis, or AF-lis) because of adverse winds; the seer, Calchas (KAL-kus), interpreted omens to mean that the winds would change when Agamemnon sacrificed his daughter, Iphigenia (if-i-je-$\overline{\text{NI}}$-uh). That sacrifice was made.

While the war was in progress and Agamemnon fighting before Troy, Egistheus returned to

Argos and became Clytemnestra's lover. He roused discontent among the people and became powerful.

These plays, then, develop a new idea of justice and freedom in the period in which Aeschylus lived. The first one presents the old ideas which made the tragedy of Agamemnon possible. Watch for those ideas.

The Greeks had arranged a series of beacons stretching from Troy to the Grecian mainland to be kindled as a token of victory over Troy. It is with their imminent flaming that the play opens.

The translations of the *Oresteia* are made by the twentieth-century scholar, George Thomson.

Characters:

Watchman
Chorus of Old Men
Clytemnestra
Herald
Agamemnon
Cassandra
Aegisthus
Captain of the Guard

The scene is the entrance to the palace of the Atreidae. Before the doors stand shrines of the gods.
[*A* WATCHMAN *is posted on the roof.*]

Watchman:
I've prayed God to release me from sentry duty
All through this long year's vigil, like a dog
Couched on the roof of Atreus, where I study
Night after night the pageantry of this vast
Concourse of stars, and moving among them like
Noblemen the constellations that bring
Summer and winter as they rise and fall.
And I am still watching for the beacon signal
All set to flash over the sea the radiant
News of the fall of Troy. So confident
Is a woman's spirit, whose purpose is a man's.
Every night, as I turn in to my stony bed,
Quilted with dew, not visited by dreams,
Not mine—no sleep, fear stands at my pillow
Keeping tired eyes from closing once too often;
And whenever I start to sing or hum a tune,
Mixing from music an antidote to sleep,
It always turns to mourning for the royal house,
Which is not in such good shape as it used to be
But now at last may the good news in a flash
Scatter the darkness and deliver us. [*The beacon flashes.*]
O light of joy, whose gleam turns night to day,
O radiant signal for innumerable
Dances of victory! Ho there! I call the queen,
Agamemnon's wife, to raise with all the women
Alleluias of thanksgiving through the palace
Saluting the good news, if it is true
That Troy has fallen, as this blaze portends:
Yes, and I'll dance an overture myself.
My master's dice have fallen out well, and I
Shall score three sixes for this nightwatching. [*A pause.*]
Well, come what will, may it soon be mine to grasp
In this right hand my master's, home again! [*Another pause.*]
The rest is secret. A heavy ox has trodden
Across my tongue. These walls would have tales to tell
If they had mouths. I speak only to those
Who are in the know, to others—I know nothing.
[*The* WATCHMAN *goes into the palace. Women's cries are heard. Enter* CHORUS OF OLD MEN.]

Chorus:
It is ten years since those armed prosecutors of Justice, Menelaus and Agamemnon, twin-sceptred in God-given sovranty, embarked in the thousand ships crying war, like eagles with long wings beating the air over a robbed mountain nest, wheeling and screaming for their lost children. Yet above them some god, maybe Apollo or Zeus, overhears the sky-dweller's cry and sends after the robber a Fury. [CLYTEMNESTRA *comes out of the palace and unseen by the elders places offerings before the shrines.*] Just so the two kings were sent by the greater king, Zeus, for the sake of a promiscuous woman to fight Paris, Greek and Trojan locked fast together in the dusty betrothals of battle. And however it stands with them now, the end is unalterable; no flesh, no wine can appease God's fixed indignation.

As for us, with all the able-bodied men enlisted and gone, we are left here leaning our strength on a staff; for, just as in infancy, when the marrow is still unformed, the War-god is not at his post, so it is in extreme old age, as the leaves fall fast, we walk on three feet, like dreams in the daylight. [*They see* CLYTEMNESTRA.]

O Queen, what news? what message sets light to the altars? All over the town the shrines are ablaze with unguents drawn from the royal stores and the flames shoot up into the night sky. Speak, let us hear all that may be made public, so healing the anxieties that have gathered thick in our hearts; let the gleam of good news scatter them! [CLYTEMNESTRA *goes out to tend the other altars of the city.*]

Strength have I still to recall that sign which greeted the two kings
Taking the road, for the prowess of song is not yet spent.
I sing of two kings united in sovranty, leading
Armies to battle, who saw two eagles
Beside the palace
Wheel into sight, one black, and the other was white-tailed,
Tearing a hare with her unborn litter.
Ailinon cry, but let good conquer!

Shrewdly the priest took note and compared each eagle with each king,
Then spoke out and prefigured the future in these words:
"In time the Greek arms shall demolish the fortress of Priam;
Only let no jealous God, as they fasten
On Troy the slave's yoke,
Strike them in anger; for Artemis[1] loathes the rapacious
Beagles of Zeus that have slaughtered the frail hare.
Ailinon cry, but let good conquer!
O Goddess, gentle to the tender whelp of fierce lions
As to all young life of the wild,
So now fulfil what is good in the omen and mend what is faulty.
And I appeal unto the Lord Apollo,
Let not the north wind hold the fleet storm-bound,

---

1. Artemis is the goddess of the hunt and all wild things. In this context, the hare is the city of Troy.

Driving them on to repay that feast with another,
Inborn builder of strife, feud that fears no man, it is still there,
Treachery keeping the house, it remembers, revenges, a child's death!"
Such, as the kings left home, was the seer's revelation.
Ailinon cry, but let good conquer!

Zeus, whoe'er he be, if so it best
Please his ear to be addressed,
So shall he be named by me.
All things have I measured, yet
None have found save him alone,
Zeus, if a man from a heart heavy-laden
Seek to cast his cares aside.

Long since lived a ruler of the world,[2]
Puffed with martial pride, of whom
None shall tell, his day is done;
Also, he who followed him
Met his master and is gone.
Zeus the victorious, gladly acclaim him;
Perfect wisdom shall be yours;

Zeus, who laid it down that man
Must in sorrow learn and through
Pain to wisdom find his way.
When deep slumber falls, remembered wrongs
Chafe the bruised heart with fresh pangs, and no
Welcome wisdom meets within.
Harsh the grace dispensed by powers immortal,
Pilots of the human soul.

Even so the elder prince,[3]
Marshal of the thousand ships,
Rather than distrust a priest,
Torn with doubt to see his men
Harbor-locked, hunger-pinched, hard-oppressed,
Strained beyond endurance, still
Watching, waiting, where the never-tiring
Tides of Aulis ebb and flow:

And still the storm blew from mountains far north,
With moorings windswept and hungry crews pent
In rotting hulks,
With tackling all torn and seeping timbers,
Till Time's slow-paced, enforced inaction
Had all but stripped bare the bloom of Greek manhood.
And then was found but one
Cure to allay the tempest—never a blast so bitter—
Shrieked in a loud voice by the priest, "Artemis!" striking the Atreidae with dismay, each with his staff smiting the ground and weeping.

And then the king spoke, the elder, saying:
"The choice is hard—hard to disobey him,
And harder still
To kill my own child, my palace jewel,
With unclean hands before the altar
Myself, her own father, spill a maid's pure blood.
I have no choice but wrong.
How shall I fail my thousand ships and betray my comrades?
So shall the storm cease, and the men eager for war clamor for that virginal blood righteously! So pray for a happy outcome!"

And when he bowed down beneath the harness
Of cruel coercion, his spirit veering
With sudden sacrilegious change,
He gave his whole mind to evil counsel.
For man is made bold with base-contriving
Impetuous madness, first cause of much grief.
And so then he slew his own child
For a war to win a woman
And to speed the storm-bound fleet from the shore to battle.

She cried aloud "Father!" yet they heard not;
A girl in first flower, yet they cared not,
The lords who gave the word for war.
Her father prayed, then he bade his vassals
To seize her where swathed in folds of saffron
She lay, and lift her up like a yearling
With bold heart above the altar,
And her lovely lips to bridle
That they might not cry out, cursing the House of Atreus,
With gags, her voice sealed with brute force and crushed.
And then she let fall her cloak
And cast at each face a glance that dumbly craved compassion;
And like a picture she would but could not greet
Her father's guests, who at home
Had often sat when the meal was over,
The cups replenished, with all hearts enraptured
To hear her sing grace with clear unsullied voice for her loving father.

The end was unseen and unspeakable.
The task of priestcraft was done.
For Justice first chastens, then she presses home her lesson.
The morrow must come, its grief will soon be here,
So let us not weep today.
It shall be made known as clear as daybreak.
And so may all this at last end in good news,
For which the queen prays, the next of kin and stay of the land of Argos. [CLYTEMNESTRA *appears at the door of the palace.*]
Our humble salutations to the queen!
Hers is our homage, while our master's throne
Stands empty. We are still longing to hear
The meaning of your sacrifice. Is it good news?

Clytemnestra:
Good news! With good news may the morning rise
Out of the night—good news beyond all hope!
My news is this: The Greeks have taken Troy.

Chorus:
What? No, it cannot be true! I cannot grasp it.

Clytemnestra:
The Greeks hold Troy—is not that plain enough?

Chorus:
Joy steals upon me and fills my eyes with tears.

Clytemnestra:
Indeed, your looks betray your loyalty.

---

2. The reference here is Uranus and Kronos, both kings of the gods. Zeus led a successful revolt against Kronos so that Zeus could become king.

3. This refers to the beginning of the Trojan War when the Greek fleet was delayed in the harbor of Aulis. In order to appease Artemis and secure favorable winds, Agamemnon, "the elder prince," followed the prophecy of the seer, Calchas, and sacrificed his daughter, Iphigenia.

Chorus:
What is the proof? Have you any evidence?

Clytemnestra:
Of course I have, or else the Gods have cheated me.

Chorus:
You have given ear to some beguiling dream.

Clytemnestra:
I would not come screaming fancies out of my sleep.

Chorus:
Rumors have wings—on these your heart has fed.

Clytemnestra:
You mock my intelligence as though I were a girl.

Chorus:
When was it? How long is it since the city fell?

Clytemnestra:
In the night that gave birth to this dawning day.

Chorus:
What messenger could bring the news so fast?

Clytemnestra:
The God of Fire, who from Ida sent forth light
And beacon by beacon passed the flame to me.
From the peak of Ida first to the cliff of Hermes
On Lemnos, and from there a third great lamp
Was flashed to Athos, the pinnacle of Zeus;
Up, up it soared, luring the dancing fish
To break surface in rapture at the light;
A golden courier, like the sun, it sped
Post-haste its message to Macistus, thence
Across Euripus, till the flaming sign
Was marked by the watchers on Messapium,
And thence with strength renewed from piles of heath
Like moonrise over the valley of Asopus,
Relayed in glory to Cithaeron's heights,
And still flashed on, not slow the sentinels,
Leaping across the lake from peak to peak,
It passed the word to burn and burn, and flung
A comet to the promontory that stands
Over the Gulf of Saron, there it swooped
Down to the Spider's Crag above the city,
Then found its mark on the roof of this house of Atreus,
That beacon fathered by Ida's far-off fires.
Such were the stages of our torch relay,
And the last to run is the first to reach the goal.
That is my evidence, the testimony which
My lord has signaled to me out of Troy.

Chorus:
Lady, there will be time later to thank the Gods.
Now I ask only to listen: speak on and on.

Clytemnestra:
Today the Greeks have occupied Troy.
I seem to hear there a very strange street-music.
Pour oil and vinegar into one cup, you will see
They do not make friends. So there two tunes are heard.
Slaves now, the Trojans, brothers and aged fathers,
Prostrate, sing for their dearest the last dirge.
The others, tired out and famished after the night's looting,
Grab what meal chance provides, lodgers now
In Trojan houses, sheltered from the night frosts,
From the damp dews delivered, free to sleep
Off guard, off duty, a blissful night's repose.
Therefore, provided that they show due respect
To the altars of the plundered town and are not
Tempted to lay coarse hands on sanctities,
Remembering that the last lap—the voyage home—
Lies still ahead of them, then, if they should return
Guiltless before God, the curses of the bereaved
Might be placated—barring accidents.
That is my announcement—a message from my master.
May all end well, and may I reap the fruit of it!

Chorus:
Lady, you have spoken with a wise man's judgment.
Now it is time to address the gods once more
After this happy outcome of our cares.

Thanks be to Zeus and to gracious Night, housekeeper of heaven's embroidery, who has cast over the towers of Troy a net so fine as to leave no escape for old or young, all caught in the snare! All praise to Zeus, who with a shaft from his outstretched bow has at last brought down the transgressor!

"By Zeus struck down!" The truth is all clear
With each step plainly marked. He said, Be
It so, and so it was. A man denied once
That heaven pays heed to those who trample
Beneath the feet holy sanctities. He lied wickedly;
For God's wrath soon or late destroys all sinners filled
With pride, puffed up with vain presumption,
And great men's houses stocked with silver
And gold beyond measure. Far best to live
Free of want, without grief, rich in the gift of wisdom.
Glutted with gold, the sinner kicks
Justice out of his sight, yet
She sees *him* and remembers.

As sweet temptation lures him onwards
With childlike smile into the death-trap
He cannot help himself. His curse is lit up
Against the darkness, a bright baleful light.
And just as false bronze in battle hammered turns black and shows
Its true worth, so the sinner time-tried stands condemned.
His hopes take wing, and still he gives chase, with foul crimes branding all his people.
He cries to deaf heaven, none hear his prayers.
Justice drags him down to hell as he calls for succor.
Such was the sinner Paris, who
Rendered thanks to a gracious
Host by stealing a woman.

She left behind her the ports all astir
With throngs of men under arms filing onto shipboard;
She took to Troy in lieu of dowry death.
A light foot passed through the gates and fled,
And then a cry of lamentation rose.
The seers, the king's prophets, muttered darkly:
"Bewail the king's house that now is desolate,
Bewail the bed marked with print of love that fled!"
Behold, in silence, without praise, without reproach,
They sit upon the ground and weep.
Beyond the wave lies their love;
Here a ghost seems to rule the palace!
Shapely the grace of statues,
Yet they can bring no comfort,
Eyeless, lifeless and loveless.

Delusive dream shapes that float through the night
Beguile him, bringing delight sweet but unsubstantial;

For, while the eye beholds the heart's desire,
The arms clasp empty air, and then
The fleeting vision fades and glides away
On silent wing down the paths of slumber.
The royal hearth is chilled with sorrows such as these,
And more; in each house from end to end of Greece
That sent its dearest to wage war in foreign lands
The stout heart is called to steel itself
In mute endurance against
Blows that strike deep into the heart's core:
Those that they sent from home they
Knew, but now they receive back
Only a heap of ashes.

The God of War holds the twin scales of strife,
Heartless gold-changer trafficking in men,
Consigning homeward from Troy a jar of dust fire-refined,
Making up the weight with grief,
Shapely vessels laden each
With the ashes of their kin.
They mourn and praise them saying, "He
Was practiced well in sword and spear,
And he, who fell so gallantly—
All to avenge another man's wife":
It is muttered in a whisper
And resentment spreads against each of the royal warlords.
They lie sleeping, perpetual
Owners each of a small
Holding far from their homeland.

The sullen rumors that pass mouth to mouth
Bring the same danger as a people's curse,
And brooding hearts wait to hear of what the night holds from sight.
Watchful are the Gods of all
Hands with slaughter stained. The black
Furies wait, and when a man
Has grown by luck, not justice, great,
With sudden turn of circumstance
He wastes away to nothing, dragged
Down to be food in hell for demons.
For the heights of fame are perilous.
With a jealous bolt the Lord Zeus in a flash shall blast them.
Best to pray for a tranquil
Span of life and to be
Neither victor nor vanquished.

—The news has set the whole town aflame.
Can it be true? Perhaps it is a trick.
—Only a child would let such fiery words
Kindle his hopes, then fade and flicker out.
—It is just like a woman
To accept good news without the evidence.
—An old wives' tale, winged with a woman's wishes,
Spreads like wildfire, then sinks and is forgotten.

We shall soon know what the beacon signifies,
Whether it is true or whether this joyful daybreak
Is only a dream sent to deceive us all.
Here comes a messenger breathless from the shore,
Wearing a garland and covered in a cloud
Of dust, which shows that he has news to tell,
And not in soaring rhetoric of smoke and flame,
But either he brings cause for yet greater joy,
Or else,—no, let us abjure the alternative.
Glad shone the light, as gladly break the day!

[*Enter* HERALD]

Herald:
O joy! Argos, I greet you, my fatherland!
Joy brings me home after ten years of war.
Many the shattered hopes, but this has held.
Now I can say that when I die my bones
Will lie at rest here in my native soil.
I greet you joyfully, I greet the Sun,
Zeus the All-Highest, and the Pythian King,[4]
Bending no more against us his fatal shafts,
As he did beside Scamander—that was enough,
And now defend us, Savior Apollo; all
The Gods I greet, among them Hermes, too,
Patron of messengers, and the spirits of our dead,
Who sent their sons forth, may they now prepare
A joyful welcome for those whom war has spared.
Joy to the palace and to these images
Whose faces catch the sun, now, as of old,
With radiant smiles greet your sovran lord,
Agamemnon, who brings a lamp to lighten you
And all here present, after having leveled
Troy with the mattock of just-dealing Zeus,
Great son of Atreus, master and monarch, blest
Above all living men. The brigand Paris
Has lost his booty and brought down the house of Priam.

Chorus:
Joy to you, Herald, welcome home again!

Herald:
Let me die, having lived to see this day!

Chorus:
Your yearning for your country has worn you out.

Herald:
So much that tears spring to the eyes for joy.

Chorus:
Well, those you longed for longed equally for you.

Herald:
Ah yes, our loved ones longed for our safe return.

Chorus:
We have had many anxieties here at home.

Herald:
What do you mean? Has there been disaffection?

Chorus:
Never mind now. Say nothing and cure all.

Herald:
Is it possible there was trouble in our absence?

Chorus:
Now, as you said yourself, it would be a joy to die.

Herald:
Yes, all has ended well. Our expedition
Has been successfully concluded, even though in part
The issue may be found wanting. Only the Gods
Prosper in everything. If I should tell you all
That we endured on shipboard in the night watches,
Our lodging the bare benches, and even worse
Ashore beneath the walls of Troy, the rains
From heaven and the dews that seeped
Out of the soil into lice-infested blankets;
If I should tell of those winters, when the birds
Dropped dead and Ida heaped on us her snows;
Those summers, when unruffled by wind or wave

4. Apollo.

The sea slept breathless under the glare of noon—
But why recall that now? It is all past,
Yes, for the dead past never to stir again.
Ah, they are all gone. Why count our losses? Why
Should we vex the living with grievance for the dead?
Goodbye to all that for us who have come back!
Victory has turned the scale, and so before
This rising sun let the good news be proclaimed
And carried all over the world on wings of fame:
"These spoils were brought by the conquerors of Troy
And dedicated to the Gods of Greece."
And praise to our country and to Zeus the giver
And thanks be given. That is all my news.
[CLYTEMNESTRA *appears at the palace door.*]

Chorus:
Thank God that I have lived to see this day!
This news concerns all, and most of all the queen.

Clytemnestra:
I raised my alleluia hours ago,
When the first messenger lit up the night,
And people mocked me saying, "Has a beacon
Persuaded you that the Greeks have captured Troy?
Truly a woman's hopes are lighter than air."
But I still sacrificed, and at a hundred
Shrines throughout the town the women chanted
Their endless alleluias on and on,
Singing to sleep the sacramental flames,
And now what confirmation do I need from you?
I wait to hear all from my lord, for whom
A welcome is long ready. What day is so sweet
In a woman's life as when she opens the door
To her beloved, safe home from war? Go and tell him
That he will find, guarding his property,
A wife as loyal as he left her, one
Who in all these years has kept his treasuries sealed,
Unkind only to enemies, and knows no more
Of other men's company than of tempering steel. [*Exit.*]

Herald:
Such a protestation, even though entirely true,
Is it not unseemly on a lady's lips?

Chorus:
Such is her message, as you understand,
Full of fine phrases plain to those who know.
But tell us now, what news have you of the king's
Co-regent, Menelaus? Is he too home again?

Herald:
Lies cannot last, even though sweet to hear.

Chorus:
Can you not make your news both sweet and true?

Herald:
He and his ships have vanished. They are missing.

Chorus:
What, was it a storm that struck the fleet at sea?

Herald:
You have told a long disaster in a word.

Chorus:
Has no one news whether he is alive or dead?

Herald:
Only the Sun, from whom the whole earth draws life.

Chorus:
Tell us about the storm. How did it fall?

Herald:
A day of national rejoicing must not be marred
By any jarring tongue. A messenger who comes
With black looks bringing the long prayed-against
Report of total rout, which both afflicts
The state in general and in every household leaves
The inmates prostrate under the scourge of war—
With such a load upon his lips he may fitly
Sing anthems to the Furies down in hell;
But when he greets a prospering people with
News of the war's victorious end—how then
Shall I mix foul with fair and find words to tell you
Of the blow that struck us out of that angry heaven?
Water and Fire, those age-old enemies,
Made common cause against the homebound fleet.
Darkness had fallen, and a northerly gale
Blew up and in a blinding thunderstorm
Our ships were tossed and buffeted hull against hull
In a wild stampede and herded out of sight;
Then, at daybreak, we saw the Aegean in blossom
With a waving crop of corpses and scattered timbers.
Our ship came through, saved by some spirit, it seems,
Who took the helm and piloted her, until
She slipped under the cliffs into a cove.
There, safe at last, incredulous of our luck,
We brooded all day, stunned by the night's disaster.
And so, if any of the others have survived,
They must be speaking of us as dead and gone.
May all yet end well! Though it is most to be expected
That Menelaus is in some great distress,
Yet, should some shaft of sunlight spy him out
Somewhere among the living, rescued by Zeus,
Lest the whole house should perish, there is hope
That he may yet come home. There you have the truth.

Chorus:
Tell us who invented that
Name so deadly accurate?
Was it one who presaging
Things to come divined a word
Deftly tuned to destiny?
Helen—hell indeed she carried
To men, to ships, to a proud city, stealing
From the silk veils of her chamber, sailing seaward
With the Zephyr's breath behind her;
And they set forth in a thousand ships to hunt her
On the path that leaves no imprint,
Bringers of endless bloodshed.

So, as Fate decreed, in Troy,
Turning into keeners kin,
Furies, instruments of God's
Wrath, at last demanded full
Payment for the stolen wife;
And the wedding song that rang out
To greet the bride from beyond the broad Aegean
Was in time turned into howls of imprecation
From the countless women wailing
For the loved ones they had lost in war for her sake,
And they curse the day they gave that
Welcome to war and bloodshed.

An old story is told of an oxherd who reared at his hearth a lion-cub, a pet for his children,
Pampered fondly by young and old with dainty morsels begged at each meal from his master's table.

But Time showed him up in his true nature after his kind—a beast savaging sheep and oxen,
Mad for the taste of blood, and only then they knew what they had long nursed was a curse from heaven.
And so it seemed then there came to rest in Troy
A sweet-smiling calm, a clear sky, seductive,
A rare pearl set in gold and silver,
Shaft of love from a glancing eye.
She is seen now as an agent
Of death sent from Zeus, a Fury
Demanding a bloody bride-price. [*Enter* CLYTEMNESTRA]

From ancient times people have believed that when
A man's wealth has come to full growth it breeds
And brings forth tares and tears in plenty.
No, I say, it is only wicked deeds
That increase, fruitful in evil.
The house built on justice always
Is blest with a happy offspring.

And yet the pride bred of wealth often burgeons anew
In evil times, a cloud of deep night,
Spectre of ancient crimes that still
Walks within the palace walls,
True to the dam that bore it.

But where is Justice? She lights up the smoke-darkened hut.
From mansions built by hands polluted
Turning to greet the pure in heart,
Proof against false praise, she guides
All to its consummation. [*Enter* AGAMEMNON *in a chariot followed by another chariot carrying* CASSANDRA[5] *and spoils of war.*]

Agamemnon, conqueror, joy to our king! How shall my greeting neither fall short nor shoot too high? Some men feign rejoicing or sorrow with hearts untouched; but those who can read man's nature in the book of the eyes will not be deceived by dissembled fidelity. I declare that, when you left these shores ten years ago to recover with thousands of lives one woman, who eloped of her own free will, I deemed your judgment misguided; but now in all sincerity I salute you with joy. Toil happily ended brings pleasure at last, and in time you shall learn to distinguish the just from the unjust steward.

Agamemnon:
First, it is just that I should pay my respects
To the land of Argos and her presiding Gods,
My partners in this homecoming as also
In the just penalty which I have inflicted on
The city of Troy. When the supreme court of heaven
Adjudicated on our cause, they cast
Their votes unanimously against her, though not
Immediately, and so on the other side
Hope hovered hesitantly before it vanished.
The fires of pillage are still burning there
Like sacrificial offerings. Her ashes
Redolent with riches breathe their last and die.
For all this it is our duty to render thanks
To the celestial powers, with whose assistance
We have exacted payment and struck down
A city for one woman, forcing our entry
Within the Wooden Horse, which at the setting
Of the Pleiads like a hungry lion leapt
Out and slaked its thirst in royal blood.
As to your sentiments, I take due note
And find that they accord with mine. Too few
Rejoice at a friend's good fortune. I have known
Many dissemblers swearing false allegiance.
One only, though he joined me against his will,
Once in the harness, proved himself a staunch
Support, Odysseus, be he now alive or dead.
All public questions and such as concern the Gods
I shall discuss in council and take steps
To make this triumph lasting; and if here or there
Some malady comes to light, appropriate
Remedies will be applied to set it right.
Meanwhile, returning to my royal palace,
My first duty is to salute the Gods
Who led me overseas and home again.
Victory attends me; may she remain with me!

Clytemnestra:
Citizens of Argos, councillors and elders,
I shall declare without shame in your presence
My feelings for my husband. Diffidence
Dies in us all with time. I shall speak of what
I suffered here, while he was away at the war,
Sitting at home, with no man's company,
Waiting for news, listening to one
Messenger after another, each bringing worse
Disasters. If all his rumored wounds were real,
His body was in shreds, shot through and through.
If he had died—the predominant report—
He was a second Geryon, an outstretched giant
With three corpses and one death for each,
While I, distraught, with a knot pressing my throat,
Was rescued forcibly, to endure still more.
And that is why our child is not present here,
As he should be, pledge of our marriage vows,
Orestes. Let me reassure you. He lives
Safe with an old friend, Strophius, who warned me
Of various dangers—your life at stake in Troy
And here a restive populace, which might perhaps
Be urged to kick a man when he is down.
As for myself, the fountains of my tears
Have long ago run dry. My eyes are sore
After so many nights watching the lamp
That burnt at my bedside always for you.
If I should sleep, a gnat's faint whine would shatter
The dreams that were my only company.
But now, all pain endured, all sorrow past,
I salute this man as the watchdog of the fold,
The stay that saves the ship, the sturdy oak
That holds the roof up, the longed-for only child,
The shore despaired-of sighted far out at sea.
God keep us from all harm! And now, dearest,
Dismount, but not on the bare ground! Servants,
Spread out beneath those feet that have trampled Troy
A road of royal purple, which shall lead him
By the hand of Justice into a home unhoped-for,
And there, when he has entered, our vigilant care
Shall dispose of everything as the Gods have ordained.

Agamemnon:
Lady, royal consort and guardian of our home,
I thank you for your words of welcome, extended
To fit my lengthy absence; but due praise
Should rather come from others; and besides,
I would not have effeminate graces unman me
With barbarous salaams and beneath my feet
Purple embroideries designed for sacred use.

5. kă-SĂN´-druh

Honor me as a mortal, not as a god.
Heaven's greatest gift is wisdom. Count him blest
Who has brought a long life to a happy end.
I shall do as I have said, with a clear conscience.

Clytemnestra:
Yet tell me frankly, according to your judgment.

Agamemnon:
My judgment stands. Make no mistake about that.

Clytemnestra:
Would you not in time of danger have vowed such an act?

Agamemnon:
Yes, if the priests had recommended it.

Clytemnestra:
And what would Priam have done, if he had won?

Agamemnon:
Oh, he would have trod the purple without a doubt.

Clytemnestra:
Then you have nothing to fear from wagging tongues.

Agamemnon:
Popular censure is a potent force.

Clytemnestra:
Men must risk envy in order to be admired.

Agamemnon:
A contentious spirit is unseemly in a woman.

Clytemnestra:
Well may the victor yield a victory.

Agamemnon:
Do you set so much store by your victory?

Clytemnestra:
Be tempted, freely vanquished, victor still!

Agamemnon:
Well, if you will have it, let someone unlace
These shoes, and, as I tread the purple, may
No far-off god cast at me an envious glance
At the prodigal desecration of all this wealth!
Meanwhile, extend your welcome to this stranger.
Power tempered with gentleness wins God's favor.
No one is glad to be enslaved, and she
Is a princess presented to me by the army,
The choicest flower culled from a host of captives.
And now, constrained to obey you, setting foot
On the sacred purple, I pass into my home.

Clytemnestra:
The sea is still there, nothing can dry it up,
Renewing out of its infinite abundance
Unfailing streams of purple and blood-red dyes.[6]
So too this house, the Gods be praised, my lord.
Has riches inexhaustible. There is no counting
The robes *I* would have vowed to trample on,
Had some oracle so instructed, if by such means
I could have made good the loss of one dear soul.[7]
So now your entry to your hearth and home
Is like a warm spell in the long winter's cold,
Or when Zeus from the virgin grape at last
Draws wine, coolness descends upon the house
(For then from the living root the new leaves raise
A welcome shelter against the burning Dog-Star)
As man made perfect moves about his home.
[*Exit* AGAMEMNON.]
Zeus, perfecter of all things, fulfil my prayers
And fulfil also your own purposes! [Exit]

Chorus:
What is this delirious dread,
Ominous, oracular,
Droning through my brain with unrelenting
Beat, irrepressible prophet of evil?
Why can I not cast it out
Planting good courage firm
On my spirit's empty throne?
In time the day came
When the Greeks with anchors plunged
Moored the sloops of war, and troops
Thronged the sandy beach of Troy.

So today my eyes have seen
Safe at last the men come home.
Still I hear the strain of stringless music,
Dirge of the Furies, a choir uninvited
Chanting in my heart of hearts.
Mortal souls stirred by God
In tune with fate divine the shape
Of things to come; yet
Grant that these forebodings prove
False and bring my fears to naught.

If a man's health be advanced over the due mean,
It will trespass soon upon sickness, who stands
Next neighbor, between them a thin wall.
So does the vessel of life
Launched with a favoring breeze
Suddenly founder on reefs of destruction.
Caution seated at the helm
Casts a portion of the freight
Overboard with measured throw;
So the ship may ride the storm.
Furrows enriched each season with showers from heaven
Banish hunger from the door.
But if the red blood of a man spatters the ground, dripping and deadly, then who
Has the magical power to recall it?
Even the healer who knew
Spells to awaken the dead,
Zeus put an end to his necromancy.
Portions are there preordained,
Each supreme within its own
Province fixed eternally.
That is why my spirit groans
Brooding in fear, and no longer it hopes to unravel
Mazes of a fevered mind.
[*Enter* CLYTEMNESTRA.]

Clytemnestra:
You, too, Cassandra, come inside! The merciful
Zeus gives you the privilege to take part
In our domestic sacrifice and stand
Before his altar among the other slaves there.
Put by your pride and step down. Even Heracles
Submitted once to slavery, and be consoled
In serving a house whose wealth has been inherited
Over so many generations. The harshest masters
Are those who have snatched their harvest out of hand.
You shall receive here what custom prescribes.

Chorus:
She is speaking to you. Caught in the net, surrender.

---

6. The purple dye was extracted from seaweed. It was very rare, therefore very expensive; a color reserved for the gods.
7. Iphigenia.

Clytemnestra:
If she knows Greek and not some barbarous language,
My mystic words shall fill the soul within her.

Chorus:
You have no choice. Step down and do her will.

Clytemnestra:
There is no time to waste. The victims are
All ready for the knife to render thanks
For this unhoped-for joy. If you wish to take part,
Make haste, but, if you lack the sense to understand,—
[*To the* CHORUS.]
Speak to her with your hands and drag her down.

Chorus:
She is like a wild animal just trapped.

Clytemnestra:
She is mad, the foolish girl. Her city captured,
Brought here a slave, she will be broken in.
I'll waste no words on her to demean myself. [*Exit.*]

Cassandra:
Oh! oh! Apollo!

Chorus:
What blasphemy, to wail in Apollo's name!

Cassandra:
Oh! oh! Apollo!

Chorus:
Again she cries in grief to the god of joy!

Cassandra:
Apollo, my destroyer! a second time!

Chorus:
Ah, she foresees what is in store for her.
She is now a slave, and yet God's gift remains.

Cassandra:
Apollo, my destroyer! What house is this?

Chorus:
Do you not know where you have come, poor girl?
Then let us tell you. This is the House of Atreus.

Cassandra:
Yes, for its very walls smell of iniquity,
A charnel house that drips with children's blood.[8]

Chorus:
How keen her scent to seize upon the trail!

Cassandra:
Listen to them as they bewail the foul
Repast of roast meat for a father's mouth!

Chorus:
Enough! Reveal no more! We know it all.

Cassandra:
What is it plotted next? Horror unspeakable,
A hard cross for kinsfolk.
The hoped-for savior is far away.

Chorus:
What does she say? This must be something new.

Cassandra:
Can it be so—to bathe one who is travel-tired,
And then smiling stretch out
A hand followed by a stealthy hand!

Chorus:
She speaks in riddles, and I cannot read them.

Cassandra:
What do I see? A net!
Yes, it is she, his mate and murderess!
Cry alleluia, cry, angels of hell, rejoice,
Fat with blood, dance and sing!

Chorus:
What is the Fury you have called upon?
Helpless the heart faints with the sinking sun.
Closer still draws the stroke.

Cassandra:
Ah, let the bull[9] beware!
It is a robe she wraps him in, and strikes!
Into the bath he slumps heavily, drowned in blood.
Such her skilled handicraft.

Chorus:
It is not hard to read her meaning now.
Why does the prophet's voice never have good to tell,
Only cry woes to come?

Cassandra:
Oh, pitiful destiny! Having lamented his,
Now I lament my own passion to fill the bowl.
Where have you brought me? Must I with him die?

Chorus:
You sing your own dirge, like the red-brown bird
That pours out her grief-stricken soul,
Itys, Itys! she cries, the sad nightingale.

Cassandra:
It is not so; for she, having become a bird,
Forgot her tears and sings her happy lot,
While I must face the stroke of two-edged steel.

Chorus:
From whence does this cascade of harsh discords
Issue, and where will it at last be calmed?
Calamity you cry—O where must it end?

Cassandra:
O wedding day, Paris accurst of all!
Scamander,[10] whose clear waters I grew beside!
Now I must walk weeping by Acheron.

Chorus:
Even a child could understand.
The heart breaks, as these pitiful cries
Shatter the listening soul.

Cassandra:
O fall of Troy, city of Troy destroyed!
The king's rich gifts little availed her so
That she might not have been what she is now.

Chorus:
What evil spirit has possessed
Your soul, strumming such music upon your lips
As on a harp in hell?

Cassandra:
Listen! My prophecy shall glance no longer
As through a veil like a bride newly-wed,
But bursting towards the sunrise shall engulf
The whole world in calamities far greater

---

8. She refers to Thyestes' banquet. See introduction.
9. Agamemnon.
10. Scamander is a river near Troy; Acheron (AK-e-ron) is the river of the underworld.

Than these. No more riddles, I shall instruct,
While you shall verify each step, as I
Nose out from the beginning this bloody trail.
Upon this roof—do you see them?—stands a choir—
It has been there for generations—a gallery
Of unmelodious minstrels, a merry troop
Of wassailers drunk with human blood, reeling
And retching in horror at a brother's outraged bed.
Well, have I missed? Am I not well-read in
Your royal family's catalogue of crime?

Chorus:
You come from a far country and recite
Our ancient annals as though you had been present.

Cassandra:
The Lord Apollo bestowed this gift on me.

Chorus:
Was it because he had fallen in love with you?

Cassandra:
I was ashamed to speak of this till now.

Chorus:
Ah yes, adversity is less fastidious.

Cassandra:
Oh, but he wrestled strenuously for my love.

Chorus:
Did you come, then, to the act of getting child?

Cassandra:
At first I consented, and then I cheated him.

Chorus:
Already filled with his gift of prophecy?

Cassandra:
Yes, I forewarned my people of their destiny.

Chorus:
Did your divine lover show no displeasure?

Cassandra:
Yes, the price I paid was that no one listened to me.

Chorus:
Your prophecies seem credible enough to us.

Cassandra:
Oh!
Again the travail of the prophetic trance
Runs riot in my soul. Do you not see them
There, on the roof, those apparitions—children
Murdered by their own kin, in their hands
The innards of which their father ate—oh
What a pitiable load they carry! For that crime
Revenge is plotted by the fainthearted lion,[11]
The stay-at-home, stretched in my master's bed
(Being his slave, I must needs call him so),
Lying in wait for Troy's great conqueror.
Little he knows what that foul bitch with ears
Laid back and rolling tongue intends for him
With a vicious snap, her husband's murderess.
What abominable monster shall I call her—
A two-faced amphisbaene or Scylla that skulks
Among the rocks to waylay mariners,
Infernal sea-squib locked in internecine
Strife—did you not hear her alleluias
Of false rejoicing at his safe return?
Believe me or not, what must be will be, and then
You will pity me and say, She spoke the truth.

Chorus:
The feast of Thyestes I recognized, and shuddered,
But for the rest my wits are still astray.

Cassandra:
Your eyes shall see the death of Agamemnon.

Chorus:
No, hush those ill-omened lips, unhappy girl!

Cassandra:
There is no Apollo present, and so no cure.

Chorus:
None, if you speak the truth; yet God forbid!

Cassandra:
Pray God forbid, while they close in for the kill!

Chorus:
What man is there who would plot so foul a crime?

Cassandra:
Ah, you have altogether misunderstood,

Chorus:
But how will he do it? That escapes me still.

Cassandra:
And yet I can speak Greek only too well.

Chorus:
So does Apollo, but his oracles are obscure.

Cassandra:
Ah, how it burns me up! Apollo! Now
That lioness[12] on two feet pours in the cup
My wages too, and while she whets the blade
For him promises to repay my passage money
In my own blood. Why wear these mockeries,
This staff and wreath, if I must die, then you
Shall perish first and be damned. Now we are quits!
Apollo himself has stripped me, looking upon me
A public laughingstock, who has endured
The name of witch, waif, beggar, castaway,
So now the god who gave me second sight
Takes back his gift and dismisses his servant,
Ready for the slaughter at a dead man's grave.
Yet we shall be avenged. Now far away,
The exile[13] shall return, called by his father's
Unburied corpse to come and kill his mother.
Why weep at all this? Have I not seen Troy fall,
And those who conquered her are thus discharged.
I name this door the gate of Hades: now
I will go and knock, I will take heart to die.
I only pray that the blow may be mortal,
Closing these eyes in sleep without a struggle,
While my life blood ebbs quietly away.

Chorus:
O woman, in whose wisdom is so much grief,
How, if you know the end, can you approach it
So gently, like an ox that goes to the slaughter?

Cassandra:
What help would it be if I should put it off?

Chorus:
Yet, while there is life there's hope—so people say.

Cassandra:
For me no hope, no help. My hour has come.

---

11. Aegisthus.
12. Clytemnestra.
13. Orestes.

Chorus:
You face your end with a courageous heart.

Cassandra:
Yes, so they console those whom life has crossed.

Chorus:
Is there no comfort in an honorable death?

Cassandra:
O Priam, father, and all your noble sons! [*She approaches the door, then draws back.*]

Chorus:
What is it? Why do you turn back, sick at heart?

Cassandra:
Inside there is a stench of dripping blood.

Chorus:
It is only the blood of their fireside sacrifice.

Cassandra:
It is the sort of vapor that issues from a tomb.
I will go now and finish my lament
Inside the house. Enough of life! O friends!
I am not scared. I beg of you only this:
When the day comes for them to die, a man
For a man, woman for woman, remember me!

Chorus:
Poor soul condemned to death, I pity you.

Cassandra:
Yet one word more, my own dirge for myself.
I pray the Sun, on whom I now look my last,
That he may grant to my master's avengers
A fair price for the slave-girl slain at his side.
O sad mortality! when fortune smiles,
A painted image; and when trouble comes,
One touch of a wet sponge wipes it away. [*Exit.*]

Chorus:
And her case is even more pitiable than his.
Human prosperity never rests but always craves more, till blown up with pride it totters and falls. From the opulent mansions pointed at by all passersby none warns it away, none cries. "Let no more riches enter!" To him was granted the capture of Troy, and he has entered his home as a god, but now, if the blood of the past is on him, if he must pay with his own death for the crimes of bygone generations, then who is assured of a life without sorrow?

Agamemnon:
Oh me!

Chorus:
Did you hear?

Agamemnon:
Oh me, again!

Chorus:[14]
It is the King. Let us take counsel!
1 I say, raise a hue and cry!
2 Break in at once!
3 Yes, we must act.
4 *They* spurn delay.
5 They plot a tyranny.
6 Must we live their slaves?
7 Better to die.
8 Old men, what can we do?
9 We cannot raise the dead.
10 His death is not yet proved.
11 We are only guessing.
12 Let us break in and learn the truth!
[*The doors are thrown open and* CLYTEMNESTRA *is seen standing over the bodies of* AGAMEMNON *and* CASSANDRA, which are laid out on a purple robe.]

Clytemnestra:
All that I said before to bide my time
Without any shame I shall now unsay. How else
Could I have plotted against an enemy
So near and seeming dear and strung the snare
So high that he could not jump it? Now the feud
On which I have pondered all these years has been
Fought out to its conclusion. Here I stand
Over my work, and it was so contrived
As to leave no loophole. With this vast dragnet
I enveloped him in purple folds, then struck
Twice, and with two groans he stretched his legs,
Then on his outspread body I struck a third blow,
A drink for Zeus the Deliverer of the dead.
There he lay gasping out his soul and drenched me
In these deathly dew-drops, at which I cried
In sheer delight like newly-budding corn
That tastes the first spring showers. And so,
Venerable elders, you see how the matter stands.
Rejoice, if you are so minded. I glory in it.
With bitter tears he filled the household bowl;
Now he has drained it to the dregs and gone.

Chorus:
How can you speak so of your murdered king?

Clytemnestra:
You treat me like an empty-headed woman.
Again, undaunted, to such as understand
I say—commend or censure, as you please—
It makes no difference—here is Agamemnon,
My husband, dead, the work of this right hand,
Which acted justly. There you have the truth.

Chorus:
Woman, what evil brew have you devoured to take
On you a crime that cries out for a public curse?
Yours was the fatal blow, banishment shall be yours,
Hissed and hated of all men.

Clytemnestra:
Your sentence now for me is banishment,
But what did you do then to contravene
His purpose, when, to exorcise the storms,
As though picking a ewe-lamb from his flocks,
Whose wealth of snowy fleeces never fails
To increase and multiply, he killed his own
Child, born to me in pain, my best-beloved?
Why did you not drive *him* from hearth and home?
I bid you cast at me such menaces
As make for mastery in equal combat
With one prepared to meet them, and if, please God,
The issue goes against you, suffering
Shall school those grey hairs in humility.

---

14. To the best of our knowledge, this is the first time in any Greek play when the chorus-members have spoken as individuals. Some translations show the passage as a crescendo through the seventh speech; then a lapse into a do-nothing attitude. What does this movement show about the relation of the chorus to the tradition-ridden, fatalistic society?

Chorus:
You are possessed by some spirit of sin that stares
Out of your bloodshot eyes matching your bloody hands.
Dishonored and deserted of your kind, for this
Stroke you too shall be struck down.

Clytemnestra:
Listen! By Justice, who avenged my child,
By the Fury to whom I vowed this sacrament,
No thought of fear shall enter through this door
So long as the hearth within is kindled by
Aegisthus, faithful to me now as always.
Low lies the man who insulted his wedded wife,
The darling of the Chryseids at Troy,
And stretched beside him this visionary seer,
Whom he fondled on shipboard, both now rewarded,
He as you see, and she swanlike has sung
Her dying ditty, his tasty side dish, for me
A rare spice to add relish to my joy.

Chorus:
Oh, for the gift of death
To bring the long sleep that knows no waking,
Now that my lord and loyal protector
Breathes his last. For woman's sake
Long he fought overseas,
Now at home falls beneath a woman's hand.
Helen, the folly-beguiled, having ravaged the city of Troy,
She has set on the curse of Atreus
A crown of blood beyond ablution.

Clytemnestra:
Do not pray for death nor turn your anger against one woman as the slayer of thousands!

Chorus:
Demon of blood and tears
Inbred in two women single-hearted!
Perched on the roof he stands and preens his
Sable wings, a carrion-crow
Loud he croaks, looking down
Upon the feast spread before him here below.

Clytemnestra:
Ah now you speak truth, naming the thrice-fed demon, who, glutted with blood, craves more, still young in his hunger.

Chorus:
When will the feast be done?
Alas, it is the will of Zeus,
Who caused and brought it all to pass.
Nothing is here but was decreed in heaven.

Clytemnestra:
It was not my doing, nor am I Agamemnon's wife, but a ghost in woman's guise, the shade of the banqueter whom Atreus fed.

Chorus:
How is the guilt not yours?
And yet the crimes of old may well
Have had a hand, and so it drives
On, the trail of internecine murder.

Clytemnestra:
What of *him*? Was the guilt not his, when he killed the child that I bore him? And so by the sword he has fallen.

Chorus:
Alas, the mind strays. The house is falling.
A storm of blood lays the walls in ruins.
Another mortal stroke for Justice' hand
Will soon be sharpened.
Oh me, who shall bury him, who sing the dirge?
Who shall intone at the tomb of a blessed spirit
A tribute pure in heart and truthful?

Clytemnestra:
No, I'll bury him, but without mourners. By the waters of Acheron Iphigenia is waiting for him with a kiss.

Chorus:
The charge is answered with countercharges.
The sinner must suffer: such is God's will.
The ancient curse is bringing down the house
In self-destruction.

Clytemnestra:
That is the truth, and I would be content that the spirit of vengeance should rest, having absolved the house from its madness.

[*Enter* AEGISTHUS *with a bodyguard.*]

Aegisthus:
Now I have proof that there are Gods in heaven,
As I gaze on this purple mesh in which
My enemy lies, son of a treacherous father.
His father, Atreus, monarch of this realm,
Was challenged in his sovran rights by mine,
Thyestes, his own brother, and banished him
From hearth and home. Later he returned
A suppliant and found sanctuary, indeed
A welcome; for his brother entertained him
To a feast of his own children's flesh, of which
My father unsuspecting took and ate.
Then, when he knew what he had done, he fell
Back spewing out the slaughtered flesh and, kicking
The table to the floor, with a loud cry
He cursed the House of Pelops. That is the crime
For which the son lies here. And fitly too
The plot was spun by me; for as a child
I was banished with my father, until Justice
Summoned me home. Now let me die, for never
Shall I live to another sight so sweet.

Chorus:
Aegisthus, if it was you who planned this murder,
Then be assured, the people will stone you for it.

Aegisthus:
Such talk from the lower benches! Even in dotage
Prison can teach a salutary lesson.
Better submit, or else you shall smart for it.

Chorus:
You woman, who stayed at home and wallowed in
His bed, you plotted our great commander's death!

Aegisthus:
Orpheus led all in rapture after him.[15]
Your senseless bark will be snuffed out in prison.

Chorus:
You say the plot was yours, yet lacked the courage
To raise a hand but left it to a woman!

Aegisthus:
As his old enemy, I was suspect.
Temptation was the woman's part. But now

15. That is: You are not Orpheus, whose music caused people to follow him.

I'll try my hand at monarchy, and all
Who disobey me shall be put in irons
And starved of food and light till they submit.

Chorus:
Oh, if Orestes yet beholds the sun,
May he come home and execute them both!

Aegisthus:
Ho, my guards, come forward, you have work to do.

Captain of the Guard:
Stand by, draw your swords!

Chorus:
We are not afraid to die.

Aegisthus:
Die! We'll take you at your word.

Clytemnestra:
Peace, my lord, and let no further wrong be done.
Captain, sheathe your swords. And you, old men,
Go home quietly. What has been, it had to be.
Scars enough we bear, now let us rest.

Aegisthus:
Must I stand and listen to their threats?

Chorus:
Men of Argos never cringed before a rogue.

Aegisthus:
I shall overtake you yet—the day is near.

Chorus:
Not if Orestes should come home again.

Aegisthus:
Vain hope, the only food of castaways.

Chorus:
Gloat and grow fat, blacken justice while you dare!

Aegisthus:
All this foolish talk will cost you dear.

Chorus:
Flaunt your gaudy plumes and strut beside your hen!

Clytemnestra:
Pay no heed to idle clamor. You and I,
Masters of the house, shall now direct it well.

Exercises

1. It might be interesting to read through the speeches of the Chorus without any reference to the other speeches or action of the play. What is your impression of their attitude toward life in general? Do you find many examples of their speaking proverbial wisdom? It is one theme of this discussion of the Greeks that in their early cultural development they were bound by tradition and nature. Does this speaking in proverbs have any relation to this theme?
2. Cassandra, of course, is trying to arouse the Chorus to action. Quite aside from the mythical problem of the curse of Apollo which caused everyone to disbelieve her prophecies, can you see any other reason why she cannot get these men to act? For example, why, when she was left alone in the chariot, knowing that she faced death as soon as she entered the palace, did she not run away? Certainly the members of the Chorus would not stop her.
3. Below is given a chart dealing with the levels of human freedom of action. It might be interesting to place the characters somewhere above or below the dividing line. Where would you place the Chorus throughout the play? Do they stand still, or does their position fluctuate? Where would you place Cassandra? Agamemnon? Clytemnestra?
4. When the Chorus is telling of the death of Iphigenia, they speak of her "swathed in folds of saffron." Later they say, "Night . . . who has cast over the towers of Troy a net so fine." Still later, Agamemnon walks on a purple "web," or "net." Why did Aeschylus use this image throughout the play? Does it have any significance beyond its literal meaning?
5. Notice that *Agamemnon* has its beginning in the darkness in the country town of Mycenae. *The Eumenides*, the third play of the trilogy, ends in the bright sunlight of Athens. Does this symbolism have any significance?

The area of conduct in which men are free to accomplish their purposes and desires. {

The Dividing Line ______________________

A not-quite-human level where men's ideas of justice are bound by tradition and nature. {

Eumenides

Aeschylus

This is the third play of the *Oresteia*. In the second one *(Choephori*, or *The Libation Bearers*), Orestes has returned to Argos, recognized his sister, Electra, and the two of them have planned and carried out the murder of Aegisthus and Clytemnestra. In the second play, the two ideas of justice became more apparent, for Orestes felt qualms about the murder of his mother. His sense of filial duty in carrying out revenge, as well as the fact that Apollo had commanded him to the deed, triumphed over his own conscience. Immediately after the murder he was set upon by the old hags, goddesses descended from the blood of Uranus, whose duty it was to pursue those who had killed their own kindred.

The old idea of justice, revenge or retaliation,

was presented in *Agamemnon;* we see in *Eumenides*[1] the development of a new idea of justice and freedom for the city of Athens. Watch how this is handled. When you have finished the play, stop a while and think about the ways in which men can live under this new concept.

Characters: *Prophetess*
Apollo
Orestes (oh-RES-teez)
Ghost of Clytemnestra (kly-tem-NES-tra)
Chorus of Furies
Athena
Escort of Women

Before the temple of Apollo at Delphi.
[*Enter the* PRIESTESS.]

Priestess:
First among all the gods to whom this prayer
Shall be addressed is the first of prophets, Earth;[2]
And next her daughter, Themis, who received
The oracular shrine from her; third, another
Daughter, Phoebe, who having settled here
Bestowed it as a birthday gift, together
With her own name, on Phoebus; whereupon,
Leaving his native isle of Delos and landing
In Attica, he made his way from there
Attended by the sons of Hephaestus, who tamed
The wilderness and built a road for him;
And here Zeus, having inspired him with his art,
Set him, the fourth of prophets, on this throne,
His own son and interpreter, Apollo.
Together with these deities I pay
Homage to Athena and to the nymphs that dwell
In the Corycian caves on the rugged slopes
Of Parnassus,[3] where Dionysus led
His troop of frenzied Bacchants to catch and kill
King Pentheus like a mountain-hare; and so,
After calling on Poseidon and the springs
Of Pleistus, watering this valley, and last
On Zeus the All-Highest, who makes all things perfect,
I take my seat on the oracular throne,
Ready to be consulted. Let all Greeks
Approach by lot according to the custom
And I shall prophesy to them as God dictates. [*She enters the temple, utters a loud cry, and returns.*]
O horror, horror! I have been driven back
Strengthless, speechless, a terror-struck old woman,
By such a sight as was never seen before.
Entering the shrine I saw at the navel-stone
In the posture of a suppliant a man
Who held an olive-branch and an unsheathed sword
In hands dripping with blood; and all round him,
Lying fast asleep, a gruesome company
Of women—yet not women—Gorgons rather;
And yet not Gorgons; them I saw once in a picture
Of the feast of Phineus: these are different.
They have no wings, and are all black, and snore,
And drips ooze from their eyes, and the rags they wear
Unutterably filthy. What country could
Have given such creatures birth, I cannot tell.
Apollo is the master of this house,
So let him look to it, healer, interpreter,
Himself of other houses purifier.
[*The inside of the temple is revealed, as described, with* APOLLO *and* HERMES *standing beside* ORESTES.]

Apollo:
I will keep faith, at all times vigilant,
Whether at your side or far away, and never
Mild to your enemies, whom you now see
Subdued by sleep, these unloved virgins, these
Children hoary with age, whose company
Is shunned by God and man and beast, being born
For evil, just as the abyss from which they come
Is evil, the bottomless pit of Tartarus.
Yet you must fly before them, hotly pursued,
Past island cities and over distant seas,
Enduring all without faltering, until
You find sanctuary in Athena's citadel,
And there, embracing her primeval image, you
Shall stand trial, and after healing words
From me, who commanded you to kill your mother,
You shall be set free and win your salvation.

Orestes:
O Lord Apollo, you have both wisdom and power,
And, since you have them, use them on my behalf!

Apollo:
Remember, endure and have no fear! And you,
Hermes, go with him, guide him, guard his steps,
An outcast from mankind, yet blest of Zeus.
[*Exeunt* HERMES *and* ORESTES. *Enter the ghost of* CLYTEMNESTRA.]

Clytemnestra:
Oho! asleep! What good are you to me asleep?
While I, deserted and humiliated,
Wander, a homeless ghost. I warn you that
Among the other spirits of the dead
(The taunt of murder does not lose its sting
In the dark world below) I am the accused
And not the accuser, with none to defend me,
Brutally slain by matricidal hands.
Look on these scars, and remember all
The wineless offerings which I laid upon
The hearth for you at many a solemn midnight—
All now forgotten, all trampled underfoot!
And *he* is gone! Light as a fawn he skipped
Out of your snare and now he laughs at you.
Oh hear me! I am pleading for my soul!
O goddesses of the underworld, awake!
I, Clytemnestra, call you now in dreams!

Chorus:
Mu!

Clytemnestra:
Ah, you may mew, but he is fled and gone.
He has protectors who are no friends of mine.

Chorus:
Mu!

---

1. you-MEN-i-deez
2. Earth, Themis, Phoebe, and Phoebus Apollo are the gods who have prophesied at the Oracle of Delphi.
3. Mount Parnassus stands beside Delphi. King Pentheus of Thebes was killed by the female worshippers of Dionysus either here or on Mount Kithaeron.

Clytemnestra:
Still so drowsy, still so pitiless?
Orestes has escaped, the matricide!

Chorus:
Oh, oh!

Clytemnestra:
Still muttering and mumbling in your sleep!
Arise, do evil! is not that your task?

Chorus:
Oh, oh!

Clytemnestra:
How sleep and weariness have made common cause
To disenvenom the foul dragon's rage!

Chorus:
Oh, oh! where is the scent? Let us mark it down!

Clytemnestra:
Yes, you may bay like an unerring hound,
But still you are giving chase only in your dreams.
What are you doing? Rise, slothful slugabeds,
Stung by the scourge of my rebukes, arise
And blow about his head your bloody breath,
Consume his flesh in bellyfuls of fire!
Come on, renew the chase and hunt him down! *[Exit.]*

Chorus:
We have been put to shame! What has befallen us?
The game has leapt out of the snare and gone.
In slumber laid low, we slip the prey.

Aha, son of Zeus! pilferer, pillager!
A God, to steal away the matricide!
A youth to flout powers fixed long ago!

In dream I felt beneath the heart a swift
Charioteer's sharp lash.
Under the ribs, under the flank
It rankles yet, red and sore,
Like the public scourger's blow.

This is the doing of the younger gods.
Dripping with death, red drops
Cover the heel, cover the head.
Behold the earth's navel-stone
Thick with heavy stains of blood!

His own prophetic cell he has himself defiled.
Honoring mortal claims, reckless of laws divine,
And dealing death to Fates born of old.
He injures us and yet *him* he shall never free,
Not in the depths of hell, never shall he have rest
But suffer lasting torment below.

Apollo:
Out, out! Be off, and clear this holy place
Of your foul presence, or else from my golden bow
Shall spring a snake of silver and bite so deep
That from your swollen bellies you shall spew
The blood which you have sucked! Your place is where
Heads drop beneath the axe, eyes are gouged out,
Throats slit, and men are stoned, limbs lopped, and boys
Gelded, and a last whimper heard from spines
Spiked writhing in the dust. Such celebrations,
Which fill heaven with loathing, are your delight.
Off with you, I say, and go unshepherded,
A herd shunned with universal horror!

Chorus:
O Lord Apollo, hear us in our turn!
You are not an abettor in this business.
You are the culprit. On you lies the whole guilt.

Apollo:
Explain yourselves. How do you make that out?

Chorus:
It was at your command that he killed his mother.

Apollo:
I commanded him to take vengeance for his father.

Chorus:
So promising the acceptance of fresh blood.

Apollo:
I promised to absolve him from it here.

Chorus:
Why do you insult the band that drove him here?

Apollo:
This mansion is not fit for your company.

Chorus:
But this is the task that has been appointed to us.

Apollo:
What is this privilege that you are so proud of?

Chorus:
To drive all matricides from hearth and home.

Apollo:
And what of a woman who has killed her husband?

Chorus:
That is not manslaughter within the kin.

Apollo:
So then you set at naught the marriage-bond
Sealed by Zeus and Hera, and yet what tie
Is stronger, joined by Fate and watched over
By Justice, than the joy which Aphrodite
Has given to man and woman? If you let those
Who violate that covenant go unpunished,
You have no right to persecute Orestes.
Why anger here, and there passivity?
On this in time Athena shall pass judgment.

Chorus:
We shall give chase and never let him go.

Apollo:
Pursue him then, and make trouble for yourselves.

Chorus:
No words of yours can circumscribe our powers.

Apollo:
I would not have your powers even as a gift.

Chorus:
Then take your proud stand by the throne of Zeus.
Meanwhile a mother's blood is beckoning to us,
And we must go and follow up the trail.

Apollo:
And I will still safeguard the suppliant.
A wrong unheard-of in heaven and on earth
Would be his protest, if I should break faith.
[*A year passes. Before a shrine of Athena at Athens. Enter* ORESTES.]

Orestes:
O Queen Athena, I have come here in obedience
To the Lord Apollo. Grant me sanctuary,
An outcast, yet with hands no longer sullied, for
The edge of my pollution has been worn

Off on countless paths over land and sea;
And now, in accordance with his word, present
Before your image, I entreat you to
Receive me here and pass the final judgment.

Chorus:
Step where our dumb informer leads the way;
For as the hounds pursue a wounded fawn,
So do we dog the trail of human blood.
How far we have traveled over land and sea,
Faint and footsore but never to be shaken off!
He must be somewhere here, for I smell blood.

—Beware, I say, beware!
Look on all sides for fear he find some escape!
—Ah, here he is, desperate,
Clasping that image awaiting trial.
—It cannot be! The mother's blood
That he has spilt is irrecoverable.
—Ravenous lips shall feed upon his living flesh
And on his blood—a lush pasturage.
—And others shall he see in hell, who wronged
Parents, guests or gods;
For Hades is a stern inquisitor of souls,
Recording all things till the hour of judgment.

Orestes:
Taught by long suffering, I have learnt at what
Times it is right to keep silence and when
To break it, and in this matter a wise
Instructor has charged me to speak. The stain
Of matricide has been washed out in the flow
Of swine's blood by Apollo. I could tell
Of many who have given me lodging and no
Harm has befallen them from my company;
And now with lips made pure I call upon
Athena to protect me and so join
Our peoples as allies for all time to come.
Wherever she may be, on Libyan shores
Or by the stream of Trito, where she came
To birth, or like a captain keeping watch
On the heights of Phlegra against some enemy,
O may she come—far off, she can still hear me—
And from my sufferings deliver me!

Chorus:
Neither Apollo nor Athena can
Save your soul from perdition, a feast for fiends.
Have you no answer? Do you spurn us so,
Fattened for us, our consecrated host?

Let us dance and declare in tune with this grim music
the laws which it is ours to enforce on the life of man.
It is only those that have blood on their hands who need
fear us at all, but from them without fail we exact
retribution.

Mother Night, your children cry! Hear, black Night!
It is ours to deal by day and dark night judgment.
The young god Apollo has rescued the matricide!
    Over the blood that has been shed
    Maddening dance, melody desperate. deathly,
    Chant to bind the soul in hell,
    Spell that parches flesh to dust.

This the Fates who move the whole world through
Have assigned to us, a task for all future ages,
To keep watch on all hands that drip red with kindred blood.
    Over the blood that has been shed
    Maddening dance, melody desperate, deathly,
    Chant to bind the soul in hell,
    Spell that parches flesh to dust.

Such are the powers appointed us from the beginning,
None of the Gods of Olympus to eat with us, while we
Take no part in the wearing of white—no,
Other pleasures are our choice—
    Wrecking the house, hunting the man,
    Hard on his heels ever we run,
    And though his feet be swift we waste and wear him out.

Hence it is thanks to our zealous endeavor that from such
Offices Zeus and the Gods are exempted, and yet he
Shuns us because we are covered in blood, not
Fit to share his majesty.
    Wrecking the house, hunting the man,
    Hard on his heels ever we run,
    And though his feet be swift we waste and wear him out.

Glories of men, how bright in the day is their splendor,
Yet shall they fade in the darkness of hell,
Faced with our grisly attire and dancing
Feet attuned to sombre melodies.
    Nimble the feet leap in the air,
    Skip and descend down to the ground,
    Fugitive step suddenly tripped up in fatal confusion.

Caught without knowing he stumbles, his wickedness blinds him,
Such is the cloud of pollution that hangs
Over him and on his house, remembered
Many generations after him.
    Nimble the feet leap in the air,
    Skip and descend down to the ground,
    Fugitive step suddenly tripped up in fatal confusion.
Our task is such. With long memories
We keep constant watch on human sin.
What others spurn is what we prize,

Our heaven their hell, a region of trackless waste,
Both for the quick and dead, for blind and seeing too.

What wonder then that men bow in dread
At these commandments assigned to us
By Fate—our ancient privilege?
We are not without our own honors and dignities,
Though we reside in hell's unfathomable gloom. [*Enter* ATHENA.]

Athena:
I heard a distant cry, as I was standing
Beside Scamander to take possession of
The lands which the Achaean princes have
Bestowed on my people in perpetuity;
And thence I have made my way across the sea
In wingless flight; and now, as I regard
Before my shrine this very strange company,
I cannot but ask, in wonder, not in fear,
Who you may be. I address you all in common,
This stranger here who is seated at my image,
And you, who are not human in appearance
Nor yet divine; but rather than speak ill
Without just cause let me receive your answer.

Chorus:
Daughter of Zeus, your question is soon answered.
We are the dismal daughters of dark Night,
Called Curses in the palaces of hell.

Athena:
I know your names then and your parentage.

Chorus:
And now let us inform you of our powers.

Athena:
Yes, let me know what office you perform.

Chorus:
We drive the matricide from hearth and home.

Athena:
Where? In what place does his persecution end?

Chorus:
A place where joy is something quite unknown.

Athena:
Is that your hue and cry against this man?

Chorus:
Yes, because he dared to kill his mother.

Athena:
Was he driven to it perhaps against his will?

Chorus:
What force could drive a man to matricide?

Athena:
It is clear there are two parties to this case.

Chorus:
We challenged him to an ordeal by oath.

Athena:
You seem to seek only the semblance of justice.

Chorus:
How so? Explain, since you are so rich in wisdom.

Athena:
Do not use oaths to make the wrong prevail.

Chorus:
Then try the case yourself and give your judgment.

Athena:
Will you entrust the verdict to my charge?

Chorus:
Yes, a worthy daughter of a worthy father.

Athena:
Stranger, what is your answer? Tell us first
Your fatherland and family and what
Misfortune overtook you, and then answer
The charge against you. If you have taken your stand
Here as a suppliant with full confidence
In the justice of your cause, now is the time
To render on each count a clear reply.

Orestes:
O Queen Athena, first let me remove one doubt.
I am not a suppliant seeking purification.
I was already cleansed before I took
This image in my arms, and I can give
Evidence of this. The manslayer is required
To keep silent until he has been anointed
With sacrificial blood. That has been done,
And I have traveled far over land and sea
To wear off the pollution. So, having set
Your mind at rest, let me tell you who I am.
I come from Argos, and my father's name—
For asking me that I thank you—was Agamemnon,
The great commander, with whom not long ago
You wiped out Troy. He died an evil death,
Murdered on his return by my blackhearted
Mother, who netted him in a bath of blood.
And therefore I, restored from banishment,
In retribution for my father's death,
I killed my mother; and yet not I alone—
Apollo too must answer for it, having
Warned me what anguish would afflict me if
I should fail to take vengeance on the guilty.
Whether it was just or not, do you decide.

Athena:
This is too grave a case for mortal minds,
Nor is it right that I should judge an act
Of blood shed with such bitter consequences,
Especially since you have come to me
As one already purified, who has done no wrong
Against this city. But your opponents here
Are not so gentle, and, if their plea
Should be rejected, the poison dripping from
Their angry bosoms will devastate my country.
The issue is such that, whether I let them stay
Or turn them out, it is fraught with injury.
But be it so. Since it has come to this,
I will appoint judges for homicide,
A court set up in perpetuity.
Do you prepare your proofs and witnesses,
Then I, having selected from my people
The best, will come to pass a final judgment.[*Exit.*]

Chorus:
Now the world shall see the downfall of old commandments made
Long ago, if the accurst matricide should win his case.
Many a bitter blow awaits parents from their own children in the times to come.

We who had the task to watch over human life shall now
Cease to act, giving free rein to deeds of violence.
Crime shall spread from house to house like a plague, and whole cities shall be desolate.

Then let no man stricken cry
Out in imprecation, "Oh
Furies!" Thus shall fathers groan,
Thus shall mothers weep in vain,
Since the house of righteousness
Lies in ruins, overthrown.

Times there are when fear is good,
Keeping watch within the soul.
Needful too are penalties.
Who of those that have not nursed
Wholesome dread within them can
Show respect to righteousness?

Choose a life despot-free yet restrained by rule of law.
God has appointed the mean as the master in all things.
Wickedness breeds pride, but from wisdom is brought forth
Happiness prayed for by all men.

So, we say, men must bow down before the shrine of Right.
Those who defy it shall fail; for the ancient commandments
Stand—to respect parents and honor the stranger.
Only the righteous shall prosper.
The man who does what is right by choice, not constraint,
Shall prosper always; the seed of just men shall never perish.
Not so the captain who ships a load of ill-gotten gains.
Caught in the gathering storm his proud sail shall be torn from the masthead.

He cries to deaf ears, no longer able to ride
The gale and meanwhile his guardian spirit is close beside him
And scoffs to see him despair of ever again making port,
Dashed on the reefs of Justice, unlooked-on and unlamented.

[*Enter* ATHENA *with the* JUDGES, *followed by citizens of Athens.*]

Athena:
Herald, give orders to hold the people back,
Then sound the trumpet and proclaim silence.
For while this new tribunal is being enrolled,
It is right that all should ponder on its laws,
Both the litigants here whose case is to be judged,
And my whole people: for all generations. [*Enter* APOLLO.]

Chorus:
Apollo, what is there here that concerns you?
We say you have no authority in this matter.

Apollo:
I come both as a witness, the accused
Having been a suppliant at my sanctuary
And purified of homicide at my hands,
And also to be tried with him, for I too
Must answer for the murder of his mother.
Open the case, and judge as you know how.

Athena:
The case is open. You shall be first to speak. [*To the* CHORUS.]
The prosecutors shall take precedence
And first inform us truthfully of the facts.

Chorus:
Many in number, we shall be brief in speech.
We beg you to answer our questions one by one.
First, is it true that you killed your mother?

Orestes:
I killed her. That is true, and not denied.

Chorus:
So then the first of the three rounds is ours.

Orestes:
You should not boast that you have thrown me yet.

Chorus:
Next, since you killed her, you must tell us how.

Orestes:
Yes, with a drawn sword leveled at the throat.

Chorus:
Who was it who impelled or moved you to it?

Orestes:
The oracle of this God who is my witness.

Chorus:
The God of prophecy ordered matricide?

Orestes:
Yes, and I have not repented it to this day.

Chorus:
You *will* repent it, when you have been condemned.

Orestes:
My father shall defend me from the grave.

Chorus:
Having killed your mother, you may well trust the dead!

Orestes:
She was polluted by a double crime.

Chorus:
How so? Explain your meaning to the judges.

Orestes:
She killed her husband and she killed my father.

Chorus:
She died without bloodguilt, and you still live.

Orestes:
Why did you not hunt her when she was alive?

Chorus:
She was not bound by blood to the man she killed.

Orestes:
And am I then bound by blood to my mother?

Chorus:
Abandoned wretch, how did she nourish you
Within the womb? Do you repudiate
The nearest and dearest tie of motherhood?

Orestes:
Apollo, give your evidence. I confess
That I did this deed as I have said.
Pronounce your judgment: was it justly done?

Apollo:
Athena's appointed judges, I say to you,
Justly, and I, as prophet, cannot lie.
Never from my prophetic shrine have I
Said anything of city, man or woman
But what my father Zeus has commanded me.
This plea of mine must override all others,
Since it accords with our great father's will.

Chorus:
Your argument is, then, that Zeus commanded you
To charge Orestes with this criminal act
Regardless of the bond between son and mother?

Apollo:
It is not the same, to murder a great king,
A woman too to do it, and not in open
Fight like some brave Amazon, but in such
Manner as I shall now inform this court.
On his return from battle, bringing home
A balance for the greater part of good,
She welcomed him with fine words and then, while
He bathed, pavilioned him in a purple robe
And struck him down and killed him—a man and king
Whom the whole world had honored. Such was the crime
For which she paid. Let the judges take note.

Chorus:
According to your argument Zeus gives
Precedence to the father; yet Zeus it was
Who cast into prison his own father Kronos.
Judges, take note, and ask him to explain.

Apollo:
Abominable monsters, loathed by gods
And men, do you not understand that chains
Can be unfastened and prison doors unlocked?
But once the dust has drunk a dead man's blood,
He can never rise again—for that no remedy
Has been appointed by our almighty Father,
Although all else he can overturn at will
Without so much effort as a single breath.

Chorus
See what your plea for the defendant means.
Is this not what he did—to spill his mother's
Blood on the ground? And shall he then be allowed
To live on in his father's house? What public
Altar can he approach and where find fellowship?

Apollo:
The mother is not a parent, only the nurse
Of the seed which the true parent, the father,
Commits to her as to a stranger to
Keep it with God's help safe from harm. And I
Have proof of this. There can be a father
Without a mother. We have a witness here,
This daughter of Olympian Zeus, who sprang
Armed from her father's head, a goddess whom
No goddess could have brought to birth. Therefore,
Out of goodwill to your country and your people
I sent this suppliant to seek refuge with you,
That you, Athena, may find in him and his
A faithful ally for all time to come.

Athena:
Enough has now been spoken. Are you agreed
That I call on the judges to record
Their votes justly according to their conscience?

Apollo:
Our quiver is empty, every arrow spent.
We wait to hear the issue of the trial.

Athena:
And has my ruling your approval too?

Chorus:
Sirs, you have heard the case, and now declare
Judgment according to your solemn oath.

Athena:
Citizens of Athens, hear my declaration
At this first trial in the history of man.
This great tribunal shall remain in power
Meeting in solemn session on this hill,
Where long ago the Amazons encamped
When they made war on Theseus, and sacrificed
To Ares—hence its name:[4] Here reverence
For law and inbred fear among my people
Shall hold their hands from evil night and day,
Only let them not tamper with the laws,
But keep the fountain pure and sweet to drink.
I warn you not to banish from your lives
All terror but to seek the mean between
Autocracy and anarchy; and in this way
You shall possess in ages yet unborn
An impregnable fortress of liberty
Such as no people has throughout the world.
With these words I establish this tribunal
Grave, quick to anger, incorruptible,
And always vigilant over those that sleep.
Let the judges now rise and cast their votes.[5]

Chorus:
We charge you to remember that we have
Great power to harm, and vote accordingly.

Apollo:
I charge you to respect the oracles
Sanctioned by Zeus and see that they are fulfilled.

Chorus:
By interfering in what is not your office
You have desecrated your prophetic shrine.

Apollo:
Then was my Father also at fault when he
Absolved Ixion, the first murderer?

Chorus:
Keep up your chatter, but if our cause should fail,
We shall lay on this people a heavy hand.

Apollo:
Yes, you will lose your case, and then you may
Spit out your poison, but it will do no harm.

Chorus:
Insolent youth mocks venerable age.
We await the verdict, ready to let loose
Against this city our destructive rage.

Athena:
The final judgment rests with me, and I
Announce that my vote shall be given to Orestes.
No mother gave me birth, and in all things
Save marriage I commend with all my heart
The masculine, my father's child indeed.
Therefore I cannot hold in higher esteem
A woman killed because she killed her husband.
If the votes are equal, Orestes wins.
Let the appointed officers proceed
To empty the urns and count the votes.

Orestes:
O bright Apollo, how shall the judgment go?

Chorus:
O black mother Night, are you watching this?

Orestes:
My hour has come—the halter or the light.

Chorus:
And ours—to exercise our powers or perish.

Apollo:
Sirs, I adjure you to count carefully.
If judgment errs, great harm will come of it,
Whereas one vote may raise a fallen house.

Athena:
He stands acquitted on the charge of bloodshed,
The human votes being equally divided.

Orestes:
Lady Athena, my deliverer,
I was an outcast from my country, now
I can go home again and live once more
In my paternal heritage, thanks to you
And to Apollo and to the third, the Savior,
Who governs the whole world. Before I go
I give my word to you and to your people
For all posterity that no commander
Shall lead an Argive army in war against
This city. If any should violate this pledge,
Out of the graves which shall then cover us
We would arise with adverse omens to
Obstruct and turn them back. If, however,
They keep this covenant and stand by your side,
They shall always have our blessing. And so farewell!
May you and your people always prevail
Against the assaults of all your enemies! [*Exit.*]

---

4. The hill and the court which met on it were called the Areopagus (air-ee-OP-uh-gus).
5. It is understood that the members of the jury are dropping their votes into an urn during the next eight speeches.

Chorus:
Oho, you junior gods, since you have trod under foot
The laws of old and robbed us of our powers,
We shall afflict this country
With damp contagion, bleak and barren, withering up the soil,
Mildew on bud and birth abortive. Venomous pestilence
Shall sweep your cornlands with infectious death.
To weep?—No! To work? Yes! To work ill and lay low the people!
So will the maids of Night mourn for their stolen honors.

Athena:
Let me persuade you to forget your grief!
You are not defeated. The issue of the trial
Has been determined by an equal vote.
It was Zeus himself who plainly testified
That Orestes must not suffer for what he did.
I beg you, therefore, do not harm my country,
Blasting her crops with drops of rank decay
And biting cankers in the early buds.
Rather accept my offer to stay and live
In a cavern on this hill and there receive
The adoration of my citizens.

Chorus:
Oho, you junior gods, etc.

Athena:
No, *not* dishonored, and therefore spare my people!
I too confide in Zeus—why speak of that?—
And I alone of all the Olympian gods
Know of the keys which guard the treasury
Of heaven's thunder. But there is no need of that.
Let my persuasion serve to calm your rage.
Reside with me and share my majesty;
And when from these wide acres you enjoy
Year after year the harvest offerings
From couples newly-wed praying for children,
Then you will thank me for my intercession.

Chorus:
How can you treat us so?
Here to dwell, ever debased, defiled!
Hear our passion, hear, black Night!
For the powers once ours, sealed long, long ago
Have by the junior gods been all snatched away.

Athena:
You are my elders, and therefore I indulge
Your passion. And yet, though not so wise as you,
To me too Zeus has granted understanding.
If you refuse me and depart, believe me,
This country will yet prove your heart's desire,
For as the centuries pass so there will flow
Such glory to my people as will assure
To all divinities worshipped here by men
And women gathered on festive holidays
More honors than could be yours in any other
City throughout the world. And so, I beg you,
Keep from my citizens the vicious spur
Of internecine strife, which pricks the breast
Of manhood flown with passion as with wine!
Abroad let battle rage for every heart
That is fired with love of glory—that shall be theirs
In plenty. So this is my offer to you—
To give honor and receive it and to share
My glory in this country loved by heaven.

Chorus:
How can you, etc.

Athena:
I will not weary in my benedictions,
Lest it should ever be said that you, so ancient
In your divinity, were driven away
By me and by my mortal citizens.
No, if Persuasion's holy majesty,
The sweet enchantment of these lips divine,
Has power to move you, please, reside with me.
But, if you still refuse, then, since we have made
This offer to you, it would be wrong to lay
Your hands upon us in such bitter rage.
Again, I tell you, it is in your power to own
This land attended with the highest honors.

Chorus:
Lady Athena, what do you offer us?

Athena:
A dwelling free of sorrow. Pray accept.

Chorus:
Say we accept, what privileges shall we have?

Athena:
No family shall prosper without your grace.

Chorus:
Will you ensure us this prerogative?

Athena:
I will, and bless all those that worship you.

Chorus:
And pledge that assurance for all time to come?

Athena:
I need not promise what I will not perform.

Chorus:
Your charms are working, and our rage subsides.

Athena:
Here make your dwelling, where you shall win friends.

Chorus:
What song then shall we chant in salutation?

Athena:
A song of faultless victory—from land and sea,
From skies above let gentle breezes blow
And breathing sunshine float from shore to shore;
Let crops and cattle increase and multiply
And children grow in health and happiness,
And let the righteous prosper; for I, as one
Who tends flowers in a garden, cherish fondly
The seed that bears no sorrow. That is your part,
While I in many a battle shall strive until
This city stands victorious against all
Its enemies and renowned throughout the world.

Chorus:
We accept; we agree to dwell with you
Here in Athens, which by grace of Zeus
Stands a fortress for the gods,
Jeweled crown of Hellas. So
With you now we join in prayer
That smiling suns and fruitful soils unite to yield
Lifelong joy, fortune fair,
Light and darkness reconciled.

Athena:
For the good of my people I have given homes in the city

to these deities,[6] whose power is so great and so slowly appeased; and, whenever a man falls foul of them, apprehended to answer for the sins of his fathers, he shall be brought to judgment before them, and the dust shall stifle his proud boast.

Chorus:
Free from blight may the early blossom deck
Budding trees, and may no parching drought
Spread across the waving fields.
Rather Pan in season grant
From the flocks and herds a full
Return from year to year, and from the rich
Store which these gods vouchsafe
May the Earth repay them well!

Athena:
Guardians of my city, listen to the blessings they bring, and remember that their power is great in heaven and hell, and on earth too they bring to some glad music and to some lives darkened with weeping.

Chorus:
Free from sudden death that cuts
Short the prime of manhood, blest
In your daughters too, to whom
Be granted husband and home, and may the dread Fates
Keep them safe, present in every household,
Praised and magnified in every place!

Athena:
Fair blessings indeed from powers that so lately were averted in anger, and I thank Zeus and the spirit of persuasion that at last there is no strife left between us, except that they vie with me in blessing my people.

Chorus:
Peace to all, free from that
Root of evil, civil strife!
May they live in unity,
And never more may the blood of kin be let flow!
Rather may all of them bonded together
Feel and act as one in love and hate!

Athena:
From these dread shapes, so quick to learn a new music, I foresee great good for my people, who, if only they repay their favors with the reverence due, shall surely establish the reign of justice in a city that will shine as a light for all mankind.

[*Enter* ESCORT OF WOMEN, *carrying crimson robes and torches.*]

Chorus:
Joy to you all in your justly appointed riches,
Joy to all the people blest
With the Virgin's love, who stands
Next beside her Father's throne!
Wisdom man has learnt at last.
Under her protection this
Land enjoys the grace of Zeus.

Athena:
Joy to you also, and now let me lead you in torchlight to your new dwelling place! Let solemn oblations speed you in joy to your home beneath the earth, and there imprison all harm while still letting flow your blessings!

Chorus:
Joy to you, joy, yet again we pronounce our blessing,
Joy to all the citizens,
Gods and mortals both alike.
While you hold this land and pay
Homage to our residence,
You shall have no cause to blame
Chance and change in human life.

Athena:
I thank you for your gracious salutations,
And now you shall be escorted in the light
Of torches to your subterranean dwelling,
Attended by the sacristans of my temple
Together with this company of girls
And married women and others bowed with years.
Women, let them put on these robes of crimson,
And let these blazing torches light the way,
That the goodwill of our new co-residents
Be shown in the manly prowess of your sons!

[*The* CHORUS *put on the crimson robes and a procession is formed led by young men in armor, with the* CHORUS *and the escort following, and behind them the citizens of Athens. The rest is sung as the procession moves away.*]

Chorus of the Escort:
Pass on your way, O powers majestic,
Daughters of darkness in happy procession!
People of Athens, hush, speak fair!

Pass to the caverns of earth immemorial
There to be worshipped in honor and glory!
People of Athens, hush, speak fair!

Gracious and kindly of heart to our people,
Come with us, holy ones, hither in gladness,
Follow the lamps that illumine the way!
O sing at the end alleluia!

Peace to you, peace of a happy community,
People of Athens! Zeus who beholds all
Watches, himself with the Fates reconciled.
O sing at the end alleluia!

Exercises

1. Of course all that one has to do to understand this play almost completely is to understand the difference in the meaning of the word *justice* as it is first used in the play by the Furies and as it is used by Athena in her last speech of the play. That difference in meaning is worth analyzing in class. To do so, here are some questions which may guide your discussion:
   a. Insofar as the structure of the play is concerned—and its significance—why can Orestes leave when two-thirds of the play is over?
   b. The Furies insist that *fear* is a necessary part of the idea of justice that people hold. How right are they?
   c. The real turning point of the play probably comes when Athena gives her final instructions to the jury:

      Here reverence
      For law and inbred fear among my people

6. This is the transition of the awful goddesses from the *Erinyes* (The Furies) to the *Eumenides* (the Gracious Ones).

Shall hold their hands from evil night and day,
Only let them not tamper with the laws,
But keep the fountain pure and sweet to drink.
I warn you not to banish from your lives
All terror but to seek the mean between
Autocracy and anarchy; and in this way
You shall possess in ages yet unborn
An impregnable fortress of liberty. . .

What principles are involved in this statement?

d. The actual role of the Eumenides (as they are changed from the Furies) is never made entirely clear. From the evidence in the play itself, what seems to be their role in the maintenance of a new type of justice?

2. What difference in the lives of the people of Athens will be found as they change from the old idea of justice to the new? In what way will the new idea allow for personal freedom?

Pericles' Memorial Oration

This portion of Pericles' (PAIR-ĭ-kleez) famous oration is taken from the history of the Peloponnesian War as written by Thucydides (thoo-SĬD-ĭ-deez). Pericles made this address at the public funeral of a group of Athenian young men who had been killed in the war.

As a method of study, you might ask yourself what questions about human life had been raised previously in the plays of Aeschylus. In the *Agamemnon* the chorus railed against great wealth or great action, insisting that the most humble life was the best. In *Eumenides* we observed the question of whether justice should be by reason or by stern revenge within the family. The question of the conflict between maturing man and an absolute god who ruled through fear had been raised. Other questions which we have not yet seen in the literature, but which were present in the Greek mind (and in our own) are whether the state needs to protect itself by universal military training or not, and whether a life of cultural pursuits does not enfeeble people in a nation. Perhaps the greatest question for our time and theirs is whether a democracy can really function. The argument on the one side is that an absolute government gets things done quickly and efficiently, while in a democracy, people talk so much that they have no time for action.

You will find some of the answers in which the Athenians believed in the following selection.

. . . Before I praise the dead, I should like to point out by what principles of action we rose to power, and under what institutions and through what manner of life our empire became great. For I conceive that such thoughts are not unsuited to the occasion, and that this numerous assembly of citizens and strangers may profitably listen to them.

Our form of government does not enter into rivalry with the institutions of others. We do not copy our neighbors, but are an example to them. It is true that we are called a democracy; for the administration is in the hands of the many and not of the few. But while the law secures equal justice to all alike in their private disputes, the claim of excellence is also recognized; and when a citizen is in any way distinguished, he is preferred to the public service, not as a matter of privilege , but as the reward of merit. Neither is poverty a bar, but a man may benefit his country whatever be the obscurity of his condition. There is no exclusiveness in our public life, and in our private intercourse we are not suspicious of one another, nor angry with our neighbor if he does what he likes; we do not put on sour looks at him, which though harmless are not pleasant. While we are thus unconstrained in our private intercourse, a spirit of reverence pervades our public acts: we are prevented from doing wrong by respect for authority and for the laws; having an especial regard to those which are ordained for the protection of the injured, as well as to these unwritten laws which bring upon the transgressor of them the reprobation of the general sentiment.

And we have not forgotten to provide for our weary spirits many relaxations from toil; we have regular games and sacrifices throughout the year; at home the style of our life is refined; and the delight which we daily feel in all these things helps to banish melancholy. Because of the greatness of our city the fruits of the whole earth flow in upon us; so that we enjoy the goods of other countries as freely as of our own.

Then again, our military training is in many respects superior to that of our adversaries. Our city is thrown open to the world; and we never expel a foreigner, or prevent him from seeing or learning anything of which the secret, if revealed to an enemy, might profit him. We rely not upon management of trickery, but upon our own hearts and hands. And in the matter of education whereas they from early youth are always undergoing laborious exercises which are to make them brave, we live at ease, and yet are equally ready to face the perils which they face. . . .

If, then, we prefer to meet danger with a light heart but without laborious training, and with a courage which is gained by habit and not enforced by law, are we not greatly the gainers? Since we do not anticipate the pain, although, when the hour comes, we can be as brave as those who never allow themselves to rest; and thus too our city is equally admirable in peace and in war. For we are lovers of the beautiful, yet simple in our tastes, and we cultivate the mind without loss of manliness. Wealth we employ, not for talk and ostentation, but when there is a real use for it. To avow poverty with us is no disgrace; the true disgrace is in doing nothing to avoid it. An Athenian citizen does not neglect the State because he takes care of his own household; and even those of us who are engaged in business have a very fair idea of politics. We alone regard a man who takes no interest in public affairs, not as a harmless but as a useless character; and if few of us are originators, we are all sound judges, of a policy. The great impediment to action is, in our opinion, not discussion, but the want of that knowledge which is gained by discussion preparatory to action. For we have a peculiar power of thinking before we act, and of acting too; whereas other men are courageous from ignorance but hesitate upon reflection. And they are surely to be esteemed the bravest spirits, who, having the clearest sense both of the pains and the pleasures of life, do not on that account shrink from danger. In doing good, again we are unlike others; we make our friends by conferring, not by receiving favors. Now he who confers a favor is the firmer friend, because he would fain by kindness keep alive the memory of an obligation; but the recipient is colder in his feelings, because he knows that in requiting another's generosity he will not be winning gratitude, but only paying a debt. We alone do good to our neighbors not upon a calculation of interest, but in the confidence of freedom and in a frank and fearless spirit.

To sum up: I say that Athens is the school of Hellas, and that the individual Athenian in his own person seems to have the power of adapting himself to the most varied forms of action with the utmost versatility and grace. This is no passing and idle word, but truth and fact; and the assertion is verified by the position to which these qualities have raised the State. For in the hour of trial, Athens alone among her contemporaries is superior to the report of her. No enemy who comes against her is indignant at the reverses which he sustains at the hands of such a city; no subject complains that his masters are unworthy of him. And we shall assuredly not be without witnesses: there are mighty monuments of our power, which will make us the wonder of this and of succeeding ages; we shall not need the praises of Homer or of any other panegyrist, whose poetry may please for the moment although his representation of the facts will not bear the light of day. For we have compelled every land and every sea to open a path for our valor, and have everywhere planted eternal memorials of our friendship and of our enmity. Such is the city for whose sake these men nobly fought and died: they could not bear the thought that she might be taken from them; and every one of us who survive should gladly toil on her behalf.

Exercises

1. The chorus of *Agamemnon* cautions against the evils of wealth. We, too, have a proverb about money and evil. How have the Greeks grown since Aeschylus wrote of the earlier populace? How would Pericles argue with our own proverb?
2. What stand would Pericles take on the question of universal military training?
3. Here is raised an old question about men of words and men of action. It is frequently said that the democratic ways are terribly slow because people spend their time talking and never act. Is a compromise between words and action possible?
4. Why does Pericles speak of the individual Athenian when he is making a summary of the government?

Oedipus the King

Sophocles

This play is perhaps the best known of all the Greek tragedies since it was taken by Aristotle in his volume, *Poetics*, as a model for this form of drama. All of the classic elements of tragedy are here: a man of great stature who falls from high station to low because of a fatal flaw in his personality; the unity of time (one day) and of place (the exterior of the royal palace at Thebes); the calling forth of the emotions of pity and fear in the spectator; and the final sense of catharsis. This last might be defined as the sense that the action has worked itself out to its one inevitable conclusion. In doing so, the emotions of pity and fear are purged in the spectator, so that he is left at peace. We feel that the ending, though tragic, is right, and that there is no more to be said or done.

In order to understand the play, one should know some of the mythology which lies in its background. The city of Thebes was founded by Cadmus, as we are reminded frequently in the speeches. The history which follows is not of immediate concern until we come to the reign of King Laius (LIE-oos) and his queen, Jocasta. Two things happened at that time. First, Laius set out on a journey and was murdered on the road by unknown assailants. In the meantime a fearful monster known as the Sphinx (to whom frequent references are made in the play) established itself outside the gate of Thebes and demanded a yearly tribute from the city. This was to continue until someone could solve the riddle which the Sphinx proposed to every passer-by. The riddle, we might think, is a simple one, for it was the old one, "What goes on four legs in the morning, on two legs at noon, and on three legs in the evening?" The answer, of course, is *Man*. The riddle and its answer in this play are symbolic of the idea that the one who could solve the riddle knew the nature of man.

To the city at this time came a young man, Oedipus, supposedly the son of the king and queen of Corinth. The Sphinx posed her riddle and he gave the right answer readily, thus freeing the city of the monster and the tribute she demanded. The king being dead, the people of the city chose Oedipus as their king. As was the custom, he married Jocasta who bore him two sons and two daughters. It is several years after this when the play begins.

One question that this play might bring up in the mind of a spectator is whether Oedipus is the victim of fate, or whether he is a man with free will whose character is his fate and produces his doom. Probably one will not find a clear answer to this question. In this connection one might ask what is the fatal flaw in Oedipus' character. Is it his sudden anger? Is it his impulsiveness in all of his actions, an impulsiveness which might be of great value to a ruler who must make quick decisions? Or is it his search for truth which will not be turned aside even when his wife and the chorus suggest that he should leave well enough alone? This last, again, would be a good quality in most men. Another interesting point is that of clear vision: Oedipus sees all things clearly; Tiresias is blind and sees truth with a sort of inner sight. Which one beholds more clearly? And why is the wound which Oedipus inflicts upon himself not only *an* appropriate one but *the* appropriate one?

This modern translation is made by Theodore Howard Banks.

Characters:

Oedipus, King of Thebes *(ED-i-pus, or EED-i-pus)*
Jocasta, Queen of Thebes, wife and mother of *Oedipus (joe-KAST-uh)*
Creon, brother of *Jocasta*
Tiresias, a prophet *(tie-REE-see-us)*
Boy, attendant of *Tiresias*
Priest of Zeus
Shepherd
First Messenger, from Corinth
Second Messenger
Chorus of Theban elders
Attendants

Scene: *Before the doors of the palace of* OEDIPUS *Thebes. A crowd of citizens are seated next to the two altars at the sides. In front of one of the altars stands the* PRIEST OF ZEUS. [*Enter* OEDIPUS.]

Oedipus:
Why are you here as suppliants, my children,
You in whose veins the blood of Cadmus flows?
What is the reason for your boughs of olive,
The fumes of incense, the laments and prayers
That fill the city? Because I thought it wrong,
My children, to depend on what was told me,
I have come to you myself, I, Oedipus,
Renowned in the sight of all. [*to* PRIEST] Tell me—you are
Their natural spokesman—what desire or fear
Brings you before me? I will gladly give you
Such help as is in my power. It would be heartless
Not to take pity on a plea like this.

Priest:
King Oedipus, you see us, young and old,
Gathered about your altars: some, mere fledglings
Not able yet to fly; some, bowed with age;
Some, priests, and I the priest of Zeus among them;
And these, who are the flower of our young manhood.
The rest of us are seated—the whole city—
With our wreathed branches in the market places,
Before the shrines of Pallas, before the fire
By which we read the auguries of Apollo.
Thebes, as you see yourself, is overwhelmed
By the waves of death that break upon her head.
No fruit comes from her blighted buds; her cattle
Die in the fields; her wives bring forth dead children.
A hideous pestilence consumes the city,
Striking us down like a god armed with fire,
Emptying the house of Cadmus, filling full
The dark of Hades with loud lamentation.
I and these children have not thronged your altars
Because we hold you equal to the immortals,
But because we hold you foremost among men,
Both in the happenings of daily life
And when some visitation of the gods
Confronts us. For we know that when you came here,
You freed us from our bondage, the bitter tribute
The Sphinx wrung from us by her sorceries.
And we know too that you accomplished this
Without foreknowledge, or clue that we could furnish.
We think, indeed, some god befriended you,
When you renewed our lives. Therefore, great king,
Glorious in all men's eyes, we now beseech you
To find some way of helping us, your suppliants,
Some way the gods themselves have told you of,
Or one that lies within our mortal power;
For the words of men experienced in evil
Are mighty and effectual. Oedipus!
Rescue our city and preserve your honor,
Since the land hails you as her savior now
For your past service. Never let us say
That when you ruled us, we were lifted up
Only to be thrown down. Restore the state
And keep it forever steadfast. Bring again
The happiness and good fortune you once brought us.
If you are still to reign as you reign now,
Then it is better to have men for subjects
Than to be king of a mere wilderness,
Since neither ship nor town has any value
Without companions or inhabitants.

Oedipus:
I pity you, my children. Well I know
What hopes have brought you here, and well I know
That all of you are suffering. Yet your grief,
However great, is not so great as mine.
Each of you suffers for himself alone,
But my heart feels the heaviness of my sorrow,
Your sorrow, and the sorrow of all the others.
You have not roused me. I have not been sleeping.
No. I have wept, wept long and bitterly,
Treading the devious paths of anxious thought;
And I have taken the only hopeful course
That I could find. I have sent my kinsman, Creon,
Son of Menoeceus, to the Pythian home[1]
Of Phoebus Apollo to find what word or deed
Of mine might save the city. He has delayed
Too long already, his absence troubles me;
But when he comes, I pledge myself to do
My utmost to obey the god's command.

Priest:
Your words are timely, for even as you speak
They sign to me that Creon is drawing near.

Oedipus:
O Lord Apollo! Grant he may bring to us
Fortune as smiling as his smiling face.

Priest:
Surely he brings good fortune. Look! The crown
Of bay leaves that he wears is full of berries.

Oedipus:
We shall know soon, for he is close enough
To hear us. Brother, son of Menoeceus, speak!
What news? What news do you bring us from the god?
[*Enter* CREON]

Creon:
Good news. If we can find the fitting way
To end this heavy scourge, all will be well.

---

1. That is, the oracle at Delphi.

Oedipus:
That neither gives me courage nor alarms me.
What does the god say? What is the oracle?

Creon:
If you wish me to speak in public, I will do so.
Otherwise let us go in and speak alone.

Oedipus:
Speak here before everyone. I feel more sorrow
For their sakes than I feel for my own life.

Creon:
Then I will give the message of Lord Phoebus:
A plain command to drive out the pollution
Here in our midst, and not to nourish it
Till our disease has grown incurable.

Oedipus:
What rite will purge us? How are we corrupted?

Creon:
We must banish a man, or have him put to death
To atone for the blood he shed, for it is blood
That has brought this tempest down upon the city.

Oedipus:
Who is the victim whose murder is revealed?

Creon:
King Laius, who was our lord before you came
To steer the city on its proper course.

Oedipus:
I know his name well, but I never saw him.

Creon:
Laius was killed, and now we are commanded
To punish his killers, whoever they may be

Oedipus:
How can they be discovered? Where shall we look
For the faint traces of this ancient crime?

Creon:
In Thebes, the god said. Truth can be always found:
Only what is neglected ever escapes.

Oedipus:
Where was King Laius murdered? In his home,
Out in the fields, or in some foreign land?

Creon:
He told us he was journeying to Delphi.
After he left, he was never seen again.

Oedipus:
Was no one with King Laius who saw what happened?
You could have put his story to good use.

Creon:
The sole survivor fled from the scene in terror,
And there was only one thing he was sure of.

Oedipus:
What was it? A clue might lead us far
Which gave us even the faintest glimmer of hope.

Creon:
He said that they were violently attacked
Not by one man but by a band of robbers.

Oedipus:
Robbers are not so daring. Were they bribed
To commit this crime by some one here in Thebes?

Creon:
That was suspected. But in our time of trouble
No one appeared to avenge the death of Laius.

Oedipus:
But your King was killed! What troubles could you have had
To keep you from searching closely for his killers?

Creon:
We had the Sphinx. Her riddle made us turn
From mysteries to what lay before our doors.

Oedipus:
Then I will start fresh and again make clear
Things that are dark. All honor to Apollo
And to you, Creon, for acting as you have done
On the dead King's behalf. So I will take
My rightful place beside you as your ally,
Avenging Thebes and bowing to the god.
Not for a stranger will I dispel this taint,
But for my own sake, since the murderer,
Whoever he is, may strike at me as well.
Therefore in helping Laius I help myself.
Come, children, come! Rise from the altar steps,
And carry away those branches. Summon here
The people of Cadmus. Tell them I mean to leave
Nothing undone. So with Apollo's aid
We may at last be saved—or meet destruction.
[*Exit* OEDIPUS]

Priest:
My children, let us go. The King has promised
The favor that we sought. And may Lord Phoebus
Come to us with his oracles, assuage
Our misery, and deliver us from death.
[*Exeunt. Enter* CHORUS]

Chorus:
The god's great word, in whose sweetness we ever rejoice,
    To our glorious city is drawing nigh,
Now, even now, from the gold of the Delphic shrine.
    What next decree will be thine,
Apollo, thou healer, to whom in our dread we cry?
    We are anguished, racked, and beset by fears!
What fate will be ours? One fashioned for us alone,
  Or one that in ancient time was known
  That returns once more with the circling years?
Child of our golden hope, O speak, thou immortal voice!

Divine Athene, daughter of Zeus, O hear![2]
    Hear thou, Artemis! Thee we hail,
Our guardian goddess throned in the market place.
    Apollo, we ask thy grace.
Shine forth, all three, and the menace of death will fail.
  Answer our call! Shall we call in vain?
If ever ye came in the years that have gone before,
  Return, and save us from plague once more,
  Rescue our city from fiery pain!
Be your threefold strength our shield. Draw near to us now, draw near!
  Death is upon us. We bear a burden of bitter grief.
There is nothing can save us now, no device that our thought can frame.
    No blossom, no fruit, no harvest sheaf

---

2. These appeals to the gods are understandable chiefly as cries of despair. Ares, referred to in line 188, is the God of War and here chiefly suggests destruction. Bacchus, or Dionysus (line 200), was the patron god of Thebes, and his devotees, the bacchantes, held wild revels in the streets of the city.

Springs from the blighted and barren earth.
Women cry out in travail and bring no children to birth;
But swift as a bird, swift as the sweep of flame,
Life after life takes sudden flight
To the western god, to the last, dark shore of night.
Ruin has fallen on Thebes. Without number her children are dead;
Unmourned, unattended, unpitied, they lie polluting the ground.
Grey-haired mothers and wives new-wed
Wail at the altars everywhere,
With entreaty, with loud lament, with clamor filling the air.
And songs of praise to Apollo, the healer, resound.
Athene, thou knowest our desperate need.
Lend us thy strength. Give heed to our prayer, give heed!

Fierce Ares has fallen upon us. He comes unarrayed for war,
Yet he fills our ears with shrieking, he folds us in fiery death.
Grant that he soon may turn in headlong flight from our land,
Swept to the western deep by the fair wind's favoring breath,
Or swept to the savage sea that washes the Thracian shore.
We few who escape the night are stricken down in the day.
O Zeus, whose bolts of thunder are balanced within thy hand,
Hurl down thy lightning upon him! Father, be swift to slay!
Save us, light-bringing Phoebus! The shower of thine arrows let fly;
Loose them, triumphant and swift, from the golden string of thy bow!

O goddess, his radiant sister, roaming the Lycian glade,
Come with the flash of thy fire! Artemis, conquer our foe!
And thou, O wine-flushed god to whom the Bacchantes cry,
With thy brilliant torch ablaze amid shouts of thy maenad train,
With thy hair enwreathed with gold, O Bacchus, we beg thine aid
Against our destroyer Ares, the god whom the gods disdain!
[*Enter* OEDIPUS]

Oedipus:
You have been praying. If you heed my words
And seek the remedy for your own disease,
The gods will hear your prayers, and you will find
Relief and comfort. I myself know nothing
About this story, nothing about the murder,
So that unaided and without a clue
I could not have tracked it down for any distance.
And because I have only recently been received
Among you as a citizen, to you all,
And to all the rest, I make this proclamation:
Whoever knows the man who killed King Laius,
Let him declare his knowledge openly.
If he himself is guilty, let him confess
And go unpunished, except for banishment.
Or if he knows the murderer was an alien,
Let him by speaking earn his due reward,
And thanks as well. But if he holds his tongue,
Hoping to save himself or save a friend,
Then let him hear what I, the King, decree
For all who live in Thebes, the land I rule.
No one shall give this murderer shelter. No one
Shall speak to him. No one shall let him share
In sacrifice or prayer or lustral rites.
The door of every house is barred against him.
The god has shown me that he is polluted.
So by this edict I ally myself
With Phoebus and the slain. As for the slayer,
Whether he had accomplices or not,
This is my solemn prayer concerning him:
May evil come of evil; may he live
A wretched life and meet a wretched end.
And as for me, if I should knowingly
Admit him as a member of my household,
May the same fate which I invoked for others
Fall upon me. Make my words good, I charge you,
For love of me, Apollo, and our country
Blasted by the displeasure of the gods.
You should not have left this guilt unpurified,
Even without an oracle to urge you,
When a man so noble, a man who was your King,
Had met his death. Rather, it was your duty
To seek the truth. But now, since it is I
Who hold the sovereignty that once was his,
I who have wed his wife, who would have been
Bound to him by the tie of having children
Born of one mother, if he had had a child
To be a blessing, if fate had not struck him down—
Since this is so, I intend to fight his battle
As though he were my father.[3] I will leave
Nothing undone to find his murderer,
Avenging him and all his ancestors.
And I pray the gods that those who disobey
May suffer. May their fields bring forth no harvest,
Their wives no children; may the present plague,
Or one yet worse, consume them. But as for you,
All of you citizens who are loyal to me,
May Justice, our champion, and all the gods
Show you their favor in the days to come.

Chorus:
King Oedipus, I will speak to avoid your curse.
I am no slayer, nor can I point him out.
The question came to us from Phoebus Apollo;
It is for him to tell us who is guilty.

Oedipus:
Yes. But no man on earth is strong enough
To force the gods to act against their will.

Chorus:
There is; I think, a second course to follow.

Oedipus:
If there is yet a third, let me know that.

Chorus:
Tiresias, the prophet, has the clearest vision
Next to our Lord Apollo. He is the man
Who can do most to help us in our search.

Oedipus:
I have not forgotten. Creon suggested it,
And I have summoned him, summoned him twice.
I am astonished he is not here already.

---

3. This whole passage is filled with dramatic irony: that is, the audience understands the words in another sense than the speaker means them.

Chorus:
The only rumors are old and half-forgotten.

Oedipus:
What are they? I must find out all I can.

Chorus:
It is said the King was killed by travelers.

Oedipus:
So I have heard, but there is no eye-witness.

Chorus:
If fear can touch them, they will reveal themselves
Once they have heard so dreadful a curse as yours.

Oedipus:
Murderers are not terrified by words.

Chorus:
But they can be convicted by the man
Being brought here now, Tiresias. He alone
Is godlike in his knowledge of the truth.
[*Enter* TIRESIAS,[4] *led by a* BOY.]

Oedipus:
You know all things in heaven and earth, Tiresias:
Things you may speak of openly, and secrets
Holy and not to be revealed. You know,
Blind though you are, the plague that ruins Thebes.
And you, great prophet, you alone can save us.
Phoebus has sent an answer to our question,
An answer that the messengers may have told you,
Saying there was no cure for our condition
Until we found the killers of King Laius
And banished them or had them put to death.
Therefore, Tiresias, do not begrudge your skill
In the voice of birds or other prophecy,
But save yourself, save me, save the whole city,
Save everything that the pestilence defiles.
We are at your mercy, and man's noblest task
Is to use all his powers in helping others.

Tiresias:
How dreadful a thing, how dreadful a thing is wisdom,
When to be wise is useless! This I knew
But I forgot, or else I would never have come.

Oedipus:
What is the matter? Why are you so troubled?

Tiresias:
Oedipus, let me go home. Then you will bear
Your burden, and I mine, more easily.

Oedipus:
Custom entitles us to hear your message.
By being silent you harm your native land.

Tiresias:
You do not know when, and when not to speak.
Silence will save me from the same misfortune.

Oedipus:
If you can be of help, then all of us
Kneel and implore you not to turn away.

Tiresias:
None of you know the truth, but I will never
Reveal my sorrow—not to call it yours.

Oedipus:
What are you saying? You know and will not speak?
You mean to betray us and destroy the city?

Tiresias:
I refuse to pain you. I refuse to pain myself.
It is useless to ask me. I will tell you nothing.

Oedipus:
You utter scoundrel! You would enrage a stone!
Is there no limit to your stubbornness?

Tiresias:
You blame my anger and forget your own.

Oedipus:
No one could help being angry when he heard
How you dishonor and ignore the state.

Tiresias:
What is to come will come, though I keep silent.

Oedipus:
If it must come, your duty is to speak.

Tiresias:
I will say no more. Rage to your heart's content.

Oedipus:
Rage? Yes, I will rage! I will spare you nothing.
In the plot against King Laius, I have no doubt
That you were an accomplice, yes, almost
The actual killer. If you had not been blind,
I would have said that you alone were guilty.

Tiresias:
Then listen to my command! Obey the edict
That you yourself proclaimed and never speak,
From this day on, to me or any Theban.
You are the sinner who pollutes our land.

Oedipus:
Have you no shame? How do you hope to escape
The consequence of such an accusation?

Tiresias:
I have escaped. My strength is the living truth.

Oedipus:
This is no prophecy. Who taught you this?

Tiresias:
You did. You forced me to speak against my will.

Oedipus:
Repeat your slander. Let me learn it better.

Tiresias:
Are you trying to tempt me into saying more?
I have spoken already. Have you not understood?

Oedipus:
No, not entirely. Give your speech again.

Tiresias:
I say you are the killer, you yourself.

Oedipus:
Twice the same insult! You will pay for it.

Tiresias:
Shall I say more to make you still more angry?

Oedipus:
Say what you want to. It will make no sense.

---

4. Tiresias is a blind prophet, a priest of Apollo. He seems to have been almost infinitely old, and was both masculine and feminine. Consequently his wisdom was almost without bounds. Priests often made their prophecies after observing flights of birds, listening to the cries of birds, observing the entrails of sacrificial animals, etc.

Tiresias:
You are living in shame with those most dear to you,
As yet in ignorance of your dreadful fate.

Oedipus:
Do you suppose that you can always use
Language like that and not be punished for it?

Tiresias:
Yes. I am safe, if truth has any strength.

Oedipus:
Truth can save anyone excepting you,
You with no eyes, no hearing, and no brains!

Tiresias:
Poor fool! You taunt me, but you soon will hear
The self-same insults heaped upon your head.

Oedipus:
You live in endless night. What can you do
To me or anyone else who sees the day?

Tiresias:
Nothing. I have no hand in your destruction.
For that, Apollo needs no help from me.

Oedipus:
Apollo! Is this your trick, or is it Creon's?

Tiresias:
Creon is guiltless. The evil is in you.

Oedipus:
How great is the envy roused by wealth, by kingship,
By the subtle skill that triumphs over others
In life's hard struggle! Creon, who has been
For years my trusted friend, has stealthily
Crept in upon me anxious to seize my power,
The unsought gift the city freely gave me.
Anxious to overthrow me, he has bribed
This scheming mountebank, this fraud, this trickster,
Blind in his art and in everything but money!
Your art of prophecy! When have you shown it?
Not when the watch-dog of the gods was here,
Chanting her riddle. Why did you say nothing,
When you might have saved the city? Yet her puzzle
Could not be solved by the first passer-by.
A prophet's skill was needed, and you proved
That you had no such skill, either in birds
Or any other means the gods have given.
But I came, I, the ignorant Oedipus,
And silenced her. I had no birds to help me.
I used my brains. And it is I you now
Are trying to destroy in the hope of standing
Close beside Creon's throne. You will regret
This zeal of yours to purify the land,
You and your fellow-plotter. You seem old;
Otherwise you would pay for your presumption.

Chorus:
Sir, it appears to us that both of you
Have spoken in anger. Anger serves no purpose.
Rather we should consider in what way
We best can carry out the god's command.

Tiresias:
King though you are, I have a right to answer
Equal to yours. In that I too am king.
I serve Apollo. I do not acknowledge
You as my lord or Creon as my patron.
You have seen fit to taunt me with my blindness.
Therefore I tell you this: you have your eyesight
And cannot see the sin of your existence,
Cannot see where you live or whom you live with,
Are ignorant of your parents, bring disgrace
Upon your kindred in the world below
And here on earth. And soon the double lash
Of your mother's and father's curse will drive you headlong
Out of the country, blinded, with your cries
Heard everywhere, echoed by every hill
In all Cithaeron. Then you will have learned
The meaning of your marriage, learned in what harbor,
After so fair a voyage, you were shipwrecked.
And other horrors you could never dream of
Will teach you who you are, will drag you down
To the level of your children. Heap your insults
On Creon and my message if you choose to.
Still no one ever will endure the weight
Of greater misery than will fall on you.

Oedipus:
Am I supposed to endure such talk as this,
Such talk from him? Go, curse you, go! Be quick!

Tiresias:
Except for your summons I would never have come.

Oedipus:
And I would never have sent for you so soon
If I had known you would prove to be a fool.

Tiresias:
Yes, I have proved a fool—in your opinion,
And yet your parents thought that I was wise.

Oedipus:
What parents? Wait! Who was my father? Tell me!

Tiresias:
Today will see your birth and your destruction.

Oedipus:
You cannot speak unless you speak in riddles!

Tiresias:
And yet how brilliant you are in solving them!

Oedipus:
You sneer at me for what has made me great.

Tiresias:
The same good fortune that has ruined you.

Oedipus:
If I have saved the city, nothing else matters.

Tiresias:
In that case I will go. Boy, take me home.

Oedipus:
Yes, let him take you. Here, you are in the way.
Once you are gone, you will give no further trouble.

Tiresias:
I will not go before I have said my say,
Indifferent to your black looks. You cannot harm me.
And I say this: the man whom you have sought,
Whom you have threatened, whom you have proclaimed
The killer of King Laius—he is here.
Now thought an alien, he shall prove to be
A native Theban, to his deep dismay.
Now he has eyesight, now his wealth is great;
But he shall make his way to foreign soil
Blinded, in beggary, groping with a stick.
In his own household he shall be shown to be

The father of his children—and their brother,
Son to the woman who bore him—and her husband,
The killer and the bedfellow of his father.
Go and consider this; and if you find
That I have been mistaken, you can say
That I have lost my skill in prophecy.
[*Exeunt* OEDIPUS *and* TIRESIAS.]

Chorus:
What man is this the god from the Delphic rock denounces,
Whose deeds are too shameful to tell, whose murderous hands are red?
Let his feet be swifter now than hooves of horses racing
The storm-clouds overhead.
For Zeus's son, Apollo, leaps in anger upon him,
Armed with lightning to strike and slay;
And the terrible Fates, unflagging, relentless,
Follow the track of their prey.

The words of the god have flashed from the peaks of snowy Parnassus,
Commanding us all to see this killer as yet unknown.
Deep in the tangled woods, through rocks and caves he is roaming
Like a savage bull, alone.
On his lonely path he journeys, wretched, broken by sorrow,
Seeking to flee from the fate he fears;
But the voice from the center of earth that doomed him
Inescapably rings in his ears.
Dreadful, dreadful those words! We can neither approve nor deny them.
Shaken confounded with fears, we know not what to say.
Nothing is clear to us, nothing—what is to come tomorrow,
Or what is upon us today.
If the prophet seeks revenge for the unsolved murder of Laius,
Why is Oedipus charged with crime?
Because some deep-rooted hate divides their royal houses?
The houses of Laius and Oedipus, son of the King of Corinth?
There is none that we know of, now, or in ancient time.

From Zeus's eyes and Apollo's no human secret is hidden;
But man has no test for truth, no measure his wit can devise.
Tiresias, indeed, excels in every art of his office,
And yet we too may be wise.
Though Oedipus stands accused, until he is proven guilty
We cannot blacken his name;
For he showed his wisdom the day the winged maiden faced him.
He triumphed in that ordeal, saved us, and won our affection.
We can never believe he stooped to an act of shame.
[*Enter* CREON.]

Creon:
Thebans, I come here outraged and indignant,
For I have learned that Oedipus has accused me
Of dreadful crimes. If, in the present crisis,
He thinks that I have wronged him in any way,
Wronged him in word or deed, then let my life
Come to a speedy close. I cannot bear
The burden of such scandal. The attack
Ruins me utterly, if my friends, and you,
And the whole city are to call me traitor.

Chorus:
Perhaps his words were only a burst of anger,
And were not meant as a deliberate insult.

Creon:
He *did* say that I plotted with Tiresias?
And that the prophet lied at my suggestion?

Chorus:
Those were his words. I cannot guess his motive.

Creon:
Were his eyes clear and steady? Was his mind
Unclouded, when he brought this charge against me?

Chorus:
I cannot say. To see what princes do
Is not our province. Here come the King himself.
[*Enter* OEDIPUS.]

Oedipus:
So you are here! What brought you to my door?
Impudence? Insolence? You, my murderer!
You, the notorious stealer of my crown!
Why did you hatch this plot? What kind of man,
By heaven, what kind of man, could you have thought me?
A coward or a fool? Did you suppose
I would not see your trickery take shape,
Or when I saw it, would not counter it?
How stupid you were to reach for royal power
Without a troop of followers or rich friends!
Only a mob and money win a kingdom.

Creon:
Sir, let me speak. When you have heard my answer,
You will have grounds on which to base your judgment.

Oedipus:
I cannot follow all your clever talk.
I only know that you are dangerous.

Creon:
That is the issue. Let me explain that first.

Oedipus:
Do not explain that you are true to me.

Creon:
If you imagine that a blind self-will
Is strength of character, you are mistaken.

Oedipus:
As you are, if you strike at your own house,
And then expect to escape all punishment.

Creon:
Yes, you are right. That would be foolishness.
But tell me, what have I done? How have I harmed you?

Oedipus:
Did you, or did you not, urge me to summon
Tiresias, that revered, that holy prophet?

Creon:
Yes. And I still think my advice was good.

Oedipus:
Then answer this: how long ago was Laius—

Creon:
Laius! Why how am I concerned with him?

Oedipus:
How many years ago was Laius murdered?

Creon:
So many they cannot easily be counted.

Oedipus:
And was Tiresias just as cunning then?

Creon:
As wise and honored as he is today.

Oedipus:
At that time did he ever mention me?

Creon:
Not in my hearing. I am sure of that.

Oedipus:
And the murderer—a thorough search was made?

Creon:
Yes, certainly, but we discovered nothing.

Oedipus:
Then why did the man of wisdom hold his tongue?

Creon:
I cannot say. Guessing is not my habit.

Oedipus:
One thing at least you need not guess about.

Creon:
What is it? If I know it, I will tell you.

Oedipus:
Tiresias would not have said I murdered Laius,
If you two had not put your heads together.

Creon:
You best know what he said. But now I claim
The right to take my turn in asking questions.

Oedipus:
Very well, ask. You never can find me guilty.

Creon:
Then answer this: my sister is your wife?

Oedipus:
I cannot deny that fact. She is my wife.

Creon:
And in your rule she has an equal share?

Oedipus:
She has no wish that goes unsatisfied.

Creon:
And as the third I stand beside you both?

Oedipus:
True. That position proves your treachery.

Creon:
No. You would see, if you thought the matter through
As I have done. Consider. Who would choose
Kingship and all the terrors that go with it,
If, with the same power, he could sleep in peace?
I have no longing for a royal title
Rather than royal freedom. No, not I,
Nor any moderate man. Now I fear nothing.
Every request I make of you is granted,
And yet as king I should have many duties
That went against the grain. Then how could rule
Be sweeter than untroubled influence?
I have not lost my mind. I want no honors
Except the ones that bring me solid good.
Now all men welcome me and wish me joy.
Now all your suitors ask to speak with me,
Knowing they cannot otherwise succeed.
Why should I throw away a life like this
For a king's life? No one is treacherous
Who knows his own best interests. To conspire
With other men, or to be false myself,
Is not my nature. Put me to the test.
First, go to Delphi. Ask if I told the truth
About the oracle. Then if you find
I have had dealings with Tiresias, kill me.
My voice will echo yours in passing sentence.
But base your verdict upon something more
Than mere suspicion. Great injustice comes
From random judgments that bad men are good
And good men bad. To throw away a friend
Is, in effect, to throw away your life,
The prize you treasure most. All this, in time,
Will become clear to you, for time alone
Proves a man's honesty, but wickedness
Can be discovered in a single day.

Chorus:
Sir, that is good advice, if one is prudent.
Hasty decisions always lead to danger.

Oedipus:
When a conspiracy is quick in forming,
I must move quickly to retaliate.
If I sat still and let my enemy act,
I would lose everything that he would gain.

Creon:
So then, my banishment is what you want?

Oedipus:
No, not your banishment. Your execution.

Creon:
I think you are mad. **Oe.:** I can protect myself.

Creon:
You should protect me also. **Oe.:** You? A traitor?

Creon:
Suppose you are wrong? **Oe.:** I am the King. I rule.

Creon:
Not if you rule unjustly. **Oe.:** Thebes! Hear that!

Creon:
Thebes is my city too, as well as yours.

Chorus:
No more, no more, sirs! Here is Queen Jocasta.
She comes in time to help make peace between you.
[*Enter* JOCASTA.]

Jocasta:
Oedipus! Creon! How can you be so foolish?
What! Quarrel now about a private matter
When the land is dying? You should be ashamed.
Come, Oedipus, come in. Creon, go home.
You make a trivial problem too important.

Creon:
Sister, your husband has made dreadful threats.
He claims the right to have me put to death
Or have me exiled. He need only choose.

Oedipus:
Yes. I have caught him at his treachery,
Plotting against the person of the King.

Creon:
If I am guilty, may it be my fate
To live in misery and to die accursed.

Jocasta:
Believe him, Oedipus, believe him, spare him—
I beg you by the gods—for his oath's sake,
For my sake, for the sake of all men here.

Chorus:
Consent, O King. Be gracious. Hear us, we beg you.

Oedipus:
What shall I hear? To what shall I consent?

Chorus:
Respect the evidence of Creon's wisdom,
Respect the oath of innocence he has taken.

Oedipus:
You know what this means? **Ch.:** Yes. **Oe.:** Tell me again what you ask for

Chorus:
To yield, to relent.
He is your friend and swears he is not guilty.
Do not act in haste, convicting him out of hand.

Oedipus:
When you ask for this, you ask for my destruction;
You sentence me to death or to banishment.
Be sure that you understand.

Chorus:
No, by Apollo, no!
If such a thought has ever crossed my mind,
Then may I never find
A friend to love me or a god to save;
And may dark doom pursue me to the grave.
My country perishes, and now new woe
Springs from your quarrel, one affliction more
Has come upon us, and my heart is sore.

Oedipus:
Let him go free, even though that destroys me.
I shall be killed, or exiled in disgrace.
Not his appeal but yours aroused my pity.
I shall hate him always, no matter where he is.

Creon:
You go beyond all bounds when you are angry,
And are sullen when you yield. Natures like yours
Inflict their heaviest torments on themselves.

Oedipus:
Go! Go! Leave me in peace! **Cr.:** Yes, I will go.
You have not understood, but in the sight
Of all these men here I am innocent.

[*Exit* CREON.]

Chorus:
Take the King with you, Madam, to the palace.

Jocasta:
When I have learned what happened, we will go.

Chorus:
The King was filled with fear and blind suspicion.
Creon resented what he thought injustice.

Jocasta:
Both were at fault? **Ch.:** Both **Joc.:** Why was the King suspicious?

Chorus:
Do not seek to know.
We have said enough. In a time of pain and trouble
Inquire no further. Let the matter rest.

Oedipus:
Your well-meant pleading turned me from my purpose,
And now you come to this. You fall so low
As to think silence best.

Chorus:
I say again, O King,
No one except a madman or a fool
Would throw aside your rule.
For you delivered us; your single hand
Lifted the load from our belovéd land.
When we were mad with grief and suffering,
In our extremity you found a way
To save the city, as you will today.

Jocasta:
But tell *me* Oedipus, tell *me*, I beg you,
Why you were so unyielding in your anger.

Oedipus:
I will, Jocasta, for I honor you
More than I do the elders. It was Creon's plotting.

Jocasta:
What do you mean? What was your accusation?

Oedipus:
He says I am the murderer of King Laius.

Jocasta:
Did he speak from first-hand knowledge or from hearsay?

Oedipus:
He did not speak at all. His lips are pure.
He bribed Tiresias, and that scoundrel spoke.

Jocasta:
Then you can rid your mind of any fear
That you are guilty. Listen to me. No mortal
Shares in the gods' foreknowledge. I can give you
Clear proof of that. There came once to King Laius
An oracle—I will not say from Phoebus,
But from his priest—saying it was his fate
That he should be struck down by his own child,
His child and mine. But Laius, as we know,
Was killed by foreign robbers at a place
Where three roads came together. As for the child,
When it was only three days old, its father
Pierced both its ankles, pinned its feet together,
And then gave orders that it be abandoned
On a wild mountainside. so in this case
Phoebus did not fulfill his oracle. The child
Was not its father's murderer, and Laius
Was not the victim of the fate he feared,
Death at his son's hands, although just that fate
Was what the seer predicted. Pay no heed
To prophecies. Whatever may be needful
The god himself can show us easily.

Oedipus:
What have you said, Jocasta? What have you said?
The past comes back to me. How terrible!

Jocasta:
Why do you start so? What has happened to you?

Oedipus:
It seemed to me—I thought you said that Laius
Was struck down where three roads came together.

Jocasta:
I did. That was the story, and still is.

Oedipus:
Where was it that this murder was committed?

Jocasta:
In Phocis, where the road from Thebes divides,
Meeting the roads from Daulia and Delphi.

Oedipus:
How many years ago did this occur?

Jocasta:
The news of it was published here in Thebes
Not long before you came to be our king.

Oedipus:
Is this my fate? Is this what the gods decreed?

Jocasta:
What have I said that has so shaken you?

Oedipus:
Do not ask me yet. Tell me about King Laius.
What did he look like? Was he young or old?

Jocasta:
His build was not unlike yours. He was tall.
His hair was just beginning to turn grey.

Oedipus:
I cannot bear the thought that I called down
A curse on my own head unknowingly.

Jocasta:
What is it Oedipus? You terrify me!

Oedipus:
I dread to think Tiresias had clear eyesight;
But tell me one thing more, and I will know.

Jocasta:
And I too shrink, yet I will answer you.

Oedipus:
How did he travel? With a few men only,
Or with his guards and servants, like a prince?

Jocasta:
There were five of them in all, with one a herald.
They had one carriage in which King Laius rode.

Oedipus:
It is too clear, too clear! Who told you this?

Jocasta:
The only servant who escaped alive.

Oedipus:
And is he still here now, still in the palace?

Jocasta:
No. When he came home and found Laius dead
And you the reigning king, he pleaded with me
To send him where the sheep were pasturing,
As far as possible away from Thebes.
And so I sent him. He was worthy fellow
And, if a slave can, deserved a greater favor.

Oedipus:
I hope it is possible to get him quickly.

Jocasta:
Yes, that is easy. Why do you want to see him?

Oedipus:
Because I am afraid, deadly afraid
That I have spoken more than I should have done.

Jocasta:
He shall come. But Oedipus, have I no right
To learn what weighs so heavily on your heart?

Oedipus:
You shall learn everything, now that my fears
Have grown so great, for who is dearer to me
Than you, Jocasta? Whom should I speak to sooner,
When I am in such straits? King Polybus
Of Corinth was my father. Meropé,
A Dorian, was my mother. I myself
Was foremost among all the citizens,
Till something happened, strange, but hardly worth
My feeling such resentment. As we sat
One day at dinner, a man who had drunk too much
Insulted me by saying I was not
My father's son. In spite of being angry,
I managed to control myself. Next day
I asked my parents, who were both indignant
That he had leveled such a charge against me.
This was a satisfaction, yet the thing
Still rankled, for the rumor grew widespread.
At last I went to Delphi secretly.
Apollo gave no answer to my question
But sent me off, anguished and terrified,
With fearful prophecies that I was fated
To be my mother's husband, to bring forth
Children whom men could not endure to see,
And to take my father's life. When I heard this
I turned and fled, hoping to find at length
Some place where I would know of Corinth only
As a far distant land beneath the stars,
Some place where I would never have to see
The infamies of this oracle fulfilled.
And as I went on, I approached the spot
At which you tell me Laius met his end.
Now this, Jocasta, is the absolute truth.
When I had come to where the three roads fork,
A herald met me, walking before a carriage,
Drawn by two colts, in which a man was seated,
Just as you said. The old man and the herald
Ordered me off the road with threatening gestures.
Then as the driver pushed me to one side,
I struck him angrily. And seeing this,
The old man, as I drew abreast, leaned out
And brought his driver's two-pronged goad down hard
Upon my head. He paid a heavy price
For doing that. With one blow of my staff
I knocked him headlong from his chariot
Flat on his back. Then every man of them
I killed. Now if the blood of Laius flowed
In that old stranger's veins, what mortal man
Could be more wretched, more accursed than I?
I whom no citizen or foreigner
May entertain or shelter, I to whom
No one may speak, I, I who must be driven
From every door. No other man has cursed me,
I have brought down this curse upon myself.
The hands that killed him now pollute his bed!
Am I not vile, foul, utterly unclean?
For I must fly and never see again
My people or set foot in my own land,
Or else become the husband of my mother
And put to death my father Polybus,
To whom I owe my life and my upbringing.

Men would be right in thinking that such things
Have been inflicted by some cruel fate.
May the gods' high and holy majesty
Forbid that I should see that day. No! No!
Rather than be dishonored by a doom
So dreadful may I vanish from the earth.

Chorus:
Sir, these are terrible things, but there is hope
Until you have heard what the one witness says.

Oedipus:
That is the one remaining hope I have,
To wait for the arrival of the shepherd

Jocasta:
And when he *has* arrived, what can he do?

Oedipus:
He can do this. If his account agrees
With yours, I stand acquitted of this crime.

Jocasta:
Was what I said of any consequence?

Oedipus:
You said his story was that robbers killed
King Laius. If he speaks of the same number,
Then I am not the murderer. One man
Cannot be several men. But if he says
One traveler, single-handed, did the deed,
Beyond all doubt the evidence points to me.

Jocasta:
I am quite certain that was what he said.
He cannot change now, for the whole of Thebes
Heard it, not I alone. In any case,
Even supposing that his story *should*
Be somewhat different, he can never make
Laius's death fulfill the oracle.
Phoebus said plainly Laius was to die
At my son's hands. However, that poor child
Certainly did not kill him, for it died
Before its father. I would not waste my time
In giving any thought to prophecy.

Oedipus:
Yes, you are right. And yet have someone sent
To bring the shepherd here. Make sure of this.

Jocasta:
I will, at once. Come, Oedipus, come in.
I will do nothing that you disapprove of.
[*Exeunt* OEDIPUS *and* JOCASTA.]

Chorus:
May piety and reverence mark my actions;
May every thought be pure through all my days.
May those great laws whose dwelling is in heaven
Approve my conduct with their crown of praise:
Offspring of skies that overarch Olympus,
Laws from the loins of no mere mortal sprung,
Unslumbering, unfailing, unforgetting,
Filled with a godhead that is ever young.

Pride breeds the tyrant. Insolent presumption,
Big with delusive wealth and false renown,
Once it has mounted to the highest rampart
Is headlong hurled in utter ruin down.
But pour out all thy blessings, Lord Apollo,
Thou who alone hast made and kept us great,
On all whose sole ambition is unselfish,
Who spend themselves in service to the state.
Let that man be accursèd who is proud,
In act unscrupulous, in thinking base,
Whose knees in reverence have never bowed,
In whose hard heart justice can find no place,
Whose hands profane life's holiest mysteries,
How can he hope to shield himself for long
From the gods' arrows that will pierce him through?
If evil triumphs in such ways as these,
Why should we seek, in choric dance and song,
To give the gods the praise that is their due?

I cannot go in full faith as of old,
To sacred Delphi or Olympian vale,
Unless men see that what has been foretold
Has come to pass, that omens never fail.
All-ruling Zeus, if thou art King indeed,
Put forth thy majesty, make good thy word,
Faith in these fading oracles restore!
To priest and prophet men pay little heed;
Hymns to Apollo are no longer heard;
And all religion soon will be no more.
[*Enter* JOCASTA.]

Jocasta:
Elders of Thebes, I thought that I should visit
The altars of the gods to offer up
These wreaths I carry and these gifts of incense.
The King is overanxious, overtroubled.
He is no longer calm enough to judge
The present by the lessons of the past,
But trembles before anyone who brings
An evil prophecy. I cannot help him.
Therefore, since thou art nearest, bright Apollo,
I bring these offerings to thee. O, hear me!
Deliver us from this defiling curse.
His fear infects us all, as if we were
Sailors who saw their pilot terrified.
[*Enter* MESSENGER.]

Messenger:
Sirs, I have come to find King Oedipus.
Where is his palace, can you tell me that?
Or better yet, where is the King himself?

Chorus:
Stranger, the King is there, within his palace.
This is the Queen, the mother of his children.

Messenger:
May all the gods be good to you and yours!
Madam, you are a lady richly blessed.

Jocasta:
And may the gods requite your courtesy.
But what request or message do you bring us?

Messenger:
Good tidings for your husband and your household.

Jocasta:
What is your news? What country do you come from?

Messenger:
From Corinth. And the news I bring will surely
Give you great pleasure—and perhaps some pain.

Jocasta:
What message can be good and bad at once?

Messenger:
The citizens of Corinth, it is said,
Have chosen Oedipus to be their King.

Jocasta:
What do you mean? Their King is Polybus.

Messenger:
No, madam. Polybus is dead and buried.

Jocasta:
What! Dead! The father of King Oedipus?

Messenger:
If I speak falsely, let me die myself.

Jocasta [*to* ATTENDANT.]
Go find the King and tell him this. Be quick!
What does an oracle amount to now?
This is the man whom Oedipus all these years
Has feared and shunned to keep from killing him,
And now we find he dies a natural death!
[*Enter* OEDIPUS.]

Oedipus:
My dear Jocasta, why have you sent for me?

Jocasta:
Listen to this man's message, and then tell me
What faith you have in sacred oracles.

Oedipus:
Where does he come from? What has he to say?

Jocasta:
He comes from Corinth and has this to say:
The King, your father, Polybus is dead.

Oedipus [*to* MESSENGER.]
My father! Tell me that again yourself.

Messenger:
I will say first what you first want to know.
You may be certain he is dead and gone.

Oedipus:
How did he die? By violence or sickness?

Messenger:
The scales of life tip easily for the old.

Oedipus:
That is to say he died of some disease.

Messenger:
Yes, of disease, and merely of old age.

Oedipus:
Hear that, Jocasta! Why should anyone
Give heed to oracles from the Pythian shrine,
Or to the birds that shriek above our heads?
They prophesied that I must kill my father.
But he is dead; the earth has covered him.
And I am here, I who have never raised
My hand against him—unless he died of grief,
Longing to see me. Then I might be said
To have caused his death. But as they stand, at least,
The oracles have been swept away like rubbish.
They are with Polybus in Hades, dead.

Jocasta:
Long ago, Oedipus, I told you that.

Oedipus:
You did, but I was blinded by my terror.

Jocasta:
Now you need take these things to heart no longer.

Oedipus:
But there is still my mother's bed to fear.

Jocasta:
Why should you be afraid? Chance rules our lives,
And no one can foresee the future, no one.
We live best when we live without a purpose
From one day to the next. Forget your fear
Of marrying your mother. That has happened
To many men before this in their dreams.
We find existence most endurable
When such things are neglected and forgotten.

Oedipus:
That would be true, Jocasta, if my mother
Were not alive; but now your eloquence
Is not enough to give me reassurance.

Jocasta:
And yet your father's death is a great comfort.

Oedipus:
Yes, but I cannot rest while she is living.

Messenger:
Sir, will you tell me who it is you fear?

Oedipus:
Queen Meropé, the wife of Polybus.

Messenger:
What is so terrible about the Queen?

Oedipus:
A dreadful prophecy the gods have sent us.

Messenger:
Are you forbidden to speak of it, or not?

Oedipus:
It may be told. The Lord Apollo said
That I was doomed to marry my own mother,
And shed my father's blood with my own hands.
And so for years I have stayed away from Corinth,
My native land—a fortunate thing for me,
Though it is very sweet to see one's parents.

Messenger:
Was that the reason you have lived in exile?

Oedipus:
Yes, for I feared my mother and my father.

Messenger:
Then since my journey was to wish you well,
Let me release you from your fear at once.

Oedipus:
That would deserve my deepest gratitude.

Messenger:
Sir, I *did* come here with the hope of earning
Some recompense when you had gotten home.

Oedipus:
No. I will never again go near my home.

Messenger:
O son, son! You know nothing. That is clear—

Oedipus:
What do you mean, old friend? Tell me, I beg you.

Messenger:
If that is why you dare not come to Corinth.

Oedipus:
I fear Apollo's word would be fulfilled.

Messenger:
That you would be polluted through your parents?

Oedipus:
Yes, yes! My life is haunted by that horror.

Messenger:
You have no reason to be horrified.

Oedipus:
I have no reason! Why? They are my parents.

Messenger:
No. You are not the son of Polybus.

Oedipus:
What did you say? Polybus not my father?

Messenger:
He was as much your father as I am.

Oedipus:
How can that be—my father like a stranger?

Messenger:
But he was *not* your father, nor am I.

Oedipus:
If that is so, why was I called his son?

Messenger:
Because he took you as a gift, from me.

Oedipus:
Yet even so, he loved me like a father?

Messenger:
Yes, for he had no children of his own.

Oedipus:
And when you gave me, had you bought or found me?

Messenger:
I found you in the glens of Mount Cithaeron.

Oedipus:
What could have brought you to a place like that?

Messenger:
The flocks of sheep that I was tending there.

Oedipus:
You went from place to place, hunting for work?

Messenger:
I did, my son. And yet I saved your life.

Oedipus:
How? Was I suffering when you took me up?

Messenger:
Your ankles are the proof of what you suffered.

Oedipus:
That misery! Why do you speak of that?

Messenger:
Your feet were pinned together, and I freed them.

Oedipus:
Yes. From my cradle I have borne those scars.

Messenger:
They are the reason for your present name.[5]

Oedipus:
Who did it? Speak! My mother, or my father?

Messenger:
Only the man who gave you to me knows.

Oedipus:
Then you yourself did not discover me.

Messenger:
No. A man put you in my arms, some shepherd.

Oedipus:
Do you know who he was? Can you describe him?

Messenger:
He was, I think, one of the slaves of Laius.

Oedipus:
The Laius who was once the King of Thebes?

Messenger:
Yes, that is right. King Laius was his master.

Oedipus:
How could I see him? Is he still alive?

Messenger:
One of his fellow Thebans would know that.

Oedipus:
Does anyone here know who this shepherd is?
Has anyone ever seen him in the city
Or in the fields? Tell me. Now is the time
To solve this mystery once and for all.

Chorus:
Sir, I believe the shepherd whom he means
Is the same man you have already sent for.
The Queen, perhaps, knows most about the matter.

Oedipus:
Do you, Jocasta? You know the man we summoned.
Is he the man this messenger spoke about?

Jocasta:
Why do you care? What difference can it make?
To ask is a waste of time, a waste of time!

Oedipus:
I cannot let these clues slip from my hands.
I must track down the secret of my birth.

Jocasta:
Oedipus, Oedipus! By all the gods,
If you set any value on your life,
Give up this search! I have endured enough.

Oedipus:
Do not be frightened. Even if my mother
Should prove to be a slave, and born of slaves,
This would not touch the honor of your name.

Jocasta:
Listen, I beg you! Listen! Do not do this!

Oedipus:
I cannot fail to bring the truth to light.

Jocasta:
I know my way is best for you, I know it!

Oedipus:
I know your best way is unbearable.

Jocasta:
May you be saved from learning who you are!

Oedipus:
Go, someone. Bring the shepherd. As for her,
Let her take comfort in her noble birth.

Jocasta:
You are lost! Lost! That is all I can call you now!
That is all I will ever call you, ever again!
[*Exit* **JOCASTA.**]

Chorus:
What wild grief, sir, has driven the Queen away?

5. The name *Oedipus* means "swollen foot."

Evil, I fear, will follow from her silence,
A storm of sorrow that will break upon us.

Oedipus:
Then let it break upon us I must learn
My parentage, whatever it may be.
The Queen is proud, far prouder than most women,
And feels herself dishonored by my baseness.
But I shall not be shamed. I hold myself
The child of Fortune, giver of all good.
She brought me forth. And as I lived my life,
The months, my brothers, watched the ebb and flow
Of my well-being. Never could I prove
False to a lineage like that, or fail
To bring to light the secret of my birth.

Chorus:
May Phoebus grant that I prove a true prophet!
My heart foreknows what the future will bring:
At tomorrow's full moon we shall gather, in chorus
To hail Cithaeron, to dance and sing
In praise of the mountain by Oedipus honored,
Theban nurse of our Theban King.

What long-lived nymph was the mother who bore you?
What god whom the joys of the hills invite
Was the god who begot you? Pan? or Apollo?
Or Hermes, Lord of Cylené's height?
Or on Helicon's slope did an oread place you
In Bacchus's arms for his new delight?

Oedipus:
Elders, I think I see the shepherd coming
Whom we have sent for. Since I never met him,
I am not sure, yet he seems old enough,
And my own slaves are the men bringing him.
But you, perhaps, know more of this than I,
If any of you have seen the man before.

Chorus:
Yes, it is he. I know him, the King's shepherd,
As true a slave as Laius ever had.
[*Enter* SHEPHERD.]

Oedipus:
I start with you, Corinthian. Is this man
The one you spoke of? **Mess.:** Sir, he stands before you.

Oedipus:
Now you, old man. Come, look me in the face.
Answer my questions. You were the slave of Laius?

Shepherd:
Yes, but not bought. I grew up in his household.

Oedipus:
What was the work that you were given to do?

Shepherd:
Sheep-herding. I have always been a shepherd.

Oedipus:
Where was it that you took your sheep to pasture?

Shepherd:
On Mount Cithaeron, or the fields near by.

Oedipus:
Do you remember seeing this man there?

Shepherd:
What was he doing? What man do you mean?

Oedipus:
That man beside you. Have you ever met him?

Shepherd:
No, I think not. I cannot recollect him.

Messenger:
Sir, I am not surprised, but I am sure
That I can make the past come back to him.
He cannot have forgotten the long summers
We grazed our sheep together by Cithaeron,
He with two flocks, and I with one—three years.
From spring to autumn. Then, for the winter months,
I used to drive my sheep to their own fold,
And he drove his back to the fold of Laius.
Is that right? Did it happen as I said?

Shepherd:
Yes, you are right, but it was long ago.

Messenger:
Well then, do you remember you once gave me
An infant boy to bring up as my own?

Shepherd:
What do you mean? Why do you ask me that?

Messenger:
Because the child you gave me stands before you.

Shepherd:
Will you be quiet? Curse you! Will you be quiet?

Oedipus [*to* Shepherd]**:**
You there! You have no reason to be angry.
You are far more to blame in this than he.

Shepherd:
What have I done, my Lord? What have I done?

Oedipus:
You have not answered. He asked about the boy.

Shepherd:
Sir, he knows nothing, nothing at all about it.

Oedipus:
And you say nothing. We must make you speak.

Shepherd:
My Lord, I am an old man! Do not hurt me!

Oedipus [*to* Guards]**:**
One of you tie his hands behind his back.

Shepherd:
Why do you want to know these fearful things?

Oedipus:
Did you, or did you not, give him that child?

Shepherd:
I did. I wish that I had died instead.

Oedipus:
You will die now, unless you tell the truth.

Shepherd:
And if I speak, I will be worse than dead.

Oedipus:
You seem to be determined to delay.

Shepherd:
No. No! I told you that I had the child.

Oedipus:
Where did it come from? Was it yours or not?

Shepherd:
No, it was not mine. Someone gave it to me.

Oedipus:
Some citizen of Thebes? Who was it? Who?

Shepherd:
Oh! Do not ask me that! Not that, my Lord!

Oedipus:
If I must ask once more, you are a dead man.

Shepherd:
The child came from the household of King Laius.

Oedipus:
Was it a slave's child? Or of royal blood?

Shepherd:
I stand on the very brink of speaking horrors.

Oedipus:
And I of hearing horrors—but I must.

Shepherd:
Then hear. The child was said to be the King's.
You can best learn about this from the Queen.

Oedipus:
The Queen! She gave it to you? **Shep.:** Yes, my Lord.

Oedipus:
Why did she do that? **Shep.:** So that I should kill it.

Oedipus:
Her own child? **Shep.:** Yes, she feared the oracles.

Oedipus:
What oracles? **Shep.:** That it must kill its father.

Oedipus:
Then why did you give it up to this old man?

Shepherd:
I pitied the poor child. I thought the man
Would take it with him back to his own country.
He saved its life only to have it come
At last to this. If you should be the man
He says you are, you were born miserable.

Oedipus:
All true! All, all made clear! Let me no longer
Look on the light of day. I am known now
For what I am—I, cursed in being born,
Cursed in my marriage, cursed in the blood I shed.
[*Exit* OEDIPUS.]

Chorus:
Men are of little worth. Their brief lives last
A single day.
They cannot hold elusive pleasure fast;
It melts away.
All laurels wither; all illusions fade;
Hopes have been phantoms, shade on air-built shade,
Since time began.
Your fate, O King, your fate makes manifest
Life's wretchedness. We can call no one blessed,
No, not one man.

Victorious, unerring, to their mark
Your arrows flew.
The Sphinx with her curved claws, her riddle dark,
Your wisdom slew.
By this encounter you preserved us all,
Guarding the land from death's approach, our tall,
Unshaken tower.
From that time, Oedipus, we held you dear,
Great King of our great Thebes, without a peer
In place and power.

But now what sadder story could be told?
A life of triumph utterly undone!
What fate could be more grievous to behold?
Father and son
Both found a sheltering port, a place of rest,
On the same breast.
Father and son both harvested the yield
Of the same bounteous field.
How could that earth endure such dreadful wrong
And hold its peace so long?
All-seeing time condemned your marriage lot;
In ways you least expected bared its shame—
Union wherein begetter and begot
Were both the same.
This loud lament, these tears that well and flow,
This bitter woe
Are for the day you rescued us, O King,
From our great suffering;
For the new life and happiness you gave
You drag down to the grave.
[*Enter* SECOND MESSENGER.]

Second Messenger:
Most honored elders, princes of the land,
If you are true-born Thebans and still love
The house of Labdacus,[6] then what a burden
Of sorrow you must bear, what fearful things
You must now hear and see! There is no river—
No, not the stream of Ister or of Phasis—
That could wash clean this house from the pollution
It hides within it or will soon bring forth:
Horrible deeds not done in ignorance,
But done deliberately. The cruelest evils
Are those that we embrace with open eyes.

Chorus:
Those we already know of are enough
To claim our tears. What more have you to tell?

Second Messenger:
It may be briefly told. The Queen is dead.

Chorus:
Poor woman! oh, poor woman! How? What happened?

Second Messenger:
She killed herself. You have been spared the worst,
Not being witnesses. Yet you shall learn
What her fate was, so far as I remember.
When she came in, almost beside herself,
Clutching her hair with both her hands, she rushed
Straight to her bedroom and slammed shut the doors
Behind her, screaming the name of Laius—
Laius long dead, but not her memory
Of their own child, the son who killed his father,
The son by whom his mother had more children.
She cursed the bed in which she had conceived
Husband by husband, children by her child,
A dreadful double bond. Beyond this much
I do not know the manner of her death,
For with a great cry Oedipus burst in,
Preventing us from following her fate
To its dark end. On him our gaze was fixed,
As in a frenzy he ran to and fro,
Calling: 'Give me a sword! Give me a sword!
Where is that wife who is no wife, that mother,

6. Labdacus was a grandson of Cadmus and the father of Laius.

That soil where I was sower and was sown?'
And as he raved, those of us there did nothing,
Some more than mortal power directed him.
With a wild shriek, as though he had some sign,
He hurled himself against the double doors,
Forcing the bars out of their loosened sockets,
And broke into his room. There was the Queen,
Hanged in a noose, still swinging back and forth.
When he saw this, the King cried out in anguish,
Untied the knotted cord in which she swung,
And laid the wretched woman on the ground.
What happened then was terrible to see.
He tore the golden brooches from her robe,
Lifted them up as high as he could reach,
And drove them with all his strength into his eyes,
Shrieking, 'No more, no more shall my eyes see
The horrors of my life—what I have done,
What I have suffered. They have looked too long
On those whom they ought never to have seen.
They never knew those whom I longed to see.
Blind, blind! Let them be blind! 'With these wild words
He stabbed and stabbed his eyes. At every blow,
The dark blood dyed his beard, not sluggish drops,
But a great torrent like a shower of hail.
A two-fold punishment of two-fold sin
Broke on the heads of husband and of wife.
Their happiness was once true happiness,
But now disgrace has come upon them, death,
Sorrow, and ruin, every earthly ill
That can be named. Not one have they escaped.

Chorus:
Is he still suffering? Has he found relief?

Second Messenger:
He calls for someone to unbar the doors
And show him to all Thebes, his father's killer,
His mother's—no, I cannot say the word;
It is unholy, horrible. He intends
To leave the country, for his staying here
Would bring down his own curse upon his house.
He has no guide and no strength of his own.
His pain is unendurable. This too
You will see. They are drawing back the bars.
The sight is loathsome and yet pitiful.
[*Enter* OEDIPUS.]

Chorus:
Hideous, hideous! I have seen nothing so dreadful,
Ever before!
I can look no more.
Oedipus, Oedipus! What madness has come upon you?
What malignant fate
Has leaped with its full weight.
Has struck you down with an irresistible fury,
And born you off as its prey?
Poor wretch! There is much that I yearn
To ask of you, much I would learn;
But I cannot. The sight of you fills me with horror!
I shudder and turn away.

Oedipus:
Oh, Oh! What pain! I cannot rest in my anguish!
Where am I? Where?
Where are my words? They die away as I speak them,
Into thin air.
What is my fate to be?

Chorus:
A fate too fearful for men to hear of, for men to see.

Oedipus:
Lost! Overwhelmed by the rush of unspeakable darkness!
It smothers me in its cloud.
The pain of my eyes is piercing.
The thought of my sins, the horrors that I have committed,
Racks me without relief.

Chorus:
No wonder you suffer, Oedipus, no wonder you cry aloud
Under your double burden of pain and grief.

Oedipus:
My friend, my friend! How steadfast you are, how ready
To help me in my great need!
I feel your presence beside me.
Blind as I am, I know your voice in the blackness
Of my long-lasting night.

Chorus:
How could you put out your eyes, still another infamous deed?
What god, what demon, induced you to quench their light?

Oedipus:
It was Apollo, my friends, who brought me low,
Apollo who crushed me beneath this unbearable burden;
But it was my hand, mine, that struck the blow.
Why should I see? What sight could have given me pleasure?

Chorus:
These things are as you say.

Oedipus:
What is there now to love? What greeting can cheer me?
Lead me away,
Quickly, quickly! O lead me out of the country
To a distant land! I am beyond redemption
Accursed, beyond hope lost, the one man living
Whom all the gods most hate.

Chorus:
Would we had never heard of your existence,
Your fruitless wisdom and your wretched fate.

Oedipus:
My curses be upon him, whoever freed
My feet from the cruel fetters, there on the mountain,
Who restored me from death to life, a thankless deed.
My death would have saved my friends and me from anguish.

Chorus:
I too would have had it so.

Oedipus:
Then would I never have been my father's killer.
Now all men know
That I am the infamous son who defiled his mother,
That I shared the bed of the father who gave me being.
And if there is sorrow beyond any mortal sorrow,
I have brought it upon my head.

Chorus:
I cannot say that you have acted wisely.
Alive and blind? You would be better dead.

Oedipus:
Give me no more advice, and do not tell me
That I was wrong. What I have done is best.

For if I still had eyesight when I went
Down to the underworld, how could I bear
To see my father and my wretched mother?
After the terrible wrong I did them both,
It would not have been punishment enough
If I had hanged myself. Or do you think
That I could find enjoyment in the sight
Of children born as mine were born? No! No!
Nor in the sight of Thebes with its towered walls
And sacred statues of the gods. For I—
Who is so wretched?—I, the foremost Theban,
Cut myself off from this by my own edict
That ordered everyone to shun the man
Polluting us, the man the gods have shown
To be accursed, and of the house of Laius.
Once I laid bare my shame, could I endure
To look my fellow-citizens in the face?
Never! Never! If I had found some way
Of choking off the fountain of my hearing,
I would have made a prison of my body,
Sightless and soundless. It would be sweet to live
Beyond the reach of sorrow. Oh, Cithaeron!
Why did you give me shelter rather than slay me
As soon as I was given to you? Then
No one would ever have heard of my begetting.
Polybus, Corinth, and the ancient house
I thought my forebears'! You reared me as a child.
My fair appearance covered foul corruption,
I am impure, born of impurity.
Oh, narrow crossroad where the three paths meet!
Secluded valley hidden in the forest,
You that drank up my blood, my father's blood
Shed by my hands, do you remember all
I did for you to see? Do you remember
What else I did when I came here to Thebes?
Oh marriage rites! By which I was begotten,
You then brought forth children by your own child,
Creating foulest blood-relationship:
An interchange of fathers, brothers, sons,
Brides, wives, and mothers—the most monstrous shame
Man can be guilty of. I should not speak
Of what should not be done. By all the gods,
Hide me, I beg you, hide me quickly somewhere
Far, far away. Put me to death or throw me
Into the sea, out of your sight forever.
Come to me, friends, pity my wretchedness.
Let your hands touch me. Hear me. Do not fear,
My curse can rest on no one but myself.

Chorus:
Creon is coming. He is the one to act
On your requests, or to help you with advice.
He takes your place as our sole guardian.

Oedipus:
Creon! What shall I say? I cannot hope
That he will trust me now, when my past hatred
Has proved to be so utterly mistaken.
[*Enter* CREON.]

Creon:
I have not come to mock you, Oedipus,
Or to reproach you for any evil-doing.
[*to* ATTENDANTS] You there. If you have lost all your respect
For men, revere at least the Lord Apollo,
Whose flame supports all life. Do not display
So nakedly pollution such as this,
Evil that neither earth nor holy rain
Nor light of day can welcome. Take him in,
Take him in, quickly. Piety demands
That only kinsmen share a kinsman's woe.

Oedipus:
Creon, since you have proved my fears were groundless,
Since you have shown such magnanimity
To one so vile as I, grant my petition.
I ask you not for my sake but your own.

Creon:
What is it that you beg so urgently?

Oedipus:
Drive me away at once. Drive me far off.
Let me not hear a human voice again.

Creon:
I have delayed only because I wished
To have the god reveal to me my duty.

Oedipus:
But his command was certain: put to death
The unholy parricide. And I am he.

Creon:
True. But as things are now, it would be better
To find out clearly what we ought to do.

Oedipus:
An oracle for a man so miserable?

Creon:
Yes. Even you will now believe the god.

Oedipus:
I will. Creon, I charge you with this duty.
Accept it, I entreat you. Give to her
Who lies within such burial as you wish,
For she belongs to you. You will perform
The proper obsequies. But as for me,
Let not my presence doom my father's city,
But send me to the hills, to Mount Cithaeron,
My mountain, which my mother and my father
Chose for my grave. So will I die at last
By the decree of those who sought to slay me.
And yet I know I will not die from sickness
Or anything else. I was preserved from death
To meet some awful, some mysterious end.
My own fate does not matter, only my children's.
Creon, my sons need give you no concern,
For they are men, and can find anywhere
A livelihood. But Creon, my two girls!
How lost, how pitiable! They always ate
Their daily bread with me, at my own table,
And had their share of everything I touched.
Take care of them! O Creon, take care of them!
And one thing more—if I could only touch them
And with them weep. O prince, prince, grant me this!
Grant it, O noble Creon! If I touched them,
I could believe I saw them once again.
[*Enter* ISMENE *and* ANTIGONE.]

What! Do I hear my daughters? Hear them sobbing?
Has Creon had pity on me? Has he sent them,
My children, my two darlings? Is it true?

Creon:
Yes. I have had them brought. I knew how much
You used to love them, how you love them still.

Oedipus:
May the gods bless you, Creon, for this kindness;

And may they guard you better on your journey
Than they have guarded me. Children, where are you?
Come to your brother's hands, the hands that made
Your father's clear eyes into what these are—
Your father, who saw nothing and knew nothing,
Begetting you where he had been conceived.
I cannot see you, but I weep for you,
Weep for the bitter lives that you must lead
Henceforward. Never, never will you go
To an assembly with the citizens,
Or to a festival, and take your part.
You will turn back in tears. And when you come
To the full bloom of womanhood, what man
Will run the risk of bringing on himself
Your shame, my daughters, and your children's shame?
Is there one evil, one, that is not ours?
'Your father killed his father; he begot
Children of his own mother; she who bore you
Bore him as well.' These are the taunts, the insults
That you will hear. Who, then, will marry you?
No one, my children. Clearly it is your fate
To waste away in barren maidenhood.
Creon, Creon, their blood flows in your veins.
You are the only father left to them;
They have lost both their parents. Do not let them
Wander away, unmarried, destitute,
As miserable as I. Have pity on them,
So young, so utterly forlorn, so helpless
Except for you. You are kind-hearted. Touch me
To tell me that I have your promise. Children,
There is so much, so much that I would say,
If you were old enough to understand it,
But now I only teach you this one prayer:
May I be given a place in which to live,
And may my life be happier than my father's.

Creon:
Come, come with us. Have done with further woe.

Oedipus:
Obedience is hard. **Cr.:** No good in life endures beyond its season.

Oedipus:
Do you know why I yield? **Cr.:** When I have heard your reason I will know.

Oedipus:
You are to banish me. **Cr.:** The gods alone can grant you that entreaty.

Oedipus:
I am hated by the gods. **Cr.:** Then their response to you will not be slow.

Oedipus:
So you consent to this? **Cr.:** I say no more than I have said already.

Oedipus:
Come, then, lead me away. **Cr.:** Not with your children. You must let them go.

Oedipus:
Creon, not that, not that! **Cr.:** You must be patient. Nothing can restore
Your old dominion. You are King no more.

[*Exeunt* CREON, OEDIPUS, ISMENE, *and* ANTIGONE.]

Chorus:
Behold him, Thebans: Oedipus, great and wise,
Who solved the famous riddle. This is he
Whom all men gazed upon with envious eyes,
Who now is struggling in a stormy sea,
Crushed by the billows of his bitter woes.
Look to the end of mortal life. In vain
We say a man is happy, till he goes
Beyond life's final border, free from pain.

Two Questions for Consideration

1. The first question which arises after reading the *Oedipus* is whether the king is brought to his doom through the workings of an inexorable fate, whether he is brought low because of a flaw in his own character, or whether the downfall is the result of the interweaving of the two forces. Can you find evidence in the play itself to support any of these positions?
2. One scholar has suggested that the play was written as an admonition to the increasingly atheistic people of Athens that the gods were powerful. Do you find evidence in the play to support or deny this statement as the central theme of the play?

The Allegory of the Cave

Plato

This story represents Plato's idea about absolute reality in the universe, and the world that appears to our senses. What should the student of philosophy, who glimpses reality, do? This is taken from Book VII of the *Republic.* Socrates and Glaucon (GLOW [as in how] kon) are talking.

And now, I said, let me show in a figure how far our nature is enlightened or unenlightened;—Behold! human beings living in an underground den, which has a mouth open towards the light and reaching all along the den; here they have been from their childhood, and have their legs and necks chained so that they cannot move and can only see before them, being prevented by the chains from turning round their heads. Above and behind a fire is blazing at a distance, and between the fire and the prisoners there is a raised way, like the screen which marionette players have in front of them, over which they show the puppets.

I see.

And do you see, I said, men passing along the wall carrying all sorts of vessels, and statues and figures of animals made of wood and stone and various materials, which appear over the wall? Some of them are talking, others silent.

You have shown me a strange image, and they are strange prisoners.

Like ourselves, I replied; and they see only their own shadows, or the shadows of one another, which the fire throws on the opposite wall of the cave?

True, he said; how could they see anything but the shadows if they were never allowed to move their heads?

And of the objects which are being carried in like manner they would only see the shadows?

Yes, he said.

And if they were able to converse with one another, would they not suppose that they were naming what was actually before them?

Very true.

And suppose further that the prison had an echo which came from the other side, would they not be sure to fancy when one of the passers-by spoke that the voice which they heard came from the passing shadow?

No question, he replied.

To them, I said, the truth would be literally nothing but the shadows of the images.

That is certain.

And now look again, and see what will naturally follow if the prisoners are released and disabused of their error. At first, when any of them is liberated and compelled suddenly to stand up and turn his neck round and walk and look towards the light, he will suffer sharp pains; the glare will distress him, and he will be unable to see the realities of which in his former state he had seen the shadows; and then conceive someone saying to him, that what he saw before was an illusion, but that now, when he is approaching nearer to being and his eye is turned towards more real existence, he has a clearer vision,—what will be his reply? And you may further imagine that his instructor is pointing to the objects as they pass and requiring him to name them—will he not be perplexed? Will he not fancy that the shadows which he formerly saw are truer than the objects which are now shown to him?

Far truer.

And if he is compelled to look straight at the light, will he not have a pain in his eyes which will make him turn away to take refuge in the objects of vision which he can see, and which he will conceive to be in reality clearer than the things which are now being shown to him?

True, he said.

And suppose once more, that he is reluctantly dragged up a steep and rugged ascent, and held fast until he is forced into the presence of the sun himself, is he not likely to be pained and irritated? When he approaches the light his eyes will be dazzled, and he will not be able to see anything at all of what are now called realities.

Not all in a moment, he said.

He will require to grow accustomed to the sight of the upper world. And first he will see the shadows best, next the reflections of men and other objects in the water, and then the objects themselves; then he will gaze upon the light of the moon and the stars and the spangled heaven; and he will see the sky and the stars by night better than the sun or the light of the sun by day?

Certainly.

Last of all he will be able to see the sun,[1] and not mere reflections of it in the water, but he will see it in its own proper place, and not in another; and he will contemplate it as it is.

Certainly.

He will then proceed to argue that this is it which gives the season and the years, and is the guardian of all that is in the visible world, and in a certain way the cause of all things which he and his fellows have been accustomed to behold?

Clearly, he said, he would first see the sun and then reason about it.

And when he remembered his old habitation, and the wisdom of the den and his fellow-prisoners, do you not suppose that he would congratulate himself on the change and pity them?

Certainly, he would.

And if they were in the habit of conferring honours among themselves on those who were quickest to observe the passing shadows and to remark which of them went before, and which followed after, and which were together; and who were therefore best able to draw conclusions as to the future, do you think that he would care for such honors and glories, or envy the possessors of them? Would he not say with Homer,

"Better to be the poor servant of a poor master," and to endure anything, rather than think as they do and live after their manner?

Yes, he said, I think that he would rather suffer anything than entertain these false notions and live in this miserable manner.

Imagine once more, I said, such a one coming suddenly out of the sun to be replaced in his old situation; would he not be certain to have his eyes full of darkness?

To be sure, he said.

And if there were a contest, and he had to compete in measuring the shadows with the prisoners who had never moved out of the den, while his sight was still weak, and before his eyes had become steady (and the time which would be needed to acquire this new habit of sight might be very considerable), would he not be ridiculous? Men would say of him that up he went and came back without his eyes; and that it was better not even to think of ascending; and if any one tried to loose another and lead him up to the light, let them only catch the offender, and they would put him to death.

No question, he said.

This entire allegory, I said, you may now append, dear Glaucon, to the previous argument; the prison-house is the world of sight, the light of the fire is the sun, and you will not misapprehend me if you interpret the journey upwards to be the ascent of the soul into the intellectual world according to my poor belief, which, at your desire, I have expressed—whether rightly or wrongly God knows. But whether true or false, my opinion is that in the world of knowledge the idea of good appears last of all, and is seen only with an effort; and when seen, is also inferred to be the universal author of all things beautiful and right, parent of light and of the lord of light in this visible world, and the immediate source of reason and truth in the intellectual; and that this is the power upon which he who would act rationally either in public or private life must have his eye fixed.

I agree, he said, as far as I am able to understand you.

Moreover, I said, you must not wonder that those who attain to this beatific vision are unwilling to descend to human affairs; for their souls are ever hastening into the upper world where they desire to dwell; which desire of theirs is very natural, if our allegory may be trusted.

Yes, very natural.

And is there anything surprising in one who passes from divine contemplations to the evil state of man, misbehaving himself in a ridiculous manner; if, while his eyes are blinking and before he has become accustomed to the surrounding darkness, he is compelled to fight in courts of law,

---

1. Imagine that the sun is Plato's idea of The Good.

or in other places, about the images or the shadows of images of justice, and is endeavoring to meet the conceptions of those who have never yet seen absolute justice?

Anything but surprising, he replied.

Anyone who has common sense will remember that the bewilderments of the eyes are of two kinds, and arise from two causes, either from coming out of the light or from going into the light, which is true of the mind's eye, quite as much as of the bodily eye; and he who remembers this when he sees anyone whose vision is perplexed and weak, will not be too ready to laugh; he will first ask whether that soul of man has come out of the brighter life, and is unable to see because unaccustomed to the dark, or having turned from darkness to the day is dazzled by excess of light.

The business of us who are the founders of the State will be to compel the best minds to attain that knowledge which we have already shown to be the greatest of all—they must continue to ascend until they arrive at the good; but when they have ascended and seen enough we must not allow them to do as they do now.

What do you mean?

I mean that they remain in the upper world; but this must not be allowed; they must be made to descend again among the prisoners in the den, and partake of their labors and honors, whether they are worth having or not.

A Question

Why does Plato insist that the one who has gone through all of the difficulties involved in coming to see and know the true light *must* return to the cave, that he must even partake of the labors and honors of the people in the cave, even though he recognizes that these are foolish?

Phaedo

Plato

The scene of this dialogue is a small town in the Peloponnesus to which Phaidon (Phaedo) has gone some time after the death of Socrates in 399 B.C. Here he encounters Echecrates, a former student of Socrates. Echecrates asks Phaedo about the death, and the remainder of the dialogue ensues. Except in a few instances which are so designated, Phaedo is the speaker, recounting all of the conversation of Socrates' last day.

The central problem of this dialogue is the fate of the soul after the death of the body, and in the discussion Socrates touches on most of the doctrines which he had developed during his lifetime. Some of the ideas which the reader might notice are these: (1) the idea of the separateness of soul and body; (2) the "Platonic" virtues; (3) the doctrine of opposites and of the ebb and flow of all things from their opposites; (4) the concept of the soul's recollection as evidence of the preexistence of the soul; (5) the whole thought about reincarnation of the soul; (6) and the concept that the soul is not simply a harmony of the various qualities which make up the body.

You might also notice the extent to which Socrates builds his philosophy on the thought of earlier philosopher-scientists, particularly the Eleatics.

The speakers in this dialogue are Phaedo (FEED-oh),) Echecrates (ek-uh-KRA-teez), Socrates, Cebes (SEE-beez), Simmias (SIM-ee-us), and Crito (KRI-toe).

The translation is that of the twentieth-century scholar, W.H.D. Rouse.

Echecrates:

Were you there yourself, Phaidon, with Socrates, on the day when he took the poison in prison, or did you hear about it from someone?

Phaidon:

I was there myself, Echecrates.

Echecrates:

Then what was it our friend said before his death? And how did he end? I should be glad to hear. You see no one at all from our part of the world[1] goes now to visit in Athens, and no visitor has come to us from there this long time who might be able to tell us properly what happened; all they could say was, he took the poison and died; no one could tell us anything about the other details.

Phaidon:

Then you never heard how things went at the trial?

Echecrates:

Yes, somebody did bring news of that, and we were surprised how long it seemed between the sentence and his death. Why was that, Phaidon?

Phaidon:

It was just a piece of luck, Echecrates; for the day before the trial it so happened that the wreath was put on the poop of the ship which the Athenians send to Delos.

Echecrates:

What ship is that?

Phaidon:

That is the ship, as the Athenians say, in which Theseus once went off to Crete with those "twice seven," you know, and saved them and saved himself.[2] The Athenians vowed to Apollo then, so it is said, that if the lives of these were saved, they would send a sacred mission every year to Delos; and they do send it still, every year ever since that, to honour the god. As soon as the mission has begun, then, it is their law to keep the city pure during that time, and to put no one to death before the ship arrives at Delos and comes back again here; this often takes some time, when the winds happen to delay them. The beginning of the mission is when the priest of Apollo lays a wreath on the poop of the ship, and this happened, as I say, the day before the trial. Accordingly Socrates had a long time in prison between the trial and his death.

---

1. Phlius, a small town in the Peloponnesus (Morea) about sixty miles from Athens.
2. In Athenian legend; Athens because of a past misdeed had to send seven youths and seven maidens every ninth year to King Minos in Crete to be devoured by the Minotaur. Theseus of Athens went to Crete and killed the monster.

Echecrates:

Then what about the death itself, Phaidon? What was said or done, and which of his friends were with him? Or did the magistrates forbid their presence, and did he die alone with no friends there?

Phaidon:

Oh no, friends were with him, quite a number of them.

Echecrates:

That's just what I want to know; please be so kind as to tell me all about it as clearly as possible, unless you happen to be busy.

Phaidon:

Oh, I have plenty of time, and I will try to tell you the whole story; indeed, to remember Socrates, and what he said himself, and what was said to him is always the most precious thing in the world to me.

Echecrates:

Well, Phaidon, those who are going to hear you will feel the same; pray try to tell the whole story as exactly as you can.

Phaidon:

I must say I had the strangest feeling being there. I felt no pity, as one might, being present at the death of a dear friend; for the man seemed happy to me, Echecrates, in bearing and in speech. How fearlessly and nobly he met his end! I could not help thinking that divine providence was with that man as he passed from this world to the next, and on coming there also it would be well with him, if ever with anyone that ever was. For this reason I felt no pity at all, as one might at a scene of mourning; and yet not the pleasure we used to have in our philosophic discussions. The conversation was certainly of that sort, but I really had an extraordinary feeling, a strange mixture of pleasure and pain at once, when I remembered that then and there that man was to make his end. And all of us who were present were very much in the same state, sometimes laughing, sometimes shedding tears, and one of us particularly, Apollodoros—no doubt you know the man and his ways.

Echecrates:

Oh yes, of course.

Phaidon:

Well, he behaved quite as usual, and I was broken down myself, and so were others.

Echecrates:

But who were they, Phaidon?

Phaidon:

Of our countrymen[3] there was this Apollodoros I have mentioned, and Critobulos and his father, and, besides, Hermogenes and Epigenes and Aischines and Antisthenes; there was also Ctesippos the Paianian and Menexenos, and others of our countrymen; but Plato was ill, I think.

Echecrates:

Were any foreigners present?

Phaidon:

Yes, Simmias the Theban and Cebes and Phaidondes; and from Megara, Eucleides and Terpsion.

Echecrates:

Oh, were not Aristippos and Cleombrotos present?

Phaidon:

No, they were said to be in Aegina.

Echecrates:

Was anyone else there?

Phaidon:

I think these are about all who were present.

Echecrates:

Very well; tell me, what did you talk about?

Phaidon:

I will try to tell you the whole story from the beginning. You see we had been accustomed during all the former days to visit Socrates, myself and the rest. We used to gather early at the court where the trial had been, for that was near the prison. We always waited until the prison was opened, passing the time together, for it was not opened early; and when it was opened we went in to Socrates and generally spent the day with him. That day, however, we gathered earlier than usual; for the day before, after we left the prison in the evening, we learnt that the ship had come in from Delos; so we warned one another to come as early as possible, to the usual place. We came early, then, and the porter who used to answer the door came out to us, and told us to wait and not to go in till he gave the word; for, he said, "The Eleven[4] are knocking off his fetters and informing him that he must die today."

After a short while he came back and told us to go in. So we went in, and found Socrates just released, and Xanthippe,[5] you know her, with his little boy, sitting beside him. Then when Xanthippe saw us, she cried out in lamentation and said as women do, "O Socrates! Here is the last time your friends will speak to you and you to them!"

Socrates glanced at Criton and said quietly, "Please let someone take her home, Criton."

Then some of Criton's people led her away crying and beating her breast. Socrates sat up on his bed, and bent back his leg and rubbed it with his hand, and said while he rubbed it, "How strange a thing it seems, my friends, that which people call pleasure! And how wonderful is its relation to pain, which they suppose to be its opposite; both together they will not come to a man, yet if he pursues one of the pair, and catches it, he is almost compelled to catch the other, too; so they seem to be both hung together from one head. I think that Aesop would have made a fable, if he had noticed this; he would have said they were at war, and God wanted to make peace between them and could not, and accordingly hung them together by their heads to the same thing, and therefore whenever you get one, the other follows after. That's just what it seems like to me; first came the pain in my leg from the irons, and here seems to come following after it, pleasure."

Cebes took up here, and said, "Upon my word, Socrates, I am much obliged to you for reminding me. About your poems, I mean, when you put into verse Aesop's fables, and the prelude for Apollo; many people have asked me, for example Euenos, the other day, what on earth put it in your mind to make those poems after you came into prison, although you never made any before. Then if you care that I should be able to answer Euenos, next time he asks me, and I'm sure he will, tell me what to say."

---

3. Athenians.
4. In charge of the prison and of executions.
5. Socrates' wife.

"Tell him then, Cebes," he said, "just the truth: that I did not want to rival him or his creations when I did it, for I knew it would not be easy; but I was trying to find out the meaning of certain dreams, and getting it off my conscience, in case they meant to command me to attempt that sort of composition. The dreams went like this: In my past life, the same dream often used to come to me, in different shapes at different times, but saying the same thing, 'Socrates, get to work and compose music!'[6] Formerly I took this to mean what I was already doing; I thought the dream was urging and encouraging me, as people do in cheering on their own men when they are running a race, to compose—which, taking philosophy to be the highest form of composition, I was doing already; but now after the trial, while the festival was putting off my execution, I thought that, if the dream should really command me to work at this common kind of composition, I ought not to disobey the dream but to do so. For it seemed safer not to go away before getting it off my conscience by composing poetry, and so obeying the dream. So first of all I composed in honour of the god[7] whose festival this was; after the god, I considered that a poet must compose fiction if he was to be a poet, not true tales, and I was no fiction-monger, and therefore I took the fictions that I found to my hand and knew, namely Aesop's, and composed the first that came. Then tell Euenos that, Cebes, and bid him farewell, and tell him to follow me as soon as he can, if he is sensible. I am going away, as it seems, today; for so the Athenians command."

"What advice, Socrates," he said, "to give to Euenos! I have often met the man; from what I have seen of him so far he will be the last man to obey!"

"Why," said he, "is not Euenos a philosopher?"

"I think so," said Simmias.

"Then Euenos will be willing enough, and so will everyone who goes properly into the subject. But perhaps he will not do violence to himself; for they say that is not lawful."

As he spoke, he let down his legs on to the ground, and sat thus during the rest of the talk. Then Cebes asked him, "What do you mean, Socrates, by saying, that it is not lawful for a man to do violence to himself, but that the philosopher would be willing to follow the dying?"

"Why, Cebes," he said, "have not you and Simmias heard all about such things from Philolaos, when you were his pupils?"

"Nothing clear, Socrates."

"Well truly, all I say myself is only from hearsay; however, what I happen to have heard I don't mind telling you. Indeed, it is perhaps most proper that one who is going to depart and take up his abode in that world should think about the life over there and say what sort of life we imagine it to be: for what else could one do with the time till sunset?"

"Well then, why pray do they say it is not lawful for a man to take his own life, my dear Socrates? I have already heard Philolaos myself, as you asked me just now, when he was staying in our parts, and I have heard others too, and they all said we must not do that; but I never heard anything clear about it."

"Well, go on trying," said Socrates, "and perhaps you may hear something. It might perhaps seem surprising to you if in this one thing, of all that happens to a human being, there is never any exception—if it never chances to a man amongst the other chances of his life that sometimes for some people it is better to die than to live; but it does probably seem surprising to you if those people for whom it *is* better to die may not rightly do this good to themselves, but must wait for some other benefactor."

And Cebes answered, with a light laugh. "True for ye, by Zeus!" using his native Doric.

"Indeed, put like this," said Socrates, "it would seem unreasonable; but possibly there is a grain of reason in it. At least, the tale whispered in secret about these things is that we men are in a sort of custody, and a man must not release himself or run away, which appears a great mystery to me and not easy to see through. But I do think, Cebes, it is right to say the gods are those who take care of us, and that we men are one of the gods' possessions—don't you think so?"

"Yes, I do," said Cebes.

"Then," said he, "if one of your own possessions, your slave, should kill himself, without your indicating to him that you wanted him to die, you would be angry with him, and punish him if there were any punishment?"

"Certainly," said he.

"Possibly, then, it is not unreasonable in that sense, that a man must not kill himself before God sends on him some necessity, like that which is present here now."

"Yes indeed, that seems likely," said Cebes. "But you said just now, Socrates, that philosophers ought cheerfully to be willing to die; that does seem unreasonable, at least if there is reason in what we have just said, that God is he who cares for us and we are his possessions. That the wisest men should not object to depart out of this service in which we are overseen by the best overseers there are, gods, there is no reason in that. For I don't suppose a wise man thinks he will care better for himself when he is free. But a foolish man might well believe that he should run away from an owner; and he would not remember that from a good one he ought not to run away but to stay as long as he could, and so he would thoughtlessly run away, while the man of sense would desire always to be with one better than himself. Indeed, in this case, Socrates, the opposite of what was said would be likely: It is proper that wise men should object to die, and foolish men should be glad."

Socrates, hearing this, was pleased, I thought, at the way Cebes dealt with the matter; and, glancing away at us, he said, "Cebes is always on the hunt for arguments, and won't believe straight off whatever one says."

And Simmias added, "But I tell you, Socrates, I think I now see something in what Cebes says, myself; for what could men want, if they are truly wise, in running away from owners better than themselves, and lightly shaking them off? And I really think Cebes is aiming his argument at you, because you take it so easily to leave both us and good masters, as you admit yourself, gods!"

"Quite right," said he. "I think I must answer this before you just as if you were a court!"

"Exactly," said Simmias.

"Very well," said he, "I will try to convince you better than I did my judges. I believe, my dear Simmias and Cebes, that I shall pass over first of all to other gods, both wise and good, secondly to dead men better than those in

6. "Music" included poetry.
7. Apollo.

this world; and if I did not think so, I should do wrong in not objecting to death; but, believing this, be assured that I hope I shall find myself in the company of good men, although I would not maintain it for certain; but that I shall pass over to gods who are very good masters, be assured that if I would maintain for certain anything else of the kind, I would with certainty maintain this. Then for these reasons, so far from objecting, I have good hopes that something remains for the dead, as has been the belief from time immemorial, and something much better for the good than for the bad."

"Then," said Simmias, "do you mean to keep this idea to yourself and go away with it, or will you give us a share? This good find seems to be a case of findings is sharings[8] between us, and don't forget you are on your defence, to see if you can convince us."

"Well, I'll try," he said.

"But first I see Criton here has been wanting to say something ever so long; let's ask what it is."

"Only this," Criton said, "the man who is to give you the poison keeps telling me to advise you not to talk too much. He says people get hotter by talking, and nothing like that ought to accompany the poison; otherwise people who do that often have to take two or three potions."

And Socrates said, "Oh, let him be; he must just be ready to give me two, or three if necessary."

"I guessed as much," said Criton, "but he keeps bothering me."

"Oh, let him be," said he. "Now then, I want to give the proof at once, to you as my judges, why I think it likely that one who has spent his life in philosophy should be confident when he is going to die, and have good hopes that he will win the greatest blessings in the next world when he has ended: so Simmias and Cebes my judges, I will try to show how this could be true.

"The fact is, those who tackle philosophy aright are simply and solely practising dying, practising death, all the time, but nobody sees it. If this is true, then it would surely be unreasonable that they should earnestly do this and nothing else all their lives, yet when death comes they should object to what they had been so long earnestly practising."

Simmias laughed at this, and said, "I don't feel like laughing just now, Socrates, but you have made me laugh. I think the many if they heard that would say, 'That's a good one for the philosophers!' And other people in my city would heartily agree that philosophers are really suffering from a wish to die, and now they have found them out, that they richly deserve it!"

"That would be true, Simmias," said Socrates, "except the words 'found out.' For they have not found out in what sense the real philosophers wish to die and deserve to die, and what kind of death it is. Let us say good-bye to them," he went on, "and ask ourselves: Do we think there is such a thing as death?"

"Certainly," Simmias put in.

"Is it anything more than the separation of the soul from the body?" said Socrates. "Death is, that the body separates from the soul, and remains by itself apart from the soul, and the soul, separated from the body, exists by itself apart from the body. Is death anything but that?"

"No," he said, "that is what death is."

"Then consider, my good friend, if you agree with me here, for I think this is the best way to understand the question we are examining. Do you think it the part of a philosopher to be earnestly concerned with what are called pleasures, such as these—eating and drinking, for example?"

"Not at all," said Simmias.

"The pleasures of love, then?"

"Oh no."

"Well, do you suppose a man like that regards the other bodily indulgences as precious? Getting fine clothes and shoes and other bodily adornments—ought he to price them high or low, beyond whatever share of them it is absolutely necessary to have?"

"Low, I think," he said, "if he is a true philosopher."

"Then in general," he said, "do you think that such a man's concern is not for the body, but as far as he can he stands aloof from that and turns towards the soul?"

"I do."

"Then firstly, is it not clear that in such things the philosopher as much as possible sets free the soul from communion with the body, more than other men?"

"So it appears."

"And I suppose, Simmias, it must seem to most men that he who has no pleasure in such things and takes no share in them does not deserve to live, but he is getting pretty close to death if he does not care about pleasures which he has by means of the body."

"Quite true, indeed."

"Well then, what about the actual getting of wisdom? Is the body in the way or not, if a man takes it with him as companion in the search? I mean, for example, is there any truth for men in their sight and hearing? Or as poets are forever dinning into our ears, do we hear nothing and see nothing exactly? Yet if these of our bodily senses are not exact and clear, the others will hardly be, for they are all inferior to these, don't you think so?"

"Certainly," he said.

"Then," said he, "when does the soul get hold of the truth? For whenever the soul tries to examine anything in company with the body, it is plain that it is deceived by it."

"Quite true."

"Then is it not clear that in reasoning, if anywhere, something of the realities becomes visible to it?"

"Yes."

"And I suppose it reasons best when none of these senses disturbs it, hearing or sight, or pain, or pleasure indeed, but when it is completely by itself and says good-bye to the body, and so far as possible has no dealings with it, when it reaches out and grasps that which really is."

"That is true."

"And is it not then that the philosopher's soul chiefly holds the body cheap and escapes from it, while it seeks to be by itself?"

"So it seems."

"Let us pass on, Simmias. Do we say there is such a thing as justice by itself, or not?"

"We do say so, certainly!"

"Such a thing as the good and beautiful?"

"Of course!"

"And did you ever see one of them with your eyes?"

"Never," said he.

"By any other sense of those the body has did you ever grasp them? I mean all such things, greatness, health,

8. A proverb.

strength, in short everything that really is the nature of things whatever they are: Is it through the body that the real truth is perceived? Or is this better—whoever of us prepares himself most completely and most exactly to comprehend each thing which he examines would come nearest to knowing each one?"

"Certainly."

"And would he do that most purely who should approach each with his intelligence alone, not adding sight to intelligence, or dragging in any other sense along with reasoning, but using the intelligence uncontaminated alone by itself, while he tries to hunt out each essence uncontaminated, keeping clear of eyes and ears and, one might say, of the whole body, because he thinks the body disturbs him and hinders the soul from getting possession of truth and wisdom when body and soul are companions—is not this the man, Simmias, if anyone, who will hit reality?"

"Nothing could be more true, Socrates," said Simmias.

"Then from all this," said Socrates, "genuine philosophers must come to some such opinion as follows, so as to make to one another statements such as these: 'A sort of direct path, so to speak, seems to take us to the conclusion that so long as we have the body with us in our enquiry, and our soul is mixed up with so great an evil, we shall never attain sufficiently what we desire, and that, we say, is the truth. For the body provides thousands of busy distractions because of its necessary food; besides, if diseases fall upon us, they hinder us from the pursuit of the real. With loves and desires and fears and all kinds of fancies and much rubbish, it infects us, and really and truly makes us, as they say, unable to think one little bit about anything at any time. Indeed, wars and factions and battles all come from the body and its desires, and from nothing else. For the desire of getting wealth causes all wars, and we are compelled to desire wealth by the body, being slaves to its culture; therefore we have no leisure for philosophy, from all these reasons. Chief of all is that if we do have some leisure, and turn away from the body to speculate on something, in our searches it is everywhere interfering, it causes confusion and disturbance, and dazzles us so that it will not let us see the truth; so in fact we see that if we are ever to know anything purely we must get rid of it, and examine the real things by the soul alone; and then, it seems, after we are dead, as the reasoning shows, not while we live, we shall possess that which we desire, lovers of which we say we are, namely wisdom. For if it is impossible in company with the body to know anything purely, one thing of two follows: either knowledge is possible nowhere, or only after death; for then alone the soul will be quite by itself apart from the body, but not before. And while we are alive, we shall be nearest to knowing, as it seems, if as far as possible we have no commerce or communion with the body which is not absolutely necessary, and if we are not infected with its nature, but keep ourselves pure from it, until God himself shall set us free. And so, pure and rid of the body's foolishness, we shall probably be in the company of those like ourselves, and shall know through our own selves complete incontamination, and that is perhaps the truth. But for the impure to grasp the pure is not, it seems, allowed. 'So we must think, Simmias, and so we must say to one another, all who are rightly lovers of learning; don't you agree?"

"Assuredly, Socrates."

"Then," said Socrates, "if this is true, my comrade, there is great hope that when I arrive where I am travelling, there if anywhere I shall sufficiently possess that for which all our study has been pursued in this past life. So the journey which has been commanded for me is made with good hope, and the same for any other man who believes he has got his mind purified, as I may call it."

"Certainly," replied Simmias.

"And is not purification really that which has been mentioned so often in our discussion, to separate as far as possible the soul from the body, and to accustom it to collect itself together out of the body in every part, and to dwell alone by itself as far as it can, both at this present and in the future, being freed from the body as if from a prison?"

"By all means," said he.

"Then is not this called death—a freeing and separation of soul from body?"

"Not a doubt of that," said he.

"But to set it free, as we say, is the chief endeavour of those who rightly love wisdom, nay of those alone, and the very care and practice of the philosophers is nothing but the freeing and separation of soul from body, don't you think so?"

"It appears to be so."

"Then, as I said at first, it would be absurd for a man preparing himself in his life to be as near as possible to death, so to live, and then when death came, to object?"

"Of course."

"Then in fact, Simmias," he said, "those who rightly love wisdom are practising dying, and death to them is the least terrible thing in the world. Look at it in this way: If they are everywhere at enmity with the body, and desire the soul to be alone by itself, and if, when this very thing happens, they shall fear and object—would not that be wholly unreasonable? Should they not willingly go to a place where there is good hope of finding what they were in love with all through life (and they loved wisdom), and of ridding themselves of the companion which they hated? When human favourites and wives and sons have died, many have been willing to go down to the grave, drawn by the hope of seeing there those they used to desire, and of being with them; but one who is really in love with wisdom and holds firm to this same hope, that he will find it in the grave, and nowhere else worth speaking of—will he then fret at dying and not go thither rejoicing? We must surely think, my comrade, that he will go rejoicing, if he is really a philosopher; he will surely believe that he will find wisdom in its purity there and there alone. If this is true, would it not be most unreasonable, as I said just now, if such a one feared death?"

"Unreasonable, I do declare," said he.

"Then this is proof enough," he said, "that if you see a man fretting because he is to die, he was not really a philosopher, but a philosoma—not a wisdom-lover but a body-lover. And no doubt the same man is money-lover and honours-lover, one or both."

"It certainly is so, as you say," he replied.

"Then, Simmias," he said, "does not what is called courage belong specially to persons so disposed as philosophers are?"

"I have no doubt of it," said he.

"And the same with temperance, what the many call temperance, not to be agitated about desires but to hold them lightly and decently; does not this belong to those alone who hold the body lightly and live in philosophy?"

"That must be so," he said.

"You see," said he, "if you will consider the courage and temperance of others, you will think it strange."

"How so, Socrates?"

"You know," said he, "that everyone else thinks death one of the greatest evils?"

"Indeed I do," he said.

"Then is it not fear of greater evils which makes the brave endure death, when they do?"

"That is true."

"Then fear, and fearing, makes all men brave, except philosophers. Yet it is unreasonable to become brave by fear and cowardice!"

"Certainly."

"And what of the decent men? Are they not in the same case? A sort of intemperance makes them temperate! Although we say such a thing is impossible, nevertheless with that self-complacent temperance they are in a similar case; because they fear to be deprived of other pleasures, and because they desire them, they abstain from some because they are mastered by others. They say, of course, intemperance is 'to be ruled by pleasures'; yet what happens to them is, to master some pleasures and to be mastered by others, and this is much the same as what was said just now, that in a way intemperance has made them temperate."

"So it seems."

"Bless you, Simmias! This is hardly an honest deal in virtue—to trade pleasure for pleasure, and pain for pain, and fear for fear, and even greater for less, as if they were current coin; no, the only honest currency, for which all these must be traded, is wisdom, and all things are in truth to be bought with this and sold for this.[9] And courage and temperance and justice and, in short, true virtue, depend on wisdom, whether pleasure and fear and all other such things are added or taken away. But when they are deprived of wisdom and exchanged one for another, virtue of that kind is no more than a make-believe,[10] a thing in reality slavish and having no health or truth in it; and truth is in reality a cleansing from all such things, and temperance and justice and courage, and wisdom itself, are a means of purification. Indeed, it seems those who established our mystic rites were no fools; they in truth spoke with a hidden meaning long ago when they said that whoever is uninitiated and unconsecrated when he comes to the house of Hades will lie in mud, but the purified and consecrated when he goes there will dwell with gods. Indeed, as they say in the rites, 'Many are called but few are chosen,[11] and these few are in my opinion no others than those who have loved wisdom in the right way. One of these I have tried to be by every effort in all my life, and I have left nothing undone according to my ability; if I have endeavoured in the right way, if we have succeeded at all, we shall know clearly when we get there; very soon, if God will, as I think. There is my defence before you gentlemen on the bench, Simmias and Cebes, showing that in leaving you and my masters here, I am reasonable in not fretting or being upset, because I believe that I shall find there good masters and good comrades. So if I am more convincing to you in my defence than I was to Athenian judges, I should be satisfied."

When Socrates had thus finished, Cebes took up the word: "Socrates," he said, "on the whole I think you speak well; but that about the soul is a thing which people find very hard to believe. They fear that when it parts from the body it is nowhere any more; but on the day when a man dies, as it parts from the body, and goes out like a breath or a whiff of smoke, it is dispersed and flies away and is gone and is nowhere any more. If it existed anywhere, gathered together by itself, and rid of these evils which you have just described, there would be great and good hope, Socrates, that what you say is true; but this very thing needs no small reassurance and faith, that the soul exists when the man dies, and that it has some power and sense."

"Quite true," said Socrates, "quite true, Cebes; well, what are we to do? Shall we discuss this very question, whether such a thing is likely or not?"

"For my part," said Cebes, "I should very much like to know what your opinion is about it."

Then Socrates answered, "I think no one who heard us now could say, not even a composer of comedies, that I am babbling nonsense and talking about things I have nothing to do with! So if you like, we must make a full enquiry.

"Let us enquire whether the souls of dead men really exist in the house of Hades or not. Well, there is the very ancient legend which we remember, that they are continually arriving there from this world, and further that they come back here and are born again from the dead. If that is true, and the living are born again from the dead, must not our souls exist there? For they could not be born again if they did not exist; and this would be sufficient proof that it is true, if it should be really shown that the living are born from the dead and from nowhere else. But if this be not true, we must take some other line."

"Certainly," said Cebes.

"Then don't consider it as regards men only," he said; "if you wish to understand more easily, think of all animals and vegetables, and, in a word, everything that has birth, let us see if everything comes into being like that, always opposite from opposite and from nowhere else; whenever there happens to be a pair of opposites, such as beautiful and ugly, just and unjust, and thousands of others like these. So let us enquire whether everything that has an opposite must come from its opposite and from nowhere else. For example, when anything becomes bigger, it must, I suppose, become bigger from being smaller before."

"Yes."

"And if it becomes smaller, it was bigger before and became smaller after that?"

"True," he said.

"And again, weaker from stronger, and slower from quicker?"

"Certainly."

"Very well, if a thing becomes worse, is it from being better, and more just from more unjust?"

"Of course."

"Have we established that sufficiently, then, that everything comes into being in this way, opposite from opposite?"

"Certainly."

"Again, is there not the same sort of thing in them all, between the two opposites two becomings, from the

9. Plato's text is doubtful here, and in the next two sentences.
10. σκιαγραφα literally, a shadow-drawing.
11. The Greek means "Wand-bearers are many, inspired mystics are few."

first to the second, and back from the second to the first; between greater and lesser increase and diminution, and we call one increasing and the other diminishing?"

"Yes," he said.

"And being separated and being mingled, growing cold and growing hot, and so with all; even if we have sometimes no names for them, yet in fact at least it must be the same everywhere, that they come into being from each other, and that there is a becoming from one to the other?"

"Certainly," said he.

"Well then," he said, "is there something opposite to being alive, as sleeping is opposite to being awake?"

"There is," he said.

"What?"

"Being dead," he said.

"Well, all these things come into being from each other, if they are opposites, and there are two becomings between each two?"

"Of course."

"Then," said Socrates, "I will speak of one of the two pairs that I mentioned just now, and its becomings; you tell me about the other. My pair is sleeping and being awake, and I say that being awake comes into being from sleeping and sleeping from being awake, and that their becomings are falling asleep and waking up. Is that satisfactory?"

"Quite so."

"Then you tell me in the same way about life and death. Do you not say that to be alive is the opposite of to be dead?"

"I do."

"And that they come into being from each other?"

"Yes."

"From the living, then, what comes into being?"

"The dead," he said.

"And what from the dead?"

"The living, I must admit."

"Then from the dead, Cebes, come living things and living men?"

"So it appears," he said.

"Then," said he, "our souls exist in the house of Hades."

"It seems so."

"Well, of the two becomings between them, one is quite clear. For dying is clear, I suppose, don't you think so?"

"Oh yes," said he.

"Then what shall we do?" he said. "Shall we refuse to grant in return the opposite becoming; and shall nature be lame in this point? Is it not a necessity to grant some becoming opposite to dying?"

"Surely it is," he said.

"What is that?"

"Coming to life again."

"Then," said he, "if there is coming to life again, this coming to life would be a being born from the dead into the living."

"Certainly."

"It is agreed between us, then, in this way also that the living are born from the dead, no less than the dead from the living: and since this is true, there would seem to be sufficient proof that the souls of the dead must of necessity exist somewhere, whence we assume they are born again."

"It seems to me, Socrates," he answered, "from our admissions that must of necessity be true."

"Another way of looking at this, Cebes," he said, "shows, as I think, that we were right to make those admissions. If opposites did not return back continually to replace opposites, coming into being just as if going round in a circle, but if birth were something going direct from the opposite once only into the exact opposite and never bent back and returned back again to its original, be sure that in the end all things would get the same form and go through the same process, and becomings would cease."

"How do you mean?" he asked.

"What I mean is nothing difficult to understand," said he. "For example, if there were falling asleep, but waking up did not return back in its place, coming into being from the sleeping, be sure that in the end Endymion[12] would be nowhere and this would show his story to be nonsense, because everything else would be in the same state as he, fast asleep. And if everything were combined and nothing split up, the result would be the Chaos of Anaxagoras, 'all things together.' In the same way, my dear Cebes, if everything died that had any life, and when it died, the dead things remained in that state and never came to life again, is it not absolutely necessary that in the end all things would be dead and nothing alive? For if the living things came into being from things other than the dead, and the living died, all things must be swallowed up in death, and what device could possibly prevent it?"

"Nothing could possibly prevent it, Socrates, and what you say I think perfectly true."

"Yes, Cebes," he said, "I think this is all perfectly true, and we are not deceived in admitting what we did; but in fact coming to life again is really true, and living persons are born from the dead, and the souls of the dead exist."[13]

"Another thing," said Cebes, putting in, "you know that favourite argument of yours, Socrates, which we so often heard from you, that our learning is simply recollection: that also makes it necessary, I suppose, if it is true, that we learnt at some former time what we now remember; but this is impossible unless our soul existed somewhere before it was born in this human shape. In this way also the soul seems to be something immortal."

Then Simmias put in, "But, Cebes, what are the proofs of this? Remind me, for I don't quite remember now."

"There is one very beautiful proof," said Cebes, "that people, when asked questions, if they are properly asked, say of themselves everything correctly; yet if there were not knowledge in them, and right reason, they would not be able to do this. You see, if you show someone a diagram or anything like that, he proves most clearly that this is true."

Socrates said, "If you don't believe this, Simmias, look at it in another way and see whether you agree. You disbelieve, I take it, how what is called learning can be recollection?"

"Disbelieve you," said Simmias, "not I! I just want to have an experience of what we are now discussing—recollection. I almost remember and believe already from what Cebes tried to say; yet none the less I should like to hear how *you* were going to put it."

"This is how," he answered. "We agree, I suppose,

12. The Moon fell in love with Endymion, most beautiful of men, and kept him in a perpetual sleep on Mt. Latmos, so that she could embrace him nightly.

13. Socrates' theory of a conservation of life is somewhat like our familiar theory of the conservation of energy.

that if anyone remembers something he must have known it before at some time."

"Certainly," he said.

"Then do we agree on this also, that when knowledge comes to him in such a way, it is recollection? What I mean is something like this: If a man has seen or heard something or perceived it by some other sense, and he not only knows that, but thinks of something else of which the knowledge is not the same but different, is it not right for us to say he remembered that which he thought of?"

"How do you mean?"

"Here is an example: Knowledge of a man and knowledge of a lyre are different."

"Of course."

"Well, you know about lovers, that when they see a lyre or a dress or anything else which their beloved uses, this is what happens to them: they know the lyre, and they conceive in the mind the figure of the boy whose lyre it is? Now this is recollection; just as when one sees Simmias, one often remembers Cebes, and there would be thousands of things like that."

"Thousands, indeed!" said Simmias.

"Then is that sort of thing," said he, "a kind of recollection? Especially when one feels this about things which one had forgotten because of time and neglect?"

"Certainly," he said.

"Very well then," said Socrates. "When you see a horse in a picture, or a lyre in a picture, is it possible to remember a man? And when you see Simmias in a picture, to remember Cebes?"

"Yes indeed."

"Or when you see Simmias in a picture, to remember Simmias himself?"

"Oh yes," said he. ("These being either like or unlike?"

"Yes."

"It makes no difference," he said. "Whenever, seeing one thing, from sight of this you think of another thing whether like or unlike, it is necessary," he said, "that that was recollection."

"Certainly.")[14]

"Does it not follow from all this that recollection is both from like and from unlike things?"

"It does."

"But when a man remembers something from like things, must this not necessarily occur to him also—to reflect whether anything is lacking or not from the likeness of what he remembers?"

"He must."

"Consider then," he said, "if this is true. We say, I suppose, there is such a thing as the equal, not a stick equal to a stick, or a stone to a stone, or anything like that, but something independent which is alongside all of them, the equal itself, equality; yes or no?"

"Yes indeed," said Simmias, "upon my word, no doubt about it."

"And do we understand what that is?"

"Certainly," he said. "Where did we get the knowledge of it? Was it not from such examples as we gave just now, by seeing equal sticks or stones and so forth, from these we conceived that, which was something distinct from them? Don't you think it is distinct? Look at it this way also: Do not the same stones or sticks appear equal to one person and unequal to another?"

"Certainly."

"Well, did the really-equals ever seem unequal to you, I mean did equality ever seem to be inequality?"

"Never, Socrates."

"Then those equal things," said he, "are not the same as the equal itself."

"Not at all, I think, Socrates."

"Yet from these equals," he said, "being distinct from that equal, you nevertheless conceived and received knowledge of that equal?"

"Very true," he said.

"Well," said he, "how do we feel about the sticks as compared with the real equals we spoke of just now; do the equal sticks seem to us to be as equal as equality itself, or do they fall somewhat short of the essential nature of equality; or nothing short?"

"They fall short," he said, "a great deal."

"Then we agree on this: When one sees a thing, and thinks, 'This which I now see wants to be like something else—like one of the things that are, but falls short and is unable to be such as that is, it is inferior,' it is necessary, I suppose, that he who thinks thus has previous knowledge of that which he thinks it resembles but falls short of?"

"That is necessary."

"Very well, do we feel like that or not about equal things and the equal?"

"Assuredly we do."

"It is necessary then that we knew the equal before that time when, first seeing the equal things, we thought that all these aim at being such as the equal, but fall short."

"That is true."

"Well, we go on to agree here also: we did not and we could not get a notion of the equal by any other means than by seeing or grasping, or perceiving by some other sense. I say the same of equal and all the rest."

"And they are the same, Socrates, for what the argument wants to prove."

"Look here, then; it is from the senses we must get the notion that all these things of sense aim at that which is the equal, and fall short of it; or how do we say?"

"Yes."

"Then before we began to see and hear and use our other senses, we must have got somewhere knowledge of what the equal is, if we were going to compare with it the things judged equal by the senses and see that all things are eager to be such as that equal is, but are inferior to it."

"This is necessary from what we agreed, Socrates."

"Well, as soon as we were born we saw and heard and had our other senses?"

"Certainly."

"Then, we say, we must have got knowledge of the equal before that?"

"Yes."

"Before we were born, then, it is necessary that we must have got it."

"So it seems."

"Then if we got it before we were born and we were born having it, we knew before we were born and as soon as we were born, not only the equal and the greater and the less but all the rest of such things? For our argument now is no more about the equal than about the beautiful itself,

14. The bracketed passage has been transposed from 74 C-D of the Greek text, where it would appear to be meaningless.

and the good itself, and the just and the pious, and I mean everything which we seal with the name of 'that which is,' the essence, when we ask our questions and respond with our answers in discussion. So we must have got the proper knowledge of each of these before we were born."

"That is true."

"And if having got the knowledge, in each case, we have not forgotten, we must continue knowing this and know it through life; for to know is, having got knowledge of something, to keep it and not to lose it; dropping knowledge, Simmias, is what we call forgetfulness, isn't it?"

"Just so, Socrates," he said.

"But, I think, if we got it before birth, and lost it at birth, and if afterwards, using our senses about these things, we recover the knowledge which once before we had, would not what we call learning be to recover our own knowledge? And this we should rightly call recollection?"

"Certainly."

"For, you see, it has been shown to be possible that a man perceiving something, by sight or hearing or some other sense, thinks, from this perception, of some other thing which he has forgotten, to which he compares this as being like or unlike. So as I say, there is choice of two things: either we were all born knowing them and we all know them throughout life; or afterwards those who we say learn just remember, and nothing more, and learning would be recollection."

"That is certainly true, Socrates."

"Which do you choose then, Simmias? Were we born knowing, or do we remember afterwards what we had got knowledge of before?"

"I can't choose all at once, Socrates."

"Another question, then; you can choose, and have some opinion about this. When a man knows anything, could he give an account of what he knows or not?"

"He must be able to do that, Socrates."

"Do you think that all could give account of the matters we have been discussing?"

"I would that they could," said Simmias, "but so far from that, I fear that tomorrow at this time there may be no one left in the world able to do that properly."

"Then, Simmias, you don't think that all know them?"

"Oh, no!"

"Then are they trying to remember what they once learnt?"

"It must be so."

"When did our souls get the knowledge of these things? For surely it is not since we became human beings."

"Certainly not."

"Then before."

"Yes."

"So, Simmias, our souls existed long ago, before they were in human shape, apart from bodies, and then had wisdom."

"Unless, indeed, we get all these knowledges at birth, Socrates; for this time is still left."

"Very well, my comrade; at what other time do we lose them? For we are not born having them, as we admitted just now. Do we lose them at the very same time as we get them? Can you suggest any other time?"

"Oh no, Socrates, I did not see I was talking nonsense."

"Is this the case then, Simmias?" he asked. "If all these exist which we are always harping on, the beautiful and the good and every such essence; and if we refer to these essences all the things which our senses perceive, finding out that the essences existed before and are ours now, and compare our sensations with them, it necessarily follows that, just as these exist, so our soul must have existed before our birth; but if they do not exist, this argument will be worthless. Is this true, and is there equal necessity that these things exist and our souls did before our birth, or if they do not exist, neither did our souls?"

"I am quite convinced, Socrates," said Simmias, "that there is the same necessity; our argument has found an excellent refuge when it maintains equally that our soul exists before we are born, and the essences likewise which you speak of. Nothing is clearer to me than this, that all such things exist most assuredly, beauty and good and the others which you named; and I think it has been sufficiently proved."

"And what thinks Cebes?" said Socrates. "We must convince Cebes too."

"It is good enough for him," said Simmias, "as I believe; but he is the most obstinate man in the world at disbelieving what is said; however, I believe he really is convinced that our soul existed before our birth.

"Yet will it exist after death too?" he went on. "I don't think myself that has been proved yet, Socrates. We are confronted still with what Cebes said just now: Can it be that when the man dies his soul is scattered abroad and that is the end of it, as so many say? For supposing it is composed from somewhere or other, and comes into existence before it even enters a human body; what hinders it, when it has entered and finally got rid of that body, from ending at that moment also, and being itself destroyed?"

"Well said, Simmias," said Cebes. "It does seem that half of what ought to be proved has been proved, that our soul exists before our birth; it must also be proved that when we die it will exist no less than before our birth, if the proof is to be completed."

"It has been proved already, my dear Simmias and Cebes," said Socrates, "if you choose to combine this argument with what we agreed to before it, that all the living comes from the dead. For if the soul exists before, and if it is necessary that when coming into life and being born it comes from death and from nothing else at all, it must certainly be necessary that it exists even when one dies, since it must be born again. Well then, what you said has in fact been proved already. Still, I think you and Cebes would be glad to investigate this argument yet further, and you seem to me to have the fear which children have—that really, when it leaves the body, the wind blows it away and scatters it, especially if anyone dies not in calm weather but in a great tempest."

Cebes laughed, and said, "Then think we are afraid of that, Socrates," he said, "and try to convince us against it; or better, don't think *we* are afraid, but imagine there is a kind of child in us which has such fears; then let us try to persuade this child not to fear death as if it were a bogey."

"No," said Socrates, "you must sing incantations over it every day, until you charm it out."

"My dear Socrates," he said, "where shall we get a good charmer of such things, since you are leaving us?"

"Hellas is a big place, my dear Cebes," he replied, "and there are many good men in it, and there are many barbarian nations too; and you must search through them all looking for such a charmer; you must spare neither money nor pains, since you could not spend money on anything more important. And you must not forget to search among yourselves; for perhaps you could not easily find any better able than yourselves to do that."

"Oh, that shall be done, of course," said Cebes; "but let us go back to where we left off—if you would like to."

"But certainly I should like to," he said; "of course I should!"

"That's well said," said Cebes.

"Very well then," said Socrates, "we must ask ourselves what sorts of things properly undergo this; I mean, what sorts of things are dissolved and scattered, for what sorts we must fear such an end, and for what not; next we must consider which sort the soul belongs to. We shall know then whether to be confident or fearful for our own soul."

"True," he said.

"Isn't it to the composite, which is by nature compounded, that dissolution is proper—I mean it is dissolved just as it was composed? And, on the other hand, an uncompounded thing, if indeed such exists, is least of all things naturally liable to dissolution?"

"That seems to me correct," said Cebes.

"Then what is always the same and in the same state is likely to be the uncompounded, but what is always changing and never keeps in the same state is likely to be the compounded?"

"I think so."

"Let us turn to what we have discussed already," he said. This essence which we describe in all our questions and answers as existing—is it always in the same state or does it change? I mean the equal itself, the beautiful itself, everything which exists by itself, that which is—does it admit of any changes whatever? Or is it true that each thing that so exists, being of one form and itself alone, is always in the same state, and never admits of any change whatever in any way or at any time or in any place?"

"It must necessarily be always in the same state," said Cebes.

"And what of the many particulars, men or horses or dresses or what you will, things equal or beautiful and so forth, all that have the same name as those essences? Are they always in the same state; or, quite opposite to the essences, are they not constantly changing in themselves and in relation to each other, and, one might say, never keep in the same state?"

"That again is right," said Cebes, "they never keep in the same state."

"These, then, you could touch or see or perceive by the other senses, but those which continue in the same state cannot be grasped by anything except intellectual reasoning, and such things are unseen[15] and not visible?"

"Certainly that is true," he said.

"Shall we lay down, then, that there are two kinds of existing things, one visible, one unseen?"

"Yes," he said.

"And the unseen is always in the same state, but the visible constantly changing?"

"Yes to that also," he said.

"Now come," said he, "in ourselves one part is body and one part soul?"

"Just so," he said.

"Then which kind do we say the body would be more like and akin to?"

"The visible," he said, "that is clear to anyone."

"And the soul—is it visible, or unseen?"

"Not visible to mankind at least, Socrates," he said.

"But when we say visible and not visible, we mean to human senses, don't we?"

"Yes, we do."

"Then what of the soul—do we say that is visible or invisible?"

"Not visible."

"Unseen, then?"

"Yes."

"Then soul is more like to the unseen, and body to the visible."

"It surely must be."

"Now you remember that we were saying some time ago that the soul, when it has the body to help in examining things, either through sight or hearing or any other sense—for to examine something through the body means through the senses—then it is dragged by the body towards what is always changing, and the soul goes astray and is confused and staggers about like one drunken because she is taking hold of such things."

"Certainly."

"But when she examines by herself, she goes away yonder to the pure and everlasting and immortal and unchanging; and being akin to that, she abides ever with it, whenever it becomes possible for her to abide by herself. And there she rests from her wanderings, and while she is amongst those things she is herself unchanging because what she takes hold of is unchanging: and this state of the soul has the name of wisdom?"

"Most excellent and true, Socrates."

"Then which of the two kinds is she more like and more akin to, judging from what we said before and what we are saying now?"

"Everyone, even the most ignorant, would admit, I think, Socrates," he said, "from that way of reasoning, that soul is wholly and altogether more like the unchanging than the changing."

"And the body?"

"More like the changing."

"Look at it in this way also: When soul and body are together, our nature assigns the body to be slave and to be ruled, and the soul to be ruler and master; now, then, further, which of the two seems to be like the divine, and which like the mortal? Don't you think the divine is naturally such as to rule and to guide, and the mortal such as to be ruled and to be a slave?"

"I do."

"Then which is the soul like?"

"It is clear, Socrates, that the soul is like the divine, and the body like the mortal."

"Consider now, Cebes, whether it follows from all that we have said, that the soul is most like the divine and immortal and intellectual and simple and indissoluble and self-unchangeable, but on the contrary, the body is most like the human and mortal and manifold and unintellectual and dissoluble and ever-changing. Can we say anything to contradict that, my dear Cebes, or is that correct?"

"We cannot contradict it."

---

15. The word used is αειδη unseen or without form. Plato introduces it here because it sounds significantly like the word Αιδη Hades, suggesting that the unchanging essences are immaterial and belong to the other world.

"Very well. This being so, is it not proper to the body to be quickly dissolved, but on the contrary to the soul to be wholly indissoluble or very nearly so?"

"Of course."

"You understand, then," he said, "that when the man dies, the visible part of him, the body—that which lies in the visible world, and which we call the corpse, for which it is proper to dissolve and disappear—does not suffer any of this at once but instead remains a good long time, and if a man dies with his body in a nice condition and age, a very long time. For if the body is shrivelled up and mummified like the mummies in Egypt it lasts almost whole, for an incredibly long time. And some portions of the body, even when it decays, bones and sinews and so forth, may almost be called immortal."

"Yes."

"But the soul, the 'unseen' part of us, which goes to another place noble and pure and unseen like itself, a true unseen Hades, to the presence of the good and wise God, where, if God will, my own soul must go very soon—shall our soul, then, being such and of such nature, when released from the body be straightway scattered by the winds and perish, as most men say? Far from it, my dear Simmias! This is much more likely: If it is pure when it gets free, and drags nothing of the body with it, since it has no communion with the body in life if it can help it, but avoids the body and gathers itself into itself, since it is always practising this—here we have nothing else but a soul loving wisdom rightly, and in reality practising death—don't you think this would be a practice of death?"

"By all means."

"Then, being thus, it goes away into the unseen, which is like itself, the divine and immortal and wise, where on arrival it has the opportunity to be happy, freed from wandering and folly and fears and wild loves and all other human evils, and, as they say of the initiated, really and truly passing the rest of time with the gods. Is that what we are to say, Cebes?"

"Yes indeed," said Cebes.

"But if contrariwise, I think, if it leaves the body polluted and unpurified, as having been always with it and attending it and in love with it and bewitched by it through desires and pleasures, so that it thinks nothing to be true but the bodily—what one could touch and see and drink and eat and use for carnal passion; if what is darksome to the eyes and 'unseen' but intellectual and to be caught by philosophy, if this, I say, it is accustomed to hate and fear and flee; do you think a soul in that state will get away pure and incorrupt in itself?"

"By no possible means whatever," he said.

"No, I think it is interpenetrated by the bodily, which the association and union with it of the body has by constant practice made ingrained."

"Exactly."

"A heavy load, my friend, we must believe that to be, heavy and earthy and visible; and such a soul with this on board is weighed down and dragged back into the visible world, by fear of the unseen, Hades so-called, and cruises[16] about restless among tombs and graves, where you know shadowy apparitions of souls have often been seen, phantoms such as are produced by souls like this, which have not been released purely, but keep something of the visible, and so they are seen."

"That is likely, Socrates."

"Indeed it is likely; and likely that these are not the souls of the good, but souls of the mean, which are compelled to wander about such places as a penalty for their former way of life, which was evil; and wander they must until by desire for the bodily which is always in their company they are imprisoned once more in a body. And they are imprisoned, as is likely, into the same habits which they had practised in life before."

"What sort of habits do you mean, Socrates?"

"It is likely, for example, that those who have practised gluttony and violence and drunkenness and have not taken heed to their ways enter the bodies of asses and suchlike beasts, don't you think so?"

"Very likely indeed."

"Those, again, who have preferred injustice and tyrannies and robberies, into the bodies of wolves and hawks and kites; or where else do we say they would go?"

"No doubt," said Cebes, "they pass into creatures like these."

"Then it is clear," said he, "that the rest go wherever they do go, to suit their own likenesses and habits?"

"Quite clear, of course," he said.

"Then of these the happiest people," he said, "and those who go to the best place, are those who have practised the public and political virtues which they call temperance and justice, got from habit and custom without philosophy and reason?"

"How are these happiest, pray?"

"Why, isn't it likely that they pass into another similar political and gentle race, perhaps bees or wasps or ants; or even into the same human race again, and that there are born from them decent men?"

"Yes, that is likely."

"But into the family of gods, unless one is a philosopher and departs wholly pure, it is not permitted for any to enter, except the lover of learning. Indeed, it is for the sake of this purity, Simmias and Cebes, my two good comrades, that those who truly seek wisdom steadfastly abstain from all bodily desires and refuse to give themselves over to them, not from having any fear of ruin of their home or of poverty, as the money-loving multitude has; and again, not from being afraid of dishonour, or a bad reputation for wickedness, as the honour-lovers and power-lovers are; that is why these abstain from them."

"No, Socrates," said Cebes, "that would not be proper."

"Not at all, by heaven," said he. "Therefore those who care at all for their own soul and do not live just serving[17] the body say good-bye to everyone of that kind and walk not after guides who know not where they are going; for they themselves believe they must not act contrary to philosophy, and its deliverance and purification, and so they turn to philosophy and follow by the way she leads them."

"How, Socrates?"

"I will tell you," he said.

"The lovers of learning understand," said he, "that philosophy found their soul simply imprisoned in the body and welded to it, and compelled to survey through this as if through prison bars the things that are, not by itself through itself, but wallowing in all ignorance; and she saw that the danger of this prison came through desire, so that the prisoner himself would be chief helper in his own im-

16. Literally "rolls about" (like a ship at sea).
17. This word is doubtful in the Greek text.

prisonment. As I say then, lovers of learning understand that philosophy, taking possession of their soul in this state, gently encourages it and tries to free it, by showing that surveying through the eyes is full of deceit, and so is perception through the ears and the other senses; she persuades the soul to withdraw from these, except so far as there is necessity to use them, and exhorts it to collect itself together and gather itself into itself, and to trust nothing at all but itself, and only whatever of the realities each in itself the soul itself by itself can understand; but that whatever of what varies with its environs the soul examines through other means, it must consider this to be no part of truth; such a thing, philosophy tells it, is a thing of the senses and of the visible, but what it sees itself is a thing of the intellect and of the 'unseen.' So the soul of the true philosopher believes that it must not oppose this deliverance, and therefore abstains from pleasures and desires and griefs and fears as much as possible, counting that when a man feels great pleasure or fear or pain or desire, he suffers not only the evil that one might think (for example, being ill or squandering money through his desires), but the greatest and worst of all evils, which he suffers and never counts."

"What is that, Socrates?" asked Cebes.

"That the soul of every man suffers this double compulsion: At the same time as it is compelled to feel great pleasure or pain about anything, it is compelled also to believe that the thing for which it specially feels this is most clearly real and true, when it is not. These are generally the visible things, aren't they?"

"Certainly."

"Then in this state especially the soul is imprisoned by the body?"

"Pray how?"

"Because each pleasure and pain seems to have a nail, and nails the soul to the body and pins it on and makes it bodily, and so it thinks the same things are true which the body says are true. For by having the same opinion as the body, and liking the same things, it is compelled, I believe, to adopt the same ways and the same nourishment, and to become such as never could come pure to the house of Hades, but would always go forth infected by the body; so it would fall again quickly into another body and there be sown and grown, and therefore would have neither part nor lot in communion with the divine and pure and simple."

"Most true, indeed," said Cebes.

"So then it is for these reasons, Cebes, that those who rightly love learning are decent and brave, not for the reasons which the many give; what do you think?"

"Certainly not."

"No indeed. Such would be the reasoning of the philosopher. His soul would not think it right that philosophy should set her free, and that while being set free she herself should surrender herself back again in bondage to pleasures and pains, and so perform the endless task of a Penelope unweaving the work of her loom.[18] No, she thinks she must calm these passions; and, following reason and keeping always in it, beholding the true and the divine and the certain, and nourishing herself on this, his soul believes that she ought to live thus, as long as she does live, and when she dies she will join what is akin and like herself, and be rid of human evils. After nurture of this kind there is nothing to fear, my dear Simmias and Cebes, and she need not expect in parting from the body to be scattered about and blown away by the winds, and to be gone like a bird and be nowhere anymore."

There was a long silence after Socrates had ended; Socrates himself was deep in these thoughts, or appeared to be, and so were most of us. But Cebes and Simmias whispered together a bit, and when Socrates noticed them he said, "What's the matter? Surely you don't think our argument has missed anything? Indeed, there are a good many suspicions and objections, if one is to go through it thoroughly. If, then, you are considering something else, I say nothing; but if you are at all puzzled about what we have been saying, don't hesitate to speak yourselves. Go through it, and see if you think it might have been improved; and take me with you through it again if you think I can help you any more at all in your difficulties."

Simmias answered, "Well then, Socrates, I will tell you the truth. We have been puzzled for a long time, both of us, and each pushes on the other and bids him ask; because we wish to hear and don't want to be a nuisance, in case you are feeling unhappy about the present misfortune!"

Socrates laughed gently as he heard this, and said. "Bless me, my dear Simmias! Surely I could hardly persuade others that I don't think the present fortune a misfortune, when I can't persuade even you, but you fear I am more fretful now than I have been in my past life. Apparently it seems to you that I'm a worse prophet than the swans. When they perceive that they must die, you know, they sing more and better than they ever did before, glad to be going away into the presence of that god whose servants they are. But men tell lies against them because they fear death themselves, and they say that the swans are mourning their death and singing a dirge for sorrow; men don't take into account that no bird ever sings when it is hungry or cold or feels any other pain, not the swallow or the hoopoe or even the nightingale, which they say all sing a dirge for sorrow. But I don't believe those birds do sing in sorrow, nor do the swans, but these, I think, because they belong to Apollo, are prophets and know beforehand the good things in the other world, and sing and rejoice on that day far more than ever before. Indeed I think myself that I am the swans' fellow-slave, and sacred to the same god, and I think I have prophecy from my master no less than they have, and I depart from life no more dispirited than they do. No, as far as that matters, you should speak and ask what you will, so long as we have leave of the Athenian Board of Eleven."

"Good," said Simmias, "then I will speak out, and tell you my difficulty, and Cebes too, where he does not accept all you have said. For I think, as perhaps you do, Socrates, that to know the plain truth about such matters in this present life is impossible, or at least very difficult; but only a very soft man would refuse to test in every possible way what is said about them, and would give up before examining them all over till he was tired out. I think a man's duty is one of two things: either to be taught or to find out where the truth is, or if he cannot, at least to take the best possible human doctrine and the hardest to disprove, and to ride on this like a raft over the waters of life and take the risk; unless he could have a more seaworthy vessel to carry him more safely and with less danger, some

---

18. Penelope prolonged her task for three years by unweaving at night what she wove by day. *Odyssey* xix. Bodily indulgence is unweaving and the soul would have to weave it up again.

divine doctrine to bring him through. So now I will not be ashamed to ask, since you tell me yourself to do it; and I shall not blame myself afterwards because I did not now say what I think. Well, my opinion is, Socrates, when I consider what has been said in my own mind and with Cebes here, that it is not quite satisfactory."

Socrates said, "Perhaps, my comrade, your opinion is true. But say where it is not satisfactory."

"Here," said he: "That one could say the same about harmony[19] and a harp with strings; that the harmony is invisible and bodiless and all-beautiful and divine on the tuned harp; but the harp itself and the strings are bodies and bodily and composite and earthy and akin to the mortal. So when someone breaks the harp, or cuts and bursts the strings, suppose he should maintain by the same argument as yours that it is necessary the harmony should still exist and not perish; for it would be just as impossible that the harp should still exist when the strings are broken, and the strings should still exist which are of mortal kind, as that the harmony should perish—harmony, which is of the same kith and kin as the divine and immortal, perishing before the mortal; no, he would say, the harmony must necessarily exist somewhere, and wood and strings must rot away first, before anything could happen to the harmony! Well, Socrates, I think you yourself must have noticed that we conceive the soul to be something like this—that our body being tuned and held together by hot and cold and dry and wet and suchlike, our soul is a kind of mixture and harmony of these very things, when they are well and harmoniously mixed together. If, then, our soul is a kind of harmony, it is plain that when the body is slackened inharmoniously or too highly strung, by diseases and other evils, the soul must necessarily perish, although it is most divine, just as the other harmonies do, those in sounds and those in all the works of craftsmen, but the relics of each body will remain until it rots or is burnt. Then consider what we must answer to this argument, if anyone claims that the soul is a mixture of the things in the body, and at what is called death, it is the first to perish."

Socrates gazed at us with his eyes wide open, as he usually did, and said, smiling, "What Simmias says is quite fair. Then if any of you is readier than I am, why didn't he reply? I think he tackles the question neatly. But before the answer comes, I think we ought to hear Cebes first, what fault he, too, has to find with our argument. Then there will be a little time and we can consider what to say; afterwards, when we have heard them, we ought to agree with them if they seem to be in tune with us, or if not, we should continue as before to defend our doctrine. Come along, Cebes," he said, "speak! What worried you?"

"I'll tell you," said Cebes. "I think the argument is where it was, and has the same objection which I made before. That our soul existed before it came into this form, I do not retract; it was a nice, neat proof, and quite satisfactory, if I may say so without offence; but that when we are dead the soul will still exist somewhere, I can't say the same of that. However, I do not agree with the objection of Simmias, that the soul is not stronger and much longer-lasting than the body; for I think it is very far superior in all those respects. 'Well,' the argument might say to me, 'why do you still disbelieve? You can see when the man is dead the weaker part still existing, and don't you think the longer-lasting must necessarily survive during this time?' Well, see if you think anything of this answer of mine; really, it seems that I also want a simile, like Simmias. I think all this is very much the same as saying as follows of a weaver who died old: The man is not dead but exists somewhere safe and sound, and here is a proof one might offer—here is the cloak which he wove himself, and used to wear, safe and sound, and it has not perished. If someone disbelieved, one might ask him, 'Which kind of thing is longer-lasting, a man, or a cloak in use and wear?' If the answer was, 'A man lasts longer than a cloak,' one might imagine that this proved that the man was certainly safe and sound, since the shorter-lasting thing had not perished. But I don't think that is right, Simmias; just consider what I have to say now. Everyone would understand that such an argument is silly; for this weaver had woven and worn out many such cloaks and died later than all except the last, when he died before it, yet for all that a man is neither inferior to a cloak nor weaker. Soul and body might admit of the same simile, and one might fairly say the same about them, I think, that the soul is long-lasting, the body weaker and shorter-lasting; but one might say more, that each of the souls wears out many bodies, especially if it lives many years. For if the body wastes and perishes while the man still lives, but the soul always weaves anew what is worn away, it would, however, be necessary that when the soul perished it would happen to be wearing the last body and it would perish before this last only, and when the soul perished, the body would show at once the nature of its weakness and would quickly rot and vanish in decay. This argument, then, is not yet enough to give confidence that when we die our soul exists somewhere. For if one should grant your supporter even more than what you say, and admitted to him not only that our souls existed in the time before our birth, but that nothing hindered the souls of some of us from still existing when we die, and continuing to exist, and from being born and dying again and again, for so strong is its nature that the soul endures being born many times: one might admit that, and yet never admit that it does not suffer in these many births, and at last in one of its deaths does not perish outright. But one might say that no one knows which death and dissolution of the body brings death of the soul; for it is impossible for anyone of us to distinguish it beforehand. Now if this is correct, it follows that anyone who is confident about death is foolish in his confidence, unless he can show that the soul is wholly immortal and imperishable; for if he cannot show this, it is necessary that he who is about to die must always fear for his soul lest at the present separation from the body it may utterly perish."

When we had heard these two we were very unhappy, as we told one another afterwards. We had been firmly convinced by the earlier arguments, and now we seemed to be thrown back by the speakers into confusion and disbelief; we distrusted not only the earlier arguments but those which were coming, and we thought that either we were worthless judges, or else there could be nothing to trust in the whole thing.

Echecrates:

By heaven, Phaidon, I feel with you. As I heard you tell such a story, I felt like asking myself, "Then what argument can we trust any longer?" That one seemed quite convincing when Socrates spoke, but now it has fallen into distrust. This notion has a wonderful hold of me and always did, that our soul is a kind of harmony, and when you

19. Or tune.

spoke of it I was, one might say, reminded that I had once thought so too. Now again we must start from the beginning, for I very much want another argument to persuade me that the soul of the dead does not die with him. Tell me this in heaven's name, how did Socrates follow up the discussion? Was he also put out like the rest of you? Did he show it or not? If not, did he quietly defend the reasoning? And did he defend it enough, or too little? Tell us the whole story as exactly as you can.

Phaidon:

Well, I must say, Echecrates, I always wondered at Socrates, but I never wondered at him more than when I was with him then. To have something to say was perhaps no novelty in that man; but what most surprised me was, how pleasant and friendly and respectful he was in welcoming the speculations of the young men, and then how sharply he saw how we were affected by what was said, and then how well he treated us, and rallied us like a lot of beaten runaways, and headed us back to follow the argument and examine it along with him.

Echecrates:

Well, how?

Phaidon:

I will tell you. I happened to be sitting on his right hand, on a low stool beside his bed, and his seat was much higher than mine. Then he stroked my head and pinched together the hair on my neck—he used occasionally to play with my hair—and said, "Tomorrow perhaps, Phaidon, you'll cut off this pretty hair."[20]

"It seems like it, Socrates," I said.

"Well, you won't, if you will listen to me."

"But why?" said I.

"Today," he said, "you shall cut off this, and I mine, at least if our argument comes to its latter end and we can't bring it to life again. In fact if I were you, and if the argument escaped me, I would swear an oath like the Argives,[21] never to let my hair grow long again till I renew the fight with Simmias and Cebes and beat their argument."

"But Socrates," I said, "two to one! Not even Heracles could be a match for two, as they say!"[22]

"Then," he said, "call me in as your Ioleos, while there is daylight still."

"I call you to help, then," said I, "not as Heracles did to Ioleos; but like an Ioleos to Heracles."

"That will be the same thing," he said. "But first let us be careful against a danger."

"What is the danger?" said I.

"Don't let us be 'misologues,' hating argument as misanthropes hate men; the worst disease one can have is to hate arguments. Misology and misanthropy come in the same way. Misanthropy is put on from believing someone too completely without discrimination, and thinking the man to be speaking the truth wholly and wholesomely, and then finding out soon afterwards that he is bad and untrustworthy and quite different; when this happens often to a man, especially from those he thought to be his closest and truest friends, at last, after so many knocks, he hates everybody, and believes there is no soundness in anyone at all. Haven't you noticed that happening?"

"Oh yes," I said.

"Then that is an ugly thing," he said, "and it is clear such a man tries to deal with men when he has no skill in human affairs. For if he had that technical skill when he dealt with them, he would take them as they are, and believe that the very good and very bad are few, but most are betwixt and between."

"What do you mean?" I asked.

"As with very big and very small men. Don't you think the rarest thing is to find a very big or a very small man, or dog, or anything else? So with quick and slow, ugly and handsome, white and black? Don't you see that in all these the extremes are few and rare, but the betweens plenty and many?"

"Oh, yes, indeed," I said.

"Then," said he, "if there were a competition in wickedness, there, too, the prize-winners would be few?"

"Quite likely," I said.

"Yes, quite likely," said he, "but in that respect arguments are not like men. I have been following your lead so far, but I think the likeness lies in this: when a person without technical skill in words believes an argument to be true, and soon afterwards thinks it false, sometimes when it is and sometimes when it is not, and so again one person after another—and especially those who spend their time arguing against each other—you know that in the end they think they are the wisest men in the world, and that they alone understand how there is nothing sound and wholesome either in practical affairs or in arguments, but all real things are just like a Euripos,[23] a tide moving up and down and never remaining the same."

"That is truly stated indeed," I said.

"Then, Phaidon," he said, "it would be a pitiable disease, when there *is* an argument true and sound and such as can be understood, if through the pain of meeting so many which seem sometimes to be true and sometimes not, instead of blaming himself and his own clumsiness a man should in the end gladly throw the blame from himself upon the arguments, and for the rest of his life should continually hate and abuse them, and deprive himself of the truth and the knowledge of what is real."

"Yes, I do declare," said I, "it would be pitiable."

"First, then, let us be careful," he said, "and let us not admit into our souls the belief that there really is no health or soundness in arguments. Much rather let us think that we are not sound ourselves, let us be men and take pains to become sound: you and the others to prepare you for all your coming life, I to prepare myself for death. For in fact as regards this very matter I am just now no philosopher, I am a philovictor—I want to win, as much as the most uneducated men do. Such men, you know, when there is difference of opinion, care nothing how the truth stands in a question, but do their very best to make their audience believe whatever they have laid down. Just now I am the same as they are, with only one difference: I shall do my very best to convince of the truth—not my audience, except by the way, but to convince myself that what seems true to me is perfectly true. For, my dear comrade, see how selfishly I reckon it up! If what I say is really true, then it is well to be convinced; but if for the dead nothing remains,

20. In mourning for Socrates.
21. Herodotos, I. 82. They swore not to let their hair grow till they reconquered Thyreai.
22. A proverb. Heracles was fighting the hydra, and saw a crab coming up to help the hydra. He then called in Ioleos.
23. The strait between Euboia and the mainland, where there are several "tides" or currents of water every day.

then at least for just this time before death, I shall not be disagreeable to you here by lamentations. And this ignorance[24] of mine will not last, which would be an evil thing, but very soon it will perish. Thus prepared, then," he said, "my dear Simmias and Cebes, I proceed to the question; but you, if you please, do not be anxious about Socrates, not a bit, but be very anxious about truth; if you think I say anything true, agree with me, and if not, oppose me with all your might, that my eagerness may not deceive both myself and you—I don't want to be like a bee and leave my sting in you when I go.

"Forward, now," he went on. "First remind me what you said, if I don't seem to remember. Simmias, as I think, disbelieves, and fears that the soul, although something more divine and beautiful than the body, may perish before the body like a sort of harmony. Cebes I thought admitted with me that soul was at least longer-lasting than body, but everyone must doubt whether the soul has already worn out many bodies, and now, leaving the last body, it may perish itself; and death may be just this, the destruction of soul, since body is perishing continually and never stops. Are not these the matters which we must consider, Simmias and Cebes?" Both agreed to this. "Well, do you reject all the earlier arguments, or only some?"

"Some only," they replied.

"And what of that one," said he, "when we said learning was recollection, and that therefore our soul must exist somewhere before being imprisoned in the body?"

"That one," said Cebes, "seemed to me wonderfully convincing, and I abide by it now as by no other argument."

"Yes, and so do I, too," said Simmias, "and I should be surprised if I could ever think otherwise about that."

Socrates answered, "Well, my good friend from Thebes," he said, "you must think otherwise, if the notion holds that harmony is a thing composite, and soul is a harmony arising from all the elements strung and tuned in the body. For you will not allow yourself to say that a composite harmony existed before the elements from which it had to be composed—eh, Simmias?"

"Oh dear me no, Socrates!"

"You perceive then," said he, "that this is what you really affirm, when you say that the soul existed before it came into human shape and body, and that it existed composed of things which did not exist. But see, harmony is not such a thing as you likened it to; no, first the harp and the strings and their tones not yet harmonised come into being, and last of all the harmony is composed, and it is first to perish. Then how will your argument be in tune[25] with that?"

"It will not," said Simmias.

"And yet," said he, "it ought to be in tune with the argument about harmony, if with any at all."

"So it ought," said Simmias.

"Then your argument," he said, "is not in tune. But look here: Which of the two do you choose—is learning recollection, or is the soul a harmony?"

"I much rather choose the first," said he. "Perhaps the other came without proof from a likely comparison that looked good, which makes most people pleased with it; but I am conscious that arguments proved from likelihood are humbugs, and if we are not careful they deceive us, in geometry and everything else. But the argument about recollection and learning has been shown to stand on a good foundation. What was said, I think, was that our soul existed before coming into the body just as that essence exists which has the name of 'real being.' This I have accepted, I am convinced, with right and sufficient reason. I must therefore refuse now, as it seems, to accept for myself or anyone else that account of the soul which calls it a harmony."

"Very well, Simmias," said he. "What do you think of this: Is it proper for a harmony, or any other composite thing, to exist in any other state than the state of its component parts?"

"No," he said.

"Again, it cannot do, or be done to, anything else than they do or are done to?" He said no. "Then it is proper that a harmony does not lead the things which compose it, but follows?" He agreed. "Then a harmony cannot be moved and cannot sound or do anything else in opposition to its own parts?"

"Impossible," he said.

"Well, is not each harmony naturally so much a harmony according as it is harmonised?"

"I don't understand," he said.

"Listen," said he, "if it is more harmonised and more intensely, supposing that to be possible, would it be more a harmony and more intense, and if less harmonised and less intensely, would it be less a harmony and less intense?"

"Certainly."

"Is this true, then, of soul—that even in the smallest degree one soul can be more intensely and more completely, or less intensely and less completely, that very thing, a soul, than another is?"

"Not in the least," he said.

"Very well, then," he said, "in God's name: Is it said that one soul has sense and virtue and is good, but another has folly and wickedness and is bad, and is this true?"

"Quite true," he said.

"Then what will they say, those who lay down that soul is harmony, what will they say these things are which are in the souls, virtue and vice? Will they say these are yet another harmony, and a discord? And say that one soul is harmonised, the good one, and, being itself harmony, has in it another harmony, but the other is discordant itself and has in it no other harmony?"

"I can't say," said Simmias, "but it is clear that one who laid that down would say something of that kind."

"But we agreed before," said Socrates, "that one soul is not more or less soul than other; that means it is agreed that one is not more or less harmony than another, nor to a greater or less degree that another. Is that so?"

"Certainly."

"But that which is neither more nor less harmony has been neither more nor less harmonised. Is that true?"

"That is true."

"When it is neither more nor less harmonised, can it partake of harmony to a greater or less degree, or only the same?"

"The same."

"Then soul, since one is no more than another what we actually mean by soul, consequently is neither more nor less harmonised?"

24. Another reading is "folly."
25. Literally, "sing together," i.e., accord.

"Just so."

"In this condition, it would have no greater share of discord or harmony?"

"No, indeed."

"Then in this condition one would not partake of vice or virtue more than another, if vice is discord and virtue harmony?"

"No more."

"Rather I think, Simmias, according to right reasoning, no soul will partake of vice, if it is really harmony; for harmony which is wholly this very thing harmony could never partake of discord."

"Never, surely."

"Nor could soul partake of vice, if it is wholly soul."

"How could it, after what we admitted?"

"By this our reasoning then, all souls of all living creatures will be equally good, if they are equally and actually souls."

"I think so, Socrates," he said.

"Do you think that is correct," said he, "and do you think our argument would have come to this state, if the foundation were right, that is, that soul is harmony?"

"Not in the least," he said.

"Well now," said Socrates, "of all that there is in man, would you say anything rules but soul, especially a wise one?"

"No, not I."

"A soul which gives way to the feelings of the body, or one that even opposes them? I mean something like this—suppose fever be in the body and thirst, would you say soul drags it in the opposite way, so as not to drink, and if hunger be in it, not to eat? And we see the soul opposing the body in thousands of other things, don't we?"

"We do."

"Well then; did we not moreover agree earlier, that if it be indeed a harmony it would never sound a tune opposing the elements from which it arises, according as they are strung tight or loose, and twangled, and however else they are treated? It must follow these, it could never lead them?"

"Yes," he said, "we did agree. Of course."

"Very well: Don't we see it now doing the very opposite, leading all the things from which it is said to be composed, and opposing almost always all through life, a tyrant in every way, punishing them sometimes harshly and with bodily pain, that is, through gymnastic and physic, sometimes gently, giving now threats and now advice, talking to desires and angers and fears just as if it was different from them and they from it? Remember, too, Homer's lines in the Odyssey, where he says somewhere of Odysseus[26]

Striking his chest, he thus reproached his heart,
My heart, bear up! You have borne worse than this!

Do you think when he composed this he regarded the soul as a kind of harmony, something to be led by the body's feelings?—surely not, but as something able to lead these and play the tyrant, something much more divine than a harmony!"

"Yes indeed, Socrates, I agree," he said.

"Then, my good sir," he said, "it is quite wrong altogether to say that the soul is a harmony; for it appears we should contradict Homer, the divine poet, and ourselves too."

"Just so," he said.

"So much for that, then," said Socrates. "Our Theban Harmonia[27] has been appeased, it seems, pretty well; but what of Cadmos? My dear Cebes," he said, "how shall we appease Cadmos? What argument will do?"

"You'll find one, I think," said Cebes; "this one at least, against the harmony, was amazingly unexpected. When Simmias was telling what he was puzzled about, I wondered very much if anyone could deal with his argument at all, and to my surprise it couldn't stand your argument's first attack. I shouldn't wonder if the same happened to the argument of Cadmos."

"My good man," said Socrates, "don't tempt Providence, or some evil eye may overturn the argument which is coming. But God will care for that; let us charge into the fray like Homeric heroes, and try if there's anything in your contention. This is the sum of what you seek: You demand that it be proved that our soul is imperishable and immortal, if a student of philosophy, being about to die, and being confident, and believing that after death he will be better off in that world than if he had lived to the end a different life, is not to be found foolish and senseless in this confidence. But to show that the soul is something strong and godlike and existed before we were born men, all this you say may be no more than to indicate, not immortality, but that the soul is something long-lasting, and that it existed somewhere before for an immeasurable time, and knew and did many things; but it is not really any more immortal, but in fact its entry into the body of a man was the beginning of destruction for it, like a disease; it lives this life in distress, and last of all, at what is called death, it perishes. So there is no difference at all, you say, whether it comes once into the body or often, at least as regards our feeling of fear; for fear is proper, if one is not senseless, for him that knows not and cannot prove that the soul is immortal. That is very much what you say, Cebes; and I repeat it often on purpose that nothing may escape us; pray add or subtract if you wish."

And Cebes replied, "No, there is nothing I wish to add or subtract now; that is what I do say."

Socrates was silent for some time, thinking to himself; then he said, "That is no trifle you seek, Cebes; we are bound to discuss generally the cause of generation and destruction. If you allow me, I will run through my own experience in these matters. Then if anything of what I shall say seems useful, you shall use it to prove whatever you may say."

"By all means," Cebes said.

"Then listen, and I will tell you. When I was a young man, Cebes, I was most amazingly interested in the lore which they call natural philosophy. For I thought it magnificent to know the causes of everything, why it comes into being and why it is destroyed and why it exists; I kept turning myself upside down to consider things like the following: Is it when hot and cold get some fermentation in them, as some said,[28] that living things are bred? Is it the blood by which we think,[29] or air[30] or fire;[31] or whether it is none of these, but the brain is what provides the senses of hearing and sight and smell, and from these arise memory and opinion, and from memory and opinion in

26. *Odyssey* xx. 17.
27. Wife of Theban Cadmos in Greek story.
28. Anaximandros, Anaxagoras and others.
29. Empedocles.
30. Anaximenes.
31. Heracleitos.

tranquility comes knowledge; again I considered the destructions of these things, and what happens about heaven and earth. At last I believed myself as unfitted for this study as anything could be. I will tell you a sufficient proof: I found myself then so completely blinded by this study that I unlearned even what I used to think that I knew—what I understood clearly before, as I thought and others thought—about many other things and particularly as to the reason why man grows. I used to think that this was clear to all—by eating and drinking; for when from his foods flesh was added to flesh, and bones to bones, and in the same way the other parts each had added to them what was their own, then what was the little mass before became great later, and so the small man became big. That is what I believed then; isn't it a natural opinion?"

"I think so," said Cebes.

"Look next at this, then. I believed that when a big man stood by a small man, it was correct enough to suppose that he was bigger by the head, and so horse and horse; more clearly still, I thought ten was greater than eight because two was added to it, and the two-cubit bigger than the one-cubit because it overreached it by half."

"But now," said Cebes, "what do you think about them?"

"I'm very far, I swear, from thinking I know the cause of any of these things, for I can't agree with myself, even when one is added to one, either that the one to which it was added has become two, or the one which was added has become two, or that the one added and the one it was added to become two, by the adding of the one to the other; for I am surprised that when they were apart from each other each was one and they were not then two, but when they approached each other this was the cause of their becoming two, the meeting, their being near together. Or again, if a one is cut in half I cannot be convinced any longer that this, the cutting, was the cause of its becoming two; then it was because they were brought close together and one was added to the other, now because one is taken away and separated from the other. Nor can I even convince myself any longer that I know how the one is generated, or in a word how anything else is generated or perishes or exists; I can't do it by this kind of method, but I am muddling along with another of my own[32] and I don't allow this one at all.

"Well, I heard someone reading once out of a book, by Anaxagoras he said, how mind is really the arranger and cause of all things; I was delighted with this cause, and it seemed to me in a certain way to be correct that mind is the cause of all, and I thought that if this is true, mind arranging all things places everything as it is best. If, therefore, one wishes to find out the cause of anything, how it is generated or perishes or exists, what one ought to find out is how it is best for it to exist or to do or feel everything; from this reasoning, then, all that is proper for man to seek about this and everything is only the perfect and the best; but the same man necessarily knows the worse, too, for the same knowledge includes both. Reasoning thus, then, I was glad to think I had found a teacher of the cause of things after my own mind in Anaxagoras: I thought he would show me first whether the earth is flat or round, and when he had shown this, he would proceed to explain the cause and the necessity, by showing that it was better that it should be such; and if he said it was in the middle of the universe, he would proceed to explain how it was better for it to be in the middle; and if he would explain all these things to me, I was prepared not to want any other kind of cause. And about the sun too I was equally prepared to learn in the same way, and the moon and stars besides, their speed as compared with one another, their turnings, and whatever else happens to them, how these things are better in each case for them to do or to be done to. For I did not believe that, when he said all this was ordered by mind, he would bring in any other cause for them than that it was best they should be as they are. So I thought that, when he had given the cause for each and for all together, that which is best for each, he would proceed to explain the common good of all; and I would not have sold my hopes for anything, but I got his books eagerly as quick as I could, and read them, that I might learn as soon as possible the best and the worse.

"Oh, what a wonderful hope! How high I soared, how low I fell! When as I went on reading I saw the man using mind not at all; and stating no valid causes of the arrangement of all things, but giving airs and ethers[33] and waters as causes, and many other strange things. I felt very much as I should feel if someone said, 'Socrates does by mind all he does'; and then, trying to tell the causes of each thing I do, if he should say first that the reason why I sit here now is, that my body consists of bones and sinews, and the bones are hard and have joints between them, and the sinews can be tightened and slackened, surrounding the bones along with flesh and the skin which holds them together; so when the bones are uplifted in their sockets, the sinews slackening and tightening make me able to bend my limbs now, and for this cause I have bent together and sit here; and if next he should give you other such causes of my conversing with you, alleging as causes voices and airs and hearings and a thousand others like that, and neglecting to give the real causes. These are that since the Athenians thought it was better to condemn me, for this very reason I have thought it better to sit here, and more just to remain and submit to any sentence they may give. For, by the Dog! these bones and sinews, I think, would have been somewhere near Megara or Boeotia long ago, carried there by an opinion of what is best, if I had not believed it better and more just to submit to any sentence which my city gives than to take to my heels and run. But to call such things causes is strange indeed. If one should say that unless I had such things, bones and sinews and all the rest I have, I should not have been able to do what I thought best, that would be true; but to say that these, and not my choice of the best, are the causes of my doing what I do (and when I act by mind, too!), would be a very far-fetched and slovenly way of speaking. For it shows inability to distinguish that the real cause is one thing, and that without which the cause could not be a cause is another thing. This is what most people seem to me to be fumbling after in the dark, when they use a borrowed name for it and call it cause! And so one man makes the earth remain under the sky, if you please, by putting a rotation about the earth; another thinks it is like the bottom of a flat kneading-trough and puts the air underneath to support it; but they never look for the power which has placed things so that they are in the best possible state, nor do they think it has a divine

32. The logical method.

33. Air is the lower air about the earth, ether the upper air of heaven.

strength, but they believe they will some time find an Atlas[34] more mighty and more immortal and more able than ours to hold all together, and really they think nothing of the good which must necessarily bind and hold all things together. How glad I should be to be anyone's pupil in learning what such a cause really is! But since I have missed this, since I could not find it myself or learn it from another, would you like me to show you, Cebes," he said, "how I managed my second voyage in search for the cause?"

"Would I not!" said he: "more than anything else in the world!"

"Well then," he said, "it occurred to me after all this—and it was then I gave up contemplating the realities—that I must be careful not to be affected like people who observe and watch an eclipse of the sun. What happens to them is that some lose their sight, unless they look at his reflection in water or something of that sort. This passed through my mind, and I feared that I might wholly blind my soul by gazing at practical things[35] with my eyes and trying to grasp them by each of the senses. So I thought I must take refuge in reasoning, to examine the truth of the realities. There is, however, something not like in my image; for I do not admit at all that one who examines the realities by reasoning makes use of images, more than one who examines them in deeds and facts. Well anyway, this is how I set out; and laying down in each case the reasoning which I think best fortified, I consider as true whatever seems to harmonise with that, both about causes and about everything else, and as untrue whatever does not. But I wish to make it clearer, for I think you do not understand yet."

"Indeed I do not," said Cebes, "not well."

"Well, this is what I mean," he said, "nothing new, but the same as I have been saying all this time in our conversation, and on other occasions. I am going to try to show you the nature of the cause, which I have been working out. I shall go back to the old song and begin from there, supposing that there exists a beautiful something all by itself, and a good something and great and all the rest of it; and if you grant this and admit it, I hope from these to discover and show you the cause, that the soul is something immortal."

"I grant it to you," said Cebes; "pray be quick and go on to the end."

"Then consider," he said, "what follows, and see if you agree with me. What appears to me is, that if anything else is beautiful besides beauty itself, what makes it beautiful is simply that it partakes of that beauty; and so I say with everything. Do you agree with such a cause?"

"I agree," said he.

"Very well," he said, "I can no longer recognise or understand all those clever causes we heard of; and if any one tells me that anything is beautiful because it has a fine flowery colour or shape or anything like that, I thank him and let all that go; for I get confused in all those, but this one thing I hold to myself simply and completely, and foolishly perhaps, that what makes it beautiful is only that beauty, whether its presence or a share in it or however it may be with the thing, for I am not positive about the manner, but only that beautiful things are beautiful by that beauty. For this I think to be the safest answer to give to myself or anyone else, and clinging to this I think I shall never fall, but it is a safe answer for me and everyone else, that by that beauty all beautiful things are beautiful. Don't you think so?"

"I do."

"And by greatness the great things are great, and the greater greater, and by smallness small things are small?"

"Yes."

"So you would not accept it if you were told that one person was greater than another by a head, or less by the same, but you would protest that you say every greater is greater than another because of greatness alone, and the smaller is smaller by reason of smallness alone; you would fear, I think, that a contradictory reasoning might meet you if you said someone is greater or less by a head, first that the same thing is making the greater greater and the lesser lesser, and next that a small thing like a head is making the greater greater, which is a monstrosity—that a small thing should make anyone great. Would you not fear that?"

And Cebes said, with a laugh, "I should!"

"So," said he, "you would not dare to say that ten is more than eight by two, but you would say it is more by number and because of number?—and the two-cubit measure greater than the cubit not by half, but by length? For you would fear the same each time."

"Certainly," he said.

"Well, if one has been added, you would be careful not to say the addition caused the two, or if one is divided, the division caused the two. And you would shout that you do not know how each thing comes to be, except by partaking of its own proper essence, whatever each partakes of; in these examples, you see for instance no other cause for becoming two but partaking of twohood, and whatever is to be two must partake of this, and of onehood whatever is to be one, while these splittings and addings and such niceties you would just bow to and let them go, leaving cleverer men than you to answer. For you would be frightened of your own shadow, as people say, your inexperience, and you would cling to that safe supposition,[36] and so you would answer. If anyone should attack the supposition itself, you would let him be and would not answer, until you examined the consequences to see if they were in agreement or discord together; and when you must give account of that supposition itself, you would do it in the same way by supposing another supposition, whichever seemed best of the higher suppositions, until you came to something satisfactory; at the same time you would not make a muddle like the dialecticians, by confusing arguments about the beginning with arguments about the consequences of the beginning, if you wished to find out something of reality. For those people, perhaps, think and care nothing at all about this; they are clever enough to make a mess of the whole business and yet to be pleased with themselves; but if you are a true philosopher, I believe you would do as I say."

"Very true," said Simmias and Cebes together.

Echecrates:

Reasonable too, I do declare, Phaidon. Amazingly clear he makes it, as anyone with a grain of sense can see.

Phaidon:

Yes indeed, Echecrates, and all of them thought so who were present.

34. The Titan who upheld the heavens.
35. Natural phenomena, etc.
36. i.e., the "safe answer."

Echecrates:

So do we who were not present, but are hearing of it now. But what was said after that?

Phaidon:

As I think, when this was granted, and all agreed that each of these ideal qualities has a kind of existence, and the particular things that partake of them get their name from them, next he asked: "Well then," said he, "if that is what you agree, when you say Simmias is bigger than Socrates, and smaller than Phaidon, you say that both are in Simmias, both bigness and smallness?"

"I do."

"But all the same you agree that for Simmias to overtop Socrates is not true as the words describe it. For Simmias, I suppose, does not naturally overtop Socrates by being Simmias, but by the bigness which he happens to have; nor does he overtop Socrates because Socrates is Socrates, but because Socrates has smallness as against the other's bigness."

"True."

"Nor again is he overtopped by Phaidon because Phaidon is Phaidon, but because Phaidon has bigness as against the smallness of Simmias?"

"That is right."

"Thus, then, Simmias has the title of being both small and great, being between both, in the first case submitting his smallness for the other's bigness to surpass, in the second offering his bigness which surpasses the other's smallness. At the same time," he said, smiling, "I seem to speak like a lawyer's deed, but that is very much how things are." He said yes. "I say this," he added, "because I want you to agree with me. For it appears to me that bigness itself never consents to be big and small at the same time, and not only that, even the bigness in us never accepts smallness and will not be surpassed; but one of two things, it must either depart and retreat whenever its opposite, smallness, comes near, or else must perish at its approach; it does not consent to submit and receive the smallness, and so to become other than what it was. Just so I, receiving and submitting to smallness, am still the man I am, I'm still this same small person; but the bigness in me, being big, has not dared to become small! In the same way, the smallness in us does not want to become or be big, nor does any other of the opposites, being still what it was, want to become and be the opposite; but either it goes away or it is destroyed in this change."

"Certainly," said Cebes, "that is what I think."

One of those present, hearing this, said—I do not clearly remember who it was—"Good heavens, didn't we admit in our former discussion the very opposite of what we are saying now—that the greater came from the less and the less from the greater, and in fact this is how opposites are generated, from opposites? Now it seems to be said that this could never be."

Socrates bent down his head to listen, and said, "Spoken like a man! I thank you for reminding me, but you don't understand the difference between what we are saying now and what we said then. For then we said that the practical opposite thing is generated from its practical opposite, but now we are saying that the opposite quality itself could never become the quality opposite to itself, either in us or in nature. Then, my friend, we were speaking of things which have opposites, these being named by the name of their (opposite) qualities, but now we are speaking of the opposite qualities themselves, from which being in the things, the things are named: those qualities themselves, we say, could never accept generation from each other." Then, with a glance at Cebes, he added, "Is it possible that you too, Cebes, were disturbed by what our friend spoke of?"

"No, not by this," replied Cebes, "but I don't deny that I get disturbed a good deal."

"Well, then, are we agreed," said Socrates, "simply on this, that nothing will ever be opposite to itself?"

"Quite agreed," he said.

"Here is something else," he said, "see if you will agree to this. You speak of hot and cold?"

"Yes."

"Is it the same as fire and snow?"

"Not at all."

"But the hot is something other than fire, and the cold other than snow?"

"Yes."

"Well, I suppose you agree that snow receiving fire (to use our former way of putting it) will never be what it was, snow, and also be hot, but when the hot approaches it will either retreat from it or be destroyed."

"Certainly."

"Fire, also, when the cold approaches, will either go away from it or be destroyed, but it will never endure to receive the coldness and still be what it was, fire, and cold too."

"True," said he.

"Then it is possible," he said, "with some such things, that not only the essence is thought worthy of the same name forever, but something else also is worthy, which is not that essence but which, when it exists, always has the form of that essence. Perhaps it will be a little clearer as follows. Odd numbers must always be called odd, I suppose, mustn't they?"

"Yes."

"Of all things do we use this name only for oddness, for that is what I ask, or is there something else, not oddness, but what must be called always by that name because its nature is never to be deserted by oddness? For example, triplet and so forth. Now consider the triplet: Don't you think it should be called always both by its own name and also by the name of odd, although oddness is not the same as triplet? Still it is the nature of triplet and quintet and half of all the numbers, that each of them is odd although it is not the same thing as oddness; so also two and four and all the other row of numbers are each of them always even, although none is the same thing as evenness; do agree?"

"Of course," he said.

"Now attend, this is what I want to make clear. It seems that not only those real opposites do not receive each other, but also things which not being opposites of each other yet always have those real opposites in them, these also do not look like things which receive that reality which is opposite to the reality in them, but when it approaches they either are destroyed or retire. We shall say, for example, that a triplet will be destroyed before any such thing happens to it, before it remains and becomes even, while it is still three?"

"Certainly," said Cebes.

"Nor, again," he said, "is twin the opposite of triplet."

"Not at all."

"Then not only the opposite essences do not remain

at the approach of each other, but some other things do not await the approach of the opposites."

"Very true," he said.

"Then shall we distinguish what sorts of things these are," he said, "if we can?"

"Certainly."

"Then, Cebes, would they be those which compel whatever they occupy not only to get their own essence but also the essence of some opposite?"

"How so?"

"As we said just now. You know, I suppose, that whatever the essence of three occupies must necessarily be not only three but odd."

"Certainly."

"And the essence opposite to that which does this we say could never come near such a thing."

"It could not."

"And what has done this? Was not it oddness?"

"Yes."

"And opposite to this is the essence of even?"

"Yes."

"Then the essence of even will never approach three."

"No."

"So three has no part in the even."

"None."

"Then the triplet is uneven."

"Yes."

"Now for my distinction. What things, not being opposite to something, yet do not receive the opposite itself which is in that something? For instance now, the triplet is not the opposite to the even, yet still does not receive it because it always brings the opposite against it; and a pair brings the opposite against the odd, and fire against cold, and so with very many others. Just look then, if you distinguish thus, not only the opposite does not receive the opposite, but that also which brings anything opposite to whatever it approaches never receives the opposite to that which it brings. Recollect once more; there's no harm to hear the same thing often. Five will not receive the essence of even, or its double ten the essence of odd; yet this same double will not receive the essence of odd, although it is not opposite to anything. Again, one and a half and other such things with a half in them will not receive the essence of whole, nor will one-third and all such fractions, if you follow and agree with me in this."

"I do agree certainly, and I follow."

"Once more, then," he said, "go back to the beginning. And don't answer the questions I ask, till I show you how. I want something more than the first answer I mentioned, the safe one; I see a new safety from what we have been saying now. If you ask me what must be in any body if that body is to be hot, I will not give you that safe answer, the stupid answer, 'Heat,' but a more subtle answer from our present reasoning, 'Fire'; or if you ask what must be in a body if it is to be diseased, I will not answer 'Disease,' but 'Fever'; or if you ask what must be in a number if it is to be odd, I will not say 'Oddness,' but 'Onehood,' and so forth. Now then, do you know clearly enough what I want?"

"Oh yes," he said.

"Answer then," said he, "what must be in a body if it is to be living?"

"Soul," said he.

"Is this always true?"

"Of course," he said.

"Well now, whatever the soul occupies, she always comes to it bringing life?"

"She does, indeed," he said.

"Is there an opposite to life, or not?"

"There is."

"What?"

"Death."

"Then soul will never receive the opposite to that which she brings, as we have agreed already."

"Most assuredly," said Cebes.

"Well, what name did we give just now to that which did not receive the essence of the even?"

"Uneven," he said.

"And what name to that which does not receive what is just, or to that which does not receive music?"

"Unmusical," he said, "and unjust the other."

"Very well. What do we call that which does not receive death?"

"Immortal," he said.

"And the soul does not receive death?"

"No."

"Then the soul is a thing immortal?"

"It is," he said.

"Very well," said he. "Shall we say this has been proved? Or what do you think?"

"Proved, and amply proved, Socrates."

"Now then, Cebes," he said, "if the uneven were necessarily imperishable, would not three be imperishable?"

"Of course."

"And if the not-hot were necessarily imperishable, when someone brought a hot thing to snow, the snow would retire safe and unmelted? For it would not be destroyed, nor would it remain and receive the heat."

"Quite true," he said.

"So also if the not-cold were imperishable, when something cold was brought to fire, the fire would not be quenched or destroyed, but it would go away safe."

"That is necessary," he said.

"And is it equally necessary to say that of the immortal? If the immortal is also imperishable, it is impossible for the soul to be destroyed when death comes to it; for death it will never receive, by our argument, and it will never be dead, just as we showed that the three would never be even, nor the odd be even nor indeed would fire, or the heat in the fire, ever be cold. But someone might say, 'The odd will not become even, when the even comes near, as we have agreed, but what is to hinder is being destroyed and an even being made instead?' In answer to the man who said that, we could not maintain that it is not destroyed; for the uneven is not imperishable; since if that had been granted us we could easily maintain that when the even approached, the odd, and the three, go clean off; and we could do the same about fire and heat and all the rest, couldn't we?"

"Certainly."

"So about the immortal, if we agree that this is imperishable, the soul would be imperishable as well as immortal; but if we do not, we need a new argument."

"There's no need of that in this case," said he, "nothing could escape destruction if the immortal, which is everlasting, could be destroyed."

"God himself, I think," said Socrates, "and the very essence of life, and whatever else is immortal, would be admitted by all never to suffer destruction."

"Yes, admitted by all indeed," he said, "by men of course and still more, I think, by the gods."

"Then, since the immortal is also imperishable, the soul if it is immortal would be imperishable too?"

"That must certainly be."

"So when death approaches a man, the mortal in him dies, as it seems, but the immortal part goes away undestroyed, giving place to death."

"So it seems."

"Then beyond all doubt, Cebes," he said, "soul is immortal and imperishable, and in fact our souls will exist in the house of Hades."

"I have nothing else to say to the contrary, Socrates," he answered, "and I cannot disbelieve you in any way."

"But now if Simmias has something to say, or anyone else, it is well not to be silent. I don't know what better opportunity we could have; we can't put it off now; there is only this chance if anyone wishes to say or hear more about such matters as this."

"No, indeed," said Simmias, "I can't find anything myself to disbelieve after what has been said. But in the momentous matter which we are discussing, I do distrust human weakness, and I am compelled to have a little incredulity in my mind about what we say."

"Not only that, Simmias," said Socrates; "you are quite right, and you ought still to scrutinise our first suppositions and see if you can trust them; and if you test them sufficiently, you will follow our reasoning, I think, as well as it is possible for man to follow it; and if only this be made clear, you will seek nothing further."

"True," he said.

"Well, here is something more, gentlemen," said Socrates, "that we ought to understand. If the soul is immortal, she needs care, not only for the time which we call life, but for all time, and the danger indeed would seem to be terrible if one is ready to neglect her. For if death were release from everything, a great blessing it would be for evil men to be rid of the body and their own wickedness along with the soul. But since, as things are, she appears to be immortal, there could be no escape from evil for her and no salvation, except that she should become as good and wise as possible. For when the soul comes to Hades she brings with her nothing but her education and training; and this is said to do the greatest help or hurt to the dead man at the very beginning of his course thither. What men say is this. At death the guardian spirit of each, to whom each was allotted for life, undertakes to lead each to a certain place; there those gathered must stand their trial, and then pass on to the house of Hades with the guide whose duty it is to conduct them hence to that place. When they have met there what they must meet with, and remained such time as they should, another guide again brings them back after many long periods of time. The journey is not as Telephos describes in Aeschylus, for he says that a simple way leads to Hades, but this appears to me neither simple nor single. If so, there would be no need of guides, for no one could miss one way to anywhere. But really, it seems to have many breaks and branches; I judge by the pious offerings made to the dead among us.[37] The wise and decent soul follows and understands the circumstances; but the soul which has desire for the body, as I said once before, flutters about it for a long time and about the visible world, resisting much and suffering much, and the appointed spirit drags her away by force not easily. When she comes where the others are, the unpurified soul, which has done deeds like herself, which has touched unjust murders, or done other such deeds which are akin to these and are the acts of kindred souls, is avoided by all; each one turns from her and will neither be fellow-traveller nor guide, but she wanders by herself in complete helplessness, until certain times come: when they come she is carried by necessity to her proper dwelling place. But the soul which has passed through life purely and decently finds gods for fellow-travellers and leaders, and each soul dwells in her own proper dwelling place. There are many wonderful regions in the earth, and the earth itself is not of such a quality or such a size as it is thought to be by those who are accustomed to describe the earth, so a certain man has convinced me."

Then Simmias asked, "What is this you say, Socrates? I have heard much about the earth myself, but not this story that convinced you. So I should be very glad to hear it."

He answered, "Why indeed, Simmias, I am afraid I lack a Glaucos' handbook[38] to tell you all that! But truly I think it is too hard for Glaucos' book, and besides my not perhaps being equal to it, at the same time even if I understood it, my life, Simmias, seems to me insufficient for such a long story. But what I believe to be the shape of the earth and its regions, I can tell you, there's nothing to hinder that."

"Well," said Simmias, "that will do."

"I believe, then," said he, "that first, if it is round and in the middle of the heavens, it needs nothing to keep it from falling, neither air nor any other such necessity, but the uniformity of the heavens,[39] themselves alike all through, is enough to keep it there, and the equilibrium of earth itself; for a thing in equilibrium and placed in the middle of something which is everywhere alike will not incline in any direction, but will remain steady and in like condition. First I believe that," he said.

"Quite right too," said Simmias.

"Next, I believe it is very large indeed, and we live in a little bit of it between the Pillars of Heracles[40] and the river Phasis,[41] like ants or frogs in a marsh, lodging round the sea, and that many other people live in many other such regions. For there are everywhere about the earth many hollows of all sorts in shape and size, into which have collected water and mist and air; but the earth itself is pure and lies in the pure heavens where the stars are, which is called ether by most of those who are accustomed to explain such things; of which all this is a sediment, which is always collecting into the hollows of the earth. We then, who lodge in its hollows, know nothing about it, and think we are living upon the earth; as if one living deep on the bottom of the sea should think he was at the top, and, seeing through the water sun and stars, should think the sea was heaven, but from sluggishness and weakness should never come to the surface and never get out and peep up out of the sea into this place, or observe how much more

37. Food and the like were laid on shrines where roads joined; he therefore assumes that the roads below were like that.

38. A proverb: probably some discoverer or inventor.

39. The universe is homogeneous and of one density, so there is no reason why the earth should move this way or that.

40. Mts. Calpe and Abyla, on the straits of Gibraltar; Calpe is the modern Rock of Gibraltar.

41. The river Rion which flows into the eastern part of the Black Sea.

pure and beautiful it is than his own place, and should never have heard from anyone who saw it. This very thing has happened to us; for we live in a hollow of the earth and think we live on the surface, and call the air heaven, thinking that the stars move through that and that is heaven; but the fact is the same, from weakness and sluggishness we cannot get through to the surface of the air, since if a man could come to the top of it, and get wings and fly up, he could peep over and look, just as fishes here peep up out of the sea and look round at what is here, so he could look at what is there, and if his nature allowed him to endure the sight, he could learn and know that that is the true heaven and the true light and the true earth. For this earth and the stones and all the place here are corrupted and corroded, as things in the sea are by the brine so that nothing worth mention grows in the sea, and there is nothing perfect there, one might say, but caves and sand and infinite mud and slime wherever there is any earth, things worth nothing at all as compared with the beauties we have; but again those above as compared with ours would seem to be much superior. But if I must tell you a story, Simmias, it is worth hearing what things really are like on the earth under the heavens."

"Indeed, Socrates," said Simmias, "we should be glad to hear this story."

"It is said then, my comrade," he went on, "that first of all the earth itself looks from above, if you could see it, like those twelve-patch leathern balls,[42] variegated, with strips of colour of which the colours here, such as are used by painters, are a sort of specimens; but there the whole earth is made of such as these, and much brighter and purer than these; one is sea purple wonderfully beautiful, one is like gold, the white is whiter than chalk or snow, and the earth is made of these and other colours, more in number and more beautiful than any we have seen. For indeed the very hollows full of water and mist present a colour of their own as they shine in the variety of other colours, so that the one whole looks like a continuous coloured pattern. Such is the earth, and all that grows in it is in accord, trees and flowers and fruits; and again mountains and rocks in like manner have their smoothness and transparency and colours more beautiful, and the precious stones which are so much valued here are just chips of those, sard and jaspers and emerald and so forth, but there every single one is such and they are still more beautiful. The cause of that is that those stones are pure and not corroded or corrupted as ours are by the rot and brine of stuff which has gathered here, which bring ugliness and disease on stones and earth and everything else, living creatures and plants. But the real earth is adorned with all these and with gold and silver and all such things as these. For there they are clearly to be seen, being many in number and large and all over the earth, so that to see it is a sight for happy spectators. Animals there are on it many and various, and men too, some living inland, some round the air as we do round the sea, some in islands surrounded by the flowing air near the mainland; in a word, what water and sea are to us for our use, the air is to them, and what the air is to us, ether is to them. The seasons have such temperature that the people there are free from disease and live a much longer time than we do, and in sight and hearing and intelligence and so forth they are as different from us as air is different from water and ether from air in purity. Groves of the gods also they have and sanctuaries, and the gods really dwell in them, and there are between them and the gods voices and prophecies and perceptions and other such communions; sun and moon and stars are seen by them as they are, and their happiness in all other respects is according.

"This, then, is the nature of the whole earth and all that is about it; but there are many regions in it and hollows of it all round, some deeper and spreading wider than the one we live in, some deeper but having their gap smaller than ours, some again shallower in depth than ours and wider; but these are all connected together by tunnels in many places narrower or wider, and they have many passages where floods of water run through from one to another as into a mixing-bowl, and huge rivers ever flowing underground both of hot waters and cold, where also are masses of fire and great rivers of fire, and many rivers of liquid mud, some clearer, some muddier, like the rivers of mud which run in Sicily before the lava[43] and the lava itself. And each of these regions is filled with this, according as the overflow comes in each case. All these things are moved up and down by a sort of seesaw which there is in the earth, and the nature of this seesaw movement is this. One of the chasms in the earth is largest of all, and, besides, it has a tunnel which goes right through the earth, the same which Homer speaks of when he says,

> Far, far away, where is the lowest pit
> Beneath the earth,[44]

and which elsewhere he and many other poets have called Tartaros. For into this chasm all the rivers flow together, and from this again they flow out, and they are each like the earth through which they flow. The cause which makes all the streams run out from there and run in is that this fluid has no bottom or foundation to rest on. So it seesaws and swells up and down, and the air and wind about it do the same; for they follow with it, both when the rivers move towards that side of the earth, and when they move towards this side, and just as the breath always goes in and out when men breathe, so there, too, the wind is lifted up and down with the liquid and makes terrible tempests both coming in and going out. Therefore whenever the water goes back into the place which is called 'down,' it rushes in along those rivers and fills them up like water pumped in; but when, again, it leaves that part and moves this way, it fills up our region once more, and when the rivers are filled they flow through the channels and through the earth, and, coming each to those places where their several paths lead, they make seas and lakes and rivers and fountains. After that they sink into the earth again, some passing round larger regions and more numerous, some round fewer and smaller, and plunge again into Tartaros, some far below their source, some but little, but all below the place where they came out. Some flow in opposite where they tumbled out, some in the same place; and there are others which go right round the earth in a circle, curling about it like serpents once or many times, and then fall and discharge as low down as possible. It is possible from each side to go down as far as the centre, but no farther, for beyond that the opposite part is uphill from both sides.

42. Leathern balls with coloured patches. He is thinking also of the twelve Signs of the Zodiac, hence twelve.

43. From Mount Etna in eruption.

44. Iliad viii, 14.

"All these rivers are large, and they are of many kinds; but among these many are four in especial. The greatest of these, and the outermost, running right round, is that called Ocean; opposite this and flowing in the contrary direction is Acheron, the River of Pain, which flows through a number of desert places, and also flowing under the earth comes to the Acherusian Lake, to which come the souls of most of the dead, and when they have remained there certain ordained times, some longer and some shorter, they are sent out again to birth in living creatures. The third of these rivers issues forth in the middle, and near its issue it falls into a large region blazing with much fire, and makes a lake larger than our[45] sea, boiling with water and mud; from there it moves round turbid and muddy, and rolls winding about the earth as far as another place at the extreme end of the Acherusian Lake, without mingling with the water; when it has rolled many times round it falls into a lower depth than Tartaros. This is what they call Pyriphlegethon, the River of Burning Fire, and its lava streams blow up bits of it wherever they are found on the earth. Opposite this again the fourth river discharges at first into a region terrible and wild, it is said, all having the colour of dark blue; this they call the Stygian, the River of Hate, and the lake which the river makes they call Styx. But the river, falling into this and receiving terrible powers in the water, plunges beneath the earth and, rolling round, moves contrary to Pyriphlegethon and meets it in the Acherusian Lake on the opposite side. The water of this, too, mixes with none, but this also goes round and falls into Tartaros opposite to Pyriphlegethon. The name of this, as the poets say, is Cocytos, the River of Wailing.

"Such is the nature of the world. So when the dead come to the place whither the spirit conveys each, first the judges divide them into those who have lived well and piously, and those who have not. And those who are thought to have been between the two travel to the Acheron, then embark in the vessels which are said to be there for them, and in these come to the lake, and there they dwell, being purified from their wrongdoings; and after punishment for any wrong they have done they are released, and receive rewards for their good deeds each according to his merit. But those who are thought to be incurable because of the greatness of their sins, those who have done many great acts of sacrilege or many unrighteous and lawless murders or other such crimes, these the proper fate throws into Tartaros whence they never come out. Those who are thought to have committed crimes curable although great, if they have done some violence to father or mother, say, from anger, and have lived the rest of their lives in repentance, or if they have become manslaughterers in some other such way, these must of necessity be cast into Tartaros; but when they have been cast in and been there a year the wave throws them out, the manslaughterers by way of Cocytos, the patricides and matricides by way of Pyriphlegethon; and when they have been carried down to the Acherusian Lake, there they shriek and call to those whom they slew or treated violently, and, calling on them, they beg and beseech them to accept them and let them go out into the lake; if they win consent, they come out and cease from their sufferings; if not, they are carried back into Tartaros and from there into the rivers again, and they never cease from this treatment until they win the consent of those whom they wronged: for this was the sentence passed on them by the judges. But those who are thought to have lived in especial holiness, they are those who are set free and released from these places here in the earth as from a prison house, and come up into the pure dwelling place and are settled upon earth. Of these same, again, those who have purified themselves enough by philosophy live without bodies altogether forever after, and come into dwellings even more beautiful than the others, which it is not easy to describe nor is there time enough at this present. But for the reasons which we have given, Simmias, we must do everything so as to have our share of wisdom and virtue in life; for the prize is noble and the hope great.

"No sensible man would think it proper to rely on things of this kind being just as I have described; but that, since the soul is clearly immortal, this or something like this at any rate is what happens in regard to our souls and their habitations—that this is so seems to me proper and worthy of the risk of believing; for the risk is noble. Such things he must sing like a healing charm to himself, and that is why I have lingered so long over the story. But these are the reasons for a man to be confident about his own soul, when in his life he has bidden farewell to all other pleasures, the pleasures and adornments of the body, thinking them alien and such as do more harm than good, and has been earnest only for the pleasure of learning; and having adorned the soul with no alien ornaments, but with her own—with temperance and justice and courage and freedom and truth, thus he awaits the journey to the house of Hades, ready to travel when the doom ordained shall call. You indeed," he said, "Simmias and Cebes and all, hereafter at some certain time shall each travel on that journey: but me—'Fate calls me now,' as a man might say in a tragedy, and it is almost time for me to travel towards the bath; for I am sure you think it better to have a bath before drinking the potion, and to save the women the trouble of washing a corpse."

When he had spoken, Criton said, "Ah well, Socrates, what injunctions have you for these friends or for me, about your children or anything else? What could we do for you to gratify you most?"

"What I always say, Criton," he said, "nothing very new: Take good care of yourselves, and you will gratify me and mine and yourselves whatever you do, even if you promise nothing now. But if you neglect yourselves, and won't take care to live your lives following the footsteps, so to speak, of both this last conversation and those we have had in former times, you will do no good even if you promise ever so much at present and ever so faithfully."

"Then we will do our best about that," he said; "but how are we to bury you?"

"How you like," said he, "if you catch me and I don't escape you." At the same time, laughing gently and looking towards us, he said, "Criton doesn't believe me, my friends, that this is I, Socrates now talking with you and laying down each of my injunctions, but he thinks me to be what he will see shortly, a corpse, and asks, if you please, how to bury me! I have been saying all this long time, that when I have drunk the potion, I shall not be here then with you; I shall have gone clear away to some bliss of the blest, as they call it. But he thinks I am talking nonsense, just to console myself, yes and you too. Then go bail for me to Criton," he said, "the opposite of the bail he gave to those judges. He gave bail that I would remain; you please, give bail that I will not remain after I die, but I shall get off clear and clean, that Criton may take it more easily, and

45. The Mediterranean.

may not be vexed by seeing my body either being burnt or buried; don't let him worry for me and think I'm in a dreadful state, or say at the funeral that he is laying out or carrying out or digging in Socrates. Be sure, Criton, best of friends," he said, "to use ugly words not only is out of tune with the event, but it even infects the soul with something evil. Now, be confident and say you are burying my body, and then bury it as you please and as you think would be most according to custom."

With these words, he got up and retired into another room for the bath, and Criton went after him, telling us to wait. So we waited discussing and talking together about what had been said, or sometimes speaking of the great misfortune which had befallen us, for we felt really as if we had lost a father and had to spend the rest of our lives as orphans. When he had bathed, and his children had been brought to see him—for he had two little sons, and one big—and when the women of his family had come, he talked to them before Criton and gave what instructions he wished. Then he asked the women and children to go, and came back to us. It was now near sunset, for he had spent a long time within. He came and sat down after his bath, and he had not talked long after this when the servant of the Eleven came in, and standing by him said, "O Socrates! I have not to complain of you as I do of others, that they are angry with me, and curse me, because I bring them word to drink their potion, which my officers make me do! But I have always found you in this time most generous and gentle, and the best man who ever came here. And now too, I know well you are not angry with me, for you know who are responsible, and you keep it for them. Now you know what I came to tell you, so farewell, and try to bear as well as you can what can't be helped."

Then he turned and was going out, with tears running down his cheeks. And Socrates looked up at him and said, "Farewell to you also, I will do so." Then, at the same time turning to us, "What a nice fellow!" he said. "All the time he has been coming and talking to me, a real good sort, and now how generously he sheds tears for me! Come along, Criton, let's obey him. Someone bring the potion, if the stuff has been ground; if not, let the fellow grind it."

Then Criton said, "But Socrates, I think the sun is still over the hills, it has not set yet. Yes, and I know of others who, having been told to drink the poison, have done it very late; they had dinner first and a good one, and some enjoyed the company of any they wanted. Please don't be in a hurry, there is time to spare."

But Socrates said, "Those you speak of have very good reason for doing that, for they think they will gain by doing it; and I have good reasons why I won't do it. For I think I shall gain nothing by drinking a little later, only that I shall think myself a fool for clinging to life and sparing when the cask's empty.[46] Come along," he said, "do what I tell you, if you please."

And Criton, hearing this, nodded to the boy who stood near. The boy went out, and after spending a long time, came in with the man who was to give the poison[47] carrying it ground ready in a cup. Socrates caught sight of the man and said, "Here, my good man, you know about these things; what must I do?"

"Just drink it," he said, "and walk about till your legs get heavy, then lie down. In that way the drug will act of itself."

At the same time, he held out the cup to Socrates, and he took it quite cheerfully, Echecrates, not a tremble, not a change in colour or looks; but looking full at the man under his brows, as he used to do, he asked him. "What do you say about this drink? What of a libation to someone[48] Is that allowed, or not?"

He said, "We only grind so much as we think enough for a moderate potion."

"I understand," he said, "but at least, I suppose, it is allowed to offer a prayer to the gods and that must be done, for good luck in the migration from here to there. Then that is my prayer, and so may it be!"

With these words he put the cup to his lips and, quite easy and contented, drank it up. So far most of us had been able to hold back our tears pretty well; but when we saw him begin drinking and end drinking, we could no longer. I burst into a flood of tears for all I could do, so I wrapped up my face and cried myself out; not for him indeed, but for my own misfortune in losing such a man and such a comrade. Criton had got up and gone out even before I did, for he could not hold the tears in. Apollodoros had never ceased weeping all this time, and now he burst out into loud sobs, and by his weeping and lamentations completely broke down every man there except Socrates himself. He only said, "What a scene! You amaze me. That's just why I sent the women away, to keep them from making a scene like this. I've heard that one ought to make an end in decent silence. Quiet yourselves and endure."

When we heard him we felt ashamed and restrained our tears. He walked about, and when he said that his legs were feeling heavy, he lay down on his back, as the man told him to do; at the same time the one who gave him the potion felt him, and after a while examined his feet and legs; then pinching a foot hard, he asked if he felt anything; he said no. After this, again, he pressed the shins; and, moving up like this, he showed us that he was growing cold and stiff. Again he felt him, and told us that when it came to his heart, he would be gone. Already the cold had come nearly as far as the abdomen, when Socrates threw off the covering from his face—for he had covered it over—and said, the last words he uttered, "Criton," he said, "we owe a cock to Asclepios;[49] pay it without fail."

"That indeed shall be done," said Criton. "Have you anything more to say?"

When Criton had asked this, Socrates gave no further answer, but after a little time, he stirred, and the man uncovered him, and his eyes were still. Criton, seeing this, closed the mouth and eyelids.

This was the end of our comrade, Echecrates, a man, as we would say, of all then living we had ever met, the noblest and the wisest and most just.

---

46. There's a proverb:

> Cask full or failing, drink; but in between
> Spare if you like; sparing at bottom's mean.
>
> —Hesiod, *Works and Days*, 368

47. The poison was hemlock.
48. The custom was for the butler to spill a drop into the cup which the drinker then spilt on the ground as a libation with a prayer; then the butler filled and the man drank.
49. A thank-offering to the god of healing. The cock is the poor man's offering. The touching beauty and restraint of this account is heightened still more, if Plato, who was ill and unable to be present at the death of his dearest friend, took this last request to have been made for his sake.

Some Questions for Discussion

1. What is Socrates' argument against suicide?
2. Notice carefully the distinction which Socrates makes between soul and body. With this in mind, why does he say that the philosopher has sought death throughout his life?
3. In the proof of the immortality of the soul, state clearly the doctrine of opposites, both of opposite things and opposite processes. What is Socrates' proof of immortality based on this doctrine? In his discussion of the doctrine of learning, how does he draw upon the idea of reality as Idea or Essence? (see "The Allegory of the Cave"). How does he try to prove immortality with this doctrine?
4. Granting the existence of the soul before birth, how can we be sure that it continues to exist after death? Reconstruct the arguments here.
5. What is Socrates' picture of the good soul in Hades?
6. Can you state Simmias' objection to the preceding argument when he argues that the soul may be like a harmony?
7. What is the implication of Simmias' question that the soul is like a weaver and the body like a series of coats which he weaves? Now follow very carefully Socrates refutation of these two questions, particularly the second one. Do you notice any contradiction or seeming contradiction in Socrates' argument here and his earlier discussion of the doctrine of opposites? Is this a real contradiction, or can it be explained?

The Bacchae

Euripides

The Bacchae (BOCK-ee) is probably more "contemporary" than most of the twentieth-century literature presented in volume 2 of this text. It was one of the last two plays that Euripides wrote after he had exiled himself from "civilized" Athens to Macedonia.

In the myth, Dionysus was the son of Zeus by the mortal woman, Semele, daughter of Cadmus, the first king of Thebes. Semele uttered the wish to see Zeus in all his glory as the god of lightning, and, as her wish was granted, she was blasted by the lightning-stroke. The unborn god, Dionysus, was saved from his mother's womb and hidden by Zeus (in his thigh) until the time of his birth.

Euripides follows the belief that the worship of Dionysus moved through Asia before it took root in Greece. This is the account that Dionysus gives of himself as he comes to his native city of Thebes to inaugurate his cult in Hellas, bringing with him a chorus of Asian women.

The conventional interpretation of this play is that a person or a society must recognize the fact that the human personality contains much of the Dionysiac (irrational and emotional) element, and must give this part of the character adequate expression in order to develop a healthy individual or culture. This healthy group is represented by the Asian women. Certainly Pentheus is a caricature of the "rational" man, particularly as he stands amid what seem to be the ruins of his palace and carries on his discussion with the god, not even noticing the chaos around him. Perhaps Pentheus, the traditional rational Greek, deserves punishment, but what of Agave, Cadmus, and the others who have accepted the god and honored him?

This modern translation is by Philip Vellacott.

Characters

Dionysus (die-uh-NIE-sus)
Chorus of Oriental women, devotees of Dionysus
Teiresias (tie-REE-see-us), *a blind seer*
Cadmus (KAD-mus), *founder of Thebes, and formerly king*
Pentheus (PEN-thee-us), *his grandson, now king of Thebes*
A Guard attending Pentheus
A Herdsman
A Messenger
Agaue (ah-GAH-vee), *daughter of Cadmus and mother of Pentheus*

Scene: Before the palace of Pentheus in Thebes. At one side of the stage is the monument of Semele (SEM-uh-lee); *above it burns a low flame, and around it are the remains of ruined and blackened masonry.*

[Dionysus enters on stage right. He has a crown of ivy, a thyrsus[1] in his hand, and a fawnskin draped over his body. He has long flowing hair and a youthful, almost feminine beauty.]

Dionysus:

I am Dionysus, son of Zeus. My mother was
Semele, Cadmus' daughter. From her womb the fire
Of a lightning-flash delivered me. I have come here
To Thebes and her two rivers, Dirce and Ismenus,
Veiling my godhead in a mortal shape. I see
Here near the palace my mother's monument, that records
Her death by lightning. Here her house stood; and its ruins
Smoulder with the still living flame of Zeus's fire—
The immortal cruelty Hera wreaked upon my mother.
Cadmus does well to keep this ground inviolable,
A precinct consecrated in his daughter's name;
And I have decked it round with sprays of young vine-leaves.
From the fields of Lydia and Phrygia,[2] fertile in gold,

---

1. A thyrsus is a light stick of reed or fennel with fresh strands of ivy twined about it. It was carried by every devotee of Dionysus.
2. These are the names of Asian countries in which the worship of Dionysus has been accepted in its progress toward Greece (Hellas).

I travelled first to the sun-smitten Persian plains,
The walled cities of Bactria, the harsh Median country,
Wealthy Arabia, and the whole tract of the Asian coast
Where mingled swarms of Greeks and Orientals live
In vast magnificent cities; and before reaching this,
The first city of Hellas I have visited,
I had already, in all those regions of the east,
Performed my dances and set forth my ritual
To make my godhead manifest to mortal men.

The reason why I have chosen Thebes as the first place
To raise my Bacchic shout,[3] and clothe all who respond
In fawnskin habits, and put my thyrsus in their hands—
The weapon wreathed with ivy-shoots—my reason is this:
My mother's sisters said—what they should have been the last
To say—that I, Dionysus, was not Zeus's son;
That Semele, being with child—they said—by some mortal,
Obeyed her father's prompting, and ascribed to Zeus
The loss of her virginity; and they loudly claimed
That this lie was the sin for which Zeus took her life.

Therefore I have driven those same sisters mad, turned them
All frantic out of doors; their home now is the mountain;
Their wits are gone. I have made them bear the emblem of
My mysteries; the whole female population of Thebes,
To the last woman, I have sent raving from their homes.
Now, side by side with Cadmus' daughters, one and all
Sit roofless on the rocks under the silver pines.
For Thebes, albeit reluctantly, must learn in full
This lesson, that my Bacchic worship is a matter
As yet beyond her knowledge and experience;
And I must vindicate my mother Semele
By manifesting myself before the human race
As the divine son whom she bore to immortal Zeus.

Now Cadmus has made over his throne and kingly honours
To Pentheus, son of his eldest daughter Agaue. He
Is a fighter against gods, defies me, excludes me from
Libations, never names me in prayers. Therefore I will
Demonstrate to him, and to all Thebes, that I am a god.

When I have set all in order here, I will pass on
To another place, and manifest myself. Meanwhile
If Thebes in anger tries to bring the Bacchants home
By force from the mountain, I myself will join that army
Of women possessed and lead them to battle. That is why
I have changed my form and taken the likeness of a man.
Come, my band of worshippers, women whom I have brought

From lands of the east, from Tmolus,[4] bastion of Lydia,
To be with me and share my travels! Raise the music
Of your own country, the Phrygian drums invented by
Rhea[5] the Great Mother and by me. Fill Pentheus' palace
With a noise to make the city of Cadmus turn and look!
—And I will go to the folds of Mount Cithaeron,[6] where
The Bacchants are, and join them in their holy dance.
[DIONYSUS *goes out towards the mountain. The* CHORUS *enter where* DIONYSUS *entered, from the road by which they have travelled.*

Chorus:

From far-off lands of Asia, *Strope 1*
From Tmolus the holy mountain,
We run with the god of laughter;
Labour is joy and weariness is sweet,
And our song resounds to Bacchus!

Who stands in cur path? *Antistrophe 1*
Make way, make way!
Who in the house? Close every lip,
Keep holy silence, while we sing
The appointed hymn to Bacchus!

Blest is the happy man *Strophe 2*
Who knows the mysteries the gods ordain,
And sanctifies his life,

Joins soul with soul in mystic unity,
And, by due ritual made pure,
Enters the ecstasy of mountain solitudes;
Who observes the mystic rites
Made lawful by Cybele[7] the Great Mother;
Who crowns his head with ivy,
And shakes aloft his wand in worship of Dionysus.

On, on! Run, dance, delirious, possessed!
Dionysus comes to his own;
Bring from the Phrygian hills to the broad streets of Hellas
The god, child of a god,
Spirit of revel and rapture, Dionysus!

Once, on the womb that held him *Antistrophe 2*
The fire-bolt flew from the hand of Zeus;
And pains of child-birth bound his mother fast,
And she cast him forth untimely,
And under the lightning's lash relinquished life;
And Zeus the son of Cronos
Ensconced him instantly in a secret womb
Chambered within his thigh,
And with golden pins closed him from Hera's sight.

So, when the Fates had made him ripe for birth,
Zeus bore the bull-horned god
And wreathed his head with wreaths of writhing snakes;
Which is why the Maenads[8] catch
Wild snakes, nurse them and twine them round their hair.

O Thebes, old nurse that cradled Semele, *Strope 3*
Be ivy garlanded, burst into flower
With wreaths of lush bright-berried bryony,
Bring sprays of fir, green branches torn from oaks,
Fill soul and flesh with Bacchus' mystic power;
Fringe and bedeck your dappled fawnskin cloaks

With wooly tufts and locks of purest white.
There's a brute wildness in the fennel-wands—
Reverence it well. Soon the whole land will dance
When the god with ecstatic shout
Leads his companies out
To the mountain's mounting height
Swarming with riotous bands
Of Theban women leaving

3. Dionysus is also known by the name of Bacchus (his worshippers are Bacchantes), and also by the name of Bromius.
4. An Asian mountain in Lydia.
5. The earth mother, wife of Kronus. Notice the alliance between the female fertility-worship and that of Dionysus.
6. kee-the-RON. A mountain just outside the city of Thebes.
7. KI-buh-lee. The original earth mother, wife of the first god, Uranus.
8. MEE-nad. Another name for the female worshippers of Dionysus.

Their spinning and their weaving
Stung with the maddening trance
Of Dionysus!

O secret chamber the Curetes knew![9] *Antistrophe 3*
O holy cavern in the Cretan glade
Where Zeus was cradled, where for our delight
The triple-crested Corybantes[10] drew
Tight the round drum-skin, till its wild beat made
Rapturous rhythm to the breathing sweetness
Of Phrygian flutes![11] Then divine Rhea found
The drum could give her Bacchic airs completeness;
From her, the Mother of all,
The crazy Satyrs[12] soon,
In their dancing festival
When the second year comes round,
Seized on the timbrel's tune
To play the leading part
In feasts that delight the heart
Of Dionysus.

O what delight is in the mountains! *Epode*
There the celebrant,[13] wrapped in his sacred fawnskin,
Flings himself on the ground surrendered,
While the swift-footed company streams on;
There he hunts for blood, and rapturously
Eats the raw flesh of the slaughtered goat,
Hurrying on to the Phrygian or Lydian mountain heights.
Possessed, ecstatic, he leads their happy cries;
The earth flows with milk, flows with wine,
Flows with nectar of bees;
The air is thick with a scent of Syrian myrrh.
The celebrant runs entranced, whirling the torch
That blazes red from the fennel-wand in his grasp,
And with shouts he rouses the scattered bands,
Sets their feet dancing,
As he shakes his delicate locks to the wild wind.
And amidst the frenzy of song he shouts like thunder:
'On, on! Run, dance, delirious, possessed!
You, the beauty and grace of golden Tmolus,
Sing to the rattle of thunderous drums,
Sing for joy,
Praise Dionysus, god of joy!
Shout like Phrygians, sing out the tunes you know,
While the sacred pure-toned flute
Vibrates the air with holy merriment,
In time with the pulse of the feet that flock
To the mountains, to the mountains!'
And, like a foal with its mother at pasture,
Runs and leaps for joy every daughter of Bacchus.
[*Enter* TEIRESIAS. *Though blind, he makes his way unaided to the door, and knocks.*

Teiresias:
Who keeps the gate? Call Cadmus out, Agenor's son,
Who came from Sidon here to build these walls of Thebes.[14]
Go, someone, say Teiresias is looking for him.
He knows why; I'm an old man, and he's older still—
But we agreed to equip ourselves with Bacchic wands
And fawnskin cloaks, and put on wreaths of ivy-shoots.
[*Enter* CADMUS]

Cadmus:
Dear friend, I knew your voice, although I was indoors,
As soon as I heard it—the wise voice of a wise man.
I am ready. See, I have all that the god prescribes.
He is my daughter's son; we must do all we can
To exalt and honour him. Where shall we go to dance
And take our stand with others, tossing our grey heads?
You tell me what to do, Teiresias. We're both old,
But you're the expert. [*He stumps about, beating his thyrsus on the ground.*] I could drum the ground all night
And all day too, without being tired. What joy it is
To forget one's age!

Teiresias:
I feel exactly the same way,
Bursting with youth! I'll try it—I'll dance with the rest.

Cadmus:
You don't think we should go to the mountain in a coach?

Teiresias:
No, no. That would not show the god the same respect.

Cadmus:
I'll take you there myself then—old as we both are.

Teiresias:
The god will guide us there, and without weariness.

Cadmus:
Are we the only Thebans who will dance to him?

Teiresias:
We see things clearly; all the others are perverse.

Cadmus:
We're wasting time; come, take my hand.

Teiresias:
Here, then; hold tight.

Cadmus:
I don't despise religion. I'm a mortal man.

Teiresias:
We have no use for theological subtleties.
The beliefs we have inherited, as old as time,
Cannot be overthrown by any argument,
Not by the most inventive ingenuity.
It will be said, I lack the dignity of my age,
To wear this ivy-wreath and set off for the dance.
Not so; the god draws no distinction between young
And old, to tell us which should dance and which should not.
He desires equal worship from all men; his claim
To glory is universal; no one is exempt.

Cadmus:
Teiresias, I shall be your prophet, since you are blind.
Pentheus, to whom I have resigned my rule in Thebes,

---

9. The reference here is to the cave on the island of Crete where Zeus was hidden from his father and raised to manhood (or godhood).
10. kore-uh-BAN-teez. The priests of Cybele.
11. Flutes. The aulos, the reedy, two-pronged musical instrument used in conjunction with Greek tragedies and Dionysian rites (see Chap. 8).
12. SAYT-ur. Half-animal gods; part of the worship of Dionysus.
13. The celebrant. Dionysus and the Chorus comprise the typical group of Bacchic worshippers, a male leader with a devoted band of women and girls. The leader flings himself on the ground in the climax of ecstasy when the power of the god enters into him and he becomes possessed.
14. Cadmus was the original king of Thebes. He planted the dragon's teeth from which grew a group of warriors who built the city. Pentheus' father, Echion (ee-KEY-on), who is referred to later in the play, was one of the warriors who grew from the dragon's teeth.

Is hurrying here towards the palace. He appears
Extremely agitated. What news will he bring?
[*Enter* PENTHEUS. *He addresses the audience, without at first noticing* CADMUS *and* TEIRESIAS, *who stand at the opposite side of the stage.*

Pentheus:
I happen to have been away from Thebes; reports
Of this astounding scandal have just been brought to me.
Our women, it seems, have left their homes on some pretence
Of Bacchic worship, and now are gadding about
On the wooded mountain-slopes, dancing in honour of
This upstart god Dionysus, whoever he may be.
Amidst these groups of worshippers, they tell me, stand
Bowls full of wine; and our women go creeping off
This way and that to lonely places and give themselves
To lecherous men. They are Maenad priestesses, if you please!
Aphrodite supplants Bacchus in their ritual.
Well, those I've caught, my guards are keeping safe; we've tied
Their hands, and lodged them at state expense. Those still at large
On the mountain I am going to hunt out; and that
Includes my own mother Agaue and her sisters
Ino and Autonoe. Once they're fast in iron fetters,
I'll put a stop to this outrageous Bacchism.

They tell me, too, some oriental conjurer
Has come from Lydia, a magician with golden hair
Flowing in scented ringlets, his face flushed with wine,
His eyes lit with the charm of Aphrodite;[15] and he
Entices young girls with his Bacchic mysteries,
Spends days and nights consorting with them. Once let me
Get that fellow inside my walls—I'll cut his head
From his shoulders; that will stop him drumming with his thyrsus,
Tossing his long hair. *He's* the one—this foreigner—
Who says Dionysus is a god; who says he was
Sewn up in Zeus's thigh. The truth about Dionysus
Is that he's dead, burnt to a cinder by lightning
Along with his mother, because she said Zeus lay with her.
Whoever the man may be, is not his arrogance
An outrage? Has he not earned a rope around his neck?
[PENTHEUS *turns to go, and sees* CADMUS *and* TEIRESIAS.]

Why, look! Another miracle! Here's Teiresias
The prophet—in a fawnskin; and my mother's father—
A Bacchant with a fennel-wand! Well, there's a sight
For laughter! [*But he is raging, not laughing*]

Sir, I am ashamed to see two men
Of your age with so little sense of decency.
Come, you're my grandfather: throw down that ivy-wreath,
Get rid of that thyrsus!—*You* persuaded him to this,
Teiresias. By introducing a new god, you hope
To advance your augurer's business, to collect more fees
For inspecting sacrifices. Listen: your grey hairs
Are your protection; otherwise you'd be sitting now
In prison with all these crazy females, for promoting
Pernicious practices. As for women, I tell you this:
Wherever the sparkle of sweet wine adorns their feasts,
No good will follow from such Bacchic ceremonies.

Chorus:
Have you no reverence, Sir, no piety? Do you mock
Cadmus, who sowed the dragon-seed of earth-born men?
Do you, Echion's son, dishonour your own race?

Teiresias:
When a good speaker has a sound case to present,
Then eloquence is no great feat. Your fluent tongue
Promises wisdom; but the content of your speech
Is ignorant. Power and eloquence in a headstrong man
Spell folly; such a man is a peril to the state.

This new god, whom you ridicule—no words of mine
Could well express the ascendancy he will achieve
In Hellas. There are two powers, young man, which are supreme
In human affairs: first, Demeter[16] —the same goddess
Is also Earth; give her which name you please—and she
Supplies mankind with solid food. After her came
Dionysus, Semele's son; the blessing he procured
And gave to men is counterpart to that of bread:
The clear juice of the grape. When mortals drink their fill
Of wine, the sufferings of our unhappy race
Are banished, each day's troubles are forgotten in sleep.
There is no other cure for sorrow. Dionysus,
Himself a god, is thus poured out in offering
To the gods, so that through him come blessings on mankind.
And do you scorn this legend, that he was sewn up
In Zeus's thigh? I will explain the truth to you.
When Zeus snatched Dionysus from the lightning-flame
And took the child up to Olympus as a god,
Hera resolved to cast him out of heaven. But Zeus
Found such means to prevent her as a god will find.
He took a fragment of the ether that surrounds
The earth, fashioned it like a child, presented it
To Hera as a pledge[17] to soothe her jealousy,
And saved Dionysus from her. Thus, in time, because
The ancient words for 'pledge' and 'thigh' are similar,
People confused them, and the 'pledge' Zeus gave to Hera
Became transformed, as time went on, into the tale
That Dionysus was sewn up in Zeus's thigh.

And this god is a prophet; the Bacchic ecstasy
And frenzy hold a strong prophetic element.
When he fills irresistibly a human body
He gives those so possessed power to foretell the future.
In Ares' province too Dionysus has his share;
Sometimes an army, weaponed and drawn up for battle,
Has fled in wild panic before a spear was raised.
This too is an insanity sent by Dionysus.

Ay, and the day will come when, on the very crags
Of Delphi,[18] you shall see him leaping, amidst the blaze
Of torches, over the twin-peaked ridge, waving aloft
And brandishing his Bacchic staff, while all Hellas
Exalts him. Pentheus, pay heed to my words. You rely
On force; but it is not force that governs human affairs.
Do not mistake for wisdom that opinion which
May rise from a sick mind. Welcome this god to Thebes,

15. af-ro-DIE-tee. The goddess of love and beauty.
16. di-MEET-ur. The third personification of the earth goddess.
17. The ancient word for pledge: the translation necessarily expands the original. *Homeros* means "pledge," and *meros* means thigh.
18. Delphi was the shrine sacred to Apollo, a god of the rational Greeks. The twin-peaked ridge is Mount Parnassus, the home of the Muses.

Offer libations to him, celebrate his rites,
Put on his garland. Dionysus will not compel
Women to be chaste, since in all matters self-control
Resides in our own natures. You should consider this;
For in the Bacchic ritual, as elsewhere, a woman
Will be safe from corruption if her mind is chaste.

Think of this too: when crowds stand at the city gates
And Thebes extols the name of Pentheus, you rejoice;
So too, I think, the god is glad to receive honour.

Well, I at least, and Cadmus, whom you mock, will wear
The ivy-wreath and join the dancing—we are a pair
Of grey heads, but this is our duty; and no words
Of yours shall lure me into fighting against gods.
For a most cruel insanity has warped your mind;
While drugs may well have caused it, they can bring no cure.

Chorus:
What you have said, Teiresias, shows no disrespect
To Apollo; at the same time you prove your judgment sound
In honouring Dionysus as a mighty god.

Cadmus:
My dear son, Teiresias has given you good advice.
Don't stray beyond pious tradition; live with us.
Your wits have flown to the winds, your sense is foolishness.
Even if, as you say, Dionysus is no god,
Let him have *your* acknowledgment; lie royally,
That Semele may get honour as having borne a god,
And credit come to us and to all our family.

Remember, too, Actaeon's miserable fate—
Torn and devoured by hounds which he himself had bred,
Because he filled the mountains with the boast that he
Was a more skilful hunter than Artemis herself.
Don't share his fate, my son! Come, let me crown your head
With a wreath of ivy; join us in worshipping this god.

Pentheus:
Keep your hands off! Go to your Bacchic rites, and don't
Wipe off your crazy folly on me. But I will punish
This man who has been your instructor in lunacy.
Go, someone, quickly to his seat of augury,
Smash it with crowbars, topple the walls, throw all his things
In wild confusion, turn the whole place upside down,
Fling out his holy fripperies to the hurricane winds!
This sacrilege will sting him more than anything else.
The rest of you—go, comb the country and track down
That effeminate foreigner, who plagues our women with
This new disease, fouls the whole land with lechery;
And once you catch him, tie him up and bring him here
To me; I'll deal with him. He shall be stoned to death.
He'll wish he'd never brought his Bacchic rites to Thebes.
[*Exit* PENTHEUS]

Teiresias:
Foolhardy man! You do not know what you have said.
Before, you were unbalanced; now you are insane.
Come, Cadmus; let us go and pray both for this man,
Brutish as he is, and for our city, and beg the god
To show forbearance. Come, now, take your ivy staff
And let us go. Try to support me; we will help
Each other. It would be scandalous for two old men
To fall; still, we must go, and pay our due service
To Dionysus, son of Zeus. Cadmus, the name
Pentheus means *sorrow*. God grant he may not bring sorrow
Upon your house. Do not take that as prophecy;
I judge his acts. Such foolish words bespeak a fool.
[*Exeunt* TEIRESIAS *and* CADMUS.]

Chorus:
Holiness, Queen of heaven,
Holiness, golden-winged ranging the earth,
Do you hear his blasphemy?
Pentheus dares—do you hear?—to revile the god of joy,
The son of Semele, who when the gay-crowned feast is set.
Is named among gods the chief;
Whose gifts are joy and union of soul in dancing,
Joy in music of flutes,
Joy when sparkling wine at feasts of the gods
Soothes the sore regret,
Banishes every grief,
When the reveller rests, enfolded deep
In the cool shade of ivy-shoots,
On wine's soft pillow of sleep.

The brash, unbridled tongue, *Antistrophe 1*
The lawless folly of fools, will end in pain.
But the life of wise content
Is blest with quietness, escapes the storm
And keeps its house secure.
Though blessed gods dwell in the distant skies,
They watch the ways of men.
To know much is not to be wise.
Pride more than mortal hastens life to its end;
And they who in pride pretend
Beyond man's limit, will lose what lay
Close to their hand and sure.
I count it madness, and know no cure can mend
The evil man and his evil way.

O to set foot on Aphrodite's island, *Strophe 2*
On Cyprus, haunted by the Loves, who enchant
Brief life with sweetness; or in that strange land
Whose fertile river carves a hundred channels
To enrich her rainless sand;
Or where the sacred pastures of Olympus slant
Down to Pieria, where the Muses dwell—
Take me, O Bromius, take me and inspire
Laughter and worship! There our holy spell
And ecstasy are welcome; there the gentle band
Of Graces have their home, and sweet Desire.
Dionysus, son of Zeus, delights in banquets; *Antistrophe 2*
And his dear love is Peace, giver of wealth,
Saviour of young men's lives—a goddess rare!
In wine, his gift that charms all griefs away,
Alike both rich and poor may have their part.
His enemy is the man who has no care
To pass his years in happiness and health,
His days in quiet and his nights in joy,
Watchful to keep aloof both mind and heart
From men whose pride claims more than mortals may.
The life that wins the poor man's common voice,
His creed, his practice—this shall be my choice.

[*Some of the guards whom* PENTHEUS *sent to arrest* DIONYSUS *now enter with their prisoner.* PENTHEUS *enters from the palace.*]

Guard:
Pentheus, we've brought the prey you sent us out to catch;
We hunted him, and here he is. But, Sir, we found

The beast was gentle; made no attempt to run away,
Just held his hands out to be tied; didn't turn pale,
But kept his florid colour, smiling, telling us
To tie him up and run him in; gave us no trouble
At all, just waited for us. Naturally I felt
A bit embarrassed. 'You'll excuse me, Sir,' I said,
'I don't want to arrest you; it's the king's command.'

Another thing, sir—those women you rounded up
And put in fetters in the prison, those Bacchants;
Well, they're all gone, turned loose to the glens; and there they are,
Frisking about, calling on Bromius their god.
The fetters simply opened and fell off their feet;
The bolts shot back, untouched by mortal hand; the doors
Flew wide. Master, this man has come here with a load
Of miracles. Well, what happens next is your concern.

Pentheus:
Untie this man's hands. [*The* GUARD *does so*] He's securely in the trap.
He's not so nimble-footed as to escape me now.

Well, friend: your shape is not unhandsome—for the pursuit
Of women, which is the purpose of your presence here.
You are no wrestler, I can tell from these long curls
Cascading most seductively over your cheek.
Your skin, too, shows a whiteness carefully preserved;
You keep away from the sun's heat, walk in the shade,
So hunting Aphrodite with your lovely face.

Ah, well; first tell me who you are. What is your birth?

Dionysus:
Your question's easily answered, it is no secret.
Perhaps you have heard of Tmolus, a mountain decked with flowers.

Pentheus:
A range that curves round Sardis? Yes, I know of it.

Dionysus:
That is my home. I am a Lydian by birth.

Pentheus:
How comes it that you bring these rituals to Hellas?

Dionysus:
Dionysus, son of Zeus, himself instructed me.

Pentheus:
Is there a Lydian Zeus, then, who begets new gods?

Dionysus:
I speak of Zeus who wedded Semele here in Thebes.

Pentheus:
Did he possess you in a dream, or visibly?

Dionysus:
Yes, face to face; he gave these mysteries to me.

Pentheus:
These mysteries you speak of: what form do they take?

Dionysus:
To the uninitiated that must not be told.

Pentheus:
And those who worship—what advantage do they gain?

Dionysus:
It is not for you to learn; yet it is worth knowing.

Pentheus:
You bait your answer well, to arouse my eagerness.

Dionysus:
His rituals abhor a man of impious life.

Pentheus:
You say you saw him face to face: what was he like?

Dionysus:
Such as he chose to be. I had no say in that.

Pentheus:
Still you side-track my question with an empty phrase.

Dionysus:
Just so. A prudent speech sleeps in a foolish ear.

Pentheus:
Is Thebes the first place where you have introduced this god?

Dionysus:
No; every eastern land dances these mysteries.

Pentheus:
No doubt. Their moral standards fall far below ours.

Dionysus:
In this they are superior; but their customs differ.

Pentheus:
Do you perform these mysteries by night or day?

Dionysus:
Chiefly by night. Darkness promotes religious awe.

Pentheus:
For women darkness is deceptive and impure.

Dionysus:
Impurity can be pursued by daylight too.

Pentheus:
You must be punished for your foul and slippery tongue.

Dionysus:
And you for blindness and impiety to the god.

Pentheus:
How bold this Bacchant is! A practised pleader too.

Dionysus:
Tell me my sentence. What dread pain will you inflict?

Pentheus:
I'll start by cutting of your delicate long hair.

Dionysus:
My hair is sacred; I preserve it for the god.

Pentheus:
And next, that thyrsus in your hand—give it to me.

Dionysus:
Take it from me yourself; it is the god's emblem.

Pentheus:
I'll lock you up in prison and keep you there.

Dionysus:
The god
Himself, whenever I desire, will set me free.

Pentheus:
Of course—when you, with all your Bacchants, call to him!

Dionysus:
He is close at hand here, and sees what is done to me.

Pentheus:
Indeed? Where is he, then? Not visible to my eyes.

Dionysus:
Beside me. You, being a blasphemer, see nothing.

Pentheus [*to the* GUARDS]:
Get hold of him; he's mocking me and the whole city.

Dionysus [*to the* GUARDS]:
Don't bind me, I warn you. [*To* PENTHEUS] I am sane, and you are mad.

Pentheus:
My word overrules yours. [*To the* GUARDS] I tell you, bind him fast.

Dionysus:
You know not what you are saying, what you do, nor who
You are.[19]

Pentheus:
Who? Pentheus, son of Echion and Agaue.

Dionysus:
Your name points to calamity. It fits you well.

Pentheus:
Take him away and shut him in my stables, where
He can stay staring at darkness.—You can dance in there!
As for these women you've brought as your accomplices,
I'll either send them to the slave-market to be sold,
Or keep them in my own household to work the looms;
And that will stop their fingers drumming on tambouriness!

Dionysus:
I'll go. Nothing can touch me that is not ordained.
But I warn you: Dionysus, who you say is dead,
Will come in swift pursuit to avenge this sacrilege.
You are putting *him* in prison when you lay hands on me.
[GUARDS *take* DIONYSUS *away to the stables;* PENTHEUS *follows.*]

Chorus:
Dirce, sweet and holy maid, *Strophe*
Acheloüs' Theban daughter,
Once the child of Zeus was made
Welcome in your welling water,
When the lord of earth and sky
Snatched him from the undying flame,
Laid him safe within his thigh,
Calling loud the infant's name:
'Twice-born Dithyrambus! Come,
Enter here your father's womb;
Bacchic child, I now proclaim
This in Thebes shall be your name.'
Now, divine Dirce, when my head is crowned
And my feet dance in Bacchus' revelry—
Now you reject me from your holy ground.
Why should you fear me? By the purple fruit
That glows in glory on Dionysus' tree,
His dread name yet shall haunt your memory!

Oh, what anger lies beneath *Antistrophe*
Pentheus' voice and sullen face—
Offspring of the dragon's teeth,
And Echion's earth-born race,
Brute with bloody jaws agape,
God-defying, gross and grim,
Slander of his human shape!
Soon he'll chain us limb to limb—
Bacchus' servants! Yes, and more:
Even now our comrade lies
Deep on his dark prison floor.
Dionysus! Do your eyes
See us? O son of Zeus, the oppressor's rod
Falls on your worshippers; come, mighty god,
Brandish your golden thyrsus and descend
From great Olympus; touch this murderous man,
And bring his violence to a sudden end!

Where are you, Dionysus? Leading your dancing bands *Epode*
Over the mountain slopes, past many a wild beast's lair,
Or on Corycian crags, with the thyrsus in their hands?
Or in the wooded coverts, maybe, of Olympus, where
Orpheus once gathered the trees and mountain beasts,
Gathered them with his lyre, and sang an enchanting air.
Happy vale of Pieria! Bacchus delights in you;
He will cross the flood and foam of the Axius river, and there
He will bring his whirling Maenads, with dancing and with feasts,
Cross the father of waters, Lydias, generous giver
Of wealth and luck, they say, to the land he wanders through,
Whose famous horses graze by the rich and lovely river.
[*Suddenly a shout is heard from inside the building—the voice of* DIONYSUS.]

Dionysus:
Io, Io! Do you know my voice, do you hear?
Worshippers of Bacchus! Io. Io!

Chorus:
Who is that? Where is he?
The shout of Dionysus is calling us!

Dionysus:
Io, Io! hear me again:
I am the son of Semele, the son of Zeus!

Chorus:
Io, Io, our lord, our lord!
Come, then, come to our company, lord of joy!

Dionysus:
O dreadful earthquake, shake the floor of the world!

Chorus [*with a scream of terror*]:
Pentheus' palace is falling, crumbling in pieces! [*They continue severally.*]
—Dionysus stands in the palace; bow before him!
—We bow before him.—See how the roof and pillars
Plunge to the ground!—Bromius is with us,
He shouts from prison the shout of victory!
[*The flame on Semele's tomb grows and brightens.*]

Dionysus:
Fan to a blaze the flame the lightning lit;
Kindle the conflagration of Pentheus' palace!

Chorus:
Look, look, look!
Do you see, do you see the flame of Semele's tomb,
The flame that lived when she died of the lightning-stroke?
[*A noise of crashing masonry is heard.*]
Down, trembling Maenads! Hurl yourselves to the ground.
Your god is wrecking the palace, roof to floor;
He heard our cry—he is coming, the son of Zeus!
[*The doors open and* DIONYSUS *appears.*]

Dionysus:
Women of Asia, why do you cower thus, prostrate and terrified?

---

19. Compare this speech with that of Teiresias as he predicts the fate of Oedipus in Sophodes' *Oedipus the King.*

Surely you could hear Dionysus shattering Pentheus' palace? Come,
Lift yourselves up, take good courage, stop this trembling of your limbs!

Chorus:
We are saved! Oh, what a joy to hear your Bacchic call ring out!
We were all alone, deserted; you have come, and we rejoice.

Dionysus:
Were you comfortless, despondent, when I was escorted in,
Helpless, sentenced to be cast in Pentheus' murky prison-cell?

Chorus:
Who could help it? What protector had we, once deprived of you?
Tell us now how you escaped the clutches of this wicked man.

Dionysus:
I alone, at once, unaided, effortlessly freed myself.

Chorus:
How could that be? Did not Pentheus bind your arms with knotted ropes?

Dionysus:
There I made a mockery of him. He thought he was binding me;
But he neither held nor touched me, save in his deluded mind.
Near the mangers where he meant to tie me up, he found a bull;
And he tied his rope round the bull's knees and hooves, panting with rage,
Dripping sweat, biting his lips; while I sat quietly by and watched.
It was then that Dionysus shook the building, made the flame
On his mother's tomb flare up. When Pentheus saw this, he supposed
The whole place was burning. He rushed this way, that way, calling out
To the servants to bring water; every slave about the place
Was engaged upon this futile task. He left it presently,
Thinking I had escaped; snatched up his murderous sword, darted indoors.
Thereupon Dionysus—as it seemed to me; I merely guess—
Made a phantom hover in the courtyard. Pentheus flew at it,
Stabbing at the empty sunlight, thinking he was killing *me*.
Yet a further humiliation Bacchus next contrived for him:
He destroyed the stable buildings. Pentheus sees my prison now
Lying there, a heap of rubble; and the picture grieves his heart.
Now he's dazed and helpless with exhaustion. He has dropped his sword.
He, a man, dared to take arms against a god. I quietly walked
Out of the palace here to join you, giving Pentheus not a thought.
But I hear his heavy tread inside the palace. Soon, I think,
He'll be out here in the forecourt. After what has happened now,
What will he have to say? For all his rage, he shall not ruffle *me*.
It's a wise man's part to practise a smooth-tempered self-control.

[*Enter* PENTHEUS.]

Pentheus:
This is outrageous. He has escaped—that foreigner.
Only just now I had him locked up and in chains.
[*He sees* DIONYSUS *and gives an excited shout.*]
He's there! Well, what's going on now? How did you get out?
How dare you show your face here at my very door?

Dionysus:
Stay where you are. You are angry; now control yourself.

Pentheus:
You were tied up inside there. How did you escape?

Dionysus:
I said—did you not hear?—that I should be set free—

Pentheus:
By whom? You're always finding something new to say.

Dionysus:
By him who plants for mortals the rich-clustered vine.

Pentheus:
The god who frees his worshippers from every law.

Dionysus
Your insult to Dionysus is a compliment.

Pentheus [*to attendant* GUARDS]:
Go round the walls and tell them to close every gate.

Dionysus:
And why? Or cannot gods pass even over walls?

Pentheus:
Oh, you know everything—save what you ought to know.

Dionysus:
The things most needful to be known, those things I know.
But listen first to what this man has to report;
He comes from the mountain, and he has some news for you.
I will stay here; I promise not to run away.

[*Enter a* HERDSMAN.]

Herdsman:
Pentheus, great king of Thebes! I come from Mount Cithaeron,
Whose slopes are never free from dazzling shafts of snow.

Pentheus:
And what comes next? What urgent message do you bring?

Herdsman:
I have seen the holy Bacchae, who like a flight of spears
Went streaming bare-limbed, frantic, out of the city gate.
I have come with the intention of telling you, my lord,
And the city, of their strange and terrible doings—things
Beyond all wonder. But first I would learn whether
I may speak freely of what is going on there, or
If I should trim my words. I fear your hastiness,
My lord, your anger, your too potent royalty.

Pentheus:
From me fear nothing. Say all that you have to say;
Anger should not grow hot against the innocent
The more dreadful your story of these Bacchic rites,
The heavier punishment I will inflict upon
This man who enticed our women to their evil ways.

Herdsman:
At dawn today, when first the sun's rays warmed the earth,

My herd of cattle was slowly climbing up towards
The high pastures; and there I saw three separate
Companies of women. The leader of one company
Was Autonoe; your mother Agaue was at the head
Of the second, Ino of the third; and they all lay
Relaxed and quietly sleeping. Some rested on beds
Of pine-needles, others had pillows of oak-leaves.
They lay just as they had thrown themselves down on the ground,
But modestly, not—as you told us—drunk with wine
Or flute-music, seeking the solitary woods
For the pursuit of love.
When your mother Agaue
Heard the horned cattle bellowing, she stood upright
Among the Bacchae, and called to them to stir themselves
From sleep; and they shook off the strong sleep from their eyes
And leapt to their feet. They were a sight to marvel at
For modest comeliness; women both old and young,
Girls still unmarried. First they let their hair fall free
Over their shoulders; some tied up the fastenings
Of fawnskins they had loosened; round the dappled fur
Curled snakes that licked their cheeks. Some would have in their arms
A young gazelle, or wild wolf-cubs, to which they gave
Their own white milk—those of them who had left at home
Young children newly born, so that their breasts were full.
And they wore wreathes of ivy-leaves, or oak, or flowers
Of bryony. One would strike her thyrsus on a rock,
And from the rock a limpid stream of water sprang.
Another dug her wand into the earth, and there
The god sent up a fountain of wine. Those who desired
Milk had only to scratch the earth with finger-tips,
And there was the white stream flowing for them to drink,
While from the thyrsus a sweet ooze of honey dripped.
Oh! if you had been there and seen all this, you would
Have offered prayers to this god whom you now condemn.
We herdsmen, then, and shepherds gathered to exchange
Rival reports of these strange and extraordinary
Performances; and one, who had knocked about the town,
And had a ready tongue, addressed us: 'You who live
On the holy mountain heights,' he said, 'shall we hunt down
Agaue, Pentheus' mother, and bring her back from these
Rituals, and gratify the king? What do you say?'
This seemed a good suggestion; so we hid ourselves
In the leafy bushes, waiting. When the set time came,
The women began brandishing their wands, preparing
To dance, calling in unison on the son of Zeus,
'Iacchus! Bromius!' And with them the whole mountain,
And all the creatures there, joined in the mystic rite
Of Dionysus, and with their motion all things moved.

Now, Agaue as she danced passed close to me; and I
At once leapt out from hiding, bent on capturing her.
But she called out, 'Oh, my swift-footed hounds, these men
Are hunting us. Come, follow me! Each one of you
Arm herself with the holy thyrsus, and follow me!'

So we fled, and escaped being torn in pieces by
Those possessed women. But our cattle were there, cropping
The fresh grass; and the women attacked them, with their bare hands.
You could see one take a full-uddered bellowing young heifer
And hold it by the legs with her two arms stretched wide;
Others seized on our cows and tore them limb from limb;
You'd see some ribs, or a cleft hoof, tossed high and low;
And rags of flesh hung from pine-branches, dripping blood.
Bulls, which one moment felt proud rage hot in their horns,
The next were thrown bodily to the ground, dragged down
By hands of girls in thousands; and they stripped the flesh
From the bodies faster than you could wink your royal eyes.

Then, skimming bird-like over the surface of the ground,
They scoured the plain which stretches by Asopus' banks
And yields rich crops for Thebes; and like an enemy force
They fell on Hysiae and Erythrae, two villages
On the low slopes of Cithaeron, and ransacked them both;
Snatched babies out of the houses; any plunder which
They carried on their shoulders stayed there without straps—
Nothing fell to the ground, not bronze or iron; they carried
Fire on their heads, and yet their soft hair was not burnt.
The villagers, enraged at being so plundered, armed
Themselves to resist; and then, my lord, an amazing sight
Was to be seen. The spears those men were throwing drew
No blood; but the women, hurling a thyrsus like a spear,
Dealt wounds; in short, those women turned the men to flight.
There was the power of a god in that. Then they went back
To the place where they had started from, to those fountains
The god had caused to flow for them. And they washed off
The blood; and snakes licked clean the stains, till their cheeks shone.

So, master, whoever this divinity may be,
Receive him in this land. His powers are manifold;
But chiefly, as I hear, he gave to men the vine
To cure their sorrows; and without wine, neither love
Nor any other pleasure would be left for us.

Chorus:
I shrink from speaking freely before the king; yet I
Will say it: there is no greater god than Dionysus.

Pentheus:
This Bacchic arrogance advances on us like
A spreading fire, disgracing us before all Hellas.
We must act now. [*To the* HERDSMAN] Go quickly to the Electran gate;
Tell all my men who carry shields, heavy or light,
All riders on fast horses, all my archers with
Their twanging bows, to meet me there in readiness
For an onslaught on these maniacs. This is beyond
All bearing, if we must let women so defy us.

Dionysus:
You refuse, Pentheus, to give heed to what I say
Or change your ways. Yet still, despite your wrongs to me,
I warn you: stay here quietly; do not take up arms
Against a god. Dionysus will not tolerate
Attempts to drive his worshippers from their holy hills.

Pentheus:
I'll not have you instruct me. You have escaped your chains;
Now be content—or must I punish you again?

Dionysus:
I would control my rage and sacrifice to him
If I were you, rather than kick against the goad.
Can you, a mortal, measure your strength with a god's?

Pentheus:
I'll sacrifice, yes—blood of women, massacred
Wholesale, as they deserve, among Cithaeron's glens.

Dionysus:
Your army will be put to flight. What a disgrace
For bronze shields to be routed by those women's wands!

Pentheus:
How can I deal with this impossible foreigner?
In prison or out, nothing will make him hold his tongue.

Dionysus:
My friend, a happy settlement may still be found.

Pentheus:
How? must I be a slave to my own slave-women?

Dionysus:
I will, using no weapons, bring those women here.

Pentheus:
Hear that, for the gods' sake! You're playing me some trick.

Dionysus:
What trick?—if I am ready to save you by my skill.

Pentheus:
You've planned this with them, so that the rituals can go on.

Dionysus:
Indeed I have planned this—not with them, but with the god.

Pentheus:
Bring out my armour, there!—That is enough from you.

Dionysus [*with an authoritative shout*]:
Wait! [*Then quietly*] Do you want *to see*
Those women, where they sit together, up in the hills?

Pentheus:
Why, yes; for that, I'd give a weighty sum of gold.

Dionysus:
What made you fall into this great desire to see?

Pentheus:
It would cause me distress to see them drunk with wine.

Dionysus:
Yet you would gladly witness this distressing sight?

Pentheus:
Of course—if I could quietly sit under the pines.

Dionysus:
They'll track you down, even if you go there secretly.

Pentheus:
Openly, then. Yes, what you say is very true.

Dionysus:
Then shall I lead you? You will undertake to go?

Pentheus:
Yes, lead me there at once; I am impatient.

Dionysus:
Then,
You must first dress yourself in a fine linen gown.

Pentheus:
Why in a linen gown? Must I then change my sex?

Dionysus:
In case they kill you, if you are seen there as a man.

Pentheus:
Again you are quite right. How you think of everything!

Dionysus:
It was Dionysus who inspired me with that thought.

Pentheus:
Then how can your suggestion best be carried out?

Dionysus:
I'll come indoors with you myself and dress you.

Pentheus:
What?
Dress me? In woman's clothes? But I would be ashamed.

Dionysus:
Do you want to watch the Maenads? Are you less eager now?

Pentheus:
What kind of dress did you say you would put on me?

Dionysus:
First I'll adorn your head with locks of flowing hair.

Pentheus:
And after that? What style of costume shall I have?

Dionysus:
A full-length robe; and on your head shall be a snood.

Pentheus:
Besides these, is there anything else you'll put on me?

Dionysus:
A dappled fawnskin round you, a thyrsus in your hand.

Pentheus:
I could not bear to dress myself in woman's clothes.

Dionysus:
If you join battle with the Maenads, blood will flow.

Pentheus:
You are right; I must first go to spy on them.

Dionysus:
That way
Is better than inviting force by using it.

Pentheus:
And how shall I get through the town without being seen?

Dionysus:
We'll go by empty streets; I will show you the way.

Pentheus:
The Maenads must not mock me; better anything
Than that. Now I'll go in, and think how best to act.

Dionysus:
You may do so. My preparations are all made.

Pentheus:
I'll go in, then; and either I'll set forth at the head
Of my armed men—or else I'll follow your advice.
[*Exit* PENTHEUS.]

Dionysus:
Women, this man is walking into the net. He will
Visit the Bacchae; and there death shall punish him.

Dionysus!—for you are not far distant—all is now
In your hands. Let us be revenged on him! And first
Fill him with wild delusions, drive him out of his mind.
While sane, he'll not consent to put on woman's clothes;
Once free from the curb of reason, he will put them on.
I long to set Thebes laughing at him, as he walks
In female garb through all the streets; to humble him
From the arrogance he showed when first he threatened me.

Now I will go, to array Pentheus in the dress
Which he will take down with him to the house of Death,
Slaughtered by his own mother's hands. And he shall know
Dionysus, son of Zeus, in his full nature God,
Most terrible, although most gentle, to mankind.
[DIONYSUS *follows* PENTHEUS *into the palace.*]

Chorus:

O for long nights of worship, gay *Strophe*
With the pale gleam of dancing feet,
With head tossed high to the dewy air—
Pleasure mysterious and sweet!
O for the joy of a fawn at play
In the fragrant meadow's green delight,
Who has leapt out free from the woven snare,
Away from the terror of chase and flight,
And the huntsman's shout, and the straining pack,
And skims the sand by the river's brim
With the speed of wind in each aching limb,
To the blessed lonely forest where
The soil's unmarked by a human track,
And leaves hang thick and the shades are dim.

What prayer should we call wise? *Refrain*
What gift of Heaven should man
Count a more noble prize,
A prayer more prudent, than
To stretch a conquering arm
Over the fallen crest
Of those who wished us harm?
And what is noble every heart loves best.

Slow, yet unfailing, move the Powers *Antistrophe*
Of heaven with the moving hours.
When mind runs mad, dishonours God,
And worships self and senseless pride,
Then Law eternal wields the rod.
Still Heaven hunts down the impious man,
Though divine subtlety may hide
Time's creeping foot. No mortal ought
To challenge Time—to overbear
Custom in act, or age in thought.
All men, at little cost, may share
The blessing of a pious creed;
Truths more than mortal, which began
In the beginning, and belong
To very nature—these indeed
Reign in our world, are fixed and strong.

What prayer should we call wise? *Refrain*
What gift of heaven should man
Count a more noble prize,
A prayer more prudent, than
To stretch a conquering arm
Over the fallen crest
Of those who wished us harm?
And what is noble every heart loves best.

Blest is the man who cheats the stormy sea *Epode*
And safely moors beside the sheltering quay;
So, blest is he who triumphs over trial.
One man, by various means, in wealth or strength
Outdoes his neighbour; hope in a thousand hearts
Colours a thousand different dreams; at length
Some find a dear fulfilment, some denial.
But this I say,
That he who best
Enjoys each passing day
Is truly blest.

[*Enter* DIONYSUS. *He turns to call* PENTHEUS.]

Dionysus:

Come, perverse man, greedy for sights you should not see,
Eager for deeds you should not do—Pentheus! Come out
Before the palace and show yourself to me, wearing
The garb of a frenzied Bacchic woman, and prepared
To spy on your mother and all her Bacchic company.
[*Enter* PENTHEUS *dressed as a Bacchic devotee. He is dazed and entirely subservient to* DIONYSUS.]

You are the very image of one of Cadmus' daughters.

Pentheus:

Why now! I seem to see two suns; a double Thebes;
Our city's wall with seven gates appears double.
[DIONYSUS *takes* PENTHEUS *by the hand and leads him forward.*]

You are a bull I see leading me forward now;
A pair of horns seems to have grown upon your head.
Were you a beast before? You have become a bull.

Dionysus:

The god then did not favour us; he is with us now,
We have made our peace with him; you see as you should see.

Pentheus:

How do I look? Tell me, is not the way I stand
Like the way Ino stands, or like my mother Agaue?

Dionysus:

Looking at you, I think I see them both. Wait, now;
Here is a curl has slipped out of its proper place,
Not as I tucked it carefully below your snood.

Pentheus:

Indoors, as I was tossing my head up and down
Like a Bacchic dancer, I dislodged it from its place.

Dionysus:

Come, then; I am the one who should look after you.
I'll fix it in its place again. There; lift your head.

Pentheus:

You dress me, please; I have put myself in your hands now.

Dionysus:

Your girdle has come loose; and now your dress does not
Hang, as it should, in even pleats down to the ankle.

Pentheus:

That's true, I think—at least by the right leg, on this side;
But on the other side the gown hangs well to the heel.

Dionysus:

You'll surely count me chief among your friends, when you
Witness the Maenads' unexpected modesty.

Pentheus:

Ought I to hold my thyrsus in the right hand—so,
Or in the left, to look more like a Bacchanal?

Dionysus:

In the right hand; and raise it at the same time as
Your right foot. I am glad you are so changed in mind.

Pentheus:

Could I lift up on my own shoulders the whole weight
Of Mount Cithaeron, and all the women dancing there?

Dionysus:

You could, if you so wished. The mind you had before
Was sickly; now your mind is just as it should be.

Pentheus:
Shall we take crowbars? Or shall I put my shoulder under
The rocks, and heave the mountain up with my two arms?

Dionysus:
Oh, come, now! Don't destroy the dwellings of the nymphs,
And the quiet places where Pan sits to play his pipes.

Pentheus:
You are right. We ought not to use force to overcome
Those women. I will hide myself among the pines.

Dionysus:
Hide—yes, you'll hide, and find the proper hiding-place
For one who comes by stealth to spy on Bacchic rites.

Pentheus:
Why, yes! I think they are there now in their hidden nests,
Like birds, all clasped close in the sweet prison of love.

Dionysus:
What you are going to watch for is this very thing!
Perhaps you will catch them—if you are not first caught yourself.

Pentheus:
Now take me through the central streets of Thebes; for I
Am the one man among them all that dares do this.

Dionysus:
One man alone, you agonise for Thebes; therefore
It is your destined ordeal that awaits you now.
Come with me; I will bring you safely to the place;
Another shall conduct you back.

Pentheus:
My mother—yes?

Dionysus:
A sight for all to witness.

Pentheus:
To this end I go.

Dionysus:
You will return borne high—

Pentheus:
Royal magnificence!

Dionysus:
In your own mother's arms.

Pentheus:
You insist that I be spoiled.

Dionysus:
One kind of spoiling.

Pentheus:
Yet I win what I deserve.

[*Exit* PENTHEUS.]

Dionysus:
Pentheus, you are a man to make men fear; fearful
Will be your end—an end that shall lift up your fame
To the height of heaven.
Agaue, and you her sisters, daughters of Cadmus,
Stretch out your hands! See, I am bringing this young man
To his great battle; and I and Bromius shall be
Victors. What more shall happen, the event will show.

[*Exit* DIONYSUS.]

Chorus:
Hounds of Madness, fly to the mountain, fly *Strophe*
Where Cadmus' daughters are dancing in ecstasy!
Madden them like a frenzied herd stampeding,
Against the madman hiding in woman's clothes
To spy on the Maenad's rapture!
First his mother shall see him craning his neck
Down from a rounded rock or a sharp crag.
And shout to the Maenads, 'Who is the man, you Bacchae,
Who has come to the mountain, come to the mountain spying
On the swift wild mountain—dances of Cadmus' daughters?
Which of you is his mother?
No, that lad never lay in a woman's womb;
A lioness gave him suck, or a Libyan Gorgon!'

Justice, now be revealed! Now let your sword
Thrust—through and through—to sever the throat
Of the godless, lawless, shameless son of Echion,
Who sprang from the womb of Earth!

See! With contempt of right, with a reckless rage *Antistrophe*
To combat your and your mother's mysteries, Bacchus,
With maniac fury out he goes, stark mad,
For a trial of strength against *your* invincible arm!
His proud purposes death shall discipline.
He who unquestioning gives the gods their due,
And knows that his days are as dust, shall live untouched.
I have no wish to grudge the wise their wisdom;
But the joys *I* seek are greater, outshine all others,
And lead our life to goodness and loveliness:
The joy of the holy heart
That night and day is bent to honour the gods
And disown all custom that breaks the bounds of right.

Justice, now be revealed! Now let your sword
Thrust—through and through—to sever the throat
Of the godless, lawless, shameless son of Echion,
Who sprang from the womb of Earth!

[*Then with growing excitement, shouting in unison, and dancing to the rhythm of their words.*]

Come, Dionysus! *Epode*
Come, and appear to us!
Come like a bull or a
Hundred-headed serpent,
Come like a lion snorting
Flame from your nostrils!
Swoop down, Bacchus, on the
Hunter of the Bacchae;
Smile at him and snare him;
Then let the stampeding
Herd of the Maenads
Throw him and throttle him,
Catch, trip, trample him to death!

[*Enter a* MESSENGER.]

Messenger:
O house that once shone glorious throughout Hellas, home
Of the old Sidonian king who planted in this soil
The dragon's earth-born harvest! How I weep for you!
Slave though I am, I suffer with my master's fate.

Chorus:
Are you from the mountain, from the Bacchic rites? What news?

Messenger:
Pentheus, son of Echion, is dead.

Chorus:
Bromius, lord! Your divine power is revealed!

Messenger:
What, woman? What was that you said? Do you exult
When such a cruel fate has overtaken the king?

Chorus:
I am no Greek.
I sing my joy in a foreign tune.
Not any more do I cower in terror of prison!

Messenger:
Do you think Thebes has no men left who can take command?

Chorus:
Dionysus commands *me;*
Not Thebes, but Dionysus.

Messenger:
Allowance must be made for you; yet, to rejoice
At the accomplishment of horrors, is not right.

Chorus:
Tell us everything, then: this tyrant king
Bent on cruelty—how did he die?

Messenger:
When we had left behind the outlying parts of Thebes
And crossed the river Asopus, we began to climb
Toward the uplands of Cithaeron, Pentheus and I—
I went as his attendant—and the foreigner
Who was our guide to the spectacle we were to see.
Well, first we sat down in a grassy glade. We kept
Our footsteps and our talk as quiet as possible,
So as to see without being seen. We found ourselves
In a valley full of streams, with cliffs on either side.
There, under the close shade of branching pines, the Maenads
Were sitting, their hands busy at their happy tasks;
Some of them twining a fresh crown of ivy-leaves
For a stripped thyrsus; others, gay as fillies loosed
From painted yokes, were singing holy Bacchic songs,
Each answering other. But the ill-fated Pentheus saw
None of this; and he said, 'My friend, from where we stand
My eyes cannot make out these so-called worshippers;
But if I climbed a towering pine-tree on the cliff
I would have a clear view of their shameful practices.'

And then I saw that foreigner do an amazing thing.
He took hold of a pine-tree's soaring, topmost branch,
And dragged it down, down, down to the dark earth. It was bent
In a circle as a bow is bent, as a wheel's curve,
Drawn with a compass, bends the rim to its own shape;
The foreigner took that mountain-pine in his two hands
And bent it down—a thing no mortal man could do.
Then seating Pentheus on a high branch, he began
To let the tree spring upright, slipping it through his hands
Steadily, taking care he should not be flung off.
The pine-trunk, straightened, soared into the soaring sky,
Bearing my master seated astride, so that he was
More visible to the Maenads than they were to him.
He was just coming into view on his high perch,
When out of the sky a voice—Dionysus, I suppose;
That foreigner was nowhere to be seen—pealed forth:
'Women, here is the man who made a mock of you,
And me, and of my holy rites. Now punish him.'
And in the very moment the voice spoke, a flash
Of dreadful fire stretched between earth and high heaven.

The air fell still. The wooded glade held every leaf
Still. You could hear no cry of any beast. The women,
Not having caught distinctly what the voice uttered,
Stood up and gazed around. Then came a second word
Of command. As soon as Cadmus' daughters recognised
The clear bidding of Bacchus, with the speed of doves
They darted forward, and all the Bacchae after them.
Through the torrent-filled valley, over the rocks, possessed
By the very breath of Bacchus they went leaping on.
Then, when they saw my master crouched high in the pine,
At first they climbed the cliff which towered opposite,
And violently flung at him pieces of rocks, or boughs
Of pine-trees which they hurled as javelins; and some
Aimed with the thyrsus; through the high air all around
Their wretched target missiles flew. Yet every aim
Fell short, the tree's height baffled all their eagerness;
While Pentheus, helpless in this pitiful trap, sat there.
Then, with a force like lightning, they tore down branches
Of oak, and with these tried to prize up the tree's roots.
When all their struggles met with no success, Agaue
Cried out, 'Come, Maenads, stand in a circle round the tree
And take hold of it. We must catch this climbing beast,
Or he'll disclose the secret dances of Dionysus.'
They came; a thousand hands gripped on the pine and tore it
Out of the ground. Then from his high perch plunging, crashing
To the earth Pentheus fell, with one incessant scream
As he understood what end was near.

His mother first,
As priestess, led the rite of death, and fell upon him.
He tore the headband from his hair, that his wretched mother
Might recognise him and not kill him. 'Mother,' he cried,
Touching her cheek, 'it is I, your own son Pentheus, whom
You bore to Echion. Mother, have mercy; I have sinned,
But I am still your own son. Do not take my life!'

Agaue was foaming at the mouth; her rolling eyes
Were wild; she was not in her right mind, but possessed
By Bacchus, and she paid no heed to him. She grasped
His right arm between wrist and elbow, set her foot
Against his ribs, and tore his arm off by the shoulder.
It was no strength of hers that did it, but the god
Filled her, and made it easy. On the other side
Ino was at him, tearing at his flesh; and now
Autonoe joined them, and the whole maniacal horde.
A single and continuous yell arose—Pentheus
Shrieking as long as life was left in him, the women
Howling in triumph. One of them carried off an arm,
Another a foot, the boot still laced on it. The ribs
Were stripped, clawed clean; and women's hands, thick red with blood,
Were tossing, catching, like a plaything, Pentheus' flesh.

His body lies—no easy task to find—scattered
Under hard rocks, or in the green woods. His poor head—
His mother carries it, fixed on her thyrsus-point,
Openly over Cithaeron's pastures, thinking it
The head of a young mountain-lion. She has left her sisters
Dancing among the Maenads, and herself comes here
Inside the walls, exulting in her hideous prey,
Shouting to Bacchus, calling him her fellow-hunter,
Her partner in the kill, comrade in victory.
But Bacchus gives her bitter tears for her reward.

Now I will go. I must find some place far away
From this horror, before Agaue returns home.
A sound and humble heart that reverences the gods
Is man's noblest possession; and the same virtue
Is wisest too, I think, for those who practise it.

[*Exit the* MESSENGER.]

Chorus:
Let us dance a dance to Bacchus, shout and sing
For the fall of Pentheus, heir of the dragon's seed,
Who hid his beard in a woman's gown,
And sealed his death with the holy sign
Of ivy wreathing a fennel-reed,
When bull led man to the ritual slaughter-ring.
Frenzied daughters of Cadmus, what renown
Your victory wins you—such a song
As groans must stifle, tears must drown!

Emblem of conquest, brave and fine!—
A mother's hand, defiled
With blood and dripping red
Caresses the torn head
Of her own murdered child!

But look! I see her—there, running towards the palace—
Agaue, Pentheus' mother, her eyes wildly rolling.
Come, welcome them—Dionysus' holy company.

[AGAUE *appears, frenzied and panting, with* PENTHEUS' *head held in her hand. The rest of her band of devotees, whom the* CHORUS *saw approaching with her, do not enter; but a few are seen standing by the entrance, where they wait until the end of the play.*]

Agaue:
Women of Asia! Worshippers of Bacchus!

[AGAUE *tries to show them* PENTHEUS' *head; they shrink from it.*]

Chorus:
Why do you urge me? Oh!

Agaue:
I am bringing home from the mountains
A vine-branch freshly cut,
For the gods have blessed our hunting.

Chorus:
We see it . . . and welcome you in fellowship.

Agaue:
I caught him without a trap,
A lion-cub, young and wild.
Look, you may see him: there!

Chorus:
Where was it?

Agaue:
On Cithaeron;
The wild and empty mountain—

Chorus:
Cithaeron!

Agaue:
. . . spilt his life-blood.

Chorus:
Who shot him?

Agaue:
I was first;
All the women are singing,
'Honour to great Agaue!'

Chorus:
And then—who next?

Agaue:
Why, Cadmus' . . .

Chorus:
What—Cadmus?

Agaue:
Yes, his daughters—
But after me, after me—
Laid their hands to the kill.
To-day was a splendid hunt!
Come now, join in the feast!

Chorus:
What, wretched woman? *Feast?*

Agaue: [*tenderly stroking the head as she holds it*]: This calf is young: how thickly
The new-grown hair goes crisping
Up to his delicate crest!

Chorus:
Indeed, his long hair makes him
Look like some wild creature.

Agaue:
The god is a skilled hunter?
And he poised his hunting women,
And hurled them at the quarry.

Chorus:
True, our god is a hunter.

Agaue:
Do you praise me?

Chorus:
Yes, we praise you.

Agaue:
So will the sons of Cadmus . . .

Chorus:
And Pentheus too, Agaue?[20]

Agaue:
Yes he will praise his mother
For the lion-cub she killed.

Chorus:
Oh, fearful!

Agaue:
Ay, fearful!

Chorus:
You are happy?

Agaue:
I am enraptured;
Great in the eyes of the world,
Great are the deeds I've done,
And the hunt that I hunted there!

Chorus:
Then show it, poor Agaue—this triumphant spoil
You've brought home; show it to all the citizens of Thebes.

---

20. *And Pentheus too, Agaue?* the chorus are physically shocked by the sight of Agaue and her prey; but their attitude does not change to pity. Agaue has been (in their view, justly) punished for her blasphemy against Dionysus, by being tricked into performing the usual Bacchic rite of slaughter, not upon the usual victim, a beast, but upon a man, and that her own son. She is now an abhorred and polluted creature, unfit for the company of the 'pure' Bacchae. Hence, though they welcome the punishment of Pentheus, their tone towards Agaue is one not of admiration but of contempt. This line in particular indicates the complete absence of pity.

Agaue:
Come, all you Thebans living within these towered walls,
Come, see the beast we, Cadmus' daughters, caught and killed;
Caught not with nets or thonged Thessalian javelins,
But with our own bare arms and fingers. After this
Should huntsmen glory in their exploits, who must buy
Their needless tools from armourers? We with our hands
Hunted and took this beast, then tore it limb from limb.

Where is my father? Let old Cadmus come. And where
Is my son Pentheus? Let him climb a strong ladder
And nail up on the cornice of the palace wall
This lion's head that I have hunted and brought home.
[*Enter* CADMUS *with attendants bearing the body of PENTHEUS.*]

Cadmus:
Come, men, bring your sad burden that was Pentheus. Come,
Set him at his own door. By weary, endless search
I found his body's remnants scattered far and wide
About Cithaeron's glens, or hidden in thick woods.
I gathered them and brought them here.

I had already
Returned with old Teiresias from the Bacchic dance,
And was inside the walls, when news was brought me of
My daughters' terrible deed. I turned straight back; and now
Return, bringing my grandson, whom the Maenads killed.
I saw Autonoe, who bore Actaeon to Aristaeus,
And Ino with her, there among the trees, still rapt
In their unhappy frenzy; but I understood
That Agaue had come dancing on her way to Thebes—
And there indeed she is, a sight for misery!

Agaue:
Father! Now you may boast as loudly as you will
That you have sired the noblest daughters of this age!
I speak of all three, but myself especially.
I have left weaving at the loom for greater things,
For hunting wild beasts with my bare hands. See this prize,
Here in my arms; I won it, and it shall be hung
On your palace wall. There, father, take it in your hands.
Be proud of my hunting; call your friends to a feast; let them
Bless you and envy you for the splendour of my deed.

Cadmus:
Oh, misery unmeasured, sight intolerable!
Oh, bloody deed enacted by most pitiful hands!
What noble prize is this you lay at the gods' feet,
Calling the city, and me, to a banquet? Your wretchedness
Demands the bitterest tears; but mine is next to yours.
Dionysus has dealt justly, but pursued justice
Too far; born of my blood, he has destroyed my house.

Agaue:
What an ill-tempered creature an old man is! How full
Of scowls! I wish my son were a great hunter like
His mother, hunting beasts with the young men of Thebes;
But *he* can only fight with gods. Father, you must
Correct him.—Will not someone go and call him here
To see me, and to share in my great happiness?

Cadmus:
Alas, my daughters! If you come to understand
What you have done, how terrible your pain will be!
If you remain as you are now, though you could not
Be happy, at least you will not feel your wretchedness.

Agaue:
Why not happy? What cause have I for wretchedness?

Cadmus:
Come here. First turn your eyes this way. Look at the sky.

Agaue:
I am looking. Why should you want me to look at it?

Cadmus:
Does it appear the same to you, or is it changed?

Agaue:
Yes, it is clearer than before, more luminous.

Cadmus:
And this disturbance of your mind—is it still there?

Agaue:
I don't know what you mean; but—yes, I feel a change;
My mind is somehow clearer than it was before.

Cadmus:
Could you now listen to me and give a clear reply?

Agaue:
Yes, father. I have forgotten what we said just now.

Cadmus:
When you were married, whose house did you go to then?

Agaue:
You gave me to Echion, of the sown race, they said.

Cadmus:
Echion had a son born to him. Who was he?

Agaue:
Pentheus. His father lay with me; I bore a son.

Cadmus:
Yes; and whose head is that you are holding in your arms?

Agaue:
A lion's—so the women said who hunted it.

Cadmus:
Then look straight at it. Come, to look is no great task.
[AGAUE *looks; and suddenly screams.*]

Agaue:
What am I looking at? What is this in my hands?

Cadmus:
Look at it steadily; come closer to the truth.

Agaue:
I see—O gods, what horror! Oh, what misery!

Cadmus:
Does this appear to you to be a lion's head?

Agaue:
No! I hold Pentheus' head in my accursed hand.

Cadmus:
It is so. Tears have been shed for him, before you knew.

Agaue:
But who killed him? How did he come into my hands?

Cadmus:
O cruel hour, that brings a bitter truth to light!

Agaue:
Tell me—my heart is bursting, I must know the rest.

Cadmus:
It was you, Agaue, and your sisters. You killed him.

Agaue:
Where was it done? Here in the palace? Or where else?

Cadmus:
Where, long ago, Actaeon was devoured by hounds.

Agaue:
Cithaeron, But what evil fate took Pentheus there?

Cadmus:
He went to mock Dionysus and your Bacchic rites.

Agaue:
Why were we on Cithaeron? What had brought us there.

Cadmus:
You were possessed. All Thebes was in a Bacchic trance.

Agaue:
Dionysus has destroyed us. Now I understand.

Cadmus:
He was insulted. You refused to call him god.

Agaue:
Father, where is the beloved body of my son?

Cadmus:
Here. It was I who brought it, after painful search.

Agaue:
And are his limbs now decently composed?

Cadmus:
Not yet.
We came back to the city with all possible haste.

Agaue:
How could I touch his body with these guilty hands?

Cadmus:
Your guilt, my daughter, was not heavier than his.

Agaue:
What part did Pentheus have, then, in my insanity?

Cadmus:
He sinned like you, refusing reverence to a god.
Therefore the god has joined all in one ruin—you,
Your sisters, Pentheus—to destroy my house and me.
I have no son; and now, my unhappy child, I see
This son of yours dead by a shameful, hideous death.
You were the new hope of our house, its bond of strength,
Dear grandson. And Thebes feared you; no one dared insult
Your old grandfather if he saw you near; you would
Teach him his lesson. But now I shall live exiled,
Dishonoured—I, Cadmus the great, who planted here,
And reaped, that glorious harvest of the Theban race.

O dearest son—yes, even in death you shall be held
Most dear—you will never touch my beard again, and call
Me Grandfather, and put your arm round me and say,
'Who has wronged you or insulted you? Who is unkind,
Or vexes or disturbs you? Tell me, Grandfather,
That I may punish him.' Never again. For me
All that remains is pain; for you, the pity of death;
For your mother, tears; torment for our whole family.

If any man derides the unseen world, let him
Ponder the death of Pentheus, and believe in gods.

Chorus:
I grieve for your fate, Cadmus; though your grandson's death
Was justly merited, it falls cruelly on you.

Agaue:
Father, you see how one disastrous day has shattered
My whole life . . .

[At this point the two MSS on which the text of this play depends show a lacuna of considerable extent; it covers the end of this scene, in which Agaue mourns over Pentheus' body, and the appearance of Dionysus manifested as a god. The MSS resume in the middle of a speech by Dionysus. A number of quotations by ancient authors, together with less than 20 lines from *Christus Patiens* (an anonymous A.D. 4th-century work consisting largely of lines adapted from Greek tragedies) make it possible to attempt a guess at the content of the missing lines. Since this play is often performed, it seems worthwhile to provide here a usable text. In the lines that follow, the words printed in italics are mere conjecture, and have no value except as a credible completion of the probable sense; while those in Roman type represent the sources available from *Christus Patiens* and elsewhere.]

. . . my whole life, *turned my pride to shame, my happiness*
To horror. Now my only wish is to compose
My son's body for burial, and lament for him;
And then die. But this is not lawful; for my hands
Are filthy with pollution of their own making.
When I have spilt the blood I bore, and torn the flesh
That grew in my own womb, how can I after this
Enfold him to my breast, or chant his ritual dirge?
And yet, I beg you, pity me, and let me touch
My son, and say farewell to that dear body which
I cherished, and destroyed unknowing. It is right
That you should pity, for your hands are innocent.

Cadmus:
My daughter, you and I and our whole house are crushed
And broken by the anger of this powerful god.
It is not for me to keep you from your son. Only
Be resolute, and steel your heart against a sight
Which must be fearful to any eyes, but most of all
To a mother's. (To attendants) Men, put down your burden on the ground
Before Agaue, and remove the covering.

Agaue:
Dear child, how cruel, how unnatural are these tears,
Which should have fallen from your eyes on my dead face.
Now I shall die with none to mourn me. This is just;
For in my pride I did not recognise the god,
Nor understand the things I ought to have understood.
You too are punished for the same impiety;
But which is the more terrible, your fate or mine,
I cannot tell. Since you have suffered too, you will
Forgive both what I did, not knowing what I did,
And what I do now, touching you with unholy hands—
At once your cruellest enemy and your dearest friend.

I place your limbs as they should lie; I kiss the flesh
That my own body nourished and my own care reared
To manhood. Help me, father; lay his poor head here.
Make all exact and seemly, with what care we can.
O dearest face, O young fresh cheek? O kingly eyes,
Your light now darkened! O my son! See, with this veil
I now cover your head, your torn and bloodstained limbs.

Take him up, carry him to burial, a king
Lured to a shameful death by the anger of a god.
[*Enter* DIONYSUS.]

Chorus:
But look! Who is this, rising above the palace door?
It is he—Dionysus comes himself, no more disguised
As mortal, but in the glory of his divinity!

Dionysus:
Behold me, a god great and powerful, Dionysus,
The son whom Theban Semele bore to immortal Zeus.
I come to the city of seven gates, to famous Thebes,
Whose people slighted me, denied my divinity,
Refused my ritual dances. Now they reap the fruit
Of impious folly. The royal house is overthrown;
The city's streets tremble in guilt, as every Theban
Repents too late his blindness and his blasphemy.
Foremost in sin was Pentheus, who not only scorned
My claims, but put me in fetters and insulted me.
Therefore death came to him in the most shameful way,
At his own mother's hands. This fate he justly earned;
No god can see his worship scorned, and hear his name
Profaned, and not take vengeance to the utmost limit.
Thus men may learn that gods are more powerful than they.

Agaue and her sisters must immediately
Depart from Thebes; their exile will be just penance
For the pollution which this blood has brought on them.
Never again shall they enjoy their native land;
That such defilement ever should appear before
The city's altars, is an offence to piety.

Now, Cadmus, hear what suffering Fate appoints for you.
[Here the MSS resume.]

You shall transmute your nature, and become a serpent.
Your wife Harmonia, whom her father Ares gave
To you, a mortal, likewise shall assume the nature
Of beasts, and live a snake. The oracle of Zeus
Foretells that you, at the head of a barbaric horde,
Shall with your wife drive forth a pair of heifers yoked,
And with your countless army destroy many cities;
But when they plunder Loxias' oracle, they shall find
A miserable homecoming. However, Ares shall
At last deliver both you and Harmonia,
And grant you immortal life among the blessed gods.

I who pronounce these fates am Dionysus, begotten
Not by a mortal father, but by Zeus. If you
Had chosen wisdom, when you would not, you would have lived
In wealth and safety, having the son of Zeus your friend.

Cadmus:
Have mercy on us, Dionysus. We have sinned.

Dionysus:
You know too late. You did not know me when you should.

Cadmus:
We acknowledge this; but your revenge is merciless.

Dionysus:
And rightly; I am a god, and you insulted me.

Cadmus:
Gods should not be like mortals in vindictiveness.

Dionysus:
All this my father Zeus ordained from the beginning.

Agaue:
No hope, father. Our harsh fate is decreed: exile.

Dionysus:
Then why put off a fate which is inevitable?
[*Exit* DIONYSUS.]

Cadmus:
Dear child, what misery has overtaken us all—
You, and your sisters, and your old unhappy father!
I must set forth from home and live in barbarous lands;
Further than that, it is foretold that I shall lead
A mixed barbarian horde to Hellas. And my wife,
Harmonia, Ares' daughter, and I too, must take
The brutish form of serpents; and I am to lead her thus
At the head of an armed force, to desecrate the tombs
And temples of our native land. I am to reach
No respite from this curse; I may not even cross
The downward stream of Acheron to find peace in death.

Agaue:
And I in exile, father, shall live far from you.

Cadmus:
Poor child, why do you cling to me, as the young swan
Clings fondly to the old, helpless and white with age?

Agaue:
Where can I turn for comfort, homeless and exiled?

Cadmus:
I do not know. Your father is little help to you.

Agaue:
Farewell, my home; farewell the land I know.
Exiled, accursed and wretched, now I go
Forth from this door where first I came a bride.

Cadmus:
Go, daughter, find some secret place to hide
Your shame and sorrow.

Agaue:
Father, I weep for you.

Cadmus:
I for your suffering, and your sisters' too.

Agaue:
There is strange tyranny in the god who sent
Against your house this cruel punishment.

Cadmus:
Not strange: our citizens despised his claim,
And you, and they, put him to open shame.

Agaue:
Father, farewell.

Cadmus:
Poor child! I cannot tell
How you can *fare well;* yet I say, Farewell.

Agaue:
I go to lead my sisters by the hand
To share my wretchedness in a foreign land.
[*She turns to the Theban women who have been waiting at the edge of the stage.*]
Come, see me forth.
Gods, lead me to some place
Where loath'd Cithaeron may not see my face,
Nor I Cithaeron. I have had my fill
Of mountain-ecstasy; now take who will
My holy ivy-wreath, my thyrsus-rod,
All that reminds me how I served this god!
[*Exit, followed by* CADMUS.]

Chorus:
Gods manifest themselves in many forms,
Bring many matters to surprising ends;
The things we thought would happen do not happen;
The unexpected God makes possible:
And that is what has happened here to-day.

[*Exeunt.*]

One Question for Discussion

In a world governed by a god like Dionysus, where is justice? How can men plan their lives?

UNIT III

ROME: The International Culture

CHAPTER 9

Rome: The Failure of Professionalism

■ Contrasts between the Greek view of life and the Roman are easy to find. For example, when Greece had beaten back the Persians in 480 B.C. and had embarked on the glorious fifth century in Athens, the dramatist Aeschylus in a number of plays developed the theme of the nobility of the human spirit, and suggested the ways in which that nobility might be preserved. When Rome had conquered Carthage in the second Punic War, and had become the ruler of the entire Mediterranean area, the artistic spokesman was the writer of comedy Plautus (PLAW-tus), who borrowed his form from the second-rate Greek comic writers and wrote a number of plays full of already-stock-characters for the pure amusement of his audiences; plays which are about as subtle in their appeal as a kick with a frozen boot.

Or, when Pericles set forth the Athenian ideal in his Funeral Oration, he spoke with greatest pride of the individual Athenian who could adapt himself to all types of activity with the utmost versatility and grace. In a roughly similar time the Roman Augustus boasted that he had found Rome a city of brick, and had left it a city of marble. The Greek praised the wonder of the human personality; the Roman praised physical things and physical accomplishments.

But one can make other contrasts. The greatness of Periclean Athens lasted for only about fifty years. Rome, through its legal system, established peace within the borders of its great empire from about the time of the accession of Augustus in 31 B.C. until the death of Marcus Aurelius (aw-REE-lee-us) in A.D. 180. If we take warfare on the borders—in Britain, Germany, along the Danube, in faraway Asia, and Africa—as a necessary condition of great empire, the establishment of a body of law which could maintain peace within the boundaries for more than two centuries is a magnificent practical achievement of Rome which the Greeks, with their fierce independence could never approach.

Or, in Rome, women were granted equality with their husbands, and the strength and virtue of the Roman matron is a tradition (even though that female strength in the ruling houses often expressed itself in poison for her husband). Greek women, with the exception of a few courtesans, lived as second- or third-class citizens.

Such comparisons could be made almost indefinitely. Both civilizations, until their later years at least, were rational and trusted their minds rather than their emotions or their faith to lead them toward their idea of truth. But how differently rationalism can proceed! The Greeks in their philosophic speculation asked the ultimate question, "Why?" The Romans simply asked, "How can we get the job done?" The latter is the pragmatic approach. The Greek question leads to the abstract speculation of the great philosophers; the Roman query results in big government, big army, big buildings. Greek art, whether it be sculpture or literature, takes a natural object and creates an abstraction of it, seeking its essential characteristic, its inner truth. Roman art, sculpture in particular, takes a natural object and renders it exactly as seen by the eye with almost total naturalism. The Romans answered their question of how to get the job done by deciding that it would be best and most efficiently done by experts, by professionals. The Greek method encouraged the amateur to develop his personality in varied activities. History shows that neither is the completely "right" answer, but in terms of our search for personal freedom, Roman professionalism seems to have been an almost complete failure.

SOME LANDMARKS OF ROMAN HISTORY

The traditional date for the founding of Rome is 753 B.C. At that time it was a village on the strategically situated Palatine (PAL-uh-tine) Hill; a village which, under the rule of the almost legendary kings, notable among whom were the Tarquins who were Etruscans and brought much Greek skill and craftsmanship to the growing Roman state, rapidly extended its influence to other villages on the neighboring hills. The kings were expelled in 509 B.C., and a republic established with the senate as the governing body.

The republic lasted from 509 B.C. to the reign of Julius Caesar in 48 B.C. and its early years constitute the great age when all the virtues which the later Romans revered guided the lives of the people. In their religion they worshipped a number of gods which had no physical embodiment; they were gods who sanctified boundaries, a god which embodied fortune, a god which was responsible for the fructifying of the earth, a god, Janus (hence our month of January), which looked both outward and inward from the portals of the house to ward off outside enemies and preserve harmony within. These are all very practical gods, each with a job to do in a society which was agricultural. This was a society based primarily on the family-sized farm, and upon the Roman as citizen-farmer-soldier with most of the puritan virtues of frugality, complete honesty, loyalty, and hard work. Such qualities lead almost inevitably to material success but not necessarily to personal freedom.

Prosperity did come to the republic and with it the establishment of government and military success, first in Italy and later throughout the Mediterranean world. The governing power was first entrusted to the senate, originally the advisers to the kings, and essentially a body of the aristocracy. The actual administration of the law was put into the hands of two consuls of equal power. Later, a growing number of common people, the Plebeians (pluh-BEE-uns), demanded a voice in the government, and were given an officer, the tribune, who, at first, merely presented the opinion of the commoners to the senate, but later were given power to nullify the acts of the consuls. During this time, too, various assemblies came into being: the assembly curiata (the assembly of the tribes) which was convened to gather the opinion of the common people, and the assembly centuriata (an assembly based on military groups). These assemblies, together with the original officers and others (praetors, aediles, censors) continued throughout the entire history of Rome with a varied extension and diminution of power. A further necessary step in government came at the same time as the appointment of tribunes, for the law had always been a collection of customs which were simply remembered by the senate and the consuls. In 451 B.C. a body of ten men was appointed to collect and write down a legal code—the Twelve Tables of Law—which had the same effect as Draco's Code in Greece. From that time forth, the law was known to all people.

Militarily the Roman virtues led to a gradual conquest of almost all of Italy, Sicily, Corsica, and Spain. Here the Romans came into contact with the Greek cities which had long been established throughout the Mediterranean world and, in particular the city of Carthage, once a Phoenician colony, which had surpassed its mother city as the chief commercial and trading center of the area. The total destruction of Carthage was accomplished in three wars, but, for all practical purposes it was made a dependent of Rome at the end of the second war in 201 B.C. Later, in the Macedonian Wars, Rome took over most of the great empire which had once belonged to Alexander.

This conquest brought the downfall of the Roman virtues which had brought the original success. In the first place, Rome captured hundreds of thousands of slaves who were brought to Italy where, slave labor being cheaper than free labor, they supplanted the small independent farmers who had been the backbone of Roman society. In the second place, many of the small farmers came to the city of Rome, where they became a vast army of unemployed, ready to sell their votes to any wealthy family who would supply them with bread and free shows. In Caesar's time this proletariat numbered 320,000 in the city of Rome alone. A third great problem was general misgovernment, particularly in the provinces, for the provincial governors were usually ambitious political or military men who would serve for a year or two in a province to make enough money to further their ambitions at home. Taxes in the provinces were usually farmed out; that is, a group of investors in Rome would simply buy from the Roman government the right to tax in a certain area. Then the investment company would send its own agents out to collect taxes—as much as the traffic would bear—to recoup their original investment and make a very substantial profit. As a result, in Italy, one sees in retrospect the unhealthy situation of a fairly small number of extremely wealthy people, a very large number of the extremely poor, and a very small stable middle class. The fact is that Rome still had a city-state government, with which it was attempting to govern the world. The machine simply wasn't big enough for the task which confronted it.

The last century of the republic was a century of civil war between generals who had made conquests in the provinces and returned to attempt to take over the central government. Two or three times high-minded men, such as the brothers Gracchi (GRAK-ee) and Sulla, attempted to reform the government, send out colonies to reduce the rabble in the city, and in other ways to return to the older virtues of the republic, but the body politic was so diseased that these remedies never effected a permanent cure.

Julius Caesar was the one man who could comprehend realistically the problems of empire rather than attempting to return to the old life of the republic. Though he had only five years from the time when he crossed the Rubicon and marched on Rome to the time of his assassination (49-44 B.C.), and even though most of those years were spent in military campaigns in Spain, North Africa and Egypt, and in Asia, yet he did much to reform the government. He sent many of the unemployed in Rome to colonies in the provinces, and completely changed the debt laws to afford relief to the growing class of debtors. In order to further spread out the population, he established a law that a landowner had to employ one free laborer for each two slaves on the great estates. He limited the term of office for provincial governors to one or two years, and did much else to stabilize the life of his time. One can only speculate on what he might have accomplished had he not been killed. After his death, civil war again broke out which ended at the Battle of Actium, where Antony was defeated and Octavian, Caesar's nephew, took the title of Caesar Augustus.

The empire continued from this time until the "fall of Rome," which one can date in the fifth century, either in A.D. 410 when Alaric the Goth captured the city of Rome, or in A.D. 455 when the Vandals sacked the city, or at some other convenient episode in the 400s. Actually the people at the time never knew that Rome fell; they simply felt that they were in a disruptive time in history, and it is only in retrospect that such dates can be established.

Following Augustus we have a long line of emperors, some good, some atrocious. Fortunately the government, composed of a group of political professionals, was strong enough to endure through the reigns of a Caligula, a Nero, a Domitian, or even the year A.D. 69 when Rome had four emperors. From A.D. 96 to 180, we find the high point of empire with the reign of five effective and competent emperors in succession: Nerva, Trajan (TRAY-jun), Hadrian, Antoninus Pius (an-tuh-NI-nus pious), and Marcus Aurelius. Following this last ruler, the emperorship largely became the property of the army, with the legions supporting any general who would offer the largest benefits to the military. The problems which all the emperors faced were very much the same: an increasing national debt because of military expense, a declining population in Italy, a growing disinclination to take public office in the cities outside Rome (the officers were held responsible for paying the cities' taxes to the central government, and with increasing rural poverty no one wanted to bankrupt himself by holding office), and growing rebellion on the borders of the empire. A vast population movement from the north and east pushed Germanic, Gothic, and Vandal peoples west and south until they overran all of Italy and Spain. While all of this was in progress, two events occurred which are of historical importance for us. The first was the Christianizing of the entire Empire by Constantine I in the year A.D. 337, and the division of the Roman Empire into an eastern and western empire under the same ruler. During the last years of his life Constantine had rebuilt the ancient city of Byzantium which he rechristened Constantinople, from which he ruled the eastern half of the empire. The western half was administered from Rome (and briefly from Milan) until the year A.D. 404 when the imperial residence was moved to the city of Ravenna on the Adriatic coast. From this new capital the influence of Byzantium was to spread through Europe in the very early Middle Ages.

THE ACHIEVEMENT OF ROME

Probably the greatest single achievement of Rome was the establishment of a system of law under which the whole of a vast empire stretching from the north of England to the Tigris and Euphrates rivers could be governed. This law is a tribute to the clear-sightedness of a number of the rulers who saw that no single, hard-and-fast rule could be acceptable to such a variety of peoples as were found in the empire. For this reason a relatively few basic lines of justice were laid down which would prevail throughout the world and, for the rest, local laws and customs were allowed to remain, or were altered slightly to conform to the basic rules and concept of justice. Thus, when the empire conquered a territory, the people seldom felt a violent wrench from their established ways, their accustomed codes of conduct. This body of law, constantly revised, was finally codified under the eastern emperor, Justinian, during the years A.D. 529 to 537. This code is the final monument and summary of the best that Rome had meant.

Laws are not all that Rome has left. Good roads stretching all through the Western world are another of its legacies. Travel during Roman times was faster and more comfortable than at any time until the nineteenth century. Aqueducts carrying water both for drinking and for irrigation were another triumph. A number of these remain as a monument to the engineering skill of these people, the best known at Nîmes in France. A triumph that has vanished is the irrigation system in Northern Africa which made a fertile land out of the desert, an accomplishment which has never been equaled.

The Romans were also great builders of cities. Rome itself, and many provincial cities boasted great baths where as many as 1,600 people could bathe at the same time (and these structures also contained libraries, exercise rooms, and other facilities for recreation). Most of the cities had good-sized stadiums (of which the Colosseum at Rome is the best known), temples to various gods abounded, and the great forums, like Trajan's Forum in Rome, beautified many cities. Law courts (basilicas), apartment houses, and triumphal arches were common features of the Roman city. Parenthetically, it became the custom in Rome to allow a "triumph" to any general who killed 5,000 of the enemy, and it was not uncommon for a military leader to make war on fairly peaceful tribes so that he could make his quota and return to the city for a highly publicized entry, complete with a triumphal arch under which the captive slaves were marched as a symbol of their subjugation (under the yoke) to Rome.

Most of the successes of Rome which have been listed above are physical things: buildings, roads, stadiums, and temples. The provincial roads were usually built by the soldiers who occupied more-or-less permanent camps throughout the empire. The other structures, real triumphs of engineering skill, were built with slave labor under the direction of engineers. We know comparatively little about the life of the average Roman, but it must have been dull and pointless. Particularly in the later centuries of the empire, tradesmen were frozen by law to their jobs, and a young man had to follow the trade of his father; the free farmers were reduced to serfdom and were permanently attached to the land which they cultivated. Political activities were carried on by professional politicians, usually members of the great families or military leaders. Most of the arts were carried on by professionals; indeed, a considerable business in Rome lay in the copying of Greek sculpture by Greek slaves. Even in athletics, the average Roman was a spectator, and the sporting events were colossal productions: fights between professional gladiators in which the loser or losers were killed in the arena; wild animal "hunts" in the Colosseum, and even naval battles, for the circus could be flooded to a depth sufficient to float small ships. How deeply the tastes of the time had sunk is revealed by the use of condemned criminals at the end of some of the dramatic tragedies in the theater so that when the play called for a death the killing could actually be performed on the stage.

The writers of satire from the time of Nero (see Petronius's "Dinner at Trimalchio's" for instance) describe the banquets of the wealthy in which the practice had grown up of taking emetics during the meal so that the banqueter could eat more and more. Imperial Rome, particularly in its later stages, developed a worship of bigness for its own sake, and a demand for more and more violent stimuli to sate jaded appetites.

In the midst of this, one must not lose sight of the fact that the traditional "noble Roman" did exist. These were men, usually of the old aristocracy, who lived by the virtues of duty and simplicity; frequently they were followers of the stoic philosophy. Devoted to the state and to their own dignity, they made the empire run smoothly in the midst of general degradation. The fact is that the Romans had no use for the human values so loved by the Greeks, so eloquently expressed in the curved lines of the Parthenon which were adapted meticulously to the human eye. Even the best of the Romans gave themselves and their lives to materialistic and pragmatic practical values.

ROMAN RELIGION AND PHILOSOPHY

Early Roman religion, as we have said, consisted of a worship of spirits appropriate to the life of simple farmers. With the growth of an empire and the development of great cities, such gods were no longer adequate. Fairly early, the entire pantheon of Greek gods was adopted and given Roman names; thus Zeus became Jupiter; Hera, Juno; Poseidon, Neptune, etc. With the exception of Jupiter, who became identified with the Roman State, the rather playful gods of the Greeks did not fit the Roman temperament. After Augustus most of the emperors were deified by an act of the senate, the emperor was identified with the Idea of the State, and emperor worship became the official religion of the Roman empire. Although all people within the empire were required to participate in this worship, it required little more than a ceremonial burning of incense at the altar of empire on stated occasions, and local people were allowed to retain their local customs of worship. (Early Christians were regarded as subversive because they would not follow the ritual of Emperor worship.) Except for the earliest rural faith, none of these religious beliefs satisfied what seems to be a deeply felt need in most people for some answers to the ultimate questions of life. Consequently Rome was flooded with a variety of religions, cults, and philosophies which were found in the parts of the conquered world.

The Greek philosophies of stoicism and epicureanism are found in Rome as early as the second century B.C.

Epicureanism is based on the materialistic atomism of the early Greek philosopher, Democritus, as formalized by Epicurus (e-pee-KURE-us). Very briefly, it views the universe as one of constant change, the basis of which is the material atoms falling together and apart, and guided by a force called Necessity or Accident. For the Romans, the ethical and moral results of this belief are of greatest importance. In such a universe, the human being has no soul, and his body is composed of atoms which may fall apart at any moment. How can one live well? Clearly the goal for life is happiness now, for there may be no tomorrow. On the other hand, since accident controls everything, there is at least a fifty-fifty chance that there will be a tomorrow. Any excess for today may produce misery in that hypothetical tomorrow. Therefore, moderation becomes the way of life of the good epicurean. In this way, one enjoys moderate happiness today and takes out insurance that he will also be able to have the same middle-road delight tomorrow.

Some brief quotations from Epicurus illustrate the type of moderation which he favored: "Pleasure is the beginning and the end of the blessed life." "Prudence is the pursuit of pleasure." "The wise man will avoid public life and power, for this produces enemies; instead he will live unnoticed so that he will have no enemies." "Eat little for fear of indigestion; drink little for fear of the morning after; eschew politics and love and all violently passionate activities; do not give hostages to fortune by marriage and having children. Above all, live so as to avoid fear." Epicurus held that two of the greatest sources of fear were religion and the dread of death. Although many people think of religion as a consolation, for Epicurus it was the opposite. Supernatural interference with the course of nature seemed to him a source of terror, and immortality fatal to the hope of any release from pain.

The Latin poet and philosopher, Lucretius (loo-KREE-shus; (96-55 B.C.), in his long poem, *De Rerum Natura* ("On the Nature of Things"), explained the workings of the universe as seen by the epicurean. The poem hardly makes exciting reading, but it is interesting in the careful explanation of the ways in which all the phenomena of the world come into being in perfectly rational and materialistic ways. Horace (65-8 B.C.) the writer of odes, exemplifies the philosophy in his way of life, and sets down the moral and ethical results of epicureanism in his poetry. Horace had become the friend of Maecenas (mee-CEE-nus), one of the richest men of the time, and the benefactor gave the poet a small farm on the Sabine hills. Here Horace spent much of his mature life, celebrating the simple pleasures—such as a simple home-cooked meal in the open air—attended by only five slaves. In his odes he preached moderation in all things, warning against the inconvenience of poverty, and also against important position, for, he warns, the lightning strikes the tallest pines and the highest mountains. The chief pleasure of Horace is his measured sense of humor, for, as a very worldly man, he saw all of the foibles of his time, laughed at many of them, and unashamedly participated in a goodly number.

Stoicism had its beginning in the changing world which Heracleitus envisioned and was fully developed by Aristotle, who became the patron saint of the stoics. Such a world is guided by a great Reason or Logos. Most of the great Romans were followers of this philosophy or religion, for stoicism in Rome did become a religion rather than a speculation into the nature of the universe. The great Intelligence became God, and philosophic inquiry was turned to a statement of guidelines for a good and noble life. What were those ethical and moral guidelines?

Let us start with the guiding Logos which is in all things and surrounds all things, and directs every change that occurs in the world. If this be present, then nothing in nature is irrational or out of order, and a man's first obligation is to accept everything that happens, and to do his duty within the framework of intelligently guided events. Thus the Emperor Marcus Aurelius, who would have preferred the contemplative, philosophic life, accepted his responsibility more seriously than most emperors and spent most of the years of his reign on the Danubian frontier fighting the tribesmen who attacked Rome. This was his duty, and he pursued it vigorously in spite of personal inclinations. In the same way Epictetus (ep-ik-TEE-tus), another stoic, was born a slave and remained in that condition because the great intelligence had placed him in that spot in the world order.

A second of the great teachings of stoicism lay in the idea of the brotherhood of all men. The argument here is that since the great intelligence is within each person, and each one is a necessary part of the rational scheme of things, then all men are brothers in the changing universe. This belief furnished the basis for Roman law, for the great compilers of that law were stoics, and their monument is the legal system which attempted to bring justice to every man.

The impact of this philosophy can best be felt when one reads some of the writings of Marcus Aurelius, for the emperor found time in the fever-ridden swamps of the Danube to jot down a whole series of little paragraphs and essays which were collected in a volume called the *Meditations.* Here are some of his thoughts:

> Whatever this is that I am, it is a little flesh and breath, and the ruling part. Throw away thy books; no longer distract thyself: it is not allowed; but as if thou wast now dying despise the flesh, it is blood and bones and a network, a contexture of nerves, veins and arteries. See the breath also, what kind of a thing it is; air, and not always the same, but every moment sent out and again sucked in. The third then is the ruling part: consider thus: Thou art an old man; no longer let this be a slave, no longer be either dissatisfied with thy present lot, or shrink from the future.
>
> Every moment think steadily as a Roman and a man to do what thou hast in hand with perfect and simple dignity, and feeling of affection, and freedom, and justice; and to give thyself relief from all other thoughts. And thou wilt give thyself relief, if thou doest every act of thy life, as if it were the last, laying aside all carelessness and passionate aversion from the commands of reason, and all hypocrisy, and self-love, and discontent with the portion which has been given to thee. Thou seest how few the things are, the which if a man lays hold of, he is able to live a life which flows in quiet, and is like the existence of the gods; for the gods on their part will require nothing more from him who observes these things.
>
> Of the human life the time is a point, and the substance is in a flux, and the perception dull, and the composition of the whole body subject to putrefaction, and the soul of a whirl, and fortune hard to divine, and fame a thing devoid of judgment. And to say all in a word, everything which belongs to the body is a stream, and what belongs to the soul is a dream and vapour, and life is a warfare and a stranger's sojourn and after-fame is oblivion. What, then is that which is able to conduct a man? One thing, and only one—philosophy. But this consists in keeping the spirit within a man free from violence and unharmed, superior to pains and pleasures, doing nothing without a purpose, nor yet falsely and with hypocrisy, not feeling the need of another man's doing or not doing anything; and besides, accepting all that happens, and all that is allotted, as coming from thence, wherever it is, from whence he himself came; and finally waiting for death with a cheerful mind, as being nothing else than a dissolution of the elements of which every living being is compounded. But if there is no harm to the elements themselves in each continually changing into another, why should a man have any apprehension about the change and dissolution of all the elements? For it is according to nature, and nothing is evil which is according to nature.

A third of the imported Greek philosophies was neoplatonism. This, it will be seen, became even more of a religion than did stoicism, and in its picture of an afterlife offers comfort to those people of Rome who found little satisfaction or self-fulfillment in life on earth. It emphasizes spiritual qualities as well as ethics.

This new faith originated with the doctrines of Plato, and came to Rome from the Academy, the still flourishing school in Athens which was founded by Plato. The neoplatonists started with the concept of ideas as the only reality. The belief in the essence of the good is almost the same as belief in God.

Now, said the neoplatonists, men can never know ideas in their pure form. For example, we must always appreciate and know beauty in some of its manifestations in a beautiful person, a beautiful landscape, or a beautiful picture, but we can never imagine pure beauty apart from one of these things. To use another example, we can never imagine pure mind. We can only approach a knowledge of the mind as we see people acting as their mind dictates. That is, we see only the manifestations of mind; never the reality. So it is with Good (God, or Pure Idea), they said. For the reasons mentioned, the only reality, Pure Idea, is something which men can never conceive of on earth. The goal for man, then, is to approach as near as possible to an understanding of reality while he is on earth so that he may be fit to enter the City of Good upon his death and finally contemplate the True Reality.

Here, then, is the beginning of a true religion. It is dualistic, for it makes a distinction which can never be bridged between earth and heaven, flesh and spirit. With neoplatonism begins the idea of salvation and eternal life for those people who have lived this present life in contemplation and desire for true wisdom. The influence of this idea on Christianity can scarcely be overemphasized, for it was St. Augustine, a neoplatonist in his youth, who built the foundation of doctrine for the early Roman Catholic Church in his great volume, *The City of God.*

Epicureanism, stoicism, and neoplatonism: these three all present high-minded, intellectual answers to questions about a proper way of life. But one can imagine that to the average, nonintellectual Roman, troubled about the hollowness of his life, they brought little help, for they are all too intellectual, too cold, for the man in the street. He needed a faith that was more immediate and which would provide a mental and emotional catharsis here and now. A great number of other cults came to Rome to meet this need. One of these cults was Mithraism, brought in from Persia. This cult represented the world as a part of a conflict between the power of good (light) and darkness. The good god, Ahuramazda, identified with the sun, could not be known by human powers, but an intercessor, Mithra, had been provided for the salvation of man. In his concern for man and his suffering, Mithra is a Prometheus-like figure. The religion offers seven definite steps of initiation, one of which is baptism in the blood of a sacred bull. If the individual follows these steps, he is assured of a new life, and of a permanent and happy after-life. The practice of baptism always suggests the washing away of the guilt of an old life and the rebirth into a new one.

Perhaps more important than Mithraism was the cult of Isis, brought in from Egypt, but closely associated with the worship of Dionysus. In each case the God had been put to death and had been resurrected to bring salvation to mankind. In both Mithraism and the cult of Isis, the idea of a new life was particularly important to the Romans, since, during the late empire, many of them must have been convinced of the pointlessness of this life. Both of these last cults, along with neoplatonism, have some of the qualities of Christianity which was eventually to triumph and to become the state religion of Rome and the chief spiritual influence in the Western world. It is of such importance, however, that it will be considered in a later chapter.

THE BEST OF THE ROMAN IDEAL

Artistically and creatively, Rome reached its peak during the reign of Augustus. Virgil and Horace both lived during these years. The great orator, Cicero, had just died, and the passionate poet, Catullus (kuh-TUL-us), had died only a few years before. Virgil, by the way, was almost adopted by Christianity, and during the Middle Ages was the only classic author who was read, largely because of his Fourth Eclogue, in which he celebrated the birth of a child who, he predicted, would bring the world back to the Golden Age. His fame, however, is not with such early works as this, but rests on his great epic poem, the *Aeneid* (iNEE-id).

To cut through the superficial judgments which one may make about the *Aeneid* is difficult. The first such judgment is that the poem provided "instant mythology" for the Roman empire, for it was apparent to Virgil that much of the greatness of Athenian life resulted from the tradition furnished by Homer's *Iliad* and *Odyssey.* Virgil knew these poems well and patterned his epic upon them to give Rome the same kind of golden past which Greece had had, and to provide inspiration for the carrying on of great and noble works. Too clearly the reader gets the picture of Virgil thinking to himself, "Tomorrow we are going to start the old tradition of Roman greatness."

A second quick judgment is that the *Aeneid* presents a picture of the tired businessman as epic hero, and somehow, the over-thoughtful, rather pompous figure of the middle-aged Aeneas (i-NEE-us) falls short of the glory-bound Achilles or Hector, and especially the wily and resourceful Odysseus.

The good reader will accept these first judgments and then feel beyond them. The *Aeneid is* literature as propaganda for a great nation. But what's the matter with propaganda for a good cause? The hero is middle-aged and has gained the wisdom of maturity. Aeneas sees clearly that a kind of sadness underlies all heroic acts, and that many things which men do result from choices which are forced upon them. Compared with Homer, Virgil loses much in dash; what he gains is a sad and chastened wisdom.

The poem recounts the legend of the founding of Rome by the Trojan hero, Aeneas, after the fall of Troy to Agamemnon and the Greeks. Aeneas, commanded by Jupiter and Aeneas' goddess mother, escaped from Troy with his aged father, his son Ascanius (a-SKAY-nee-us; also called Ilus, and later Iulus to relate him to the Julian line of Caesars), and with the household gods which are to be the gods of the new city, Rome. The voyage is full of epic incident, storms at sea, battles, rather pleasant interludes, and the final war on Italian soil to conquer the kingdom of Latium and arrange for the marriage which will produce the Roman line.

Only two or three incidents need be mentioned to suggest the flavor of the epic. At the first of the book Aeneas, storm-tossed, landed on the shore near Carthage where he and his companions were made welcome by Dido (DIE-dough), the queen of the city. As he recounted his adventures, Dido fell in love with him, and he with her. So satisfying was the affair that Aeneas lingered for a long time, while Dido tried to persuade him to settle there and make Carthage the city which he was supposed to found. Aeneas, prodded by his stoic sense of duty, knew that he must push on, and so, one morning before daybreak, he and his companions set sail. Aeneas as a person hated his decision, but he was honor-bound to make it; Dido was so devastated that she had a great funeral pyre built and committed suicide in the flames. One of the ironies of the poem lies in the meeting of the lovers in the underworld in Book VI, when Aeneas tries to rekindle their love and she turns against him. Aeneas knew all there was to know about the founding of cities, but he understood little about the human heart.

Another of the little incidents occurs when the Trojans land on Sicily. The land is so beautiful that a number of Aeneas' group suggest that the city be founded there, but the hero knows that this is not the place, so he allows some of his party to stay while he again sails away to make war and cause death so that the city might be properly founded. Once again he realized the tragedy of his choice, but Duty, stern daughter of the voice of god, would not let him make the easy choice.

Many other events could be cited to illustrate the same point. Aeneas' chief adversary in Italy is a hero named Turnus, a thoroughly noble person; probably a better man than Aeneas. Turnus was patterned on the character of Hector in the *Iliad.* Turnus must be destroyed, and Aeneas does it. Hector, too, had to be killed. The difference is that Achilles, the youthful hero, fought his battle fiercely and killed his enemy in passion. Aeneas simply knew that the better man must be killed, and he did the job in full knowledge and for a greater good (the founding of the city of Rome) than would be accomplished by the saving of one good man.

Such is the tone of the whole poem except for some interludes such as the funeral games for Anchises when Virgil allows himself to relax and enjoy the deeds of physical strength and skill. The *Aeneid*, like the stoic philosophy, sees duty as the highest way of life, and the true Roman hero places duty above all other human values. Virgil wonderfully gave Rome its best and highest creed, when in the underworld, Anchises told his son, Aeneas:

> Others, no doubt, will better mould the bronze
> To the semblance of soft breathing, draw from marble,
> The living countenance; and others plead
> With greater eloquence, or learn to measure,
> Better than we, the pathways of the heaven,
> The risings of the stars: remember, Roman,
> To rule the people under law, to establish
> The way of peace, to battle down the haughty,
> To spare the meek. Our fine arts, these, forever.

This was the highest of the Roman ideal. While it sacrificed much in the realm of human value, while it denigrated such qualities as imagination and joy, it furnished a noble code of conduct as long as the Romans adhered to it.

Bibliography

General History and Interpretation

1. F.C. Bourne. *A History of the Romans.* Boston: D.C. Heath and Company. A recent general history, very readable.
2. Edith Hamilton. *The Roman Way*, Mentor. Furnishes a nice contrast with her *Greek Way*, and gives some excellent comment on Latin literature.
3. J.W. Mackail. *Virgil and His Meaning to the World of Today.*

Roman Literature

1. Catullus, *Poems.* Here one can see a passionate side of the Roman character which is not presented in *The Search.* Use one of several modern translations.
2. Moses Hadas, ed., *The Essential Works of Stoicism.* Bantam Books, Inc.
3. Ovid, *The Metamorphoses* and *The Art of Love* have been translated by Rolfe Humphries.
4. Virgil, *The Aeneid.* The student might want to see what comes before and after Book VI. Of several contemporary translations, the Humphries or the C. Day Lewis are excellent.

CHAPTER 10

Roman Art and Music: The Arts of Megalopolis

■ The City is one of the largest and most populous on the face of the earth. Throughout the world it is known and heralded as a great political, cultural, and artistic center, a city offering every pleasure known to man. From it well-constructed roads lead to every major city on the continent; its bridges, towers, fantastic network of waterways and sewers work to provide its inhabitants with comforts they take for granted but which less privileged people envy and try desperately to emulate. The City has huge governmental and business buildings; an abundance of theaters, stadiums, libraries, amphitheaters, and other pleasure palaces; and beautiful places of worship for the many religions which are practiced there. These buildings are designed by the leading architects of the world in almost every style attempted by previous cultures as well as the avant-garde styles of the day and are built by large laboring forces directed by skilled engineers; they are structurally sound buildings, immense space enclosures, but often an undistinguished, concrete, basic structure is hidden under glamorous facings of marble, brick, and sculptural ornamentation.

Citizens of the City dwell in mansions filled with luxuries of all descriptions and staffed by highly trained servants; tract homes which are ample and comfortable enough for a family's basic comforts, but incredibly repetitious and monotonous in design and aesthetic expression; apartment houses which are large compartmentalized palaces; and mile upon mile of tenements of meanest description. It is a city of complete contrasts: beauty and ugliness, richness and squalor, comforts and miseries, learning and illiteracy, culture and barbarism.

The City is New York. The City was ancient Rome.

ROMAN ARCHITECTURE

In the eighteenth century a young American genius visited Nîmes in Southern France and was overwhelmed by the Maison Carrée (MAY-sown Car-RAY, Fig. 61), a small marble temple built there by the Romans in 16 B.C. He studied this ancient monument by the bright light of the day and the soft light of the moon; with meticulous care he measured its columns, produced numerous sketches and diagrams, wrote glowing descriptions, and committed its image to memory. When Thomas Jefferson returned to Virginia, he designed many plantation houses and public buildings in which he incorporated portions of this antique building. And from Jefferson, who must be recognized as one of America's foremost architects, generations of our architects found inspiration which would lead them first to Rome and then to Greece. The classic world lives on in America in state capitols, university buildings, banks, football stadiums, palatial and tract homes. Although very few of these buildings share the harmony of aesthetic and utilitarian qualities of Monticello (MON-te-CHEL-lo), inspired in great part by the Pantheon, or the Virginia State Capitol, where the Roman temple form was first used in an American public building, they are ubiquitous and considered as American as apple pie á la mode.

Figure 61. Maison Carrée at Nîmes, 16 B.C. (Marburg—Art Reference Bureau).

Jefferson was a classicist in law, political theory, and in architecture, and it is often assumed that his legal and political enthusiasms led him to a romantic enthusiasm for Roman architecture, a style that many contemporary critics and historians decry, especially when comparing it with Greek architecture. But one can look at Roman architecture with the unjaded eye of Jefferson who had never seen the Parthenon or any other building from the classic civilizations except the Maison Carrée, but who was thoroughly familiar with the writings of the Roman architect Vitruvius (first century B.C.). The ancient Romans devised an architecture of space enclosure which combined pragmatism and romanticism in unique, sometimes vulgar, combinations, but always with great facility, enthusiasm, and bravado. Americans, essentially, have been committed to a similar architectural development.

The Maison Carrée was a smaller and earlier version of the great Corinthian temple that the Emperor Hadrian had built in Trajan's Forum and hundreds similar to it were to be found throughout the Roman Empire. At first glance, it seems quite similar to a late Hellenistic temple, for it is based on the post and lintel system, is compact and rectangular in form, and has fluted Corinthian columns. In all this it is Greek, and the Romans would not have denied their indebtedness. What is Roman about the temple is the podium on which the building stands high and aloof over the flat land, the single flight of steps which lead to its large, commodious portico, and the absence of the Greek ambulatory. Instead of a long series of columns in a peristyle about the temple, the Romans attached columns to three sides of the cella, indicating that their chief purpose was embellishment rather than structural. These engaged columns, used in every major Roman building, indicate Roman appreciation of decoration, of art for art's sake; they are lovely testimony to the Roman sense of what is beautiful and proper, even if it served no useful purpose.

An example of a completely utilitarian construction project is a Roman aqueduct which has been in almost constant use since the first century A.D., the Pont du Gard (PONE-d-you-gar) near Nîmes (Fig. 62). To bring an adequate supply of water from its source 25 miles away, a system of underground and overground concrete channels was constructed and the system included this massive, 902′ long, tri-level bridge and aqueduct which crosses a valley at a height of 160′. The broad lower arches support the bridge and the upper levels of large and small arches support the concrete water channel. This structure is a magnificent feat of engineering, especially since no mortar was used in the original construction of the arches. Additionally, it creates a pleasing aesthetic effect because of its simplicity, and its echoing arches provide a subtle play of repetition in diversity. The Pont du Gard was but one of thousands of bridges, aqueducts, and roads which were built by the pragmatic, comfort-loving Romans—and but one of many such structures still in use.

Figure 62. Pont du Gard, Nîmes, first century A.D. (Photographie Giraudon).

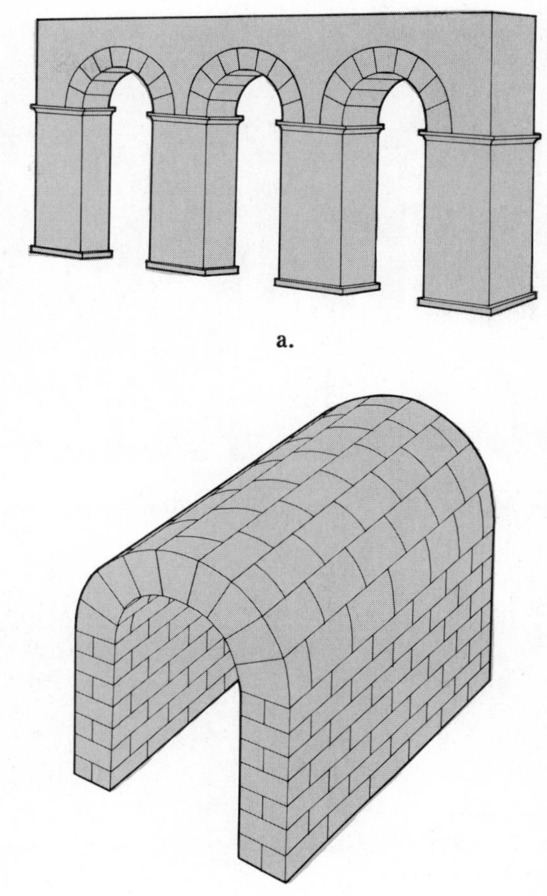

Figure 63. Semicircular arch arcade (a); semicircular arch vault (b).

Rome made a great and lasting contribution to the development of the rounded arch and vault as an architectural principle. The arch and vault were not invented by the Romans but probably were adapted from Greek or Oriental sources, for they had been used for undistinguished structures such as gates, storage areas, and sewers in Greece and Asia Minor. It was the Roman, however, who first exploited the arch and vault principle on massive scale, particularly in public buildings. The arch and vault principle can be seen easily in Figure 63. The great merit of the arch is that it provides a means of spanning a large space while decentralizing or spreading the weight-force thrusts of the material above it. When, as in the Pont du Gard, arches are placed side by side in a series, they constitute an arcade which can span large land or water areas, and the lateral thrust at the haunches of each arch is counteracted by the thrusts of the neighboring arches. When extended along its axis, the arch becomes a vault called a barrel or tunnel vault, as is shown by the triumphal arches of ancient Rome and nineteenth-century America. A dome is formed when arches completely span a space by intersecting each other around a central axis. Thus was formed the dome of the Roman Pantheon.

The Pantheon (PAN-the-on; Fig. 64), the best-preserved building surviving from the ancient world, is considered to be one of the world's finest and most impressive domed buildings, and it is the only pagan temple of classical antiquity which is still a place of worship—from pagan temple it became Christian church in the early Christian era and thereby escaped ruin. Its exterior today is not impressive, for buildings of all descriptions impose closely upon it from almost every side; its marble facing, described as rich and colorful, has disappeared, along with the bronze plates from the portico ceiling and the gilded bronze tiles that covered the entire exterior of the drum and dome. Moreover, through the ages the street in front of it has risen, thus submerging the steps leading to its porch which formerly was part of an impressive rectangular, colonnaded arcade. The missing embellishments must have made the Pantheon more distinguished in antiquity than it is today, but the strange combination of a rectangular portico with a circular cella always has been awkward and detrimental to the aesthetic appeal of the exterior. It is necessary to reconstruct the exterior of the Pantheon to see it in full splendor, but such is not the case in viewing the interior, which is awe-inspiring. Architecture often has been defined as the art of enclosing space—and this is the most significant interior of antiquity, perhaps of all time, and undoubtedly the greatest evidence of Roman architectural vision and engineering skill. The painting of the interior (Fig. 65) by Giovanni Pannini, an eighteenth-century painter noted for his architectural views, is more helpful than any photograph in illustrating this interior, which the Romans meant

Figure 64. Pantheon, Rome, c. A.D. 120 (Anderson—Art Reference Bureau).

Figure 65. Giovanni Paolo Pannini, "The Interior of the Pantheon," National Gallery of Art, Washington, D.C. Samuel H. Kress Collection.

to be shrine and abode for the seven planetary gods. The interior is based on the union of a cylinder and a hemisphere over a circular ground plan. The top of the dome is 143′ high, and that is the exact diameter of the interior floor. A round opening in the ceiling, 29′ in diameter, is the sole source of light. This oculus, or eye to or from the heavens, creates illumination that bathes the varicolored marble walls and floor in thousands of variations according to the vagaries of the weather. A less pleasing and common function is that it allows rain into the building; however the original drainage system still functions.

The dome's interior surface has coffers or indented panels which lighten the weight of the concrete and brick dome and furnish decoration even now, but once were centered with sparkling, gilded stars. Indeed, the dome was meant to leave the impression of a starry sky, further enhancing the original concept of this building as a home of the gods. That the Romans had a unique and unexcelled sense of unity and space, and the ability to produce this space in visual terms, is made manifest in the Pantheon.

The Colosseum (Fig. 66) has a concrete core with miles of vaulted corridors and stairways which are more essential to the purpose of the building

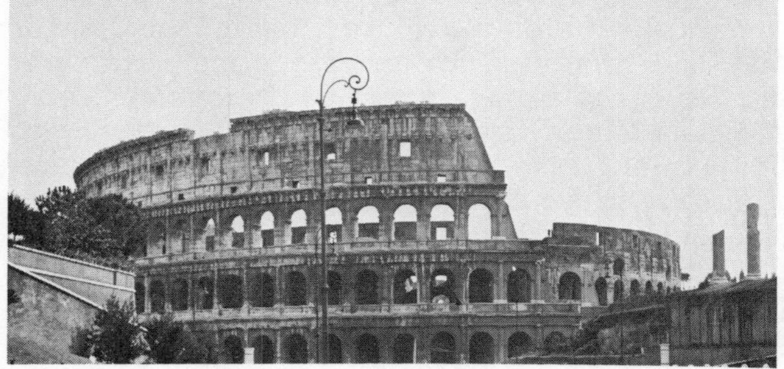

Figure 66. Colosseum, Rome. Long axis: 620′; short axis: 513′; height: 160′ (Archives, Wm. C. Brown Company Publishers).

and more Roman in spirit than its magnificent facade which is much admired. The sectional diagram (Fig. 67) of the great bowl indicates clearly that the building had a network of intersecting barrel-vaulted corridors and stairways organized efficiently to enable the 50,000 or more spectators to fill or empty the building in a matter of minutes. The façade reveals Roman practicality again, for the three rows of superimposed and open archways not only buttress each other, but also lighten the exterior wall and admit light into the labyrinth.

Novelists and filmmakers have delighted in producing stories in which Emperor Nero sends Christians to horrible martyrdoms in this pagan structure. Although, according to tradition, some Christians did die there before Christianity became the state religion in the fourth century, the Colosseum was inaugurated in A.D. 80, twelve years

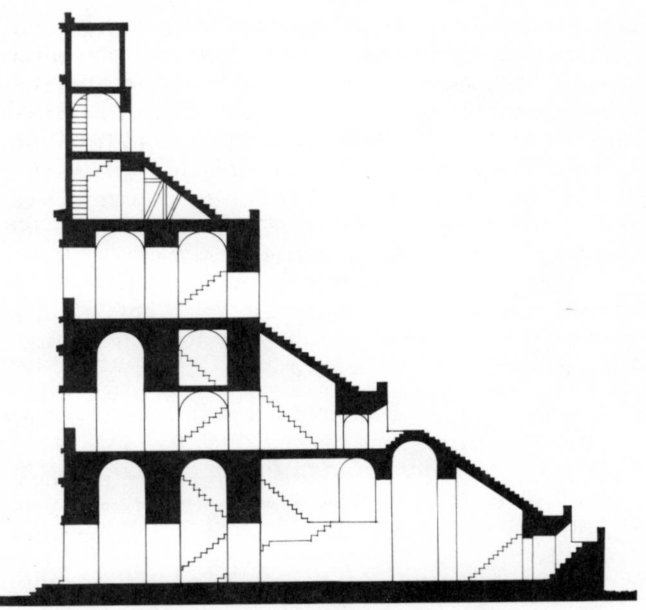

Figure 67. Schematic sectional view of Colosseum.

Figure 68. Colosseum (interior) (Robert C. Lamm).

after Nero's death and the regular use of the building was for sporting spectacles. The Christian martyrs died in the Circus Maximus, a much larger, wooden structure which was completely destroyed early in the Christian era. Nevertheless, Christianity has taken its revenge on this noble edifice, for its present deteriorated condition was not caused by war, climate, or weak construction, but by church leaders and other builders who confiscated its rich marble facing and tons of its stone for church and private construction throughout Rome. In fact, for centuries a Christian church stood in the middle of this vast bowl. Today in this area only a substructure of rooms and corridors remain, the "below the scenes" mechanical area for the Roman amphitheater (Fig. 68).

Even in the Colosseums's present state, the grand conception and professional competence of Roman architects and engineers is evident. Greek architects built their theaters on a hillside; if no hillside was available, there was no theater. The Romans doubled the semicircular Greek theater and made it into a full circle; by using arch and vault construction, they raised this semicircle four stories, to approximately 161′. To add strength to the walls pierced with open arches, they constructed the walls of concrete made from rubble, volcanic dust, lime, and water. And for beauty, they faced this giant ovalar bowl with multicolored marble. For decorative purposes, also, the three Greek orders of columns and their variants are superimposed on the successive stories or levels: the engaged columns on the lower level are Doric, actually a local variant known as the Tuscan Order; those on the second level are Ionic; the third level features the Corinthian; and on the fourth level there is another variant, this time of the Corinthian in flat, engaged piers or pilasters. Thus as the building ascends, the forms, orders, and walls grow lighter. The facade presents exciting contrasts and horizontals, open arches and solid walls, conflicting forms brought together in imposing harmony and utility.

The Colosseum and Pantheon are spectacular structures which impressed the ancients as deeply as they impress us. In studying the artistic achievement of any culture, often it is advisable to compare similar forms or structures to see the changes and differences which these forms or structures manifested over a long period. Rome had innumerable monumental arches which were erected to celebrate and record the victories and achievements of great leaders. It is not necessary to illustrate and discuss all arches extant to arrive at a very obvious conclusion. A comparison of the Arch of Titus (Fig. 69), c. A.D. 81, and the Arch of Constantine (Fig. 70), c. A.D. 315, proves that the Roman style changed drastically in less than two hundred years. The Arch of Titus is simple, fairly well-proportioned, although too heavy for its delicate, engaged Corinthian columns and other structural embellishments. The Arch of Titus clearly and simply indicates that it is a symbol of the yoke inflicted upon the conquered. In contrast, Constantine's Arch is much larger, more elaborate, and completely covered with architectural and sculptural embellishments. *Horror vacui* (horror VAK-you-e: abhorence of undecorated space) has set in and the structure and its basic symbolic purpose disappear under the most confusing facing in the history of

Figure 69. Arch of Titus, Rome, c. A.D. 81 (Robert C. Lamm).

Figure 70. Arch of Constantine, Rome, c. A.D. 312-315 (Anderson—Art Reference Bureau).

art. The Arch of Titus may be likened to a short historical essay recounting an event and pointing a moral, the Arch of Constantine to a catechism which tries to describe and define everything, and all that in terms of the spirit rather than the flesh. Constantine's Arch is the last of the noteworthy Roman monuments and reflects the apparent waning of the Roman's ability to cope with his world in a lucid and succinct manner.

The Roman achievement in architecture should not be dismissed lightly, for it acts upon us today. The following summary of Roman architectural achievements is impressive:

1. development of the rounded arch and vault as a vital structural principle,
2. the achievement of significant interiors—architecture as space enclosure,
3. extensive development and use of engineering skills,
4. the development of concrete as a building material,
5. a daring involvement with verticality without eliminating horizontal elements,
6. emphasis on the utilitarian, luxurious, and propagandistic aspects of architecture.

ROMAN SCULPTURE

Sculpture was as ubiquitous in the Roman world as are signboards in contemporary United States. Streets, public buildings, and the homes of the aristocrats were filled with portrait busts; life-sized, full-length portraits in bronze or marble; free-standing statues and reliefs of the gods of all the major religions; masterpieces confiscated from Greece and Egypt by victorious generals; superb, mediocre, and horrible copies of Greek works of all periods by Roman artisans who produced them in mass quantities; and bas-relief jewelry of all sorts in a multitude of materials. It is fashionable today to scoff at Roman sculpture, but most of the Greek marbles enthroned and venerated in the world's greatest museums are Roman copies. The real difference lies in the fact that the Greeks had the urge to create while the Romans usually were content to copy.

It was in portraiture and historical narrative that the Roman sculptor showed his unique ability—sometimes genius—and his sense of Roman tradition. The "Roman Patrician with Busts of His Ancestors" (Fig. 71), c. 30 B.C., is a persuasive likeness, a visual document of a facial text, at once as straightforward and unflattering as a passport photo. This unnamed gentleman is holding busts of deceased members of his family, most likely his father and grandfather. At the death of a prominent member of a family, a death mask of wax

Figure 71. "Roman Patrician with Busts of His Ancestors," c. 300 B.C. Capitoline Museum, Rome (Alinari—Art Reference Bureau).

Figure 72. "Augustus of Primaporta," c. 20 B.C. (courtesy Vatican Museums).

was made to be preserved in a family shrine and to be carried in funeral processions. The spirit of the family, the continuous father-image, is monumentalized in this work. For the tradition-minded Roman these concepts were more important than idealization of features.

The commanding statue of the Emperor Augustus from Primaporta (Fig. 72), c. 20 B.C., shows unmistakable non-Roman influences. The pose and general form recall the work of Polycleitos and the commanding gesture derives from pictorial art of the Near East. It is known, however, that this is a rather objective portrait, for Roman coins and reliefs of this period depicted these same features of Augustus with monotonous regularity. The successful tactile rendering of the emperor's consular costume of leather, metal, and cloth give a feeling of actuality and immediacy which the Romans prized, but which the ancient Greeks would have considered banal. The commanding gesture will become a stock device for artists through the centuries for depicting emperors, dictators, all men of secular authority. But Augustus was more than the law: he was the divine ruler. Michelangelo will depict Christ in this manner in the "Last Judgment" of the Sistine Chapel. The "Augustus of Primaporta" is an outstanding example of a didactic art form which has been and probably always will be in the service of state and church.

The only monumental equestrian statue extant from the ancient world is that of Marcus Aurelius (Fig. 73), now presiding majestically in the Piazza del Campidoglio which was designed by Michelangelo to honor this unique work. Again we are aware, not only of the stoic emperor's unflattered and unidealized features, but of his role as all-conquering lord of the earth. This work is at once a portrait and a propaganda device.

In the genre of historical narrative, few sculptors have been as ambitious and as successful as the anonymous creator of Trajan's Column (Fig. 74) erected between A.D. 106-13 to celebrate the military victories of Emperor Trajan. This marble column is 125′ high and has a continuous five-foot spiral band in relief covering its surface. This relief

Figure 73. Equestrian statue of Marcus Aurelius, A.D. 161-180. Piazza del Campidoglio, Rome (Anderson—Art Reference Bureau).

Figure 74. Trajan's column, Rome, A.D. 106-113 (Anderson—Art Reference Bureau).

band, if unwound, would be 656′ long, much longer than the Parthenon frieze. To "read" this narrative it is necessary to walk around and around the column, but very soon it is impossible to continue the story without binoculars. How and if this story was completely read by the Romans has never been explained satisfactorily. Perhaps slaves were stationed at the foot of the monument to deliver illuminating lectures and sell guide books. We do know that the columnar narration is very similar to that of the Roman scroll or rotolus, the book of those days. Emperor Trajan appears time and time again in the 150 episodes which blend into each other—the visual experience is somewhat similar to watching a movie, or for very visually-minded people, of reading an historical novel. This type of presentation is called "continuous narration" and must be differentiated from the "simultaneous narration" of the Parthenon frieze where all action of one given moment at a specific place is frozen into one form. The classical Greek unities were not appreciated by the Romans who excelled in history and biography, the didactic tools of imperial government. A detail from the bottom of the column (Fig. 75) shows use of symbolism in that a river god represents the Danube; geographic logis-

Figure 75. Detail of Trajan's column (Alinari—Art Reference Bureau).

tic, and political recording in a matter-of-fact way; abbreviation of landscape to stage sets; and abandonment of foreshortening and perspective space in order to make the personnel and their activities the prime interest in an explicit way while maintaining visual continuity.

By the early fourth century, Roman portraiture had changed drastically from that of Republican and Augustan Rome, as can be seen in a comparison of the "Augustus of Primaporta" and the head of the first Christian Emperor, "Constantine the Great" (Fig. 76). The eight-foot head of Constantine is no physical likeness, but a symbol of imperial majesty and spiritual self. Even in relation to this gigantic head, the eyes are extremely large, pronounced, and dramatically outlined by heavy brows and cheekbones. Constantine is depicted not as a mere man, nor even as a handsome and commanding emperor, but as an exalted being, separate and unique in power, authority, and vision. He is other-worldly, and this conceptual quality is basic to early Christian and Byzantine art which is developing at this time.

A fifth-century Consular Dyptych (DIP-tick)

Figure 76. "Constantine the Great," early fourth century A.D. Capitoline Museum, Rome (Hirmer Fotoarchiv München).

Figure 77. Dyptych of Consul Boethius, c. A.D. 487. Brescia Museum (Alinari—Art Reference Bureau).

depicting the consul Boethius (beau-E-thi-us; Fig. 77), although a miniature in fact and miniscule in comparison with the bust of Constantine, is similar to it in that the artist has denied the physical reality of Boethius and emphasized his authority and spirit. Costume, body, and space are reduced to a vital line pattern that is more emotional and decorative than representational. Boethius and Augustus are alike only in that they share the commanding arm gesture, the symbol of authority. At the risk of seeming pretentious and precious, it can be said of the Augustus that here is depicted a man with supreme authority and of the Boethius that here is depicted supreme authority who happens to be a man.

The Latin word for dignity is "gravitas," which calls to mind the words "grave," "heavy," "serious," "pedantic," "didactic." These words do apply to most of Roman sculpture, which has political purpose, and contrasts sharply with the more purely aesthetic and humanitarian concepts that derive from the Greek "arete." But, let us be reminded, the Roman sculptor could be gay, light, charming, vulgar, even common. The "Dionysus Sarcophagus" (sar-COUGH-a-gus) of the early third century (Fig. 78) depicts a joyous scene in which the handsome god of drink and debauchery presides over his frolicking followers in an area where grapes and vines abound. This is a Dionysian revel or, if you prefer, an orgy (a rather mild one). This panel is part of a sarcophagus, a word which means "flesh-eater in Latin and is a sculptured box which served as a tomb. Was the Roman who ordered this

Figure 78. Dionysus sarcophagus, c. A.D. 200 (The Walters Art Gallery).

tomb the same kind of a man as the Roman patrician and were either of them in any ways similar to Augustus or Constantine? This is a difficult question to answer, for stylistic changes are indicative of changes in the way man sees himself and lives. A detailed study of Roman sculpture, however, would indicate that all the works depicted had at least some counterparts in every century of the Roman era. That there was a change of emphasis from the strict representational or objective view to the emotional, other-worldly, subjective view during this era is also obvious. The Roman sculptor seldom produced work of highest merit, but he did capture the rapid changes in attitudes, philosophy, and spirit of the Roman world.

ROMAN PAINTING

In A.D. 79 the cities of Pompeii (pom-PAY-e) and Herculaneum (her-cue-LAY-knee-am) were destroyed and buried during the eruption of Mt. Vesuvius (ve-SOO-vee-us). Since the eighteenth century, archaeologists have been excavating these Roman resort centers and have discovered numerous murals and mosaics, almost the entire corpus of paintings and murals extant from the ancient world. These works have been labeled Greek, Hellenistic, or Roman in countless eulogistic but quite unconvincing accounts. It is known that the Greeks held their paintings and painters in higher regard than their sculpture and sculptors, and it is known that the Romans were highly indebted to the Greeks for illusionistic techniques of architectural perspective, foreshortening, and modeling. But as to what is essentially Greek, Hellenistic, or Roman in these works must be considered problematical and perhaps is an idle question; nevertheless, they are in the Roman period.

The painting of "Hercules Discovering the Infant Telephus in Arcadia" (Fig. 79), which was found in the Basilica of Herculaneum, lacks unity of vision and accomplishment, but is reproduced here to indicate various interests and capabilities of

Figure 79. "Hercules Discovering the Infant Telephus in Arcadia," wall painting from Herculaneum, c. A.D. 70. National Museum, Naples (Alinari—Art Reference Bureau).

the painter in the classical world. Hercules, the great mythological hero of antiquity, is depicted nude as a powerful man of great bulk and highly developed muscles, modeled in a manner reminiscent of Hellenistic sculpture. The lion is painted in an impressionistic manner with sketchy, agitated dabs, while the doe is precisely and gracefully outlined. The very classically-conceived woman is the personification of Arcadia, a mythical geographic area where nature is idyllic, unsophisticated, and man lives in stoic harmony with it. All the figures in this work exist within a sharply controlled, three-dimensional space. Although the presentation of individual forms varies and the subject matter is difficult to read without a guide, it is evident that classical painters had an immense range of technical skills, a highly involved formal vocabulary (that is, conventions for use of light, color, shapes, and lines), and a diverse literary repertory (stories, themes, and motifs drawn from literature and oral tradition). These qualities they shared with contemporary architects and sculptors. It is a safe assumption that Roman painters produced works equivalent in quality to the Pantheon and the "Augustus of Primaporta."

ROMAN MUSIC

Roman musical activities as described by Cicero, Seneca, Quintilianus and others occupied a rather important place in Roman life. The Romans had nothing original to contribute to music nor are there any extant musical documents or theoretical treatises; they were content to use the brass instruments of the Etruscans and the whole of Greek musical culture.

More instruments were used because there were more activities for which musical instruments had specific functions. The buccina, lituus, and tuba were all trumpetlike instruments associated with warfare and royal courts, functions reserved for trumpets until well into the seventeenth century. The hydraulis,[1] originally a pipe organ of clear and delicate tone, was used in connection with gladiatorial contests, but with vastly increased air pressure, resulting in a strident tone and a reputed range of three miles.[2]

Roman and Greek dramas still used music, although the performers were usually Greek. The aulos (called *tibia* in Latin) and kithara continued to be employed as they were in Greece, along with several varieties of percussion instruments. Nero, who should be mentioned in connection with music, had coins minted depicting him as a kithara player.

In summary, musical culture in Rome displays the same preoccupation with practicality and utility which characterizes the Roman Empire in general. Rome excelled in law, government, economics, engineering, and the art of warfare, and built a mighty empire. The Greek empire of mind and spirit was taken over for what it was worth which, in the final analysis, was very little to the Romans and very much to later generations.

Bibliography

1. Maiuri, Amedeo. *Roman Painting.* New York: Skira, 1953. A superb volume abounding with magnificent color illustrations.
2. Smith, E. Baldwin. *Architectural Symbolism in Imperial Rome and the Middle Ages.* Princeton: Princeton University Press, 1956. Impressive work making architecture more comprehensible in terms of politics, economics, and religion.
3. Strong, Eugenie S. *Art in Ancient Rome.* 2 vols., New York: Scribner's, 1928. Covers all aspects of Roman art. A good book for investigation of special interests.
4. Robertson, Donald S. *Handbook of Greek and Roman Architecture.* New York: Cambridge University Press, 1943 (available in paperback edition).
5. Wheeler, Mortimer. *Roman Art and Architecture.* New York: Frederick A. Praeger, Inc., 1964 (available in paperback). Lucid, comprehensive account of Roman visual arts which students may find most helpful.

Literary Selections

The Lower World (The Aeneid, Book VI.)

Virgil (Publius Virgilius Maro)

In the story of the journey of Aeneas (i-NEE-us), the Trojan hero has fled from Troy, and, after a great storm at sea which was caused by Juno, he and his people landed on the coast of North Africa. They made their way to Carthage, a land ruled by Queen Dido (DIE-doe). In her court he told the story of the last days of the Trojan War and of the fall of Troy. He told how he gathered a group around him including his aged father, Anchises (an-KI-sees), son Ascanius (A-SKAY-nee-us), and the household gods and fled from the coast of Asia Minor. He also told of their subsequent wanderings and of the death of Anchises.

In the meantime Dido has fallen in love with Aeneas, and he, as much as his duty will allow, with her. Fearful of what might come of this, Aeneas and his band fled to Sicily, and Dido built a great funeral pyre and cast herself upon it. In Sicily Aeneas left a good part of his group who were tired of wandering, and with a select band he pushed on to fulfill his destiny—the founding of the City of

1. Hydraulis (Greek, *hydor,* "water"; *aulos,* "pipe"), invented c. 300 B.C. Actually a pipe organ with air pressure maintained through hydraulic pressure.
2. The association of hydraulis with gladiatorial contests, especially those with assorted Christians and lions, delayed for many centuries the introduction of the pipe organ into Christian services. In general, the Roman manner of music caused this art form to have a lowly reputation among the early Christians.

TIME CHART FOR ROMAN CULTURE

Time	Government and Politics	Philosophy and Religion	Literature and Art
1000-500 B.C.	Period of kings, senate, and comitia curiata.	Worship of Janus, Tellus, and Vesta. A bargain religion.	
509 B.C.	Senate and comitia centuriata. Plebeian quest for equality: 1. Valerian Law—509 2. Office of Tribune—494 3. Twelve Tables—449 4. Comitia Tributa established 5. Plebiscites passed by comitia became law—287		Plautus 254-184 B.C. Terence 190-159 B.C.
270 B.C.	Italy united by Rome. Rome proceeds with world conquest. Punic Wars 264-146. Conquest under Republic ends 133.	The beginnings of Eastern cults, philosophies, and religions in Rome.	
133-49 B.C.	Critical period for Republic. Masses degenerate and flock to the city. Civil conflicts between rival generals and dictators.	Lucretius states Epicurean philosophy for Rome.	Cicero 106-43 B.C. Caesar 100-44 B.C. Lucretius 98-44 B.C. Catullus 87-54 B.C.
49 B.C.	Julius Caesar conquers Rome. Reforms of Caesar.		
30 B.C.	Octavius becomes first Roman emperor with title "Augustus."	Emperor worship. Seneca writes full statement of Stoicism.	Period of great architecture starts. Virgil 70-19 B.C. Horace 65-68 B.C.
14-69 A.D. 69-96 A.D. 96-180 A.D. 180-	The Julian Caesars. The Flavian Caesars. The Antoninus Caesars. The Army takes control. Central authority collapses.	The best people seek refuge in Epicureanism, Stoicism, Christianity, Judaism, Gnosticism, and in mystery cults. Complete formulation of Neo-Platonism as religion.	Livy 59 B.C. to A.D. 17 Ovid 43 B.C. to A.D. 17 Petronius d.—66 A.D. Martial 38-102 A.D. Juvenal 60-140 A.D. Marcus Aurelius 121-180 A.D. Plotinus 205-270 A.D.
337 A.D.	Constantine rules. Empire split between Constantinople and Rome.	Christianity becomes state religion.	
410 A.D. or 476 A.D.	Conventional date for fall of Rome. Alaric sacks city.	Great church fathers.	

Rome. The group arrived in Italy after Palinurus (pal-uh-NOOR-us), the steersman, was lost overboard. Long before, Aeneas had been told that he should consult the Cumaean (kyoo-MEE-an si-bil) Sibyl, a prophetess of Apollo, on his arrival, and that he should visit the underworld where he would meet the spirit of his father. This visit is presented here in full. After the visit the little group sailed up the Tiber and established a village and fort. They became engaged in a war with the Italian hero, Turnus, and finally vanquished him. Then Aeneas was ready to follow his destiny further by marrying Lavinia, daughter of King Latinus (la-TIE-nus), and establishing the Roman Empire.

The selection given here presents the best of the Roman spirit. Notice first the difficulty of Aeneas' mission; yet his sense of duty drives him on. Notice the pathos which this professional spirit evokes in the meeting with Dido's spirit. Pride of race and family are present as Anchises points out the spirits who are to return to earth to found the great Roman families. Virgil is, for all practical purposes, writing the *Social Register* for the Rome of his own time. Finally one should notice the nine lines in which Anchises gives what seems to be the highest statement of the Roman ideal.

Since Dante used Virgil as his guide through Hell and Purgatory, it is interesting to note Virgil's influence on the *Divine Comedy*.

The translation given here was made by the twentieth-century poet and scholar, Rolfe Humphries.

Mourning for Palinurus, he drives the fleet
To Cumae's coast-line; the prows are turned, the anchor
Let down, the beach is covered by the vessels.
Young in their eagerness for the land in the west,
They flash ashore; some seek the seeds of flame
Hidden in veins of flint, and others spoil
The woods of tinder, and show where water runs.
Aeneas, in devotion, seeks the heights
Where stands Apollo's temple, and the cave
Where the dread Sibyl dwells, Apollo's priestess,
With the great mind and heart, inspired revealer
Of things to come. They enter Diana's grove,
Pass underneath the roof of gold.

The story
Has it that Daedalus fled from Minos' kingdom,[1]
Trusting himself to wings he made, and travelled
A course unknown to man, to the cold north,
Descending on this very summit; here,
Earth-bound again, he built a mighty temple,
Paying Apollo homage, the dedication
Of the oarage of his wings. On the temple doors
He carved, in bronze, Androgeos' death, and the payment
Enforced on Cecrops' children, seven sons
For sacrifice each year: there stands the urn,
The lots are drawn—facing this, over the sea,
Rises the land of Crete: the scene portrays
Pasiphae in cruel love, the bull
She took to her by cunning, and their offspring,
The mongrel Minotaur, half man, half monster,
The proof of lust unspeakable; and the toil
Of the house is shown, the labyrinthine maze
Which no one could have solved, but Daedalus
Pitied a princess' love, loosened the tangle,
Gave her a skein to guide her way. His boy,
Icarus, might have been here, in the picture,
And almost was—his father had made the effort
Once, and once more and dropped his hands; he could not
Master his grief that much. The story held them;
They would have studied it longer, but Achates[2]
Came from his mission; with him came the priestess,
Deiphobe, daughter of Glaucus, who tends the temple
For Phoebus and Diana; she warned Aeneas:
"It is no such sights the time demands; far better
To offer sacrifice, seven chosen bullocks,
Seven chosen ewes, a herd without corruption."
They were prompt in their obedience, and the priestess
Summoned the Trojans to the lofty temple

The rock's vast side is hollowed into a cavern,
With a hundred mouths, a hundred open portals,
Whence voices rush, the answers of the Sibyl.
They had reached the threshold, and the virgin cried:
"It is time to seek the fates; the god is here,
The god is here, behold him." And as she spoke
Before the entrance, her countenance and color
Changed, and her hair tossed loose, and her heart was heaving,
Her bosom swollen with frenzy; she seemed taller,
Her voice not human at all, as the god's presence
Drew nearer, and took hold on her. "Aeneas,"
She cried, "Aeneas, are you praying?
Are you being swift in prayer? Until you are,
The house of the gods will not be moved, nor open
Its mighty portals." More than her speech, her silence
Made the Trojans cold with terror, and Aeneas
Prayed from the depth of his heart: "Phoebus Apollo,
Compassionate ever, slayer of Achilles
Through aim of Paris' arrow, helper and guide
Over the seas, over the lands, the deserts,
The shoals and quicksands, now at last we have come
To Italy, we hold the lands which fled us:
Grant that thus far, no farther, a Trojan fortune
Attend our wandering. And spare us now,
All of you, gods and goddesses, who hated
Troy in the past, and Trojan glory. I beg you,
Most holy prophetess, in who foreknowing
The future stands revealed, grant that the Trojans—
I ask with fate's permission—rest in Latium
Their wandering storm-tossed gods. I will build a temple,
In honor of Apollo and Diana,
Out of eternal marble, and ordain
Festivals in their honor, and for the Sibyl
A great shrine in our kingdom, and I will place there

1. Daedalus (DED-uh-lus) was a mythical artist and inventor. Imprisoned by King Minos of Crete, he constructed wings for himself and his son Icarus (IK-ar-us) and flew away. Icarus flew too near the sun and melted the wax wings. The other pieces of sculpture mentioned here show other incidents in Daedalus' life.

2. The companion of Aeneas (a-KOT-eez).

The lots and mystic oracles for my people
With chosen priests to tend them. Only, priestess,
This once, I pray you, chant the sacred verses
With your own lips; do not trust them to the leaves,[3]
The mockery of the rushing wind's disorder."

But the priestess, not yet subject to Apollo,
Went reeling through the cavern, wild, and storming
To throw the god, who presses, like a rider,
With bit and bridle and weight, tames her wild spirit,
Shapes her to his control. The doors fly open,
The hundred doors, of their own will, fly open,
And through the air the answer comes:—"O Trojans,
At last the dangers of the sea are over;
That course is run, but graver ones are waiting
On land. The sons of Dardanus[4] will reach
The kingdom of Lavinia[5]—be easy
On that account—the sons of Dardanus, also,
Will wish they had not come there. War, I see,
Terrible war, and the river Tiber foaming
With streams of blood. There will be another Xanthus,
Another Simois,[6] and Greek encampment,
Even another Achilles, born in Latium,
Himself a goddess' son. And Juno further
Will always be there: you will beg for mercy,
Be poor, turn everywhere for help. A woman
Will be the cause once more of so much evil,
A foreign bride, receptive to the Trojans,
A foreign marriage. Do not yield to evil,
Attack, attack, more boldly even than fortune
Seems to permit. An offering of safety,—
Incredible!—will come from a Greek city."

So, through the amplifiers of her cavern,
The hollow vaults, the Sibyl cast her warnings,
Riddles confused with truth; and Apollo rode her,
Reining her rage, and shaking her, and spurring
The fierceness of her heart. The frenzy dwindled,
A little, and her lips were still. Aeneas
Began:—"For me, no form of trouble, maiden,
Is new, or unexpected; all of this
I have known long since, lived in imagination.
One thing I ask: this is the gate of the kingdom,
So it is said, where Pluto reigns, the gloomy
Marsh where the water of Acheron[7] runs over.
Teach me the way from here, open the portals
That I may go to my beloved father,
Stand in his presence, talk with him. I brought him,
Once, on these shoulders, through a thousand weapons
And following fire, and foemen. He shared with me
The road, the sea, the menaces of heaven,
Things that an old man should not bear; he bore them,
Tired as he was. And he it was who told me
To come to you in humbleness. I beg you
Pity the son, the father. You have power,
Great priestess, over all; it is not for nothing
Hecate[8] gave you this dominion over
Avernus' groves. If Orpheus could summon
Eurydice from the shadows with his music,
If Pollux could save his brother, coming, going,
Along this path,—why should I mention Theseus,
Why mention Hercules?[9] I, too, descended
From the line of Jupiter." He clasped the altar,
Making his prayer, and she made answer to him:
"Son of Anchises, born of godly lineage,
By night, by day, the portals of dark Dis[10]
Stand open: it is easy, the descending
Down to Avernus. But to climb again,
To trace the footsteps back to the air above,
There lies the task, the toil. A few, beloved
By Jupiter, descended from the gods,
A few, in whom exalting virtue burned,
Have been permitted. Around the central woods
The black Cocytus glides, a sullen river;
But if such love is in your heart, such longing
For double crossing of the Stygian lake,
For double sight of Tartarus, learn first
What must be done. In a dark tree there hides
A bough, all golden, leaf and pliant stem,
Sacred to Proserpine.[11] This all the grove
Protects, and shadows cover it with darkness.
Until this bough, this bloom of light, is found,
No one receives his passport to the darkness
Whose queen requires this tribute. In succession,
After the bough is plucked, another grows,
Gold-green with the same metal. Raise the eyes,
Look up, reach up the hand, and it will follow
With ease, if fate is calling; otherwise,
No power, no steel, can loose it. Furthermore,
(Alas, you do not know this!), one of your men
Lies on the shore, unburied, a pollution
To all the fleet, while you have come for counsel
Here to our threshold. Bury him with honor;
Black cattle slain in expiation for him
Must fall before you see the Stygian kingdoms,
The groves denied to living men."

Aeneas,
With sadness in his eyes, and downcast heart,
Turned from the cave, and at his side Achates
Accompanied his anxious meditations.
They talked together: who could be the comrade
Named by the priestess, lying there unburied?
And they found him on dry sand; it was Misenus,[12]
Aeolus' son, none better with the trumpet
To make men burn for warfare. He had been
Great Hector's man-at-arms; he was good in battle

---

3. The prophecies of this Cumaean Sibyl were usually written on leaves which the winds in the cave might scatter and confuse (v. Book III).
4. The mythical founder of Troy.
5. The daughter of the Italian King Latinus. Aeneas was later to marry her to establish his kingdom.
6. Rivers near Troy that ran with blood during the Trojan War.
7. This is the river (AK-uh-ron) that leads to Hades. Other rivers in the lower world are the Styx, which forms a boundary for the region, Cocytus (kō-SĪ-tus), and Phlegethon (FLEǴ-uh-thon), which serves as a barrier between the mild punishments and the more severe.
8. Hecate (HEK-uh-tee) is a very powerful goddess who, among many responsibilities, controlled the spirits of the dead. Avernus is a very deep pool surrounded by gloomy woods. Its depth and gloom inspired the idea that it led to the underworld.
9. All of these are the names of mythical heroes who had descended into Hades and returned.
10. Dis is another name for the underworld.
11. Proserpine (prō-SUR-pi-nee), as wife of Pluto, is queen of the underworld.
12. mi-SEEN-us.

With spear as well as horn, and after Hector
Had fallen to Achilles, he had followed
Aeneas, entering no meaner service.
Some foolishness came over him; he made
The ocean echo to the blare of his trumpet
That day, and challenged the sea-gods to a contest
In martial music, and Triton, jealous, caught him,
However unbelievable the story,
And held him down between the rocks, and drowned him
Under the foaming waves. His comrades mourned him,
Aeneas most of all, and in their sorrow
They carry out, in haste, the Sibyl's orders,
Construct the funeral altar, high as heaven,
They go to an old wood, and the pine-trees fall
Where wild beasts have their dens, and holm-oak rings
To the stroke of the axe, and oak and ash are riven
By the splitting wedge, and rowan-trees come rolling
Down the steep mountain-side. Aeneas helps them,
And cheers them on; studies the endless forest,
Takes thought, and prays: "If only we might see it,
That golden bough, here in the depth of the forest,
Bright on some tree. She told the truth, our priestess,
Too much, too bitter truth, about Misenus."
No sooner had he spoken than twin doves
Came flying down before him, and alighted
On the green ground. He knew his mother's birds,[13]
And made his prayer, rejoicing,—"Oh, be leaders,
Wherever the way, and guide me to the grove
Where the rich bough makes rich the shaded ground.
Help me, O goddess-mother!" And he paused,
Watching what sign they gave, what course they set.
The birds flew on a little, just ahead
Of the pursuing vision; when they came
To the jaws of dank Avernus, evil-smelling,
They rose aloft, then swooped down the bright air,
Perched on the double tree, where the off-color
Of gold was gleaming golden through the branches.
As mistletoe, in the cold winter, blossoms
With its strange foliage on an alien tree,
The yellow berry gilding the smooth branches,
Such was the vision of the gold in leaf
On the dark holm-oak, so the foil was rustling,
Rattling, almost, the bract in the soft wind
Stirring like metal. Aeneas broke it off
With eager grasp, and bore it to the Sibyl.

Meanwhile, along the shore, the Trojans mourned,
Paying Misenus' dust the final honors.
A mighty pyre was raised, of pine and oak,
The sides hung with dark leaves, and somber cypress
Along the front, and gleaming arms above.
Some made the water hot, and some made ready
Bronze caldrons, shimmering over fire, and others
Lave and anoint the body, and with weeping
Lay on the bier his limbs, and place above them
Familiar garments, crimson color; and some
Take up the heavy burden, a sad office,
And, as their fathers did, they kept their eyes
Averted, as they brought the torches nearer.
They burn gifts with him, bowls of oil, and viands,
And frankincense; and when the flame is quiet
And the ashes settle to earth, they wash the embers
With wine, and slake the thirsty dust. The bones
Are placed in a bronze urn by Corynaeus,
Who, with pure water, thrice around his comrades
Made lustral cleansing, shaking gentle dew
From the fruitful branch of olive; and they said
Hail and farewell! And over him Aeneas
Erects a mighty tomb, with the hero's arms,
His oar and trumpet, where the mountain rises
Memorial for ever, and named Misenus.

These rites performed, he hastened to the Sibyl.
There was a cavern, yawning wide and deep,
Jagged, below the darkness of the trees,
Beside the darkness of the lake. No bird
Could fly above it safely, with the vapor
Pouring from the black gulf (the Greeks have named it
Avernus, or A-Ornos, meaning *birdless*),
And here the priestess for the slaughter set
Four bullocks, black ones, poured the holy wine
Between the horns, and plucked the topmost bristles
For the first offering to the sacred fire,
Calling on Hecate, a power in heaven,
A power in hell. Knives to the throat were driven,
The warm blood caught in bowls. Aeneas offered
A lamb, black-fleeced, to Night and her great sister,
A sterile heifer for the queen; for Dis
An altar in the night, and on the flames
The weight of heavy bulls, the fat oil pouring
Over the burning entrails. And at dawn,
Under their feet, earth seemed to shake and rumble,
The ridges move, and bitches bay in darkness,
As the presence neared. The Sibyl cried a warning,
"Keep off, keep off, whatever is unholy,
Depart from here! Courage, Aeneas; enter
The path, unsheathe the sword. The time is ready
For the brave heart." She strode out boldly, leading
Into the open cavern, and he followed.

Gods of the world of spirit, silent shadows,
Chaos and Phlegethon, areas of silence,
Wide realms of dark, may it be right and proper
To tell what I have heard, this revelation
Of matters buried deep in earth and darkness!

Vague forms in lonely darkness, they were going
Through void and shadow, through the empty realm
Like people in a forest, when the moonlight
Shifts with a baleful glimmer, and shadow covers
The sky, and all the colors turn to blackness.
At the first threshold, on the jaws of Orcus,
Grief and avenging Cares have set their couches,
And pale Diseases dwell, and sad Old Age,
Fear, evil-counselling Hunger, wretched Need,
Forms terrible to see, and Death, and Toil,
And Death's own brother, Sleep, and evil Joys,
Fantasies of the mind, and deadly War,
The Furies' iron chambers, Discord, raving,
Her snaky hair entwined in bloody bands.
An elm-tree loomed there, shadowy and huge,
The aged boughs outspread, beneath whose leaves,
Men say, the false dreams cling, thousands on thousands.
And there are monsters in the dooryard, Centaurs,
Scyllas, of double shape, the beast of Lerna,
Hissing most horribly, Briareus,
The hundred-handed giant, a Chimaera
Whose armament is fire, Harpies, and Gorgons,
A triple-bodied giant. In sudden panic

---

13. Aeneas' mother was Venus.

Aeneas drew his sword, the edge held forward,
Ready to rush and flail, however blindly,
Save that his wise companion warned him, saying
They had no substance, they were only phantoms
Flitting about, illusions without body.

From here, the road turns off to Acheron,
River of Hell; here, thick with muddy whirling,
Cocytus boils with sand. Charon[14] is here,
The guardian of these mingling waters, Charon,
Uncouth and filthy, on whose chin the hair
Is a tangled mat, whose eyes protrude, are burning,
Whose dirty cloak is knotted at the shoulder.
He poles a boat, tends to the sail, unaided,
Ferrying bodies in his rust-hued vessel.
Old, but a god's senility is awful
In its raw greenness. To the bank come thronging
Mothers and men, bodies of great-souled heroes,
Their life-time over, boys, unwedded maidens,
Young men whose fathers saw their pyres burning,
Thick as the forest leaves that fall in autumn
With early frost, thick as the birds to landfall
From over the seas, when the chill of the year compels them
To sunlight. There they stand, a host, imploring
To be taken over first. Their hands, in longing
Reach out for the farther shore. But the gloomy boatman
Makes choice among them, taking some, and keeping
Others far back from the stream's edge. Aeneas,
Wondering, asks the Sibyl, "Why the crowding?
What are the spirits seeking? What distinction
Brings some across the livid stream, while others
Stay on the farther bank?" She answers, briefly:
"Son of Anchises, this is the awful river,
The Styx,[15] by which the gods take oath; the boatman
Charon; those he takes with him are the buried,
Those he rejects, whose luck is out, the graveless.
It is not permitted him to take them over
The dreadful banks and hoarse-resounding waters
Till earth is cast upon their bones. They haunt
These shores a hundred restless years of waiting
Before they end postponement of the crossing."
Aeneas paused, in thoughtful mood, with pity
Over their lot's unevenness; and saw there,
Wanting the honor given the dead, and grieving,
Leucaspis, and Orontes, the Lycian captain,
Who had sailed from Troy across the stormy waters,
And drowned off Africa, with crew and vessel,
And there was Palinurus, once his pilot,
Who, not so long ago, had been swept over,
Watching the stars on the journey north from Carthage.
The murk was thick; Aeneas hardly knew him,
Sorrowful in that darkness, but made question:
"What god, O Palinurus, took you from us?
Who drowned you in the deep? Tell me. Apollo
Never before was false, and yet he told me
You would be safe across the seas, and come
Unharmed to Italy; what kind of promise
Was this, to fool me with?" But Palinurus
Gave him assurance:—"It was no god who drowned me,
No falsehood on Apollo's part, my captain,
But as I clung to the tiller, holding fast
To keep the course, as I should do, I felt it
Wrenched from the ship, and I fell with it, headlong.
By those rough seas I swear, I had less fear
On my account than for the ship, with rudder
And helmsman overboard, to drift at the mercy
Of rising seas. Three nights I rode the waters,
Three nights of storm, and from the crest of a wave,
On the fourth morning, sighted Italy,
I was swimming to land, I had almost reached it, heavy
In soaking garments; my cramped fingers struggled
To grasp the top of the rock, when barbarous people,
Ignorant men, mistaking me for booty,
Struck me with swords; waves hold me now, or winds
Roll me along the shore. By the light of heaven
The lovely air, I beg you, by your father,
Your hope of young Iulus,[16] bring me rescue
Out of these evils, my unconquered leader!
Cast over my body earth—you have the power—
Return to Velia's harbor,—or there may be
Some other way—your mother is a goddess,
Else how would you be crossing this great river,
This Stygian swamp?—help a poor fellow, take me
Over the water with you, give a dead man
At least a place to rest in." But the Sibyl
Broke in upon him sternly:—"Palinurus,
Whence comes this mad desire? No man, unburied,
May see the Stygian waters, or Cocytus,
The Furies' dreadful river; no man may come
Unbidden to this bank. Give up the hope
That fate is changed by praying, but hear this,
A little comfort in your harsh misfortune:
Those neighboring people will make expiation,
Driven by signs from heaven, through their cities
And through their countryside; they will build a tomb,
Thereto bring offerings yearly, and the place
Shall take its name from you, Cape Palinurus."
So he was comforted a little, finding
Some happiness in the promise.

And they went on,
Nearing the river, and from the stream the boatman
Beheld them cross the silent forest, nearer,
Turning their footsteps toward the bank. He challenged:—
"Whoever you are, O man in armor, coming
In this direction, halt where you are, and tell me
The reason why you come. This is the region
Of shadows, and of Sleep and drowsy Night;
I am not allowed to carry living bodies
In the Stygian boat; and I must say I was sorry
I ever accepted Hercules and Theseus
And Pirithous, and rowed them over the lake,
Though they were sons of gods and great in courage.
One of them dared to drag the guard of Hell,
Enchained, from Pluto's throne, shaking in terror,
The others to snatch our queen from Pluto's chamber."
The Sibyl answered briefly: "No such cunning
Is plotted here; our weapons bring no danger.
Be undisturbed: the hell-hound in his cavern
May bark forever, to keep the bloodless shadows
Frightened away from trespass; Proserpine,
Untouched, in pureness guard her uncle's threshold.
Trojan Aeneas, a man renowned for goodness,
Renowned for nerve in battle, is descending

14. KARE-on.
15. STICKS.
16. This is Aeneas' son, also known as Ascanius.

To the lowest shades; he comes to find his father.
If such devotion has no meaning to you,
Look on this branch at least, and recognize it!"
And with the word she drew from under her mantle
The golden bough; his swollen wrath subsided.
No more was said; he saw the bough, and marvelled
At the holy gift, so long unseen; came sculling
The dark-blue boat to the shore, and drove the spirits,
Lining the thwarts, ashore, and cleared the gangway,
And took Aeneas aboard; as that big man
Stepped in, the leaky skiff groaned under the weight,
And the strained seams let in the muddy water,
But they made the crossing safely, seer and soldier,
To the far margin, colorless and shapeless,
Grey sedge and dark-brown ooze. They heard the baying
Of Cerberus,[17] that great hound, in his cavern crouching,
Making the shore resound, as all three throats
Belled horribly; and serpents rose and bristled
Along the triple neck. The priestess threw him
A sop with honey and drugged meal; he opened
The ravenous throat, gulped, and subsided, filling
The den with his huge bulk. Aeneas, crossing
Passed on beyond the bank of the dread river
Whence none return.

A wailing of thin voices[18]
Came to their ears, the souls of infants crying,
Those whom the day of darkness took from the breast
Before their share of living. And there were many
Whom some false sentence brought to death. Here Minos[19]
Judges them once again; a silent jury
Reviews the evidence. And there are others,
Guilty of nothing, but who hated living,
The suicides. How gladly, now, they would suffer
Poverty, hardship, in the world of light!
But this is not permitted; they are bound
Nine times around by the black unlovely river;
Styx holds them fast.

They came to the Fields of
Mourning,
So-called, where those whom cruel love had wasted
Hid in secluded pathways, under myrtle,
And even in death were anxious. Procris, Phaedra,
Eriphyle, displaying wounds her son
Had given her, Caeneus, Laodamia,
Caeneus, a young man once, and now again
A young man, after having been a woman.
And here, new come from her own wound, was Dido,[20]
Wandering in the wood. The Trojan hero,
Standing near by, saw her, or thought he saw her,
Dim in the shadows, like the slender crescent
Of moon when cloud drifts over. Weeping, he greets her:—
"Unhappy Dido, so they told me truly
That your own hand had brought you death. Was I—
Alas!—the cause? I swear by all the stars,
By the world above, by everything held sacred
Here under the earth, unwillingly, O queen,
I left your kingdom. But the gods' commands,
Driving me now through these forsaken places,
This utter night, compelled me on. I could not
Believe my loss would cause so great a sorrow.
Linger a moment, do not leave me; whither,
Whom, are you fleeing? I am permitted only
This last word with you."

But the queen, unmoving
As flint or marble, turned away, her eyes
Fixed on the ground: the tears were vain, the words,
Meant to be soothing, foolish; she turned away,
His enemy forever, to the shadows
Where Sychaeus, her former husband, took her
With love for love, and sorrow for her sorrow.
And still Aeneas wept for her, being troubled
By the injustice of her doom; his pity
Followed her going.

They went on. They came
To the farthest fields, whose tenants are the warriors,
Illustrious throng. Here Tydeus came to meet him,
Parthenopaeus came, and pale Adrastus,
A fighter's ghost, and many, many others,
Mourned in the world above, and doomed in battle,
Leaders of Troy, in long array; Aeneas
Sighed as he saw them: Medon; Polyboetes,
The priest of Ceres; Glaucus; and Idaeus
Still keeping arms and chariot; three brothers,
Antenor's sons; Thersilochus; a host
To right and left of him, and when they see him,
One sight is not enough; they crowd around him,
Linger, and ask the reasons for his coming.
But Agamemnon's men, the Greek battalions,
Seeing him there, and his arms in shadow gleaming,
Tremble in panic, turn to flee for refuge,
As once they used to, toward their ships, but where
Are the ships now? They try to shout, in terror;
But only a thin and piping treble issues
To mock their mouths, wide-open.

One he knew
Was here, Deiphobus,[21] a son of Priam,
With his whole body mangled, and his features
Cruelly slashed, and both hands cut, and ears
Torn from his temples, and his nostrils slit
By shameful wounds. Aeneas hardly knew him,
Shivering there, and doing his best to hide
His marks of punishment; unhailed, he hailed him:—
"Deiphobus, great warrior, son of Teucer,
Whose cruel punishment was this? Whose license
Abused you so? I heard, it seems a story
Of that last night, how you had fallen, weary
With killing Greeks at last; I built a tomb,
Although no body lay there, in your honor,
Three times I cried, aloud, over your spirit,
Where now your name and arms keep guard. I could not,
Leaving my country, find my friend, to give him
Proper interment in the earth he came from."
And Priam's son replied:—"Nothing, dear comrade,
Was left undone; the dead man's shade was given
All ceremony due. It was my own fortune
And a Spartan woman's[22] deadliness that sunk me

---

17. SIR-bur-us.
18. Here and about 190 lines later you might compare the sins and their punishments with the disposition Dante makes of the souls in Hell in Canto XI of the *Inferno*.
19. MI-nus.
20. Dido, Queen of Carthage, filled with rage and guilt had committed suicide when Aeneas sailed away from her city.
21. dee-IF-uh-bus.
22. This is Helen of Troy. Vergil believes that she was married to Deiphobus after Paris' death.

Under these evils; she it was who left me
These souvenirs. You know how falsely happy
We were on that last night; I need not tell you.
When that dread horse came leaping over our walls,
Pregnant with soldiery, she led the dancing,
A solemn rite, she called it, with Trojan women
Screaming their bacchanals; she raised the torches
High on the citadel; she called the Greeks.
Then—I was worn with trouble, drugged in slumber,
Resting in our ill-omened bridal chamber,
With sleep as deep and sweet as death upon me—
Then she, that paragon of helpmates, deftly
Moved all the weapons from the house; my sword,
Even, she stole from underneath my pillow,
Opened the door, and called in Menelaus,
Hoping, no doubt, to please her loving husband,
To win forgetfulness of her old sinning.
It is quickly told: they broke into the chamber,
The two of them, and with them, as accomplice,
Ulysses came, the crime-contriving bastard.
O gods, pay back the Greeks; grant the petition
If goodness asks for vengeance! But you, Aeneas,
A living man—what chance has brought you here?
Vagrant of ocean, god-inspired,—which are you?
What chance has worn you down, to come, in sadness,
To these confusing sunless dwelling-places?"

While they were talking, Aurora's rosy car
Had halfway crossed the heaven; all their time
Might have been spent in converse, but the Sibyl
Hurried them forward:—"Night comes on, Aeneas;
We waste the hours with tears. We are at the cross-road,
Now; here we turn to the right, where the pathway leads
On to Elysium, under Pluto's ramparts.
Leftward to Tartarus, and retribution,
The terminal of the wicked, and their dungeon."
Deiphobus left them, saying, "O great priestess,
Do not be angry with me; I am going;
I shall not fail the roll-call of the shadows.
Pride of our race, go on; may better fortune
Attend you!" and, upon the word, he vanished.

As he looked back, Aeneas saw, to his left,
Wide walls beneath a cliff, a triple rampart,
A river running fire, Phlegethon's torrent,
Rocks roaring in its course, a gate, tremendous,
Pillars of adamant, a tower of iron,
Too strong for men, too strong for even gods
To batter down in warfare, and behind them
A Fury, sentinel in bloody garments,
Always on watch, by day, by night. He heard
Sobbing and groaning there, the crack of the lash,
The clank of iron, the sound of dragging shackles.
The noise was terrible; Aeneas halted,
Asking, "What forms of crime are these, O maiden?
What harrying punishment, what horrible outcry?"
She answered:—"O great leader of the Trojans,
I have never crossed that threshold of the wicked;
No pure soul is permitted entrance thither,
But Hecate, by whose order I was given
Charge of Avernus' groves, my guide, my teacher,
Told me how gods exact the toll of vengeance.
The monarch here, merciless Rhadamanthus,
Punishes guilt, and hears confession; he forces
Acknowledgment of crime; no man in the world,
No matter how cleverly he hides his evil,
No matter how much he smiles at his own slyness,
Can fend atonement off; the hour of death
Begins his sentence. Tisiphone, the Fury,
Leaps at the guilty with her scourge; her serpents
Are whips of menace as she calls her sisters.
Imagine the gates, on jarring hinge, rasp open,
You would see her in the doorway, a shape, a sentry,
Savage, implacable. Beyond, still fiercer,
The monstrous Hydra dwells; her fifty throats
Are black, and open wide, and Tartarus
Is black, and open wide, and it goes down
To darkness, sheer deep down, and twice the distance
That earth is from Olympus. At the bottom
The Titans crawl, Earth's oldest breed, hurled under
By thunderbolts; here lie the giant twins,
Aloeus' sons, who laid their hands on heaven
And tried to pull down Jove; Salmoneus here
Atones for high presumption,—it was he
Who aped Jove's noise and fire, wheeling his horses
Triumphant through his city in Elis, cheering
And shaking the torch, and claiming divine homage,
The arrogant fool, to think his brass was lightning,
His horny-footed horses beat out thunder!
Jove showed him what real thunder was, what lightning
Spoke from immortal cloud, what whirlwind fury
Came sweeping from the heaven to overtake him.
Here Tityos, Earth's giant son, lies sprawling
Over nine acres, with a monstrous vulture
Gnawing, with crooked beak, vitals and liver
That grow as they are eaten; eternal anguish,
Eternal feast. Over another hangs
A rock, about to fall; and there are tables
Set for a banquet, gold with royal splendor,
But if a hand goes out to touch the viands,
The Fury drives it back with fire and yelling.
Why name them all, Pirithous, the Lapiths,
Ixion? The roll of crime would take forever.
Whoever, in his lifetime, hated his brother,
Or struck his father down; whoever cheated
A client, or was miserly—how many
Of these there seem to be!—whoever went
To treasonable war, or broke a promise
Made to his lord, whoever perished, slain
Over adultery, all these, walled in,
Wait here their punishment. Seek not to know
Too much about their doom. The stone is rolled,
The wheel keeps turning; Theseus forever
Sits in dejection; Phlegyas, accursed,
Cries through the halls forever: *Being warned,*
Learn justice; reverence the gods! The man
Who sold his country is here in hell; the man
Who altered laws for money; and a father
Who knew his daughter's bed. All of them dared,
And more than dared, achieved, unspeakable
Ambitions. If I had a hundred tongues,
A hundred iron throats, I could not tell
The fullness of their crime and punishment."
And then she added:—"Come: resume the journey,
Fulfill the mission; let us hurry onward.
I see the walls the Cyclops made, the portals
Under the archway, where, the orders tell us,
Our tribute must be set." They went together
Through the way's darkness, came to the doors, and halted,
And at the entrance Aeneas, having sprinkled
His body with fresh water, placed the bough

Golden before the threshold. The will of the goddess
Had been performed, the proper task completed.

They came to happy places, the joyful dwelling,
The lovely greenery of the groves of the blessed.
Here ampler air invests the fields with light,
Rose-colored, with familiar stars and sun.
Some grapple on the grassy wrestling-ground
In exercise and sport, and some are dancing,
And others singing; in his trailing robe
Orpheus strums the lyre; the seven clear notes
Accompany the dance, the song. And heroes
Are there, great-souled, born in the happier years,
Ilus,[23] Assaracus; the city's founder,
Prince Dardanus. Far off, Aeneas wonders,
Seeing the phantom arms, the chariots,
The spears fixed in the ground, the chargers browsing,
Unharnessed, over the plain. Whatever, living,
The men delighted in, whatever pleasure
Was theirs in horse and chariot, still holds them
Here under the world. To right and left, they banquet
In the green meadows, and a joyful chorus
Rises through groves of laurel, whence the river
Runs to the upper world. The band of heroes
Dwell here, all those whose mortal wounds were suffered
In fighting for the fatherland; and poets,
The good, the pure, the worthy of Apollo;
Those who discovered truth and made life nobler;
Those who served others—all, with snowy fillets
Binding their temples, throng the lovely valley.
And these the Sibyl questioned, most of all
Musaeus,[24] for he towered above the center
Of that great throng:—"O happy souls, O poet,
Where does Anchises dwell? For him we come here,
For him we have traversed Erebus' great rivers."
And he replied:—"It is all our home, the shady
Groves, and the streaming meadows, and the softness
Along the river-banks. No fixed abode
Is ours at all; but if it is your pleasure,
Cross over the ridge with me; I will guide you there
By easy going." And so Musaeus led them
And from the summit showed them fields, all shining,
And they went on over and down.

Deep in a valley of green, father Anchises
Was watching, with deep earnestness, the spirits
Whose destiny was light, and counting them over,
All of his race to come, his dear descendants,
Their fates and fortunes and their works and ways,
And as he saw Aeneas coming toward him
Over the meadow, his hands reached out with yearning,
He was moved to tears, and called:—"At last, my son,—
Have you really come, at last? and the long road nothing
To a son who loves his father? Do I, truly,
See you, and hear your voice? I was thinking so,
I was hoping so, I was counting off the days,
And I was right about it. O my son!
What a long journey, over land and water,
Yours must have been! What buffeting of danger!
I feared, so much, the Libyan realm would hurt you."
And his son answered:—"It was your spirit, father,
Your sorrowful shade, so often met, that led me
To find these portals. The ships ride safe at anchor,
Safe in the Tuscan sea. Embrace me, father;
Let hand join hand in love; do not forsake me."
And as he spoke, the tears streamed down. Three times
He reached out toward him, and three times the image
Fled like the breath of the wind or a dream on wings.

He saw, in a far valley, a separate grove
Where the woods stir and rustle, and a river,
The Lethe,[25] gliding past the peaceful places,
And tribes of people thronging, hovering over,
Innumberable as the bees in summer
Working the bright-hued flowers, and the shining
Of the white lilies, murmuring and humming.
Aeneas, filled with wonder, asks the reason
For what he does not know, who are the people
In such a host, and to what river coming?
Anchises answers:—"These are spirits, ready
Once more for life; they drink of Lethe's water
The soothing potion of forgetfulness.
I have longed, for long, to show them to you, name them,
Our children's children; Italy discovered,
So much the greater happiness, my son."
"But, O my father, is it thinkable
That souls would leave this blessedness, be willing
A second time to bear the sluggish body,
Trade Paradise for earth? Alas, poor wretches,
Why such a mad desire for light?" Anchises
Gives detailed answer: "First, my son, a spirit
Sustains all matter heaven and earth and ocean,
The moon, the stars; mind quickens mass, and moves it.
Hence comes the race of man, of beast, of winged
Creatures of air, of the strange shapes which ocean
Bears down below his mottled marble surface.
All these are blessed with energy from heaven;[26]
The seed of life is a spark of fire, but the body
A clod of earth, a clog, a mortal burden.
Hence humans fear, desire, grieve, and are joyful,
And even when life is over, all the evil
Ingrained so long, the adulterated mixture,
The plagues and pestilences of the body
Remain, persist. So there must be a cleansing,
By penalty, by punishment, by fire,
By sweep of wind, by water's absolution,
Before the guilt is gone. Each of us suffers
His own peculiar ghost. But the day comes
When we are sent through wide Elysium,
The Fields of the Blessed, a few of us, to linger
Until the turn of time, the wheel of ages,
Wears off the taint, and leaves the core of spirit
Pure sense, pure flame. A thousand years pass over
And the god calls the countless host to Lethe
Where memory is annulled, and souls are willing
Once more to enter into mortal bodies."

The discourse ended; the father drew his son
And his companion toward the hum, the center
Of the full host; they came to rising ground
Where all the long array was visible,
Anchises watching, noting, every comer.
"Glory to come, my son, illustrious spirits
Of Dardan lineage, Italian offspring,
Heirs of our name, begetters of our future!

---

23. These are all ancestors of Aeneas, all former kings of Troy.
24. A mythical poet and singer.
25. LEE-thee.
26. You might compare this with Dante's ideas on the same thing. See, for example, Purgatory, Cantos XVI and XVIII.

These I will name for you and tell our fortunes:
First, leaning on a headless spear, and standing
Nearest the light, that youth, the first to rise
To the world above, is Silvius; his name
Is Alban; in his veins Italian blood
Will run with Trojan; he will be the son
Of your late age; Lavinia will bear him,
A king and sire of kings; from him our race
Will rule in Alba Longa.[27] Near him, Procas,
A glory to the Trojan race; and Capys,
And Numitor, and Silvius Aeneas,
Resembling you in name, in arms, in goodness,
If ever he wins the Alban kingdom over.
What fine young men they are! What strength, what prowess!
The civic oak already shades their foreheads.
These will found cities, Gabii, Fidenae,
Nomentum; they will crown the hills with towers
Above Collatia, Inuus fortress, Bola,
Cora, all names to be, thus far ungiven.

"And there will be a son of Mars; his mother
Is Ilia, and his name is Romulus,
Assaracus' descendant. On his helmet
See, even now, twin plumes; his father's honor
Confers distinction on him for the world.
Under his auspices Rome, that glorious city,
Will bound her power by earth, her pride by heaven,
Happy in hero sons, one wall surrounding
Her seven hills, even as Cybele, riding
Through Phrygian cities, wears her crown of towers,
Rejoicing in her offspring, and embracing
A hundred children of the gods, her children,
Celestials, all of them, at home in heaven.
Turn the eyes now this way; behold the Romans,
Your very own. These are Iulus' children,
The race to come. One promise you have heard
Over and over: here is its fulfillment,
The son of a god, Augustus Caesar, founder
Of a new age of gold, in lands where Saturn
Ruled long ago; he will extend his empire
Beyond the Indies, beyond the normal measure
Of years and constellations, where high Atlas
Turns on his shoulders the star-studded world.
Maeotia[28] and the Caspian seas are trembling
As heaven's oracles predict his coming,
And all the seven mouths of Nile are troubled
Not even Hercules, in all his travels,
Covered so much of the world, from Erymanthus
To Lerna; nor did Bacchus, driving his tigers
From Nysa's summit. How can hesitation
Keep us from deeds to make our prowess greater?
What fear can block us from Ausonian land?

"And who is that one yonder, wearing the olive,
Holding the sacrifice? I recognize him,
That white-haired king of Rome, who comes from Cures,
A poor land, to a mighty empire, giver
Of law to the young town. His name is Numa.
Near him is Tullus; he will rouse to arms
A race grown sluggish, little used to triumph.
Beyond him Ancus, even now too boastful,
Too fond of popular favor. And then the Tarquins,
And the avenger Brutus, proud of spirit,
Restorer of the balance. He shall be
First holder of the consular power; his children
Will stir up wars again, and he, for freedom
And her sweet sake, will call down judgment on them,
Unhappy, however future men may praise him,
In love of country and intense ambition.

"There are the Decii,[29] and there the Drusi,
A little farther off, and stern Torquatus,
The man with the axe, and Camillus, the regainer
Of standards lost. And see those two, resplendent
In equal arms, harmonious friendly spirits
Now, in the shadow of night, but if they ever
Come to the world of light, alas, what warfare,
What battle-lines, what slaughter they will fashion,
Each for the other, one from Alpine ramparts
Descending, and the other ranged against him
With armies from the east, father and son
Through marriage, Pompey and Caesar. O my children,
Cast out the thoughts of war, and do not murder
The flower of our country. O my son,
Whose line descends from heaven, let the sword
Fall from the hand, be leader in forbearing!

"Yonder is one who, victor over Corinth,
Will ride in triumph home, famous for carnage
Inflicted on the Greeks; near him another,
Destroyer of old Argus and Mycenae
Where Agamemnon ruled; he will strike down
A king descended from Achilles; Pydna
Shall be revenge for Pallas' ruined temple,
For Trojan ancestors. Who would pass over,
Without a word, Cossus, or noble Cato,
The Gracchi, or those thunderbolts of warfare,
The Scipios, Libya's ruin, or Fabricius
Mighty with little, or Serranus, ploughing
The humble furrow; My tale must hurry on:
I see the Fabii next, and their great Quintus
Who brought us back an empire by delaying.
Others, no doubt, will better mould the bronze[30]
To the semblance of soft breathing, draw, from marble,
The living countenance; and others plead
With greater eloquence, or learn to measure,
Better than we, the pathways of the heaven,
The risings of the stars: remember, Roman,
To rule the people under law, to establish
The way of peace, to battle down the haughty,
To spare the meek. Our fine arts, these, forever."

Anchises paused a moment, and they marvelled,
And he went on:—"See, how Marcellus triumphs,
Glorious over all, with the great trophies
Won when he slew the captain of the Gauls,
Leader victorious over leading foeman.
When Rome is in great trouble and confusion
He will establish order, Gaul and Carthage
Go down before his sword, and triple trophies
Be given Romulus in dedication."

---

27. One of the earliest of the Italian cities, near Rome. Supposedly founded by Ascanius.
28. These names merely signify that the empire will extend from one end to the other of the known world.
29. These are the names of families who produced famous men in Rome's history.
30. Probably these nine lines are a better expression of the best of the Roman spirit than can be found in any other place.

There was a young man going with Marcellus,
Brilliant in shining armor, bright in beauty,
But sorrowful, with downcast eyes. Aeneas
Broke in, to ask his father: "Who is this youth
Attendant on the hero? A son of his?
One of his children's children? How the crowd
Murmurs and hums around him! what distinction,
What presence, in his person! But dark night
Hovers around his head with mournful shadow.
Who is he, father?" And Anchises answered:—
"Great sorrow for our people! O my son,
Ask not to know it. This one fate will only
Show to the world; he will not be permitted
Any long sojourn. Rome would be too mighty,
Too great in the gods' sight, were this gift hers.
What lamentation will the field of Mars
Raise to the city! Tiber, gliding by
The new-built tomb, the funeral state, bear witness!
No youth from Trojan stock will ever raise
His ancestors so high in hope, no Roman
Be such a cause for pride. Alas for goodness,
Alas for old-time honor, and the arm
Invincible in war! Against him no one,
Whether on foot or foaming horse, would come
In battle and depart unscathed. Poor boy,
If you should break the cruel fates; if only—
You are to be Marcellus. Let me scatter
Lilies, or dark-red flowers, bringing honor
To my descendant's shade; let the gift be offered,
However vain the tribute."

So through the whole wide realm they went together,
Anchises and his son; from the fields of air
Learning and teaching of the fame and glory,
The wars to come, the toils to face, or flee from,
Latinus' city and the Latin peoples,
The love of what would be.

There are two portals,
Twin gates of Sleep, one made of horn, where easy
Release is given true shades, the other gleaming
White ivory, whereby the false dreams issue
To the upper air. Aeneas and the Sibyl
Part from Anchises at the second portal.
He goes to the ships, again, rejoins his comrades,
Sails to Caieta's harbor, and the vessels
Rest on their mooring-lines.

Eclogue IV

Virgil (Pubilius Virgilius Maro)

Virgil's *Fourth Eclogue* (EK-log, a pastoral or idyllic poem), known as the "Pollio" from the name of the friend to whom it was addressed, and known also as "The Messianic Eclogue," was written in 40 B.C. to commemorate the birth of a child; but the identity of the child has eluded the scholars—there is no agreement among them. However, the high praise and the mystical allusions of the poet, strongly reminiscent of the very phrases of Isaiah in his prophecies of the Messiah, have connected the poem in the minds of many with the coming of the Christ. Early Christians found in the Eclogue corroboration of the Biblical prophecies, and thought of Virgil, consequently, as a "virtuous Pagan," one to whom had been vouchsafed some gleams of the advent of Christ. Virgil's reputation as a good, even holy, man, grew as the Middle Ages remembered his poem; his reputation increased, in folklore, as a magician and seer—possibly because of his birthplace, where witchcraft, necromancy, and magic were always a matter of popular concern. So strong was his reputation as a foreteller of Christ's birth that Dante saw fit to make him his "guide, philosopher, and friend" in the *Divine Comedy;* he was led by Virgil as far as the pagan could take him, to the very entrance of the earthly Paradise.

The student would do well to refresh his memory of the verses of Isaiah, especially in Chapters vii, ix, and xi, that have to do with vines and briers, "unto us a child is born," the concord among living things, and the like. There is no evidence that Virgil was acquainted with the writings of the Hebrew prophet.

Pastoral Muses of Sicily,
now let us sing a loftier song;
not all are pleased with country themes
of orchard trees and lowly shrubs:
if we sing in pastoral style,
let it be a style still worthy of a consul's ear!

Now, even now, the last great age is coming in,
foretold in the Cumaean Sybil's book;
The great cycle of the ages starts anew,
as from the beginning;
Astraea returns, the maiden Justice;
the Golden Age of Saturn comes again;
a new generation is sent us from high heaven.

Diana,—Lucina, Light-Bringer—chaste goddess,
look favorably upon the coming birth,
the child for whom the old bad Iron Race yields
to a new Golden one, rising over all the world:
your brother Apollo begins his reign.

Pollio, in your term of office, even while you are consul,
this Wonder of Time will begin his being;

Line 1—"Pastoral"—it is interesting to note that the more sophisticated the civilization, the more urban and artificial the life of time, the greater the appeal of pastoral poetry, "the simple life," "back to nature." Vergil's age is a case in point; torn with the dissensions of civil strife and the growing importance of metropolitan Rome, the Italy of his day found satisfaction in "getting away from it all" thru the medium of the pastoral.

Line 9—"the cycle of the ages"—it is unnecessary to go into the ancient (Etruscan?) notion that the world-cycle moved thru successive stages back to a point identical with the beginning; the "Platonic Year," when even the stars and planets would return to their position as at Creation. Suffice it to say, Vergil does have some sort of cycle of world history in mind; the Ages of Gold, Silver, Brass, and Iron, returning eventually to a new Golden Age.

Line 19—"Pollio"—C. Asinus Pollio, Vergil's friend to whom the Eclogue is addressed, was a well-known public figure of the times; a general and adherent of Julius Caesar, he became consul in 40 B.C., and concluded the peace treaty between Octavian and Antony, known as the Treaty of Brundisium. It has been suggested (but not proved) that the child of the Eclogue may have been one of Pollio's sons.

the majestic months commence their progress;
under your leadership, Pollio.
even if traces remain of our human guilt,
new times will free earth from its abiding terror.

This child will live like a god;
he will see gods and heroes mingling together,
and himself will be seen of them a god and a hero;
he will rule over a world made peaceful,
with ancestral virtues.

For you, little child, the earth untilled
will pour forth, as your first birthday-gifts,
her plants and herbs; twining ivy,
and valerian, and the arum lily,
intermingling with the gay acanthus.

Of themselves the goats, untended, will return home,
their udders swollen with milk;
the herds will have no fear of mighty lions;
your very cradle will run over with lovely flowers.
The serpent will die, poison's treacherous plant
will die;
Oriental spice will spring up everywhere.

When you are old enough to read of great men,
and the deeds of your fathers before you,
when you understand the meaning of manliness,
then will the harvest field turn yellow with volunteer
grain,
the reddening grape-cluster hang in the place of the
profitless bramble,
and tough old oaks will drip with honey-dew.

(Even then will linger some last vestiges
of the wickedness of man;
the lusting passion that delights
to dare the sea with ships,
to ring towns about with high walls,
to scar the earth with furrows:
there will still be another Tiphys,
piloting a new Argo that carries its chosen heroes;
there will still be wars; once again
some great Achilles will be sent against another
Troy . . .)

But when the maturing years find you fully grown,
then even the trader will abandon the sea;
no pine-masted vessels will barter wares;
instead, everywhere the whole earth
will of itself yield all things needful.
No more will the ground suffer the harrow,
nor the vine the pruning-hook;
the stalwart plowman will remove the yoke from his
oxen.

Wool will not have to learn the deception of lying dyes,
for the ram in the meadows will himself
change the color of his fleece,
sometimes to soft purple, like the murex,
sometimes to saffron yellow;
of its own volition
crimson will clothe the grazing lamb.

"Run on, such times as these!"
—thus say the Gray Sisters over their spindles,
agreeing in the fixed decree of destiny.

Go on, little child, to great honors;
your hour is at hand, dear offspring of divinity,
great fulfillment of Jove.

See, earth bows its vaulted weight,
the lands, the expanse of the sea, even the deep
heavens;
see how everything rejoices in the time that is to be!

With you for my theme, Orpheus, singer of Thrace, could
not overcome me,
though he were helped by his mother Calliope;
nor Linus, howevermuch comely Apollo, his father,
assisted him;
even Pan, if Arcadia his homeland judged him with
me,
even Pan, with Arcadia judging, would admit himself beaten!

Begin, then, little boy, by greeting your mother with a
smile;
she has waited thru the long weariness of many
months.
Learn to smile, little child—
for one whom his parents have not smiled upon
no god deems worthy of his table, nor goddess of
her couch.

On the Nature of Things

Titus Lucretius Carus

In the following passage, Lucretius discusses the rise of ambition, of republican forms of government, of religions, the discovery of metals, of garments, of agriculture, of singing and dancing, and finally of the total development of luxurious civilization. Notice how carefully he suggests a materialistic origin for all of these things.

At several points during the selection he makes general statements about the nature of men and of human motives. Can you piece these together to discover Lucretius' basic thoughts about human nature and human motives, and about the nature of the best life? From these would you say that the author was essentially an optimist, a pessimist, or something in between? Compare the ideas with some of those expressed by Cicero and by Marcus Aurelius.

More and more every day men who excelled in intellect and were of vigorous understanding, would kindly show others how to exchange their former way of living for new methods. Kings began to build towns and lay out a citadel as a place of strength and of refuge for themselves, and divided cattle and lands and gave to each man in proportion to his personal beauty and strength and intellect; for beauty and vigorous strength were much esteemed. Afterwards wealth was discovered and gold found out,

Line 54—"Tiphys"—the pilot of the Argo: Jason and the Argonauts, sailing after the Golden Fleece, suggest to the reader at once adventurousness and cupidity, bravery and selfishness.

Line 84—Orpheus, Linus, and Pan; the greatest singers of classical antiquity.

Line 89—the ending is apparently a mildly humorous good luck charm: "Smile, baby, so that your parents will smile at you; unwanted, unwelcome children are Bad Luck, but smiling, happy, wanted ones are blessed."

which soon robbed of their honors strong and beautiful alike, for men however valiant and beautiful of person generally follow in the train of the richer man. But were a man to order his life by the rules of true reason, a frugal subsistence joined to a contented mind is for him great riches; for never is there any lack of a little. But men desired to be famous and powerful, in order that their fortunes might rest on a firm foundation and they might be able by their wealth to lead a tranquil life; but in vain, since in their struggle to mount up to the highest dignities they rendered their path one full of danger; and even if they reach it, yet envy like a thunderbolt sometimes strikes and dashes men down from the highest point with ignominy into noisome Tartarus; since the highest summits and those elevated above the level of other things are mostly blasted by envy as by a thunderbolt, so that far better it is to obey in peace and quiet than to wish to rule with power supreme and be the master of kingdoms. Therefore let men wear themselves out to no purpose and sweat drops of blood, as they struggle on along the straight road of ambition, since they gather their knowledge from the mouths of others and follow after things from hearsay rather than the dictates of their own feelings; and this prevails not now nor will prevail by and by any more than it has prevailed before.

Kings therefore being slain, the old majesty of thrones and proud sceptres were overthrown and laid in the dust, and the glorious badge of the sovereign head bloodstained beneath the feet of the rabble mourned for its high prerogative; for that is greedily trampled on which before was too much dreaded. It would come then in the end to the lees of uttermost disorder, each man seeking for himself empire and sovereignty. Next a portion of them taught men to elect legal officers, and drew up codes, to induce men to obey the laws. For mankind, tired out with a life of brute force, lay exhausted from its feuds; and therefore the more readily it submitted of its own free will to laws and stringent codes. For as each one moved by anger took measures to avenge himself with more severity than is now permitted by equitable laws, for this reason men grew sick of a life of brute force. Thence fear of punishment mars the prizes of life; for violence and wrong enclose all who commit them in their meshes and do mostly recoil on him whom they began; and it is not easy for him who by his deeds transgresses the terms of the public peace to pass a tranquil and a peaceful existence. For though he eludes God and man, yet he cannot but feel a misgiving that his secret can be kept forever; seeing that many by speaking in their dreams or in the wanderings of disease have often we are told betrayed themselves and have disclosed their hidden deeds of evil and their sins.

And now what cause has spread over great nations the worship of the divinities of the gods and filled towns with altars and led to the performance of stated sacred rites, rites not in fashion on solemn occasions and in solemn places, from which even now is implanted in mortals a shuddering awe which raises new temples of the gods over the whole earth and prompts men to crowd them on festive days, all this is not so difficult to explain in words. Even then in sooth the races of mortal men would see in waking mind glorious forms, would see them in sleep of yet more marvellous size of body. To these then they would attribute sense, because they seemed to move their limbs and to utter lofty words suitable to their glorious aspects and surpassing powers. And they would give them life everlasting, because their face would appear before them and their form abide; yes, and yet without all this because they would not believe that beings possessed of such powers could lightly be overcome by any force. And they would believe them to be pre-eminent in bliss, because none of them was ever troubled with the fear of death, and because at the same time in sleep they would see them perform many miracles, yet feel on their part no fatigue from the effort. Again they would see the system of heaven and the different seasons of the years come round in regular succession, and could not find out by what cause this was done; therefore they would seek a refuge in handing over all things to the gods and supposing all things to be guided by their nod. And they placed in heaven the abodes and realms of the gods, because night and moon are seen to roll through heaven; moon, day and night, and night's austere constellations and night-wandering of the sky and flying bodies of flame, clouds, sun, rains, snow, winds, lightnings, hail, and rapid rumblings and loud threatful thunderclaps.

O hapless race of men, when that they charged the gods with such acts and coupled with them bitter wrath! What groanings did they then beget for themselves, what wounds for us, what tears for our children's children! No act is it of piety to be often seen with veiled head to turn to a stone and approach every altar and fall prostrate on the ground and spread out the palms before the statues of the gods and sprinkle the altars with much blood of beasts and link vow on vow, but rather to be able to look on all things with a mind at peace. For when we turn our gaze on the heavenly quarters of the great upper world and ether fast above the glittering stars, and direct our thoughts to the courses of the sun and moon, then into our breasts burdened with other ills that fear as well begins to exalt its reawakened head, the fear that we may haply find the power of the gods to be unlimited, able to wheel the bright stars in their varied motion; for lack of power to solve the question troubles the mind with doubts, whether there was ever a birth-time of the world, and whether likewise there is to be any end; how far the walls of the world can endure this strain of restless motion; or whether gifted by the grace of gods with an everlasting existence they may glide on through a never-ending tract of time and defy the strong powers of immeasurable ages. Again who is there whose mind does not shrink into itself with fear of the gods, whose limbs do not cower in terror, when the parched earth rocks with the appalling thunder-stroke and rattling runs through the great heaven? Do not people and nations quake, and proud monarchs shrink into themselves smitten with fear of the gods, lest for any foul transgression or overweening work the heavy time of reckoning has arrived at its fullness? When, too, the utmost fury of the headstrong wind passes over the sea and sweeps over its waters the commander of a fleet together with his mighty legions and elephants, does he not draw near with vows to seek the mercy of the gods and ask in prayer with fear and trembling a lull in the winds and propitious gales; but all in vain, since often caught up in the furious hurricane he is borne none the less to the shoals of death? So constantly does some hidden power trample on human grandeur and is seen to tread under its heel and make sport for itself of the renowned rods and cruel axes.[1] Again when the whole earth rocks under their feet and towns tumble with the shock or doubtfully threaten to fall, what wonder that mortal men

1. A bundle of rods enclosing an axe was the emblem of magisterial authority at Rome.

abase themselves and make over to the gods in things here on earth high prerogatives and marvellous powers, sufficient to govern all things?

To proceed, copper and gold and iron were discovered and at the same time weighty silver and the substance of lead, when fire with its heat had burnt up vast forests on the great hills, either by a discharge of heaven's lightning, or else because men waging with one another a forest-war had carried fire among the enemy in order to strike terror, or because drawn on by the goodness of the soil they would wish to clear rich fields, and bring the country into pasture, or else to destroy wild beasts and enrich themselves with the booty; for hunting with pitfall and with fire came into use before the practice of enclosing the lawn with nets and stirring it with dogs. Whatever the fact is, from whatever cause the heat of flame had swallowed up the forests with a frightful crackling from their very roots and had thoroughly baked the earth with fire, there would run from the boiling veins and collect into the hollows of the ground a stream of silver and gold, as well as of copper and lead. And when they saw these afterwards cool into lumps and glitter on the earth with a brilliant gleam, they would lift them up attracted by the bright and polished lustre, and they would see them to be moulded in a shape the same as the outline of the cavities in which each lay. Then it would strike them that these might be melted by heat and cast in any form or shape soever, and might by hammering out be brought to tapering points of any degree of sharpness and fineness, so as to furnish them with tools and enable them to cut the forests and hew timber and plane smooth the planks, and also to drill and pierce and bore, and they would set about these works just as much with silver and gold at first as with the overpowering strength of stout copper, but in vain, since their force would fail and give way and not be able like copper to stand the severe strain. At that time copper was in higher esteem and gold would be neglected on account of its uselessness, with its dull blunted edge; now copper lies neglected, gold has mounted up to the highest place of honor. Thus time as it goes round changes the seasons of things. That which was in esteem, falls at length into utter disrepute; and then another thing mounts up and issues out of its degraded state and every day is more and more coveted and blossoms forth high in honor when discovered and is in marvelous repute with men.

And now to find out by yourself in what way the nature of iron was discovered. Arms of old were hands, nails, and teeth, and stones and boughs broken off from the forest, and flame and fire, as soon as they had become known. Afterwards the force of iron and copper was discovered, and the use of copper was known before that of iron, as its nature is easier to work and it is found in greater quantity. With copper they would labor the soil of the earth, with copper stir up the billows of war and deal about the wide gaping wounds and seize cattle and lands; for everything defenseless and unarmed would readily yield to them with arms in hand. Then by slow steps the sword of iron gained ground and the make of the copper sickle became a by-word; and with iron they began to plough through the earth's soil, and the struggles of wavering war were rendered equal . . . .

A garment tied on the body was in use before a dress of woven stuff. Woven stuff comes after iron, because iron is needed for weaving a web; and in no other way can such finely polished things be made, as heddles and spindles, shuttles and ringing yarnbeams. And nature impelled men to work up the wool before womankind; for the male sex in general far excells the other in skill and is much more ingenious; until the rugged countrymen so upbraided them with it, that they were glad to give it over into the hands of the women and take their share in supporting hard toil, and in such hard work hardened body and hands.

But nature parent of things was herself the first model of sowing and first gave rise to grafting, since berries and acorns dripping from the trees would put forth in due season swarms of young shoots underneath; and hence also came the fashion of inserting grafts in their stocks and planting in the ground young saplings over the fields. Next they would try another and yet another kind of tillage for their loved piece of land and would see the earth better the wild fruits through genial fostering and kindly cultivation, and they would force the forests to recede every day higher and higher up the hillside and yield the ground below to tilth, in order to have on the uplands and plains, meadows, tanks, runnels, cornfields, and glad vineyards, and allow a gray-green strip of olives to run between and mark divisions, spreading itself over hillocks and valleys and plains; just as you now see richly dight with varied beauty all the ground which they lay out and plant with rows of sweet fruit-trees, and enclose all round with plantations of other goodly trees.

But imitating with the mouth the clear notes of birds was in use long before men were able to sing in tune smooth-running verses and give pleasure to the ear. And the whistlings of the zephyr through the hollows of reeds first taught peasants to blow into hollow stalks. Then step by step they learned sweet plaintive ditties, which the pipe pours forth pressed by the fingers of the players, heard through pathless woods and forests and lawns, through the unfrequented haunts of shepherds and abodes of unearthly calm. These things would soothe and gratify their minds when sated with food; for then all things of this kind are welcome. Often therefore stretched in groups on the soft grass beside a stream of water under the boughs of a high tree at no great cost they would pleasantly refresh their bodies, above all when the weather smiled and the seasons of the year painted the green grass with flowers. Then went round the jest, the tale, the peals of merry laughter; for the peasant muse was then in its glory; then frolick mirth would prompt to entwine head and shoulders with garlands plaited with flowers and leaves, and to advance in the dance out of step and move the limbs clumsily and with clumsy feet beat mother earth; which would occasion smiles and peals of merry laughter, because all these things then from their greater novelty and strangeness were in high repute, and the wakeful found a solace for want of sleep in this, in drawing out a variety of notes and going through tunes and running over the reeds with curving lip; whence even at the present day watchmen observe these traditions and have lately learned to keep the proper tune; and yet for all this receive not a jot more of enjoyment than erst the rugged race of sons of earth received. For that which we have in our hands, if we have known before nothing pleasanter, pleases above all and is thought to be the best;[2] and as a rule the later discovery of something better spoils the taste

2. Notice throughout this piece the philosophic generalization which Lucretius makes. Try reading them together without the intervening descriptions and see if you can get a fairly complete picture of his philosophy.

for the former things and changes the feelings in regard to all that has gone before. Thus began distaste for the acorn, thus were abandoned those sleeping places strawn with grass and enriched with leaves. The dress too of wild beasts' skin fell into neglect; though I can fancy that in those days it was found to arouse such jealousy that he who first wore it met his death by an ambuscado, and after all it was torn in pieces among them and drenched in blood, was utterly destroyed and could not be turned to any use. In those times therefore skins, now gold and purple plague men's lives with cares and wear them out with war. And in this methinks the greater blame rests with us; but us it harms not in the least to do without a robe of purple, spangled with gold and large figures, if only we have a dress of the people to protect us. Mankind therefore ever toils vainly and to no purpose wastes life in groundless cares, because sure enough they have not learnt what is the true end of getting and up to what point genuine pleasure goes on increasing: this by slow degrees has carried life out into the deep sea and stirred up from their lowest depths the mighty billows of war.

But those watchful guardians sun and moon traversing with their light all around the great revolving sphere of heaven taught men that the seasons of the year came round and that the system was carried on after a fixed plan and fixed order.

Already they would pass their life fenced about with strong towers, and the land, portioned out and marked off by boundaries, be tilled; the sea would be filled with ships scudding under sail; towns have auxiliaries and allies as stipulated by treaty, when poets began to consign the deeds of men to verse; and letters had not been invented long before. For this reason our age cannot look back to what has gone before, save where reason points out any traces.

Ships and tillage, walls, laws, roads, dress, and all such like things, all the prizes, all the elegancies too of life without exception, poems, pictures, and chiselling of fine-wrought statues, all these things practiced together with the acquired knowledge of the untiring mind taught men by slow degrees as they advanced on the way step by step. Thus time by degrees brings each several thing forth before men's eyes and reason raises it up into the borders of light; for things must be brought to light one after the other and in due order in the different arts, until these have reached their highest point of development.

Some Odes of Horace

Here are some questions to think about as you read the odes which follow: As you know, Horace was an Epicurean. In the poems "To Licinius Mureana," "To Leuconoe," and "To His Servant," what specific points of that philosophy are mentioned? "To Aristius Fuscus" is a sort of love poem (Lalage was Horace's current girl friend). How warm was Horace's passion? In the poem "To Postumus" we get at least one of the ideas expressed in the book of Ecclesiastes in the Bible. What do the two writers have in common? What comments have you about the kind of life Horace leads and advocates in these poems? The names of people in these poems are not very important. One may think of each poem as a letter written to a friend.

To Licinius Mureana

Receive, dear friend, the truths I teach;
So shalt thou live beyond the reach
Of adverse Fortune's power;
Not always tempt the distant deep,
Nor always timorously creep
Along the treacherous shore.

He that holds fast the golden mean,
And lives contentedly between
The little and the great,
Feels not the wants that pinch the poor,
Nor plagues that haunt the rich man's door,
Embittering all his state.

The tallest pines feel most the power
Of wintry blasts; the loftiest tower
Comes heaviest to the ground;
The bolts that spare the mountain's side,
His cloud-capt eminence divide,
And spread the ruin round.

The well informed philosopher
Rejoices with a wholesome fear,
And hopes, in spite of pain;
If winter bellow from the north,
Soon the sweet spring comes dancing forth,
And nature laughs again.

What if thine heaven be overcast?
The dark appearance will not last;
Expect a brighter sky.
The god, that strings the silver bow,
Awakes sometimes the Muses too,
And lays his arrows by.

If hindrances obstruct thy way,
Thy magnanimity display,
And let thy strength be seen;
But oh! if Fortune fill thy sail
With more than a propitious gale,
Take half thy canvas in.

To Aristius Fuscus

The man, my friend, whose conscious heart
With virtue's sacred ardour glows,
Nor taints with death th' envenomed dart,
Nor needs the guard of Moorish bows.

O'er icy Caucasus he treads,
O'er torrid Afric's faithless sands
Or where the famed Hydaspes spreads
His liquid wealth through barbarous lands.

For while in Sabine forest charmed
By Lalage, too far I strayed,
Me—singing careless and unarmed—
A furious wolf approached—and fled.

No beast more dreadful ever stained
Apulia's spacious wilds with gore,
No beast more fierce Numidia's land
(The lion's thirsty parent) bore.

Place me where no soft summer gale
Among the quivering branches sighs,

Where clouds condensed for ever veil
With horrid gloom the frowning skies.

Place me beneath the burning zone,
A clime denied to human race,
My flame for Lalage I'll own;
Her voice, her smiles, my song shall grace.

To Leuconoe

Strive not, Leuconoe, to know what end
The gods above to me or thee will send;
Nor with astrologers consult at all,
That thou mayest better know what can befall;
Whether thou liv'st more winters, or thy last
Be this, which Tyrrhen waves 'gainst rock do cast.
Be wise! drink free, and in so short a space
Do not protracted hopes of life embrace,
Whilst we are talking, envious time doth slide:
This day's thine own; the next may be denied.

To His Servant

Nay, nay, my boy—'tis not for me,
This studious pomp of Eastern luxury;
Give me no various garlands—fine
With linden twine,
Nor seek, where latest lingering blows
The solitary rose.
Earnest I beg—add not with toilsome pain,
One far-sought blossom to the myrtle plain,
For sure, the fragrant myrtle bough
Looks seemliest on thy brow;
Nor me mis-seems, while, underneath the vine,
Close interweaved, I quaff the rosy wine.

To Postumus

How swiftly glide our flying years!
Alas! nor piety, nor tears
Can stop the fleeting day;
Deep-furrowed wrinkles, posting age,
And death's unconquerable rage,
Are strangers to delay.

Though every day a bull should bleed
To Pluto, bootless were the deed,
The monarch tearless reigns,

Where vulture-tortured Tityus lies,
And triple Geryon's monstrous size
The gloomy wave detains.

Whoever tastes of earthly food
Is doomed to pass the joyless flood.
And hear the Stygian roar;
The sceptred king, who rules the earth,
The labouring hind, of humbler birth,
Must reach the distant shore.

The broken surge of Adria's main,
Hoarse-sounding, we avoid in vain,
And Mars in blood-stained arms;
The southern blast in vain we fear,
And autumn's life-annoying air
With idle fears alarms;

For all must see Cocytus flow,
Whose gloomy water sadly slow
Strays through the dreary soil.
The guilty maids, an ill-famed train!
And, Sisyphus, thy labours vain,
Condemned to endless toil.

Your pleasing consort must be left,
And you of villas, lands, bereft,
Must to the shades descend;
The cypress only, hated tree!
Of all thy much-loved groves, shall thee
Its short-lived lord, attend.

Then shall your worthier heir discharge,
And set th' imprisoned casks at large,
And dye the floor with wine,
So rich and precious, not the feasts
Of holy pontiffs cheer their guests
With liquor more divine.

Given below are two of Horace's Odes, translated into the language of the mid-twentieth century. How modern they sound. Perhaps the idea of the first one, addressed to his former mistress, Pyrrha, is that it is better to have loved and lost than to have loved and kept. The second is a more conventional Epicurean thought. The translations were made by E.D. Graham and M.A. Crane.

1.

On the bulletin board there's a picture of me
Luckily saved from disaster at sea
Donating my gear to the God of the Ocean.

Tonight, some boy smelling of after-shave lotion
Is making a play for you, Pyrrha, my fair,
Trying that innocent look with your hair.

His turn will come soon to complain of foul weather
If he thinks that after you're going together
You'll stay bland and easy as on this first date

Until you up anchor, all dinghys look great.

2.

The peace that the sailor seeks in the storm
And the rest that's the warrior's aim
Can't be purchased with wealth in any form
Nor, Grosphus, with power or fame.
The pauper who wants only what he can afford
Sleeps soundly. But he who would fly
To new fortunes, although he hastens aboard
Speedy vessels, sees his troubles stand by.

Fools nourish dreams of perfect joy;
I'll take less, having witnessed a hero
Die young and watched rotting old age destroy
Tithonus, reduced to a jibbering zero.
It may be *I* have just those things that *you* need
Amidst your horses, fine clothing, and cattle—
Subsistence, and joy from the poems I read,
And no jealous mob doing me battle.

UNIT IV

Judaism and Christianity: The Star and The Cross

Faith, Hope and Love: The Judeo-Christian Tradition

CHAPTER 11

■ It was pointed out in the preceding unit on Rome that life in the later years of the empire was a matter of increasing disillusionment and pessimism. Epicureanism is grounded on pessimism; stoicism is at best a resignation to the evil of the world; popular cults provided little abiding satisfaction. The discontent and dissatisfaction were not found only among thinkers and philosophers, but were shared by the common people. A Roman epitaph found rather frequently reveals the spirit of cynicism and disillusion; it reads

> I was not
> I was
> I am not
> I do not care

One could scarcely go further in general world-weariness; yet the sentiment was not uncommon.

There were two conflicting tendencies during the period and earlier. One was the general disbelief in the old Olympian religion, and a cynical attitude toward emperor-worship; the intellectual element in the population was skeptical about religion in general. The other was, contradictorily, the appeal of mystical cults and religions, usually of Oriental origin: Mithraism, the worship of Isis, the cult of Cybele, and the like. However much scoffing or indifferent disregard there may have been at the upper level of society, the poor and uneducated were ready for the emotional appeal of any religiosity that softened their uncertainties and insecurities; there was need for comfort and reassurance.

The genius of the Greeks was intellectual rather than moral or spiritual, and the Romans had little to add on the latter score to what they inherited from the Greeks. Both peoples had advocated the life lived according to reason. For a Plato, an Aristotle, a Cato, such a life could be worthy and satisfying, but not many men in any generation are of such caliber, and even those few are often felt to be wanting in human warmth. At best, the God whom Aristotle finds the sum of perfection is cold, distant, and aloof from the affairs of men: a noble concept, but, again, lacking warmth.

Reason, important as it is, has never been the only tool in man's possession. Call it emotion, belief, faith, there is something that is not in the same category. No man will seriously give six good reasons why he loves his beloved, for love is not "reasonable." That is not to say that it is necessarily contrary to reason; it simply moves in another category. That "something" beyond reason may be considered the compulsion of a moral ideal, or a yearning for spiritual satisfaction; it is more pronounced in some men than in others, but hardly ever totally absent in any individual. It is precisely such a range of human experience that the perhaps overly-intellectualized philosophical traditions of Greece and Rome failed to satisfy.

While the Greek and Roman cultures were developing—cultures devoted to two forms of rationalism—a third and entirely different type of society had come into being in Palestine. A vast amount of pure intellectual power has gone into the development of Jewish doctrine, but the core of Judaism is faith, as faith is different from, though not opposed to reason. The Hebrew religion in itself, and as it has had wider influence through Christianity, wove another strand into the great amalgam which we call Western civilization.

Judaism has its beginnings as far back in history as we know, and it has survived into the present with an ever-growing body of new thought.

The history of the Jews and the early thinking of their great leaders are preserved in the Bible (the Christian Old Testament), in the Talmud—one edition compiled about A.D. 400, another about A.D. 500, in the Torah, which is the written covenant between God and the people of Israel, and in a great number of commentaries by ancient and modern Jewish scholars.

The father of Judaism was Abraham, a man who lived originally in Ur, a city in the valley of the Euphrates Valley, but who, about the eighteenth century B.C. led the Jews eastward to Canaan on the eastern shore of the Mediterranean. On this nomadic journey the original covenant was revealed to him and his people. The founder of the religion was Moses, to whom the laws were given on Sinai. Greatly simplified, the articles of this covenant and the laws may be stated in this way:

First, there is but one God, Jaweh, who existed before all things, who created all things—good and what we call evil, although God is clearly identified with the good, and who will exist when the universe has vanished.

Second, God chose the Jews as his people, the elect, as a nation of priests, set apart from the world because of their priesthood, yet serving in the world for its ultimate redemption and that of all its people.

Third, the people were given the land of Israel in which they were to live and rule as a nation devoted entirely to the religious ideal. Throughout all subsequent history—when the Jews have been dispersed throughout the world—the yearning to return to their promised land has been a central drive in Hebraic character.

Fourth, since God is an ethical and moral Being, the duty of his people is to conform to the divine in every act of life.

This covenant was reaffirmed with later leaders, Isaac and Jacob, and gloriously restated at Mount Sinai after Moses had led the Jews from their period of slavery in Egypt. At this time Moses received the commandments, which with other revelations from God constitute the Torah, or The Law, for the Hebrews. The written Torah, handwritten on parchment scrolls, is preserved in all synagogues, where its study is the center of worship, for Torah is not just a set of laws, but the revelation of God himself.

The history of the people after the exodus from Egypt is recounted in the subsequent books of the Bible with the rule of the Judges, and then of the Kings: Saul, David, and Solomon. In the rule of David, Jerusalem was established as the capital of the land, and under Solomon the great Temple was constructed where the Ark of the Covenant was kept, the heart of all Jewish worship.

During the years following the reign of Solomon, the country of Israel suffered all the fortunes and misfortunes of the various small middle-Eastern kingdoms during the conquests of the Persians, the Greeks and the Macedonians. The faith suffered, too, as a number of forms of idolatry sprang up in opposition to, or in addition to Judaism. Hence the great succession of prophets, starting with Elijah and continuing for centuries. Theologically, the most important of these was Ezekiel, who prophesied during the time of the Babylonian captivity (586-530 B.C.) when the people were far from home, when their city and their temple had been destroyed. He preached the universality of the faith, and of the personal relationship between the individual Jew and his God. This message tended to diminish the nationalism of the Hebrews by showing that God existed wherever the people were, and that the city and the Temple were not indispensable. Thus Judaism tended to become a more universal religion.

The Jews were returned from their Babylonian captivity, Jerusalem rebuilt, and the Temple consecrated in 516 B.C. About the year 398 B.C. the Torah was reestablished, with the six hundred and thirteen commandments given to Moses on

Mount Sinai. A modern conservative, Rabbi Louis Finkelstein has written of the Jewish way of life as it is presented in the Torah as follows:

> Judaism is a way of life that endeavors to transform virtually every human action into a means of communion with God. Through this communion with God, the Jew is enabled to make his contribution to the establishment of the Kingdom of God and the brotherhood of man on earth. So far as its adherents are concerned, Judaism seeks to extend the concept of right and wrong to every aspect of their behavior. Jewish rules of conduct apply not merely to worship, ceremonial and justice between man and man, but also to such matters as philanthropy, personal friendships and kindnesses, intellectual pursuits, artistic creation, courtesy, the preservation of health and the care of diet.[1]

It is only natural that a religion which deals with all aspects of an individual's existence should develop many laws, and from the fourth century B.C. onwards, the rabbinical scholars devoted themselves to developing interpretations of these commandments. At the same time two religious-political parties rose in Jerusalem, the Pharisees and the Sadducees, the former stressing the universal nature of Judaism, the latter stressing Jewish nationalism. And, throughout the period, the spiritual nature of the faith expanded and contracted, as one would expect in the history of any nation.

It was during one of the times of contraction of the spiritual quality of the Hebrew faith that Jesus lived and taught a reformed doctrine. In his time, Judaism had become a highly legalistic religion which expressed itself in the letter rather than the spirit of the law. In relation to the Jews of his time, Jesus announced that he had come to fulfill the meaning of the law farther than it had ever been extended. This is the significance of his statement in the Sermon on the Mount:

> Think not that I have come to abolish the law and the prophets: I have come not to abolish them but to fulfill them. For truly, I say to you, till heaven and earth pass away, not an iota, not a dot, will pass from the law until all is accomplished. . . . For I tell you, unless your righteousness exceeds that of the scribes and Pharisees, you will never enter the kingdom of heaven.

Before and during the time of Christ, the political future of Israel as a nation was completely bound up with the development of the Roman Empire. The Emperor Titus destroyed the city of Jerusalem, and the Jews of Palestine were virtually exterminated following their revolt during the reign of Hadrian. One may add, not parenthetically, that the strength of the Hebrew faith is vividly shown in such trials. The Jews have been enslaved by the Egyptians and the Babylonians, captured and dispersed by the Romans, and persecuted throughout the world from ancient times on up through the Nazi exterminations in the twentieth century. Yet the Jews cling to their religion, which remains as one of the great faiths of the world, and a civilizing and humanizing force in a world moving toward greater and greater dehumanization. The Book of Job, following p. 000 reveals the deep philosophic questioning of the Jewish people under the sorest of trials and their triumphant faith.

SOME OF THE TEACHINGS OF JESUS

Jesus was born in the year we now call 4 B.C., or possibly 6 B.C., and the time was ripe for his message of hope and love. He preached for only three years, but for two thousand years since that time, whether men have believed his teachings or not, whether they have acted upon them or not, men throughout what was once called "Christendom" have been hearing the teachings of Jesus. What are the cardinal points of that teaching? These: that One God (a Personal Spirit, not an abstract idea nor a "principle") is not only the Creator, but the living Father of all men; that all men are consequently the sons of God, and as a result all men are brothers; that as sons of God men are capable of better lives than they lead; that their human inadequacies, imperfections, and shortcomings (their "sinfulness") can be forgiven if they are repentant; that life is eternal, and death is not extinction; that "all the Law and the Prophets" hangs upon the joint commandment "Love thy God, and thy neighbor as thyself"; and that the intention, the act of the personality, is of greater importance than the deed, the act of the person.

Not the least of the appeals of Christianity is the joy and hope which it carries with it because of its doctrine of Christ as Redeemer. Theologically, one of several explanations of this may be stated in this way: because of the sin of Adam, mankind as a whole carried with it the taint of original sin, a sort of moral disease. But God, loving man, sought to redeem him. This was accomplished through the mystery of Incarnation in which God became man, taking to himself all of man's inherent guilt. Then, in Christ's mortal death, as man, the guilt is atoned, and man is set free. The possibility of man's salvation and eternal life with God from that moment on, lies before each man. In a world-weary and guilt-ridden time like that of the late Roman Empire, even as in our own time, such a possibility can bring hope and joy to the believer.

---

1. Louis Finkelstein, *The Jews: Their History, Culture, and Religion.* (New York: Harper and Brothers, 1949), vol. 2, p. 1739.

All of these teachings affect the world of here and now, for Christianity is a "social" religion; that is, its effects are seen in the daily acts of people in relation to other people. It is not essentially a religion in which the believers isolate themselves from others and seek individual salvation through private contemplation. It is a religion of involvement for most Christians. Love must prompt the worshipper to present acts of love, mercy, and compassion as evidence of an inward change. The act of the believer in Christ cannot wait upon another world. If three words could be used to sum up this teaching, those three, with their many implications, might be those Jesus addressed to Peter: "Feed my sheep."

Out of these teachings emerged certain concepts deeply rooted in the modern world. One was the gradual emergence of the importance of the human personality, a basic fundamental for democracy, carrying a religious sanction weightier than the speculations of the philosophers. The worth and dignity of the individual soul, and its responsibility to itself, has been a shaping influence in Western thought.

It is small wonder that Christianity spread from an obscure, remote province of the Roman Empire practically throughout the known world within the first century of its existence; its message of hope, joy, salvation, and a merciful and loving God in a world that knew only the sterner aspects of justice made its welcome assured. Encompassing the whole of life, and able to take to itself the good things of any civilization, Christianity could appropriate to itself the best of Greek thought, as well as the most notable product of Rome: its law and organization. With the passage of time, it produced such diverse offshoots as the elegance and beauty of Chartres Cathedral and the horror and brutality of the Inquisition; but its impact upon the Western world is fundamental.

It is not the purpose of this portion of the text to expound Christian doctrine, nor to attempt its interpretation. This brief section seeks only to present some of the words of Jesus as they are reported in the Gospels, and to let them speak for themselves.

Bibliography

1. *The Bible.* Obviously the best source of information for both Judaism (The Old Testament) and Christianity (The New Testment). The writers personally prefer the King James Version, but recommend a modern translation like the Revised Standard Version, New York, 1946, 1952.

2. Mary Ellen Chase. *The Bible and the Common Reader.* The Macmillan Company, 1945. In conjunction with the Bible reading, this book is recommended so that the student can be aware of the background and purposes of the various books.

3. Arthur Herzberg, ed. *Judaism.* New York: George Braziller, Inc. A systematic account of Jewish belief with appropriate quotations from Jewish scholars from early times to the present.

4. James Michener. *The Source.* A fictional history of Judaism from preagricultural times to the present. If you are the kind of person, who, when he wants to read a short story, whips through *War and Peace* in a couple of hours, *The Source* gives an emotional identification with the Jew which is not found elsewhere.

Early Christian and Byzantine Art

CHAPTER 12

■ Christianity, like Judaism and Islam, is Semitic in origin. Consequently, God's commandment to Moses, "Thou shall not make unto thee any graven image, or any likeness of anything that is in the heaven above, or that is in the earth beneath, or that is in the water under the earth," has been considered by many as applicable to Christianity. Since the beginnings of Christianity religious fundamentalists have asserted that there can be no such thing as Christian art; even early liberal Church leaders allowed art to exist and develop primarily because they recognized its didactic and educational value. For at least three reasons, all fundamental to the development of Western art, strict observance of the pictorial prohibition was not enforced by the Church for many centuries, then only sporadically, never universally.

First, even in Judaism the prohibition was not strictly observed by the Jews who were dispersed after the destruction of Jerusalem by Titus in A.D. 79. Often, the farther removed from Jerusalem were the Jewish communities, the less orthodox the congregations were likely to be, especially in matters relating to two-dimensional art.

Second, in the international missionary activity of the apostles and their successors, most of the converts were illiterate, or could not read Hebrew or Greek, the languages in which the Old Testament was available and in which the Gospels were being written. Even with a literate audience, books or manuscripts were incredibly expensive and not available to most congregations. The chief means for the propagation of Christianity were oral and pictorial. Pope Gregory the Great spoke on this subject when he said, "Pictures are used in the church in order that those who are ignorant of letters may, by merely looking at the walls, read there what they are unable to read in books." The

Figure 80. Orans, c. A.D. 300. Catacombs of St. Priscilla, Rome (Hirmer Fotoarchiv München).

Second Council of Nicaea (ni-SEE-ah) in 787 finally gave official sanction to Christian art, but immediately and for centuries afterward, rules were established as to the use of colors for the robes of the various biblical personages, attitudes they had to assume in set scenes, attributes and symbols which had to be used in reference to the depiction of each saint and especially to Jesus. Early Christian, Romanesque, and Gothic painting and sculpture were created fundamentally as literary, didactic arts, although the genius of the artists was so great that our appreciation of their works is based primarily on their visual appeal.

Third, the early Christians were influenced by the cosmopolitan Graeco-Roman concepts of beauty. Classicism has always been a factor involved in Christian art, though its influence decreased in proportion to the distance from Rome and Constantinople. The religious art of the medieval and succeeding periods will be a visual composite of Semitic, classic and barbarian religious, philosophic, and aesthetic conceptions with emphasis changing and concepts conflicting from one historical period to another.

EARLY CHRISTIAN ART IN ROME

It is generally assumed that during the early Islamic occupation of Asia Minor and Egypt, the earliest strongholds of Christianity, most Christian art was destroyed. The earliest and most significant Christian art is found in the Roman catacombs. Names, epitaphs, symbols, and simple scenes abound in frescoes in these subterranean tombs, but they are difficult to see or appreciate because they are small, very abstract, and generally very badly executed. Neither client nor artist was overly concerned with beauty; in fact, orthodox or strict Christians were mainly concerned in conveying a simple message or prayer that would be understood by other Christians and, above all, by God.

The most common representation in the catacombs was that of an "orans" (OR-ans; Fig. 80), a female figure presented in complete frontality, standing with arms raised in prayer or supplication. It has been stated that the orans depicted the soul of the deceased praying for salvation and/or giving homage to God. More likely the orans is simply the personification of prayer and reflects the Hellenistic use of personification in female form of abstract ideas such as Arcadia in the painting "Hercules Discovering the Infant Telephus in Arcadia" from Herculaneum (Fig. 79). The orantes figures are paralleled in early Christian literature by prayers—orations—supplicating spiritual purity, religious fortitude, and eternal salvation. It is significant, also, that the most favored religious scenes portrayed from the Old Testament are the stories such as those of Jonah and the whale, Noah and the ark, the Israelites in the Red Sea, and three youths in the fiery furnace and scenes depicting the miracles of Christ from the Gospels, including the Last Supper, which is the Eucharist miracle. This typology, that is, the establishment of visual relationships between persons and events of the Old and New Testaments, was purposeful in that all scenes are concerned with God's intervention to provide salvation through miracles—through the Eucharist eternal salvation is guaranteed.

Most Old Testament figures in the catacomb frescoes are portrayed in the orant position. The "Three Youths in the Fiery Furnace" (Fig. 81) stand calmly in the flames as if absolutely assured their supplication will be answered. And the artist who painted this trio did no more than paint bulbous torsos with sticklike arms and thin legs projecting from a small field of red strokes. Realistic details, modeling of forms, and space illusion were unnecessary, for the story was well-known and the scene was merely a symbolic sketch which revealed the message and prayer. "The Good Shepherd" (Fig. 82) appears frequently in catacomb frescoes and has been a commonly used representation of Jesus throughout the centuries, but it had its Greek

Figure 81. "Three Youths in the Fiery Furnace," c. A.D. 300. Catacombs of St. Priscilla, Rome (Hirmer Fotoarchiv München).

prototype in archaic cult figures such as the "Calf-Bearer" (Fig. 15) and in even more similar Roman renderings of Aristaeus (are-is-TIE-us), the Roman god of gardens, who was usually depicted carrying a lamb on his shoulders. Classical prototypes can be found for most characterizations, poses and even symbols; but an even more important fact to remember is that these scenes, forms, and symbols will persist, albeit with changes, into other historical periods, including our own.

In addition to the orantes and salvation scenes, catacomb art made wide use of simple symbols such as the anchor representing hope, the dove of peace, the palm designating victory through martyrdom, and the fish which was dually symbolic, representing the Lord's Supper and an anagram upon a Greek phrase, the initial letters of which form the Greek word "icthys" or "fish." The phrase translated reads "Jesus Christ, the Son of God, Saviour" (Fig. 83). Each tomb usually was inscribed with the deceased's name and a modest epitaph—that those epitaphs were usually in Greek might be somewhat indicative of popularity of the new religion among the Easterners and slaves in Rome, individuals who were acquainted with both

Figure 82. "The Good Shepherd," c. A.D. 250. Catacombs of St. Callixtus, Rome (Hirmer Fotoarchiv München).

Ιησους
Χριστος
Θεου
'Υιος
Σωτηρ

Figure 83. Anagram as derived from Greek for "Jesus Christ, the Son of God, Savior."

Roman and Greek art and who changed and used it in the service of Christianity.

It is sometimes startling for contemporaries, who have been brought up with exposure to an abundance of paintings depicting the Crucifixion, to learn that the Crucifixion was not among the subjects depicted in catacombs and was not a common subject in Christian art for many centuries. Crucifixion was the most ignoble method of execution used by the Romans, a way of death for those judged guilty of foul and heinous crimes. For early Christians the cross, a simple geometric form, provided sufficient symbolic strength to obviate portraying this distasteful scene. Probably the earliest extant crucifixion scene produced for a public place is a small, wooden, low-relief panel on one of the west doors of the Church of Santa Sabina in Rome (Fig. 84). This door dates from approximately 430 and the "Crucifixion" is the simplest of the richly carved scenes presented, as if the artist produced it with reluctance. Likewise, the early Christians refrained from producing three-dimensional sculpture, probably because sculpture is truly "graven" and antique sculpture had been used extensively as idols. Two very rare three-dimensional sculptures survive from fourth century Rome and are noteworthy for quality, symbolic associations and style of presentation. "The Good Shepherd" (Fig. 85), a 39" high marble work is classical in pose, reminiscent of the catacomb "Good Shepherd" painting (Fig. 82) and is as detailed as the finest Hellenistic genre sculpture. The shepherd, of course, is Christ, the sheep the congregation of the faithful. The statue of "Christ En-

Figure 84. "Crucifixion," from the door of the Church of Santa Sabina, Rome, c. A.D. 430 (Hirmer Fotoarchiv München).

Figure 85. "Good Shepherd," c. A.D. 350. Lateran Museum, Rome (Hirmer Fotoarchiv München).

throned" (Fig. 86) depicts Christ as a young, beardless philosopher and/or emperor. His features, clothing, and gestures are classical; the concept of the bearded Christ is Syrian in origin and did not become accepted universally until the Romanesque period. The beardless Christ presentation seems un-Christian to contemporaries because we have learned to accept a Christ form (which has an ample number of variations to preclude monotony) entirely different from these works. But to the early Christians, who were not concerned with likeness but with symbolic meanings, these figures

Figure 86. "Christ Enthroned," c. A.D. 350-360. National Museum, Rome (Hirmer Fotoarchiv München).

were so emphatically representative of Christ that they could in no way be misconstrued as idols. Nevertheless, their existence was unusual, bordered on idolatry, and we could easily believe that they were heathen idols dating from the early Christian era if very similar figures did not appear in high relief on innumerable early Christian sarcophagi.

By the middle of the third century, important church leaders were entombed in rather simple stone sarcophagi, but the practice did not gain wide usage until Christianity was legalized in the fourth century. The sculptors of early Christian sarcophagi drew heavily from pagan sources and from catacomb paintings. For a hypothetical example of the former, it would have been quite easy for the sarcophagus salesmen to sell a work depicting the garden god Aristaeus in a setting of a vineyard where chubby cupids were picking grapes. All he would have had to do was convince his Christian customer that Aristaeus was the Good Shepherd, the grapes symbolic of the Eucharist, and the cupids baby angels. Might this not have been true of the Lateran sarcophagus of "The Good Shepherd and the Vintage" (Fig. 87)?

A superb sarcophagus with sculpture derived from catacomb paintings is the so-called "Jonah Sarcophagus" (Fig. 88) from the late third century. The Jonah story is depicted in continuous narration, a series of successive episodes in which our hero appears three times and the wiggly-waggly serpentine whale twice. Reading from left to right: Jonah is cast naked into the swirling sea by the sailors and heads directly into the mouth of the waiting whale; then the generous whale disgorges Jonah; and finally Jonah sleeps nude under a

Figure 87. "Good Shepherd and the Vintage," sarcophagus, c. A.D. 350-400. Lateran Museum, Rome (Hirmer Fotoarchiv München).

Figure 88. "The Jonah Sarcophagus," c. A.D. 300. Lateran Museum, Rome (Hirmer Fotoarchiv München).

protective arbor of gourds. It is interesting to note that within the Jonah cycle, Noah appears in a tiny box floating on the sea; and in the upper left-hand corner Jesus addresses himself to a tiny mummy standing in front of a tomb, thus paralleling the raising of Lazarus with the stories of Noah and Jonah.

By the middle of the fourth century, sarcophagi began to emphasize New Testament scenes, as is evidenced in the "Sarcophagus of the Roman Prefect Junius Bassus" (Fig. 89). The front panel illustrated is divided into ten relief units on two levels with each unit separated from the next by a highly decorated column. In the top register we see:

a. The Sacrifice of Isaac
b. The Arrest of St. Peter
c. Christ Enthroned between St. Peter and St. Paul
d-e. Christ before Pilate

In the bottom register we see:

a. The Misery of Job
b. Adam and Eve after the Fall
c. Christ's Entry into Jerusalem
d. Daniel in the Lion's Den
e. St. Paul led to his Martyrdom

This complex series is subject to many interpretations. For example, the sacrifice of Abraham prefigures the sacrifice of Christ; the Abraham, Daniel, and Job episodes show the suffering of man and remind us of God's intervention; the fall of Adam and Eve states the condition of mankind which is saved by Christ's triumphs, the earthly triumphal entry into Jerusalem and the eternal triumph of the resurrected Christ the Law-Giver; and we could go on and on. The artist included only a suggestion to which the faithful brought their knowledge and faith for personal interpretation.

The detail of the central scenes (Fig. 90) shows clearly that Christ is again presented as the emperor or young philosopher-type amazingly similar to the three-dimensional work discussed previously (Fig. 86). An amusing and completely pagan intrusion into the scene of "Christ giving the Law to Peter and Paul" is the figure of the pagan sky god Caelus, who holds the firmament upon which Christ rests his left foot; "Christ's Entry into Jerusalem" is interesting in that the artist thought it significant to include a man throwing his cloak before the feet of the donkey, thereby affirming Christ's regal status. The difficult idea to accept about early Christian and all medieval religious art is that every detail, figure, form, and attitude has theological implications and that, beyond the obvious analogies between the Old and New Testaments, Christian art became as institutionalized as the art of the Roman Empire.

After the Edict of Milan in 313 which legalized Christianity, Emperor Constantine encouraged the construction of new, large churches throughout the empire. Of Constantine's major Roman buildings, only St. John Lateran survives, but it has undergone so many renovations that it hardly resembles the original structure. St. Paul's Outside the Walls, one of the greatest churches of the fourth century, was destroyed by fire in 1823 but reconstructed by 1854 and serves as an outstanding example of an early basilica (bah-SIL-i-ka). All Christian basilicas derive from the antique basilica, which was a "royal hall," a synthesis of marketplace, legal center, and private home. Whereas the pagan basilica had its entrance on its longitudinal sides, Christians shifted the entrances to the

Figure 89. "The Sarcophagus of the Roman Prefect Junius Bassus," c. A.D. 359. Vatican Museums (Hirmer Fotoarchiv München).

shorter and usually western end, thus orienting the building along a longitudinal axis. An eighteenth-century etching of "St. Paul's Outside the Walls" by Piranesi (Fig. 91) and a schematic floor plan (Fig. 92) show better than a camera the basic structure of the basilica, which now is more than just a place of assembly (the original basilica), for it is also the sacred House of God. The internal space was divided into a large central area called the *nave* (as in *nav[y]*), because it seemed to resemble a ship, *navis* (the ship of souls), flanked by two side aisles (wings) on each side. The nave and aisles join a secondary nave, the *transept* (TRAN-sept), which was at right angles to the nave proper. The resulting cruciform floor plan form is the Latin Cross which became a characteristic of most Christian churches in the West. Behind the transept was a semicircular space called an *apse* (as in *lapse*) in which the altar was placed on a raised platform. The nave was covered with an A-shaped truss-roof and, at a level well below the nave roof, the aisles were covered by lean-to truss roofs so that clerestory (or clearstory) windows could be set in the upper nave wall to light the church. Columns joined by round arches supported the walls consisting of a triforium (tri-FO-ri-um), usually painted or covered with mosaics, and a clerestory area which held windows made of alabaster or oiled parchment. Aesthetically the basilica interior is very complex and exciting, for there is no single point from which one can grasp the space at once. One "learns" the space by moving in it to the altar,

Figure 90. Detail from "The Sarcophagus of Junius Bassus." Vatican Museums (Hirmer Fotoarchiv München).

Figure 91. Interior, St. Paul's Outside the Walls, Rome, begun A.D. 386. (Etching by Giambattista Piranesi, 1749; courtesy Anonymous Collector.)

which is the physical and spiritual goal. The constant change of light and space as one moves about a basilica gives this architectural form a diversity, while the repetition of columns and arches marching down the length of the nave and aisles provides a sense of rhythm, order, and direction.

The basilica was an obvious choice for religious use by the Christians because it enclosed a large space which could hold an immense congregation, often thousands of worshippers. In addition to the interior space, most of the larger churches were fronted by an open courtyard called an *atrium* (A-tree-um) which was flanked on three sides by an arcaded, covered *ambulatory* (as *ambulance*) and on the fourth side by a porch called the *narthex* (NAR [as in *mar*] thex) which led to the front doors of the church. The atrium derived from Roman house plans and eventually became the cloister of the medieval monastery. Whereas the early Christian basilica was very plain on the outside (usually brick and rubble constructions only slightly adorned with stucco), the interior surfaces were embellished with colors and textures in structural materials and adorned with marble paneling, paintings, and mosaics.

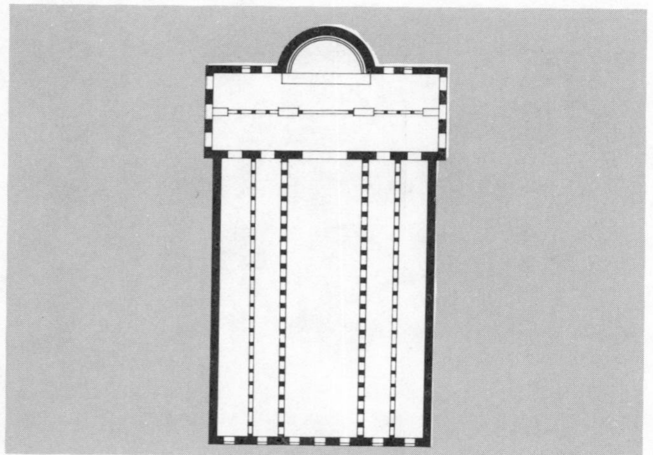

Figure 92. Schematic floor plan of St. Paul's, Rome.

Very little early Christian mural painting has survived and what remains is inferior in quality to the mosaics, which are brilliant and incredibly beautiful. It is almost impossible to describe mosaics of the early Christian and Byzantine periods because contemporary mosaics are not only inferior but very different. The early mosaics were composed of colored glass, marble, or ceramic called *tesserae* (TESS-er-aye) which were cut into somewhat cubic shapes, but not in uniform sizes. Moreover the transparent glass tesserae were often backed with gold leaf. These tesserae were inserted into a plaster surface in established patterns but each was set at slightly varying angles. Because of the variety of shapes, angles, and the fractured surfaces of the glass pieces, the mosaic scene reflects and refracts light at thousands of different angles, giving an effect which is brilliant and shimmering. When paintings were used instead of mosaics it was done in unimportant places or because mosaics were too costly.

The apse mosaic in the church of Santa Pudenziana (Fig. 93) depicts Christ enthroned and raised above the apostles. In the background are buildings representing the Heavenly Jerusalem and in the sky are winged representations of the four evangelists: the lion of St. Mark, the ox of St. Luke, the eagle of St. John, and the winged man of St. Matthew. The origin of the evangelical symbols is not known, but already at the beginning of the fifth century these symbols are fully developed and accepted. Despite the fact that it is much renovated, this mosaic is of particular importance because the monumental enthronement of Christ asserts his authority and implies the institutional authority of the Church. This scene was not meant to be read as a historical event, but as a complex essay on salvation which was assured by Christ's death on the cross, of which we have been informed by the evangelists, and which can be assured to each of us through the Church which represents God on earth.

The Church of Santa Maria Maggiore, built in the fifth century, presents what is believed to be the oldest cycle of evangelical and biblical mosaics. The Old Testament story of the "Crossing of the Red Sea" (Fig. 94) is crowded on one side with Egyptian soldiers pouring out of a high and narrow gate which overwhelms the schematic representation of the city and on the other side with Israelites who are gathered together in a pyramid of heads. Between these awkwardly executed groups is the sea in which a few soldiers and horses flounder and on which numerous shields float.

Figure 93. "Christ Teaching the Apostles in the Heavenly Jerusalem," mosaic in the apse of Santa Pudenziana, Rome, c. A.D. 401-407 (Hirmer Fotoarchiv München).

Although the depiction is ungainly at best, the point of God's intervention is dramatically stated. In Santa Maria Maggiore another scene depicts on two levels the encounter of Abraham with the three celestial visitors at Mamre and his subsequent vision of the Trinity (Fig. 95). The artist of these scenes was concerned with providing some illusion of space and modeling of figures—in fact, there are strong classical elements, especially in drapery handling. On the lower level, Sarah prepares food which Abraham sets before the three young men whose celestial status is marked by halos. On the upper level, Abraham bows before his visitors, who now appear in a vision but this time the central figure is completely surrounded by an oval field of light called an *aureole* (OH-ray-ol). This trio represents the Holy Trinity and the central figure in the aureole is Jesus who is usually depicted in this manner in "Transfigurations." The representation of the three celestial visitors is common in the West into the Gothic period and in Byzantine world even today. In fact in Byzantine art this representation is the chief means of depicting the Trinity. A comparison of the two scenes illustrated from Santa Maria Maggiore indicates that artists of different backgrounds worked together on many of the huge art projects of the early Christian era and

Figure 94. "Crossing of the Red Sea," mosaic from the second quarter of fifth century A.D. in the Church of Santa Maria Maggiore, Rome (Alinari—Art Reference Bureau).

Figure 95. "Abraham and the Celestial Visitors," mosaic from the second quarter of fifth century A.D. in the Church of Santa Maria Maggiore, Rome (Alinari—Art Reference Bureau).

accounts for the diversity of quality and styles to be seen within one building and the difficulty in ascribing definite stylistic designations at early stages of artistic development. The stylistic boundaries of early Christian art in the West and early Christian art in the East or Byzantium vary from historian to historian as, in truth, they varied from artist to artist.

Before leaving Rome, let us study a mosaic fragment from the Oratory of Pope John VII which depicts this gentle pontiff with a square halo (Fig. 96). The halo or nimbus is a round symbol of light placed around the heads of saints to indicate their holiness, although rulers were given imperial halos to symbolize their exalted status even if they behaved outrageously. Pope John, with his large melancholy eyes and excessively long nose, was given a square halo to indicate that although he was still alive, he was a good man and a cinch to become a saint.

BYZANTINE ART

It is impossible to establish a clear-cut demarcation between the early Christian art of Rome and that of other parts of the empire until the sixth century and even then it is often very difficult to do so because there was constant exchange of artists and ideas among the main Mediterranean communities. The term *Byzantine art* refers not only to the art of the Eastern empire, which was established when Constantine moved the capital of the empire from Rome to Constantinople between A.D. 323 and 329, but also to an art style, basically that of late antiquity, which remained essentially static except for the addition of a few Greek and Oriental elements. Early Christian art in the West, on the other hand, fell heir to the civilization of antiquity, but transformed itself drastically through many successive artistic styles.

When Hagia Sophia (HA-ah-a SO-fee-ah; "Church of Holy Wisdom") was consecrated on A.D. December 27, 537, the energetic and proud Emperor Justinian exclaimed "O Solomon, I have excelled thee!" Undoubtedly it was the architectural triumph of his age and is still to be considered among man's greatest architectural achievements. Its architects, Anthemius of Tralles and Isidorus of Miletus, labored from 522 to 537 to create this masterpiece which combines the longitudinal axis of an early Christian basilica and a square central crossing crowned by a huge dome abutted on the east and west ends by half-domes. The massive exterior (Fig. 97) rises by slow stages to the crown of the dome 182′6″ above the ground, and stands out

Figure 96. "Pope John VII," mosaic fragment from Oratory of John VII. Vatican Museums (Alinari—Art Reference Bureau).

Figure 97. Anthemius of Tralles and Isidorus of Miletus, Hagia Sophia, A.D. 532-537, Istanbul (Hirmer Fotoarchiv München).

clearly, for its diameter is slightly over 108′. In every respect it is larger than the Pantheon.

The interior of Hagia Sophia (Fig. 98) is of breath-taking beauty for the dome seems to float as it rests upon a closely spaced ring of forty windows. In fact the entire building is flooded with light which also penetrates from the hundreds of windows in its thin, shell-like walls. Today this great monument is a Turkish mosque and most of its walls are covered with plaster and paint, but under those prosaic materials are millions of brilliant tessarae in lovely pictures and ornamental schemes which once played a lively game of light reflection and refraction. The illusion of spaciousness is confirmed, even increased, by the great open space of the nave itself which is over 100′ wide and 200′ long. The main space enclosure, in length, width, and height, is one of the largest ever achieved.

The central dome actually rests on four arches which carry its weight to the great piers at the corners of the square vault. Concave spherical triangles called *pendentives* (pen-DEN-tiv) make the transition from the square to the circular rim of the dome. The use of pendentives in Hagia Sophia is the earliest example of this architectural device used in a monumental building and became a basic feature of Byzantine architecture. Hagia Sophia was one of the earliest Byzantine buildings, but it is also undoubtedly the greatest.

The most concentrated and probably richest array of Byzantine monuments from the Age of Justinian is found not in Constantinople, but in Ravenna (rah-VEN-ah), Italy, which was the capital of the Western and the Ostrogothic Empires in the fifth century and the main center of Byzantine control in Italy during most of Justinians's reign. Moreover, the monuments of Ravenna reflect the highest achievements of many different conflicting art styles and philosophies which were contemporaneous and concentrated in a relatively small area.

The mosaic of "The Good Shepherd" (Fig. 99) from the Mausoleum of the Empress Galla Placidia is one of the oldest and most aesthetically pleasing in this former imperial community. The scene is in a lunette (lew-NET), a semicircular wall surface of a vaulted room; in this case the vault is covered with a magnificent mosaic representing a cobalt-blue sky sparkling with stars of golds, blues, greens, and whites patterned like luxuriant flowers and jeweled crosses. At the center of the lunette a majestic Good Shepherd dressed in gold and blue, with huge golden halo and slender cross, watches

Figure 98. Interior, Hagia Sophia (Hirmer Fotoarchiv München).

Figure 99. Mosaic of "The Good Shepherd" in the tomb of Galla Placidia, c. A.D. 450, Ravenna (Hirmer Fotoarchiv München).

over six attentive sheep who balance him in pyramid formation, three on each side. There is no mistaking this shepherd for a Greek votive figure or Roman garden god, for he is represented as King of Kings and holds a cross with knobbed ends signifying his supreme accomplishment. Often overlooked in this work are the funnel-shaped tubes that run along the foot of the mosaic immediately over the gold border. They represent foot lights and indicate that this scene was portrayed as a liturgical drama or tableau.

The most "Byzantine" of the many religious buildings in Ravenna is the octagonal domed church of San Vitale (San-vi-TALL-e; Fig. 100). Its exterior usually has been criticized as being excessively plain and unimpressive. This is nonsense. Rather, its exterior should be acclaimed for subtlety in a complex organization. Its plain red brick facing creates quiet horizontal patterns which unify the numerous walls and buttresses which move in angular patterns on three levels about a central core. Within each wall area, windows break the solidity of the brick in rhythmic pattern. This exterior is as moving and vital as those of most Baroque buildings but, unlike the Baroque, form and structural function are here united. Whereas the exterior is restrained and subtle, the interior is a veritable jewel box (Fig. 101). Its walls are faced with rich polychromed marble, pierced marble screens, and adorned with hundreds of decorative and pictorial mosaics of the highest quality; its floors are of marble mosaic and many of the columns are carved alabaster. San Vitale is a highly-developed example of the "central-type" church, that is, a church with a central and circular nave (actually octagonal in this case) surmounted by an octagonal drum on which the round dome rests. The transition from the octagonal drum to the round dome was accomplished by using *squinches* (skwinch), small apselike vaults which are placed across the angles formed by the octagonal walls. One of the most impressive features of this church is not only that it has an aisle nearly completely surrounding the nave, but also that there is a vaulted triforium gallery over this aisle which opens into the high nave. Indeed San Vitale is a

Colorplate 8. **Emperor Justinian and His Suite,** San Vitale, Ravenna
Courtesy Art Reference Bureau.

Figure 100. San Vitale, Ravenna, c. A.D. 525-547 (Hirmer Fotoarchiv München).

compact and intimate church which functioned for the court somewhat like a small but luxurious theatre.

Two of the world's most famous and justly celebrated mosaics are located in the apse of San Vitale facing the altar from opposite sides. They are the depictions of "The Emperor Justinian and His Courtiers" (Pl. 8) and "The Empress Theodora and Her Retinue" (Fig. 102). These panels are enclosed in decorative framework of incredible sumptuousness, as if their imperial subject matter puts them in a special class; also, the ceremonial character of these works differs greatly from the biblical narratives presented throughout the rest of the church. The Justinian panel depicts the Emperor with military bodyguards, ministers, and Archbishop Maximianus along with his clerical assistants. Justinian stands in the center of the scene: he is depicted in strict frontality, garbed in ceremonial robe and crowned both with the imperial diadem and a halo, for he represented Caesaro-Papism, the unity of the spiritual force of the church and the temporal power of the state. Maximianus holds a giant pectoral cross, the symbol of his power as the spiritual and temporal guardian of Ravenna. One of the soldiers bears a shield with the Chrismon insignia, the monogram of the Greek letters Chi (χ) and Rho (ρ), which together form the abbreviation for Christ as well as, allegorically, becoming a combination of the cross and shepherd's crook representing Christ's death and pastoral mission. Symbols, simple and complex, abound, testifying to the omnipotent power of Christ and his vice-regent on earth. Justinian, his power, mission, and glory, thus heralded, gazes at the viewer with masklike inscrutability and his feet tread on air.

Empress Theodora is pictured with her retinue in the narthex or atrium as they prepare to enter the church which had been commissioned by the imperial couple. A courtier pushes aside a curtain at a doorway and the Empress begins to advance, carrying her gift of a gold chalice embedded with precious jewels. Her ceremonial gown deserves special notice for it is decorated with a depiction of the Magi bringing their offerings to the Infant Jesus—this is meant to suggest a parallelism with her own activity. For this ritual occasion Theodora wears a huge diadem from which ropes of large

Figure 101. Interior, view toward the apse, San Vitale, Ravenna (Hirmer Fotoarchiv München).

Figure 102. "The Empress Theodora and Her Retinue," mosaic in San Vitale, c. A.D. 547 (Hirmer Fotoarchiv München).

pearls depend over her shoulders and bosom. Theodora started her public life as a circus girl and, if her biographers are to be credited, she quickly advanced into a more lucrative albeit immoral profession before attracting Justinian's attention and winning his love. The wages of her sin seem to have been very high, for Theodora became Empress, mandatory of God, and her portrait is one of the most beautiful and enduring in the history of art.

All the figures in these panels were acclaimed as excellent likenesses, although their bodies are flattened, devoid of weight and substance, dematerialized. These are spiritualized representations. And it is this quality in these works, produced through the almost magical powers of an extremely talented artist, that affirms the supermundane quality of the event and makes all the symbolic claims of temporal and spiritual authority seem God-ordained.

The Age of Justinian marks the zenith of Byzantine art. In 726 an imperial edict forbade religious images and divided the realm into two hostile groups: the *iconoclasts* (i-CON-o-klast—"image-destroyers"), who insisted on literal interpretation of the biblical veto against images, and the *iconophiles* (i-CON-o-file—"image-lovers"), who finally managed to have the edict reversed in 843.

Although it would be possible to discuss Byzantine art since the seventh century at great length, it must be recognized that all the basic Christian and classical elements from which Byzantine art derived had been firmly established by 726—what followed were variations and refinements, not vital changes nor advances. It is to the West we must turn again to see the rise of the great and vigorous medieval art styles, the Romanesque and the Gothic.

BYZANTINE EPILOGUE

Russia, the Balkans, Sicily, and even Alaska can boast of impressive church buildings in the Byzantine style. Only two will be discussed here which are extremely well-known and indicate the mutations and deviations the Byzantine architectural style affords. St. Mark's Cathedral in Venice dates from the eleventh century and differs from Hagia Sophia in that the basic Greek Cross form is clearly visible from within and that in addition to the central dome, each arm of the cross is capped by a full dome. From the exterior, and especially from the air (Fig. 103), St. Mark's with its five

Figure 103. St. Mark's (aerial view), Venice, begun 1063 (Alinari—Art Reference Bureau).

domes, each encased in wood covered by gilt copper sheeting and topped by ornate lanterns, is very impressive. One of the most fantastic, highly imaginative Byzantine churches is the sixteenth-century Cathedral of St. Basil adjoining the Kremlin in Moscow (Fig. 104). The abundance of domes of all shapes and sizes seems to make it the ancestor of Disneyland. Although both St. Mark's Cathedral and the Cathedral of St. Basil have gay and colorful exteriors lacking the dignity of Hagia Sophia, they do convey the sense of the miraculous which, after all, does not have to be austere and somber.

After the victory of the iconophiles in 843, Byzantine painting and mosaic blended the spiritual ideal of beauty promoted in Justinian's time with an enthusiasm for the traditions and forms of classical Greek art. Perhaps the finest examples of the Second Golden Age of Byzantine art are to be found in the monastery church at Daphne (DAF-knee), Greece. In the "Crucifixion" mosaic (Fig. 105), Christ, Mary, and St. John have a classical dignity and express a gentle, controlled pathos in their facial expressions and gestures. This is a work that combines the compassion of humanism with the didactic assertion of dogma. The depiction of "Christ Pantocrator" (pan-ta-KRAT-or; Fig. 106) on the dome of this church is one of the least amiable portrayals of Christ ever produced, but one that maintains the concept of "God Almighty, the Omnipotent Lawgiver" which appeared in the apse of San Pudenziano in the fourth century and had its human counterpart in the San Vitale depiction of Emperor Justinian.

Very few painted icons survive from before the seventeenth century. Fortunately, many works by Andrei Rublev (active 1370, d. 1427-30), who is considered to be the greatest Russian master and the Byzantine equivalent of Giotto, have been preserved. His most famous work is "The Old Testament Trinity" (Fig. 107), the trio of celestial visitors who honored Abraham at Mamre. With Rublev, Byzantine painting reached the heights of decorative elegance and simplicity; unlike Giotto who began a new era in Western painting and was followed by generations of artists who took his work as an inspiration for working in new directions, Rublev was repeatedly copied and slavishly imitated. His works marked the end of development. Rublev and other master painters, sculptors, and architects carried on the Byzantine tradition in Russia where it flourished until the Revolution of 1917.

Figure 104. Cathedral of St. Basil, 1554-1560, Moscow (Marburg—Art Reference Bureau).

Figure 105. "Crucifixion," mosaic, c. 1100, Monastery Church, Daphnē, Greece (Alinari—Art Reference Bureau.)

Figure 106. "Christ Pantocrater," dome mosaic, eleventh century, Monastery Church, Daphnē, Greece (Marburg—Art Reference Bureau).

Figure 107. Andrei Rublev, "Old Testament Trinity," c. 1410-20. Tretyakov Gallery, Moscow (Marburg—Art Reference Bureau).

Bibliography

1. Grabar, André. *Byzantine Painting.* New York: Skira International Corp., 1953. The text is somewhat advanced for the beginning student, but well worth the challenge. The title is misleading, for most of the book is devoted to mosaics. The illustrations, all in color, make this book one of the most beautiful ever published.
2. Grabar, André and Nordenfalk, Carl. *Early Medieval Painting.* New York: Skira International Corp., 1964. Again a superb book, the text a little difficult, perhaps because the material is unfamiliar to most laymen. The reproductions are amazing in fidelity and beauty.
3. Morey, Charles Rufus. *Early Christian Art,* 2nd ed. Princeton: Princeton University Press, 1953. This book is the classic work in this area of study. Read its text while referring to illustrations used in any of the other books listed in this Bibliography for a truly enjoyable, informative, and valuable experience.
4. Volbach, Wolfgang F. and Hirmer, Max. *Early Christian Art.* New York: Harry N. Abrams, Inc., 1962. Short, excellent, succinct text; 258 superb photographs of key works, many of which are especially valuable as the works are generally known only through old and inadequate reproductions. Highly recommended.

Selections from the Bible

The Book of Job

The problem of human suffering, particularly the suffering of the innocent, the just, and the good has confused mankind since the beginning of time, particularly when men believe in a just and benevolent God. The Book of Job, written sometime after the seventh century B.C. tackles this problem as few books do. The author is unknown (indeed there is a strong possibility that the prose, prologue, and epilogue were originally a unit, and that the poetic drama is an interpolation), and the hero, Job, may or may not have been a historical character. It seems probable that the book is addressed to all of Israel after some one of the frequent persecutions of the Jews. Perhaps the author is attempting to explain to his people the nature of their suffering. If one considers the final answer from a completely rational point of view—as the Greeks, the Romans, and twentieth-century Americans would—one is left unsatisfied, for the attempt to probe God's secrets with the unaided human mind has seldom brought satisfactory results. If the reader can somehow translate his questioning into the realm of faith and mystery, an intuitive understanding may be reached.

From verses 1-5 in Chapter 1, we must accept the fact that Job is a completely good man, and totally loyal to God. Job's comforters hold to an old religious concept of a simple cause-and-effect relationship between God and man: if man is upright, God will reward him; if he is evil, God will punish him. The generation gap is quite apparent when the youth, Elihu, speaks in Chapter 32 and begins to introduce a totally new idea of the nature of the God-man relationship; an idea which is developed as God speaks out of the whirlwind.

The reader should not expect a logical development of ideas up to Chapter 32. Rather, Job's searing doubts are explored with ever-greater intensity, and the arguments for the old religious idea are reiterated by the three comforters. Although this is not a drama in the strict sense of the word, the reader should try to imagine the tone of voice of the speakers. Notice, for example, the timid way in which Eliphaz begins his argument in Chapter 4 after sitting on the ground for seven days and seven nights, or how Bildad's argument in Chapter 25 sputters to a quick conclusion. What is Elihu's tone after listening to the lengthy discussions of the old man?

1 There was a man in the land of Uz, whose name was
Job; and that man was blameless and upright, one who
feared God, and turned away from evil. 2 There were born
to him seven[1] sons and three daughters. 3 He had seven
thousand sheep, three thousand camels, five hundred yoke
of oxen, and five hundred she-asses, and very many servants; so that this man was the greatest of all the people of
the east. 4 His sons used to go and hold a feast in the house
of each on his day; and they would send and invite their
three sisters to eat and drink with them. 5 And when the
days of the feast had run their course, Job would send and
sanctify them, and he would rise early in the morning and
offer burnt offerings according to the number of them all;
for Job said, "It may be that my sons have sinned, and
cursed God in their hearts." Thus Job did continually.

6 Now there was a day when the sons of God came to
present themselves before the LORD, and Satan also came
among them. 7 The LORD said to Satan, "Whence have
you come?" Satan answered the LORD, "From going to
and fro on the earth, and from walking up and down on it."
8 And the LORD said to Satan, "Have you considered my
servant Job, that there is none like him on the earth, a
blameless and upright man, who fears God and turns away
from evil?" 9 Then Satan answered the LORD, "Does Job
fear God for nought? 10 Hast thou not put a hedge about
him and his house and all that he has, on every side? Thou
hast blessed the work of his hands, and his possessions have
increased in the land. 11 But put forth thy hand now, and
touch all that he has, and he will curse thee to thy face."
12 And the LORD said to Satan, "Behold, all that he has is
in your power; only upon himself do not put forth your
hand." So Satan went forth from the presence of the
LORD.

---

1. The use of the symbolic numbers 3 and 7 suggests a wider significance of the dialogue than to the plight of only one man.

13 Now there was a day when his sons and daughters
were eating and drinking wine in their eldest brother's
house; 14 and there came a messenger to Job, and said,
"The oxen were plowing and the asses feeding beside them;
15 and the Sabeans fell upon them and took them, and slew
the servants with the edge of the sword; and I alone have
escaped to tell you." 16 While he was yet speaking, there
came another, and said, "The fire of God fell from heaven
and burned up the sheep and the servants, and consumed
them; and I alone have escaped to tell you." 17 While he
was yet speaking, there came another, and said, "The Chal-
deans formed three companies, and made a raid upon the
camels and took them, and slew the servants with the edge
of the sword; and I alone have escaped to tell you."
18 While he was yet speaking, there came another, and said,
"Your sons and daughters were eating and drinking wine in
their eldest brother's house; 19 and behold, a great wind
came across the wilderness, and struck the four corners of
the house, and it fell upon the young people, and they are
dead; and I alone have escaped to tell you."

20 Then Job arose, and rent his robe, and shaved his
head, and fell upon the ground, and worshiped. 21 And he
said, "Naked I came from my mother's womb, and naked
shall I return; the LORD gave, and the LORD has taken
away; blessed be the name of the LORD."

22 In all this Job did not sin or charge God with
wrong.

2 Again there was a day when the sons of God came to
present themselves before the LORD, and Satan also
came among them to present himself before the LORD.
2 And the LORD said to Satan, "Whence have you come?"
Satan answered the LORD, "From going to and fro on the
earth, and from walking up and down on it." 3 And the
LORD said to Satan, "Have you considered my servant Job,
that there is none like him on earth, a blameless and upright
man, who fears God and turns away from evil? He still
holds fast his integrity, although you moved me against
him, to destroy him without cause." 4 Then Satan answered the LORD, "Skin for skin! All that a man has he
will give for his life. 5 But put forth thy hand now, and
touch his bone and his flesh, and he will curse thee to thy
face." 6 And the LORD said to Satan, "Behold, he is in
your power; only spare his life."

7 So Satan went forth from the presence of the
LORD, and afflicted Job with loathsome sores from the
sole of his foot to the crown of his head. 8 And he took a
potsherd with which to scrape himself, and sat among the
ashes. 9 Then his wife said to him, "Do you still hold fast
your integrity? Curse God, and die."

10 But he said to her, "You speak as one of the foolish women would speak. Shall we receive good at the hand
of God, and shall we not receive evil?" In all this Job did
not sin with his lips.

11 Now when Job's three friends heard of all this evil
that had come upon him, they came each from his own
place, Eliphaz the Temanite, Bildad the Shuhite, and
Zophar the Naamathite.[2] They made an appointment together to come to condole with him and comfort him.
12 And when they saw him from afar, they did not recognize him; and they raised their voices and wept; and they
rent their robes and sprinkled dust upon their heads toward
heaven. 13 And they sat with him on the ground seven days
and seven nights, and no one spoke a word to him, for they
saw that his suffering was very great.

3 After this Job opened his mouth and cursed the day
of his birth.
2 And Job said:
3 "Let the day perish wherein I was born,
and the night which said,
'A man-child is conceived.'
4 Let that day be darkness!
May God above not seek it,
nor light shine upon it.
5 Let gloom and deep darkness claim it.
Let clouds dwell upon it;
let the blackness of the day terrify it.
6 That night—let thick darkness seize it!
let it not rejoice among the days of the year,
let it not come into the number of the months.
7 Yea, let that night be barren;
let no joyful cry be heard in it.
8 Let those curse it who curse the day,
who are skilled to rouse up Leviathan.
9 Let the stars of its dawn be dark;
let it hope for light, but have none,
nor see the eyelids of the morning;
10 because it did not shut the doors of my mother's womb,
nor hide trouble from my eyes.
11 "Why did I not die at birth,
come forth from the womb and expire?
12 Why did the knees receive me?
Or why the breasts, that I should suck?
13 For then I should have lain down and been quiet;
I should have slept; then I should have been at rest,
14 with kings and counselors of the earth
who rebuilt ruins for themselves,
15 or with princes who had gold,
who filled their houses with silver.
16 Or why was I not as a hidden untimely birth,
as infants that never see the light?
17 There the wicked cease from troubling
and there the weary are at rest.
18 There the prisoners are at ease together;
they hear not the voice of the taskmaster.
19 The small and the great are there,
and the slave is free from his master.
20 "Why is light given to him that is in misery,
and life to the bitter in soul,
21 who long for death, but it comes not,
and dig for it more than for hid treasures;
22 who rejoice exceedingly,
and are glad, when they find the grave?
23 Why is light given to a man whose way is hid,
whom God has hedged in?
24 For my sighing comes as my bread,
and my groanings are poured out like water.
25 For the thing that I fear comes upon me,
and what I dread befalls me.
26 I am not at ease, nor am I quiet;
I have no rest; but trouble comes."

4 Then Eliphaz the Temanite answered:
2 "If one ventures a word with you, will you be
offended?
Yet who can keep from speaking?

---

2. EL-i-faz the TEE-man-ite, BIL-dad the SHOE-hite, ZO (rhyme with so)—far the NAY-ay-muh-thite.

3 Behold, you have instructed many,
and you have strengthened the weak hands.
4 Your words have upheld him who was stumbling,
and you have made firm the feeble knees.
5 But now it has come to you, and you are impatient;
it touches you, and you are dismayed.
6 Is not your fear of God your confidence,
and the integrity of your ways your hope?
7 "Think now, who that was innocent ever perished?
Or where were the upright cut off?
8 As I have seen, those who plow iniquity
and sow trouble reap the same.
9 By the breath of God they perish,
and by the blast of his anger they are consumed.
10 The roar of the lion, the voice of the fierce lion,
the teeth of the young lions, are broken.
11 The strong lion perishes for lack of prey,
and the whelps of the lioness are scattered.
12 "Now a word was brought to me stealthily,
my ear received the whisper of it.
13 Amid thoughts from visions of the night,
when deep sleep falls on men,
14 dread came upon me, and trembling,
which made all my bones shake.
15 A spirit glided past my face;
the hair of my flesh stood up.
16 It stood still,
but I could not discern its appearance.
A form was before my eyes;
there was silence, then I heard a voice:
17 'Can mortal man be righteous before God?[3]
can a man be pure before his Maker?
18 Even in his servants he puts no trust,[4]
and his angels he charges with error;
19 how much more those who dwell in houses of clay,
whose foundation is in the dust,
who are crushed before the moth.
20 Between morning and evening they are destroyed;
they perish for ever without any regarding it.
21 If their tent-cord is plucked up within them,
do they not die, and that without wisdom?'

5 "Call now; is there any one who will answer you?
To which of the holy ones will you turn?
2 Surely vexation kills the fool,
and jealousy slays the simple.
3 I have seen the fool taking root,
but suddenly I cursed his dwelling.
4 His sons are far from safety,
they are crushed in the gate,
and there is no one to deliver them.
5 His harvest the hungry eat,
and he takes it even out of thorns;
and the thirsty pant after his wealth.
6 For affliction does not come from the dust,
nor does trouble sprout from the ground;
7 but man is born to trouble
as the sparks fly upward.
8 "As for me, I would seek God,
and to God would I commit my cause;
9 who does great things and unsearchable,
marvelous things without number:
10 he gives rain upon the earth
and sends waters upon the fields;
11 he sets on high those who are lowly,
and those who mourn are lifted to safety.
12 He frustrates the devices of the crafty,
so that their hands achieve no success.
13 He takes the wise in their own craftiness;
and the schemes of the wily are brought to a quick end.
14 They meet with darkness in the daytime,
and grope at noonday as in the night.
15 But he saves the fatherless from their mouth,
the needy from the hand of the mighty.
16 So the poor have hope,
and injustice shuts her mouth.
17 "Behold, happy is the man whom God reproves;
therefore despise not the chastening of the Almighty.
18 For he wounds, but he binds up;
he smites, but his hands heal.
19 He will deliver you from six troubles;
in seven there shall no evil touch you.
20 In famine he will redeem you from death,
and in war from the power of the sword.
21 You shall be hid from the scourge of the tongue,
and shall not fear destruction when it comes.
22 At destruction and famine you shall laugh,
and shall not fear the beasts of the earth.
23 For you shall be in league with the stones of the field,
and the beasts of the field shall be at peace with you.
24 You shall know that your tent is safe,
and you shall inspect your fold and miss nothing.
25 You shall know also that your descendants shall be many,
and your offspring as the grass of the earth.
26 You shall come to your grave in ripe old age,
as a shock of grain comes up to the threshing floor in its season.
27 Lo, this we have searched out; it is true.
Hear, and know it for your good."

Then Job answered:
6 2 "O that my vexation were weighed,
and all my calamity laid in the balances!
3 For then it would be heavier than the sand of the sea;
therefore my words have been rash.
4 For the arrows of the Almighty are in me;
my spirit drinks their poison;
the terrors of God are arrayed against me.
5 Does the wild ass bray when he has grass,
or the ox low over his fodder?
6 Can that which is tasteless be eaten without salt,
or is there any taste in the slime of the purslane?
7 My appetite refuses to touch them;
they are as food that is loathsome to me.
8 "O that I might have my request,
and that God would grant my desire;
9 that it would please God to crush me,
that he would let loose his hand and cut me off!
10 This would be my consolation;
I would even exult in pain unsparing;
for I have not denied the words of the Holy one.
11 What is my strength, that I should wait?
And what is my end, that I should be patient?

---

3. Read here, "Can mortal man be more just than his maker?"
4. The words *he* and *his* refer to God.

12 Is my strength the strength of stones,
or is my flesh bronze?
13 In truth I have no help in me,
and any resource is driven from me.
14 "He who withholds kindness from a friend
forsakes the fear of the Almighty.
15 My brethren are treacherous as a torrent-bed,
as freshets that pass away,
16 which are dark with ice,
and where the snow hides itself.
17 In time of heat they disappear;
when it is hot, they vanish from their place.
18 The caravans turn aside from their course;
they go up into the waste, and perish.
19 The caravans of Tema look,
the travelers of Sheba hope.
20 They are disappointed because they were confident;
they come thither and are confounded.
21 Such you have now become to me;
you see my calamity, and are afraid.
22 Have I said, 'Make me a gift'?
Or, 'From your wealth offer a bribe for me'?
23 Or, 'Deliver me from the adversary's hand'?
Or, 'Ransom me from the hand of oppressors'?
24 "Teach me, and I will be silent;
make me understand how I have erred.
25 How forceful are honest words!
But what does reproof from you reprove?
26 Do you think that you can reprove words,
when the speech of a despairing man is wind?
27 You would even cast lots over the fatherless,
and bargain over your friend.
28 "But now, be pleased to look at me;
for I will not lie to your face.
29 Turn, I pray, let no wrong be done.
Turn now, my vindication is at stake.
30 Is there any wrong on my tongue?
Cannot my taste discern calamity?

7 "Has not man a hard service upon earth,
and are not his days like the days of a hireling?
2 Like a slave who longs for the shadow,
and like a hireling who looks for his wages,
3 so I am allotted months of emptiness,
and nights of misery are apportioned to me.
4 When I lie down I say, 'When shall I arise?'
But the night is long,
and I am full of tossing till the dawn.
5 My flesh is clothed with worms and dirt;
my skin hardens, then breaks out afresh.
6 My days are swifter than a weaver's shuttle,
and come to their end without hope.
7 "Remember that my life is a breath;
my eye will never again see good.
8 The eye of him who sees me will behold me no more;
while thy eyes are upon me, I shall be gone.
9 As the cloud fades and vanishes,
so he who goes down to Sheol does not come up;
10 he returns no more to his house,
nor does his place know him any more.
11 "Therefore I will not restrain my mouth;
I will speak in the anguish of my spirit;
I will complain in the bitterness of my soul.
12 Am I the sea, or a sea monster,
that thou settest a guard over me?
13 When I say, 'My bed will comfort me,
my couch will ease my complaint.'
14 then thou dost scare me with dreams
and terrify me with visions.
15 so that I would choose strangling
and death rather than my bones.
16 I loathe my life; I would not live for ever.
Let me alone, for my days are a breath.
17 What is man, that thou dost make so much of him,
and that thou dost set thy mind upon him,
18 dost visit him every morning,
and test him every moment?
19 How long wilt thou not look away from me,
nor let me alone till I swallow my spittle?
20 If I sin, what do I do to thee, thou watcher of men?
Why hast thou made me thy mark?
Why have I become a burden to thee?
21 Why dost thou not pardon my transgression
and take away my iniquity?
For now I shall lie in the earth;
thou wilt seek me, but I shall not be."

8 Then Bildad the Shuhite answered:
2 "How long will you say these things,
and the words of your mouth be a great wind?
3 Does God pervert justice?
Or does the Almighty pervert the right?
4 If your children have sinned against him,
he has delivered them into the power of their transgression.
5 If you will seek God
and make supplication to the Almighty,
6 if you are pure and upright,
surely then he will rouse himself for you
and reward you with a rightful habitation.
7 And though your beginning was small,
your latter days will be very great.
8 "For inquire, I pray you, of bygone ages,
and consider what the fathers have found;
9 for we are but of yesterday, and know nothing,
for our days on earth are a shadow.
10 Will they not teach you, and tell you,
and utter words out of their understanding?
11 "Can papyrus grow where there is no marsh?
Can reeds flourish where there is no water?
12 While yet in flower and not cut down,
they wither before any other plant.
13 Such are the paths of all who forget God;
the hope of the godless man shall perish.
14 His confidence breaks in sunder,
and his trust is a spider's web.
15 He leans against his house, but it does not stand;
he lays hold of it, but it does not endure.
16 He thrives before the sun,
and his shoots spread over his garden.
17 His roots twine about the stoneheap;
he lives among the rocks.
18 If he is destroyed from his place,
then it will deny him, saying, 'I have never seen you.'
19 Behold, this is the joy of his way;
and out of the earth others will spring.
20 "Behold, God will not reject a blameless man,
nor take the hand of evildoers.
21 He will yet fill your mouth with laughter,
and your lips with shouting.

22 Those who hate you will be clothed with shame,
and the tent of the wicked will be no more."

9 Then Job answered:
2 "Truly I know that it is so:
But how can a man be just before God?
3 If one wished to contend with him,
one could not answer him once in a thousand times.
4 He is wise in heart, and mighty in strength
—who has hardened himself against him, and succeeded?—
5 he who removes mountains, and they know it not,
when he overturns them in his anger;
6 who shakes the earth out of its place,
and its pillars tremble;
7 who commands the sun, and it does not rise;
who seals up the stars;
8 who alone stretched out the heavens,
and trampled the waves of the sea;
9 who made the Bear and Orion,
the Pleiades and the chambers of the south;
10 who does great things beyond understanding,
and marvelous things without number.
11 Lo, he passes by me, and I see him not;
he moves on, but I do not perceive him.
12 Behold, he snatches away; who can hinder him?
Who will say to him, 'What doest thou'?
13 "God will not turn back his anger;
beneath him bowed the helpers of Rahab.
14 How then can I answer him,
choosing my words with him?
15 Though I am innocent, I cannot answer him;
I must appeal for mercy to my accuser.
16 If I summoned him and he answered me,
I would not believe that he was listening to my voice.
17 For he crushes me with a tempest,
and multiplies my wounds without cause;
18 he will not let me get my breath,
but fills me with bitterness.
19 If it is a contest of strength, behold him!
If it is a matter of justice, who can summon him?
20 Though I am innocent, my own mouth would condemn me;
though I am blameless, he would prove me perverse.
21 I am blameless; I regard not myself;
I loathe my life.
22 It is all one; therefore I say,
he destroys both the blameless and the wicked.
23 When disaster brings sudden death,
he mocks at the calamity of the innocent.
24 The earth is given into the hand of the wicked;
he covers the faces of its judges—
if it is not he, who then is it?
25 "My days are swifter than a runner;
they flee away, they see no good.
26 They go by like skiffs of reed,
like an eagle swooping on the prey.
27 If I say, 'I will forget my complaint,
I will put off my sad countenance, and be of good cheer,'
28 I become afraid of all my suffering
for I know thou wilt not hold me innocent.
29 I shall be condemned;
why then do I labor in vain?
30 If I wash myself with snow
and cleanse my hands with lye,
31 yet thou wilt plunge me into a pit,
and my own clothes will abhor me.
32 For he is not a man, as I am, that I might answer him,
that we should come to trial together.[5]
33 There is no umpire between us,
who might lay his hand upon us both.
34 Let him take his rod away from me,
and let not dread of him terrify me.
35 Then I would speak without fear of him,
for I am not so in myself.

10 "I loathe my life;
I will give free utterance to my complaint;
I will speak in the bitterness of my soul.
2 I will say to God, Do not condemn me;
let me know why thou dost contend against me.
3 Does it seem good to thee to oppress,
to despise the work of thy hands
and favor the designs of the wicked?
4 Hast thou eyes of flesh?
Dost thou see as man sees?
5 Are thy days as the days of man,
or thy years as man's years,
6 that thou dost seek out my iniquity
and search for my sin,
7 although thou knowest that I am not guilty,
and there is none to deliver out of thy hand?
8 Thy hands fashioned and made me;
and now thou dost turn about and destroy me.
9 Remember that thou hast made me of clay;
and wilt thou turn me to dust again?
10 Didst thou not pour me out like milk
and curdle me like cheese?
11 Thou didst clothe me with skin and flesh,
and knit me together with bones and sinews.
12 Thou hast granted me life and steadfast love;
and thy care has preserved my spirit.
13 Yet these things thou didst hide in thy heart;
I know that this was thy purpose.
14 If I sin, thou dost mark me,
and dost not acquit me of my iniquity.
15 If I am wicked, woe to me!
If I am righteous, I cannot lift up my head,
for I am filled with disgrace
and look upon my affliction.
16 And if I lift myself up, thou dost hunt me like a lion,
and again work wonders against me;
17 thou dost renew thy witnesses against me,
and increase thy vexation toward me;
thou dost bring fresh hosts against me."
18 "Why didst thou bring me forth from the womb?
Would that I had died before any eye had seen me,
19 and were as though I had not been,
carried from the womb to the grave.
20 Are not the days of my life few?
Let me alone, that I may find a little comfort
21 before I go whence I shall not return,
to the land of gloom and deep darkness.
22 the land of gloom and chaos,
where light is as darkness."

---

5. Here begins one of Job's recurring themes: He would like to face God and have what amounts to a legal trial. What picture of God does Job hold?

11 Then Zophar the Na'amathite answered:
[2] "Should a multitude of words go unanswered,
and a man full of talk be vindicated?
[3] Should your babble silence men,
and when you mock, shall no one shame you?
[4] For you say, 'My doctrine is pure,
and I am clean in God's eyes.'
[5] But oh, that God would speak,
and open his lips to you,
[6] and that he would tell you the secrets of wisdom!
For he is manifold in understanding.
Know then that God exacts of you less than your guilt deserves.
[7] "Can you find out the deep things of God?
Can you find out the limit of the Almighty?
[8] It is higher than heaven—what can you do?
Deeper than Sheol[6]—what can you know?
[9] Its measure is longer than the earth,
and broader than the sea.
[10] If he passes through, and imprisons,
and calls to judgment, who can hinder him?
[11] For he knows worthless men;
when he sees iniquity, will he not consider it?
[12] But a stupid man will get understanding,
when a wild ass's colt is born a man.
[13] "If you set your heart aright,
you will stretch out your hands toward him.
[14] If iniquity is in your hand, put it far away,
and let not wickedness dwell in your tents.
[15] Surely then you will lift up your face without blemish;
you will be secure, and will not fear.
[16] You will forget your misery;
you will remember it as waters that have passed away.
[17] And your life will be brighter than the noonday;
its darkness will be like the morning.
[18] And you will have confidence, because there is hope;
you will be protected and take your rest in safety.
[19] You will lie down, and none will make you afraid;
many will entreat your favor.
[20] But the eyes of the wicked will fail;
all way of escape will be lost to them,
and their hope is to breathe their last."

12 Then Job answered:
[2] "No doubt you are the people,
and wisdom will die with you.
[3] But I have understanding as well as you;
I am not inferior to you.
Who does not know such things as these?
[4] I am a laughingstock to my friends;
I, who called upon God and he answered me,
a just and blameless man, am a laughingstock.
[5] In the thought of one who is at ease there is contempt for misfortune;
it is ready for those whose feet slip.
[6] The tents of robbers are at peace,
and those who provoke God are secure,
who bring their god in their hand.
[7] "But ask the beasts, and they will teach you;
the birds of the air, and they will tell you;
[8] or the plants of the earth, and they will teach you;
and the fish of the sea will declare to you.
[9] Who among all these does not know
that the hand of the LORD has done this?
[10] In his hand is the life of every living thing
and the breath of all mankind.
[11] Does not the ear try words
as the palate tastes food?
[12] Wisdom is with the aged,
and understanding in length of days.
[13] "With God are wisdom and might;
he has counsel and understanding.
[14] If he tears down, none can rebuild;
if he shuts a man in, none can open.
[15] If he withholds the waters, they dry up;
if he sends them out, they overwhelm the land.
[16] With him are strength and wisdom;
the deceived and the deceiver are his.
[17] He leads counselors away stripped,
and judges he makes fools.
[18] He looses the bonds of kings,
and binds a waistcloth on their loins.
[19] He leads priests away stripped,
and overthrows the mighty.
[20] He deprives of speech those who are trusted,
and takes away the discernment of the elders.
[21] He pours contempt on princes,
and looses the belt of the strong.
[22] He uncovers the deeps out of darkness,
and brings deep darkness to light.
[23] He makes nations great, and he destroys them:
he enlarges nations, and leads them away.
[24] He takes away understanding from the chiefs of the people of the earth,
and makes them wander in a pathless waste.
[25] They grope in the dark without light;
and he makes them stagger like a drunken man.

13 "Lo, my eye has seen all this,
my ear has heard and understood it.
[2] What you know, I also know;
I am not inferior to you.
[3] But I would speak to the Almighty,
and I desire to argue my case with God.
[4] As for you, you whitewash with lies;
worthless physicians are you all.
[5] Oh that you would keep silent,
and it would be your wisdom!
[6] Hear now my reasoning,
and listen to the pleadings of my lips.
[7] Will you speak falsely for God,
and speak deceitfully for him?
[8] Will you show partiality toward him,
will you plead the case for God?
[9] Will it be well with you when he searches you out?
Or can you deceive him, as one deceives a man?
[10] He will surely rebuke you
if in secret you show partiality.
[11] Will not his majesty terrify you,
and the dread of him fall upon you?
[12] Your maxims are proverbs of ashes,
your defences are defences of clay.
[13] "Let me have silence, and I will speak,
and let come on me what may.
[14] I will take my flesh in my teeth,
and put my life in my hand.
[15] Behold, he will slay me; I have no hope;
yet I will defend my ways to his face.
[16] This will be my salvation,
that a godless man shall not come before him.

---

6. SHEE-ol, the word for the Hebrew underworld.

17 Listen carefully to my words,
and let my declaration be in your ears.
18 Behold, I have prepared my case;
I know that I shall be vindicated.
19 Who is there that will contend with me?
For then I would be silent and die.
20 Only grant two things to me,
then I will not hide myself from thy face:
21 withdraw thy hand far from me,
and let not dread of thee terrify me.
22 Then call, and I will answer;
or let me speak, and do thou reply to me.
23 How many are my iniquities and my sins?
Make me know my transgression and my sin.
24 Why dost thou hide thy face,
and count me as thy enemy?
25 Wilt thou frighten a driven leaf
and pursue dry chaff?
26 For thou writest bitter things against me,
and makest me inherit the iniquities of my youth.
27 Thou puttest my feet in the stocks,
and watchest all my paths;
thou settest a bound to the soles of my feet.
28 Man wastes away like a rotten thing,
like a garment that is moth-eaten.

14 "Man that is born of a woman
is of few days, and full of trouble.
2 He comes forth like a flower, and withers;
he flees like a shadow, and continues not.
3 And dost thou open thy eyes upon such a one
and bring him into judgment with thee?
4 Who can bring a clean thing out of an unclean?
There is not one.
5 Since his days are determined,
and the number of his months is with thee,
and thou hast appointed his bounds that he cannot pass,
6 look away from him, and desist,
that he may enjoy, like a hireling, his day.
7 "For there is hope for a tree,
if it be cut down, that it will sprout again,
and that its shoots will not cease.
8 Though its root grow old in the earth,
and its stump die in the ground,
9 yet at the scent of water it will bud
and put forth branches like a young plant.
10 But man dies, and is laid low;
man breathes his last, and where is he?
11 As waters fail from a lake,
and a river wastes away and dries up,
12 So man lies down and rises not again;
till the heavens are no more he will not awake,
or be roused out of his sleep.
13 Oh that thou wouldest hide me in Sheol,
that thou wouldest conceal me until thy wrath be past,
that thou wouldest appoint me a set time, and remember me!
14 If a man die, shall he live again?
All the days of my service I would wait,
till my release should come.
15 Thou wouldest call, and I would answer thee;
thou wouldest long for the work of thy hands.
16 For then thou wouldest number my steps,
thou wouldest not keep watch over my sin;
17 my transgression would be sealed up in a bag,
and thou wouldest cover over my iniquity.
18 "But the mountain falls and crumbles away,
and the rock is removed from its place;
19 the waters wear away the stones;
the torrents wash away the soil of the earth;
so thou destroyest the hope of man.
20 Thou prevailest for ever against him, and he passes;
thou changest his countenance, and sendest him away.
21 His sons come to honor, and he does not know it;
they are brought low, and he perceives it not.
22 He feels only the pain of his own body,
and he mourns only for himself."

15 Then Elíphaz the Témanite answered:
2 "Should a wise man answer with windy knowledge,
and fill himself with the east wind?
3 Should he argue in unprofitable talk,
or in words with which he can do no good?
4 But you are doing away with the fear of God,
and hindering meditation before God,
5 For your iniquity teaches your mouth,
and choose the tongue of the crafty.
6 Your own mouth condemns you, and not I;
your own lips testify against you.
7 "Are you the first man that was born?
Or were you brought forth before the hills?
8 Have you listened in the council of God?
And do you limit wisdom to yourself?
9 What do you know that we do not know?
What do you understand that is not clear to us?
10 Both the grayhaired and the aged are among us,
older than your father.
11 Are the consolations of God too small for you,
or the word that deals gently with you?
12 Why does your heart carry you away,
and why do your eyes flash,
13 that you turn your spirit against God,
and let such words go out of your mouth?
14 What is man, that he can be clean?
Or he that is born of a woman, that he can be righteous?
15 Behold, God puts no trust in his holy ones,
and the heavens are not clean in his sight;
16 how much less one who is abominable and corrupt,
a man who drinks iniquity like water!
17 "I will show you, hear me;
and what I have seen I will declare
18 (what wise men have told,
and their fathers have not hidden,
19 to whom alone the land was given,
and no stranger passed among them).
20 The wicked man writhes in pain all his days,
through all the years that are laid up for the ruthless.
21 Terrifying sounds are in his ears;
in prosperity the destroyer will come upon him.
22 He does not believe that he will return out of darkness,
and he is destined for the sword.
23 He wanders abroad for bread, saying, 'Where is it?'
He knows that a day of darkness is ready at his hand;
24 distress and anguish terrify him;
they prevail against him, like a king prepared for battle.
25 Because he has stretched forth his hand against God,
and bids defiance to the Almighty,

26 running stubbornly against him
with a thick-bossed shield;
27 because he has covered his face with his fat,
and gathered fat upon his loins,
28 and has lived in desolate cities,
in houses which no man should inhabit,
which were destined to become heaps of ruins;
29 he will not be rich, and his wealth will not endure,
nor will he strike root in the earth;
30 he will not escape from darkness;
the flame will dry up his shoots,
and his blossom will be swept away by the wind.
31 Let him not trust in emptiness, deceiving himself;
for emptiness will be his recompense.
32 It will be paid in full before his time,
and his branch will not be green.
33 He will shake off his unripe grape, like the vine,
and cast off his blossom, like the olive tree.
34 For the company of the godless is barren,
and fire consumes the tents of bribery.
35 They conceive mischief and bring forth evil
and their heart prepares deceit."

16 Then Job answered:
2 "I have heard many such things;
miserable comforters are you all
3 Shall windy words have an end?
Or what provokes you that you answer?
4 I also could speak as you do,
if you were in my place;
I could join words together against you,
and shake my head at you.
5 I could strengthen you with my mouth,
and the solace of my lips would assuage your pain.
6 "If I speak, my pain is not assuaged,
and if I forbear, how much of it leaves me?
7 Surely now God has worn me out;
he has made desolate all my company.
8 And he has shriveled me up,
which is a witness against me;
and my leanness has risen up against me,
it testifies to my face.
9 He has torn me in his wrath, and hated me;
he has gnashed his teeth at me;
my adversary sharpens his eyes against me.
10 Men have gaped at me with their mouth,
they have struck me insolently upon the cheek,
they mass themselves together against me.
11 God gives me up to the ungodly,
and casts me into the hands of the wicked.
12 I was at ease, and he broke me asunder;
he seized me by the neck and dashed me to pieces;
13 He set me up as his target,
his archers surround me.
He slashes open my kidneys, and does not spare;
he pours out my gall on the ground.
14 He breaks me with breach upon breach;
he runs upon me like a warrior.
15 I have sewed sackcloth upon my skin,
and have laid my strength in the dust.
16 My face is red with weeping,
and on my eyelids is deep darkness;
17 although there is no violence in my hands,
and my prayer is pure.
18 "O earth, cover not my blood,
and let my cry find no resting place.
19 Even now, behold, my witness is in heaven,
and he that vouches for me is on high.
20 My friends scorn me;
my eye pours out tears to God,
21 that he would maintain the right of a man with God,
like that of a man with his neighbor.
22 For when a few years have come
I shall go the way whence I shall not return.

17 My spirit is broken, my days are extinct,
the grave is ready for me.
2 Surely there are mockers about me,
and my eye dwells on their provocation.
3 "Lay down a pledge for me with thyself;
who is there that will give surety for me?
4 Since thou hast closed their minds to understanding,
therefore thou wilt not let them triumph.
5 He who informs against his friends to get a share of their property,
the eyes of his children will fail.
6 "He has made me a byword of the peoples,
and I am one before whom men spit.
7 My eye has grown dim from grief,
and all my members are like a shadow.
8 Upright men are appalled at this,
and the innocent stirs himself up against the godless.
9 Yet the righteous holds to his way,
and he that has clean hands grows stronger and stronger.
10 But you, come on again, all of you,
and I shall not find a wise man among you.
11 My days are past, my plans are broken off,
the desires of my heart.
12 They make night into day;
'The light,' they say, 'is near to the darkness.'
13 If I look for Shoel as my house,
if I spread my couch in darkness,
14 if I say to the pit, 'You are my father,'
and to the worm, 'My mother,' or 'My sister,'
15 where then is my hope?
Who will see my hope?
16 Will it go down to the bars of Sheol?
Shall we descend together into the dust?"

18 Then Bildad the Shuhite answered:
2 "How long will you hunt for words?
Consider, and then we will speak.
3 Why are we counted as cattle?
Why are we stupid in your sight?
4 You who tear yourself in your anger,
shall the earth be forsaken for you,
or the rock be removed out of its place?
5 "Yea, the light of the wicked is put out,
and the flame of his fire does not shine.
6 The light is dark in his tent,
and his lamp above him is put out.
7 His strong steps are shortened
and his own schemes throw him down
8 For he is cast into a net by his own feet,
and he walks on a pitfall.
9 A trap seizes him by the heel,
a snare lays hold of him.
10 A rope is hid for him in the ground,
a trap for him in the path.
11 Terrors frighten him on every side,
and chase him at his heels.

12 His strength is hunger-bitten,
and calamity is ready for his stumbling.
13 By disease his skin is consumed,
the first-born of death consumes his limbs.
14 He is torn from the tent in which he trusted,
and is brought to the king of terrors.
15 In his tent dwells that which in none of his;
brimstone is scattered upon his habitation.
16 His roots dry up beneath,
and his branches wither above.
17 His memory perishes from the earth,
and he has no name in the street.
18 He is thrust from light into darkness,
and driven out of the world.
19 He has no offspring or descendant among his people,
and no survivor where he used to live.
20 They of the west are appalled at his day,
and horror seizes them of the east.
21 Surely such are the dwellings of the ungodly,
such is the place of him who knows not God."

19 Then Job answered:
2 "How long will you torment me,
and break me in pieces with words?
3 These ten times you have cast reproach upon me;
are you not ashamed to wrong me?
4 And even if it be true that I have erred,
my error remains with myself.
5 If indeed you magnify yourselves against me,
and make my humiliation an argument against me,
6 know then that God has put me in the wrong,
and closed his net about me.
7 Behold, I cry out, 'Violence!' but I am not answered;
I call aloud, but there is no justice.
8 He has walled up my way, so that I cannot pass,
and he has set darkness upon my paths.
9 He has stripped from me my glory,
and taken the crown from my head.
10 He breaks me down on every side, and I am gone,
and my hope has he pulled up like a tree.
11 He has kindled his wrath against me,
and counts me as his adversary.
12 His troops come on together;
they have cast up siegeworks against me,
and encamp round about my tent.
13 "He has put my brethren far from me,
and my acquaintances are wholly estranged from me.
14 My kinsfolk and my close friends have failed me;
the guests in my house have forgotten me;
15 my maidservants count me as a stranger;
I have become an alien in their eyes.
16 I call to my servant, but he gives me no answer;
I must beseech him with my mouth.
17 I am repulsive to my wife,
loathsome to the sons of my own mother.
18 Even young children despise me;
when I rise they talk against me.
19 All my intimate friends abhor me,
and those whom I loved have turned against me.
20 My bones cleave to my skin and to my flesh,
and I have escaped by the skin of my teeth.
21 Have pity on me, have pity on me, O you my friends,
for the hand of God has touched me!
22 Why do you, like God, pursue me?
why are you not satisfied with my flesh?
23 "Oh that my words were written!
Oh that they were inscribed in a book!
24 Oh that with an iron pen and lead
they were graven in rock for ever!
25 For I know that my Redeemer lives,
and at last he will stand upon the earth;
26 and after my skin has been thus destroyed,
then without my flesh I shall see God,
27 whom I shall see on my side,
and my eyes shall behold, and not another.
My heart faints within me!
28 If you say, 'How we will pursue him!'
and, 'The root of the matter is found in him';
29 be afraid of the sword,
for wrath brings the punishment of the sword,
that you may know there is a judgment."

20 Then Zophar the Na'amathite answered:
2 "Therefore my thoughts answer me,
because of my haste within me.
3 I hear censure which insults me,
and out of my understanding a spirit answers me.
4 Do you not know this from of old,
since man was placed upon earth,
5 that the exulting of the wicked is short,
and the joy of the godless but for a moment?
6 Though his height mount up to the heavens,
and his head reach to the clouds,
7 he will perish for ever like his own dung;
those who have seen him will say, 'Where is he?'
8 He will fly away like a dream, and not be found;
he will be chased away like a vision of the night.
9 The eye which saw him will see him no more,
nor will his place any more behold him.
10 His children will seek the favor of the poor,
and his hands will give back his wealth.
11 His bones are full of youthful vigor,
but it will lie down with him in the dust.
12 "Though wickedness is sweet in his mouth,
though he hides it under his tongue,
13 though he is loath to let it go,
and holds it in his mouth,
14 yet his good is turned in his stomach;
it is the gall of asps within him.
15 He swallows down riches and vomits them up again;
God casts them out of his belly.
16 He will suck the poison of asps;
the tongue of a viper will kill him.
17 He will not look upon the rivers,
the streams flowing with honey and curds.
18 He will give back the fruit of his toil,
and will not swallow it down;
from the profit of his trading
he will get no enjoyment.
19 For he has crushed and abandoned the poor,
he has seized a house which he did not build.
20 "Because his greed knew no rest,
he will not save anything in which he delights.
21 There was nothing left after he had eaten;
therefore his prosperity will not endure.
22 In the fulness of his sufficiency he will be in straits;
all the force of misery will come upon him.
23 To fill his belly to the full
God will send his fierce anger into him,
and rain it upon him as his food.

24 He will flee from an iron weapon;
a bronze arrow will strike him through.
25 It is drawn forth and comes out of his body,
the glittering point comes out of his gall;
terrors come upon him.
26 Utter darkness is laid up for his treasures;
a fire not blown upon will devour him;
what is left in his tent will be consumed.
27 The heavens will reveal his iniquity,
and the earth will rise up against him.
28 The possessions of his house will be carried away,
dragged off in the day of God's wrath.
29 This is the wicked man's portion from God,
the heritage decreed for him by God."

21 Then Job answered:
2 "Listen carefully to my words,
and let this be your consolation.
3 Bear with me, and I will speak,
and after I have spoken, mock on.
4 As for me, is my complaint against man?
Why should I not be impatient?
5 Look at me, and be appalled,
and lay your hand upon your mouth.
6 When I think of it I am dismayed,
and shuddering seizes my flesh.
7 Why do the wicked live,
reach old age, and grow mighty in power?
8 Their children are established in their presence,
and their offspring before their eyes.
9 Their houses are safe from fear,
and no rod of God is upon them.
10 Their bull breeds without fail;
their cow calves, and does not cast her calf.
11 They send forth their little ones like a flock,
and their children dance.
12 They sing to the tambourine and the lyre,
and rejoice to the sound of the pipe.
13 They spend their days in prosperity,
and in peace they go down to Sheol.
14 They say to God, 'Depart from us!
We do not desire the knowledge of thy ways.
15 What is the Almighty, that we should serve him?
And what profit do we get if we pray to him?'
16 Behold, is not their prosperity in their hand?
The counsel of the wicked is far from me.
17 "How often is it that the lamp of the wicked is put out?
That their calamity comes upon them?
That God distributes pains in his anger?
18 That they are like straw before the wind,
and like chaff that the storm carries away?
19 You say, 'God stores up their iniquity for their sons.'
Let him recompense it to themselves, that they may
know it.
20 Let their own eyes see their destruction,
and let them drink of the wrath of the Almighty.
21 For what do they care for their houses after them,
when the number of their months is cut off?
22 Will any teach God knowledge,
seeing that he judges those that are on high?
23 One dies in full prosperity,
being wholly at ease and secure,
24 his body full of fat
and the marrow of his bones moist.
25 Another dies in bitterness of soul,
never having tasted of good.
26 They lie down alike in the dust,
and the worms cover them.
27 "Behold, I know your thoughts,
and your schemes to wrong me.
28 For you say, 'Where is the house of the prince?
Where is the tent in which the wicked dwelt?'
29 Have you not asked those who travel the roads,
and do you not accept their testimony
30 that the wicked man is spared in the day of calamity,
that he is rescued in the day of wrath?
31 Who declares his way to his face,
and who requites him for what he has done?
32 When he is borne to the grave,
watch is kept over his tomb.
33 The clods of the valley are sweet to him;
all men follow after him,
and those who go before him are innumerable.
34 How then will you comfort me with empty nothings?
There is nothing left of your answers but falsehood."

22 Then Eli´phaz the Te´manite answered:
2 "Can a man be profitable to God?
Surely he who is wise is profitable to himself.
3 Is it any pleasure to the Almighty if you are righteous,
or is it gain to him if you make your ways blameless?
4 Is it for your fear of him that he reproves you,
and enters into judgment with you?
5 Is not your wickedness great?
There is no end to your iniquities.
6 For you have exacted pledges of your brothers for nothing,
and stripped the naked of their clothing.
7 You have given no water to the weary to drink,
and you have withheld bread from the hungry.
8 The man with power possessed the land,
and the favored man dwelt in it.
9 You have sent widows away empty,
and the arms of the fatherless were crushed.
10 Therefore snares are round about you,
and sudden terror overwhelms you;
11 your light is darkened, so that you cannot see,
and a flood of water covers you.
12 "Is not God high in the heavens?
See the highest stars, how lofty they are!
13 Therefore you say, 'What does God know?
Can he judge through the deep darkness?
14 Thick clouds enwrap him, so that he does not see,
and he walks on the vault of heaven.'
15 Will you keep to the old way
which wicked men have trod?
16 They were snatched away before their time;
their foundation was washed away.
17 They said to God, 'Depart from us,'
and 'What can the Almighty do to us?'
18 Yet he filled their houses with good things—
but the counsel of the wicked is far from me.
19 The righteous see it and are glad;
the innocent laugh them to scorn,
20 saying, 'Surely our adversaries are cut off,
and what they left the fire has consumed.'
21 "Agree with God, and be at peace;
thereby good will come to you.
22 Receive instruction from his mouth,
and lay up his words in your heart.
23 If you return to the Almighty and humble yourself,
if you remove unrighteousness far from your tents,

24 if you lay gold in the dust,
and gold of Ophir among the stones of the torrent bed,
25 and if the Almighty is your gold,
and your precious silver;
26 then you will delight yourself in the Almighty,
and lift up your face to God.
27 You will make your prayer to him, and he will hear you;
and you will pay your vows.
28 You will decide on a matter, and it will be established
for you,
and light will shine on your ways.
29 For God abases the proud,
but he saves the lowly.
30 He delivers the innocent man;
you will be delivered through the cleanness of your
hands."

23 Then Job answered:
2 "Today also my complaint is bitter
his hand is heavy in spite of my groaning.
3 Oh, that I knew where I might find him,
that I might come even to his seat!
4 I would lay my case before him
and fill my mouth with arguments.
5 I would learn what he would answer me,
and understand what he would say to me.
6 Would he contend with me in the greatness of his power?
No; he would give heed to me.
7 There an upright man could reason with him,
and I should be acquitted for ever by my judge.
8 "Behold, I go forward, but he is not there;
and backward, but I cannot perceive him;
9 on the left hand I seek him, but I cannot behold him;
I turn to the right hand, but I cannot see him.
10 But he knows the way that I take;
when he has tried me, I shall come forth as gold.
11 My foot has held fast to his steps;
I have kept his way and have not turned aside.
12 I have not departed from the commandment of his lips;
I have treasured in my bosom the words of his mouth.
13 But he is unchangeable and who can turn him?
What he desires, that he does.
14 For he will complete what he appoints for me;
and many such things are in his mind.
15 Therefore I am terrified at his presence;
when I consider, I am in dread of him.
16 God has made my heart faint;
the Almighty has terrified me;
17 for I am hemmed in by darkness,
and thick darkness covers my face.

24 "Why are not times of judgment
kept by the Almighty,
and why do those who know him
never see his days?
2 Men remove landmarks;
they seize flocks and pasture them.
3 They drive away the ass of the fatherless;
they take the widow's ox for a pledge.
4 They thrust the poor off the road;
the poor of the earth all hide themselves.
5 Behold, like wild asses in the desert
they go forth to their toil,
seeking prey in the wilderness
as food for their children.
6 They gather their fodder in the field
and they glean the vineyard of the wicked man.
7 They lie all night naked, without clothing,
and have no covering in the cold.
8 They are wet with the rain of the mountains,
and cling to the rock for want of shelter.
9 (There are those who snatch the fatherless child from
the breast,
and take in pledge the infant of the poor.)
10 They go about naked, without clothing;
hungry, they carry the sheaves;
11 among the olive rows of the wicked they make oil;
they tread the wine presses, but suffer thirst.
12 From out of the city the dying groan,
and the soul of the wounded cries for help;
yet God pays no attention to their prayer.
13 "There are those who rebel against the light,
who are not acquainted with its way,
and do not stay in its path.
14 The murderer rises in the dark,
that he may kill the poor and needy;
and in the night he is as a thief.
15 The eye of the adulterer also waits for the twilight,
saying, 'No eye will see me';
and he disguises his face.
16 In the dark they dig through houses;
by day they shut themselves up;
they do not know the light.
17 For deep darkness is morning to all of them;
for they are friends with the terrors of deep darkness.
18 "You say, 'They are swiftly carried away upon the face
of the waters;
their portion is cursed in the land;
no treader turns toward their vineyards.
19 Drought and heat snatch away the snow waters;
so does Sheol those who have sinned.
20 The squares of the town forget them;
their name is no longer remembered;
so wickedness is broken like a tree.'
21 "They feed on the barren childless woman,
and do no good to the widow.
22 Yet God prolongs the life of the mighty by his power;
they rise up when they despair of life.
23 He gives them security, and they are supported;
and his eyes are upon their ways.
24 They are exalted a little while, and then are gone;
they wither and fade like the mallow;
they are cut off like the heads of grain.
25 If it is not so, who will prove me a liar,
and show that there is nothing in what I say?"

25 Then Bildad the Shuhite answered:
2 "Dominion and fear are with God;
he makes peace in his high heaven.
3 Is there any number to his armies?
Upon whom does his light not arise?
4 How then can man be righteous before God?
How can he who is born of woman be clean?
5 Behold, even the moon is not bright
and the stars are not clean in his sight;
6 how much less man, who is a maggot,
and the son of man, who is a worm!"

26 Then Job answered:
2 "How you have helped him who has no power!
How you have saved the arm that has no strength.

3 How you have counseled him who has no wisdom,
and plentifully declared sound knowledge!
4 With whose help have you uttered words,
and whose spirit has come forth from you?
5 The shades below tremble,
the waters and their inhabitants.
6 Sheol is naked before God,
and Abaddon has no covering.
7 He stretches out the north over the void,
and hangs the earth upon nothing.
8 He binds up the waters in his thick clouds,
and the cloud is not rent under them.
9 He covers the face of the moon,
and spreads over it his cloud.
10 He has described a circle upon the face of the waters
at the boundary between light and darkness.
11 The pillars of heaven tremble,
and are astounded at his rebuke.
12 By his power he stilled the sea;
by his understanding he smote Rahab.
13 By his wind the heavens were made fair;
his hand pierced the fleeing serpent.
14 Lo, these are but the outskirts of his ways;
and how small a whisper do we hear of him!
But the thunder of his power who can understand?"

27 And Job again took up his discourse, and said:
2 "As God lives, who has taken away my right,
and the Almighty, who has made my soul bitter.
3 as long as my breath is in me,
and the spirit of God is in my nostrils;
4 my lips will not speak falsehood,
and my tongue will not utter deceit.
5 Far be it from me to say that you are right;
till I die I will not put away my integrity from me.
6 I hold fast my righteousness, and will not let it go;
my heart does not reproach me for any of my days.
7 "Let my enemy be as the wicked,
and let him that rises up against me be as the unrighteous.
8 For what is the hope of the godless when God cuts him off,
when God takes away his life?
9 Will God hear his cry,
when trouble comes upon him?
10 Will he take delight in the Almighty?
Will he call upon God at all times?
11 I will teach you concerning the hand of God?
what is with the Almighty I will not conceal.
12 Behold, all of you have seen it yourselves;
why then have you become altogether vain?
13 "This is the portion of a wicked man with God,
and the heritage which oppressors receive from the Almighty:
14 If his children are multiplied, it is for the sword;
and his offspring have not enough to eat.
15 Those who survive him the pestilence buries,
and their widows make no lamentation.
16 Though he heap up silver like dust,
and pile up clothing like clay;
17 he may pile it up, but the just will wear it,
and the innocent will divide the silver.
18 The house which he builds is like a spider's web,
like a booth which a watchman makes.
19 He goes to bed rich, but will do so no more;
he opens his eyes, and his wealth is gone.
20 Terrors overtake him like a flood;
in the night a whirlwind carries him off.
21 The east wind lifts him up and he is gone;
it sweeps him out of his place.
22 It hurls at him without pity;
he flees from its power in headlong flight.
23 It claps its hands at him,
and hisses at him from its place.

28 "Surely there is a mine for silver,
and a place for gold which they refine.
2 Iron is taken out of the earth,
and copper is smelted from the ore.
3 Men put an end to darkness,
and search out to the farthest bound
the ore in gloom and deep darkness.
4 They open shafts in a valley away from where men live;
they are forgotten by travelers,
they hang afar from men, they swing to and fro.
5 As for the earth, out of it comes bread;
but underneath it is turned up as by fire.
6 Its stones are the place of sapphires,
and it has dust of gold.
7 "That path no bird of prey knows,
and the falcon's eye has not seen it.
8 The proud beasts have not trodden it;
the lion has not passed over it.
9 "Man puts his hand to the flinty rock,
and overturns mountains by the roots.
10 He cuts out channels in the rocks,
and his eye sees every precious thing.
11 He binds up the streams so that they do not trickle,
and the thing that is hid he brings forth to light.
12 "But where shall wisdom be found?
And where is the place of understanding?
13 Man does not know the way to it,
and it is not found in the land of the living.
14 The deep says, 'It is not in me,'
and the sea says, 'It is not with me.'
15 It cannot be gotten for gold,
and silver cannot be weighed as its price.
16 It cannot be valued in the gold of Ophir,
in precious onyx or sapphire.
17 Gold and glass cannot equal it,
nor can it be exchanged for jewels of fine gold.
18 No mention shall be made of coral or of crystal;
the price of wisdom is above pearls.
19 The topaz of Ethiopia cannot compare with it,
nor can it be valued in pure gold.
20 "Whence then comes wisdom?
And where is the place of understanding?
21 It is hid from the eyes of all living,
and concealed from the birds of the air.
22 Abaddon and Death say,
'We have heard a rumor of it with our ears.'
23 "God understands the way to it,
and he knows its place.
24 For he looks to the ends of the earth,
and sees everything under the heavens.
25 When he gave to the wind its weight,
and meted out the waters by measure;
26 when he made a decree for the rain,
and a way for the lightning of the thunder;
27 then he saw it and declared it;
he established it, and searched it out.

28 And he said to man,
'Behold, the fear of the Lord, that is wisdom;
and to depart from evil is understanding.' "

29 And Job again took up his discourse, and said:
2 "Oh, that I were as in the months of old,
as in the days when God watched over me;
3 when his lamp shone upon my head,
and by his light I walked through darkness;
4 as I was in my autumn days,
when the friendship of God was upon my tent;
5 when the Almighty was yet with me,
when my children were about me;
6 when my steps were washed with milk,
and the rock poured out for me streams of oil!
7 When I went out to the gate of the city,
when I prepared my seat in the square,
8 the young men saw me and withdrew,
and the aged rose and stood;
9 the princes refrained from talking,
and laid their hand on their mouth;
10 the voice of the nobles was hushed,
and their tongue cleaved to the roof of their mouth.
11 When the ear heard, it called me blessed,
and when the eye saw, it approved;
12 because I delivered the poor who cried,
and the fatherless who had none to help him.
13 The blessing of him who was about to perish came upon me,
and I caused the widow's heart to sing for joy.
14 I put on righteousness, and it clothed me;
my justice was like a robe and a turban.
15 I was eyes to the blind,
and feet to the lame.
16 I was a father to the poor,
and I searched out the cause of him whom I did not know.
17 I broke the fangs of the unrighteous,
and made him drop his prey from his teeth.
18 Then I thought, 'I shall die in my nest,
and I shall multiply my days as the sand,
19 my roots spread out to the waters,
with the dew all night on my branches,
20 my glory fresh with me,
and my bow ever new in my hand.'
21 "Men listened to me, and waited,
and kept silence for my counsel.
22 After I spoke they did not speak again,
and my word dropped upon them.
23 They waited for me as for the rain;
and they opened their mouths as for the spring rain.
24 I smiled on them when they had no confidence;
and the light of my countenance they did not cast down.
25 I chose their way, and sat as chief,
and I dwelt like a king among his troops,
like one who comforts mourners.

30 "But now they make sport of me,
men who are younger than I,
whose fathers I would have disdained
to set with the dogs of my flock.
2 What could I gain from the strength of their hands,
men whose vigor is gone?
3 Through want and hard hunger
they gnaw the dry and desolate ground;
4 they pick mallow and the leaves of bushes,
and to warm themselves the roots of the broom.
5 They are driven out from among men;
they shout after them as after a thief.
6 In the gullies of the torrents they must dwell,
in holes of the earth and of the rocks.
7 Among the bushes they bray;
under the nettles they huddle together.
8 A senseless, a disreputable brood,
they have been whipped out of the land.
9 "And now I have become their song,
I am a byword to them.
10 They abhor me, they keep aloof from me;
they do not hesitate to spit at the sight of me.
11 Because God has loosed my cord and humbled me,
they have cast off restraint in my presence.
12 On my right hand the rabble rise,
they drive me forth,
they cast up against me their ways of destruction.
13 They break up my path,
they promote my calamity;
no one restrains them.
14 As through a wide breach they come;
amid the crash they roll on.
15 Terrors are turned upon me;
my honor is pursued as by the wind,
and my prosperity has passed away like a cloud.
16 "And now my soul is poured out within me;
days of affliction have taken hold of me.
17 The night racks my bones,
and the pain that gnaws me takes no rest.
18 With violence it seizes my garment;
it binds me about like the collar of my tunic.
19 God has cast me into the mire,
and I have become like dust and ashes.
20 I cry to thee and thou dost not answer me;
I stand, and thou dost not heed me.
21 Thou hast turned cruel to me;
with the might of thy hand thou dost persecute me.
22 Thou liftest me up on the wind, thou makest me ride on it,
and thou tossest me about in the roar of the storm.
23 Yea, I know that thou wilt bring me to death,
and to the house appointed for all living.
24 "Yet does not one in a heap of ruins stretch out his hand,
and in his disaster cry for help?"
25 Did not I weep for him whose day was hard?
Was not my soul grieved for the poor?
26 But when I looked for good, evil came;
and when I waited for light, darkness came.
27 My heart is in turmoil, and is never still;
days of affliction come to meet me.
28 I go about blackened, but not by the sun;
I stand up in the assembly, and cry for help.
29 I am a brother of jackals,
and a companion of ostriches.
30 My skin turns black and falls from me,
and my bones burn with heat.
31 My lyre is turned to mourning,
and my pipe to the voice of those who weep.

31 "I have made a covenant with my eyes;
how then could I look upon a virgin?
2 What would be my portion from God above,
and my heritage from the Almighty on high?

3 Does not calamity befall the unrighteous,
and disaster the workers of iniquity?
4 Does not he see my ways,
and number all my steps?
5 "If I have walked with falsehood,
and my foot has hastened to deceit;
6 (Let me be weighed in a just balance,
and let God know my integrity!)
7 if my step has turned aside from the way,
and my heart has gone after my eyes,
and if any spot has cleaved to my hands;
8 then let me sow, and another eat;
and let what grows for me be rooted out.
9 "If my heart has been enticed to a woman,
and I have lain in wait at my neighbor's door;
10 then let my wife grind for another,
and let others bow down upon her.
11 For that would be a heinous crime;
that would be an iniquity to be punished by the judges;
12 for that would be a fire which consumes unto Abaddon,
and it would burn to the root all my increase.
13 "If I have rejected the cause of my manservant or my maidservant,
when they brought a complaint against me;
14 what then shall I do when God rises up?
When he makes inquiry, what shall I answer him?
15 Did not he who made me in the womb make him?
And did not one fashion us in the womb?
16 "If I have withheld anything that the poor desired,
or have caused the eyes of the widow to fail,
17 or have eaten my morsel alone,
and the fatherless has not eaten of it
18 (for from his youth I reared him as a father,
and from his mother's womb I guided him);
19 if I have seen any one perish for lack of clothing,
or a poor man without covering;
20 if his loins have not blessed me,
and if he was not warmed with the fleece of my sheep;
21 if I have raised my hand against the fatherless,
because I saw help in the gate;
22 then let my shoulder blade fall from my shoulder,
and let my arm be broken from its socket.
23 For I was in terror of calamity from God,
and I could not have faced his majesty.
24 "If I have made gold my trust,
or called fine gold my confidence;
25 if I have rejoiced because my wealth was great,
or because my hand had gotten much;
26 if I have looked at the sun when it shone,
or the moon moving in splendor,
27 and my heart has been secretly enticed,
and my mouth has kissed my hand;
28 this also would be an iniquity to be punished by the judges,
for I should have been false to God above.
29 "If I have rejoiced at the ruin of him that hated me,
or exulted when evil overtook him
30 (I have not let my mouth sin
by asking for his life with a curse);
31 if the men of my tent have not said,
'Who is there that has not been filled with his meat?'
32 (the sojourner has not lodged in the street;
I have opened my doors to the wayfarer);
33 if I have concealed my transgressions from men,
by hiding my iniquity in my bosom,
34 because I stood in great fear of the multitude,
and the contempt of families terrified me,
so that I kept silence, and did not go out of doors—
35 Oh, that I had one to hear me!
(Here is my signature! let the Almighty answer me!)
Oh, that I had the indictment written by my adversary!
36 Surely I would carry it on my shoulder;
I would bind it on me as a crown;
37 I would give him an account of all my steps;
like a prince I would approach him.
38 "If my land has cried out against me,
and its furrows have wept together;
39 if I have eaten its yield without payment,
and caused the death of its owners;
40 let thorns grow instead of wheat, and
foul weeds instead of barley."

The words of Job are ended.

32 So these three men ceased to answer Job, because he
was righteous in his own eyes. 2 Then Elihu the son
of Barachel the Buzite, of the family of Ram, became
angry. He was angry at Job because he justified himself
rather than God; 3 he was angry also at Job's three friends
because they had found no answer, although they had declared Job to be in the wrong. 4 Now Elihu had waited to
speak to Job because they were older than he. 5 And when
Elihu saw that there was no answer in the mouth of these
three men, he became angry.

6 And Elihu the son of Barachel the Buzite answered:
"I am young in years,
and you are aged;
therefore I was timid and afraid
to declare my opinion to you.
7 I said, 'Let days speak,
and many years teach wisdom.'
8 But it is the spirit in a man,
the breath of the Almighty,
that makes him understand.
9 It is not the old that are wise,
nor the aged that understand what is right.
10 Therefore I say, 'Listen to me;
let me also declare my opinion.'
11 "Behold, I waited for your words,
I listened for your wise sayings,
while you searched out what to say.
12 I gave you my attention,
and, behold, there was none that confuted Job,
or that answered his words, among you.
13 Beware lest you say, 'We have found wisdom;
God may vanquish him, not man.'
14 He has not directed his words against me,
and I will not answer him with your speeches.
15 "They are discomfited, they answer no more;
they have not a word to say.
16 And shall I wait, because they do not speak,
because they stand there, and answer no more?
17 I also will give my answer;
I also will declare my opinion.
18 For I am full of words,
the spirit within me constrains me.
19 Behold, my heart is like wine that has no vent;
like new wineskins, it is ready to burst.

20 I must speak, that I may find relief;
I must open my lips and answer.
21 I will not show partiality to any person
or use flattery toward any man.
22 For I do not know how to flatter,
else would my Maker soon put an end to me.

33 "But now, hear my speech, O Job,
and listen to all my words.
2 Behold, I open my mouth;
the tongue in my mouth speaks.
3 My words declare the uprightness of my heart,
and what my lips know they speak sincerely.
4 The spirit of God has made me,
and the breath of the Almighty gives me life.
5 Answer me, if you can;
set your words in order before me; take your stand.
6 Behold, I am toward God as you are;
I too was formed from a piece of clay.
7 Behold, no fear of me need terrify you;
my pressure will not be heavy upon you.
8 "Surely, you have spoken in my hearing,
and I have heard the sound of your words.
9 You say, 'I am clean, without transgression;
I am pure, and there is no iniquity in me.
10 Behold, he finds occasions against me,
he counts me as his enemy;
11 he puts my feet in the stocks,
and watches all my paths.'
12 "Behold, in this you are not right. I will answer you.
God is greater than man.
13 Why do you contend against him,
saying, 'He will answer none of my words'?
14 For God speaks in one way,
and in two, though man does not perceive it.
15 In a dream, in a vision of the night,
when deep sleep falls upon men,
while they slumber on their beds,
16 then he opens the ears of men,
and terrifies them with warnings,
17 that he may turn man aside from his deed,
and cut off pride from man;
18 he keeps back his soul from the Pit,
his life from perishing by the sword.
19 "Man is also chastened with pain upon his bed,
and with continual strife in his bones;
20 so that his life loathes bread,
and his appetite dainty food.
21 His flesh is so wasted away that it cannot be seen;
and his bones which were not seen stick out.
22 His soul draws near the Pit,
and his life to those who bring death.
23 If there be for him an angel,
a mediator, one of the thousand,
to declare to man what is right for him;
24 and he is gracious to him, and says,
'Deliver him from going down into the Pit,
I have found a ransom;
25 let his flesh become fresh with youth;
let him return to the days of his youthful vigor.'
26 Then man prays to God, and he accepts him,
he comes into his presence with joy.
27 He recounts to men his salvation,
and he sings before men, and says:
'I sinned, and perverted what was right,
and it was not requited to me.
28 He has redeemed my soul from going down into the Pit,
and my life shall see the light.'
29 "Behold, God does all these things,
twice, three times, with a man,
30 to bring back his soul from the Pit,
that he may see the light of life.
31 Give heed, O Job, listen to me;
be silent, and I will speak.
32 If you have anything to say, answer me
speak, for I desire to justify you.
33 If not, listen to me;
be silent, and I will teach you wisdom."

34 Then Elihu said:
2 "Hear my words, you wise men,
and give ear to me, you who know;
3 for the ear tests words
as the palate tastes food.
4 Let us choose what is right;
let us determine among ourselves what is good.
5 For Job has said, 'I am innocent,
and God has taken away my right;
6 in spite of my right I am counted a liar;
my wound is incurable, though I am without transgression.'
7 What man is like Job,
who drinks up scoffing like water,
8 who goes in company with evildoers
and walks with wicked men?
9 For he has said, 'It profits a man nothing
that he should take delight in God.'
10 "Therefore, hear me, you men of understanding,
far be it from God that he should do wickedness,
and from the Almighty that he should do wrong.
11 For according to the work of a man he will requite him,
and according to his ways he will make it befall him.
12 Of a truth, God will not do wickedly,
and the Almighty will not pervert justice.
13 Who gave him charge over the earth
and who laid on him the whole world?
14 If he should take back his spirit to himself,
and gather to himself his breath,
15 all flesh would perish together,
and man would return to dust.
16 "If you have understanding, hear this;
listen to what I say.
17 Shall one who hates justice govern?
Will you condemn him who is righteous and mighty,
18 who says to a king, 'Worthless one,'
and to nobles, 'Wicked man';
19 who shows no partiality to princes,
nor regards the rich more than the poor,
for they are all the work of his hands?
20 In a moment they die;
at midnight the people are shaken and pass away,
and the mighty are taken away by no human hand.
21 "For his eyes are upon the ways of a man,
and he sees all his steps.
22 There is no gloom or deep darkness
where evildoers may hide themselves.
23 For he has not appointed a time for any man
to go before God in judgment.
24 He shatters the mighty without investigation,
and sets others in their place.
25 Thus, knowing their works,
he overturns them in the night, and they are crushed.

26 He strikes them for their wickedness
in the sight of men,
27 because they turned aside from following him,
and had no regard for any of his ways,
28 so that they caused the cry of the poor to come to him,
and he heard the cry of the afflicted—
29 When he is quiet, who can condemn?
When he hides his face, who can behold him?
whether it be a nation or a man?—
30 that a godless man should not reign,
that he should not ensnare the people.
31 "For has any one said to God,
'I have borne chastisement; I will not offend any more;
32 teach me what I do not see:
if I have done iniquity, I will do it no more'?
33 Will he then make requital to suit you,
because you reject it?
For you must choose, and not I;
therefore declare what you know.
34 Men of understanding will say to me,
and the wise man who hears me will say:
35 'Job speaks without knowledge,
his words are without insight.'
36 Would that Job were tried to the end,
because he answers like wicked men.
37 For he adds rebellion to his sin;
he claps his hands among us,
and multiplies his words against God."

35 And Elihu said:
2 "Do you think this to be just?
Do you say, 'It is my right before God,'
3 that you ask, 'What advantage have I?
How am I better off than if I had sinned?'
4 I will answer you
and your friends with you.
5 Look at the heavens, and see;
and behold the clouds, which are higher than you.
6 If you have sinned, what do you accomplish against him?
And if your transgressions are multiplied, what do you do to him?
7 If you are righteous, what do you give to him;
or what does he receive from your hand?
8 Your wickedness concerns a man like yourself,
and your righteousness a son of man.
9 "Because of the multitude of oppressions people cry out;
they call for help because of the arm of the mighty.
10 But none says, 'Where is God my Maker,
who gives songs in the night,
11 who teaches us more than the beasts of the earth,
and makes us wiser than the birds of the air?'
12 There they cry out, but he does not answer,
because of the pride of evil men.
13 Surely God does not hear an empty cry,
nor does the Almighty regard it.
14 How much less when you say that you do not see him,
that the case is before him, and you are waiting for him!
15 And now, because his anger does not punish,
and he does not greatly heed transgression,
16 Job opens his mouth in empty talk,
he multiplies words without knowledge."

36 And Elihu continued, and said:
2 "Bear with me a little, and I will show you,
for I have yet something to say on God's behalf.
3 I will fetch my knowledge from afar,
and ascribe righteousness to my Maker.
4 For truly my words are not false;
one who is perfect in knowledge is with you.
5 "Behold, God is mighty, and does not despise any;
he is mighty in strength of understanding.
6 He does not keep the wicked alive,
but gives the afflicted their right.
7 He does not withdraw his eyes from the righteous.
but with kings upon the throne
he sets them for ever, and they are exalted.
8 And if they are bound in fetters
and caught in the cords of affliction,
9 then he declares to them their work
and their transgressions, that they are behaving arrogantly.
10 He opens their ears to instruction,
and commands that they return from iniquity.
11 If they hearken and serve him,
they complete their days in prosperity,
and their years in pleasantness.
12 But if they do not hearken, they perish by the sword,
and die without knowledge.
13 "The godless in heart cherish anger;
they do not cry for help when he binds them.
14 They die in youth,
and their life ends in shame.
15 He delivers the afflicted by their affliction,
and opens their ear by adversity.
16 He also allured you out of distress
into a broad place where there was no cramping,
and what was set on your table was full of fatness.
17 "But you are full of the judgment on the wicked;
judgment and justice seize you.
18 Beware lest wrath entice you into scoffing;
and let not the greatness of the ransom turn you aside.
19 Will your cry avail to keep you from distress,
or all the force of your strength?
20 Do not long for the night,
when peoples are cut off in their place.
21 Take heed, do not turn to iniquity,
for this you have chosen rather than affliction.
22 Behold, God is exalted in his power;
who is a teacher like him?
23 Who has prescribed for him his way,
or who can say, 'Thou hast done wrong'?
24 "Remember to extol his work,
of which men have sung.
25 All men have looked on it;
man beholds it from afar.
26 Behold, God is great, and we know him not;
the number of his years is unsearchable.
27 For he draws up the drops of water,
he distils his mist in rain
28 which the skies pour down,
and drop upon man abundantly.
29 Can any one understand the spreading of the clouds,
the thunderings of his pavilion?
30 Behold, he scatters his lightning about him,
and covers the roots of the sea.
31 For by these he judges peoples;
he gives food in abundance.

32 He covers his hands with the lightning,
and commands it to strike the mark.
33 Its crashing declares concerning him,
who is jealous with anger against iniquity.

37 "At this also my heart trembles,
and leaps out of its place.
2 Hearken to the thunder of his voice
and the rumbling that comes from his mouth.
3 Under the whole heaven he lets it go,
and his lightning to the corners of the earth.
4 After it his voice roars;
he thunders with his majestic voice
and he does not restrain the lightnings when his voice is heard.
5 God thunders wondrously with his voice;
he does great things which we cannot comprehend.
6 For to the snow he says, 'Fall on the earth';
and to the shower and the rain, 'Be strong.'
7 He seals up the hand of every man,
that all men may know his work.
8 Then the beasts go into their lairs,
and remain in their dens.
9 From its chamber comes the whirlwind,
and cold from the scattering winds.
10 By the breath of God ice is given,
and the broad waters are frozen fast.
11 He loads the thick cloud with moisture;
the clouds scatter his lightning.
12 They turn round and round by his guidance,
to accomplish all that he commands them
on the face of the habitable world.
13 Whether for correction, or for his land,
or for love, he causes it to happen.
14 "Hear this, O Job;
stop and consider the wondrous works of God.
15 Do you know how God lays his command upon them,
and causes the lightning of his cloud to shine;
16 Do you know the balancings of the clouds,
the wondrous works of him who is perfect in knowledge,
17 you whose garments are hot
when the earth is still because of the south wind?
18 Can you, like him, spread out the skies,
hard as a molten mirror?
19 Teach us what we shall say to him;
we cannot draw up our case because of darkness.
20 Shall it be told him that I would speak?
Did a man ever wish that he would be swallowed up?
21 "And now men cannot look on the light
when it is bright in the skies,
when the wind has passed and cleared them.
22 Out of the north comes golden splendor;
God is clothed with terrible majesty.
23 The Almighty—we cannot find him;
he is great in power and justice,
and abundant righteousness he will not violate.
24 Therefore men fear him;
he does not regard any who are wise in their own conceit."

38 Then the LORD answered Job out of the whirlwind:
2 "Who is this that darkens counsel by
words without knowledge?
3 Gird up your loins like a man,
I will question you, and you shall declare to me.
4 "Where were you when I laid the foundation of the earth?
Tell me, if you have understanding.
5 Who determined its measurements—surely you know!
Or who stretched the line upon it?
6 On what were its bases sunk,
or who laid its cornerstone,
7 when the morning stars sang together,
and all the sons of God shouted for joy?
8 "Or who shut in the sea with doors,
when it burst forth from the womb;
9 when I made clouds its garment,
and thick darkness its swaddling band,
10 and prescribed bounds for it,
and set bars and doors,
11 and said, 'Thus far shall you come, and no farther,
and here shall your proud waves be stayed'?
12 "Have you commanded the morning since your days began,
and caused the dawn to know its place,
13 that it might take hold of the skirts of the earth,
and the wicked be shaken out of it?
14 It is changed like clay under the seal,
and it is dyed like a garment.
15 From the wicked their light is withheld,
and their uplifted arm is broken.
16 "Have you entered into the springs of the sea,
or walked in the recesses of the deep?
17 Have the gates of death been revealed to you,
or have you seen the gates of deep darkness?
18 Have you comprehended the expanse of the earth?
Declare, if you know all this.
19 "Where is the way to the dwelling of light,
and where is the place of darkness,
20 that you may take it to its territory
and that you may discern the paths to its home?
21 You know, for you were born then,
and the number of your days is great!
22 "Have you entered the storehouses of the snow,
or have you seen the storehouses of the hail,
23 which I have reserved for the time of trouble,
for the day of battle and war?
24 What is the way to the place where the light is distributed,
or where the east wind is scattered upon the earth?
25 "Who has cleft a channel for the torrents of rain,
and a way for the thunderbolt,
26 to bring rain on a land where no man is,
on the desert in which there is no man;
27 to satisfy the waste and desolate land,
and to make the ground put forth grass?
28 "Has the rain a father,
or who has begotten the drops of dew?
29 From whose womb did the ice come forth,
and who has given birth to the hoarfrost of heaven?
30 The waters become hard like stone,
and the face of the deep is frozen.
31 "Can you bind the chains of the Pleiades,
or loose the cords of Orion?
32 Can you lead forth the Mazzaroth in their season,
or can you guide the Bear with its children?
33 Do you know the ordinances of the heavens?
Can you establish their rule on the earth?
34 "Can you lift up your voice to the clouds,
that a flood of waters may cover you?

35 Can you send forth lightnings, that they may go
and say, to you, 'Here we are'?
36 Who has put wisdom in the clouds,
or given understanding to the mists?
37 Who can number the clouds by wisdom?
Or who can tilt the waterskins of the heavens,
38 when the dust runs into a mass
and the clods cleave fast together?
39 "Can you hunt the prey for the lion,
or satisfy the appetite of the young lions,
40 when they crouch in their dens,
or lie in wait in their covert?
41 Who provides for the raven its prey,
when its young ones cry to God,
and wander about for lack of food?

39 "Do you know when the mountain goats bring forth?
Do you observe the calving of the hinds?
2 Can you number the months that they fulfil,
and do you know the time when they bring forth.
3 when they crouch, bring forth their offspring,
and are delivered of their young?
4 Their young ones become strong, they grow up in the open;
they go forth, and do not return to them.
5 "Who has let the wild ass go free?
Who has loosed the bonds of the swift ass,
6 to whom I have given the steppe for his home,
and the salt land for his dwelling place?
7 He scorns the tumult of the city;
he hears not the shouts of the driver.
8 He ranges the mountains as his pasture,
and he searches after every green thing.
9 "Is the wild ox willing to serve you?
Will he spend the night at your crib?
10 Can you bind him in the furrow with ropes,
or will he harrow the valleys after you?
11 Will you depend on him because his strength is great,
and will you leave to him your labor?
12 Do you have faith in him that he will return,
and bring your grain to your threshing floor?
13 "The wings of the ostrich wave proudly;
but are they the pinions and plumage of love?
14 For she leaves her eggs to the earth,
and lets them be warmed on the ground,
15 forgetting that a foot may crush them,
and that the wild beast may trample them.
16 She deals cruelly with her young, as if they were not hers;
though her labor be in vain, yet she has no fear;
17 because God has made her forget wisdom,
and given her no share in understanding.
18 When she rouses herself to flee,
she laughs at the horse and his rider.
19 "Do you give the horse his might?
Do you clothe his neck with strength?
20 Do you make him leap like the locust?
His majestic snorting is terrible.
21 He paws in the valley, and exults in his strength;
he goes out to meet the weapons.
22 He laughs at fear, and is not dismayed;
he does not turn back from the sword.
23 Upon him rattle the quiver,
the flashing spear and the javelin.
24 With fierceness and rage he swallows the ground;
he cannot stand still at the sound of the trumpet.
25 When the trumpet sounds, he says 'Aha!'
He smells the battle from afar,
the thunder of the captains, and the shouting.
26 "Is it by your wisdom that the hawk soars,
and spreads his wings toward the south?
27 Is it at your command that the eagle mounts up
and makes his nest on high?
28 On the rock he dwells and makes his home
in the fastness of the rocky crag.
29 Thence he spies out the prey;
his eyes behold it afar off.
30 His young ones suck up blood;
and where the slain are, there is he."

40 And the LORD said to Job:
2 "Shall a faultfinder contend with the Almighty?
He who argues with God, let him answer it."
3 Then Job answered the LORD:
4 "Behold, I am of small account; what shall I answer thee?
I lay my hand on my mouth.
5 I have spoken once, and I will not answer;
twice, but I will proceed no further."
6 Then the LORD answered Job out of the whirlwind:
7 "Gird up your loins like a man;
I will question you, and you declare to me.
8 Will you even put me in the wrong?
Will you condemn me that you may be justified?
9 Have you an arm like God,
and can you thunder with a voice like his?
10 "Deck yourself with majesty and dignity;
clothe yourself with glory and splendor.
11 Pour forth the overflowings of your anger,
and look on every one that is proud, and abase him.
12 Look on every one that is proud, and bring him low;
and tread down the wicked where they stand.
13 Hide them all in the dust together;
bind their faces in the world below.
14 Then will I also acknowledge to you,
that your own right hand can give you victory.
15 "Behold, Behemoth,[7]
which I made as I made you;
he eats grass like an ox.
16 Behold, his strength in his loins,
and his power in the muscles of his belly.
17 He makes his tail stiff like a cedar;
the sinews of his thighs are knit together.
18 His bones are tubes of bronze,
his limbs like bars of iron.
19 "He is the first of the works of God;
let him who made him bring near his sword!
20 For the mountains yield food for him
where all the wild beasts play.
21 Under the lotus plants he lies,
in the covert of the reeds and in the marsh.
22 For his shade the lotus trees cover him;
the willows of the brook surround him.
23 Behold, if the river is turbulent he is not frightened;
he is confident though Jordan rushes against his mouth.
24 Can one take him with hooks,
or pierce his nose with a snare?

7. Behemoth is the hippopotamus.

41 "Can you draw out Leviathan[8] with a fishhook,
or press down his tongue with a cord?
2 Can you put a rope in his nose,
or pierce his jaw with a hook?
3 Will he make many supplications to you?
Will he speak to you soft words?
4 Will he make a covenant with you
to take him for your servant for ever?
5 Will you play with him as with a bird,
or will you put him on leash for your maidens?
6 Will traders bargain over him?
Will they divide him up among the merchants?
7 Can you fill his skin with harpoons,
or his head with fishing spears?
8 Lay hands on him;
think of the battle; you will not do it again!
9 Behold, the hope of a man is disappointed;
he is laid low even at the sight of him.
10 No one is so fierce that he dares to stir him up.
Who then is he that can stand before me?
11 Who has given to me, that I should repay him?
Whatever is under the whole heaven is mine.
12 "I will not keep silence concerning his limbs,
or his mighty strength, or his goodly frame.
13 Who can strip off his outer garment?
Who can penetrate his double coat of mail?
14 Who can open the doors of his face?
Round about his teeth is terror.
15 His back is made of rows of shields,
shut up closely as with a seal.
16 One is so near to another
that no air can come between them.
17 They are joined one to another;
they clasp each other and cannot be separated.
18 His sneezings flash forth light,
and his eyes are like the eyelids of the dawn.
19 Out of his mouth go flaming torches;
sparks of fire leap forth.
20 Out of his nostrils comes forth smoke,
as from a boiling pot and burning rushes.
21 His breath kindles coals,
and a flame comes forth from his mouth.
22 In his neck abides strength,
and terror dances before him.
23 The folds of his flesh cleave together,
firmly cast upon him and immovable.
24 His heart is hard as a stone,
hard as the nether millstone.
25 When he raises himself up the mighty are afraid;
at the crashing they are beside themselves.
26 Though the sword reaches him, it does not avail;
nor the spear, the dart, or the javelin.
27 He counts iron as straw,
and bronze as rotten wood.
28 The arrow cannot make him flee;
for him slingstones are turned to stubble.
29 Clubs are counted as stubble;
he laughs at the rattle of javelins.
30 His underparts are like sharp potsherds;
he spreads himself like a threshing sledge on the mire.
31 He makes the deep boil like a pot;
he makes the sea like a pot of ointment.
32 Behind him he leaves a shining wake;
one would think the deep to be hoary.
33 Upon earth there is not his like,
a creature without fear.
34 He beholds everything that is high;
he is king over all the sons of pride."

42 Then Job answered the LORD:
2 "I know that thou canst do all things,
and that no purpose of thine can be thwarted.
3 'Who is this that hides counsel without knowledge?'
Therefore I have uttered what I did not understand,
things too wonderful for me, which I did not know.
4 'Hear, and I will speak;
I will question you, and you declare to me.'
5 I had heard of thee by the hearing of the ear,
but now my eye sees thee;
6 therefore I despise myself,
and repent in dust and ashes."

7 After the LORD had spoken these words to Job,
the LORD said to Eliphaz the Temanite: "My wrath is
kindled against you and against your two friends; for you
have not spoken of me what is right, as my servant Job has.
8 Now therefore take seven bulls and seven rams, and go to
my servant Job, and offer up for yourselves a burnt offering; and my servant Job shall pray for you, for I will
accept his prayer not to deal with you according to your
folly; for you have not spoken of me what is right, as my
servant Job has." 9 So Eliphaz the Temanite and Bildad the
Shuhite and Zophar the Naamathite went and did what the
LORD had told them; and the LORD accepted Job's
prayer.

10 And the LORD restored the fortunes of Job, when
he had prayed for his friends; and the LORD gave Job twice
as much as he had before. 11 Then came to him all his
brothers and sisters and all who had known him before, and
ate bread with him in his house; and they showed him
sympathy and comforted him for all the evil that the
LORD had brought upon him; and each of them gave him a
piece of money and a ring of gold. 12 And the LORD
blessed the latter days of Job more than his beginning; and
he had fourteen thousand sheep, six thousand camels, a
thousand yoke of oxen, and a thousand she-asses. 13 He
had also seven sons and three daughters. 14 And he called
the name of the first Jemimah; and the name of the second
Keziah; and the name of the third Keren-hap puch. 15 And
in all the land there were no women so fair as Job's daughters; and their father gave them inheritance among their
brothers. 16 And after this Job lived a hundred and forty
years, and saw his sons, and his sons' sons, four generations.
17 And Job died, an old man, and full of days.

Some Topics for Discussion

1. The reader might question the role of Satan at the first of the book. As one of the children of God, what force does he represent? A force for evil, almost as powerful as God himself? The scene with Satan is almost duplicated in the "Prologue in Heaven" of Goethe's *Faust*.
2. One of the central arguments of Job's comforters is that the wicked are always destroyed, while the good prosper. In Chapter 21 Job answers this argument. What is the basis for the argument of the comforters? What is the basis for Job's final answer?

8. Leviathan in this context is the crocodile.

3. In all the discussion up to Elihu's outburst the four men are searching for something not understood in the governing of the world. Sometimes this takes the form of sinfulness, which Job does not recognize, sometimes a question about the ways of God in determining the course of the universe. Using this search for the "something not understood" as a key question, follow all of the speeches.
4. How does Elihu's rebuke to the old men foreshadow the revelation given from God in the voice out of the whirlwind? Question very carefully God's answer to the problem which is faced in the book. What is he really saying?
5. Do you find that the final rewarding of Job with the two-fold return of everything that he has lost a satisfactory conclusion to the book?
6. This Hebrew book and the play *Oedipus the King* have much in common in that both represent the downfall of a good man through the intervention of God or gods. Do you see any difference in the spirit of the inquiry between the Hebrew and the Greek exploration of the problem?

The Sermon on the Mount

(Matthew 5-7)

Seeing the crowds, he went up on the mountain, and when he sat down his disciples came to him. And he opened his mouth and taught them, saying:

"Blessed are the poor in spirit, for theirs is the kingdom of heaven.

"Blessed are those who mourn, for they shall be comforted.

"Blessed are the meek, for they shall inherit the earth.

"Blessed are those who hunger and thirst for righteousness, for they shall be satisfied.

"Blessed are the merciful, for they shall obtain mercy.

"Blessed are the pure in heart, for they shall see God.

"Blessed are the peacemakers, for they shall be called sons of God.

"Blessed are those who are persecuted for righteousness' sake, for theirs is the kingdom of heaven.

"Blessed are you when men revile you and persecute you and utter all kinds of evil against you falsely on my account. Rejoice and be glad, for your reward is great in heaven, for so men persecuted the prophets who were before you.

"You are the salt of the earth; but if salt has lost its taste, how can its saltness be restored? It is no longer good for anything except to be thrown out and trodden under foot by men.

"You are the light of the world. A city set on a hill cannot be hid. Nor do men light a lamp and put it under a bushel, but on a stand, and it gives light to all in the house. Let your light so shine before men, that they may see your good works and give glory to your Father who is in heaven.

"Think not that I have come to abolish the law and the prophets; I have come not to abolish them but to fulfill them. For truly, I say to you, till heaven and earth pass away, not an iota, not a dot, will pass from the law until all is accomplished. Whoever then relaxes one of the least of these commandments and teaches men so, shall be called least in the kingdom of heaven; but he who does them and teaches them shall be called great in the kingdom of heaven. For I tell you, unless your righteousness exceeds that of the scribes and Pharisees, you will never enter the kingdom of heaven.

"You have heard that it was said to the men of old, 'You shall not kill; and whoever kills shall be liable to judgment.' But I say to you that every one who is angry with his brother shall be liable to judgment; whoever insults his brother shall be liable to the council, and whoever says, 'You fool!' shall be liable to the hell of fire. So if you are offering your gift at the altar, and there remember that your brother has something against you, leave your gift there before the altar and go; first be reconciled to your brother, and then come and offer your gift. Make friends quickly with your accuser, while you are going with him to court, lest your accuser hand you over to the judge, and the judge to the guard, and you be put in prison; truly, I say to you, you will never get out till you have paid the last penny.

"You have heard that it was said, 'You shall not commit adultery.' But I say to you that every one who looks at a woman lustfully has already committed adultery with her in his heart. If your right eye causes you to sin, pluck it out and throw it away; it is better that you lose one of your members than that your whole body be thrown into hell. And if your right hand causes you to sin, cut it off and throw it away; it is better that you lose one of your members than that your whole body go into hell.

"It was also said, 'Whoever divorces his wife, let him give her a certificate of divorce.' But I say to you that every one who divorces his wife, except on the ground of unchastity, makes her an adulteress; and whoever marries a divorced woman commits adultery.

"Again you have heard that it was said to the men of old, 'You shall not swear falsely, but shall perform to the Lord what you have sworn.' But I say to you, do not swear at all, either by heaven, for it is the throne of God, or by the earth, for it is his footstool, or by Jerusalem, for it is the city of the great King. And do not swear by your head, for you cannot make one hair white or black. Let what you say be simply 'Yes' or 'No'; anything more than this comes from evil.

"You have heard that it was said, 'An eye for an eye and a tooth for a tooth.' But I say to you, Do not resist one who is evil. But if any one strikes you on the right cheek, turn to him the other also; and if any one would sue you and take your coat, let him have your cloak as well; and if any one forces you to go one mile, go with him two miles. Give to him who begs from you, and do not refuse him who would borrow from you.

"You have heard that it was said, 'You shall love your neighbor and hate your enemy.' But I say to you, Love your enemies and pray for those who persecute you, so that you may be sons of your Father who is in heaven; for he makes his sun rise on the evil and on the good, and sends rain on the just and on the unjust. For if you love those who love you, what reward have you? Do not even the tax collectors do the same? And if you salute only your brethren, what more are you doing than others? Do not even the Gentiles do the same? You, therefore, must be perfect, as your heavenly Father is perfect.

"Beware of practicing your piety before men in order to be seen by them; for then you will have no reward from your Father who is in heaven.

"Thus, when you give alms, sound no trumpet before you, as the hypocrites do in the synagogues and in the streets, that they may be praised by men. Truly, I say to you, they have their reward. But when you give alms, do not let your left hand know what you right hand is doing, so that your alms may be in secret; and your Father who sees in secret will reward you.

"And when you pray, you must not be like the hypocrites; for they love to stand and pray in the synagogues and at the street corners, that they may be seen by men. Truly, I say to you, they have their reward. But when you pray, go into your room and shut the door and pray to your Father who is in secret; and your Father who sees in secret will reward you.

"And in praying do not heap up empty phrases as the Gentiles do; for they think that they will be heard for their many words. Do not be like them, for your Father knows what you need before you ask him. Pray then like this:

'Our Father who art in heaven,
Hallowed be thy name.
Thy kingdom come,
Thy will be done,
    On earth as it is in heaven.
Give us this day our daily bread;
And forgive us our debts,
    As we also have forgiven our debtors;
And lead us not into temptation,
    But deliver us from evil.'

"For if you forgive men their trespasses, your heavenly Father also will forgive you; but if you do not forgive men their trespasses, neither will your Father forgive your trespasses.

"And when you fast, do not look dismal, like the hypocrites, for they disfigure their faces that their fasting may be seen by men. Truly, I say to you, they have their reward. But when you fast, anoint your head and wash your face, that your fasting may not be seen by men but by your Father who is in secret; and your Father who sees in secret will reward you.

"Do not lay up for yourselves treasures on earth, where moth and rust consume and where thieves break in and steal, but lay up for yourselves treasures in heaven, where neither moth nor rust consumes and where thieves do not break in and steal; for where your treasure is, there will your heart be also.

"The eye is the lamp of the body. So, if your eye is sound, your whole body will be full of light; but if your eye is not sound, your whole body will be full of darkness. If then the light in you is darkness, how great is the darkness!

"No one can serve two masters; for either he will hate the one and love the other, or he will be devoted to the one and despise the other. You cannot serve God and mammon.

"Therefore I tell you, do not be anxious about your life, what you shall eat or what you shall drink, nor about your body, what you shall put on. Is not life more than food, and the body more than the clothing? Look at the birds of the air: they neither sow nor reap nor gather into barns, and yet your heavenly Father feeds them. Are you not of more value than they? And which of you by being anxious can add one cubit to his span of life? And why be anxious about clothing? Consider the lilies of the field, how they grow; they neither toil nor spin; yet I tell you, even Solomon in all his glory was not arrayed like one of these. But if God so clothes the grass of the field, which today is alive and tomorrow is thrown into the oven, will he not much more clothe you, O men of little faith? Therefore do not be anxious, saying, 'What shall we eat?' or 'What shall we drink?' or 'What shall we wear?' For the Gentiles seek all these things; and your heavenly Father knows that you need them all. But seek first his kingdom and his righteousness, and all these things shall be yours as well.

"Therefore do not be anxious about tomorrow, for tomorrow will be anxious for itself. Let the day's own trouble be sufficient for the day.

"Judge not, that you be not judged. For with the judgment you pronounce you will be judged, and the measure you give will be the measure you get. Why do you see the speck that is in your brother's eye, but do not notice the log that is in your own eye? Or how can you say to your brother, 'Let me take the speck out of your eye,' when there is the log in your own eye? you hypocrite, first take the log out of your own eye, and then you will see clearly to take the speck out of your brother's eye.

"Do not give dogs what is holy; and do not throw your pearls before swine, lest they trample them underfoot and turn to attack you.

"Ask, and it will be given you; seek, and you will find; knock, and it will be opened to you. For every one who asks receives, and he who seeks finds, and to him who knocks it will be opened. Or what man of you, if his son asks him for a loaf, will give him a stone? Or if he asks for a fish, will give him a serpent? If you then, who are evil, know how to give good gifts to your children, how much more will your Father who is in heaven give good things to those who ask him? So whatever you wish that men would do to you, do so to them; for this is the law and the prophets.

"Enter by the narrow gate; for the gate is wide and the way is easy, that leads to destruction, and those who enter by it are many. For the gate is narrow and the way is hard, that leads to life, and those who find it are few.

"Beware of false prophets, who come to you in sheep's clothing but inwardly are ravenous wolves. You will know them by their fruits. Are grapes gathered from thorns, or figs from thistles? So, every sound tree bears good fruit, but the bad tree bears evil fruit. A sound tree cannot bear evil fruit, nor can a bad tree bear good fruit. Every tree that does not bear good fruit is cut down and thrown into the fire. Thus you will know them by their fruits.

"Not every one who says to me, 'Lord, Lord,' shall enter the kingdom of heaven, but he who does the will of my Father who is in heaven. On that day many will say to me, 'Lord, Lord, did we not prophesy in your name, and cast out demons in your name, and do many mighty works in your name?' And then will I declare to them, 'I never knew you; depart from me, you evil-doers.'

"Every one then who hears these words of mine and does them will be like a wise man who built his house upon the rock; and the rain fell, and the floods came, and the winds blew and beat upon that house, but it did not fall, because it had been founded on the rock. And everyone who hears these words of mine and does not do them will be like a foolish man who built his house upon the sand; and the rain fell, and the floods came, and the winds blew and beat against the house, and it fell; and great was the fall of it."

And when Jesus finished these sayings, the crowds were astonished at his teaching, for he taught them as one who had authority, and not as their scribes.

Five Parables

I

(Matthew 18:23-35)

"Therefore the kingdom of heaven may be compared to a king who wished to settle accounts with his servants. When he began the reckoning, one was brought to him who owed him ten thousand talents; and as he could not pay, his lord ordered him to be sold, with his wife and children and all that he had, and payment to be made. So the servant fell on his knees, imploring him, 'Lord, have patience with me, and I will pay you everything.' And out of pity for him the lord of that servant released him and forgave him the debt. But that same servant, as he went out, came upon one of his fellow servants who owed him a hundred denarii; and seizing him by the throat he said, 'Pay what you owe.' So his fellow servant fell down and besought him, 'Have patience with me, and I will pay you.' He refused and went and put him in prison till he should pay the debt. When his fellow servants saw what had taken place, they were greatly distressed, and they went and reported to their lord all that had taken place. Then his lord summoned him and said to him, 'You wicked servant! I forgave you all that debt because you besought me; and should not you have had mercy on your fellow servant, as I had mercy on you?' And in anger his lord delivered him to the jailers, till he should pay all his debt. So also my heavenly Father will do to every one of you, if you do not forgive your brother from your heart."

II

(Matthew 20:1-16)

"For the kingdom of heaven is like a householder who went out early in the morning to hire laborers for his vineyard. After agreeing with the laborers for a denarius a day, he sent them into his vineyard. And going out about the third hour he saw others standing idle in the market place; and to them he said, 'You go into the vineyard too, and whatever is right I will give you.' So they went. Going out again about the sixth hour and the ninth hour, he did the same. And about the eleventh hour he went out and found others standing; and he said to them, 'Why do you stand here idle all day?' They said to him, 'Because no one has hired us.' He said to them, 'You go into the vineyard too.' And when evening came, the owner of the vineyard said to his steward, 'Call the laborers and pay them their wages, beginning with the last, up to the first.' And when those hired about the eleventh hour came, each of them received a denarius. Now when the first came, they thought they would receive more; but each of them also received a denarius. And on receiving it they grumbled at the householder, saying, "These last worked only one hour, and you have made them equal to us who have borne the burden of the day and the scorching heat.' But he replied to one of them, 'Friend, I am doing you no wrong; did you not agree with me for a denarius? Take what belongs to you, and go; I choose to give to this last as I give to you. Am I not allowed to do what I chose with what belongs to me? Or do you begrudge my generosity?" So the last will be first, and the first last."

III

(Luke 10:30-37)

"A man was going down from Jerusalem to Jericho and he fell among robbers, who stripped him and beat him, and departed, leaving him half-dead. Now by chance a priest was going down that road; and when he saw him he passed by on the other side. So likewise a Levite, when he came to the place and saw him, passed by on the other side. But a Samaritan, as he journeyed, came to where he was; and when he saw him, he had compassion, and went to him and bound up his wounds, pouring on oil and wine; then he set him on his own beast and brought him to an inn, and took care of him. And the next day he took out two denarii and gave them to the innkeeper, saying, 'Take care of him; and whatever more you spend, I will repay you when I come back.' Which of these three, do you think, proved neighbor to the man who fell among the robbers?" He said, "The one who showed mercy on him." And Jesus said to him, "Go and do likewise."

IV

(Luke 15:11-32)

"There was a man who had two sons; and the younger of them said to his father, 'Father, give me the share of property that falls to me.' And he divided his living between them. Not many days later, the younger son gathered all he had and took his journey into a far country, and there he squandered his property in loose living. And when he had spent everything, a great famine arose in that country, and he began to be in want. So he went and joined himself to one of the citizens of that country, who sent him into his fields to feed swine. And he would gladly have fed on the pods that the swine ate; and no one gave him anything. But when he came to himself he said, 'How many of my father's hired servants have bread enough and to spare, but I perish here with hunger! I will arise and go to my father, and I will say to him, "Father, I have sinned against heaven and before you; I am no longer worthy to be called your son; treat me as one of your hired servants." ' And he arose and came to his father. But while he was yet at a distance, his father saw him and had compassion, and ran and embraced him and kissed him. And the son said to him, 'Father, I have sinned against heaven and before you; I am no longer worthy to be called your son.' But the father said to his servants, 'Bring quickly the best robe, and put it on him; and put a ring on his hand, and shoes on his feet; and bring the fatted calf and kill it, and let us eat and make merry; for this my son was dead, and is alive again; he was lost, and is found.' And they began to make merry.

"Now his elder son was in the field; and as he came and drew near to the house, he heard music and dancing. And he called one of the servants and asked what this meant. And he said to him, 'Your brother has come, and your father has killed the fatted calf, because he has received him safe and sound.' But he was angry and refused to go in. His father came out and entreated him, but he answered his father, 'Lo, these many years I have served you, and I never disobeyed your command; yet you never gave me a kid, that I might make merry with my friends. But when this son of yours came, who has devoured your living with harlots, you killed for him the fatted calf!' And he said to him, 'Son, you are always with me, and all that is mine is yours. It was fitting to make merry and be glad, for this your brother was dead, and is alive; he was lost, and is found.' "

V

(Matthew 25:14-30)

"For it [the Kingdom of Heaven] will be as when a man going on a journey called his servants and entrusted to them his property; to one he gave five talents, to another two, to another one, to each according to his ability. Then he went away. He who had received the five talents went at once and traded with them; and he made five talents more. So too, he who had the two talents made two talents more. But he who had received the one talent, went and dug in the ground and hid his master's money. Now after a long time the master of those servants came and settled accounts with them. And he who had received the five talents came forward, bringing five talents more, saying, 'Master, you delivered to me five talents; here I have made five talents more.' His master said to him, 'Well done, good and faithful servant; you have been faithful over a little, I will set you over much; enter into the joy of your master.' And he also who had the two talents came forward, saying, 'Master, you delivered to me two talents; here I have made two talents more.' His master said to him, 'Well done, good and faithful servant; you have been faithful over a little, I will set you over much; enter into the joy of your master.' He also who had received the one talent came forward, saying, 'Master, I knew you to be a hard man, reaping where you did not sow, and gathering where you did not winnow; so I was afraid, and I went and hid your talent in the ground. Here you have what is yours.' But his master answered him, 'You wicked and slothful servant! You knew that I reap where I have not sowed, and gather where I have not winnowed? Then you ought to have invested my money with the bankers, and at my coming I should have received what was my own with interest. So take the talent from him, and give it to him who has the ten talents. For to every one who has will more be given, and he will have abundance; but from him who has not, even what he has will be taken away. And cast the worthless servant into the outer darkness; there men will weep and gnash their teeth.' "

Exercises

The East has always been fond of teaching by parable, the brief narrative that by comparison provides a way of getting at a truth. It is not quite like an algebraic problem, to be solved by substituting terms: "x = y, a = b," and the like. It is rather a way of stimulating the imagination, of getting at the point by *insight.* Jesus was following an ancient, well-established tradition in teaching by parables. These stories must be understood on an exceedingly literal level; they mean what they say; but they do not stop there—the mind goes on to seize upon the inherent likenesses, the points to be compared. Here are some questions over the parables in the text.

1. "The Wicked Servant." What prompted the action of the servant's lord, at the beginning and at the end? What is the specific fault of the servant? What was the point that Jesus was trying to convey?
2. "The Vineyard." Imagine a disciple of Plato, who wrote the whole treatise of *The Republic* in order to consider the question "What is Justice?", commenting upon this story. In two or three sentences, what would his opinion be? Imagine a disciple of Jesus trying to answer, again in two or three sentences. Where is the point of departure between the two?
3. "The Good Samaritan." Why does Jesus make a *Samaritan* the subject of his tale? In trying to modernize it, what word would you pick instead? (On second thought—better *not* answer that question!) What fault or shortcoming among his contemporaries was Jesus pointing out?
4. "The Prodigal Son." It is always tempting to feel a great deal of sympathy for the elder brother in this story. When you do so (or when you side with the workers in the vineyard who had worked all day), what *basis* of judgment are you using. How does this measuring rod of what is just differ from that of Jesus?
5. "The Talents." Which of the other parables is this most like? As a story it is harsh and forbidding; how would you answer the argument that it does not portray a merciful and loving God?

UNIT V

The Age of Faith

Building Medieval Walls

CHAPTER 13

■ The so-called Middle Ages extend for approximately a thousand years from about A.D. 450 to about 1450. Furthermore, they divide themselves sharply at about the year 1000, for reasons which will become apparent. This long period constitutes an amalgamation of various cultures—some features of the Arabic and Moslem, the Eastern civilization which had its source in Byzantium (Constantinople), and principally the crude northern way of life of Germany and the Scandanavian countries—into the old Graeco-Roman institutions. As such, the gestation of the Middle Ages constitutes an almost new start for Western culture, with only a memory of past glories, with written records which lay dormant for centuries, and with the Roman Church as foci of centralizing forces. The rather glorious medieval culture which reached maturity during the twelfth and thirteenth centuries represents a fusion of seemingly contradictory ways of life, and of opposition in ways of feeling and thought. Once again we can witness a testimony to the toughness of the human spirit which lives, survives, changes itself, and finally triumphs over darkness and confusion, expressing itself in magnificent symbols of new growth.

We have already said that Rome "fell" sometime in the fifth century—the arbitrary dates of 410 or 476 do not make much difference. It should be remarked, however, that the average Roman citizen living at the time did not know that Rome had fallen. Life went on much as it had before; life got tougher and tougher, but the government and the Emperor, whether he be Italian or Ostrogoth, were still there. For example, the philosopher, Boethius, who wrote the famous *Consolations of Philosophy* in 524, the year of his death, held the office of Roman consul about fifty years after the final "official" date for the fall of Rome.

As a matter of fact, the power of Rome dwindled until it was virtually nonexistent. For centuries the Roman legions had been replaced by barbarian mercenaries, and Rome, unable to defend its borders, either pulled back the soldiers who had been stationed on the extreme boundaries of the empire or allowed them to become integrated with the local peoples. An ever-increasing number of tribesmen were settled in Italy when the original Italian peoples deserted the land. The capital of the Empire was moved, once to Milan and later to Ravenna, and under the Emperor Constantine the empire was split into an eastern and a western section, with a growing sense of independence in each area. The "fall" was simply a slow disintegration of power, not a sudden cataclysm. But as civil power failed, the Church gained in strength until it became the great unifying power in Western civilization. The development of this power needs to be considered.

THE EARLY CHURCH: ST. AUGUSTINE

Christianity had its source in the teachings of Christ, but it became an institutionalized church largely through the efforts of two men. The first of these was the apostle Paul, who traveled widely and kept up a very active correspondence with the communities of Christians throughout the Roman world. Largely through his efforts the various congregations in the important cities were held together. After his work, a centralized doctrine and a widely accepted institution for the preservation and the propagation of the faith was still lacking. This last work was accomplished in large measure by St. Augustine (354-430).

Augustine was a North African, very well educated in the arts of logic and dialectic in his native town of Thagaste and in Carthage. The chief Christianizing influence on the young man was his mother, Monica, who admonished him and prayed for him so much that she must have been a real millstone around the neck of the high-spirited young man. He was not baptized until he came under the influence of St. Ambrose and other Christians in Milan in 387. The following year he returned to North Africa, where he founded a monastic order, was made Bishop of Hippo in 396, and spent the rest of his life in that post, writing and preaching in defense of the faith against various heretical groups and against pagans, particularly those who attacked Christianity after the sack of Rome in the year 410. His greatest work, *The City of God*, was written in part as a refutation of the pagan claim that Rome's failure resulted from the Christian influence.

All of his life Augustine was a searcher for a firm belief. As a young man he became a Manichaean, a sect with a strong dualistic belief in a power of good and a power of evil conflicting in the world and in man. His logical mind, however, could not accept all of the doctrine of this sect, and later, in Rome, he became a skeptic, a believer in nothing, not even his own existence. Finally he read the writings of the neoplatonists and was strongly influenced by them, so much so that he regarded his neoplatonic period as the most important stepping stone to his acceptance of Christianity, for his final doctrine incorporated much of neoplatonism. This was in Milan where he was serving as a municipally appointed teacher (his students in Carthage had been too unruly for him to put up with; in Rome the students were better, but they seldom paid their tuition), where his mother had joined him, and where he heard the preaching of St. Ambrose and established friendships with a number of devout Christians. One day he experienced an almost mystic conversion and was baptized in 387. Although he preferred to lead a contemplative life, his later duties as Bishop of Hippo forced him into vigorous activity as a supporter of the Roman Church against the Manichaeans, and the Arian and Donatist heretical sects. While conducting this defense, his doctrines established themselves.

Many books have been written about the whole body of Augustine's philosophy. Here we shall give only a very summary treatment of his ideas about the nature of God, of the creation, of free will, his philosophy of history, and the infallibility of the Church, for these beliefs provide the backbone for European civilization up to the late Middle Ages.

Earlier in our study we have made the point that a culture is based upon the idea of Reality which is held by that culture. According to Augustine, God was the only reality who created the world out of nothingness. This God was a mystic being, not an intellectual principle as was the case with the neoplatonists, so that knowledge of God and life in him was available to all human beings, whether they were philosophers or not. Although Augustine regarded his own early philosophic speculations as stepping stones to belief, he felt that his conversion came about through the grace of God, not through man's own efforts, and that this grace is available to all men. For Augustine and all believers throughout the Middle Ages, union with God is the only true goal and the only true happiness for man.

The process of creation-from-nothingness took place because of two aspects of the mind of God, roughly corresponding to the Platonic essences, but with significant differences. One such aspect corresponds to the eternal truths, such as the truth that the sum of the angles of a triangle always equals 180°. Such truths, existing before creation and after the destruction of the world, constitute the basic patterns and harmonies of the universe. Another aspect of God's mind consists of the "seminal (or seed) reasons" for created things. These are the patterns which acquire physical substance and form the visible things of the world: the visible men, trees, earth, and the myriad things which are apparent to our senses. These sense-apparent things exist in time; they rise, disintegrate, and pass away, and because of their transitory nature are the least important of God's creations.

Implicit in the last statement is Augustine's dualistic concept of time. He believed in a direct flow of time in which man's activities (never repeating themselves in spiral or circular patterns) moved upward toward eventual perfections, toward the godlike. The flow of time and all the changes which occur within it is characteristic of man's world. God, however, with all the attributes of his Mind, dwells in eternity, which is really a timeless instant. In this realm past and future have no meaning; all is present.

In this way, Augustine reconciled the problem of God's foreknowledge of all events and man's free will. He asserted that man, with the exception of original sin which could be washed away with baptism, had free will; yet God knew every event that would take place. How does one avoid fatalism and the idea of predestination if all of a man's actions are known in advance? The answer is that God's seeing all things as present-time allows for foreknowledge in what *we* call time, yet the "seeing" of things does not influence them. All events are simultaneous for God, and thus He can know them without influencing them. Man's vision is shackled by past, present, and an inscrutible future, but in his temporal world, he has complete free will.

In his attitude toward the body and the whole world of matter, Augustine is somewhat ambivalent. If this world is a creation of God, it must be good. On the other hand, a concern with lust or the acquisition of worldly goods, turns a person away from God. His thought here was strongly influenced by Platonic doctrine (see *The Phaedo*, for example), but not entirely. He believed that the physical things of the world are all passing away and changing. For example, in *The City of God* he makes the point that in Rome in 410 many people lost all of their worldly possessions, yet the Christian remained happy since his "possessions" were in his spirit and could not be taken away. The conclusion is that a concern with worldly things is a concern with nothing, since these things are ephemeral. The only vital concern is with the things of the spirit, which have their existence in the realm of eternity. This type of thought is not completely dualistic in that it does not despise the flesh and the things of the world, yet it tends in that direction. Many later Christian thinkers were to turn completely against the world and the flesh, asserting even more strongly than Plato and Augustine that these things were traps for the mind and the spirit of mankind. Much of the puritanical thought of our time comes from this basic reasoning.

Augustine in the first complete formulation of a Christian philosophy of history viewed the story of man as a conflict between two cities. (He used the word *city* as we might use the word *community* in such a phrase as the "business community.") One of these was the City of God, the other the City of Satan. In the beginning, when time was created, he stated, everything belonged to the good city, yet with the revolt of the angels and Satan's expulsion from heaven, the other city came into being. From that time until the birth of Christ, almost all of mankind belonged to the City of Satan. Only a few Hebrews who had faith in the coming of a Savior belonged to the City of God. With Christ's coming for the redemption of man, and with the formation of the Church, the membership in the two cities was more sharply divided, since all members of the City of God were also members of the Church. This, he was careful to assert, did not work conversely—all members of the Church were not necessarily members of God's City. The end of history will come with the Last Judgment and the final and complete separation of the two cities. The saved will be reclothed in their perfect bodies and take their place with God; the damned will undergo eternal torture with Satan. Since the members of the good city are already known to God, we find here the basis for the doctrine of the elect, a doctrine which was to be completely enunciated by Calvin after the Reformation.

This philosophy of history has at least one other important consequence. If the original members of the City of God are to be found only among the Hebrews, they alone knew truth. Thus all pagan learning, that of the Greeks, for example, is falsehood, and is not to be studied. Such a doctrine did much to discourage learning during the early Middle Ages.

Augustine was not only an abstract philosopher, but a very busy administrator as Bishop of Hippo, and a propagandist for the Roman Church. In this respect he was faced with the problem of the efficacy of the sacraments when performed by priests who belonged to heretical sects or who led impure lives. His judgment in the matter was that the efficacy of the sacraments (and one must remember that only through the sacraments did one find salvation) lay in the office of the priesthood, not in the man who performed them. The basis for this decision rested in the argument that if the benefit of the sacraments lay in the quality of the man who performed them, then men themselves would be placed in judgment of God's grace. The promulgation of this doctrine did much to establish the concept of the infallibility of the Church, since its power was inherent within its offices. This power, it was argued, descended directly from the apostles who were the original bishops of the church. From them it passed to other bishops, and from the bishops to the priests through the "laying on of hands." Through this act, the power to administer the sacraments was given and could not be revoked.

Sometime after the death of Augustine final authority of the Church in Rome was achieved, for the bishops of Rome had asserted their supremacy over the other bishops. The argument for this was that St. Peter had founded the Church in Rome, and that he was Christ's spiritual successor. Biblical authority was given for this claim from Christ's words concerning Peter, "Upon this rock *(petras)* will I build my church." Leo, Bishop of Rome from 440 to 461, first made this claim to ecclesiastical authority, and Pope Gregory the Great, slightly more than a century later, was such an able diplomat and churchman that the primacy of the Pope became universally accepted for the Western Church.

These were the moves that established a body of doctrine incorporating the infallibility of the Church, and a strong and revered institution which was able to maintain its authority throughout the troubled and confused years of the early Middle Ages as the only source of order throughout all of Europe. Very early the church was divided into two branches: the regular clergy (from the Latin *regula* or *rule*) composed of the monks and those who retreated from the active life, and the secular clergy, the Pope, the bishops and parish priests who lived among men and sought to lead them to a better life. During the time of the decline of the Roman authority, a very great number of men, particularly among the intellectual class, retreated from the world to live and work in the communal life of monasteries leading the contemplative existence. This is not an unusual phenomenon during any time of cultural upheaval, including our own.

FEUDALISM AND MANORIALISM

Following the withdrawal of Roman military and governmental stability, people of Western Europe had to find ways by which they could govern themselves with some semblance of justice, and by which they could make a living. The governmental system, feudalism, did not develop fully until the tenth century, but it can be described here as the slowly evolving political system of the Middle Ages. Manorialism, the economic arrangement by which the people made a living, actually had its beginning during late Roman times when the peasants were forced to stay on the land and became serfs. Furthermore, the two systems, at the lowest level—the demesne, or land-holding of a single knight—are so intertwined that they are scarcely distinguishable.

In its essence, feudalism is simply an arrangement by which the whole territory of the former empire was divided up in small enough units so that a single man could rule each one. It also created a fighting society, since the lords constantly raided adjoining territories, and all of them were subject to the forays of the northern tribes from Germany and Scandanavia.

In what had once been the civilized Roman Empire we find a number of kings who lacked both the money and power to hold their kingdoms together. These rulers proceeded to split up their kingdoms among the nobility, the highest ranking of which were the barons. The barons accepted the land from the king, and in return swore allegiance to him and agreed to furnish a certain number of fighting men when the kingdom was attacked. Thus a baron became a *vassal* of the king. But since the barons also lacked power to administer their lands, they took vassals under them, further subdividing the land. This successive division of land continued down to the knight who owned one estate or demesne which consisted of a village and the rather extensive farm-lands which surrounded it. Each member of the nobility was thus a despotic ruler over the land which he actually controlled, subject only to the oaths of loyalty which he took to the lord immediately over him. One knight could control his one small village and the farms which surrounded it, and provide some form of rough justice for the inhabitants.

The manorial system was simply the sum total of the life within one of these villages. Here, unless he was away at war, resided the lord in his manor house. A priest took care of the spiritual needs of the community, and the church and parish house usually occupied the center of the village. In addition to these buildings, one usually found a community bake-oven, a wine-press, and a mill for grinding grain. The farming land (one can assume that an average demesne comprised about a thousand acres) was divided into three main sections, two of which were planted each year, the third allowed to lie fallow. The lord retained a certain area as his personal property (though it was farmed by the serfs), the priest was given a small allotment of land, a section was retained as a common woodland, and another section was used as a common meadow. Each farmer or serf was given certain strips of land in each of the three fields—each strip was usually an eighth of a mile in length and about seventeen feet wide. The serf and his family were "attached" to the land, that is, they could not leave, but neither could they be turned away. The serf gave a certain portion of his produce to the lord and was also obligated to work a certain number of days on the lord's land. The lord, in his turn, was obliged to protect his villagers and to provide justice, though he was the only judge in the case of disputes, and his word was final.

The manorial system gives us a picture of a poverty-stricken and almost totally isolated life. All of the bare necessities were provided within the single manor, and the serf scarcely ever traveled beyond it. No news of the world came in except when the lord returned from a war, or when an occasional itinerant peddler came through. One can safely assume that none of the peasants could read, and formal education was unknown. Life on the manor slowed to the regular round of work, religious holidays, births, marriages and deaths. Life was maintained, but at the lowest possible level. Little wonder that the people came to regard this world as a vale of tears and that they lived in anticipation of a glorious after-life in heaven.

CHARLEMAGNE

Only one event of great political (and humanistic) importance occurred during the early Middle Ages. This was the rule of Charlemagne from 768 to 814. While this span of almost a half century can scarcely be called a "renaissance," it did provide a spark of light and culture in an otherwise dark period of almost five centuries, and because of it, perhaps, the light of civilization was not entirely extinguished.

Charles was the second of the Carolingian Kings of the Franks, and his father had already gained the support of the Roman Church by defeating the Lombards in Italy and granting a very considerable area of land to the Papacy. When Charles came to the throne he set about to expand and solidify the kingdom of the Franks, fighting the Moslems in Spain, the Norsemen up to the border of Denmark, and against the Lombards in Italy. The Battle of Roncevaux in 778 in which Charles' knight, Count Roland, was ambushed and killed furnished the kernel for the great cycle of songs and stories relating to the exploits of Charles. In return for this warring activity against the pagans, and as a shrewd political move, the Pope crowned Charles as "Emperor of the Romans" on Christmas day in the year 800.

Important as these political events are, they cannot be our main concern. The significant factor here is that Charles had a great respect for learning and brought scholars from all Europe to his court at Aachen (Aix-la-Chapelle). The architecture of this court itself is a landmark in Western culture, for Charles had been to Ravenna where he had seen the magnificent architecture and the gleaming mosaics, the ideas for which had come directly from Byzantium. The chapel at Aachen is a copy of the church of St. Vitale in Ravenna, and it did much to introduce Eastern ideas of beauty to the Western world.

Most important of all in this revival of learning was the establishment of the Palace School. To direct it, Charles imported the English scholar Alcuin, from the cathedral school at York, and in addition to teaching and directing the school itself, Alcuin collected a considerable number of manuscripts of ancient learning and revived the monastic practice of copying manuscripts both for the palace library and for distribution to other seats of learning. While little original thought was generated in the Palatine School, this act to preserve learning was to be of importance to later centuries.

Under Charles, all of Italy, northern Spain, all of modern France, and southern Germany were united under a single rule, though Charles did not attempt to impose a single code of law on the diverse people. He did, however, have all of his counties inspected regularly to see that the lands were well governed and that justice was administered. Further than that he strengthened even further the power of the Church, since he forcibly Christianized all of the pagans whom he conquered. One consequence of his being crowned as emperor by the Pope lay in the development of the idea that the Church was superior to all secular authority, an idea that was to give all sorts of trouble in later centuries.

After Charlemagne's death in 814, and the short rule of his ineffective son Louis the Pious, his empire was divided among his three grandsons, none of whom was able to continue the tradition that he had inherited. The empire rapidly fell apart, particularly under the invasions of the Norsemen, the Vikings, who ravaged all of Europe and even sailed to the continent which was later to be named America.

THE ASSIMILATION OF CULTURES

Early in this chapter it was pointed out that the most important development during the early Middle Ages was the digestion of several very different and opposed cultures. No one can deny that the old classic tradition of Greece and Rome had run its full course and was no longer fruitful. If life was to become meaningful, new ideas, new ways of life, new blood needed to be transfused into the cultural body. The dark period from the fifth to the tenth centuries, full of doubt, confusion, warfare, and death was the result of these clashing cultures, but, in the long run (since we do not have to live in those times) it was essential in terms of the change to a new culture.

In the main, Byzantine and Moslem cultures remained as storehouses which would be drawn upon by European civilization in the later Middle Ages. Except for a brief conquest of Italy and North Africa under the Eastern emperor, Justinian, and the influence which we have already noted during the rule of Charlemagne, Byzantium was chiefly important as a bastion against eastern infringement upon Europe by the Persians, and by the Slavic and Magyar peoples who settled in what is now Hungary, the Balkans, and southern Russia. These peoples were Christianized and civilized chiefly by missionaries from the Eastern Catholic Church. Another and rather unusual influence of the East came through the Christianizing of Ireland according to the Eastern ritual. For a time at least, Ireland enjoyed a higher and more enlightened culture than did the rest of Europe, and subtle influences of this civilization reached the mainland.

The rise of the Moslems was much more evident in that Islamic culture and religion seriously threatened to engulf all of Europe. Originally the Arabs were an uncultured polytheistic people, and they, in themselves, did little to produce enlightenment, but under the general peace and stability of their rule, Hellenistic, Persian, and Syrian art and intellect were permitted to expand.

Mohammed was born in Mecca about the year 570 and worked as a merchant there until his then unpopular religious beliefs forced him to flee the city in 622. This last date is accepted as the beginning of the Moslem faith. Very soon after this flight he returned to Mecca in triumph and succeeded in converting many Arabs to his belief.

Mohammed regarded his religious insight as an extension and culmination of the Judeo-Christian tradition, and the faith shares much with those two religious beliefs. Islam stresses the oneness of God and the equality of all men before God. For this reason it developed no priesthood and no central institutional authority other than the political rulers, the caliphs, under whose rule and warlike spirit the faith was propagated. Particularly important for the development of Western culture was the Muslim banning of statues and images, which was to send many refugee artists to Europe when the Muslims captured Constantinople in 1453.

The Arabs, united for the first time in their new religious belief, set out to conquer most of the world, and were remarkably successful. Very early they overran Persia and the lands to the east, including India. They also occupied Egypt and all of North Africa, and by 720 had conquered all of Spain. They crossed the Pyrenees and invaded France. Here they were met by Charles Martel, grandfather of Charlemagne, near the city of Poitiers in 732 and driven back to Spain. Much of Charlemagne's time was spent fighting in Spain in his attempt to drive the Moors out of Europe.

The contribution of Islam lay not in the wars, but in the peace and prosperity which followed them. Trade routes were opened clear to China so that material goods and immaterial ideas flowed freely through the Islamic world. They were great builders, synthesizing the Roman dome with features of Persian architecture to produce the pointed dome which we usually associate with Islamic construction. Because images were banned for religious reasons, they developed decorative forms based on geometric designs which we now call *arabesques.* Most important of all, learning flourished under the rule of these people, and such great universities as those at Cairo and Toledo came into being, both preserving older knowledge and developing new. The works of Plato and Aristotle were translated into Arabic and studied with great zeal; mathematics was developed, particularly with the use of the Arabic system of numbers rather than the clumsy Roman system, and the study of medicine was greatly advanced. All this amounts to the fact that while Italy and northern Europe were slogging along in the mud, a very high culture flourished in Asia, Africa, and Spain. One is tempted to wonder whether Charles Martel's victory in 732 was a victory after all. The riches of this culture were not to be known in Europe until after the crusades.

By far the greatest cultural fusion in the early Middle Ages was that of the Celto-Germanic peoples of the north with the Graeco-Romans of the south. We have already become well acquainted with the balanced and intellectual culture of the Greeks and Romans, whose horizontal-linear architecture and predictable designs in art and architecture give a clue, at least, to their reposeful, rational character. We have already seen, too, that many of the northern people had come into the Roman empire either by invitation, infiltration, or military conquest. But these people were vastly different in basic character from the Romans. Their architectural line was energetic, vertical, and angular; their decorations were twisted and unpredictable. Just about the time of the removal of Roman authority we witness a great folk-wandering of these peoples, with tribes from the east pressing upon the Germanic tribes, and they, in turn, moving outward both as colonizers and as warlike raiders through all of the continent of Europe. This restless movement of peoples was to continue for centuries, with an inevitable clash and subsequent fusion of the two cultures.

The basic social organization of these

northern peoples was the *comitatus*, which was the banding together of a group of fighting men under the leadership of a warrior chieftain. The men pledged their loyalty and their strength to the chief, and he, in turn, promised to give them rewards from captured plunder. Thus in the early Germanic poem of *Beowulf*, both the hero and another leader, Hrothgar, are frequently called "ring-givers" from their roles as leaders distributing gold to their fighting men. Once the comitatus was formed, it had only one function: to fight, to capture, and to plunder. The dragonships of the Norsemen were frequent and fearful visitors in England and all Europe.

But there is another aspect to these people which is revealed in their religion. The contemporary philosopher, Lewis Mumford, has spoken of the Graeco-Romans as "pessimistic of the body and optimistic for the soul," and of the Celto-Germanic peoples as optimistic of the body but pessimistic for the spirit. The distinction is a valid one. The classic and Christian southern peoples regarded life here on earth only as a short period of pain and sorrow to be followed, they hoped, by a joyous after-life in heaven. The Celto-Germanics ate greatly, drank deeply, raped widely, but were ultimately pessimistic about the afterlife. Theirs was perhaps the only religion which pictures the ultimate defeat of the "good" gods by the forces of evil and darkness.

The Norsemen worshipped a group of anthropomorphic "good" gods who lived in a celestial residence called Valhalla. Wotan was the king of the gods; the most active, certainly, was Thor, the thunder god. Baldur represented the idea of beauty, springtime, and warmth; Loki was the trickster. Even in the heavenly abode the pessimistic nature of these gods appears, for, through a trick of Loki's, Baldur was slain. For the fighting men on earth, an afterlife among the gods was promised, but far different from any heaven conceived of by Christians, Moslems, or Jews. If a warrior were killed in battle, semidivine maidens (the Valkyrie) swooped over the battlefield to take him to Valhalla. Here the hero simply continued his earthly life of fighting, eating, and drinking.

For the gods and heroes, however, an awful fate was predicted, for Valhalla was surrounded by the land of the giant Jotuns, probably representing the cold and the darkness of the northern climate. The gods and the Jotuns were engaged in constant small warfare and trickery, but in the Norse religion, the future held a great battle between the two forces, with the Jotuns winning and bringing about the downfall of the gods. Thus the ultimate and total pessimism of the spirit of the Scandinavian-Germanic people.

The difference between the Graeco-Roman and the Celto-Germanic personalities has been suggested earlier with a comparison between the structural line and the type of ornamentation which each found beautiful and which, therefore, may give a clue to the differences in character. A comparison between the type of literature which each culture produced may strengthen our awareness of the clash of cultures. No better example of the Graeco-Roman literature of the very early Middle Ages can be found than Boethius's *Consolation of Philosophy*. Boethius, one remembers, was a Roman consul, serving under the Roman emperor (actually an Ostrogoth) Theodoric. The *Consolation* was written in the year 524 when he was languishing in prison awaiting death after being accused by his emperor of treason.

Boethius gives his work the form of a highly rational dialogue between himself as a man who is deeply distressed by his fate in the world, and a vision of philosophy as a stately woman. The dialogue is interspersed with poetical passages which serve to sum up the previous discussion and form a bridge into their next topic. The subjects for discussion range from the nature of fortune and chance, of happiness, the existence of evil, of free will, and the paradox of man's free will and an all-knowing God. In reading the whole discussion, one is reminded of a Socratic dialogue, and, indeed, Boethius draws heavily on Platonic thought. While the ideas themselves are not new, the reader is constantly aware of a classic coolness and dignified withdrawal from the passions of life. Perhaps a brief quotation may make this clear. The excerpt is drawn from book III, prose X. Philosophy speaks first:

> "But it has been conceded that the highest Good is happiness?"
>
> "Yes," I said.
>
> "Therefore," she said, "it must be confessed that God is Happiness itself."
>
> "I cannot gainsay what you premised before," said I, "and I perceive that this follows necessarily from those premises."
>
> "Look, then," she said, "whether the same proposition is not proved more strongly by the following argument: there cannot be two different highest Goods. For it is clear that where there are two different goods the one cannot be the other; wherefore neither one can be the perfect Good while each is wanting to the other. And that which is not perfect is manifestly not the highest; therefore, if two things are the highest Good, they can by no means be different. Further, we have concluded that both God and happiness are the highest Good; therefore the highest Deity must be identical with the highest happiness."
>
> "No conclusion," said I, "could be truer in fact or stronger in theory or worthier of God."
>
> "Over and above this," she said, "let me give you a corollary such as geometricians are wont to do when they wish to derive a deduction from the propositions they have demonstrated. Since men become happy by attaining happiness, and happiness is

identical with divinity, it is plain that they become happy by attaining divinity. And as men become just by attaining justice and wise by attaining wisdom, so by the same reasoning they become godlike by attaining divinity. Every happy man, then, is God-like; but, while there is nothing to prevent as many men as possible from being God-like, only one is God by nature: men are God-like by participation."[1]

Nothing could be more urbane, civilized, classic, or rational than the discussion cited above. To become aware of the difference in spirit between this and the Celto-Germanic personality, one may look briefly at two of the hero-epics from the northern people. *Beowulf* and the *Nibelungenlied* will serve as examples. The very sound of the harsh lines, much smothered and rounded in modern English translation, reveals something of the masculine vigor of the people. Consider, for example, the alliteration of crashing consonants in the line, "Bit his bone-frame, drank blood from his veins." This is a far cry from the epics of Greece and Rome in its very tone.

The story of Beowulf is almost equally harsh. It tells of Beowulf, a warrior from the south of Sweden who went to the court of his uncle in Denmark. There he slew a monster, Grendel, who had been devastating the uncle's kingdom. As a trophy of the fight, Beowulf brought home the arm and shoulder of the monster as it had been wrenched from the giant's torso. Following the victory, a great banquet was held in the hero's honor. Having eaten and drunk until they could hold no more, Beowulf and his men lay down on the floor of the banquet hall, their war gear hanging by them, for the night's rest. But when all was quiet, Grendel's mother entered the hall, killed some of the men, and took the bloody arm and shoulder of her son back to the home which she had beneath the waters of a dismal fen.

On the next morning Beowulf set out and tracked Grendel's mother to the shore of a swamp. Fearlessly he donned his armor and plunged into the water, down to the opening of the cave. Here he grappled with the hag-monster and finally killed her with a weapon forged by the giants of old.

The last episode of the poem tells of Beowulf's last days when, as king or chief of his Swedish tribe, his own land was threatened by a dragon. As a warrior hero and leader, he went forth, killed the dragon, and was mortally wounded himself. The poem ends with his funeral pyre as a Viking chieftain, and the construction of his tomb as a monument which would serve as a landmark for Viking ships at sea.

Beowulf was never tender, never kind, never sympathetic. When his friends were slain in battle or in the great hall of Heorot, he never wept for them or extolled their virtues. Rather he swore vengeance and went forth to do it. He was the mighty warrior, the great adventurer. Such was the Germanic hero.

Another example is at once older and younger; it is the German tale called the *Niebelungenlied*, or "Song of the Niblungs." It was not written down in its present form until the 1200s, but its materials hark back to the days of Attila the Hun, in the fifth century. The Scandinavian version of the tale is known as the *Volsungasaga;* Wagner freely adapted the tale in his four music-dramas, *The Ring of the Niblungen.*

The epic is concerned with the hero Siegfried, who loved Kriemhild, sister of the Burgundian king, Gunther. In order to win her, Siegfried promised his help in Gunther's wooing of Brunhild, the warlike queen of a distant country. By magical means Siegfried assisted him in the feats of strength that won her. On their wedding night, Brunhild tied Gunther up in knots, and hung him behind the door; again it was Siegfried who came to the rescue, and on the second night, wrapped in his cloak of invisibility, wrestled with her and subdued her, without Brunhild's being aware that her adversary was Siegfried, not Gunther. How he took from her then a ring and a girdle, giving them to Kriemhild; how the two queens quarreled; how Kriemhild, in haughty anger, revealed the trick of Bunhild's conquest; and how Brunhild plotted revenge, is quickly recounted; the climax of the first part is the treacherous murder of Siegfried by Hagen, the loyal henchman of Gunther, and the villain of the piece. The last half of the story concerns Kriemhild's revenge against the Burgundians. Married, after many years, to Etzel (Attila), King of the Huns, she invites the Burgundians to visit her, and there follows a general massacre in which they are all slain, including Kriemhild.

One sees in these epics the warrior's world of the first half of the medieval period, its spirit of adventure, courage, bravery, harshness, and blood.

Perhaps these examples help one to visualize the difference between the character of the two peoples who encountered each other during the early Middle Ages. So important was it that Dorothy Sayers in her introduction to the translation of the *Divine Comedy* attributes the origin of the two great political factions which tore Italy apart in late medieval times, the Guelfs and the Ghibellines, to this cultural difference. She contents that the Ghibellines represented the descendants of the northern stock with all of their vigorous energy, and that the Guelfs were essentially the native Italian land-owning, placid southern people.

Be that as it may, by the tenth century the two cultures achieved a physical amalgamation.

1. Boethius, *The Consolation of Philosophy*, ed. James J. Buchanan (New York: Frederick Ungar Publishing Co., Inc., 1957), pp. 31-32.

Many of the northerners had moved to the south, had become Christianized, and had given up some of their savage ways. The Angles and Saxons settled in England, other Norsemen took over the great province of Normandy in France. Throughout all of Europe the Germanic people settled and took land, so that the northern chieftain moved into the already evolving feudal system, becoming a baron or a count, a duke or a knight, holding land from his suzerain and granting fiefs to those under him. It was still a warlike society, the difference being chiefly in its fairly settled nature. The leader gave up his wooden hall for a castle built of stone. The highest virtue became a masculine loyalty between the lord and his vassals. The *Song of Roland* furnishes a good example of this new civilization. This minor epic was written in French about the time of the first crusade (the 1090s), but the written version simply records a hero-story that had been sung and recited concerning the events that happened (legendarily) three centuries before in the days of Charlemagne. The persons of the story are Franks, the Germanic conquerors who gave their name to France; the central figure is Roland, the emperor's nephew. The great event of the poem is the ambush by Saracens of the rear guard of Charlemagne's army in the passes of the Pyrenees at Roncevaux. The ambush was arranged by Roland's treacherous kinsmen Ganelon, inspired by envy and revenge. Roland and his companion Oliver, together with the militant Archbishop Turpin, are the last survivors of the Frankish host; they too are killed, facing overwhelming odds. One of the best-known episodes is that of Roland's refusal to blow his ivory horn (oliphant), despite the urging of Oliver, to recall Charlemagne's host before the battle begins; when he realizes that he and his Franks are doomed, he does at last blow three mighty blasts that Charlemagne hears, thirty leagues away, and the Emperor returns to rout the Saracens and avenge the death of Roland and his companions. The epic concludes with the trial and punishment of Ganelon.

It is a truly feudal poem, full of the vigorous, active, restless spirit of the northern warrior. Roland is the man-at-arms, the warrior, unsoftened by the chivalry of later knighthood; he is a splendid barbarian, courageous in the face of overwhelming odds, loyal to his friends, utterly devoted to God, his spiritual overlord, and to Charlemagne, his temporal one. He is blood-brother to his earlier northern kinsman, Beowulf: both heroes represent the all-out, do-or-die, "go-for-broke" spirit of the heroic age.

There are many magnificent scenes: the pathetic one in which the wounded Oliver, dazed and blinded by blood, strikes his best friend Roland, and the two are immediately reconciled; the striking one in which Roland tries to shatter his sword, "Durendal," against a rock lest it fall into pagan hands; for its hilt is a reliquary, with sacred and precious relics in it. Let us read only the one, the 176th stanza or "laisse" of the poem:

> Count Roland lies under a pine tree,
> Towards Spain has he turned his face.
> Many things he recalls to remembrance:
> How many lands, hero-like, he has won;
> Sweet France; the men of his lineage;
> Charlemagne his lord, who reared him.
> At this he sighs and weeps, nor can he restrain himself.
> But he does not wish to go into oblivion;
> He confesses his fault, and prays God's mercy:
> "True Father, Who never lies,
> Who raised St. Lazarus from the dead,
> Who preserved Daniel from the lions,
> Keep my soul from all dangers,
> Despite all the sins I have committed in my life!"
> He raises towards God the glove from his right hand;
> St. Gabriel from his hand receives it.
> On his arms his head falls back;
> His hands clasped, he goes to his end.
> God sends his angel Cherubin
> And St. Michael of the Peril;
> Together with these comes St. Gabriel.
> The count's soul they carry into Paradise.

The similarities and differences between this story and that of *Beowulf* are immediately apparent. Roland, with its heavy Christian overlay, is much more "civilized" than the early epic. But it is still a very masculine, savagely militaristic poem, extolling the glories of war, or bravery, and of loyalty. Not least interesting in the poem is the role of the Archbishop Turpin, who is a great Church leader, at least in title. Throughout the battle, however, he ranges through the ranks of fighting men, wielding his great mace (at this time it was illegal for a churchman to wield a sword) and breaking heads with the best of them. We see here a new role of the church, with churchmen active in feudal society, holding great areas of land, and as much concerned with battle and secular affairs as with the religious life. The final act of Roland reveals much of the spirit of the time, for his offer of his glove to God is the very act of pledging loyalty to a feudal lord. Roland, always a vassal of Charlemagne, has now accepted a new suzerain in God, and the acceptance of the glove signifies God's acceptance of Roland as a vassal in the celestial feudal system.

SUMMARY

It is almost symbolic that the people of the early Middle Ages built walls around their villages; wooden palisades in the early days, later, with feudalism, the walls were constructed of stone and the lord's house and the whole village became a fortified castle. The total way of life at the time parallels these narrow fortifications, for early medieval man built fortifications of equal strength around his person and his mind.

His universe was based on the Catholic Church, which allowed no questioning of itself or of its actions. Further, the Church through a narrowing of the Augustinian doctrine, took a very dim view of all worldly pleasure and practically forbade any questioning of the physical world which surrounded men. Science as we know it was lost completely, so that the physical world was a closed book, to be interpreted only as a vague shadow of the mind and intention of God. Life here and now was viewed as a brief and transitory journey through a dismal land, with true life and true happiness coming after death. Furthermore (particularly apparent in the morality play of *Everyman*), the only way to reach the blissful afterlife lay in the faithful acceptance of the doctrines and the sacraments of the Church.

The economic system of manorialism bound the greatest part of the population to the thousand acres or so of the manor itself. They could not escape, they seldom traveled beyond the limits of the single demesne. Food, clothing, and every physical comfort was limited to what the single manor could produce. Not even the mind could escape the narrow confines, since reading was almost unknown and news from the world outside almost never penetrated the manor.

The political system of feudalism was equally narrowing. Justice lay entirely in the hands of the feudal lord or, more often, his deputy. Except for the specific obligations of serf to lord and vassal to suzerain, which were generally known and accepted, the law was made up on the spot, and the individual never knew what to expect.

The narrow confines of Church, manorialism, and feudalism provided the walls which closed in upon the human spirit. Creativity and freedom of thought were almost unknown. But, with the withdrawal of Roman protection, and with all the dangers from bands of marauders, these walls provided protection for the individual. If the ordinary serf could not live well, he could live safely.

Perhaps Elinor Wylie's twentieth-century poem "Sanctuary" expresses the same problem:

> This is the bricklayer; hear the thud
> Of his heavy load dumped down on stone,
> His lustrous bricks are brighter than blood,
> His smoking mortar whiter than bone.
>
> Set each sharp-edged, fire-bitten brick
> Straight by the plumb-line's shivering length;
> Make my marvelous wall so thick
> Dead nor living may shake its strength.
>
> Full as a crystal cup with drink
> Is my cell with dreams, and quiet, and cool. . .
> Stop, old man! You must leave a chink;
> How can I breathe? *You can't, you fool!*

But the human spirit is never content with mere security. Particularly with the gaining of a little freedom as it did in the tenth century, it clamors for more and more room for expansion. (Perhaps we witness this same phenomenon with the black-American in the twentieth century.) The seeds which were to grow and eventually break down the narrow walls of the Middle Ages were already planted. Some of the directions for that growth may be indicated.

First, the human spirit has never long been content *not* to examine the world around it. The varied forms of the world, its beauties, and reason for being demand attention. Both art and science express this quest for an exploration of the world of the senses.

Second, the two personality types of Europe, the rational Graeco-Roman and the emotional and energetic Germanic lived side by side but not in unison by the year 1000. Some form of synthesis between these two personality types, almost exactly opposite each other, needed to be found.

Third, a problem limited largely to politics: the question of supremacy of church or state demanded settlement. At a time when the secular power was so weak as to be almost nonexistent, the Church could and did assert its authority over kings and lords. But with the growth of the powers of the world, a struggle was bound to arise; a struggle that would demand a synthesis and compromise, not necessarily a total victory of one side over the other.

Fourth, and perhaps most important of all, men demand and need joy in the present life, but this was sternly denied by the Church. A desire for immediate physical and intellectual pleasure in life now would necessarily conflict with the doctrine that life here was nothing, the afterlife was everything. The pull of life as opposed to the Church-dictated pull of death was bound to tear the human personality apart until some synthesis could be effected.

These are the latent problems which one sees at the end of the early Middle Ages. Their solutions will be dealt with in subsequent chapters.

Bibliography

General

Kenneth Clark. *Civilization.* This sophisticated and urbane book might well be a companion piece to *The Search* from this point on through the discussion of the twentieth century. It will not be listed in succeeding bibliographies, but Clark's comments on art and life are greatly worth having.

Philosophy

1. St. Augustine. *Confessions.* Edward Pusey trans. Pocket Books, 1957.

2. Boethius. *Consolations of Philosophy*. James Buchanan, trans. Frederick Ungar Publishing Co., Inc., 1957.

3. Frederick Coplestone. *A History of Philosophy*. vol. 1.

4. Anne Freemantle, ed. *The Age of Belief* (through Chap. 5). Mentor Books. The two histories of philosophy listed here present some pretty tough reading for the student, but so does all pure philosophy, and medieval thought in particular.

5. Henry Osborn Taylor. *The Medieval Mind*. The Macmillan, Co., 1950. A brilliant study of all aspects of medieval life and thought. Also recommended for the next chapter.

Literature

The Song of Roland. The Isabel Butler translation (Houghton Mifflin Company) is a standard; Dorothy Sayers has a new translation (Penguin Books, Inc.).

Beowulf and many of the other early Germanic stories make for interesting reading.

The Late Middle Ages: Expansion and Synthesis

CHAPTER 14

■ It is impossible to pinpoint any particular reason for the liberation of a whole social structure, but as we look back over the centuries we know that it happened in eleventh-century Europe. Perhaps not the least of the reasons was a release from a sense of doom; the end of the world had been predicted for the year 1000 and the prediction was widely believed by the peasantry. One must imagine the wonder of a whole culture when people woke up on New Year's morning of the year 1001, pinched themselves, and found that they were still alive in the flesh, and felt the pangs of hunger, not for spiritual food, but for a very physical breakfast. Such a reprieve may have been one of the causative factors in the general awakening of Europe. The people were still in the Middle Ages; God was still the accepted Reality, but what a difference was soon to be discovered in the lives and the thoughts of men and women!

The difference expresses itself in various ways. One can notice the change from the masculine code of feudalism to the feminine code of chivalry, closely associated with the rising Cult of the Virgin which became the dominant popular religious force in late medieval times. Another factor to be considered is the rise of cities. The crusades, still another leavening influence, brought about an increasing knowledge of the relatively luxurious life of Islamic culture. Within the new cities we also witness the revival of humanistic learning with the rise of the great universities. Last to be mentioned, though perhaps basic to the whole movement, was the philosophic ferment about the nature of reality itself, which culminated in the "Battle of Universals" in philosophic circles.

Historians attribute the rise of cities to a number of causes, all of which were probably significant. One reason lay in the increase of land available for agriculture because of the drainage of swamps, for it must be remembered that cities need agriculture to supply food. The needs of the great nobility for central fighting forces gave another impetus to the gathering of people, for, as wars became bigger and landholdings wider, the barons needed men in a central place who could be mobilized immediately. Perhaps the most important force in the development of cities was the rise of trade and commerce (though if one asks for the causative force in this development, he cannot find a specific answer except that it happened). At any rate, the itinerant peddler, traveling from manor to manor, had been known throughout the early Middle Ages. Sometime about the eleventh century, this trade became somewhat stabilized as the peddlers-become-merchants set up stalls under the protection of the great churches or abbeys, and the Church law which governed the place insured peaceful transactions. This brought about another change· if trade was to flourish, the old barter system was no longer adequate, and money was reintroduced to Europe. The nobility was quick to seize upon this change and to foster it. For centuries they had collected their feudal dues in produce and goods, but money offered them much greater freedom in carrying on their activities. They were willing, therefore, to grant charters to the cities, giving them varying degrees of freedom from feudal responsibilities in return for tax money. Thus did the towns grow, and whatever the immediate forces which made them flourish, their development was but a symptom of a general stirring of the human spirit.

Throughout Europe the word went around, "City air is free air," for in free cities the custom was established that a serf who could maintain his residence for a year and a day became a free man. The more adventurous and intelligent serfs flocked to the city. Here men of common interests—interests centered in their trades—formed themselves into guilds to regulate the quality and price of their goods and to provide insurance and a measure of social life for the members and their families.

As these guilds—first craft guilds, later merchant guilds—became wealthy, the great guild halls flanked the great church to form a quadrangle about the open market place; these became the distinguishing feature of the medieval city. After the towns were founded, came the great expansion of the merchants, plying their trade with the East and returning to Europe with the silks and spices which they were able to buy there. In 1241, nearly three centuries after the first movement toward city growth, came the great Hanseatic League, the guild of merchants of the German coastal towns, uniting to carry on their trade. The cities, already founded, formed a safe outlet for their goods. Trade could be carried on. The increase in wealth, for the Church, for the producers of goods in the craft guilds, and for the merchants was such that it found an outlet in drama, processions and parades—one answer to the need for beauty in a world which had for centuries been sparse and bare.

The crusades were another of the forces which enlightened the Middle Ages. The first crusade took place at the end of the eleventh century, and was followed by many others even into the Renaissance. The last crusade was led by Don John of Austria (1571). In carrying on these holy wars to free the Holy Land from the Moslems, various groups of crusading knights (the Knights of St. John, for example) set up permanent bases on such islands as Rhodes and Malta, and even on the eastern shores of the Mediterranean. As was noted in the consideration of the early Middle Ages, a flourishing culture and a luxurious civilization had been alive in the Near East, parts of North Africa and Spain during the first 500 years of medieval times in Europe.

While this culture had been known earlier in Europe, as a few travelers had come in contact with it, particularly in Spain, it was not until the time of the crusades that the possibility of a relatively luxurious way of life became known to many people in the West. As the soldiers returned and told the tales of things which they had seen on their travels, perhaps bringing booty and souvenirs home, as is the ancient custom of soldiers in all time, the demand for a better way of life spread throughout Europe.

One of the most interesting transformations was that from feudalism to chivalry, a movement from a masculine to a feminine code of behavior. Feudalism, according to the historian, Henry Adams, was the code of men-at-arms. With these later Middle Ages, however, and especially in France, women succeeded to rule in the matter of ethics and behavior. The man was away from home for great stretches of time, trading, at the wars, wherever the affairs of the time called him. Women took over the manners of the time, manners which had been crude and rough under man's domination. If we must have a name by which to fix this movement in our memory, Adams gives us that of Eleanor of Aquitaine (1122-1202), Queen of France and Queen of England, and her daughter, Mary of Champagne and her granddaughter, Blanche of Castile. Certainly it was these women who established the Courts of Love, courts which were to write legal-sounding codes in all matters of etiquette. It was here that the rough codes of feudalism were transformed into gentler modes of living and belief. This change may be seen in the contrast between Roland's lament over the fallen Franks at Roncevaux, representative of the ideals of feudalism, and the lament over the dead Lancelot, representative of the chivalrous knight. Roland, surveying the field of death where lie his comrades in arms, says:

> Lords and barons, now may God have mercy upon you, and grant Paradise to all your souls that you may rest among the blessed flowers. Man never saw better men of arms that ye were. Long and well, year in and year out, have you served me, and many wide lands have ye won for the glory of Charles. Was it to such an end that he nourished you? O France, fair land, today art thou made desolate by rude slaughter. Ye Frankish barons, I see you die through me, yet I can do naught to save and defend you. May God, who knows no lie, aid you!

Yet when Lancelot, the almost perfect knight of chivalry, lies dead, we hear the following lament:

> Thou wert the courtliest knight that ever bare shield, and thou were the truest friend to thy lover that ever bestrode horse, and thou wert the truest lover among sinful men that ever loved woman, and thou wert the kindest man that ever struck with sword, and thou wert the goodliest person that ever came among the crowd of knights, and thou wert the meekest man and the gentlest that ever are in hall among ladies, and thou wert the sternest knight to thy mortal foe that ever put spear in breast.

From this we see the transformation from a fighting code to a courtly and courteous one. Both are found in the lament over Lancelot, but the virtues of mildness, of love, and of humility always stand before the virtues of strength or the recognition of human weakness.

While many are aware that the elaborate codes of courtly love were but a fancy icing over very real illicit love affairs, one must remember that aristocratic marriages were arranged almost entirely for political purposes, and that the knights stayed away from home for years, yet the codes themselves worked toward a civilizing of barbaric Europe. The curious problem of the love triangle as told in Chaucer's "Franklin's Tale," and the highly civilized solution as told by the Franklin illustrate the benign influence of the feminine mystique in the Middle Ages.

Closely allied to the development of chivalry was the development of beauty and warmth within the Church. As has already been pointed out, the official doctrine of the Church was a vast intellectual monument. It centered in the Trinity—the Father, the Son, and the Holy Ghost—a Three who were always One, administering the cold and rigid justice which was found in the development of doctrine from the time of Augustine. For sinful men, justice is the last thing to be desired, and the medieval man, ridden by the absolutism of the time, was convinced that he was sinful. He sought not justice, but mercy; and for mercy he could only turn to the Woman, the Mother. Thus, as a part of the domination of woman which we have already noticed, developed the Cult of the Virgin.

This was the time of the building of cathedrals, and the power of the cult, almost an obsession with the people of the time, is shown in the number of cathedrals dedicated to Mary. Indeed, in France, one asks not how to get to the cathedral, but how to get to Notre Dame, the church of "Our Lady." The two are almost synonymous. As Adams points out:

> The measure of this devotion [to the Virgin], which proves to any religious American mind, beyond possible cavil, its serious and practical reality, is the money it cost. According to statistics, in the single century between 1170 and 1270, the French built 80 cathedrals and nearly five hundred churches of the cathedral class, which would have cost, according to an estimate made in 1840, more than five thousand millions to replace. Five thousand million francs is a thousand million dollars,[1] and this covered only the great churches of a single century. . . . The share of this capital which was—if one may use a commercial figure—invested in the Virgin cannot be fixed . . . but in a spiritual and artistic sense, it was almost the whole. . . .
>
> Expenditure like this rests invariably on an economic idea. . . . In the thirteenth [century] they trusted their money to the Queen of Heaven because of their belief in her power to repay it with interest in the life to come.

Therein lay the power of the Virgin in bringing human understanding and human sympathy into the cold philosophic structure of Church doctrine. While the philosophers wrangled about the nature of the universal substance, the common man found his comfort and a release of his pent-up energies in the addition of a Person with human sympathy and warmth to the austere Trinity. Such faith reveals itself in the great body of stories of the mysteries of the Virgin, one of the most widely-known and touching of which is "Our Lady's Juggler," given on p. 387.

Most important of all in terms of basic way life were the continual attacks and modifications of the doctrine of the Church itself, for the Church insisted upon absolute authority. In spite of his early philosophic gropings, St. Augustine had finally said, "I believe in order that I may know." Thus *faith* in the Scripture and the writings of the early churchmen and total submission to these sources was the first necessity for Christian life. Knowledge came second, and if at any point the doctrine seemed contrary to reason or inexplicable by it, the doctrine was to be believed and intellect was to be denied.

Upon this basis was built the great structure of Christian Scholasticism, the way of thought of

1. This in the money values of 1840. If we multiplied the figure by twenty, it would still be low for the 1970s.

the late Middle Ages. Most simply, Scholasticism can be explained in this way: If a thinker had any question for which he wanted an answer, he went first to the Bible and the writings of the Church Fathers to discover all the passages which pertained to his subject. This was his only source for basic data; experimentation in the world of his senses was not permitted. Then, as a second step, he used Aristotelian logic to work on his source material. Such logic is built upon the three part syllogism: a major premise: *All men are mortal;* a minor premise: *Socrates is a man;* a conclusion: *therefore Socrates is mortal.* Then this conclusion can be used as a major or minor premise in further syllogisms until the thinker reaches an answer to his problem.[2]

As early as the ninth century the conflict between faith and reason had been pointed up by John Scotus Erigena who insisted that both reason and the Scriptures had come from God, and that there could be no conflict between them. After his time, the Church's stand on faith alone had been reaffirmed, particularly by Anselm of Canterbury in the eleventh century.

This reaffirmation was not to stand unchallenged for long. In the late eleventh century a philosophic conflict broke out which was called the Battle of Universals. The "battle" involved a lengthy philosophic dispute, greatly simplified here, about the nature of reality. Twentieth-century students may view this as a dry wrangle between a number of ivory-tower philosophers, but it was not. In the first place it has been pointed out that the idea of reality which is held at any time determines the nature of civilization, and that a change in this idea will bring about a change in the way people think and live. We are dealing with thinkers as important to their time as Einstein and Freud have been to ours. Second, the philosophers were important Churchmen, and since the Church was the central institution of the time, any change in its position would and did have a very great effect on life itself. True, the peasant on the farm or the craftsman in his shop neither knew or cared about the Battle of Universals, but the men concerned in it were the men who made and moved society as a whole.

To see the nature of this "battle" we may remember that one of the strongest foundations of Church doctrine was a Christian adaptation of the neoplatonist belief that reality was permanent, unchanging, without any body or material substance, existing in the Mind of God. This position sprang from Plato's belief in essences, forms, or ideas as the ultimate reality. Thus body and substance, all physical things which change were only illusory shadows, imperfect copies, of the Idea (see Plato's "Allegory of the Cave" for a full explanation). According to this accepted doctrine, the human body was to be disregarded and a study of the physical world wasted time which should be spent seeking eternal truths. This neoplatonic, Augustinian doctrine was accepted by the "Establishment" up to the eleventh century, and became known as the *Realist* position.

The philosopher Roscellinus first challenged this doctrine and established what was called the *Nominalist* position, very close to the belief of most people today. He said that physical things were the only reality. For example, each sense-apparent tree is real and as far as trees are concerned, no higher reality exists. The question then arises, "How can we know the 'idea' tree?" Certainly we know these insubstantial ideas, for we can speak of trees, or men, or elephants or justice when no specific one is present to our senses. Roscellinus answered that these "ideas" were only names (hence the word *Nominalist*), and that we form the idea as a generalization only after experience with a great number of individual things. We experience, he said, specific examples of elms, pines, palms, and all kinds of trees. In our mind we then generalize and form the "idea" tree so that we can talk about the species—and understand each other—in the middle of the ocean, with no specific tree within a thousand miles.

The two positions in the battle were thus established, as opposite as any two opposites can be. William of Champeaux stoutly defended the Realist position, the standard doctrine of the Church. If he should fail, the Church itself would be in danger, and indeed it was.

A middle position was suggested by the brilliant thinker Peter Abelard, probably the most popular teacher in the early University of Paris. (Abelard is shown as a hero for the twentieth century as well as a brilliant thinker of the eleventh and twelfth centuries in the contemporary play, *Abelard and Heloise.*) Abelard had studied with both Roscellinus and William of Champeaux and knew their arguments thoroughly and, as a matter of interest, he defeated William in a public debate on the nature of the universals. (Henry Adams in *Mont-St. Michel and Chartres* gives an imaginary debate between the two which is not too difficult

2. The modern student tends to scoff at this type of reasoning until he remembers that *every* culture sets similar limits to its thought process. For example, in the early twentieth century, the searcher for truth drew the basic material for his investigation from the world of the senses (he was not encouraged to go outside of this realm) and then used the scientific method to refine his raw data and find answers to his questions. The type of knowledge found through the use of this technique of research is totally different from that found in the Middle Ages, but the limitations are equally severe. A God-centered society results from one method, a completely materialistic society comes from the other. The present failure of our materialistic culture testifies to some limitations of our way of thought.

to follow.) Abelard's compromise became known as the *Conceptualist* position, and anticipates an Aristotelian view of the problem even before the whole body of Aristotle's works was known to Europe. The Conceptualist view can be stated rather quickly, for it will become much better developed with the work of St. Thomas a century or so later. Briefly, Abelard held that the *idea* is *real*, but that it does not exist either before a particular physical thing or after it. That is, reality as idea exists only in the physical, sense-apparent object.

Abelard's intellectual daring was condemned by the Church, but the Battle of Universals was debated without conclusion for a century. The Realist, the Nominalist, and the Conceptualist positions remained at loggerheads and were a sore point in Church doctrine until the great synthesis which was to be made by St. Thomas who established what was to become the official dogma of the Church.

Abelard not only developed one of the sides in the Battle of Universals, but he threw another bombshell into the religious thought of the time when he published his book *Sic et non* ("Yes and No"). On remembers that the source of all knowledge at the time lay in the Scriptures and the writings of the early commentators on the Bible, the Church Fathers. In *Sic et non* Abelard proposed a number of important religious questions, then, in opposite columns set down what the Fathers had written on the subject. In doing so, he demonstrated that one could find contradictory answers in this body of writings. If this body was the source of knowledge, and if contradictions existed within it, as Abelard clearly showed, how wrong must conclusions be which were based on this writing. The whole way of thought of Scholasticism was threatened if its original source of knowledge was self-contradictory, and all answers to questions which had been derived by the method must be suspect.

Still another fire broke out in the structure of the Church with the rediscovery of all of Aristotle's works in the last part of the twelfth century. Because his logic had been universally used as the method of thinking, Aristotle, though a pagan, was perhaps the most venerated name among all of the world's philosophers throughout the early Middle Ages, but only his work on logic was known to the philosophers of the time. About the year 1200 almost the entire body of his works was brought into Europe in a curious form. Aristotle had written in Greek, Syrian scholars had translated him into Syriac, then Arabic writers had converted those translations into Arabic. Finally, through the Moslems in Spain, the body of thought was discovered, turned into medieval Latin and made available to Europe. The discovery of this whole body of scientific knowledge posed several touchy questions, but the most important was that it revealed that Aristotle had developed a very complete knowledge of the world by investigation and classifying *physical* things. The Church had stood against any studies of the physical world, yet here was a man more revered by scholars than were most of the saints, who had developed his knowledge by such investigation. The impact was about as great as if we discovered that one of our most revered scientists received his knowledge and made his discoveries by consulting a witch doctor. What was the Church to do?

The first reaction was to ban the newly discovered works entirely, and in 1210 and for the next few years we have records of the books being banned at the University of Paris. The discovery of the books was sufficiently well known, however, that they could not so conveniently be done away with. The next step was the publication of "authorized" versions from which all of Aristotle's ideas which were directly contradictory to Church doctrine had been expurgated. Since the minds of the scholars were hungry for new material, this step did not work either, and finally the entire body of knowledge was made available to the scholars of the late Middle Ages.

The church had preached complete otherworldliness and disdained earthly knowledge except as it seemed to be a symbol or testimony of Scriptural knowledge and heavenly life. Yet these books revealed that the most revered mind of the Middle Ages had dissected animals to discover similarities and differences between species; had classified plants according to their structure. Thus another problem was presented, demanding synthesis if the Church was to maintain its authority.

The rise of the universities is the last of the symptoms of new life which we will consider here. Actually their origin is very obscure, for we have little knowledge of them until their formal charters were issued. In Christian Europe (as different from Spain) the University of Salerno, which specialized in medicine, was probably the earliest, for we have records of its existence in the middle of the eleventh century, yet situated in southern Italy, it had little influence on the general dawn of culture. The University of Bologna with its great law school was given a formal grant of rights in 1158; the University of Paris was granted a royal charter in 1200 and a Papal license in 1231. Oxford was formed in the twelfth century when a group of teachers and students seceded from Paris, and Cambridge came into being somewhat later when a dissident group left Oxford. The growth was so rapid that by the end of the Middle Ages we find eighty universities scattered throughout Europe. The actual founding dates for the universities are of relatively little importance since it is probable that schools had existed in connection with cathedrals and abbeys where the universities were founded at least a century before formal charters were granted; this, at least, was the case with the University of Paris, which had a long history as the Cathedral School of Notre Dame before it was licensed as a university. Nor did the schools have a smooth course throughout; the occasion for the Papal license of the University of Paris in 1231 was the reopening of the University which had been closed for two years following a riot between students and the city authorities. Few things are new under the sun!

The universities were simply guilds of scholars and teachers, at first with no campus and no buildings. Classes were held in any rooms available, usually in churches. Original charters and agreements consisted of regulations limiting rental charges for rooms, the price of books (usually rented, too, since the hand-copied manuscripts were rare and expensive), the number of classes a student had to attend to be considered officially as a student (usually two a week), and the number of lectures and their length that a professor had to give in order to collect his fees. Many students and professors wandered all over Europe from one university to another, living the life of vagabonds, beggars, thieves, and drunkards, and the songs of the wandering scholars (the goliards) testify to their worldly interests. Of course, then, as now, we have records only of the students who got into trouble or who composed poetry; most of the serious ones who only worked and studied remain anonymous.

This was a new group of people who had been unknown in the early Middle Ages. They were eager for all sorts of knowledge and questing for experience. Their motto may well have been Abelard's famous teaching, "for by doubting we come to inquiry, by inquiry we discover the truth." These people would not tolerate a culture which walled itself in by authority and allowed no questioning of that authority. Here, as in most areas of life in the late Middle Ages we see life bursting out at the seams.

At the end of the preceding chapter we saw that medieval man by the year 1000 had shut himself up in the narrow walls of his authoritarian church, of feudalism and manorialism. These provided a good measure of physical and mental safety, but little room in which to move about. With the rise of cities, the growth of the feminine influence in society and the Cult of the Virgin, and with all of the intellectual ferment which involved the philosophers and was propagated in the universities, we see men breaking down the narrow walls to search for knowledge in the physical world rather than the world of ancient books; from their crusades they learned that life here on this earth could be beautiful, an idea enhanced by the civilizing effects of chivalry, courtly love, and the Cult of the Virgin. In the ferment of city life and in the idea-ferment of the universities all established modes of existence were questioned. This questioning is revealed in the literature of the time.

MAN'S QUESTIONS AS SEEN IN EARLY LITERATURE

The morality play of *Everyman* was perhaps the best-known literary work in the mid-Middle Ages, for it was played in all the cities and in every town and hamlet throughout Europe. It is interesting that the Churchmen felt the necessity of presenting this drama so widely. Could they have felt the need for a strong reinforcement of the teachings of the old puritanical way of life? Writing such as this comes out only when the ideas which it teaches are threatened. What does it teach? The events of life which bring pleasure are evil, it tells us. Knowledge will carry us as far as the grave, as will our five wits, and even our beauty; only our good deeds and our penance will go with us beyond that event. The entrance to heaven is kept, not by angels, but by an accountant who takes the record book of the individual, posts and makes double entries, and comes forth with the verdict: eternal bliss or eternal damnation. There is no middle ground. Finally, the conception of a way of life in *Everyman* denies the human personality, since the individual has no chance to set his own purposes. The purpose is established from outside by the celestial accountants, and the fear of death is ever-present to frighten the individual into obedience.

A delightful contrast to *Everyman* points up the conflict between the dismal view of that drama as it is opposed by complete delight here and now in the *chant-fable*, *Aucassin and Nicolette*. If one has much imagination, he smiles with pleasure at the sensuous description of Nicolette, or the piling up of ludicrous incidents: Aucassin riding forth to battle like every stereotype of the medieval knight, only to forget what he should be doing, and ending as a captive; or again, falling off his horse and breaking his collar bone. Meanwhile Nicolette hides behind a bush and waits until he drags himself most painfully into her little bower before she gives him comfort and love which is more potent than penicillin. One could list many incidents, or call attention to the gracefulness of the verse as opposed to the tumbling-potatoes-on-the-floor rhythms of *Everyman*. The *chant-fable* not only speaks of the joy of life, it *is* that joy. The two as a side-by-side contrast ask the question, "Which way is this civilization to go?"

Chaucer, in his "Prologue to the Canterbury Tales," illustrates this problem, though his tone and outlook are essentially realistic. While he is not seeking to illustrate anything, while he is trying only to describe an assortment of people with their too human weakness, yet he poses the problem nevertheless. The basic nature of the gathering of the pilgrims is a case in point. The pilgrimage to the Shrine of St. Thomas is, or should be, a religious exercise. Yet these people, or some of them, at any rate, seem to be there for an extended picnic, and nothing else. In the characters, again, we see the division of personality. On the one hand we have the poor and virtuous Parson; on the other we see the Friar, the Summoner, and the Pardoner, who are devoted entirely to the gratification of the flesh, and all of whom exploit their religious affiliation to make these gratifications possible.

In some instances we see the city men, the new class of merchants, lawyers, doctors, and guildsmen. Their aim is profit, and they will not be stopped by nice concerns of religion in order to achieve their purpose. They partake of the upsurging spirit which denies the balance of the old Graeco-Roman tradition. Still another interesting group is composed of the knight, his son, and the prioress, who represent the ideals of chivalry, and of a religion which is turning from fear to beauty for its attractiveness. Chaucer draws no moral from this collection of people, nor does he attempt to state a problem with the exactness of a mathematician or a social worker. What does the reader make of this collection of medieval men and women?

Nowhere is the spiritual conflict of the time better illustrated than in the student songs, for the universities themselves were products of the new and stirring life. The pulls upon the personality are particularly evident in one of the student creeds in which the dying goliard burlesques the creed of the Church. With almost savage vigor he takes each word of the Church's creed and turns it to a flaunting of his vices. Then the student faces the last moment and is gripped by a fear of the unknown to which he is committing himself: a fear which is supported by 500 years of religious tradition. With an anguish which strikes home to the reader, he commits his soul of God and begs for the last sacrament of the Church.

THE MEDIEVAL SYNTHESIS

To summarize the conflicts in the late Middle Ages, which have been suggested, the clash of the times came about in new secular ways of thinking and living which challenged the older religious and mystic ways. Where was the art that could bring these together in a new synthesis? Where were the men who could define new relationships between men and the universe, men and God, the individual man and society as a whole? Where could be found artists to suggest new purposes for life since the old were so sorely challenged?

It would seem that this new synthesis came about in three places. In philosophy, it was St. Thomas Aquinas who built a new philosophic structure which could accommodate the divergent points of view. In art, the medieval Gothic cathedral furnished a synthesis at the point when the artist's skill and the function came together. Chartres Cathedral is the prime example of such a structure. In literature, the new balance was suggested by Dante Alighieri in *The Divine Comedy*. Let us look briefly at the ways in which the synthesis was achieved in these three forms.

It cannot be our purpose here to go into detail in a discussion of the doctrines of St. Thomas. Rather, we shall here show how he reconciled some of the contradictions of the time. In discussing Thomas' thought, one can scarcely avoid using the symbol of the equilateral triangle as a representation of the individual person, of the nation, and of the universe, for all of his ideas seem to shape themselves around that symbol. It was no accident that this is also the symbol of the Trinity of God; it may have been accident that it is also a shape which suggests both stability and upward motion. In its visual form it unifies the energy of the Celto-Germanic spirit with the desire for stability of the Graeco-Roman.

In Thomas' unification of Aristotelian thought with that of the Church, he accepted the central Aristotelian doctrine, similar to that of the conceptualists. This doctrine was that matter and form (or idea) cannot exist separately. Matter, he said, had only potentiality, that is the possibility of being itself, until it was entered into by the idea of the thing. Then it became that thing. For example, "clay" is not "brick," nor is there "brick" without "clay"; but when "clay," which has only potentiality by itself, is joined with the form or idea of "brick," then the "brick" exists. Next, he said, lower forms of existence are only matter in the formation of higher forms. And everything, he said, was moving, changing, growing, turning into something else. This movement is the movement toward perfection, which is God. Thus the First Mover, God, does not move things from behind, but is the purpose toward which all things are moving. Since things must desire the thing toward which they move, then the motive force is the love of God.

This argument involves the most important of Thomas's proofs of the existence of God. (He proposed five such proofs, bearing out his belief that all things accepted by faith could be proved by reason.) His most famous proof is that of motion. Very briefly stated, this proof proceeds in this way: We see motion. If there is motion, there must be a mover. If we think backward; for example, I roll a stone; something causes me to move to roll it; but something causes the mover which moves me, etc., we have an endless and infinite series of movers. On the other hand, consider the first mover as a force which attracts rather than pushes from behind. Then we can come to a first "attracting force" (like a magnet) which sets all other things in motion. This First Mover, or, if you will, the Unmoved Mover is God, pulling all things toward himself.

Furthermore, in the idea that both *form* and *matter* are necessary for reality, Thomas brought together the conflicting arguments in the Battle of Universals. Here we may consider the question of whether form (or Idea) has existence *before*, or only *in* a specific thing, and whether it exists *after* the specific has vanished. All three, said Thomas. The Idea exists (as potentiality) before the thing; it exists in the thing, and in its continuing progress upward, it exists after the particular thing. Thus, borrowing heavily from the Conceptualist view, he brought the three positions into harmony.

It was with the doctrine of lower and higher forms, all in motion toward perfection, that Thomas brought together the conflict between the growing desire of people for natural knowledge and the doctrine of the Church that such knowledge was a study of nothingness, for, said Thomas, the highest human studies are philosophy and law. He considered philosophy as a study of the humanly knowable laws for the discipline of the spirit, and law, of course, as the study of the rules for the governing of man's physical nature. Both, according to the Aristotelian concept of reality, are necessary and equal. To reach a knowledge of these subjects, a study of all forms and all matter is necessary. It is in this way that men attain their highest perfection—through knowledge.

Then, he continued, there is another realm of knowledge, complementary to philosophy. This is theology, which has its source in God. It cannot be understood through natural learning, but only by revelation. The two, however, are not opposed to each other. Rather, a knowledge of philosophy leads to the possibility of receiving revelation and revelation presupposes a knowledge of philosophy. Finally, he said that true knowledge, the union with the divine science, came only after death. It was the duty of man, therefore, during his lifetime to acquire as much natural knowledge as possible that he might be fit to receive the final revelation of God after his death.

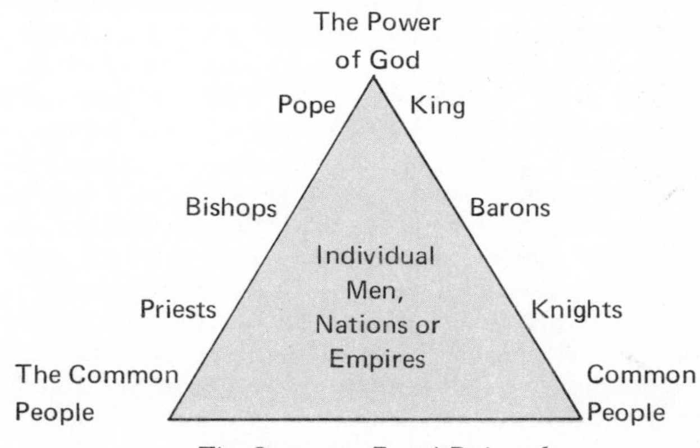

The Separate, Equal Roles of Church and State

The settlement of the opposition of Church and State came with a justification of feudalism on the basis of the lower forms constantly seeking the higher. However, in the governing of man he believed Church and State equal, with both the King and the Pope receiving their power directly from God. It was the duty of the king to administer God's laws for the physical nature of man; of the Pope and the Church to administer the law for the spirit of man. This solution, which justified the status quo, ran contrary to the secular spirit of the time and the growing nationalism. Thomas's argument would not stand for long against the moving social and political forces.

The pull of life and death, perhaps the greatest question of all, was solved by St. Thomas, first with the Aristotelian doctrine of matter and form existing only when they were together and in each other. With this, and with Thomas' insistence that natural knowledge, gained through the use of human senses, was necessary for the perfection of the human being, he banished the dualism which had existed since the time of Augustine and the idea of the City of God. Hereafter, both man's body and soul were necessary for his earthly perfection, the one as important as the other.

Thus it was that the Middle Ages, in this final great synthesis, found freedom and opened the way for man to develop himself, like the medieval city, outside of its early walls, yet still in keeping with the fundamental pattern. The way for science

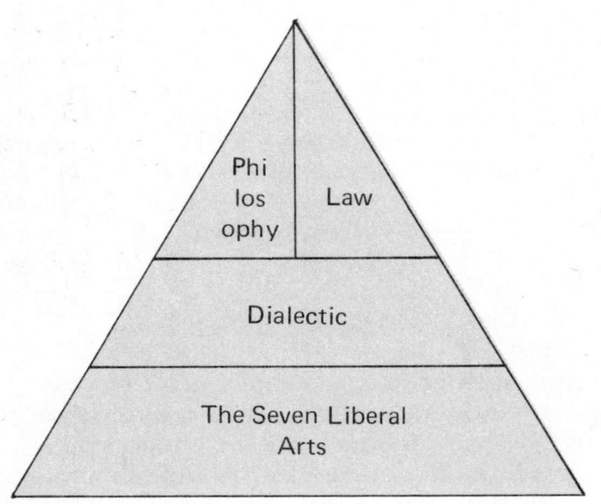

Thomas' Plan of Education

was now open, hate for the body was banished, the state was recognized as one of the forms of order leading to the highest order, that of the kingdom of God.

Without becoming too technical, this may suggest the kind of synthesis which was made in philosophy. For the common man, however, the involved thinking of philosophers has little meaning. In the Middle Ages, it was the common man, as well as the serious thinker, who needed a solution to the problems which were splitting his personality.

For this common man, it is probable that the Gothic cathedral effected this synthesis. The thrust of the cathedral was upward. Standing before it, the beholder's eye moved up its great towers, impelled by the pointed arches, until the eye reached the spire which directed it even farther upward—toward heaven. In this way was the need for the other-worldly satisfied. So, too, did the figures in the stained-glass windows tell the stories of the Bible and the lives of saints and satisfy the religious needs of the time. It is foolish to argue that the common man could "read" the stories told in the windows. Even with opera glasses we cannot clearly read the upper pictures. However, the profuse beauty of colored light, like the echo of the unintelligible Latin ecclesiastical chants echoing through the arches, filled the onlooker with a sense of beauty and awe.

So there was more to the cathedral than lessons, for here was beauty. Not only did the windows preach the gospel, but their colors also brought joy to the beholder. The pageantry of the church was a thing of splendor made colorful by the rich garments of the bishop and those who assisted him at the mass, by the heaviness of the incense, and by the chant of the choir. All these brought richness to the life of the medieval man who sought such satisfaction in his day-to-day living. Even the task of building these cathedrals, a great communal effort shared alike by nobility, wealthy burghers, and the common men, furnished a creative outlet for the energies of these people of the Middle Ages.

Architecturally, the Gothic cathedral furnished a symbol of balance between classic and energetic. It achieved balanced tension and unity, yet it had the thrust, the upward push, which we have remarked as characteristic of the northern personality. The elongated statuary of the portals, the pointed arches, the flying buttresses, beautiful in themselves and symbolic of the desire to go upward beyond the limits which wall and column could support, all these are marks of the Gothic.

Among the thousands of symbols connected with the Gothic cathedral, one significance of the tower deserves mention. The lower, heavy square tower represented earthly life. The spire signified man's aspiration toward the divine. And finally, the elevation of the eye from the last point of physical stone toward the sky suggested man's union with God. The architect of the old tower at Chartres had the right idea when he created a transition between the square tower and the octagonal spire which is almost imperceptible. In a truly Thomistic sense, the things of this world blend perfectly with those of the next; the physical and the spiritual are united. The transition triumphs both as architecture and as symbol of the best thought of the time.

In one other aspect the cathedral was the symbol of the synthesis of the Middle Ages, for it was here that the Cult of the Virgin reached its height. The sudden flowering of this cult may be ascribed to the sense of sin which obsessed the people, convinced as they were of their moral deformity from Adam, and of their weakness to withstand the pulls of the world around them. For them, the justice of the Trinity was a thing to flee from, and they fell back upon the mercy of the Mother. Miracles were needed to insure their salvation, and a whole body of literature has grown up to tell of the miracles wrought by the Gracious Lady. To quote Adams:

> To peasants, and beggars, and people in trouble, this sense of her power and calm is better than active sympathy. People who suffer beyond the formulas of expression—who are crushed into silence, and beyond pain—want no display of emotion—no bleeding heart—no weeping at the foot of the Cross—no hysterics—no phrases! They want to see God, and to know that He is watching over His own. How many women are there, in this mass of thirteenth century suppliants, who have lost children? Probably nearly all, for the death rate is very high in the conditions of medieval life. There are thousands of such women here, for it is precisely this class who come most; and probably every one of them has looked up to Mary in her great window, and has felt actual certainty, as though she saw with her own eyes—there in heaven, while she looked—her own lost baby playing with the Christ-child at the Virgin's knee, as much at home as the saints, and much more at home than the kings. Before rising from her knees, every one of these women will have bent down and kissed the stone pavement in gratitude for Mary's mercy. The earth, she says, is a sorry place, and the best of it is bad enough . . . but there above is Mary in heaven who sees and hears me as I see her, and who keeps my little boy till I come; so I can wait with patience, more or less! Saints and prophets and martyrs are all very well, and Christ is very sublime and just, but Mary knows!

This worship of the woman brought comfort, solace, and understanding. For the nobleman, the joys of the world could be called courtesy and courteous love, all devoted to the woman and eventually to the Virgin. Here, for the man of noble birth, the natural desires could be regulated and channeled, put in the corsets of correct manners which were dictated by the great ladies and their courts of love. And for the common man, the juggler, there was something else. There was escape from justice by throwing himself on mercy and upon the hope and expectation of miracles. The sins and errors which could in no way escape justice might be atoned through the mercy of the Mother of God. Even more, here we find a spiritual democracy; an outlet for the conscious or unconscious desire for equality within the unequal feudal system. This, of course, was a new desire for men, one which had risen in the Middle Ages since the growth of cities; the possibility of freedom and equality had dawned upon the mind of men who previously had assumed inequality to be the natural order. Men were not yet ready for equality on earth, however, but in the Virgin's sight, the juggler doing his tricks for her amusement was as important as the learned friar writing books according to the rules of scholasticism.

The cathedral was all these things to the common man of the Middle Ages. At the same time it provided beauty in the present life and inspiration to heaven. It curbed Gothic energy and heightened and vitalized classic stability. At its height, let us say at the time of the building of the older tower of Chartres, it represented the golden moment in the development of an art form when the artist is able to do exactly what he has to do, when he has gained freedom in his medium.

In addition to the cathedral, there were other great syntheses of medieval life. We have already spoken of the great philosophic one of St. Thomas which brought the warring doctrines of the Church together into a single firm structure. Dante's *Commedia* in the realm of literature was the other.

For the present study, the important thing about the *Commedia* was the removal of the restrictions which earlier centuries had imposed on men. The goal and final purpose of man was still the attainment of heaven and the bliss of that afterlife, but man was left free to achieve this goal through his own power and the discipline of his own will. Dante's God was no accountant, such as we found in *Everyman.* Rather He was perfect wisdom, which, in Dante's mind, was almost synonymous with love. Man's purpose and goal, like the enteleche of Aristotle was perfect union with this God. For Dante, this heavenly state is man's true home, which he must ever earn anew because of Adam's sin. Furthermore, man, while he is alive, cannot know the wisdom, or order, or love of God; for salvation, the final union is still a matter of God's grace rather than a result of man's effort. It is as if God's wisdom is a different category of wisdom from that of human beings, one to which people may aspire, but to which they can be admitted only by the will of God.

While men may not achieve union with God through their own efforts, they may prepare themselves for it by gaining the maturity which comes with earthly wisdom. This mature nature is called innocence by Dante, by which he meant the happy state of Adam before the fall. It is for this reason that Dante places the Garden of Eden, the Earthly Paradise, at the top of the mountain of Purgatory. It is here that men, after having attained their full maturity, the sum total of human wisdom, may await the act of God which will transport them into the category beyond.

Dante's concept differs in another way from that of the author of *Everyman.* In that grim sermon-drama, man is drawn to God through fear. With Dante, mankind is a part of God's order, which is love; so it is through the pull of love that man works toward his great purpose. And with Dante, man has free will; the great choice is left squarely with him. On earth he may make his choice, and his choice, expressed in faith and works, becomes his destiny in the afterlife.

What are the choices? Since the way of God is discipline and orderliness, the way of Satan is disorder and lack of proportion. God himself is perfect freedom, and the way toward him is the constant increase of one's personal freedom. Essential sin is the loss of freedom. This idea can be illustrated with the simple and not *too* sinful example of smoking—or any other addiction.

At first—in relation to cigarettes—the individual is ignorant, knowing neither the pleasures or the harms of smoking. So, for one reason or another, he tries one. *The act in itself is not sinful,* nor are subsequent experiences with smoking. The person always says, "I can quit any time." And, for a time that is true. A time comes, however, when given a choice of smoking or not smoking, the true addict will always choose to smoke; he has lost the power to say no, and if cigarettes are denied him, he will end up climbing the wall. Thus he has sacrificed one aspect of his freedom of choice, and this, for Dante, is sin. Godlike freedom is the ability to say yes, no, or any of the choices between. Sin is loss of that ability, and in Dante's Hell we see that the degree of sin is measured by the extent to which the person consciously twists his body or his intellect away from free choice. The person who loses hope of making free choices is destined for Hell, and the inscription which Dante envisions over the mouth of Hell, "Abandon hope, all ye that enter here," is an expression of the state which the condemned ones have reached. In their choice, they have abandoned all hope and all desire to be anything or anywhere else. The punishments which Dante saw for the souls in Hell are symbolic of the nature which they have made for themselves. With the body removed, in other words, we see them exactly as they have made themselves to be. Step by descending step we traverse the cone of Hell, in each lower depth viewing the souls who are deeper and deeper in sin. Step by descending step we see these souls deprived of more and more freedom, until at the very bottom of the pit we find Satan, the greatest sinner all, deprived of movement, frozen, as he is, in ice. So is he bound by his sins.

Emerging with Dante at the base of the mountain of Purgatory, we find another picture. Here are the souls who have erred, who have somehow strayed in their earthly lives from the path of wisdom. The difference is that these people still have hope; they aspire toward their own true selves and toward God. Their labors are difficult as they expiate their sin, but through all the labor they are joyous, for they know that the end will be full wisdom and maturity, the Garden of Eden, and the state of Earthly Paradise. It is of utmost importance to realize that each soul decides for itself when it is completely purged of any sin and is ready to move upward to another cornice of the mountain. The decision is never made by an angel or any other outside force. So free of envy are all the souls on the mountain that they chant *Gloria in excelsis* in unison when an individual moves upward.

Finally in Heaven, and guided by Beatrice, Dante receives instruction in theology, the science of God. It is here that he sees the perfect order of the whole universe, both of men and of angels. He sees the Church and its officers as the guardians of man's spirit and he sees the kings' importance to God, for they maintain temporal order on earth. Here, too, he finds freedom, as opposed to the ever-increasing bondage which he witnessed in Hell, for in Heaven, though the souls are symbolically assigned to different spheres as a result of their different capacities for joy and love, yet they are actually free to pass through all the spheres and to approach the throne of God itself. There is no bondage here. In the final Cantos of the *Paradiso*, Dante comes as close as any human being can to communicating the mystic union of the soul with God as actual living experience.

Is this only a poem of death, or does Dante have something to say for men-alive? We believe that he has much to say to us. He says that men must make their choice, for which they have their own wills. If they choose wisely, they will choose a life of order and discipline. Throughout their life, they will gain knowledge, for that and its resultant wisdom will make men free. Finally, he tells us, man's studies should turn to philosophy and law, the fields of knowledge which represent the best possible concepts of order on earth; the former disciplines and instructs the spirit, the latter has the same function in man's temporal dealings with other men. This life will be one which is joyously led, and which leads to the final realization of the true self when, by the will of God, the soul is united with the perfect wisdom.

What has Dante brought together here? In the first place, he envisions a life at once balanced and aspiring. These are the Gothic and classic elements of the Middle Ages. He brings together the desire for broad worldly knowledge and religion, for his poem itself is scientific according to the science of his time, and he counsels the widest possible earthly knowledge as a necessary condition for heavenly bliss. He brings together the pulls of life and death, for his concept of the full life is one which is joyous and in which men use their full powers, yet use them as they aspire to the greatest possible happiness and freedom both now and in the hereafter. Finally, he unites the rival claims of pope and king as he sees each, working God's will and God's order on earth, each in his own way and in his own place.

This is the final answer of the Middle Ages to the great question of man's search for freedom. It started with the building of walls, for men needed their protection. It has progressed through the stage where men found their walls no longer necessary for protection and found them cramping in the human desire for the good life. It emerges in a great synthesis in which human nature is free, by nature divine, but in which men have freedom of choice. The *Commedia* unites body and soul, in that the process of discipline, which the individual must choose for himself, is the discipline which must occur in the present life; a discipline, which in its order, produces freedom here and prepares the spirit for freedom in the afterlife. Particularly in the cathedrals and in the *Commedia* do we see the artist at work, proposing new answers to the great questions of mankind. It is upon these answers that the institutions are to be reshaped, and upon them that a new pattern for existence is to be built.

What was the nature of human freedom within this new design? The period of synthesis during the late Middle Ages was brief. Dante lived from 1265 to 1321. St. Thomas lived from 1225 to 1274. Chartres dates from the thirteenth century. Yet by the middle of the fifteenth century, the Renaissance had burst upon Europe. The forces which had challenged the old walls of life which had been built during the Dark Ages (the years 500 to 1000) were too strong to be held in check, and the secular spirit was to go ahead to new triumphs. But in those 200 years, we can witness a new freedom toward which many world-weary people of the twentieth century look back with longing. It is worthy of at least a brief examination.

The single and fundamental characteristic of medieval freedom lies in the sense of unity which furnished strict rules for all types of human behavior, and yet which furnished complete individual freedom to create within those rules. This seems to be a paradox, a contradiction. At least it can be seen as a most delicate balance between individual aspiration and endeavor and community solidarity which offers stability.

Perhaps better than anywhere else, this balance can be seen in the art of the late Middle Ages. Consider, for example, the cathedral. Its pattern was extremely strict. It must be oriented with the altar toward the east. It must be cruciform. Each part of the structure carried some symbolic meaning, so that the symbols must be exactly treated. All this was a part of the strict rule which governed art and life in the period of balance.

Yet consider the freedom of the individual within this rule. The stonecarver was free to do as he wanted. If he wanted to carve little fat angels or animals which he had seen or imagined, that was his decision. One sees much of this type of work on the miserere seats in the choir stall. Here a woodcarver thought that it would be fun to carve a pig playing a fiddle. No sooner thought of than started! Or somewhere else, the carver wished to caricature a fat burgher of the town. He could do it because he was a free man, working within the limits of the grand design. These were no machine-made units to be put up as they came from the machine. They were the work of free and independent craftsmen.

This same freedom within strict limits is found in all spheres of activity during the late Middle Ages. For example, the craftsman necessarily belonged to his guild. It was the association which regulated the quality of his work, the price which could be charged, and many other things. Beyond that, the guild served as an insurance and burial society for its members, a social group, and a dramatic society, since the mystery and miracle plays which amused and inspired the city-dwellers were functions of the guilds. The guild hall was not only a place of business, but was also a social center where banquets, weddings, and balls were held. The guild also regulated very strictly the membership within itself, and established stringent rules for the training of the craftsmen. All these point to the strict communal regulation of the individual.

But within those limits, the member of a guild, the shoemaker, let us say, was absolutely free. He had his own shop, which was part of his home. He did his work only on order, so that when there was no business, he could lock up and take the members of his family, together with the apprentices and journeymen in his shop, and go for an outing in the country. Furthermore, and one suspects that this is the important aspect of the whole system, each pair of shoes was an individual creation. The pride of craft and of creation entered into all of the work which was done, and the master craftsman developed a sense of pride in each item of his work. The very fact that he did the whole job, from heel to toe, from sole to the very top of the uppers, gave him a sense of responsibility and of pride.

The story of "Our Lady's Juggler" reveals the same type of freedom within religion. The Catholic creed was strict, and its rules were absolute. But within them men were free. There was sufficient opportunity for individual practice of the religious observances to satisfy each person. Dante's idea of freedom as participation in the wisdom, the order, and the love of God are of great importance here. The man who was not free was the one who, by his own choices, had rendered himself inhuman in outward form and in nature. The order of God, however, was of sufficient latitude that men could make a comfortable life within it. In addition to this, there was the one provision of the Christian scheme of things which has always been a source of strength for that faith. This was the idea that a mistake does not mean inevitable damnation. Such an error may need purging, but it is only when one comes to a conscious desire for the way of evil that one is damned.

The concept of freedom in this period of balance in the Middle Ages, then, was one in which all the forces of the culture grouped themselves around the individual to give him support. Yet they did not hamper his freedom, his individuality, or his creativity as long as he stayed within the rules of that culture.

This balance, like all others which we have seen, is too delicate to last. Within a brief time, the secular forces which we have seen born during the Middle Ages were to triumph, breaking down the new designs which had been made by St. Thomas, by the architects of the great cathedrals, and by Dante. The fundamental beliefs of the culture were to change in a new epoch which we call the Renaissance.

Bibliography

General

H.O. Taylor. *The Medieval Mind.*

Philosophy

Anne Freemantle, ed. *The Age of Belief* (Chap. 6 to the end).

Literature

1. Chaucer. *The Canterbury Tales.* The student will

enjoy reading all the tales and their introductions, but if a selection must be made, we recommend "The Knight's Tale," the "Franklin's Tale," and the "Reve's Tale" as samples of different types of medieval literature.

2. Dante. *Divine Comedy*. The "Purgatory" and "Paradise." After an exploration of the possibilities for evil in the human soul (Hell), it is good to see the way of redemption and the soul's potentiality for good, culminating in the mystic union with God.

   One can easily find a whole library of scholarly works on Dante; Dorothy Sayers' *Further Papers on Dante* is very helpful.

3. St. Francis. *The Little Flowers of St. Francis*. L. Sherley-Price, trans., Baltimore, Md: Penguin Books, Inc. The universal empathy of this mystic saint is revealed in these poems.

The Medieval Synthesis in Art

CHAPTER 15

■ The thousand years of European history between 450 and 1450 has often been called the "Dark Ages" or the medieval period of Western civilization. Antiquity, or Graeco-Roman culture, began this period and the Renaissance, or revival of antiquity, ended it. Of course the entire concept of "medieval" implies that classical culture was dormant for a thousand years while Europe floundered in barbarism, that the period was without a culture or art of any significance. In many respects this interpretation is incorrect: the Graeco-Roman tradition never died; the late medieval period saw a cultural development that was as vital in its time and as influential for our time as the Graeco-Roman culture; the so-called Renaissance was as much evolutionary as revolutionary in its development from the Gothic or late medieval culture.

Previously we have discussed the Graeco-Roman artistic traditions which by the fourth century showed drastic changes caused by the military, economic, and political disintegration of the Roman Empire and, above all, by the growth of Christianity. Throughout the medieval period many scholars, artists, and emperors were deeply conscious of the great Mediterranean cultures, sought in many ways to preserve much of the Graeco-Roman heritage and, in the case of Charlemagne, pursued a conscious policy of classical revival. The fact that the Frankish emperor sought to "revive" classical traditions indicates that classicism was at best a secondary force in early medieval society. This book, however, testifies to the potency and endurance of the Carolingian achievement, for it is printed in letters whose shapes derive from Carolingian writing which was developed, partially, in order to transcribe and transmit the work of great Latin writers. Manuscript paintings, too, were often based on Roman or Greek models and should be considered as visual counterparts of classical texts. Even the Byzantine heritage is seen in Charlemagne's court church at Aachen (AH-ken) which was modeled on St. Vitale in Ravenna. It is difficult to find many significant artistic monuments that strongly reflect the Graeco-Roman or Byzantine cultures during the early Middle Ages (450-1000); it is equally difficult to find many significant art works of any kind from this period. European culture was, indeed, at low ebb during this time. What is important to understand is that the barbaric peoples were introducing vital and new elements throughout this era. In the eleventh through the fifteenth centuries, Roman, Byzantine, and barbarian artistic and philosophic elements would reach high degrees of influence under the aegis of Christianity to produce the medieval synthesis known as Gothic art.

THE EARLY MIDDLE AGES 450-1000

At the time of its greatest expansion, the Roman Empire did not extend into Ireland, which was then occupied by the Celts, and had only limited control of western Europe north of the Alps where the Germanic peoples engaged the Roman legions in almost constant warfare. The decline of the Western Roman empire and the concomitant rise of Germanic power, so clearly evident as early as the fifth century, caused an almost complete dissolution of classicism or Mediterranean culture as the center of gravity of European civilization shifted northward. Unfortunately, perhaps, the artistic achievement of these new masters of Europe had not advanced beyond the Iron Age.

The Celtic and Germanic peoples had no monumental art tradition of architecture, substantive sculpture, or figurative painting. For centuries they had been a nomadic people whose art was primarily utilitarian and decorative, an art which found its greatest expression in metalwork such as military gear and personal ornamentation. This metalwork of highly refined, even exquisite, craftsmanship in a variety of materials and techniques, and probably derived from the metalwork of ancient Persia and Scythia (southern Russia), featured a combination of abstract geometric and organic shapes in the so-called "animal style." When these barbarian people settled in western Europe, these forms were transformed into artistic expression in stone, wood, and especially the painting in illuminated manuscripts.

Monumental art, it must be emphasized, usually is produced in urban centers, towns and cities where there is an affluent upper-class with leisure time to provide patronage. The Germanic and Celtic peoples developed very few towns because their economy and social structure were primarily rural. The main patron of art during the early Middle Ages was the Church. It was in the great Irish monasteries that the barbaric style reached its highest development and this fact is of great significance to the development of Western culture, including Western art. Ireland, it must be noted, was Christianized in the fifth century by English missionaries, who thus brought to that island its first significant contact with Graeco-Roman civilization. But the Irish, who were barbaric, rural Celts, never became Rome-oriented, and they established their church on a system similar to the monastic system practiced in Egypt. In Italy the bishops succeeded to the political powers of the Roman government which was chiefly urban in character and, thus, Christianity there developed about the urban centers. In Ireland the abbot was the master of the rural monastic establishment which became the seat of religion and learning, the cultural center. Moreover, from 600 to 800 the Irish engaged in enthusiastic missionary activity in northern Britain, France, the low countries, and central Europe, establishing thousands of monasteries based on the Irish model.

During this Golden Age of Ireland, Irish monasteries produced countless Bibles and other Christian books which were disseminated throughout Europe—and in all these works the artistic embellishment was geometric abstraction and organic, not figurative. There is no doubt that the Irish saw books and manuscripts with figures painted in the Roman manner, but they chose to illustrate the Word of God with the finest decorative art in history. From Lindisfarne (LIN-dis-farne), a monastery founded by Irishmen in Saxon England, comes one of the finest and most complex works in the history of book illustration, the *Lindisfarne Gospels* c. 700. The "Cross Page" (Fig. 108) is incredibly dense with intertwined dragons and serpents called *lacertines* (lines which upon close inspection are animal bodies) arranged with precision to achieve exact symmetry within the geometric frame and set against a background of an even more complicated pattern. This page is a miniature maze of shapes and colors with mirror-image effects, all produced with the precision of printed TV circuitry. Above all, it is beautiful adornment with a vitality seldom seen in figurative art.

The *Book of Kells* is the best known of the Irish books and the most sophisticated example of decorative illustration. In the "Monogram Page" (Fig. 109) of the *Kells* manuscript, it is relatively easy to separate the trumpet and spiral forms from the complicated interlacings. Close inspection reveals rather humorous animal and human representations which, however, are very abstract, thus preventing conflict with the overall decorative unity. Obviously overall design, rich and lavish in color, is meant to appeal to the eye without having to mean

Figure 108. "Cross Page," *Lindisfarne Gospels,* c. A.D. 700. British Museum, London (courtesy Art Reference Bureau).

Figure 109. "Monogram Page" from the *Book of Kells,* c. A.D. 800. (Reproduced by permission of the Board of Trinity College, Dublin.)

or represent anything. In comparison with the essential horizontal patterns of Greek decoration as seen in Greek pottery, Celto-Germanic manuscript pages are very dynamic, restless, and mystical.

The covers of these books were also richly decorated. Enamel work in which colored glass is fused with metal was held in high favor as were covers made of gold and silver, engraved with patterns or even figures and then encrusted with precious or semiprecious jewels set in elaborate patterns. "The Crucifixion" cover of the *Lindau Gospels* (LIN-dow) c. 870 (Fig. 110) is of gold, with the figures of angels and Christ raised from the surface and delineated with very moving, expressive lines. Some of the gems are set right into the gold, but the major stones are placed on claw feet or arcaded turret settings which allow light to penetrate under the stones to increase their brilliance.

This love of embellishment, the use of precious metals, semiprecious and precious gems, was not confined to books, but was extended to the priests' vestments, all ceremonial objects used in the mass such as chalices, ciboriums, crosses, candlesticks, incense burners, bells, cruets, and

Figure 110. Upper cover of the binding of the *Lindau Gospels,* c. A.D. 870. The Pierpont Morgan Library, New York.

reliquaries. In the treasure vaults of European churches one can see these containers in shapes of arms, hands, feet, even heads, in gold and silver encrusted with jewels. To indicate the overwhelmingly spiritual value of the Word, a relic or a ceremony, all religious objects were painstakingly created with elaborate use of the most precious substances on earth.

As most princes or political rulers in the West during the early Middle Ages were no more than illiterate, peripatetic military chieftains, the bishop's church and palace or the monastery often served as a political and religious center. The Church was the chief patron of the arts which were considered utilitarian, as they were made in and for the service of God. Although most of the artistic production of the Church during the early Middle Ages was produced by monks, talented freemen and serfs were encouraged to artistic activity. As practically all the schools were monastic, however, training was chiefly for the production of religious materials. Little secular art, except personal ornamentation, was produced. Because of this background the Carolingian Renaissance is of extreme importance. Charlemagne established his capital at Aachen, brought to it not only religious scholars and artists, but encouraged an interest in reviving the art and culture of the Roman empire. He was not exceptionally successful, for his models dated from late or Christian antiquity and even these were imperfectly understood by his artists. Nevertheless, in the emperor's *scriptoria* (skrip-TOR-ia; writing rooms), scribes and illuminators copied classic authors and paintings, and murals, reliefs, and mosaics modeled on classic works were produced in abundance by artists he brought to his capital from Rome, Constantinople, Ravenna, Ireland, and other art centers. Perhaps it is incorrect to state that classic models were imperfectly understood by the Carolingian artists, because every so-called revival of classicism stresses different aspects of it—and the court of Charlemagne was militantly Christian, not pagan. In Carolingian art we see a combination of classic forms and Christian subject matter and symbols; the basic purpose of this art was to assert the spiritual nature of man rather than the humanistic. A manuscript page from the *Gospel Book of Archbishop Ebbo of Rheims* (Fig. 111), painted shortly after Charlemagne's death, depicts "St. Mark" in figurative terms that derive from a classic model, but the saint is drawn so that the drapery twirls about his torso in lines every bit as vital and moving as those in an Irish manuscript. Mark is not a scholar writing a book; he is a man seized with divine inspiration, a transmitter of the Sacred Text. This painting shows the crude beginnings of the synthesis of classicism and barbarism which will find glorious culmination in the Gothic cathedral.

Figure 111. "St. Mark" from the *Gospel Book of Archbishop Ebbo of Rheims,* c. A.D. 816-835. Municipal Library, Epernay, France (Photo, Giraudon).

No building better exemplifies the northern, barbaric spirit in architecture than the Stave Church of Norway (Fig. 112). The architectural principle of its construction is relatively simple. Four ship's masts were placed in a square or rectangle extending through the roof to support a sharply pointed tower. Around this skeleton the remainder of the structure and the walls were built of wood panels in a frame braced by ship-ribbing construction. The result looks like an arrow shot straight into the air. One can make the point that in a climate where there is much snow, slanting roofs are necessary—but not *that* slanting. This was the architect's idea of beauty—no classicist he.

Another interesting feature of the Stave Church is the exterior decoration of long animal heads in wood flung out vertically from the gables. Usually when there is such decoration, it has utilitarian function, as in the case with gargoyles which serve as rain spouts on the Gothic Church. On the Stave Church no such function is apparent, but these forms derive from the protective animal figures at the helm of Viking vessels and supposedly were used for purely decorative purposes. Above all, the Stave Church is essentially a vertical build-

Figure 112. Norwegian stave church (Archives, Wm. C. Brown Company Publishers).

ing, a construction of broken vertical lines that point to heaven and to infinity, thus illustrating the religious emotionalism of the people who found this artistic expression beautiful.

ROMANESQUE ART: 1000-1200

By A.D. 1000 the Church was the fortress of God in theory and fact. The Empire of the Middle Ages was rent by the feudal system: kings, princes, dukes, and even lowly squires challenged all centralized secular power; the unifying and vital force of society was the Church and the Pope was the true suzerain of Christendom. The pagan Viking and Magyar warriors were now Christian warriors developing feudal states in Normandy, Scandinavia, and Hungary. The great Caliphate of Cordova was beginning to disintegrate and by the end of the Middle Ages, Ferdinand and Isabella rid the Iberian peninsula of the Moslems by sword and conversion. Europe, at last, felt somewhat safe from the Moslems and barbarians and in 1095 Pope Urban was able to reassert the political and economic power of Europe when he raised the international army of the First Crusade. The Church was the authoritarian and militant force for the consolidation of medieval culture.

Throughout the turmoil of the early medieval period, the Church had encouraged an apocalyptic mood of escapism, a yearning for the better life after death, and in the process had established a spiritual and social hegemony because it promised the ultimate security. It is not surprising, then, that the Church, not the court or state, was the chief patron for art of the period, and that the church edifice became the prime artistic expression of the age.

In the eleventh century there was an increase in church construction that extended throughout Europe and into Asia Minor, from Scotland to Portugal to Jerusalem. The Clunaic (CLUE-nay-ick) Order alone built nearly a thousand monastic churches; in the next century the Cistercian Order built over seven hundred; and soon every hamlet, village, town, and city in the West had a church. Of course, Christianity has continued to be extremely beneficient to the building trade right to modern times, but the church construction of the Romanesque period was a conspicuous increase from that of the preceding centuries. Many historians consider all buildings based in any way on Roman tradition which were erected from the fall of Rome to the beginning of the Gothic period to be Romanesque. Insofar as they are thinking of buildings which are round-arched, solid, and heavy, rather like the Roman buildings, the terminology is fair enough. But the early medieval period saw architectural movements sponsored by the court, during Carolingian times for example, and this architecture was limited to imperial cities. In the eleventh century, Romanesque architecture sprang up all over Western Europe and was primarily monastic church construction. Unlike the earlier pre-Romanesque or proto-Romanesque buildings, religious or secular, the true Romanesque architecture of the eleventh and twelfth centuries had stone or brick vaults instead of wooden roofs and exteriors decorated with architectural ornament and sculpture. The sources for the Romanesque church were the Roman basilica for the floor plan of nave, aisles, transept, and apse; the Roman baths for the groined vault; and Roman architecture in general for the semicircular arch.

The Romanesque church was usually the chief building of a complicated and large monastic establishment which included dormitories, refectories, kitchens, chapels, storerooms, bathrooms, schools, infirmaries, scriptoria, hostelries, stables—all the buildings of a self-contained community. Many monasteries housed hundreds of monks. Thus the churches had to be large to contain them and even larger to mirror the religious convictions which made church a palace for the King of Kings. Moreover, these churches often were or became the centers of towns. As the town and monastic community grew, the church had to provide ample space for community meetings and altars where each ordained monk and each priest could say mass. Soon little chapels were extended all around the apse to produce an architectural arrangement called a *chevet* (SHEV-ay). Bells called the community to prayer and bell towers began to appear at the ends of the façade. The church grew larger and larger throughout the Romanesque period as new or enlarged architectural units became necessary.

At the same time that the floor plan was enlarged, the buildings took on a vertical construction which was more daring than any building that the Romans built. Why? Obviously great height in a building is not necessary to accommodate a crowd. The simple answer is, for symbolical purposes. The church was the House of God; it should reach into the heavens; it should dominate the town, the earth. Also, the early Christian basilica was a relatively low building with a wooden roof; low wooden roofs often caught fire, since the chief means of illuminating these large buildings were candles and lamps. Thus, the stone or brick vault became an essential feature of the church—and a new problem developed. Stone roofs are heavy and need strong, solid support; therefore, walls were made thicker and the number of windows reduced to keep those walls solid and strong. Inevitably, added structural support was needed to keep walls from buckling under the immense weight of the stone vaults, and buttresses, brick or stone props built up against the walls, were added for reinforcement.

The Romanesque church developed logically in view of the physical and spiritual needs of the community. In fact the ribbed vaults, flying buttresses, and stained glass windows which are considered the distinguishing marks of the Gothic church were developed during the Romanesque period in various parts of Europe, although they did not become commonplace until the Gothic era. The Gothic architectural style is nothing more than a continuation of the Romanesque and the academic subdivisions of art historians would have been incomprehensible to medieval builders. What the traveler of the period would have noted were regional differences in the use of materials which make a French Romanesque church quite different from an Italian one and both quite different from a German one. Each geographic area used building materials common to its locale. Thus Romanesque in France is usually of limestone blocks, in Germany and the Netherlands of brick, and in Italy rubble and stone faced with marble.

The medieval period was the great age for the collection of relics and reliquaries. Every community, monastery, and church vied to obtain body parts or objects associated with the saints and, especially, Christ. These objects naturally were considered to be holy and were said to have effected miracles. Erasmus tells us that by his time there were sufficient pieces of the True Cross in Europe to build a warship—and he was not exaggerating. Some churches boasted of hundreds of relics; monasteries would send a mob of monks to kidnap a coveted item; and St. Louis bankrupted France to purchase the Crown of Thorns. The abbey church of La Madeleine (MAD-e-len) at Vézelay (VEY-za-lay) still is the chief repository for the relics of Magdalen; Canterbury had the body of Thomas à Becket (BECK-it); Amiens (aw-MYEN) the head of John the Baptist; and Santiago de Compostela (san-ti-AW-go day compo-STEL-ah) in northwestern Spain, the body of the Apostle St. James.

Not only were the churches eager to obtain relics as an aid to the greater sanctification of their premises and as potential curatives for the various ills of the community, but also to attract pilgrims. Let us recognize the sincere belief of those who believe in the sanctity and efficacy of relics, but admit that during the Middle Ages relics also were a tourist attraction, a boon for the commercial activity of the monastery and the town which would be envied by any contemporary Chamber of Commerce. Canterbury was "the place to visit" for every pious and social Englishman, as Chaucer tells us in *The Canterbury Tales*. The most important pilgrimage city of the Middle Ages was Rome and the most important pilgrimage church was Santiago de Compostela, which was built to approximately its present form between 1071 and 1112. Throughout Europe, pilgrimage routes were established leading from one great reliquary to another, for the church building in itself must be considered a reliquary. Thousands of pilgrims traveled these routes, visiting churches and obtaining special absolutions, divine favor, spiritual and social comfort. To the monastery, church, and town alike they brought prosperity, for they left behind money which they had paid for candles, masses, food, lodging, and entertainment. Pilgrimages, in effect, were the beginning of the modern travel business.

The social-economic-political history of the Middle Ages is as inextricably bound to the Church as was religion itself. This rather long disquisition on these elements has been included to give you an idea of the importance of the Church and the church building in medieval life. No photograph or series of photographs of Romanesque churches can convey the meaning of these buildings nor the communicative potency that made them especially beautiful to medieval man.

The Church of La Madeleine at Vézelay

(1096-1132) is the largest surviving Romanesque abbey or monastic church in France. Although there is no monastic Romanesque church which can be said to be typical, the style varying from one geographic area to another, La Madeleine has many characteristics common to this type of edifice and some which are outstanding examples. The facade (Fig. 113) might not seem imposing in the reproduction, until it is realized that the church stands at the top of a high hill commanding the village, which grew about it like a massive citadel. Like a military fortress, it is massive, heavy, and solid in appearance. The three portals are rather small, with rounded arches; the façade has little architectural or sculptural ornamentation, and the building would have appeared completely squat had not the southwest tower been extended to carry a strong vertical accent to the sky. A view of the tower from the side (Fig. 114) indicates how the verticality of the tower echoes and accentuates the vertical buttresses which reinforce the thick wall which, in turn, is broken only by very small windows. The view of the chevet (Fig. 115) shows well how the simple round apse known to the Romans and early Christians was changed by the addition of apsidial chapels. Although this unit is the most fenestrated part of the church, it still seems heavy and bound to the ground.

Figure 114. View of south wall and tower, Ste.-Madeleine, Vézelay (Robert C. Lamm).

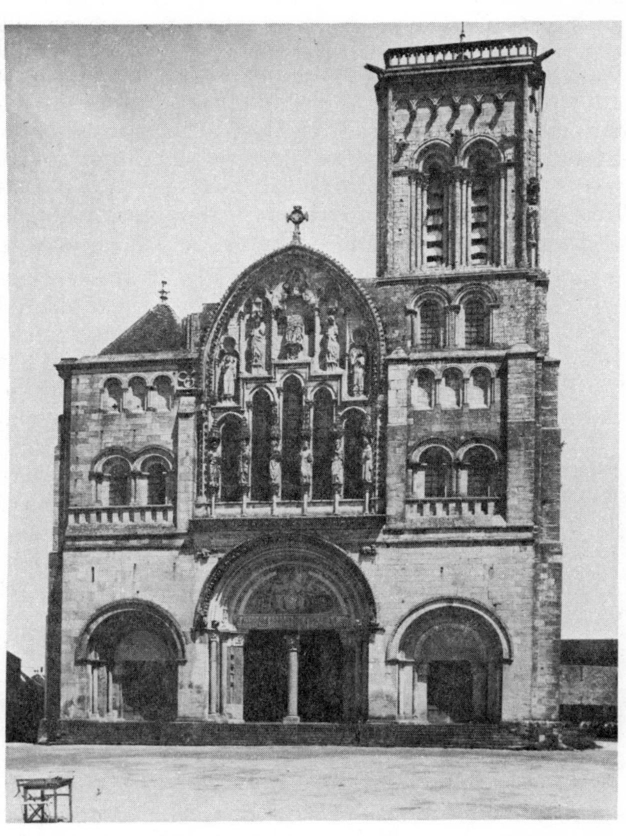

Figure 113. Façade, Ste.-Madeleine, Vézelay, c. 1096-1132 (Robert C. Lamm).

Figure 115. Chevet, Ste.-Madeleine, Vézelay (Robert C. Lamm).

Abbey churches generally were very plain on the exterior, almost devoid of ornamentation and sculpture. Their primary function was to serve the monastic community, not the secular; therefore, the main ornamentation was confined to the interior of the building where the Lord's subjects could pay him homage in divine services that went on day and night, year after year. Nevertheless, in the tympanums of the façade portal (Fig. 116) there is a rather simple depiction of the "Last Judgment," one of the most widely represented relief themes of the Romanesque era, which was still gripped with a millennarium psychosis. Passing through the central portal and entering the narthex, one is confronted with one of the most magnificant and beautiful tympanums in art (Fig. 117). The nave portal is wide and the tympanum of "The Mission of the Apostles" is huge, so large that the entrance is divided by a central post a *trumeau* (TRUE-mo), which aids in supporting the lintel and the semicircular tympanum above it. In iconography and composition "The Mission of the Apostles" (Fig. 118) is incredibly complex, for its sculptor drew its subject matter from the Bible, Isidore of Seville's *Etymologies*, the signs of the zodiac, scenes from everyday life, and *bestiaries* (BES-ti-air-ease), books recounting the lore, symbolism and features of actual and imaginary animals. The basic motif is very simple: the central and dominating figure is Christ, from whose hands emanate rays of the Holy Spirit to book-carrying apostles—the mission is given the apostles to spread the Word of God and transmit divine mercy to mankind. This subject had special relevance in this age of crusades for, in effect, it proclaims the duty of all Christians to carry the Gospel throughout the earth. On the lintel is carved a parade of people representing the heathen nations, including half-naked savages with

Figure 117. Central portal of narthex, Ste.-Madeleine, Vézelay (Robert C. Lamm).

Figure 116. Central portal of façade, Ste.-Madeleine, Vézelay (Robert C. Lamm).

Figure 118. "The Mission of the Apostles," tympanum of central portal of the narthex, Ste.-Madeleine, Vézelay, 1120-1132 (Photo, Bulloz).

bow and arrow, who are in need of spiritual guidance and sustenance. In the series of archivolts (ARE-ka-volts), the group of relief bands which frame the tympanum, are twelve fruits representing the months, men performing tasks appropriate for each month, and the signs of the zodiac. These representations were meant to remind man of the limited time he has in which to attain salvation and that preaching of the faith is unlimited in time. The hundreds of figures, secondary motifs, and complex symbols in this portal are so brilliantly unified that a learned theologian as well as a master sculptor must be assumed to have participated in its creation.

It is significant that this superb sculpture is in relief, for Romanesque artists found their models in the drawings and illuminated manuscripts of the monastic libraries. Conscientious viewing of "The Mission of the Apostles" reveals that the figures of Christ and the apostles are delineated with clear, sharp, swirling lines, that the figures are attenuated, twisted, and other-worldly. Romanesque sculpture is very unlike classical Roman sculpture in that it is symbolic rather than naturalistic, emotional rather than restrained, based on two-dimensional models and concepts rather than upon three-dimensional ones. Nevertheless, this era produced the first monumental sculpture since antiquity. Most Romanesque sculpture was carved out of sandstone or limestone, soft material easily adapted to the demands of pictorial forms and plasticity peculiar to Romanesque church art.

Figure 119. Interior, Ste.-Madeleine, Vézelay (Robert C. Lamm).

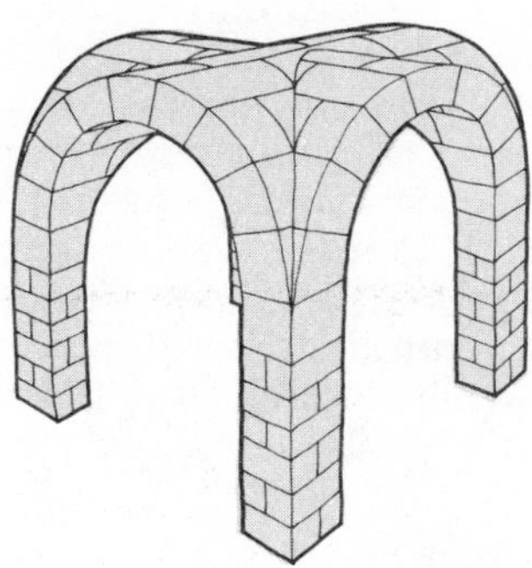

Figure 120. Schematic drawing of cross-vault.

Entering the nave at Vézelay (Fig. 119), one is struck by its great height (about 90′), the groin vaults, and round transverse arches or ribs strikingly banded in colored stones. It is obvious that for every pier, arch, and section of the vault each stone was cut exactly to achieve a near-perfect integration of function, structure, and decoration. Many Romanesque churches had tunnel vaults such as those used in the Colosseum. Such a tunnel vault has a great weakness in that it is an unbroken series of arches pressed together, one behind the other, which—if it is not to be weakened structurally—must be lighted or opened at the ends only. Every window or door in the wall reduces its ability to absorb the weight and thrust of the arch. At Vézelay and in most Romanesque churches the tunnel vault is intersected at right angles by another tunnel vault of the same size and a "groin vault" or "cross-vault" is formed (Fig. 120). This vaulting system used at a high level, as in Vézelay, allows a great deal of illumination from clerestory windows into the nave and concentrates the thrust of the vault along the groins to the piers at the corners of the bay. Many Romanesque churches and almost all Gothic churches used ribs along the groins of the vaults to reduce the quantity of centering (temporary wooden supports used while building) and to develop a thinner vault, consequently reducing thrust and mass throughout the building. The development of Romanesque and Gothic architectural styles is inextricably bound with vault-rib-buttress construction. The fluid and well-articulated pier, arch, and vault construction of Vézelay signifies a very early phase of medieval architectural development, but Vézelay is one of the most unified and harmonious buildings of the Middle Ages.

Figure 121. Sculptured capital, Ste.-Madeleine, Vézelay (Robert C. Lamm).

Hundreds of sculptured capitals depicting Biblical scenes, incidents from the lives of the saints, allegories, and complete fantasy (perhaps unexplained Christian symbolism or emerging secularism?) are among the chief glories of Vézelay (Fig. 121). Delightful demons, decorative vegetation, and animated saints participate in visual sermons which delight contemporaries because of their decorative and naive qualities, but probably instilled the fear of hell among the medieval monks who knew these stories well. One monk, at least, did not appreciate all the beautiful and complex symbolism of Romanesque painting, sculpture, architecture, the richness of vestments and ceremonial utensils. That monk was St. Bernard of Clairvaux (BARE-nard of clare-VO), the principal spokesman of the Cistercian (sis-TUR-shun) order founded in 1098. The Cistercians were great monastery and church builders, but they were opposed to the Clunaic visual luxury and erected plain, uniform buildings from which they excluded sculpture, paintings, all elements which might be considered ostentatious—even bell towers. St. Bernard complained to a Clunaic abbot of "the vast height of your churches, their immoderate length, their superfluous breadth, the curious carvings and paintings which attract the worshipper's gaze and hinder his attentions." Obviously an inner demon called Aesthetics beset St. Bernard, for he said "at the very sight of these costly yet marvelous vanities men are kindled to offer gifts rather than to pray. . . What, think you is the purpose of all this? The compunction of penitents, or the admiration of beholders?" It is paradoxical that in 1146 St. Bernard preached and began the Second Crusade in the midst of the glories of La Madeleine of Vézelay.

The trumeau figure of the prophet Jeremiah from the Church of St. Pierre in Moissac (MWA-zak; Fig. 122) and the prophet Isaiah at Souillac (SUE-ee-yak; Fig. 123), both completed early in the twelfth century by anonymous sculptors, are supreme works of artistic achievement. The gentle, attenuated Jeremiah, distinguished with precisely-rendered strands of hair flowing from his forehead down his back and over his shoulders, a beard falling over his chest, and a giant mustache that divides his sad face, strains to emerge from the

Figure 122. Trumeau figure of the "Prophet Jeremiah," Church of St. Pierre, Moissac, early twelfth century (Photo Giraudon).

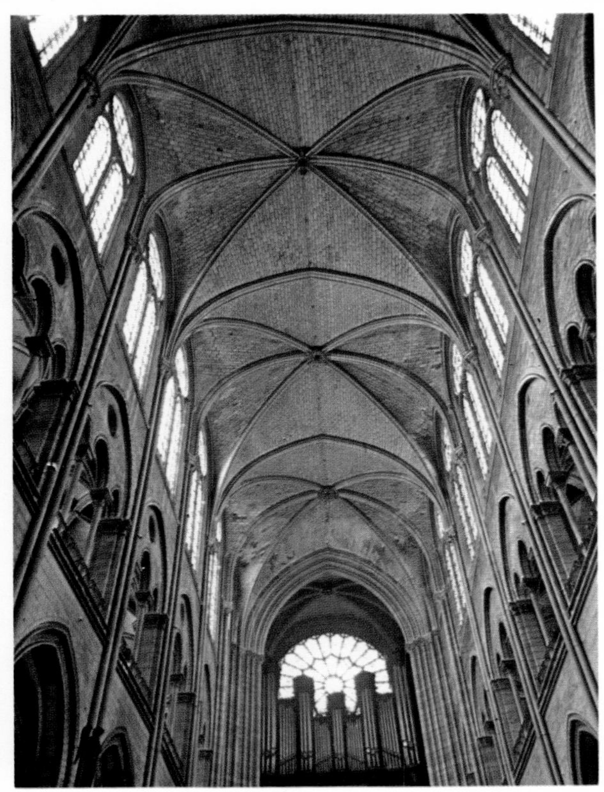

Colorplate 9. **Nave,** Notre Dame Cathedral, Paris
Courtesy Robert Lamm.

Colorplate 10. **South Rose Window and Lancets,** Chartres Cathedral
Courtesy Robert Lamm.

Colorplate 11. **Tree of Jesse Window,** Chartres Cathedral
Courtesy Robert Lamm.

Colorplate 12. **The Calling of the Apostles Peter and Andrew**—*Duccio di Buoninsegna*

Courtesy The National Gallery of Art, Washington, D.C. Samuel H. Kress Collection.

Colorplate 13. **The Annunciation**—*Simone Martini* (and *Leppo Memmi,* side panels)

Courtesy Uffizi Gallery, Florence.

Colorplate 14. **The Annunciation**—*Jan van Eyck*

Courtesy The National Gallery of Art, Washington, D.C. Andrew Mellon Collection.

Figure 123. "Prophet Isaiah," Abbey Church of Souillac, early twelfth century (Photo, Bulloz).

block in which he is carved. He is an Atlas in travesty whose delicate form is completely incapable of supporting the mass of masonry above him. Yet he expresses all the spiritual vigor and nervous tension of the saints El Greco painted in the sixteenth century. The Isaiah of Souillac is carved with even greater virtuosity. Although stone-bound, his hands grip one side of the block as he dances like a dervish, with drapery folds and body movements

Figure 124. Mont-St. Michel, France, c. 1020-c. 1521 (Bulloz—Art Reference Bureau).

often in wild contrast. He is the prophet singing and dancing in exaltation of the coming of the Lord.

Romanesque art, in all its manifestations, finds its unity in architecture. Solid, heavy, dark as the Romanesque buildings may be, they express also Romanesque contradictions of dimensions and stress, Romanesque exaggeration of nervous tension and ecstatic expression. The Romanesque church is in truth the Fortress of God where the apocalyptic vision is ever called to mind. The Benedictine Abbey, monastic church and lovely village which comprise the architectural complex of Mont-St. Michel beautifully exemplifies this concept. Mont-St. Michel was begun about 1020 by Abbot Hildebert and Richard II of Normandy, grandfather of William the Conqueror, and completed in the sixteenth century when Henry VIII was on the English throne and Francis I was King of the French. For five centuries, while abbot succeeded abbot, crusade followed crusade, building on the promontory continued. Mont-St. Michel, thus, is a glorious mixture of Norman, Norman Romanesque, Transitional, Early, and late Gothic architecture. It is customary and necessary to divide the Middle Ages into periods, styles, and the like; but it is necessary, too, to remember that the period was unified in Christianity. The soaring height of Mont-St. Michel typifies the architectural movement which to a great extent symbolized Christianity throughout the Middle Ages.

GOTHIC ARCHITECTURE 1200-1450

The term *Gothic cathedral* evokes in all of us a clear and definite mental image. Perhaps no other monument of a culture so radically different from our own is as much a part of contemporary life as the Gothic cathedral. This plastic expression of the religious and intellectual order of the Middle Ages is intact and in use today. It is still the center of nearly every northern European city and, in dubious imitations, of many cities and college campuses in the United States as well.

Of course it is arbitrary to set the dates for Gothic architecture as 1200 to 1450, for all basic structural elements of the Gothic were developed and used during the Romanesque period and are still in use today. All architectural elements find their prototypes in early history and all architectural styles of any aesthetic value manage to persist, although as secondary or tertiary styles, when a new or "modern" style is in ascendency. The Gothic style was at its peak from the thirteenth through the fifteenth centuries and, most significantly, this is the period of the great rise of cities in western Europe. Whereas the Romanesque church was a monastic establishment and usually built in the countryside where small villages developed about it, the Gothic cathedral was from the beginning an urban building. It was usually built in the center of the city, often on the same spot where a Romanesque church or pagan temple had once stood, and it became the city's glory and chief community center. The cathedral was not only the seat of the bishop, but the theater, classroom, concert hall, court, and general meeting place for the citizenry. And, because it was a secular as well as religious center, it had to combine in its structure, sculpture, and stained glass diverse elements and motifs to meet the needs of the entire community, whereas the monastic church was designed primarily for the religious needs of a unified religious community.

A visitor to any great Gothic cathedral cannot help but be impressed by these monuments of soaring stone reaching upwards to touch infinity. Notre Dame (NO-tra dahm) of Paris (Fig. 125), built between 1163 and 1200, is probably the best known of all Gothic cathedrals, although not the most highly regarded. Nevertheless, its dimensions are most impressive: its facade is 135′ wide and 141′ high to the start of the towers which are 207′ high (about twenty stories); it is 360′ long and its vault is 110′ high; its floor plan runs to approximately 65,000 square feet and its cubic dimensions are approximately seven and three-quarter million cubic feet. Above its transept crossing rises a giant pointed spire, its flèche (flesh), which pierces the heavens. Viewing the side or back of the building from a distance (Fig. 126), the flèche with its decorative crockets and finials looks ethereal and daring in the sky and the flying buttresses projecting from the apse seem like a pattern of gossamar wings supporting the building. In the interior one is impressed by the great height and space of the nave

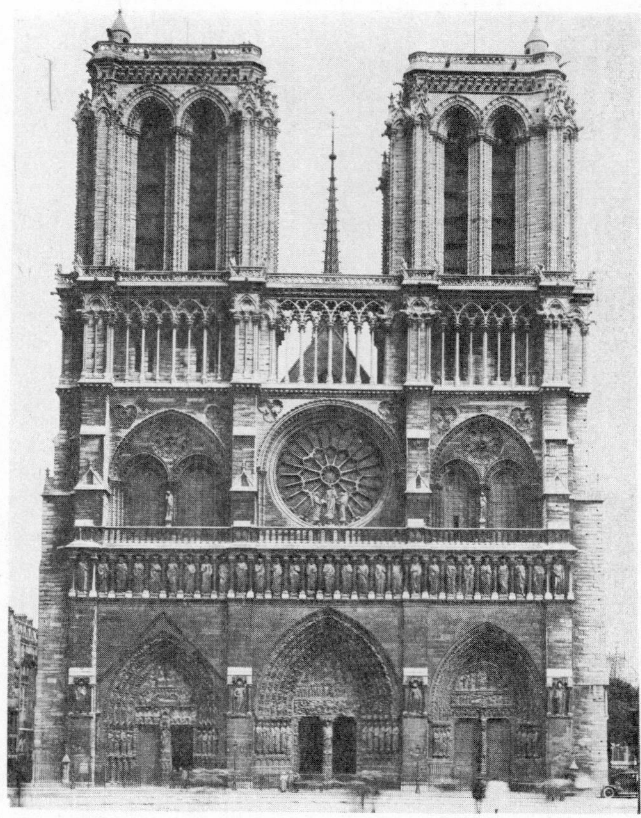

Figure 125. West façade, Notre Dame, Paris, c. 1163-c. 1200 (Photo, Bulloz).

Figure 126. Notre Dame (view from the southeast), Paris (Hirmer Fotoarchiv München).

(Fig. 127, pl. 9), the heavy columns of the nave arcade which ponderously march to the great transept crossing, and the altar in the huge choir. Even

Figure 127. Nave and choir, Notre Dame, Paris (Photo, Bulloz).

before the sense of spaciousness and height has been completely recognized, one becomes aware of the immense numbers of large stained-glass windows, which break through the solidity of the walls, the innumerable columns, ribs, and arches; and even as one is experiencing aesthetic shock and pleasure, he might wonder how was this building constructed? What holds it together? What does it mean?

An architect or art historian might ask these same questions in the following way:

1. How can a building be constructed as tall as possible (in order to come literally as near to heaven as it can and surpass in height the cathedrals of neighboring cities)?
2. If the height is increased, how can the weight be handled so the wall does not buckle?
3. How can light be admitted into so vast a structure without weakening the walls?
4. How can so massive a building not only be constructed without becoming monotonous, but be made to serve the joint purpose of beauty and edification?

The first question was answered when builders discovered the advantage of the pointed arch over the rounded arch. The principle of the arch is of mutual support; the two halves lean upon each other so that the very force which would cause either to fall is utilized to hold them upright. But the flatter the arch, the greater the lateral thrust at the springline, that is, the greater sidewise push at the point it begins to turn upward. With the pointed arch, the lateral thrust is reduced; the push of its weight continues more nearly downward. Hence the more pointed the arch, the less tendency there is to push its supporting pier outwards, and the less need consequently to make the pier massive and heavy (Fig. 128). Moreover the pointed arch has the added advantage of having no fixed diameter and, thus, can be used to span any space, with the crowns of each intersecting pointed arch easily being made to rise to the same height. A quick comparison of Romanesque and Gothic cross-vaulting should be beneficial. The groins of the cross-vaulting are usually ribbed and carry the thrust of the vault. When semicircular ribs are used in a cross-vault over an oblong bay (Fig. 129a), the arches and ribs of the short side of the bay, those of the long side, and those of the diagonal side are of different sizes, necessitating awkward raising or depressing of the supporting columns or piers. With

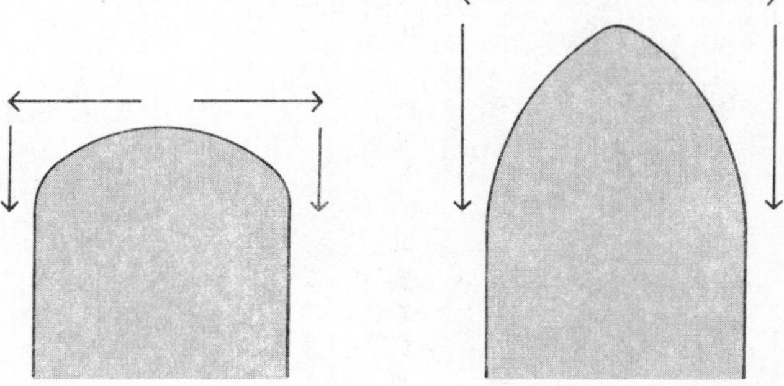

Figure 128. Schematic drawing of Romanesque and Gothic arch thrusts.

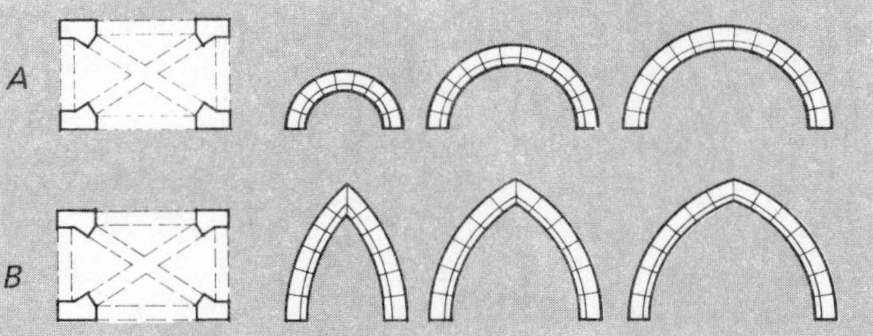

Figure 129. Cross-vault of semicircular arches over an oblong bay (a); cross-vault of pointed arches over an oblong bay (b).

the use of the pointed arch and the pointed rib, all crowns can be raised to the same height (Fig. 129b) without distortions being necessitated elsewhere. Thus with the pointed arch and subsequent pointed rib, mechanical difficulty is resolved and aesthetic appeal is increased.

Second, the pointed arch and rib obviously do not eliminate weight and thrust, but distribute them differently. The ribs actually carry much of the weight of the vault and in later Gothic buildings each bay often will have a proliferation of ribs which will carry thrusts to the ground by means of innumerable supports attached to the basic piers. Also, the Gothic style deals with the problem of propping or buttressing the piers of the pointed arch from the outside by means of another pointed arch known as the "flying buttress." At the springline of the pointed arch, the thrust is carried through the flying buttress outward and downward to heavy piers outside the inner wall. Such support leaves space for windows in the upper walls of the nave.

Third, since most of the weight and thrust is carried by the massive piers of the nave, as well as by attached and flying buttresses, there is little need for masonry in much of the walls of a Gothic cathedral. Indeed, these too can be perforated and lightened by use of the pointed arch, leaving room for the tall slender windows that are characteristic of the Gothic style.

Finally, huge edifices like the cathedrals, for which there was no ready-made formula and which were evolving in form according to local needs, could have been dull, factory like structures, mechanically sound but aesthetically uninteresting. That they are not is one of the triumphs of the Gothic spirit in art. Rigidly limited by the nature of materials (stone, wood, glass), and held strictly by the uncompromising laws of mechanics, the Gothic builders managed to assert a remarkable degree of individuality within limitations. These limitations cannot be overemphasized, for the thrusts and counterthrusts of medieval building were so sensitively calibrated that moving one stone out of position could cause a building to collapse. Nevertheless the Gothic builder showed exceptional individuality and freedom of play. Do the outside piers supporting the flying buttress need weight for the downward thrust that is their function? Very well: but let that weight be disguised by piling on their tops (adding still further to the downward thrust!) the heaven-pointing spires of crockets and finials, carrying the eye ever upward and adding a touch of delicacy through lacy carving. Do the lines of the balustrade or cornice need relief from a too horizontal emphasis? Let them be decorated with grotesque figures (Fig. 130) which not only break the horizontal, but

Figure 130. Grotesques and a gargoyle, tower terrace, Notre Dame, Paris (Photo, Alinari-Giraudon).

which, according to popular legend, protect the church from the demons which ever assault it. And wherever stone can be cut or wood carved into beauty, let the lessons of nature, the symbols of God's world, occupy the eye and the mind of the beholder.

The Cathedral of Chartres (SHAR-tr) is considered by most critics to be the finest example of Gothic architecture (Fig. 131). This is a building of classical dignity in which the builders gave fullest expression to Gothic culture. Most of Chartres Cathedral was built between 1194 and 1260, although parts of the west façade are from the Romanesque church built in 1145 and the north tower was completed in 1507. Although the basic Gothic cathedral usually was completed within twenty-five to fifty years, many were added to for centuries, some even left uncompleted, and some, such as the one begun in Milan in 1386, are still under construction. The towers of Notre Dame of Chartres have tall tapering spires that show different expressions of the Gothic spirit of aspiration. In the older (south) tower and spire the transition from the square base tower to the octagonal form of the spire is accomplished without ostentation, and the simple spire rising in sloping lines to a

Figure 131. West façade, Chartres Cathedral, c. 1145-c. 1507 (Photo, W. Turk).

Figure 132. Portals of west façade, c. 1145-1170, Chartres Cathedral (Hirmer Fotoarchiv München).

Figure 133. Jamb statues, west portal, Chartres Cathedral (Hirmer Fotoarchiv München).

point is dignified, somber, and very much in keeping with the spirit of the lower façade. The new (north) spire is slimmer, more complex and intricate in design, and expresses the flamboyant spirit of late Gothic culture.

The portals of the west façade (Fig. 132) are more elaborately decorated with sculpture than any Romanesque church but, unlike the Romanesque, they are in more harmonious relation to the structure of the building. Emphasis on symmetry and clarity replaces the dense crowding of Romanesque work; the jamb figures (Fig. 133) are elongated but essentially have their own axis and could, therefore, be detached from their supports. Here we see a revolutionary development, a step toward the re-establishment of monumental sculpture in the round. It is interesting to note that these sculptures of the west façade were part of the old Romanesque church of Chartres and date from c. 1145-70. Consequently they must be considered late Romanesque or, preferably, proto-Gothic. A representation of St. Theodore (Fig. 134) from the south portal of Chartres c. 1215-20 is almost classical with its highly idealized face, the gentle S-curve of the body. The tenderness of expression, the

Figure 134. Jamb statues including the warrior saint, "Saint Theodore," south transept portal, Chartres Cathedral, c. 1215-1220 (Hirmer Fotoarchiv München).

Figure 135. Nave (looking east), Chartres Cathedral, 1194-1220 (Robert C. Lamm).

great emphasis on the detail of the brave Christian warrior's armor, the linear patterns of his tunic, and the columnar verticality of his body mark this as an early Gothic sculpture of highest quality.

The nave (Fig. 135) of Chartres is truly impressive in size: 130′ long, 53′ wide, 122′ high. The height is especially astounding, but civic rivalry caused the nave of Amiens to be 140′ high and that of Beauvais (beau-VAY) to soar to 157′. What makes Chartres exceptionally impressive is that the walls, instead of being mere carriers of the weight of the superstructure, now exist mainly as a framework for the glass. It is often said that no one "knows" Chartres until he has visited it every day for a year. This seems very true, because the intensity of light varies by season and time of day and the filtered light is constantly changing in this building which, from the interior, gives the impression of being all windows. One hundred and seventy-five glass panels surviving from the Middle Ages provide a wealth of pure color and convey the emotional exaltation that must have inspired medieval man to create this mighty edifice dedicated to the Queen of Heaven. No church in Christendom exalts Mary to the degree that is proclaimed at Chartres, although most Gothic cathedrals are dedicated to Notre Dame, Our Lady. The Cult of the Virgin and the code of courtly love developed at the same time and, undoubtedly, were intertwined in the development of the social manners of the age. Mary is the multifoliate rose of the "rose windows" (pl. 10); she sits enthroned in majesty in the central panel of the apse over the high altar. All of the 4,000 saints, angels, prophets, tradespeople, and craftsmen featured in the windows of Chartres are members of her court. Throughout the year, especially on her feast days, crowds of pilgrims paid her homage. Chartres became a great pilgrimage church in the Middle Ages because it had two great relics, the skull of St. Anne, and the veil of Mary given to Charlemagne by the Byzantine Empress Irene; it is a pilgrimage place still today for devout Christians who aspire one day to come into Mary's eternal presence and for those who wish to experience this magnificent church with its unsurpassed stained glass windows.

The chief architect of Notre Dame of Chartres must have been an unusual man, for he subordinated all masonry elements to the windows of the interior and the sculpture of the exterior. In doing so, however, he showed prescience of the current art dogma that material and structure need not be confined to certain limited purposes. It is necessary to recognize that the glass panels and sculpture of Chartres do not exist separately, but are an integral part of the entire building. The glass designer had to divide the window space with mullions, carved stone posts that divide the windows into parts, by stone tracery to frame small glass panels, and by fine strips of lead that hold the small pieces of glass in place. The light that penetrates the stained glass and provides the polychromatic effect makes the glass appear transparent, and makes the lead, stone, and iron dividers become opaque black lines that separate the colors. Like mosaics, stained glass varies in brilliance according to the brilliance of the light and does not lighten the building as much as it sets the mood of the interior. For example, the window of "The Tree of Jesse" (pl. 11) is composed principally of blue glass and the south "Rose Window" primarily of red glass, a contrast of warm and cool colors. The predominance of one because of the position of the light source at any time helps determine the general atmospheric and spiritual mood.

It is important to recognize that in the twelfth and thirteenth centuries light was considered by philosophers and theologians to be the source and essence of all visual beauty. Thomas Aquinas spoke of luminosity as the chief characteristic of the beautiful. According to the platonizing metaphysics of the Middle Ages, light is the most noble of natural phenomena, the least material, the closest approximation to pure form and the prime principle of order and value. Dante's "Paradise" is a political and mystical exposition of medieval light metaphysics—the divine light penetrates the universe according to its dignity. In the physical light which illuminates the Gothic cathedral, the mystical reality becomes palpable to the senses.

In the heart of Paris there stands a small reliquary church, much restored in the ninteenth century, but built by the Saint and King Louis IX to house the Crown of Thorns he had purchased from the Byzantine Emperor in 1239, virtually bankrupting France to do so. When this holy relic arrived at a southern French seaport, Louis and his entire court were there to receive it, and from there the king carried it on foot to Paris to show his reverence and humility. By 1248 St. Louis had his Sainte Chapelle (Holy Chapel) ready to receive this most important of all earthly crowns. It is a small church, or combination of two churches on two levels (Fig. 136), with a large portal on both levels and the upper crowned by a huge semicircular stained glass window. A side view (Fig. 137) shows the intense verticality of this small building with its buttresses and flèche rising heavenwards, in Gothic aspiration. The interior of the lower church

Figure 136. Façade, Sainte Chapelle, Paris, c. 1243-1248 (Robert C. Lamm).

Figure 137. Side view, Sainte Chapelle, Paris (Robert C. Lamm).

Figure 138. Interior, upper chapel, Sainte Chapelle, Paris (Robert C. Lamm).

is richly painted—walls, ceilings, and other architectural units in bright golds, blues, greens, and reds—but the second and upper church, which contained the giant reliquary, is a jewel box of stained glass (Fig. 138). The walls disappear and light in all its manifestations floods the exalted reliquary. The original glass of Sainte Chapelle could hardly be more beautiful than the present windows, two-thirds of which are nineteenth-century restorations. A student entering the church astounded her professor by crying, "Oh, my God!" until he realized that the aesthetic and spiritual effect had been immediate.

Like the Romanesque monastic church, the Gothic cathedral varied from region to region, country to country, according to the materials at hand and the needs of the community. Moreover, the Gothic style was in constant evolution. How tempting it would be to write of the multitowered, fairyland Gothic Cathedral of Milan, the cathedrals featuring the "flamboyant" style of the late Gothic in France and Belgium, and the fluent perpendicular style in England. But the basic Gothic style originated in France and the Gothic cathedral of Notre Dame of Amiens (1220-1529) in many respects marks the culmination of the best ideas of its predecessors. Although its interior is beautiful in that it is unified into an organic entity with each space flowing into one another about slender vertical supports, it is the façade (Fig. 139), completed between 1220 and 1288, which commands our attention. Four huge buttresses sharply divide the façade into three vertical sections; the cavernous central portal announces the broad nave, as the smaller portals do the aisles; the central rose window indicates the front of the high nave. With clarity the architects of Amiens revealed the inner structure by external design. In all this Amiens is not strikingly different from Notre Dame of Chartres or Notre Dame of Paris, but the sheer profusion of ornament and sculpture on the façade defies reason. Christ, Mary, and all the saints are here; their clothing is sculpted in such detail that the various textures of cloth seldom have been rendered with such astounding fidelity in stone. Pinnacles rise everywhere; arches and moldings break up flat surfaces; canopies overhang statues;

Figure 139. Façade, Notre Dame of Amiens, c. 1220-1259 (Hirmer Fotoarchiv München).

finials and crockets decorate and crown pinnacles, canopies, arches; and the inevitable signs of the zodiac, personifications of the virtues and vices, and the occupations of the month find their places in this profusion of carving. Even today when light strikes this facade, a glittering effect occurs which denies the materiality of the wall. In the Middle Ages this entire moving surface was painted with bright colors and gilded with gold. How overwhelming this façade must have been to the medieval man—how fitting an entrance to the huge, seemingly limitless interior which glowed with the vibrant light through the multicolored stained glass during the day and by thousands of candles and lamps at night.

It has been customary to call the Gothic cathedral a Bible in stone. It was a Bible, an encyclopedia, all the theology, mythology, and thought of the time—a synthesis of medieval knowledge and faith. All men do not know the Bible, understand the complexities of formal philosophy and theology, nor did the average man of the Middle Ages. Every man understands the medieval cathedral according to the degree of his knowledge and faith. No building, before or since, has had so much spiritual and secular sustenance to offer to men of every degree.

LATE GOTHIC PAINTING

Stained glass windows were an integral part of Gothic architecture and obviated the necessity for painting, except as architectural decoration, in the Gothic cathedral. During the twelfth and thirteenth centuries, stained glass and relief sculpture served the pictorial purposes which once had been served by mosaics and frescoes in early Christian, Byzantine, and Romanesque churches. Large-scale mural painting was virtually nonexistent during the Gothic heyday except in Italy, where fenestration seldom was as extensive as in northern Europe. The fact that in Italy light is stronger and daylight is of longer duration than in the north might be of some significance. More important, however, is the fact that Italy always maintained close contact with Byzantium, never fully accepting the Gothic. As a result, panel painting, frescoes, and mosaics were kept very much alive on Italian soil. This Byzantine influence grew even stronger after the conquest of Constantinople by the armies of the Fourth Crusade in 1204. The combination of Gothic and neo-Byzantine influences in painting produced in the fourteenth century two forceful styles in Italy which would be of crucial importance for the development of Western painting.

A Florentine painter named Cimabue (CHIM-a-boo-a; 1240?-1302) was renowned for his skill as a fresco and tempera painter. (Fresco paintings are made on fresh, wet plaster with pigments suspended in water; tempera paintings are usually painted on panels with pigments mixed with egg yolk. Both painting techniques are difficult because drying time is very rapid and it is virtually impossible to correct errors without completely redoing areas in which a change is desired.) Probably his most famous painting is "Madonna Enthroned" (Fig. 140), painted in Florence between 1280 and 1290. The mere size of the huge tempera panel, 12′7 1/2″ × 7′4″, distinguishes it from Byzantine icons, which were never painted on such a scale. The gable shape of the picture and the throne on

Figure 140. Cimabue, "Madonna Enthroned," c. 1280-90. Uffizi Gallery, Florence (Alinari—Art Reference Bureau).

which the Madonna rests, of course, are Gothic in origin, as is the general verticality of the composition. The rigid, angular draperies, the rather flat bodies depicted in a very shallow space, the severity of poses and expressions, and the hieratic exposition of the motif are derived from Byzantium. All of Cimabue's work shows a remarkable blending of the two diverse styles, but the primary significance of this type of work is symbolic. Nevertheless, Cimabue's sense of monumental scale had a profound influence upon his pupil Giotto (JOT-toe; 1266-1336).

Giotto is called the "Father of Western Painting" because he established the illusionary qualities of space, tactility (bulk), movement, and human expression, qualities which the majority of painters since have had to use as thesis or antithesis. He is considered to be a great artist not just because of his innovations, but because of the excellence of his work. His indebtedness to Cimabue is obvious in the "Madonna Enthroned" (Fig. 141), which he painted about 1310. Yet even acknowledging the debt, this painting has a unity of vision and a humanism completely lacking in Cimabue's work. Giotto endowed his Madonna, the Christ Child, and the adoring angels with tactile or bulk quality: that is, they give the illusion of weight, solidity, and dimension. In fact, the figures have a three-dimensional reality like sculpture in the round and, in contrast, Cimabue's figures appear similar to very low relief. Although Giotto's Madonna is an unattractive giantess who, if rising quickly, would break through the top of her throne and the painting itself, we are keenly aware of her tangibility. Also Giotto creates an illusion of space in which the figures can move, crowded though it may be, and even allows a space in front of the throne where we might enter the scene. Admittedly this illusion of space is somewhat inaccurate and inconsistent compared with Renaissance perspective, but a new sense of reality was created.

Figure 141. Giotto, "Madonna Enthroned," c. 1310. Uffizi Gallery, Florence (Alinari—Art Reference Bureau).

Despite the impressive qualities of this panel painting, Giotto's reputation rests upon his frescoes; he painted large-scale fresco cycles of the Life of Christ in Padua and in Florence, and of the life of St. Francis in Assisi (ah-SEE-see). "The Lamentation" fresco from the Arena Chapel in Padua (Fig. 142) must of necessity serve to illustrate Giotto's other momentous achievements: the introduction of human expression and the establishment of the picture plane so that the viewer is on the same ground as the painted images. In the "Lamentation" the human participants are frozen in gestures and attitudes that bespeak the anguish of Christ's mother and followers. And in the heavens small angels bellow their grief and strain their bodies with forced tensions and frantic movements. The very controlled emotion of the bulky, earth-bound humans gives the scene classic restraint, while the angels echo and intensify their emotions to convey the full impact of the scene. Such an understanding of the psychology of human emotions, be it of the humans depicted or of the viewers, had never been so strikingly portrayed or evoked in painting. Moreover, Giotto makes us participants in the scene rather than observers by having the scene take place in the foreground so that the viewer's eye-level falls on the lower half of the picture. Picture space, here, is conceived as continuous with the viewer's space. Thus Giotto's painting achievements may be summarized as the creation of superb illusions of tactile qualities, existence and movement in space, psychological understanding of subject and viewer, and the establishment of a continuity of space between viewer and painting.

Giotto amalgamated in his painting the Greek manner of Byzantine art, the monumental manner of Cimabue, and Gothic sculptural three-

Figure 142. Giotto, "The Lamentation," c. 1305-1306. Arena Chapel, Padua (Alinari—Art Reference Bureau).

dimensional qualities. To all of these technical achievements he brought humanity, a sense of man's awareness of his emotion and place in the world. It is difficult for us to realize or believe that Giotto's contemporaries saw these works as the ultimate reality that could be produced in art, that it is claimed that people even walked into these works because Giotto's illusionism was so "real" for its time. But, remember that reality, or the illusion of reality, changes from epoch to epoch.

Giotto frequently is called the first Renaissance painter and, indeed, the Italian Renaissance did preserve his achievements and mined the unexplored potential in tactility, space, movement, and human expression. Nevertheless, Giotto, like Dante, his friend and fellow Florentine, was a medieval man, brought up and sustained by medieval society whose goals and attitudes are reflected in his masterpieces. He was a widely-traveled, well-paid, bourgeois artisan who was renowned for his painting, mosaics, sculpture, and architecture. He was not a classicist, philosopher, antiquarian, or conscious revolutionary. His art must be regarded as the consummation and culmination of medieval artistic thought, not as a departure from it.

In Sienna two artists of importance appear in the thirteenth century whose work, much different from that of Giotto and Cimabue, received international recognition in their lifetimes and was greatly instrumental in forming what is known as the "International Style." Duccio (due-CHE-oh) (c. 1255-c.1319) mastered the Byzantine style but endowed it with fluid line of grace and delicacy which made him the most elegant painter of his time. His "Rucellai (RUE-ka-lie) Madonna" (Fig. 143), painted about 1285, is highly decorative through intricate folds of background drapery, liberal use of gold, delicacy of line in garments and

Figure 143. Duccio, "Rucellai Madonna," c. 1285. Santa Maria Novella, Florence (Alinari—Art Reference Bureau).

figure delineation. Duccio's entire concept of the Madonna is dreamlike and other-worldly in comparison to Cimabue's majestic Madonna and Giotto's huge earth-mother. Duccio's "The Calling of the Apostles Peter and Andrew" (pl. 12) depicts a world of golden sky and transparent blue sea, where a refined, tall and elegant Christ, gently beckons to simple but stately fishermen. The sea is transparent, and delicately drawn fish swim before our eyes. It is a lovely world, the world of Duccio, and this is the world the popes at Avignon, the kings and princes of the north will have their artists emulate in the first "International Style" of painting.

It was a fellow Sienese who carried Duccio's style to the north, the extremely talented Simone Martini (see-MO-nay mar-TEA-knee; 1284-1344). For years he painted for the papal court at Avignon and amalgamated in his work the most graceful elements of Duccio's Byzantine style and the Gothic style of refinement as expressed in late Gothic architecture. His "Annunciation" (pl. 13) epitomizes the courtly style. The frame of the annunciation scene is completely Gothic, replete with crockets and finials; the background is Byzantine, with gold leaf signifying eternity and infinity. The Angel Gabriel kneels before a startled Virgin Mary and his bright wings fit nicely into the arcade above him, his plain cloak swirls gracefully in a nonexistent breeze, and he gently raises his right hand in salute as the words "Hail Mary, full of grace . . ." leave his lips and travel to Mary. The Virgin draws back daintily from her elegant visitor, as she somewhat reticently receives his message. Both Mary and Gabriel are delineated in gentle curvilinear patterns. Between the Divine Messenger and Virgin Mary is an elegant vase from which beautiful white lilies emerge, an image that is at once visually beautiful and symbolic of Mary's purity. The entire work is as delicately executed, painting and frame, as the finest art of the goldsmith; the conception is aristocratic, courtly, not hieratic. This is a work of Gothic-Byzantine lyricism, perhaps comparable to the courtly sonnets of Petrarch who also served the pope in Avignon.

The "International Style" was international in that it combined attributes of Byzantine and Gothic forms, was promulgated through the princely courts, both religious and secular, where concepts of grace and delicacy, of refinement and love of harmonious color found sympathic response from wealthy clients who sought, from the arts, aesthetic pleasure even more than spiritual enlightenment.

Book and manuscript illumination was the leading form of painting in northern Europe at the time of the International Style, although panel painting was growing in importance. Probably the most famous of late Gothic illuminated books is the *Tres Riches Heures du Duc de Berry*, (tray reech urs due duke da BARE-ee) illustrated by Pol de Limbourg (paul da LIM-burg) and two of his brothers. They were Flemish artists who served the great Duke who was wealthier than his brother the King of France and a greater art patron. The *Tres Riches Heures* was a combination calendar and prayer book in which the Limbourgs depicted man, peasant and noble in the panorama of life of the early fifteenth century. These illustrations were complicated and detailed scenes (probably painted with the assistance of a magnifying glass) showing man at work and play, in the fields on palaces, as the seasons passed. One illustration must suffice to give an idea of the loving attention the Limbourgs gave to every detail. "February" (Fig. 144) is an especially interesting and unusual miniature, for it represents the earliest snow landscape in the history of Western art: the sheep are huddled together in the fold, birds scratch for food in the farmyard which a peasant woman crosses while blowing on her hands to keep away the chill. In the left foreground we see into the interior of the small cottage (the painter obligingly omitted the front

Figure 144. The Limbourg brothers, "February" from *Les Très Riches Heures du* Duc de Berry, 1413-1416. Musée Condé, Chantilly, France (Photo, Bulloz).

wall for our benefit) where three seated women lift their skirts as they toast their feet before a fire. In the middle section of the painting a serf chops down a tree and in the far distance another drives his laden donkey along a narrow trail to the village. Every object—the thatching of the fence, the snow-topped beehives, the smoke rising from the chimney—is painted with minute fidelity to visual appearance. "February" and all other illustrations in the *Tres Riches Heures* are as complicated, detailed, and full of intertwining and intermingling forms, lines, and patterns as the Celtic manuscripts of the early Middle Ages. Now, however, this love of detail and complexity is expended upon depicting *this* world and is no longer subservient to symbolical and supernatural meanings. Not that supermundane connections are lacking, but these works are first and above all a copy of nature; and although these presentations are far from photographic and are suffused with the delicacy of line and color basic to the International Style, they represent the beginnings of bourgeois naturalistic portrait, genre, and landscape tradition which will be discussed in Volume 2 of this text.

The invention of oil painting by Flemish artists around 1400 caused an artistic revolution equal in importance to the innovations of Giotto in the techniques of illusion. In oil painting, pigments are mixed with slow-drying oils, thus allowing the artist greater flexibility than they have when they are working with fast-drying tempera and fresco painting. Moreover, oil painting permits the smooth reworking of the same area over and over again. Illusionistic effects of singular subtlety, richness, and enamel-like luminosity and extremely detailed work are possible. Moreover, oil painting done on a panel (later on canvas) can be independent of architectural forms and is easily movable. This latter characteristic combined with basically naturalistic subject matter proved irresistible to the growing bourgeois class of the late Gothic period and painting became a common object of household furnishings.

Jan van Eyck (Yaun van Ike; c.1390-1441) did not invent or discover oil painting as so many writers claim, but he was among the first to discover its vast artistic possibilities and to use it in conquest of visible reality. "Giovanni Arnolfini (zhoe-VAHN-knee ar-nol-FEE-knee) and his Bride" (Fig. 145) is a masterpiece of clinical observation and rendition of light, bulk, texture, and a subtle analysis of the personalities of the young couple. The painting depicts the Italian silk merchant Arnolfini and his Flemish wife reciting their wedding vows—and in the mirror on the background wall we see reflections of two persons, probably Jan van Eyck and a servant. On the wall over this mirror, the painter inscribed in Latin, "Jan van Eyck was here, 1434." Thus the artist recorded and signed the nuptial contract.

Of course, the painting is laden with symbolism: the lighted candle symbolizes the presence of God; the dog is Fido, or in those days Fides—the symbol of fidelity; the couple has shed their shoes while speaking their marriage vows to indicate they are standing on hallowed ground; almost every object in the painting has symbolical meaning and purpose. The symbolism, however, is secondary to the visual scene which contains still lifes, portraits, and even the Stations of the Cross which adorn the frame of the convex mirror.

Perhaps some of you have a vague memory of having seen Arnolfini before. It is altogether possible that this portrait of the long-nosed, sallow-skinned businessman dwarfed by his great beaver hat inspired Tenniel's illustrations of the Mad Hatter in *Alice's Adventures in Wonderland.* Mrs. Arnolfini is demure, thoughtful and, as students enjoy pointing out, seemingly pregnant. Probably the portrait was completed some time after the marriage. Also this type of dress, which emphasizes

Figure 145. Jan van Eyck, "Giovanni Arnolfini and His Bride" (Reproduced by courtesy of the Trustees, The National Gallery, London).

fecundity as an attribute of beauty, was very modish in the early fifteenth century. Still, there is reason to think that van Eyck was being realistic, for on the post of the chair beside the bed appears the carved figure of St. Margaret, the protectress of women in childbirth.

Even when van Eyck painted purely religious scenes such as "The Annunciation" (pl. 14), the sense of immediacy and reality is emphasized through his simulation of a multitude of textures, of the play of light for naturalistic atmospheric effects, and rich and high saturation of colors (even at low values) which give the entire painting a rich enamel-like quality. Note the heavy, patterned and jeweled cloak of Angel Gabriel and the obvious delight he has in delivering his message; note, also, that Mary is depicted as an attractive Flemish girl who raises her hands in wonder as if to say "Oh goodness, me!" The total impression is captivating because, despite the perfection displayed in every detail, the scene obviously is of this world.

It would be impossible to even write a generalized study of the greatest monument of early Flemish painting, "The Ghent (GENT—hard g) Altarpiece" in a few paragraphs, but every student deserves to be introduced to the northern equivalent of Michelangelo's ceiling painting in the Sistine Chapel. In basic form the altarpiece is a tryptych (TRIP-tick, a central painting with two hinged wings), with each unit having four panels. In addition, the back sides of the wings are painted, thus the altarpiece compromises twenty parts of assorted shapes, sizes, and subjects. This work was completed by Jan van Eyck in 1432, but started by his brother Hubert around 1425. We shall not attempt to attribute individual panels, but confine ourselves to studying the subject matter and especially intriguing technical bits of information. When the altarpiece is completely closed (Fig. 146) the upper section shows an "Annunciation" taking place in a large room, with Gabriel and the Virgin being separated by two panels of room space containing no furnishings but having windows through which we see sections of the City of Ghent. In a display of virtuosity the artist has painted onto the canvas shadows that would appear to be caused by the frame. The two center

Figure 146. Hubert and Jan van Eyck, "The Ghent Altarpiece" (closed), completed in 1432, St. Bavon, Ghent (copyright A.C.L. Bruxelles).

panels on the lower level feature grey-painted statues of St. John the Evangelist and St. John the Baptist. The saints are flanked by glowing naturalistic portraits of Jodocus Vydt and his wife Isabella Borluut who commissioned this work for their burial chapel. The two St. Johns painted as statues (grisailles—gree-ZAY-uh) serve as keys to the story within: one was the forerunner of the Lamb of God, the other was the apostle and mystic who was given the Apocalyptic Revelation.

When the doors of the altar are open (Fig. 147), van Eyck's vision of paradise is revealed in

Figure 147. "The Ghent Altarpiece" (open) (copyright A.C.L. Bruxelles).

full splendour. The lower central panel depicts the apocalyptic vision of the mystic lamb on the altar on which is inscribed "Behold the Lamb of God which taketh away the sins of the world," and "Jesus, the Way, the Truth, and the Life." This heaven is full of exotic trees and flowers, buildings which indicate that heaven is very much like Flanders. Before the altar are the evangelists reading their books and behind them are kings, prophets, and doctors of the church. On the other side kneel the simply-robed apostles, behind whom are popes and bishops in rich robes. The wings which flank the "Adoration of the Lamb" are filled with hermit saints, pilgrims, judges, and knights. In the background we see St. Agnes with her lamb, St. Barbara with her tower, and St. Ursula leading her company of martyred virgins. The entire lower series shows all good people paying respect to the Lamb of God and the symbols of His Passion.

In the center upper panel, God sits in majesty, a young, authoritative image crowned with the papal tiara. On His left sits the Queen of Heaven, Mary, eternally young and beautiful; on His right is John the Baptist. This central group is flanked by a chorus of angels on one side and angelic musicians on the other. The fifteenth century was a period of impressive church music and at that time Flanders was the music center of Europe. This art, like painting, was encouraged by the Dukes of Burgundy. Masses written by Jacob Obrecht (YAH-cub o-BREGHT), an early Flemish composer and teacher of the humanist Erasmus (ah-RAZ-muss), were played and sung throughout Flanders. Organs and instrumental music came into use in Flemish churches at this time and it is not surprising, therefore, that one angel plays an organ, one a harp, and another a vielle, an early form of the viol (the predecessor of the violin family).

In the pair of half panels which complete the upper wings of the altarpiece, the painter introduced nude figures of Adam and Eve, the first monumental nude figures in northern art. They are part of the story, for their sin (mankind's sin) made the sacrifice of the Lamb of God necessary. These realistic nudes are painted at a different level than the other figures in the upper panels, which are viewed from the normal line of vision: Adam and Eve are seen from below and one can look at the sole of Adam's right foot. They alone of all figures in the inner section of the altarpiece are contained in niches—they are outside the glorious company of heaven.

The painting has numerous inscriptions, symbols in tiles and fabrics, juxtaposition of figures, a complexity of stories and allegories—it is the synthesis of Gothic thought and vision in painting. The spiritual elements are conveyed in natural forms, which the van Eycks recognized had beauty in themselves.

It is tempting to write about other great Flemish master painters of the fifteenth century: the sculpturesque Van der Weyden, the very human Petrus Christus, and especially the demon-ridden Hieronymus Bosch. But it is a temptation that must be resisted. It is important, however, to mention that Jan van Eyck, like Giotto, was a learned, well-traveled, respected bourgeois. The Duke of Burgundy, Philip the Good, used Van Eyck as a diplomat, sent him to Portugal to arrange a political marriage alliance, and served as godfather to his son. The Gothic artist was no serf or monastery-enslaved monk. He was a man of the world, a world in which there had been a synthesis of spiritualism and secularism, of various art forms and styles, a synthesis which was the foundation for the modern world.

BIBLIOGRAPHY

Adams, Henry. *Mont St. Michel and Chartres.* American Institute of Architects, 1904. Any edition of the often reproduced work will please the romantic reader. Nineteenth-century prose and romanticism at its finest.*

Conant, Kenneth John. *Carolingian and Romanesque Architecture, 800-1200.* Baltimore: Pelican History of Art, Penguin Books, Inc., 1959.* Includes all important monuments of the period, excellent descriptions and clear definitions of architectural terms.

Dupont, J. and Gnudi, C. *Gothic Painting.* New York: Skira, Inc., 1954. Superb colored illustrations.

Evans, Joan, *Art in Medieval France.* New York: Oxford University Press, 1948. Comprehensive study written with clarity and charm.

Friedlander, Max J. *Early Netherlandish Paintings from Van Eyck to Breugel.* London: Phaidon Press, 1956. Well-written, well-illustrated and comprehensive.

Grabar, André and Nordenfalk, Carl. *Early Medieval Painting.* New York: Skira, Inc., 1957. A beautifully illustrated book. The text is difficult without previous study of the subject.

Mâle, Émile. *Religious Art in France in the Thirteenth Century.* New York: Dutton, 1913. Any book written by Mâle will give the reader hours of pleasure and fascinating information. Mâle is especially charming when he is very esoteric and controversial. He even argues with himself.

——. *Religious Art from the Twelfth to the Eighteenth Century.* New York: Pantheon Books, Inc., 1948.* A very diversified study of monuments, symbols, social life, and believe-it-or-nots. One of the most charming books in paperback editions.

Nordenfalk, Carl. *Romanesque Painting.* New York: Skira, Inc., 1958. Beautiful color illustrations of paintings unfamiliar to most art-lovers in the United States. Text is difficult but rewarding.

Panofsky, Erwin. *Early Netherlandish Painting.* 2 vols. New Haven: Harvard University Press, 1954. Definitive, exhaustive and exhausting unless taken in small doses. Very rewarding.

Pevsner, Nikolaus. *An Outline of European Architecture.* 6th ed. Baltimore: Penguin Books, Inc., 1960.* The true beginner's guide.

Pope-Hennessy, John. *Introduction to Italian Sculpture.* 3 vols. London: Phaidon Press, 1955-62. A superb, easy-to-read, history which is much more than an introduction for it covers Medieval, Renaissance, and Baroque sculpture. Hundreds of fine black and white photographs.

Simson, Otto G. von. *The Gothic Cathedral.* New York: Pantheon Books, Inc., 1956.* All aspects of the Gothic cathedral are discussed in depth.

Swarzenski, Hanns. *Monuments of Romantic Art.* Chicago: University of Chicago Press, 1954. All aspects of Romanesque discussed with clarity. Fine photographs, especially of small metalwork and carving.

*Paperback.

Music in Medieval Life

CHAPTER 16

■ Only the Christian Church stood firm amidst the general confusion after the failure of Roman professionalism and the crumbling of secular authority. Along with the withdrawal to monastic life there was a movement to put the house in order, to reform and stabilize the organization of the Church and to impose order on the great diversity of religious practices.

Pope Gregory I (590-604) was responsible for the organization and codification of the church's liturgical music (music associated with public worship). The unwieldy mass of traditional music, much of it of uncertain (pagan) origin, was reduced to a single large collection of melodies suitable for Christian worship. Because of the ravages of time and the fallibility of human memory (the music codified by Gregory was transmitted by oral tradition) most of the liturgical music known today was composed during and after the so-called Carolingian Renaissance which began under the Frankish king Charlemagne.

SACRED MUSIC

The Christian Church, with its teachings, liturgy, priesthood, lands and buildings was an inseparable part of the medieval world, though it was not the whole of medieval life. In an age in which God was the ultimate reality, people needed not only their religious faith but the complicated apparatus (dogma, doctrine, discipline) which organized Christianity built through the centuries and which ensured almost absolute dependence upon the Church—for the Church needed the people, all of the people. Whether through rational instruction, emotional appeal, or just plain fear of eternal damnation and/or social ostracism (or varying combinations of these), the Church commanded the loyalty of everyone from the lowliest of serfs to powerful (but frequently illiterate) noblemen, not to mention the few members of a small but ever-increasing educated class.

Music of the Church performed an indispensable function in imparting to the faithful a feeling of sublime reverence. The texts of the Latin mass were almost totally incomprehensible to the vast majority of the congregation, even though the average person had some knowledge of the general import of the divine service. Conversely, the Latin chants of the choir of monks had a direct impact upon the emotions; the undulating flow of the music resounded throughout the resonant stone churches and evoked in the worshippers strong feelings amounting to a mystical communion with the world of the spirit, an exalted world above and beyond the pain and sorrow of earthly existence. Even today, when performed in a medieval church by a good choir, these same chants somehow manage to move believers and nonbelievers alike to a sense of awe and reverence. If these old chants can elevate avowed non-Christians to a state of suspended disbelief, one can begin to feel the effect they must have had upon devout Christians of an earlier age.

Gregorian chant[1] is the term usually applied to the nearly 3,000 melodies which comprise the liturgical chant of the Roman Catholic church. Plainsong probably derives from Greek and Jewish sources. Some of the oriental characteristics can be traced to Jewish synagogue music, but similar characteristics appear in the music of ancient Greece.

The repertory of Gregorian chant falls into the two main classes of *mass* and *office*. The *mass* is the most solemn of Roman services. It represents the commemoration and symbolic repetition of the mystery of Christian life, death, resurrection and salvation. Matins, Vespers, Compline, etc., are among the other daily services, which are referred to as *offices*.

The mass consists of the *proper*, in which the texts vary according to the liturgical calendar, and the *ordinary*, which uses the same texts throughout the church year. Both proper and ordinary have texts which are recited or chanted by the celebrants (clergy) or sung by the choir.[2] The complete mass is outlined here (italics indicate the sung portions of the text).

THE MASS

ORDINARY (same text)	*PROPER* (changing texts)
	1. *Introit*
2. *Kyrie*	
3. *Gloria*	
	4. Oratio (prayers, collect)
	5. Epistle
	6. Gradual
	7. *Alleluia* (or *Tract* during Lent)
	8. Gospel
9. *Credo*	
	10. *Offertory*
	11. Secret
	12. Preface
13. *Sanctus*	
14. Canon	
15. *Agnus dei*	
	16. *Communion*
	17. Post-communion
18. *Ite missa est* (or *Benedicamus Domino)*	

Although modernization of the mass permits the universal incorporation of indigenous modern languages (in place of some of the Latin), increased layman participation and congregational singing, the essential structure remains.

CHURCH MODES

The melodies of Gregorian chant are analyzed by a theoretical system called the eight church modes (or ecclesiastical modes), a process similar to the Greater Perfect System, but in a much more simplified form. The eight church modes (also called the eight tones) helped categorize a body of music which had been in constant use for many centuries. Early Christian scholars tried to pattern their modal theory on the Greek model, but ended up with quite a different system because of misconceptions based upon an inadequate knowledge of Greek music.

The ecclesiastical or *church modes*, as they are usually called, exist today, not only because of the continuing tradition of Gregorian chant, but more importantly because thousands of secular melodies from folk songs to classical music to contemporary popular music are *modal*, for example, *Greensleeves*, *I Wonder As I Wander*,[3] the beginning of the second movement of Brahms' *Fourth Symphony*, and numerous songs written by various rock groups. The medieval church modes are alive and well and a simplified explanation of just what they were (and still are) will assist in some understanding of a body of music over fourteen centuries old.

Medieval musicians (usually monks) knew something about the Greek Greater Perfect System but nothing of its complexities and very little of its practical application. As a result, they literally

---

1. Also called *plainsong* or occasionally, but more properly, *Roman chant*.
2. High mass includes music; low mass usually does not.
3. A spiritual which is based in part on the middle section of Chopin's *Fantaisie Impromptu*, which later inspired a popular song entitled *I'm Always Chasing Rainbows*.

turned the Greek System upside down by reversing the Greek names for the modes and by running their modal scales from low pitch to high pitch. One illustration will suffice:

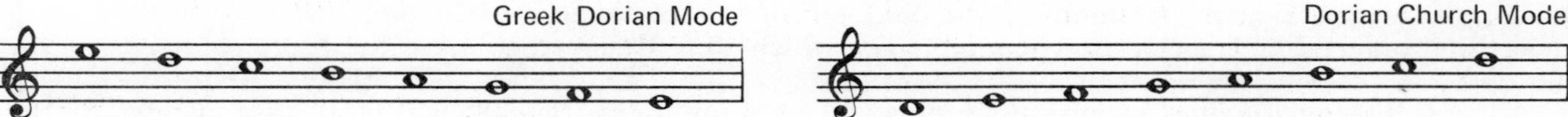

There are four basic church modes plus one variant of each for a total of eight modes, as opposed to the seven different Greek modes. However, the four related church modes (Hypodorian, Hypophrygian, Hypolydian, Hypomixolydian) sound more or less like the four basic sets of pitches. The myriad possibilities of Greek music (100,000 or more potential varities of the *same* melody) have been reduced to a single, church-approved tuning system and four sanctioned sets of pitches from which composers could derive their melodies.[4] The modes illustrated below have a Greek name plus a number which served the practical purposes of brevity and precision. These are so-called *authentic* modes. Modes 2, 4, 6, and 8 are referred to as *plagal* modes.

Church Modes

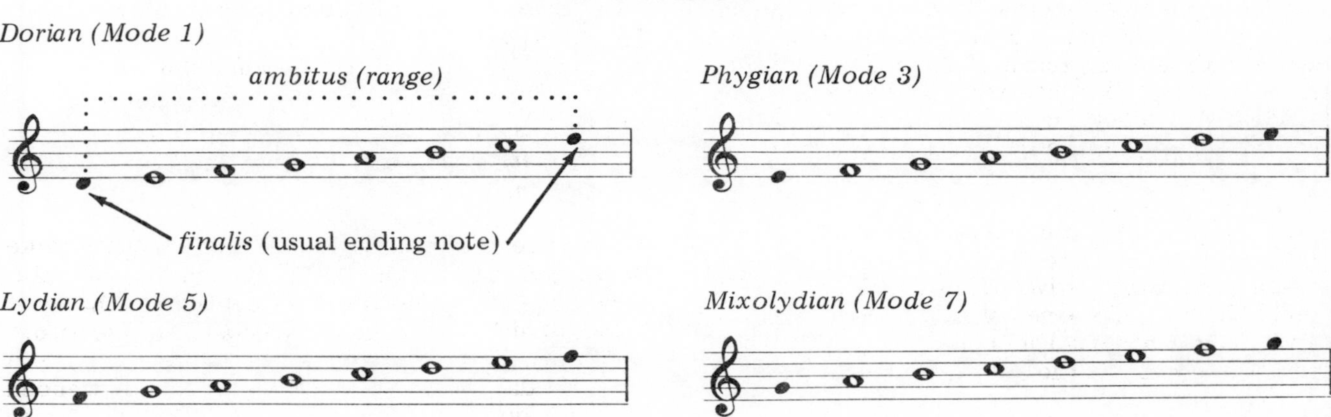

The difference in sound (and mood) between the church modes and later scale patterns is illustrated by the following three versions of the beginning of the old English song *Greensleeves.* The first version is based on the major mode or scale (see n. 15 in this chapter) which has been in common use since the seventeenth century. Version number two is the one frequently but erroneously associated with the Christmas carol *What Child Is This?* and is in the minor mode (again refer to n. 15). The third version presents the song in its original Dorian mode.

Three Versions of Greensleeves

4. Whether melodies are derived from existing scales or whether theoretical scale systems, such as the church modes, are based upon existing music is a circular argument analogous to the problem of the chicken and the egg.

The reasons for the drastic differences between Greek and Christian liturgical music are not difficult to analyze. Greek music performed many functions and served many masters; church music had one function and served one master. Greek music was both vocal and instrumental; liturgical music was entirely vocal for several centuries. (Instruments were banned because, in part, of unpleasant associations of instrumental music with pagan Roman ceremonies.) In brief, all of the exotic flavor of Greek vocal and instrumental music was reduced to a body of vocal melodies which were designed to serve the liturgical needs of the church.

The following *Alleluias* which can be sung at Communion illustrate all eight modes as indicated by the Arabic numerals. All should be sung fairly rapidly in a smoothly flowing manner. The small notes following large notes ( ) are sung very lightly. A dash over a note indicates a slight prolongation ( ). A slight stress is indicated by a vertical dash under a note ( ). There is no unanimity of opinion about the singing of plainsong nor do these examples display all the possibilities of performance practices; however, these eight short examples do illustrate both the complete modal system and a few of the characteristics of chant. All Alleluias are *melismatic*, several notes to a syllable, and many are of probable Jewish and/or Oriental origin. The 8 below the treble clef sign indicates that the notes will all sound an octave lower.[5]

Gregorian Chant: *Alleluias*[6]

MEDIEVAL NOTATION

The prescribed notation for Gregorian chant is still the system developed during the Middle Ages. "For the proper execution of the chant, the manner of forming the notes and of linking them together, established by our forefathers and in constant and universal use in the Middle Ages, is of great importance and is recommended still as the norm for modern editions."[7]

5. For listening procedures for medieval music see, "Listening Outline (second stage)" at the end of this chapter.
6. *The Liber Usualis,* edited by the Benedictines of Solesmes, published by the Society of St. John the Evangelist, Desclée & Cie., printers to the Holy See and the Sacred Congregation of Rites, Tournai (Belgium), p. 96-97.
7. *Ibid.*, p. x.

Below is the previously cited Alleluia for Communion (Dorian mode) in medieval notation followed by the same chant in modern notation. These two examples obviously represent different stages of development of the same system. Because of the unique characteristics of plainsong, the old notation is entirely adequate.

Gregorian Chant: *Alleluia*[8]

Sacred monophonic music of the Middle Ages includes *Gregorian chant*, variations of chant such as *tropes* and *sequences*, and music associated with liturgical drama such as the *conductus.*

GREGORIAN CHANT

Gregorian chant is *monophonic* (unison only), nonmetrical, and rhythmically flexible because it is bound to the word rhythms of the text. Traditionally it is sung by a male soloist and a male chorus without accompaniment (a capella).

The fluid and supple melodies of plainsong display a great range of melodic types and characteristics. In general, though there are many exceptions, the *range* is no more than one note larger than an octave (ninth). The melodic motion is usually stepwise (conjunct), and, except for the octave, large skips are quite rare.

Most chants are sung to prose texts, with the great majority of these from the psalms. Other Scriptural texts are used, especially in Canticles, Introits and Graduals. The most significant non-Scriptural prose texts are in the ordinary of the mass: Kyrie, Gloria, Credo, Sanctus, Agnus Dei. In regard to text setting, the melodies fall into three main classes: *syllabic* (one note to each syllable), *neumatic* (two to four notes to a syllable), and *melismatic* (still more notes to a syllable).

Following is the first item of Mass IV (also called *Missa Cunctipotens*), an example of tenth-century plainsong. The text is Greek, with *Kyrie eleison* (Lord have mercy on us) sung three times (for the Holy

Gregorian Chant Kyrie IV: *Cunctipotens*[9]

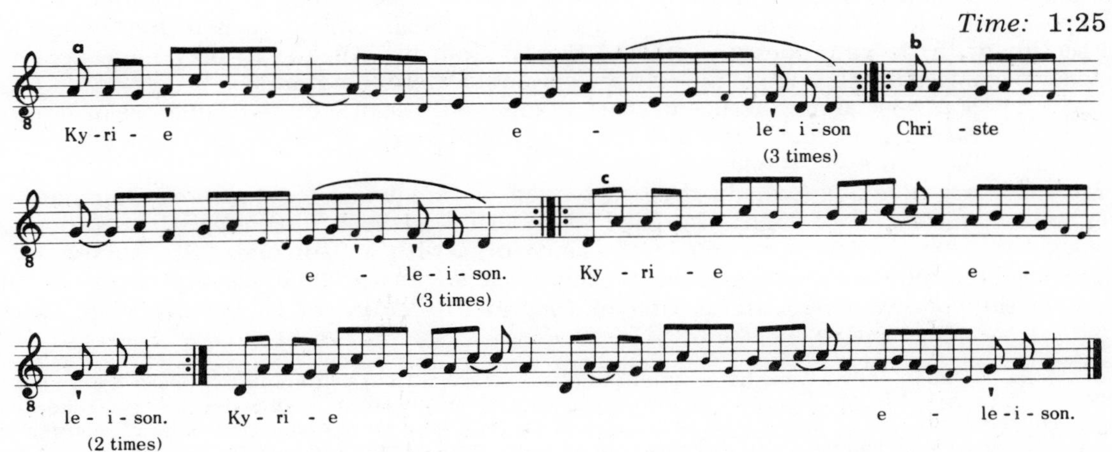

8. *Ibid.*, p. 96.
9. *Ibid.*, p. 25.

Trinity), *Christe eleison* (Christ have mercy on us) sung three times, followed by three *Kyrie eleisons.* The chant is in mode 1 (Dorian) and is melismatic. The double dots before and after the double bars indicate that the section is to be repeated. Modal melodies do not always follow the "rules" by ending on the prescribed *finalis*, as is the case here. In terms of its musical form, the piece falls into three distinct sections which can be labeled a-b-c. All three sections have a note pattern of a-a-g-a at the beginning (commencing on the second note of section c) and sections a and b have identical cadences (ending patterns) of seven notes. Because there is no clear repetition of musical material the sectional pattern is a-b-c.

Tropes

A *trope* (Latin, *tropus*, "figure of speech") is a textual addition to an authorized text. Explanatory sentences and even whole poems were inserted between words of the original text. The longer melismatic passages which lent themselves to this procedure consequently became syllabic chants. The practice of troping reached its height during the Romanesque period, the ninth through thirteenth centuries.

Some historians explain troping as a natural desire toward continuing creativity in the face of unchanging texts authorized centuries earlier by Pope Gregory I. Another possible and practical explanation would consider troping as a method for remembering complicated melismatic passages. During the ninth century, and earlier, choirs had to sing the liturgy by memory after having learned the melodies by rote from monks who were sent out to the monasteries. At this time, music notation was in a low state of development and could provide only an approximation of the actual notes to be sung. Trying to remember a melody with many notes and few words must have been as trying for ninth-century musical amateurs as it is today.[10]

Troping was used most often with items of the Ordinary: Kyrie tropes, Gloria tropes and so forth. As troping became widespread it tended to overshadow some of the authorized texts with the consequence that all tropes were abolished by the Council of Trent (1543-63).

Following is the first part (section a) of the Kyrie IV illustrated on the preceding page. Notes added to or removed from the original melody are indicated by parentheses.

Kyrie-Trope: *Omnipotens*[11]

Time: :15

Om - ni - po-tens ge - ni - tor, De - us om - ni - um cre - a - tor: e - lei - son.

A single Kyrie Eleison (Lord have mercy) now reads, in translation: "Omnipotent Father, Lord creator of all: have mercy upon us."

Sequences

A sequence is actually the oldest form of trope, an Alleluia trope. Many Alleluias are of Oriental origin (at least in part) and end with a long melisma on the last syllable, which is where the sequence is added. This final section with its new poetry is then detached from the Alleluia to become a separate body of music. Extensive changes in the original melody are common after separation.

The sequence is of special importance because it apparently signified the beginnings of music composition as such. Commencing during the ninth century there gradually emerged from feudal society the creative individual, the composer, the artist.

A large repertory of sequences and rhymed sequences threatened for a time to dominate traditional Gregorian chant. The Council of Trent also tried to abolish sequences, but met with such opposition that four sequences were permitted to remain in the repertory (with a fifth one, "Stabat Mater," added in 1727). The oldest of the surviving sequences is the so-called Easter Sequence by Wipo (c. 1000-1050). Reproduced on the following page is the first of four main sections of the sequence, in Dorian mode.

10. Guido of Arezzo (c. 995-1050) a Benedictine monk who, among other things, attempted to teach the liturgy to choirs of monks exclaimed in despair: "In our times, of all men, singers are the most foolish . . . marvelous singers, and singer's pupils, though they sing every day for a hundred years, will never sing one antiphon, not even a short one, of themselves, without a master, losing enough time in singing to have learned thoroughly both sacred and secular letters." Oliver Strunk, *Source Readings in Music History* (New York: W.W. Norton & Company, Inc.), p. 117.
11. A. Schubiger, *Die Sangerschule von St. Gallen* (1858), p. 40.

Sequence: *Victimae paschali laudes*[12]

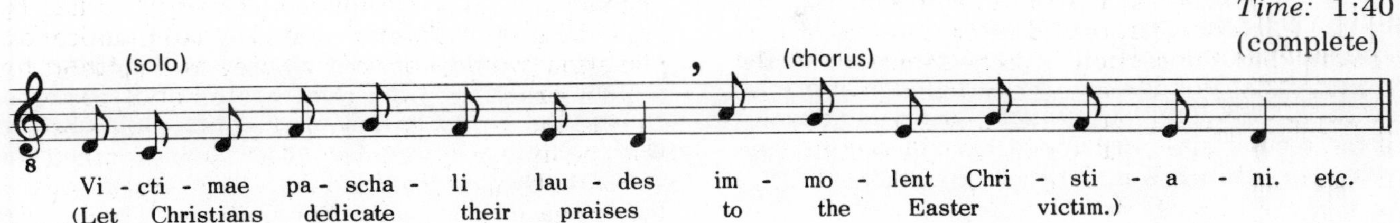
Time: 1:40
(complete)
(solo)
(chorus)
Vi - cti - mae pa - scha - li lau - des im - mo - lent Chri - sti - a - ni. etc.
(Let Christians dedicate their praises to the Easter victim.)

LITURGICAL DRAMA

Liturgical drama developed during the tenth and eleventh centuries from Introit tropes for Easter and Christmas. These biblical stories with dialogue, action, and music were presented *inside* the church, although they were never part of the official liturgy. They continued to enlarge during the twelfth and thirteenth centuries while being gradually moved outside to a church porch. By the fourteenth century, liturgical drama developed into enormously popular "mysteries" (corruption of Latin, *ministerium*, service) which were performed in the public squares and eventually on the wagons of the guilds.

The following excerpt from "The Play of the Three Kings" dates from about the late eleventh century. Some of the melodies were borrowed from plainsong but some music was undoubtedly composed for the occasion. The mode is Dorian and the style, befitting a public performance in which the text should be understood, is mostly syllabic.

Liturgical Drama: *Infantem Vidimus*[13]

Time: :35
Shepherds
Boys
In - fan - tem vi - di - mus. Qui sunt hi, quos stel -
(We have seen the Infant. Who are those whom the
la du - cit nos a - de - un - tes, in - au - di - ta fe - ren - tes?
star leads, approaching us and bearing strange things?
Magi
Nos su - mus quos cer - ni - tes re - ges Thar - sis et A - ra - bum et Sa -
We are those whom you see – the Kings of Tharsis, Arabia,
ba, do - na of - fe - ren - tes Chri - sto Re - gi - na - to Do - mi - no.
and Saba, offering gifts to Christ the King, the new-born Lord.)

12. *The Liber Usualis,* p. 780.
13. Dom P. Schubiger, O.S.B., "Das liturgische Drama des Mittelalters and seine Musik," *Musikalische Spicilegien* (Berlin, 1876), p. 44 (citing Einsiedeln, *Stiftsbibliothek,* No. 367).

The *conductus*, a generic term for Latin lyric poetry of the twelfth and thirteenth centuries, is associated with the production of liturgical drama. It was sung as important characters in the play processed on and off the stage, for example, the Virgin Mary "conducted" on stage by an appropriate song. The conductus was the Latin counterpart of the secular style developed by troubadours and trouvères (see below under secular music).

Following is a *conductus* from "The Play of Daniel" in which the Virgin Mary rides into the cathedral on an ass. The mode is Mixolydian (mode 7) and the style syllabic. A regular rhythmic organization replaces the free-flowing lines of plainsong, tropes and sequences. The conductus is *metrical* (quadruple meter in this case) as befits its function as processional music. Of the seven verses, only the first verse is quoted.

Conductus: *Song of the Ass*[14]

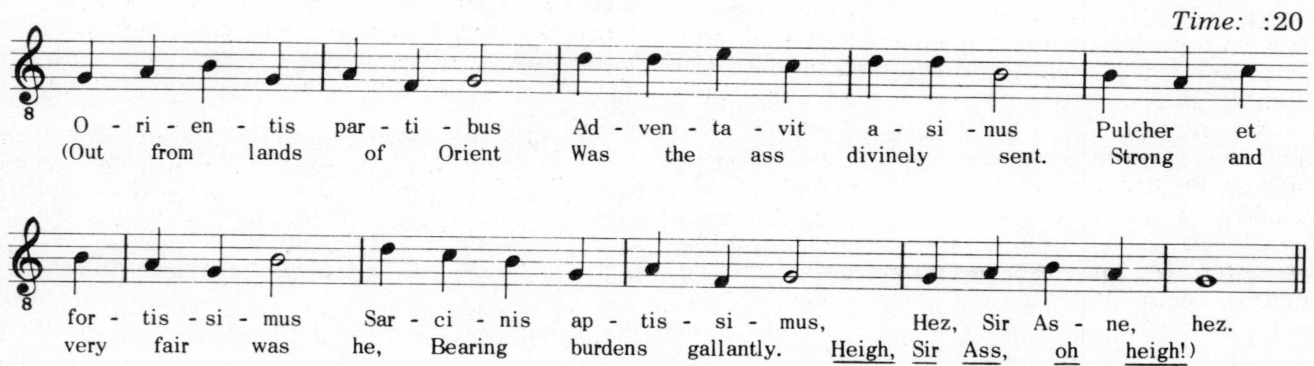

SECULAR MUSIC

If we are to evaluate secular music of the Middle Ages strictly on the basis of surviving manuscripts, we would have to conclude that there was no secular music prior to the appearance of the first troubadour songs in c. A.D. 1050. In point of fact, sacred music was written down by scholarly monks while secular music was not. The almost total dominance of the medieval Church assured the preservation of accumulated knowledge which the Church deemed important, and this did not include, among other things, secular music. Folk music survived as it always has (prior to modern recording techniques) solely as an oral tradition; people sang and played notes that were never written down.

The *profession* of music could be practiced only in the Church (choirs, choirmasters, organists, composers) while the *practice* of music must have existed, as it has in every society, in the everyday lives of people, in their marrying, burying, working, fighting, and dancing.

Troubadours

The *troubadours*, the aristocratic poet-musicians of Provence (southern France), began a tradition around A.D. 1050 which spread into northern France *(trouvères)* and Germany *(minnesingers)* before finally dying out with the *meistersingers* of sixteenth-century Germany. In a manner of speaking however, the troubadour tradition has never died out. Its origins are obscure but are certainly bound up with the age of chivalry and the crusades.

The institutions of chivalry probably began in the eleventh century as an occupation for the lower warrior class: the knights. At a time when the worst disorders of the so-called Dark Ages had ended, these warriors had little to occupy their attention since most were illiterate and theirs was a barren, isolated world of activities confined mainly to eating, drinking and fighting. Pope Urban II's call for the First Crusade in 1095 ultimately propelled Europe out of its cultural, economic and political isolation. Bored barons now had a Holy War on which to expend their energies. While the men were warring on the infidels, their women were quietly increasing their own importance in daily affairs outside the castle, which led to the development of the Virgin Cult in which women were credited with the idealized virtues of the Virgin Mary.

14. G.M. Dreves, *Analecta hymnica xx*, 217, 257; H.C. Greene, *Speculum* vi.

The troubadours sang mostly of courtly love, of beautiful and virtuous ladies and brave and daring knights. Accompanied by a professional musician of the lower classes *(jongleur* or *minstrel)*, the troubadour roamed the countryside singing of love and romance and carrying the news, in song, between villages, manor houses, chateaux and castles.

Troubadour songs are generally *strophic*, using the same melody for each verse. Contrary to the smoothly flowing music of Gregorian chant, secular music was usually constructed of a series of phrases, which is just another way of saying that words and music move in a manner comparable to a paragraph, that is, phrases flow together to make sentences and sentences add up to a completed idea or paragraph. A musical phrase is a partial idea which may lead to a completion of the thought which an English teacher would call a sentence and musicians would call a musical period. Musical phrases can be arbitrarily designated with lower case letters (a, b, etc.) and musical periods (sentences or sections) can be labeled with capital letters (A, B, etc.).

Identification of phrases and periods in music is simply a practical way for the nonmusician to listen to music in a reasonably intelligent manner. Because we cannot tell where music is going until it has arrived at its destination, the understanding of the structure or form of a composition has been proven to be the easiest and best way to approach music for both nonmusician and professional musician alike. Once listeners learn to identify musical phrases and periods, they can begin to *move along* with the music and thus approach some comprehension of the total composition.

The following troubadour song is a case in point. It is composed of four different phrases called *a, b, c, d* (indicated by the dotted line), some of which are repeated to make a total of seven phrases. These seven phrases are grouped into three larger sections or musical *periods* and designated as A-A-B. The following will indicate the basic structure of the piece; the lower-case letter stands for the *phrase structure*, and the capital letters indicate the larger groupings of musical periods which identify the overall *form* (structure) of the piece: A A B / *ab, ab, cdb.* All troubadour *cansos*, and there are many, have an A-A-B form. The piece on the following page has a further unifying factor called the *motive* (indicated by brackets and the number 1). A motive can be defined as the smallest unit of musical thought, usually three or four notes, and is a means by which the composer can unify his composition and thus bring ever more order into his structure. The language of all troubadour songs is Provençal, the vernacular of medieval southern France (Provence).

As in the case with some of the secular music of the time, the mode of this composition does not conform to any of the patterns of the church modes. This particular piece has a strong tendency towards what would be called a *major scale* (c-d-e-f-g-a-b-c).[15]

Trouvères

By mid-twelfth century the troubadour influence had spread to northern France, where Blondel de Nesles, minstrel to Richard-the-Lion-Hearted, was one of the great *trouvères.* Trouvère *chansons*, like the troubadour songs, were monophonic and probably unaccompanied. The chansons, however, were more clearly defined in their rhythmic and formal structures and in general more refined and elegant.

The following chanson is a *virelai* which has contrasting rotating patterns of words and music. The verse pattern (words) of eight phrases can be described as *ab cd ef ab* or, in larger units: A B C A / *ab cd ef ab*. The A section functions as a *refrain* which begins and ends the song. The music also has eight phrases, with a phrase structure of *ab cc ab ab.* Using larger units this can be described as A B A A / *ab cc ab ab*. There is a characteristic rhythmic pattern which appears twelve times: ♫♩♩. This virelai, in common with many trouvère songs, uses a scale of f-g-a-b♭-c-d-e-f. This can only be described as a clearcut *major mode* (see n. 15).

15. The *major mode* differs from the church modes in two respects: 1. it has a *fixed* pattern of tones and semitones, and 2. there is only *one* major mode. In other words, a piece is in major or it is not.

A major scale is composed of two equal tetrachords (T-T-S) joined by a whole step:

C Major F Major

The alter ego of the major is the *minor mode*, the other basic structure which makes up the so-called *major-minor system* which, during the seventeenth century, superseded the church modes. In the major-minor system all music is in either major or in minor. The eight church modes are reduced, in other words, to two: major or minor.

C major

C minor

Troubadour Canso: *Be m'an perdut*[16]

16. C. Appel, *Bernart von Ventadorn* (Halle, 1915), Plate ix (citing Milan manuscript *Chansonnier G*, folio 14).

Trouvere *Virelai: Or la truix*[17]

Minnesingers

The German *minnesinger* tradition began about a century after the appearance of the first troubadour songs in Provençe and persisted long after French secular music had changed to other forms. In medieval German, *minne* means "love," but most *minnelieder* (literally "love songs") texts incline toward rather melancholy narration with small concern for the amorous life. In keeping with German conservatism, minnelieder make less use of regular meters and more use of the church modes. The favorite form was the *barform* (A-A-B), or exactly the same form used by troubadour *cansos* and trouvère *ballades.*[18]

Goliards

The *goliards* of the tenth through thirteenth centuries were wandering students, vagabonds, defrocked monks, minstrels, rascals, artists and dreamers, the medieval equivalent of all those disenchanted with today's Establishment, regardless of age. Only one goliard melody was written in a musical notation which could be deciphered, but

17. Bodleian Oxford, Douce 308, folio 226 and 237.

18. *Barform* is from the medieval German name, i.e., a "bar" has a form of A-A-B. The form is as old as the ancient Greek modes and persists to the present day, particularly in Lutheran chorales, for example, "A Mighty Fortress Is Our God." The same form is also used in the poetry of the *blues.*

large collections of their poetry have been preserved, including the famous collection called "Carmina Burana." A sampling of the opening lines of a few poems from "Carmina Burana" clearly indicates the themes of most of their poetry:

"O fortune, variable as the moon"

"I lament fortune's blows"

"Were the world all mine from the sea to the Rhine, I would gladly forsake it all if the Queen of England were in my arms"

"In rage and bitterness I talk to myself"

"I am the Abbot of Cluny, and I spend my time with drinkers"

"When we are in the tavern we don't care who has died"

"The God of Love flies everywhere"

"When a boy and a girl are alone together"

"Sweetest boy I give myself completely to you"

"Hail to thee, most beautiful"[19]

HARMONY

Fully developed *harmonic* or *homophonic* music is a singular contribution made by Western civilization, just as jazz is America's unique contribution to music. The music of the Middle and Far East and of Africa emphasizes melody, *timbre* (tone color) and rhythm (particularly in Africa). Since no other culture has developed music in a *vertical* sense (harmony, chords, melody plus accompaniment, etc.), one wonders why Western musicians turned from the single melodic line to simultaneous melodies and eventually to the progression of vertical grouping of tones which are called chords or harmony. The answer would seem to lie in the very rigidity of the church mode system. Composers had at their disposal only one sanctioned tuning system (the Pythagorean) and only four basic modes. Boredom is perhaps responsible for more change (and sometimes progress) than one would ever dream and boredom seems to be a motivating factor in the development of harmony. After centuries of manipulating a limited number of notes in a limited number of patterns, *someone* (unrecorded by history) conceived of the possibility of writing *simultaneous* melodies.

At some unknown time and place during the eighth or ninth centuries (probably), experiments were begun which led to new directions in music. What would happen if there were two or even three melodies sung at the same time? Text, rhythm, mode and timbre could possibly remain the same, but there would be one or more additional melodies. And so began the crude attempts at what became, by the sixteenth century, a vast repertory of complex and sophisticated music consisting essentially of four, six, or even eight plainsongs sung simultaneously, and all skillfully blended to become the magnificent choral music of the High Renaissance.

The technique of writing simultaneous melodies is called *counterpoint*, and the resulting musical style is *polyphony*. *Counterpoint* (Latin, *punctus contra punctum*, "note against note") is the skill involved in combining melodies, of putting note against note. *Polyphony* (Greek, *poly*, "many"; *phonos*, "voice") is a style of composition in which two or more melodies are sung or sounded together. The one-voice (monophonic) chant becomes a many-voiced composition (polyphonic).

Polyphony can be described as the *horizontal* aspect of harmony:

melody 1
melody 2
melody 3

There is also a *vertical* harmony present in all polyphonic music, inasmuch as notes are actually sounded together:

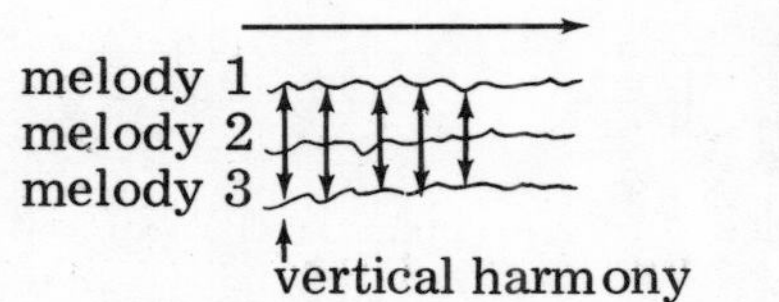

horizontal harmony (polyphony)

Emphasis on the vertical relationships of harmony did not develop until the seventeenth century.

ORGANUM

Early polyphonic music was called *organum*, possibly in reference to the fact that the music was an "organized" addition to plainsong. Composers selected melodies from the liturgy and added notes below at a fixed interval.

Strict Organum

Organum of the Fifth: Beginning with a chant in Dorian mode, for example, composers added a second voice a fifth below. The two voices then moved in parallel lines throughout, in *parallel fifths*.

Of course they also experimented with *Organum of the Fourth* (the other "acceptable" interval permitted by medieval music theorists), and from

19. Hans Spanke, "Der Codex Buranus als Liederbuch," *Zeitschrift fur Musikwissenschaft* xiii (1931), p. 241.

there to *Composite Organum*, which was simply a duplicating of the two existing voices until, for the first time in the history of music, a rudimentary kind of four-part harmony was realized.

The practice of strict organum probably did not last too long, because composers sought ways of freeing the added melody from its strict dependence on the original chant. Their experiments included three different ways of achieving some independence for the added voice: *parallel*, *free* and *melismatic* organum.

Parallel Organum

The voices began together (in unison) after which the original plainsong moved up until it was a fourth above the organal voice and the two voices could move in parallel fourths. The voices came together to make a unison at cadences. This combined oblique and parallel motion can be diagrammed as follows:

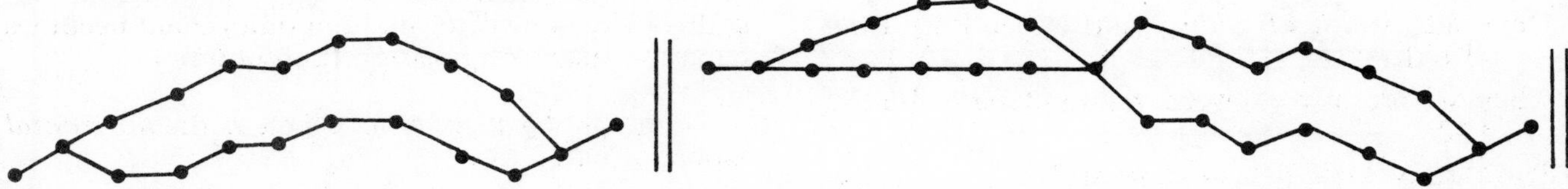

and notated as follows (verses 1 and 2 are sung with the first line of music followed by verses 3 and 4 with the second line):

Parallel Organum
Sequence: *Rex caeli, Domine*[20]

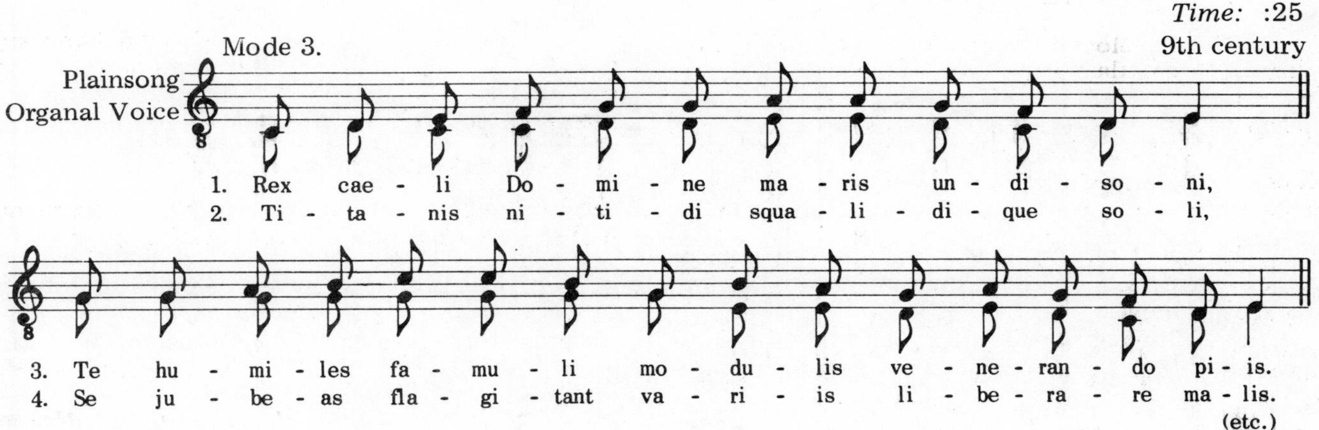

Free Organum

In their search for ways in which to make the added melody more independent of the original, composers exploited the idea of *contrary motion*, referred to at the time as *free organum*. When the plainsong rose in pitch, the *organal* voice (added melody) would go down in pitch, and vice versa, a procedure still endemic to polyphonic music. This free organum technique can be seen diagrammed on the following page.

The search for at least two independent melodic lines was hampered by the lack of a precise rhythmic notation. Pitches could be fixed but their relative duration was quite subjective. The practical problem is simply stated: How can two independent melodic lines be sung simultaneously and still stay together?

Melismatic Organum

Melismatic organum (in addition to parallel and free organum) represents another partial solution to this problem. The procedure was not complicated but the final result was necessarily dependent upon the ability of the composer to write an interesting new melody which was compatible with the original plainsong. The preexisting plainsong was slowed down while the organal voice sang a number of notes *(melismas)* against each drawn-out note of plainsong. In actual practice a director would perhaps point to those singing the *tenor* part (Latin *tenere*, "to hold") to indicate when they should shift to their next long

20. M. Gerbert, *Scriptores* i (St. Blaise, 1784), p. 167.

Free Organum (Contrary Motion)
Trope: *Agnus Dei*[21]

Time: :40
12th century

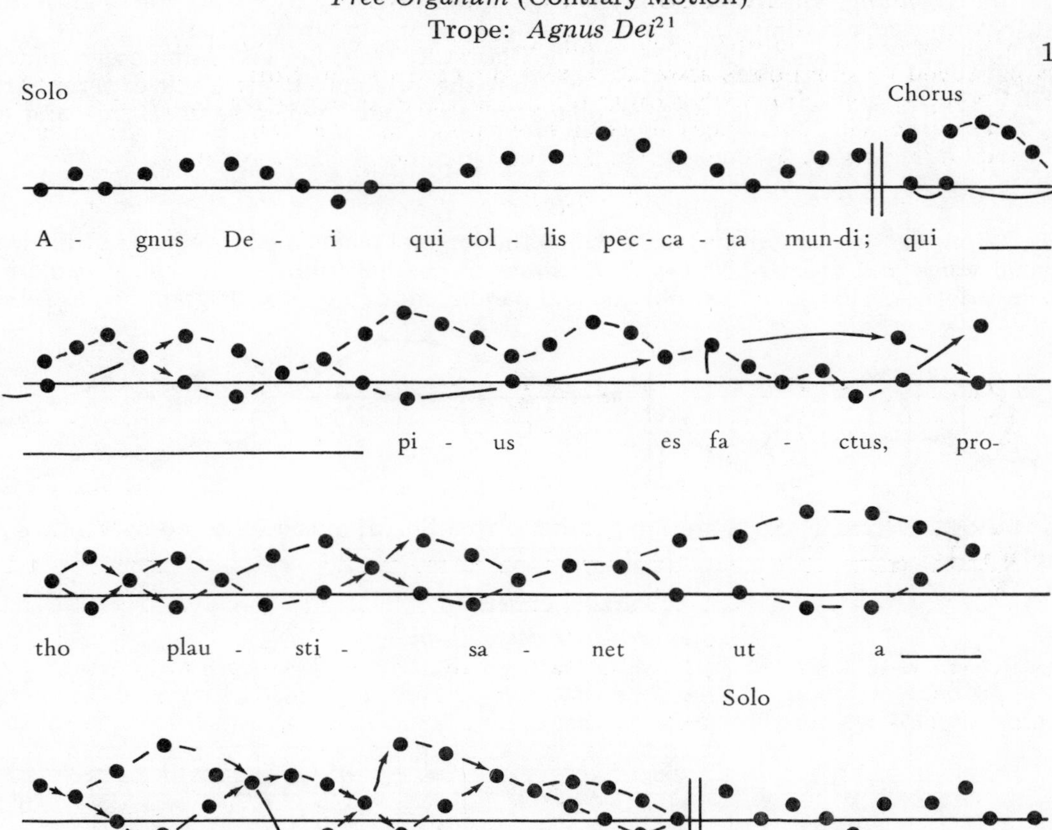
Solo
Chorus
A - gnus De - i qui tol - lis pec - ca - ta mun-di; qui
pi - us es fa - ctus, pro-
tho plau - sti - sa - net ut a
Solo
ctus: mi - se - re - re no - bis.

note. The effect of a rapid, elaborate melody combined with a slow, sonorous tenor is very striking because of the new melodic freedom combined with the variety of overtones produced by the combination of the two lines of music.

The following portion of a melismatic organum (in diagram form) has eighty-five notes in the florid melismas of the organal voice against only eight notes in the tenor:

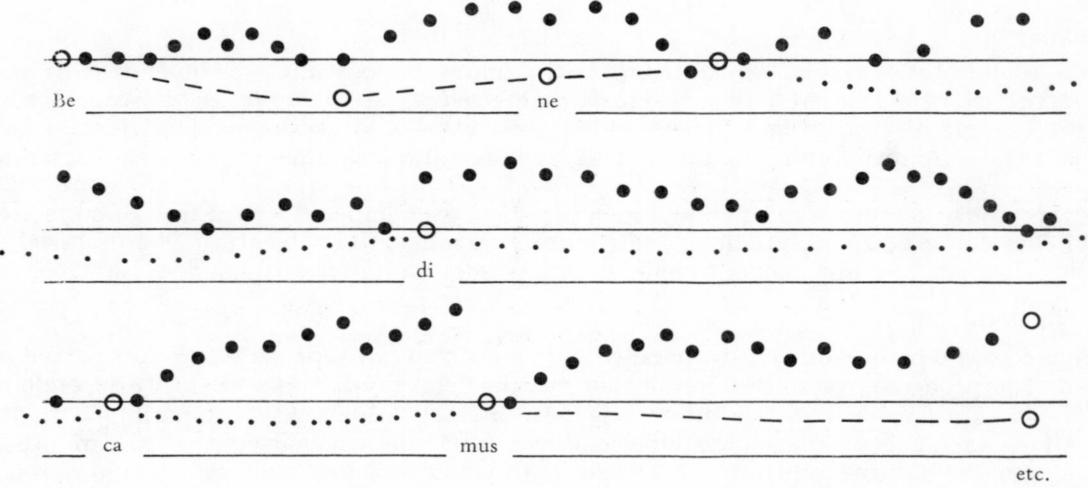
Be ne
di
ca mus
etc.

21. Besseler, *Die Musik des Mittelalters* (Potsdam, 1931), p. 95.
22. F. Ludwig, transcription in G. Adler, *Handbuch der Musikgeschichte* (Frankfurt am Main, 1924), p. 148.

DEVELOPMENT OF POLYPHONY

Beginning with the twelfth-century, polyphonic writing underwent rapid development. The notation of rhythm was improved by composers associated with the cathedral of Notre Dame in Paris as they began writing three-part compositions. Borrowing rhythmic modes from poetry (trochaic, iambic, dactylic, etc.), they wrote metrical music with two voices above an elongated tenor. The tenor was now so drawn-out that it was usually played by an organ, the only instrument which could sustain the notes.

Organum: *Alleluya (Nativitas)*[23]

Time: 2:00
(Complete)
Perotin (12th century)

Organs were used extensively in Byzantium during the early Middle Ages (along with kitharas and aulos) and were probably introduced into the Western church during the ninth century. Since about the tenth century pipe organs have been the principal instrument for church music.

MOTET

The *motet*, one of the most important forms of sacred music, was developed in the thirteenth century. The text given in the example below in the tenor indicates only the source of the borrowed plainsong because the line is now played by an instrument. Above the tenor is a composed line with its own set of words, hence the name *motetus* (French *le mot*, "the word"). The top voice, or *triplum* (treble) also had its own set of words which could be a different poem or even a different language. Increasing secularization led to motets such as the one illustrated with variations on the same love song (with borrowings from a

Motet
School of Notre Dame: *En non Diu! Quant voi; Eius in Oriente*[24]

Time: 1:00
(Complete)

23. Y. Rokseth, *Polyphonies du XIIIe siècle* (Paris, 1935).
24. *Ibid.*

trouvère song) sung in French by the *Triplum* and *Motetus.* The preferred consonances are still unison, P4, P5 and P8, but these apply only between adjoining voices. Strong dissonances against the third voice are common. The piece is in Dorian mode because the original plainsong was in mode 1. Titles of motets are given by using the opening lines of all three texts including the line that is played rather than sung. The meter is compound duple.

SECULAR POLYPHONIC MUSIC

Secular influences became increasingly strong during the thirteenth and fourteenth centuries of the Gothic period. In addition to the secular texts of the motets, there were polyphonic settings of the old troubadour-trouvère melodies and a growing literature of instrumental music for dancing. The *estampie* (Provencal, *estamper*, "to stamp") was the most popular dance of the Gothic Age and also one of the oldest forms of instrumental music. It appeared in both monophonic and polyphonic versions. The monophonic *estampie* was usually performed by *pipe* and *tabor.*

The *pipe* was a *flageolet,* or small flute with three tone holes. It was held by the left hand and played by blowing directly into the mouthpiece. With his other hand the instrumentalist played a *tabor*, or small drum, and thus functioned as a one-man dance band.

The following monophonic *ductia* (shortened version of the *estampie*) is in the standard triple meter and *aa bb cc* form of the dance. The brackets above the numerals 1 and 2 are first and second endings. After the twelve-bar section *a* is played completely through the first ending, the section is repeated from the beginning, played through the second ending (omitting the first ending), and continued on into the next section.

Each of the three sections *(a, b, c)* is composed of three phrases of four bars each (4 + 4 + 4). Each section is repeated to give the complete form of *aa bb cc.*

Ductia: *Danse Royale*[25]

Time: 1:05
13th century

Sacred music emphasized vocal music with or without instrumental accompaniment, but secular music exploited every instrument which became available.

Instruments introduced into Gothic secular music, because of the crusades, included imports of Near Eastern origin such as the lute, gittern, rebec, shawm, and bagpipe. The lute is a plucked string instrument with a pear-shaped body and a mellow resonant tone. It became the most popular instrument of the Renaissance.

The gittern (Greek *kithara*) was a plucked string instrument with a boxlike body and a sharp bright tone. It was replaced by the vihuela da mano and in the fifteenth century by the Spanish guitar.

25. P. Aubry, *Estampies et danses royales* (1906), p. 14.

Both the lute and gittern are mentioned for the first time in the thirteenth century epic poem *La Roman de la Rose.*

The rebec (Arabian *rabab*) was a bowed string instrument, or fiddle. Its most important characteristic was the sustained tone produced by bowing. Later developments led through the vielle to the viol to the modern violin.

The shawm, a loud double-reed instrument, was a relative of the aulos. In conjunction with trumpets it was used mostly for ceremonial music. It was eventually replaced by the milder-toned oboe.

The bagpipe, of probable ancient Oriental or Near Eastern origin, appears in most cultures and was the ubiquitous instrument of the Middle Ages.

During the late fourteenth century the flageolet was replaced by a more developed form called the recorder, which, in turn, was supplanted by the modern flute four centuries later.

Below is a two-part estampie with the parts labeled only as Cantus Superior and Cantus Inferior. They were to be played by any instruments that were available, a common practice in instrumental music until the eighteenth century. A partial key signature is used because the lower voice used b-flats while the upper part did not. The piece is in the major mode on f (F Major). The form of the complete piece is *a-b-c-c-c*, of which only section *a* is given. It has two phrases of eight bars each (8 + 8).

The small note with a diagonal line through its stem (/) in the example is called a grace note. It is an ornamental embellishment of the melody and is played very rapidly. It is considered to have no time value, although it does take a portion of the time value of the note which precedes it.

Estampie: Instrumental Dance[26]

THE POLYPHONIC MASS

As musical styles developed and flourished during the Gothic period, individual composers achieved international reputations. Guillaume de Machaut, almost equally gifted as poet and composer of both sacred and secular music was one of the first of the highly gifted artists who prepared the way for the so-called Renaissance man. He was the first to write a complete polyphonic setting of the ordinary of the Mass, a practice which was followed by every major composer through the sixteenth century and by many composers up to the present day.

26. Wooldridge, *Early English Harmonyi* (London, 1897), Pl. 19.

The *tenor* of masses and motets is now referred to as the *cantus firmus* (fixed song). In its use as a basis for composition, this preexisting melody still stands as a kind of medieval authority for the composition of polyphonic sacred music. In many cases, however, the *cantus firmus* is derived from a secular melody and the authority reduced to a convention, thus reflecting the waning of ecclesiastical control.

The selection below from Machaut's setting of the Mass illustrates several musical techniques:

1. *Syncopation.* This term refers to the deliberate disturbance of a normal beat and/or accent pattern. This is achieved by placing accents in unexpected places and/or by removing them from expected places. In a grouping of 8 eighth notes, the expected accents would be on 1 and 5.

The rhythmic pattern below in measures two and four avoids the expected accent on the 5th eighth

note (because of the tie) and shifts it over to the 6th eighth note (tied to the 7th eighth note) to give an off-beat accent to the music.

2. *Triadic harmony.* The *triad* is a harmonic construction, or *chord* which is made up of two or more superimposed thirds, for example, a third added above a bottom note (called the *root*) and another third added on top of that:

The two thirds total up to a fifth (3 + 3 = 5!) because the note in the middle is counted twice. *Tertiary harmony* (chords built in thirds) became the norm for composers until well into the twentieth century. In the Machaut piece, triads are used in the middle of phrases and sections. The open chord

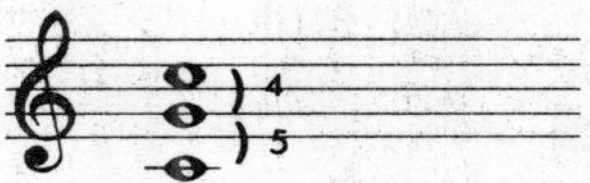

of fifth plus fourth is standard for beginning and ending sections but another century will see this open sound filled in to become a *triad* (plus an octave duplication for four part harmony):

3. *Cadences. Cadences* of this period frequently use a *double leading tone.* Two voices lead into the final chord by means of the smallest interval of a *half step* (semitone). In measures 6 and 7 e is a *leading tone* moving to f, and b leads to c: The symbol 𝄐 is called a *fermata* and indicates a pause of indefinite length.

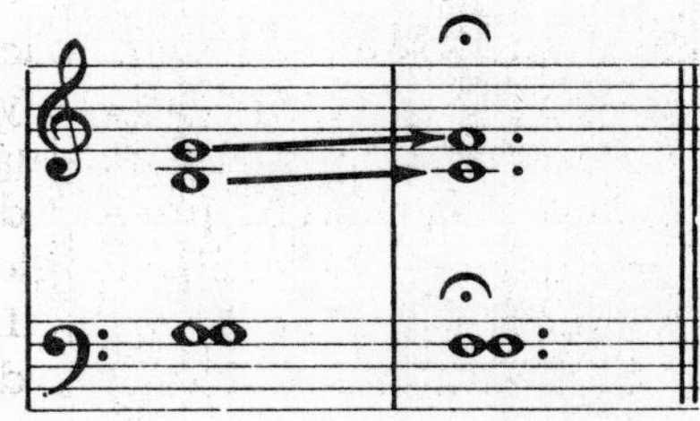

The following portion of the *Agnus Dei* is sung by the upper three voices and accompanied by an instrument on the *contratenor* part (as indicated by the absence of text). The mixed vocal-instrumental texture is characteristic of pre-Renaissance music.

Following is an outline of the major developments in music during the Middle Ages. The chart is of course greatly simplified in order to indicate

Mass: *Agnus Dei*[27]

Time: 1:20
(Complete)
Guillaume de Machaut (c. 1300-c. 1377)

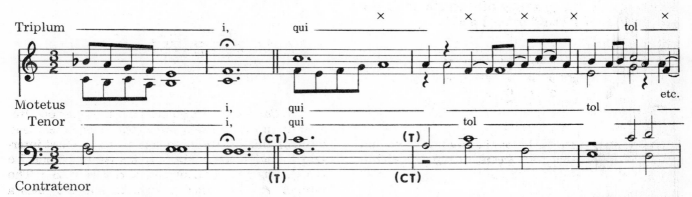

X = *triad.* (The notes of a triad may be moved up an octave without essentially affecting the triad sound, as in the first chord of measure 2).

general trends rather than details. Each period, style, and so forth begins approximately with the first letter of the word or phrase, although there is no necessity for pinpointing precise dates even when they are known. Dotted lines indicate either prior development leading up to a specific musical instrument or, as with monasticism, the dissolution or waning influence of the institution. Arrows indicate continuing development or, as with the connection between feudalism and chivalry, one institution developing out of another.

However pretentious this statement may appear, music can provide not only the "sound" of the Middle Ages but can even provide a rather comprehensive history of medieval Christianity and medieval society in general. We can, in a manner of speaking, "see" medieval life by studying its art, architecture, crafts, tapestries and illuminated manuscripts. We can "experience" medieval life by reading its epics, sagas, *chansons de geste*, lyrical poetry, and romances.

Of course "seeing" and "experiencing" medieval life has certain drawbacks. Pictures of art and architecture simply will not suffice; the actual works of art must be visited and viewed, preferably in their original location rather than in some European or American museum. For most people the literature must be read in translation, with a resultant loss of direct experience. Music, however, is akin to a universal language in that, when properly performed, it can bring alive the panorama of medieval life from Gregorian chant to liturgical drama, the age of chivalry in the songs of troubadours and trouvères, the whole development of architecture through the Gothic style, and much more.

The development of polyphonic music is just one case in point. Gregorian chant was comfortable

27. H. Besseler, *Die Musik des Mittelalters und der Renaissance* (Bucken, *Handbuch der Musikwissenschaft*), Potsdam, 1931, p. 149.

DEVELOPMENT OF MEDIEVAL MUSIC

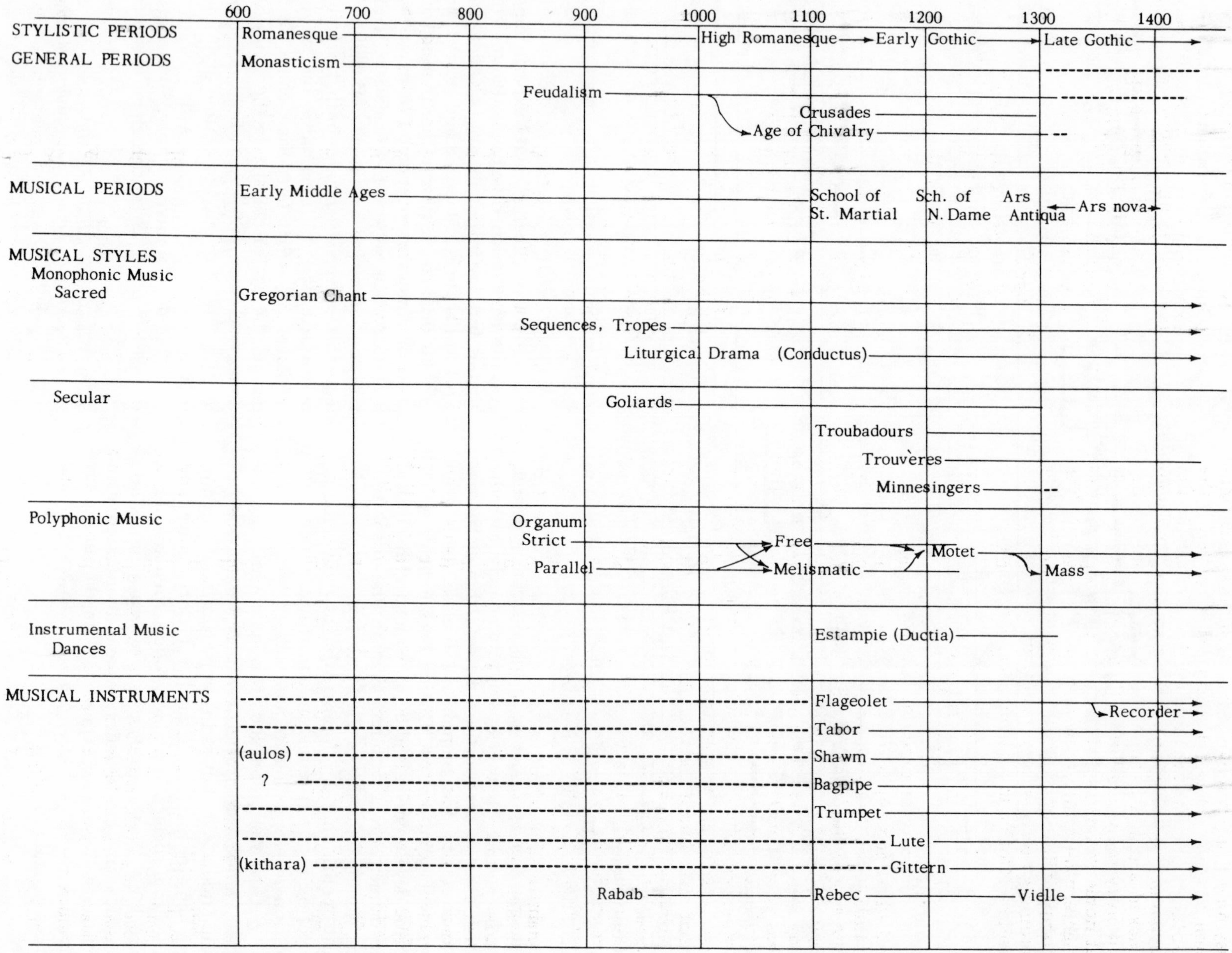

	600	700	800	900	1000	1100	1200	1300	1400
STYLISTIC PERIODS	Romanesque				High Romanesque	Early Gothic		Late Gothic	
GENERAL PERIODS	Monasticism								
			Feudalism						
					Crusades				
					Age of Chivalry				
MUSICAL PERIODS	Early Middle Ages					School of St. Martial	Sch. of N. Dame		
							Ars Antiqua	Ars nova	
MUSICAL STYLES Monophonic Music Sacred	Gregorian Chant								
			Sequences, Tropes						
				Liturgical Drama (Conductus)					
Secular				Goliards					
						Troubadours			
						Trouvères			
						Minnesingers			
Polyphonic Music			Organum: Strict		Free		Motet		
			Parallel		Melismatic			Mass	
Instrumental Music Dances						Estampie (Ductia)			
MUSICAL INSTRUMENTS						Flageolet		Recorder	
						Tabor			
	(aulos)					Shawm			
	?					Bagpipe			
						Trumpet			
						Lute			
	(kithara)					Gittern			
				Rabab		Rebec	Vielle		

and proper in the monasteries but Romanesque churches demanded and received polyphonic music to fill an ever-growing interior space. The dynamic, asymmetrical, complex mass of interreacting tension of stone walls and soaring vaulting that is the Gothic cathedral has its aural counterpart in the dynamic, asymmetrical, complex and tension-packed art that is Gothic polyphonic music. The intensity and vitality of Gothic music is completely at home in Chartres and utterly out of place in an eighteenth-century drawing room. It is perhaps this compatibility of dynamic space and sound that has prompted architectural historians to refer to architecture (Gothic in particular) as "frozen music."

SUMMARY

At whatever time one chooses to date the so-called Middle Ages, one fact is reasonably clear: music generally served one master—the Church. By the end of the Middle Ages (Gothic period) music had returned to its pre-Christian function of serving many masters. One would suspect that music has *always* met the needs of the people but the evidence during the early Middle Ages indicates an organized religion (Christianity) in full control of music as an aid to worship. However, the very fact that the church appropriated music for its own purposes in no way indicates that the people relinquished the practice of music—such an idea is inconceivable, considering the many thousands of years during which music has served as a fundamental form of human expression.

The Church was more or less literate and maintained a continuing compilation of written music. The practice of secular music among the masses can be only a strong probability. Nevertheless, the Gothic era saw the rise of *notated* secular music and thus a perceptible shift away from wholly liturgical music and a movement toward a fully rounded musical life. The lack of a practical notation did retard the development of secular music, thus making it a late bloomer in medieval art. By the fourteenth century, however, music was written and performed at a level comparable to the achievements of the other arts.

LISTENING OUTLINE (SECOND STAGE)

Note: This outline should be considered as a guide to listening; it represents the *maximum* of things to listen for. There is no expectation that everyone or even anyone can actually hear all these items; however, one can follow the music with the outline and learn to systematize and objectify listening procedures.

1. Listening Outline
   a. Medium and Number of Performers
      (1) Vocal (specify voice parts)
          Text
      (2) Instrumental (specify instruments)
      (3) Combination (specify)
   b. Texture
      (1) Monophonic, homophonic, polyphonic, combination
      (2) Number of actual parts or voices (not necessarily the same as the number of performers)
   c. Construction
      (1) Characteristic intervals (melodic and/or harmonic)
      (2) Characteristic harmonies
      (3) Types of cadences (Landini, Burgundian, other)
          (a) Intermediate
          (b) Final
   d. Form
      (1) Sacred, secular
      (2) Music: through-composed, barform, other
      (3) Text: through-composed, repeated, strophic, verse-refrain, other
   e. Tonality
      (1) Modal
      (2) Major-minor
   f. Notation (determined from the score)
      (1) Clef, time signature, tempo indication (if any)
   g. Miscellaneous
2. Conclusions
   a. Possible Period: Ancient (600 B.C.-A.D. 100); Roman (100-600); Romanesque (600-1000); High Romanesque (1000-1150); Early Gothic (1150-1350); Late Gothic (1350-1450).
   b. Possible Style: Greek song, Gregorian chant sequence, trope, liturgical drama, conductus, troubadour song, trouvère song, minnesinger song, goliard song, estampie, strict organum, parallel organum, free organum, melismatic organum, motet, mass movement.
   c. Possible National Origin: Greece, Rome, western Europe, northern France, southern France (Provence), Germany, Italy, other.

Record List

1. Gregorian Chant, "Eight Alleluias," apparently not recorded.
2. Gregorian Chant, "Kyrie IV: Cunctipotens," not recorded.
3. Kyrie-Trope: "Omnipotens," not recorded.
4. Sequence, "Victimae paschali laudes," *Masterpieces* (see Record List for Chapter 3).

5. Liturgical Drama: "Infantem vidimus," *Treasury of Early Music*, 4 volumes, Haydn Society 9100/9103; S-9100/9103 (referred to as *Treasury).*
6. Conductus: "Song of the Ass." *The Jolly Minstrels: Minstrel Tunes, Songs and Dances of the Middle Ages on Authentic Instruments*, Vanguard VCS-10049.
7. Troubadour Canso: "Be m'an perduct," *Treasury*.
8. Trouvère Virelai: "Or la truix," *Masterpieces.*
9. Parallel Organum, Sequence: "Rex caeli Domino," *Masterpieces.*
10. Free Organum; Trope: "Agnus Dei," *Masterpieces.*
11. Melismatic Organum: "Benedicamus Domino," *Masterpieces.*
12. Perotin, Organum: "Alleluya (Nativitas)," *Masterpieces.*
13. School of Notre Dame, Motet: "En non Diu! Quant voi; Eius in Oriente," *Masterpieces.*
14. Ductia: "Danse Royale," *The Jolly Minstrels.*
15. Estampie: "Instrumental Dance," *Masterpieces.*
16. Machaut, Mass: "Agnus Dei," *Masterpieces.*

Also Recommended

Music of Medieval France, Sacred and Secular (1200-1400), Bach Guild BG-656.

Ten Centuries of Music, 10-DGG KL-52/61; SKL-152/161.

Bibliography

Liber Usualis. Desclee & Cie. Tournai, Belgium, 1952. The complete liturgical music (Gregorian chant) of the Roman Catholic church.

Seay, Albert. *Music in the Medieval World.* Prentice-Hall, Inc. (paperback), 1965, 182 pp. A survey text intended more for amateurs than professional musicians.

Strunk, Oliver. *Source Readings in Music History From Classical Antiquity Through the Romantic Era.* W.W. Norton & Company, Inc., 1950, 919 pp. Useful primary material about music excerpted from the writings of Clement of Alexander, St. Basil, St. Jerome, St. Augustine, Boethius, Cassiodorus, Odo of Cluny, Guido of Arezzo and others.

Thomson, James C. *Music Through the Renaissance.* Wm. C. Brown Company Publishers (paperback), 1965, 165 pp. A brief, illustrated survey of music from primitive peoples through the sixteenth century. Condensed and simplified for the nonmusician.

Walter, Don C. *Men and Music in Western Culture.* Appleton-Century-Crofts (paperback), 1969, 244 pp. A very general survey from 3000 B.C. to the present day. Designed to give nonmusicians a broad overview of the importance of music in the life of man.

Time Chart for the Middle Ages

Maps Showing a Few Significant Territorial Changes	Important Political, Historical, and Military Events	Philosophical Events	Art, Music, and Literature
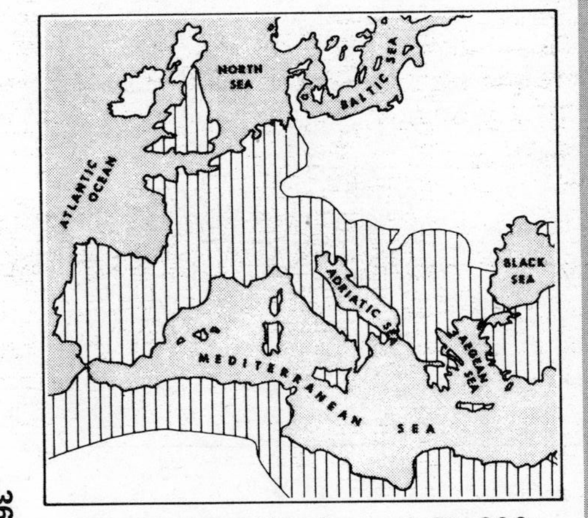 The Roman Empire c. A.D. 300	375-500—Great invasions of Roman Empire by northern and eastern tribes. Asiatic Huns harry Germanic peoples	354-430—Augustine formulated doctrine of Church based on Neo-Platonism	
	395—Roman Empire split between East (Capitol: Constantinople) and West (Capitol: Rome or Ravenna)	395—Christianity becomes Roman state religion under Emperor Constantine	
	410-476—Conventional dates for the fall of Rome. The city captured by tribes of Visigoths and Vandals		
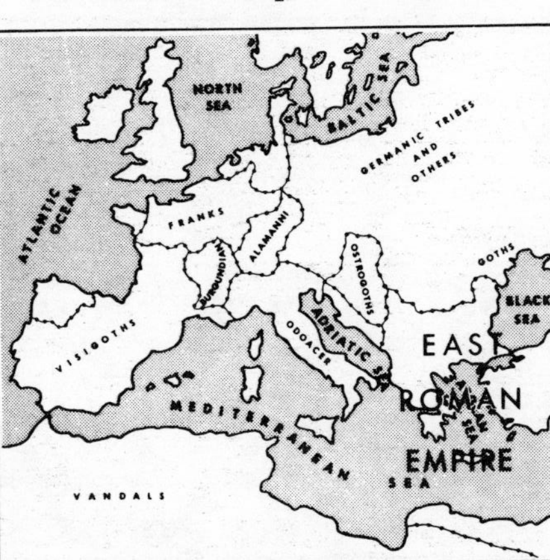 Invasions of the Roman Empire c. A.D. 500	465-511—Clovis established line of Frankish kings and (496) becomes Christian	480-524—Boethius, "Consolations of Philosophy" expresses Roman world-weariness in a Christian—classical synthesis	
	509-604—Pope Gregory defends Rome against invaders—establishes political power of the Church		509-604—Pope Gregory establishes Gregorian Chant (plain song)

Time Chart for the Middle Ages (cont.)

Maps Showing a Few Significant Territorial Changes	Important Political, Historical, and Military Events	Philosophical Events	Art, Music, and Literature
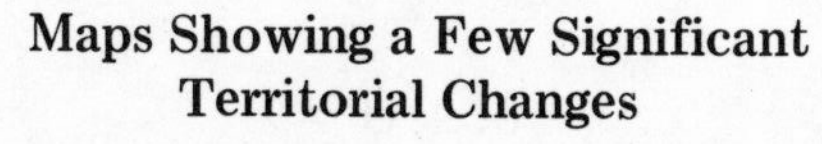	570-632—Life of Mohammed		
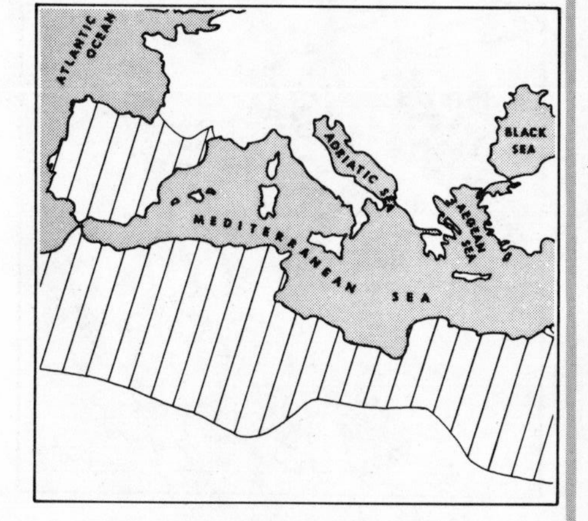 ATLANTIC OCEAN, BLACK SEA, ADRIATIC SEA, MEDITERRANEAN SEA, AEGEAN SEA	597—St. Augustine's mission to England		700—Beginning of Romanesque architecture developed from basilica
	600-650—First development of Feudalism from northern tribal customs		
	732—Battle of Poitiers, Mohammedans checked in France, driven back to Spain		
	751—Pepin becomes King of Franks; establishes Carolingian rulers	781—Charlemagne's Palace School established. Start of revival of learning	
Spread of Mohammedanism c. A.D. 732	800—Charlemagne crowned Roman Emperor by Pope. Establishes precedent for Papal authority.		
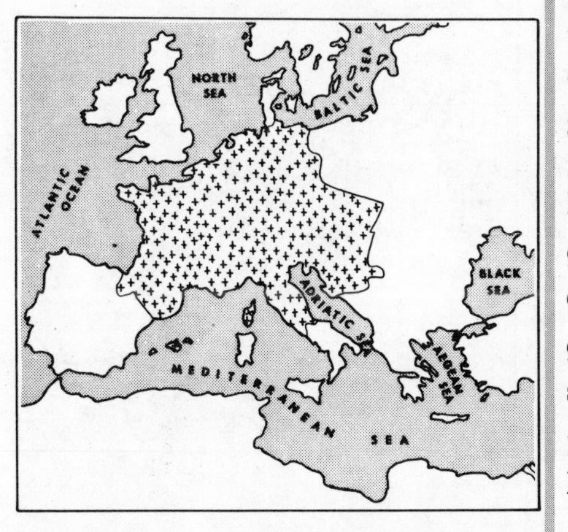 NORTH SEA, BALTIC SEA, ATLANTIC OCEAN, BLACK SEA, ADRIATIC SEA, MEDITERRANEAN SEA, AEGEAN SEA	850-900—Decline of Frankish Kingdom. Further invasion of Northmen		c.900—Organum in music discussed by Odo of Cluny
	900—Feudalism fully established in Europe		900—Approximate beginning of stave architecture in Norway
	900-1000—Towns begin to spring up in Europe		
	1066—Norman invasion of England		
Charlemagne's Empire c. A.D. 800			

Time Chart for the Middle Ages (cont.)

Maps Showing a Few Significant Territorial Changes

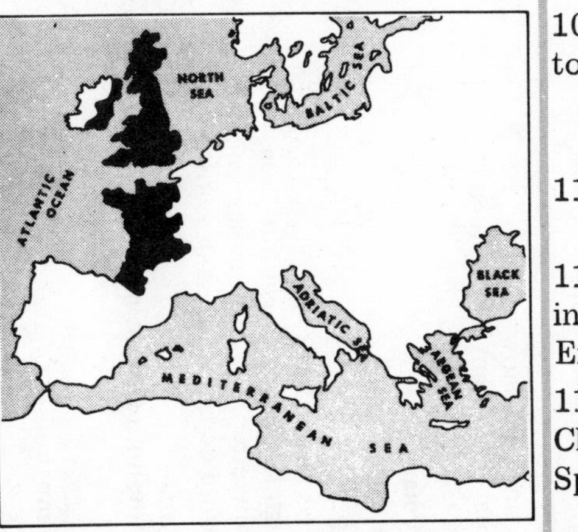

English and French Territories about 1154

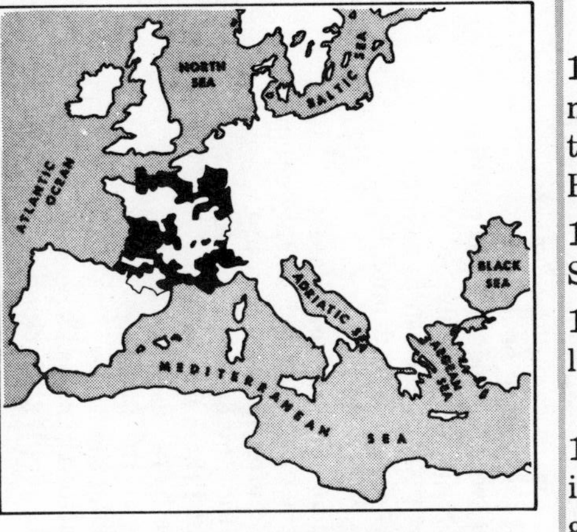

English and French Territories about 1453

Important Political, Historical, and Military Events	Philosophical Events	Art, Music, and Literature
1077—Emperor Henry IV bows to Pope at Canossa	1000-1100—The Battle of Universals; Realist-Nominalist Controversy	1000-1100—Full development of Romanesque architecture
1100-1300—Period of Crusades	1079-1142—Peter Abelard teaches in Paris, "Sic et Non"	1022-1084—Building of Abbey of Mont Saint Michel almost as we know it
1154-1189—Rule of Henry II in England. Establishment of English common law	1200—The first trickle of the main body of Aristotle's works enters Europe	1087-1127—First known troubador—but secular music was already well-established
1150 onwards—Half Spain in Christian hands. Unification of Spain continues	1270—Formal founding of University of Paris. For at least 200 years groups of students had collected at Bologna, Salerno, etc.	1194—The beginning of building of the present Chartres Cathedral. The height of Gothic style
1215—Magna Carta—law superior to king	1270—Introduction of all of Aristotle's works in Europe	1170-1270—In France alone 80 cathedrals. 500 great churches built, almost all devoted to the Virgin. The height of the Cult of the Virgin
1272—Rudolf of Hapsburg made Austrian king—start of the rise of the House of Hapsburg	1214-1294—Roger Bacon bases knowledge on study of physical world	1240-1302—Cimabue, begins to paint figures naturalistically
1291—Revolt of Swiss Cantons. Start of democratic Switzerland	1225-1274—Thomas Aquinas establishes Church doctrine on Aristotelian principles	1265-1321—Dante achieves "medieval synthesis" in "The Divine Comedy"
1295—English parliament established		1276-1327—Painter Giotto continues trend toward naturalism
1302—Estates General founded in France. A hint of democratic government		1300 onwards—Musical development of counterpoint, polyphony. Improvement of system of musical notation
1337 to about 1440—Hundred Years War. England loses French lands. Great steps towards unification of both countries		1313-1375—Boccaccio 1340-1400—Geoffrey Chaucer "The Canterbury Tales"

Literary Selections

Everyman

Characters

Everyman, God (Adonai), Death, Messenger, Fellowship, Cousin, Kindred, Goods, Good-Deeds, Discretion, Strength, Five-Wits, Beauty, Knowledge, Confession, Angel, Doctor.

HERE BEGINNETH A TREATISE HOW THE HIGH FATHER OF HEAVEN SENDETH DEATH TO SUMMON EVERY CREATURE TO COME AND GIVE ACCOUNT OF THEIR LIVES IN THIS WORLD AND IS IN MANNER OF A MORAL PLAY.

Messenger:
I pray you all give your audience,
And hear this matter with reverence,
By figure a moral play—
The *Summoning of Everyman* called it is,
That of our lives and ending shows
How transitory we be all day.
This matter is wondrous precious,
But the intent of it is more gracious,
And sweet to bear away.
The story saith,—Man, in the beginning,
Look well, and take good heed to the ending,
Be you never so gay!
Ye think sin in the beginning full sweet,
Which in the end causeth thy soul to weep,
When the body lieth in clay.
Here shall you see how *Fellowship* and *Jollity*,
Both *Strength*, *Pleasure*, and *Beauty*,
Will fade from thee as flower in May.
For ye shall hear, how our heaven king
Calleth *Everyman* to a general reckoning:
Give audience, and hear what he doth say.

God:
I perceive here in my majesty,
How that all creatures be to me unkind,
Living without dread in worldly prosperity:
Of ghostly sight the people be so blind,
Drowned in sin, they know me not for their God;
In worldly riches is all their mind,
They fear not my rightwiseness, the sharp rod;
My law that I shewed, when I for them died,
They forget clean, and shedding of my blood red;
I hanged between two, it cannot be denied;
To get them life I suffered to be dead;
I healed their feet, with thorns hurt was my head:
I could do no more than I did truly,
And now I see the people do clean forsake me.
They use the seven deadly sins damnable;
As pride, covetise, wrath, and lechery,
Now in the world be made commendable;
And thus they leave of angels the heavenly company;
Everyman liveth so after his own pleasure,
And yet of their life they be nothing sure:
I see the more that I them forbear
The worse they be from year to year;
All that liveth appaireth[1] fast,
Therefore I will in all the haste
Having a reckoning of Everyman's person
For and I leave the people thus alone
In their life and wicked tempests,
Verily they will become much worse than beasts;
For now one would by envy another up eat;
Charity they all do clean forget.
I hoped well that Everyman
In my glory should make his mansion,
And thereto I had them all elect;
But now I see, like traitors deject,
They thank me not for the pleasure that I to them meant
Nor yet for their being that I them have lent;
I proffered the people great multitude of mercy,
And few there be that asketh it heartily;
They be so combered with worldly riches,
That needs of them I must do justice,
On Everyman living without fear.
Where art thou, Death, thou mighty messenger?

Death:
Almighty God, I am here at your will,
Your commandment to fulfil.

God:
Go thou to Everyman,
And show him in my name
A pilgrimage he must on him take,
Which he in no wise may escape;
And that he bring with him a sure reckoning
Without delay or any tarrying.

Death:
Lord, I will in the world go run over all,
And cruelly outsearch both great and small;
Every man will I beset that liveth beastly
Out of God's laws, and dreadeth not folly:
He that loveth riches I will strike with my dart,
His sight to blind, and from heaven to depart,
Except that alms be his good friend,
In hell for to dwell, world without end.
Lo, yonder I see Everyman walking;
Full little he thinketh on my coming;
His mind is on fleshly lusts and his treasure,
And great pain it shall cause him to endure
Before the Lord Heaven King.
Everyman, stand still; whither art thou going
Thus gaily? Hast my Maker forgot?

Everyman:
Why askst thou?
Wouldest thou wete?[2]

Death:
Yea, sir, I will show you;
In great haste I am sent to thee
From God out of his majesty.

Everyman:
What, sent to me?

Death:
Yea, certainly.
Though thou have forget him here,
He thinketh on thee in the heavenly sphere,
As, or we depart, thou shalt know.

Everyman:
What desireth God of me?

---

1. Is impaired.
2. Know.

Death:
That shall I show thee;
A reckoning he will needs have
Without any longer respite.

Everyman:
To give a reckoning longer leisure I crave;
This blind matter troubleth my wit.

Death:
On thee thou must take a long journey:
Therefore thy book of count with thee thou bring;
For turn again thou can not by no way,
And look thou be sure of thy reckoning:
For before God thou shalt answer, and show
Thy many bad deeds and good but a few;
How thou hast spent thy life, and in what wise,
Before the chief lord of paradise.
Have ado that we were in that way,
For, wete thou well, thou shalt make none attournay.[3]

Everyman:
Full unready I am such reckoning to give.
I know thee not: what messenger art thou?

Death:
I am Death, that no man dreadeth.
For every man I rest and no man spareth;
For it is God's commandment
That all to me should be obedient.

Everyman:
O Death, thou comest when I had thee least in mind,
In thy power it lieth me to save,
Yet of my good will I give thee, if ye will be kind,
Yea, a thousand pound shalt thou have,
And defer this matter till another day.

Death:
Everyman, it may not be by no way;
I set not by gold, silver, nor riches,
Ne by pope, emperor, king, duke, ne princes.
For and I would receive gifts great,
All the world I might get;
But my custom is clean contrary.
I give thee no respite: come hence, and not tarry.

Everyman:
Alas, shall I have no longer respite?
I may say Death giveth no warning:
To think on thee, it maketh my heart sick,
For all unready is my book of reckoning.
But twelve year and I might have abiding,
My counting book I would make so clear,
That my reckoning I should not need to fear.
Wherefore, Death, I pray thee, for God's mercy,
Spare me till I be provided of remedy.

Death:
Thee availeth not to cry, weep, and pray:
But haste thee lightly that you were gone the journey.
And prove thy friends if thou can.
For, wete thou well, the tide abideth no man,
And in the world each living creature
For Adam's sin must die of nature.

Everyman:
Death, if I should this pilgrimage take,
And my reckoning surely make,
Show me, for saint charity,
Should I not come again shortly?

Death:
No, Everyman; and thou be once there,
Thou mayst never more come here,
Trust me verily.

Everyman:
O gracious God, in the high seat celestial,
Have mercy on me in this most need;
Shall I have no company from this vale terrestrial
Of mine acquaintance that way me to lead?

Death:
Yea, if any be so hardy,
That would go with thee and bear thee company.
Hie thee that you were gone to God's magnificence,
Thy reckoning to give before his presence.
What, weenest thou thy life is given thee,
And thy worldly goods also?

Everyman:
I had wend so, verily.

Death:
Nay, nay; it was but lent thee;
For as soon as thou art go,
Another awhile shall have it, and then go therefro
Even as thou has done.
Everyman, thou art mad; thou hast thy wits five,
And here on earth will not amend thy life,
For suddenly I do come.

Everyman:
O wretched caitiff, whither shall I flee,
That I might scape this endless sorrow!
Now, gentle Death, spare me till to-morrow,
That I may amend me
With good advisement.

Death:
Nay, thereto I will not consent,
Nor no man will I respite,
But to the heart suddenly I shall smite
Without any advisement.
And now out of thy sight I will me hie;
See thou make thee ready shortly,
For thou mayst say this is the day
That no man living may scape away.

Everyman:
Alas, I may well weep with sighs deep;
Now have I no manner of company
To help me in my journey, and me to keep;
And also my writing is full unready.
How shall I do now for to excuse me?
I would to God I had never be gete![4]
To my soul a full great profit it had be;
For now I fear pains huge and great.
The time passeth; Lord, help that all wrought;
For though I mourn it availeth nought.
The day passeth, and is almost a-go;
I wot not well what for to do.
To whom were I best my complaint to make?
What, and I to Fellowship thereof spake,
And showed him of this sudden chance?
For in him is all mine affiance;
We have in the world so many a day
Be on good friends in sport and play.

---

3. Mediator.
4. Been gotten, been born.

I see him yonder, certainly;
I trust that he will bear me company;
Therefore to him will I speak to ease my sorrow.
Well met, good Fellowship, and good morrow!

Fellowship:
Everyman, good morrow by this day.
Sir, why lookest thou so piteously?
If any thing be amiss, I pray thee, me say,
That I may help to remedy.

Everyman:
Yea, good Fellowship, yea.
I am in great jeopardy.

Fellowship:
My true friend, show to me your mind;
I will not forsake thee, unto my life's end,
In the way of good company.

Everyman:
That was well spoken, and lovingly.

Fellowship:
Sir, I must needs know your heaviness;
I have pity to see you in any distress;
If any have ye wronged he shall revenged be,
Though I on the ground be slain for thee—
Though that I know before that I should die.

Everyman:
Verily, Fellowship, gramercy.

Fellowship:
Tush! by thy thanks I set not a straw;
Show me your grief, and say no more.

Everyman:
If I my heart should to you break,
And then you to turn your mind from me,
And would not me comfort, when you hear me speak,
Then should I ten times sorrier be.

Fellowship:
Sir, I say as I will do in deed.

Everyman:
Then be you a good friend at need:
I have found you true here before.

Fellowship:
And so ye shall evermore;
For, in faith, and thou go to Hell,
I will not forsake thee by the way!

Everyman:
Ye speak like a good friend; I believe you well;
I shall deserve it, and I may.

Fellowship:
I speak of no deserving, by this day.
For he that will say and nothing do
Is not worthy with good company to go;
Therefore show me the grief of your mind,
As to your friend most loving and kind.

Everyman:
I shall show you how it is;
Commanded I am to go a journey,
A long way, hard and dangerous,
And give a strait count without delay
Before the high judge Adonai.[5]
Wherefore I pray you, bear me company,
As ye have promised, in this journey.

Fellowship:
That is matter indeed! Promise is duty,
But, and I should take such a voyage on me,
I know it well, it should be to my pain:
Also it make me afeard, certain.
But let us take counsel here as well as we can,
For your words would fear a strong man.

Everyman:
Why, ye said, If I had need,
Ye would me never forsake, quick nor dead,
Though it were to hell truly.

Fellowship:
So I said, certainly,
But such pleasures be set aside, thee sooth to say:
And also, if we took such a journey,
When should we come again?

Everyman:
Nay, never again till the day of doom.

Fellowship:
In faith, then will not I come there!
Who hath you these tidings brought?

Everyman:
Indeed, Death was with me here.

Fellowship:
Now, by God that all hath bought,
If Death were the messenger,
For no man that is living today
I will not go that loath journey—
Not for the father that begat me!

Everyman:
Ye promised other wise, pardie.

Fellowship:
I wot well I say so truly
And yet if thou wilt eat, and drink, and make good cheer,
Or haunt to women, the lusty company,
I would not forsake you, while the day is clear,
Trust me verily!

Everyman:
Yea, thereto ye would be ready;
To go to mirth, solace, and play
Your mind will sooner apply
Than to bear me company in my long journey.

Fellowship:
Now, in good faith, I will not that way.
But and thou wilt murder, or any man kill,
In that I will help thee with a good will!

Everyman:
O that is a simple advice indeed!
Gentle fellow, help me in my necessity;
We have loved long, and now I need,
And now, gentle Fellowship, remember me.

Fellowship:
Whether ye have loved me or no,
By Saint John, I will not with thee go.

Everyman:
Yet I pray thee, take the labour, and do so much for me
To bring me forward, for saint charity,
And comfort me till I come without the town.

---

5. God.

Fellowship:
Nay, and thou would give me a new gown,
I will not a foot with thee go;
But and you had tarried I would not have left thee so.
And as now, God speed thee in thy journey,
For from thee I will depart as fast as I may.

Everyman:
Whither away, Fellowship? Will you forsake me?

Fellowship:
Yea, by my fay, to God I betake thee.

Everyman:
Farewell, good Fellowship; for this my heart is sore;
Adieu for ever, I shall see thee no more.

Fellowship:
In faith, Everyman, farewell now at the end;
For you I will remember that parting is mourning.

Everyman:
Alack! shall we thus depart indeed?
Our Lady, help, without any more comfort,
Lo, Fellowship forsaketh me in my most need:
For help in this world whither shall I resort?
Fellowship herebefore with me would merry make;
And now little sorrow for me doth he take.
It is said, in prosperity men friends may find,
Which in adversity be full unkind.
Now whither for succour shall I flee,
Sith that Fellowship hath forsaken me?
To my kinsmen I will truly,
Praying them to help me in my necessity:
I believe that they will do so,
For kind will creep where it may not go.
Where be ye now, my friends and kinsmen?

Kindred:
Here be we now at your commandment.
Cousin, I pray you show us your intent
In any wise, and not spare.

Cousin:
Yea, Everyman, and to us declare
If ye be disposed to go any whither,
For wete you well, we will live and die together.

Kindred:
In wealth and woe we will with you hold,
For over his kin a man may be bold.

Everyman:
Gramercy, my friends and kinsmen kind.
Now shall I show you the grief of my mind:
I was commanded by a messenger,
That is an high king's chief officer;
He bade me go a pilgrimage to my pain,
And I know well I shall never come again;
Also I must give a reckoning straight,
For I have a great enemy, that hath me in wait,
Which intendeth me for to hinder.

Kindred:
What account is that which ye must render?
That would I know.

Everyman:
Of all my works I must show
How I have lived and my days spent;
Also of ill deeds, that I have used
In my time, sith life was me lent;
And of all virtues that I have refused.
Therefore I pray you go thither with me,
To help to make mine account, for saint charity.

Cousin:
What, to go thither? Is that the matter?
Nay, Everyman, I had liefer fast bread and water
All this five year and more.

Everyman:
Alas, that ever I was bore![6]
For now shall I never be merry
If that you forsake me.

Kindred:
Ah, sir; what, ye be a merry man!
Take good heart to you, and make no moan.
But one thing I warn you, by Saint Anne,
As for me, ye shall go alone.

Everyman:
My Cousin, will you not with me go?

Cousin:
No, by our Lady; I have the cramp in my toe.
Trust not to me, for, so God me speed,
I will deceive you in your most need.

Kindred:
It availeth not us to tice.
Ye shall have my maid with all my heart;
She loveth to go to feasts, there to be nice,
And to dance, and abroad to start:
I will give her leave to help you in that journey,
If that you and she may agree.

Everyman:
Now show me the very effect of your mind.
Will you go with me, or abide behind?

Kindred:
Abide behind? Yea, that I will and I may!
Therefore farewell until another day.

Everyman:
How should I be merry or glad?
For fair promises to me make,
But when I have most need, they me forsake.
I am deceived; that maketh me sad.

Cousin:
Cousin Everyman, farewell now,
For verily I will not go with you;
Also of mine own an unready reckoning
I have to account; therefore I make tarrying.
Now, God keep thee, for now I go.

Everyman:
Ah, Jesus, is all come hereto?
Lo, fair words maketh fools feign;
They promise and nothing will do certain.
My kinsmen promised me faithfully
For to abide with me steadfastly,
And now fast away do they flee:
Even so Fellowship promised me.
What friend were best me of to provide?
I lose my time here longer to abide.
Yet in my mind a thing there is:—
All my life I have loved riches;
If that my goods now help me might,

---

6. Born.

He would make my heart full light.
I will speak to him in this distress.—
Where art thou, my Goods and riches?

Goods:
Who calleth me? Everyman? What haste thou hast!
I lie here in corners, trussed and piled so high,
And in chests I am locked so fast,
Also sacked in bags, thou mayst see with thine eye,
I cannot stir; in packs low I lie.
What would ye have, lightly me say.

Everyman:
Come hither, Good, in all the haste thou may,
For of counsel I must desire thee.

Goods:
Sir, and ye in the world have trouble or adversity,
That can I help you to remedy shortly.

Everyman:
It is another disease that grieveth me;
In this world it is not, I tell thee so.
I am sent for another way to go,
To give a straight account general
Before the highest Jupiter of all;
And all my life I have had joy and pleasure in thee.
Therefore I pray thee go with me,
For, peradventure, thou mayst before God Almighty
My reckoning help to clean and purify;
For it is said ever among,
That money maketh all right that is wrong.

Goods:
Nay, Everyman, I sing another song,
I follow no man in such voyages;
For and I went with thee
Thou shouldst fare much the worse for me;
For because on me thou did set thy mind,
Thy reckoning I have made blotted and blind
That thine account thou cannot make truly;
And that hast thou for the love of me.

Everyman:
That would grieve me full sore,
When I should come to that fearful answer.
Up, let us go thither together.

Goods:
Nay, not so, I am too brittle, I may not endure;
I will follow no man one foot, be ye sure.

Everyman:
Alas, I have thee loved, and had great pleasure
All my life-days on good and treasure.

Goods:
That is to thy damnation without lesing,
For my love is contrary to the love everlasting
But if thou had me loved moderately during,
As, to the poor give part of me,
Then shouldst thou not in this dolour be,
Nor in this great sorrow and care.

Everyman:
Lo, now was I deceived or I was ware,
And all I may wyte[7] my spending of time.

Goods:
What, weenest thou that I am thine?

Everyman:
I had wend so.

Goods:
Nay, Everyman, I say no;
As for a while I was lent thee,
A season thou hast had me in prosperity;
My condition is man's soul to kill;
If I save one, a thousand I do spill;
Weenest thou that I will follow thee?
Nay, from this world, not verily.

Everyman:
I had wend otherwise.

Goods:
Therefore to thy soul Good is a thief;
For when thou art dead, this is my guise
Another to deceive in the same wise
As I have done thee, and all to his soul's reprief.

Everyman:
O false Good, cursed thou be!
Thou traitor to God, that has deceived me,
And caught me in thy snare.

Goods:
Marry, thou brought thyself in care,
Whereof I am glad,
I must needs laugh, I cannot be sad.

Everyman:
Ah, Good, thou hast had long my heartly love;
I gave thee that which should be the Lord's above.
But wilt thou not go with me in deed?
I pray thee truth to say.

Goods:
No, so God me speed,
Therefore farewell, and have good day.

Everyman:
O, to whom shall I make moan
For to go with me in that heavy journey?
First Fellowship said he would with me gone;
His words were very pleasant and gay,
But afterward he left me alone.
Then spake I to my kinsmen all in despair,
And also they gave me words fair,
They lacked no fair speaking,
But all forsake me in the ending.
Then went I to my Goods that I loved best,
In hope to have comfort, but there had I least:
For my Goods sharply did me tell
That he bringeth many into hell.
Then of myself I was ashamed,
And so I am worthy to be blamed;
Thus may I well myself hate,
Of whom shall I now counsel take?
I think that I shall never speed
Till that I go to my Good-Deed,
But alas, she is so weak,
That she can neither go nor speak,
Yet will I venture on her now.—
My Good-Deeds, where be you?

Good-Deeds:
Here I lie cold on the ground;
Thy sins hath me sore bound,
That I cannot stir.

---

7. Blame.

Everyman:
O, Good-Deeds, I stand in fear;
I must you pray of counsel,
For help now should come right well.

Good-Deeds:
Everyman, I have understanding
That ye be summoned account to make
Before Messias, of Jerusalem King;
And you by me[8] that journey what[9] you will I take.

Everyman:
Therefore I come to you, my moan to make;
I pray you, that ye will go with me.

Good-Deeds:
I would full fain, but I cannot stand verily.

Everyman:
Why, is there anything on you fall?

Good-Deeds:
Yea, sir, I may thank you of all;
If ye had perfectly cheered me,
Your book of account now full ready had be.
Look, the books of your works and deeds eke;
Oh, see how they lie under the feet,
To your soul's heaviness.

Everyman:
Our Lord Jesus, help me!
For one letter here I can not see.

Good-Deeds:
There is a blind reckoning in time of distress!

Everyman:
Good-Deeds, I pray you, help me in this need,
Or else I am for ever damned indeed;
Therefore help me to make reckoning
Before the redeemer of all thing,
That king is, and was, and ever shall.

Good-Deeds:
Everyman, I am sorry of your fall,
And fain would I help you, and I were able.

Everyman:
Good-Deeds, your counsel I pray you give me.

Good-Deeds:
That shall I do verily;
Though that on my feet I may not go,
I have a sister, that shall with you also,
Called Knowledge, which shall with you abide,
To help you to make that dreadful reckoning.

Knowledge:
Everyman, I will go with thee, and be thy guide,
In thy most need to go by thy side.

Everyman:
In good condition I am now in every thing,
And am wholly content with this good thing;
Thanked be God my Creator.

Good-Deeds:
And when he hath brought thee there,
Where thou shalt heal thee of thy smart,
Then go you with your reckoning and your Good-Deeds together
For to make you joyful at heart
Before the blessed Trinity.

Everyman:
My Good-Deeds, gramercy;
I am well content, certainly,
With your words sweet.

Knowledge:
Now go we together lovingly,
To Confession, that cleansing river.

Everyman:
For joy I weep; I would we were there;
But, I pray you, give me cognition
Where dwelleth that holy man, Confession.

Knowledge:
In the house of salvation:
We shall find him in that place,
That shall us comfort by God's grace.
Lo, this is Confession; kneel down and ask mercy,
For he is in good conceit with God almighty.

Everyman:
O glorious fountain that all uncleanness doth clarify,
Wash from me the spots of vices unclean,
That on me no sin may be seen;
I come with Knowledge for my redemption,
Repent with hearty and full contrition;
For I am commanded a pilgrimage to take,
And great accounts before God to make.
Now, I pray you, Shrift, mother of salvation,
Help my good deeds for my piteous exclamation.

Confession:
I know your sorrow well, Everyman;
Because with Knowledge ye come to me,
I will you comfort as well as I can,
And a precious jewel I will give thee,
Called penance, wise voider of adversity;
Therewith shall your body chastised be,
With abstinence and perseverance in God's service:
Here shall you receive that scourge of me,
Which is penance strong, that ye must endure,
To remember thy Savior was scourged for thee
With sharp scourges, and suffered it patiently;
So must thou, or thou scape that painful pilgrimage;
Knowledge, keep him in this voyage,
And by that time Good-Deeds will be with thee.
But in any wise, be sure of mercy,
For your time draweth fast, and ye will saved be;
Ask God mercy, and He will grant truly,
When with the scourge of penance man doth him bind,
The oil of forgiveness then shall he find.

Everyman:
Thanked be God for his gracious work!
For now I will my penance begin;
This hath rejoiced and lighted my heart,
Though the knots be painful and hard within.

Knowledge:
Everyman, look your penance that ye fulfil,
What pain that ever it to you be,
And Knowledge shall give you counsel at will,
How your accounts ye shall make clearly.

Everyman:
O eternal God, O heavenly figure,
O way of rightwiseness, O goodly vision,

8. If you go by me.
9. With.

Which descended down in a virgin pure
Because he would Everyman redeem,
Which Adam forfeited by his disobedience:
O blessed Godhead, elect and high-divine,
Forgive my grievous offence;
Here I cry thee mercy in this presence.
O ghostly treasure, O ransomer and redeemer
Of all the world, hope and conductor,
Mirror of joy, and founder of mercy,
Which illumineth heaven and earth thereby,
Hear my clamorous complaint, though it late be;
Receive my prayers; unworthy in this heavy life,
Though I be, a sinner most abominable,
Yet let my name be written in Moses' table;
O Mary, pray to the Maker of all thing,
Me for to help at my ending,
And save me from the power of my enemy,
For Death assaileth me strongly;
And, Lady, that I may be means of thy prayer
Of your Son's glory to be partaker,
By the means of his passion I it crave,
I beseech you, help my soul to save.—
Knowledge, give me the scourge of penance;
My flesh therewith shall give a quittance:
I will now begin, if God give me grace.

Knowledge:
Everyman, God give you time and space:
Thus I bequeath you in the hands of our Saviour,
Thus may you make your reckoning sure.

Everyman:
In the name of the Holy Trinity,
My body sore punished shall be:
Take this, body, for the sin of the flesh;
Also thou delightest to go gay and fresh,
And in the way of damnation thou did me bring;
Therefore suffer now strokes and punishing.
Now of penance I will wade the water clear,
To save me from purgatory, that sharp fire.

Good-Deeds:
I thank God, now I can walk and go;
And am delivered of my sickness and woe.
Therefore with Everyman I will go, and not spare;
His good works I will help him to declare.

Knowledge:
Now, Everyman, be merry and glad;
Your Good-Deeds cometh now; ye may not be sad;
Now is your Good-Deeds whole and sound,
Going upright upon the ground.

Everyman:
My heart is light, and shall be evermore;
Now will I smite faster than I did before.

Good-Deeds:
Everyman, pilgrim, my special friend,
Blessed be thou without end;
For thee is prepared the eternal glory.
Ye have me made whole and sound,
Therefore I will bide by thee in every stound.[10]

Everyman:
Welcome, my Good-Deeds; now I hear thy voice,
I weep for very sweetness of love.

Knowledge:
Be no more sad, but ever rejoice,
God seeth thy living in his throne above;
Put on this garment to thy behove,
Which is wet with your tears,
Or else before God you may it miss,
When you to your journey's end come shall.

Everyman:
Gentle Knowledge, what do you it call?

Knowledge:
It is a garment of sorrow:
From pain it will you borrow;
Contrition it is,
That getteth forgiveness;
It pleaseth God passing well.

Good-Deeds:
Everyman, will you wear it for your heal?

Everyman:
Now blessed be Jesu, Mary's Son!
For now have I on true contrition.
And let us go now without tarrying;
Good-Deeds, have we clear our reckoning?

Good-Deeds:
Yea, indeed I have it here.

Everyman:
Then I trust we need not fear;
Now, friends, let us not part in twain.

Knowledge:
Nay, Everyman, that will we not, certain.

Good-Deeds:
Yet must thou lead with thee
Three persons of great might.

Everyman:
Who should they be?

Good-Deeds:
Discretion and Strength they hight,
And thy Beauty may not abide behind.

Knowledge:
Also ye must call to mind
Your Five-wits as for your counsellors.

Good-Deeds:
You must have them ready at all hours.

Everyman:
How shall I get hither?

Knowledge:
You must call them all together,
And they will hear you incontinent.

Everyman:
My friends, come hither and be present,
Discretion, Strength, my Five-wits, and Beauty.

Beauty:
Here at your will we be all ready.
What will ye that we should do?

Good-Deeds:
That ye would with Everyman go,
And help him in his pilgrimage,
Advise you, will ye with him or not in that voyage?

Strength:
We will bring him all thither,
To his help and comfort, ye may believe me.

10. Season.

Discretion:
So will we go with him all together.

Everyman:
Almighty God, loved thou be,
I give thee laud that I have hither brought
Strength, Discretion, Beauty, and Five-wits; lack I nought;
And my Good-Deeds, with Knowledge clear,
All be in my company at my will here;
I desire no more to my business.

Strength:
And I, Strength, will by you stand in distress,
Though thou would in battle fight on the ground.

Five-Wits:
And though it were through the world round,
We will not depart for sweet nor sour.

Beauty:
No more will I unto death's hour,
Whatsoever thereof befall.

Discretion:
Everyman, advise you first of all;
Go with a good advisement and deliberation;
We all give you virtuous monition
That all shall be well.

Everyman:
My friends, hearken what I will tell:
I pray God reward you in his heavenly sphere.
Now hearken, all that be here
For I will make my testament
Here before you all present.
In alms half my good I will give with my hands twain
In the way of charity, with good intent,
And the other half still shall remain
In quiet to be returned there it ought to be.
This I do in despite of the fiend of hell
To go quite out of his peril
Ever after and this day.

Knowledge:
Everyman, hearken what I say;
Go to priesthood, I you advise,
And receive of him in any wise
The holy sacrament and ointment together;
Then shortly see ye turn again hither;
We will all abide you here.

Five-Wits:
Yea, Everyman, hie you that ye ready were,
There is no emperor, king, duke, ne baron,
That of God hath commission,
As hath the least priest in the world being;
For of the blessed sacraments pure and benign,
He beareth the keys and thereof hath the cure
For man's redemption, it is ever sure;
Which God for our soul's medicine
Gave us out of his heart with great pine;
Here in this transitory life, for thee and me
The blessed sacraments seven there be.
Baptism, confirmation, with priesthood good,
And the sacrament of God's precious flesh and blood,
Marriage, the holy extreme unction, and penance;
These seven be good to have in remembrance,
Gracious sacraments of high divinity.

Everyman:
Fain would I receive that holy body
And meekly to my ghostly father I will go.

Five-Wits:
Everyman, that is the best that ye can do:
God will you to salvation bring,
For priesthood exceedeth all other thing;
To us Holy Scripture they do teach,
And converteth man from sin heaven to reach;
God hath to them more power given,
Than to any angel that is in heaven;
With five words he may consecrate
God's body in flesh and blood to make,
And handleth his maker between his hands;
The priest bindeth and unbindeth all bands,
Both in earth and in heaven;
Thou ministers all the sacraments seven;
Though we kissed thy feet thou were worthy;
Thou art surgeon that cureth sin deadly:
No remedy we find under God
But all only priesthood.
Everyman, God gave priests that dignity,
And setteth them in his stead among us to be;
Thus be they above angels in degree.

Knowledge:
If priests be good it is so surely;
But when Jesus hanged on the cross with great smart
There he gave, out of his blessed heart,
The same sacrament in great torment:
He sold them not to us, that Lord Omnipotent.
Therefore Saint Peter the apostle doth say
That Jesu's curse hath all they
Which God their Saviour do buy or sell,
Or they for any money do take or tell.
Sinful priests giveth the sinners example bad;
Their children sitteth by other men's fires, I have heard;
And some haunteth women's company,
With unclean life, as lusts of lechery:
These be with sin made blind.

Five-Wits:
I trust to God no such may we find;
Therefore let us priesthood honour,
And follow their doctrine for our souls' succour;
We be their sheep, and they shepherds be
By whom we all be kept in surety.
Peace, for yonder I see Everyman come,
Which hath made true satisfaction.

Good-Deeds:
Methinketh it is he indeed.

Everyman:
Now Jesu be our alder speed.[11]
I have received the sacrament for my redemption,
And then mine extreme unction:
Blessed be all they that counselled me to take it!
And now, friends, let us go without longer respite;
I thank God that ye have tarried so long.
Now set each of you on this rod your hand,
And shortly follow me:
I go before, there I would be; God be our guide.

---

11. Speed in help of all.

Strength:
Everyman, we will not from you go,
Till ye have gone this voyage long.

Discretion:
I, Discretion, will bide by you also.

Knowledge:
And though this pilgrimage be never so strong,
I will never part you fro:
Everyman, I will be as sure by thee
As ever I did by Judas Maccabee.

Everyman:
Alas, I am so faint I may not stand,
My limbs under me do fold;
Friends, let us not turn again to this land,
Not for all the world's gold,
For into this cave must I creep
And turn to the earth and there to sleep.

Beauty:
What, into this grave? Alas!

Everyman:
Yea, there shall you consume more and less.

Beauty:
And what, should I smother here?

Everyman:
Yea, by my faith, and never more appear.
In this world live no more we shall,
But in heaven before the highest Lord of all.

Beauty:
I cross out all this; adieu by Saint John;
I take my cap in my lap and am gone.

Everyman:
What, Beauty, whither will ye?

Beauty:
Peace, I am deaf; I look not behind me,
Not and thou would give me all the gold in thy chest.

Everyman:
Alas, whereto may I trust?
Beauty goeth fast away hie;
She promised with me to live and die.

Strength:
Everyman, I will thee also forsake and deny;
Thy game liketh me not at all.

Everyman:
Why, then ye will forsake me all.
Sweet Strength, tarry a little space.

Strength:
Nay, sir, by the rood of grace
Though thou weep till thy heart brast.

Everyman:
Ye would ever bide by me, ye said.

Strength:
Yea, I have you far enough conveyed;
Ye be old enough, I understand,
Your pilgrimage to take on hand;
I repent me that I hither came.

Everyman:
Strength, you to displease I am to blame;
Will you break promise that is debt?

Strength:
In faith, I care not;
Thou art but a fool to complain,
You spend your speech and waste your brain;
Go thrust thee into the ground.

Everyman:
I had wend surer I should you have found.
He that trusteth in his Strength
She him deceiveth at the length.
Both Strength and Beauty forsaketh me,
Yet they promised me fair and lovingly.

Discretion:
Everyman, I will after Strength be gone,
As for me I will leave you alone.

Everyman:
Why, Discretion, will ye forsake me?

Discretion:
Yea, in faith, I will go from thee,
For when Strength goeth before
I follow after evermore.

Everyman:
Yet I pray thee, for the love of the Trinity,
Look in my grave once piteously.

Discretion:
Nay, so nigh will I not come.
Farewell, every one!

Everyman:
O all thing faileth, save God alone;
Beauty, Strength, and Discretion;
For when Death bloweth his blast,
They all run from me full fast.

Five-Wits:
Everyman, my leave now of thee I take;
I will follow the other, for here I thee forsake.

Everyman:
Alas! then may I wail and weep,
For I took you for my best friend.

Five-Wits:
I will no longer thee keep;
Now farewell, and there an end.

Everyman:
O Jesu, help, all hath forsaken me!

Good-Deeds:
Nay, Everyman, I will bide with thee,
I will not forsake thee indeed;
Thou shalt find me a good friend at need.

Everyman:
Gramercy, Good-Deeds; now may I true friends see;
They have forsaken me every one;
I loved them better than my Good-Deeds alone.
Knowledge, will ye forsake me also?

Knowledge:
Yea, Everyman, when ye to death do go:
But not yet for no manner of danger.

Everyman:
Gramercy, Knowledge, with all my heart.

Knowledge:
Nay, yet I will not from hence depart,
Till I see where ye shall be come.

Everyman:
Methinketh, alas, that I must be gone
To make my reckoning and my debts pay,
For I see my time is nigh spent away.
Take example, all ye that this do hear or see,
How they that I loved best do forsake me,
Except my Good-Deeds that bideth truly.

Good-Deeds:
All earthly things is but vanity:
Beauty, Strength, and Discretion, do man forsake,
Foolish friends and kinsmen, that fair spake,
All fleeth save Good-Deeds, and that am I.

Everyman:
Have mercy on me, God most mighty;
And stand by me, thou Mother and Maid, holy Mary.

Good-Deeds:
Fear not, I will speak for thee.

Everyman:
Here I cry God mercy.

Good-Deeds:
Short our end, and minish our pain;
Let us go and never come again.

Everyman:
Into thy hands, Lord, my soul I commend;
Receive it, Lord, that it be not lost;
As thou be boughtest, so me defend,
And save me from the fiend's boast,
That I may appear with that blessed host
That shall be saved at the day of doom.
In manus tuas—of might's most
For ever—*commendo spiritum meum.*[12]

Knowledge:
Now hath he suffered that we all shall endure;
The Good-Deeds shall make all sure.
Now hath he made ending;
Methinketh that I hear angels sing
And make great joy and melody,
Where Everyman's soul received shall be.

Angel:
Come, excellent elect spouse to Jesu:
Hereabove thou shalt go
Because of thy singular virtue:
Now the soul is taken the body fro;
Thy reckoning is crystal-clear.
Now shalt thou into the heavenly sphere,
Unto the which all ye shall come
That liveth well before the day of doom.

Doctor:
This moral men may have in mind;
Ye hearers, take it of worth, old and young,
And forsake pride, for he deceiveth you in the end,
And remember Beauty, Five-wits, Strength, and Discretion,
They all at the last do Everyman forsake,
Save his Good-Deeds, there doth he take.
But beware, and they be small
Before God, he hath not help at all.
None excuse may be there for Everyman:
Alas, how shall he do then?
For after death amends may no man make,
For then mercy and pity do him forsake.
If his reckoning be not clear when he do come,
God will say—*ite maledicti in ignem aeternum.*[13]
And he that hath his account whole and sound,
High in heaven he shall be crowned;
Unto which place God brings us all thither
That we may live body and soul together.
Thereto help the Trinity,
Amen, say ye, for saint Charity.

THUS ENDETH THIS MORALL PLAY OF EVERYMAN.

Aucassin and Nicolette

Who will deign to hear the song,
Solace of a captive's wrong,
Telling how two children met,
Aucassin and Nicolette;
How by grievous pains distraught,
Noble deeds the varlet wrought
For his love, and her bright face!
Sweet my rhyme, and full of grace,
Fair my tale, and debonair.
He who lists—though full of care,
Sore astonied, much amazed,
All cast down, by men mispraised,
Sick in body, sick in soul,
Hearing, shall be glad and whole,
So sweet the tale.[1]

Now they say and tell and relate:

How the Count Bougars of Valence made war on Count Garin of Beaucaire, war so great, so wonderful, and so mortal, that never dawned the day but that he was at the gates and walls and barriers of the town, with a hundred knights and ten thousand men-at-arms, on foot and on horse. So he burned the Count's land, and spoiled his heritage, and dealt death to his men. The Count Garin of Beaucaire was full of years, and frail; he had long outworn his day. He had no heir, neither son nor daughter, save one only varlet, and he was such as I will tell you. Aucassin was the name of the lad. Fair he was, and pleasant to look upon, tall and shapely of body in every whit of him. His hair was golden, and curled in little rings about his head; he had grey and dancing eyes, a clear, oval face, a nose high and comely, and he was so gracious in all good graces that nought in him was found to blame, but good alone. But love, that high prince, so utterly had cast him down, that he cared not to become knight, neither to bear arms, nor to tilt at tourneys, nor yet to do aught that it became his name to do.

His father and his mother spake him thus, "Son, don now thy mail, mount thy horse, keep thy land, and render aid to thy men. Should they see thee amongst them, the better will the men-at-arms defend their bodies and their substance, thy fief[2] and mine."

"Father," said Aucassin, "why speakest thou in such fashion to me? May God give me nothing of my desire if I

12. Into your hands I commend my spirit.
13. Be damned to the eternal fire.
1. Don't look for "deeper meanings" in this piece, nor take it too seriously. It is included in this book as a comparison with *Everyman* to show the two conflicting moods of the Middle Ages. The names are pronounced oh-kak-SAN and nĭ-koh-LET.
2. Fief—the demesne of the Count.

become knight, or mount to horse, or thrust into the press to strike other or be smitten down, save only that thou give me Nicolette, my sweet friend, whom I love so well."

"Son," answered the father, "this may not be. Put Nicolette from mind. For Nicolette is but a captive maid, come hither from a far country, and the Viscount of this town bought her with money from the Saracens, and set her in this place. He hath nourished and baptized her, and held her at the font. On a near day he will give her to some young bachelor, who will gain her bread in all honor. With this what has thou to do? Ask for a wife, and I will find thee the daughter of a king, or a count. Were he the richest man in France, his daughter shalt thou have, if so thou wilt."

"Faith, my father," said Aucassin, "what honor of this world would not Nicolette, my very sweet friend, most richly become! Were she Empress of Byzantium or of Allemaigne, or Queen of France or England, low enough would be her degree, so noble is she, so courteous and debonair, and gracious in all good graces."

Now is sung:

Aucassin was of Beaucaire,
Of the mighty castle there,
But his heart was ever set
On his fair friend, Nicolette.
Small he heeds his father's blame,
Or the harsh words of his dame:
"Fool, to weep the livelong day,
Nicolette trips light and gay.
Scouring she from far Carthage,
Bought of Paynims for a wage.
Since a wife beseems thee good,
Take a wife of wholesome blood."
"Mother, nought for this I care,
Nicolette is debonair;
Slim the body, fair the face,
Make my heart a lighted place;
Love has set her as my peer,
Too sweet, my dear."

Now they say and tell and relate:

When the Count Garin of Beaucaire found that in nowise could he withdraw Aucassin his son from the love of Nicolette, he sought out the Viscount of the town, who was his man, and spake him thus, "Sir Count, send Nicolette your godchild straightly from this place. Cursed be the land wherefrom she was carried to this realm; for because of her I lose Aucassin, who will not become knight, nor do aught that it becometh knight to do. Know well that, were she once within my power, I would hurry her to the fire; and look well to yourself for you stand in utmost peril and fear."

"Sire," answered the Viscount, "this lies heavy upon me, that ever Aucassin goes and he comes seeking speech with my ward. I have bought her with my money, and nourished and baptized her, and held her at the font. Moreover, I am fain to give her to some young bachelor, who will gain her bread in all honor. With this Aucassin your son had nought to do. But since this is your will and your pleasure, I will send her to so far a country that nevermore shall he see her with his eyes."

"Walk warily," replied the Count Garin, "for great evil easily may fall to you of this." So they went their ways.

Now the Viscount was a very rich man, and had a rich palace standing within a garden. In a certain chamber of an upper floor he set Nicolette in ward, with an old woman to bear her company, and to watch; and he put there bread and meat and wine and all things for their need. Then he placed a seal upon the door, so that none might enter in, nor issue forth, save only that there was a window looking on the garden, strictly close, whereby they breathed a little fresh air.

Now is sung:

Nicolette is prisoned fast,
In a vaulted chamber cast,
Shaped and carven wondrous well,
Painted as by miracle.
At the marble casement stayed
On her elbow leaned the maid;
Golden showed her golden hair,
Softly curved her eyebrows rare,
Fair her face, and brightly flushed,
Sweeter maiden never blushed.
In the garden from her room
She might watch the roses bloom,
Hear the birds make tender moan;
Then she knew herself alone.
"'Lack, great pity 'tis to place
Maid in such an evil case.
Aucassin, my liege, my squire,
Friend, and dear, and heart's desire,
Since thou dost not hate me quite,
Men have done me foul despite,
Sealed me in this vaulted room,
Thrust me to this bitter doom.
But by God, Our Lady's Son,
Soon will I from here begone,
So it be won."

Now they say and tell and relate:

Nicolette was prisoned in the chamber, as you have heard and known. The cry and the haro[3] went through all the land that Nicolette was stolen away. Some said that she had fled the country, and some that the Count Garin of Beaucaire had done her to death. Whatever man may have rejoiced, Aucassin had no joy therein, so he sought out the Viscount of the town and spake him thus, "Sir Viscount, what have you done with Nicolette, my very sweet friend, the thing that most I love in all the world? Have you borne her off, or hidden her from my sight? Be sure that should I die hereof, my blood will be required of you, as is most just, for I am slain of your two hands; since you steal from me the thing that most I love in all the world."

"Fair sire," answered the Viscount, "put this from mind. Nicolette is a captive maid whom I brought here from a far country. For her price I trafficked with the Saracens, and I have bred and baptized her, and held her at the font. I have nourished her duly, and on a day will give her to some young bachelor who will gain her bread in honorable fashion. With this you have nought to do; but only to wed the daughter of some count or king. Beyond this, what profit would you have, had you become her lover, and taken her to be your bed? Little enough would be your gain therefrom, for your soul would lie tormented

3. Protest against injustice.

in Hell all the days of all time, so that to Paradise never should you win."

"In Paradise what have I to do? I care not to enter, but only to have Nicolette, my very sweet friend, whom I love so dearly well. For into Paradise go none but such people as I will tell you of. There go those aged priests, and those old cripples, and the maimed, who all day long and all night cough before the altars, and in the crypts beneath the churches; those who go in worn old mantles and old tattered habits; who are naked, and barefoot, and full of sores; who are dying of hunger and of thirst, of cold and of wretchedness. Such as these enter in Paradise, and with them have I nought to do. But in Hell will I go. For to Hell go the fair clerks and the fair knights who are slain in the tourney and the great wars, and the stout archer and the loyal man. With them will I go. And there go the fair and courteous ladies, who have friends, two or three, together with their wedded lords. And there pass the gold and the silver, the ermine and all rich furs, harpers and minstrels, and the happy of the world. With these will I go, so only that I have Nicolette, my very sweet friend, by my side."

"Truly," cried the Viscount, "you talk idly, for never shall you see her more; yea, and if perchance you spoke together, and your father heard thereof, he would burn both me and her in one fire and yourself might well have every fear."

"This lies heavy upon me," answered Aucassin. Thus he parted from the Viscount making great sorrow.

Now is sung:

Aucassin departed thus
Sad at heart and dolorous;
Gone is she, his fairest friend,
None may comfort give or mend,
None by counsel make good end.
To the palace turned he home,
Climbed the stair, and sought his room.
In the chamber all alone
Bitterly he made his moan,
Presently began to weep
For the love he might not keep.
"Nicolette, so gent, so sweet,
Fair the faring of thy feet,
Fair thy laughter, sweet thy speech,
Fair our playing each with each,
Fair thy clasping, fair thy kiss,
Yet it endeth all in this.
Since from me my love is ta'en
I misdoubt that I am slain;
Sister, sweet friend."

Now they say and tell and relate:

Whilst Aucassin was in the chamber lamenting Nicolette, his friend, the Count Bougars of Valence, wishful to end the war, pressed on his quarrel, and setting his pikemen and horsemen in array, drew near the castle to take it by storm. Then the cry arose and the tumult; and the knights and the men-at-arms took their weapons, and hastened to the gates and the walls to defend the castle, and the burgesses climbed to the battlements, flinging quarrels[4] and sharpened darts upon the foe. Whilst the siege was so loud and perilous, the Count Garin of Beaucaire sought the chamber where Aucassin lay mourning, assotted upon[5] Nicolette, his very sweet friend, whom he loved so well.

"Ha, son," cried he, "craven art thou and shamed, that seest thy best and fairest castle so hardly beset. Know well that if thou lose it, thou art a naked man. Son, arm thyself lightly, mount the horse, keep thy land, aid thy men, hurtle into the press. Thou needest not to strike together, neither to be smitten down, but if they see thee amongst them, the better will they defend their goods and their bodies, thy land and mine; and thou art so stout and strong that very easily thou canst do this thing, as is but right."

"Father," answered Aucassin, "what sayest thou now? May God give me naught that I require of Him if I become a knight, or mount to horse, or thrust into the press to strike knight or to be smitten down, save only thou givest me Nicolette, my sweet friend, whom I love so well!"

"Son," replied the father, "this can never be. Rather will I suffer to lose my heritage, and go bare of all, than that thou shouldst have her, either as woman or as dame."

So he turned without farewell; but when Aucassin saw him part, he stayed him, saying, "Father, come now; I will make a true bargain with thee."

"What bargain, fair son?"

"I will arm me, and thrust into the press on such bargain as this: that if God bring me again safe and sound, thou wilt let me look on Nicolette, my sweet friend, so long that I may have with her two words or three, and kiss her only one time."

"I pledge my word to this," said the father. Of this covenant had Aucassin much joy.

Now is sung:

Aucassin the more was fain
Of the kiss he sought to gain,
Rather than his coffers hold
A hundred thousand marks of gold.
At the call his squire drew near,
Armed him fast in battle gear;
Shirt and hauberk donned the lad,
Laced the helmet on his head,
Girt his golden-hilted sword—
Came the war-horse at his word—
Gripped the buckler and the lance,
At the stirrups cast a glance;
Then, most brave from plume to heel,
Pricked the charger with the steel,
Called to mind his absent dear,
Passed the gateway without fear
Straight to the fight.

Now they say and tell and relate:

Aucassin was armed and horsed as you have heard. God, how bravely showed the shield about his neck, the helmet on his head, and the fringes of the baldric upon his left thigh! The lad was tall and strong, slender and comely to look upon; and the steed he bestrode was great and speedy, and fiercely had he charged clear of the gate. Now think not that he sought spoil of oxen and cattle, nor to smite others and himself escape. Nay, but of all this he took no heed. Another was with him; and he thought so dearly upon Nicolette, his fair friend, that the reins fell from his hand, and he struck never a blow. Then the charger, yet smarting from the spur, bore him into the battle, amidst the

4. Square-headed crossbow-bolt.
5. Infatuated with.

thickest of the foe, so that hands were laid upon him from every side, and he was made prisoner. Thus they spoiled him of shield and lance, and forthwith led him from the field a captive, questioning amongst themselves by what death he should be slain.

When Aucassin marked their words, "Ha, God!" cried he. "Sweet Creature, these are my mortal foes who lead me captive, and who soon will smite off my head; and when my head is smitten, never again may I have fair speech with Nicolette, my sweet friend, whom I hold so dear. Yet have I a good sword; and my horse is yet unblown. Now if I defend me not for her sake, may God keep her never, should she love me still!" The varlet was hardy and stout, and the charger he bestrode was right fierce. He plucked forth his sword, and smote suddenly on the right hand and on the left, cutting sheer through nasal and headpiece, gauntlet and arm, making such ruin around him as the wild boar deals when brought to bay by hounds in the wood, until he had struck down ten knights, and hurt seven more, and won clear of the *melee*, and rode back at utmost speed, sword in his hand.

The Count Bougars of Valence heard tell that his men were about to hang Aucassin, his foe, in shameful wise, so he hastened to the sight; and Aucassin passed him not by. His sword was yet in hand, and struck the Count so fiercely upon the helm that the headpiece was cleft and shattered upon the head. So bewildered was he by the stroke that he tumbled to the ground, and Aucassin stretched forth his hand, and took him, and led him captive by the nasal of the helmet, and delivered him to his father. "Father," said Aucassin, "behold the foe who wrought such war and mischief upon you! Twenty years hath this war endured, and none was there to bring it to an end."

"Fair son," replied his father, "better are such deeds as this than foolish dreams!"

"Father," returned Aucassin, "preach me no preachings; but carry out our bargain."

"Ha! What bargain, fair son?"

"How now, father, hast thou returned from the market? By my head, I will remember—whosoever may forget—so close is it to my heart! Didst thou not bargain with me, when I armed me and fared into the press, that if God brought me again safe and sound, thou wouldst grant me sight of Nicolette, my sweet friend, so long that I might have with her two words or three, and kiss her once? Such was the bargain; so be thou honest dealer."

"I!" cried the father. "God aid me never, should I keep such terms. Were she here, I would set her in the flames; and thou thyself might well have every fear."

"Is this the very end?" said Aucassin.

"So help me God," said his father, "yea!"

"Certes," said Aucassin, "grey hairs go ill with a lying tongue."

"Count of Valance," said Aucassin, "thou art my prisoner?"

"Sire," answered the Count, "it is verily and truly so."

"Give me thy hand," said Aucassin.

"Sire, as you wish!" So each took the other's hand.

"Plight me thy faith," said Aucassin, "that so long as thou drawest breath, never shall pass a day but thou shalt deal with my father in shameful fashion, either in goods or in person, if so thou canst."

"Sire, for God's love make me not a jest, but name me a price for my ransom. Whether you ask gold or silver, steed or palfrey, pelt or fur, hawk or hound, it shall be paid."

"What!" said Aucassin; "art thou not my prisoner?"

"Truly, sire," said the Count Bougars.

"God aid me never," quoth Aucassin, "but I send thy head flying, save thou plight me such faith as I said."

"In God's name," cried he, "I plight such affiance as seems most meet to thee." He pledged his troth; so Aucassin set him upon a horse, and brought him into a place of surety, himself riding by his side.

Now is sung:

When Count Garin knew his son
Aucassin still loved but one,
That his heart was ever set
Fondly on fond Nicolette,
Straight a prison he hath found,
Paved with marble, walled around,
Where in vault beneath the earth
Aucassin made little mirth,
But with wailing filled his cell
In such wise as now I tell
"Nicolette, white lily-flow'r,
Sweetest lady found in bow'r,
Sweet as grape that brimmeth up
Sweetness in the spiced cup,
On a day this chanced to you:
Out of Limousin there drew
One, a pilgrim, sore adread—
Lay in pain upon his bed,
Tossed, and took with fear his breath,
Very dolent, near to death—
Then you entered, pure and white,
Softly to the sick man's sight,
Raised the train that swept adown,
Raised the ermine-bordered gown
Raised the smock, and bared to him,
Daintily, each lovely limb.
Then a wondrous thing befell.
Straight he rose up, sound and well,
Left his bed, took cross in hand,
Sought again his own dear land.
Lily-flow'r, so white, so sweet,
Fair the faring of thy feet,
Fair thy laughter, fair thy speech,
Fair our playing each with each!
Sweet thy kisses, soft thy touch!
All must love thee overmuch.
'Tis for thee that I am thrown
In this vaulted cell alone;
'Tis for thee that I attend
Death, that comes to make an end—
For thee, sweet friend!

Now they say and tell and relate:

Aucassin was set in prison as you have heard tell, and Nicolette for her part was shut in the chamber. It was in the time of summer heat, in the month of May, when the days are warm, long and clear, and the night still and serene. Nicolette lay one night sleepless on her bed, and watched the moon shine brightly through the casement, and listened to the nightingale plain in the garden. Then she bethought her of Aucassin, her friend, whom she loved so well. She called also to mind the Count Garin of Beaucaire, her mortal foe, and feared greatly to remain, lest her hiding-place should be told to him, and she be put to death in some shameful fashion. She made certain that the old woman who held her in ward was sound asleep. So she rose, and wrapped herself in a very fair silk mantle, the best she had, and taking the sheets from her bed and the towels of her bath, knotted them together to make so long a rope as she was able, tied it about a pillar of the window, and slipped down into the garden. Then she took her skirt in both hands, the one before, and the other behind, and kilted her lightly against the dew which lay thickly upon the grass, and so passed through the garden. Her hair was golden, with little lovelocks; her eyes blue and laughing; her face most dainty to see, with lips more vermeil than ever was rose or cherry in the time of summer heat; her teeth white and small; her breasts so firm that they showed beneath her vesture like two rounded nuts. So frail was she about the girdle that your two hands could have spanned her, and the daisies that she brake with her feet in passing showed altogether black against her instep and her flesh, so white was the fair young maiden.

She came to the postern, and unbarring the gate, issued forth upon the street of Beaucaire, taking heed to keep within the shadows, for the moon shone very bright, and thus she fared until she chanced upon the tower where her lover was prisoned. The tower was buttressed with pieces of wood in many places, and Nicolette hid herself amongst the pillars, wrapped close in her mantle. She set her face to a crevice of the tower, which was old and ruinous, and there she heard Aucassin weeping within, making great sorrow for the sweet friend whom he held so dear; and when she had hearkened awhile, she began to speak.

Now is sung:

Nicolette, so bright of face,
Leaned within this buttressed place,
Heard her lover weep within,
Marked the woe of Aucassin.
Then in words her thought she told:
"Aucassin, fond heart and bold,
What avails thine heart should ache
For a Paynim maiden's sake?
Ne'er may she become thy mate,
Since we prove thy father's hate,
Since thy kinsfolk hate me too;
What is left for me to do?
Nothing, but to seek the strand,
Pass o'er sea to some far land."
Shore she then one golden tress,
Thrust it in her love's duress;
Aucassin hath seen the gold
Shining bright in that dark hold,
Took the lock at her behest,
Kissed and placed it in his breast;
Then once more his eyes were wet
    For Nicolette.

Now they say and tell and relate:

When Aucassin heard Nicolette say that she would fare into another country, he was filled with anger. "Fair sweet friend," said he, "this be far from thee, for then wouldst thou have slain me. And the first man who saw thee, if so he might, would take thee forthwith and carry thee to his bed, and make thee his leman. Be sure that if thou wert found in any man's bed, save it be mine, I should not need a dagger to pierce my heart and slay me. Certes, no; wait would I not for a knife; but on the first wall or the nearest stone would I cast myself, and beat out my brains altogether. Better to die so foul a death as this than know thee to be in any man's bed, save mine."

"Aucassin," said she, "I doubt that thou lovest me less than thy words; and that my love is fonder than thine."

"Alack," cried Aucassin, "fair sweet friend, how can it be that thy love should be so great? Woman can not love man, as man loves woman; for woman's love is in the glance of her eye, and the blossom of her breast, and the tip of the toe of her foot; but the love of man is set deep in the hold of his heart, from whence it can not be torn away."

Whilst Aucassin and Nicolette were thus at odds together, the town watch entered the street, bearing naked swords beneath their mantles, for Count Garin had charged them strictly, once she were taken, to put her to death. The warder from his post upon the tower marked their approach, and as they drew near, heard them speaking of Nicolette, menacing her with death.

"God," said he, "it is great pity that so fair a damsel should be slain, and a rich alms should I give if I could warn her privily, and so she escape the snare; for of her death Aucassin, my liege, were dead already, and truly this were a piteous case."

Now is sung:

Brave the warder, full of guile,
Straight he sought some cunning wile:
Sought and found a song betime,
Raised this sweet and pleasant rhyme.
"Lady of the loyal mind,
Slender, gracious, very kind,
Gleaming head and golden hair,
Laughing lips and eyes of vair!
Easy, Lady, 'tis to tell
Two have speech who love full well.
Yet in peril are they met,
Set the snare, and spread the net.
Lo, the hunters draw this way,
Cloaked, with privy knives, to slay.
Ere the huntsmen spy the chase[6]
Let the quarry haste apace
    And keep her well."

Now they say and tell and relate:

"Ah," said Nicolette, "may the soul of thy father and of thy mother find sweetest rest, since in so fair and courteous a manner hast thou warned me. So God please, I will indeed keep myself close, and may He keep me too."

She drew the folds of her cloak about her, and crouched in the darkness of the pillars till the watch had passed beyond; then she bade farewell to Aucassin, and bent her steps to the castle wall. The wall was very ruinous, and mended with timber, so she climbed the fence, and went her way till she found herself between wall and moat. Gazing below, she saw the fosse was very deep and perilous, and the maid had great fear.

"Ah, God," cried she, "sweet Creature, should I fall, my neck must be broken; and if I stay, tomorrow shall I be taken, and men will burn my body in a fire. Yet were it

6. Quarry.

better to die, now, in this place, than to be made a show tomorrow in the market."

She crossed her brow, and let herself slide down into the moat, and when she reached the bottom, her fair feet and pretty hands, which had never learned that they could be hurt, were so bruised and wounded that the blood came from them in places a many; yet knew she neither ill nor dolor because of the mightiness of her fear. But if with pain she had entered in, still more it cost her to issue forth. She called to mind that it were death to tarry, and by chance found there a stake of sharpened wood, which those within the keep had flung forth in their defense of the tower. With this she cut herself a foothold, one step above the other, till with extreme labor she climbed forth from the moat. Now the forest lay but the distance of two bolts from a crossbow, and ran some thirty leagues in length and breadth; moreover, within were many wild beasts and serpents. She feared these greatly, lest they should do her a mischief; but presently she remembered that should men lay hands upon her, they would lead her back to the city to burn her at the fire.

Now is sung:

Nicolette the fair, the fond,
Climbed the fosse and won beyond;
There she kneeled her, and implored
Very help of Christ the Lord.
"Father, King of majesty,
Where to turn I know not, I.
So, within the woodland gloom
Wolf and boar and lion roam,
Fearful things, with rav'ning maw,
Rending tusk and tooth and claw.
Yet, if all adread I stay,
Men will come at break of day,
Treat me to their heart's desire,
Burn my body in the fire.
But by God's dear majesty
Such a death I will not die;
Since I die, ah, better then
Trust the boar than trust to men.
Since all's evil, men and beast,
Choose I the least."

Now they say and tell and relate:

Nicolette made great sorrow in such manner as you have heard. She commended herself to God's keeping, and fared on until she entered the forest. She kept upon the fringes of the woodland, for dread of the wild beasts and reptiles; and hiding herself within some thick bush, sleep overtook her, and she slept fast until six hours of the morn, when shepherds and herdsmen came from the city to lead their flocks to pasture between the wood and the river. The shepherds sat by a clear, sweet spring, which bubbled forth on the outskirts of the greenwood, and spreading a cloak upon the grass, set bread thereon. Whilst they ate together, Nicolette awoke at the song of the birds and the laughter, and hastened to the well.

"Fair children," said she, "God have you in His keeping."

"God bless you also," answered one who was more fluent of tongue than his companions.

"Fair child," said she, "do you know Aucassin, the son of Count Garin of this realm?"

"Yes, we know him well."

"So God keep you, pretty boy," said she, "as you tell him that within this wood there is a fair quarry for his hunting; and if he may take her, he would not part with one of her members for a hundred golden marks, nor for five hundred, nay, nor for aught that man can give."

Then looking upon her steadfastly, their hearts were troubled, the maid was so beautiful. "Will I tell him?" cried he who was readier of words than his companions. "Woe to him who speaks of it ever, or tells Aucassin what you say. You speak not truth but faery, for in all this forest there is no beast neither stag, nor lion, nor boar—one of whose legs would be worth two pence, or three at very best, and you talk of five hundred marks of gold! Woe betide him who believes your story, or shall spread it abroad! You are a fay, and no fit company for such as us; so pass upon your road."

"Ah, fair child," answered she, "yet you will do as I pray; for this beast is the only medicine that may heal Aucassin of his hurt. And I have here five sous in my purse; take them, and give him my message. For within three days must he hunt this chase and if within three days he find not the quarry, never may he cure him of his wound."

"By my faith," cried he, "we will take the money and if he comes this way, will give him your message; but certainly we will not go and look for him."

"As God pleases!" answered she. So she bade farewell to the shepherds, and went her way.

Now is sung:

Nicolette, as you heard tell,
Bade the shepherd lads farewell;
Through deep woodlands warily
Fared she 'neath the leafy tree,
Till the grass-grown way she trod
Brought her to a forest road,
Whence, like fingers on a hand,
Forked sev'n paths throughout the land.
There she called to heart her love,
There bethought her she would prove
Whether true her lover's vows.
Plucked she then young sapling boughs,
Grasses, leaves that branches yield,
Oak shoots, lilies of the field—
Built a lodge with frond and flow'r—
Fairest mason, fairest bow'r!
Swore then, by the truth of God,
Should her lover come that road,
Nor for love of her who made
Dream a little in its shade,
'Spite his oath, no true love, he
Nor fond heart, she!

Now they say and tell and relate:

Nicolette builded the lodge, as you have heard; very pretty it was and very dainty, and well furnished, both outside and in, with a tapestry of flowers and of leaves. Then she withdrew herself a little way from the bower, and hid within a thicket to spy what Aucassin would do. And the cry and the haro went through all the realm that Nicolette was lost; some had it that she was stolen away, and others that Count Garin had done her to death. Whoever had joy thereof, Aucassin had little pleasure. His father, Count Garin, brought him out of his prison, and sent letters to the lords and ladies of those parts bidding them to a very rich feast, so that Aucassin, his son, might cease to dote. When the feast was at its merriest, Aucassin leaned against the musicians' gallery, sad and all discomforted. No laugh had he for any jest, since she whom most he loved was not amongst the ladies set in hall.

A certain knight marked his grief, and coming presently to him, said, "Aucassin, of such fever as yours, I, too, have been sick. I can give you good counsel, if you are willing to listen."

"Sir knight," said Aucassin, "great thanks! Good counsel, above all things, I would hear."

"Get to horse," said he; "take your pleasure in the woodland amongst flowers and bracken and the songs of the birds. Perchance (who knows?) you may hear some word of which you will be glad."

"Sir knight," answered Aucassin, "great thanks! This will I do." He left the hall privily, and went down-stairs to the stable where was his horse. He caused the charger to be saddled and bridled, then put foot in stirrup, mounted, and left the castle, riding till he entered the forest, and so by adventure came upon the well whereby the shepherd lads were sitting; and it was then about three hours after noon. They had spread a cloak upon the grass, and were eating their bread, with great mirth and jollity.

Now is sung:

Round about the well were set
Martin, Robin, Esmeret—
Jolly shepherds, gaily met—
Frulin, Jack, and Aubriet.
Laughed the one, "God keep in ward
Aucassin, our brave young lord—
Keep besides the damsel fair,
Blue of eye and gold of hair,
Gave us wherewithal to buy
Cate and sheath-knife presently,
Horn and quarter-staff and fruit,
Shepherd's pipe and country flute;
God make him well!"

Now they say and tell and relate:

When Aucassin marked the song of the herdboys he called to heart Nicolette, his very sweet friend, whom he held so dear. He thought she must have passed that way, so he struck his horse with the spurs and came quickly to the shepherds.

"Fair children, God keep you!"

"God bless you!" replied he who was readier of tongue than his fellows.

"Fair children," said he, "tell over again the song that you told but now."

"We will not tell it," answered he who was more fluent of speech than the others. "Sorrow be his who sings it to you, fair sir!"

"Fair children," returned Aucassin, "do you not know me?"

"Oh, yes; we know that you are Aucassin, our young lord. But we are not your men; we belong to the Count."

"Fair children, sing me the song once more, I pray you!"

"By the Wounded Heart, what fine words! Why should I sing for you if I have no wish to do so? Why, the richest man in all the land—saving the presence of Count Garin—would not dare to drive my sheep and oxen and cows from out his wheatfield or his pasture, for fear of losing his eyes! Wherefore, then, should I sing for you if I have no wish to do so?"

"God keep you, fair children; yet you will do this thing for me. Take ten sous that I have in my purse."

"Sire, we will take the money; but I will not sing for you, since I have sworn not to do so. But I will tell it in plain prose, if such be your pleasure."

"As God pleases!" answered Aucassin. "Better the tale in prose than no story at all!"

"Sire, we were in this glade between six and nine of the morn, and were breaking our bread by the well, just as we are doing now, when a girl came by, the loveliest thing in all the world, so fair that we doubted her a fay, and she brimmed our wood with light. She gave us money, and made a bargain with us that if you came here we would tell you that you must hunt in this forest; for in it is such a quarry that if you may take her you would not part with one of her members for five hundred silver marks, nor for aught that man can give. For in the quest is so sweet a salve that if you take her you shall be cured of your wound; and within three days must the chase be taken, for if she be not found by then, never will you see her more. Now go to your hunting if you will, and if you will not, let it go; for truly have I carried out my bargain with her."

"Fair children," cried Aucassin, "enough have you spoken; and may God set me on her track!"

Now is sung:

Aucassin's fond heart was moved
When this hidden word he proved
Sent him by the maid he loved.
Straight his charger he bestrode,
Bade farewell, and swiftly rode
Deep within the forest dim,
Saying o'er and o'er to him:
"Nicolette, so sweet, so good,
'Tis for you I search this wood—
Antler'd stag nor boar I chase—
Hot I follow on your trace.
Slender shape and deep blue eyes,
Dainty laughter, low replies,
Fledge the arrow in my heart.
Ah, to find you—ne'er to part!
Pray God give so fair an end,
Sister, sweet friend!"

Now they say and tell and relate:

Aucassin rode through the wood in search of Nicolette, and the charger went right speedily. Do not think that the spines and the thorns were pitiful to him. Truly, it was not so; for his raiment was so torn that the least tattered of his garments could scarcely hold to his body, and the blood ran from his arms and legs and flanks in forty places, or at least in thirty, so that you could have followed after him by the blood which he left upon the grass. But he thought so fondly of Nicolette, his sweet friend, that he felt neither ill nor dolor. Thus all day long he searched the forest in his fashion, but might learn no news of her, and when it drew towards dusk, he commenced to weep because he had heard nothing. He rode at adventure down an old grass-grown road, and looking before him, saw a young man standing, such as I will tell you. Tall he was, and marvelously ugly and hideous. His head was big and blacker than smoked meat; the palm of your hand could easily have gone between his two eyes; he had very large cheeks and a monstrous flat nose with great nostrils; lips redder than uncooked flesh; teeth yellow and foul; he was shod with shoes and gaiters of bull's hide, bound about the leg with ropes to well above the knee; upon his back was a rough cloak; and he stood leaning on a huge club. Aucassin urged his steed towards him, but was all afeared when he saw him as he was.

"Fair brother, God keep you."

"God bless you too," said he.

"As God keeps you, what do you here?"

"What is that to you?" said he.

"Truly, naught," answered Aucassin. "I asked with no wish to do you wrong."

"And you, for what cause do you weep?" asked the other, "and make such heavy sorrow? Certainly, were I so rich a man as you are, not the whole world should make me shed a tear."

"Do you know me, then?" said Aucassin.

"Yes, well I know you to be Aucassin, the son of the Count, and if you will tell me why you weep, well, then I will tell what I do here."

"Certes," said Aucassin, "I will tell you with all my heart. I came this morning to hunt in the forest, and with a white grey-hound, the swiftest in the whole world. I have lost him, and that is why I weep."

"Hear him," cried he, "by the Sacred Heart, and you make all this lamentation for a filthy dog! Sorrow be his who shall esteem you more. Why, there is not a man of substance in these parts who would not give you ten or fifteen or twenty hounds—if so your father wishes—and be right glad to make you the gift. But for my part I have full reason to weep and cry aloud."

"And what is your grief, brother?"

"Sire, I will tell you. I was hired by a rich farmer to drive his plough, with a yoke of four oxen. Now three days ago, by great mischance, I lost the best of my bullocks, Roget, the very best ox in the plough. I have been looking for him ever since, and have neither eaten nor drunk for three days; since I dare not go back to the town, because men would put me into prison, as I have no money to pay for my loss. Of all the riches of the world I have nought but the rags upon my back. My poor old mother, too, who had nothing but one worn-out mattress, why, they have taken that from under her, and left her lying on the naked straw. That hurts me more than my own trouble. For money comes and money goes; if I have lost today, why, I may win tomorrow; and I will pay for my ox when pay I can. Not for this will I wring my hands. And you—you weep aloud for a filthy cur. Sorrow take him who shall esteem you more."

"Certes, thou art a true comforter, fair brother, and blessed may you be. What is the worth of your bullock?"

"Sire, the villein demands twenty sous for his ox. I can not beat the price down by a single farthing."

"Hold out your hand," said Aucassin; "take these twenty sous which I have in my purse, and pay for your ox."

"Sire," answered the hind, "many thanks, and God grant you find that for which you seek."

So they parted from each other, and Aucassin rode upon his way. The night was beautiful and still, and so he fared along the forest path until he came to the seven cross-roads where Nicolette had builded her bower. Very pretty it was, and very dainty, and well furnished both outside and in, ceiling and floor, with arras and carpet of freshly plucked flowers; no sweeter habitation could man desire to see. When Aucassin came upon it, he reined back his horse sharply, and the moonbeams fell within the lodge.

"Dear God," cried Aucassin, "here was Nicolette, my sweet friend, and this has she builded with her fair white hands. For the sweetness of the house and for love of her, now will I dismount, and here will I refresh me this night."

He withdrew his foot from the stirrup, and the charger was tall and high. He dreamed so deeply on Nicolette, his very sweet friend, that he fell heavily upon a great stone, and his shoulder came from its socket. He knew himself to be grievously wounded, but he forced him to do all that he was able, and fastened his horse with the other hand to a thorn. Then he turned on his side, and crawled as best he might into the lodge. Looking through a crevice of the bower, he saw the stars shining in the sky, and one brighter than all the others, so he began to repeat—

Now is sung:

Little Star I gaze upon
Sweetly drawing to the moon.
In such golden haunt is set
Love, and bright-haired Nicolette.
God hath taken from our war
Beauty, like a shining star.
Ah, to reach her, though I fell
From her Heaven to my Hell!
Who were worthy such a thing,
Were he emperor or king?
Still you shine, oh perfect Star,
  Beyond, afar.

Now they say and tell and relate:

When Nicolette heard Aucassin speak these words, she hastened to him from where she was hidden near by. She entered in the bower, and clasping her arms about his neck, kissed and embraced him straitly. "Fair sweet friend, very glad am I to find you."

"And you, fair sweet friend, glad am I to meet." So they kissed, and held each other fast, and their joy was lovely to see.

"Ah, sweet friend," cried Aucassin, "it was but now that I was in grievous pain with my shoulder, but since I hold you close I feel neither sorrow nor wound."

Nicolette searched his hurt, and perceived that the shoulder was out of joint. She handled it so deftly with her white hands and used such skillful surgery, that by the grace of God (who loveth all true lovers) the shoulder came back to its place. Then she plucked flowers, and fresh grass and green leafage, and bound them tightly about the setting with the hem torn from her shift, and he was altogether healed.

"Aucassin," said she, "Fair sweet friend, let us take thought together as to what must be done. If your father beats the wood tomorrow, and men take me, whatever may chance to you, certainly I shall be slain."

"Certes, fair sweet friend, the sorer grief would be mine. But so I may help, never shall you come to his hands." So he mounted to horse, and setting his love before him, held her fast in his arms, kissing her as he rode, and thus they came forth to the open fields.

Now is sung:

Aucassin, that loving squire,
Dainty fair to heart's desire,
Rode from out the forest dim
Clasping her he loved to him.
Placed upon the saddlebow
There he kissed her, chin and brow,
There embraced her, mouth and eyes.
But she spake him, sweetly wise:
"Love, a term to dalliance;
Since for us no home in France
See we Rome or far Byzance?"
"Sweet my love, all's one to me,
Dale or woodland, earth or sea;
Nothing care I where we ride
So I hold you at my side."
So, enlaced, the lovers went,
Skirting town and battlement,
Rocky scaur,[7] and quiet lawn;
Till one morning, with the dawn,
Broke the cliffs down to the shore,
Loud they heard the surges roar,
Stood by the sea.

(From this point Aucassin and Nicolette were separated. After some adventures Aucassin returned to his home where he became Count of Beaucaire. Nicolette was taken to Carthage where she was recognized as the king's daughter and was to be married to a Moorish Prince. She ran away, however, and made her way to Beaucaire disguised as a minstrel.)

Now is sung:

'Neath the keep of strong Beaucaire
On a day of summer fair,
At his pleasure, Aucassin
Sat with baron, friend and kin.
Then upon the scent of flow'rs,
Song of birds, and golden hours,
Full of beauty, love, regret,
Stole the dream of Nicolette,
Came the tenderness of years;
So he drew apart in tears.
Then there entered to his eyes
Nicolette, in minstrel guise,
Touched the viol with the bow,
Sang as I will let you know.
"Lords and ladies, list to me,
High and low, of what degree;
Now I sing, for your delight,
Aucassin, that loyal knight,
And his fond friend, Nicolette.
Such the love betwixt them set
When his kinsfolk sought her head,
Fast he followed where she fled.
From their refuge in the keep
Paynims bore them o'er the deep.
Nought of him I know to end.
But for Nicolette, his friend,
Dear she is, desirable,
For her father loves her well;
Famous Carthage owns him king,
Where she has sweet cherishing.
Now, as lord he seeks for her,
Sultan, Caliph, proud Emir.
But the maid of these will none,
For she loves a dansellon,
Aucassin, who plighted troth.
Sworn has she some pretty oath
Ne'er shall she be wife or bride,
Never lie at baron's side
Be he denied."

Now they say and tell and relate:

When Aucassin heard Nicolette sing in this fashion, he was glad at heart; so he drew her aside, and asked, "Fair sweet friend," said Aucassin, "know you nought of this Nicolette, whose ballad you have sung?"

"Sire, truly, yea; well I know her for the most loyal of creatures, and as the most winning and modest of maidens born. She is daughter to the King of Carthage, who took her when Aucassin also was taken, and brought her to the city of Carthage, till he knew for certain that she was his child, whereat he rejoiced greatly. Any day he would give her for husband one of the highest kings in all Spain; but rather would she be hanged or burned than take him, however rich he be."

"Ah, fair sweet friend," cried the Count Aucassin, "if you would return to that country and persuade her to have speech with me here, I would give you of my riches more than you would dare to ask of me or to take. Know that for love of her I choose not to have a wife, however proud her race, but I stand and wait; for never will there be wife of mine if it be not she, and if I knew where to find her I should not need to grope blindly for her thus."

"Sire," answered she, "if you will do these things, I will go and seek her for your sake, and for hers too; because to me she is very dear."

He pledged his word, and caused her to be given twenty pounds. So she bade him farewell, and he was weeping for the sweetness of Nicolette. And when she saw his tears, "Sire," said she, "take it not so much to heart; in so short a space will I bring her to this town, and you shall see her with your eyes."

When Aucassin knew this, he rejoiced greatly. So she parted from him, and fared in the town to the house of the Viscountess, for the Viscount, her godfather, was dead. There she lodged, and opened her mind fully to the lady on all the business; and the Viscountess recalled the past, and knew well that it was Nicolette whom she had cherished. So she caused the bath to be heated, and made her take her ease for fully eight days. Then Nicolette sought an herb that was called celandine, and washed herself therewith, and became so fair as she had never been before. She arrayed her in a rich silken gown from the lady's goodly store, and seated herself in the chamber on a rich stuff of broidered sendal; then she whispered the dame, and begged her to fetch Aucassin, her friend. This she did. When she reached the palace, lo, Aucassin in tears, making great sorrow for the long tarrying of Nicolette, his friend; and the lady called to him, and said, "Aucassin, behave not so wildly; but come with me, and I will show you that thing you love best in all the world; for Nicolette, your sweet friend, is here from a far country to seek her love." So Aucassin was glad at heart.

7. Isolated cliff.

Now is sung:

When he learned that in Beaucaire
Lodged his lady, sweet and fair,
Aucassin arose, and came
To her hostel, with the dame;
Entered in, and passed straightway
To the chamber where she lay.
When she saw him, Nicolette
Had such joy as never yet;
Sprang she lightly to her feet,
Swiftly came with welcome meet.
When he saw her, Aucassin
Oped both arms, and drew her in,
Clasped her close in fond embrace,
Kissed her eyes and kissed her face.
In such greeting sped the night,
Till, at dawning of the light,
Aucassin, with pomp most rare,
Crowned her Countess of Beaucaire.
Such delight these lovers met,
Aucassin and Nicolette.
Length of days and joy did win,
Nicolette and Aucassin;
Endeth song and tale I tell
With marriage bell.

Songs and Poems of the Wandering Scholars

The pull of life was strong in the time when new ideas were breaking down the old medieval walls. And students (even those who were to become learned clergymen) were much the same in those days as they are now.

Gaudeamus Igitur

Let us live, then, and be glad
While young life's before us!
After youthful pastime had,
After old age, hard and sad,
Earth will slumber o'er us.

Where are they who in this world
Ere we kept, were keeping?
Go ye to the gods above;
Go to hell; inquire thereof;
They are not; they are sleeping.

Brief is life, and brevity
Briefly shall be ended;
Death comes like a whirlwind strong,
Bears us with his blast along;
None shall be defended.

Live this university,
Men that learning nourish;
Live each member of the same,
Long live all that bear its name,
Let them ever flourish!

Live the commonwealth also,
And the men that guide it!
Live our town in strength and health,
Founders, patrons, by whose wealth
We are here provided!

Live all gods! A health to you,
Melting maids and beauteous;
Live the wives and women too,
Gentle, loving, tender, true,
Good, industrious, duteous!

Perish cares that pule and pine!
Perish envious blamers!
Die the Devil, thine and mine!
Die the starch-neck Philistine!
Scoffers and defamers!

Lauriger Horatius

Horace with your laurel crowned,
Truly have you spoken;
Time, a-rush with leap and bound,
Devours and leaves us broken.

Where are now the flagons, full
Of sweet wine, honey-clear?
Where the smiles and shoves and frowns
Of blushing maiden dear?

Swift the young grape grows and swells;
So do comely lasses!
Lo, on the poet's head, the snows
Of the Time that passes!

What's the good of lasting fame,
If people think it sinful
Here and now to kiss a dame
And drink a jolly skinful!

A Goliard's Creed

"A *goliard* is dying; the priest sent for in haste speaks comfortable words; have comfort, good son; let him but recite his Credo."[1]

That I will, Sir, and hear me now.

Credo—in dice I well believe,
That got me often bit and sup,
And many a time hath had me drunk,
And many a time delivered me
From every stich and every penny.

In Deum—never with my will
Gave Him a thought nor ever will.
The other day I took a shirt
From a ribald and I diced it,
And lost, and never gave it back.
If I die, he can have mine.

Put it in writing, 'tis my will,
I would not like it were forgot.
Patrem—at St. Denis in France,
Good sir, I had a father once,
Omnipotentem in his having,
Money and horses and fine wearing,
And by the dice that thieveth all things
I lost and gamed it all away . . . .

Creatorem who made all
I've denied—He has His will
Of me now, I know I'm dying,
Nothing here but bone and hide.

---

1. The Creed being recited is as follows: I believe (credo) in God (in Deum) the Father (Patrem), Omnipotent (Omnipotentem), the Creator (Creatorem) of heaven (coeli) and earth (et terrae) . . . and in the resurrection (et . . . resurrectionem) of the body (corporis) and life everlasting (vitam aeternam). Amen.

Coeli—of Heaven ever think?
Nay, but the wine that I could drink.

Et terrae—there was all my joy. . . .
(The burlesque recitation goes on to the final phrase)

Et corporis—the body's lust
I do perform. Sir Priest, I chafe
At thinking of that other life.
I tell you, 'tis not worth a straw.
And I would pray to the Lord God
That He will in no kind of way
Resurrectionem make of me,
So long as I may drench the place
With good wine where I'll be laid
And so pray I of all my friends
That if I can't, themselves will do't,
And leave me a full pot of wine
Which I may to the Judgment bring.

Vitam aeternam wilt Thou give,
O Lord God? wilt Thou forgive
All my evil, well I know it,

Amen. Priest, I now am through with't.
Through with life. Death hath its pain.
Too much . . . . too much . . . . This agony . . . .
I'm dying. I to God commend you.
I ask it of you—Pray for me."

Our Lady's Juggler

In this simple story one can see the hold and the charm of the Cult of the Virgin, especially for the simple people for whom chivalry on the one hand and philosophy on the other had no meaning.

In the days of King Louis there lived a poor juggler by the name of Barnabas, a native of Compiegne, who wandered from city to city performing tricks of skill and prowess.

On fair days he would lay down in the public square a worn and aged carpet, and after having attracted a group of children and idlers by certain amusing remarks which he had learned from an old juggler, and which he invariably repeated in the same fashion without altering a word, he would assume the strangest postures and balance a pewter plate on the tip of his nose. At first the crowd regarded him with indifference, but when, with his hands and head on the ground he threw into the air and caught with his feet six copper balls that glittered in the sunlight, or when, throwing himself back until his neck touched his heels, he assumed the form of a perfect wheel and in that position juggled with twelve knives, he elicited a murmur of admiration from his audience, and small coins rained on his carpet.

Still, Barnabas of Compiegne, like most of those who exist by their accomplishments, had a hard time making a living. Earning his bread by the sweat of his brow, he bore rather more than his share of those miseries we are all heir to through the fault of our Father Adam.

Besides, he was unable to work as much as he would have liked, for in order to exhibit his wonderful talents, he required—like the trees—the warmth of the sun and the heat of the day. In winter time he was no more than a tree stripped of its leaves, in fact, half-dead. The frozen earth was too hard for the juggler. Like the cicada mentioned by Marie de France, he suffered during the bad season from hunger and cold. But, since he had a simple heart, he suffered in silence.

He had never thought much about the origin of wealth nor about the inequality of human conditions. He firmly believed that if this world was evil the next could not but be good, and this faith upheld him. He was not like the clever fellows who sell their souls to the devil; he never took the name of God in vain; he lived the life of an honest man, and though he had no wife of his own, he did not covet his neighbor's, for woman is the enemy of strong men, as we learn by the story of Samson which is written in the Scriptures.

Verily, his mind was not turned in the direction of carnal desire, and it caused him far greater pain to renounce drinking than to forgo the pleasure of women. For, though he was not a drunkard, he enjoyed drinking when the weather was warm. He was a good man, fearing God, and devout in his adoration of the Holy Virgin. When he went into a church he never failed to kneel before the image of the Mother of God and to address her with his prayer:

"My Lady, watch over my life until it shall please God that I die, and when I am dead, see that I have the joys of Paradise."

One evening, after a day of rain, as he walked sad and bent with his juggling balls under his arm and his knives wrapped up in his old carpet seeking some barn where he might go supperless to bed, he saw a monk going in his direction, and respectfully saluted him. As they were both walking at the same pace, they fell into conversation.

"Friend," said the monk, "how does it happen that you are dressed all in green? Are you perchance going to play the part of the fool in some mystery?"[1]

"No, indeed, father," said Barnabas. "My name is Barnabas, and my business is that of juggler. It would be the finest calling in the world if I could eat every day."

"Friend Barnabas," answered the monk, "be careful what you say. There is no finer calling than the monastic. The priest celebrates the praise of God, the Virgin, and the saints; the life of a monk is a perpetual hymn to the Lord."

And Barnabas replied: "Father, I confess I spoke like an ignorant man. My estate cannot be compared to yours, and though there may be some merit in dancing and balancing a stick with a denier[2] on top of it on the end of your nose, it is in no wise comparable to your merit. Father, I wish I might, like you, sing the Office every day, especially the Office of the Very Holy Virgin, to whom I am specially and piously devoted. I would willingly give up the art by which I am known from Soissons to Beauvais, in more than six hundred cities and villages, in order to enter the monastic life."

The monk was touched by the simplicity of the juggler, and as he was not lacking in discernment, he recognized in Barnabas one of those well-disposed men of whom Our Lord has said, "Let peace be with them on earth." And he made answer therefore:

"Friend Barnabas, come with me and I will see that you enter the monastery of which I am the Prior. He who led Mary the Egyptian through the desert put me across your path in order that I might lead you to salvation."

Thus did Barnabas become a monk. In the monastery which he entered, the monks celebrated most magnificently

1. Mystery—one of the religious dramas of the time.
2. Denier—a small coin.

the Cult of the Holy Virgin, each of them bringing to her service all the knowledge and skill which God had given him.

The Prior, for his part, wrote books, setting forth, according to the rules of scholasticism, all the virtues of the Mother of God. Brother Maurice copied these treatises with a cunning hand on pages of parchment, while Brother Alexandre decorated them with delicate miniatures representing the Queen of Heaven seated on the throne of Solomon, with four lions on guard at the foot of it. Around her head, which was encircled by a halo, flew seven doves, the seven gifts of the Holy Spirit: fear, piety, knowledge, power, judgment, intelligence, and wisdom. With her were six golden-haired virgins: Humility, Prudence, Retirement, Respect, Virginity, and Obedience. At her feet two little figures, shining white and quite naked, stood in suppliant attitudes. They were souls imploring, not in vain, Her all-powerful intercession for their salvation. On another page Brother Alexandre depicted Eve in the presence of Mary, that one might see at the same time sin and its redemption, woman humiliated, and the Virgin exalted. Among the other much prized pictures in his book were the Well of Living Waters, the Fountain, the Lily, the Moon, the Sun, and the Closed Garden, of which much is said in the Canticle; the Gate of Heaven and the City of God. These were all images of the Virgin.

Brother Marbode, too, was one of the cherished children of Mary. He was ever busy cutting images of stone, so that his beard, his eyebrows, and his hair were white with the dust, and his eyes perpetually swollen and full of tears. But he was a hardy and a happy man in his old age, and there was no doubt that the Queen of Paradise watched over the declining days of Her child. Marbode represented Her seated in a pulpit, Her forehead encircled by a halo, with an orb of pearls. He was at great pains to make the folds of Her robe cover the feet of Her of whom the prophet has said, "My beloved is like a closed garden."

At times he represented Her as a graceful child, and Her image seemed to say, "Lord, Thou art My Lord!"

There were also in the monastery poets who composed prose writings in Latin and hymns in honor of the Most Gracious Virgin Mary; there was, indeed, one among them—a Picard—who translated the Miracles of Our Lady into rimed verses in the vulgar tongue.

Perceiving so great a competition in praise and so fine a harvest of good works, Barnabas fell to lamenting his ignorance and simplicity.

"Alas!" he sighed as he walked by himself one day in the little garden shaded by the monastery wall, "I am so unhappy because I cannot, like my brothers, give worthy praise to the Holy Mother of God to whom I have consecrated all the love in my heart. Alas, I am a stupid fellow, without art, and for your service, Madame, I have no edifying sermons, no fine treatises nicely prepared according to the rules, no beautiful paintings, no cunningly carved statues, and no verses counted off by feet and marching in measure! Alas, I have nothing."

Thus did he lament and abandon himself to his misery.

One evening when the monks were talking together by way of diversion, he heard one of them tell of a monk who could not recite anything but the *Ave Maria.* He was scorned for his ignorance, but after he died there sprang from his mouth five roses, in honor of the five letters in the name Maria. Thus was his holiness made manifest.

In listening to this story, Barnabas was conscious once more of the Virgin's beneficence, but he was not consoled by the example of the happy miracle, for his heart was full of zeal and he wanted to celebrate the glory of his Lady in Heaven.

He sought for a way in which to do this, but in vain, and each day brought him greater sorrow, until one morning he sprang joyously from his cot and ran to the chapel, where he remained alone for more than an hour. He returned thither again after dinner, and from that day onward he would go into the chapel every day the moment it was deserted, passing the greater part of the time which the other monks dedicated to the pursuit of the liberal arts and the sciences. He was no longer sad and he sighed no more. But such singular conduct aroused the curiosity of the other monks, and they asked themselves why Brother Barnabas retired alone so often, and the Prior, whose business it was to know everything that his monks were doing, determined to observe Barnabas. One day, therefore, when Barnabas was alone in the chapel, the Prior entered in company with two of the oldest brothers, in order to watch, through the bars of the door, what was going on within.

They saw Barnabas before the image of the Holy Virgin, his head on the floor and his feet in the air, juggling with six copper balls and twelve knives. In honor of the Holy Virgin he was performing the tricks which had in former days brought him the greatest fame. Not understanding that he was thus putting his best talents at the service of the Holy Virgin, the aged brothers cried out against such sacrilege. The Prior knew that Barnabas had a simple soul, but he believed that the man had lost his wits. All three set about to remove Barnabas from the chapel, when they saw the Virgin slowly descend from the altar and, with a fold of her blue mantle, wipe the sweat that streamed over the juggler's forehead.

Then the Prior, bowing his head down to the marble floor, repeated these words:

"Blessed are the pure in heart, for they shall see God."

"Amen," echoed the brothers, bowing down to the floor.

The Prolog to the Canterbury Tales

Geoffrey Chaucer

Chaucer gives us here a picture of some of the people of the late Middle Ages. Notice the shrewdness of his description: small references which reveal interesting qualities of the characters which one is apt to miss. The selection is included to give more than an interesting description of a group of people. A whole panorama of the late Middle Ages is presented.

When April with its sweet and welcome showers
The drought of March has pierced, and to the flowers
And every vein of growing things has sent
Life-giving moisture, wholesome nourishment;
When Zephyr,[1] too, has with his own sweet breath
Revived again in every wood and heath
The tender shoots, and when the northering sun

1. Zephyr—the west wind: here, the life-giving breath of Spring.

Has half his course into the Ram[2] now run,
And little song-birds make their melody
That sleep all thru the night with open eye
—So Nature urges them with her commands—
Then people long to go in pilgrim bands,
And palmers[3] once again to seek far strands
And distant shrines, well known in many lands:
Especially, from every county's end
Of England, Canterbury-ward they wend,
The holy blessed martyr[4] there to seek
Who was their help when they were ill or weak.

It happened in that season, on a day,
In Southwerk at the Tabard as I lay,
Ready my pilgrimage to undertake
To Canterbury, for my own soul's sake,
At night there came into that hostelry
Some nine-and-twenty in a company
Of various folk, who came by chance to fall
Into one group, and pilgrims were they all;
To Canterbury they all planned to ride.
The chambers and the stables there were wide,
And we were lodged in comfort, with the best.
And very soon—the sun now gone to rest—
So had I spoken with them, every one,
That I was of their fellowship anon,
And planned with them quite early to arise
To take our way, as I shall you advise:

—Nevertheless, while I have time and space,
Before I further in this story pace,
It seems to me both sensible and sound
To tell you in detail of all I found
About each one, just as it seemed to me,
And what they were, and what was their degree,
And tell what kind of costume they were in;
And at a knight, then, will I first begin.

Knight

A knight there was, a worthy man,
Who from the time when that he first began
To ride on quests, had well loved chivalry,
Truth and honor, freedom and courtesy.
Full worthy was this man in his lord's war,
And therein had he ridden—none so far—
Thru Christendom, and heathen lands no less,
Always honored for his worthiness.
At Alexandria was he when it was won;
Many a time he had the board begun[5]
Above all other guests, in distant Prussia;
In Latvia[6] he fought, again in Russia,
No Christian man so oft, of his degree.
Against the Moors in Spain he fought, and he
In Africa and Asia Minor warred
Against the infidel; his mighty sword
Found service all about the Inland Sea;
At any noble action, there he'd be.
At mortal battles had he been—fifteen;
And for the faith he fought, at Tramyssene,
In tourney thrice, and each time slew his foe.
And this same worthy knight had been also
At one time with the lord of Palatye
Against another heathen land—Turkey;
And every time he held the topmost prize.
And yet, with all his courage, he was wise—
His conduct, meek as that of any maid.
No villainy had this man ever said
In all his life to any sort of wight.
He was a true, a perfect, gentle knight.

—But, to tell you briefly his array,
His horse was good, but certainly not gay;
He wore a fustian garment (a gypoun)
All rust-and-armor stained (his haubergeon),
For he had just completed the last stage
Of travel, and at once made pilgrimage.

Squire

With him was his son, a fine young Squire,
A lover and a lusty bachelor,
With locks as curly as if laid in press;
Near twenty years of age he was, I guess.
His stature was of ordinary length,
But agile, and revealing a great strength.
And he had ridden in the cavalry
In Flanders, in Artois, and Picardy,
And born him well, within his life's short space,
In hope that he might win his lady's grace.
Fancily clad in fashion's newest whim,
—One thought of flowering fields, on seeing him!—
Singing he was, or whistling, all the day:
He was as fresh as is the month of May.
His gown was short, with sleeves both long and wide;
He knew just how to sit a horse and ride,
To make up songs, and fit the words aright,
To joust, and dance, and draw, and even write.
So hot he loved (at least, so goes the tale)
He slept o'nights less than the nightingale!
Courteous was he, meek, in service able,
And carved before his father at the table.

Yeoman

A yeoman had he—no other servants, tho,
As at that time; it pleased him to ride so—
And he was clad in coat and hood of green.
A sheaf of peacock arrows, bright and keen,
Under his belt he carried, gay but grim;
(He well knew how to keep his gear in trim—
His arrow never drooped with feathers low)
And in his hand he bore a mighty bow.
His head was cropped; his face the sun had burned;
Of woodcraft, every subtle trick he'd learned.
Upon his arm a bracer gay he wore
And by his side a sword and buckler bore,
And on the other side, a dagger gay,
As sharp as point of spear, well sheathed away.
A Christopher medal gleamed upon his breast;

---

2. Ram—the third sign of the zodiac, which the sun enters c. March 12 and leaves c. April 11 to enter Taurus. Chaucer is only saying that April is well-advanced; the date is about April 18.

3. Palmers—pilgrims who had visited the Holy Lands bore palms as token of their pilgrimage.

4. Martyr—Thomas a Becket, murdered in the cathedral at Canterbury in 1170, was canonized in 1173. His shrine was the great national shrine, and many stories of miraculous cures were told of it.

5. He sat in the seat of honor, at the head of the table: a mark of distinction and worth.

6. Probably he had fought in Latvia or Lithuania, with the Order of Teutonic Knights. Chaucer lists by name other scenes of the Knights's exploits: the main point is, they were associated with fighting for the faith rather than for gain. The Knight is very nearly the ideal knight of chivalry.

His horn's green sling was hung across his chest.
He must have been a forester, I guess.

Prioress

There was also a nun, a Prioress,
Whose smile was sweetly simple, but not coy;[7]
Her greatest oath was but by good St. Loy;
And she was known as Madam Eglantine.
Full well she sang the services divine
Intoning thru her nose right properly.
And French she spoke, both well and carefully,
But Stratford-fashion, if the truth be told;
Parisian French she knew not—hers was old.
Her table-manners were well taught, withal;
She never from her lips let morsels fall,
Nor wet her fingers in the sauce too deep;
She knew just how to lift her food, to keep
A single drop from falling on her breast.
In etiquette she found the greatest zest.
Her upper lip she always wiped so clean
That in her cup there never could be seen
A speck of grease, when she had drunk her fill;
Fine manners at the table were her will.
And truly she was fond of harmless sport,
Pleasant, friendly, and of good report;
She took great pains the court to imitate,
Her manner formal, an affair of state;
For she would have men do her reverence.
But now, to tell about her moral sense,
So kindly was she and so piteous,
She wept, if ever that she saw a mouse
Caught in a trap, if it were dead, or bled.
Some little dogs she had, and these she fed
With roasted meat, or milk and good white bread.
But sore she wept if one of them were dead,
Or if men hit one with a stick, to smart;
And all for her was conscience, tender heart.
Becomingly her wimple fell in pleat;
As blue as glass her eyes, her nose right neat;
Her mouth was very small, and soft, and red;
But certainly she had a fine forehead;
It was almost a span in breadth, I'd say—
She was not under-sized, in any way!
Quite stylish was the cloak the lady wore;
About her arm small coral beads she bore,
And they were interspersed with gauds[8] of green,
And therefrom hung a brooch of golden sheen,
Whereon was written first a crowned "A,"
And after, "Amor Vincit Omnia."
She had another nun, for company,
Who was her chaplain; and her priests were three.

Monk

A monk there was—th' administrative sort—
Outrider,—hunting was his favorite sport—
A manly man, to be an abbott able.
Full many a fancy horse he had in stable,
And when he rode, men could his bridle hear
Jingling in the whistling wind as clear
And just as loud as does the chapel-bell
Where this good lord was Keeper of the Cell.
The rule of Maurus or St. Benedict[9]
This monk considered old and over-strict.
He'd rather let the old things go their way.
And follow fashions of a newer day.
For texts he didn't give a well-plucked hen
That say that hunters are not holy men,
Nor that a monk who leaves his cloister's bounds
Is like a fish that's out of water—zounds!
—Why shouldn't monks go out of cloister?
Texts like that aren't worth an oyster!
And I said his views were good thereon.
Why should he study till his wits were gone
Upon a book in cloister, like a clerk,
Or labor with his hands, always at work,
As old St. Austin[10] bids? What good is served?
Let Austin have his work to him reserved!
And so this monk his hunting much preferred.
Greyhounds had he, swift as any bird;
In riding, and in hunting of the hare,
Was his delight—and for no cost he'd spare.
I saw his sleeves were fur-trimmed at the hand,
Expensively, the finest in the land;
And, to fasten up his hood beneath his chin.
He had a rich, elaborate, golden pin;
A love-knot in the larger end there was.
His head was bald, and shone as bright as glass;
As if anointed shone his ruddy face.
He was a lord right fat, and in good case.
His eyes were staring, rolling in his head,
Gleaming like the furnace-fires red.
His boots were supple, and his horse was great;
Now certainly, he was a fine prelate!
He was not pale as some poor starveling ghost.
A fat swan loved he best of any roast.
His palfrey was as brown as any berry.

Friar

A friar there was, a wanton man and merry;
A Limiter,[11] a most impressive one;
Indeed in all four orders there was none
Who knew so much of small talk, fine language;
And he had made right many a marriage
Of young girls at his own expense and hire;
A pillar of his order was this friar!
Familiar and full well beloved was he
With franklins[12] over all in his county,
For as confessor he had won renown
Far more than curates had in their possession
—His order licensed him to hear confession.
His hearing of confession was a pleasure,
His absolution always within measure;
The penance he imposed was never stern—
If something for himself he'd thereby earn!
For when to his poor order gifts were given,
It must be sign the givers were well shriven;
For such gifts, said this friar for his part,

7. Chaucer says her smiling *was* coy: but in his day the word meant "bashful," "modest," "retiring."
8. Gauds—the large Paternoster beads marking off the sections of a rosary.
9. St. Benedict and his disciple Maurus, founders of the Benedictine Order; St. Benedict established the famous monastery at Monte Cassino in 529.
10. St. Augustine, Bishop of Hippo, was a great proponent of labor as part of the monastic life.
11. A "Limiter" was a friar licensed to beg within a definite ("limited") region.
12. Franklins were landholders of free, but not of noble, birth; they ranked below the gentry.

Show clearly that a man is changed at heart.
For many men are hardened, it appears,
So that they find no outlet thru their tears;
Instead of tears and useless weeping, then,
The silver that they give will save such men.
He always kept his tippet[13] stuffed with knives
And pins to give to young attractive wives.
Certainly he had a merry note;
He knew well how to sing, and play a rote,[14]
At song-fests he would win the prize outright.
As any lily flower his neck was white.
And like a champion wrestler he was strong.
All the taverns, as he went along,
And every hostler, and barmaid, he knew,
Better than outcasts and the beggar-crew;
Because, to such a worthy man as he,
It was not fitting, you will all agree,
To have acquaintance with such worthless wretches;
Such contact brings no profit, nothing fetches. . . .
There is no gain in dealing with *canaille*,[15]
But with rich men, of social station high.
And thus, whenever profit would arise,
This friar was humble, courteous, and wise.
So virtuous a man was nowhere found;
And what a beggar, as he made his round!
Why, if a widow had no shoe to show,
So pleasant was his "In principio . . .[16]
He'd have the widow's mite, before he went!
His income always went beyond his rent.
And he could play around like any whelp;
On love-days[17] he knew how to be of help.
He was not like a needy monk or scholar,
Threadbare, shabby, down to his last dollar;
But he was like a great man or a pope.
Of finest woolen was his semicope,[18]
That rounded like a bell out of its mold.
He lisped a little, if the truth he told,
To make his speech sound sweeter on his tongue;
And in his harping, after he had sung,
His twinkling eyes shone in his head as bright
As do the stars on cold and frosty night.
This worthy Limiter was called Hubert.

Merchant

The merchant, next:—with forked beard, and girt
In livery, high on his horse he sat,
Upon his head a Flemish beaver hat;
His boots were clasped up in the latest mode;
He spoke in serious fashion as he rode,
Referring always to his gains in gold.
He wished, he said, to have the sea patrolled
From Middleburgh across to Orewell.[19]
A money-changer, he could buy or sell;
This worthy man knew how his wits to set:
No one ever knew he was in debt,
So well he managed all the deals he made,
His sales and bargains, and his tricks of trade.
He was a worthy man, in every way;
But what his name, I never heard men say!

Clerk

A clerk of Oxford rode with us also,
Who turned to logic-study long ago;
His horse was lean and skinny as a rake,
And he was not so fat, I'll undertake!
But hollow-looking, hungry evermore;
Quite threadbare were the shabby clothes he wore,
For he had found as yet no benefice,
Nor was so worldly as to hold office.
For he had rather have, at his bed's head,
A score of books, all bound in black or red,
Of Aristotle and philosophy
Than rich robes, fiddle, or gay psaltery.
And yet philosophy, if truth be told,
Had brought him in but very little gold,
But all that willing friends to him had lent
On books and learning eagerly he spent;
When friends helped with his schooling, then for those
He'd pray in earnest, for their souls' repose.
Of study he took every care and heed;
Not a word he spoke more than was need;
Then what he said was formal, reverent,
Short and to the point, of high intent;
Pertaining unto virtue was his speech;
And gladly would he learn, and gladly teach.

Sergeant-at-law

A sergeant of the law, who used to go
Full many a time to St. Paul's portico,[20]
There was also, of richest excellence;
Discreet he was and of great reverence.
—At least he seemed so, for his words were wise.
He often sat as justice in assize,[21]
By full commission or in his own right.
His learning and his fame were more than slight,
So he had fees, and robes, abundantly.
Nowhere a greater purchaser[22] than he.
Provisions of the law so well he knew
That none could quibble with the deeds he drew.
But no one does as much as this man does—
And yet, he seemed much busier than he was . . .
From William's day[23] he knew each court decision
In every case, by heart, and with precision.
His documents were drawn up so that none
Could find a fault or loop-hole—not a one;
The Statutes he'd recite, and all by rote.
He rode quite simply in a medley coat,
Girt with a belt of striped silk. No more
I have to tell of what this Sergeant wore.

---

13. Tippet—a long scarf; a handy substitute for pockets.
14. Rote—a stringed instrument, sometimes played with a bow, sometimes with a fixed wheel like a hurdy-gurdy.
15. Canaille—riff-raff, rabble.
16. "In principio . . ."—the beginning of the Last Gospel. These verses were thought to have supernatural powers, and were used as greeting, blessing, and the like.
17. "Love-days" were days set aside for settlement of disputes by arbitration; the clergy were often the judges.
18. A short cape or cloak.
19. The port of Middleburgh, just off the coast of Netherlands, was just opposite the English port of Harwich (then called "Orewell"). The merchant was probably engaged (among other things!) in the wool trade, and desired protection for his shipping.
20. The porch of St. Paul's Cathedral was a traditional meeting-place for lawyers.
21. Assize: session of the court.
22. Purchaser—a buyer of land. Does Chaucer imply that the Sergeant is desirous of becoming a landed gentleman, or that he is a land-speculator?
23. The Sergeant knew the law clear back to the conquest—the statutes of William the Conqueror.

Franklin

With him a franklin rode, whose beard was white
As any daisy, and his face was bright
And ruddy: sanguine, one would call the man.
He loved a wine-sop as the day began.
He liked to live in comfort and in joy;
Truly, he was Epicurus' boy,
Who stoutly held that comfort—that is, pleasure—
Was of happiness the only measure.
A householder, and a great, was he;
He was St. Julian[24] in his own country.
His bread and ale were uniformly fine;
No man was better stocked than he with wine;
Baked meats were never lacking at his place—
Both fish and flesh—or he'd have felt disgrace!
It snowed in his house both of meat and drink,
Of every good thing that a man can think.
According to the season of the year,
So changed his food, and all his table-cheer;
Fat partridges he kept on his preserve,
And fishponds stocked, his table well to serve.
Woe to the cook, unless his sauce were fine,
And sharp and tasty, and the meal on time!
His covered table was not put away
But stood in readiness the live-long day.
At session,[25] he was lord—no man stood higher—
And many a time he served as Knight-of-Shire.
He wore a knife, and purse—made all of silk—,
Hung from his girdle, white as morning milk.
He'd served as sheriff, and county auditor;
Nowhere was a more worthy vavasour.[26]

The Five Tradesmen

A haberdasher, and a carpenter,
A weaver, dyer, and an arras-maker,
—All these were clad in the same livery
Of one great dignified fraternity;
All fresh and new the gear they wore, it seemed;
Not with brass their knives and trimmings gleamed,
But silver, and fine work in every part;
Their belts and purses were in style, and smart.
Important citizens, enough, were all
These men, to sit on dais in guild-hall,
And anyone of them, it's safe to state,
Was wise enough to be a magistrate;
They certainly had goods enough, and rent;
And, I'm sure, their wives would give assent,
For otherwise they would have been in blame;
It's good to hear a "Madam" with one's name,
And lead the way at church, and to be seen
With mantle borne, as royal as a queen!

Cook

A cook was in their party, to prepare
Their favorite dishes, foods both rich and rare:
Chickens, marrow-bones, and tarts well-flavored.
Many a draught of London ale he'd savored.
He knew how to roast, boil, broil, and fry,
Make soups and sauces hot, and bake a pie.
A pity was it, so it seemed to me,
That on his shin an ulcerous sore had he.
His blanc-mange[27] would be rated with the best.

Shipman

A shipman was there, living far to west
—For all I know he came from Dartmouth town.
He rode as best he could a nag; his gown
Of falding[28] rough hung clear down to his knee;
A dagger hanging on a lace had he
About his neck, beneath his arm and down.
Hot summer suns had made his hue all brown;
A boon companion was this salty tar.
He'd helped himself to many a good wine jar
From Bordeaux, while below his owners slept.
Fine scruple was a thing he never kept.
In sea-fights, if he got the upper hand,
By water he sent them home to every land.
But no man, in his skill to reckon tides,
His streams, his chance and all besides,
His harbors, and his moons, and navigation;
From Hull to Carthage had his reputation.
Bold he was, but wise, in undertaking;
Many a tempest set his beard to shaking!
And he knew all the havens as they were
From Gotland to the Cape of Finisterre,[29]
And every creek in Brittany and Spain.
His barge was called the good ship "Madeleine."

Physician

A doctor of physic, known both far and near,
Was with us; nowhere could you find his peer,
In surgery or physic; what is more,
Well-grounded in astrology's deep lore,
He treated patients for the better part
By horoscope and such-like magic art.
For he knew how to forecast, by his spell,
The ascendant planets that would make them well.
He knew the cause of every malady,
Whether of cold or hot or moist or dry,[30]
Where engendered, from what humor traced;
He was a doctor of much skill and taste.
The cause once known, and of the source once sure,
He quickly brought the sick man to his cure.
And he had ready his apothecaries
To send him potent drugs and lectuaries[31]—
For each assisted other, gold to gain;
Their friendship was no new one, that is plain!
—This doctor knew old Esculapius,
The Greek Deiscorides, and ancient Rufus,
Hippocrates, Galen, Hali the Saracen,
Serapion, and Rhazes, Avicen,
Averroes, Bernard, Constantine,

24. St. Julian is the patron saint of hospitality.
25. These were probably sessions of the Justices of the Peace, not the big assizes.
26. Vavasour—a substantial landholder.
27. Not like the modern pudding, but a compound of minced capon, almonds, cream, sugar, and flour!
28. Falding—coarse woolen cloth with shaggy nap.
29. That is, from Sweden to the western tip of France.
30. The reference is to the theory of the "bodily humors," or fluids, and their effect on the health and temperament of the person.
31. Lectuaries—more properly, electuaries. Medicine in a sticky or sirupy base, originally meant to be "licked up" by the patient!

Gatesden, Gilbert, John the Damascene.[32]
And in his diet temperate was he;
It was not full of superfluity,
But wholesome, one of healthful nourishment.
Bible-study was not this man's bent.
He dressed in costly colors, red and blue,
With taffeta and silken linings, too;
And yet he was a man to hate expense.
He kept what he had earned in pestilence;
And since, in physic, gold's a cordial, he
Found gold was what he loved especially!

Wife of Bath

A goodwife came from Bath, that ancient city,
But she was rather deaf; and that's a pity.
Her skill in making cloth, I hear, was such
That, as they say, she wove "to beat the Dutch."[33]
In all the parish never a woman came
To offering before this worthy dame—
But if there did, so much enraged was she
That she lost all her Christian charity!
Her kerchiefs were of finest weave, and dear;
They must have weighed a full ten pounds, or near,
That on a Sunday covered up her head.
Her hose[34] were fancy-fine, of scarlet red,
And tightly tied, her shoes were soft and new.
Her face was bold, and fair, and red of hue.
She was a worthy woman all her life;
To husbands five this woman had been wife,
Not counting other company in youth;
There's no need now to speak of that, in truth!
Three times to Jerusalem she'd been;
Full many a distant stream her feet were in . . .
To Rome she'd been, and gone to far Boulogne,
In Spain to Santiago, to Cologne;
She knew a lot of wandering by the way.
Gap-toothed this goodwife was, the truth to say.
Easily her ambling horse she sat,
With flowing wimple—on her head a hat
As broad as is a buckler or a shield;
A foot-mantle left her ample hips concealed;
And on her feet she wore well-sharpened spurs.
The gift of laughter and of fun was hers.
Love's remedies she knew, and not by chance;
She knew first-hand the art of that old dance.

Parson

A good religious man went on this ride,
A parish priest, who served the countryside;
Poor in money, rich in holy work,
A very learned scholar was this clerk.
The gospel of Our Lord he strove to preach,
And tried his poor parishioners to teach.
Benign he was, hard-working, diligent,
In adverse seasons patiently content,
As he had proved on more than one occasion.
He did not threaten excommunication
When poor folk could not pay their tithes; instead,
The little that he had he'd share, his bread
As well as money, with a cheerful heart.
Contentment with a little was his art.
Tho wide his parish, houses far asunder,
He'd not neglect, in spite of rain or thunder,
The afflicted in mind, body, or estate,
The farthest in his parish, small or great;
Staff in hand, he'd visit them, on foot.
This fine example to his flock he put,
That first he acted; afterward he taught.
From out the Gospel these words he had caught.
This figure he had added thereunto:
"If fine gold rust, what shall poor iron do?"
For if the priest be foul, in whom we trust,
No wonder if the ignorant people rust;
A shame it is, and brings the priest to mock—
A shitty shepherd, tending a clean flock!
Rather should a priest example give,
By his clean living, how his sheep should live.
He never set his benefice to hire
And left his sheep encumbered in the mire,
Running up to London, to St. Paul's,
Singing paid requiems within those walls;
Nor in some brotherhood withdrew, alone;
But caring for his flock he stayed at home,
So that no wolf his helpless sheep might harry;
He was a shepherd, not a mercenary.
A virtuous man and holy was he, then,
Not arrogant in scolding sinful men,
Not haughty in his speech, or too divine,
But prudent in his teaching and benign.
To draw the folk to heaven by kindliness
And good example was his business.
But then, if any one were obstinate,
Whoever he was, of high or low estate,
He'd scold him sharply, raise a mighty row;
Nowhere was there a better priest, I vow.
No hankering after pomp and reverence,
No putting on of airs, and no pretence;
The lore of Christ and His apostles true
He taught; but what he preached, he'd do.

Plowman

With him there was a plowman, his own brother,
Who'd loaded many a cart with dung; no other
Was a worker good and true as he,
Living in peace and perfect charity.
God he loved best, with his entire soul,
At all times, whether he knew joy or dole;
And next, as Christ commands, he loved his neighbor.
For he would thresh, or ditch, or dig, and labor
For Jesus' sake, without a thot of pay,
To help poor folk, if in his power it lay.
Cheerfully, in full, his tithes he paid
Both on his goods, and what by work he made.
In tabard clad, he rode an old gray mare.
—(A miller and a reeve were also there,
A summoner, also, and a pardoner,
A manciple and I—that's all there were.)

Miller

The miller was a big and hefty lout,
Brawny, burly, big of bone, and stout.

---

32. This impressive list is to indicate that the doctor was thoroughly versed in all the medical authorities, ancient and "modern." It seems curious to a modern reader to find among his qualifications that he is an excellent astrologer.
33. Chaucer says "She passed hem of Ypres and of Gaunt"—the Low Countries were famous for textiles.
34. Not stockings, but gaiters or leggings.

Against all comers, as events turned out,
He won the ram[35] at every wrestling-bout,
Stocky, broad-shouldered, in build a battering-ram,
There was no door he couldn't tear from jamb
Or break it, running at it with his head.
His beard like any sow or fox was red,
And broad as any spade, and cut off short,
Right atop his nose he had a wart;
In it stood a little tuft of hairs,
Red as the bristles in an old sow's ears.
As for his nostrils, they were black and wide;
A sword and buckler bore he by his side.
His big mouth like a furnace needed stoking:
He was a jesting clown whose bawdy joking
Mostly ran to sin: it wasn't nice.
From the grain he ground he'd steal—and then toll thrice;
Good millers have a golden thumb, it's said . . .
A white coat, and a blue hood on his head,
He wore; and with his bagpipe's merry sound
He cheered us as we started, outward-bound.

Manciple

There was a manciple[36] from the Inns of Court[37]
To whom all purchasers could well resort
To learn to buy supplies in large amount;
For whether he bought by cash, or on account,
He watched his dealings with so close an eye
That he came out ahead in every try.
Now is it not indeed by God's own grace
That he, uneducated, could outface
His masters—that heap of learned men?
His employers numbered three times ten,
Legal experts, with good sense endowed:
—There must have been a dozen in the crowd
Worthy to be stewards of rent or land
Of any lord in England, to help him stand
Within his income, if he only would,
In honor, out of debt, all to the good,
Or help him live as sparsely as desired:
Why, they could help a county, as required,
In any kind of case that might befall:—
And yet this manciple could beat them all.

Reeve

The reeve, a scrawny, peevish man was he;
His beard was shaved as close as close could be;
His hair was shorn off short around his ears,
His top docked like a priest's, so it appears.
His legs were very long and very lean,
Thin as a stick; no calf could there be seen.
He managed well the granary and bin;
No auditor could get ahead of him.
And he could estimate, by drought and rain,
The yield he could expect of seed and grain.
His lord's sheep, cows, and other stock,
The swine and horses, and the poultry-flock,
Were wholly in his hands to manage well,
And on his oath the reckoning to tell,
Ever since his lord reached twenty years.
No man could ever find him in arrears.
There was no agent, shepherd, hired hand,
Whose tricks he didn't know or understand;
They feared him, everyone, as they feared death.
His dwelling place stood fair upon the heath,
But sheltered was his place with green trees' shade.
Far better bargains than his lord he made;
Richly he had feathered his own nest.
He knew the way to please his master best,
By giving him, or lending, his own goods,
And getting not mere thanks, but coats and hoods.
In youth, he'd learned a trade—he was a wright;
In carpentry he was a skillful wight.
This reeve's good horse rode at an easy trot;
A dapple-gray he was; his name was Scot.
His long surcoat of Persian blue was made,
And by his side he bore a rusty blade.
Of Norfolk was this reeve of whom I tell,
From just outside a town called Baldeswell.
He tucked up all his garments like a friar,
And rode the hindmost: Such was his desire.

Summoner

A summoner[38] was there with us in that place,
Who had a fire-red cherubic face,
All pimply, full of whelks; his eyes were narrow,
And he was hot and lecherous as a sparrow,
With black and scabby brows, and scanty beard:
His was the sort of face that children feared.
There was no mercury nor brimstone, salve
Of tartar, lead, or borax, that could have
The strength to rid him of the lumps and knobs
Disfiguring his face in ugly gobs;
These acneous pimples covered both his cheeks.
And he was fond of garlic, onions, leeks;
He loved to drink strong wine, as red as blood;
Then spoke and cried as one demented would.
And having drunk his wine, and feeling gay,
Then not a word but Latin would he say;
—He knew a few expressions—two or three—
That he had picked up, out of some decree—
No wonder, for he heard it every day:
And everybody knows that even a jay
Can learn to call out "Wat!" as well as the Pope!
But when he tried with other things to cope,
His slender stock of learning would give out:
"Questio quid juris!"[39] he would shout.
He was a noble rascal, and a kind;
A better fellow would be hard to find.
He would arrange it, for a quart of wine,
For a friend of his to keep a concubine
The whole year thru, and never get in trouble;
Oh, he was very good at dealings double!
And if he liked a person whom he saw,
He'd teach that person not to stand in awe
Nor fear, for what he did, the archdeacon's curse—
Why, does a man's soul live within his purse?
Yet purse alone can suffer penalty:
"Purse is the archdeacon's hell," said he.
(But well I know he lied in saying so;
Such curses ought the guilty men forego.

---

35. The customary wrestling prize.
36. Steward, or purchasing agent.
37. The lodgings of the lawyers.
38. Process-server or bailiff for the ecclesiastical court, usually presided over by the archdeacon.
39. "The question is, what part of the law applies?"—a lawyer's technicality.

As absolution saves, so curses slay;
From all *Significavits*,[40] stay away!)
And at his mercy, in his tender charge,
Were young folks of the diocese at large;
He knew their secrets; they were easily led.
He had set a garland on his head
So large it would have served for an ale-stake.[41]
A buckler he had made him of a cake.

Pardoner

With him a noble pardoner rode, his pal
And peer (his patron-house was Ronceval),[42]
Who straight from Rome had come—or so said he—
And loud he sang, "Come hither, love, to me!"
The summoner added, in the bass, a ground:
No trumpet had one half so loud a sound.
The pardoner had yellow hair, like wax,
That hung as limp as does a bunch of flax;
Stringily his locks hung from his head,
So that his shoulders were all overspread,
But thin it lay, in hanks there, one by one.
No hood he wore; he left it off, for fun,
Trussed up in his bag. It seemed to him
That thus he rode in fashion's latest whim,
Uncovered—save for cap—his head all bare.
Staring eyes he had, just like a hare.
A vernicle he'd sewed upon his cap.
His wallet lay before him, in his lap,
Brimful of pardons, hot from Rome, please note!
Small the voice he had, just like a goat.
He had no beard: nor ever would, in truth:
As it were fresh-shaved, his face was smooth;
I think he was a gelding—or a mare.
But of his trade, from Berwyck clear to Ware
Was never such a pardoner as this lad!
In his bag a pillow-case he had
Which—so he claimed—was once Our Lady's veil—
He said he had a fragment of the sail
That once St. Peter used, in days of yore,
Before Our Lord gave him new work, ashore!
He had a cross of latten,[43] set with stones,
And in a glass jar carried some pig's bones.
But with these silly "relics," when he spied
Some simple priest out in the country-side,
On such a day more money would he win
Than in two months the parson could fetch in;
And thus, with flattery and lying mock,
He'd fool the priest and all his simple flock.
But give the devil his due; for, when all's past,
In church he was a great ecclesiast;
Well knew he how to read a Bible story,
But especially well he sang the offertory;
For well he knew that when the song was sung,
He then would preach, and sharpen up his tongue,
To win their money from the gullible crowd;
That's why he sang so merrily and loud.
Now I've told you briefly, clause by clause,
The state, the number and array and cause
In which assembled was this company
In Southwerk at this noble hostelry
That's called the Tabard Inn, right near the Bell.

(And that is all that this book has to tell:
But Reader, while your interest still prevails,
Go read the rest of Chaucer's Canterbury Tales.)

The Divine Comedy

Dante Alighieri

At the outset, let us agree that reading the *Commedia* is no easy task. Dante himself recognized this when, in writing to a friend and patron, he said:

> The meaning of this work is not simple . . . for we obtain one meaning from the letter of it, and another from that which the letter signifies; and the first is called *literal*, but the other *allegorical* or *mystical* . . . .
>
> The subject of the whole work, then, taken in the literal sense is "the state of the soul after death straightforwardly affirmed," for the development of the whole work hinges on and about that. But, if, indeed, the work is taken *allegorically*, its subject is: "Man, as by good or ill deserts, in the exercise of his free choice, he becomes liable to rewarding or punishing justice."

On two scores, the rewards of reading the *Commedia* justify the effort. First, it represents the finest statement of the medieval synthesis that we have; it is comparable to Chartres Cathedral or the *Summa Theologica* of St. Thomas. Second, and more important, it presents one of the half-dozen very great insights into the nature and meaning of human life in all of literature or art. It is meaningful to us in the twentieth century not only as a great historical document, but as living literature.

Its form represents as tight a discipline as we know in literature, for it takes its shape around the number three. It is written in *terza rima*, a form preserved in the translations taken from the Hell and Purgatory as excerpts from those sections are given here. It is written in three great sections: Hell, Purgatory, and Heaven. Within the first of these sections we find one introductory canto, followed by thirty-three more cantos, and in each of the following sections thirty-three cantos are to be found. The sum is the number one hundred, the perfect and complete number.

Insofar as its meaning is concerned, the great poem will speak for itself, aided by the notes. We must understand, however, that Dante accepts the idea that all of nature is in motion, following the laws, the love, and the wisdom of God. Of all the orders of being, man alone has both free will and the potentiality of turning from the way of God. With free will comes the responsibility of choosing and accepting the consequences of choice. No man can say that he is the irresponsible victim of heredity or environment. With the gift of intellect and

40. *Significavit*—the opening word in a summons to appear before the ecclesiastical court.
41. Ale was advertised by a bunch of greens, hanging on a stake or pole above the door.
42. A London hospital.
43. Cheap metal.

free will; each man must assume the full weight of making choices, and he must, as well, accept the idea that his choices are important and that they do make a difference for others, and most particularly for himself.

The translation was made by the twentieth-century writer and Dante scholar, Dorothy Sayers.

THE GREATER IMAGES

DANTE in the *story* is always himself—the Florentine poet, philosopher, and politician, and the man who loved Beatrice. In the *allegory*, he is the image of every Christian sinner, and his pilgrimage is that which every soul must make, by one road or another, from the dark and solitary Wood of Error to the City of God.

VIRGIL is in the *story* the shade of the poet who, in the *Aeneid*, celebrated the origin and high destiny of the Roman Empire and its function in unifying the civilized world. In the Middle Ages he was looked upon as having been an unconscious prophet of Christianity and also (in popular tradition) as a great "White Magician," whose natural virtue gave him power among the dead. Dante's portrait of him has preserved traces of these medieval fancies, and also agrees very well with what we know of the gentle and charming characteristics of the real Virgil. In the *allegory*, Virgil is the image of Human Wisdom—the best that man can become in his own strength without the especial grace of God. He is the best of human philosophy, the best of human morality; he is also poetry and art, the best of human feeling and imagination. Virgil, as the image of these things, cannot himself enter Heaven or bring anyone else there (art and morality and philosophy cannot be made into substitutes for religion), but he can (and they can), under the direction of the Heavenly Wisdom, be used to awaken the soul to a realization of its own sinfulness, and can thereafter accompany and assist it towards that state of natural perfection in which it is again open to receive the immediate operation of Divine Grace.

BEATRICE remains in the *story* what she was in real life: the Florentine girl whom Dante loved from the first moment that he saw her, and in whom he seemed (as is sometimes the case with lovers) to see Heaven's glory walking the earth bodily. Because, for him, she was thus in fact the vehicle of the Glory—the earthly vessel in which the divine experience was carried—she is, in the *allegory*, from time to time likened to, or equated with, those other "God-bearers": the Church, and Divine Grace in the Church; the Blessed Virgin; even Christ Himself. She is the image by which Dante perceives all these, and her function in the poem is to bring him to that state in which he is able to perceive them directly; at the end of the *Paradiso* the image of Beatrice is—not replaced by, but—taken up into the images, successively, of the Church Triumphant; of Mary, the historic and universal God-bearer; and of God, in whom Image and Reality are one and the same. Beatrice thus represents for every man that person—or, more generally that experience of the Not-self—which by arousing his adoring love, has become for him the God-bearing image, the revelation of the presence of God.

HELL in the *story* is the place or condition of lost souls after death; it is pictured as a huge funnel-shaped pit, situated beneath the Northern Hemisphere and running down to the centre of the earth. In the *allegory*, it is the image of the deepening possibilities of evil within the soul. Similarly, the sinners who there remain fixed forever in the evil which they have obstinately chosen are also images of the perverted choice itself. For the *story*, they are historical or legendary personages, external to Dante (and to us); for the *allegory* they figure his (and our) disordered desires, seen and known to us as we plunge ever deeper into the hidden places of the self: every condemned sinner in the poem is thus the image of a self-condemned sin (actual or potential) in every man. Neither in the *story* nor in the *allegory* is Hell a place of punishment to which anybody is arbitrarily *sent:* it is the condition to which the soul reduces itself by a stubborn determination to evil, and in which it suffers the torment of its own perversions.

We must be careful to distinguish between Hell itself, taken literally, and the *vision of Hell* which is offered to Dante. Hell itself is not remedial; the dead who have chosen the "eternal exile" from God, and who thus experience the reality of their choice, cannot profit by that experience. In that sense, no living soul can enter Hell, since, however great the sin, repentance is always possible while there is life, even to the very moment of dying.[1] But the *vision of Hell*, which is remedial, is the soul's self-knowledge in all its evil potentialities—"the revelation of the nature of impenitent sin."[2]

PURGATORY in the *story*, as in Catholic theology, is the place or condition of redeemed souls after death, and is imagined by Dante as a lofty mountain on an island in the Southern Hemisphere. On its seven encircling cornices, the souls are purged successively of the taint of the seven deadly sins, and so made fit to ascend into the presence of God in Paradise. In the *allegory*, it is the image of repentance, by which the soul purges the guilt of sin in *this* life; and, similarly, the blessed spirits who willingly embrace its purifying pains figure the motions of the soul, eagerly confessing and making atonement for its sins.

PARADISE, in the same way, is, in the *story*, the place or condition, after death, of beatified souls in Heaven. Dante pictures it, first, under the figure of the ten Heavens of medieval astronomy and, secondly, under that of the Mystical Rose. He explains that, although the souls are shown as enjoying ascending degrees of bliss in the ten successive Heavens, all these are, in reality, one Heaven; nor is the bliss unequal, each soul being filled, according to its capacity, with all the joy it is able to experience. In the *allegory*, Paradise is the

1. Unless, indeed, the will is so hardened in sin that the power to repent is destroyed, in which case the condition of the soul, even in this world, is literally a "living hell." Dante deals with this possibility in Canto XXXIII.

2. See P.H. Wicksteed: *From Vita Nuova to Paradiso*, from which the last few words are quoted.

image of the soul in a state of grace, enjoying the foretaste of the Heaven which it knows to be its true home and city; and in the inhabitants of Paradise we may recognize the figure of the ascending stages by which it rises to the contemplation of the Beatific Vision.

THE EMPIRE AND THE CITY. Throughout the poem, we come across various images of the Empire of the City (Florence, Rome, and other cities of Italy, as well as the City and Empire of Dis in Hell, and the Eternal City or Heavenly Rome in Paradise). All these may be taken as expressing, in one way or another, what today we should perhaps more readily think of as the Community. Indeed, the whole *allegory* may be interpreted politically, in the widest sense of the word, as representing the way of salvation, not only for the individual man, but for Man-in-community. Civilizations, as well as persons, need to know the Hell within them and purge their sins before entering into a state of Grace, Justice, and Charity and so becoming the City of God on earth.

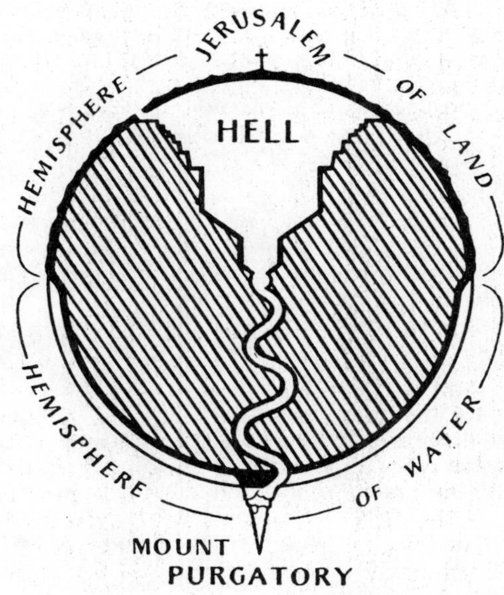

CANTO I

THE STORY. *Dante finds that he has strayed from the right road and is lost in a Dark Wood. He tries to escape by climbing a beautiful Mountain, but is turned aside, first by a gambolling Leopard, then by a fierce Lion, and finally by a ravenous She-Wolf. As he is fleeing back into the Wood, he is stopped by the shade of Virgil, who tells him that he cannot hope to pass the Wolf and ascend the Mountain by that road. One day a Greyhound will come and drive the Wolf back to Hell; but the only course at present left open to Dante is to trust himself to Virgil, who will guide him by a longer way, leading through Hell and Purgatory. From there, a worthier spirit than Virgil (Beatrice) will lead him on to see the blessed souls in Paradise. Dante accepts Virgil as his "master, leader, and lord," and they set out together.*

Midway this way of life we're bound upon,
I woke to find myself in a dark wood,
Where the right road was wholly lost and gone.

Ay me! how hard to speak of it—that rude 4
And rough and stubborn forest! the mere breath
Of memory stirs the old fear in the blood;

It is so bitter, it goes nigh to death; 7
Yet there I gained such good, that, to convey
The tale, I'll write what else I found therewith.

How I got into it I cannot say, 10
Because I was so heavy and full of sleep
When first I stumbled from the narrow way;

But when at last I stood beneath a steep 13
Hill's side, which closed that valley's wandering maze
Whose dread had pierced me to the heart-root deep,

Then I looked up, and saw the morning rays 16
Mantle its shoulder from that planet bright
Which guides men's feet aright on all their ways;

And this a little quieted the affright 19
That lurking in my bosom's lake had lain
Through the long horror of that piteous night.

And as a swimmer, panting, from the main 22
Heaves safe to shore, then turns to face the drive
Of perilous seas, and looks, and looks again,

So, while my soul yet fled, did I contrive 25
To turn and gaze on that dread pass once more
Whence no man yet came ever out alive.

Weary of limb I rested a brief hour, 28
Then rose and onward through the desert hied,
So that the fixed foot always was the lower;

And see! not far from where the mountain-side 31
First rose, a Leopard, nimble and light and fleet,
Clothed in a fine furred pelt all dapple-dyed,

Came gambolling out, and skipped before my feet, 34
Hindering me so, that from the forthright line
Time and again I turned to beat retreat.

The morn was young, and in his native sign 37
The Sun climbed with the stars whose glitterings
Attended on him when the Love Divine

I. 1: *midway*: i.e., at the age of 35, the middle point of man's earthly pilgrimage of three-score and ten years.
I. 17: *that planet bright*: the Sun. In medieval astronomy, the Earth was looked upon as being the centre of the universe, and the sun counted as a planet. In the *Comedy*, the Sun is often used as a figure for "the spiritual sun, which is God." (Dante: *Convivio*, iv. 12.)
I. 27: *whence no man yet came ever out alive*: Dante, as we shall see, is by no means "out" as yet; nor will he be, until he has passed through the "death unto sin."
I. 30: *so that the fixed foot always was the lower*: i.e., he was going uphill. In walking, there is always one fixed foot and one moving foot; in going uphill, the moving foot is brought *above*, and in going downhill *below*, the fixed foot.
I. 37: *in his native sign*: According to tradition, the Sun was in the Zodiacal sign of Aries (the Ram) at the moment of the creation. The Sun is in Aries from 21 March to 21 April: therefore the "sweet season" is that of spring. Later, we shall discover that the day is Good Friday, and that the moon was full on the previous night. These indications do not precisely correspond to the actual Easter sky of 1300; Dante has merely described the astronomical phenomena typical of Eastertide.

First moved those happy, prime-created things:
So the sweet season and the new-born day
Filled me with hope and cheerful augurings

Of the bright beast so speckled and so gay;
Yet not so much but that I fell to quaking
At a fresh sight—a Lion in the way.

I saw him coming, swift and savage, making
For me, head high, with ravenous hunger raving
So that for dread the very air seemed shaking.

And next, a Wolf, gaunt with the famished craving
Lodged ever in her horrible lean flank,
The ancient cause of many men's enslaving;—

She was the worst—at that dread sight a blank
Despair and whelming terror pinned me fast,
Until all hope to scale the mountain sank.

Like one who loves the gains he has amassed,
And meets the hour when he must lose his loot,
Distracted in his mind and all aghast,

Even so was I, faced with that restless brute
Which little by little edged and thrust me back,
Back, to that place wherein the sun is mute.

Then, as I stumbled headlong down the track,
Sudden a form was there, which dumbly crossed
My path, as though grown voiceless from long lack

Of speech; and seeing it in that desert lost,
"Have pity on me!" I hailed it as I ran,
"Whate'er thou art—or very man, or ghost!"

It spoke: "No man, although I once was man;
My parents' native land was Lombardy
And both by citizenship were Mantuan.

Sub Julio born, though late in time, was I,
And lived at Rome in good Augustus' days,
When the false gods were worshipped ignorantly.

Poet was I, and tuned my verse to praise
Anchises' righteous son, who sailed from Troy
When Ilium's pride fell ruined down ablaze.

But thou—oh, why run back where fears destroy
Peace? Why not climb the blissful mountain yonder,
The cause and first beginning of all joy?"

"Canst thou be Virgil? thou that fount of splendour
Whence poured so wide a stream of lordly speech?"
Said I, and bowed my awe-struck head in wonder;

"Oh honour and light of poets all and each,
Now let my great love stead me—the bent brow
And long hours pondering all thy book can teach!

Thou art my master, and my author thou,
From thee alone I learned the singing strain,
The noble style, that does me honour now.

See there the beast that turned me back again—
Save me from her, great sage—I fear her so,
She shakes my blood through every pulse and vein."

"Nay, by another path thou needs must go
If thou wilt ever leave this waste," he said,
Looking upon me as I wept, "for lo!

The savage brute that makes thee cry for dread
Lets no man pass this road of hers, but still
Trammels him, till at last she lays him dead.

Vicious her nature is, and framed for ill;
When crammed she craves more fiercely than before;
Her raging greed can never gorge its fill.

With many a beast she mates, and shall with more,
Until the Greyhound come, the Master-hound,
And he shall slay her with a stroke right sore.

He'll not eat gold nor yet devour the ground;
Wisdom and love and power his food shall be,
His birthplace between Feltro and Feltro found;

Saviour he'll be to that low Italy
For which Euryalus and Nisus died,
Turnus and chaste Camilla, bloodily.

He'll hunt the Wolf through cities far and wide,
Till in the end he hunt her back to Hell,
Whence Envy first of all her leash untied.

But, as for thee, I think and deem it well
Thou take me for thy guide, and pass with me
Through an eternal place and terrible

Where thou shalt hear despairing cries, and see
Long-parted souls that in their torments dire
Howl for the second death perpetually.

II. 63-4: *as though grown voiceless from long lack of speech*: i.e., the form is trying to speak to Dante, but cannot make itself heard. From the point of view of the *story*, I think this means that, being in fact that of a ghost, it cannot speak until Dante has established communication by addressing it first. *Allegorically*, we may take it in two ways: (1) on the historical level, it perhaps means that the wisdom and poetry of the classical age had been long neglected; (2) on the spiritual level, it undoubtedly means that Dante had sunk so deep into sin that the voice of reason, and even of poetry itself, had become faint and almost powerless to recall him.

I. 70: *sub Julio*: under Julius (Caesar). Virgil was born in 70 B.C. and had published none of his great poems before the murder of Julius in 44 B.C., so that he never enjoyed his patronage.

I. 87: *the noble style*: Dante, in 1300, was already a poet of considerable reputation for his love-lyrics and philosophic odes, though he had not as yet composed any narrative verse directly modelled upon the *Aeneid*. When he says that he owes to Virgil the "*bello stilo* which has won him honour," he can scarcely be referring to the style of his own *prose* works, whether in Latin or Italian, still less to that of the as yet unwritten *Comedy*. Presumably he means that he had studied to imitate, in his poems written in the vernacular, the elegance, concise power, and melodious rhythms of the Virgilian line.

I. 105: *between Feltro and Feltro*: This is a much-debated line. If the Greyhound represents a political "saviour," it may mean that his birthplace lies between Feltre in Venetia and Montefeltro in Romagna (i.e., in the valley of the Po). But some commentators think that "feltro" is not a geographical name at all, but simply that of a coarse cloth (felt, or frieze); in which case Dante would be expecting salvation to come from among those who wear the robe of poverty, and have renounced "gold and ground"—i.e., earthly possessions. We should perhaps translate: "In cloth of frieze his people shall be found."

I. 106: *low Italy*: The Italian word is *umile*, humble, which may mean either "low-lying," as opposed to "high Italy" among the Alps, or "humiliated," with reference to the degradation to which the country had been brought. In either case, the classical allusions which follow show that Dante meant Rome.

I. 114: *an eternal place and terrible*: Hell.

I. 117: *the second death*: this might mean "cry for a second death to put an end to their misery," but more probably means "cry out because of the pains of Hell," in allusion to *Rev.* xx. 14.

Next, thou shalt gaze on those who in the fire
Are happy, for they look to mount on high,
In God's good time, up to the blissful quire;

To which glad place, a worthier spirit than I
Must lead thy steps, if thou desire to come,
With whom I'll leave thee then, and say good-bye;

For the Emperor of that high Imperium
Wills not that I, once rebel to His crown,
Into that city of His should lead men home.

Everywhere is His realm, but there His throne,
There is His city and exalted seat:
Thrice-blest whom there He chooses for His own!"

Then I to him: "Poet, I thee entreat,
By that great God whom thou didst never know,
Lead on, that I may free my wandering feet

From these snares and from worse; and I will go
Along with thee, St. Peter's Gate to find,
And those whom thou portray'st suffering so."

So he moved on; and I moved on behind.

THE IMAGES. *The Dark Wood* is the image of Sin or Error—not so much of any specific act of sin or intellectual perversion as of that spiritual condition called "hardness of heart," in which sinfulness has so taken possession of the soul as to render it incapable of turning to God, or even knowing which way to turn.

The Mountain, which on the mystical level is the image of the Soul's Ascent to God, is thus on the moral level the image of Repentance, by which the sinner returns to God. It can be ascended directly from "the right road," but not from the Dark Wood, because there the soul's cherished sins have become, as it were, externalized, and appear to it like demons or "beasts" with a will and power of their own, blocking all progress. Once lost in the Dark Wood, a man can only escape by so descending into himself that he sees his sin, not as an external obstacle, but as the will to chaos and death within him (Hell). Only when he has "died to sin" can he repent and purge it. Mount Purgatory and the Mountain of Canto I are, therefore, really one and the same mountain, as seen on the far side, and on this side, of the "death unto sin."

The Beasts. These are the images of sin. They may be identified with Lust, Pride, and Avarice respectively, or with the sins of Youth, Manhood, and Age; but they are perhaps best thought of as the images of the three *types* of sin which, if not repented, land the soul in one or other of the three main divisions of Hell (*v.* Canto XI).

The gay *Leopard* is the image of the self-indulgent sins—*Incontinence;* the fierce *Lion,* of the violent sins—*Bestiality;* the *She-Wolf* of the malicious sins, which involve *Fraud.*

The Greyhound has been much argued about. I think it has both an historical and a spiritual significance. Historically, it is perhaps the image of some hoped-for political saviour who should establish the just World-Empire. Spiritually, the Greyhound, which has the attributes of God ("wisdom, love, and power"), is probably the image of the reign of the Holy Ghost on earth—the visible Kingdom of God for which we pray in the Lord's Prayer (cf. *Purg.* xi. 7-9).

CANTO II

THE STORY. *Dante's attempts to climb the Mountain have taken the whole day and it is now Good Friday evening. Dante has not gone far before he loses heart and "begins to make excuse." To his specious arguments Virgil replies flatly: "This is mere cowardice"; and then tells how Beatrice, prompted by St. Lucy at the instance of the Virgin Mary herself, descended into Limbo to entreat him to go to Dante's rescue. Thus encouraged, Dante pulls himself together, and they start off again.*

Day was departing and the dusk drew on,
Loosing from labour every living thing
Save me, in all the world; I—I alone—

Must gird me to the wars—rough travelling,
And pity's sharp assault upon the heart—
Which memory shall record, unfaltering;

Now, Muses, now, high Genius, do your part!
And Memory, faithful scrivener to the eyes,
Here show thy virtue, noble as thou art!

I soon began: "Poet—dear guide—'twere wise
Surely, to test my powers and weigh their worth
Ere trusting me to this great enterprise.

Thou sayest, the author of young Silvius' birth,
Did to the world immortal, mortal go,
Clothed in the body of flesh he wore on earth—

Granted; if Hell's great Foeman deigned to show
To *him* such favour, seeing the vast effect,
And what and who has destined issue—no,

That need surprise no thoughtful intellect,
Since to Rome's fostering city and empery
High Heaven had sealed him as the father-elect;

Both these were there established, verily,
To found that place, holy and dedicate,
Wherein great Peter's heir should hold his See;

So that the deed thy verses celebrate
Taught him the road to victory, and bestowed
The Papal Mantle in its high estate.

II. 118-19: *those who in the fire are happy*: the redeemed in Purgatory.
I. 134: *St. Peter's Gate*: the gate by which redeemed souls are admitted to Purgatory (*Purg.* ix. 76 *sqq.*); not the gate of Heaven.
I. 7: Canto I forms, as it were, a prologue to the whole *Divine Comedy.* The actual *Inferno* (Hell) begins with Canto II; and here we have the invocation which, in each of the three books, prefaces the journey to Hell, Purgatory, and Paradise respectively. It is addressed, in the classic manner, to the Muses, to Genius, and to Memory, the Mother of the Muses. (As the story proceeds, Dante will invoke higher, and still higher aid; till the final invocation towards the end of the *Paradiso,* is made to God, the "supreme light" Himself.)
I. 13: *the author of young Silvius' birth*: Aeneas; the allusion is to the sixth book of the *Aeneid,* which describes how Aeneas visits Hades and is told that he is to settle in Italy and so bring about the foundation of Rome, the seat both of the Empire and the Papacy.
I. 16: *Hell's great Foeman*: God.

Thither the Chosen Vessel, in like mode,
Went afterward, and much confirmed thereby
The faith that sets us on salvation's road.

But how should *I* go there? Who says so? Why?
I'm not Aeneas, and I am not Paul!
Who thinks me fit? Not others. And not I.

Say I submit, and go—suppose I fall
Into some folly? Though I speak but ill,
Thy better wisdom will construe it all."

As one who wills, and then unwills his will,
Changing his mind with every changing whim,
Till all his best intentions come to nil,

So I stood havering in that moorland dim,
While through fond rifts of fancy oozed away
The first quick zest that filled me to the brim.

"If I have grasped what thou dost seem to say,"
The shade of greatness answered, "these doubts breed
From sheer black cowardice, which day by day

Lays ambushes for men, checking the speed
Of honourable purpose in mid-flight,
As shapes half-seen startle a shying steed.

Well then, to rid thee of this foolish fright,
Hear why I came, and learn whose eloquence
Urged me to take compassion on thy plight.

While I was with the spirits who dwell suspense,
A Lady summoned me—so blest, so rare,
I begged her to command my diligence.

Her eyes outshone the firmament by far
As she began, in her own gracious tongue,
Gentle and low, as tongues of angels are:

'O courteous Mantuan soul, whose skill in song
Keeps green on earth a fame that shall not end
While motion rolls the turning spheres along!

A friend of mine, who is not Fortune's friend,
Is hard beset upon the shadowy coast;
Terrors and snares his fearful steps attend,

Driving him back; yea, and I fear almost
I have risen too late to help—for I was told
Such news of him in Heaven—he's too far lost.

But thou—go thou! Lift up thy voice of gold;
Try every needful means to find and reach
And free him, that my heart may rest consoled.

Beatrice am I, who thy good speed beseech;
Love that first moved me from the blissful place
Whither I'd fain return, now moves my speech.

Lo! when I stand before my Lord's bright face
I'll praise thee many a time to Him.' Thereon
She fell on silence; I replied apace:

'Excellent lady, for whose sake alone
The breed of men exceeds all things that dwell
Closed in the heaven whose circles narrowest run

To do thy bidding pleases me so well
That were't already done, I should seem slow;
I know thy wish, and more needs not to tell.

Yet say—how can thy blest feet bear to know
This dark road downward to the dreadful centre,
From that wide room which thou dost yearn for so?'

'Few words will serve (if thou desire to enter
Thus far into our mystery),' she said,
'To tell thee why I have no fear to venture.

Of hurtful things we ought to be afraid,
But of no others, truly, inasmuch
As these have nothing to give cause for dread;

My nature, by God's mercy, is made such
As your calamities can nowise shake,
Nor these dark fires have any power to touch.

Heaven hath a noble Lady, who doth take
Ruth of this man thou goest to disensnare
Such that high doom is cancelled for her sake.

She summoned Lucy to her side, and there
Exhorted her: "Thy faithful votary
Needs thee, and I commend him to thy care."

Lucy, the foe to every cruelty,
Ran quickly and came and found me in my place
Beside ancestral Rachel, crying to me:

"How now, how now, Beatrice, God's true praise!
No help for him who once they liegeman was,
Quitting the common herd to win thy grace?

Dost thou not hear his piteous cries, alas?
Dost thou not see death grapple him, on the river
Whose furious rage no ocean can surpass?"

When I heard that, no living wight was ever
So swift to seek his good or flee his fear
As I from that high resting-place to sever

And speed me down, trusting my purpose dear
To thee, and to thy golden rhetoric
Which honours thee, and honours all who hear.'

She spoke; and as she turned from me the quick
Tears starred the lustre of her eyes, which still
Spurred on my going with a keener prick.

I. 28: *the Chosen Vessel*: St. Paul (*Acts* ix. 15). His vision of Hell is described in the fourth-century apocryphal book known as *The Apocalypse of Paul*, which Dante had evidently read. (See M.R. James: *The Apocryphal New Testament.*) There is probably also an allusion to 2 *Cor.* xii. 2.

I. 52: *the spirits who dwell suspense*: those of the virtuous pagans, who taste neither the bliss of salvation nor the pains of damnation, but dwell forever suspended between the two, in Limbo, the uppermost circle of Hell. (We shall meet them in Canto IV.)

I. 70: Of all this passage, Charles Williams says: "Beatrice has to ask [Virgil] to go; she cannot command him, though she puts her trust in his 'fair speech.' Religion itself cannot order poetry about; the grand art is wholly autonomous . . . We should have been fortunate if the ministers of religion and poetry had always spoken to each other with such courtesy as these." (*The Figure of Beatrice*, p. 112.)

I. 78: *the heaven whose circles narrowest run*: The heaven of the Moon, the smallest and nearest to the Earth.

I. 91: *my nature, by God's mercy, is made such*: The souls of the blessed can still pity the self-inflicted misery of the wicked, but they can no longer be hurt or infected by it: "the action of pity will live for ever; the passion of pity will not." (C.S. Lewis: *The Great Divorce*, p. 111, where the subject is handled in a very illuminating way.)

I. 102: *ancestral Rachel*: Leah and Rachel, the two wives of Jacob, figure respectively the active and the contemplative life.

I. 107: *the river:* no literal river is intended; it is only a metaphor for human life.

Therefore I sought thee out, as was her will, 118
And brought thee safe off from that beast of prey
Which barred thee from the short road up the hill.

What ails thee then? Why, why this dull delay? 121
Why bring so white a liver to the deed?
Why canst thou find no manhood to display

When three such blessed ladies deign to plead 124
Thy cause at that supreme assize of right,
And when my words promise thee such good speed?"

As little flowers, which all the frosty night 127
Hung pinched and drooping, lift their stalks and fan
Their blossoms out, touched by the warm white light,

So did my fainting powers; and therewith ran 130
Such good, strong courage round about my heart
That I spoke boldly out like a free man:

"O blessed she that stooped to take my part! 133
O courteous thou, to obey her true-discerning
Speech, and thus promptly to my rescue start!

Fired by thy words, my spirit now is burning 136
So to go on, and see this venture through.
I find my former stout resolve returning.

Forward! henceforth there's but one will for two, 139
Thou master, and thou leader, and thou lord."
I spoke; he moved; so, setting out anew,

I entered on that savage path and froward. 142

THE IMAGES. *Mary, The Blessed Virgin,* whom the Church calls *Theotokos* (Mother of God), is the historical and universal God-bearer, of whom Beatrice, like any other God-bearing image, is a particular type. Mary is thus, in an especial and supreme manner, the vessel of Divine Grace, as experienced in, and mediated through, the redeemed creation. (Note that the name of Mary, like the name of Christ, is never spoken in Hell.)

Lucia (St. Lucy), a virgin martyr of the third century, is the patron saint of those with weak sight, and chosen here as the image of Illuminating Grace. Mary, Beatrice, and Lucia are a threefold image of Divine Grace in its various manifestations.

Virgil's Mission. Dante is so far gone in sin and error that Divine Grace can no longer move him directly; but there is still something left in him which is capable of responding to the voice of poetry and of human reason; and this, under Grace, may yet be used to lead him back to God. In this profound and beautiful image, Dante places Religion, on the one hand, and human Art and Philosophy, on the other, in their just relationship.

CANTO III

THE STORY. *Arriving at the gate of Hell, the Poets read the inscription upon its lintel. They enter and find themselves in the Vestibule of Hell, where the Futile run perpetually after a whirling standard. Passing quickly on, they reach the river Acheron. Here the souls of all the damned come at death to be ferried across by Charon, who refuses to take the living body of Dante till Virgil silences him with a word of power. While they are watching the departure of a boatload of souls the river banks are shaken by an earthquake so violent that Dante swoons away.*

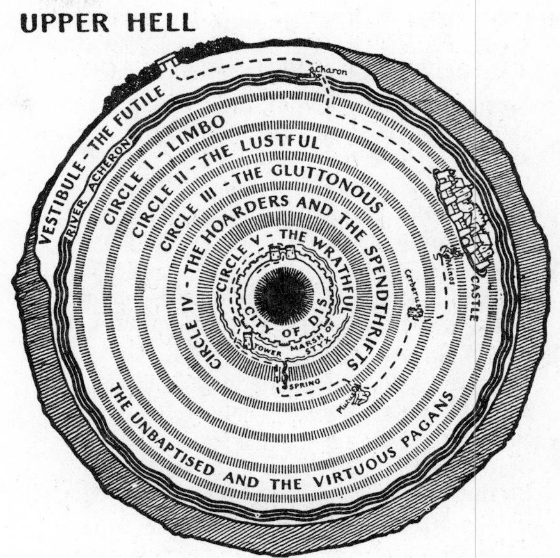

INCONTINENCE – THE SINS OF THE LEOPARD

THROUGH ME THE ROAD TO THE CITY OF DESOLATION,
THROUGH ME THE ROAD TO SORROWS DIUTURNAL,
THROUGH ME THE ROAD AMONG THE LOST CREATION.

JUSTICE MOVED MY GREAT MAKER; GOD ETERNAL 4
WROUGHT ME: THE POWER, AND THE UNSEARCHABLY
HIGH WISDOM, AND THE PRIMAL LOVE SUPERNAL.

I. 120: *the short road up the hill*: this line shows clearly that the "blissful Mountain" and Mount Purgatory are in reality one and the same; since the Beasts prevent Dante from taking "the short road," he is obliged to go by the long road—i.e., through Hell—to find the mountain again on the other side of the world.

I. 1: *the City of Desolation* (*la citta dolente*; lit.: the sorrowful city). Hell, like Heaven, is represented under the figure sometimes of a city, and sometimes of an empire. Later on (Canto IX) we shall come to the actual city itself, which has its fortifications on the edge of the Sixth Circle, and comprises the whole of Nether Hell. At present we are only in Upper Hell, forming as it were the suburbs of the city and made up of the Vestibule and the first five circles.

II. 4-6: *power . . . wisdom supreme and primal love*: the attributes of the Trinity. "If there is God, if there is freewill, then man is able to choose the opposite of God. Power, Wisdom, Love, gave man freewill; therefore Power, Wisdom, Love, created the gate of hell and the possibility of hell." (Charles Williams: *The Figure of Beatrice*, p. 113.)

NOTHING ERE I WAS MADE WAS MADE TO BE
SAVE THINGS ETERNE, AND I ETERNE ABIDE;
LAY DOWN ALL HOPE, YOU THAT GO IN BY ME.

These words, of sombre colour, I descried
Writ on the lintel of a gateway; "Sir,
This sentence is right hard for me," I cried.

And like a man of quick discernment: "Here
Lay down all thy distrust," said he, "reject
Dead from within thee every coward fear;

We've reached the place I told thee to expect,
Where thou shouldst see the miserable race,
Those who have lost the good of intellect."

He laid his hand on mine, and with a face
So joyous that it comforted my quailing,
Into the hidden things he led my ways.

Here sighing, and here crying, and loud railing
Smote on the starless air, with lamentation,
So that at first I wept to hear such wailing.

Tongues mixed and mingled, horrible execration,
Shrill shrieks, hoarse groans, fierce yells and hideous blether
And clapping of hands thereto, without cessation

Made tumult through the timeless night, that hither
And thither drives in dizzying circles sped,
As whirlwind whips the spinning sands together.

Whereat, with horror flapping round my head:
"Master, what's this I hear? Who can they be,
These people so distraught with grief?" I said.

And he replied: "The dismal company
Of wretched spirits thus find their guerdon due
Whose lives knew neither praise nor infamy;

They're mingled with that caitiff angel-crew
Who against God rebelled not, nor to Him
Were faithful, but to self alone were true;

Heaven cast them forth—their presence there would dim
The light; deep Hell rejects so base a herd,
Lest sin should boast itself because of them.

Then I: "But, Master, by what torment spurred
Are they driven on to vent such bitter breath?"
He answered: "I will tell thee in a word:

This dreary huddle has no hope of death,
Yet its blind life trails on so low and crass
That every other fate it envieth.

No reputation in the world it has,
Mercy and doom hold it alike in scorn—
Let us not speak of these; but look, and pass."

So I beheld, and lo! an ensign borne
Whirling, that span and ran, as in disdain
Of any rest; and there the folk forlorn

Rushed after it, in such an endless train,
It never would have entered in my head
There were so many men whom death had slain.

And when I'd noted here and there a shade
Whose face I knew, I saw and recognized
The coward spirit of the man who made

The great refusal; and that proof sufficed;
Here was that rabble, here without a doubt,
Whom God and whom His enemies despised.

This scum, who'd never lived, now fled about
Naked and goaded, for a swarm of fierce
Hornets and wasps stung all the wretched rout

Until their cheeks ran blood, whose slubbered smears,
Mingled with brine, around their footsteps fell,
Where loathly worms licked up their blood and tears.

Then I peered on ahead, and soon quite well
Made out the hither bank of a wide stream,
Where stood much people. "Sir," said I, "pray tell

Who these are, what their custom, why they seem
So eager to pass over and be gone—
If I may trust my sight in this pale gleam."

And he to me: "The whole shall be made known;
Only have patience till we stay our feet
On yonder sorrowful shore of Acheron."

Abashed, I dropped my eyes; and, lest unmeet
Chatter should vex him, held my tongue, and so
Paced on with him, in silence and discreet,

To the riverside. When from the far bank lo!
A boat shot forth, whose white-haired boatman old
Bawled as he came: "Woe to the wicked! Woe!

Never you hope to look on Heaven—behold!
I come to ferry you hence across the tide
To endless night, fierce fires and shramming cold.

And thou, the living man there! stand aside
From these who are dead!" I budged not, but abode;
So, when he saw me hold my ground, he cried:

"Away with thee! for by another road
And other ferries thou shalt make the shore,
Not here; a lighter skiff must bear thy load."

Then said my guide: "Charon, why wilt thou roar
And chafe in vain? Thus it is willed where power
And will are one; enough; ask thou no more."

I. 8: *things eterne*: In Canto XXXIV Dante tells how Hell was made when Satan fell from Heaven: it was created "for the devil and his angels" (*Matt.* XXV. 41) and before it nothing was made except the "eternal things," i.e., the Angels and the Heavens.

I. 9: *lay down all hope*: For the soul that literally enters Hell there is no return, nor any passage to Purgatory and repentance. Dante is naturally disturbed (I. 12) by this warning. But what he is entering upon, while yet in this life, is not Hell but the vision of Hell, and for him there is a way out, provided he keeps his hope and faith. Accordingly, Virgil enjoins him (II. 14-15) to reject doubt and fear.

I. 18: *the good of intellect*: In the *Convivio* Dante quotes Aristotle as saying: "truth is the good of the intellect." What the lost souls have lost is not the intellect itself, which still functions mechanically, but the *good* of the intellect: i.e., the knowledge of God, who is Truth. (For Dante, as for Aquinas, "intellect" does not mean what we call, colloquially, "braininess": it means the whole "reasonable soul" of man.)

I. 16: *the great refusal*: Probably Celestine V, who, in 1294, at the age of 80, was made Pope, but resigned the papacy five months later. His successor was Pope Boniface VIII, to whom Dante attributed many of the evils which had overtaken the Church.

II. 91-2: *another road and other ferries*: souls destined for Heaven never cross Acheron; they assemble at the mouth of Tiber and are taken in a boat piloted by an angel to Mount Purgatory at the Antipodes (*Purg.* ii). Charon recognizes that Dante is a soul in Grace (see II. 127-9).

This shut the shaggy mouth up of that sour
Infernal ferryman of the livid wash,
Only his flame-ringed eyeballs rolled a-glower.

But those outwearied, naked souls—how gash
And pale they grew, chattering their teeth for dread,
When first they felt his harsh tongue's cruel lash.

God they blaspheme, blaspheme their parents' bed,
The human race, the place, the time, the blood,
The seed that got them, and the womb that bred;

Then, huddling hugger-mugger, down they scud,
Dismally wailing, to the accursed strand
Which waits for every man that fears not God.

Charon, his eyes red like a burning brand,
Thumps with his oar the lingerers that delay,
And rounds them up, and beckons with his hand.

And as, by one and one, leaves drift away
In autumn, till the bough from which they fall
Sees the earth strewn with all its brave array,

So, from the bank there, one by one, drop all
Adam's ill seed, when signalled off the mark,
As drops the falcon to the falconer's call.

Away they're borne across the waters dark,
And ere they land that side the stream, anon
Fresh troops this side come flocking to embark.

Then said my courteous master: "See, my son,
All those that die beneath God's righteous ire
From every country come here every one.

They press to pass the river, for the fire
Of heavenly justice stings and spurs them so
That all their fear is changed into desire;

And by this passage, good souls never go;
Therefore, if Charon chide thee, do thou look
What this may mean—'tis not so hard to know."

When he thus said, the dusky champaign shook
So terribly that, thinking on the event,
I feel the sweat pour off me like a brook.

The sodden ground belched wind, and through the rent
Shot the red levin, with a flash and sweep
That robbed me of my wits, incontinent;

And down I fell, as one that swoons on sleep.

THE IMAGES. *Hell-Gate.* High and wide and without bars (*Inf.* viii. 126), the door "whose threshold is denied to none" (*Inf.* xiv. 87) always waits to receive those who are astray in the Dark Wood. Anyone may enter if he so chooses, but if he does, he must abandon hope, since it leads nowhere but to the *Citta Dolente*, the City of Desolation. In the *story*, Hell is filled with the souls of those who died with their wills set to enter by that gate; in the *allegory*, these souls are the images of sin in the self or in society.

The Vestibule was presumably suggested to Dante by the description in *Aeneid* vi. (where, however, it is tenanted by rather a different set of people). It does not, I think, occur in any previous Christian eschatology. Heaven and Hell being states in which choice is permanently fixed, there must also be a state in which the refusal of choice is itself fixed, since to refuse choice is in fact to choose indecision. The Vestibule is the abode of the weather-cock mind, the vague tolerance which will neither approve nor condemn, the cautious cowardice for which no decision is ever final. The spirits rush aimlessly after the aimlessly whirling banner, stung and goaded, as of old, by the thought that, in doing anything definite whatsoever, they are missing doing something else.

Acheron, "the joyless," first of the great rivers of Hell whose names Dante took from Virgil and Virgil from Homer.

Charon, the classical ferryman of the dead. Most of the monstrous organisms by which the functions of Hell are discharged are taken from Greek and Roman mythology. They are neither devils nor damned souls, but the images of perverted appetites, presiding over the circles appropriate to their natures.

CANTO IV

THE STORY. *Recovering from his swoon, Dante finds himself across Acheron and on the edge of the actual Pit of Hell. He follows Virgil into the First Circle—the Limbo where the Unbaptized and the Virtuous Pagans dwell "suspended," knowing no torment save exclusion from the positive bliss of God's presence. Virgil tells him of Christ's Harrowing of Hell, and then shows him the habitation of the great men of antiquity—poets, heroes, and philosophers.*

A heavy peal of thunder came to waken me
Out of the stunning slumber that had bound me,
Startling me up as though rude hands had shaken me.

I rose, and cast my rested eyes around me,
Gazing intent to satisfy my wonder
Concerning the strange place wherein I found me.

Hear truth: I stood on the steep brink whereunder
Runs down the dolorous chasm of the Pit,
Ringing with infinite groans like gathered thunder.

Deep, dense, and by no faintest glimmer lit
It lay, and though I strained my sight to find
Bottom, not one thing could I see in it.

"Down must we go, to that dark world and blind,"
The poet said, turning on me a bleak
Blanched face; "I will go first—come thou behind."

I. 126: *all their fear is changed into desire*: This is another of the important passages in which Dante emphasizes that Hell is the soul's choice. The damned fear it and long for it, as in this life a man may hate the sin which makes him miserable, and yet obstinately seek and wallow in it.

I. 7: *I stood on the steep brink*: It is disputed how Dante passed Acheron; the simplest explanation is that Charon, obedient to Virgil's "word of power," ferried him across during his swoon. Technically speaking, Dante had to describe a passage by boat in Canto VIII, and did not want to anticipate his effects; I think, however, he had also an allegorical reason for omitting the description here (see Canto VII. *Images: Path down Cliff*). Note that the "peal of thunder" in I. 1 is not that which followed the lightning-flash at the end of Canto III, but (I. 9) the din issuing from the mouth of the Pit—an orchestra of discord, here blended into one confused roar, which, resolved into its component disharmonies, will accompany us to the bottom circle of Hell.

Then I, who had marked the colour of his cheek: 16
"How can I go, when even thou art white
For fear, who art wont to cheer me when I'm weak?"

But he: "Not so; the anguish infinite 19
They suffer yonder paints my countenance
With pity, which thou takest for affright;

Come, we have far to go; let us advance." 22
So, entering, he made me enter, where
The Pit's first circle makes circumference.

We heard no loud complaint, no crying there, 25
No sound of grief except the sound of sighing
Quivering for ever through the eternal air;

Grief, not for torment, but for loss undying, 28
By women, men, and children sighed for so,
Sorrowers thick—thronged, their sorrows multiplying.

Then my good guide: "Thou dost not ask me who 31
These spirits are," said he, "whom thou perceivest?
Ere going further, I would have thee know

They sinned not; yet their merit lacked its chiefest 34
Fulfilment, lacking baptism, which is
The gateway to the faith which thou believest;

Or, living before Christendom, their knees 37
Paid not aright those tributes that belong
To God; and I myself am one of these.

For such defects alone—no other wrong— 40
We are lost; yet only by this grief offended:
That, without hope, we ever live, and long."

Grief smote my heart to think, as he thus ended, 43
What souls I knew, of great and sovran
Virtue, who in that Limbo dwelt suspended.

"Tell me, sir—tell me, Master," I began 46
(In hope some fresh assurance to be gleaning
Of our sin-conquering Faith), "did any man

By his self-merit, or on another leaning, 49
Ever fare forth from hence and come to be
Among the blest?" He took my hidden meaning.

"When I was newly in this state," said he, 52
"I saw One come in majesty and awe,
And on His head were crowns of victory.

Our great first father's spirit He did withdraw, 55
And righteous Abel, Noah who built the ark,
Moses who gave and who obeyed the Law,

King David, Abraham the Patriarch, 58
Israel with his father and generation,
Rachel, for whom he did such deeds of mark,

With many another of His chosen nation; 61
These did He bless; and know, that ere that day
No human soul had ever seen salvation."

While he thus spake, we still made no delay, 64
But passed the wood—I mean, the wood (as 'twere)
Of souls ranged thick as trees. Being now some way—

Not far—from where I'd slept, I saw appear 67
A light, which overcame the shadowy face
Of gloom, and made a glowing hemisphere.

'Twas yet some distance on, yet I could trace 70
So much as brought conviction to my heart
That persons of great honour held that place.

"O thou that honour'st every science and art, 73
Say, who are these whose honour gives them claim
To different customs and a sphere apart?"

And he to me: "Their honourable name, 76
Still in thy world resounding as it does,
Wins here from Heaven the favour due to fame."

Meanwhile I heard a voice that cried out thus: 79
"Honour the most high poet! his great shade,
Which was departed, is returned to us."

It paused there, and was still; and lo! there made 82
Toward us, four mighty shadows of the dead,
Who in their mien nor grief nor joy displayed.

"Mark well the first of these," my master said, 85
"Who in his right hand bears a naked sword
And goes before the three as chief and head;

Homer is he, the poets' sovran lord; 88
Next, Horace comes, the keen satirical;
Ovid the third; and Lucan afterward.

Because I share with these that honourable 91
Grand title the sole voice was heard to cry
They do me honour, and therein do well."

Thus in their school assembled I, even I, 94
Looked on the lords of loftiest song, whose style
O'er all the rest goes soaring eagle-high.

When they had talked together a short while 97
They all with signs of welcome turned my way,
Which moved my master to a kindly smile;

And greater honour yet they did me—yea, 100
Into their fellowship they deigned invite
And make me sixth among such minds as they.

So we moved slowly onward toward the light 103
In talk 'twere as unfitting to repeat
Here, as to speak there was both fit and right.

And presently we reached a noble seat— 106
A castle, girt with seven high walls around,
And moated with a goodly rivulet

O'er which we went as though upon dry ground; 109
With those wise men I passed the sevenfold gate
Into a fresh green meadow, where we found

Persons with grave and tranquil eyes, and great 112
Authority in their carriage and attitude,
Who spoke but seldom and in voice sedate.

So here we walked aside a little, and stood 115
Upon an open eminence, lit serene
And clear, whence one and all might well be viewed.

Plain in my sight on the enamelled green 118
All those grand spirits were shown me one by one—
It thrills my heart to think what I have seen!

---

l. 53: *I saw One come*: The episode, based upon I *Peter* iii. 19, of Christ's descent into Limbo to rescue the souls of the patriarchs (the "Harrowing of Hell") was a favourite subject of medieval legend and drama. The crucifixion is reckoned as having occurred in A.D. 34, when Virgil had been dead fifty-three years. Note that the name of Christ is never spoken in Hell—He is always referred to by some periphrasis.

l. 55: *our great first father*: Adam.

l. 106: *a noble seat*: The scene is, I think, a medievalized version of the Elysian Fields, surrounded by "many-watered Eridanus." (*Aen.* vi. 659.) Detailed allegorical interpretations of the seven gates, walls, etc., have no great value.

I saw Electra, saw with her anon
Hector, Aeneas, many a Trojan peer,
And hawk-eyed Caesar in his habergeon;

I saw Camilla and bold Penthesilea,
On the other hand; Latinus on his throne
Beside Lavinia his daughter dear;

Brutus, by whom proud Tarquin was o'erthrown,
Marcia, Cornelia, Julia, Lucrece—and
I saw great Saladin, aloof, alone.

Higher I raised my brows and further scanned,
And saw the Master of the men who know
Seated amid the philosophic band;

All do him honour and deep reverence show;
Socrates, Plato, in the nearest room
To him; Diogenes, Thales and Zeno,

Democritus, who held that all things come
By chance; Empedocles, Anaxagoras wise,
And Heraclitus, him that wept for doom;

Dioscorides, who named the qualities,
Tully and Orpheus, Linus, and thereby
Good Seneca, well-skilled to moralize;

Euclid the geometrician, Ptolemy,
Galen, Hippocrates, and Avicen,
Averroës who made the commentary—

Nay, but I tell not all that I saw then;
The long theme drives me hard, and everywhere
The wondrous truth outstrips my staggering pen.

The group of six dwindles to two; we fare
Forth a new way, I and my guide withal,
Out from that quiet to the quivering air,

And reach a place where nothing shines at all.

THE IMAGES. After those who refused choice come those without opportunity of choice. They could not, that is, choose Christ; they could, and did choose human virtue, and for that they have their reward. (Pagans who chose evil by their own standards are judged by these standards—cf. *Rom.* ii. 8-15—and are found lower down.) Here again, the souls "have what they chose"; they enjoy that kind of after-life which they themselves imagined for the virtuous dead; their failure lay in not imagining better. They are lost (as Virgil says later, *Purg.* vii. 8) because they "had not faith"—primarily the Christian Faith, but also, more generally, faith in the nature of things. The *allegory* is clear: it is the weakness of Humanism to fall short in the imagination of ecstasy; at its best it is noble, reasonable, and cold, and however optimistic about a balanced happiness in this world, pessimistic about a rapturous eternity. Sometimes wistfully aware that others claim the experience of this positive bliss, the Humanist can neither accept it by faith, embrace it by hope, nor abandon himself to it in charity. Dante discusses the question further in the *Purgatory* (esp. Cantos VII and XXII) and makes his full doctrine explicit in *Paradise*, Cantos XIX-XX.

CANTO V

THE STORY. *Dante and Virgil descend from the First Circle to the Second (the first of the Circles of Incontinence). On the threshold sits Minos, the judge of Hell, assigning the souls to their appropriate places of torment. His opposition is overcome by Virgil's word of power, and the Poets enter the Circle, where the souls of the Lustful are tossed for ever upon a howling wind. After Virgil has pointed out a number of famous lovers, Dante speaks to the shade of Francesca da Rimini, who tells him her story.*

From the first circle thus I came descending
To the second, which, in narrower compass turning,
Holds greater woe, with outcry loud and rending.

There in the threshold, horrible and girning,
Grim Minos sits, holding his ghastly session,
And, as he girds him, sentencing and spurning;

For when the ill soul faces him, confession
Pours out of it till nothing's left to tell;
Whereon that connoisseur of all transgression

Assigns it to its proper place in hell,
As many grades as he would have it fall,
So oft he belts him round with his own tail.

Before him stands a throng continual;
Each comes in turn to abye the fell arraign;
They speak—they hear—they're whirled down one and all.

"Ho! thou that comest to the house of pain,"
Cried Minos when he saw me, the appliance
Of his dread powers suspending, "think again

How thou dost go, in whom is thy reliance;
Be not deceived by the wide open door!"
Then said my guide: "Wherefore this loud defiance?

Hinder not thou his fated way; be sure
Hindrance is vain; thus it is willed where will
And power are one; enough; ask now no more."

And now the sounds of grief begin to fill
My ear; I'm come where cries of anguish smite
My shrinking sense, and lamentation shrill—

A place made dumb of every glimmer of light,
Which bellows like tempestuous ocean birling
In the batter of a two-way wind's buffet and fight.

I. 121: *Electra etc.*: Pride of place is given to the Trojans, founders of the Roman line; (Julius) Caesar is grouped with them as a descendant of Aeneas.

I. 129: *Saladin*: His inclusion here, along with Lucan, Averroës, and other A.D. personages who were not, strictly speaking, without opportunity of choice, perhaps tacitly indicates Dante's opinion about all those who, though living in touch with Christianity and practising all the moral virtues, find themselves sincerely unable to accept the Christian revelation.

I. 131: *the Master of the men who know*: Aristotle.

I. 6: *as he girds him, sentencing*: as Dante explains in II. 11-12, Minos girds himself so many times with his tail to indicate the number of the circle to which each soul is to go (cf. Canto XXVII. 124 and note).

I. 28: *a place made dumb of every glimmer of light*—(cf. Canto I. 60, "wherein the sun is mute"): Nevertheless, Dante is able to see the spirits. This is only one of many passages in which the poet conveys to us that the things he perceives during his journey are not perceived altogether by the mortal senses, but after another mode. (In *Purg.* xxi. 29, Virgil explains to another spirit that Dante "could not come alone, because he does not see after our manner, wherefore I was brought forth from Hell to guide him.") So, in the present case, Dante recognizes that the darkness is total, although he can see in the dark.

The blast of hell that never rests from whirling 31
Harries the spirits along in the sweep of its swath,
And vexes them, for ever beating and hurling.

When they are borne to the rim of the ruinous path 34
With cry and wail and shriek they are caught by the gust,
Railing and cursing the power of the Lord's wrath.

Into this torment carnal sinners are thrust, 37
So I was told—the sinners who make their reason
Bond thrall under the yoke of their lust.

Like as the starlings wheel in the wintry season 40
In wide and clustering flocks wing-borne, wind-borne,
Even so they go, the souls who did this treason,

Hither and thither, and up and down, outworn, 43
Hopeless of any rest—rest, did I say?
Of the least minishing of their pangs forlorn.

And as the cranes go chanting their harsh lay, 46
Across the sky in long procession trailing,
So I beheld some shadows borne my way,

Driven on the blast and uttering wail on wailing; 49
Wherefore I said: "O Master, art thou able
To name these spirits thrashed by the black wind's flailing?"

"Among this band," said he, "whose name and fable 52
Thou seek'st to know, the first who yonder flies
Was empress of many tongues, mistress of Babel.

She was so broken to lascivious vice 55
She licensed lust by law, in hopes to cover
Her scandal of unnumbered harlotries.

This was Semiramis; 'tis written of her 58
That she was wife to Ninus and heiress, too,
Who reigned in the land the Soldan now rules over.

Lo! she that slew herself for love, untrue 61
To Sychaeus' ashes. Lo! tost on the blast,
Voluptuous Cleopatra, whom love slew.

Look, look on Helen, for whose sake rolled past 64
Long evil years. See great Achilles yonder,
Who warred with love, and that war was his last.

See Paris, Tristram see!" And many—oh, wonder 67
Many—a thousand more, he showed by name
And pointing hand, whose life love rent asunder.

And when I had heard my Doctor tell the fame 70
Of all those knights and ladies of long ago,
I was pierced through with pity, and my head swam.

"Poet," said I, "fain would I speak those two 73
That seem to ride as light as any foam,
And hand in hand on the dark wind drifting go."

And he replied: "Wait till they nearer roam, 76
And thou shalt see; summon them to thy side
By the power of the love that leads them, and they will come."

So, as they eddied past on the whirling tide, 79
I raised my voice: "O souls that wearily rove,
Come to us, speak to us—if it be not denied."

And as desire wafts homeward dove with dove 82
To their sweet nest, on raised and steady wing
Down-dropping through the air, impelled by love,

So these from Dido's flock came fluttering 85
And dropping toward us down the cruel wind,
Such power was in my affectionate summoning.

"O living creature, gracious and so kind, 88
Coming through this black air to visit us,
Us, who in death the globe incarnadined,

Were the world's King our friend and might we thus 91
Entreat, we would entreat Him for thy peace,
That pitiest so our pangs dispiteous!

Hear all thou wilt, and speak as thou shalt please, 94
And we will gladly speak with thee and hear,
While the winds cease to howl, as they now cease.

There is a town upon the sea-coast, near 97
Where Po with all his streams comes down to rest
In ocean; I was born and nurtured there.

Love, that so soon takes hold in the gentle breast, 100
Took this lad with the lovely body they tore
From me; the way of it leaves me still distrest.

Love, that to no loved heart remits love's score, 103
Took me with such great joy of him, that see!
It holds me yet and never shall leave me more.

106

I. 61: *she that slew herself for love*: Dido.

I. 88: *O living creature*: The speaker is Francesca da Rimini. Like many of the personages in the *Comedy*, she does not directly name herself, but gives Dante particulars about her birthplace and history which enable him to recognize her. She was the daughter of Guido Vecchio di Polenta of Ravenna, and aunt to Guido Novello di Polenta, who was Dante's friend and host during the latter years of his life; so that her history was of topical interest to Dante's readers. For political reasons, she was married to the deformed Gianciotto, son of Malatesta da Verrucchio, lord of Rimini, but fell in love with his handsome younger brother Paolo, who became her lover. Her husband, having one day surprised them together, stabbed them both to death (1285).

I. 94: *hear all thou wilt*: Tender and beautiful as Dante's handling of Francesca is, he has sketched her with a deadly accuracy. All the good is there; the charm, the courtesy, the instant response to affection, the grateful eagerness to please; but also all the evil; the easy yielding, the inability to say No, the intense self-pity.

Of this, the most famous episode in the whole *Comedy*, Charles Williams writes: "It is always quoted as an example of Dante's tenderness. So, no doubt, it is, but it is not here for that reason. . . . It has a much more important place; it presents the first tender, passionate, and half-excusable consent of the soul to sin. . . . [Dante] so manages the description, he so heightens the excuse, that the excuse reveals itself as precisely the sin . . . the persistent parleying with the occasion of sin, the sweet prolonged laziness of love, is the first surrender of the soul to Hell—small but certain. The formal sin here is the adultery of the two lovers; the poetic sin is their shrinking from the adult love demanded of them, and their refusal of the opportunity of glory," (*The Figure of Beatrice*, p. 118).

I. 97: *a town upon the sea-coast*: Ravenna.

I. 102: *the way of it leaves me still distrest*: Either (1) the way of the murder, because the lovers were killed in the very act of sin and so had no time for repentance; or (2) the way in which their love came about. The story went that Paolo was sent to conduct the marriage negotiations, and that Francesca was tricked into consenting by being led to suppose that he, and not Gianciotto, was to be her bridegroom. In the same way, in the Arthurian romances, Queen Guinevere falls in love with Lancelot when he is sent to woo her on King Arthur's behalf; and it is this parallel which makes the tale of Lancelot so poignant for her and Paolo.

Love to a single death brought him and me; 106
Cain's place lies waiting for our murderer now."
These words came wafted to us plaintively.

Hearing those wounded souls, I bent my brow 109
Downward, and thus bemused I let time pass,
Till the poet said at length: "What thinkest thou?"

When I could answer, I began: "Alas! 112
Sweet thoughts how many, and desire how great,
Brought down these twain unto the dolorous pass!"

And then I turned to them: "Thy dreadful fate, 115
Francesca, makes me weep, it so inspires
Pity," said I, "and grief compassionate.

Tell me—in that time of sighing-sweet desires, 118
How, and by what, did love his power disclose
And grant you knowledge of your hidden fires?"

Then she to me: "The bitterest woe of woes 121
Is to remember in our wretchedness
Old happy times; and this thy Doctor knows;

Yet, if so dear desire thy heart possess 124
To know that root of love which wrought our fall,
I'll be as those who weep and who confess.

One day we read for pastime how in thrall 127
Lord Lancelot lay to love, who loved the Queen;
We were alone—we thought no harm at all.

As we read on, our eyes met now and then, 130
And to our cheeks the changing colour started,
But just one moment overcame us—when

We read of the smile, desired of lips long-thwarted, 133
Such smile, by such a lover kissed away,
He that may never more from me be parted

Trembling all over, kissed my mouth. I say 136
The book was Galleot, Galleot the complying
Ribald who wrote; we read no more that day."

While the one spirit thus spoke, the other's crying 139
Wailed on me with a sound so lamentable,
I swooned for pity like as I were dying.

And, as a dead man falling, down I fell. 142

The Images. *The Circles of Incontinence.* This and the next three circles are devoted to those who sinned less by deliberate choice of evil than by failure to make resolute choice of the good. Here are the sins of self-indulgence, weakness of will, and easy yielding to appetite—the "Sins of the Leopard."

The Lustful. The image here is sexual, though we need not confine the *allegory* to the sin of unchastity. Lust is a type of *shared* sin; at its best, and so long as it remains a sin of incontinence only, there is mutuality in it and exchange: although, in fact, mutual indulgence only serves to push both parties along the road to Hell, it is not, in intention, wholly selfish. For this reason Dante, with perfect orthodoxy, rates it as the least hateful of the deadly sins. (Sexual sins in which love and mutuality have no part find their place far below.)

Minos, a medievalized version of the classical Judge of the Underworld (see *Aen.* vi. 432). He may image an accusing conscience. The souls are damned on their own confession, for, Hell being the place of self-knowledge in sin, there can be no more self-deception here. (Similarly, even in the circles of Fraud, all the shades tell Dante the truth about themselves; this is poetically convenient, but, given this conception of Hell, it must be so.) The *literally* damned, having lost "the good of the intellect," cannot profit by their self-knowledge; *allegorically,* for the living soul, this vision of the Hell in the self is the preliminary to repentance and restoration.

The Black Wind. As the lovers drifted into self-indulgence and were carried away by their passions, so now they drift for ever. The bright, voluptuous sin is now seen *as it is*—a howling darkness of helpless discomfort. (The "punishment" for sin is simply the sin itself, experienced without illusion—though Dante does not work this out with mathematical rigidity in every circle.)

CANTO VI

THE STORY. *Dante now finds himself in the Third Circle, where the Gluttonous lie wallowing in the mire, drenched by perpetual rain and mauled by the three-headed dog Cerberus. After Virgil has quieted Cerberus by throwing earth into his jaws, Dante talks to the shade of Ciacco, a Florentine, who prophesies some of the disasters which are about to befall Florence, and tells him where he will find certain other of their fellow-citizens. Virgil tells Dante what the condition of the spirits will be, after the Last Judgment.*

When consciousness returned, which had shut close
The doors of sense, leaving me stupefied
For pity of those sad kinsfolk and their woes,

New sufferings and new sufferers, far and wide, 4
Where'er I move, or turn myself, or strain
My curious eyes, are seen on every side.

I am now in the Third Circle: that of rain— 7
One ceaseless, heavy, cold, accursed quench,
Whose law and nature vary never a grain;

Huge hailstones, sleet and snow, and turbid drench 10
Of water sluice down through the darkened air,
And the soaked earth gives off a putrid stench.

Cerberus, the cruel, misshapen monster, there 13
Bays in his triple gullet and doglike growls
Over the wallowing shades; his eyeballs glare

A bloodshot crimson, and his bearded jowls 16
Are greasy and black; pot-bellied, talon-heeled,
He clutches and flays and rips and rends the souls.

---

l. 107: *Cain's place*: Caina, so called after Cain; the first ring of the lowest circle in Hell, where lie those who were treacherous to their own kindred, (Canto XXXII).

l. 123: *thy Doctor*: Virgil (see l. 70). Dante is probably thinking of Aeneas' words to Dido: *infandum, regina, jubes renovare dolorem* . . . (O queen, thou dost bid me renew an unspeakable sorrow . . .),*Aeneid* ii. 3.

l. 137: *the book was Galleot*: In the romance of *Lancelot du Lac*, Galleot (or Galehalt) acted as intermediary between Lancelot and Guinevere, and so in the Middle Ages his name, like that of Pandarus in the tale of *Troilus and Cressida,* became a synonym for a go-between. The sense of the passage is: "The book was a pander and so was he who wrote it."

l. 7: *I am now in the Third Circle*: Once again, Dante does not say how he got here: we may suppose that Virgil carried or assisted him down before he had wholly recovered his senses.

They howl in the rain like hounds; they try to shield 19
    One flank with the other; with many a twist and squirm,
    The impious wretches writhe in the filthy field.

When Cerberus spied us coming, the great Worm, 22
    He gaped his mouths with all their fangs a-gloat,
    Bristling and quivering till no limb stood firm.

At once my guide, spreading both hands wide out, 25
    Scooped up whole fistfuls of the miry ground
    And shot them swiftly into each craving throat.

And as a ravenous and barking hound 28
    Falls dumb the moment he gets his teeth on food,
    And worries and bolts with never a thought beyond,

So did those beastly muzzles of the rude 31
    Fiend Cerberus, who so yells on the souls, they're all
    Half deafened—or they would be, if they could.

Then o'er the shades whom the rain's heavy fall 34
    Beats down, we forward went; and our feet trod
    Their nothingness, which seems corporeal.

These all lay grovelling flat upon the sod; 37
    Only, as we went by, a single shade
    Sat suddenly up, seeing us pass that road.

"O thou that through this Hell of ours art led, 40
    Look if thou know me, since thou wast, for sure,"
    Said he, "or ever I was unmade, made."

Then I to him: "Perchance thy torments sore 43
    Have changed thee out of knowledge—there's no trusting
    Sight, if I e'er set eyes on thee before.

But say, who are thou? brought by what ill lusting 46
    To such a pass and punishment as, meseems,
    Worse there may be, but nothing so disgusting?"

"Thy native city," said he, "where envy teems 49
    And swells so that already it brims the sack,
    Called me her own in the life where the light beams.

Ciacco you citizens nicknamed me—alack! 52
    Damnable gluttony was my soul's disease;
    See how I waste for it now in the rain's wrack.

And I, poor sinner, am not alone: all these 55
    Lie bound in the like penalty with me
    For the like offence." And there he held his peace,

And I at once began: "Thy misery 58
    Moves me to tears, Ciacco, and weighs me down.
    But tell me if thou canst, what end may be

In store for the people of our distracted town. 61
    Is there one just man left? And from what source
    To such foul head have these distempers grown?"

And he: "Long time their strife will run its course, 64
    And come to bloodshed; the wood party thence
    Will drive the other out with brutal force;

But within three brief suns their confidence 67
    Will have a fall, and t'other faction rise
    By help of one who now sits on the fence;

And these will lord it long with arrogant eyes, 70
    Crushing their foes with heavy loads indeed,
    For all their bitter shame and outraged cries.

Two righteous men there are, whom none will heed; 73
    Three sparks from Hell—Avarice, Envy, Pride—
    In all men's bosoms sowed the fiery seed."

His boding speech thus ended; so I cried: 76
    "Speak on, I beg thee! More, much more reveal!
    Tegghiaio, Farinata—how betide

Those worthy men? and Rusticucci's zeal? 79
    Arrigo, Mosca, and the rest as well
    Whose minds were still set on the public weal?

Where are they? Can I find them? Prithee tell— 82
    I am consumed with my desire to know—
    Feasting in Heaven, or poisoned here in Hell?"

He answered: "With the blacker spirits below, 85
    Dragged to the depth by other crimes abhorred;
    There shalt thou see them, if so deep thou go.

But when to the sweet world thou art restored, 88
    Recall my name to living memory;
    I'll tell no more, nor speak another word."

Therewith he squinted his straight gaze awry, 91
    Eyed me awhile, then, dropping down his head,
    Rolled over amid that sightless company.

---

l. 22: *Worm*: This, in Old English as in Italian (*vermo*), is simply a word for a monster, cf. the fairy-tale of "The Laidly Worm of Spindleston Heugh," where it denotes a dragon.

l. 26: *whole fistfuls of the miry ground*: To throw something into his mouth was the traditional way of appeasing this particular guardian of Hell—hence the phrase "to give a sop to Cerberus." In *Aeneid* vi, the Sibyl who guides Aeneas through Hades brings a number of cakes for the purpose. Here Virgil, not having made this provision, makes use of the first substitute that comes to hand.

l. 49: *thy native city*: Florence.

l. 52: *Ciacco you citizens nicknamed me*: The word means "pig," and, according to Boaccaccio, was the nickname of a Florentine gentleman notorious for his gluttony.

l. 61: *our distracted town*: i.e., Florence.

l. 64: *long time their strife will run its course*: This is the first of a number of passages dealing (under the guise of prophecy) with political events in Italy, and especially in Florence, which took place after the supposed date of the Vision (1300). It refers to the struggle between the two Guelf parties (the Blacks and the Whites), and to final expulsion of the Whites (including Dante) from Florence.

l. 65: *the wood party*: the Whites. The adjective *selvaggia* means either the "woodland" party (because certain of its leaders had come into Florence from the surrounding country) or the "savage" (i.e., uncultivated party) (as opposed to the more aristocratic Blacks). The English word "wood," which formerly had the meaning "mad, wild, savage," is thus a fairly exact equivalent of the ambiguous Italian.
The two parties "came to bloodshed" at the May-Day Festival of 1300, and the expulsion of the Black leaders took place shortly after. The Blacks returned in November 1301, with the help of Boniface VIII (the "sitter on the fence," l. 69), who till then had shown no decided preference for either party. The first decree banishing the Whites was published in January 1302, and the last in the latter half of the same year—all "within three suns" of the time at which Ciacco is supposed to be speaking.

l. 73: *two righteous men*: Dante is usually credited with meaning himself and his friend Guido Cavalcanti; but he does not say so, and we need not found a charge of self-righteousness on what he has not said.

ll. 78-80: *Tegghiaio . . . Mosca*: The persons named are all distinguished Florentines. We shall meet Farinata in Canto X, Tegghiaio and Rusticucci in Canto XVI, and Mosca in Canto XXVIII. Arrigo is not mentioned again.

Then spake my guide: "He'll rouse no more," he said,
"Till the last loud angelic trumpet's sounding;
For when the Enemy Power shall come arrayed

Each soul shall seek its own grave's mournful mounding,
Put on once more its earthly flesh and feature,
And hear the Doom eternally redounding."

Thus with slow steps I and my gentle teacher,
Over that filthy sludge of souls and snow,
Passed on, touching a little upon the nature

Of the life to come. "Master," said I, "this woe—
Will it grow less, or still more fiercely burning
With the Great Sentence, or remain just so?"

"Go to," said he, "hast thou forgot thy learning,
Which hath it: The more perfect, the more keen,
Whether for pleasure's or for pain's discerning?

Though true perfection never can be seen
In these damned souls, they'll be more near complete
After the Judgment than they yet have been."

So, with more talk which I need not repeat,
We followed the road that rings that circle round,
Till on the next descent we set our feet;

There Pluto, the great enemy, we found.

THE IMAGES. *The Gluttonous:* The surrender to sin which began with mutual indulgence leads by an imperceptible degradation to solitary self-indulgence. Of this kind of sin, the Gluttons are chosen as the image. Here is no reciprocity and no communication; each soul grovels alone in the mud, without heeding his neighbours—"a sightless company," Dante calls them.

The Rain. Gluttony (like the other self-indulgences it typifies) often masquerades on earth as a warm, cosy, and indeed jolly kind of sin; here it is seen as it is—a cold sensuality, a sodden and filthy spiritual wretchedness.

Cerberus. In the *story*, Cerberus is the three-headed dog familiar to us from Homer and Virgil and the tale of the Twelve Labours of Hercules, who guards the threshold of the classical Hades. For the *allegory*, he is the image of uncontrolled appetite; the Glutton, whose appetite preyed upon people and things, is seen to be, in fact, the helpless prey on which that appetite gluts itself.

CANTO VII

THE STORY. *At the entrance to the Fourth Circle, the poets are opposed by Pluto, and Virgil is again obliged to use a "word of power." In this circle, the Hoarders and the Spendthrifts roll huge rocks against one another, and here Virgil explains the nature and working of Luck (or Fortune). Then, crossing the circle, they descend the cliff to the Marsh of Styx, which forms the Fifth Circle and contains the Wrathful. Skirting its edge, they reach the foot of a tower.*

"*Papè Satan, papè Satan aleppe,*"
Pluto 'gan gabble with his clucking tongue;
My all-wise, gentle guide, to me unhappy

Said hearteningly: "Let no fears do thee wrong;
He shall not stay thy journey down this steep;
His powers, whate'er they be, are not so strong."

Then, turning him, and letting his glance sweep
O'er that bloat face: "Peace, thou damned wolf!" said he,
"Go, choke in thine own venom! To the deep,

Not without cause, we go. I say to thee,
Thus it is willed on high, where Michaël
Took vengeance on the proud adultery."

Then, as the sails bellying in the wind's swell
Tumble a-tangle at crack of the snapping mast,
Even so to earth the savage monster fell;

And we to the Fourth Circle downward passed,
Skirting a new stretch of the grim abyss
Where all the ills of all the world are cast.

God's justice! Who shall tell the agonies,
Heaped thick and new before my shuddering glance?
Why must our guilt smite us with strokes like this?

As waves against the encountering waves advance
Above Charybdis, clashing with toppling crest,
So must the folk here dance and counter-dance.

More than elsewhere, I saw them thronged and pressed
This side and that, yelling with all their might,
And shoving each a great weight with his chest.

They bump together, and where they bump, wheel right
Round, and return, trundling their loads again,
Shouting: "Why chuck away?" "Why grab so tight?"

Then round the dismal ring they pant and strain
Back on both sides to where they first began
Still as they go bawling their rude refrain;

And when they meet, then each re-treads his span,
Half round the ring to joust in the other list;
I felt quite shocked, and like a stricken man.

"Pray tell me, sir," said I, "all this—what is't?
Who are these people? On our left I find
Numberless tonsured heads; was each a priest?"

I. 96: *the Enemy Power*: This is the strangest and most terrible periphrasis used for Christ in these circles of the damned, who have chosen to know all goodness as antagonism and judgment.

I. 106: *Thy learning*: the philosophy of Aristotle, as incorporated in the theology of St. Thomas Aquinas. The souls will be "more perfect" after the Last Judgment because they will then be reunited to their bodies.

I. 115: *Pluto*: god of the wealth that springs from the soil, naturally came to be regarded as an "underground" deity, and from early times was apt to be identified with Hades (Dis). Dante, however, distinguishes him from Dis (Satan), and while making him an infernal power, retains his primitive character as a symbol of riches. There is perhaps also a fusion with Plutus, the "god of wealth" mentioned by Phaedrus. "The great enemy" is probably an allusion to I *Tim.* vi. 10.

I. 1: *Papè Satan aleppe*: Various attempts have been made to interpret this cryptic remark, but none of them is very convincing. One may safely conjecture that it is meant as an invocation to the Devil, and it is as well to leave it at that. Cf. Nimrod's jargon in Canto XXXI.

I. 12: *where Michaël took vengeance on the proud adultery*: The reference is to the Archangel Michael's war upon the rebellious angels (*Rev.* xii. 7-9). "Adultery" is used in the Biblical sense of unfaithfulness to God—as in "whoring after strange gods" (*Deut.* xxxi. 16, etc., and similar passages). "Proud," because Satan and his angels fell through pride.

I. 23: *Charybdis*: famous whirlpool near Messina.

"In life," said he, "these were so squint of mind
As in the handling of their wealth to use
No moderation—none, in either kind;

That's plain, from their shrill yelpings of abuse
At the ring's turn, where opposite degrees
Of crime divide them into rival crews.

They whose pates boast no hairy canopies
Are clerks—yea, popes and cardinals, in whom
Covetousness hath made its masterpiece."

"Why, sir." said I, "surely there must be some
Faces I know in all this gang, thus brought
By these defilements to a common doom."

"Nay," he replied, "that is an empty thought;
Living, their minds distinguished nothing; dead,
They cannot be distinguished. In this sort

They'll butt and brawl for ever; when from bed
The Last Trump wakes the body, these will be
Raised with tight fists, and those stripped, hide and head.

Hoarding and squandering filched the bright world's glee
Away, and set them to this tourney's shock,
Whose charms need no embroidered words from me.

See now, my son, the fine and fleeting mock
Of all those goods men wrangle for—the boon
That is delivered into the hand of Luck;

For all the gold that is beneath the moon,
Or ever was, could not avail to buy
Repose for one of these weary souls—not one."

"Master, I would hear more of this," said I;
"What is this Luck, whose talons take in hand
All life's good things that go so pleasantly?"

Then he: "Ah, witless world! Behold the grand
Folly of ignorance! Make thine ear attendant
Now on my judgment of her, and understand.

He whose high wisdom's over all transcendent
Stretched forth the Heavens, and guiding spirits supplied,
So that each part to each part shines resplendent,

Spreading the light equal on every side;
Likewise for earthly splendours He saw fit
To ordain a general minister and guide,

By whom vain wealth, as time grew ripe for it,
From race to race, from blood to blood, should pass,
Far beyond hindrance of all human wit.

Wherefore some nations minish, some amass
Great power, obedient to her subtle codes,
Which are hidden, like the snake beneath the grass.

For her your science finds no measuring-rods;
She in her realm provides, maintains, makes laws,
And judges, as do in theirs the other gods.

Her permutations never know truce nor pause;
Necessity lends her speed, so swift in fame
Men come and go, and cause succeeds to cause.

Lo! this is she that hath so curst a name
Even from those that should give praise to her—
Luck, whom men senselessly revile and blame;

But she is blissful and she does not hear;
She, with the other primal creatures gay,
Tastes her own blessedness, and turns her sphere.

Come! to more piteous woes we must away;
All stars that rose when I set out now sink,
And the High Powers permit us no long stay."

So to the further edge we crossed the rink,
Hard by a bubbling spring which, rising there,
Cuts its own cleft and pours on down the brink.

Darker than any perse its waters were,
And keeping company with the ripples dim
We made our way down by that eerie stair.

A marsh there is called Styx, which the sad stream
Forms when it finds the end of its descent
Under the grey, malignant rock-foot grim;

And I, staring about with eyes intent,
Saw mud-stained figures in the mire beneath,
Naked, with looks of savage discontent,

At fisticuffs—not with fists alone, but with
Their heads and heels, and with their bodies too,
And tearing each other piecemeal with their teeth.

"Son," the kind master said, "here may'st thou view
The souls of those who yielded them to wrath;
Further, I'd have thee know and hold for true

That others lie plunged deep in this vile broth,
Whose sighs—see there, wherever one may look—
Come bubbling up to the top and make it froth.

Bogged there they say: 'Sullen were we—we took
No joy of the pleasant air, no joy of the good
Sun; our hearts smouldered with a sulky smoke;

I. 73:*sqq.*: *He whose high wisdom*: This is the first of the series of great discourses in which Dante gradually unfolds the plan of the spiritual and physical universe. The "guiding spirits" mentioned here are the celestial intelligences (angels) who control the heavenly spheres. *Luck* or *Fortune* is here conceived as a similar ministering spirit, whose function it is to control and distribute wealth and opportunity upon the earth. Virgil describes her under the familiar classical figure of a goddess with a wheel, or sphere, whose turning brings about the ups-and-downs of disaster and prosperity. By this figure Dante does not deny free will, or ascribe the course of history to blind chance: he says (*De Monarchia*, xii. 70): " . . . fortune, which agency we better and more rightly call the divine providence."

I. 87: *the other gods*: i.e., the angels. Dante several times uses this name for them, and not only when Virgil is speaking.

I. 89: *necessity lends her speed*: Here again Dante does not mean that, in the pagan phrase, "the gods themselves are subject to necessity," but merely that, such is the brevity of human life, the changes of fortune must needs be swift.

I. 95: *primal creatures*: the celestial Intelligences, who were created, with the heavens themselves, directly by God, and not through secondary agencies (i.e., they were not evolved or generated).

I. 98: *all stars that rose . . . now sink*: All the stars that were rising when Virgil first met Dante on Good Friday evening have passed the zenith and begun to set; i.e., it is now past midnight. (So long as the poets are descending into Hell the time is never indicated by the sun, but always by the changes of the night sky.)

I. 101: *a bubbling spring*: This is the water of the river Acheron, which, after forming a complete circle about Hell, runs underground beneath the first four circles, and now emerges again to pour down the cliff and form the river and marsh of Styx (see map).

Sullen we lie here now in the black mud.'
This hymn they gurgle in their throats, for whole
Words they can nowise frame." Thus we pursued

Our path round a wide arc of that ghast pool,
Between the soggy marsh and arid shore,
Still eyeing those who gulp the marish foul,

And reached at length the foot of a tall tower.

THE IMAGES. *The Hoarders and the Spendthrifts.* Mutual indulgence has already declined into selfish appetite; now, that appetite becomes aware of the incompatible and equally selfish appetites of other people. Indifference becomes mutual antagonism, imaged here by the antagonism between hoarding and squandering.

The Joust. Note the reappearance of community in a perverted form: these irrational appetites are united, after a fashion, by a common hatred, for the waging of a futile war. So nations, political parties, business combines, classes, gangs, etc., sometimes display a spurious comradeship in opposition.

The Wrathful. Community in sin is unstable: it soon disintegrates into an anarchy of hatred, all against all. Dante distinguishes two kinds of Wrath. The one is active and ferocious; it vents itself in sheer lust for inflicting pain and destruction—on other people, on itself, on anything and everything it meets. The other is passive and sullen, the withdrawal into a black sulkiness which can find no joy in God or man or the universe.

The Marsh. Both kinds of Wrath are figured as a muddy slough; on its surface, the active hatreds rend and snarl at one another; at the bottom, the sullen hatreds lie gurgling, unable even to express themselves for the rage that chokes them. This is the last of the Circles of Incontinence. This savage self-frustration is the end of that which had its tender and romantic beginnings in the dalliance of indulged passion.

The Path down the Cliff. For the first time, Dante's passage from one circle to the other is described in detail. We are not told at what precise point in the wilderness he found Hell-gate; one may encounter it at any moment. The crossing of Acheron—the image of the assent to sin—is made unconsciously. From Limbo to the Second Circle—from the lack of imagination that inhibits the will to the false imagination that saps it—the passage is easy and, as it were, unnoticed. From the Second Circle to the Third—from mutuality to separateness—the soul is carried as though in a dream. From the Third to the Fourth Circle the way is a little plainer—for as one continues in sin one becomes uneasily aware of inner antagonisms and resentments, though without any clear notion how they arise. But as antagonism turns to hatred, the steps of the downward path begin to be fearfully apparent. From this point on the descent is mapped out with inexorable clarity.

Styx—the name means "hateful"—is the second of the four chief rivers of Hell. It economically does double duty as the Fifth Circle and as the boundary between Upper and Nether Hell.

CANTO VIII

THE STORY. *From the watch-tower on the edge of the marsh a beacon signals to the garrison of the City of Dis that Dante and Virgil are approaching, and a boat is sent to fetch them. Phlegyas ferries them across Styx. On the way they encounter Filippo Argenti, one of the Wrathful, who is recognized by Dante and tries to attack him. They draw near to the red-hot walls of the City and after a long circuit disembark at the gate. Virgil parleys with the Fallen Angels who are on guard there, but they slam the gate in his face. The two poets are obliged to wait for Divine assistance.*

I say, continuing, that ere we came
To the tower's foot, our eyes had long been led
To its summit, by two twinkling points of flame

Which we saw kindled there; while, far ahead,
And almost out of eyeshot, we espied
An answering beacon's flicker. So I said,

Turning to the well of wisdom at my side;
"What does it say? What does that other light
Wink back? Who make these signals?" He replied:

"Already across the water heaves in sight
What's to be looked for from the signal's waft,
So it be not veiled from thee by the blight

Of these marsh mists." I looked; and never shaft
So swift from bowstring sped through the thin air
As through those turbid waves a little craft

Came skimming toward us; one sole mariner
Guided its course, who shouted from the prow:
"Oho, thou wicked spirit! So thou art there!"

"Nay, Phlegyas, Phlegyas," said my lord, "peace now!
This time thou criest in vain; we are no meat
For thee—thou hast but to ferry us o'er the slough."

As one who hears of some outrageous cheat
Practised on him, and fumes and chokes with gall,
So Phlegyas, thwarted, fumed at his defeat.

So then my guide embarked, and at his call
I followed him; and not till I was in
Did the boat seem to bear a load at all.

When we were set, the ancient vessel then
Put forth at once, cleaving the water's grime
Deeper than her wont, our voyage to begin;

And as we ran the channel of the dead slime
There started up at me a mud-soaked head,
Crying: "Who are thou, come here before thy time?"

"Tho' I come," said I, "I stay not; thou who art made
So rank and beastly, who art thou?" "Go to;
Thou seest that I am one who weep," he said.

And I: "Amid the weeping and the woe,
Accursed spirit, do thou remain and rot!
I know thee, filthy as thou art—I know."

I. 3: *two twinkling points of flame*: to signal the approach of two passengers.
I. 18: *thou wicked spirit*: Phlegyas addresses only one of the poets; presumably because he (*a*) sees that Dante is not a shade, and (*b*) suspects Virgil of having brought him there for a felonious purpose (cf. Cantos IX. 54 and XII. 90).
I. 26: *not till I was in*: because of Dante's mortal weight.

Then he stretched out both hands to clutch the boat,
But the master was on his guard and thrust him back,
Crying: "Hence to the other dogs! Trouble him not!"

And after, laid his arms about my neck
And kissed my face and said: "Indignant soul,
Blessed is the womb that bare thee! This bold jack

Was an arrogant brute in the world, nor in his whole
Life can remembrance find one sweetening touch;
So must his raging spirit writhe here and roll.

Many who strut like kings up there are such
As here shall wallow hog-like in the mud,
Leaving behind nothing but foul reproach."

"Master," said I, "I tell thee, it were good
If I might see this villain soused in the swill
Before we have passed the lake—Oh, that I could!"

And he made answer: "Thou shalt gaze thy fill
Or ever thou set eyes on the far shore;
Herein 'tis fitting thou shouldst have thy will."

And soon I saw him set upon so sore
By the muddy gang, with such a pulling and hauling,
That I still praise and thank my God therefor.

"Have at Filippo Argenti!" they were bawling;
"Loo! loo!" The shade of the fierce Florentine
Turned on himself, biting with his teeth and mauling.

There left we him, as doth this tale of mine;
For on my ears there smote a wailing cry,
And I craned forward, eager to divine

Its meaning. "See, my son! it now draws nigh,"
Said my good lord, "the city named of Dis,
With its sad citizens, its great company."

And I: "Already I see its mosques arise
Clear from the valley yonder—a red shell,
As though drawn out of glowing furnaces."

And he replied: "The flames unquenchable
That fire them from within thus make them burn
Ruddy, as thou seest, in this, the nether Hell."

We now were come to the deep moats, which turn
To gird that city all disconsolate,
Whose walls appeared as they were made of iron.

A long way round we had to navigate
Before we came to where the ferryman
Roared: "Out with you now, for here's the gate!"

Thousand and more, thronging the barbican,
I saw, of spirits fallen from Heaven, who cried
Angrily: "Who goes there? why walks this man,

Undead, the kingdom of the dead?" My guide,
Wary and wise, made signs to them, to show
He sought a secret parley. Then, their pride

Abating somewhat, they called out: "Why, so!
Come thou within, and bid that fellow begone—
That rash intruder on our realm below.

Let him wend back his foolish way alone;
See if he can; for thou with us shalt stay
That through this nighted land hast led him on."

Reader, do but conceive of my dismay,
Hearing these dreadful words! It seemed quite plain
I nevermore should see the light of day.

"O Master dear, that seven times over again
Hast brought me safely through," said I, "and freed
From all the perils that in my path have lain,

Leave me not utterly undone! Indeed,
If we may not go forward, pray let's quit,
And hasten back together with all good speed!"

Then said my lord and leader: "Fear no whit;
There's none at all can stay our steps, nor make thee
Forbear the pass: such Power hath granted it.

Wait for me here; to cheerful thoughts betake thee;
Feed thy faint heart with hope, and calm thy breast,
For in this underworld I'll not forsake thee."

My gentle father's gone! I'm left distrest,
Abandoned here! Horrid perhapses throng
My doubtful mind, where yeas and noes contest.

His proffered terms I could not hear. Not long
He'd stood in talk with them, when suddenly
They all rushed jostling in again headlong,

---

l. 45: *blessed is the womb that bare thee*: It is important to understand this passage, since otherwise we may feel that Virgil is blasphemously encouraging Dante in very cruel and unchristian behaviour. We must distinguish here between the *literal* and *allegorical* meanings, which the poem fuses into a single image.

1. *Literally.* In Hell the soul is fixed eternally in that which it has chosen; it cannot, that is, enjoy there the good which it has rejected. Therefore, the reaction it calls forth from Dante can be no more than the reflection of what it has in itself. Thus Francesca calls forth that same easy pity which betrayed her to lust; Ciacco, the perfunctory pity which is all that the egotist can spare for his neighbours; the Hoarders and Spendthrifts, *because* they made no distinctions in life, are indistinguishable in eternity (Canto VII. 53, 54). But the Wrathful have rejected pity and chosen cruelty; therefore they can receive no pity, and goodness can only manifest itself to them as wrath, since they have chosen to know it so.
2. *Allegorically.* In the *vision* of Hell, the soul knows itself in a state of sin. Up to this moment Dante has only wondered, grieved, pitied, or trembled; now, for the first time, he sees (in the image of the damned soul) sin as it is—vile, degraded, and dangerous—and turns indignantly against it. For whatever inadequate and unworthy reasons, he accepts judgment and places himself on God's side. It is the first feeble stirring of the birth of Christ within the soul, and Virgil accordingly hails it with words that were used of Christ Himself. (*Luke* xi. 27.)

l. 61: *Filippo Argenti*: a Florentine knight of the Adimari family, of very violent temper, and so purse-proud that he is said to have had his horse shod with silver (hence the nickname "Argenti"). The Adimari were of the opposite faction to Dante and bitterly opposed his recall from banishment.

l. 68: *the city named of Dis*: i.e., named after Dis or Pluto, the King of Hell. Virgil uses the classical name; Dante, as a Christian, calls him Beelzebub, Satan, or Lucifer.

l. 70: *mosques*: Mohammedanism was looked on—correctly enough—by the Middle Ages as being a Christian heresy (see Canto XXVIII), and immediately inside the walls of Dis we shall, in fact, find the Circle of the Heretics. More generally, the "mosques" indicate that the City is devoted to a perverse and infidel cult.

l. 72: *glowing furnaces*: It is only in Nether Hell, below the walls of Dis, that we encounter any torment by fire.

l. 83: *spirits fallen from Heaven*: These are the rebel angels of Christian tradition; the classical monsters continue right down to the bottom of Hell, but here, in the Circles of the perverted will, we find also the more malignant spirits who knew the true God and opposed Him.

Leaving him outside. So the enemy
Slammed the gate in my master's face; who thus
Turned him, and came with slow steps back to me.

His eyes were downcast, and his anxious brows
Shorn of all boldness. Sighing he said: "What's here?
Who dares forbid me the Mansions Dolorous?"

And then aloud to me: "Have thou no fear
Though I be wroth; I'll win this trial of power,
Whatever hindrance they contrive in there.

Their truculence is no new thing; once before
'Twas tried at a less secret gate, whereon
No bars remain for ever. Above that door

Thou sawest the dead title. And now comes one,
This side already treading the steep abyss
And guardless passing all the circles down,

That shall unbar to us the gates of Dis."

THE IMAGES. *Phlegyas* in Greek mythology was a king of Boeotia, son of Ares the war-god by a human mother. His daughter Coronis was loved by Apollo; whereupon Phlegyas in his rage set fire to Apollo's temple. Apollo killed him with his arrows, and he was condemned to torment in Hades, (see *Aen.* vi. 618). He is thus an appropriate ferryman to ply between the Circle of the Wrathful and the City of the Impious.

The City of Dis. This comprises the whole of Nether Hell, and its ramparts, moated by the Styx, form a complete circle about the Pit, (see map). The sins tormented within the City are those in which the will is actively involved (the sins of Violence and Fraud), and its iron walls are the image of a rigid and determined obstinacy in ill-doing.

Virgil's Repulse at the Gate. Humanism is always apt to underestimate, and to be baffled by, the deliberate will to evil. Neither is it any sure protection against Heresy. The *allegory* is further developed in the next canto.

CANTO IX

THE STORY. *Dante, alarmed by Virgil's anxiety, tactfully inquires of him whether he really knows the way through Hell, and gets a reassuring answer. The Furies appear and threaten to unloose Medusa. A noise like thunder announces the arrival of a Heavenly Messenger, who opens the gates of Dis and rebukes the demons. When he has departed, the Poets enter the City and find themselves in a great plain covered with the burning tombs of the Heretics.*

Seeing my face, and what a coward colour
It turned when he came back, my guide was quick
To put away his own unwonted pallor.

He stood and leaned intent, as who should prick
His ear to hear, for far one could not see,
So black the air was, and the fog so thick.

"Nay, somehow we must win this fight," said he;
"If not . . . That great self-proffered aid is lent;
But oh! how long his coming seems to be!"

I saw too clearly how his first intent
Was cloaked by what came after; what he said
Was not what he'd designed, but different.

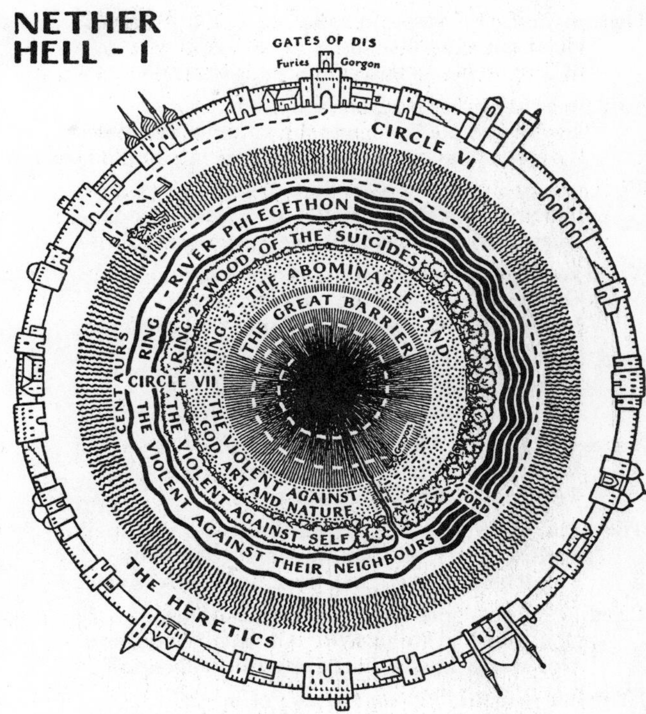

HERESY : VIOLENCE – THE SINS OF THE LION

But none the less his speech increased my dread—
For maybe I pieced out the broken phrase
To a worse ending than was in his head.

"Did any ever, descending from that place
Where loss of hope remains their only woe,
Thread to its depth this hollow's dreary maze?"

I put this question. He replied: "Although
'Tis rare that one of us should come this way
Or undertake the journey I now go,

Yet once before I made it, truth to say,
Conjured by cruel Erichtho, she whose spell
Wont to call back the shades to their dead clay.

I was not long stripped of my mortal shell
When she compelled me pass within yon wall
To fetch a spirit from Judas' circle of Hell;

That is the deepest, darkest place of all,
And farthest from high Heaven's all-moving gyre;
I know the way; take heart—no ill shall fall.

---

l. 125: *a less secret gate*: the gate of Hell, when the devils sought to oppose Christ's entrance into Limbo.
l. 127: *the dead title*: the inscription over Hell-gate (Canto III. 1-6).
l. 8: *that great self-proffered aid is lent*: How Virgil summons this aid or knows of its coming is not stated; presumably he is aware that the help of Him who harrowed Hell is always available for a Christian soul in need.
l. 16: *descending from that place*, etc.: i.e., from Limbo.
l. 29: *high Heaven's all-moving gyre:* i.e., the *Primum Mobile,* the highest of the revolving heavens, which imparts motion to all the rest.

On every side, the vast and reeking mire 31
Surrounds this city of the woe-begot,
Where now's no entering, save with wrath and ire . . ."

And he went on, saying I know not what, 34
For my whole being was drawn up with my eyes
To where the tower's high battlements burned red-hot:

For there of a sudden I saw three shapes arise, 37
Three hellish Furies, boltered all with blood;
Their form and bearing were made woman-wise;

Vivid green hydras girt them, and a brood 40
Of asps and adders, each a living tress,
Writhed round the brows of that fell sisterhood.

And, knowing well those handmaids pitiless 43
Who serve the Queen of everlasting woe:
"Behold," said he, "the fierce Erinyes.

There on the right Alecto howls, and lo! 46
Megaera on the left; betwixt them wails
Tisiphone." And he was silent so.

They beat their breasts, and tore them with their nails, 49
Shrieking so loud that, faint and tremulous,
I clutched the poet; and they, with fiercer yells,

Cried: "Fetch Medusa!", glaring down on us, 52
"Turn him to stone! Why did we not requite—
Woe worth the day!—the assault of Theseus?"

"Turn thee about, and shut thine eyelids tight; 55
If Gorgon show her face and thou thereon
Look once, there's no returning to the light."

Thus cried the master; nor to my hands alone 58
Would trust, but turned me himself, and urgently
Pressed my palms close and covered them with his own.

O you whose intellects keep their sanity, 61
Do you mark well the doctrine shrouded o'er
By the strange verses with their mystery.

Then o'er that dull tide came the crash and roar 64
Of an enormous and appalling sound,
So that the ground shuddered from shore to shore;

A sound like the sound of a violent wind, around 67
The time of opposing heats and the parched weather,
When it sweeps on the forest and leaps with a sudden bound,

Shattering and scattering the boughs hither and thither; 70
Superb with a tower of dust for harbinger
It goes, while the wolves and herdsmen flee together.

He loosed my eyes: "Now look," said he, "see there, 73
Yonder, beyond the foam of the ancient lake,
Where the harsh marsh mist hangs thickest upon the air."

And as the frogs, spying the foeman snake, 76
Go squattering over the pond, and dive, and sit
Huddled in the mud, even so I saw them break

Apart, whole shoals of ruined spirits, and flit 79
Scudding from the path of one who came to us,
Walking the water of Styx with unwet feet.

His left hand, moving, fanned away the gross 82
Air from his face, nor elsewise did he seem
At all to find the way laborious.

And when I saw him, right well did I deem 85
Him sent from Heaven, and turned me to my guide,
Who signed me to be still and bow to him.

What scorn was in his look! He stood beside 88
The gate, and touched it with a wand; it flew
Open; there was no resistance; all stood wide.

"Outcasts of Heaven, despicable crew," 91
Said he, his feet set on the dreadful sill,
"Why dwells this foolish insolence in you?

Why kick against the pricks of that great Will 94
Whose purpose never can be overborne,
And which hath oft increased your sorrows still?

Or say, what boots it at the Fates to spurn? 97
Think how your Cerberus tried it, and yet bears
The marks of it on jowl and throttle torn."

Then back he went by those foul thoroughfares, 100
And unto us said nothing, but appeared
Like one much pressed with weightier affairs

Than the cares of those before him. So we stirred 103
Our footsteps citywards with hearts reposed,
Safely protected by the heavenly word.

Through the great ward we entered unopposed, 106
And I, being all agog to learn what state
Of things these huge defensive works enclosed,

Gazed round, the moment I had passed the gate, 109
And saw a plain, stretched spacious on both sides,
Filled with ill woes and torments desolate.

For as at Arles, where soft the slow Rhone slides, 112
Or as at Pola, near Quarnaro's bay,
That fences Italy with its washing tides,

The ground is all uneven with the array, 115
On every hand, of countless sepulchres,
So here; but in a far more bitter way:

For strewn among the tombs tall flames flared fierce, 118
Heating them so white-hot as never burned
Iron in the forge of any artificers.

The grave-slabs all were thrown back and upturned, 121
And from within came forth such fearful crying,
'Twas plain that here sad tortured spirits mourned.

"O Sir," said I, "who are the people lying 124
In these grim coffers, whose sharp pains disclose
Their presence to the ear by their sad sighing?"

I. 44: *the Queen of everlasting woe*: Proserpine, or Persephone, queen of the classical underworld.
I. 54: *the assault of Theseus*: Theseus, king of Athens, tried to carry off Persephone from Hell; he failed, but was rescued by Hercules. The Furies mean that, if they had succeeded in punishing Theseus, other living men would have been deterred from venturing into the underworld, and they had better make an example of Dante.
I. 88: *what scorn was in his look!* In Hell, God's power is experienced only as judgment, alien and terrible.
I. 97: *what boots it at the Fates to spurn?* The Angel uses two forms of speech—one Christian, "that great Will," the other classical, "the Fates"—to denote the Divine power. The evil powers which he is addressing belong both to the Christian and to the pre-Christian mythology.
I. 98: *Cerberus*: As the last of his labours, Hercules brought Cerberus out of Hell, mauling his throat in the process.
I. 112: *Arles*: where in Dante's time the Rhone spread into a stagnant lake, contains many ancient tombs, said to be those of Charlemagne's soldiers slain in battle against the Saracens at Aleschans. *Pola* (on the Adriatic) is said to have formerly contained about 700 tombs of Slavonians, buried on the seashore.

And he: "The great heresiarchs, with all those,
Of every sect, their followers; and much more
The tombs lie laden than thou wouldst suppose.

Here like with like is laid; and their flames roar
More and less hot within their monuments."
Then we moved onward, and right-handed bore

Between those fires and the high battlements.

THE IMAGES. *The Furies (Erinyes)* in Greek mythology were the avenging goddesses who haunted those who had committed great crimes. In the *allegory*, they are the image of the fruitless remorse which does not lead to penitence.

Medusa was a *Gorgon* whose face was so terrible that anyone who looked upon it was turned to stone. In the *allegory*, she is the image of the despair which so hardens the heart that it becomes powerless to repent.

The Heavenly Messenger. He is, I think, the image of Divine revelation, (*a*) stirring the conscience, (*b*) safeguarding the mind against false doctrine.

The Heretics. See next canto.

CANTO X

THE STORY. *As the Poets are passing along beneath the city walls, Dante is hailed by Farinata from one of the burning tombs, and goes to speak to him. Their conversation is interrupted by Cavalcante dei Cavalcanti with a question about his son. Farinata prophesies Dante's exile and explains how the souls in Hell know nothing of the present, though they can remember the past and dimly foresee the future.*

Thus onward still, following a hidden track
Between the city's ramparts and the fires,
My master goes, and I go at his back.

"O sovran power, that through the impious gyres,"
Said I, "dost wheel me as thou deemest well,
Speak to me, satisfy my keen desires.

Those that find here their fiery burial,
May they be seen? for nothing seems concealed;
The lids are raised, and none stands sentinel."

And he: "All these shall be shut fast and sealed
When from Jehoshaphat they come anew,
Bringing their bodies now left far afield.

And hereabouts lie buried, close in view,
Epicure and his followers—they who hold
That when the body dies the soul dies too.

Hence that demand thou choosest to unfold
May here and now be fully satisfied,
Likewise thy hidden wish, to me untold."

"Alas," said I, "from thee I'd never hide
One single thought, save that short speech is sweet,
As thou hast warned me once or twice, dear guide."

"O Tuscan, walking thus with words discreet
Alive through the city of fire, be it good to thee
To turn thee hither awhile, and stay thy feet.

Thy native accent proves thee manifestly
Born of the land I vexed with so great harm—
A noble land, and too much vext, maybe."

This summons threw me into such alarm,
Coming suddenly from a tomb, that in my dread
I shrank up close against my escort's arm.

"Come, come, what art thou doing? Turn round," he said;
"That's Farinata—look! he's risen to sight,
And thou canst view him all, from waist to head."

Already my eyes were fixed on his; upright
He had lifted him, strong-breasted, stony-fronted,
Seeming to hold all Hell in deep despite;

And my good guide, with ready hands undaunted
Thrusting me toward him through the tombs apace,
Said: "In thy speech precision is what's wanted."

I reached the vault's foot, and he scanned my face
A little while, and then said, with an air
Almost contemptuous: "What's thy name and race?"

Being anxious to obey, I did not care
To make a mystery, but told all out;
He raised his brows a trifle, saying: "They were

Foes to me always, stubborn, fierce to flout
Me and my house and party; I was quick
To chase them, twice I put them to the rout."

"Quite true; and by that same arithmetic,"
Said I, "they rallied all round and came back twice;
Your side, it seems have not yet learnt the trick."

Just then, close by him, I saw slowly rise
Another shadow, visible down to the chin;
It had got to its knees, I think. It moved its eyes

I. 11: *Jehoshaphat*: The belief that the Valley of Jehoshaphat would be the scene of the Last Judgment was derived from *Joel* iii. 2, 12.

I. 18: *thy hidden wish, to me untold*: Virgil can often read Dante's thoughts, and sometimes seems to take a Sherlock-Holmes-like pleasure in surprising him by doing so. He knows that Dante's question covers an unspoken wish to see certain distinguished Florentines who had been followers of the school of Epicurus.

II. 22-7: *O Tuscan . . . thy native accent*: Dante is recognized as a Tuscan by his idiom and as a Florentine by his accent.

I. 32: *Farinata*: This is Farinata degli Uberti, the famous leader of the Ghibellines in Florence, about whom Dante had already inquired of Ciacco (Canto VI. 78). After he and his party were banished in 1250, they allied themselves with the Siennese and, in 1260, lured the Florentine Guelfs into an ambush and defeated them with appalling slaughter at Montaperti, near the river Arbia.

The Guelfs, among whom were Dante's ancestors, fled from Florence. They never forgave Farinata, and when they returned to power, they razed the Uberti palaces to the ground and pronounced relentless decrees of exile against the whole family. Farinata was condemned for heresy in 1283.

II. 48-51: *twice . . . to the rout . . . they came back twice*: The first rout of the Guelfs was in 1248 and their first return in 1251. The second rout was at Montaperti in 1260, and the second and final return in 1266, after the Battle of Benevento, which extinguished the Ghibellines' hope of ever regaining power in Florence. (Note how Farinata's pride instantly evokes a corresponding pride in Dante.)

I. 53: *another shadow*: Cavalcante dei Cavalcanti, a Guelf knight, noted, like Farinata, for his Epicureanism. His son, Guido Cavalcanti, was a fellow-poet and friend of Dante and son-in-law to Farinata.

Round about me, as though it sought to win 55
Sight of some person in my company;
At last, when all such hope lay quenched within,

It wept: "If thy grand art has made thee free 58
To walk at large in this blind prison of pain,
Where is my son? why comes he not with thee?"

"I come not of myself," I answered plain, 61
"He that waits yonder leads me on this road,
For whom, perhaps, your Guido felt disdain."

The words he used, together with his mode 64
Of torment, were sufficient to betray
His name, as thus my pointed answer showed.

He leapt upright, crying: "What? what dost thou say? 67
He felt? why felt? are life and feeling o'er?
Looks he no longer on the pleasant day?"

Then, seeing me hesitate awhile before 70
I made reply, he let himself suddenly fall
Backward again, and showed his face no more.

But that great-hearted spirit, at whose call 73
I'd stayed my steps, his countenance did not move,
Nor bent his neck, nor stirred his side at all.

"And if," he spoke straight on where we broke off, 76
"If they have missed the trick of it, I burn
Less in this bed than with the thought thereof.

But thou, ere fifty times the light return 79
To that queen's face who reigneth here below,
Shalt find out just what that trick costs to learn.

But tell me why, as thou dost hope to go 82
Back to the light, thy people make decrees
So harsh against our house, and hate us so."

"That field of havoc and bloody butcheries," 85
I answered him, "when Arbia's stream ran red,
Have filled our temple with these litanies."

He sighed before he spoke, and shook his head: 88
"'Faith, I was not alone there, nor had gone
In with the rest without good cause," he said;

"But when they made agreement, every one, 91
To wipe out Florence, and I stood to plead
Boldly for her—ay, there I was alone."

"Now, so may rest come some time to your seed," 94
Said I, "pray solve me this perplexity,
Which ties my brains in a tight knot indeed.

It seems you can foresee and prophesy 97
Events that time will bring, if I hear right,
But with things present, you deal differently."

"We see," said he, "like men who are dim of sight, 100
Things that are distant from us; just so far
We still have gleams of the All-Guider's light.

But when these things draw near, or when they are, 103
Our intellect is void, and your world's state
Unknown, save some one bring us news from there.

Hence thou wilt see that all we can await 106
Is the stark death of knowledge in us, then
When time's last hour shall shut the future's gate."

At this my conscience smote me; I again 109
Addressed him: "Tell that fallen shade, I pray,
His son still walks the world of living men;

If I was silent when he asked me, say 112
'Twas only that my wits were in a worry,
Snared by that error which you've swept away."

And now my guide was calling me to hurry, 115
Wherefore I urged the shade, with greater haste,
To say who else was in that cemetery.

"I lie," said he, "with thousands; in this chest 118
The second Frederick lies; our ranks include
The Cardinal; I will not name the rest."

He spoke, and sank; returning to where stood 121
The ancient poet, I pondered what they meant,
Those words which seemed to bode me little good.

Then he moved on, and later, as we went, 124
"Why so distraught?" said he. I set to work
Answering his question to his full content.

Sagely he bade me: "See thou mind and mark 127
Those adverse warnings; now to what I say—"
And here he raised his finger—"prithee, hark!

When thou shalt stand bathed in the glorious ray 130
Of her whose blest eyes see all things complete
Thou'lt learn the meaning of thy life's whole way."

I. 58: *thy grand art* (lit.: "genius"): Cavalcante thinks that if poetical genius has enabled Dante to visit Hell in the flesh, his own poet-son should have been able to accompany his friend.

I. 63: *your Guido felt disdain*: either because Guido, as a modern, despised classical poetry; or because, as a Guelf, he disliked Virgil's imperialism; or because, as a sceptic, he had no use for Virgil's religious piety: or all three. The passage has been much disputed. Note that, in speaking to Farinata and Cavalcante, Dante shows his respect by using the formal "you" in place of the familiar "thou."

I. 70: *seeing me hesitate*: Dante is taken aback at finding that Cavalcante does not know whether Guido is alive or dead, and so does not answer immediately.

I. 80: *queen . . . here below:* Proserpine, also identified with Hecate and Diana; the Moon. Fifty lunar months from the date of the vision (April 1300) bring us to the summer of 1304. Dante was banished in 1302, and the efforts of the White Guelfs to return to Florence were finally frustrated in July 1304.

I. 87: *these litanies*: This may mean that prayers were offered in church for the downfall of the Ghibellines, or else that, when the Guelfs were in power, the decrees of exile were formally signed and published in the church of St. John.

I. 92: *to wipe out Florence*: After Montaperti, the wholesale destruction of Florence was voted by all the Ghibelline leaders except Farinata, who, drawing his sword, cried out that if they attempted it he was ready to lay down a thousand lives, if he had them, in defence of his native city; and Florence was accordingly spared.

I. 108: *when time's last hour shall shut the future's gate*: "When earthly time ceases there will be nothing to know—nothing but the sin of the past and that sin in the present. . . . Charity has already failed here; presently prophecies and tongues and knowledge are to cease too." (Charles Williams: *The Figure of Beatrice*, p. 127.) Farinata's explanation clears up Dante's perplexity, and he hastens to convey to Cavalcante that his son is still alive. Guido's death was, however, so near in time that it had become veiled (I. 103) from the knowledge of the damned.

I. 119: *the second Frederick*: the Emperor Frederick II (1194-1250).

I. 120: *the Cardinal*: Ottaviano degli Ubaldini.

I. 131: *her whose blest eyes*: Beatrice, under whose guidance Dante, in the Heaven of Mars, has the course of his life revealed to him by his ancestor Cacciaguida (*Para.* xvi).

With that, leaving the wall, we turned our feet
Towards the centre, by a path that ran
Down to a vale, whose fumes rose high to greet

Our nostrils, even where the descent began.

THE IMAGES. *The Heretics.* "It is necessary to remember what Dante meant by heresy. He meant an obduracy of the mind; a spiritual state which defied, consciously, 'a power to which trust and obedience are due'; an intellectual obstinacy. A heretic, strictly, was a man who knew what he was doing; he accepted the Church, but at the same time he preferred his own judgment to that of the Church. This would seem to be impossible, except that it is apt to happen in all of us after our manner." (Charles Williams: *The Figure of Beatrice*, p. 125.)

The tombs of the intellectually obdurate—iron without and fire within—thus fittingly open the circles of Nether Hell: the circles of deliberately willed sin.

CANTO XI

THE STORY. *While the Poets pause for a little on the brink of the descent to the Seventh Circle, Virgil explains to Dante the arrangement of Hell.*

Where a great cliff fell sheer, its beetling brow
Ringed with huge jagged rocks, we reached the brink
O'erhanging the still ghastlier dens below;

And here so overpowering was the stink
The deep Abyss threw off, that we withdrew
Staggered, and for a screen were forced to shrink

Behind a massive vault where, plain to view,
Stood writ: "I hold Pope Anastasius,
Lured by Photinus from the pathway true."

"We'll wait awhile," the master said, "that thus
Our senses may grow used to this vile scent,
And after that, it will not trouble us."

And I: "But let's not lose the time so spent;
Think now what compensation thou canst find."
"Surely," he answered, "such was my intent.

See now, my son: three narrowing circles wind
Within these cliffs," thus he took up the tale,
"Each under each, like those we've left behind.

Damned spirits fill them all; thou canst not fail
To know them at a glance, though, if I state
How and for what they're here pent up in jail.

Of all malicious wrong that earns Heaven's hate
The end is injury; all such ends are won
Either by force or fraud. Both perpetrate

Evil to others; but since man alone
Is capable of fraud, God hates that worst;
The fraudulent lie lowest, then, and groan

Deepest. Of these three circles, all the first
Holds violent men; but as threefold may be
Their victims, in three rings they are dispersed.

God, self, and neighbour—against all these three
Force may be used; either to injure them
Or theirs, as I shall show convincingly.

Man on his neighbour may bring death or mayhem
By force; or damage his chattels, house, and lands
By harsh extortions, pillage, or fire and flame;

So murderers, men who are violent of their hands,
Robbers and plunderers, all find chastisement
In the first ring, disposed in various bands.

Against themselves men may be violent,
And their own lives or their own goods destroy;
So they in the second ring in vain repent

Who rob themselves of your world, or make a toy
Of fortune, gambling and wasting away their purse,
And turn to weeping what was meant for joy.

Those men do violence to God, who curse
And in their hearts deny Him, or defame
His bounty and His Natural Universe;

So the third ring sets its seal on the double shame
Of Sodom and of Cahors, and on the speech
Of the froward heart, dishonouring God's great name.

Fraud, which gnaws every conscience, may be a breach
Of trust against the confiding, or deceive
Such as repose no confidence; though each

Is fraud, the latter sort seems but to cleave
The general bond of love and Nature's tie;
So the second circle opens to receive

Hypocrites, flatterers, dealers in sorcery,
Panders and cheats, and all such filthy stuff,
With theft, and simony and barratry.

---

l. 8: *Pope Anastasius*: Anastasius II (Pope 496-8); incurred the imputation of heresy by giving communion to Photinus, a deacon of Thessalonica in communion with the Church of Constantinople, which was at this time at odds with the Western Church over the definition of the union of the two natures in Christ's one person. Dante probably got his information directly or indirectly from the *Liber Pontificalis*, a source hostile to Anastasius (see Duchesne's edition, vol. i, p. 258).

l. 16: *three narrowing circles*: i.e., the Circle of *Violence* (Circle 7) and the two Circles of *Fraud* (Circles 8 and 9). Virgil begins by describing that part of Nether Hell which still lies ahead. The circles get narrower as the Pit deepens.

l. 22: *malicious wrong*: the phrase "malicious" is here used generally to cover both Violence and Fraud; i.e., all deliberately injurious behaviour.

ll. 28-51: These lines describe the Circle of *Violence* (Circle 7), with its three component Rings devoted respectively to violence against (*i*) others, (*ii*) self, (*iii*) God.

l. 41: *their own lives or their own goods*: Property is regarded, in accordance with Roman Law, as an extension of the personality. Consequently, to damage or destroy one's own or one's neighbour's goods is a sin of the same type as the damage and destruction of one's own or one's neighbour's body. Similarly (ll. 46-8), blasphemy against God's creation is blasphemy against God, for the creation belongs to Him.

l. 49: *the double shame of Sodom and of Cahors*: Sodomy (homosexual vice) is so named from *Genesis* xix. The "shame of Cahors" is Usury—so called from Cahors in the South of France, notorious for its many usurers in Dante's time. Ring iii thus punishes three sorts of violence against God: Sodomy, Usury, and Blasphemy.

ll. 52-66: Virgil now goes on to describe, successively, the two Circles of *Fraud.* There are two kinds of Fraud: the one (Fraud Simple, Circle 8) only betrays the confidence of humanity in general; the other (Fraud Complex, Circle 9) in addition betrays the confidence of those who had special reason to trust, and is, therefore, not merely fraudulent but treacherous.

l. 57: *the second circle*: i.e., the *second* in Nether Hell; the *first* Circle of *Fraud*; Circle 8 in the general scheme.

Fraud of the other sort forgets both love
Of kind, and that love too whence is begot
The special trust that's over and above;

So, in the smallest circle, that dark spot,
Core of the universe and throne of Dis,
The traitors lie; and their worm dieth not."

"Master," said I, "how clear thy discourse is!
It makes this gulf's arrangement plain as plain,
With all its inmates; I quite follow this;

But tell me: all those others, whom the rain
Beats, and the wind drives, and the sticky mire
Bogs, and those brawlers with their shrill campaign—

Why dwell not they in the city red with fire
If to God's wrath they too are fallen a prey?
Or if not, wherefore is their plight so dire?"

"What error has seduced thy reason, pray?"
Said he, "thou art not wont to be so dull;
Or are thy wits woolgathering miles away?

Dost thou not mind the doctrine of thy school—
Those pages where the *Ethics* tells of three
Conditions contrary to Heaven's will and rule,

Incontinence, vice, and brute bestiality?
And how incontinence offends God less
Than the other two, and is less blameworthy?

If thou wilt think on what this teaching says,
Bearing in mind what sort of sinners dwell
Outside the city, and there endure distress,

Thou'lt see why they lie separate from these fell
Spirits within, and why God's hammer-blow
Of doom smites them with weight less terrible."

"O Sun that healest all dim sight, thou so
Dost charm me in resolving of my doubt,
To be perplexed is pleasant as to know.

Just once again," said I, "turn thee about
To where thou spak'st of usury as a crime
Against God's bounty—ravel me that knot out."

"Not in one place," said he, "but many a time
Philosophy points out to who will learn,
How Nature takes her course from the Sublime

Intellect and Its Art; note that; then turn
The pages of thy *Physics*, and not far
From the beginning, there shalt thou discern

How your Art, as it best can, follows her
Like a pupil with his master; we may call
This art of yours God's grandchild, as it were.

By Art and Nature, if thou well recall
How Genesis begins, man ought to get
His bread, and make prosperity for all.

But the usurer contrives a third way yet,
And in herself and in her follower, Art,
Scorns Nature, for his hope is elsewhere set.

Follow me now; I think we should depart;
Horizon-high the twinkling Fishes swim,
And the Wain's right over Caurus; we must start

Onward and downward, over the chasm's rim."

THE IMAGES. The only image here is that of Hell itself. Dante's classification of sins is based chiefly on Aristotle, with a little assistance from Cicero. Aristotle divided wrong behaviour into three main kinds: (A) *Incontinence* (uncontrolled appetite); (B) *Bestiality* (perverted appetite); (C) *Malice* or *Vice* (abuse of the specifically human faculty of reason). Cicero declared that all injurious conduct acted by either (a) *Violence* or (b) *Fraud.* Combining these two classifications, Dante obtains three classes of sins: I. *Incontinence;* II. *Violence* (or *Bestiality*); III. *Fraud* (or *Malice*). These he subdivides and arranges in 7 Circles: 4 of Incontinence, 1 of Violence, and 2 of Fraud.

To these purely ethical categories of wrong *behaviour* he, as a Christian, adds 2 Circles of wrong *belief:* 1 of *Unbelief* (Limbo) and 1 of *Mischief* (the Heretics), making 9 Circles in all. Finally, he adds the Vestibule of the Futile, who have neither faith nor works; this, not being a Circle, bears no number.

Thus we get the 10 main divisions of Hell. In other books of the *Comedy* we shall find the same numerical scheme of 3, made up by subdivision to 7; plus 2 (= 9); plus 1 (= 10). Hell, however, is complicated by still further subdivision. The Circle of *Violence* is again divided into 3 Rings; the Circle of Fraud Simple into 10 Bowges; and the Circle of Fraud Complex into 4 Regions. So that Hell contains a grand total of 24 divisions (see section map).

I. 61: *fraud of the other sort*: i.e., the treacherous sort—Circle 9.
I. 65: *Dis:* the classical king of Hades: i.e., Satan.
II. 68 *sqq.: this gulf*: i.e., Nether Hell. Dante now asks about the people whom he had already seen in Upper Hell, and why they are not punished within the City of Dis. Virgil reminds him of the seventh chapter of Aristotle's *Ethics*, where incontinence is said to be less reprehensible than bestiality or malice, and treachery the worst conduct of all.
II. 95 *sqq.: usury as a crime against God's bounty*: Dante's thought in this passage (which is that of the Medieval Church) is of such urgent relevance to-day that it is worth while to disentangle it from his (to us) rather odd and unfamiliar phraseology. What he is saying is that there are only two sources of real wealth: Nature and Art—or, as we should put it, Natural Resources and the Labour of Man. The buying and selling of Money as though it were a commodity creates only a spurious wealth, and results in injury to the earth (Nature) and the exploitation of labour (Art). The attitude to men and things which this implies is a kind of blasphemy; since Art derives from Nature, as Nature derives from God, so that contempt of them is contempt of Him.
I. 101: *thy Physics*: i.e., the *Physics* of Aristotle (ii. 2).
I. 107: *how Genesis begins*: "And the Lord God took the man, and put him into the garden of Eden" [put the resources of Nature at his disposal] "to dress it and to keep it" [that he might preserve and cultivate them by his art and labour]. (*Gen.* ii 15.)
I. 113: *the twinkling Fishes*, etc.: Virgil again indicates the time by describing the position of the unseen stars. The Wain (the Plough, or Great Bear) is lying right over the abode of Caurus, the north-west wind, and the constellation of Pisces (the Fishes) is just rising over the horizon. This is the zodiacal sign which immediately precedes Aries (the Ram); and since the signs rise at two-hourly intervals, and the Sun is in Aries (Canto I. 37), it is now two hours before sunrise on Holy Saturday—i.e., about 4 A.M.

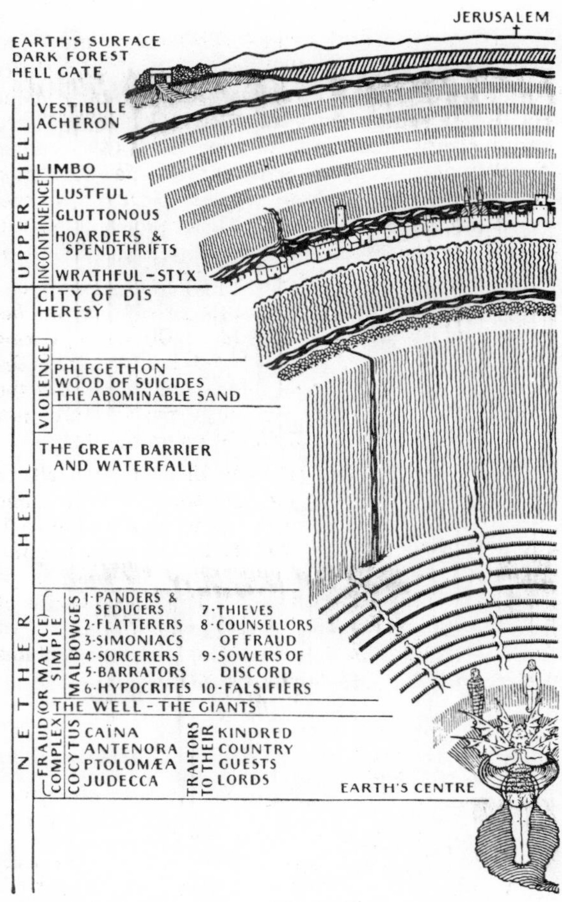

CANTO XII

THE STORY. *At the point where the sheer precipice leading down to the Seventh Circle is made negotiable by a pile of tumbled rock, Virgil and Dante are faced by the Minotaur. A taunt from Virgil throws him into a fit of blind fury, and while he is thrashing wildly about, the Poets slip past him. Virgil tells Dante how the rocks were dislodged by the earthquake which took place at the hour of Christ's descent into Limbo. At the foot of the cliff they come to Phlegethon, the river of boiling blood, in which the Violent against their Neighbours are immersed, and whose banks are guarded by Centaurs. At Virgil's request, Chiron, the chief Centaur, sends Nessus to guide them to the ford and carry Dante over on his back. On the way, Nessus points out a number of notable tyrants and robbers.*

The place we came to, to descend the brink from,
Was sheer crag; and there was a Thing there—making,
All told, a prospect any eye would shrink from.

Like the great landslide that rushed downward, shaking 4
The bank of Adige on this side Trent,
(Whether through faulty shoring or the earth's quaking)

So that the rock, down from the summit rent 7
Far as the plain, lies strewn, and one might crawl
From top to bottom by that unsure descent,

Such was the precipice; and there we spied, 10
Topping the cleft that split the rocky wall,
That which was wombed in the false heifer's side,

The infamy of Crete, stretched out a-sprawl; 13
And seeing us, he gnawed himself, like one
Inly devoured with spite and burning gall.

Then cried my Wisdom: "How now, hellion! 16
Thinkst thou the Duke of Athens comes anew,
That slew thee in the upper world? Begone,

Monster! not guided by thy sister's clue 19
Has this man come; only to see and know
Your punishments, he threads the circle through."

Then, as a bull pierced by the mortal blow 22
Breaks loose, and cannot go straight, but reels in the ring
Plunging wildly and staggering to and fro,

I saw the Minotaur fall a-floundering, 25
And my wary guide called: "Run! run for the pass!
Make good thy going now, while his rage has its fling."

So down we clambered by that steep crevasse 28
Of tumbled rock; and oft beneath my tread
The stones slipped shifting with my unwonted mass.

I went bemused; wherefore: "Perchance thy head 31
Puzzles at this great fissure here, watched o'er
By the furious brute I quelled just now," he said.

"I'd have thee know, when I went down before, 34
That other time, into Deep Hell this way,
The rock had not yet fallen; but now for sure

'Twas thus, if I judge rightly: on the day 37
When that great Prince to the First Circle above
Entered, and seized from Dis the mighty prey,

Shortly ere He came, the deep foul gulf did move 40
On all sides down to the centre, till I thought
The universe trembled in the throes of love.,

---

l. 5: *the bank of Adige*: Dante likens the fall of rock to the Slavini di Marco on the Adige between Trent and Verona. An early commentator (Benvenuto da Imola) says that the comparison is very apt, since before the landslide the bank was as sheer as the wall of a house and absolutely unscalable; but afterwards it was just possible to scramble down it.

l. 13: *the infamy of Crete*: the Minotaur was the offspring of Pasiphae (wife of Minos, king of Crete), who became enamoured of a beautiful bull, and was brought to him in the effigy of a cow ("the false heifer") made for her by the cunning artificer Daedalus. Minos kept the Minotaur in the labyrinth at Cnossos. Later, having waged a successful war against Athens, he compelled the Athenians to send him a yearly tribute of seven youths and seven maidens to be devoured by the monster. The Minotaur was slain by Theseus, "the Duke of Athens," who made his way back from the labyrinth by the aid of a clue of thread given to him by Ariadne, daughter of Minos and Pasiphaë.

l. 34: *when I went down before*: Virgil's previous journey (Canto IX. 22) was made before the death of Christ.

l. 39: *the mighty prey*: i.e., the souls of the patriarchs (Canto IV. 55 *sqq.*).

l. 42: *the universe trembled in the throes of love*, etc.: Empedocles taught that the universe was held together in tension by discord among the elements; but that from time to time the motions of the heavens brought about a state of harmony (love). When this happened, like matter flew to like, and the universe was once more resolved into its original elements and so reduced to chaos.

Whereby, as some believe, the world's been brought 43
Oft-times to chaos; in that moment, here
And elsewhere, was these old rocks' ruin wrought.

But now look to the vale, for we draw near 46
The river of blood, where all those wretches boil
Whose violence filled the earth with pain and fear."

O blind, O rash and wicked lust of spoil, 49
That drives our short life with so keen a goad,
And steeps our life eternal in such broil!

I saw a river, curving full and broad 52
Arcwise, as though the whole plain's girth embracing.
Just as my guide had told me on the road;

And 'twixt the bank and it came centaurs racing 55
By one and one, their bows and quivers bearing
As when through the woods of the world they went a-chasing.

They checked their flight to watch us downward faring, 58
And three of the band wheeled out and stood a-row,
Their bows and chosen arrows first preparing;

And one cried out from far: "Hey! whither go 61
You on the cliff there? What's your penalty?
Speak where you stand; if not, I draw the bow."

The master shouted back: "That word shall be 64
For Chiron there; headstrong thou dost remain,
And so thou ever wast—the worse for thee."

Then, nudging me: "That's Nessus, who was slain 67
For fair Deïanira, and in the aftermath
With his own blood avenged his blood again.

Gazing upon his breast, betwixt them both, 70
Achilles' tutor, the great Chiron, stands;
The third is Pholus, once so full of wrath.

All round the fosse they speed in myriad bands, 73
Shooting at every soul that tries to lift
Higher out of the blood than doom demands."

We were near them now, those creatures snell and swift, 76
And Chiron took an arrow, and with the notch
Put back upon his jaws his snowy drift

Of beard, and having freed his great mouth: "Watch," 79
Said he to those who stood with him; "mark you
How the feet of the one behind move what they touch?

Those of the dead are not used so to do," 82
And my good guide, now standing at his breast
Where the two natures join, replied: "Quite true,

He is alive; so, on his lonely quest, 85
Needs must I lead him through the vales of night;
Necessity brings him here, not sport nor jest;

From the singing of alleluias in the light 88
Came she who laid on me this novel charge;
The man's no poacher, I'm no thievish sprite.

Now by the power that moves my steps at large 91
On this wild way, lend us a courier
Whom we may follow by the river's marge,

To show us where the ford is, and to bear 94
This other upon his back across the tide,
For he's no spirit to walk the empty air."

Then Chiron turned on his right flank, and cried: 97
"Wheel round and guide them, Nessus; if you're met
By another patrol, see that it stands aside."

So with this trusty escort, off we set 100
Along the bank of the bubbling crimson flood,
Whence the shrieks of the boiled rose shrill and desperate.

There saw I some—plunged eyebrow—deep they stood; 103
And the great centaur said to me: "Behold
Tyrants, who gave themselves to ravin and blood.

Here they bewail oppressions manifold; 106
Alexander's here; Dionysius too, whose brute
Fury long years vexed Sicily uncontrolled.

That forehead there, with locks as black as soot, 109
Is Azzolino, and that fair-haired one
Obizzo d'Este, he whose light was put

Out, up above there, by his stepson son." 112
I turned here to the poet, who said, "Why, yes,
He first, I second now, must guide thee on."

Further along, the centaur checked his pace 115
Beside a second gang, who seemed to start
Far as the throat from the stream's boiling race.

He showed one shade set by itself apart, 118
Saying: "There stands the man who dared to smite,
Even in the very bosom of God, the heart

They venerate still on Thames." Next, reared upright 121
Both head and chest from the stream, another horde
Appeared, full many known to me by sight.

---

l. 47: *river of blood*: Phlegethon.

l. 62: *what's your penalty?* The Centaurs mistake Dante and Virgil for damned souls going to their allotted place of torment.

l. 65: *Chiron*: the great Centaur to whom Achilles, Peleus, Theseus, and other Greek heroes went to be tutored. He was famous for his skill in hunting, gymnastics, medicine, music, and prophecy, and was accounted the wisest and most just of the Centaurs. Accordingly, though placing him among the guardians of Phlegethon, Dante has given him the most amiable character of all the inhabitants of Hell.

l. 67: *Nessus*: This Centaur attempted to carry off Deïanira, the wife of Hercules, while taking her over a river on his back. Hercules killed him with an arrow, and the dying Nessus told Deïanira to take some of his blood, since it would act upon Hercules as a love-charm. Deïanira did so, and later, fearing that Hercules was falling in love with another woman, put on him a shirt steeped in the blood of Nessus. The blood was poisonous and, after suffering intolerable agonies, Hercules placed himself on a pyre of wood and had himself burned to death.

l. 72: *Pholus*: Little is known of him except that he also was killed by Hercules. The three Centaurs possibly typify three passions which may lead to violence: wrath, lust, and the will to dominate.

l. 88: *from the singing of alleluias . . . came she*: i.e.,Beatrice.

l. 90: *no poacher, and . . . no thievish sprite*: Virgil means that he and Dante have not come, like Theseus or Orpheus, to try and rob Hell of any of its victims.

l. 112: *stepson son:* Actually his son; Dante calls him "stepson" because of his unnatural behaviour.

l. 120: *the heart they venerate still on Thames*: Prince Henry, son of Richard, Duke of Cornwall, and nephew to Henry III of England, was killed in the Cathedral at Viterbo, during High Mass ("in the very bosom of God"), by Guy, son of Simon de Montfort (1270). A statue of him, holding in its right hand the casket containing his heart, is said to have been placed on London Bridge.

Thus shallow and shallower still the red blood poured 124
Till it was only deep enough to cook
The feet; and here it was we passed the ford.

And the centaur said to me: "Now, prithee, look: 127
Just as, this side, it ever grows less deep,
On that, I'd have thee know, the boiling brook

Lowers its rocky bed, down-shelving steep, 130
Until it comes full circle, and joins its ring
There where the tyrants are condemned to weep.

Here doth the heavenly justice rack and wring 133
Pyrrhus and Sextus; here it overbears
That scourge of earth called Attila the King;

And here for ever it milks the trickling tears 136
Squeezed by the scald from those rough highwaymen
The Pazzian and Cornetan Riniers."

With this he turned and crossed the ford again. 139

THE IMAGES. *The Circle of Violence.* From now to the end of Canto XVII we are in the circle devoted to *Violence* or *Bestiality* (the "sins of the Lion") which, together with the Circle of the Heretics, makes up the first division of Nether Hell.

The Minotaur and The Centaurs. In this and the next ring we find demon-guardians compounded of man and brute. They are the types of perverted appetite—the human reason subdued to animal passion. The Minotaur had the body of a man and the head of a bull; the Centaurs were half-man, half-horse.

Phlegethon—"the fiery"—is the third chief river of Hell. Like Acheron and Styx, it forms a complete circuit about the abyss, and it is deep at one side and shallow at the other. The sinners whose fiery passions caused them to shed man's blood are here plunged in that blood-bath for ever.

CANTO XIII

THE STORY. *The Poets enter a pathless Wood. Here Harpies sit shrieking among the withered trees, which enclose the souls of Suicides. Pier delle Vigne tells Dante his story, and also explains how these shades come to be changed into trees and what will happen to their bodies at the Last Day. The shades of two Profligates rush through the wood, pursued and torn by black hounds. Dante speaks to a bush containing the soul of a Florentine.*

Ere Nessus had regained the bank beyond
We'd pushed into a forest, where no mark
Of any beaten path was to be found.

No green here, but discoloured leaves and dark, 4
No tender shoots, but writhen and gnarled and tough,
No fruit, but poison-galls on the withered bark.

Wild beasts, from tilth and pasture slinking off 7
'Twixt Cecina and Corveto, never come
To lurk in scrub so tangled or so rough.

There the foul Harpies nest and are at home, 10
Who chased the Trojans from the Strophades
With dismal outcry ominous of doom.

Wide-winged like birds and lady-faced are these, 13
With feathered belly broad and claws of steel;
And there they sit and shriek on the strange trees.

And the good master thus began: "'Twere well, 16
Ere going further, thou shouldst understand,
Thou'rt now in the second ring, and shalt be, till

Thou comest to the abominable sand. 19
But now, look well, and see a thing whose telling
Might kill my credit with thee out of hand."

Already all round I heard a mournful wailing, 22
But, seeing none to wail, I stopped short, blinking
Bewilderedly, as though my wits were failing.

I think he must have thought that I was thinking 25
That all these voices through the boles resounding
Were those of folk who from our gaze hid shrinking,

Because he said: "If from these boughs abounding 28
Thou wilt pluck off one small and single spray,
Thy thoughts will stagger at their own dumbfounding."

So I put forth my hand a little way, 31
And broke a branchlet from a thorn-tree tall;
And the trunk cried out: "Why tear my limbs away?"

Then it grew dark with blood, and therewithal 34
Cried out again: "Why dost thou rend my bones?
Breathes there no pity in thy breast at all?

We that are turned to trees were human once; 37
Nay, thou shouldst tender a more pious hand
Though we had been the souls of scorpions."

As, when you burn one end of a green brand, 40
Sap at the other oozes from the wood,
Sizzling as the imprisoned airs expand,

So from that broken splint came words and blood 43
At once: I dropped the twig, and like to one
Rooted to the ground with terror, there I stood.

"O wounded soul," my sage replied anon, 46
"Might I have brought him straightway to believe
The thing he'd read of in my verse alone,

Never had he lifted finger to mischieve 49
Thee thus; but 'twas incredible; so I
Prompted his deed, for which myself must grieve.

But tell him who thou wast, that he may try 52
For some amends, to right thee with mankind
When, by permission, he returns on high."

To this the trunk made answer: "Words so kind 55
Tempt me to speech; nor take it in ill part
If at some length I'm lured to speak my mind.

---

l. 131: *until it comes full circle*: Apparently Dante and Virgil have made the full half-circle of Phlegethon, from the deep side where the tyrants stand to the shallow ford.

l. 2: *we'd pushed into a forest*: Note that the three rings of Circle 7 are all on the same level.

l. 8: *'twixt Cecina and Corveto*: Cecina (a river in the province of Volterra) and Corveto (a small town on the river Marta) mark the boundaries of the Tuscan Maremma, where, in Dante's time, there were many dense forests full of wild animals.

l. 19: *the abominable sand*: Ring iii (see Canto XIV).

l. 48: *the thing he had read of in my verse alone*: i.e., in the *Aeneid* (iii 22 *sqq.*). (This famous episode of the bleeding tree has been frequently imitated, not only by Dante, but notably also by Ariosto, Tasso, and Spenser.)

I am he that held both keys of Frederick's heart, 58
To lock and to unlock; and well I knew
To turn them with so exquisite an art,

I kept his counsel and let few men through; 61
Loyal to my glorious charge did I remain,
And sacrificed my sleep and my strength too.

But that great harlot which can ne'er refrain 64
From Caesar's household her adulterous eyes,
The vice of kings' courts and their common bane,

Inflamed all hearts against me, and these likewise, 67
Flaming, inflamed Augustus to distrust,
Till my glad honours turned to obloquies.

So, in a scornful spirit of disgust, 70
And thinking to escape from scorn by death,
To my just self I made myself unjust;

But by these strange new roots my trunk beneath, 73
Never to my most honourworthy lord,
I swear to you, was I found false of faith;

And if to that bright world indeed restored 76
One of you goes, oh, heal my memory,
Which lies and bleeds from envy's venomed sword."

He paused there; and the poet said to me: 79
"While he is mute, let not this moment go,
But speak, and ask what more seems good to thee."

And I: "Ask thou, whate'er thou think'st will do 82
My hunger good and satisfy me well;
I cannot ask, pity unhearts me so."

Wherefore: "So may this man prove liberal," 85
Thus he resumed, "thine errand to perform,
Imprisoned spirit, do thou be pleased to tell

How souls get cramped into this knotty form, 88
And, if thou canst, if any shall do off
These limbs one day and find release therefrom."

At this the trunk blew hard, and the windy puff 91
After this wise soon whistled into speech:
"You shall be answered with brief words enough.

When the wild soul leaps from the body, which 94
Its own mad violence forces it to quit,
Minos dispatches it down to the seventh ditch.

It falls in the wood; no place is picked for it, 97
But as chance carries it, there it falls to be,
And where it falls, it sprouts like a corn of wheat,

And grows to a sapling, and thence to a wild tree; 100
Then the Harpies feed on its leaves, and the sharp bite
Gives agony, and a vent to agony.

We shall take our flight, when all souls take their flight, 103
To seek our spoils, but not to be rearrayed,
For the spoils of the spoiler cannot be his by right;

Here shall we drag them, to this gloomy glade; 106
Here shall they hang, each body evermore
Borne on the thorn of its own self-slaughtering shade."

Thinking the trunk might wish to tell us more, 109
We stood intent, when suddenly there came crashing
On our astonished ears a wild uproar,

As the huntsman hears the boar and the chase dashing 112
Down on his post like the noise of a hurricane,
With trampling of beasts and all the branches smashing.

And lo! on the left of us came two that ran 115
Naked and torn, with such a furious burst
As snapped to flinders every forest fan.

"O death, come now, come quickly!" thus the first; 118
And the second, finding himself outstripped in the rush,
Cried: "Lano, thy legs were not so nimble erst

At the jousts of Toppo." So in the last push, 121
His breath failing perhaps, he shot sidelong
And made one group of himself and a thick bush.

And filling the woods behind them came a throng 124
Of great black braches, fleet of foot and grim,
And keen as greyhounds fresh-slipped from the thong;

They seized the skulker, and set their teeth in him, 127
And rent him piecemeal, and away they went
Carrying the wretched fragments limb by limb.

Then my guide drew me by the hand, and bent 130
His steps to the poor bush, left mangled there,
Gasping vain protests through each bleeding rent.

"O Jacomo," it cried, "of Sant' Andrea, 133
Why make a screen of me? What was the good?
Am I to blame for thy misspent career?"

Then said my gentle master when he stood 136
Beside it: "Who wast thou, that through such tattered
Wounds sighest out thy grief mingled with blood?"

"O spirits, who come in time to see me battered 139
Thus shamefully, and all my foliage torn,"
It said, "bring back the leaves that lie there scattered,

I. 58: *he that held both keys of Frederick's heart*: Pier delle Vigne, for many years chief counsellor to the Emperor Frederick II (mentioned in Canto X). Accused of conspiring against his master, he was disgraced, imprisoned, and blinded, and in despair took his own life.

I. 64: *that great harlot*: i.e., Envy (see I. 78).

I. 68: *Augustus*: i.e., Caesar = the Emperor.

I. 77: *heal my memory*: The fact that Dante places Pier in the Wood of the Suicides, and not among the traitors at the bottom of the Pit, shows that he believed him to have been falsely accused.

I. 102: *a vent to agony*: The trees can only utter when broken and bleeding. The Harpies, by tearing the leaves, make wounds from which issue the wails that puzzled Dante (II. 22-7).

I. 105: *the spoils of the spoiler cannot be his by right*: (lit.: "it is not just that a man should have what he takes from himself")—Dante treats suicide as a kind of self-robbery (Canto XI. 43). Here he means, I think, that a robber cannot have a just title to the goods he has plundered.

I. 107: *here shall they hang*: Nowhere, perhaps, does Dante assert more clearly than in this moving and terrible image his conviction of the intimate and unbreakable bond between spirit and flesh. The Suicides willed the death of the flesh, but they cannot be rid of it: their eternity is an eternity of that death. (The absurd charge of heretically denying the resurrection of the body was brought against Dante on the strength of these lines, but only by those to whom the language of poetic imagery is a sealed book.)

I. 115: *two that ran*: "The first" is Lano of Siena; he belonged to a club of young rakes (referred to again in Canto XXIX), who sold up all their estates and "blued" the proceeds within twenty months. Lano then threw away his life in an encounter between the Sienese and Aretines at a ford called Pieve del Toppo (1288). "The second" is a Paduan, Jacomo di Sant' Andrea, who, not content with such pranks as playing ducks and drakes with gold pieces on the Lagoon at Venice, had a pleasant way of burning down his own and other people's houses for the fun of it. He is said to have been put to death in 1239 by Ezzelino.

Gather them close beneath the shrub forlorn.
My city was she that for the Baptist changed
Her ancient patron, wherefore on her scorn

Still by his art he makes himself avenged;
Yea, did not Arno's bridge even now retain
Some image of the guardian she estranged,

Those citizens who built her walls again
On the ashes left by Attila, had been baffled
Wholly, and all their labour spent in vain;

I am one that made my own roof-tree my scaffold."

THE IMAGES. *The Wood.* This forms the Second Ring of the Circle of the Violent, and contains the souls of those who wantonly destroyed their own lives or their own goods, "turning to weeping what was meant for joy" (Canto XI. 45).

The Harpies. Here again we have a mixture of brute and human. The Harpies had the bodies of birds, long claws, and the faces of women pale with hunger. When Aeneas and his companions came to the Islands of the Strophades, the Harpies swooped down upon their food, devouring and defiling it (*Aen.* iii. 209 *sqq.*). They are the image of the "will to destruction."

The Bleeding Trees. The sin of Suicide is, in an especial manner, an insult to the body; so, here, the shades are deprived of even the semblance of the human form. As they refused life, they remain fixed in a dead and withered sterility. They are the image of the self-hatred which dries up the very sap of energy and makes all life infertile.

The Profligates. These are very different from the "Spendthrifts" of Canto VII, who were merely guilty of extravagance. The profligates here were men possessed by a depraved passion, who dissipated their goods for the sheer wanton lust of wreckage and disorder. They may be called the image of "gambling-fever"—or, more generally, the itch to destroy civilization, order, and reputation.

CANTO XIV

THE STORY. *In a desert of Burning Sand, under a rain of perpetual fire, Dante finds the Violent against God, Nature, and Art. The Violent against God lie supine, facing the Heaven which they insulted; among these is Capaneus, blasphemous and defiant in death as in life. The Poets pick their way carefully between the forest and the hot sand till they come to the edge of a boiling, red stream. Here Virgil explains the origin of all the rivers of Hell.*

Love of my native place with kind constraint
Moving me, I brought back the scattered leaves
To him whose voice already was grown faint;

Then on we went, to reach the bound which cleaves
The second ring from the third, and saw appear
A terrible art which justice here conceives.

I say, to make all this new matter clear,
We reached a plain which spurns all foliage
And every live plant from its surface sere.

The doleful wood garlands it like a hedge,
As the sad moat garlands the wood around;
And here we stayed our steps 'twixt edge and edge.

An arid, close-packed sand, in fashion found
Not otherwise than that which once was trod
By Cato's marching feet, such was the ground.

Fearful indeed art thou, vengeance of God!
He that now reads what mine own eyes with awe
Plainly beheld, well may he dread thy rod!

Great herds of naked spirits here I saw,
Who all most wretchedly bewailed their lot,
Seeming subjected to a diverse law.

Some on the ground lay supine in one spot,
And some upon their hunkers squatted low,
Others roamed ceaselessly and rested not;

Most numerous were the rovers to-and-fro;
Of those that lay, the numbers were more small,
But much the loudest were their cries of woe.

And slowly, slowly dropping over all
The sand, there drifted down huge flakes of fire,
As Alpine snows in windless weather fall.

Like as Alexander, in those torrider
Regions of Ind, saw flaming fireballs shed
Over his host, floating to earth entire,

So that his men and he took pains to tread
The soil, trampling the blaze out with their feet,
Since it was easier quenched before it spread,

Even so rained down the everlasting heat,
And, as steel kindles tinder, kindled the sands,
Redoubling pain; nor ever ceased the beat

And restless dance of miserable hands,
Flapping away, now this side and now that,
The raw smart of the still-fresh-biting brands.

---

l. 143: *my city*: Florence. Her "ancient patron" was Mars. When the Florentines were converted to Christianity they built the Church of St. John Baptist on the site of the temple of Mars, and stowed the heathen statue away in a tower near the Arno. After the burning of the city by Totila (whom Dante, misled by some of the chroniclers, seems to have confused with Attila), the mutilated remains of the god were recovered from the river and set up on the Ponte Vecchio; and but for this, so the superstition ran, Florence could never have been rebuilt. Even so, it was said, Mars continued to vex the faithless city with continued internecine strife. But Dante may be covertly reproaching the Florentines with abandoning martial pursuits and concentrating on amassing the florins stamped with the Baptist's image.

l. 151: *one that made my own roof-tree my scaffold:* The speaker has been variously identified. Florence seems to have had a kind of "suicide-wave" about Dante's time; his son Jacopo observes that it is a special vice of the Florentines to hang themselves, "just as the people of Arezzo are given to throwing themselves down wells."

l. 3: *whose voice already was grown faint*: The small broken twigs were already clotted with blood, and the bush had no voice left.

l. 15: *Cato's marching feet*: The march of Cato of Utica through the Libyan desert in 47 B.C. is described in Lucan's *Pharsalia* ix. 411 *sqq*.

ll. 22 *sqq.*: *some lay . . . some squatted . . . others roamed*: the Violent against God, Art, and Nature respectively.

l. 31: *like as Alexander*: Dante seems to have taken this story about Alexander the Great from Albertus Magnus (*De Meteoris*), who in turn took it, with certain alterations, from the spurious *Letter of Alexander to Aristotle about the Marvels of the Indies*.

I thus began: "Master, strong to frustrate 43
All hostile things, save only indeed those grim
Fiends who opposed our entrance at the gate,

Who is the shade that lies, mighty of limb, 46
Contorted and contemptuous, scorning the flame,
So that the rain seems not to ripen him?"

But he himself, soon as he heard me frame 49
This question to my guide about him, cried:
"That which in life I was, in death I am.

Though Jove tire out his armourer, who supplied 52
His wrathful hand with the sharp thunder-stone
That in my last day smote me through the side;

Though he tire all the rest out, one by one, 55
In Mongibel's black stithy, and break them quite,
Crying, 'To aid! Vulcan, lay on, lay on!'

As once before he cried at Phlegra's fight; 58
Yea, though he crush me with his omnipotence,
No merry vengeance shall his heart delight."

Then my guide spoke out with a vehemence 61
Such as I never had heard him use before:
"O Capaneus, since thy proud insolence

Will not be quenched, thy pains shall be the more; 64
No torment save thine own hot rage could be
A fitting cautery to thy rabid sore."

Then said with milder mouth, turning to me: 67
"This was one of the seven kings who pressed
The siege of Thebes; he held, and seemingly

Still holds, God light, and flouts Him with a jest; 70
Yet, as I told him, his mad mouthings make
A proper brooch for such a brazen breast.

Now follow me, and look to it that thou take 73
No step upon the burning sand, but keep
Thy feet close back against the woodland brake."

Silent we came where, from that forest deep, 76
A little brook poured forth a bubbling jet
Whose horrid redness makes my flesh still creep.

It was like that stream of the Bulicame, set 79
Apart and shared by the women of the town;
And straight out over the sand ran the rivulet.

Its bed, and both its shelving banks, and the crown 82
Of the margins left and right, were turned to stone;
Which made me think that here our path led down.

"Of all the marvels I as yet have shown 85
Thine eyes, since first we entered by that door
Of which the threshold is denied to none,

Nothing we've seen deserves thy wonder more 88
Than this small stream which, flowing centreward,
Puts out all flames above its either shore."

Thus said my guide; whom I at once implored 91
Since he'd so whet my appetite to taste
His food, immediately to spread the board.

"Far off amid the sea there lies a waste 94
Country," said he, "called Crete, beneath whose king,
Once on a long-lost time, the world was chaste.

A mount is there, named Ida; many a spring 97
Laughed through its ferns of yore and the valleys smiled—
Forsaken now, like some old, mouldering thing.

There Rhea once found safe cradling for her child, 100
And to hide his cries, lest danger come to pass,
Let fill the hills with Corybant clamours wild.

A great old man stands under the mountain's mass; 103
Toward Damietta he keeps his shoulders holden,
And he looks on Rome as though on a looking-glass.

He towers erect, and his head is purely golden, 106
Of the silver fine his breast and arms and hands,
Of brass down to the cleft his trunk is moulden,

And thence to the ground his legs are iron bands, 109
Save that the right foot's baked of the earthen clay,
And that is the foot upon which he chiefly stands.

All but the gold is cracked, and from the splay 112
Of that great rift run tears gathering and dripping,
Till out through the cavern floor they wear their way

Into this vale, from rock to rock down-dipping, 115
Making Acheron, Styx and Phlegethon; then they take
Their downward course, by this strait conduit slipping,

II. 51 *sqq.*: *that which in life* I *was.*, etc.: This is Capaneus, who took part in the war of the "Seven against Thebes." While scaling the city wall, he boasted that not even Jove could stop him, and was struck with a thunder-bolt. Dante read about him in the *Thebaïd* of Statius (the poet whom he afterwards meets in Purgatory).

I. 52: *his armourer*: Vulcan, the blacksmith of the gods, who had his forge in Mongibello (Mount Etna).

I. 58: *Phlegra's fight*: the battle in which the rebellious Titans were overthrown by the gods (see Canto XXXI. 91 *sqq.*).

I. 70: *still holds God light*: Note again the double vocabulary (as in Canto IX. 94-9). Capaneus says "Jove;" Virgil says "God," meaning the same thing. The heathen are judged by their own standards.

I. 77: *a small brook*: This is the effluent of Phlegethon, which, after crossing the Wood of the Suicides, now runs across the Third Ring to plunge over the edge of the Pit. It has the property of petrifying the sand which forms its bed.

I. 79: *the Bulicame*: a hot sulphur-spring of reddish colour near Viterbo, part of whose waters were specially portioned off for use in the prostitutes' quarter.

I. 90: *puts out all flames*: The steam from the boiling river forms a cloud above the banks and quenches the flames. (Canto XV. l.)

II. 95-6: *beneath whose king, . . . the world was chaste*: i.e., in the fabled "Golden Age" of Saturn, the mythical king of Crete.

I. 100: *Rhea*: wife of Saturn and mother by him of Jupiter. It had been prophesied to Saturn that he would be dethroned by his own son, and he therefore devoured all his children as soon as they were born. Rhea deceived him by wrapping a stone in swaddling-clothes, and fled with Jupiter to Mount Ida; when the child cried, she caused the Corybants (Bacchantes) to make a wild clamour so that Saturn should not hear him.

II. 103 *sqq.*: *a great old man*, etc.: This *allegory* of the successively degenerating periods of history is founded in *Daniel* ii. 32 *sqq.*; the four ages of man (gold, silver, brass, iron) are taken from Ovid: *Metamorphoses* i 89 *sqq.* Only the Golden Age gave no cause for tears. The feet of iron and clay may be respectively the Empire and the Church. The statue stands in the middle of the Mediterranean (the centre of civilization), looking from the old civilization of the East (Damietta) to the new civilization of the West (Rome).

To where there is no more downward; there they make 118
Cocytus; and what that's like I need not tell;
For thine own eyes shall look on Cocytus lake."

Then I to him: "But, Master, if this rill 121
Flows from our world, why is it only found
Here on this bank, nor elsewhere visible?"

And he to me: "Thou knowest, the place is round; 124
Though thou hast come a good long way, 'tis true,
Still wheeling leftward toward the Pit's profound,

Thou hast not yet turned the full circle through; 127
So why put on such a bewildered air
If now and then we come upon something new?"

And I again: "Where's Lethe, sir? and where 130
Is Phlegethon? The first thou leav'st aside,
Tracing the second to that water there."

"Thy questions all delight me," he replied, 133
"But for the one—thyself canst answer it:
Think of the boiling of the blood-red tide.

And Lethe thou shalt see, far from this Pit, 136
Where go the souls to wash them in its flood,
Their guilt purged off, their penitence complete."

He added: "Come; it's time to leave the wood; 139
See that thou follow closely where I tread;
The margins burn not, they shall make our road,

And all the fires are quenched there overhead." 142

THE IMAGES. *The Sand.* "In these circles of the Violent the reader is peculiarly conscious of a sense of sterility. The bloody river, the dreary wood, the harsh sand, which compose them, to some extent are there as symbols of unfruitfulness" (Charles Williams: *The Figure of Beatrice*, p. 129). The images of the sand and burning rain are derived from the doom of Sodom and Gomorrah, (*Gen.* xix. 24).

The Blasphemers. Capaneus the Blasphemer is chosen as the particular image of Violence against God: he is an image of Pride, which makes the soul obdurate under judgment. The arrangement of Hell, being classical, allots no special place to Pride (held by Christianity to be the root of all sin), but it offers a whole series of examples of Pride, each worse than the last, as the Pit deepens. Farinata's pride is dark and silent; that of Capaneus is loud and defiant, but not yet so wholly ignoble as that of Vanni Fucci (Canto XXV. 1), far down in the Eighth Circle.

CANTO XV

THE STORY. *While crossing the Sand upon the dyke banking Phlegethon, Dante sees the Violent against Nature, who run perpetually, looking towards the human body against which they offended. He meets his old teacher, Brunetto Latini, whom he addresses with affectionate regret and deep gratitude for past benefits. Brunetto predicts Dante's ill-treatment at the hands of the Florentines.*

Now the hard margin bears us on, while steam
From off the water makes a canopy
Above, to fend the fire from bank and stream.

Just as the men of Flanders anxiously 4
'Twixt Bruges and Wissant build their bulwarks wide
Fearing the thrust and onset of the sea;

Or as the Paduans dyke up Brenta's tide 7
To guard their towns and castles, ere the heat
Loose down the snows from Chiarentana's side,

Such fashion were the brinks that banked the leat, 10
Save that, whoe'er he was, their engineer
In breadth and height had builded them less great.

Already we'd left the wood behind so far 13
That I, had I turned back to view those glades,
Could not have told their whereabouts; and here,

Hurrying close to the bank, a troop of shades 16
Met us, who eyed us much as passers-by
Eye one another when the daylight fades

To dusk and a new moon is in the sky, 19
And knitting up their brows they squinnied at us
Like an old tailor at the needle's eye.

Then, while the whole group peered upon me thus, 22
One of them recognized me, who caught hard
At my gown's hem, and cried: "O marvellous!"

When he put out his hand to me, I stared 25
At his scorched face, searching him through and through,
So that the shrivelled skin and features scarred

Might not mislead my memory: then I knew: 28
And, stooping down to bring my face near his,
I said: "What, you here, Ser Brunetto? you!"

And he: "My son, pray take it not amiss 31
If now Brunetto Latini at thy side
Turn back awhile, letting this troop dismiss."

I. 118: *no more downward*: the centre of the earth and of gravity. Cocytus (Canto XXXIV) is the last of the infernal rivers.

II. 130 *sqq.*: *Lethe and . . . Phlegethon*: Virgil explains that Dante has already seen Phlegethon—it is the river of the tyrants, though its name was not mentioned in Canto XII. *Lethe* (the river of forgetfulness) flows to the Centre from the Earthly Paradise on Mount Purgatory on the other side of the world.

II. 4 *sqq.*: Dante compares the dykes to those built in the Low Countries to keep out the sea, and to the embankments made by the Paduans along the river Brenta to prevent flooding in spring, when the river is swollen by melted snow from Chiarentana (probably Carenzana, a mountain in the Trentino).

I. 11: *their engineer*: God is, of course, the supreme Architect of Hell (Canto III. 4-6); but the constructional details would be supposed to be carried out by some one of the "Intelligences" who are His ministers. As we see from I. 23, the top of the dyke was about a man's height from the sand.

I. 29: *to bring my face near his*: another reading, perhaps even more attractive, has: "And reached my hand down to that face of his, Saying . . ."

I. 30: *Ser Brunetto*: Messer Brunetto Latini (*c.* 1220-94) was a Florentine Guelf, a man of considerable learning. An early commentator says "that he was a neighbour of Dante and taught him a great many things; that he did not care for the soul, as he was altogether worldly; that he sinned greatly in unnatural crime, and scoffed much at the things of God and Holy Church" (Vernon). He wrote in French a prose encyclopedia called *Le Livre dou Tresor* or *Thesaurus* (see I. 119), and an abridged version in Italian verse, *Il Tesoretto*. Though he was an influence in Dante's early life, he was not a "tutor" or "schoolmaster," but a man holding public office in the state, till he was banished with other Guelfs after the Battle of Montaperti.

"With all my heart I beg you to," I cried; 34
"Or I'll sit down with you, as you like best,
If he there will permit—for he's my guide."

"Oh, son," said he, "should one of our lot rest 37
One second, a hundred years he must lie low,
Nor even beat the flames back from his breast.

Therefore go on; I at thy skirts will go, 40
And then rejoin my household, who thus race
Forever lost, and weeping for their woe."

I durst not venture from the road to pace 43
Beside him, so I walked with down-bent head,
Like some devout soul in a holy place.

He thus began: "What chance or fate has led 46
Thy footsteps here before thy final day?
And who is this that guides thee?" So I said:

"Up in the sunlit life I lost my way 49
In a dark vale, before my years had come
To their full number. Only yesterday

At morn I turned my back upon its gloom; 52
This other came, found me returning there,
Stopped me, and by this path now leads me home."

And he made answer: "Follow but thy star; 55
Thou canst not fail to win the glorious haven,
If in glad life my judgment did not err.

Had I not died so soon, I would have given 58
Counsel and aid to cheer thee in thy work,
Seeing how favoured thou hast been by heaven.

But that ungrateful, that malignant folk 61
Which formerly came down from Fiesole,
And still is grained of mountain and hewn rock,

For thy good deeds will be thine enemy— 64
With cause; for where the bitter sloes are rooted
Is no fit orchard for the sweet fig-tree.

A blind people, and always so reputed, 67
Proud, envious, covetous, since times remote;
Cleanse off their customs lest thou be polluted.

Fortune has honours for thee—of such note, 70
Both sides will seek to snatch thee and devour;
But yet the good grass shall escape the goat.

Let Fiesole's wild beasts scratch up their sour 73
Litter themselves from their rank native weed,
Nor touch the plant, if any such can flower

Upon their midden, in whose sacred seed 76
Survives the Roman line left there to dwell
When this huge nest of vice began to breed."

I answered him: "Might I have had my will, 79
Believe me, you'd not yet been thrust apart
From human life; for I keep with me still,

Stamped on my mind, and now stabbing my heart, 82
The dear, benign, paternal image of you,
You living, you hourly teaching me the art

By which men grow immortal; know this too: 85
I am so grateful, that while I breathe air
My tongue shall speak the thanks which are your due.

Your words about my future I'll write fair, 88
With other texts, to show to a wise lady
Who'll gloss them, if I ever get to her.

This much I'd have you know: I can stand steady, 91
So conscience chide not, facing unafraid
Whatever Fortune brings, for I am ready.

Time and again I've heard these forecasts made; 94
The whims of Luck shall find me undeterred,
So let her ply her wheel, the churl his spade."

And when my master's ear had caught that word 97
He turned right-face-about, and looked me straight
In the eyes and said: "Well-heeded is well-heard."

Yet none the less I move on in debate 100
With Ser Brunetto, asking him whose fame
In all his band is widest and most great.

"Some," he replies, "it will be well to name; 103
The rest we must pass over, for sheer dearth
Of time—'twould take too long to mention them.

All these, in brief, were clerks and men of worth 106
In letters and in scholarship—none more so;
And all defiled by one same taint on earth.

In that sad throng goes Francis of Accorso, 109
And Priscian; could thy hunger have been sated
By such scabbed meat, thou mightest have seen also

Him whom the Servant of servants once translated 112
From Arno to Bacchiglione, where he left
The body he'd unstrung and enervated.

I would say more, but must not; for a drift 115
Of fresh dust rising from the sandy ground
Warns me to cease and make my going swift;

Here come some folk with whom I mayn't be found; 118
Keep handy my *Thesaurus*, where I yet
Live on; I ask no more." Then he turned round,

I. 56: *the glorious haven*: Brunetto seems to mistake Dante, and think that he is only aspiring to lasting fame on earth, and says that, if he himself had not died too soon, he would have helped him to achieve perfection of knowledge.

II. 61-79: According to Florentine tradition, Julius Caesar besieged Catiline in Fiesole; when the city fell, the Romans built a new one—Florence—on the Arno, to be peopled half by Fiesolans and half by Romans. Dante attributes much of the strife and disorder in Florence to this adulteration of the Roman stock by families from Fiesole and the surrounding country (see *Para* xvi. 67-9). "Blind Florentines" was a proverbial reproach, whose origin is now lost in mists of legend (cf. our "wise fools of Gotham").

I. 71: *both sides will seek to snatch thee*: i.e., Dante will be persecuted by both parties.

I. 87: *my tongue shall speak the thanks which are your due*: The episode of Brunetto Latini gives the lie to the common assertion that Dante put only his enemies in Hell. But while maintaining, on the one hand, that personal feelings cannot remove the difference in God's sight between right and wrong, he asserts, on the other, that, as between man and man, nothing can ever remove the obligation to acknowledge benefits received. "For ever and ever (derivation) must be remembered, willingly praised, and ardently published before earth and heaven. . . . Such a loyalty is necessary to the life of the City." (Charles Williams: *The Figure of Beatrice*, p. 130.)

I. 89: *to show to a wise lady*: Dante, remembering Virgil's words (Canto X. 130-32), says he will ask Beatrice to explain all these prophecies about himself.

I. 96: *the churl his spade*: Let Luck turn her wheel, and the labourer turn the soil—Dante shall remain as unmoved by the one as by the other. Virgil seems not altogether to approve this parade of indifference, and warns Dante that he will do well to heed what is said to him.

I. 112: *him whom the Servant of servants once translated*: Andrea dei Mozzi. The title "Servant of the servants of God" is one of the official titles of the Pope.

And seemed like one of those who over the flat 121
And open course in the fields beside Verona
Run for the green cloth; and he seemed, at that,

Not like a loser, but the winning runner. 124

THE IMAGES. *The Sodomites* are chosen as the image of all pervese vices which damage and corrupt the natural powers of the body. (It is here, for instance, that Dante would probably place drugtakers and the vicious type of alcoholics.) Their perpetual fruitless running forms a parallel, on a lower level, to the aimless drifting of the Lustful in Canto V.

CANTO XVI

THE STORY. *Dante is already within earshot of the waterfall at the end of the path, when he meets the shades of three distinguished Florentine noblemen and gives them news of their city. At the edge of the cliff, Virgil throws Dante's girdle into the gulf below, and in answer to this signal a strange form comes swimming up towards them.*

Already I'd reached a place where the dull thrumming
Of the water tumbling down to the circle below
Was heard ahead like the sound of a beehive's humming,

When lo! three shadows, running all in a row, 4
Broke from a company that across the sand
Was passing under the rain of the burning woe.

They came towards us, crying with one voice: "Stand, 7
Thou there, the fashion of whose dress would seem
To make thee a native of our perverted land!"

O me! the marks I saw upon every limb, 10
Branded in by the flames, old scars and new—
It makes me heartsick only to think of them.

Heedful, my teacher heard those spirits through, 13
Then turned his face my way: "Now wait," said he;
"To those the utmost courtesy is due.

Were not this place by nature arrowy 16
With fire, I'd say it was far more suitable
That thou shouldst hurry to them than they to thee."

They raised their voices again when we stood still, 19
Renewing their ancient wail; then, coming close,
The three of them formed themselves into a wheel.

Like old-time champions, stript, oiled, on their toes 22
Circling, and spying for vantage of hold and place
Before getting down to clinches and to blows,

Just so they wheeled; but each one kept his gaze 25
So fixed on me that all the time one way
The feet went, and another way the face.

"Eh, though scorn prompt thee," one began to say, 28
"Seeing our squalor, and scorched, filthy state,
From us and from our prayers to turn away,

Let our great fame yet move thee to relate 31
What man thou art, that free and dangerless
Thus through deep Hell dost move thy living feet.

He in whose tracks I tread here, nevertheless, 34
For all he now goes naked and peeled and scored,
Was nobler in degree than thou couldst guess.

Grandson to good Gualdrada was this lord, 37
He was called Guido Guerra, and his fame
In life stood high with counsel and with sword.

He that behind me treads the sand and flame 40
Was Tegghiai' Aldobrandi once; applause
Up in your world should surely greet that name.

Here, partner in their pain, am I, who was 43
Jacopo Rusticucci; of this woe
My bestial wife's the first and foremost cause."

Could I have kept the fire off, there below, 46
I'd have leapt down to them, and I declare
I think my tutor would have let me go;

But I'd have burnt and baked me so, that fear 49
Quite vanquished the good-will which made me yearn
To clasp them to my bosom then and there.

So I began: "Indeed, indeed, not scorn 52
But heartfelt grief to see your tribulation
Pierced me, too deeply to be soon outworn,

When this my lord gave me an intimation 55
Which made me think that I might look to gaze
On men like you, and of such reputation.

Truly, your city's mine; I've heard your praise— 58
Your deeds, your honoured names—rehearsed by all,
And have with love rehearsed them all my days.

I'm one who, turning from the bitter gall, 61
Seek the sweet fruit promised by my sure guide;
But to the Centre I have first to fall."

"So may thy soul these many years abide 64
Housed in thy body, and the after-light
Of fame shine long behind thee," he replied,

"Tell us if in our city still burn bright 67
Courage and courtesy, as they did of old,
Or are their embers now extinguished quite?

For Guillim Borsier', but late enrolled 70
With us, who runs in yon tormented train,
Has much distressed us by the tales he's told."

"A glut of self-made men and quick-got gain 73
Have bred excess in thee and pride, forsooth,
O Florence! till e'en now thou criest for pain."

I. 121: *and seemed like one of those who . . . run*: This foot-race, whose prize was a piece of green cloth, was instituted to celebrate a Veronese victory, and was run on the First Sunday in Lent.

I. 2: *the water tumbling down*: The effluent of all the upper rivers pours over the precipice, and runs either under or above ground across the Eighth Circle, to reappear as Cocytus in the Ninth.

I. 8: *the fashion of whose dress*: The characteristic Florentine costume—the straight gown (*lucco*) and hood (*capocchio*)—are familiar in all the pictures of Dante.

I. 21: *formed themselves into a wheel*: These shades may not stop running even for a moment (see Canto XV. 37-9) under a dire penalty, so they adopt this method of remaining abreast of Dante.

II. 37-45: The three persons named are all noble Florentine Guelfs. Tegghiaio and Rusticucci are among the "worthy men" after whom Dante inquired so anxiously of Ciacco (Canto VI. 78-80).

Just as the shades in Brunetto's group were all men of letters, these are all persons of political importance; it appears from Canto XV. 118 that the various groups were not allowed to mix.

Thus I proclaimed aloud with lifted mouth; 76
The three knew they were answered, each on each
Looking, as men look when they hear the truth.

"If thou at other times canst thus enrich 79
Men's ears," they all replied, "scot-free, as thus,
Happy art thou, that hast the gift of speech!

Wherefore, if thou escape this place of loss 82
And come to see the lovely stars again,
Then, when thou shalt rejoice to say, 'I was,'

Look that thou speak of us to living men." 85
Thereon they broke their wheel, and fled so fast,
Their legs seemed wings; you could not say *Amen*

So quickly as across the sandy vast 88
They vanished; only then my master stirred,
Choosing to go. I followed. On we passed,

And went but a short way before we heard 91
The sound of the water thundering down so close
That had we spoken we'd scarce have heard a word.

As that first river that to the eastward flows 94
From Monte Veso down to a mouth of its own,
On the left slope of the Apennines (where it goes

By the name of Acquacheta, ere running down 97
To its lower bed, and after that becomes
Known by another name at Forli town)

Resounds from the mountain-side as it drops and drums 100
At the fall above St. Benedict's, near the ground
Where a thousand people should settle and have their homes,

So plunging over a steep chasm we found 103
That dark-dyed water, bellowing with a din
Such that the ear would soon be stunned with sound.

I was wearing a rope girdle, the same wherein 106
I once, indeed, had nursed a fleeting hope
To catch the leopard with the painted skin;

Now, at my guide's command, I loosed the rope 109
And took it off, and held it out to him
All neatly wound together and coiled up.

He took it, and leaning right-hand from the brim 112
Of the Pit, he tossed it over the precipice,
So that it dropped well out from the rocky rim.

"Surely some strange and novel thing will rise," 115
Said I to myself, "to answer this strange sign
Which thus my master's following with his eyes."

Dear me! when one's with people who divine 118
More than they see, and read one's thoughts right through,
How careful one should be! My guide read mine:

"Oh, it will come," said he, "and quickly too, 121
The thing I look for; what thy fancies frame
There in thy head will soon be in thy view."

When truth looks like a lie, a man's to blame 124
Not to sit still, if he can, and hold his tongue,
Or he'll only cover his innocent head with shame;

But here I can't be silent; and by the song 127
Of this my Comedy, Reader, hear me swear,
So may my work find favour and live long,

That I beheld through that thick murky air 130
Come swimming up a shape most marvellously
Strange for even the stedfast heart to bear;

As he returns, that has gone down to free 133
The anchor from whatever's fouling it,
Or rock or other thing hid undersea,

Spreading his arms and gathering up his feet. 136

THE IMAGES. *The Rope Girdle.* Much controversy has raged about this. For the *story*, it is perhaps enough to say that something was needed to serve as a signal, and that the story-teller pitched upon this as one of the few detachable objects which his characters might be supposed to have about them. Dante, however, goes out of his way to tell us (for the first time and rather surprisingly) that he had once hoped to catch the Leopard of Canto I with the rope. The Leopard is the image of the sins of Youth, or Incontinence; and it seems likely that the girdle has something to do with Chastity—it may, e.g., symbolize some vow of chastity which failed in its object. The Circles of Incontinence are now left behind, and the girdle is therefore available for another purpose. This time it does "catch" something—a thing variegated and gay like the Leopard, but infinitely more dangerous, brought up from the Circles of Fraud. *Allegorically*, this may suggest that when the earlier and more obvious temptations seem to have departed, they may recur, disguised and more insidious, provoked by the very safeguards originally erected against them.

CANTO XVII

THE STORY. *Geryon, the monster called up from the Circles of Fraud, alights on the edge of the precipice. While Virgil talks to him, Dante goes to look at the shades of Usurers seated on the Burning Sand. The Poets then mount on Geryon's shoulders and are carried down over the Great Barrier to the Eighth Circle.*

"Behold the beast with stinging tail unfurled,
That passes mountains and breaks weapon and wall;
Behold him that pollutes the whole wide world."

Thus said my lord to me, and therewithal 4
Made him a sign to bring him to aboard
Near the path's end, but farther from the fall.

I. 76: *with lifted mouth*: Here, as again in Canto XIX, Dante marks the difference between his private speech and his prophetic speech: he lifts his head as though to proclaim the doom of Florence.
II. 79-80: The shades acclaim Dante's powers of poetic inspiration, but hint that his eloquence may some day cost him dear.
I. 84: *when thou shalt rejoice to say, "I was"*: i.e., when he will be glad to remember that he once had this terrible experience.
I. 95: *down to a mouth of its own*: The Acquacheta, which from Forli onwards is called the Montone, was in Dante's time the first river rising in the Etruscan Alps to fall direct into the Adriatic, instead of into the Po (see map below).
I. 102: *where a thousand people could settle*: This may refer to a scheme of the Conti Guidi for settling a number of their vassals in this district. (Some commentators think Dante means that the foundation of St. Benedict's could have supported many more monks than it actually did.)
I. 118: *people who divine . . . one's thoughts*: cf. Cantos X. 18, XIII. 25, etc.

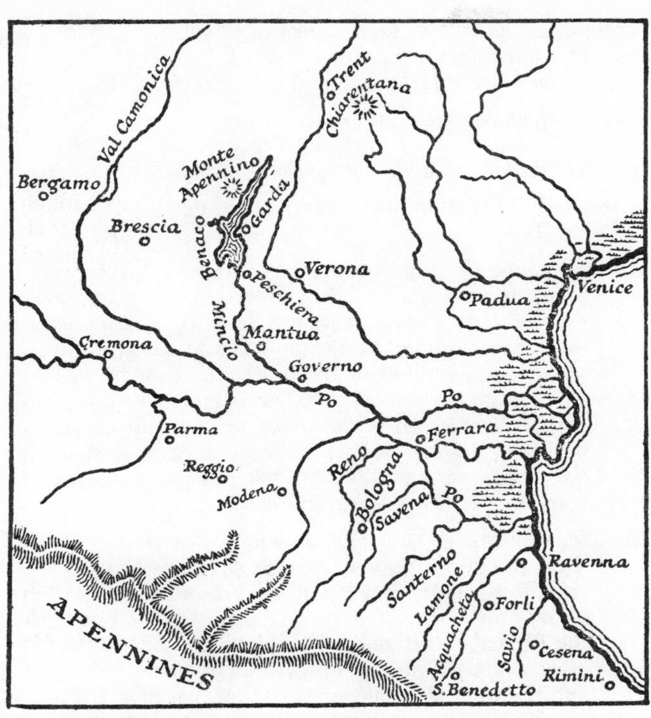

And on he came, that unclean image of Fraud,
To ground upon the hard with head and chest,
But not his tail, which still he left abroad.

His face was a just man's, it so expressed
In every line a mild benignity;
And like a wyvern's trunk was all the rest.

He had two fore-paws, shaggy arm-pit high,
Whence breast and back and both flanks shimmered off,
Painted with ring-knots and whorled tracery.

Nor Turk nor Tartar ever wrought coloured stuff
So rainbow-trammed and broidered; never wore
Arachne's web such dyes in warp and woof.

And as wherries many a time lie drawn ashore,
Half in the water, half upon the strand,
Or as the beaver plants him to wage war

At home there, in the guzzling Germans' land,
So that worst beast of beastly kind hung clipped
To the cliff whose curb of stone girdles the sand;

And all his tail quivered in the void and whipped
Upward, twisting the venomed fork in air
Wherewith, like a scorpion's tail, its point was tipped.

"Now," said my guide, "we must a little bear
Aside, and make our way towards this same
Malevolent brute that clings and crouches there."

So we descended on our right, and came
Ten paces onward, skirting the cliff's face,
To give a wide berth to the sand and flame,

And joined him thus; and when we reached the place,
I saw some folk a little way ahead
Sitting on the sand, near the empty edge of space;

Wherefore: "That thou mayst know," my master said,
"All that there is to know about this ring,
Go forward, view those shades and learn their state;

But do not linger too long parleying;
While thou art gone I'll speak the beast, and borrow
His sturdy back to speed our journeying."

So I went, all by myself, along the narrow
Outermost brink of the seventh circle, and so
Came where those people sat to dree their sorrow,

Which gushed from their eyes and made the sad tears flow;
While this way and that they flapped their hands, for ease
From the hot soil now, and now from the burning snow,

Behaving, in fact, exactly as one sees
Dogs in the summer, scuffing with snout and paw,
When they're eaten up with breeses and flies and fleas.

I looked at many thus scorched by the fiery flaw,
And though I scanned their faces with utmost heed,
There was no one there I recognized; but I saw

How, stamped with charge and tincture plain to read,
About the neck of each a great purse hung,
Whereon their eyes seemed still to fix and feed.

So as I went gazing upon the throng,
I saw a purse display, azure on or,
The gesture and form of a lion; further along

My eye pursued, and fell on one that bore
A purse of blood-red gules, which had on it
A goose whiter than curd; and yet one more

Beside him sat, who on his wallet white
Showed a blue sow in farrow; this one cried
To me: "What art thou doing in this pit?

Away! and learn (since thou hast not yet died),
My neighbour Vitaliano shall come here
To sit with me upon my left-hand side.

These Florentines keep bawling in my ear—
I'm Paduan myself—all day they shout:
'Let come, let come that knight without a peer

Who bears three goats upon his satchel stout!' "
With that he writhed his mouth awry, and made
A gross grimace, thrusting his tongue right out

---

l. 12: *a wyvern's trunk*: Dante's word is *serpente*, which means any kind of reptile, with or without legs. I have rendered it here by "wyvern"—a fabulous creature with one pair of legs and a serpent's tail.
l. 18: *Arachne's web.*
l. 21: *as the beaver plants him*: The beaver was popularly supposed to angle for fish by sitting on the shore and dropping its tail into the water by way of bait. In Dante's time it was commonly found further south than it is to-day.
l. 31: *we descended on our right*: i.e., they descended from the dyke and went along at the extreme edge of the precipice, which was of stone (l. 24) and presumably outside the limits assigned by Providence to the fiery rain.
ll. 55 *sqq.*: *stamped with charge and tincture*: The various devices upon the Usurers' purses are the arms of men and families notorious for their usury. The Paduan who speaks in ll. 64-76 is Rinaldo dei Scrovegni, and Vitaliano dei Vitaliani, whom he mentions, is also a Paduan. The rest are Florentines: one of the Gianfigliazzi family, one of the Ubbriachi, and Giovanni Buiamonte dei Becchi (the "knight without a peer").
l. 75: *a gross grimace*: to taunt Dante with the number of Florentines among the Usurers.

Like an ox licking its nose. Then I, afraid 76
To anger him who bade me make short stay
By staying longer, left that sad brigade

And went to seek my guide without delay, 79
And found him already mounted on the croup
Of the fearsome beast. "Courage!" I heard him say,

"Such is the stair by which we have to stoop; 82
I'll sit behind lest thou take harm from the tail,
So do thou mount before; be bold now—up!"

Like one with the quartan fit on him, leaden-pale 85
At the finger-nails already, and quaking faster
At the mere sight of the shade, so did I quail

Hearing him; yet his hintings of disaster 88
Shamed me to valour, as a hind may be
Bold in the presence of an honoured master.

So I climbed to those dread shoulders obediently; 91
"Only do" (I meant to say, but my voice somehow
Wouldn't come out right) "please catch hold of me."

But he that at other times had not been slow 94
In other straits to aid me, gripped me fast
In his arms the moment I mounted, and held me now

Secure; and said: "Now move thee, Geryon! cast 97
Thy circle wide, and wheel down gradually,
Think of the strange new burden that thou hast."

And as a ship slips from her berth to sea 100
Backing and backing, so did the beast begin
To leave the bank; and when he felt quite free

He turned his tail to where his breast had been, 103
Stretching it forth and wriggling like an eel,
And with his paws gathered the thick air in.

No greater fear, methinks, did any feel 106
When Phaeton dropped the chariot-reins of the sun,
Firing the sky—we see the mark there still—

Nor when poor Icarus felt the hot wax run, 109
Unfeathering him, and heard his father calling,
"Alack! alack! thou fliest too high, my son!"—

Than I felt, finding myself in the void falling 112
With nothing but air all round, nothing to show,
No light, no sight but the sight of the beast appalling.

And on he goes, swimming and swimming slow, 115
Round and down, though I only know it by feeling
The wind come up and beat on my face from below.

And now I hear on the right as we spin wheeling 118
The noise of the cataract under us horribly roaring,
And I crane my head and look down with my senses reeling.

Then the terror of alighting seemed worse than the terror of soaring;
For I heard the wails and I saw the tall fires leap,
So that for fear I shrank back trembling and cowering.

And I saw—what before I could not see—the sweep 124
And swoop of our downward flight through the grand woes,
Which now drew near on every side of the deep.

And now, as a hawk that has long hung waiting does— 127
When, without any sight at all of lure or prey,
She makes the falconer cry: "She stoops!" and goes

Dropping down weary, then suddenly wheels away 130
In a hundred circlings, and sets her far aloof
From her master, sullen and scornful—so, I say,

Geryon set us down on the bottom rough, 133
A-foot at the foot of the cliff-face that surrounded
The chasm; and having shogged our burden off,

Brisker than bolt from bow away he bounded. 136

THE IMAGES. *Geryon.* In Greek mythology, Geryon was a monster who was killed by Hercules. He was usually represented as having a human form with three heads, or three conjoined bodies; but Dante has given him a shape compounded of three natures—human, bestial, and reptile. In the *allegory*, he is the image of Fraud, with "the face of a just man" and an iridescence of beautiful colour, but with the paws of a beast and a poisonous sting in his serpent's tail—an image which scarcely calls for interpretation.

The Usurers. These, as we have seen, are the image of the Violent against Nature and the Art derived from Nature; they sit looking upon the ground, because they have sinned against that and against the labour that should have cultivated its resources. The old commentator Gelli observes brilliantly that the Sodomites and Usurers are classed together because the first make sterile the natural instincts which result in fertility, while the second make fertile that which by its nature is sterile—i.e., they "make money breed." More generally, the Usurers may be taken as types of all economic and mechanical civilizations which multiply material luxuries at the expense of vital necessities and have no roots in the earth or in humanity.

CANTO XVIII

THE STORY. *Dante now finds himself in the Eighth Circle (Malbowges), which is divided into ten trenches (bowges) containing those who committed Malicious Frauds upon mankind in general. The Poets walk along the edge of Bowge i, where Panders and Seducers run, in opposite directions, scourged by demons; and here Dante talks with Venedico Caccianemico of Bologna. As they cross the bridge over the bowge, they see the shade of Jason. Then they go on to the bridge over Bowge ii, where they see Thaïs, and Dante converses with another of the Flatterers who are here plunged in filth.*

---

l. 85: *the quartan fit*: i.e., the cold fit of the quartan ague, announcing itself by premonitory shiverings.

l. 107: *Phaeton*: the son of Phoebus; he asked his father to allow him to drive the chariot of the Sun, but was unable to control the horses, so that they started out of their course, burning the track of the Milky Way across the sky, and would have set fire to the earth, but that Jupiter intervened by killing Phaeton with a thunderbolt.

l. 109: *Icarus*: was the son of Daedalus. His father made him wings, which were fastened to his shoulders with wax. Icarus flew too near the sun, so that the wax melted and he fell into the Aegean Sea and was drowned.

NETHER HELL - 2

THE SINS OF THE WOLF

There is in Hell a region that is called
Malbowges; it is all of iron-grey stone,
Like the huge barrier-rock with which it's walled.

Plumb in the middle of the dreadful cone
There yawns a well, exceeding deep and wide,
Whose form and fashion shall be told anon.

That which remains, then, of the foul Pit's side,
Between the well and the foot of the craggy steep,
Is a narrowing round, which ten great chasms divide.

As one may see the girding fosses deep
Dug to defend a stronghold from the foe,
Trench within trench about the castle-keep,

Such was the image here; and as men throw
Their bridges outward from the fortress-wall,
Crossing each moat to the far bank, just so

From the rock's base spring cliffs, spanning the fall
Of dyke and ditch, to the central well, whose rim
Cuts short their passage and unites them all.

When Geryon shook us off, 'twas in this grim
Place that we found us; and the poet then
Turned to the left, and I moved after him.

There, on our right, more anguished shades of men,
New tortures and new torturers, I espied,
Cramming the depth of this first bowge of ten.

In the bottom were naked sinners, who, our side
The middle, moved to face us; on the other,
Along with us, though with a swifter stride.

Just as the Romans, because of the great smother
Of the Jubilee crowds, have thought of a good device
For controlling the bridge, to make the traffic smother,

So that on one side all must have their eyes
On the Castle, and go to St. Peter's; while all the throng
On the other, towards the Mount moves contrariwise.

I saw horned fiends with heavy whips and strong
Posted each side along the dismal rock,
Who scourged their backs, and drove them on headlong.

Hey! how they made them skip at the first shock!
How brisk they were to lift their legs and prance!
Nobody stayed for the second or third stroke.

And as I was going, one of them caught my glance,
And I promptly said to myself: "How now! who's he?
Somewhere or other I've seen that countenance."

I stopped short, figuring out who this might be;
And my good lord stopped too; then let me go
Back a short way, to follow him and see.

The whipped shade hung his head, trying not to show
His face; but little good he got thereby,
For: "Hey, there! thou whose eyes are bent so low,

Thy name's Venedico—or thy features lie—
Caccianemico, and I know thee well;
What wormwood pickled such a rod," said I,

"To scrub thy back?" And he: "I would not tell,
But for that voice of thine; those accents clear
Remind me of the old life, and compel

My answer. I am the man who sold the fair
Ghisola to the Marchese's lust; that's fact,
However they tell the ugly tale up there.

I. 2: *Malbowges (Malebolge)*: The Italian word *bolgia* means (*a*) a trench in the ground; (*b*) a purse or pouch. *Malebolge* can thus be interpreted as either "evil pits" or "evil pouches;" and Dante puns on this double meaning (Canto XIX. 72). There is no English word which combines the two meanings; there is, however, an old word "bowge" meaning "pouch." This makes it possible to english *Malebolge* as "Malbowges" (which is, in all probability, the form which a medieval translator would have given it), and so to retain a suggestion of the pun about "pouching."
I. 6: *shall be told anon*: see Canto XXXI.
II. 28-33: The fact that traffic control appears to Dante as a startling and ingenious novelty probably brings home to us, far more than his theology or his politics, the six hundred years which separate his times from ours. The year 1300 (the year of his vision) had been proclaimed by Pope Boniface VIII a Jubilee Year, and Rome was consequently crowded with pilgrims. For the better avoidance of congestion, the authorities (whose organization seems to have been remarkably efficient) adopted a rule of the road on the Bridge of Castello Sant' Angelo, so-called from the castle which stood at one end of it. The "Mount" at the other end was either the Janiculum or Monte Giordano. It will be noticed that in the First Bowge the rule is "keep to the right," as it is on the Continent to-day.
II. 49-50: *Venedico Caccianemico*: a Bolognese Guelf. Ghisola was his own sister, and the Marchese was Obizzo d' Este (Canto XII. 111).
I. 51: *what wormwood*: lit.: "what has got thee into such a pickle (*pungenti salse*)?" The word *salse* means "*sauce*"; but it was also the name of a place near Bologna where criminals were flogged and executed, so that Dante's sauce is punning as well as pungent. I have done my best to supply a parallel allusion of a native and contemporary kind.
I. 57: *however they tell the ugly tale*: Presumably other, whitewashing, versions of the story, less disagreeable to the feelings of the powerful d' Este family, had been assiduously put about.

I'm not alone here from Bologna; packed 58
The place is with us; one could scarcely find
More tongues saying 'Yep' for 'Yes' in all the tract

'Twixt Reno and Savena. Art inclined 61
To call for proof? What witness need I join
To the known witness of our covetous mind?"

And one of the fiends caught him a crack on the loin 64
With the lash, even as he spoke, crying: "Away,
Pander! there are no women here to coin!"

So to my escort I retraced my way, 67
And soon we came, a few steps further wending,
To where a great spur sprang from the barrier grey.

This we climbed lightly, and right-handed bending, 70
Crossed its rough crest, departing from that rout
Of shades who run their circuits never-ending.

But, coming above the part that's tunnelled out 73
To let the flogged pass under, "Stay" said he;
"Let those who go the other way about

Strike on thine eyes; just now thou couldst not see 76
Their faces, as we passed along the verge,
For they were travelling the same road as we."

So from that ancient bridge we watched the surge 79
Sweep on towards us of the wretched train
On the farther side, chased likewise by the scourge.

"Look who comes here," my good guide said again 82
Without my asking, "that great spirit of old,
Who will not shed one tear for all his pain.

Is he not still right royal to behold? 85
That's Jason, who by valour and by guile
Bore from the Colchian strand the fleece of gold.

He took his way past Lemnos, where, short while 88
Before, the pitiless bold women achieved
The death of all the menfolk of their isle;

And there the young Hypsipyle received 91
Tokens and fair false words, till, snared and shaken,
She who deceived her fellows was deceived;

And there he left her, childing and forsaken; 94
For those deceits he's sentenced to these woes,
And for Medea too revenge is taken.

And with him every like deceiver goes. 97
Suffice thee so much knowledge of this ditch
And those whom its devouring jaws enclose."

Already we'd come to where the narrow ridge 100
Crosses the second bank, and makes of it
An abutment for the arch of the next bridge.

Here we heard people in the farther pit 103
Make a loud whimpering noise, and heard them cough,
And slap themselves with their hands, and snuffle and spit.

The banks were crusted with foul scum, thrown off 106
By the fume, and caking there, till nose and eye
Were vanquished with sight and reek of the noisome stuff.

So deep the trench, that one could not espy 109
Its bed save from the topmost cliff, which makes
The keystone of the arch. We climbed; and I,

Thence peering down, saw people in the lake's 112
Foul bottom, plunged in dung, the which appeared
Like human ordure running from a jakes.

Searching its depths, I there made out a smeared 115
Head—whether clerk or lay was hard to tell,
It was so thickly plastered with the merd.

"Why stand there gloating?" he began to yell, 118
"Why stare at me more than the other scum?"
"Because," said I, "if I remember well,

I've seen thy face, dry-headed, up at home; 121
Thou art Alessio Interminei, late
Of Lucca—so, more eagerly than on some,

I look on thee." He beat his pumpkin pate, 124
And said: "The flatteries I spewed out apace
With tireless tongue have sunk me to this state."

Then said my guide: "Before we leave the place, 127
Lean out a little further, that with full
And perfect clearness thou may'st see the face

Of that uncleanly and dishevelled trull 130
Scratching with filthy nails, alternately
Standing upright and crouching in the pool.

I. 60: *"yep" (sipa) for "yes" (si)*: an allusion to the Bolognese dialect. The Savena and Reno are rivers running west and east of Bologna.

I. 63: *the known witness of our covetous mind*: The Bolognese seem to have had a reputation for venality.

II. 67 *sqq.: retraced my way*, etc.: The poets had turned left on entering Malbowges and walked along the edge of Bowge i. Then Dante retraced his steps to go after Caccianemico. Now he returns to where Virgil is waiting for him, and they continue their original course till they come to where the first rock-spur runs across their path at right angles and forms a bridge over the bowge. To cross the bridge they have to *climb* on to this spur and turn right so as to walk *along* it till they are over the spot where the rock is tunnelled out to let the bowge pass below it. From this, the crest of the arch, they look down on the sinners passing below, as one would watch trains from the middle of a railway bridge (see illustration, p. 435). Once this procedure has been clearly visualized, the reader will have very little trouble with the geography of Malbowges.

I. 86: *Jason*: the Greek hero who led the Argonauts to fetch the Golden Fleece from the hands of Aietes, king of Colchis. He was helped by the king's daughter, Medea, whom he persuaded to accompany him home to Iolcus. He married her, but afterwards deserted her for Creusa.

I. 88: *Lemnos*: When the women of Lemnos killed all the men on the island because they had brought home some Thracian concubines, Hypsipyle, the daughter of King Thosa, saved her father by a ruse (I. 93). On their way to Colchis, the Argonauts landed at Lemnos and Jason seduced Hypsipyle.

II. 100-101: *the narrow ridge*, etc.: The spur runs straight on, forming bridges over all the bowges in succession (see map, p. 431).

I. 122: *Allessio Interminei*: Little is known of him, except that he was a member of a White Guelf family, and was notorious for his oily manners.

That is the harlot Thaïs. 'To what degree,' 133
Her leman asked, 'have I earned thanks, my love?'
'O, to a very miracle,' said she.

And having seen this, we have seen enough." 136

THE IMAGES. *The Eighth and Ninth Circles.* These are the Circles of *Fraud* or *Malice*—the "Sins of the Wolf."

Malbowges. The Eighth Circle is a huge funnel of rock, round which run, at irregular intervals, a series of deep, narrow trenches called "bowges" (*bolge*). From the foot of the Great Barrier at the top to the Well which forms the neck of the funnel run immense spurs of rock (like the ribs of an umbrella) raised above the general contour of the slope and forming bridges over the bowges. The maps and the sketch on p. 431 show the arrangement, except, of course, that the distances from bowge to bowge are greater, and the rock-surfaces much steeper and craggier, than it is possible to suggest in small diagrams.

Malbowges is, I think, after a rather special manner, the image of the City in corruption: the progressive disintegration of every social relationship, personal and public. Sexuality, ecclesiastical and civil office, language, ownership, counsel, authority, psychic influence, and material interdependence—all the media of the community's exchange are perverted and falsified, till nothing remains but the descent into the final abyss where faith and trust are wholly and for ever extinguished.

The Panders and Seducers. In the Circles of Fraud (the abuse of the specifically human faculty of reason) the ministers of Hell are no longer mere embodied *appetites*, but actual devils, images of the perverted *intellect*. In the First Bowge, those who deliberately exploited the passions of others and so drove them to serve their own interests, are themselves driven and scourged. The image is a sexual one; but the Panders and Seducers *allegorically* figure the stimulation and exploitation of every kind of passion—e.g., rage or greed—by which one may make tools of other people.

The Flatterers. These, too, exploit others by playing upon their desires and fears; their especial weapon is that abuse and corruption of language which destroys communication between mind and mind. Here they are plunged in the slop and filth which they excreted upon the world. Dante did not live to see the full development of political propaganda, commercial advertisement, and sensational journalism, but he has prepared a place for them.

CANTO XIX

THE STORY. *In the Third Bowge of Malbowges, Dante sees the Simoniacs, plunged head-downwards in holes of the rock, with flames playing upon their feet. He talks to the shade of Pope Nicholas III, who prophesies that two of his successors will come to the same bad end as himself. Dante rebukes the avarice of the Papacy.*

O Simon Magus! O disciples of his!
Miserable pimps and hucksters, that have sold
The things of God, troth-plight to righteousness,

Into adultery for silver and gold; 4
For you the trump must sound now—you are come
To the bag: the third bowge has you in its hold.

Already we'd mounted over the next tomb, 7
Scaling the cliff until we reached that part
Whence a dropped line would hit the centre plumb.

O most high Wisdom, how exact an art 10
Thou showest in heaven and earth and hell's profound;
How just thy judgments, righteous as thou art!

I saw the gulley, both its banks and ground, 13
Thickset with holes, all of the selfsame size,
Pierced through the livid stone; and each was round,

Seeming nor more nor less wide to mine eyes 16
Than those in my own beautiful St. John,
Made for the priests to stand in, to baptize;

Whereof, not many years back, I broke up one, 19
To save a stifling youngster jammed in it;
And by these presents be the true facts known.

From each hole's mouth stuck out a sinner's feet 22
And legs up to the calf; but all the main
Part of the body was hid within the pit.

The soles of them were all on fire, whence pain 25
Made their joints quiver and thrash with such strong throes,
They'd have snapped withies and hempen ropes in twain.

And as on oily matter the flame flows 28
On the outer surface only, in lambent flashes,
So did it here, flickering from heels to toes.

"Master, who is that writhing wretch, who lashes 31
Out harder than all the rest of his company,"
Said I, "and whom a ruddier fire washes?"

I. 133: *Thais*: The fulsome reply here quoted really belongs, not to the historical Thaïs, the Athenian courtesan, but to a character in Terence's play, *Eunuchus*, of the same name and profession. It is mentioned by Cicero, and Dante presumably took it from him, under the impression that it was historical. Note that Thaïs is not here because she is personally a harlot; the sin which has plunged her far below the Lustful, and even below the traffickers in flesh, is the prostitution of words—the medium of *intellectual* intercourse.

I. 1: *Simon Magus*: after whom the sin of Simony is named (*Acts* viii. 9-24).

I. 17: *my own beautiful St. John*: The Church of St. John Baptist at Florence, where Dante himself was baptized, and of which he always thinks, in his exile, with homesick affection (cf. *Para.* xvi. 25;; xxv. 5). The font in the Baptistery was surrounded by holes in which the officiating priests stood, so as not to be jostled by the crowd on days when a great number of babies were being baptized at once. (There is a similar font to this day at Pisa: see sketch, p. 435.) A small boy who was playing round the font one day got jammed in one of these holes, and was extricated by Dante, who took the responsibility of breaking down the marble surround. A garbled account of this story was apparently circulated, in which Dante no doubt figured as a sacrilegious destroyer of Church property—hence his determination to put the facts on record.

"If thou wouldst have me carry thee down," said he, 34
"By the lower bank, his own lips shall afford
News of his guilt, and make him known to thee."

"Thy pleasure is my choice; for thou art lord," 37
Said I, "and knowest I swerve not from thy will;
Yea, knowest my heart, although I speak no word."

So to the fourth brink, and from thence downhill, 40
Turning to the left, we clambered; and thus passed
To the narrow and perforate bottom, my dear lord still

Loosing me not from his side, until at last 43
He brought me close to the cleft, where he who made
Such woeful play with his shanks was locked up fast.

"Oh thou, whoever thou art, unhappy shade, 46
Heels over head thus planted like a stake,
Speak if thou canst." This opening I essayed

And stood there like the friar who leans to take 49
Confession from the treacherous murderer
Quick-buried, who calls him back for respite's sake.

He cried aloud: "Already standing there? 52
Art standing there already, Boniface?
Why then, the writ has lied by many a year.

What! so soon sated with the gilded brass 55
That nerved thee to betray and then to rape
The Fairest among Women that ever was?"

Then I became like those who stand agape, 58
Hearing remarks which seem to make no sense,
Blank of retort for what seems jeer and jape.

But Virgil now broke in: "Tell him at once: 61
'I am not who thou think'st, I am not he' ";
So I made answer in obedience.

At this the soul wrenched his feet furiously, 64
Almost to spraining; then he sighed, and wept,
Saying: "Why then, what dost thou ask of me?

Art so concerned to know my name, thou'st leapt 67
These barriers just for that? Then truly know
That the Great Mantle once my shoulders wrapped.

Son of the Bear was I, and thirsted so 70
To advance the ursine litter that I pouched
Coin up above, and pouched myself below.

Dragged down beneath my head lie others couched, 73
My predecessors who simonized before,
Now in the deep rock-fissures cowering crouched.

I too shall fall down thither and make one more 76
When he shall come to stand here in my stead
Whom my first sudden question took thee for.

But already have I been planted in this bed 79
Longer with baked feet and thus topsy-turvy
Than he shall stand flame-footed on his head;

For after him from the west comes one to serve ye 82
With uglier acts, a lawless Shepherd indeed,
Who'll cover us both—fit end for soul so scurvy;

He'll be another Jason, as we read 85
The tale in Maccabees; as that controlled
His king, so this shall bend France like a reed."

I know not whether I was here too bold, 88
But in this strain my answer flowed out free:
"Nay, tell me now how great a treasure of gold

Our Lord required of Peter, ere that He 91
Committed the great Keys into his hand;
Certes He nothing asked save 'Follow Me.'

Nor Peter nor the others made demand 94
Of silver or gold when, in the lost soul's room,
They chose Matthias to complete their band.

Then bide thou there; thou hast deserved thy doom; 97
Do thou keep well those riches foully gained
That against Charles made thee so venturesome.

And were it not that I am still constrained 100
By veneration for the most high Keys
Thou barest in glad life, I had not refrained

My tongue from yet more grievous words than these; 103
Your avarice saddens the world, trampling on worth,
Exalting the workers of iniquities.

I. 34: *if thou wouldst have me carry thee down*: In this bowge (as also in Bowge x) Dante is taken down on to the floor of the ditch in order to speak to the sinners. The banks are too steep for him to descend in his mortal body unassisted, so Virgil carries him. They go right over the bridge first, and then down on the *inner* and *lower* side of the bowge, which (as Dante explains in Canto XXIII) is shorter and less steep than the upper (see sketch, p. 435).
I. 46: *whoever thou art*: The shade is Nicholas III, Pope 1277-80.
I. 50: *the treacherous murderer*: By Florentine law, assassins were executed by being planted head-downwards in a hole, which was then filled up. Dante likens his own attitude to that of the attendant priest, stooping down to hear the wretch's last confession—prolonged, to postpone the fatal moment as long as possible.
I. 53: *Boniface*: The shade thinks he is being addressed by Pope Boniface VIII. There appears to have been only one hole allotted to popes, each of whom remained with his burning feet protruding till his successor arrived to thrust him down lower and take his place.
I. 54: *the writ has lied*: Nicholas, like the other damned souls, can foresee the distant future, and, knowing that Boniface is not due to die till 1303, is amazed to find him (as he supposes) there already.
I. 57: *the Fairest among Women*: i.e., the Church, the Bride of God, identified with the "Spouse of Lebanon" (*Song of Songs*, i. 8, etc.).
I. 69: *the Great Mantle*: i.e., the Papal Mantle.
I. 70: *son of the Bear*: Nicholas was one of the Orsini family—*orsa* is the Italian for "bear"—hence the pun on the "ursine" litter.
I. 83: *a lawless Shepherd*: Pope Clement V, who came from Gascony (the West). Nicholas will hold the uppermost place for twenty-three years (1280-1303), but Boniface only for eleven (from his death in 1303 to that of Clement in 1314).
I. 85: *Jason*: See 2 *Maccabees* iv. 7 *sqq.* He bribed Antiochus Epiphanes to make him High Priest and to connive at pagan practices; similarly Clement V will rise to the papacy by the influence of Philip the Fair of France.
I. 89: *in this strain* (lit.: metre): Dante is now about to speak (as in Canto XVI) in his own character of prophetic poet, and so uses this word, and again the word "chanted" (I. 118), to mark the difference between his private and his prophetic utterance.
II. 92-3: *the great Keys . . . follow Me:Matthew* iv. 19: *John* xxi. 19.
II. 94-6: *nor Peter nor the others*, etc.: when the Apostles chose Matthias to fill the place of Judas (*Acts* i. 13-26).
II. 98-9: *those riches foully gained*: Having been thwarted in his ambitious scheme to marry his niece to Charles of Anjou, king of Sicily, Nicholas joined a conspiracy against Charles, which eventually resulted in the notorious massacre known as the Sicilian Vespers.

Pastors like you the Evangelist shewed forth,
Seeing her that sitteth on the floods committing
Fornication with the kings of the earth;

Her, the seven-headed born, whose unremitting
Witness uplifted in her ten horns thundered,
While she yet pleased her spouse with virtues fitting.

You deify silver and gold; how are you sundered
In any fashion from the idolater,
Save that he serves one god and you an hundred?

Ah, Constantine! what ills were gendered there—
No, not from thy conversion, but the dower
The first rich Pope received from thee as heir!"

While I thus chanted to him, such a sour
Rage bit him—or perhaps his conscience stirred—
He writhed and jerked his feet with all his power.

I think my guide approved of what he heard—
I think so, since he patiently attended
With a pleased smile to each outspoken word;

And after took me in both arms extended,
And, when he had clasped me close upon his breast,
Climbed back by the same road he had descended,

Nor wearied of the load that he embraced
Till he had borne me to the arch's crown
Linking the fourth and fifth banks; on that crest

He set at length his burden softly down,
Soft on the steep, rough crag where even a goat
Would find the way hard going; here was thrown

Open the view of yet another moat.

THE IMAGES. *The Simoniacs.* Simony is the sin of trafficking in holy things, e.g., the sale of sacraments or ecclesiastical offices. The sinners who thus made money for themselves out of what belongs to God are "pouched" in fiery pockets in the rock, head-downwards, because they reversed the proper order of things and subordinated the heavenly to the earthly. The image here is ecclesiastical: we need not, however, suppose that, *allegorically*, the traffic in holy things is confined to medieval people or even to modern clergymen. A mercenary marriage, for example, is also the sale of a sacrament.

CANTO XX

THE STORY. *In the Fourth Bowge of the Eighth Circle Dante sees the Sorcerers, whose heads are twisted so that they can only look behind them, and who are therefore compelled to walk backwards. Virgil tells him about the origin of Mantua. The moon is setting as the Poets leave the bowge.*

New punishments behoves me sing in this
Twentieth canto of my first canticle,
Which tells of spirits sunk in the Abyss.

I now stood ready to observe the full
Extent of the new chasm thus laid bare,
Drenched as it was in tears most miserable.

Through the round vale I saw folk drawing near,
Weeping and silent, and at such slow pace
As Litany processions keep, up here,

And presently, when I had dropped my gaze
Lower than the head, I saw them strangely wried
'Twixt collar-bone and chin, so that the face

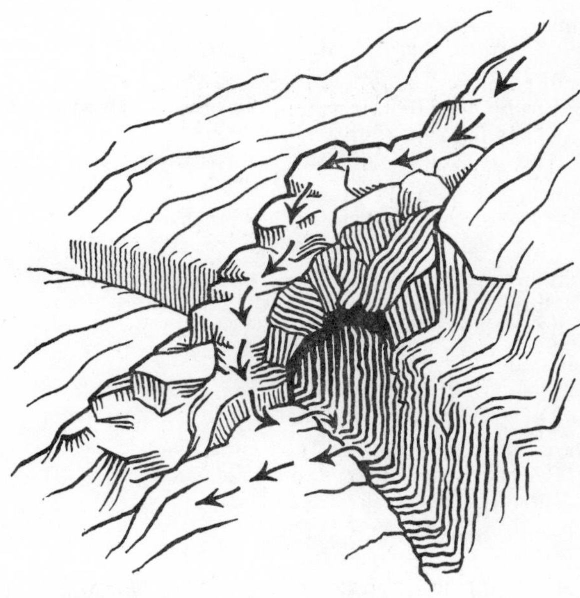

Bridge over Bowge iii, showing path taken by the poets (Canto XIX. 34 sqq. and note)

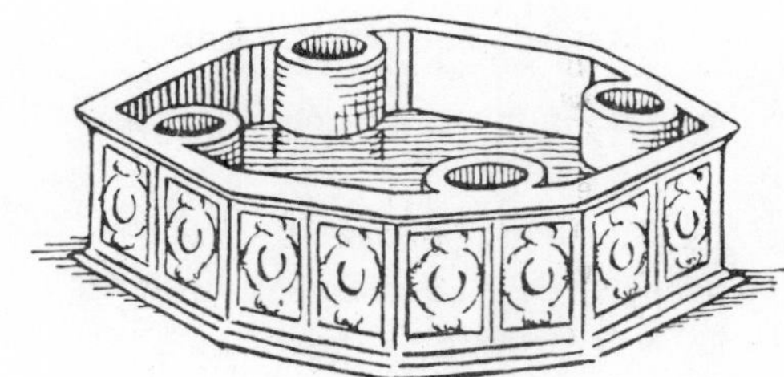

Font in the Baptistery at Pisa, showing the "holes" made for the priests to stand in (Canto XIX. 17 sqq. and note)

Of each was turned towards his own backside,
And backwards must they needs creep with their feet,
All power of looking forward being denied.

Perhaps some kind of paralytic fit
Could twist men so—such cases may have been;
I never saw it, nor can I credit it;

And, Reader, so God give thee grace to glean
Profit of my book, think if I could be left
Dry-eyed, when close before me I had seen

---

ll. 106 *sqq.: the Evangelist*, etc.: see *Revelation* xvii: The figure here is of the Church corrupted by avarice: the "seven heads" and "ten horns" are usually interpreted as signifying the Seven Sacraments and the Ten Commandments. (The attribution of the seven heads to the Woman, instead of to the Beast she sits on, is probably due to a misreading of the Vulgate.)

l. 115: *Constantine*: The allusion is to the so-called "Donation of Constantine," by which the first Christian Emperor was alleged to have transferred to the Papal See his temporal sovereignty over Italy. The document is undoubtedly a forgery; it is, however, true that it was Constantine's adoption of Christianity as the official Imperial religion which made it possible for the Church to make those claims to temporal power which led, in Dante's opinion, to so many political and ecclesiastical evils.

Our image so distorted, so bereft
Of dignity, that their eyes' brimming pools
Spilled down to bathe the buttocks at the cleft.

Truly I wept, leaned on the pinnacles
Of the hard rock; until my guide said, "Why!
And art thou too like all the other fools?

Here pity, or here piety, must die
If the other lives; who's wickeder than one
That's agonized by God's high equity?

Lift up, lift up thy head, and look upon
Him for whom once the earth gaped wide, before
The Thebans' eyes: 'Whither wilt thou begone,

Amphiaraüs? Why leavest thou the war?'
They cried; but he rushed down, and never stayed
Till he reached Minos, that o'er such hath power.

See how he makes a breast of's shoulder-blade!
Because he tried to see too far ahead,
He now looks backward and goes retrograde.

And lo you there Tiresias, who shed
His proper shape and altered every limb,
Changing his manhood for a womanhead,

So that he needs must smite the second time
His wand upon the twin and tangled snakes
To get his cock-feathers restored to him.

Aruns behind his breast back-forward makes;
In Luna's mountains, at whose foot the knave
Who dwells down in Carrara hoes and rakes,

He 'mid the white bright marbles had his cave;
There lived, and there looked out, with nought to screen
His view of starry heaven and ocean wave.

And she that veils her breasts, by thee unseen,
With her loose locks, and, viewed from where we stand,
Has on the far side all her hairy skin

Was Manto, she that searched through many a land
Ere settling in my birthplace; that's a tale
I'd like to tell—brief patience, then, command.

After her father passed beyond life's pale,
When Bacchus' city lay in bondage thralled,
Long years she wandered up hill and down dale.

High in fair Italy, where Almayn's walled
By the Alps above the Tyrol, lies and dreams
At the mountain's foot a lake, Benaco called;

For the water here of over a thousand streams,
Meseems, that lave Mount Apennine, running apace
'Twixt Garda and Val Camonica, spreads and brims

To a mere; and there in the midst of it lies a place
That the bishop of Verona, and those of Trent
And Brescia, if they passed that way, might bless.

Peschiera sits at the circling shore's descent,
'Gainst Bergamese and Brescians built for cover,
A goodly keep; there all the effluent

Benaco's bosom cannot hold, spills over,
Slipping and lipping down, and sliding so
Through verdant meads, a river and a rover—

Benaco called no more, but Mincio,
From where the water first sets head to run,
Down to Governo, where it joins the Po.

It finds a level, ere half its course is done,
And there stagnates and spreads to a marshy fen,
Rank and unwholesome in the summer sun.

Passing that road, the cruel witch-maiden
Found in the marsh firm tracts of land, which lay
Untilled and uninhabited of men;

There, shunning human contact, did she stay
With her familiar household; there she plied
Her arts; there lived; there left her empty clay.

After, scattered folk from far and wide
Drew to the spot, which lay defensibly,
Being girded by the swamp on every side.

---

l. 22: *our image so distorted*: "Dante weeps, not now for any personal discovery in Hell, but from sheer misery at the physical contortion of the human form. . . . All is gone awry; all is perverted—and so much so that his pity has here no place." (Charles Williams: *The Figure of Beatrice*, p. 136.)

l. 28: *here pity, or here piety, must die* (lit.: "Here *pieta* lives when it is wholly dead"): the word *pieta* means both "pity" and "piety"; I have had to expand Dante's epigrammatic phrase to give the full force of the equivoque.

ll. 29-30: *who's wickeder*, etc.: These two lines, again, have a double significance: they may be rendered: "Who is more wicked than (the sinner) who is (here) tormented by God's judgment?" or "Who is more wicked than one who is tormented by (i.e., passionately protests against) God's judgment (as here exhibited)?" I have no doubt that *both* meanings are intended. Pity and piety are here mutually exclusive: it is necessary to acquiesce in judgment if one is not to become (by sympathy) partaker in the sin.

The rebuke which Dante here puts into Virgil's mouth may have been suggested by passages in the fourth-century *Apocalypse of Paul*: "And I wept and said: Woe unto men! woe unto the sinners! . . . And the angel answered and said unto me: Wherefore weepest thou? Art thou more merciful than the Lord God which is blessed for ever, who hath established the judgment and left every man of his own will to choose good and evil and to do as pleaseth him?" (M.R. James: *Apocryphal New Testament*, p. 546; and see also p. 543.)

l. 34: *Amphiaraüs*: one of the "Seven against Thebes." Having foreseen his own death, he tried to escape taking part in the war; but his wife Eriphyle betrayed him, and while fleeing from the pursuit of Polynices, he was swallowed up by an earthquake (see Statius: *Thebaids* viii. 147 *sqq.*).

l. 40: *Tiresias*: a Theban prophet. In his youth he found a pair of snakes twined together and struck them with his stick to separate them: whereupon he found himself changed into a woman, and so remained for seven years, until, having similarly separated another pair of snakes, he regained his manhood (see Ovid: *Metam.* iii).

l. 46: *Aruns*: an Etruscan augur (see Lucan: *Pharsalia* i. 584-8). Luna (Luni), near the mouth of the Macra, is called by Pliny the first city in Etruria. The mountains of Carrara, above Luna, are famous for their white marble.

l. 55: *Manto*: the daughter of Tiresias. The founding of Mantua by Manto is mentioned in *Aeneid* x. 198-200.

l. 59: *Bacchus' city*: Thebes, the legendary birthplace of Bacchus.

l. 61: *Almayn*: Germany.

l. 63: *Benaco*: now called Lake Garda.

l. 65: *Mount Apennine*: not the Apennine range, but a single mountain. (See map, p. 429.)

l. 68: *the bishop of Verona . . . Trent and Brescia*: the three dioceses met on an island in the lake.

O'er those dead bones they built their city, to be 91
For her sake named that chose the place out thus,
Mantua, with no further augury.

Far more than now it once was populous, 94
Ere Casalodi's folly fell to the sword
Of Pinamonte, who was treacherous.

I charge thee then, if stories go abroad, 97
Other than this, of how my city grew,
Let no such lying tales the truth defraud."

"Master, for me thy teaching is so true 100
And so compels belief, all other tales,"
Said I, "were dust and ash compared thereto.

But tell me of this great crowd that yonder trails, 103
If any worthy of note be now in sight;
My mind harks back to that before all else."

He answered: "He whose chin-beard shows so white 106
On his brown shoulders was a memorable
Augur in Greece, what time the land was quite

Emptied of males, so that you'd scarce be able 109
To find a cradling boy; he set the time,
With Calchas, for the cutting of the first cable;

Eurypylus his name; and my sublime 112
Tragedy sings him somewhere—thou'lt recall
The place, that hast by heart the whole long rhyme.

That other there, who looks so lean and small 115
In the flanks, was Michael Scott, who verily
Knew every trick of the art magical.

Lo! Guy Bonatti; lo! Asdente—he 118
May well wish now that he had stuck to his last,
But he repents too late; and yonder see

The witch-wives, miserable women who cast 121
Needle and spindle and shuttle away for skill
With mommets and philtres; there they all go past.

But come! Cain with his thorn-bush strides the sill 124
Of the two hemispheres; his lantern now
Already dips to the wave below Seville;

And yesternight the moon was full, as thou 127
Shouldst well remember, for throughout thy stay
In the deep wood she harmed thee not, I trow."

Thus he; and while he spake we went our way. 130

THE IMAGES. *The Sorcerers.* The primary image of sorcery here is that of the fortune-tellers, who, having attempted to usurp God's prerogative by prying into the future, are now so twisted that eyes and feet face in opposite directions. More generally, there is an image of the twisted nature of all magical art, which is a deformation of knowledge, and especially of the psychic powers, to an end outside the unity of the creation in God. It is in especial the misuse of knowledge so as to dominate environment (including not only material things but the personalities of others) for the benefit of the ego. Magic to-day takes many forms, ranging from actual Satanism to attempts at "conditioning" other people by manipulating their psyches; but even when it uses the legitimate techniques of the scientist or the psychiatrist, it is distinguished from true science by the "twisted sight," which looks to self instead of to God for the source and direction of its power.

CANTO XXI

THE STORY. *In the Fifth Bowge, Barrators, who made money by trafficking in public offices, are plunged in Boiling Pitch, guarded by demons with sharp hooks. Virgil crosses the bridge and goes down to parley with the demons. Belzecue, the chief demon, says that the spur of rock which the Poets have been following was broken by an earthquake (at the moment of Christ's entry into Hell) and no longer bridges the Sixth Bowge; but he will give them an escort of ten demons to "see them safe as far as the bridge which is still unbroken." In this disagreeable company, Virgil and Dante set off along the lower brink of the Bowge.*

And so we passed along from bridge to bridge,
With other talk, whereof my Comedy
Cares not to tell, until we topped the ridge;

And there we stayed our steps awhile, to see 4
Malbowges' next ravine, and wailings all
Vain: and most marvellous dark it seemed to be.

For as at Venice, in the Arsenal 7
In winter-time, they boil the gummy pitch
To caulk such ships as need an overhaul,

Now that they cannot sail—instead of which 10
One builds him a new boat, one toils to plug
Seams strained by many a voyage, others stitch

I. 95: *Casalodi*: In 1272 the Brescian counts of Casalodi who were Guelfs, seized Mantua. Their rule was greatly resented; and Alberto di Casalodi foolishly let himself be persuaded by Pinamonte dei Buonaccorsi, a Mantuan, to appease the people by banishing all the unpopular nobles of his party. As soon as he had done so, Pinamonte put himself at the head of the citizens, and drove out the Casalodi with great slaughter.

I. 109: *emptied of males*: i.e., when all the Greeks had departed to the siege of Troy. Eurypylus is associated with Calchas in *Aen.* ii. 110 *sqq.*

I. 116: *Michael Scott*: the famous wizard of Balwearie mentioned in Scott's *Lay of the Last Minstrel.*

I. 118: *Bonatti . . . Asdente*: Bonatti of Forli was an astrologer; Asdente, a shoemaker of Parma, who set up as a soothsayer.

I. 123: *mommets and philtres*: waxen images and magic potions made of herbs. Here Dante touches on magical arts even more dangerous than soothsaying; for the philtres were used to obtain power over the wills of others, and the waxen images were pierced with nails or melted before the fire to bring about the death of the victim.

I. 124: *Cain with his thorn-bush*: i.e., the Man in the Moon (cf. Shakespeare: *M.N.D.* iii. I; V. I, where Moon appears with a lantern and a thorn-bush). The Moon is now setting; i.e., it is about 6:52 A.M. on Saturday.

Cantos XXI and XXII. The mood of these two cantos—a mixture of savage satire and tearing high spirits—is unlike anything else in the *Comedy*, and is a little disconcerting to the more solemn-minded of Dante's admirers. Artistically, this grim burlesque is of great value as an interlude in the ever-deepening descent from horror to horror; but Dante had also personal reasons for letting his pen rip at this point, since an accusation of barratry was the pretext upon which he was banished from Florence. (I have translated rather more freely here than elsewhere, in order to keep up the pace of the original.)

I. 7: *at Venice, in the Arsenal*: Venice, in the Middle Ages, was a great sea-power, and the old Arsenal, built in 1104, was one of the most important shipyards in Europe.

Canvas to patch a tattered jib or lug, 13
Hammer at the prow, hammer at the stern, or twine
Ropes, or shave oars, refit and make all snug—

So, not by fire, but by the art divine, 16
A thick pitch boiled down there, spattering the brink
With viscous glue; I saw this, but therein

Nothing; only great bubbles black as ink 19
Would rise and burst there; or the seething tide
Heave up all over, and settle again, and sink.

And while I stood intent to gaze, my guide, 22
Suddenly crying to me, "Look out! look out!"
Caught me where I stood, and pulled me to his side.

O then I turned, as one who turns about, 25
Longing to see the thing he has to shun,
Dares not, and dares, and, dashed with hideous doubt,

Casts a look back and still goes fleeing on; 28
And there behind us I beheld a grim
Black fiend come over the rock-ridge at a run.

Wow! what a grisly look he had on him! 31
How fierce his rush! And, skimming with spread wing,
How swift of foot he seemed! how light of limb!

On high-hunched shoulders he was carrying 34
A wretched sinner, hoist by haunch and hip,
Clutching each ankle by the sinew-string.

"Bridge ho!" he bawled, "Our own Hellrakership! 37
Here's an alderman of St. Zita's coming down;
Go souse him, while I make another trip

For more; they're barrators all in that good town— 40
Except Bonturo, hey?—I've packed it stiff
With fellows who'd swear black's white for half-a-crown."

He tossed him in, and over the flinty cliff 43
Wheeled off; and never did mastiff run so hot
And hard on the trail, unleashed to follow a thief.

Down bobbed the sinner, then up in a writhing knot; 46
But the fiends beneath the archway yelled as he rose up:
"No Sacred Face will help thee here! it's not

A Serchio bathing-party! Now then, toes up 49
And dive! 'Ware hooks! To save thyself a jabbing,
Stay in the pitch, nor dare to poke thy nose up!"

Then, with a hundred prongs clawing and stabbing: 52
"Go cut thy capers! Try down there to do
Subsurface deals and secret money-grabbing!"

Just so, cooks make their scullions prod the stew 55
With forks, to thrust the flesh well down within
The cauldron, lest it float above the brew.

Then the good master: "Better not be seen," 58
Said he; "so crouch well down in some embrasure
Behind a crag, to serve thee for a screen;

And whatsoever outrage or displeasure 61
They do to me, fear nothing; I have faced
Frays of this sort before, and have their measure."

He passed the bridgehead then; but when he placed 64
His foot on the sixth bank, good need had he
Of a bold front; for with such furious haste

And concentrated venom of savagery 67
As dogs rush out upon some harmless tramp
Who stops, alarmed, to falter out his plea,

Out dashed the demons lurking under the ramp, 70
Each flourishing in his face a hideous hook;
But he: "Hands off! ere grappling-iron or cramp

Touch me, send one to hear me speak; then look 73
You take good counsel, before any of you
Try to dispose of me by hook or crook!"

This checked them; and they cried: "Send Belzecue!" 76
And one moved forward, snarling as he went:
"What good does he imagine this will do?"

"Dost thou think, Belzecue, that I had bent 79
My footsteps thus far hither," the master said,
"Safe against all your harms, were I not sent

By will divine, by fates propitious led? 82
Let me pass on; 'tis willed in Heaven that I
Should guide another by this pathway dread."

At this the fiend, crestfallen utterly, 85
Let fall his grappling-iron at his feet,
Crying to the rest: "Strike not! he must go by."

My guide called up: "Thou, cowering there discreet, 88
Hid mousey-mouse among the splintery, cracked
Crags of the bridge, come down! all's safe for it."

I rose and ran to him, and sure I slacked 91
Not speed; for the fiends pressed forward, and grave doubt
Seized me, for fear they might not keep the pact.

So I once saw the footmen, who marched out 94
Under treaty from Caprona, look and feel
Nervous, with all their foes ringed round about.

I pressed close to my guide from head to heel, 97
Cringing, and keeping a sharp eye upon
Their looks, which were by no means amiable.

---

l. 35: *a wretched sinner*: One old commentator identifies him as an alderman called Martino Bottaio, who died in 1300.
l. 37: *our own Hellrakership* (lit.: *Malebranche* of our bridge): Dante calls the demons in this bowge *Malebranche* = Evil Claws, which I have rendered "Hellrakers."
l. 38: *St. Zita's*: i.e., Lucca, whose patron saint was St. Zita.
l. 41: *except Bonturo*: This is sarcasm, since Bonturo Dati was especially notorious for his barratry.
l. 48: *Sacred Face*: an ancient wooden figure of Christ, revered at Lucca, and invoked in time of need.
l. 49: *Serchio*: a river near Lucca.
l. 65: *the sixth bank*: i.e., the lower bank of the Fifth Bowge, which is also the upper bank of the Sixth.
l. 76: *Belzecue*: In Italian, *Malacoda* = Evil Tail. The names of the demons in the Fifth Bowge are thought by some to contain allusions to various Florentine officials who were Dante's enemies; but even if they do, the average English reader cannot get much fun out of it at this time of day. I have therefore Englished most of the names for the greater convenience of rhyme and metre.
l. 82: *by will divine, by fates propitious*: Notice once again the double terminology, as in Canto IX. 94-7 and Canto XIV. 52 and 70.
l. 88: *cowering there*: Dante's comic terror in this bowge is, characteristically, a double-edged gibe at himself and his accusers.
l. 95: *Caprona*: This Pisan fortress was taken by the Tuscan Guelfs in 1289, and Dante, apparently, took part in the operation.

They lowered their hooks to the ready, and, "Just for fun," 100
Says one, shall I tickle his rump for him?" "Yes, try it,"
Says another, "nick him and prick him, boy—go on!"

But the other devil, the one that stood in diet 103
Still with my escort, turned him instant round,
Saying: "Now Scaramallion! quiet, quiet!"

And then to us: "By this cliff 'twill be found 106
Impossible to proceed, for the sixth arch
Lies at the bottom, shattered to the ground.

If you're determined to pursue your march, 109
Follow the bank; a span quite free from block
Or fall, lies handy to reward your search;

But this—why, yesterday, five hours by the clock 112
From now, 'twas just twelve hundred, sixty and six
Years since the road was rent by earthquake shock.

I'm sending a squad your way, to fork and fix 115
Any rash soul who may be taking the air;
Why not go with them? They will play no tricks.

Stand forward, Hacklespur and Hellkin there!" 118
He then began, "and Harrowhound as well,
And your decurion shall be Barbiger;

Let Libbicock go too, and Dragonel, 121
Guttlehog of the tusks, and Grabbersnitch
And raving Rubicant and Farfarel

Take a good look all round the boiling pitch; 124
See these two safe, as far as to the spit
That runs unbroken on from ditch to ditch."

"Sir, I don't like the looks of this one bit," 127
Said I; "no escort, please; let's go alone,
If thou know'st how—for I've no stomach to it!

Where is thy wonted caution? Ugh! they frown, 130
They grind their teeth—dost thou not see them? Lo,
How they threat mischief, with their brows drawn down!"

But he: "I'd have thee firmer-minded; no, 133
Let them go grind and gnash their teeth to suit
Their mood; 'tis the broiled souls they glare at so."

They by the left bank wheeling chose their route; 136
But first in signal to their captain each
Thrust out his tongue; and, taking the salute,

He promptly made a bugle of his breech. 139

THE IMAGES. *The Barrators and the Pitch.* The Barrators are to the City what the Simoniacs are to the Church: they make profit out of the trust reposed in them by the community; and what they sell is justice. As the Simoniacs are imbedded in the burning rock, so these are plunged beneath the black and boiling stream, for their dealings were secret. Money stuck to their fingers: so now the defilement of the pitch sticks fast to them.

CANTO XXII

THE STORY. *As the party proceeds along the bank of the bowge, the devils fork a Barrator up out of the pitch, who tells the Poets who he is and mentions the names of some of his fellow-sinners. By a trick he eludes the devils who are preparing to tear him to pieces; whereupon his captors quarrel among themselves and two of them fall into the pitch.*

I have seen horsemen moving camp, and beating
The muster and assault, seen troops advancing,
And sometimes with uncommon haste retreating,

Seen forays in your land, and coursers prancing, 4
O Aretines! and I've beheld some grandish
Tilts run and tourneys fought, with banners dancing,

And fife and drum, and signal-flares a-brandish 7
From towers, and cars with tintinnabulation
Of bells, and things both native and outlandish;

But to so strange a trumpet's proclamation 10
I ne'er saw move or infantry or cavalry,
Or ship by sea-mark or by constellation.

Well, off we started with that bunch of devilry; 13
Queer company—but there! "with saints at church,
And at the inn with roisterers and revelry."

Meanwhile, my eyes were wholly bent to search 16
The pitch, to learn the custom of that moat
And those who wallowed in the scald and smirch.

And very like the dolphins, when they float 19
Hump-backed, to warn poor seamen of the heightening
Storm, that they may prepare to save the boat,

So now and then, to get a little slightening 22
Of pain, some miserable wretch would hulk
His back up, and pop down again like lightning.

Others lay round about like frogs, that skulk 25
At the stream's edge, just noses out of shelter,
The water hiding all their limbs and bulk,—

---

ll. 112-14: *five hours by the clock from now*, etc.: The earthquake is that which followed the Crucifixion and is mentioned by Virgil as having heralded Christ's entry into Hell and caused the landslide on the cliff between the Sixth and Seventh Circles (Canto XII. 34-45). According to the Synoptists, it took place at the ninth hour (3 P.M.); this would make the conversation with Belzecue take place five hours earlier, i.e., at 10 A.M.

l. 113: *twelve hundred, sixty and six*: The Crucifixion is reckoned as having taken place A.D. 34.

l. 125-6: *safe, as far as to the spit that runs unbroken*: As will be seen later (Canto XXIII), the safe-conduct is less valuable than it might appear, and the malicious grimaces of the demons show that they have taken these instructions in the spirit in which they were meant.

ll. 1 *sqq.: I have seen horsemen*, etc.: The Battle of Campaldino (1289) was fought between the Guelfs (headed by Florence) and the Ghibellines (headed by Arezzo). The Florentine forces, among whom Dante was, were thrown into confusion by the first charge of the Aretines; but the Guelfs rallied and eventually defeated the Ghibellines with great slaughter, and the rest of the campaign was fought on Aretine territory.

l. 6: *tilts run and tourneys fought: A tilt* was an encounter between two knights across a barrier; a *tourney* or *tournament* was an "all-in" encounter between equal parties of knights in open field.

l. 8: *cars with tintinnabulation of bells*: In Dante's time, each Italian city had a car (*carroccio*), or war-chariot. It was gaily painted, drawn by oxen, and furnished with a bell, and served as a rallying-point in battle.

ll. 19-21: *dolphins*: This common belief about dolphins is mentioned in a popular Italian version of Brunetto Latini's *Thesaurus*, and elsewhere.

Till Barbiger arrived; then, in a welter
Of fear, with unanimity quite clannish,
They shot into the hot-pot helter-skelter.

I saw—and from my memory cannot banish
The horrid thrill—one soul remain a squatter,
As one frog will at times, when others vanish;

And Grabbersnitch, the nearest truant-spotter,
Hooked him by the clogged hair, and up he came,
Looking to me exactly like an otter.

(I could pick all the fiends out now by name;
I'd watched while they were chosen, noted how
They called each other, and made sure of them.)

"Claws, claws there, Rubicant! we've got him now!
Worry him, worry him, flay him high and low!"
Yelled all the demon-guardians of the slough.

"O master, if thou canst, contrive to know
Who is this wretched criminal." I said,
"Thus fallen into the clutches of the foe."

My guide drew near to him thus hard-bested,
And asked him whence he came; he said: "Navarre;
In that same kingdom was I born and bred.

My mother placed me servant to a peer,
For he that got me was a ribald knave,
A spendthrift of himself and of his gear.

Next, I was good King Tibbald's man, and gave
My mind to jobbery; now, I job no more,
But foot the bill this hotter side the grave."

Here Guttlehog, who, like a savage boar,
Carried great tushes either side his jaws,
Let the wretch feel how deep the fangs could score.

'Twas cat and mouse—ten cats with cruel claws!
But Barbiger, with both arms seizing him,
Cried: "Back! I'll do the grabbing!" In the pause

He leered round at my lord, and said with grim
Relish: "Any further questions? Ask away!
Quick—before some one tears him limb from limb!"

So then my guide: "Name if thou canst, I pray,
Some Latian rogues among these tarry throngs."
And he: "But now, I left one such—or, nay,

One that to a near-neighbouring isle belongs;
Would I lay hid beside him still!—I'd mock
At threatening claws, and ugly tusks, and prongs."

"We've stood too much of this!" cried Libbicock,
And from his arm, making a sudden snatch,
Ripped off a sinewy gobbet with his hook.

Then Dragonel was fain to have a catch
At the dangling legs; which made their leader spin
Round with ferocious haste, and looks to match.

When they were somewhat calmer, and the din
Died down, my guide, turning to him who still
Stared upon his own mangled flesh and skin,

Asked promptly: "Who was he, whom in an ill
Hour thou didst quit, thou sayest, to seek the brink?"
"'Twas Fra Gomitta, the ineffable

Scamp of Gallura, corruption's very sink,"
Said he; "he held his lord's foes in his power,
And earned their praise—earned it right well, I think;

'The golden key,' says he, 'undid the door';
But all his jobs were jobbed; no petty jobbery
For him—he was a sovereign barrator.

With him's Don Michael Zanche, artist in robbery
From Logodor'; their tongues, going clack-clack-clack
About Sardinia, kick up a ceaseless bobbery.

O look! that fiend there grinning at me! alack,
He frightens me!—I've plenty more to tell,
But sure he'll flay my scalp or skin my back!"

Then their huge prefect turned on Farfarel,
Whose eyes were rolling in the act to pounce,
Crying: "Hop off, thou filthy bird of hell!"

"Are there no souls from other lands or towns,"
The quivering wretch went on, "you'd like to see?
Tuscans? or Lombards? I'll get them here at once.

Let but the Hellrakers draw back a wee
Bit from the shore, so that they need not fear
Reprisals, and for one poor little me

I'll fetch up seven, just sitting quietly here
And whistling, as it is our wont to do
When one pops out and finds the coast is clear."

Harrowhound shook his head and scornful threw
His snout up: "That's a dirty trick," said he,
"He's thought of, to get back beneath the brew."

"Trickster I am, and what a trick 'twill be,"
Said he who had every dodge at his command,
"Luring my neighbours to worse misery!"

Here Hellkin got completely out of hand
And burst out: "If thou stoop to hit the ditch
I need not gallop after thee by land,

I have my wings to soar above the pitch;
We'll leave the crest and hide behind the bank—
Are ten heads best, or one? We'll show thee which!"

New sport, good Reader! hear this merry prank!
The silly demons turned their eyes away—
And he who first held back now led the rank.

The Navarrese chose well the time to play;
He dug his toes in hard, then, quick as thought,
Dived; and so baulked the sportsmen of their prey.

Then all were stung with guilt, and he who taught
The rest to play the fool was angriest;
He swooped off to pursue him, shouting: "Caught!"

But all in vain; no wings could fly so fast
As fear; the quarry plunged; the hunter rose,
Skimming the surface with uplifted breast.

Just as the wild-duck, with the falcon close
Upon her, all of a sudden dives down quick,
And up he skirrs again, foiled and morose.

---

l. 44: *who is this wretched criminal*: Tradition says that this is a certain Spaniard, named Ciampolo, or Gian Polo.
l. 52: *King Tibbald*: Teobaldo II (Count Thibaut V of Champagne), king of Navarre (1253-70).
l. 65: *Latian*: a native of Lower Italy. (Dante never uses the word "Italian," but speaks only of Tuscans, Lombards, etc., in the north and Latians in the south.)
l. 67: *a near-neighbouring isle*: Sardinia.
l. 81: *Fra Gomita*: Sardinia at that time belonged to Pisa, and Gomita was judge of the province of Gallura, under Nino Visconti of Pisa, who put up with his peculations until he found that he had been bribed to let some prisoners escape, whereupon he had him hanged.
l. 88: *Michael Zanche*: Vicar of Logodoro under Enzo, king of Sardinia, who was a natural son of Frederick II. About 1290 he was murdered by his son-in-law, Branca d'Oria, whom we shall hear of in Canto XXXIII. 134-47.

Hacklespur, who was furious at the trick, 133
Went rushing after, hoping very much
The sinner would escape, that he might pick

A quarrel; so when he saw the jobber touch 136
Surface and vanish, he turned his claws on his brother—
Fiend, and they grappled over the ditch in a clutch.

But Hellkin was a hawk as good as another 139
To fight back tooth and nail; so, scratching and chewing,
They both dropped down plumb in the boiling smother.

The heat at once unlocked them; their undoing 142
Came when they tried to rise; they struggled, fluttering
With helpless wings clogged stiff by the tarry glueing.

Barbiger, who with the others stood there spluttering 145
With rage, sent four across to the farthermost
Bank with their draghooks; so the band flew scuttering

This side and that, each to some vantage-post 148
Whence they could reach their drags to the pair half-strangled
And baked already beneath the scummy crust;

And there we left them, floundering and entangled. 151

THE IMAGES. *The Tricked and Quarrelling Demons.* Though it may present an appearance of solidarity, Satan's kingdom is divided against itself and cannot stand, for it has no true order, and fear is its only discipline. Moreover, in the long run, the devil is a fool: trickery preys on trickery and cruelty on cruelty.

CANTO XXIII

THE STORY. *The angry demons pursue the Poets, who are forced to escape by scrambling down the upper bank of Bowge vi. Here they find the Hypocrites, walking in Gilded Cloaks lined with lead. They talk to two Jovial Friars from Bologna, and see the shade of Caiaphas crucified upon the ground.*

Silent, apart, companionless we went,
One going on before and one behind,
Like Friars Minor on a journey bent.

And Aesop's fable came into my mind 4
As I was pondering on the late affray—
I mean the frog-and-mouse one; for you'll find

That if with an attentive mind you lay 7
Their heads and tails together, the two things
Are just as much alike as Yes and Yea.

And, as one fancy from another springs 10
Sometimes, this started a new train of thought
Which doubled my first fears and flutterings.

I argued thus: "These demons have been brought, 13
Through us, to a most mortifying plight—
Tricked, knocked about, made fools of, set at naught;

If rage be added to their natural spite 16
They'll come for us, pursuing on our heel
Like greyhounds on the hare, teeth bared to bite."

I kept on looking backward, and could feel 19
My hair already bristling on my head;
"Master," said I, "unless thou canst conceal

Thyself and me, I'm very much afraid 22
Of the Hellrakers; they're after us; I see
And imagine it so, I can hear them now," I said.

"If I were made of looking-glass," said he, 25
"My outward image scarce could mirror thine
So jump as I mirror thine image inwardly.

Even now thy mind came entering into mine, 28
Its living likeness both in act and face;
So to one single purpose we'll combine

The two; if on our right-hand side this place 31
So slopes that we can manage to descend
To the next bowge, we'll flee the imagined chase."

Thus he resolved. He'd hardly made an end, 34
When lo! I saw them, close at hand, and making
To seize us, swooping on wide wings careened.

Then my master caught me up, like a mother, waking 37
To the roar and crackle of fire, who sees the flare,
And snatches her child from the cradle and runs, taking

More thought for him than herself, and will not spare 40
A moment even so much as to cast a shift
About her body, but flees naked and bare;

And over the flinty ridge of the great rift 43
He slithered and slid with his back to the hanging spill
Of the rock that walls one side of the next cleft.

Never yet did water run to the mill 46
So swift and sure, where the head-race rushes on
Through the narrow sluice to hit the floats of the wheel,

As down that bank my master went at a run, 49
Carrying me off, hugged closely to his breast,
Truly not like a comrade, but a son.

And his foot had scarce touched bottom, when on the crest 52
Above us, there they were! But he, at large
In the other chasm, could set his fears at rest;

For that high provident Will which gave them charge 55
Over the fifth moat, curbs them with constraint,
So that they have no power to pass its verge.

And now we saw a people decked with paint, 58
Who trod their circling way with tear and groan
And slow, slow steps, seeming subdued and faint.

l. 3: *Friars Minor*: the Franciscans.
l. 4: *Aesop's fable*: A frog offers to carry a mouse across a pond, tied to its leg. Half-way over, the frog treacherously dives, drowning the mouse. A hawk swoops down and devours both. The fable is found in most of the medieval collections attributed to Aesop. In one version the mouse escapes, and this may have been the one Dante had in mind. The mouse = Ciampolo; the frog = Hellkin; the hawk = Hacklespur.
l. 9: *Yes and Yea*: In the Italian *mo* and *issa*, two words both meaning "now."
l. 25: *looking-glass*: lit.: "leaded glass," mirrors being then made with a backing of lead. Virgil is saying that his own feelings are a perfect reflection of Dante's, both in face (appearance of alarm) and act (recoil from danger); so they will combine their fears and form a common resolution: viz. flight.
l. 31: *on our right-hand side*: They had already crossed the intervening space and were walking along the upper edge of Bowge vi.
l. 54: *the other chasm*: i.e., the Sixth Bowge.
l. 58: *decked with paint*: Some commentators think this means that the faces of the hypocrites were "made up"; but since this could hardly have been apparent to Dante at the first glance, because of the deep hoods they wore, it seems more likely that it refers to the brilliant colour of their cloaks (l. 64).

They all wore cloaks, with deep hoods forward thrown 61
Over their eyes, and shaped in fashion quite
Like the great cowls the monks wear at Cologne;

Outwardly they were gilded dazzling-bright, 64
But all within was lead, and, weighed thereby,
King Frederick's copes would have seemed feather-light.

O weary mantle for eternity! 67
Once more we turned to the left, and by their side
Paced on, intent upon their mournful cry.

But crushed 'neath that vast load those sad folk plied 70
Such slow feet that abreast of us we found
Fresh company with every changing stride.

Wherefore: "Try now to find some soul renowned 73
In name or deed, and as we forward fare,"
I begged my guide, "pray cast thine eyes around."

And, hearing the Tuscan tongue, some one, somewhere 76
Behind us cried: "Stay, stay now! slack your speed,
You two that run so fast through this dark air,

And I, maybe can furnish what you need." 79
My guide looked round, and then to me said: "Good!
Wait here, and then at his own pace proceed."

I stopped, and saw two toiling on, who showed, 82
By looks, much haste of mind to get beside me,
Though cumbered by the great load and strait road.

But when at length they reached us, then they eyed me 85
Askance for a long time before they spoke;
Then turned to each other, saying, while still they spied me:

"That one seems living—his throat moves to the stroke 88
Of the breath and the blood; besides, if they are dead,
What favour exempts them from the heavy cloak?"

And then to me: "O Tuscan, strangely led 91
To the sad college of hypocrites, do not scorn
To tell us who thou art," the spirits said.

I answered them: "I was bred up and born 94
In the great city on Arno's lovely stream,
And wear the body that I've always worn.

But who are you, whose cheeks are seen to teem 97
Such distillation of grief? What comfortless
Garments of guilt upon your shoulders gleam?"

And one replied: "Our orange-gilded dress 100
Is leaden, and so heavy that its weight
Wrings out these creakings from the balances.

Two Jovial Friars were we; our city-state 103
Bologna; Catalano was my name,
His, Loderingo; we were designate

By thine own city, to keep peace and tame 106
Faction, as one sole judge is wont to do;
What peace we kept, Gardingo can proclaim."

"Friars," I began, "the miseries that you—" 109
But broke off short, seeing one lie crucified
There on the ground, with three stakes stricken through;

Who, when he saw me, writhed himself, and sighed 112
Most bitterly in his beard; and seeing me make
A questioning sign, Friar Catalan replied:

"He thou dost gaze on, pierced by the triple stake, 115
Counselled the Pharisees 'twas expedient
One man should suffer for the people's sake.

Naked, transverse, barring the road's extent, 118
He lies; and all who pass, with all their load
Must tread him down; such is his punishment.

In this same ditch lie stretched in this same mode 121
His father-in-law, and all the Sanhedrin
Whose counsel sowed for the Jews the seed of blood." '

Then I saw Virgil stand and marvel at him 124
Thus racked for ever on the shameful cross
In the everlasting exile. He to them

Turning him, then addressed the Friars thus: 127
"May it so please you, if your rule permit,
To tell us if, on this right side the fosse,

Be any gap to take us out of it, 130
That we need not compel any of the Black
Angels to extricate us from this pit."

"Nearer than thou hop'st," the Friar answered back, 133
"There lies a rock, part of the mighty spur
That springs from the great wall, and makes a track

O'er all the cruel moats save this, for here 136
The arch is down; but you could scale the rock,
Whose ruins are piled from the floor to the barrier."

---

l. 63: *at Cologne*: Several old commentators relate a story that the monks of Cologne once grew so arrogant that they made formal request to the Pope to be allowed to wear scarlet robes, with silver girdles and spurs. To punish their pride, the Pope commanded, on the contrary, that they should wear especially ample robes of very common material. Some editors for "Cologne" read "Cluny."

l. 66: *King Frederick's copes*: Frederick II was said to have punished traitors by wrapping them in lead and throwing them into a hot cauldron.

l. 88: *his throat moves*: We may notice the various ways by which Dante's living body is distinguished from the apparent bodies of the shades: in the twilight of Hell his weight sinks Phlegyas' boat "deeper than her wont" (Canto VIII) and dislodges stones (Canto XII); his throat moves when he breathes and speaks, as here; a blow from his foot surprises the souls by its heaviness (Canto XXXII. 90); in Purgatory, where the sun shines, he alone casts a shadow (*Purg.* iii. 16 *sqq.*, etc.).

l. 92: *college of hypocrites*: The word "college" here means only "company."

l. 95: *the great city on Arno's lovely stream*: i.e., Florence.

l. 103: *Jovial Friars*: the nickname of the *Ordo militiae beatae Mariae*, a religious order of knights founded in 1261. Its objects were to promote reconciliation, protect widows and poor persons, etc.; but its rule was so lax that before long it became a scandal and was suppressed.

ll. 105-8: *designate by thine own city*: Catalano de' Malavolti (a Guelf) and Loderingo di Landolo (a Ghibelline), both from Bologna, were in 1266 appointed jointly to the office of *podesta* of Florence, in the hope that they might keep the peace and administer justice impartially; but all that came of their administration was a particularly savage anti-Ghibelline rising, in which the palaces of the Uberti, in the Gardingo, were sacked and burned.

l. 116: *counselled the Pharisees: John* xi. 49, 50.

l. 122: *his father-in-law*: Annas. (*John* xviii. 13.)

l. 124: *I saw Virgil . . . marvel at him*: Virgil had not, of course, seen Caiaphas on his previous journey through Hell (see Canto IX. 19-30), which was made before the time of Christ.

My guide stood with bent head and downward look
Awhile; then said: "He gave us bad advice,
Who spears the sinners yonder with his hook."

And the Friar: "I heard the devil's iniquities
Much canvassed at Bologna; among the rest
'Twas said, he was a liar and father of lies."

My guide with raking steps strode off in haste,
Troubled in his looks, and showing some small heat
Of anger; so I left those spirits oppressed,

Following in the prints of the beloved feet.

THE IMAGES. *The Leaden Cloaks.* The image of Hypocrisy, presenting a brilliant show and weighing like lead so as to make spiritual progress impossible, scarcely needs interpretation.

Caiaphas. This image lends itself peculiarly well to Dante's fourfold system of interpretation. (1) *Literal:* the punishment of Caiaphas after death; (2) *Allegorical:* the condition of the Jews in this world, being identified with the Image they rejected and the suffering they inflicted—"crucified for ever in the eternal exile"; (3) *Moral:* the condition in this life of the man who sacrifices his inner truth to expediency (e.g., his true vocation to money-making, or his true love to a politic alliance), and to whom the rejected good becomes at once a heaven from which he is exiled and a rack on which he suffers; (4) *Anagogical:* the state, here and hereafter, of the soul which rejects God, and which can know God only as wrath and terror, while at the same time it suffers the agony of eternal separation from God, who is its only true good.

CANTO XXIV

THE STORY. *After an arduous climb from the bottom of Bowge vi, the Poets gain the arch of the seventh bridge. They hear voices from below, but it is too dark to see anything, so they cross to the far side and go down. The Seventh Bowge is filled with monstrous reptiles, among whom are the shades of Thieves. A Thief is stung by a serpent, reduced to ashes, and then restored to his former shape. He reveals himself to be Vanni Fucci of Pistoia, tells his story, and predicts the overthrow of the Florentine Whites.*

What time the Sun, in the year's early youth,
Beneath Aquarius rinses his bright hair,
And nights begin to dwindle toward the south;

When on the ground the hoar-frost copies fair
Her snow-white sister's image, though her pen,
Soon losing temper, leaves brief traces there;

The hind, no fodder in his empty bin,
Wakes and looks forth; he sees the countryside
All white, slaps a despairing thigh, and then

Back to his cot; and nowhere can abide,
Nothing begin, but roams about the place,
Grieving, poor soul! Once more he peeps outside,

And hope revives—the world has changed its face
In that short time; away, then, to the pasture
He takes his crook, and drives his lambs to graze.

Just so I felt distressed, to see my master
So much put out; in just so brief a while
To salve my sore there came the healing plaster;

For when we reached the arch's broken pile
He turned towards me with the look I knew
First at the mountain's foot—his old, sweet smile.

Opening his arms—but seeming first to do
Some careful planning, and scanning of the rock—
He seized and lifted me; then, like a true

And conscientious workman, who takes stock,
And thinks things out ahead, expending great
Pains, he would hoist me over one big block,

And when I was up, choose out another straight,
Saying: "Now climb this spike—now this—take heed
To test it first; make sure 'twill bear thy weight."

No path was that for one in cloak of lead!
For even we—he weightless, I pushed on—
From crag to crag made arduous way indeed.

Had not the nether of those banks of stone
Been shorter than the upper—I can't tell
How he'd have fared, but I should have been done.

But since toward the mouth of the central well
Malbowges' sides form one continuous slope,
It follows that in each succeeding vale

One bank must rise and the other bank must drop;
And howsoever, we clambered till we got
To the last jag, level with the barrier-top.

My lungs were so pumped out, I just had not
Breath to go on; nor did I try, but came
Scramblingly up and sat down on the spot.

"Put off this sloth," the master said, "for shame!
Sitting on feather-pillows, lying reclined
Beneath the blanket is no way to fame—

Fame, without which man's life wastes out of mind,
Leaving on earth no more memorial
Than foam in water or smoke upon the wind.

Rise up; control thy panting breath, and call
The soul to aid, that wins in every fight,
Save the dull flesh should drag it to a fall.

I. 140: *he gave us bad advise*: Belzecue (Canto XXI. 123-6) had bidden the demons see the poets safe "as far as the unbroken bridge," which, he implied, was near at hand. But the next bridge is broken also, and it now dawns on Virgil that no "unbroken bridge" exists, and that the devil was sending them under a worthless safeguard on a fool's errand. (N.B. On the map, the poets are shown as having already passed another bridgehead unawares on their way between Bowges v and vi; this liberty being taken to gain a little more room for the lettering.)

II. 1-3: *the year's early youth,* etc.: The Sun is in Aquarius (the Water-Carrier) from 21 January to 21 February; the year is just passing out of "childhood" into early "youth"—i.e., from winter to spring. As the Sun moves daily higher into the north, the "nights" (the point of the heavens opposed to the sun) begin to pass away southward, and grow shorter.

II. 5-6: *her pen, soon losing temper*: Hoar-frost melts more quickly than snow.

II. 34-5: *the nether . . . shorter than the upper*: See diagram.

I. 42: *level with the barrier-top*: They have climbed to the top of the lower wall of the bowge, and have still to climb up the side of the spur and reach the arch of the next bridge.

More stairs remain to climb—a longer flight; 55
Merely to quit that crew suffices not;
Dost take my meaning? Act, and profit by it."

So up I scrambled, making myself out 58
Less breathless than I really felt; wherefore:
"Lead on," said I, "I'm resolute and stout."

And on we went, scaling the flinty scaur, 61
Which was rugged, narrow, and awkward in the ascent,
And very much steeper than the one before.

Not wishing to seem weak, I spoke as I went; 64
Whereon a voice rose from the ditch below,
Which sounded like a voice that was not meant

For speech; what it was saying I do not know, 67
Though already I stood on the crown of the bridge across
The moat; but whoever it was seemed angry; so

I craned to see; but the darkness was so gross 70
No living eye could pierce its heavy pall.
"Master," said I, "do please go over the fosse

To the other bank and let's descend the wall; 73
From hence I hear, but cannot understand,
And look below, but cannot see at all."

"My sole reply," said he, "to that demand 76
Is action; when a fit request is made
Silence and deeds should follow out of hand."

So over we went and down, where the bridge's head 79
Stooping to the eighth barrier, hits the brink of it,
And now at last the chasm lay displayed;

And the most loathsome welter filled the sink of it— 82
A mass of serpents, so diverse and daunting,
My blood still turns to water when I think of it.

Let the great Libyan desert cease from vaunting 85
Her cenchrid and chalydra broods, nor boast
The amphisbenes, pareas and jacules haunting

Her sands; she never spawned so vile a host 88
Of plagues, nor all the land of Ethiope,
Nor that which lies along the Red Sea coast.

Amid this cruel and repulsive crop 91
Of monsters, naked men ran terrified,
Hopeless of hiding-hole or heliotrope;

Their hands were held behind their backs and tied 94
With snakes, whose head and tail transfixed the loin,
Writhing in knots convolved on the hither side.

And lo! as one came running near our coign 97
Of vantage on the bank, a snake in a flash
Leapt up and stung him where neck and shoulder join.

Never did writer with a single dash 100
Of the pen write "o" or "i" so swift as he
Took fire, and burned, and crumbled away to ash.

But as he lay on the ground dispersedly, 103
All by itself the dust gathered and stirred
And grew to its former shape immediately.

So wise men say the sole Arabian bird, 106
The phoenix, dies and is reborn from fire
When her five-hundredth year is near expired;

Living, nor herb nor grain is food for her, 109
Only amomum and dropping incense-gums,
And her last swathings are of nard and myrrh.

As one who falls, nor knows how the fit comes, 112
By diabolic power, or oppilation
That chokes the brain with stupefying fumes,

Who, when he rises, stares in consternation 115
All round, bewildered by his late hard throes,
With rolling eyes and anguished suspiration,

So seemed that wretched sinner when he rose. 118
Stern is thy hand, Divine omnipotence,
That in thy vengeance rainest down such blows!

Then my guide asked him who he was, and whence; 121
And he: "From Tuscany I came pelting in
To this fierce gullet, and no long time since.

I loved to live as beasts live and not men, 124
Mule that I was!—Vanni Fucci, absolute
Beast; and Pistoia was my fitting den."

I told my guide: "Bid him not budge a foot, 127
But say what brought him here;—I've only seen him
An evil-tempered, bloody-minded brute."

The sinner heard; nor did he try to screen him, 130
Nor feign, but turned on me his mind and face,
Showing a dismal shame at work within him.

"That thou," said he, "shouldst catch me in this place 133
And see me so, torments me worse than leaving
The other life, and doubles my disgrace.

---

l. 55: *more stairs remain to climb*: primarily, the spur; but Virgil is probably hinting that, even when the whole descent into Hell is accomplished, there remains the steep ascent to Purgatory. To renounce sin is not all: the active work of purgation remains to be done before (if Dante takes his meaning) he can be reunited with Beatrice.
l. 63: *the one before*: i.e., the spur which they had been following from the First Bowge to the Fifth.
ll. 85 *sqq.*: *the great Libyan desert*,etc.: This list of reptilian monsters is taken from Lucan's *Pharsalia* (ix. 708-21); cf. Milton: *Paradise Lost*, x. 519-28.
l. 93: *heliotrope*: a kind of chalcedony, supposed to make the wearer invisible.
l. 94: *their hands were . . . tied*: because they had been used for "picking and stealing."
ll. 107 *sqq.*: *the phoenix*: Legend has it that there was only one phoenix in all the world. Every 500 years she built herself a nest of myrrh and spices. When this had been kindled by the heat of the Arabian sun, she fanned the flames with her wings till she was wholly consumed, and was afterwards reborn from the ashes.
l. 110: *amomum*: a genus of aromatic plants, which includes cardamoms, etc.
ll. 112 *sqq.*: *one who falls*: Dante is probably describing an epileptic fit.
l. 125: *Vanni Fucci*: This notorious ruffian was a Black Guelf from Pistoia. With two accomplices he stole the treasure of San Jacopo from the Church of San Zeno (1293). For this crime an innocent man (Rampino dei Foresi) was arrested, but Vanni Fucci (who had fled the city) laid an information against the person who had acted as receiver. The latter was hanged and Rampino set at liberty.
l. 126: *Pistoia was my fitting den*: Pistoia was infamous as the birthplace of the feud between Blacks and Whites.
l. 128: *say what brought him here*: i.e., to the Bowge of the Thieves; for Dante had only known him as a "man of blood," and might have expected to find him in the Marsh of the Wrathful or the Boiling River.

Yet answer thee I must, without deceiving:
I'm thrust so low, because I stole the treasure
Of the sacristy; for which fine piece of thieving

Others were falsely blamed and put in seizure;
But lest, if ever thou escape these drear
Abodes, this picture should afford thee pleasure,

I'll tell thee something; prick thine ears and hear:
Pistoia shall purge out the party Black;
New men, new laws in Florence shall appear;

From Valdimagra Mars shall bring a stack
Of vapour rolled in clouds turbid as night,
And with impetuous storm and tempest-wrack

Over Piceno's field all shall rage the fight,
Whence he shall suddenly rend the mists apart
Striking a blow to stagger every White;

And so I tell thee; may it break thy heart."

THE IMAGES. *The Thieves.* Two cantos are devoted to the Thieves, the full nature of whose punishment is not fully developed till we get to Canto XXV. The old commentators point out the likeness between the subtle serpent and the creeping thief; in this canto we can already see how, as in life the thief stole other men's goods, so here he is himself robbed of his very semblance. One must always remember that to the mind of the Middle Ages a man's lawful property was an extension of his personality (see Canto XI. 41, note)—an exterior body, as it were, and, like that body, a sacred trust to be used and not abused, either by himself or by others. This accounts for the severe view which Dante takes of offences against property.

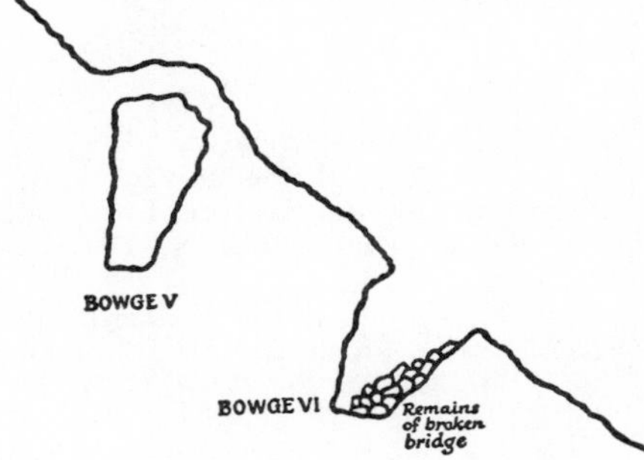

Diagram to illustrate Canto XXIV. 34–5

CANTO XXV

THE STORY. *Vanni Fucci defies God and flees, pursued by the monster Cacus. Three more spirits arrive, and the Poets watch while one of them becomes blended with the form of a reptile containing the spirit of a fourth, and the second exchanges shapes with yet another transformed Thief.*

This said, the thief lifted his hands on high,
Making the figs with both his thumbs, and shrieking:
"The fico for Thee, God! take that, say I!"

At once I liked the snakes; for one came sneaking
About his throat, and wreathed itself around
As though to say: "I will not have thee speaking";

Another wrapped his arms, and once more bound
All fast in front, knotting the coils till he
Could give no jog, they were so tightly wound.

Pistoia, O Pistoia! well were thee
To burn thyself to ashes and perish all,
Whose crimes outgo thy criminal ancestry!

Through all Hell's sable gyres funereal
I saw no spirit so proud against the Lord—
No, not that king who fell from the Theban wall—

As this; he fled without another word;
And I saw a centaur galloping in a storm
Of wrath: "Where, where's this insolent wretch?" he roared.

Maremma, methinks, breeds no such serpent-swarm
As from his crupper writhed in hideous play
To where horse-withers join with human form.

Behind his head, crouched on his shoulders, lay
A dragon with spread wings, whose bruning breath
Set fire to all that crossed him on the way.

"Lo, Cacus!" said my guide, "who dwelt beneath
Mount Aventine's high rock, and split abroad
Full many a time a lake of blood and death.

He with his brethren goes not one same road,
For when his knavish hand drew to his den
His neighbour's kine, he wrought a theft by fraud,

Whereby his crooked courses ended, when
Hercules with his club rained on him nigh
One hundred blows, whereof he felt not ten."

---

ll. 142 *sqq.*: In May 1301, the Florentine Whites assisted the Pistoian Whites to rid Pistoia of the Blacks, who then took refuge in Florence, joined the Black party there, and in November, when Charles of Valois entered the city, helped in their turn to expel the Whites from Florence. "Piceno's field" is probably the battle in which the Florentine and Lucchese Blacks, under the command of Moroello Malaspina (the "stack of vapour"), Lord of Lunigiana in the Valdimagra, captured the White stronghold of Serravalle.
l. 2: *the figs*: an obscene and insulting gesture, made by thrusting the thumb between the first and second fingers.
l. 12: *thy criminal ancestry*: alluding to the tradition that Pistoia was founded by the remnants of Catiline's army.
l. 15: *that king who fell from the Theban wall*: Capaneus (see Canto XIV. 51 and note).
l. 25: *Cacus*: This giant was not really a Centaur; Dante was probably misled by Virgil's calling him "semi-human." He stole the oxen of Geryon, which Hercules was bringing from Spain as one of his Twelve Labours, and dragged them backwards into his cave so as to leave a misleading set of hoof-prints; but Hercules heard them bellowing, killed Cacus, and recovered his property.
l. 28: *his brethren*: the Centaurs of Circle 7, Ring i (Canto XII). Cacus added theft to his crimes of bloodshed, and is therefore placed in this lower circle.
l. 33: *whereof he felt not ten*: because he died after the first nine.

While he thus spake, the centaur thundered by, 34
And at the same time, close beneath us, three
Spirits arrived, whom nor my guide nor I

Noticed, until they shouted: "Who are ye?" 37
So we broke off the tale, to pay attention
To them. Just who they were I could not see;

But, as so often haps, by intervention 40
Of chance, or other such occasion-bringer,
One of them, as they spoke, was moved to mention

Another, saying: "Why does Cianfa linger? 43
Where is he?" So, to bid my guide give ear,
From chin to nose I laid a warning finger.

Reader, if thou discredit what is here 46
Set down, no wonder; for I hesitate
Myself, who saw it all as clear as clear.

Lo! while I gazed, there darted up a great 49
Six-legged worm, and leapt with all its claws
On one of them from in front, and seized him straight;

Clasping his middle with its middle paws, 52
Along his arms it made its fore-paws reach,
And clenched its teeth tightly in both his jaws;

Hind-legs to thighs it fastened, each to each, 55
And after, thrust its tail betwixt the two,
Up-bent upon his loins behind the breech.

Ivy to oak so rooted never grew 58
As limb by limb that monstrous beast obscene
Cling him about, and close and closer drew,

Till like hot wax they stuck; and, melting in, 61
Their tints began to mingle and to run,
And neither seemed to be what it had been;

Just as when paper burns you see a dun 64
Brown hue go creeping up before the flare,
Not black as yet, although the white has gone.

The other two cried out, left gaping there: 67
"O me, Agnel! how thou art changed!" they said;
"Now 'tother nor which! nor single nor a pair!"

Two heads already had become one head, 70
We saw two faces fuse themselves, to weld
One countenance whence both the first had fled;

Into two arms the four fore-quarters swelled; 73
Legs and thighs, breast and belly, blent and knit
Such nightmare limbs as never eye beheld;

All former forms wholly extinct in it, 76
The perverse image—both at once and neither—
Reeled slowly out of sight on languid feet.

And just as a lizard, with a quick, slick slither, 79
Flicks across the highway from hedge to hedge,
Fleeter than a flash, in the battering dog-day weather,

A fiery little monster, livid, in a rage, 82
Black as any peppercorn, came and made a dart
At the guts of the others, and leaping to engage

One of the pair, it pierced him at the part 85
Through which we first draw food; then loosed its grip
And fell before him, outstretched and apart.

The stung thief stared, but no word passed his lip; 88
He stood, foot-fixed, rigid in every limb,
Yawning, as though o'ercome by fever or sleep.

He eyed the monster and the monster him; 91
From this one's mouth, from that one's wound, a trail
Of smoke poured out; meeting, they merged their stream.

Let Lucan whisht now with his wondrous tale 94
Of poor Sabellus and Nasidius,
And wait to hear the wonder that befel;

Whisht Ovid! though he metamorphosed thus 97
Cadmus and Arethusa to a snake
And fountain, I need not be envious;

He never undertook in verse to make 100
Two natures interchanging, eye to eye,
Substance and form by mutual give-and-take

For with strange corresponding symmetry, 103
The monster's tail forked to a double tine;
The shade's feet clave together, till by and by

Legs, thighs and all so fused that never a sign 106
Could be discerned of seam, or junction scarred,
Or suture anywhere along the line;

The cloven tail put on the image marred 109
And lost in the other, and the reptile's skin
Softened all over, while the man's grew hard.

I saw the arms at the arm-pits shrivel in; 112
And the brute's fore-feet, which were stubby and stout,
As the other's shortened, lengthen and grow thin.

The hind-feet, intertwined, began to sprout 115
Into the member which men keep concealed,
Whence, in the thief, two nasty paws shot out.

The smoke with counter-change of colour wheeled 118
Re-dyeing both; the hair was stript and sown
So that one head grew shag, the other peeled.

One of them rose erect and one dropped down, 121
Yet never shifting the fixed, evil stare
Wherein each made the other's face his own.

The erect one's snout bulged temple-wards, and there 124
Out of the superfluity of stuff,
From each flat cheek-bone there emerged an ear;

---

l. 35: *close beneath us*: It seems clear that the poets did not go right down to the floor of the bowge among the serpents. They either remained on the top of the bank or (as is perhaps more probable from Canto XXVI. 13-15) came part of the way down.

ll. 35-6: *three spirits*: Agnello dei Brunelleschi, Buoso degli Abati (or possibly the Buoso dei Donati mentioned in Canto XXX. 44), and Puccio dei Galigai. These, together with Cianfa dei Donati and Francesco Guercio dei Cavalcanti, who appear in the form of serpents, are the five Florentine nobles who, in this canto, confusingly exchange shapes.

ll. 49-50: *a great six-legged worm*: This is Cianfa dei Donati, the missing member of the party, who has been changed into a reptile.

l. 68: *Agnel*: This is Agnello dei Brunelleschi.

l. 82: *a little fiery monster*: This is Francesco Guercio dei Cavalcanti, whom Dante does not identify till the last line of the canto.

l. 85: *one of them*: This is Buoso degli Abati (or dei Donati).

ll. 85-6: *the part through which we first draw food*: the navel.

l. 94: *Lucan*: in his *Pharsalia*, tells how, on Cato's march through the Libyan desert, two of his soldiers were stung by serpents. One, Sabellus, dissolved away into a puddle of liquid flesh; the other, Nasidius, swelled up into a shapeless mass tthat burst his coat of mail.

l. 97: *Ovid*: See *Metamorphoses* iv. 563 *sqq.* and v. 572 *sqq.*

Part went not back, but stayed in front, whereof
The extra matter formed a nose to adorn
The face, and proper lips made thick enough.

He that lay prostrate had his features drawn
Forth to a muzzle, and inside his head
He pulled his ears, as a snail pulls her horn;

The tongue once whole and apt for speech was splayed
Into a fork; in the forked tongue the split
Closed; and the smoke subsided. Then the shade

Now brutified, fled off with hiss and spit
Along the valley; the other, in a crack,
Chattering and sputtering, sped off after it;

Then suddenly turned on it his new-made back,
Bawling to his fellow: "I'll see Buoso range,
Crawling as I crawled, all around the track!"

Thus I saw change, re-change and interchange
The seventh moat's ballast; if my pen has erred,
Pray pardon me: 'twas all so new and strange.

And though my vision was perplexed and blurred,
My mind distraught, the prompt celerity
With which those flying sinners disappeared

Was no disguise for Limping Puccio—he
Was the only one, in fact, who did not turn
Into something else, of the original three;

The other was he that made Gaville mourn.

THE IMAGES. In this canto we see how the Thieves, who made no distinction between *meum* and *tuum*—between "mine" and the "thine"—cannot call their forms or their personalities their own; for in Hell's horrible parody of exchange the "I" and the "thou" fluctuate and are lost.

CANTO XXVI

THE STORY. *Dante, with bitter irony, reproaches Florence. The Poets climb up and along the rugged spur to the arch of the next bridge, from which they see the Counsellors of Fraud moving along the floor of the Eighth Bowge, each wrapped in a tall flame. Virgil stops the twin-flame which contains the souls of Ulysses and Diomede, and compels Ulysses to tell the story of his last voyage.*

Florence, rejoice, because thy soaring fame
Beats its broad wings across both land and sea,
And all the deep of Hell rings with thy name!

Five of thy noble townsmen did I see
Among the thieves; which makes me blush anew,
And mighty little honour it does to thee.

But if toward the morning men dream true,
Thou must ere long abide the bitter boon
That Prato craves for thee, and others too;

Nay, were't already here, 'twere none too soon;
Let come what must come, quickly—I shall find
The burden heavier as the years roll on.

We left that place; and by the stones that bind
The brink, which made the stair for our descent,
My guide climbed back, and drew me up behind.

So on our solitary way we went,
Up crags, up boulders, where the foot in vain
Might seek to speed, unless the hand were lent.

I sorrowed then; I sorrow now again,
Pondering the things I saw, and curb my hot
Spirit with an unwontedly strong rein

For fear it run where virtue guide it not,
Lest, if kind star or greater grace have blest
Me with good gifts, I mar my own fair lot.

Now, thickly clustered,—as the peasant at rest
On some hill-side, when he whose rays illume
The world conceals his burning countenance least,

What time the flies go and mosquitoes come,
Looks down the vale and sees the fire-flies sprinkling
Fields where he tills or brings the vintage home—

So thick and bright I saw the eighth moat twinkling
With wandering fires, soon as the arching road
Laid bare the bottom of the deep rock-wrinkling.

Such as the chariot of Elijah showed
When he the bears avenged beheld it rise,
And straight to Heaven the rearing steeds upstrode,

For he could not so follow it with his eyes
But that at last it seemed a bodiless fire
Like a little shining cloud high in the skies,

So through that gulf moved every flaming spire;
For though none shows the theft, each, like a thief,
Conceals a pilfered sinner. To admire,

I craned so tip-toe from the bridge, that if
I had not clutched a rock I'd have gone over,
Needing no push to send me down the cliff.

II. 135-6: *the shade now brutified*: i.e., Buoso.
I. 137: *the other*: i.e., Francesco dei Cavalcanti, now restored to human form.
I. 148: *Limping Puccio* (Puccio Sciancato): this is Puccio dei Galigai. Dante did not at first (I. 39) know him, but recognized him by his limp when he ran off.
I. 151: *that made Gaville mourn*: Francesco dei Cavalcanti was killed by the inhabitants of this village in the Arno Valley, and his kinsmen avenged his death on the villagers. A summary of these various transformations may be a convenience:
(1) *Agnello*: appears as a man, and is blended with
(2) *Cianfa*, who appears as a six-legged monster.
(3) *Buoso*: appears first as a man, and changes shapes with
(4) *Francesco*, who appears first as a four-legged "lizard."
(5) *Puccio*: remains unchanged.
I. 9: *Prato*: Cardinal Nicholas of Prato was sent to Florence in 1304 by Pope Benedict XI in hopes of reconciling the hostile factions. Finding all his efforts wasted, he said, "Since you refuse to be blessed, remain accursed," and laid the city under an interdict. Various disasters which happened shortly afterwards—the collapse of a bridge, killing a vast number of people, and a terrible fire in which over 2000 houses were destroyed and many great families ruined—were attributed to the curse of the Church.
II. 20-24: Dante realizes that he, like the Counsellors, has been blessed by fate ("kind star") or Providence ("greater grace") with great intellectual gifts, and must, therefore, take particular care not to abuse them.
I. 26: *when he whose rays*, etc.: i.e., in summer, when the days are longest.
I. 28: *what time the flies go and mosquitoes come*: i.e., at dusk.
I. 35: *he the bears avenged*: Elisha. (2 Kings ii. 11-12, 23-24.)

Seeing me thus intently lean and hover, 46
My guide said: "In those flames the spirits go
Shrouded, with their own torment for their cover."

"Now thou hast told me, sir," said I, "I know 49
The truth for sure; but I'd already guessed,
And meant to ask—thinking it must be so—

Who walks in that tall fire cleft at the crest 52
As though it crowned the pyre where those great foes,
His brother and Eteocles, were placed?"

"Tormented there," said he, "Ulysses goes 55
With Diomede, for as they ran one course,
Sharing their wrath, they share the avenging throes.

In fire they mourn the trickery of the horse, 58
That opened up the gates through which the high
Seed of the Romans issued forth perforce;

There mourn the cheat by which betrayed to die 61
Deïdamia wails Achilles still;
And the Palladium is avenged thereby."

Then I: "O Master! if these sparks have skill 64
To speak, I pray, and re-pray that each prayer
May count with thee for prayers innumerable,

Deny me not to tarry a moment here 67
Until the horned flame come; how much I long
And lean to it I think thee well aware."

And he to me: "That wish is nowise wrong, 70
But worthy of high praise; gladly indeed
I grant it; but do thou refrain thy tongue

And let me speak to them; for I can read 73
The question in thy mind; and they, being Greek,
Haply might scorn thy speech and pay no heed."

So, when by time and place the twin-fire peak, 76
As to my guide seemed fitting, had come on,
In this form conjuring it, I heard him speak:

"You that within one flame go two as one, 79
By whatsoever I merited once of you,
By whatsoever I merited under the sun

When I sang the high songs, whether little or great my due, 82
Stand; and let one of you say what distant bourne,
When he voyaged to loss and death, he voyaged unto."

Then of that age-old fire the loftier horn 85
Began to mutter and move, as a wavering flame
Wrestles against the wind and is over-worn;

And, like a speaking tongue vibrant to frame 88
Language, the tip of it flickering to and fro
Threw out a voice and answered: "When I came

From Circe at last, who would not let me go, 91
But twelve months near Caieta hindered me
Before Aeneas ever named it so,

No tenderness for my son, nor piety 94
To my old father, nor the wedded love
That should have comforted Penelope

Could conquer in me the restless itch to rove 97
And rummage through the world exploring it,
All human worth and wickedness to prove.

So on the deep and open sea I set 100
Forth, with a single ship and that small band
Of comrades that had never left me yet.

Far as Morocco, far as Spain I scanned 103
Both shores; I saw the island of the Sardi,
And all that sea, and every wave-girt land.

I and my fellows were grown old and tardy 106
Or ere we made the straits where Hercules
Set up his marks, that none should prove so hardy

---

l. 54: *Eteocles*: The war of the Seven against Thebes arose from the rival claims of Eteocles and his brother Polynices, the sons of Oedipus, to the throne. They killed each other in battle, and were placed on one pyre; but, even so, such was their mutual hatred that their very flames would not mingle. (Statius: *Thebaïd* xii, 429 *sqq.*)

ll. 55-6: *Ulysses . . . Diomede*: the Greek heroes who fought against Troy. The "crafty Ulysses" (Odysseus) advised the stratagem of the Wooden Horse, by which Greek soldiers were smuggled into Troy to open the gates to the besiegers; and also the theft of the sacred statue of Pallas (the Palladium) on which the safety of Troy was held to depend. Thetis, the mother of Achilles, knowing that he would perish if he went to Troy, concealed him at the court of the king of Scyros, disguised as a woman; but he seduced the king's daughter, Deïdamia, who bore him a son. Ulysses discovered his hiding-place and persuaded him to go to Troy; whereupon Deïdamia died of grief.

ll. 74-5: *they: being Greek . . . might scorn thy speech*: The great Greek heroes would despise Dante, as an Italian (i.e., a descendant of the defeated Trojans).

l. 78: *in this form*: Virgil is also an Italian; but he has the power, which Dante has not, of compelling the spirits. We must remember that Virgil, in the Middle Ages, was thought of as a "White Magician," and though the power he uses is not what we should nowadays call "magic" in any evil sense, what follows is in fact a *formal conjuration.* Notice that, since Virgil is here only gratifying Dante's laudable curiosity, he does not use any of those great "words of power" by which he overcame the ministers of Hell in the name of high Heaven (cf. Cantos III. 95; V. 23; VII. 11, etc.), but relies on his own power, which is twofold: (1) the native virtue of a good man who, though not in the Grace of Christ, is yet fulfilling a Divine commission "under the Protection"; (2) the claim of the Poet upon the souls who are indebted to him for their fame in the world.

ll. 80-83: *"By whatsoever . . . stand and . . . say":* This is the *forma*—the form, or formula—of conjuration: a twice-repeated obsecration, "by whatsoever . . . " (naming the claim which constitutes the point of psychic contact between the master and the spirits), followed by a command: "stand . . . speak." In the next canto we shall see that the spirits cannot depart until he dismisses them (Canto XXVII. 3) and a few lines later (Canto XXVII. 21) we shall be given the *forma* of the "licence to depart."

l. 83: *one of you*: i.e., Ulysses. Notice that, unlike the other spirits with whom the poets talk, Ulysses never addresses them personally. Compelled by the conjuration, his narrative reels off automatically like a gramophone record and then stops.

The voyage of Ulysses, perhaps the most beautiful thing in the whole *Inferno,* derives from no classical source, and appears to be Dante's own invention. It may have been suggested to him by the Celtic voyages of Maelduin and St. Brendan. It influenced Tasso (*Ger. Lib.* Canto XV.), and furnished Tennyson with the theme for his poem *Ulysses.*

l. 91: *Circe*: the sorceress who detained Ulysses on his way from Troy to Ithaca, after turning several of his companions into swine (see *Odyssey*, Bk. x).

l. 92: *Caieta* (Gaeta): a town on the south coast of Italy, said to have been so named by Aeneas after his old nurse, who died and was buried there (*Aen.* vii. 1-4).

l. 96: *Penelope*: the faithful wife of Ulysses.

l. 104: *the island of the Sardi*: Sardinia.

l. 108: *his marks*: The Pillars of Hercules were looked upon as the limit of the habitable globe, and the sun was imagined setting close behind them.

To venture the uncharted distances;
Ceuta I'd left to larboard, sailing by,
Seville I now left in the starboard seas.

'Brothers,' said I, 'that have come valiantly
Through hundred thousand jeopardies undergone
To reach the West, you will not now deny

To this last little vigil left to run
Of feeling life, the new experience
Of the uninhabited world behind the sun.

Think of your breed; for brutish ignorance
Your mettle was not made; you were made men,
To follow after knowledge and excellence.'

My little speech made every one so keen
To forge ahead, that even if I'd tried
I hardly think I could have held them in.

So, with our poop shouldering the dawn, we plied,
Making our oars wings to the witless flight,
And steadily gaining on the larboard side.

Already the other pole was up by night
With all its stars, and ours had sunk so low,
It rose no more from the ocean-floor to sight;

Five times we had seen the light kindle and grow
Beneath the moon, and five times wane away,
Since to the deep we had set course to go,

When at long last hove up a mountain, grey
With distance, and so lofty and so steep,
I never had seen the like on any day.

Then we rejoiced; but soon we had to weep,
For out of the unknown land there blew foul weather,
And a whirlwind struck the forepart of the ship;

And three times round she went in a roaring smother
With all the waters; at the fourth, the poop
Rose, and the prow went down, as pleased Another,

And over our heads the hollow seas closed up."

THE IMAGES. *The Counsellors of Fraud.* The sinners in Bowge viii are not men who deceived those whom they counselled, but men who counselled others to practise fraud. The Thieves in the bowge above stole material goods; these are spiritual thieves, who rob other men of their integrity. This explains, I think, the name which Dante gives to their punishment.

The Thievish Fire: The fire which torments also conceals the Counsellors of Fraud, for theirs was a furtive sin (Lat.: *furtivus*, from *fur*, thief). And as they sinned with their tongues, so now speech has to pass through the tongue of the tormenting and thievish flame.

CANTO XXVII

THE STORY. *The spirit of Guido da Montefeltro asks for news of Romagna, and, being answered, tells his story.*

Erect and quiet now, its utterance done,
The tall flame stood; and presently, dismissed
By the sweet poet's licence, it passed on;

When lo! our eyes were drawn towards the crest
Of a new flame, coming behind its fellow,
By the strange muffled roarings it expressed.

As the Sicilian bull, first made to bellow
(And that was justice) by his cries whose tool
Tuned the vile instrument and made it mellow,

Bellowed with its victim's voice, until the bull,
Though brass throughout, appeared itself to roar,
Pierced through with torments unendurable,

So, finding at the start no way nor door
Out of the fire, the sad words were translated
Into fire's native speech; but when they wore

Their way up to the tip and had vibrated
That, with the same vibration given to them
By the tongue, as they passed out articulated,

We heard it say: "O thou at whom I aim
My voice, who saidst in speech of Lombardy:
'Go now; I vex thee with no further claim';

Though I have come a little late maybe,
Speak to me! let it not irk thee to be stayed,
For see! I burn, and yet it irks not me.

If thou into this blind realm of the dead
Art fall'n but now from those sweet Latian shores
Whence I brought all my sins here on my head,

Tell me, have the Romagnols peace or wars?
For I was of the mountains there, between
Urbino and the yoke whence Tiber pours."

Now as I leaned there still, intent and keen,
My leader touched my side, and said: "Go to;
This one is Latian, so do thou begin."

I had my answer all prepared, and so
Made no delay but carried the talk on,
Saying: "O spirit hidden there below,

---

ll. 127 *sqq.*: *the other pole*, etc.: The voyagers had crossed the equator and made so much leeway south that the Southern Celestial Pole stood high in the heavens with all its attendant constellations; consequently, not only was our Pole Star beneath the northern horizon, but the Arctic constellations (the Great and Little Bears, etc.), which in this hemisphere never set, there never rose.

l. 133: *a mountain*: This is the mountain of the Earthly Paradise, which, after Christ's Harrowing of Hell, becomes Mount Purgatory—the only land, according to Dante, in the Southern Hemisphere (see Canto XXXIV. 122-3, note).

l. 141: *as pleased Another*: i.e., as pleased God.

ll. 2-3: *dismissed by the sweet poet's licence*: These lines make it clear that the conjured spirits cannot move with the formal permission of the Master (see note, Canto XXVI. 80-83).

l. 7: *the Sicilian bull*: This instrument of torture was made by Perillus for Phalaris, the Sicilian tyrant. The victims were roasted alive in it, and their yells, issuing through the brazen mouth, were supposed to sound like the bull bellowing. Phalaris, with grisly humour, tried the invention out on Perillus (Ovid: *Ars Amat.* i. 635-6).

ll. 13-18: This rather complicated description becomes easily intelligible if one thinks how words spoken into a telephone are transmitted as electrical waves and retranslated into speech by vibrating the receiver at the other end of the line.

ll. 20-21: *who saidst in speech of Lombardy*: *"Go now,"* etc.: This is the *forma* of the "licence to depart"—*"issa ten va, più non t' adizzo"*—"now go, I vex thee no further." (The fact that Virgil uses "speech of Lombardy" shows that it was not the difference of language that would have prevented the Greeks from paying attention to Dante).

l. 29: *I was of the mountains there*: The speaker is the great Ghibelline leader, Guido da Montefeltro (1223-98) of Romagna.

Not now, nor ever, has thy Romagna known 37
Times when her tyrants' hearts were free from feud,
But open strife just now I there left none.

Ravenna stands as many a year she's stood; 40
The Eagle of Polenta, with broad vans
Stretched o'er Cervia, sits and guards his brood.

She that piled up the slaughtered hordes of France, 43
Having endured such stubborn siege and strong,
Is back beneath the Green Claws' governance.

The Mastiffs of Verrucchio old and young, 46
That mauled Montagna with such murderous mouth,
Flesh their keen teeth where they have fleshed them long.

Beside Lamone and Santerno both, 49
The cities serve the white-haired Lioncel
Who changes sides as he turns north or south.

The town where Savio bathes the city-wall, 52
Lying betwixt the mountains and the plain,
Like as she lies, so lives 'twixt free and thrall.

And now, pray tell, so may thy name remain 55
Green upon earth, who wast thou? No deny
Was made to thee; deny us not again."

So when the flame had roared confusedly 58
After its wont awhile, it started quaking
Its sharp point to and fro, and breathed reply

As follows: "If I thought that I were making 61
Answer to one that might return to view
The world, this flame should evermore cease shaking.

But since from this abyss, if I hear true, 64
None ever came alive, I have no fear
Of infamy, but give thee answer due.

A man of arms was I, turned Cordelier, 67
Thinking, thus girt, to make amends for ill,
And my whole hope had been fulfilled, I swear,

But for the High Priest—may he rot in Hell!— 70
Who thrust me back in the old evil mesh;
And how and why hearken! for I will tell.

While I was still that shape of bone and flesh 73
In which my mother moulded me at birth
My deeds were foxy and not lionish;

I knew each winding way, each covert earth, 76
And used such art and cunning in deceit
That to the ends of the world the sound went forth.

But when I reached the age when it is meet 79
For every mariner, with his port in sight,
To lower sail and gather in the sheet,

That which had pleased offended me; contrite, 82
Confessed, I took the habit; O, and these
Good means of grace had served to set me right.

But he, the Prince of the modern Pharisees, 85
Having a war to wage by Lateran—
Not against Jews, nor Moslem enemies,

For every foe he had was Christian, 88
Not one had marched on Acre, none had bought
Or sold within the realm of the Soldan—

Reckless of his High Office, setting at naught 91
Both his own priesthood and that girdle of mine
Which once made lean the wearer,—this man sought

Me out, as in Soracte Constantine 94
Sought Silvester to cure his leprosy,
Even so, as a skilled leech to medicine

The fever of his pride, he sent for me, 97
Demanding counsel; I with dubious brow
Sat mute—his words seemed drunken lunacy.

But then he said: 'Fear nothing; here and now 100
I absolve thee in advance; therefore speak out,
Teach me how to lay Palestrina low.

I. 40: *Ravenna*: The lords of Polenta, who bore an eagle on their coat of arms, ruled Ravenna from 1270 to 1441. In 1300 the head of the family was Guido Vecchio ("the elder"), uncle to Dante's friend Guido Novello ("the younger"); his territory had already been extended to cover Cervia, a town about twelve miles south of Ravenna.

I. 43: *She that piled up the . . . hordes of France*: Forli; its successful defence against French troops sent by Pope Martin IV (1282) was conducted by Guido da Montefeltro himself. In 1300 it was ruled by Sinibaldo degli Ordelaffi, whose arms were a lion, vert.

I. 46: *The Mastiffs of Verrucchio*: Malatesta and his son Malatestino of Rimini. They were Black Guelfs; Montagna dei Parcitati, whom they took prisoner (1295) and murdered, was a Ghibelline of the same city.

I. 48: *there*: in Verruchio, family seat of the lords of Rimini.

I. 50: *the white-haired Lioncel*: Mainardo Pagano (*d* 1302), whose arms were a lion, azure, on a field, argent. He was lord of Faenza on the Lamone and of Imola on the Santerno (see map, p. 173); and is said to have behaved like a Ghibelline in Romagna (to the south) and a Guelf in Tuscany (to the north).

I. 52: *where Savio bathes the city-wall*: Cesna (between Forli and Rimini) was continually changing its government, but was in 1300 comparatively free from tyranny, under the rule of its own officers.

II. 56-7: *No deny . . . deny us not*: i.e., "We have answered your question; now answer ours."

II. 61-6: Guido cannot see that Dante is alive, and supposes him to be one of the damned souls on its way to its own place (cf. Cantos XII. 62; XXVIII. 42-5, etc.). Dante does not undeceive him, but leaves the Counsellor of Fraud to his self-deception (see note on Canto VIII. 45). Generally speaking, the shades in the Circles of Fraud, unlike those in the circles above, do not want to have their stories made known in the world.

I. 67: *Cordelier*: a friar, wearing the cord of the Franciscan Order, which Guido entered in 1296.

I. 70: *the High Priest*: i.e., the Pope (Boniface VIII).

I. 86: *a war to wage by Lateran*: The long and embittered feud between Boniface and the Colonna family broke out into open warfare in 1297.

I. 89: *Acre*: the last stronghold that remained to the Christians in Palestine after the Crusades was retaken in 1291 by the Saracens with the aid of renegade Jews and of Christian merchants who treacherously supplied them with contraband of war.

I. 94: *in Soracte*: The legend was that when the Emperor Constantine was stricken with leprosy for his persecution of Christians, he summoned Pope Silvester from his refuge in Soracte, and was converted and cured by him, making the alleged "Donation of Constantine" (see Canto XIX. 115, note) as a thank-offering.

I. 102: *Palestrina* (or Penestrino): The forces of the Colonna had retired to this stronghold. On Guido's advice, the Pope offered them an amnesty, and when they had surrendered on those conditions, razed the place to the ground.

Thou knowest I have the power to open or shut 103
The gates of Heaven, for those High Keys are twain,
The Keys my predecessor cherished not.'

Then he showed weighty cause, till to refrain 106
Seemed worse than speech. 'Father, since thou straightway.'
Said I, 'dost cleanse me of the guilty stain

I must contract, why then, to hold thy sway 109
Victor triumphant in the Holy See,
Promise great things; promise, and do not pay.'

Later, I died, and Francis came for me; 112
But one of the Black Cherubs cried, 'Beware
Thou wrong me not! Hands off! He's not for thee;

He must go join my servitors down there; 115
He counselled fraud—that was his contribution
To Hell; since then I've had him by the hair.

Absolved uncontrite means no absolution; 118
Nor can one will at once sin and contrition,
The contradiction bars the false conclusion.'

O what a waking! when with fierce derision 121
He seized on wretched me, saying: 'I'll be bound
Thou didst not think that I was a logician.'

He haled me off to Minos; eight times round 124
His scaly back the monster twined his tail,
And in his rage he bit it; then he found

Against me, saying: 'Here's a criminal 127
For the thievish fire.' So was I lost, so borne
Where, as thou seest, thus clothed I walk and wail."

Its story told, the flame began to mourn 130
Anew, and sorrowing passed away from us,
Twisting and tossing with its pointed horn;

And we went on, my guide and I, to cross 133
The bridge that o'er the following chasm lies,
Where those who make division and purchase thus

A load of guilt, receive their merchandise. 136

CANTO XXVIII

THE STORY. *From the bridge over the Ninth Bowge the Poets look down upon the Sowers of Discord, who are continually smitten asunder by a Demon with a sword. Dante is addressed by Mahomet and Pier da Medicina, who send messages of warning to people on earth. He sees Curio and Mosca, and finally Bertrand de Born.*

Who, though with words unshackled from the rhymes,
Could yet tell full the tale of wounds and blood
Now shown me, let him try ten thousand times?

Truly all tongues would fail, for neither could 4
The mind avail, nor any speech be found
For things not to be named nor understood.

If in one single place were gathered round 7
All those whose life-blood in the days of yore
Made outcry from Apulia's fateful ground,

Victims of Trojan frays, and that long war 10
Whose spoil was heaped so high with rings of gold,
As Livy tells, who errs not; those that bore

The hammering brunt of battle, being bold 13
'Gainst Robert Guiscard to make stand on stand;
And they whose bones still whiten in the mould

Of Ceperan', where all the Apulian band 16
Turned traitors, and on Tagliacozzo's field
Won by old Alard, weaponless and outmanned;

If each should show his bleeding limbs unhealed, 19
Pierced, lopt and maimed, 'twere nothing, nothing whatever
To that ghast sight in the ninth bowge revealed.

No cask stove in by cant or middle ever 22
So gaped as one I saw there, from the chin
Down to the fart-hole split as by a cleaver.

His tripes hung by his heels; the pluck and spleen 25
Showed with the liver and the sordid sack
That turns to dung the food it swallows in.

I stood and stared; he saw me and stared back; 28
Then with his hands wrenched open his own breast,
Crying: "See how I rend myself! what rack

Mangles Mahomet! Weeping without rest 31
Ali before me goes, his whole face slit
By one great stroke upward from chin to crest.

All these whom thou beholdest in the pit 34
Were sowers of scandal, sowers of schism abroad
While they yet lived; therefore they now go split.

Back yonder stands a fiend, by whom we're scored 37
Thus cruelly; and over and over again
He puts us to the edge of the sharp sword

I. 105: *my predecessor*: Celestine V (see Canto III, 60, note).
I. 112: *Francis*: i.e., St. Francis of Assisi, founder of the Franciscan Order.
II. 118-20: "Contrition is necessary if the absolution is to be valid; but a man cannot be contrite for a sin at the same time that he is intending to commit it, since this involves a contradiction in logic (i.e., one cannot both will and not—will the same thing at the same time); therefore the absolution obtained in these circumstances is invalid."
I. 124: *eight times round*: indicating the Eighth Circle (see Canto V. 10-12), and adding "the Thievish Fire" to show which bowge of it.
I. 9: *Apulia's fatal ground*: The region in south-east Italy where all the wars and battles alluded to in this passage took place.
I. 10: *Trojan frays*: Wars of the Romans (Trojans) against the Samnites (343-290 B.C.); *that long war*, etc.: the Punic Wars (264-146 B.C.).
I. 11: *rings of gold*: According to Livy, so many Romans were killed at the Battle of Cannae, in the second Punic War, that three bushels of golden rings were collected from their bodies.
I. 14: *Robert Guiscard*: combated Greeks and Saracens (1015-85).
I. 16: *Ceperan(o)*: The Apulian barons, under Manfred, deserted at the pass of Ceperano, and let Charles of Anjou through to defeat Manfred at Benevento (1266).
I. 17: *Tagliacozzo*: where Charles of Anjou defeated Manfred's nephew, Conradin; by the advice of Alard de Valery, he allowed two-thirds of his army to retreat, and then, with his reserve troops, annihilated the enemy who had scattered in search of plunder.
I. 31: *Mahomet*: classed as a Christian schismatic.
I. 32: *Ali*: the nephew of Mahomet, was himself the figurehead of an internal schism within the following of the Prophet himself.

As we crawl through our bitter round of pain;
For ere we come before him to be bruised
Anew, the gashed flesh reunites its grain.

But who art thou that dalliest there bemused
Up on the rock-spur—doubtless to delay
Going to thy pangs self-judged and self-accused?"

"Nor dead as yet, nor brought here as a prey
To torment by his guilt," my master said,
"But to gain full experience of the Way

He comes; wherefore behoves him to be led—
And this is true as that I speak to thee—
Gyre after gyre through Hell, by me who am dead."

And, hearing him, stock-still to look on me
Souls by the hundred stood in the valley of stone,
And in amaze forgot their agony.

"Well, go then, thou that shalt behold the sun
Belike ere long—let Fra Dolcino know,
Unless he is in haste to follow me down,

He must well arm himself against the snow
With victuals, lest the Novarese starve him out,
Who else might find him hard to overthrow."

Thus unto me Mahomet, with one foot
Lifted to leave us; having said, he straight
Stretched it to earth and went his dreary route.

Then one with gullet pierced and nose shorn flat
Off to the very eyebrows, and who bare
Only a single ear upon his pate,

Having remained with all the rest to stare,
Before the rest opened his weasand now,
Which outwardly ran crimson everywhere,

And said: "O thou whom guilt condemns not, thou
Whom I have seen up there in Italy
Unless some likeness written in thy brow

Deceives me; if thou e'er return to see
Once more the lovely plain that slopes between
Vercelli and Marcabò, then think of me,

Of Pier da Medicina; and tell those twain,
Ser Guido and Angiolello, Fano's best,
That, if our foresight here be not all vain,

They'll be flung overboard and drowned, in the unblest
Passage near La Cattolica, by the embargo
Laid on their lives at a false lord's behest.

Neptune ne'er saw so foul a crime, such cargo
Of wickedness 'twixt Cyprus and Majorca
Ne'er passed, no pirate-crew, no men of Argo

Could show the like. That one-eyed mischief-worker
Whose land there's one here with me in this vale
Wishes he'd never seen, that smooth-tongued talker

Shall lure them to a parley, and when they sail
Deal so with them that they shall have no need
Of vow or prayer against Focara's gale."

Then I to him: "Tell me, so may I speed
Thy message up to the world as thou dost seek,
Who's he whose eyes brought him that bitter meed?"

At once he laid his hand upon the cheek
Of a fellow-shade, and pulled his jaws apart,
Saying: "Look! this is he; he cannot speak.

This outcast quenched the doubt in Caesar's heart:
'To men prepared delays are dangerous';
Thus he gave sign for civil strife to start."

O how deject to me, how dolorous
Seemed Curio, with his tongue hacked from his throat,
He that of speech was so adventurous!

And one that had both hands cut off upsmote
The bloody stumps through the thick air and black,
Sprinkling his face with many a filthy clot,

And cried: "Think, too, on Mosca, Mosca alack!
Who said: 'What's done is ended,' and thereby
For Tuscany sowed seed of ruin and wrack."

"And death to all thy kindred," added I;
Whereat, heaping despair upon despair,
He fled, like one made mad with misery.

But I remained to watch the throng, and there
I saw a thing I'd hesitate to tell
Without more proof—indeed, I should not dare,

Did not a blameless conscience stead me well—
That trusty squire that harnesses a man
In his own virtue like a coat of mail.

I. 42: *the gashed flesh reunites*: We may suppose that in all cases where damned souls are mangled or mutilated (e.g., by Cerberus in the Third Circle or by the "black braches" in the Wood of the Suicides) the shadowy flesh is thus restored; but Dante, with great artistic tact, says nothing about it until, at this point, he can use it to make a ghastly and grotesque effect. He hints at it again in Canto XXXIV. 60.

I. 56: *Fra Dolcino*: Head of a sect, the "Apostolic Brethren," rightly or wrongly condemned as schismatic. In 1305 Pope Clement V ordered a crusade against the Brethren, and after holding out for a year and a day in the hills near Novara, they were forced to surrender. Dolcino was burnt at Vercelli in 1307.

I. 76: *Pier da Medicina*: whose intrigues were instrumental in fomenting the feud between the houses of Polenta and Malatesta in Romagna. His methods were to disseminate scandal and misrepresentation—hence he is shown mutilated in the eavesdropping ear, the lying throat, and the inquisitive nose.

I. 77: *Guido* (del Cassero) *and Angiolello* (da Calignano): two noblemen of Fano, were invited to a conference at La Cattolica, on the Adriatic, by Malatestino of Rimini, who had them treacherously drowned off the headland of Focara, notorious for its dangerous winds.

I. 84: *men of Argo*: lit.: the Argolican race, i.e., the Greeks, always famous for piracy. But there may be a specific reference to the crime of Argonauts, who murdered Absyrtus and threw his body into the sea on their return from Colchis.

I. 85: *that one-eyed mischief-worker:* Malatestino of Rimini.

I. 93: *that bitter meed*: referring back to II. 86-7. It was by Curio's advice that Julius Caesar crossed the Rubicon (near Rimini), which at that time (49 B.C.) was the frontier between Italy and Cis-Alpine Gaul, and so declared war on the Republic.

I. 98: *to men prepared*, etc.: Quoted from Lucan: *Pharsalia* (i. 281).

I. 106: *Mosca*: The great Guelf-Ghibelline feud in Florence flared up over a family quarrel. Buondelmonte dei Buondelmonti, who was betrothed to a girl of the Amadei, jilted her for one of the Donati. When her kinsfolk were debating how best to avenge the slight, Mosca dei Lamberti said: "What's done is ended" (i.e., "stone dead hath no fellow"). Buondelmonte was accordingly murdered; the whole city took sides; and thenceforward Florence was distracted by the disputes of the rival factions.

Truly I saw—it seems to me I can
See still—I saw a headless trunk that sped
Running towards me as the others ran;

And by the hair it held the severed head
Swung, as one swings a lantern, in its hand;
And that caught sight of us: 'Ay me!" it said.

Itself was its own lamp, you understand,
And two in one and one in two it was,
But how—He only knows who thus ordained!

And when it reached our bridge, I saw it toss
Arm up and head together, with design
To bring the words it uttered near to us;

Which were: "O breathing soul, brought here to win
Sight of the dead, behold this grievous thing,
See if there be any sorrow like to mine.

And know, if news of me thou seek to bring
Yonder, Bertrand de Born am I, whose fell
Counsel, warping the mind of the Young King

Like Absalom with David, made rebel
Son against father, father against son,
Deadly as the malice of Achitophel.

Because I sundered those that should be one,
I'm doomed, woe worth the day! to bear my brain
Cleft from the trunk whence all its life should run;

Thus is my measure measured to me again."

THE IMAGES. *The Sowers of Discord.* Three types are shown: fomenters of (1) religious schism (Mahomet; Ali), (2) civil strife (de Medicina; Curio); (3) family disunion (Mosca; Bertrand).

They appear in the Circle of Fraud because their sin is primarily of the intellect. They are the fanatics of party, seeing the world in a false perspective, and ready to rip up the whole fabric of society to gratify a sectional egotism.

The Sundering Sword. The image here is sufficiently obvious. Note how it is adapted to suit the various types of crime.

CANTO XXIX

THE STORY. *Dante lingers, expecting to see a kinsman of his in the Ninth Bowge; but Virgil says he has already passed by unnoticed. They cross the next bridge and descend into Bowge x, where the Falsifiers lie stricken with hideous diseases. Dante talks with an old friend, Capocchio.*

My eyes were grown so maudlin with the plight
Of all these people racked with wounds and woe,
They longed to linger weeping at the sight;

But Virgil said: "How now! Why dost thou grow
Rooted to gaze? Why is thy vision drowned
Among these smitten shades? Thou didst not so

At the other moats. Dost think that thou art bound
To catalogue them all? Come, use thy wit;
Consider, this fosse is twenty-two miles round,

And already the moon is underneath our feet;
Short grows the time allowed, and on our way
There's more to see than thou hast seen as yet."

"Hadst thou but waited," I began to say,
"To find out what it was I was looking for,
I think perhaps thou wouldst have let me stay."

My guide, however, had started on before,
And I trailed after, making my reply
And adding: "Somewhere on that rocky floor,

I think, among the throng that held my eye,
A spirit of my own blood runs damnified,
Weeping the guilt that there is priced so high."

"Let not thy mind," the master then replied
"Henceforth distract itself upon that fellow;
Thou hast other things to think of—let him bide:

I saw him, close beneath the bridge's hollow,
Pointing at thee, and threatening with bent fist,
And heard him called by name Geri del Bello.

Just at that moment thou wast hard intent
On him that dwelt in Altaforte; hence
Thou didst not look his way, and so he went."

"Alas, dear Sir! his death by violence,"
Said I, "still unavenged by any of them
Who shared the affront, has rankled to this sense

Of deep resentment; wherefore, as I deem,
He went away and would not speak to me;
And all the more for that, I pity him."

Thus we talked up the cliff, till presently
The next moat's bottom came in sight,—or would
Have come in sight had there been light to see.

There, from the crossing-span's high altitude,
Malbowges' final cloister all appears
Thrown open, with its sad lay-brotherhood;

And there, such arrowy shrieks, such lancing spears
Of anguish, barbed with pity, pierced me through,
I had to clamp my hands upon my ears.

Could all disease, all dog-day plagues that stew
In Valdichiana's spitals, all fever-drench
Drained from Maremma and Sardinia, spew

Their horrors all together in one trench—
Like that, so this: suffering, and running sore
Of gangrened limbs, and putrefying stench.

---

l. 134: *Bertrand de Born*: (*c.* 1140-1215), the warrior and troubadour, was lord of Hautefort (Altaforte) in Perigord. According to his Provencal biographers, he fomented the quarrel between Henry II of England and his son Prince Henry, "the Young King" (so-called because he was crowned during his father's lifetime). For Absalom and Achitophel, see 2 *Samuel* xv-xvii. Bertrand is decapitated because to part father and son is like severing the head from the body.

l. 9: *twenty-two miles round*: Various attempts have been made to calculate the exact proportions of Malbowges from the indications in this and the next canto; but I think it is best just to bear in mind that Hell extends from a little below the Earth's surface to its centre, and that the Great Barrier comes about half-way down; and so leave imagination to fill in the details of this colossal scheme.

l. 10: *the moon is underneath our feet*: it is about 1 P.M.

l. 27: *Geri del Bello*: a cousin of Dante's father. He is said to have delighted in making mischief, and to have been killed by a member of the Sacchetti family, which he had set by the ears. The customary vendetta for his death seems not to have been carried out by his kinsmen—or, at any rate, not before 1300.

l. 29: *him that dwelt in Altaforte*: Bertrand de Born.

ll. 47-9: *Valdichiana . . . Maremma and Sardinia*: All these districts were reckoned extremely unhealthy, especially in summer; Valdichiana (in Tuscany, between the mouths of the Chiana) and Maremma being full of marshy and malarial swamps.

Down that last bank of the long cliff we bore, 52
Still turning left; and now as I drew near,
I saw more vividly to the very core

That pit wherein the High Lord's minister 55
Infallible Justice, dooms to pains condign
The falsifiers she registers down here.

No sadder sight was seen, as I divine,— 58
Even in Aegina, when wrath knew no term,
But the whole people in that air malign

Sickened, and beasts, down to the littlest worm, 61
Dropped dead, till in the end the ancient race
Had to be born anew, as poets affirm,

From seed of ants—than in that dreadful place 64
The sight of the spirits strewn through the dark valley,
Heaped here, heaped there, enduring their distress.

This on the back, and that upon the belly 67
One of another lay, while some crawled round
The dismal road, all-fours, lethargically.

So step by step we went, nor uttered sound, 70
To see and hear those sick souls in their pains,
Who could not lift their bodies from the ground.

I saw two sitting, propped like a couple of pans 73
Set to warm by the fireside, back to back,
And blotched from head to foot with scabs and blains.

And I ne'er saw curry-comb plied by ostler's jack 76
Or groom, in a frenzy because his master's waiting,
Or because he is kept up late and wants to pack

Bedwards, to match the furious rasping and grating 79
With which they curried their own hide with their nails,
Maddened by the itch that still finds no abating.

The nail went stripping down the scurfy shales, 82
Just as a scullion's knife will strip a bream,
Or any other fish with great coarse scales.

"Thou that dost take thy finger-nails to trim 85
Thy coat, and sometimes," thus my guide began
To one of these, "for pincers usest them,

Tell us, so may thy claws outlast the span 88
Of all eternity to do their task,
Is any one here within a Latian man?"

"We who confront thee in this hideous mask 91
Are Latians both," one answered in a wail,
"But who art thou? and wherefore dost thou ask?"

"I am one who comes descending, vale by vale, 94
To lead this living man," my guide averred,
"And all my business is to show him Hell."

Their mutual propping broke; startled, they stirred 97
And turned towards me trembling; others too
Turned when they caught the echo of his word.

Then my kind master courteously withdrew 100
To give me place: "Whate'er thou wilt," he said,
"Ask them." And since he urged me so to do

I thus began: "So may your names not fade, 103
In that first world, from human memory,
But live for many suns, be not afraid

To tell me who and whence you both may be, 106
Nor let your sad and shameful state prevent
Your free unfolding of yourselves to me."

"I'm Aretine, and to the stake was sent 109
By Alberto of Siena; yet," said one,
"What caused my death caused not this punishment.

It's true I told the fool one day for fun: 112
'I can take wings and fly,' and he—an ass
Full of wild whims, with addled wits, or none—

Would have me teach him how; and just because 115
I could not make him Daedalus, why, then
He had me burned, by one who, more or less,

Fathered him; but to this last bowge of ten 118
Unerring Minos doomed me for the art
Alchemic, which I practised among men."

"Was ever race so frivolous of heart," 121
Said I to the poet, "as the Sienese?
I think they could give even the French a start

And a beating." Whereupon the second of these 124
Leprous shades joined in: "Except, no doubt,
Stricca, renowned for his economies,

And Niccolò, of course, who first found out 127
How to make cloves a costly cult and passion
In the garden where such seeds take root and sprout;

Oh—and except the club where Caccia d'Ascian 130
Lost woods and vineyards, and the ingenious
Abbagliato, like a man of fashion,

Displayed his wit. Wouldst know who backs thee thus 133
Against Siena? Come, focus thy glance,
Get my face clear; thou'lt not be at a loss

To know Capocchio's shadowy countenance, 136
Transmuter of metals, alchemist, and—a feature
Which, if I eye thee hard, thou wilt at once

Recall—a most consummate ape of nature." 139

THE IMAGES. *The Falsifiers.* The Tenth Bowge shows us the images of those who falsified things, words, money, and persons. This canto deals with the falsifiers of things, typified by the Alchemists (transmuters of metals). They may be taken to figure every kind of deceiver who tampers with the basic commodities by which society lives—the adulterators of food and drugs, jerry-builders, manufacturers of

---

l. 59: *Aegina*: The story of the pestilence sent by Juno, and of how Jupiter re-peopled the island by turning ants into men, is told by Ovid (*Metam.* vii. 523-657).

l. 110: *said one*: The speaker is Griffolino d'Arezzo, a physicist, who, by promising all kinds of miracles, extracted large sums of money from a foolish young man, Albero, reputed to be the son of the Bishop of Siena. His dupe eventually complained to the Bishop, who had Griffolino burnt as a sorcerer. The offence which brings him to the Tenth Bowge is, however, not alchemy considered as a magical art (which would be punished in Bowge iv), but alchemy in its more practical application—viz. the falsification of commodities (for Daedalus, see Canto XVII. 109, note).

ll. 125 *sqq.*: *Except, no doubt, Stricca*: As in Canto XXI. 41, the "except" is ironical. The four noblemen named all belonged to the "Spendthrifts' Club" in Siena, of which Lano was also a member (see Canto XIII. 115, note). Niccolo dei Salembeni specialized in the invention of dishes prepared with costly spices.

l. 136: *Capocchio*: is said to have been a friend and fellow-student of Dante's, and to be called an "ape of nature" on account of his powers either as a draughtsman or as a mimic. If the latter, then his saying, "If I eye thee hard," perhaps means that at this point he indulged in some characteristic facial gesture which Dante could not fail to recognize—he gave him, so to speak, a "George Robey look."

shoddy, and so forth—as well, of course, as the baseness of the individual self consenting to such dishonesty.

The Valley of Disease. For the *allegory*, this is at one level the image of the corrupt heart which acknowledges no obligation to keep faith with its fellow-men; at another, it is the image of a diseased society in the last stages of its mortal sickness and already necrosing. Every value it has is false; it alternates between a deadly lethargy and a raving insanity. Malbowges began with the sale of the sexual relationship, and went on to the sale of Church and State; now, the very money is itself corrupted, every affirmation has become perjury, and every identity a lie; no medium of exchange remains, and the "general bond of love and nature's tie" (Canto XI. 56) is utterly dissolved.

CANTO XXX

THE STORY. *The shades of Myrrha and Gianni Schicchi are pointed out by Griffolino. Dante becomes intent upon a quarrel between Adam of Brescia and Sinon of Troy, and earns a memorable rebuke from Virgil.*

When Juno was incensed for Semele,
And wreaking vengeance on the Theban race,
As her sharp strokes had shown repeatedly,

So fierce a madness seized on Athamas 4
That, seeing his wife go with her two young sons
One on each arm: "Spread nets, nets at the pass,

We'll take the lioness and the whelps at once!" 7
He roared aloud; then, grasping in his wild
And pitiless clutch one of those little ones,

Baby Learchus, as he crowed and smiled, 10
He whirled him round and dashed him on a stone;
She fled, and drowned herself with the other child.

And when, by Fortune's hostile hand o'erthrown, 13
The towering pride of Troy fell to the ground,
Kingdom and king together ruining down,

Sad Hecuba, forlorn and captive bound, 16
After she'd seen Polyxena lie slain,
After, poor hapless mother, she had found

Polydorus dead by the seashore, fell insane 19
And howled like a dog, so fearfully distraught
Was she, so wrenched out of her mind with pain.

Yet Theban or Trojan furies never wrought 22
Such cruel frenzy, even in the maddened breast
Of a brute, still less in any of human sort,

As I saw in two shades, naked, pale, possessed, 25
Who ran, like a rutting boar that has made escape
From the sty, biting and savaging all the rest.

One of them fell on Capocchio, catching his nape 28
In its teeth, and dragging him prostrate, so that it made
His belly on the rough rock-bottom scour and scrape.

The Aretine, left trembling, turned dismayed 31
To me: "That's Gianni Schicchi, that hell-hound there;
He's rabid, he bites whatever he sees," he said.

"So may thou 'scape the other's teeth, declare 34
Its name," said I; "prithee be good enough—
Quick! ere it dart away and disappear."

And he: "There doth the ancient spirit rove 37
Of criminal Myrrha, who cast amorous eyes
On her own father with unlawful love,

And in a borrowed frame and false disguise 40
Went in to him to do a deed of shame;
As he that fled but now, to win the prize

'Queen of the Stable,' lent his own false frame 43
To Buoso de' Donati, and made a will
In legal form, and forged it in his name."

So when that rabid pair, on whom I still 46
Kept my gaze fixed, had passed, I turned about
To view those other spirits born for ill;

And saw one there whose shape was like a lute, 49
Had but his legs, between the groin and haunch,
Where the fork comes, been lopt off at the root.

The heavy dropsy, whose indigested bunch 52
Of humours bloats the swollen frame within,
Till the face bears no proportion to the paunch,

Puffed his parched lips apart, with stiffened skin 55
Drawn tight, as the hectic gapes, one dry lip curled
Upward by thirst, the other toward the chin.

"O you," said he, "that through this grisly world 58
Walk free from punishment—I can't think why—
Look now and hear; behold the torments hurled

On Master Adam! All that wealth could buy 61
Was mine; and now, one drop of water fills
My craving mind—one drop! O misery!

The little brooks that ripple from the hills 64
Of the green Casentin to Arno river,
Suppling their channels with their cooling rills,

---

ll. 1 *sqq.*: *when Juno was incensed,* etc.: Semele, daughter of Cadmus, king of Thebes, became by Jupiter the mother of Bacchus. Among other acts of revenge upon the royal house, Juno sent a homicidal madness upon Athamas, the husband of Semele's sister Ino (Ovid: *Metam.* iv. 512-30).

ll. 13 *sqq.*: *and when, by Fortune's hostile hand,* etc.: Hecuba was the wife of Priam, king of Troy. After the fall of the city, she and her daughter Polyxena were carried away captive to Greece. Having seen Polyxena sacrificed at the tomb of Achilles, she found on the shore the body of her son Polydorus, treacherously murdered by Polymnestor, king of Thrace, to whom she had entrusted him for safe keeping (Ovid: *Metam.* xiii. 404-575).

l. 31: *the Aretine*: i.e., Griffolino.

l. 32: *Gianni Schicchi*: a Florentine of the Cavalcanti family. When Buoso Donati (see Canto XXV. 140, note) died, his son Simone was haunted with the fear that he might have left a will restoring some of the property he had unjustly acquired. Before making the death known, he consulted Gianni Schicchi, who, being a very clever mimic, offered to dress up as Buoso and dictate a new will in Simone's favour. This he did, taking the opportunity to bequeath himself a handsome legacy and the best mare in the stables.

l. 38: *Myrrha*: The story of her crime is told by Ovid (*Metam.* x. 298 *sqq.*).

l. 42: *he that fled but now*: i.e., Gianni Schicchi: "Queen of the Stud" was the name of the mare.

l. 61: *Master Adam*: a native of Brescia who was employed by the Counts Guidi of Romena to counterfeit the gold florins of Florence. He was burnt in 1281. The coining was on a large scale, and the whole currency of Tuscany was seriously affected.

l. 65: *the green Casentin*: The Casentino is the beautiful hill district of the Upper Arno, where Romena, the castle of the Conti Guidi, was situated.

Are in my eyes and in my ears for ever; 67
And not for naught—their image dries me more
Than the disease that wastes my face's favour.

Strict, searching justice balances my score: 70
The very land I sinned in has been turned
To account, to make my sighs more swiftly pour.

Romena's there, the city where I learned 73
To falsify the Baptist's coin; up yonder,
For the offence, I was condemned and burned.

But might I here see Guido or Alexander 76
Damned, or their brother, I would not miss that sight
For all the water in the fount of Branda.

One's here already, if those mad spirits are right 79
Who circle all the track; but what's the good
Of that to me, whose legs are tied so tight?

Were I but still so active that I could 82
Drag myself only an inch in a hundred years,
I'd be on the road by now, be sure I would,

To seek out from all these sufferers 85
Disfigured and maimed, though it's half a mile across
And eleven miles round at least, from all one hears.

They brought me into this gang of ruin and loss, 88
They caused me coin the florins that brought me hither,
Whose gold contained three carats by weight of dross."

Then I to him: "What shades lie there together 91
Rolled in a heap on thy right—that abject pair
Who smoke as a washed hand smokes in wintry weather?"

"When I tumbled into this coop I found them there," 94
Said he, "and they've never given a turn or kick,
Nor will to all eternity, I dare swear.

Sinon of Troy is one, the lying Greek; 97
One, the false wife who lyingly accused
Joseph; their burning fever makes them reek."

Then, vexed belike to hear his name thus used 100
Slightingly, one of those shadows seemed to come
To life and fetched him a walloping blow, fist closed,

On the rigid belly, which thudded back like a drum; 103
So Master Adam lammed him over the face
With an arm as hard as his own, and hit him plumb.

"See now," said he, "though I cannot shift my place, 106
Because my legs are heavy, yet if need be
My arm is free, and I keep it ready, in case,"

And he: "It was not so ready and not so free 109
When they haled thee off to the fire; it was free to do
Thy dirty job of coining—there I agree."

Then he of the dropsy: "Now thou speakest true; 112
But when at Troy they called on thee to tell
The truth, thy truthfulness was less in view."

"If I spoke false, thy coins were false as well; 115
I uttered but one lie," quoth Sinon, "thou
Hast uttered more than any fiend in hell."

"Perjurer, think of the horse, think of thy vow 118
Forsworn," retorted the blown belly; "howl
For grief to think the whole world knows it now."

"Howl for the thirst that cracks thy tongue, the foul 121
Water that bloats thy paunch," the Greek replied,
"To a hedge that walls thine eyes and hides thy jowl."

To whom the coiner: "Ay, thy mouth gapes wide 124
As ever with evil words; if I feel thirst,
And watery humours stuff me up inside,

Thou burnest, and thy head aches fit to burst; 127
Hadst thou Narcissus' mirror there, we'd see
Thee lap it up and need no prompting first."

I was all agog and listening eagerly, 130
When the master said: "Yes, feast thine eyes; go on;
A little more, and I shall quarrel with thee."

And when I heard him use that angry tone 133
To me, I turned to him so on fire with shame,
It comes over me still, though all these years have flown.

And like a man who dreams a dreadful dream, 136
And dreams he would it were a dream indeed,
Longing for that which is, with eager aim

As though 'twere not; so I, speechless to plead 139
For pardon, pleaded all the while with him
By my distress, and did not know I did.

"Less shame would wash away a greater crime 142
Than thine has been"; so said my gentle guide;
"Think no more of it; but another time,

Imagine I'm still standing at thy side 145
Whenever Fortune, in thy wayfaring,
Brings thee where people wrangle thus and chide;

It's vulgar to enjoy that kind of thing." 148

THE IMAGES. *The Falsifiers.* In this canto we have the images of impersonators (falsifiers of person), perjurers (falsifiers of words), and coiners (falsifiers of money).

CANTO XXXI

THE STORY. *Dante and Virgil now reach the Well at the bottom of the abyss, round which stand the Giants, visible from the waist up above its rim. They see Nimrod and Ephialtes, and are lowered over the edge of the Well by Antaeus.*

The self-same tongue that first had wounded me,
Bringing the scarlet blood to both my cheeks,
Thus to my sore applied the remedy;

---

l. 74: *the Baptist's coin*: the Florentine florin bore the image of St. John Baptist, patron saint of the city (see Canto XIII. 143, note), on one side and a lily-flower on the other.
l. 76: *Guido or Alexander . . . or their brother* (Aghinolfo): i.e., the Conti Guidi.
l. 78: *the fount of Branda*: There was a famous fountain of this name at Siena; but Master Adam probably means the one at Romena.
l. 97: *Sinon of Troy*: the Greek spy, who, by a lying story backed up by the most solemn oaths, persuaded the Trojans to bring the Wooden Horse into Troy (see Canto XXVI. 55, note).
l. 98: *the false wife*: Potiphar's wife (*Gen.* xxxix. 6-23).
l. 128: *Narcissus' mirror*: water. Narcissus fell in love with his own reflection in a pool, and, pining away, was transformed into a flower.
l. 148: *vulgar*: The Italian word *basso* is rather stronger than the English "vulgar"—it means "base" as well; perhaps the most exact equivalent would be the colloquial use of "low."

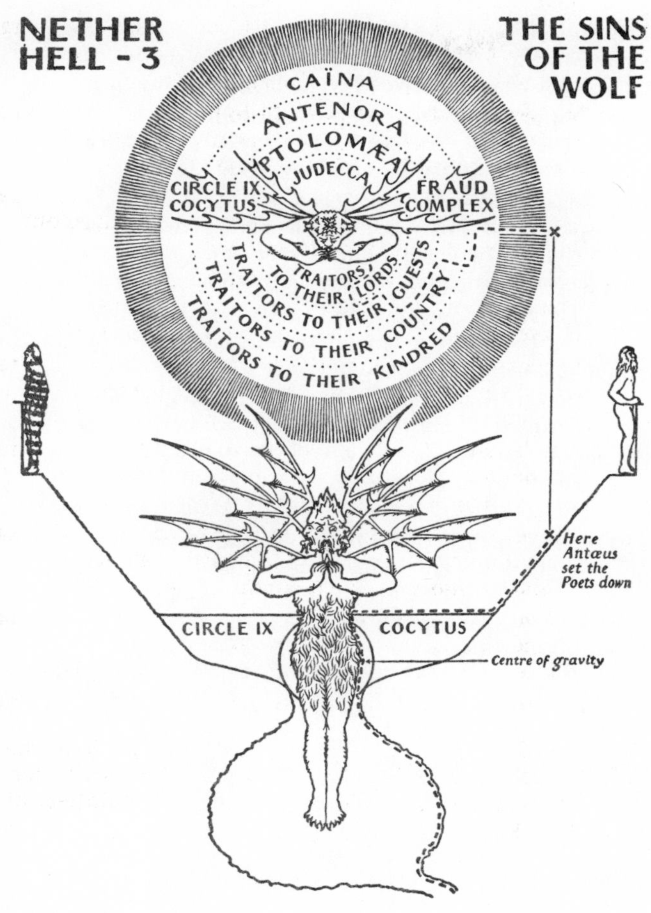

Even so, Achilles' lance was wont to mix 4
 Good gifts with ill, as erst his sire's had done,
 Hurting and healing; so the old tale speaks.

We went our way, turning our backs upon 7
 That mournful vale, up by its girdling bound,
 And silent paced across the bank of stone;

And less than day, and less than night, all round 10
 It gloomed; my eyes, strained forward on our course,
 Saw little; but I heard a high horn sound

So loud, it made all thunder seem but hoarse; 13
 Whereby to one sole spot my gaze was led,
 Following the clamour backward to its source:

When Charlemayn, in rout and ruin red, 16
 Lost all the peerage of the holy war
 The horn of Roland sounded not so dread.

And when I'd gazed that way a little more 19
 I seemed to see a plump of tall towers looming;
 "Master," said I, "what town lies on before?"

"Thou striv'st to see too far amid these glooming 22
 Shadows," said he: "this makes thy fancy err,
 Concluding falsely from thy false assuming;

Full well shalt thou perceive, when thou art there, 25
 How strangely distance can delude the eye:
 Therefore spur on thy steps the speedier."

But after that, he took me lovingly 28
 By the hand, and said: "Nay now, before we go,
 I'll tell thee, lest the strange reality

Surprise thee out of measure; therefore know, 31
 These are not towers, but giants, set in a ring,
 And hid from the navel down in the well below."

And, just as when a mist is vanishing, 34
 Little by little the eye reshapes anew
 The outlines hid by the crowded vapouring,

So, as that thick, gross air we journeyed through, 37
 Little by little drawing nigh the well,
 My error left me, and my terror grew.

As Montereggion's ring-shaped citadel 40
 Has all its circling rampart crowned with towers,
 Even so, with half their bodies the horrible

Giants, whom Jove, when the thunder rolls and lowers, 43
 Threatens from heaven, girded the well's high rim,
 Turreting it—the tall and terrible powers.

Already I made out one huge face, the dim 46
 Shoulders and breast and part of the belly, and close
 Hung at his sides, both monstrous arms of him.

Nature in truth did wisely when she chose 49
 To leave off making such vast animals
 And let Mars lack executives like those;

If she repents not elephants or whales, 52
 Whoso looks subtly at the case will find
 How prudently her judgment trims the scales;

For where the instrument of thinking mind 55
 Is joined to strength and malice, man's defence
 Cannot avail to meet those powers combined.

As large and long his face seemed, to my sense, 58
 As Peter's Pine at Rome, and every bone
 Appeared to be proportionately immense,

So that the bank which aproned him from zone 61
 To foot, still showed so much, three Friesians
 Might vainly boast to lay a finger on

---

l. 4: *Achilles' lance*: Peleus, the father of Achilles, gave to his son a lance, whose wound could be healed only by sprinkling with rust from the lance-head itself (see Ovid: *Remed. Amor.* 47-8; Chaucer, *Squire's Tale*, 231-2; Shakespeare, 2 *Hen. VI.* v. i, etc.).

l. 16: *Charlemayn*: When Charlemagne was returning from fighting the Saracens in Spain, his rearguard, led by his nephew Roland and the Twelve Peers, was betrayed to the enemy by Ganelon (see Canto XXXII. 122), and slaughtered at the Pass of Roncevaux in the Pyrenees. With almost his last breath, Roland blew his horn Olifant so loud that Charlemagne, eight miles away, heard it and returned to avenge his Peerage.

l. 40: *Montereggion*: A castle about six miles from Siena, surmounted by twelve turrets.

l. 59: *Peter's Pine*: A bronze image of a pine-tree, about 7½ ft. high, which, in Dante's time, stood under a canopy outside the old basilica of St. Peter in Rome, but was later removed to the Vatican. Much ingenuity has been expended on calculating the height of the Giants; we may take them to average 50 or 60 ft.

l. 62: *Friesians*: The men of Friesland were celebrated for their immense stature.

His hair; for from the place at which a man's 64
    Mantle is buckled, downward, you may call me
    Liar if he measured not fully thirty spans.

"*Rafel maï amech zabi almi*" 67
    The savage mouth began at once to howl,
    Such was the sweetest and the only psalm he

Could sing. "Stick to thy horn, thou stupid soul," 70
    My guide called up; "use that to vent thy breast
    When rage or other passions through thee roll.

Feel at thy neck and find the baldrick laced 73
    That girds it on thee; see, O spirit confused,
    The horn itself that hoops thy monstrous chest."

And then to me: "Himself he hath accused; 76
    That's Nimrod, by whose fault the gracious bands
    Of common speech throughout the world were loosed.

We'll waste no words, but leave him where he stands, 79
    For all speech is to him as is to all
    That jargon of his which no one understands."

So, turning to the left beside the wall, 82
    We went perhaps a cross-bow shot, to find
    A second giant, still more fierce and tall.

I do not know what master hand could bind 85
    Him thus, but there he stood, his left hand bound
    Fast down before him, and the right behind,

By an iron chain, which held him closely wound 88
    Down from the neck; and on the part displayed
    Above the brink the turns went five times round.

"So proud a spirit was this," my leader said, 91
    "He dared to match his strength against high Jove,
    And in this fashion his reward is paid.

Ephialtes is his name, who greatly strove 94
    When the giants made the gods tremble for fright;
    The arms he brandished then no longer move."

"Were it but possible, I wish my sight," 97
    Said I, "could once experience and take in
    Briareus' huge unmeasurable might."

"Not far from hence," he answered, "thou shalt win 100
    Sight of Antaeus, who speaks and wears no chain;
    And he shall bear us to the bottom of sin.

Very far off is he whom thou wouldst fain 103
    Behold; like this he's fettered, and doth look
    As this one looks, but twice as fierce again."

No terrible earthquake-trembling ever took 106
    And shook a tower so mightily as forthwith
    Huge Ephialtes in his fury shook;

And never had I been so afraid of death— 109
    For which no more was needed save the fear,
    But that I saw the chains, and dared draw breath.

So on we went; and presently drew near 112
    Antaeus; seven cloth-yards above the well,
    Without the head, his towering bulk rose sheer.

"Thou that of old within the fateful vale 115
    That made the name of Scipio ever-glorious,
    When Hannibal with all his host turned tail,

Didst ravish by thy prowess meritorious 118
    A thousand lions; thou whose aid, 'twould seem,
    Might well have made the sons of earth victorious

Hadst thou allied thee with thy brethren's team, 121
    Pray be not loth, but lower us to the deep,
    Where the great cold locks up Cocytus' stream.

Make us not go to Typhon; let not slip 124
    Thy chance to Tiryus; for this man can give
    That which is craved for here; curl not thy lip,

But stoop; for he's alive, and can retrieve 127
    Thy fame on earth, where he expects—so Grace
    Call him not early home—long years to live."

Thus spake the master; he, all eagerness, 130
    Stretched those enormous hands out to my guide
    Whence Hercules endured so great distress.

And when he felt them grasp him, Virgil cried 133
    To me: "Come here and let me take thee!" So
    He clasped me and made one bunch of us twined and tied.

As Carisenda looks, when one stands below 136
    On the leaning side, and watches a passing cloud
    Drift over against the slant of it, swimming slow,

Antaeus looked to me, as I watched him bowed 139
    Ready to stoop; and that was a moment such
    That I heartily wished we might travel another road.

But he set us lightly down in the deep whose clutch 142
    Holds Judas and holds Lucifer pent fast;
    Nor in that stooping posture lingered much,

But swung him up, as in a ship the mast. 145

---

l. 67: *Rafel maï amech zabi almi*: In view of Virgil's express warning (ll. 80-81), the strenuous efforts of commentators to make sense of this remark seem rather a waste of energy. My own impression, for what it is worth, is that if Dante did not make up this gibberish out of his own head, it may have been suggested to him by some conjuring book, for its diction and rhythm are curiously reminiscent of the garbled language of popular charms.

l. 77: *Nimrod*: "and the beginning of his kingdom was Babel" (*Gen.* x. 9-10). For the story of the building of Babel and the confusion of languages see *Genesis* xi. In making Nimrod a giant, Dante follows St. Augustine (*De Civ. Dei* xvi. 3). He is given a horn because he was "a mighty hunter before the Lord."

l. 85: *what master hand*: cf. Canto XV. 11 and note.

l. 94: *Ephialtes*: son of Neptune (the sea); one of the giants who fought against the gods, threatening to pile Mount Ossa upon Olympus, and Mount Pelion upon Ossa. They were slain by Apollo.

l. 99: *Briareus*: son of Tellus (the earth), another giant who fought against the Olympians (*Aen.* x. 565 *sqq.*). According to Homer and Virgil, he had a hundred arms and fifty heads; but Dante seems here to have followed Statius, who (*Theb.* ii. 596) merely calls him "immense," and Lucan, who (*Phars.* iv. 596) refers to "fierce Briareus."

ll. 101-21: *Antaeus*: son of Neptune and Tellus—a giant who was invincible so long as he was in contact with his mother Earth. Hercules eventually overcame him by lifting him from the ground and squeezing him to death in mid-air (see l. 132 of this canto). Antaeus is left unchained because he was not one of the giants who fought against the gods. His exploit with the lions took place near Zama in Libya, where Hannibal was defeated by Scipio. Dante took all these details about Antaeus from Lucan's *Pharsalia* (iv. 593-660).

ll. 124-5: *Typhon . . . Tityus*: two more of the sons of Tellus, who offended against Jupiter. All these earth-giants and sea-giants seem originally to have been personifications of elemental natural forces.

l. 136: *Carisenda*: a leaning tower at Bologna. When one stands beneath one of these towers and looks up, an optical illusion is produced as though it were about to fall upon one; and this illusion is strengthened if a cloud happens to be moving across in the opposite direction to the apparent movement.

THE IMAGES. *The Giants.* From the point of view of the *story*, it is easy to see that Dante placed the Giants here, not merely to furnish a means of transport from Malbowges to the depth of the Well, but, artistically, to provide a little light relief between the sickening horrors of the last bowges of Fraud Simple and the still greater, but wholly different, horrors of the pit of Treachery. But *allegorically*, what do they signify? In one sense they are images of Pride; the Giants who rebelled against Jove typify the pride of Satan who rebelled against God. But they may also, I think, be taken as the images of the blind forces which remain in the soul, and in society, when the "general bond of love" is dissolved and the "good of the intellect" wholly withdrawn, and when nothing remains but blocks of primitive mass-emotion, fit to be the "executives of Mars" and the tools of treachery. Nimrod is a braggart stupidity; Ephialtes, a senseless rage; Antaeus, a brainless vanity: one may call them the doom of nonsense, violence, and triviality, overtaking a civilization in which the whole natural order is abrogated.

CANTO XXXII

THE STORY. *The Ninth Circle is the frozen Lake of Cocytus, which fills the bottom of the Pit, and holds the souls of the Traitors. In the outermost region, Caïna, are the betrayers of their own kindred, plunged to the neck in ice; here Dante sees the Alberti brothers, and speaks with Camicion dei Pazzi. In the next, Antenora, he sees and lays violent hands on Bocca degli Abati, who names various other betrayers of their country; and a little further on he comes upon two other shades, frozen together in the same hole, one of whom is gnawing the head of the other.*

Had I but rhymes rugged and harsh and hoarse,
Fit for the hideous hole on which the weight
Of all those rocks grinds downward course by course,

I might press out my matter's juice complete;
As 'tis, I tremble lest the telling mar
The tale; for, truly, to describe the great

Fundament of the world is very far
From being a task for idle wits at play,
Or infant tongues that pipe *mamma, papa.*

But may those heavenly ladies aid my lay
That helped Amphion wall high Thebes with stone,
Lest from the truth my wandering verses stray.

O well for you, dregs of damnation, thrown
In that last sink which words are weak to tell,
Had you lived as sheep or goats in the world of the sun!

When we were down in the deep of the darkling well,
Under the feet of the giant and yet more low,
And I still gazed up at the towering walls of Hell,

I heard it said: "Take heed how thou dost go,
For fear thy feet should trample as they pass
On the heads of the weary brotherhood of woe."

I turned and saw, stretched out before my face
And 'neath my feet, a lake so bound with ice,
It did not look like water but like glass.

Danube in Austria never could disguise
His wintry course beneath a shroud so thick
As this, nor Tanaïs under frozen skies

Afar; if Pietrapan or Tambernic
Had crashed full weight on it, the very rim
Would not have given so much as even a creak.

And as with muzzles peeping from the stream
The frogs sit croaking in the time of year
When gleaning haunts the peasant-woman's dream,

So, wedged in ice to the point at which appear
The hues of shame, livid, and with their teeth
Chattering like storks, the dismal shades stood here.

Their heads were bowed toward the ice beneath,
Their eyes attest their grief; their mouths proclaim
The bitter airs that through that dungeon breathe.

My gaze roamed round awhile, and when it came
Back to my feet, found two shades so close pressed,
The hair was mingled on the heads of them.

I said: "You two, thus cramponed breast to breast,
Tell me who you are." They heaved their necks a-strain
To see me; and as they stood with faces raised,

Their eyes, which were but inly wet till then,
Gushed at the lids; at once the fierce frost blocked
The tears between and sealed them shut again.

Never was wood to wood so rigid locked
By clamps of iron; like butting goats they jarred
Their heads together, by helpless fury rocked.

Then one who'd lost both ears from off his scarred
Head with the cold, still keeping his face down,
Cried out: "Why dost thou stare at us so hard?

Wouldst learn who those two are? Then be it known,
They and their father Albert held the valley
From which the waters of Bisenzio run;

Both of them issued from one mother's belly,
Nor shalt thou find, search all Caïna through,
Two shades more fit to stand here fixt in jelly;

---

l. 10: *those heavenly ladies*: The Muses. Amphion played so bewitchingly upon the lyre that the stones of Mount Cithaeron were drawn to hear him, and built themselves up into the walls of Thebes.

l. 17: *under the feet of the giant and yet more low*: Antaeus, as we have seen, was about 50-60 ft. high; therefore his feet cannot have been more than 30 ft. or so below the edge of the well. The latter was, however, "exceeding deep" (Canto XVIII. 5), and Dante here makes it clear that they descended to a considerable depth below the feet of the giant. We must suppose that there was, first, a sheer thirty-foot drop, followed by a rather less steep descent which it was possible to negotiate on foot (see sketch, p. 457). I get the impression that Dante clambered down backwards, as one gets down a ladder; and consequently did not see where he had got to until Virgil's voice (l. 19) caused him to turn round (l. 22).

l. 27: *Tanaïs*: the Don.

l. 28: *Pietrapan or Tambernic*: Pietrapana: a corruption of Petra Apuana, a mountain in north-west Tuscany. Tambernic: either the *Frusta Gora*, near Tovarnicho, in Slavonia, or the Javornic in Carniola.

ll. 34-5: *to the point at which appear the hues of shame*: i.e., up to the neck.

l. 56: *they and their father Albert*: These are Napoleone and Alessandro degli Alberti, Counts of Mangona, who slew each other in a quarrel over their possessions in the valley of the river Bisenzio, a tributary of the Arno. One was a Guelf, the other a Ghibelline.

Not him whose breast and shadow at one blow 61
Were pierced together by the sword of Arthur,
Not Focaccia, nor this other who

So blocks me with his head I see no farther, 64
Called Sassol Mascheroni—if thou be
Tuscan, thou know'st him; and I'll tell thee, rather

Than thou shouldst plague me for more speech with thee, 67
I'm Camicion de' Pazzi, and I wait
Till Carlin come to make excuse for me."

Then I saw thousand faces, and thousands yet, 70
Made doggish with the cold; so that for dread
I shudder, and always shall, whenever I set

Eyes on a frozen pool; and as we made 73
Towards the centre where all weights down-weigh,
And I was shivering in the eternal shade,

Whether 'twas will, fate, chance, I cannot say, 76
But threading through the heads, I struck my heel
Hard on a face that stood athwart my way.

"Why trample me? What for?" it clamoured shrill; 79
"Art come to make the vengeance I endure
For Montaperti more vindictive still?"

"Master!" I cried, "wait for me! I adjure 82
Thee, wait! Then hurry me on as thou shalt choose;
But I think I know who it is, and I must make sure."

The master stopped; and while the shade let loose 85
Volleys of oaths: "Who art thou, cursing so
And treating people to such foul abuse?"

Said I; and he: "Nay, who art thou, to go 88
Through Antenora, kicking people's faces?
Thou might'st be living, 'twas so shrewd a blow."

"Living I am," said I; "do thou sing praises 91
For that; if thou seek fame, I'll give thee it,
Writing thy name with other notable cases."

"All I demand is just the opposite; 94
Be off, and pester me no more," he said;
"To try such wheedling here shows little wit."

At that I grasped the scruff behind his head: 97
"Thou'lt either tell thy name, or have thy hair
Stripped from thy scalp," I panted, "shred by shred."

"Pluck it all out," said he; "I'll not declare 100
My name, nor show my face, though thou insist
And break my head a thousand times, I swear."

I'd got his hair twined tightly in my fist 103
Already, and wrenched away a tuft or two,
He yelping, head down, stubborn to resist,

When another called: "Hey, Bocca, what's to do? 106
Don't thy jaws make enough infernal clatter
But, what the devil! must thou start barking too?"

"There, that's enough," said I, "thou filthy traitor; 109
Thou need'st not speak; but to thy shame I'll see
The whole world hears true tidings of this matter."

"Away, and publish what thou wilt!" said he; 112
"But prithee do not fail to advertise
That chatterbox there, if thou from hence go free.

He wails the Frenchmen's *argent*, treason's price; 115
'Him of Duera,' thou shalt say, 'right clear
I saw, where sinners are preserved in ice.'

And if they should inquire who else was there, 118
Close by thee's Beccaria, whose throat was cut
By Florentines; Gianni de' Soldanier

Is somewhat further on, I fancy, put 121
With Ganelon, and Tibbald, who undid
Faenza's gates when sleeping eyes were shut."

And when we'd left him, in that icy bed, 124
I saw two frozen together in one hole
So that the one head capped the other head;

And as starved men tear bread, this tore the poll 127
Of the one beneath, chewing with ravenous jaw,
Where brain meets marrow, just beneath the skull.

With no more furious zest did Tydeus gnaw 130
The scalp of Menalippus, than he ate
The brain-pan and the other tissues raw.

---

ll. 61-2: *him whose breast and shadow . . . were pierced*: Mordred the traitor, who attempted to usurp the throne of Arthur. In their last fight, Arthur smote him so fiercely that when the lance was withdrawn the sun shone through the wound and broke the shadow of his body.
l. 63: *Focaccia*: one of the Cancellieri family of Pistoia. He is said to have cut off the hand of one of his cousins and cut his uncle's throat, and thus to have started the family feud from which the Black and White Guelf factions had their origin.
l. 65: *Sassol Mascheroni*: One of the Toschi of Florence, who treacherously murdered his uncle's only son and seized the inheritance.
ll. 68-9: *Camicion de' Pazzi*: of Valdarno, murdered his kinsman Ubertino. *Carlino* dei Pazzi, another member of the family, was bribed by the Blacks to surrender the castle of Piantravigne, which he was holding for the Whites—and, having pocketed the bribe, sold it back to the Whites again. Camicion means that his own crimes will seem comparatively excusable beside that of Carlino (who is presumably destined for Antenora). It will be noticed that the shades of the Traitors, though inclined to be reticent about their own affairs, are only too eager to denounce each other, and pour out strings of names without even being asked (compare Bocca, ll. 113-23; and contrast, e.g., Farinata, Canto X. 118-20).
ll. 73-4: *as we made towards the centre*: They are now entering Antenora (l. 89). There is no line of demarcation between the regions of Cocytus, but as we go on we find the sinners plunged more deeply in the ice.
l. 81: *Montaperti*: The speaker, Bocca degli Abati, was a Ghibelline; but in the Battle of Montaperti (see Canto X. 85, note) he fought on the Guelf side and, at the most critical moment, came treacherously up behind the standard-bearer of the Florentine cavalry and cut off his hand, bringing down the standard and throwing the Florentines into a panic which lost them the day.
l. 90: *thou might'st be living*: i.e. the blow is heavier than the speaker can account for, as coming from another shade, which he supposes Dante to be.
ll. 97 *sqq.*: For the significance of Dante's ferocious behaviour, see Canto VIII. 45, note; treachery is cruel, and cruelty calls forth cruelty.
l. 114: *that chatterbox there*: Buoso da Duera; he was in command of the Ghibellines assembled to repel the French forces who were marching through Lombardy to link up with Charles of Anjou, and sold the passage of the Oglio to Guy de Montfort. Bocca uses the French word for money (*argent*) by way of rubbing in the accusation.
l. 122: *Ganelon*: see Canto XXXI. 16, note. *Tibbald*: one of the Zambrasi family of Faenza. He had a vendetta against the Lambertazzi, a Ghibelline Bolognese family who had taken refuge in Faenza, and in 1280 opened the gates of the city to the Bolognese Guelfs.
l. 130: *Tydeus*: king of Calydon, one of the "Seven against Thebes." Being himself mortally wounded by Menalippus, he yet killed his opponent, and, having ordered his head to be struck off, gnawed the scalp and tore out the brains (Statius: *Theb.* viii. 740-63).

"O thou that in such bestial wise dost sate 133
Thy rage on him thou munchest, tell me why;
On this condition," I said, "that if thy hate

Seem justified, I undertake that I, 136
Knowing who you are, and knowing all his crime,
Will see thee righted in the world on high,

Unless my tongue wither before the time." 139

THE IMAGES. *Cocytus.* Beneath the clamour, beneath the monotonous circlings, beneath the fires of Hell, here at the centre of the lost soul and the lost city, lie the silence and the rigidity and the eternal frozen cold. It is perhaps the greatest image in the whole *Inferno.* "Dante," says Charles Williams, "scatters phrases on the *difference* of the place. It is treachery, but it is also . . . cruelty; the traitor is cruel" (*The Figure of Beatrice*, p. 143). A cold and cruel egotism, gradually striking inward till even the lingering passions of hatred and destruction are frozen into immobility—that is the final state of sin. The conception is, I think, Dante's own; although the *Apocalypse of Paul* mentions a number of cold torments, these are indiscriminately mingled with the torments by fire, and their placing has no structural significance. (It is interesting, however, that in the seventeenth century, the witches who claimed to have had to do with Satan sometimes reported that he was ice-cold.)

Cocytus, the "river of mourning," is the fourth of the great infernal rivers. Caïna is named from Cain who slew his brother (*Gen.* iv.); Antenora, from Antenor of Troy who, according to medieval tradition, betrayed his city to the Greeks.

CANTO XXXIII

THE STORY. *Having heard Count Ugolino's ghastly story of his death by famine, the Poets pass on to Ptolomaea, where Fra Alberigo is cheated by Dante into telling him about himself and Branca d' Oria and others who enjoy the terrible "privilege" of Ptolomaea.*

Lifting his mouth up from the horrid feast,
The sinner wiped it on the hair that grew
Atop the head whose rear he had laid waste;

Then he began: "Thou bid'st me to renew 4
A grief so desperate that the thought alone,
Before I voice it, cracks my heart in two.

Yet, if indeed my words, like seedlings sown, 7
Shall fruit, to shame this traitor whom I tear,
Then shalt thou see me speak and weep in one.

What man thou art, or what hath brought thee here 10
I know not; but I judge thee Florentine,
If I can trust the witness of my ear.

First learn our names: I was Count Ugolin, 13
And he, Archbishop Roger; hearken well
Wherefore I use him thus, this neighbour of mine.

That once I trusted him, and that I fell 16
Into the snare that he contrived somehow,
And so was seized and slain, I need not tell.

What thou canst not have learned, I'll tell thee now: 19
How bitter cruel my death was; hear, and then,
If he has done me injury, judge thou.

A narrow loophole in the dreadful den 22
Called 'Famine' after me, and which, meseems,
Shall be a dungeon yet for many men,

Had filtered through to me the pallid gleams 25
Of many changing moons, before one night
Unveiled the future to my haunted dreams.

I saw this man, a lord and master of might, 28
Chasing the wolf and wolf-cubs on the hill
Which shuts out Lucca from the Pisans' sight.

His hounds were savage, swift and keen of skill, 31
And many a Sismund, Gualand and Lanfranc,
Like huntsmen, rode before him to the kill.

I saw how father and sons wearied and sank 34
After a short quick run; I saw the dread
Sharp teeth that tore at bleeding throat and flank.

And waking early ere the dawn was red 37
I heard my sons, who were with me, in their sleep
Weeping aloud and crying out for bread.

Think what my heart misgave; and if thou keep 40
From tears, thou art right cruel; if thou for this
Weep not, at what then art thou wont to weep?

By now they'd waked; the hour at which our mess 43
Was daily brought drew near; ill dreams had stirred
Our hearts and filled us with unquietness.

Then at the foot of that grim tower I heard 46
Men nailing up the gate, far down below;
I gazed in my sons' eyes without a word;

I wept not; I seemed turned to stone all through; 49
They wept; I heard my little Anselm say:
'Father, what's come to thee? Why look'st thou so?'

I shed no tear, nor answered, all that day 52
Nor the next night, until another sun
Rose on the world. And when the first faint ray

Stole through into that dismal cell of stone, 55
And eyeing those four faces I could see
In every one the image of my own,

---

ll. 4-9: Compare with Canto V. 121-6, and both with *Aeneid* ii. 3, 10-13.

l. 13: *Count Ugolin*: Count Ugolino della Gherardesca and his grandson, Nino dei Visconti (whom we shall meet in *Purg.* viii), were respectively the heads of the two Guelf parties which in 1288 held power in Pisa. To get rid of Nino, Ugolino allied himself with the Archbishop, Ruggieri (Roger) degli Ubaldini. But as soon as Nino was driven out, the Archbishop, seeing the Guelfs thus weakened, turned on Ugolino and imprisoned him with four of his sons and grandsons in a tower subsequently named "the Tower of Famine." There they remained till March 1289, when the Archbishop ordered the tower to be locked and the keys thrown into the river. (Dante's word [*chiavar*], however, probably means "nail up"—a sound more alarming to the prisoners.) After eight days the tower was opened and all the victims found dead of starvation.

l. 29: *the wolf and wolf-cubs*: i.e., Ugolino and his children. *The hill that shuts out Lucca* is the Monte di San Giuliano, half-way between Pisa and Lucca.

l. 32: *Sismund, Gualand and Lanfranc*: Ghibelline families of Pisa.

l. 34: *father and sons*: Actually, the youths imprisoned with Ugolino were his own two youngest sons, Gaddo and Uguccione (Hugh), and his two grandsons, Nino (surnamed *il Brigata*) and Anselm. All except Anselm were young men rather than "children" or "boys" as Dante represents them. Anselm was 15.

I gnawed at both my hands for misery;
And they, who thought it was for hunger plain
And simple, rose at once and said to me:

'O Father, it will give us much less pain
If thou wilt feed on us; thy gift at birth
Was this sad flesh, strip thou it off again.'

To spare them grief I calmed myself. Hard earth,
Hadst thou no pity? couldst thou not gape wide?
That day and next we all sat mute. The fourth,

Crept slowly in on us. Then Gaddo cried,
And dropped down at my feet: 'My father, why
Dost thou not help me?' So he said, and died.

As thou dost see me here, I saw him die,
And one by one the other three died too,
From the fifth day to the sixth. Already I

Was blind; I took to fumbling them over; two
Long days I groped there, calling on the dead;
Then famine did what sorrow could not do."

He ceased, and rolled his eyes asquint, and sped
To plant his teeth, which, like a dog's, were strong
Upon the bone, back in the wretched head.

O Pisa! scandal of all folk whose tongue
In our fair country speaks the sound of *sì*,
Since thy dull neighbours will not smite such wrong

With vengeance, move Gorgona from the sea,
Caprara move, and dam up Arno's mouth,
Till every living soul is drowned in thee!

For though Count Ugolin in very truth
Betrayed thee of thy castles, it was crime
To torture those poor children; tender youth,

O cruel city, Thebes of modern time,
Made Hugh and Il Brigata innocent
And the other two whose names are in my rhyme.

We passed; and found, as further on we went,
A people fettered in the frost's rough grip,
Flat on their backs, instead of forward bent.

There the mere weeping will not let them weep,
For grief, which finds no outlet at the eyes,
Turns inward to make anguish drive more deep;

For their first tears freeze to a lump of ice
Which like a crystal mask fills all the space
Beneath the brows and plugs the orifice.

And now, although, as from a calloused place,
By reason of the cold that pinched me so,
All feeling had departed from my face,

I felt as 'twere a wind begin to blow.
Wherefore I said: "Master, what makes it move?
Is not all heat extinguished here below?"

"Thine eyes," said he, "shall answer soon enough;
We're coming to the place from which the blast
Pours down, and thou shalt see the cause thereof."

And one of the wretched whom the frost holds fast
Cried out: "O souls so wicked that of all
The posts of Hell you hold the very last,

Rend from my face this rigid corporal,
That I may vent my stuffed heart at my eyes
Once, though the tears refreeze before they fall."

Then I: "Tell me thy name: that is my price
For help; and if I do not set thee free,
May I be sent to the bottom of the ice."

And he: "I am Friar Alberigo, he
Of the fruits of the ill garden; in this bed
Dates for my figs are given back to me."

"How now," said I, "art thou already dead?"
And in reply: "Nay, how my body fares
In the upper world I do not know," he said.

"Such privilege this Ptolomaea bears
That oft the soul falls down here ere the day
When Atropos compels it with her shears.

And, if it will persuade thee take away
These glazing tears by which my face is screened,
Know, when a soul has chosen to betray,

As I did, straight it's ousted by a fiend,
Who takes and rules the body till the full
Term of its years has circled to an end.

The soul drops down into this cistern-pool;
Belike the shade wintering behind me here
Still has a body on earth—it's probable

---

ll. 72-3: *already I was blind*: "from grief," say some commentators; but Dante knew, I think, that one of the effects of starvation is to produce blindness.

l. 75: *then famine did what sorrow could not do*: i.e., kill him.

l. 80: *speaks the sound of sì*: i.e., all who speak Italian. The various romance-languages were distinguished by the word used for "Yes," that of Northern France being the *langue d' oil (oui)*; that of Southern France, the *langue d'oc*; that of Italy, the *lingua di sì*.

ll. 82-3: *Gorgona . . . Caprara*: These two islands near the mouth of the Arno then belonged to Pisa.

ll. 85-6: *in very truth betrayed thee of thy castles*: Ugolino was accused of treachery in ceding certain Pisan strongholds to the Florentines and Lucchese. Others think he had no choice but to do so; Dante's words are ambiguous, but in any case Ugolino's treacherous conspiracy with Ruggieri against Nino, by which he betrayed both his party and his city, would have sufficed to bring him to Antenora.

l. 91: *as further on we went*: They are now passing into Ptolomaea.

l. 105: *is not all heat extinguished*: Dante knows that winds are caused by differences of temperature in the atmosphere, and wants to know how, in this region of absolute cold, there can be wind without heat. Virgil replies that he will see the cause of it later on (Canto XXXIV. 46-51).

l. 110: *O souls so wicked*: The speaker thinks that Dante and Virgil are damned souls going down to the Circle of Judecca.

l. 117: *to the bottom of the ice*: Treachery calls forth treachery; Dante knows that he *is* going to the bottom—though not in the sense the shade supposes.

ll. 118-20; *Friar Alberigo*: a "Jovial Friar" of the Manfredi family of Faenza. His younger brother, Manfred, struck him in the face in the course of a dispute. Alberigo pretended to forgive and forget, and later on invited Manfred and one of his sons to a dinner. When it was time for the dessert he called out: "Bring on the fruit!" This was the signal for armed servants to rush in and kill Manfred and his son. The "fruit of the ill garden" is probably an allusion to this. "To receive dates for one's figs" is a Tuscan expression meaning "to get back one's own with interest," "to be given tit for tat."

l. 126: *Atropos*: the Fate who cuts the thread of life.

Thou'lt know, if thou art new come down from there; 136
He is Ser Branca d' Oria; in this pit's
Cold storage he has lain this many a year."

"I think," said I, "that these are pure deceits, 139
For Branca d' Oria has by no means died;
He wears his clothes and sleeps and drinks and eats."

"Up in that moat where the Hellrakers bide," 142
He answered, "Michael Zanche'd not yet come
To boil and bubble in the tarry tide

When this man left a devil in his room, 145
In his flesh and that kinsman's flesh, whom he
Joined with himself in treachery, and in doom.

And now, do thou stretch forth thy hand to me, 148
Undo my eyes." And I undid them not,
And churlishness to him was courtesy.

O Genoa, where hearts corrupt and rot, 151
Lost to all decency! will no man hound
Thy whole tribe from the earth and purge this blot?

For with Romagna's vilest spirit I found 154
One of such rank deeds, such a Genoan,
His soul bathes in Cocytus, while on ground

His body walks and seems a living man. 157

THE IMAGES. *Ugolin and Roger* are the last of those pairs of shades who image partnership in sin. In each case, only one of them speaks. Francesca speaks of the sharing of the sin, and offers excuses for Paolo along with herself. Ulysses ignores Diomede (partnership is lost). Ugolin justifies himself at Roger's expense (treachery can share nothing but a mutual hatred). There is a deliberate parallel between the Paolo-Francesca pair and the Ugolin-Roger pair: in both cases the lines that introduce their respective stories are drawn from the same passage of Virgil, and there are other, minor, correspondences. This is Dante's way of indicating that here in the ice of Cocytus we have the last state of the corruption of love; that every devouring passion, sexual or otherwise, that sets itself against the order of God and the City, bears in itself the seeds of treachery and a devouring passion of destruction.

Ptolomaea. This third region of Cocytus is probably named after Ptolemy, captain of Jerico, who invited Simon the High Priest and his sons to a banquet and there slew them (1 *Maccabees* xvi). Here lie the Traitors to Hospitality. They who denied the most primitive of human sanctities are now almost sealed off from humanity; they cannot even weep. And they are dead to humanity before they die; that which seems to live in them on earth is only a devil in human form—the man in them has withdrawn out of reach into the cold damnation.

CANTO XXXIV

THE STORY. *After passing over the region of Judecca, where the Traitors to their Lords are wholly immersed in the ice, the Poets see Dis (Satan) devouring the shades of Judas, Brutus, and Cassius. They clamber along his body until, passing through the centre of the Earth, they emerge into a rocky cavern. From here they follow the stream of Lethe upwards until it brings them out on the island of Mount Purgatory in the Antipodes.*

"*Vexilla regis prodeunt inferni*
Encountering us; canst thou distinguish him,
Look forward," said the master, "as we journey."

As, when a thick mist breathes, or when the rim 4
Of night creeps up across our hemisphere,
A turning windmill looms in the distance dim,

I thought I saw a shadowy mass appear; 7
Then shrank behind my leader from the blast,
Because there was no other cabin here.

I stood (with fear I write it) where at last 10
The shades, quite covered by the frozen sheet,
Gleamed through the ice like straws in crystal glassed;

Some lie at length and others stand in it, 13
This one upon his head, and that upright,
Another like a bow bent face to feet.

And when we had come so far that it seemed right 16
To my dear master, he should let me see
That creature fairest once of the sons of light,

He moved him from before me and halted me, 19
And said: "Behold now Dis! behold the place
Where thou must steel thy soul with constancy."

How cold I grew, how faint with fearfulness, 22
Ask me not, Reader; I shall not waste breath
Telling what words are powerless to express;

This was not life, and yet it was not death; 25
If thou hast wit to think how I might fare
Bereft of both, let fancy aid thy faith.

The Emperor of the sorrowful realm was there, 28
Out of the girding ice he stood breast-high,
And to his arm alone the giants were

Less comparable than to a giant I; 31
Judge then how huge the stature of the whole
That to so huge a part bears symmetry.

If he was once as fair as now he's foul, 34
And dared outface his Maker in rebellion,
Well may he be the fount of all our dole.

I. 137: *Ser Branca d' Oria*: a Ghibelline of Genoa, who invited his father-in-law, Michael Zanche (see Canto XXII. 88), to a banquet and there, with the help of a nephew, murdered him. Dante says that Zanche had not yet reached the Bowge of the Barrators before the traitor's body had been taken over by a devil and his soul fallen to Ptolomaea—i.e., he was damned in the moment of committing—or perhaps even of assenting to—the treachery.

I. 146: *that kinsman*: i.e., the nephew.

I. 149: *and I undid them not*: The chorus of indignant comment about Dante's behaviour becomes so loud at this point that I feel obliged to repeat that it arises from a misunderstanding of the *allegory*, and once more refer to Canto VIII. 45, note.

I. 1: *Vexilla regis prodeunt inferni*: "The banners of the King of Hell go forth." This, with the addition of the word *inferni* (of Hell), is the first line of the Latin hymn which we know best as "The royal banners forward go."

I. 28: *fairest once of the sons of light*: referring to Satan's original status as one of the brightest of the Cherubim.

I. 28: *the Emperor*: "Dante uses the word with the full meaning of its perversion" (Charles Williams). In Canto II, he refers to God as "the Emperor of the Imperium on high"; this is the Emperor of the realm below, who gives his name to the "sorrowful City" (Canto VIII. 68).

And marvel 'twas, out-marvelling a million, 37
When I beheld three faces in his head;
The one in front was scarlet like vermilion;

And two, mid-centred on the shoulders, made 40
Union with this, and each with either fellow
Knit at the crest, in triune junction wed.

The right was of a hue 'twixt white and yellow; 43
The left was coloured like the men who dwell
Where Nile runs down from source to sandy shallow.

From under each sprang two great wings that well 46
Befitted such a monstrous bird as that;
I ne'er saw ship with such a spread of sail.

Plumeless and like the pinions of a bat 49
Their fashion was; and as they flapped and whipped
Three winds went rushing over the icy flat

And froze up all Cocytus; and he wept 52
From his six eyes, and down his triple chin
Runnels of tears and bloody slaver dripped.

Each mouth devoured a sinner clenched within, 55
Frayed by the fangs like flax beneath a brake;
Three at a time he tortured them for sin.

But all the bites the one in front might take 58
Were nothing to the claws that flayed his hide
And sometimes stripped his back to the last flake.

"That wretch up there whom keenest pangs divide 61
Is Judas called Iscariot," said my lord,
"His head within, his jerking legs outside;

As for the pair whose heads hang hitherward: 64
From the black mouth the limbs of Brutus sprawl—
See how he writhes and utters never a word;

And strong-thewed Cassius is his fellow-thrall. 67
But come; for night is rising on the world
Once more; we must depart; we have seen all."

Then, as he bade, about his neck I curled 70
My arms and clasped him. And he spied the time
And place; and when the wings were wide unfurled

Set him upon the shaggy flanks to climb, 73
And thus from shag to shag descended down
'Twixt matted hair and crusts of frozen rime.

And when we had come to where the huge thigh-bone 76
Rides in its socket at the haunch's swell,
My guide, with labour and great exertion,

Turned head to where his feet had been, and fell 79
To hoisting himself up upon the hair,
So that I thought us mounting back to Hell.

"Hold fast to me, for by so steep a stair," 82
My master said, panting like one forspent,
"Needs must we quit this realm of all despair."

At length, emerging through a rocky vent, 85
He perched me sitting on the rim of the cup
And crawled out after, heedful how he went.

I raised my eyes, thinking to see the top 88
Of Lucifer, as I had left him last;
But only saw his great legs sticking up.

And if I stood dumbfounded and aghast, 91
Let those thick-witted gentry judge and say,
Who do not see what point it was I'd passed.

"Up on thy legs!" the master said; "the way 94
Is long, the road rough going for the feet,
And at mid-terce already stands the day."

The place we stood in was by no means fit 97
For a king's palace, but a natural prison,
With a vile floor, and very badly lit.

"One moment, sir," said I, when I had risen; 100
"Before I pluck myself from the Abyss,
Lighten my darkness with a word in season.

Kindly explain; what's happened to the ice? 103
What's turned him upside-down? or in an hour
Thus whirled the sun from dusk to dawning skies?"

"Thou think'st," he said, "thou standest as before 106
Yon side the centre, where I grasped the hair
Of the ill Worm that pierces the world's core.

---

l. 38: *three faces*: The three faces, red, yellow, and black, are thought to suggest Satan's dominion over the three races of the world: the red, the European (the race of Japhet); the yellow, the Asiatic (the race of Shem); the black, the African (the race of Ham). But they are also, undoubtedly, a blasphemous anti-type of the Blessed Trinity: Hatred, Ignorance, Impotence as against Love, Wisdom, Power.

l. 46: *from under each sprang two great wings*: Satan was a fallen cherub, and retains, in a hideous and perverted form, the six wings which belong to his original rank.

ll. 51-2: *three winds . . . and froze up all Cocytus*: see Canto XXXIII. 103-108.

l. 68: *night is rising on the world*: it is about 6 P.M.

l. 74: *from shag to shag descended*: Satan's body is shaggy like that of a satyr, according to a well-known medieval convention. The poets clamber down him, feet-first, as one descends a ladder, working their way through the points where the thick pelt prevents the ice from adhering close to the surface of his body. (We must remember the enormous height of Satan—somewhere about 1000 or 1500 ft. at a rough calculation.)

l. 79: *turned head to . . . feet* etc.: They have been descending feet-first; now they turn themselves topsy-turvy and go *up* again, head-first.

l. 93: *what point it was I'd passed*: Since Dante proceeds to take the sting out of "thick-witted" by admitting that he himself was completely bewildered, we may perhaps, without offence, explain that the "point" was the centre of gravity, which was situated precisely at Satan's navel. The sketch on p. 457 will make all these geographical complexities clear.

l. 96: *mid-terce*: *Terce*, the first of the four canonical divisions of the day, lasted from sunrise (6 A.M. at the equinox) till 9 A.M.; mid-terce would therefore be about 7:30 A.M.

l. 103: *Kindly explain*: Dante wants to know (1) why Satan is apparently upside-down; (2) how it is that, having started their descent of Satan about 6 P.M., they have, after about an hour and a half of climbing, apparently arrived at the following morning. Virgil explains that (1) having passed the centre, they are now in the Southern Hemisphere, so that "up" and "down" are reversed, and (2) they are now going by southern time, so that day and night are reversed. Purgatory stands on the opposite meridian to Jerusalem; therefore Purgatory time is twelve hours behind Jerusalem time; i.e., it is now 7:30 A.M. on Holy Saturday, all over again.

l. 108: *the ill Worm:* Satan. At the centre of the Earth is a little sphere (see l. 116, and look at the sketch), and Satan's body is run through this, like a knitting-needle through an orange, with his head out at one end and his legs at the other.

So long as I descended, thou wast there; 109
But when I turned, then was the point passed by
Toward which all weight bears down from everywhere.

The other hemisphere doth o'er thee lie— 112
Antipodal to that which land roofs in,
And under whose meridian came to die

The Man born sinless and who did no sin; 115
Thou hast thy feet upon a little sphere
Of whose far side Judecca forms the skin.

When it is evening there, it's morning here; 118
And he whose pelt our ladder was, stands still
Fixt in the self-same place, and does not stir.

This side the world from out high Heaven he fell; 121
The land which here stood forth fled back dismayed,
Pulling the sea upon her like a veil,

And sought our hemisphere; with equal dread, 124
Belike, that peak of earth which still is found
This side, rushed up, and so this void was made."

There is a place low down there underground, 127
As far from Belzebub as his tomb's deep,
Not known to sight, but only by the sound

Of a small stream which trickles down the steep, 130
Hollowing its channel, where with gentle fall
And devious course its wandering waters creep.

By that hid way my guide and I withal, 133
Back to the lit world from the darkened dens
Toiled upward, caring for no rest at all,

He first, I following; till my straining sense 136
Glimpsed the bright burden of the heavenly cars
Through a round hole; by this we climbed, and thence

Came forth, to look once more upon the stars. 139

THE IMAGES. *Judecca.* The region of the Traitors to sworn allegiance is called Judecca after Judas, who betrayed Our Lord. Here, cut off from every contact and every means of expression, those who committed the final treason lie wholly submerged.

Judas, Brutus and Cassius. Judas, obviously enough, is the image of the betrayal of God. To us, with our minds dominated by Shakespeare and by "democratic" ideas, the presence here of Brutus and Cassius needs some explanation. To understand it, we must get rid of all political notions in the narrow sense. We should notice, first, that Dante's attitude to Julius Caesar is ambivalent. *Personally*, as a pagan, Julius is in Limbo (Canto IV. 123). *Politically*, his rise to power involved the making of civil war, and Curio, who advised him to cross the Rubicon, is in the Eighth Circle of Hell (Canto XXVIII. 97-102 and note). But, although Julius was never actually Emperor, he was the founder of the Roman Empire, and *by his function*, therefore, he images that institution which, in Dante's view, was divinely appointed to govern the world. Thus Brutus and Cassius, by their breach of sworn allegiance to Caesar, were Traitors to the Empire, i.e., to World-order. Consequently, just as Judas figures treason against God, so Brutus and Cassius figure treason against Man-in-Society; or we may say that we have here images of treason against the Divine and the Secular government of the world.

Dis, so Virgil calls him; Dis, or Pluto, being the name of the King of the Classical Underworld. But to Dante he is Satan or Lucifer or Beelzebub—or, as we say, the Devil. "He can see it now—that which monotonously resents and repels, that which despairs. . . . Milton imagined Satan, but an active Satan; this is beyond it, this is passive except for its longing. Shakespeare imagined treachery; this is treachery raised to an infinite cannibalism. Treachery gnaws treachery, and so inevitably. It is the imagination of the freezing of every conception, an experience of which neither life nor death can know, and which is yet quite certain, it it is willed." (Charles Williams: *The Figure of Beatrice*, p. 144.)

I. 113: *that which land roofs in*: the Northern Hemisphere, which according to St. Augustine and most medieval geographers, contained all the land in the world.

I. 114: *under whose meridian*: the meridian of Jerusalem, where Christ ("the Man born sinless") was crucified.

II. 116-17: *a little sphere*, etc.: See sketch, p. 457.

II. 121 *sqq.*: *This side the world*: i.e., the southern side. When Satan fell from Heaven, two things happened. (1) The dry land, which until then had occupied the Southern Hemisphere, fled in horror from before him, and fetched up in the Northern Hemisphere; while the ocean poured in from all sides to fill the gap. (2) the inner bowels of the Earth, to avoid contact with him, rushed upwards towards the south, and there formed the island and mountain at the top of which was the Earthly Paradise, ready for the reception of Man, and which, after Hell's Harrowing became Mount Purgatory. This, according to Dante, is the only land in the Southern Hemisphere. The hollow thus left in the middle of the Earth is the core of Hell, together with the space in which Dante and Virgil are now standing—the "tomb" of Satan. From this a winding passage leads up to the surface of the Antipodes. By this passage the river Lethe descends, and up it the poets now make their way.

I. 130: *a small stream*: This is Lethe, the river of oblivion, whose springs are in the Earthly Paradise. They are moving against it—i.e., towards recollection.

Index

A

D

E

F

G

H

I

J

N

O

Q

R

T

Z